PAULY

Advanced Econometric Methods

Thomas B. Fomby
R. Carter Hill
Stanley R. Johnson

Advanced Econometric Methods

With 26 Illustrations

Springer-Verlag
New York Berlin Heidelberg Tokyo

Thomas B. Fomby
Department of Economics
Southern Methodist University
Dallas, TX 75275
U.S.A.

R. Carter Hill
Department of Economics
University of Georgia
Brooks Hall
Athens, GA 30602
U.S.A.

Stanley R. Johnson
Departments of Economics
and Agricultural Economics
University of Missouri
217 Middlebush
Columbia, MO 65211
U.S.A.

AMS Classifications (1980): 90-01, 90A19, 62P20

Library of Congress Cataloging in Publication Data
Fomby, Thomas B.
Advanced econometric methods.
Includes bibliographical references and index.
1. Econometrics. I. Hill, R. Carter.
II. Johnson, Stanley R., 1938- . III. Title.
HB139.F65 1984 658.4'033 83-20127

Typeset by Composition House Ltd., Salisbury, England.
Printed and bound by R. R. Donnelley & Sons, Harrisonburg, Virginia.
Printed in the United States of America.

9 8 7 6 5 4 3 2 1

ISBN 0-387-90908-7 Springer-Verlag New York Berlin Heidelberg Tokyo
ISBN 3-540-90908-7 Springer-Verlag Berlin Heidelberg New York Tokyo

To
Nancy and Elizabeth
My Father
Barbara, Ben, and Peter

Preface

This book had its conception in 1975 in a friendly tavern near the School of Business and Public Administration at the University of Missouri–Columbia. Two of the authors (Fomby and Hill) were graduate students of the third (Johnson), and were (and are) concerned about teaching econometrics effectively at the graduate level. We decided then to write a book to serve as a comprehensive text for graduate econometrics. Generally, the material included in the book and its organization have been governed by the question, "How could the subject be best presented in a graduate class?" For content, this has meant that we have tried to cover "all the bases" and yet have not attempted to be encyclopedic. The intended purpose has also affected the level of mathematical rigor.

We have tended to prove only those results that are basic and/or relatively straightforward. Proofs that would demand inordinant amounts of class time have simply been referenced. The book is intended for a two-semester course and paced to admit more extensive treatment of areas of specific interest to the instructor and students. We have great confidence in the ability, industry, and persistence of graduate students in ferreting out and understanding the omitted proofs and results. In the end, this is how one gains maturity and a fuller appreciation for the subject in any case.

It is assumed that the readers of the book will have had an econometric methods course, using texts like J. Johnston's *Econometric Methods*, 2nd ed. (New York: McGraw-Hill, 1972), or *An Introduction to the Theory and Practice of Econometrics* by G. Judge, R. Hill, W. Griffiths, H. Lütkepohl, and T. Lee (New York: John Wiley, 1982). Thus, we have developed Part I of the book, on Fundamental Methodology, as a survey for the most part. We envision the book being used in conjunction with journal articles (for depth) and perhaps handbooks like *The Theory and Practice of Econometrics* by G. Judge, W. Griffiths, R. Hill, and T. Lee (New York: John Wiley, 1980) or M. Intriligator's *Econometric Models, Techniques and Applications* (Englewood Cliffs: Prentice-Hall, 1978) (for breadth). In the final section of each chapter we have provided a guide to further readings that briefly lists and describes useful related works in the area. The exercises provided with each chapter are a blend of proofs and results that replace or extend many of those in the text. Applications are included in the exercises as well. We believe strongly that students must grapple with applied econometric problems in order to appreciate the subtleties and value of econometric techniques. Of course, this means the development of an appropriate dexterity with computers and relevant software as a requirement for serious students in econometrics.

Since this book has been in process for eight years, it should surprise no one that it has gone through several stages of metamorphosis. No doubt it would continue to change if we worked on it another eight years, but enough is enough. During that time we have learned a lot about econometrics, teaching, and each other, and have increased our understanding of the growing literature in this relatively new and promising area in economics. We also have a host of people to thank for comments, suggestions, and criticisms. They include Jan Kmenta, Joe Terza, and countless diligent graduate students from whom we learned and who used various portions of the manuscript as class handouts. High on our list of people to thank is Nancy Fomby, who typed much of the manuscript (over and over as we changed things and changed them back), listened to us talk about it for these many years, and threatened us with extinction if we did not finish soon. Beverly Baker also typed portions of the manuscript. Finally, we thank Rod Ziemer for his contributed section on disequilibrium models (Section 25.4). To all these people we owe a debt of gratitude.

On April 7, 1984, just before this book goes to press, Rod Ziemer died. We deeply regret the loss of such an outstanding young scholar and friend. We feel very fortunate to have the opportunity to present his work. Rod had established himself as a prolific author. Unfortunately, his section in this book and his previous publications provide only a hint of what surely would have been a very long list of contributions to the agricultural economics and econometrics literature. We all will miss Rod dearly.

Of course, undertakings such as the development of this book require institutional support. In this connection, Southern Methodist University, the University of Georgia, the University of California–Berkeley, and the place it all started, the University of Missouri–Columbia should be acknowledged. Lastly, our colleagues at these institutions through their encouragement, criticisms, and assistance have been invaluable to us in completing this project.

Contents

PART III: SPECIAL TOPICS 281

CHAPTER 1

Introduction

1.1 The Scope and Nature of Econometrics

Econometrics is a branch of the economics discipline that brings together economic theory, mathematics, statistics, and computer science to study economic phenomena. It is both a separate field of study within economics and a powerful tool that many, if not most, economists and other social scientists use to study particular applied problems. The primary purpose of econometrics is to give empirical content to economic theory. To accomplish this, econometrics must encompass a wide range of activities. These include:

(i) precise mathematical formulation of an economic theory—mathematical economics;
(ii) development and extension of statistical and computational techniques appropriate for econometric models and data—econometric theory;
(iii) development of methods for collecting, and the actual collection of, economic data—economic statistics.

In this book we are primarily concerned with econometric theory, although in any application all three facets of econometrics have important roles.

Econometrics draws heavily from mathematical statistics, numerical analysis, and computer science, yet it is much more than just a straightforward application of techniques from these fields to economic problems. Economists, like many other social scientists, usually cannot perform controlled experiments to generate the data they analyze. Typically we are passive in the data collection phase of a project, normally using data generated by others for purposes completely unrelated to the current research. The inability to determine experimental designs for generating our data introduces uncertainty about the factors that belong in a particular economic relationship and, in fact, serves to mask the patterns and magnitudes of influence between economic variables. A primary task of the econometrician, then, is to select statistical methods that appropriately reflect how the data were actually generated by the unknown experimental design.

On the other hand, econometricians have at their disposal a rich body of economic theory. To an extent, economic theory can substitute for knowledge of the experimental design. That is, in many instances, the theory provides information about types of economic factors and variables that should be related to one another. In addition, economic theory can supply information about magnitudes and directions of effects among economic variables. Consequently, another important task of econometric method is to provide means by which nonsample information can incorporated into a modeling effort.

Unfortunately economics is not an exact science. While the theory can often indicate general types of factors that should be involved in a relationship, it is typically silent on exact mathematical form. Also, it does not go far in suggesting how variables, like "ability," "permanent income," or "expectations" should be measured. In fact, economic theory is deductive in nature. The conclusions of the theory follow logically from initial premises. There is nothing to guarantee that the economic data we observe were generated by the process described by a particular economic theory.

All of these factors suggest that the practice of econometrics is filled with uncertainty. One obvious way that uncertainty is explicitly incorporated into econometric analysis is by the addition of random terms into economic relationships, thus making deterministic models stochastic. Several reasons for the inclusion of errors or disturbance terms are often given. First, it is argued that models for empirical investigations are but approximations to the true relationships generating the data. Theories are approximations as are the models used in testing or incorporating the resulting propositions.

Sources of the approximation are of two kinds; omission of factors from consideration thought not to be especially relevant and recognition that the functional mathematical relationship chosen for application is likely not the true functional form. The random error reflects these features of the approximation. A second reason for the inclusion of an error term is that even if *all* relevant variables were included in an econometric model and the functional form were correctly specified, the relationship between the variables would not be exact because of the basic indeterminacy in the behavior of economic agents.

Finally, economists often use measured variables that do not represent exactly the factors implied by the theory. These measurement errors, caused by the use of proxy variables, also serve to make econometric representations of economic relationships inexact. These justifications are of course not mutually exclusive, and any or all may be relevant to any modeling exercise.

The inclusion of a random disturbance term in an econometric model means that for a complete specification one must not only assume the set of variables to include in an economic relationship and the mathematical form of the relationship between the variables, but as well make a set of assumptions about the probability distribution of the random disturbance. When econometric models are correctly specified, statistical theory provides the means of obtaining point and interval estimates of the parameters, testing hypotheses, and ways of evaluating the performance of those rules. If the uncertainties alluded to above lead to an incorrect model specification, then rules and procedures otherwise appropriate may no longer have their intended properties and interpretations. Accordingly, another major focus of econometric theory is the analysis of consequences of incorrect assumptions and the development of methods for detecting the presence of various misspecifications.

Reasons for undertaking the estimation of econometric models are varied. One is that economists by nature are interested in the structure of the economy and the behavior of economic agents. Giving empirical content to economic relationships allows economists to test the adequacy of their theories and, if the estimated models are not found unsuitable, provide quantitative information about economic phenomena. This quantitative information has several other functions apart from augmenting our general knowledge, however. Estimated economic relationships can serve as a basis for forecasting magnitudes of important economic variables. These forecasts may be valuable to economic policymakers who wish to predict effects or responses to changes in economic variables under their control.

1.2 The Organization of the Book

The book is divided into five parts. Part I deals with basic models, techniques, and results that will be used and referred to repeatedly. Topics covered in Part I include properties of ordinary and generalized least squares, maximum likelihood estimation, likelihood ratio test procedures, and a discussion of small and large sample hypothesis tests and properties of statistical estimators. Also, results for models with stochastic regressors and models that incorporate a variety of forms of nonsample information are introduced. Chapter 7 discusses the consequences of model building schemes that use preliminary tests and develops a nontraditional way of combining sample and nonsample information, namely the Stein-rules.

In Part II we treat generalized least squares and violations of the assumptions for the basic model of Part I. Seemingly unrelated regressions are used as the framework for developing the associated results on feasible generalized least squares. Other topics in Part II include heteroscedasticity, autocorrelation, lagged dependent variable models with autocorrelation, and unobservable variables. Part III introduces a set of special econometric topics: multicollinearity, varying and random coefficient models, pooling time-series and cross-sectional data models, models with qualitative and limited dependent variables, distributed lags and a chapter on model selection and specification.

In Part IV we treat simultaneous equations models. After an introductory chapter, we discuss identification, limited, and full information estimation, estimation of the reduced form and forecasting and dynamic properties of simultaneous equations models. In Part V, selected topics are discussed that relate primarily to simultaneous equations. These topics illustrate extensions of simultaneous equations models to incorporate qualitative or limited dependent variables, persistence hypotheses and more selected applied problems. Finally, a brief Appendix on nonlinear models is also included.

PART I
FUNDAMENTAL METHODOLOGY

The following six chapters constitute Part I of this book. These chapters are grouped together because they represent fundamental results in linear regression analysis. In particular, the methods of ordinary least squares and generalized least squares are reviewed in Chapter 2. In Chapter 3 small sample estimation theory and tests of hypotheses are developed in the context of the classical normal linear regression model. The Cramér–Rao lower bound approach to determining minimum variance unbiasedness of estimators is presented and the likelihood ratio method is used to develop a test statistic for the general linear hypothesis. Some basic asymptotic distribution theory results are presented in Chapter 4. The large sample properties of maximum likelihood estimators are discussed and it is shown that, in large samples, the usual tests of hypotheses are justified even in the presence non-normal disturbances. In Chapter 5 the conventional assumption is relaxed to allow the possibility of stochastic regressors. Under quite general conditions it is shown that the theoretical results derived in previous chapters using the nonstochastic regressors assumption largely remain intact in the more general case of stochastic regressors. In Chapter 6 various types of prior information are considered: exact linear restrictions, stochastic linear restrictions, and inequality restrictions. In addition the basic concepts of Bayesian analysis are presented and the relationship between Bayesian and sampling theory approaches to statistical inference is discussed. In Chapter 7 the properties of preliminary test estimators resulting from using tests of hypotheses in estimator choice are presented. The inadmissability of the preliminary test estimator and its risk properties are outlined and some general remarks are made about the consequences and scope of data mining via preliminary test procedures. Rounding out the chapter, Stein-rule estimation methods are shown to provide a means of addressing the inferior risk properties obtained from making estimator choice dependent upon the outcomes of tests of hypotheses.

CHAPTER 2

Review of Ordinary Least Squares and Generalized Least Squares

2.1 Introduction

The purpose of this chapter is to review the fundamentals of ordinary least squares and generalized least squares in the context of linear regression analysis. The presentation here is somewhat condensed given our objective of focusing on more advanced topics in econometrics. The results presented, though brief in form, are important and are the foundation for much to come. In the next section we present the assumptions of the classical linear regression model. In the following section the Gauss–Markov theorem is proved and the optimality of the ordinary least squares estimator is established. In Section 2.4 we introduce the large sample concepts of convergence in probability and consistency. It is shown that convergence in quadratic mean is a sufficient condition for consistency and that the ordinary least squares estimator is consistent. In Section 2.5 the generalized least squares model is defined and the optimality of the generalized least squares estimator is established by Aitken's theorem. In the next section we examine the properties of the ordinary least squares estimator when the appropriate model is the generalized least squares model. Finally, in Section 2.7 we summarize our discussion and briefly outline additional results and readings that are available.

2.2 The Classical Linear Regression Model

The classical linear regression model is a description of the population of a random variable Y. It is assumed that the observations $y_1, y_2, \ldots, y_T$ on Y constitute a random sample with a linear conditional mean made up of variables $x_1, x_2, \ldots, x_K$. More precisely,

Definition 2.2.1 (The Classical Linear Regression Model). The *classical linear regression model* is specified by

$$\mathbf{y} = X\boldsymbol{\beta} + \mathbf{e},$$

where $\mathbf{y}' = (y_1, y_2, \ldots, y_T)$, $\mathbf{e}' = (e_1, e_2, \ldots, e_T)$, $\boldsymbol{\beta}' = (\beta_1, \beta_2, \ldots, \beta_K)$,

$$X = \begin{bmatrix} x_{11} & x_{12} & \cdots & x_{1K} \\ x_{21} & x_{22} & \cdots & x_{2K} \\ & \vdots & & \\ x_{T1} & x_{T2} & \cdots & x_{TK} \end{bmatrix}$$

and the following assumptions are satisfied:

(i) X is a nonstochastic matrix of rank $K \leq T$ and, as the sample size T becomes infinitely large, $\lim_{T\to\infty}(X'X/T) = Q$, where Q is a finite and nonsingular matrix. (Note: If A is a matrix and c is a scalar, we will often write, for notational convenience, $(1/c)A = A/c$.)
(ii) The vector $\mathbf{e}$ consists of unobservable random errors which satisfy the properties $E(\mathbf{e}) = \mathbf{0}$ and $E\mathbf{ee}' = \sigma^2 I$, where $E(\cdot)$ denotes mathematical expectation.

Let us examine the details of the classical linear regression model. Foremost, the conditional mean of $\mathbf{y}$ given X is $E(\mathbf{y} | X) = X\boldsymbol{\beta}$ since by assumption $E(\mathbf{e}) = \mathbf{0}$. That is, the expected values of the random variables y_t are linear functions of the (explanatory) variables $x_{t1}, \ldots, x_{tK}$. We often call y_t the dependent variable since it (or at least its mean) is explained by the variables $x_{t1}, \ldots, x_{tK}$.

Though it is not obvious, assumption (i) limits the behavior of the regressors $x_{t1}, \ldots, x_{tK}$. For example, the size of the regressors cannot increase as fast as the index $t = 1, 2, 3, \ldots$. Also none of the regressors may become zero in the limit or collinear in the limit. For examples of these cases, the reader is referred to Exercises 2.1 and 2.2 at the end of this chapter. Also assumption (i) excludes the possibility of "exact" multicollinearity among the regressors because of the rank assumption on X. No column of X can be represented as a linear combination of the remaining columns of X.

Assumption (ii) specifies the probability distribution of the error terms. They are independent and identically distributed with zero mean and common variance σ^2.

In the next section we examine a procedure for estimating the unknown parameters (regression coefficients) $\beta_1, \beta_2, \ldots, \beta_K$ and the error variance σ^2.

2.3 Ordinary Least Squares and the Gauss–Markov Theorem

The *estimation problem* for the classical linear model consists of the need to infer values for the unknown parameters $\beta_1, \beta_2, \ldots, \beta_K$ and σ^2 given T sample observations on $y_t, x_{t1}, \ldots, x_{tK}$. The "least squares" procedure selects those values of $\beta_1, \ldots, \beta_K$ that minimize the sum of squared errors

$$S = \sum_{t=1}^{T} (y_t - \beta_1 x_{t1} - \cdots - \beta_K x_{tK})^2 = (\mathbf{y} - X\boldsymbol{\beta})'(\mathbf{y} - X\boldsymbol{\beta}). \quad (2.3.1)$$

The necessary conditions for a minimum are obtained by differentiating expression (2.3.1) with respect to $\boldsymbol{\beta}$ and setting the resulting linear equations to zero (see Exercise 2.3 for the development of vector differentiation)

$$\frac{\partial S}{\partial \boldsymbol{\beta}} = -2X'\mathbf{y} + 2X'X\hat{\boldsymbol{\beta}} = \mathbf{0}$$

or

$$X'X\hat{\boldsymbol{\beta}} = X'\mathbf{y}. \quad (2.3.2)$$

The equations in (2.3.2) are called the normal equations. Since X has rank K, $(X'X)^{-1}$ exists so that

$$\hat{\boldsymbol{\beta}} = (X'X)^{-1}X'\mathbf{y}. \quad (2.3.3)$$

The matrix of second-order derivatives, $\partial^2 S/\partial\boldsymbol{\beta}\partial\boldsymbol{\beta}' = 2X'X$, is positive definite and, thus, $\hat{\boldsymbol{\beta}}$ provides a minimum. The estimator $\hat{\boldsymbol{\beta}}$ is called the ordinary least squares estimator because the sum of squares

$$S = (\mathbf{y} - X\boldsymbol{\beta})'(\mathbf{y} - X\boldsymbol{\beta})$$

is an "ordinary" sum of squares. Later, we will see that conditions may exist whereby it is preferable to minimize a "generalized" sum of squares, $S^* = (\mathbf{y} - X\boldsymbol{\beta})'W(\mathbf{y} - X\boldsymbol{\beta})$, where W is a positive definite matrix (see Exercise 2.4 for a definition of positive definite matrices).

Before we examine the "optimality" of the ordinary least squares estimator $\hat{\boldsymbol{\beta}}$ in the classical linear regression model, let us define some terms.

Definition 2.3.1. Let $\boldsymbol{\beta}^*$ be an estimator of $\boldsymbol{\beta}$; $\boldsymbol{\beta}^*$ is *unbiased* if $E(\boldsymbol{\beta}^*) = \boldsymbol{\beta}$.

Definition 2.3.2. An unbiased estimator is *efficient* with respect to a class of estimators if it has a variance which is no greater than the variance of any other estimator in that class.

The class of estimators that we are interested in is the class of linear, unbiased estimators. A linear estimator of $\boldsymbol{\beta}$ is one which can be written as a linear transformation of the observations $\mathbf{y}$, $\boldsymbol{\beta}^* = H\mathbf{y}$. Our next task is to prove a major optimality property of the ordinary least squares estimator $\hat{\boldsymbol{\beta}}$ in the classical linear regression model.

Theorem 2.3.1 (Gauss–Markov). *Assume the properties of the classical linear regression model hold. The ordinary least squares estimator $\hat{\boldsymbol{\beta}}$ is unbiased and efficient within the class of linear, unbiased estimators.*

PROOF. The ordinary least squares estimator is

$$\hat{\boldsymbol{\beta}} = (X'X)^{-1}X'\mathbf{y}.$$

Making the substitution for $\mathbf{y}$, we obtain

$$\begin{aligned}\hat{\boldsymbol{\beta}} &= (X'X)^{-1}X'(X\boldsymbol{\beta} + \mathbf{e}) \\ &= (X'X)^{-1}X'X\boldsymbol{\beta} + (X'X)^{-1}X'\mathbf{e} \\ &= \boldsymbol{\beta} + (X'X)^{-1}X'\mathbf{e}.\end{aligned}$$

Then

$$E(\hat{\boldsymbol{\beta}}) = \boldsymbol{\beta} + (X'X)^{-1}X'E(\mathbf{e}),$$

since X is nonstochastic. Therefore,

$$E(\hat{\boldsymbol{\beta}}) = \boldsymbol{\beta} \tag{2.3.4}$$

and $\hat{\boldsymbol{\beta}}$ is unbiased.

The covariance matrix of $\hat{\boldsymbol{\beta}}$ is by definition

$$\begin{aligned}E(\hat{\boldsymbol{\beta}} - E\hat{\boldsymbol{\beta}})(\hat{\boldsymbol{\beta}} - E\hat{\boldsymbol{\beta}})' &= E(\hat{\boldsymbol{\beta}} - \boldsymbol{\beta})(\hat{\boldsymbol{\beta}} - \boldsymbol{\beta})' \\ &= E(X'X)^{-1}X'\mathbf{e}\mathbf{e}'X(X'X)^{-1} \\ &= (X'X)^{-1}X'E(\mathbf{e}\mathbf{e}')X(X'X)^{-1} \\ &= \sigma^2(X'X)^{-1}X'X(X'X)^{-1} \\ &= \sigma^2(X'X)^{-1}. \qquad (2.3.5)\end{aligned}$$

The efficiency of the ordinary least squares estimator is shown by considering an arbitrary linear function of $\mathbf{y}$, $\boldsymbol{\beta}^* = H\mathbf{y}$, as an alternative estimator of $\boldsymbol{\beta}$. Without loss of generality let H be given by

$$H = (X'X)^{-1}X' + C,$$

where C is a matrix of constants. Then

$$\boldsymbol{\beta}^* = H\mathbf{y} = HX\boldsymbol{\beta} + H\mathbf{e}$$

and

$$E\boldsymbol{\beta}^* = HX\boldsymbol{\beta}.$$

Unbiasedness requires that $HX = I$. But

$$HX = (X'X)^{-1}X'X + CX = I + CX.$$

Thus, $HX = I$ if and only if (hereafter denoted iff) $CX = 0$.

The covariance matrix of $\boldsymbol{\beta}^*$ is

$$\begin{aligned} E(\boldsymbol{\beta}^* - \boldsymbol{\beta})(\boldsymbol{\beta}^* - \boldsymbol{\beta})' &= E(H\mathbf{e}\mathbf{e}'H') \\ &= E[(X'X)^{-1}X' + C]\mathbf{e}\mathbf{e}'[X(X'X)^{-1} + C'] \\ &= \sigma^2[(X'X)^{-1}X'X(X'X)^{-1} + (X'X)^{-1}X'C' \\ &\quad + CX(X'X)^{-1} + CC'] \\ &= \sigma^2(X'X)^{-1} + \sigma^2 CC', \end{aligned}$$

since $CX = 0$. But CC' is a positive semidefinite matrix, hence the variance of $\boldsymbol{\beta}^*$ is greater than or equal to the variance of $\hat{\boldsymbol{\beta}}$ in the sense that the difference between the two covariance matrices is a positive semidefinite matrix. (See Exercise 2.4 for a definition and proof of the positive semidefiniteness of CC' and Exercise 2.10 for further interpretation.) Hence, $\hat{\boldsymbol{\beta}}$ is efficient relative to any other linear, unbiased estimator of $\boldsymbol{\beta}$. For this reason, the ordinary least squares estimator is said to possess the best, linear, unbiased (BLU) estimator property. □

A few remarks are appropriate. First, the Gauss–Markov theorem is a *small-sample* result. That is, given the assumptions of the classical linear regression model, the theorem's result is valid for *any* sample size that permits unbiased estimation ($T \geq K$). Second, notice the Gauss–Markov theorem does not require that the parametric form of the distribution of e_t be specified, e.g., e_t is not necessarily normally distributed but may be, for example, uniformly distributed. In the next chapter we examine the implications of normally distributed errors.

The remaining parameter of the classical linear regression model is the variance of the disturbances, σ^2. A natural choice for the estimator of this parameter is an average of the least squares residuals.

Theorem 2.3.2. *In the classical linear regression model, the estimator* $\hat{\sigma}^2 = \hat{\mathbf{e}}'\hat{\mathbf{e}}/(T - K)$ *is an unbiased estimator of* σ^2 *with* $\hat{\mathbf{e}} = \mathbf{y} - X\hat{\boldsymbol{\beta}}$.

Proof. The unbiasedness of $\hat{\sigma}^2$ is shown by evaluating the expectation of the sum of squared residuals.

$$\begin{aligned} \hat{\mathbf{e}} &= \mathbf{y} - X\hat{\boldsymbol{\beta}} = \mathbf{y} - X(X'X)^{-1}X'\mathbf{y} = [I - X(X'X)^{-1}X']\mathbf{y} = M\mathbf{y} \\ &= [I - X(X'X)^{-1}X'](X\boldsymbol{\beta} + \mathbf{e}) \\ &= X\boldsymbol{\beta} - X(X'X)^{-1}X'X\boldsymbol{\beta} + M\mathbf{e} = M\mathbf{e}. \end{aligned}$$

The matrix M is symmetric and idempotent ($M' = M$ and $MM = M^2 = M$) and hence tr M = rank of M, where tr denotes the trace operator. (See Exercise 2.5 for a statement of the general properties of the trace operator.)

Therefore,

$$E\hat{\mathbf{e}}'\hat{\mathbf{e}} = E(\mathbf{e}'M'M\mathbf{e}) = E(\mathbf{e}'M\mathbf{e}),$$

but $\mathbf{e}'M\mathbf{e}$ is a scalar, so

$$\begin{aligned} E(\mathbf{e}'M\mathbf{e}) &= E \operatorname{tr}(\mathbf{e}'M\mathbf{e}) \\ &= E \operatorname{tr}(M\mathbf{e}\mathbf{e}') \quad \text{(since } \operatorname{tr}(AB) = \operatorname{tr}(BA)) \\ &= \operatorname{tr} E(M\mathbf{e}\mathbf{e}') \quad \text{(since trace is a linear function)} \\ &= \operatorname{tr}(M \cdot E\mathbf{e}\mathbf{e}') \quad \text{(since } M \text{ is nonstochastic)} \\ &= \operatorname{tr}(M \cdot \sigma^2 I) \\ &= \sigma^2 \operatorname{tr} M, \end{aligned}$$

but

$$\begin{aligned} \operatorname{tr} M &= \operatorname{tr} I_T - \operatorname{tr}(X(X'X)^{-1}X') \quad \text{(since } \operatorname{tr}(A + B) = \operatorname{tr} A + \operatorname{tr} B) \\ &= \operatorname{tr} I_T - \operatorname{tr}(X'X(X'X)^{-1}) \quad \text{(since } \operatorname{tr} AB = \operatorname{tr} BA) \\ &= \operatorname{tr} I_T - \operatorname{tr} I_K = T - K. \end{aligned}$$

Thus, $E\hat{\mathbf{e}}'\hat{\mathbf{e}} = \sigma^2(T - K)$ and $E(\hat{\mathbf{e}}'\hat{\mathbf{e}})/(T - K) = \sigma^2$. □

2.4 Large Sample Properties of Ordinary Least Squares Estimators

What happens to the sampling distributions of certain estimators as the sample size becomes infinite ($T \to \infty$)? Can we infer with certainty the values of unknown population parameters if we have an infinitely large sample? These and more questions are answered by studying the large sample (asymptotic) properties of estimators.

The idea of statistical certainty in infinite samples is illustrated by the following example.

EXAMPLE 2.4.1. Let $\bar{x}_T$ denote the scalar mean of a random sample of size T from a distribution with mean μ and variance σ^2. The mean and variance of $\bar{x}_T$ are μ and σ^2/T, respectively. Consider for any fixed $\varepsilon > 0$,

$$\Pr(|\bar{x}_T - \mu| \geq \varepsilon) = \Pr\left(|\bar{x}_T - \mu| \geq \frac{c\sigma}{\sqrt{T}}\right) \quad \text{where } c = \frac{\varepsilon\sqrt{T}}{\sigma}.$$

Now consider Chebyshev's inequality, $\Pr(|z - \mu_z| \geq c\sigma_z) \leq 1/c^2$, where z is any random variable with mean μ_z and variance σ_z^2. Applying this result to our problem,

$$\lim_{T \to \infty} \Pr(|\bar{x}_T - \mu| \geq \varepsilon) \leq \lim_{T \to \infty} \frac{\sigma^2}{T\varepsilon^2} = 0.$$

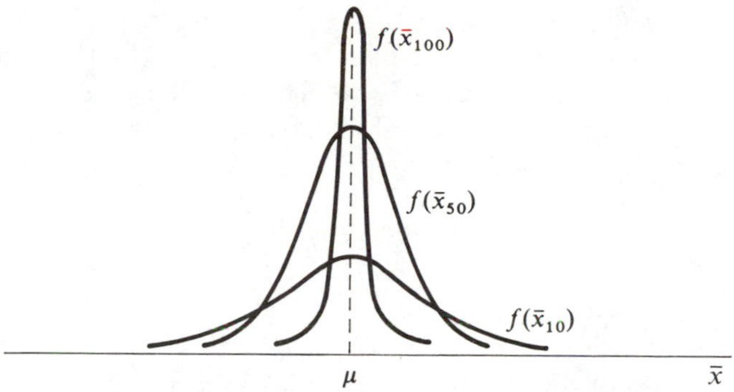

Figure 2.4.1 Illustration of convergence in probability.

Hence $\lim_{T\to\infty} \Pr(|\bar{x}_T - \mu| < \varepsilon) = 1$ and $\bar{x}_T$ converges in probability to μ if σ^2 is finite.

Convergence in probability is illustrated in Figure 2.4.1 by a collapsing of the distributions for $\bar{x}_T$ about μ.

More formally,

Definition 2.4.1. Let $\{z_T: T = 1, 2, \ldots\}$ be a sequence of random variables. The sequence is said to *converge in probability* to a constant, l, if

$$\lim_{T\to\infty} \Pr\{|z_T - l| < \varepsilon\} = 1,$$

where Pr denotes probability and ε is an arbitrary constant. The constant l is termed the *probability limit* of z_T and is denoted

$$\operatorname{plim} z_T = l.$$

The concept of convergence in probability plays a vital role in the description of large sample properties for estimators.

Definition 2.4.2. Let $\hat{\theta}_T$ be an estimator of the population parameter θ. If $\hat{\theta}_T$ converges in probability to θ, $\hat{\theta}_T$ is said to be a *consistent* estimator of θ.

In Example 2.4.1, the mean $\bar{x}_T$ from a population with finite variance is a consistent estimator of the mean μ.

We will now establish some sufficient, but not necessary, conditions for the consistency of an estimator that are easier to apply than the definition of convergence in probability. Let $\hat{\theta}_T$ be an estimator of the parameter θ based on a sample of size T. Furthermore, let

$$E(\hat{\theta}_T) = \theta + d_T,$$

where $\lim_{T\to\infty} d_T = 0$. This implies that $\lim_{T\to\infty} E(\hat{\theta}_T) = \theta$. Such an estimator is said to be *asymptotically unbiased*. Let $\operatorname{var}(\hat{\theta}_T)$ denote the variance of the estimator $\hat{\theta}_T$, $\text{var}(\hat{\theta}_T) \equiv E(\hat{\theta}_T - E(\hat{\theta}_T))^2$, and $\text{bias}^2(\hat{\theta}_T)$ denote the squared bias of the estimator $\hat{\theta}_T$, $\text{bias}^2(\hat{\theta}_T) \equiv (\hat{\theta}_T - E(\hat{\theta}_T))^2$. Assume that $\text{var}(\hat{\theta}_T)$ is such that $\lim_{T\to\infty} \text{var}(\hat{\theta}_T) = 0$. The simultaneous occurrence of asymptotic unbiasedness and vanishing asymptotic variance is termed *convergence in quadratic mean* since

$$\lim_{T\to\infty} E(\hat{\theta}_T - \theta)^2 = \lim_{T\to\infty} \text{bias}^2(\hat{\theta}_T) + \lim_{T\to\infty} \text{var}(\hat{\theta}_T) = 0.$$

By Chebychev's inequality

$$\Pr[|\hat{\theta}_T - (\theta + d_T)| < c\sqrt{\text{var}(\hat{\theta}_T)}] \geq 1 - \frac{1}{c^2}.$$

Let $c = \varepsilon/\sqrt{\text{var}(\hat{\theta}_T)}$, then

$$\Pr[|\hat{\theta}_T - (\theta + d_T)| < \varepsilon] \geq 1 - \frac{\text{var}(\hat{\theta}_T)}{\varepsilon^2}.$$

Taking the limits of both sides, and using our assumptions, gives $\text{plim}\ \hat{\theta}_T = \theta$. We summarize these results in Theorem 2.4.1.

Theorem 2.4.1 (Convergence in Quadratic Mean). *An estimator $\hat{\theta}_T$ is a consistent estimator of the parameter θ if it is asymptotically unbiased and its variance vanishes asymptotically. The converse, however, is not true.*

EXAMPLE 2.4.2. Let $x_1, x_2, \ldots, x_T$ be a random sample from a population with mean μ and variance σ^2. Show that $\bar{x}_T$ is a consistent estimator of μ.

First,

$$E(\bar{x}_T) = E\frac{1}{T}\sum_{i=1}^{T} x_i = \frac{1}{T}\sum_{i=1}^{T} Ex_i = \frac{1}{T}(T\mu) = \mu,$$

therefore, $\bar{x}_T$ is unbiased and asymptotically unbiased. Secondly,

$$\text{var}(\bar{x}_T) = \text{var}\frac{1}{T}\sum_{i=1}^{T} x_i = \frac{1}{T^2}\text{var}\left(\sum x_i\right) = \frac{1}{T^2}\sum_{i=1}^{T}\text{var}(x_i),$$

since the x_i are independent. Therefore,

$$\text{var}(\bar{x}_T) = \frac{1}{T^2}(T\sigma^2) = \frac{\sigma^2}{T}$$

and

$$\lim_{T\to\infty} \text{var}\ \bar{x}_T = \lim_{T\to\infty} \frac{\sigma^2}{T} = 0.$$

From Theorem 2.4.1, the sample mean $\bar{x}_T$ is a consistent estimator of μ.

Now, returning to the classical linear regression model, the task of the remainder of this section is to establish the consistency of the ordinary least squares estimators.

The proof of the consistency of $\hat{\boldsymbol{\beta}}$ is frequently taken much too casually. In particular, it is often claimed that $\text{plim}(X'\mathbf{e}/T) = \mathbf{0}$ follows *directly* from the fact that X is nonstochastic and uncorrelated with $\mathbf{e}$ and, therefore, consistency trivially follows. This is not the case. The limiting behavior of the moment matrix $X'X$ is an integral part of the consistency proof and must be specified carefully.

Lemma 2.4.1. $\text{plim}(X'\mathbf{e}/T) = \mathbf{0}$.

Proof. X and $\mathbf{e}$ are uncorrelated, so that $E(X'\mathbf{e}) = \mathbf{0}$. Accordingly, $X'\mathbf{e}/T$ has a zero asymptotic mean. Also $E(X'\mathbf{e}/T)(X'\mathbf{e}/T)' = (\sigma^2/T)(X'X/T)$. Therefore, the asymptotic variance of $X'\mathbf{e}/T$ vanishes as $T \to \infty$ since $\lim_{T\to\infty}(X'X/T) = Q$ holds by assumption. □

Now, using Lemma 2.4.1, a proof of the consistency of $\hat{\boldsymbol{\beta}}$ is straightforward.

Theorem 2.4.2. $\text{plim } \hat{\boldsymbol{\beta}} = \boldsymbol{\beta}$.

Proof. Recall that $\hat{\boldsymbol{\beta}}$ can be written as

$$\begin{aligned}\hat{\boldsymbol{\beta}} &= \boldsymbol{\beta} + (X'X)^{-1}X'\mathbf{e} \\ &= \boldsymbol{\beta} + (X'X/T)^{-1}(X'\mathbf{e}/T).\end{aligned}$$

Therefore

$$\begin{aligned}\text{plim } \hat{\boldsymbol{\beta}} &= \boldsymbol{\beta} + \text{plim}(X'X/T)^{-1}(X'\mathbf{e}/T) \\ &= \boldsymbol{\beta} + \lim(X'X/T)^{-1} \text{ plim}(X'\mathbf{e}/T) \\ &= \boldsymbol{\beta} + Q^{-1} \cdot \mathbf{0} = \boldsymbol{\beta}.\end{aligned}$$ □

The proof of the consistency of the estimator $\hat{\sigma}^2 = \hat{\mathbf{e}}'\hat{\mathbf{e}}/(T - K)$ of σ^2 is straightforward. Note the squares of the individual elements of $\mathbf{e}$ are independent, identically distributed random variables with mean σ^2. But Khintchine's theorem states (see, for example, Dhrymes (1974, pp. 101–102) for a proof):

Theorem 2.4.3 (Khintchine). *Let $\{z_t : t = 1, 2, \ldots\}$ be a sequence of independent identically distributed random variables with finite mean μ. Then* $\text{plim } \bar{z}_t = \mu$.

It follows that $\text{plim } \mathbf{e}'\mathbf{e}/T = \sigma^2$. Express

$$\hat{\sigma}^2 = \frac{1}{T-K}(\mathbf{e}'M\mathbf{e}) = \frac{1}{T-K}(\mathbf{e}'\mathbf{e}) - \frac{1}{T-K}(\mathbf{e}'X(X'X)^{-1}X'\mathbf{e}).$$

Now $\text{plim}(\mathbf{e}'\mathbf{e}/(T - K)) = \text{plim}(\mathbf{e}'\mathbf{e}/T) = \sigma^2$. Since $\lim_{T\to\infty}(X'X/T) = Q$ is finite and nonsingular by assumption and $\text{plim}\, X'\mathbf{e}/T = \mathbf{0}$ by Lemma 2.4.1,

$$\text{plim}\left(\frac{1}{T-K}\mathbf{e}'X\right)\left(\frac{X'X}{T}\right)^{-1}\frac{X'\mathbf{e}}{T} = 0$$

and thus $\text{plim}\,\hat{\sigma}^2 = \sigma^2$. We have just proved the following theorem.

Theorem 2.4.4. *The estimator* $\hat{\sigma}^2 = \hat{\mathbf{e}}'\hat{\mathbf{e}}/(T - K)$ *is a consistent estimator of* σ^2.

2.5 Generalized Least Squares and Aitken's Theorem

There are instances when the assumption of independent and identically distributed random errors is not tenable. For example, suppose that for observations $t = 1, 2, \ldots, T'$ the variance of e_t is σ^2 whereas for observations $T' < t \leq T$ the variance of e_t is $c\sigma^2$, where c is a *known* constant. In this case the error covariance matrix is of the form

$$E\mathbf{e}\mathbf{e}' = \sigma^2\begin{bmatrix} I_{T'} & 0 \\ 0 & cI_{(T-T')} \end{bmatrix} = \sigma^2\Omega, \tag{2.5.1}$$

where $I_{T'}$ and $I_{(T-T')}$ represent identity matrices of orders T' and $(T - T')$ respectively. Similarly, there can exist other error covariance structures which do not equal $\sigma^2 I$. More formally,

Definition 2.5.1. The *generalized least squares model* is defined by

$$\mathbf{y} = X\boldsymbol{\beta} + \mathbf{e},$$

where $\mathbf{y}$ is a $T \times 1$ vector of observations on the dependent variable, $\boldsymbol{\beta}$ is a $K \times 1$ vector of unknown coefficients and

(i) X is a $T \times K$ nonstochastic matrix of rank K of observations on the explanatory variables;
(ii) $\mathbf{e}$ is a $T \times 1$ vector of random unobservable errors with properties $E(\mathbf{e}) = \mathbf{0}$ and $E(\mathbf{e}\mathbf{e}') = \sigma^2\Omega$, where Ω is a *known* symmetric, positive definite matrix; and
(iii) $\lim_{T\to\infty}(X'\Omega^{-1}X/T) = Q_\Omega$ is finite and nonsingular.

The structure now assumed for the errors permits the possibility that they may be correlated and/or may have different variances. In either case, knowledge of the properties of the errors should be used in the estimation process. Given that the error structure $\sigma^2 I$ is erroneous, a logical conclusion would be that the ordinary least squares estimator is no longer efficient. This conclusion is formalized by *Aitken's theorem*, Aitken (1935).

Theorem 2.5.1 (Aitken's Theorem). *In the generalized least squares model the estimator*

$$\tilde{\boldsymbol{\beta}} = (X'\Omega^{-1}X)^{-1}X'\Omega^{-1}\mathbf{y}$$

is efficient among the class of linear, unbiased estimators of $\boldsymbol{\beta}$.

Proof. There exists a nonsingular matrix P such that $PP' = \Omega^{-1}$ implying that

$$P'\Omega P = I. \tag{2.5.2}$$

This follows from the diagonalization of Ω

$$A'\Omega A = \Lambda, \tag{2.5.3}$$

where A is the orthogonal matrix ($A'A = AA' = I$) whose columns are the eigenvectors (or characteristic vectors) of Ω and Λ is a diagonal matrix whose diagonal elements are the eigenvalues (or characteristic roots) of Ω. (See Exercise 2.6 for a statement and proof of this diagonalization theorem.) The required matrix is $P = A\Lambda^{-1/2}$ since

$$\begin{aligned} PP' &= A\Lambda^{-1/2}\Lambda^{-1/2}A' = A\Lambda^{-1}A' \\ &= A(A'\Omega A)^{-1}A' = AA'\Omega^{-1}AA' \\ &= \Omega^{-1}. \end{aligned}$$

Premultiplying both sides of $\mathbf{y} = X\boldsymbol{\beta} + \mathbf{e}$ by P' gives

$$P'\mathbf{y} = P'X\boldsymbol{\beta} + P'\mathbf{e},$$

$$\mathbf{y}^* = X^*\boldsymbol{\beta} + \mathbf{e}^*, \tag{2.5.4}$$

where

$$E\mathbf{e}^*\mathbf{e}^{*\prime} = EP'\mathbf{e}\mathbf{e}'P = \sigma^2 P'\Omega P = \sigma^2 I. \tag{2.5.5}$$

From the Gauss–Markov theorem (Theorem 2.3.1) the best linear unbiased estimator of $\boldsymbol{\beta}$ via the transformed model (2.5.4) is $\tilde{\boldsymbol{\beta}} = (X^{*\prime}X^*)^{-1}X^{*\prime}\mathbf{y}^* = (X'PP'X)^{-1}(P'X)'P'\mathbf{y} = (X'\Omega^{-1}X)^{-1}X'\Omega^{-1}\mathbf{y}$. □

In terms of the particular nonscalar error covariance matrix of (2.5.1) the transformation matrix P' is

$$P' = \begin{bmatrix} I_{T'} & 0 \\ 0 & \dfrac{1}{\sqrt{c}} I_{(T-T')} \end{bmatrix},$$

with

$$\Omega^{-1} = \begin{bmatrix} I_{T'} & 0 \\ 0 & \dfrac{1}{c} I_{(T-T')} \end{bmatrix}$$

and

$$\tilde{\boldsymbol{\beta}} = [(P'X)'(P'X)]^{-1}(P'X)'P'\mathbf{y} = (X'\Omega^{-1}X)^{-1}X'\Omega^{-1}\mathbf{y}.$$

Again a few remarks are appropriate. The generalized least squares estimator (sometimes called the Aitken estimator) derives its name from the fact that it minimizes the generalized sum of squares $(\mathbf{y} - X\boldsymbol{\beta})'\Omega^{-1}(\mathbf{y} - X\boldsymbol{\beta})$. The crux of the generalized least squares estimator is that $\sigma^2\Omega$ must be known up to a scalar multiple. For example, (2.5.1) is assumed known up to the scalar multiple σ^2. If, to the contrary, c were unknown, the Aitken theorem would not apply. The generalized least squares estimator would no longer be appropriate as it would depend upon unknown parameters; it would not be an estimator. The problem of unknown parameters in generalized least squares estimation will be addressed in Chapter 8.

2.6 Properties of the Ordinary Least Squares Estimators in the Context of the Generalized Least Squares Model

A comprehensive examination of error assumptions is typically a difficult task (Ramsey (1969)). This, plus the fact that ordinary least squares is more simple to apply than generalized least squares, means that in many cases ordinary least squares is mistakenly used in obtaining parameter estimates. It is important to know the properties of ordinary least squares estimators when they are based on mistaken assumptions about the covariance structure of the errors.

In particular, consider the generalized least squares model

$$\mathbf{y} = X\boldsymbol{\beta} + \mathbf{e},$$

where $E\mathbf{e}\mathbf{e}' = \sigma^2\Omega$ and Ω is a positive definite and symmetric matrix but *not* the identity matrix. Then the following results are available.

(i) The ordinary least squares estimator $\hat{\boldsymbol{\beta}} = (X'X)^{-1}X'\mathbf{y}$ is unbiased. If $\lim_{T\to\infty}(X'X/T)$ is finite and nonsingular and $\lim_{T\to\infty}(X'\Omega X/T)$ is finite, $\hat{\boldsymbol{\beta}}$ is consistent. These results follow from $E\hat{\boldsymbol{\beta}} = \boldsymbol{\beta} + E(X'X)^{-1}X'\mathbf{e} = \boldsymbol{\beta}$. Also

$$\text{plim}\ \hat{\boldsymbol{\beta}} = \boldsymbol{\beta} + \lim_{T\to\infty}\left(\frac{X'X}{T}\right)^{-1} \text{plim}\ \frac{X'\mathbf{e}}{T},$$

but $X'\mathbf{e}/T$ has zero mean and covariance matrix $\sigma^2(X'\Omega X/T^2)$. Given $\lim_{T\to\infty}(X'\Omega X/T)$ is finite and $\lim_{T\to\infty}(X'X/T)$ is finite and nonsingular, then $\text{plim}\ \hat{\boldsymbol{\beta}} = \boldsymbol{\beta}$.

(ii) The covariance matrix of $\hat{\boldsymbol{\beta}}$ is

$$\begin{aligned} E(\hat{\boldsymbol{\beta}} - \boldsymbol{\beta})(\hat{\boldsymbol{\beta}} - \boldsymbol{\beta})' &= E(X'X)^{-1}X'\mathbf{e}\mathbf{e}'X(X'X)^{-1} \\ &= \sigma^2(X'X)^{-1}X'\Omega X(X'X)^{-1}. \end{aligned}$$

Note that the covariance matrix of $\hat{\boldsymbol{\beta}}$ is no longer $\sigma^2(X'X)^{-1}$. The actual covariance matrix of $\hat{\boldsymbol{\beta}}$ may be *either* larger or smaller than the incorrect formula $\sigma^2(X'X)^{-1}$ since

$$(X'X)^{-1}X'\Omega X(X'X)^{-1} - (X'X)^{-1}$$

can be positive or negative semidefinite.

(iii) The usual estimator of σ^2, $\hat{\sigma}^2 = \hat{\mathbf{e}}'\hat{\mathbf{e}}/(T - K)$ is, in general, a biased and inconsistent estimator of σ^2 since

$$\begin{aligned} E(\hat{\mathbf{e}}'\hat{\mathbf{e}}) &= E\mathbf{e}'M\mathbf{e} \qquad (M = I - X(X'X)^{-1}X') \\ &= \operatorname{tr} EM\mathbf{e}\mathbf{e}' \\ &= \sigma^2 \operatorname{tr} M\Omega \neq \sigma^2(T - K) \end{aligned}$$

and

$$\operatorname{plim} \hat{\sigma}^2 = \sigma^2 \lim_{T\to\infty} \frac{1}{T} \operatorname{tr} M\Omega \neq \sigma^2.$$

Recall the appropriate estimator in this situation. Under the specified conditions, the best, linear, unbiased estimator of $\boldsymbol{\beta}$ is

$$\tilde{\boldsymbol{\beta}} = (X'\Omega^{-1}X)^{-1}X'\Omega^{-1}\mathbf{y}$$

which has covariance matrix $\sigma^2(X'\Omega^{-1}X)^{-1}$. An unbiased and consistent estimator of σ^2 is

$$\tilde{\sigma}^2 = \frac{\tilde{\mathbf{e}}'\Omega^{-1}\tilde{\mathbf{e}}}{T - K}, \qquad \text{where } \tilde{\mathbf{e}} = \mathbf{y} - X\tilde{\boldsymbol{\beta}}.$$

(iv) When ordinary least squares is mistakenly applied to a generalized least squares model, an estimator is generated which has variance at least as large as that of the appropriate generalized least squares estimator. This follows directly from Aitken's theorem.

Although unbiasedness and consistency in the estimation of $\boldsymbol{\beta}$ are retained when ordinary least squares is applied to a generalized least squares model, serious implications arise with respect to hypothesis testing. Importantly, incorrect use of ordinary least squares leads to invalid hypothesis testing because of biased and inconsistent estimation of the true ordinary least squares covariance matrix $\sigma^2(X'X)^{-1}X'\Omega X(X'X)^{-1}$ by $\hat{\sigma}^2(X'X)^{-1}$. From the developments in (ii) and (iii) above, the bias in using $\hat{\sigma}^2(X'X)^{-1}$ arises because $(X'X)^{-1}X'\Omega X(X'X)^{-1} \neq (X'X)^{-1}$ and $E\hat{\sigma}^2 \neq \sigma^2$. Incorrect statistical conclusions may likely occur. Goldberger (1964, pp. 239–243) and Johnston (1972, pp. 248–249) have investigated the direction of bias in ordinary least squares covariance estimators in particular (quite specialized) nonspherical cases. These results should serve as a warning to the unwitting user of ordinary least squares methods when generalized least squares methods are appropriate.

2.7 Summary and Guide to Further Readings

The major purpose of this chapter is to provide a review of the ordinary least squares and generalized least squares estimation methods. The Gauss–Markov and Aitken theorems (2.3.1 and 2.5.1) are central to the classical linear regression and generalized least squares models. Within the context of the classical linear regression model (Definition 2.2.1), the Gauss–Markov theorem establishes that the ordinary least squares estimator

$$\hat{\boldsymbol{\beta}} = (X'X)^{-1}X'\mathbf{y}$$

is the most efficient estimator among the class of unbiased estimators which are linear functions of the observation vector $\mathbf{y}$. The Aitken theorem establishes the same property for the generalized least squares estimator $\tilde{\boldsymbol{\beta}} = (X'\Omega^{-1}X)^{-1}X'\Omega^{-1}\mathbf{y}$ in the context of the generalized least squares model (Definition 2.5.1).

In analyzing the properties of the ordinary least squares estimator when the generalized least squares model is appropriate, we see that there are serious consequences when using the standard formula $\hat{\sigma}^2(X'X)^{-1}$. Since the true variance of the ordinary least squares estimator $\hat{\boldsymbol{\beta}}$ is

$$\sigma^2(X'X)^{-1}X'\Omega X(X'X)^{-1}$$

and $\hat{\sigma}^2(X'X)^{-1}$ is, in general, a biased and inconsistent estimator, statistical inferences derived by using $\hat{\sigma}^2(X'X)^{-1}$ are likely to be incorrect. It is important, therefore, to recognize when the generalized least squares model is appropriate and accordingly use the generalized least squares method rather than the ordinary least squares method.

The implications derived from Aitken's theorem are more instructive than they are practical. The difficulty with the application of the generalized least squares estimator is that the error covariance matrix Ω is usually unknown. Once Ω is estimated the properties of the generalized least squares estimator no longer hold. Then what are the properties of the (feasible) generalized least squares estimator $\hat{\tilde{\boldsymbol{\beta}}} = (X'\hat{\Omega}X)^{-1}X'\hat{\Omega}^{-1}\mathbf{y}$ that results when Ω is replaced by an estimate $\hat{\Omega}$? This question is addressed in Chapter 8. It is an extremely important question because not all economic models and data sources satisfy the conditions of the classical linear regression model. Both economic theory and the processes by which samples of data are generated often imply a generalized least squares error structure, e.g., autocorrelation, pooling time-series and cross-section data, simultaneous equations, etc.

We should note that the Gauss–Markov and Aitken theorems are important not only from the standpoint of estimating regression coefficients but also from the standpoint of prediction. Let X_* represent values of the explanatory variables for which "good" guesses of the dependent variable $\mathbf{y}_*$ are desired. The Gauss–Markov theorem guarantees that, if the classical linear regression model is appropriate, the ordinary least squares predictor

$\hat{y}_* = X_* \hat{\boldsymbol{\beta}}$ is the best, linear unbiased forecast of $\mathbf{y}_*$ (and also $E(\mathbf{y}_* | X_*)$). However, should the generalized least squares model be appropriate, the ordinary least squares predictor is no longer a best, linear, unbiased estimator. To illustrate, let y_{T+1} be a yet to be realized value of the dependent variable associated with the values of the explanatory variables, $\mathbf{x}'_{T+1}$. It is left as an exercise to show that the best, linear, unbiased predictor for the generalized least squares model is $\tilde{y}_{T+1} = \mathbf{x}'_{T+1}\tilde{\boldsymbol{\beta}} + (1/\sigma^2)\mathbf{w}'\Omega^{-1}\tilde{\mathbf{e}}$, where $\tilde{\boldsymbol{\beta}}$ is the generalized least squares estimator, $\tilde{\mathbf{e}} = (\mathbf{y} - X\tilde{\boldsymbol{\beta}})$, and $\mathbf{w} = E\mathbf{e}e_{T+1}$ (Exercise 2.8). Thus, the ordinary least squares predictor $\hat{y}_{T+1} = \mathbf{x}'_{T+1}\hat{\boldsymbol{\beta}}$ as well as the predictor $y_{T+1} = \mathbf{x}'_{T+1}\tilde{\boldsymbol{\beta}}$, though consistent, are inefficient.

Finally, let us note a few readings which are beyond the scope of our review. As Maeshiro (1980) has noted, even if Ω is known, Aitken's theorem does not apply when any of the regressors are stochastic. For example, this can occur when one of the explanatory variables is a lagged dependent variable y_{t-1}.

If it is *not* true that $Q = \lim_{T\to\infty}(X'X/T)$ is finite *and* nonsingular, the regressor matrix X is said to be *asymptotically uncooperative.* Extensive discussions of uncooperative regressors can be found in Dhrymes (1971, pp. 84–88), Theil (1971, pp. 365–366), and Schmidt (1976, pp. 86–88). One of the results of these investigations is that the presence of a time trend regressor (t) does not nullify the consistency of the ordinary least squares estimator.

2.8 Exercises

2.1. Theil (1971, p. 364) considers one form of uncooperative regressors called "extreme multicollinearity in the limit." Consider the regression $y_t = x_{t1}\beta_1 + x_{t2}\beta_2 + e_t$. Suppose that numbers c and T' exist such that $x_{t2} = cx_{t1}$ for all $t > T'$. Show that the matrix $\lim_{T\to\infty}(X'X/T)$ is singular in this case.

2.2. Consider the classical linear regression model $\mathbf{y} = X\boldsymbol{\beta} + \mathbf{e}$ except that one of the regressors is of the form $x_{ti} = \lambda^t$, $0 < \lambda < 1$. This regressor "vanishes" in that as $T \to \infty$, $x_{ti} \to 0$ with probability one. Show that the matrix $\lim_{T\to\infty}(X'X/T)$ is singular in this case.

2.3. Let v denote a scalar variable and $\mathbf{x}' = (x_1, x_2, \ldots, x_n)$ denote a $1 \times n$ vector of variables $x_1, x_2, \ldots, x_n$. Then vector differentiation of the scalar variable v with respect to the vector $\mathbf{x}$, mathematically denoted $\partial v/\partial \mathbf{x}$, is defined to be

$$\frac{\partial v}{\partial \mathbf{x}} = \left(\frac{\partial v}{\partial x_1}, \frac{\partial v}{\partial x_2}, \ldots, \frac{\partial v}{\partial x_n}\right)'.$$

With this definition prove that the following vector differentiation results hold:

(i) $\dfrac{\partial \mathbf{a}'\mathbf{x}}{\partial \mathbf{x}} = \mathbf{a}$,

(ii) $\dfrac{\partial \mathbf{x}'A\mathbf{x}}{\partial \mathbf{x}} = 2A\mathbf{x} = 2\mathbf{x}'A,$

where $\mathbf{a}' = (a_1, a_2, \ldots, a_n)$ is a $1 \times n$ vector of constants and $A = [a_{ij}]$ is a $n \times n$ symmetric matrix of constants.

2.4. Let $A = [a_{ij}]$ denote a $n \times n$ symmetric matrix of constants and $\mathbf{x}' = (x_1, x_2, \ldots, x_n)$ denote a $1 \times n$ vector of variables. Then

Definition. The quadratic form $\mathbf{x}'A\mathbf{x}$ is said to be positive definite iff $\mathbf{x}'A\mathbf{x} > 0$ for all $\mathbf{x} \neq 0$. Equivalently, the matrix A is said to be *positive definite.*

Definition. The quadratic form $\mathbf{x}'A\mathbf{x}$ is said to be *positive semidefinite* iff $\mathbf{x}'A\mathbf{x} \geq 0$ for all $\mathbf{x}$. Equivalently, the matrix A is said to be positive semidefinite.

Now prove the following proposition:

Proposition. *Let C denote a matrix of dimension $K \times T$. The matrix CC' is positive semidefinite.*

This proposition has important implications for the Gauss–Markov theorem (Theorem 2.3.1). It states that any linear combination $\mathbf{l}'\boldsymbol{\beta}$ is most efficiently estimated by ordinary least squares. That is, $\text{var}(\mathbf{l}'\boldsymbol{\beta}^*) - \text{var}(\mathbf{l}'\hat{\boldsymbol{\beta}}) = \mathbf{l}'(\sigma^2 CC')\mathbf{l} \geq 0$ since CC' is a positive semidefinite matrix. Appropriate selection of $\mathbf{l}$ confirms that $\text{var}\ \beta_i^* \geq \text{var}\ \hat{\beta}_i$ for all $i = 1, 2, \ldots, K$.

2.5. (Properties of the Trace Operator (tr)). The trace of a $n \times n$ square matrix $D = [d_{ij}]$ is defined to be $\text{tr}\ D \equiv d_{11} + d_{22} + \cdots + d_{nn}$, the sum of the diagonal elements of D. Using this definition, prove the following properties associated with the trace operator:
(i) $\text{tr}\ AB = \text{tr BA}$,
(ii) $\text{tr}(C + D) = \text{tr}\ C + \text{tr}\ D$,
where A is a $m \times n$ matrix, B is a $n \times m$ matrix, and C and D are $n \times n$ matrices.

2.6. (Diagonalization of a Symmetric Matrix.) The major proposition for this problem is

Proposition. *Let S denote a $n \times n$ symmetric matrix. Then there exists an orthogonal matrix A such that $A'SA = \Lambda$, where Λ is a diagonal matrix having the characteristic roots of S along the diagonal and the columns of A are the characteristic vectors of S.*

This proposition is proved by a sequence of lemmas, but first the following definitions are necessary.

Definition. A *characteristic vector* of S is a unit length vector ($\mathbf{x}'\mathbf{x} = 1$) which, given the linear transformation S, maps onto a scalar multiple of itself. That is, $\mathbf{x}$ is a characteristic vector of S if

$$S\mathbf{x} = \lambda\mathbf{x}.$$

Definition. The scalar λ in the above definition is the *characteristic root* associated with $\mathbf{x}$. Likewise, since $(S - \lambda I)\mathbf{x} = \mathbf{0}$, therefore $|S - \lambda I| = 0$ which is called the *characteristic equation* of the matrix S. This equation is an nth degree polynomial in λ. The zeros of this polynomial are the characteristic roots of the matrix S.

The following sequence of lemmas will provide a means for proving the above proposition. The reader is asked to prove each lemma in turn and then proceed to complete the proof of the proposition.

Lemma. *The characteristic vectors of S are orthogonal if they correspond to distinct characteristic roots.*

(Hint: Let **x** and **y** be characteristic vectors with distinct roots λ_1 and λ_2. Construct

$$\mathbf{y}'S\mathbf{x} - \mathbf{x}'S\mathbf{y} = (\lambda_1 - \lambda_2)\mathbf{x}'\mathbf{y}.$$

Show that since S is symmetric $\mathbf{x}'S\mathbf{y} = \mathbf{y}'S\mathbf{x}$. Then conclude.) From this point forward we will consider only the case where the characteristic roots of S are distinct. For the nondistinct case consult Rao (1973, p. 39).

Lemma. *Let* $\mathbf{x}_1, \mathbf{x}_2, \ldots, \mathbf{x}_n$ *denote the n characteristic vectors associated with the n distinct characteristic roots* $\lambda_1, \lambda_2, \ldots, \lambda_n$ *of the symmetric matrix S. Arrange the characteristic vectors as* $A = [\mathbf{x}_1, \mathbf{x}_2, \ldots, \mathbf{x}_n]$. *Then*

$$SA = A\Lambda,$$

where $\Lambda = \text{diag}\{\lambda_1, \lambda_2, \ldots, \lambda_n\}$ *is the diagonal matrix containing the characteristic roots of S.*

Now use the orthogonality property of A to obtain the desired result.

2.7. Let E be a $n \times n$ nonsingular matrix partitioned as

$$E = \begin{bmatrix} A & B \\ C & D \end{bmatrix},$$

where A is $n_1 \times n_1$, B is $n_1 \times n_2$, C is $n_2 \times n_1$, and D is $n_2 \times n_2$, and $n = n_1 + n_2$ suppose that A and $F = D - CA^{-1}B$ are nonsingular. Then

$$E^{-1} = \begin{bmatrix} A^{-1}(I + BF^{-1}CA^{-1}) & -A^{-1}BF^{-1} \\ -F^{-1}CA^{-1} & F^{-1} \end{bmatrix}.$$

This is called the *partitioned inverse* rule. Prove this directly by using partitioned matrix multiplication to show that $EE^{-1} = I$.

2.8. The purpose of this exercise is to show that, as discussed in the summary (Section 2.7), the best, linear, unbiased predictor of y_{T+1} in the generalized least squares model is $\tilde{y}_{T+1} = \mathbf{x}'_{T+1}\tilde{\boldsymbol{\beta}} + (1/\sigma^2)\mathbf{w}'\Omega^{-1}\tilde{\mathbf{e}}$. Given the assumptions of the generalized least squares model define a linear predictor $y^*_{T+1} = \mathbf{l}'\mathbf{y}$, where $\mathbf{l}$ is a $T \times 1$ vector of constants. If y^*_{T+1} is to be best, linear, unbiased, $\mathbf{l}$ must be chosen to minimize the prediction variance

$$\sigma^2_{y^*_{T+1}} = E(y^*_{T+1} - y_{T+1})^2$$

subject to the unbiasedness condition $E(y^*_{T+1} - y_{T+1}) = 0$.

(a) Show that the prediction error is

$$y^*_{T+1} - y_{T+1} = (\mathbf{l}'X - \mathbf{x}'_{T+1})\boldsymbol{\beta} + \mathbf{l}'\mathbf{e} - e_{T+1}.$$

(b) Show that under the unbiasedness condition $\mathbf{l}'$ must satisfy

$$\mathbf{l}'X - \mathbf{x}'_{T+1} = \mathbf{0}'.$$

(c) Given (b) show that the prediction error becomes

$$y_{T+1}^* - y_{T+1} = \mathbf{l}'\mathbf{e} - e_{T+1}.$$

(d) Based on (c) find the prediction variance.

(e) Minimize the prediction variance with respect to $\mathbf{l}$ subject to the unbiasedness condition in (b). The Lagrangian expression is

$$L = \mathbf{l}'\sigma^2\Omega\mathbf{l} - 2\mathbf{l}'(E\mathbf{e}e_{T+1}) + \sigma_{T+1}^2 - 2(\mathbf{l}'X - \mathbf{x}_{T+1}')\boldsymbol{\lambda},$$

where var $e_{T+1} = \sigma_{T+1}^2$ and $\boldsymbol{\lambda}$ is a $K \times 1$ vector of Lagrangian multipliers. (Hint: use the result in Exercise 2.7.)

(f) Verify the second-order conditions.

2.9. In Chapter 10, a generalized least squares error structure of the form

$$\frac{\sigma_u^2}{1-\rho^2}\begin{bmatrix} 1 & \rho & \cdots & \rho^{T-1} \\ \rho & 1 & & \vdots \\ \vdots & \vdots & \ddots & \rho \\ \rho^{T-1} & \rho^{T-2} & \rho & 1 \end{bmatrix} = \sigma_u^2\Omega,$$

where $-1 < \rho < 1$, will be examined. Specifically, the errors follow the rule $e_t = \rho e_{t-1} + u_t$, where the u_t are independent and identically distributed with zero mean and variance σ_u^2. This error structure is called the first-order autoregressive error process and is denoted AR(1). Using the fact that

$$\Omega^{-1} = \begin{bmatrix} 1 & -\rho & & & 0 \\ -\rho & (1+\rho^2) & -\rho & & \\ & -\rho & (1+\rho^2) & \ddots & \\ & & \ddots & \ddots & -\rho \\ 0 & & & -\rho & 1 \end{bmatrix}$$

derive the best, linear, unbiased predictor $\tilde{y}_{T+1}$ using the results of the previous exercise.

2.10. The covariance matrix of the ordinary least squares estimator $\hat{\boldsymbol{\beta}}$ is $\sigma^2(X'X)^{-1}$. The The covariance matrix of any other linear and unbiased estimator $\boldsymbol{\beta}^*$ has been shown by Theorem 2.3.1 to be equal to $\sigma^2(X'X)^{-1} + D$, where D is a positive semidefinite matrix. Show that this implies

$$\text{tr var}(\boldsymbol{\beta}^*) \geq \text{tr var}(\hat{\boldsymbol{\beta}})$$

and

$$|\text{var}(\boldsymbol{\beta}^*)| \geq |\text{var}(\hat{\boldsymbol{\beta}})|.$$

Discuss the interpretations of these variance measures as compared to the individual diagonal elements of $\sigma^2(X'X)^{-1}$.

2.11. The results presented in this chapter are general in that they hold for any design matrices X that fulfill the stated assumptions. Usually, however, regression models contain an intercept or constant term. It is customary to assign $x_{t1} = 1$ for all t so that β_1 is the intercept of the model. When this is true some additional results can be proven. Show that

(a) If one of the explanatory variables is constant, the sum of the least squares residuals, $\hat{\mathbf{e}} = \mathbf{y} - X\hat{\boldsymbol{\beta}}$, is zero.

(b) Define

$$\text{SSE} = \hat{\mathbf{e}}'\hat{\mathbf{e}}, \qquad \text{SSR} = \sum_{t=1}^{T} (\hat{y}_t - \bar{y})^2, \qquad \text{SST} = \sum_{t=1}^{T} (y_t - \bar{y})^2,$$

where $\bar{y} = \sum_{t=1}^{T} (y_t/T)$. Show that if one of the explanatory variables is a constant term then

$$\text{SST} = \text{SSR} + \text{SSE}.$$

(Hint: $\text{SST} = \mathbf{y}'\mathbf{y} - T\bar{y}^2$, $\mathbf{y}'\mathbf{y} = \hat{\mathbf{y}}'\hat{\mathbf{y}}$, then show that $\text{SSR} = \hat{\mathbf{y}}'\hat{\mathbf{y}} - T\bar{y}^2$.)

(c) The coefficient of multiple determination is *defined* as

$$R^2 = 1 - \frac{\text{SSE}}{\text{SST}}.$$

It measures the goodness of fit of the regression model. If the model contains a constant term show that:

(i) $0 \leq R^2 \leq 1$.
(ii) $R^2 = \text{SSR}/\text{SST}$.
(iii) $\sqrt{R^2}$ is the sample correlation coefficient between y_t and $\hat{y}_t$.

(d) Do the above results hold for the generalized least squares model?

2.9 References

Aitken, A. C. (1935). On least squares and linear combinations of observations. *Proceedings of the Royal Society*, Edinburgh, **55**, 42–48.

Dhrymes, P. (1971). *Distributed Lags: Problems of Estimation and Formulation*. San Francisco: Holden-Day.

Dhrymes, P. J. (1974). *Econometrics: Statistical Foundations and Applications*. New York: Springer-Verlag.

Gauss, K. F. (1821–23), *Theoria Combinationis Observationum Erroribus Minimis Obnoxiae*. French translation by J. Bertrand under title *Methode des moindres corres*. Paris: Mallet-Bachelier (1855).

Goldberger, A. (1964). *Econometric Theory*. New York: Wiley.

Johnston, J. (1972). *Econometric Methods*. New York: McGraw-Hill.

Maeshiro, A. (1980). Small sample properties of estimators of distributed lag models. *International Economic Review*, **21**, 721–733.

Markov, A. A. (1900). *Wahrscheinlichkeitsrechnung*. Leipzig: Tuebner.

Ramsey, J. B. (1969). Tests for specification errors in classical linear least squares regression analysis. *Journal of Royal Statistical Society*, B, **31**, 350–371.

Rao, C. R. (1973). *Linear Statistical Inference and Its Applications*, 2nd ed. New York: Wiley.

Schmidt, P. (1976). *Econometrics*. New York: Marcel Dekker.

Theil, H. (1971). *Principles of Econometrics*. New York: Wiley.

Wilks, S. S. (1962). *Mathematical Statistics*. New York: Wiley.

CHAPTER 3

Point Estimation and Tests of Hypotheses in Small Samples

3.1 Introduction

The ordinary least squares and generalized least squares results reviewed in Chapter 2 dealt with the efficiency of estimation methods in the classical linear regression model and the generalized least squares model. However, small sample statistical inference based on these estimators requires stronger distributional assumptions on the error terms than those made in the previous chapter. In this chapter the distributional properties of the error terms in the classical linear regression model are assumed but, in addition, the error terms are assumed to be normally distributed. This "revised" model is called the classical *normal* linear regression model. It permits maximum likelihood estimation of the parameters and the construction of likelihood ratio tests of hypotheses.

The outline of this chapter is as follows: In Section 3.2 we introduce the method of maximum likelihood estimation and then apply it to the problem of estimating $\boldsymbol{\beta}$ and σ^2 in the classical normal linear regression model. In Section 3.3 we develop a new efficiency concept, minimum variance unbiased, and describe in detail one method, the Cramér–Rao approach, for determining if candidate estimators attain this efficiency. An alternative method for determining minimum variance unbiased efficiency, the sufficient statistics approach, is also described but not in detail. The Cramér–Rao approach is used to examine the minimum variance unbiased efficiency of the ordinary least squares estimators $\hat{\boldsymbol{\beta}}$ and $\hat{\sigma}^2$. In Section 3.4 the likelihood ratio test method is introduced and applied to generate a test statistic for general linear hypotheses in the classical normal linear regression model. The concept of confidence intervals is introduced in Section 3.5 and a distinction is drawn between separate and joint tests of hypotheses. Finally, a summary of the chapter's results and a guide to further readings are contained in Section 3.6.

3.2 Maximum Likelihood Estimation

This section reviews the maximum likelihood method of point estimation. Let us start by defining the *likelihood function*.

Definition 3.2.1. Let x_t, $t = 1, 2, \ldots, T$, denote a random sample from a population characterized by the probability density function $f(x_t; \boldsymbol{\theta})$. The joint density of the random sample is called the *likelihood function* of the observations and can be written

$$L(\mathbf{x}; \boldsymbol{\theta}) = \prod_{t=1}^{T} f(x_t; \boldsymbol{\theta}).$$

The likelihood function possesses all of the properties of a joint probability density function. For example, $L(\mathbf{x}; \boldsymbol{\theta})$ integrates to one over the domain of $x_1, x_2, \ldots, x_T$, $\int L(\mathbf{x}; \boldsymbol{\theta})\, d\mathbf{x} = 1$. However, there are instances when it is useful to interpret the likelihood function in a different way. Suppose that the sample has already been drawn. Given this sample data, the value of the likelihood function depends on the parameter vector $\boldsymbol{\theta}$. Let $\tilde{\boldsymbol{\theta}}(x_1, \ldots, x_T)$ denote the vector function which maximizes the value of the likelihood function. That is,

$$L(\mathbf{x}; \tilde{\boldsymbol{\theta}}) \geq L(\mathbf{x}; \boldsymbol{\theta}^*), \tag{3.2.1}$$

where $\boldsymbol{\theta}^*$ is any other estimate of $\boldsymbol{\theta}$. The intuitive notion behind the maximum likelihood method of obtaining point estimators is that a parameter estimate that implies the largest probability of the sample drawn is more preferred than a parameter estimate that declares the sample less probable. Before the sample is drawn, the x's are random and hence $\tilde{\boldsymbol{\theta}}(x_1, \ldots, x_T)$ is also random. Thus, the solution to (3.2.1) is the maximum likelihood estimator.

Example 3.2.1. Let $x_1, \ldots, x_T$ be a random sample drawn from an $N(\mu, 1)$ population, that is,

$$f(x_t; \mu) = \frac{1}{(2\pi)^{1/2}} e^{-(x_t - \mu)^2/2}.$$

The joint density is

$$\begin{aligned} f(x_1, x_2, \ldots, x_T; \mu) = f(x_1; \mu) \cdots f(x_T; \mu) &= \frac{1}{(2\pi)^{T/2}} e^{-\Sigma (x_t - \mu)^2/2} \\ &= L(\mathbf{x}; \mu). \end{aligned}$$

Let $L^* = \ln L(\cdot)$. Since extrema are retained over the natural logarithmic transformation, $L(\cdot)$ attains its maximum at the maximum of L^* which is easier to work with. Now

$$L^* = -T/2 \ln(2\pi) - \sum (x_t - \mu)^2/2$$

and the first-order condition for a maximum with respect to the unknown parameter μ is

$$\frac{\partial L^*}{\partial \mu} = \sum (x_t - \mu) = 0,$$

which yields the maximum likelihood estimator $\tilde{\mu} = \sum x_t/T = \bar{x}$. That $\tilde{\mu}$ does indeed maximize L^*, and thus L, may be verified by noting that $(\partial^2 L^*)/(\partial \mu^2) = -T < 0$. The maximum likelihood estimator of the mean of a $N(\mu, 1)$ population is $\bar{x}$, the sample mean. Exercises 3.1 through 3.4 contain additional applications of the maximum likelihood method for finding parameter estimates.

Now consider applying the method of maximum likelihood to the linear statistical model when it is assumed that the error term follows a multivariate normal distribution. The model under consideration is explicitly defined by Definition 3.2.2.

Definition 3.2.2. The *classical normal linear regression model* satisfies the assumptions of the classical linear regression model defined in Definition 2.2.1 but in addition $\mathbf{e} \sim N(\mathbf{0}, \sigma^2 I)$.

The symbol "$\sim$" should read "is distributed as."

Major results for estimators of the parameters for the classical normal linear regression model are summarized by Theorem 3.2.1.

Theorem 3.2.1. *Let the assumptions of the classical normal linear regression model hold. The maximum likelihood estimators of* $\boldsymbol{\beta}$ *and* σ^2, $\tilde{\boldsymbol{\beta}}$ *and* $\tilde{\sigma}$, *respectively, have the following properties*:

(i) $\tilde{\boldsymbol{\beta}} \sim N(\boldsymbol{\beta}, \sigma^2(X'X)^{-1})$, *where* $\tilde{\boldsymbol{\beta}} = \hat{\boldsymbol{\beta}} = (X'X)^{-1}X'\mathbf{y}$,
(ii) $T\tilde{\sigma}/\sigma^2 = (T - K)\hat{\sigma}^2/\sigma^2 \sim \chi^2_{T-K}$, *where* $\tilde{\sigma}^2 = (T - K)\hat{\sigma}^2/T$,
(iii) $\tilde{\boldsymbol{\beta}}$ *and* $\tilde{\sigma}^2$ *(and hence* $\hat{\sigma}^2 = T\tilde{\sigma}^2/(T - K) = \hat{\mathbf{e}}'\hat{\mathbf{e}}/(T - K)$*) are mutually independent.*

Proof. The likelihood function of $\mathbf{e}$ is obtained by noting that its elements are independently distributed with identical $N(0, \sigma^2)$ distributions. The joint density of all T elements is just the product of T normal density functions with zero mean and variance σ^2 and given by

$$f(e_1, \ldots, e_T) = \prod_{t=1}^{T} \frac{1}{(2\pi\sigma^2)^{1/2}} \exp\left\{-\frac{1}{2}\left(\frac{e_t}{\sigma}\right)^2\right\}$$
$$= \frac{1}{(2\pi\sigma^2)^{T/2}} \exp\left\{-\frac{1}{2}\frac{\sum_{t=1}^{T} e_t^2}{\sigma^2}\right\}.$$

Making the change of variable to $e_t = y_t - \mathbf{x}_t'\boldsymbol{\beta}$, and noting that the absolute value of the Jacobian determinant is unity, it follows that the density for $(y_1, y_2, \ldots, y_T)$ is

$$g(y_1, y_2, \ldots, y_T) = \frac{1}{(2\pi\sigma^2)^{T/2}} \exp\left\{-\frac{1}{2}\frac{\sum (y_t - \mathbf{x}_t'\boldsymbol{\beta})^2}{\sigma^2}\right\}$$
$$= \frac{1}{(2\pi\sigma^2)^{T/2}} \exp\left\{-\frac{1}{2}\frac{(\mathbf{y} - X\boldsymbol{\beta})'(\mathbf{y} - X\boldsymbol{\beta})}{\sigma^2}\right\}.$$

(The Jacobian technique is used in mathematical statistics to derive the probability density function of transformations of random variables. Let $f(\mathbf{e})$ denote the probability density function of $\mathbf{e}$ and $g(\mathbf{y})$ the probability density function of $\mathbf{y}$. It can be shown that, under general conditions, $g(\mathbf{y}) = f(e^{-1}(\mathbf{y}))$ abs(J) where $e^{-1}(\mathbf{y})$ represents the inverse function of $\mathbf{e}$ and and abs(J) denotes the absolute value of the Jacobian, J. In turn, J is defined as the determinant of the matrix G where the (i, j)th element of G is $G_{ij} = \partial e_i/\partial y_j$. See, for example, Hogg and Craig (1970) for further elaboration.) The log likelihood is then

$$L^* = \ln L(\mathbf{y}, X; \boldsymbol{\beta}, \sigma^2) = -\frac{T}{2}\ln(2\pi) - \frac{T}{2}\ln\sigma^2 - \frac{1}{2}\frac{(\mathbf{y} - X\boldsymbol{\beta})'(\mathbf{y} - X\boldsymbol{\beta})}{\sigma^2}.$$

First-order conditions for a maximum are

$$\frac{\partial L^*(\cdot)}{\partial \boldsymbol{\beta}} = -\frac{1}{\tilde{\sigma}^2}(-X'\mathbf{y} + X'X\tilde{\boldsymbol{\beta}}) = \mathbf{0}, \tag{3.2.2}$$

$$\frac{\partial L^*(\cdot)}{\partial \sigma^2} = -\frac{T}{2\tilde{\sigma}^2} + \frac{1}{2\tilde{\sigma}^4}(\mathbf{y} - X\tilde{\boldsymbol{\beta}})'(\mathbf{y} - X\tilde{\boldsymbol{\beta}}) = 0. \tag{3.2.3}$$

Solving these $K + 1$ equations (3.2.2) and (3.2.3) for the $K + 1$ unknowns $\tilde{\boldsymbol{\beta}}$ and $\tilde{\sigma}^2$ yields

$$\tilde{\boldsymbol{\beta}} = (X'X)^{-1}X'\mathbf{y} \quad \text{and} \quad \tilde{\sigma}^2 = \frac{\hat{\mathbf{e}}'\hat{\mathbf{e}}}{T} = \frac{T-K}{T}\hat{\sigma}^2.$$

The second-order conditions for a maximum will be fulfilled if the matrix of second-order derivatives is negative definite at the point satisfying the first-order conditions. This condition is satisfied (see Exercise 3.5) and thus $\tilde{\boldsymbol{\beta}}$ and $\tilde{\sigma}^2$ are the maximum likelihood estimators.

For the distribution of $\tilde{\boldsymbol{\beta}}$ note that $\tilde{\boldsymbol{\beta}} = \boldsymbol{\beta} + (X'X)^{-1}X'\mathbf{e}$. We have already determined that $\tilde{\boldsymbol{\beta}}$ has mean $\boldsymbol{\beta}$ and covariance matrix $\sigma^2(X'X)^{-1}$ in the previous chapter. Since $\tilde{\boldsymbol{\beta}}$ is a linear combination of variables which have a multivariate normal distribution, it too has a normal distribution. □

In order to obtain the distribution of the maximum likelihood estimator of the variance the following lemma is useful:

Lemma 3.2.1. *If M is a symmetric, idempotent matrix of dimension $T \times T$ and $\mathbf{x} \sim N(\mathbf{0}, \sigma^2 I)$ then the quadratic form*

$$\frac{\mathbf{x}'M\mathbf{x}}{\sigma^2}$$

is distributed as χ^2 with $\operatorname{tr} M = m$ degrees of freedom.

PROOF. Since M is symmetric, there exists an orthogonal matrix A such that $A'MA = \Lambda$, where Λ is the diagonal matrix of eigenvalues of M (see Exercise 2.6). Since M is idempotent, $\operatorname{tr} M = m$ eigenvalues equal one and $(T - m)$ eigenvalues equal zero (see Exercise 3.6). That is, with appropriate re-ordering,

$$A'MA = \begin{bmatrix} I_m & 0 \\ 0 & 0 \end{bmatrix}.$$

Now define a new vector $\mathbf{v} = A'\mathbf{x}$, which has mean vector $E\mathbf{v} = \mathbf{0}$ and covariance matrix

$$E\mathbf{v}\mathbf{v}' = A'E\mathbf{x}\mathbf{x}'A = A'\sigma^2 IA = \sigma^2 A'A = \sigma^2 I,$$

since A is orthogonal. Then,

$$\frac{\mathbf{x}'M\mathbf{x}}{\sigma^2} = \frac{\mathbf{v}'\Lambda\mathbf{v}}{\sigma^2} = \frac{1}{\sigma^2}\mathbf{v}'\begin{bmatrix} I_m & 0 \\ 0 & 0 \end{bmatrix}\mathbf{v} = \frac{1}{\sigma^2}\sum_{i=1}^{m} v_i^2 = \sum_{i=1}^{m}\left(\frac{v_i}{\sigma}\right)^2.$$

Thus $\mathbf{x}'M\mathbf{x}/\sigma^2$ can be expressed as the sum of squares of m independent $N(0, 1)$ variables, and it has a χ^2-distribution with m degrees of freedom. □

Since

$$T\tilde{\sigma}^2/\sigma^2 = (T - K)\hat{\sigma}/\sigma^2 = \hat{\mathbf{e}}'\hat{\mathbf{e}}/\sigma^2 = \mathbf{e}'M\mathbf{e}/\sigma^2,$$

where $M = I - X(X'X)^{-1}X'$ is a symmetric idempotent matrix of rank $T - K = \operatorname{tr} M$, it follows immediately from Lemma 3.2.1 that $T\tilde{\sigma}^2/\sigma^2 = (T - K)\hat{\sigma}^2/\sigma^2$ has a χ^2-distribution with $(T - K)$ degrees of freedom. Hence $\hat{\sigma}^2$ has mean σ^2 and variance $2\sigma^4/(T - K)$, using properties of the χ^2-distribution.

Finally, to prove that $\tilde{\boldsymbol{\beta}}$ and $\tilde{\sigma}^2$ are statistically independent the following lemma is used:

Lemma 3.2.2. *Let M be defined as in Lemma 3.2.1 and B be a $m^* \times T$ matrix such that $BM = 0$. Assume $\mathbf{x} \sim N(\mathbf{0}, \sigma^2 I)$, then the linear form $B\mathbf{x}$ and the quadratic form $\mathbf{x}'M\mathbf{x}$ are distributed independently.*

PROOF. Let A be an orthogonal matrix such that $A'MA = \Lambda = \begin{bmatrix} I_m & 0 \\ 0 & 0 \end{bmatrix}$. Again define $\mathbf{v} = A'\mathbf{x}$ and partition $\mathbf{v}$ so that $\mathbf{v}_1$ and $\mathbf{v}_2$ are of dimensions m and $m^*(m + m^* = T)$, respectively. Note from Lemma 3.2.1 that

$$\mathbf{x}'M\mathbf{x} = \mathbf{v}'\begin{bmatrix} I_m & 0 \\ 0 & 0 \end{bmatrix}\mathbf{v} = \mathbf{v}_1'\mathbf{v}_1.$$

Now let $BA = D$ and partition D to correspond to the partitioning of $\mathbf{v}$, i.e., $D = [D_1 \vdots D_2]$ with D_1 and D_2 of dimension $m^* \times m$ and $m^* \times m^*$. Note that $D(A'MA) = BA(A'MA) = BMA = 0$, since it was assumed that $BM = 0$. Therefore,

$$D(A'MA) = [D_1 \vdots D_2]\begin{bmatrix} I_m & 0 \\ 0 & 0 \end{bmatrix} = 0,$$

which shows that $D_1 = 0$ and $BA = D = (0 \vdots D_2)$. Also

$$B\mathbf{x} = BAA'\mathbf{x} = D\mathbf{v} = D_2\mathbf{v}_2.$$

Now since $B\mathbf{x}$ is defined in terms of $\mathbf{v}_2$ and $\mathbf{x}'M\mathbf{x}$ in terms of $\mathbf{v}_1$, and $\mathbf{v}_1$ and $\mathbf{v}_2$ are independent, it follows that $B\mathbf{x}$ and $\mathbf{x}'M\mathbf{x}$ must also be independent. □

Now recall that

$$\tilde{\sigma}^2 = \mathbf{e}'M\mathbf{e}/T \quad \text{and} \quad \tilde{\boldsymbol{\beta}} - \boldsymbol{\beta} = (X'X)^{-1}X'\mathbf{e}, \quad \text{where } M = I - X(X'X)^{-1}X'.$$

Noting that $(X'X)^{-1}X'$ is a $K \times T$ matrix and that $(X'X)^{-1}X'M = 0$ and applying Lemma 3.2.2, we conclude that $\tilde{\boldsymbol{\beta}}$ and $\tilde{\sigma}^2$ are independently distributed random variables. This completes the proof of Theorem 3.2.1. □

The distributional properties derived in Theorem 3.2.1 provide a basis for deriving the sampling distributions of statistics used in testing general linear hypotheses in the classical normal linear regression model. Before we discuss tests of hypotheses, however, let us examine a new type of estimation efficiency.

3.3 Small Sample Estimation Theory

In the absence of any assumption about the parametric form (e.g., normal, uniform, etc.) of the distribution of $\mathbf{e}$, the derivation of an efficient class of unbiased estimators via the Gauss–Markov theorem requires the estimator to be linear, $\boldsymbol{\beta}^* = H\mathbf{y}$. The stringent linearity assumption is, in a sense, compensation for the lack of knowledge concerning the specific form of the distribution of the error term. In the presence of more explicit information, the linearity requirement can be dropped.

Thanks to work by such mathematical statisticians as Cramér, Rao, Blackwell, Fisher, Neyman, Lehmann, and Scheffé, *small sample efficiency* among unbiased estimators can be straightforwardly determined in the presence of information concerning the parent distribution of the random variable(s) under investigation. This is a powerful method. By small sample efficiency we mean that for *any given finite sample size T* (assuming sufficient degrees of freedom exist), an estimator search can be conducted which may provide an unbiased estimator that has smaller variance than any other estimator, linear or nonlinear. These estimators are called minimum variance unbiased estimators. Note that the term efficiency in this context refers to minimum variance unbiased rather than best linear unbiased. Small sample efficiency is to be contrasted with *large sample efficiency* studied in the next chapter where desirable properties of estimators are attained only as the sample size T becomes arbitrarily large.

There are two distinct methods for determining if an unbiased estimator possesses the minimum variance unbiased property; use of the Cramér–Rao lower bound or the statistical properties of completeness and sufficiency. The method of primary interest here is the Cramér–Rao lower bound as it will play a prominent role in our discussion of asymptotic sampling properties in the next chapter. A brief discussion of the completeness–sufficiency method appears at the end of this section for the purpose of comparing the two methods. After this discussion, the minimum variance unbiased efficiency of the ordinary least squares estimators $\hat{\boldsymbol{\beta}}$ and $\hat{\sigma}^2$ in the linear model is investigated using the Cramér–Rao approach.

3.3.1 Minimum Variance Unbiased Through Cramér–Rao Lower Bound Approach

The Cramér–Rao approach to determining the minimum variance unbiased efficiency of an estimator is straightforward. First, the density function of the random variable under investigation must be determined to be *regular*. That is, does the postulated density permit the use of the Cramér–Rao approach? Second, if the density is regular, a lower bound variance is determined, hereinafter called the Cramér–Rao lower bound. The variance of an unbiased estimator is then compared with the Cramér–Rao lower bound variance. If the estimator's variance equals the lower bound then it is minimum variance unbiased efficient; if not, the conclusion on the estimator's efficiency is indeterminate. In the indeterminate case, judgment has to be reserved until either another estimator is found to have a smaller variance than the present estimator or the completeness–sufficiency approach, to be discussed subsequently, is used to determine a conclusive outcome.

Before we state the famous Cramér–Rao result, let us define what it means for a density function to be regular.

Definition 3.3.1. The density function $f(x_t; \boldsymbol{\theta})$ is *regular* if the following conditions hold:

(i) The range of the random variable x_t is independent of the parameter vector $\boldsymbol{\theta}$.
(ii) The density $f(x_t; \boldsymbol{\theta})$ possesses derivatives of the first and second order with respect to $\boldsymbol{\theta}$ and these derivatives are bounded by integrable functions of x. (That is, $\partial f(x_t; \boldsymbol{\theta})/\partial\theta_i$, $\partial f(x_t; \boldsymbol{\theta})/\partial\theta_i \partial\theta_j$, and $\partial f(x_t; \boldsymbol{\theta})/\partial^2\theta_i$ exist for all i and j and, for example, $|\partial f/\partial\theta_i| \le M_i(x)$ and $E[M_i(x)] < A$ for some constant A and some function $M_i(x)$.)

These conditions are the regularity conditions for the Cramér–Rao theorem. These regularity conditions are sufficient conditions for the integral differention results in the proof (see Section 3.7). Regularity for the Cramér–Rao theorem is sometimes stated in an alternative but equivalent form. A density is said to be regular (with respect to its first derivative) if

$$E\left[\frac{\partial \ln L(\mathbf{x}; \boldsymbol{\theta})}{\partial\theta_i}\right] = \int \frac{\partial \ln L(\mathbf{x}; \boldsymbol{\theta})}{\partial\theta_i} L(\mathbf{x}; \boldsymbol{\theta})\, d\mathbf{x} = 0 \quad \text{for all } i = 1, 2, \ldots, K.$$

In practice this latter definition may be somewhat easier to check.

Now to formally state the Cramér–Rao theorem:

Theorem 3.3.1. (Cramér–Rao). *Let $x_1, x_2, \ldots, x_T$ be a random sample from the regular density $f(x_t; \boldsymbol{\theta})$. Let the likelihood function be*

$$L(\mathbf{x}; \boldsymbol{\theta}) = \prod_{t=1}^{T} f(x_t; \boldsymbol{\theta}).$$

Define the information matrix *for the random sample $\mathbf{x}' = (x_1, x_2, \ldots, x_T)$ to be*

$$I(\boldsymbol{\theta}) = -E\left[\frac{\partial^2 \ln L(\mathbf{x}; \boldsymbol{\theta})}{\partial\boldsymbol{\theta}\, \partial\boldsymbol{\theta}'}\right],$$

i.e., the ijth *element of the information matrix is*

$$I_{ij} = -E\left[\frac{\partial^2 \ln L(\mathbf{x}; \boldsymbol{\theta})}{\partial\theta_i\, \partial\theta_j}\right], \qquad i, j = 1, 2, \ldots, K.$$

Let $\hat{\boldsymbol{\theta}}$ be any unbiased estimator of $\boldsymbol{\theta}$ with covariance matrix Σ. Then the matrix $\Sigma - [I(\boldsymbol{\theta})]^{-1}$ is positive semidefinite. ($[I(\boldsymbol{\theta})]^{-1}$ is known as the Cramér–Rao lower bound matrix.)

A proof of this theorem is reserved for the appendix of this chapter (Section 3.7). The remarkable result of the Cramér–Rao theorem is that the lower bound for the variance at *any* unbiased estimator of the parameters of a regular density is $[I(\boldsymbol{\theta})]^{-1}$, *regardless of the estimation technique used to derive it*. The Cramér–Rao theorem provides a means for determining the efficiency of an unbiased estimator $\tilde{\boldsymbol{\theta}}$. If the covariance matrix of $\tilde{\boldsymbol{\theta}}$ attains the lower bound $[I(\boldsymbol{\theta})]^{-1}$, then $\tilde{\boldsymbol{\theta}}$ is minimum variance unbiased. In contrast, if the lower bound is not attained the conclusion is indeterminate. These concepts are illustrated by examining the minimum variance unbiased efficiency of the ordinary least squares estimators $\hat{\boldsymbol{\beta}}$ and $\hat{\sigma}^2$. For the interested reader, Exercises 3.7–3.10 contain other examples where the Cramér–Rao approach is useful in determining minimum variance unbiased efficiency.

3.3.2 Small Sample Efficiency of $\hat{\boldsymbol{\beta}}$ and $\hat{\sigma}^2$

The method of the previous discussion can be used to establish the result that for the classical normal linear regression model the ordinary least squares estimators $\hat{\boldsymbol{\beta}}$ and $\hat{\sigma}^2$ are minimum variance unbiased. Notice the crucial importance of the normality condition in establishing this small sample result.

First, the efficiency of $\hat{\boldsymbol{\beta}}$ will be shown through the Cramér–Rao approach.

Lemma 3.3.1. *The multivariate normal density of* $\mathbf{y}$ *is regular with respect to its first derivatives.*

PROOF. The logarithmic likelihood is

$$\ln L = -\frac{T}{2}\ln(2\pi\sigma^2) - \frac{1}{2\sigma^2}(\mathbf{y} - X\boldsymbol{\beta})'(\mathbf{y} - X\boldsymbol{\beta}).$$

Therefore,

$$\begin{aligned}\frac{\partial \ln L}{\partial \boldsymbol{\beta}} &= -\frac{1}{2\sigma^2}\frac{\partial}{\partial \boldsymbol{\beta}}(\mathbf{y}'\mathbf{y} - 2\mathbf{y}'X\boldsymbol{\beta} + \boldsymbol{\beta}'X'X\boldsymbol{\beta}) \\ &= \frac{1}{\sigma^2}(X'\mathbf{y} - X'X\boldsymbol{\beta}) = \frac{1}{\sigma^2}X'(\mathbf{y} - X\boldsymbol{\beta}), \\ \frac{\partial \ln L}{\partial \sigma^2} &= -\frac{T}{2\sigma^2} + \frac{1}{2\sigma^4}(\mathbf{y} - X\boldsymbol{\beta})'(\mathbf{y} - X\boldsymbol{\beta})\end{aligned}$$

and

$$E\left[\frac{\partial \ln L}{\partial \boldsymbol{\beta}}\right] = \mathbf{0} \quad \text{and} \quad E\left[\frac{\partial \ln L}{\partial \sigma^2}\right] = 0.$$

Hence the density is regular by definition. □

Theorem 3.3.2. *The Cramér–Rao lower bounds for the variances of* $\hat{\boldsymbol{\beta}}$ *and* $\hat{\sigma}^2$ *are* $\sigma^2(X'X)^{-1}$ *and* $2\sigma^4/T$, *respectively.*

PROOF. To form the information matrix the following results are obtained:

$$\frac{\partial^2 \ln L}{\partial \boldsymbol{\beta}\, \partial \boldsymbol{\beta}'} = -\frac{1}{\sigma^2} X'X; \; -E\left[\frac{\partial^2 \ln L}{\partial \boldsymbol{\beta}\, \partial \boldsymbol{\beta}'}\right] = \frac{X'X}{\sigma^2};$$

$$\frac{\partial^2 \ln L}{\partial^2 \sigma^2} = \frac{T}{2\sigma^4} - \frac{1}{\sigma^6}(\mathbf{y} - X\boldsymbol{\beta})'(\mathbf{y} - X\boldsymbol{\beta}); \qquad -E\left[\frac{\partial^2 \ln L}{\partial^2 \sigma^2}\right] = \frac{T}{2\sigma^4};$$

$$\frac{\partial^2 \ln L}{\partial \boldsymbol{\beta}\, \partial \sigma^2} = -\frac{1}{\sigma^4} X'(\mathbf{y} - X\boldsymbol{\beta}); \; -E\left[\frac{\partial^2 \ln L}{\partial \boldsymbol{\beta}\, \partial \sigma^2}\right] = \mathbf{0}.$$

Therefore, the information matrix is

$$I(\boldsymbol{\beta}, \sigma^2) = \begin{bmatrix} \dfrac{X'X}{\sigma^2} & \mathbf{0} \\ \mathbf{0}' & \dfrac{T}{2\sigma^4} \end{bmatrix}.$$

In turn, the Cramér–Rao lower bounds for unbiased estimators of $\boldsymbol{\beta}$ and σ^2 are the appropriate elements of $[I(\boldsymbol{\beta}, \sigma^2)]^{-1}$, namely, $\sigma^2(X'X)^{-1}$ and $2\sigma^4/T$. □

From the Cramér–Rao theorem, it follows that $\hat{\boldsymbol{\beta}}$ is a minimum variance unbiased estimator of $\boldsymbol{\beta}$ as the lower bound is attained. In contrast, however, var $\hat{\sigma}^2 = 2\sigma^4/(T - K) > 2\sigma^4/T$ and the lower bound for unbiased estimators of σ^2 is not attained. In this case the Cramér–Rao theorem does not provide verification of the efficiency of $\hat{\sigma}^2$. This question must be examined through the alternative approach of complete, sufficient statistics. In fact through this approach, it can be shown that $\hat{\sigma}^2$ is indeed minimum variance unbiased efficient. (See, for example, Schmidt (1976, p. 14).)

3.3.3 Minimum Variance Unbiased Through Complete–Sufficient Statistics Approach

From the above discussion of the minimum variance unbiased efficiency of the ordinary least squares estimators $\hat{\boldsymbol{\beta}}$ and $\hat{\sigma}^2$, it is obvious that there are instances where the use of the Cramér–Rao approach results in an indeterminate judgment as to the efficiency of an unbiased estimator. In such instances the complete–sufficient statistic approach can prove to be a useful alternative methodology. This is the case in showing that the ordinary least squares estimator $\hat{\sigma}^2$ in the classical normal linear regression model is minimum variance unbiased efficient.

A detailed discussion of the complete–sufficient statistic approach is beyond the scope of this book. For an excellent development of this method one can consult Hogg and Craig (1970) or Wilks (1962). Here the discussion is limited to a few comments comparing the two distinct approaches.

The advantage of the Cramér–Rao approach is that it is easier to comprehend and apply for the novice in mathematical statistics. The Cramér–Rao approach requires regularity and the application of one theorem, the Cramér–Rao theorem. In contrast, the complete–sufficient statistics approach requires the development of two definitions, sufficiency and completeness, and three theorems; the Fisher–Neyman factorization theorem, the Rao–Blackwell theorem, and the Lehmann–Scheffe theorem. Though intricate, the complete–sufficient statistics approach provides more definitive results. Using this approach, an unbiased estimator can be shown to be minimum variance unbiased efficient or not. There is no indeterminate outcome. Moreover, once it is established that an unbiased estimator is minimum variance unbiased efficient by this approach, uniqueness can also be claimed. That is, the complete–sufficient statistics approach allows the determination of *the* minimum variance unbiased estimator.

Obviously, the complete–sufficient statistics approach is the more powerful of the two. However, as will become obvious after the next chapter, the Cramér–Rao lower bound is of more sustaining interest in this book.

3.4 Tests of Hypotheses in Small Samples

In the previous sections the focus was on point estimation in small samples when the errors in the linear model are normally distributed. In particular the sampling distributions of the ordinary least squares estimators $\hat{\boldsymbol{\beta}}$ and $\hat{\sigma}^2$ in the classical normal linear regression model were established for any finite sample size T and it was shown (actually only asserted for $\hat{\sigma}^2$) that these same estimators are minimum variance unbiased efficient. In contrast, procedures for testing general linear hypotheses about the parameters of the classical normal linear regression model will be developed in this section. Linear hypotheses about the parameter vector $\boldsymbol{\beta}$ can be written $R\boldsymbol{\beta} = \mathbf{r}$, where R is a $J \times K$ matrix of constants with rank J ($J \leq K$) and $\mathbf{r}$ is a $J \times 1$ vector of constants. The matrix equation $R\boldsymbol{\beta} = \mathbf{r}$ then represents J linearly independent hypotheses about $\boldsymbol{\beta}$. The following examples illustrate the range of hypotheses that can be formulated in this way.

EXAMPLE 3.4.1. Suppose the hypothesis is that a single parameter, β_k, equals a constant β_k^* against the alternative $\beta_k \neq \beta_k^*$. In this case

$$R = [0 \quad 0 \quad \cdots \quad 0 \quad 1 \quad 0 \quad \cdots \quad 0] \quad \text{and} \quad \mathbf{r} = [\beta_k^*],$$

where the single nonzero element is in the kth column of R. Then $\beta_k = R\boldsymbol{\beta} = \mathbf{r} = \beta_k^*$ as desired.

EXAMPLE 3.4.2. Suppose we wish to test the joint hypotheses that $\beta_i = \beta_i^*$, $i = 1, \ldots, J; J \leq K$. Then the ith row of R would contain zeros except in the ith column, which would contain a one. The vector $\mathbf{r}$ would contain the corresponding elements β_i^*. For example, to test the joint hypothesis $\beta_1 = 0$ and $\beta_2 = 0$ against the alternative that *at least one* of the hypothesis is incorrect, the formulation is

$$\begin{bmatrix} \beta_1 \\ \beta_2 \end{bmatrix} = \begin{bmatrix} 1 & 0 & 0 & \cdots & 0 \\ 0 & 1 & 0 & \cdots & 0 \end{bmatrix} \boldsymbol{\beta} = R\boldsymbol{\beta} = \mathbf{r} = \begin{bmatrix} 0 \\ 0 \end{bmatrix}.$$

EXAMPLE 3.4.3. Single or joint tests about linear combinations of parameters also can be easily formulated. To test the hypothesis that $\beta_1 = \beta_2$, for example,

$$R = [1 \quad -1 \quad 0 \quad \cdots \quad 0] \quad \text{and} \quad \mathbf{r} = [0],$$

respectively. To test the hypothesis that $\beta_1 + \beta_2 + \cdots + \beta_K = c$, where c is a constant

$$R = [1 \quad 1 \quad \cdots \quad 1] \quad \text{and} \quad \mathbf{r} = [c].$$

The distinction between tests of a single hypothesis and joint tests of several hypotheses is important. In the former case the alternative is that the single hypothesis is not true. For joint tests the alternative $R\boldsymbol{\beta} \neq \mathbf{r}$ is that at least one of the hypotheses being considered is incorrect. In general, testing a series of single hypotheses is *not* equivalent to testing those same hypotheses jointly. The intuitive reason for this is that in a joint test of several hypotheses any single hypothesis is "affected" by the information in the other hypotheses. This distinction will be reconsidered in Section 3.5 when confidence intervals are discussed.

The method of test construction will be the likelihood ratio method proposed by Neyman and Pearson (1928). Kendall and Stuart (1973) note that likelihood ratio methods have played a role in the theory of tests analogous to that of maximum likelihood methods in the theory of estimation. The method of maximum likelihood provides a means of obtaining point estimates while the likelihood ratio method provides a means of obtaining test statistics. Though the reader is referred to Kendall and Stuart (1973, Ch. 24) for a complete discussion of likelihood ratio tests, their construction and properties, the basic notion is as follows. The likelihood ratio is

$$l = \frac{L(\hat{\omega})}{L(\hat{\Omega})}, \tag{3.4.1}$$

where $L(\hat{\omega})$ is the maximum value of the likelihood function over the reduced parameter space defined by the null hypothesis, say $H_0: R\boldsymbol{\beta} = \mathbf{r}$, and $L(\hat{\Omega})$ is the maximum value of the likelihood function over the unconstrained parameter space, i.e., the parameter space under $H_A: R\boldsymbol{\beta} \neq \mathbf{r}$. Now

$$0 \leq l \leq 1 \tag{3.4.2}$$

and l is a reasonable test statistic for H_0 as the maximum likelihood $L(\hat{\omega})$ under H_0 is a fraction of its largest possible value $L(\hat{\Omega})$. Therefore, large values of l signify that H_0 is reasonably acceptable. The critical region of the test statistic is then

$$l \leq c_\alpha, \tag{3.4.3}$$

where c_α is determined from the distribution $g(l)$ to give a test of size α, i.e.,

$$\int_0^{c_\alpha} g(l)\, dl = \alpha. \tag{3.4.4}$$

This method will be applied to general linear hypotheses $R\boldsymbol{\beta} = \mathbf{r}$ about the parameters of the classical normal linear regression model

$$\mathbf{y} = X\boldsymbol{\beta} + \mathbf{e}, \tag{3.4.5}$$

where $\mathbf{e}$ is distributed as a multivariate normal random vector with mean $\mathbf{0}$ and covariance matrix $\sigma^2 I$. The general linear hypothesis is

$$H_0\colon R\boldsymbol{\beta} = \mathbf{r} \tag{3.4.6}$$

and the alternative is

$$H_A\colon R\boldsymbol{\beta} \neq \mathbf{r}. \tag{3.4.7}$$

The likelihood function for this model is

$$L = (2\pi)^{-T/2}(\sigma^2)^{-T/2} \exp\left[-\frac{1}{2\sigma^2}(\mathbf{y} - X\boldsymbol{\beta})'(\mathbf{y} - X\boldsymbol{\beta})\right]. \tag{3.4.8}$$

The values of $\boldsymbol{\beta}$ and σ^2 which maximize the likelihood function on the entire (unrestricted) parameter space are

$$\begin{aligned} \tilde{\boldsymbol{\beta}} &= \hat{\boldsymbol{\beta}} = (X'X)^{-1}X'\mathbf{y}, \\ \tilde{\sigma}^2 &= \frac{1}{T}(\mathbf{y} - X\hat{\boldsymbol{\beta}})'(\mathbf{y} - X\hat{\boldsymbol{\beta}}). \end{aligned} \tag{3.4.9}$$

Substitution of (3.4.9) into the likelihood function (3.4.8) gives

$$L(\hat{\Omega}) = (2\pi)^{-T/2}\left[\frac{1}{T}(\mathbf{y} - X\hat{\boldsymbol{\beta}})'(\mathbf{y} - X\hat{\boldsymbol{\beta}})\right]^{-T/2} \exp[-T/2]. \tag{3.4.10}$$

The values of $\boldsymbol{\beta}$ and σ^2 which maximize the likelihood function over the parameter space constrained by $R\boldsymbol{\beta} = \mathbf{r}$ are

$$\begin{aligned} \boldsymbol{\beta}^* &= \hat{\boldsymbol{\beta}} + (X'X)^{-1}R'[R(X'X)^{-1}R']^{-1}(\mathbf{r} - R\hat{\boldsymbol{\beta}}), \\ \sigma^{2*} &= \frac{1}{T}(\mathbf{y} - X\boldsymbol{\beta}^*)'(\mathbf{y} - X\boldsymbol{\beta}^*). \end{aligned} \tag{3.4.11}$$

These results are developed in Exercise 3.11 and explicitly in Chapter 6. Substitution of these estimators back into the likelihood function (3.4.8) gives

$$L(\hat{\omega}) = (2\pi)^{-T/2}\left[\frac{1}{T}(\mathbf{y} - X\boldsymbol{\beta}^*)'(\mathbf{y} - X\boldsymbol{\beta}^*)\right]^{-T/2} \exp(-T/2). \quad (3.4.12)$$

The likelihood ratio test statistic is then

$$l = \frac{L(\hat{\omega})}{L(\hat{\Omega})} = \left[\frac{(\mathbf{y} - X\boldsymbol{\beta}^*)'(\mathbf{y} - X\boldsymbol{\beta}^*)}{(\mathbf{y} - X\hat{\boldsymbol{\beta}})'(\mathbf{y} - X\hat{\boldsymbol{\beta}})}\right]^{-T/2}.$$

The likelihood ratio test criterion calls for rejection of H_0 when $l \le c_\alpha$, or

$$l^{-2/T} = \frac{(\mathbf{y} - X\boldsymbol{\beta}^*)'(\mathbf{y} - X\boldsymbol{\beta}^*)}{(\mathbf{y} - X\hat{\boldsymbol{\beta}})'(\mathbf{y} - X\hat{\boldsymbol{\beta}})} \ge c_\alpha^{-2/T}. \quad (3.4.13)$$

Thus the null hypothesis may be rejected for large values of $l^{-2/T}$. This statistic can be put in a more convenient form by noting that

$$\begin{aligned}(\mathbf{y} - X\boldsymbol{\beta}^*)'(\mathbf{y} - X\boldsymbol{\beta}^*) &= \mathbf{y}'\mathbf{y} - 2\boldsymbol{\beta}^{*\prime}X'\mathbf{y} + \boldsymbol{\beta}^{*\prime}X'X\boldsymbol{\beta}^* \\ &= \mathbf{y}'\mathbf{y} - 2\hat{\boldsymbol{\beta}}'X'\mathbf{y} + \hat{\boldsymbol{\beta}}'X'X\hat{\boldsymbol{\beta}} + 2(\hat{\boldsymbol{\beta}} - \boldsymbol{\beta}^*)'X'\mathbf{y} \\ &\quad + \boldsymbol{\beta}^{*\prime}X'X\boldsymbol{\beta}^* - \hat{\boldsymbol{\beta}}'X'X\hat{\boldsymbol{\beta}} \\ &= (\mathbf{y} - X\hat{\boldsymbol{\beta}})'(\mathbf{y} - X\hat{\boldsymbol{\beta}}) + (\hat{\boldsymbol{\beta}} - \boldsymbol{\beta}^*)'X'X(\hat{\boldsymbol{\beta}} - \boldsymbol{\beta}^*).\end{aligned} \quad (3.4.14)$$

The result in (3.4.14) is obtained using the fact that $X'\mathbf{y} = X'X\hat{\boldsymbol{\beta}}$. Making the substitution of (3.4.14) into (3.4.13) the likelihood ratio criterion becomes

$$l^{-2/T} - 1 = \frac{(\hat{\boldsymbol{\beta}} - \boldsymbol{\beta}^*)'X'X(\hat{\boldsymbol{\beta}} - \boldsymbol{\beta}^*)}{(\mathbf{y} - X\hat{\boldsymbol{\beta}})'(\mathbf{y} - X\hat{\boldsymbol{\beta}})} \ge c_\alpha^{-2/T} - 1 = c_\alpha^*. \quad (3.4.15)$$

Moreover, using $(\boldsymbol{\beta}^* - \hat{\boldsymbol{\beta}})$ from (3.4.11), the numerator of (3.4.15) becomes

$$(\mathbf{r} - R\hat{\boldsymbol{\beta}})'[R(X'X)^{-1}R']^{-1}(\mathbf{r} - R\hat{\boldsymbol{\beta}})$$

and the likelihood ratio test rejects H_0 if

$$\frac{(\mathbf{r} - R\hat{\boldsymbol{\beta}})'[R(X'X)^{-1}R']^{-1}(\mathbf{r} - R\hat{\boldsymbol{\beta}})/J}{(\mathbf{y} - X\hat{\boldsymbol{\beta}})'(\mathbf{y} - X\hat{\boldsymbol{\beta}})/(T - K)} \ge c_\alpha^{**}. \quad (3.4.16)$$

In order to obtain the distribution of the statistic in (3.4.16) we need, in addition to Lemma 3.2.1, Lemma 3.4.1:

Lemma 3.4.1. *Let* $\mathbf{x} \sim N(\mathbf{0}, \sigma^2 I_T)$ *and* A *and* B *be symmetric matrices. Then* $Q_1 = \mathbf{x}'A\mathbf{x}/\sigma^2$ *and* $Q_2 = \mathbf{x}'B\mathbf{x}/\sigma^2$ *are independent iff* $AB = 0$, *where* 0 *is the null matrix.*

The proof of this lemma is straightforward and is left for the reader. (See Lemma 3.2.2 for a beginning.)

To obtain the distribution of (3.4.16) is then straightforward. If $\mathbf{r} = R\boldsymbol{\beta}$, $\mathbf{r} - R\hat{\boldsymbol{\beta}} = R(\boldsymbol{\beta} - \hat{\boldsymbol{\beta}}) = -R(X'X)^{-1}X'\mathbf{e}$ and the quadratic form in the numerator of (3.4.16), apart from $(1/J)$, can be written as $\mathbf{e}'A\mathbf{e}$ where

$$A = X(X'X)^{-1}R'[R(X'X)^{-1}R']^{-1}R(X'X)^{-1}X'.$$

Clearly A is symmetric and idempotent and, therefore, $\mathbf{e}'A\mathbf{e}$ is distributed as a χ^2-random variable with tr $A = J$ degrees of freedom by Lemma 3.2.1. Similarly, the quadratic form in the denominator of (3.4.16), apart from $(1/(T - K))$, can be written $\mathbf{e}'B\mathbf{e}$ where $B = I - X(X'X)^{-1}X'$ is symmetric and idempotent with rank $(T - K)$, so $\mathbf{e}'B\mathbf{e}$ is distributed as $\chi^2_{(T-K)}$. Finally A and B are independent by Lemma 3.4.1 since $AB = 0$.

Thus, under the null hypothesis, the test statistic

$$u = \frac{(\mathbf{r} - R\hat{\boldsymbol{\beta}})'[R(X'X)^{-1}R']^{-1}(\mathbf{r} - R\hat{\boldsymbol{\beta}})/J}{(\mathbf{y} - X\hat{\boldsymbol{\beta}})'(\mathbf{y} - X\hat{\boldsymbol{\beta}})/(T - K)} \tag{3.4.17}$$

has a central F-distribution with J and $T - K$ degrees of freedom since the ratio of two independent χ^2-random variables which have been divided by their degrees of freedom is an F-random variable. The likelihood ratio test of the null hypothesis (3.4.6) is to reject H_0 with type I error $= \alpha$ when $u \geq c_\alpha^{**}$ and c_α^{**} is the critical value such that

$$\int_{c_\alpha^{**}}^{\infty} F_{J,T-K}\, dF = \Pr[F_{J,T-K} \geq c_\alpha^{**}] = \alpha. \tag{3.4.18}$$

This general test statistic may be used to test any linear hypothesis which can be written in the form (3.4.6). For other examples where the likelihood ratio method can be used to develop appropriate test statistics, see Exercises 3.17–3.20.

We pause for an interpretative note. The test statistic u can be thought of in another way which provides some intuition about the nature of this test and how it works. From (3.4.14), the test statistic (3.4.17) can also be written, using (3.4.11), as

$$\begin{aligned} u &= \frac{(\hat{\boldsymbol{\beta}} - \boldsymbol{\beta}^*)'X'X(\hat{\boldsymbol{\beta}} - \boldsymbol{\beta}^*)/J}{(\mathbf{y} - X\hat{\boldsymbol{\beta}})'(\mathbf{y} - X\hat{\boldsymbol{\beta}})/(T - K)} \\ &= \frac{(\mathrm{SSE_r} - \mathrm{SSE_u})/J}{\mathrm{SSE_u}/(T - K)}, \end{aligned} \tag{3.4.19}$$

where $\mathrm{SSE_u} = (\mathbf{y} - X\hat{\boldsymbol{\beta}})'(\mathbf{y} - X\hat{\boldsymbol{\beta}})$ is the sum of squared residuals (errors) from the unrestricted model and $\mathrm{SSE_r} = (\mathbf{y} - X\boldsymbol{\beta}^*)'(\mathbf{y} - X\boldsymbol{\beta}^*)$ is the sum of squared residuals from the restricted model. Thus the test statistic u "measures" the reduction in "noise" per lost degree of freedom when moving from the restricted to the unrestricted hypothesis, relative to the basic noise per degree of freedom in the unrestricted model $\mathrm{SSE_u}/(T - K) = \hat{\sigma}^2$. The less the change in noise when the hypothesis is dropped, the more likely it is to be true. Note that while (3.4.19) is a useful expository form, (3.4.17) is computationally more efficient since $\boldsymbol{\beta}^*$ need not be calculated.

A special case of the above test is the standard t-test of a single coefficient. The test statistic for the hypothesis in Example 3.4.1 is

$$u = \frac{(\hat{\beta}_k - \beta_k^*)'(1/s^{kk})(\hat{\beta}_k - \beta_k^*)}{\hat{\sigma}^2}$$

$$= \frac{(\hat{\beta}_k - \beta_k^*)^2}{\hat{\sigma}^2 s^{kk}}, \tag{3.4.20}$$

where s^{kk} is the kth diagonal element of $(X'X)^{-1}$. The statistic in (3.4.20) has an F-distribution with 1 and $T - K$ degrees of freedom. The square root of an F-random variable with one degree of freedom in the numerator and v degrees of freedom in the denominator is a t-random variable with v degrees of freedom. Consequently, the test of the hypothesis $H_0: \beta_k = \beta_k^*$ against $H_A: \beta_k \neq \beta_k^*$ may be carried out by comparing the value of

$$t = (\hat{\beta}_k - \beta_k^*)/(\hat{\sigma}^2 s^{kk})^{1/2}$$

to the upper and lower critical values of a t-distribution with $T - K$ degrees of freedom. More general tests of a single linear hypothesis may also be conducted using the t-distribution.

3.5 Confidence Intervals

The test statistics developed above can be used to construct interval estimates and confidence regions for general linear hypotheses. For a general discussion of interval estimates see, for example, Hogg and Craig (1970). Our purpose is to use these tools to examine the difference between single and joint hypotheses. The statistic $t = (\hat{\beta}_k - \beta_k)/\text{se}(\hat{\beta}_k)$ has a t-distribution with $T - K$ degrees of freedom, where $\text{se}(\hat{\beta}_k) = (\hat{\sigma}^2 s^{kk})^{1/2}$ is the standard error of $\hat{\beta}_k$. If the upper $\alpha/2$ critical value, $\alpha \in (0, 1)$, of the t-distribution with $T - K$ degrees of freedom is denoted $t_{\alpha/2}$, then the probability that the random interval

$$[\hat{\beta}_k - t_{\alpha/2}\,\text{se}(\hat{\beta}_k), \hat{\beta}_k + t_{\alpha/2}\,\text{se}(\hat{\beta}_k)] = I_k \tag{3.5.1}$$

contains the true parameter is $1 - \alpha$. A test of the hypothesis $H_0: \beta_k = \beta_k^*$ also can be conducted by accepting H_0 if β_k^* falls within the confidence limits generated by a particular sample and rejecting H_0 otherwise.

The sampling theory approach to confidence intervals says that if the confidence coefficient is $1 - \alpha$ then $(1 - \alpha)\%$ of the confidence intervals based on a large number of samples will contain the true parameter. Thus, while it is true that

$$\Pr[\beta_k \in I_k] = \Pr[\beta_j \in I_j] = 1 - \alpha. \tag{3.5.2}$$

where I_k and I_j are random intervals constructed for β_k and β_j as in (3.5.1), it is *not* generally true that

$$\Pr[(\beta_k \in I_k), (\beta_j \in I_j)] = (1 - \alpha)^2,$$

since I_k and I_j would be constructed on the basis of the same samples and would not be independent. There are two ways to proceed. The first is to take into account the dependence and obtain

$$\Pr[(\beta_j \in I_j), (\beta_k \in I_k)] \geq 1 - 2\alpha. \tag{3.5.3}$$

See Exercise 3.15 for a proof of this result.

The second method takes a different approach. Instead of the rectangular region considered above, an ellipsoidal confidence region with an exact confidence coefficient can be determined. From (3.4.19) recall that

$$u = \frac{(\hat{\boldsymbol{\beta}} - \boldsymbol{\beta}^*)'X'X(\hat{\boldsymbol{\beta}} - \boldsymbol{\beta}^*)}{J\hat{\sigma}^2}$$

has an F-distribution with J and $T - K$ degrees of freedom. Thus if $F_\alpha(J, T - K)$ is the upper-α percentage point of the F-distribution then a $(1 - \alpha)\%$ confidence region is

$$(\hat{\boldsymbol{\beta}} - \boldsymbol{\beta})'X'X(\hat{\boldsymbol{\beta}} - \boldsymbol{\beta})/J\hat{\sigma}^2 \leq F_\alpha(J, T - K).$$

This equation is that of an ellipsoid centered at $\hat{\boldsymbol{\beta}}$. Analogous to the single parameter case, joint confidence intervals can be related to joint tests of hypotheses. For example, a joint hypothesis concerning values $\boldsymbol{\beta}$ will be rejected at the specified α-level unless the $(1 - \alpha)\%$ confidence ellipsoid contains that point. Note that it is possible to accept an hypothesis by using 95% confidence intervals *separately* yet reject the joint test or reject a hypothesis using 95% confidence intervals separately yet accept the joint test. The lesson to be learned is that the joint "message" of individual confidence intervals is no substitute for a joint confidence region in performing joint tests of hypotheses and making joint confidence statements.

3.6 Summary and Guide to Further Readings

The purpose of this chapter has been to develop the small sample estimation properties of the ordinary least squares estimators in the classical normal linear regression model as well as procedures for tests of hypotheses and the determination of confidence intervals. In particular, the estimators $\hat{\boldsymbol{\beta}} = (X'X)^{-1}X'\mathbf{y}$ and $\tilde{\sigma}^2 = (T - K)\hat{\sigma}^2/T$ are the maximum likelihood estimators and have independent distributions $N(\boldsymbol{\beta}, \sigma^2(X'X)^{-1})$ and $\sigma^2\chi^2_{T-K}/T$, respectively.

Using the Cramér–Rao approach it was shown that, given the classical normal linear regression model, the ordinary least squares estimator $\hat{\boldsymbol{\beta}}$ is minimum variance unbiased; that is, among the class of unbiased estimators, it has minimum variance. On the other hand, the Cramér–Rao approach provides an inconclusive judgment on the minimum variance unbiased efficiency of the unbiased estimator $\hat{\sigma}^2$. However, the complete-sufficient statistics approach can be used to claim its minimum variance unbiased efficiency in the classical normal linear regression model.

The likelihood ratio method was used to develop a small sample test statistic of the general linear hypothesis $R\boldsymbol{\beta} = \mathbf{r}$ in the classical normal linear regression model. This statistic involves the comparison of the unrestricted and restricted sum of squared residuals. The less the increase in the sum of squared residuals per degree of freedom due to the null hypothesis, the greater the probability that the null hypothesis is true.

Confidence intervals are a natural extension of the test statistic developed for the general linear hypothesis. However, one must be careful to distinguish between the purposes of separate and joint confidence intervals. Joint inference is improved by the use of joint confidence intervals rather than "piecing together" the results of separate confidence intervals.

Another important concept for which we did not have space to review is the power of a test. The power of a test is the probability that an incorrect null hypothesis will be rejected. As the sample size goes to infinity, the power of a test should hopefully go to one. Such a test is called a *consistent* test. Hogg and Craig (1970) provide a review of these topics as well as the definition of uniformly most powerful tests. A test is uniformly most powerful if, for any given sample size and chosen level of significance (type I error), its power is as least as great as that for all other tests. Hogg and Craig discuss the Neyman–Pearson theorem for generating such tests when they exist. Most standard references, including this book, present uniformly most powerful tests when they are available.

We end this chapter by providing a formal proof of the Cramér–Rao theorem in the next section.

3.7 Appendix: Proof of Cramér–Rao Theorem

First let us consider the case where θ is an unknown scalar parameter. Given that $L(x_1, x_2, \ldots, x_T; \theta)$ is the likelihood function, it possesses the property

$$\int_{-\infty}^{\infty} \cdots \int_{-\infty}^{\infty} L(x_1, x_2, \ldots, x_T; \theta)\, dx_1 \ldots dx_T = 1$$

or, more compactly,

$$\int L(\mathbf{x}; \theta)\, d\mathbf{x} = 1. \tag{3.7.1}$$

Differentiating (3.7.1) with respect to θ results in

$$\int \frac{\partial L(\mathbf{x};\theta)}{\partial\theta}\,d\mathbf{x} = 0, \tag{3.7.2}$$

if it is assumed that the domain of $\mathbf{x}$ is independent of θ (this permits straightforward differentiation inside the integral sign) and that the derivative $\partial L(\cdot)/\partial\theta$ exists. Equation (3.7.2) can be reexpressed as

$$\int \frac{\partial \ln L(\mathbf{x};\theta)}{\partial\theta} L(\mathbf{x};\theta)\,d\mathbf{x} = 0. \tag{3.7.3}$$

However, (3.7.3) simply states that

$$E\left[\frac{\partial \ln L(\mathbf{x};\theta)}{\partial\theta}\right] = 0, \tag{3.7.4}$$

i.e., the expectation of the derivative of the natural logarithm of the likelihood function of a random sample from a regular density is zero.

Likewise, differentiating (3.7.3) with respect to θ provides

$$\begin{aligned}&\int \frac{\partial^2 \ln L(\mathbf{x};\theta)}{\partial\theta^2} L(\mathbf{x};\theta)\,d\mathbf{x} + \int \frac{\partial \ln L(\mathbf{x};\theta)}{\partial\theta}\frac{\partial L(\mathbf{x};\theta)}{\partial\theta}\,d\mathbf{x}\\ &\quad = \int \frac{\partial^2 \ln L(\mathbf{x};\theta)}{\partial\theta^2} L(\mathbf{x};\theta)\,d\mathbf{x} + \int \left[\frac{\partial \ln L(\mathbf{x};\theta)}{\partial\theta}\right]^2 L(\mathbf{x};\theta)\,d\mathbf{x} = 0.\end{aligned} \tag{3.7.5}$$

In light of (3.7.4), (3.7.5) shows that the variance of $\partial \ln L(\mathbf{x};\theta)/\partial\theta$ is equal to minus the expectation of the second-order derivative of the likelihood function:

$$\operatorname{var}\left[\frac{\partial \ln L(\mathbf{x};\theta)}{\partial\theta}\right] = -E\left[\frac{\partial^2 \ln L(\mathbf{x};\theta)}{\partial\theta^2}\right]. \tag{3.7.6}$$

Now consider the estimator $s(\mathbf{x})$ of θ whose expectation is

$$E(s(\mathbf{x})) = \int s(\mathbf{x})L(\mathbf{x};\theta)\,d\mathbf{x}. \tag{3.7.7}$$

Differentiating (3.7.7) with respect to θ we obtain

$$\begin{aligned}\frac{\partial E(s(\mathbf{x}))}{\partial\theta} &= \int s(\mathbf{x})\frac{\partial L(\mathbf{x};\theta)}{\partial\theta}\,dx\\ &= \int s(\mathbf{x})\frac{\partial \ln L(\mathbf{x};\theta)}{\partial\theta} L(\mathbf{x};\theta)\,d\mathbf{x}\\ &= \operatorname{cov}\left[s(\mathbf{x}), \frac{\partial \ln L(\mathbf{x};\theta)}{\partial\theta}\right],\end{aligned} \tag{3.7.8}$$

the last equality holding because of (3.7.4). Since the square of the covariance is less than or equal to the product of the variances (note $[\text{cov}(X, Y)]^2 = \rho^2\sigma_x^2\sigma_y^2$ and $\rho^2 \leq 1$):

$$\left[\frac{\partial E(s(\mathbf{x}))}{\partial\theta}\right]^2 \leq \text{var}(s(\mathbf{x}))\ \text{var}\left[\frac{\partial \ln L(\mathbf{x};\theta)}{\partial\theta}\right]. \tag{3.7.9}$$

But, in light of (3.7.6),

$$\text{var}(s(\mathbf{x})) \geq \frac{\left[\dfrac{\partial E(s(\mathbf{x}))}{\partial\theta}\right]^2}{-E\left[\dfrac{\partial^2 \ln L(\mathbf{x};\theta)}{\partial\theta^2}\right]}. \tag{3.7.10}$$

If the estimator $s(\mathbf{x})$ is unbiased, $E(s(\mathbf{x})) = \theta$ and

$$\text{var}(s(\mathbf{x})) \geq \frac{1}{-E\left[\dfrac{\partial^2 \ln L(\mathbf{x};\theta)}{\partial\theta^2}\right]}. \tag{3.7.11}$$

A similar proof can be constructed for the case where $\boldsymbol{\theta}$ is a K-dimensional parameter vector and $\mathbf{s}(\mathbf{x})$ is a K-dimensional vector function (see, for example, Theil (1971, pp. 387–389) and Dhrymes (1974, pp. 125–126)). The result is

$$\text{var}(\mathbf{s}(\mathbf{x})) \geq [I(\boldsymbol{\theta})]^{-1}, \tag{3.7.12}$$

where the reciprocal of (3.7.11) has been replaced by the inverse of the information matrix, $\text{var}(\mathbf{s}(\mathbf{x}))$ is now a $K \times K$ covariance matrix and the inequality $\geq$ now means that the difference between these matrices is a positive semidefinite matrix. This imples that $\mathbf{l}'(\text{var}(\mathbf{s}(\mathbf{x})) - [I(\boldsymbol{\theta})]^{-1})\mathbf{l} \geq 0$ and, in particular, $\text{var}(s_i(\mathbf{x})) \geq I^{ii}$, where I^{ii} denotes the (i, i)th element of $[\text{I}(\theta)]^{-1}$.

3.8 Exercises

The following four exercises illustrate the use of the maximum likelihood method in determining point estimators of parameters.

3.1. Suppose we have a distribution which is $N(\theta, 1)$. For some reason we know $\theta = 0, 1$, or 2. No other values of θ are possible. We observe a random sample of size 3 and obtain $x_1 = 1$, $x_2 = 1\frac{1}{3}$ and $x_3 = 2$. Obtain a maximum likelihood estimate of θ.

3.2. Given the random sample $x_1, x_2, \ldots, x_n$ from a $N(\theta, \sigma^2)$-distribution, derive the maximum likelihood estimators of θ and σ^2. Verify the second-order conditions.

3.3. Let $x_1, x_2, \ldots, x_n$ be a random sample from each of the following probability density functions:
(a) $f(x|\theta) = \theta x^{\theta-1}, 0 < x < 1, 0 < \theta < \infty$, zero elsewhere.
(b) $f(x|\theta) = e^{-(x-\theta)}, \ \theta \leq x < \infty, \ -\infty < \theta < \infty$, zero elsewhere.

Derive the maximum likelihood estimate $\hat{\theta}$ for θ in each case given the random sample.

3.4. Derive the maximum likelihood estimate $\hat{\theta}$ for θ for each of the following discrete probability density functions.

(a)
$$f(x|\theta) = \frac{\theta^x}{x!} e^{-\theta}, \qquad \theta > 0, \quad x = 0, 1, 2, \ldots$$
(Poisson Distribution)

(b) Let $x_1, x_2, \ldots, x_n$ be a random sample of n Bernoulli trials and $x = \Sigma x_i$.
$$f(x|\theta) = \binom{n}{x}\theta^x(1-\theta)^{n-x}, \qquad 0 \leq \theta \leq 1, \quad x = 0, 1, 2, \ldots, n, \quad \text{where}$$
$$\binom{n}{x} = \frac{n!}{(n-x)!\,x!}$$
(Binomial Distribution).

3.5. Verify that the second-order conditions for a maximum in Theorem 3.2.1 are satisfied.

3.6. Prove the following matrix result.

Proposition. *If M is a symmetric, idempotent matrix of dimension $T \times T$, then* tr M *of its eigenvalues equal one while* (T − tr M) *eigenvalues equal zero. Also* tr M = rank M.

The following four exercises illustrate the use of the Cramér–Rao lower bound in determining the minimum variance unbiased efficiency of unbiased estimators.

3.7. Examine the regularity of each of the following probability density functions:
(a) $N(\theta, \sigma^2)$.
(b) Determine which probability density functions of Exercises 3.3 and 3.4 are regular with respect to their first derivatives.

3.8. Derive the Cramér–Rao lower bound variances for the parameters θ and σ^2 of the $N(\theta, \sigma^2)$-distribution given a random sample $x_1, x_2, \ldots, x_n$. Examine the efficiency of the unbiased estimators $\bar{x} = \sum x_i/n$ and $\hat{\sigma}^2 = \sum (x_i - \bar{x})^2/(n-1)$. Discuss, in particular, your conclusion concerning $\hat{\sigma}^2$. In terms of the estimation of θ, what does this imply about the efficiency of the median and midrange (the average of the largest and smallest observations) which are unbiased estimators? Does the Gauss–Markov theorem allow us to make statements concerning the relative efficiency of $\bar{x}$ versus the median and the midrange?

3.9. Derive unbiased estimators for the parameter θ in the *regular* densities of Exercises 3.3 and 3.4. Hint: Use maximum likelihood estimators as a starting point and determine if they are unbiased or instead if some function of the maximum likelihood estimator is unbiased. Examine the efficiency of each unbiased estimator using the Cramér–Rao approach.

3.10. Let $x_1, x_2, \ldots, x_n$ denote a random sample from the probability density function

$$f(x|\theta) = \frac{1}{\theta} c x^{c-1} e^{-x^c/\theta}, \qquad \theta > 0, \quad x > 0, \quad \text{zero elsewhere},$$

where c is a known positive constant.

(a) Find the maximum likelihood estimator for θ.

(b) Determine an unbiased estimator of θ.

(c) Using the Cramér–Rao lower bound approach, examine the efficiency of your unbiased estimator (part (b)). Be sure and check the regularity of the given density.

3.11. Maximize the likelihood function (3.4.8) over the parameter space $\boldsymbol{\beta}$ and σ^2 subject to the restrictions that $R\boldsymbol{\beta} = \mathbf{r}$. Your answers should verify (3.4.11). (Hint: Use Lagrangian multipliers.)

The following three exercises illustrate the use of the likelihood ratio method to determine appropriate test statistics.

3.12. Let $x_1, x_2, \ldots, x_n$ denote a random sample from a normal distribution with unknown mean θ known variance σ^2. Use the likelihood ratio method to determine an appropriate test of the hypothesis $H_0: \theta = \theta_0$ versus $H_1: \theta \neq \theta_0$. (Hint: The test statistic should be normally distributed.)

3.13. Let $x_1, x_2, \ldots, x_n$ denote a random sample from a normal distribution with both mean θ and variance σ^2 unknown. Use the likelihood ratio method to determine an appropriate test of the hypothesis $H_0: \theta = \theta_0$ versus $H_1: \theta \neq \theta_0$. (Hint: The test statistic should have a t-distribution.)

3.14. Let $x_1, x_2, \ldots, x_n$ denote a random sample from a normal distribution with both mean θ and variance σ^2 unknown. Use the likelihood ratio method to determine an appropriate test of the hypothesis $H_0: \sigma^2 = \sigma_0^2$ versus $H_1: \sigma^2 \neq \sigma_0^2$. (Hint: The test statistic should have a χ^2-distribution.)

3.15. Show the validity of (3.5.3) by using the following:

$$\begin{aligned}\Pr[(\beta_j \in I_j), (\beta_k \in I_k)] = 1 &- \Pr[(\beta_j \notin I_j), (\beta_k \in I_k)] \\ &- \Pr[(\beta_j \in I_j), (\beta_k \notin I_k)] - \Pr[(\beta_j \notin I_j), (\beta_k \notin I_k)],\end{aligned}$$

and

$$\Pr[(\beta_j \notin I_j)] = \Pr[(\beta_j \notin I_j), (\beta_k \in I_k)] + \Pr[(\beta_j \notin I_j), (\beta_k \notin I_k)]$$

and similarly for $\Pr[(\beta_k \notin I_k)]$.

3.16. Use Lemmas 3.2.1 and 3.4.1 to prove in detail that the numerator of expression (3.4.19) is a quadratic form distributed independently of the denominator.

3.17. Tests of joint hypotheses are often used to evaluate the possibility of combining different samples. Suppose we have two models given by

$$\mathbf{y}_1 = X_1\boldsymbol{\beta}_1 + \mathbf{e}_1 \quad (T_1 \text{ observations})$$

and

$$\mathbf{y}_2 = X_2\boldsymbol{\beta}_2 + \mathbf{e}_2 \quad (T_2 \text{ observations}).$$

Also assume $\mathbf{e}_1 \sim N(\mathbf{0}, \sigma^2 I_{T_1})$ and $\mathbf{e}_2 \sim N(\mathbf{0}, \sigma^2 I_{T_2})$ and that the elements of $\mathbf{e}_1$ are independent of those in $\mathbf{e}_2$. Form the R matrix for the hypothesis that $\boldsymbol{\beta}_1 = \boldsymbol{\beta}_2$. Develop the appropriate expression for the u-statistic used to make the test. This test is sometimes called the Chow test after Chow (1960).

3.18. Suppose again we have the model as specified in Exercise 3.17, but that $T_2 < K$, where K is the number of parameters in $\boldsymbol{\beta}_1$ and $\boldsymbol{\beta}_2$. Can a test be carried out for the hypothesis that $\boldsymbol{\beta}_1 = \boldsymbol{\beta}_2$? (Hint: see Fisher (1970).)

3.19. Tufte (1978) used multiple regression analysis to examine to what extent the presidential elections of 1948–1976 were affected by the political image of the incumbent party's candidate and the state of the economy in the year immediately preceding the electon. Tufte proposed the model

$$y_t = \beta_1 + \beta_2 x_{t2} + \beta_3 x_{t3} + e_t,$$

where y_t is the percentage vote for the presidential candidate of the incumbent party, x_{t3} is the net political advantage of the candidate relative to the opposing major party's candidate (this is obtained from a survey), x_{t2} is the percentage change in the real per capita disposable income in the year preceding the election and the random error e_t satisfies the properties of the classical normal linear regression model. The percentage vote is calculated using only the votes obtained by the candidate and the candidate of the opposing major party. The votes obtained by candidates of minor parties are not included. Consider the following data:

Presidential Elections, 1948–1976*

Year	"Incumbent" presidential candidate	y_t, National vote for incumbent (%)	x_{t2}, Yearly change in real per capita disposable income	x_{t3}, net presidential candidate advantage (if $x_{t3} > 0$, incumbent has advantage; if $x_{t3} < 0$ nonincumbent has advantage)
1948	Truman	52.37	3.4	+0.093
1952	Stevenson	44.59	1.1	−0.408
1956	Eisenhower	57.76	2.6	+1.146
1960	Nixon	49.91	0.0	+0.367
1964	Johnson	61.34	5.6	+1.044
1968	Humphrey	49.59	2.8	−0.353
1972	Nixon	61.79	3.3	+0.902
1976	Ford	48.89	3.3	−0.221

* SOURCE: Tufte (1978, Table 5-5, p. 121).

Using the above data, test the following hypotheses:
(a) $H_0: \beta_2 = 0; H_1: \beta_2 > 0$.
(b) $H_1: \beta_3 = 0; H_1: \beta_3 > 0$.
(c) $H_0: \beta_3 = 1; H_1: \beta_3 \neq 1$.
(d) $H_0: \beta_2 = 0$ and $\beta_3 = 0; H_1: \beta_2 \neq 0$ and/or $\beta_3 \neq 0$.
(e) $H_0: \beta_2 = \beta_3; H_1: \beta_2 \neq \beta_3$.
(f) $H_0: \beta_2 = \beta_3 = 1; H_1$: not H_0.

3.20. Nerlove (1963) analyzed the returns to scale in electricity supply on 145 electricity firms of the U.S. in the year 1955. In his analysis he specified the following cost function:

$$\ln C = \ln M + \frac{1}{r} \ln Y + \frac{a_1}{r} \ln P_L + \frac{a_2}{r} \ln P_K + \frac{a_3}{r} \ln P_F + e,$$

where C = total production costs, M = an unknown parameter, Y = output (measured in kilowatt hours), P_L = wage rate, P_K = price of capital, P_F = price of fuel, a_1, a_2, and a_3 are the output elasticities of labor, capital and fuel, respectively, $r = a_1 + a_2 + a_3$ is the returns to scale parameter and e satisfies the properties of the classical normal linear regression model. Consider the following data:

Data Concerning Group D Firms*

C	Y	P_L	P_K	P_F	C	Y	P_L	P_K	P_F
6.082	1497	1.76	168	10.3	12.620	2304	2.30	161	23.6
9.284	1545	1.80	158	20.2	12.905	2341	2.04	183	20.7
10.879	1649	2.32	177	31.9	11.615	2353	1.69	167	12.9
8.477	1668	1.80	170	20.2	9.321	2367	1.76	161	10.3
6.877	1782	2.13	183	10.7	12.962	2451	2.04	163	20.7
15.106	1831	1.98	162	35.5	16.932	2457	2.20	170	36.2
8.031	1833	1.76	177	10.3	9.648	2507	1.76	174	10.3
8.082	1838	1.45	196	17.6	18.350	2530	2.31	197	33.5
10.866	1787	2.24	164	26.5	17.333	2576	1.92	162	22.5
8.596	1918	1.69	158	12.9	12.015	2607	1.76	155	10.3
8.673	1930	1.81	157	22.6	11.320	2870	1.76	167	10.3
15.437	2028	2.11	163	24.4	22.337	2993	2.31	176	33.5
8.211	2057	1.76	161	10.3	19.035	3202	2.30	170	23.6
11.982	2084	1.77	156	21.3	12.205	3286	1.61	183	17.8
16.674	2226	2.00	217	34.3					

* SOURCE: Group D firms (Nerlove (1963, p. 196)).

(a) Using the above regression model, test the hypotheses $H_0: a_1/r + a_2/r + a_3/r = 1; H_1: a_1/r + a_2/r + a_3/r \neq 1$.
(b) Using the *restricted* reduced form cost function (i.e., the regression model above but assuming H_0 of part (a) is true)

$$(\ln C - \ln P_F) = \ln M + \frac{1}{r} \ln Y + \frac{a_1}{r} (\ln P_L - \ln P_F) + \frac{a_2}{r} (\ln P_K - \ln P_F) + e$$

test the following hypotheses (separately):

(i) $H_0: r = 1; H_1: r > 1$.

(ii) $H_0: a_1 = a_2; H_1: a_1 \neq a_2$.

(iii) $H_0: r = 1$ and $a_1 = a_2; H_1: r \neq 1$ and/or $a_1 \neq a_2$.

3.21. Consider the two aggregate savings relationships

$$s_t = \beta_1 + \beta_2 y_t + e_{t1}, \qquad t = 1947\text{–}1954,$$

$$s_t = \gamma_1 + \gamma_2 y_t + e_{t2}, \qquad t = 1955\text{–}1962,$$

where s_t = U.S. personal savings and y_t = disposable personal income. Use the Chow test (Exercise 3.17) on the following data to test whether there was a significant change in savings behavior over the two specified periods. You are testing the hypotheses $H_0: \beta_1 = \gamma_1$ and $\beta_2 = \gamma_2; H_1: \beta_1 \neq \gamma_1$ and/or $\beta_2 \neq \gamma_2$.

Year	s	y	Year	s	y
1947	4.9	168.4	1955	14.9	273.4
1948	10.6	187.4	1956	19.7	291.3
1949	6.7	187.1	1957	20.6	306.9
1950	10.8	205.5	1958	21.7	317.1
1951	14.8	224.8	1959	18.8	336.1
1952	16.0	236.4	1960	17.1	349.4
1953	17.0	250.7	1961	20.2	362.9
1954	15.6	255.7	1962	20.4	383.9

3.9 References

Chow, G. C. (1960). Tests of equality between subsets of coefficients in two linear regressions. *Econometrica*, **28**, 591–605.

Dhrymes, P. J. (1974), *Econometrics* (New York: Springer-Verlag).

Fisher, F. (1970). Tests of equality between sets of coefficients in two linear regressions: an expository note. *Econometrica*, **38**, 361–366.

Hogg, R. V. and Craig, A. T. (1970). *Introduction to Mathematical Statistics*, 3rd ed. New York: MacMillan.

Kendall, M. G. and Stuart, A. (1973). *The Advanced Theory of Statistics*, vol. 2, 3rd ed. New York: Hafner.

Nerlove, M. (1963). Returns to scale in electricity supply. In *Measurement in Economics: Studies in Mathematical Economics and Econometrics in Memory of Yehuda Grunfeld.* Edited by C. F. Christ, M. Friedman, L. A. Goodman, Z. Griliches, A. C. Harberger, N. Liviatan, J. Mincer, Y. Mundlak, M. Nerlove, D. Patinkin, L. G. Telser, and H. Theil. Stanford: Stanford University Press. Pp. 156–198.

Neyman, J. and Pearson, E. S. (1928). On the use and interpretation of certain test criteria for the purposes of statistical inference. *Biometrika*, A, **20**, 175–240 (Part I), 263–294 (Part II).

Schmidt, P. (1976). *Econometrics*. New York: Marcel Dekker.

Theil, H. (1971). *Principles of Econometrics*. New York: Wiley.
Tufte, E. (1978). *Political Control of the Economy*. Princeton, NJ: Princeton University Press.
Wilks, S. (1962). *Mathematical Statistics*. New York: Wiley.

CHAPTER 4

Large Sample Point Estimation and Tests of Hypotheses

4.1 Introduction

In the last chapter it was shown that certain properties of estimators and test statistics hold for *any* given sample size T provided appropriate assumptions are satisfied. In general, the extent of the conclusions depends upon the extent of the assumptions; best linear unbiased was provided with the assumption of independent and identically distributed errors while the additional assumption of normality of the errors lead to minimum variance unbiased efficiency and the elimination of the linearity requirement. Unfortunately, such strong results as minimum variance unbiased efficiency are not always obtainable in econometric modeling. For example, in feasible generalized least squares, lagged dependent variable models, and simultaneous equations, the derivation of small sample properties of estimators is not generally possible. Instead, the evaluation of these estimators must be based on their behavior in samples of infinite size. The idea of large sample efficiency involves new concepts yet to be discussed.

From the last chapter it was also evident that, given the classical normal linear regression model, the tests of hypotheses using the F- or t-distributions were valid for *any* given sample size T. However, these results were intimately linked to the normality assumption on the error terms. There are circumstances in economics where such an assumption cannot be justified. Using the asymptotic theory to be developed in this chapter, it will be shown that in samples of "large" size the requirement of normality is superfluous for conventional hypothesis testing.

The plan of this chapter is as follows: In Section 4.2, basic definitions and theorems in asymptotic distribution theory are developed. Also the important asymptotic properties of maximum likelihood estimators are discussed.

Section 4.3 utilizes these results to establish the asymptotic efficiency of the ordinary least squares estimators $\hat{\boldsymbol{\beta}}$ and $\hat{\sigma}^2$ under normality. In Section 4.4 it is shown that the use of t- and F-distributions for tests of hypotheses in large samples is justified even though the error terms may not be normally distributed. A summary and guide to further readings are contained in Section 4.5.

4.2 Asymptotic Distribution Theory

Motivation concerning the applicability of asymptotic distribution theory to problems in econometrics will become evident in subsequent discussions of feasible generalized least squares estimation, lagged dependent variables, and simultaneous equations. For the purpose of laying the foundation for these topics, a cursory discussion will be given. Complete treatments of asymptotic distribution theory can be found in Dhrymes (1974) and Theil (1971).

Definition 4.2.1. Let $(x_1, x_2, \ldots)$ be a sequence of random variables with cumulative distribution functions $(F_1, F_2, \ldots)$. Then the sequence $(x_1, x_2, \ldots)$ *converges in distribution* to the cumulative distribution function F if

$$\lim_{t \to \infty} F_t = F$$

for all continuity points of F.

This definition simply means that if the cumulative distribution functions of the random variables $x_1, x_2, \ldots$ converge to the cumulative distribution function F of the random variable, say, x then the limiting random variable of the sequence $x_1, x_2, \ldots$ is x with cumulative distribution function F. In the typical usage of this definition, the sequence $F_1, F_2, \ldots$ represents a sequence of sampling distributions of a particular estimator for ever increasing sample sizes. The limiting cumulative distribution function F is then the cumulative distribution function of the asymptotic distribution of the estimator in question.

The four definitions below provide an explanation of the terms consistent, uniformly, asymptotically normal and asymptotic efficiency. Examples and remarks following the definitions will illustrate their meaning.

Definition 4.2.2. Let $\hat{\boldsymbol{\theta}}_T$ be a consistent estimator of $\boldsymbol{\theta}$ and suppose $\sqrt{T}(\hat{\boldsymbol{\theta}}_T - \boldsymbol{\theta})$ converges in distribution to $N(\mathbf{0}, \Sigma)$. Then $\hat{\boldsymbol{\theta}}_T$ is said to have the asymptotic distribution $N(\boldsymbol{\theta}, \Sigma/T)$.

Definition 4.2.3. An estimator $\hat{\boldsymbol{\theta}}_T$ is defined to be *consistent uniformly asymptotically normal* when (i) it is consistent, (ii) $\sqrt{T}(\hat{\boldsymbol{\theta}}_T - \boldsymbol{\theta})$ converges in distribution to $N(\mathbf{0}, \Sigma)$, and (iii) if the convergence is uniform over any compact subset of the parameter space.

Definition 4.2.4. Let $\hat{\boldsymbol{\theta}}_T$ and $\tilde{\boldsymbol{\theta}}_T$ be consistent, uniformly, asymptotically normal estimators with asymptotic covariance matrices Σ/T and Ω/T, respectively. Then $\hat{\boldsymbol{\theta}}_T$ is said to be *asymptotically efficient relative to* $\tilde{\boldsymbol{\theta}}_T$ if the matrix $\Omega - \Sigma$ is positive semidefinite.

Definition 4.2.5. A consistent, uniformly, asymptotically normal estimator is said to be *asymptotically efficient* if it is asymptotically efficient relative to any other consistent, uniformly, asymptotically normal estimator.

Now we explore the meanings of these definitions. Why is the concept of an asymptotic distribution needed? Suppose two estimators converge in quadratic mean. Then their finite variances go to zero as $T \to \infty$. In the limit, the distributions of the estimators become *degenerate* at the population parameter. In large samples which estimator is to be preferred? The following example illustrates one way to choose.

EXAMPLE 4.2.1. Let $\bar{x}$ be the sample mean of a random sample $x_1, x_2, \ldots, x_T$ from a normal population. Then $\bar{x} \sim N(\mu, \sigma^2/T)$ and hence $\sqrt{T}(\bar{x} - \mu) \sim N(0, \sigma^2)$. Alternatively, consider the sample median, m, which is also a consistent estimator of μ. It can be shown that $\sqrt{T}(m - \mu) \sim N(0, \pi\sigma^2/2)$. The asymptotic variances of $\bar{x}$ and m are defined to be σ^2/T and $\pi\sigma^2/2T$, respectively. Since $\pi\sigma^2/2 - \sigma^2 > 0$, $\bar{x}$ is asymptotically efficient relative to m.

Under general conditions (to be discussed in Section 4.3) the ordinary least squares estimator $\hat{\boldsymbol{\beta}}$ is asymptotically efficient. Consider the alternative set of estimators

$$\frac{T - c_1}{T - c_2}\hat{\boldsymbol{\beta}},$$

where c_1 and c_2 denote arbitrary constants. These estimators are also asymptotically efficient. They have the same asymptotic distributions as $\hat{\boldsymbol{\beta}}$ (and necessarily the same asymptotic variance). Therefore, once an asymptotically efficient estimator is obtained, many estimators can be constructed which are asymptotically efficient. Unlike the unique minimum variance unbiased estimator implied by the complete–sufficient statistics approach, asymptotically efficient estimators are not unique.

If attention is restricted to the class of estimators for which $\sqrt{T}(\hat{\boldsymbol{\theta}}_T - \boldsymbol{\theta})$ is asymptotically normal then this class is referred to in the statistical literature as consistent asymptotically normal. If an estimator of this class attains the lower bound to be presented in a moment, then such an estimator is called best asymptotic normal. Unfortunately, the following example illustrates why this approach is ambiguous.

Example 4.2.2 (Rao (1973, p. 347) Credits This Example to Hodges). Let $\hat{\theta}_T$ be an estimator of the scalar parameter θ such that $\sqrt{T}(\hat{\theta}_T - \theta)$ is distributed asymptotically normal with zero mean and variance $V(\theta)$. Consider the alternative estimator

$$\hat{\theta}_T^* = \begin{cases} \gamma\hat{\theta}_T & \text{if } |\hat{\theta}_T| \leq T^{-1/4}, \\ \hat{\theta}_T & \text{if } |\hat{\theta}_T| > T^{-1/4}, \end{cases}$$

where $0 < |\gamma| < 1$. Then $\sqrt{T}(\hat{\theta}_T^* - \theta)$ is also asymptotically normal, with zero mean and variance $\gamma^2 V(0)$ if $\theta = 0$ and with the same mean but variance $V(\theta)$ when $\theta \neq 0$. As this example makes clear, given an asymptotically normal estimator $\hat{\theta}_T$, another asymptotically normal estimator can be constructed which has smaller variance than $\hat{\theta}_T$ for at least one point and the same elsewhere. This difficulty is circumvented if the admissible class of estimators is limited to those which converge to normality *uniformly* over compact subsets of the parameter space. The motivation for defining the consistent, uniformly, asymptotically normal class of estimators should now be clear, since it excludes estimators like $\hat{\theta}_T^*$.

Besides being an integral part of small sample estimation theory, the Cramér–Rao lower bound is a cornerstone of large sample (asymptotic) efficiency. This is apparent from Corollary 4.2.1 to the Cramér–Rao theorem.

Corollary 4.2.1 (Corollary to Cramér–Rao Theorem). *A sufficient condition for a consistent, uniformly, asymptotically normal estimator to be asymptotically efficient is that its asymptotic covariance equal the lower bound (hereinafter called the asymptotic Cramér–Rao lower bound)*

$$\frac{1}{T}\lim_{T\to\infty}\left[\frac{I(\boldsymbol{\theta})}{T}\right]^{-1}.$$

Proof. See Theil (1971, p. 395). □

The limit condition emphasizes the need to have sufficient assumptions in our models to assure convergence.

Theorem 4.2.1 makes it evident why maximum likelihood estimation is such a powerful tool in econometric theory. The theorem states that under general conditions, maximum likelihood estimators are (i) *consistent*, (ii) *asymptotically normal*, and (iii) *asymptotically efficient*.

Theorem 4.2.1. *Let $x_1, x_2, \ldots, x_T$ denote a random sample from the density $f(x_t; \boldsymbol{\theta})$. Let $\hat{\boldsymbol{\theta}}_T$ be the maximum likelihood estimator of $\boldsymbol{\theta}$. Then $\hat{\boldsymbol{\theta}}_T$ is a consistent estimator of $\boldsymbol{\theta}$, and $\sqrt{T}(\hat{\boldsymbol{\theta}}_T - \boldsymbol{\theta})$ has the asymptotic distribution*

$$N\left(\mathbf{0}, \lim_{T\to\infty} [I(\boldsymbol{\theta})/T]^{-1}\right)$$

if certain "regularity conditions" are satisfied.

PROOF. See Dhrymes (1974, pp. 121–123). □

The maximum likelihood regularity conditions require that: (i) the domain of the random variables x_t does not depend on the parameter vector $\boldsymbol{\theta}$; and (ii) the density $f(x_t; \boldsymbol{\theta})$ possesses derivatives of at least third order with respect to $\boldsymbol{\theta}$ which are bounded by integrable functions of $\mathbf{x}$. That is, $\partial f(x_t; \boldsymbol{\theta})/\partial\theta_i$, $\partial^2 f(x_t; \boldsymbol{\theta})/\partial\theta_i \partial\theta_j$ and $\partial^3 f(x_t; \boldsymbol{\theta})/\partial\theta_i \partial\theta_j \partial\theta_k$ exist for all i, j, $k = 1, \ldots, K$. Also, all of these derivatives are bounded as in $|\partial f/\partial\theta_i| \leq M_i(x)$ and $E[M_i(x)] < A$ for some constant A and some function $M_i(x)$. These regularity conditions differ from those of the Cramér–Rao theorem (Theorem 3.3.1) only in that the third-order derivatives are assumed to exist and are integrable.

The asymptotic covariance matrix of the maximum likelihood estimator is a function of the unknown population parameters of the model, i.e.,

$$H(\boldsymbol{\theta}) = \frac{1}{T} \lim_{T\to\infty} \left[\frac{I(\boldsymbol{\theta})}{T}\right]^{-1} = \frac{1}{T} \lim_{T\to\infty} \left\{-\frac{1}{T} E\left[\frac{\partial^2 \ln L(\mathbf{x}; \boldsymbol{\theta})}{\partial\boldsymbol{\theta}\, \partial\boldsymbol{\theta}'}\right]\right\}^{-1},$$

where $H(\boldsymbol{\theta})$ represents a matrix whose elements are functions of $\boldsymbol{\theta}$. A consistent estimator of this asymptotic covariance matrix is

$$[I(\hat{\boldsymbol{\theta}})]^{-1} = \left[-E\frac{\partial^2 \ln L(\mathbf{x}; \boldsymbol{\theta})}{\partial\boldsymbol{\theta}\, \partial\boldsymbol{\theta}'}\right]^{-1}_{\boldsymbol{\theta}=\hat{\boldsymbol{\theta}}},$$

where the notation on the right-hand side of the above expression denotes that all unknown population parameters have been replaced by their corresponding maximum likelihood estimators. Notice the absence of limits since this is a *finite* sample approximation.

The process of taking expectations in the above expressions can be tedious because the relevant functions may be highly nonlinear. Fortunately, there is a viable alternative when constructing a consistent estimator of the asymptotic covariance matrix of a maximum likelihood estimator. Under quite general conditions (see Kendall and Stuart (1973, pp. 45, 46, and 51)), it can be shown that

$$\text{plim}\left[-\frac{\partial^2 \ln L(\mathbf{x}; \boldsymbol{\theta})}{\partial\boldsymbol{\theta}\, \partial\boldsymbol{\theta}'}\right]_{\boldsymbol{\theta}=\hat{\boldsymbol{\theta}}} = -E\left[\frac{\partial^2 \ln L(\mathbf{x}; \boldsymbol{\theta})}{\partial\boldsymbol{\theta}\, \partial\boldsymbol{\theta}'}\right].$$

That is, the matrix of derivatives $-\partial^2 \ln L(\mathbf{x};\boldsymbol{\theta})/\partial\boldsymbol{\theta}\,\partial\boldsymbol{\theta}'$, with the unknown population parameters replaced by their maximum likelihood estimators is a consistent estimator of the information matrix. Therefore,

$$\left\{\left[\frac{-\partial^2 \ln L(\mathbf{x};\boldsymbol{\theta})}{\partial\boldsymbol{\theta}\,\partial\boldsymbol{\theta}'}\right]_{\boldsymbol{\theta}=\hat{\boldsymbol{\theta}}}\right\}^{-1}$$

is also a consistent estimator of the asymptotic covariance matrix of the maximum likelihood estimator. Naturally, if the exact form of the information matrix can be determined, i.e., if expectations can be evaluated, then constructing consistent estimators using it rather than the last-mentioned log likelihood form is usually preferred. The information matrix is then likely to have fewer parameters to estimate, some possibly being eliminated in the process of evaluating expectations.

Besides the properties of consistency, asymptotic normality, and asymptotic efficiency, two important *invariance* properties are very useful. These two theorems are only stated here. For proofs see Cramér (1946), Wilks (1962), and Kendall and Stuart (1973, Vol. 3).

Theorem 4.2.2 (Slutsky's Theorem). *If $\hat{\theta}$ is a consistent estimator of θ, then $g(\hat{\theta})$ is a consistent estimator of $g(\theta)$, where g is a well-defined continuous function.*

This theorem means that consistency is invariant to continuous transformation; a consistent estimator of a function is the function of the consistent estimator. Theorem 4.2.2 also applies to vector functions. If $\hat{\boldsymbol{\theta}}$ is a consistent estimator of the $K \times 1$ vector $\boldsymbol{\theta}$, then the vector function $\mathbf{g}(\hat{\boldsymbol{\theta}})$ is a consistent estimator of the vector function $\mathbf{g}(\boldsymbol{\theta})$.

The second invariance property concerns maximum likelihood estimation.

Theorem 4.2.3 (Invariance of Maximum Likelihood Estimation). *Let $\hat{\theta}_1, \hat{\theta}_2, \ldots, \hat{\theta}_K$ be the maximum likelihood estimators of $\theta_1, \theta_2, \ldots, \theta_K$. Let $\alpha_1 = \alpha_1(\theta_1, \ldots, \theta_K), \ldots, \alpha_K = \alpha_K(\theta_1, \ldots, \theta_K)$ be a set of transformations that are one-to-one. Then the maximum likelihood estimators of $\alpha_1, \ldots, \alpha_K$ are $\hat{\alpha}_1 = \alpha_1(\hat{\theta}_1, \ldots, \hat{\theta}_K), \hat{\alpha}_2 = \alpha_2(\hat{\theta}_1, \ldots, \hat{\theta}_K), \ldots, \hat{\alpha}_K = \alpha_K(\hat{\theta}_1, \ldots, \hat{\theta}_K)$.*

This theorem states that a function of a maximum likelihood estimator is the maximum likelihood estimator of the function. Also according to Theorem 4.2.1, the newly created estimators are consistent, distributed asymptotically normal, and are asymptotically efficient. Maximum likelihood estimation, as well as asymptotic efficiency, is invariant to one-to-one transformations.

The following theorem is important when interest in an economic model centers on (possibly nonlinear) functions of parameters and hypothesis tests concerning them.

Corollary 4.2.2 (Corollary to Theorem 4.2.1). *Let $\hat{\boldsymbol{\theta}}$ denote the maximum likelihood estimator of $\boldsymbol{\theta}$. Then the asymptotic covariance matrix of the (possibly nonlinear) vector function $\boldsymbol{\psi}(\hat{\boldsymbol{\theta}}) = (\psi_1(\hat{\boldsymbol{\theta}}), \ldots, \psi_K(\hat{\boldsymbol{\theta}}))'$, where the $\psi_i(\boldsymbol{\theta})$, $i = 1, 2, \ldots, K$, each represent an independent one-to-one scalar function of $\boldsymbol{\theta}$, is*

$$\frac{1}{T} G \lim_{T \to \infty} \left[-\frac{1}{T} E \frac{\partial^2 \ln L(\mathbf{x}; \boldsymbol{\theta})}{\partial \boldsymbol{\theta}\, \partial \boldsymbol{\theta}'} \right]^{-1} G',$$

where the (i, j)th *element,* $i, j = 1, 2, \ldots, K$, *of G denotes the derivative of $\psi_i(\boldsymbol{\theta})$ with respect to the* jth *element of $\boldsymbol{\theta}$. Also $\boldsymbol{\psi}(\hat{\boldsymbol{\theta}})$ is an asymptotically efficient estimator of $\boldsymbol{\psi}(\boldsymbol{\theta})$.*

Proof. See Theil (1971, p. 383). The proof of Corollary 4.2.2 involves a first-order Taylor series expansion of $\boldsymbol{\psi}(\boldsymbol{\theta})$ and the fact that $\boldsymbol{\psi}(\hat{\boldsymbol{\theta}})$ is asymptotically distributed the same as $G\hat{\boldsymbol{\theta}}$. □

This corollary is of importance when tests of hypotheses concerning the function $\boldsymbol{\psi}(\boldsymbol{\theta})$ are of interest. The estimated asymptotic covariance matrix of $\boldsymbol{\psi}(\boldsymbol{\theta})$ is that given by Corollary 4.2.2 except all unknown parameters are replaced by their corresponding maximum likelihood estimates. It should also be noted that Corollary 4.2.2 is applicable in the context of any consistent estimator $\hat{\boldsymbol{\theta}}$, not necessarily a maximum likelihood estimator, with asymptotic covariance matrix V. Then the asymptotic variance of $\boldsymbol{\psi}(\hat{\boldsymbol{\theta}})$ is GVG'. To illustrate the usefulness of Corollary 4.2.2 consider the following example.

Example 4.2.3. After simplification $y_t = \alpha\gamma + \beta\gamma x_t + (1 - \gamma)y_{t-1} + e_t$ is the lagged dependent variable model which results from the partial adjustment hypothesis (see Chapter 17). The unrestricted counterpart of the above equation is $y_t = \beta_1 + \beta_2 x_t + \beta_3 y_{t-1} + e_t$. The unrestricted coefficients are related to the original parameters by $\beta_1 = \alpha\gamma$, $\beta_2 = \beta\gamma$, and $\beta_3 = (1 - \gamma)$. On the other hand, the original parameters α, β, and γ are related to the unrestricted coefficients by $\alpha = \beta_1/(1 - \beta_3)$, $\beta = \beta_2/(1 - \beta_3)$, and $\gamma = (1 - \beta_3)$. From Corollary 4.2.2, the asymptotic variances of $\hat{\alpha} = \hat{\beta}_1/(1 - \hat{\beta}_3)$, $\hat{\beta} = \hat{\beta}_2/(1 - \hat{\beta}_3)$, and $\hat{\gamma} = (1 - \hat{\beta}_3)$ can be straightforwardly obtained (see Exercise 4.1) and the usual tests of hypotheses can be conducted on α, β, and γ. Moreover, if the e_t are independently and identically distributed $N(0, \sigma^2)$, $\hat{\alpha}$, $\hat{\beta}$, and $\hat{\gamma}$ are asymptotically efficient estimates of α, β, and γ given $\hat{\beta}_1$, $\hat{\beta}_2$, and $\hat{\beta}_3$ are the maximum likelihood estimators of β_1, β_2, and β_3.

Finally, Theorem 4.2.4 generalizes the small sample properties of the likelihood ratio statistic discussed in the previous chapter.

Theorem 4.2.4. *Assume the usual regularity conditions of maximum likelihood estimation are satisfied. Let $l = L(\hat{\omega})/L(\hat{\Omega})$ denote the likelihood ratio statistic,* *where Ω is the K-dimensional universal parameter set and ω represents the $(K - q)$-dimensional subset of Ω corresponding to the null hypothesis. Then, if the null hypothesis is true,*

$$-2 \ln l \overset{\text{asy}}{\sim} \chi_q^2,$$

where χ_q^2 denotes the χ^2-distribution with q degrees of freedom and $\overset{\text{asy}}{\sim}$ is read "is asymptotically distributed as."

PROOF. See Theil (1971, pp. 396–397). □

This asymptotic result is especially useful when the first-order maximum likelihood conditions are nonlinear and a closed form solution is not available and/or when no intuitively obvious transformation of l leads to a recognizable distribution.

Now that the basic results of asymptotic distribution theory have been summarized, we apply them in an investigation of the asymptotic efficiency of the ordinary least squares estimators $\hat{\boldsymbol{\beta}}$ and $\hat{\sigma}^2$ in the classical normal linear regression model.

4.3 Asymptotic Efficiency of $\hat{\boldsymbol{\beta}}$ and $\hat{\sigma}^2$ Under Normality

From the previous discussion it is obvious that there are two basic ways of showing that a consistent, uniformally, asymptotically normal estimator is asymptotically efficient. Either, (i) prove the estimator in question has the same asymptotic distribution as the maximum likelihood estimator, or (ii) show that the variance of the estimator attains the asymptotic Cramér–Rao lower bound. Either approach can be used in investigating the asymptotic efficiency of the ordinary least squares estimators $\hat{\boldsymbol{\beta}}$ and $\hat{\sigma}^2$ in the classical normal linear regression model (Definition 3.2.1).

Since $\hat{\boldsymbol{\beta}}$ and $\tilde{\sigma}^2 = (\mathbf{y} - X\hat{\boldsymbol{\beta}})'(\mathbf{y} - X\hat{\boldsymbol{\beta}})/T$ are maximum likelihood estimators, asymptotic efficiency follows immediately from Theorem 4.2.1 and the fact that the multivariate normal distribution satisfies the necessary regularity conditions. Notice that $\hat{\sigma}^2$ converges in the limit to the maximum likelihood estimator $\tilde{\sigma}^2$ hence $\hat{\sigma}^2$ is also asymptotically efficient.

Alternatively, consider the verification of the asymptotic efficiency of $\hat{\boldsymbol{\beta}}$ and $\hat{\sigma}^2$ through the examination of the asymptotic Cramér–Rao lower bound. From Theorem 3.3.2 the information matrix is

$$I(\boldsymbol{\beta}, \sigma^2) = \begin{bmatrix} \dfrac{X'X}{\sigma^2} & \mathbf{0} \\ \mathbf{0}' & \dfrac{T}{2\sigma^4} \end{bmatrix}.$$

Therefore,

$$\lim_{T\to\infty}\left[\frac{I(\boldsymbol{\beta},\sigma^2)}{T}\right] = \begin{bmatrix} \dfrac{Q}{\sigma^2} & \mathbf{0} \\ \mathbf{0}' & \dfrac{1}{2\sigma^4} \end{bmatrix}$$

and the asymptotic Cramér–Rao lower bound is

$$\frac{1}{T}\lim_{T\to\infty}\left[\frac{I(\boldsymbol{\beta},\sigma^2)}{T}\right]^{-1} = \frac{1}{T}\begin{bmatrix} \sigma^2 Q^{-1} & \mathbf{0} \\ \mathbf{0}' & 2\sigma^4 \end{bmatrix}.$$

Theorem 4.3.1. *The asymptotic distribution of* $\sqrt{T}(\hat{\boldsymbol{\beta}} - \boldsymbol{\beta})$ *is* $N(\mathbf{0}, \sigma^2 Q^{-1})$, *where* $Q = \lim_{T\to\infty}(X'X/T)$ *and* $\hat{\boldsymbol{\beta}}$ *is an asymptotically efficient estimator of* $\boldsymbol{\beta}$.

PROOF. For given sample size T, the distribution of $\sqrt{T}(\hat{\boldsymbol{\beta}} - \boldsymbol{\beta})$ *is*

$$N(\mathbf{0}, \sigma^2(X'X/T)^{-1}).$$

As a result, the asymptotic distribution of $\sqrt{T}(\hat{\boldsymbol{\beta}} - \boldsymbol{\beta})$ is $N(\mathbf{0}, \sigma^2 Q^{-1})$. Then the asymptotic variance of $\hat{\boldsymbol{\beta}}$ is $(\sigma^2/T)Q^{-1}$ which coincides with the Cramér–Rao lower bound. By Corollary 4.2.1, $\hat{\boldsymbol{\beta}}$ is asymptotically efficient. □

Lemma 4.3.1 (Lindberg–Levy Central Limit Theorem). *Let* $x_1, x_2, \ldots$ *be a sequence of independent and identically distributed random variables with finite mean* μ *and finite variance* σ^2. *Then the random variable*

$$z_T = \frac{1}{\sqrt{T}}\sum_{t=1}^{T}\left(\frac{x_t - \mu}{\sigma}\right)$$

converges in distribution to $N(0, 1)$.

PROOF. See Theil (1971, pp. 368–369). □

Theorem 4.3.2. *The asymptotic distribution of* $\sqrt{T}(\hat{\sigma}^2 - \sigma^2)$ *is* $N(0, 2\sigma^4)$ *and* $\hat{\sigma}^2$ *is an asymptotically efficient estimator of* σ^2.

PROOF. By Theorem 3.2.1 $(\mathbf{y} - X\hat{\boldsymbol{\beta}})'(\mathbf{y} - X\hat{\boldsymbol{\beta}})/\sigma^2 = \mathrm{SSE}/\sigma^2 \sim \chi^2_{T-K}$. Therefore, $\mathrm{SSE}/\sigma^2 = \sum_{t=1}^{T-K} v_t^2$, where the v_t are independently distributed as $N(0, 1)$ and v_t^2 are independently distributed *as* χ_1^2 with mean 1 and variance 2. By the Lindgerg–Levy theorem

$$\frac{1}{\sqrt{T-K}}\sum_{t=1}^{T-K}\left(\frac{v_t^2 - 1}{\sqrt{2}}\right) \overset{\text{asy}}{\approx} N(0, 1). \tag{4.3.1}$$

Interest centers on the asymptotic distribution of $\sqrt{T}(\hat{\sigma}^2 - \sigma^2)$. Expanding (4.3.1) and substituting $\sum_{t=1}^{T-K} v_t^2$ yields

$$\left(\frac{1}{\sqrt{2(T-K)}}\frac{\mathrm{SSE}}{\sigma^2} - \frac{\sqrt{T-K}}{\sqrt{2}}\right) \overset{\text{asy}}{\approx} N(0, 1).$$

Multiplying the left-hand side by $\sigma^2\sqrt{2}(\sqrt{T}/\sqrt{T-K})$, and noting that $\sqrt{T}/\sqrt{T-K}$ has the limiting value one, we have

$$\frac{\sigma^2\sqrt{2T}}{\sqrt{T-K}}\left(\frac{1}{\sqrt{2(T-K)}}\frac{\text{SSE}}{\sigma^2} - \frac{\sqrt{T-K}}{\sqrt{2}}\right) \overset{\text{asy}}{\approx} \sqrt{2}\sigma^2 N(0, 1).$$

Simplifying the left-hand yields

$$\sqrt{T}(\hat{\sigma}^2 - \sigma^2) \overset{\text{asy}}{\approx} N(0, 2\sigma^4).$$

Then the asymptotic variance of $\hat{\sigma}^2$ is $2\sigma^4/T$ which equals the asymptotic Cramér–Rao lower bound. By Corollary 4.2.1, $\hat{\sigma}^2$ is asymptotically efficient. □

The asymptotic efficiency of $\hat{\boldsymbol{\beta}}$ and $\hat{\sigma}^2$ depends upon their coincidence to the maximum likelihood estimators of the model at hand. These results are *totally* dependent on the assumption of normality. Given the standard linear model with homoscedastic error variances but exponential distribution, say, the asymptotic efficiency properties proven here *do not hold*. In any given model, the information matrix and corresponding Cramér–Rao lower bounds must be established anew. Equivalently, the new maximum likelihood estimates must be derived and new comparisons made.

Finally, consider the construction of a consistent estimator of the asymptotic covariance matrix for $\hat{\boldsymbol{\beta}}$ and $\hat{\sigma}^2$. Let $\boldsymbol{\theta}' = (\boldsymbol{\beta}', \sigma^2)$, then

$$\frac{\partial^2 \ln L(\mathbf{y};\boldsymbol{\theta})}{\partial\boldsymbol{\theta}\,\partial\boldsymbol{\theta}'} = \begin{bmatrix} -\dfrac{X'X}{\sigma^2} & -\dfrac{1}{\sigma^4}X'(\mathbf{y} - X\boldsymbol{\beta}) \\ \cdot & \dfrac{T}{2\sigma^4} - \dfrac{1}{\sigma^6}(\mathbf{y} - X\boldsymbol{\beta})'(\mathbf{y} - X\boldsymbol{\beta}) \end{bmatrix}.$$

Therefore,

$$-E\left[\frac{\partial^2 \ln L(\mathbf{y};\boldsymbol{\theta})}{\partial\boldsymbol{\theta}\,\partial\boldsymbol{\theta}'}\right] = \begin{bmatrix} \dfrac{X'X}{\sigma^2} & \mathbf{0} \\ \mathbf{0}' & \dfrac{T}{2\sigma^4} \end{bmatrix}.$$

A consistent estimator of the asymptotic covariance matrix of $\hat{\boldsymbol{\beta}}$ and $\hat{\sigma}^2$ is then

$$-E\left[\frac{\partial^2 \ln L(\mathbf{y};\boldsymbol{\theta})}{\partial\boldsymbol{\theta}\,\partial\boldsymbol{\theta}'}\right]^{-1}_{\boldsymbol{\theta}=\hat{\boldsymbol{\theta}}} = \begin{bmatrix} \hat{\sigma}^2(X'X)^{-1} & \mathbf{0} \\ \mathbf{0}' & \dfrac{2\hat{\sigma}^4}{T} \end{bmatrix}.$$

4.4 Nonnormal Disturbances

From the previous developments, it is obvious that the assumption of normality is an essential ingredient is small sample tests, of hypotheses and estimator properties. Given this role of normality, several questions naturally arise. Upon what general conditions can a claim of normality for disturbances in regression models be based? In the absence of normality, what properties of the linear model are retained? These questions are addressed below.

Theorem 4.4.1 (Lindberg–Feller Theorem). *Let $x_1, x_2, \ldots$ be a sequence of independent random variables with cumulative distribution functions F_i, means μ_i and variances $\sigma_i^2 \neq 0$. If*

$$z_t = \frac{\sum_{i=1}^t (x_i - \mu_i)}{c_t},$$

where

$$c_t = \left(\sum_{i=1}^t \sigma_i^2\right)^{1/2},$$

the necessary and sufficient condition for

(i) *z_t to converge in distribution to a $N(0, 1)$ variable and*

(ii) $$\lim_{t \to \infty} \max_{1 \le i \le t} \frac{\sigma_i}{c_t} = 0$$

is that, for every $\varepsilon > 0$

$$\lim_{t \to \infty} \frac{1}{c_t^2} \sum_{i=1}^t \int_{|x-\mu_i| > \varepsilon c_t} (x - \mu_i)^2 \, dF_i(x) = 0.$$

PROOF. See Gnedenko (1962). □

Under appropriate conditions, the above theorem can be applied to the distribution of the error terms in linear econometric models. Assume $\varepsilon_1, \varepsilon_2, \ldots, \varepsilon_p$ are omitted effects, where p is sufficiently large, with means μ_i and variances σ_i^2. Note that the ε_i do not have to be identically distributed or normal. Then the error term e can be thought of as $e = \varepsilon_1 + \varepsilon_2 + \cdots + \varepsilon_p$ and will have an approximate normal distribution with mean $\mu = \sum \mu_i$ and variance $\sigma^2 = \sum \sigma_i^2$. Note that, if $\mu \neq 0$, the usual assumption $E(e) = 0$ leads to the conventional interpretation that the intercept, at least in part, represents the mean of the omitted effects.

Now assume the conditions of the above theorem do not hold. Suppose, for example, that the number of neglected factors is not large and arise from asymmetric distributions or, possibly from the *a priori* reasoning underlying the model at hand, normality is not tenable. Though normality may not be tenable, suppose the error terms retain the property of being independently and identically distributed with zero mean and finite variance. What results remain intact?

From theoretical results developed earlier in the chapter, it is evident that $\hat{\boldsymbol{\beta}}$ is best linear unbiased, consistent, and has covariance matrix $\sigma^2(X'X)^{-1}$ while $\hat{\sigma}^2$ is unbiased and consistent. However, $\hat{\boldsymbol{\beta}}$ does not have a normal distribution, $(T - K)\hat{\sigma}^2/\sigma^2$ does not have a χ^2-distribution and neither $\hat{\boldsymbol{\beta}}$ or $\hat{\sigma}^2$ are minimum variance unbiased or asymptotically efficient. Moreover, the small sample tests (t and F) of hypotheses developed using normality are no longer valid. Of course, if the particular nonnormal distribution of $\mathbf{e}$ is known, then it might be possible to work out the sampling distributions for $\hat{\boldsymbol{\beta}}$ and $\hat{\sigma}^2$ and hence confidence intervals. Whether or not this can be done depends upon the tractibility of the postulated distribution.

Fortunately, however, all is not lost. It can be shown that the usual test procedures previously discussed are still *asymptotically* valid in the case that the e_t are independent and identically distributed with zero mean and constant variance σ^2, the error specification of the classical linear regression model. Given this result, the need to establish the validity of the homoscedastic error assumption becomes quite important.

Lemma 4.4.1. *Assume the elements of* $\mathbf{e}$ *are independent and identically distributed with zero mean and finite variance* σ^2. *If the elements of* X *are uniformly bounded in the sense that* $|x_{ti}| \leq c$ *for all* i, c *being a finite constant, and if*

$$\lim_{T \to \infty} \frac{X'X}{T} = Q$$

is finite and nonsingular, then

$$\frac{1}{\sqrt{T}} X'\mathbf{e} \overset{\text{asy}}{\sim} N(\mathbf{0}, \sigma^2 Q).$$

Proof. See Schmidt (1976, pp. 56–60) and Theil (1971, pp. 380–381). □

Theorem 4.4.2. *In the presence of the conditions of Lemma* 4.4.1

$$\sqrt{T}(\hat{\boldsymbol{\beta}} - \boldsymbol{\beta}) \overset{\text{asy}}{\sim} N(\mathbf{0}, \sigma^2 Q^{-1}).$$

Proof.

$$\begin{aligned}\sqrt{T}(\hat{\boldsymbol{\beta}} - \boldsymbol{\beta}) &= \sqrt{T}[(X'X)^{-1}X'\mathbf{e}] \\ &= \left(\frac{X'X}{T}\right)^{-1} \cdot \frac{1}{\sqrt{T}} X'\mathbf{e}.\end{aligned}$$

From Lemma 4.4.1, $(1/\sqrt{T})X'\mathbf{e} \overset{\text{asy}}{\sim} N(\mathbf{0}, \sigma^2 Q)$ and by assumption

$$\lim_{T \to \infty} \left(\frac{X'X}{T}\right)^{-1} = Q^{-1},$$

therefore, $\sqrt{T}(\hat{\boldsymbol{\beta}} - \boldsymbol{\beta}) \overset{\text{asy}}{\sim} N(\mathbf{0}, \sigma^2 Q^{-1} Q Q^{-1}) = N(\mathbf{0}, \sigma^2 Q^{-1})$. □

Theorem 4.4.2 shows that, when the error terms $\mathbf{e}$ are independent and identically distributed with zero mean and finite variance, the ordinary least squares estimator $\hat{\boldsymbol{\beta}}$ has the same asymptotic distribution whether or not the disturbances are normal. Notice that in the absence of normality nothing can be claimed about asymptotic efficiency. The parent distribution of $\mathbf{e}$ must be given and the maximum likelihood estimates determined before asymptotic efficiency can be claimed. As in the small sample efficiency case where, relative to best linear unbiased, the more general minimum variance unbiased result can be claimed in the presence of normality, knowledge concerning the form of the error distribution allows the stronger claim of asymptotic efficiency. These results are quite intuitive given that, in general, the more that is known about a process, the more definitive the deduced conclusions.

In the following two theorems it is shown that the usual t- and F-tests of hypotheses are *asymptotically* valid under general conditions.

Theorem 4.4.3. *Assume the elements of* $\mathbf{e}$ *are independent and identically distributed with zero mean and finite variance, and that* Q *is finite and nonsingular. Let* $\mathbf{R}'$ *denote a known* $1 \times K$ *vector,* r *a known scalar, and* $\hat{\boldsymbol{\beta}}$ *the ordinary least squares estimator. Then under the null hypothesis that* $\mathbf{R}'\boldsymbol{\beta} = r$,

$$\frac{\mathbf{R}'\hat{\boldsymbol{\beta}} - r}{(\hat{\sigma}^2\mathbf{R}'(X'X)^{-1}\mathbf{R})^{1/2}} \overset{\text{asy}}{\approx} N(0, 1).$$

Proof. Under the null hypothesis, $\mathbf{R}'\boldsymbol{\beta} = r$,

$$\mathbf{R}'\hat{\boldsymbol{\beta}} - r = \mathbf{R}'(\hat{\boldsymbol{\beta}} - \boldsymbol{\beta})$$

and the test statistic is equivalent to

$$\frac{\sqrt{T}\,\mathbf{R}'(\hat{\boldsymbol{\beta}} - \boldsymbol{\beta})}{(\hat{\sigma}^2\mathbf{R}'(X'X/T)^{-1}\mathbf{R})^{1/2}}.$$

From Theorem 4.4.2, $\sqrt{T}(\hat{\boldsymbol{\beta}} - \boldsymbol{\beta}) \overset{\text{asy}}{\approx} N(\mathbf{0}, \sigma^2 Q^{-1})$, and, therefore, for the numerator

$$\sqrt{T}(\mathbf{R}'(\hat{\boldsymbol{\beta}} - \boldsymbol{\beta})) \overset{\text{asy}}{\approx} N(\mathbf{0}, \sigma^2\mathbf{R}'Q^{-1}\mathbf{R}).$$

In the denominator as plim $\hat{\sigma}^2 = \sigma^2$ and $\lim_{T\to\infty}(X'X/T)^{-1} = Q^{-1}$,

$$(\hat{\sigma}^2\mathbf{R}'(X'X/T)^{-1}\mathbf{R})^{1/2} \overset{\text{asy}}{\approx} (\sigma^2\mathbf{R}'Q^{-1}\mathbf{R})^{1/2}.$$

Asymptotically speaking, the statistic is a standard normal random variable. □

Notice that the above result is only asymptotically valid. Equivalently, the usual t_{T-K}-distribution can be used, asymptotically, for statistical inference purposes, since the t-distribution and $N(0, 1)$-distribution converge as the number of degrees of freedom approaches infinity. Whether it is better to use the $N(0, 1)$-distribution or t-distribution in *small samples* is an open question.

Theorem 4.4.4. *Let the elements of* $\mathbf{e}$ *be independent and identically distributed with zero mean and finite variance* σ^2, *and* $\lim_{T\to\infty}(X'X/T) = Q$ *be a finite and nonsingular matrix. Let* R *be a known* $J \times K$ *matrix of rank* $J(0 < J \leq K)$ *and* $\mathbf{r}$ *a known* $J \times 1$ *vector. Then under the null hypothesis,* $R\boldsymbol{\beta} = \mathbf{r}$,

$$\frac{(\mathbf{r} - R\hat{\boldsymbol{\beta}})'[R(X'X)^{-1}R']^{-1}(\mathbf{r} - R\hat{\boldsymbol{\beta}})/J}{\hat{\sigma}^2} \overset{\text{asy}}{\approx} \frac{\chi_J^2}{J}.$$

Proof. See Schmidt (1976, pp. 63–64). □

This test is only asymptotically valid. The $F_{J,T-K}$-distribution can be used in lieu of the χ_J^2/J-distribution as they converge as the number of observations approaches infinity. As before, it is still an open question as to which distribution is to be preferred in small samples.

In summary, the conventional tests of hypotheses in the classical normal linear regression model are also appropriate for the classical linear regression model without normality (see Definition 2.2.1) given a "large" sample size.

4.5 Summary and Guide to Further Readings

The concept of the asymptotic Cramér–Rao lower bound allows the comparison of the relative efficiency of two estimators though they may have no determinable small sample properties. This method of comparison proves very helpful in many of the econometric models to be addressed here and elsewhere. Under certain fairly unrestrictive regularity conditions, maximum likelihood estimators are consistent and asymptotically efficient among the class of consistent, uniformly, asymptotically normal estimators. These sweeping properties, as well as the invariance property of maximum likelihood estimators, lend credence to the claim that the maximum likelihood method is the centerpiece of econometric methods.

Other principal results in the chapter include: the proof that the ordinary least squares estimators $\hat{\boldsymbol{\beta}}$ and $\hat{\sigma}^2$ are asymptotically efficient estimators in the presence of normally distributed error terms; the relaxation of the normality requirement for tests of hypotheses in large samples; a theorem which allows asymptotic tests of nonlinear functions; and the asymptotic likelihood ratio test.

This chapter has provided a comprehensive introduction to asymptotic distribution theory. Detailed presentations of proofs for theorems in this chapter are better left for a thorough study in mathematical statistics. The interested reader would benefit from reviewing the properties of characteristic functions in Cramér (1946) and Wilks (1962) and their application to proofs of, for example, Khintchine's theorem (Theorem 2.4.3) and the Lindberg–Levy central limit theorem (Theorem 4.3.1). An in-depth development of the asymptotic properties of the maximum likelihood estimators can be found in Dhrymes (1974, pp. 114–130).

4.6 Exercises

4.1. Derive the form of the G matrix of Corollary 4.2.2 for Example 4.2.3. Construct a consistent estimate of the asymptotic covariance matrix of $\hat{\alpha}$, $\hat{\beta}$, and $\hat{\gamma}$.

The following three exercises illustrate the usefulness of Corollary 4.2.2.

4.2. Given the Cobb–Douglas production function

$$Y = a_0 K^{a_1} L^{a_2} \mu,$$

where $Y \equiv$ output, $K \equiv$ capital, $L \equiv$ labor, and μ is a stochastic error term, the corresponding reduced form cost function is

$$C = \gamma Y^{1/r} P_{\mathrm{K}}^{a_1/r} P_{\mathrm{L}}^{a_2/r} v$$

where $C =$ total cost of production, $Y \equiv$ output, $P_{\mathrm{K}} \equiv$ price of capital, $P_{\mathrm{L}} \equiv$ price of labor, $\gamma = r(a_0 a_1^{a_1} a_2^{a_2})^{-1/2}$, $v = \mu^{-1/r}$ and $r = a_1 + a_2$. Taking natural logarithms yields

$$\ln C = \ln \gamma + \frac{1}{r} \ln Y + \frac{a_1}{r} \ln P_{\mathrm{K}} + \frac{a_2}{r} \ln P_{\mathrm{L}} + \ln v.$$

Imposing the restriction $a_1/r + a_2/r = 1$ results in the estimation equation

$$(\ln C - \ln P_{\mathrm{L}}) = \ln \gamma + \frac{1}{r} \ln Y + \frac{a_1}{r} (\ln P_{\mathrm{K}} - \ln P_{\mathrm{L}}) + \ln v.$$

In conventional form we have

$$y_t = \beta_1 + \beta_2 x_{t2} + \beta_3 x_{t3} + e_t,$$

where $\beta_1 = \ln \gamma$, $\beta_2 = 1/r$, $\beta_3 = a_1/r$, $e_t = \ln v$, $x_{t2} = \ln Y$, and

$$x_{t3} = (\ln P_{\mathrm{K}} - \ln P_{\mathrm{L}}).$$

Assume that that classical linear regression assumptions hold, the e_t are independent and identically distributed with zero mean and variance σ^2, and $\lim_{T\to\infty}(X'X/T) = Q$ is finite and nonsingular.

(a) Describe how you would estimate the returns to scale $r = a_1 + a_2$ and how you would conduct a test of the hypotheses: $H_0: r = 1$ versus $H_1: r \neq 1$.

(b) Check below the properties of your estimate of r given the conditions imposed.

Without normality of e_t		With normality of e_t	
	$\hat{r}$		$\hat{r}$
consistent		consistent	
best, linear, unbiased		best, linear, unbiased	
minimum variance unbiased		minimum variance unbiased	
asymptotically efficient		asymptotically efficient	

(c) Describe how you would estimate the output elasticity of capital, a_1, and how you would conduct a test of the hypotheses: $H_0: a_1 = 0.5$ versus $H_1: a_1 \neq 0.5$.

(d) Repeat part (b) but with respect to your estimate of a_1.

4.3. Consider the constant-elasticity-of-substitution production function

$$Q_i = c[\alpha K_i^{-\rho} + (1 - \alpha)L_i^{-\rho}]^{-v/\rho} e^{\xi_i},$$

where c is the efficiency parameter, α is the distribution parameter, ρ is the substitution parameter, v is the returns to scale parameter, Q_i, K_i, and L_i are output, capital, and labor, and ξ_i is an independent and identically distributed error term with zero mean and variance σ^2. By taking natural logarithms, we obtain

$$\ln Q_i = \ln c - \frac{v}{\rho} \ln[\alpha K_i^{-\rho} + (1 - \alpha)L_i^{-\rho}] + \xi_i.$$

Assume that ρ is not far from zero and apply a Taylor series approximation at $\rho = 0$. The result is

$$\ln Q_i = \ln c + v\alpha \ln K_i + v(1 - \alpha) \ln L_i$$
$$-\tfrac{1}{2}\rho v\alpha(1 - \alpha)[\ln K_i - \ln L_i]^2 + \xi_i.$$

Suppose the parameter of interest is the substitution parameter ρ. (Note: $\sigma = 1/(1 + \rho)$ is the elasticity of substitution.)

(a) Explain how you would obtain an estimate of ρ.

(b) Describe how you would test the hypotheses: $H_0: \rho = 0$ versus $H_1: \rho \neq 0$.

(c) Check below the properties of your estimate of ρ given the conditions imposed.

Without normality of ξ_i	$\hat{\rho}$	With normality of ξ_i	$\hat{\rho}$
consistent		consistent	
best, linear, unbiased		best, linear, unbiased	
minimum variance unbiased		minimum variance unbiased	
asymptotically efficient		asymptotically efficient	

(d) Establish estimates for the other parameters: c, α, and v. What are the properties of these estimates, first, without normality of ξ_i, and then, with normality of ξ_i?

4.4. Consider the long-run cost minimizing expansion path relation

$$(K/L)_t = [(\beta_0/\alpha_0)e^{(\lambda_1 - \lambda_2)t}]^{1-\sigma}(w/r)_t^{\sigma} e^{u_t},$$

where K = capital, L = labor, w = wage rate, r = rental rate, β_0 and α_0 are initial factor shares of labor and capital, σ = elasticity of substitution between capital and labor, $\lambda_1 = (\dot{\beta}/\beta)$ and $\lambda_2 = (\dot{\alpha}/\alpha)$ are the constant proportional rates of labor and capital augmentation and u_t is an independent and identically distributed error term with zero mean and variance σ^2. The statistical counterpart of the above expansion path is

$$y_t = \gamma_1 + \gamma_2 x_{t2} + \gamma_3 x_{t3} + u_t, \qquad t = 1, 2, \ldots, T,$$

where $y_t = \ln(K/L)_t$, $x_{t2} = \ln(w/r)_t$, $x_{t3} = t$, $\gamma_1 = (1 - \sigma)\ln(\beta_0/\alpha_0)$, $\gamma_2 = \sigma$ and $\gamma_3 = (1 - \sigma)(\lambda_1 - \lambda_2)$. Suppose the parameters of interest are σ and $(\lambda_1 - \lambda_2)$.

(a) Describe how you would estimate σ and $(\lambda_1 - \lambda_2)$.

(b) Describe how you would *jointly* test the hypotheses $H_0: \sigma = \lambda_1 - \lambda_2 = 0$ versus H_1: not H_0.

(c) Describe how you would test the hypotheses of neutral technical change $(\lambda_1 - \lambda_2 = 0)$ versus nonneutral technical change.

(d) Check below the properties of the estimates σ and $(\lambda_1 - \lambda_2)$ given the conditions imposed

Without normality

	$\hat{\sigma}$	$\widehat{\lambda_1 - \lambda_2}$
consistent		
best, linear, unbiased		
minimum variance unbiased		
asymptotically efficient		

With normality

	$\hat{\sigma}$	$\widehat{\lambda_1 - \lambda_2}$
consistent		
best, linear, unbiased		
minimum variance unbiased		
asymptotically efficient		

4.5. Show that for the general linear hypothesis $R\boldsymbol{\beta} = \mathbf{r}$, the u-statistic of (3.4.17) provides a test which is asymptotically equivalent to using the result that

$$-2 \ln l \overset{\text{asy}}{\sim} \chi_J^2.$$

4.6. One may write a Frontier Production function in the following manner

$$y_t = \alpha + \sum_{i=1}^{K} \beta_i x_{ti} - e_t$$

where the assumptions of the classical linear regression model hold except $e_t \geq 0$. That is, the e_t are independently and identically distributed with finite mean $m > 0$ and variance σ^2. Notice that the e_t cannot be normally distributed.

(a) Show that $(\alpha - m)$ and the β_i can be consistently estimated by ordinary least squares.

(b) Are the usual tests of hypotheses involving the β_i justified in small samples? large samples? Why?

(c) Is ordinary least squares appropriate for estimating the "frontier" $y_t = \alpha + \sum_{i=1}^{K} \beta_i x_{ti}$?

4.7 References

Cramér, H. (1946). *Mathematical Methods of Statistics.* Princeton, NJ: Princeton University Press.

Dhrymes, P. J. (1974). *Econometrics.* New York: Springer-Verlag.

Gnedenko, B. (1962). *The Theory of Probability.* New York: Chelsea.

Kendall, M. G. and Stuart, A. (1973). *The Advanced Theory of Statistics*, vol. 2, 3rd ed. New York: Hafner.

Rao, C. R. (1973). *Linear Statistical Inference and Its Application*, 2nd ed. New York: Wiley.

Schmidt, P. (1976). *Econometrics.* New York: Marcel Dekker.

Theil, H. (1971). *Principles of Econometrics.* New York: Wiley.

Wilks, S. (1962). *Mathematical Statistics.* New York: Wiley.

CHAPTER 5
Stochastic Regressors

5.1 Introduction

To this point we have considered the linear statistical model $\mathbf{y} = X\boldsymbol{\beta} + \mathbf{e}$, where the regressors X are treated as fixed in repeated samples. In many cases, however, this assumption is not tenable. The explanatory variables economists and other social scientists use are often generated by stochastic processes beyond their control. In this chapter we consider the consequences of relaxing the fixed X assumption under two distinct circumstances. In the first instance multivariate normality is assumed. That is, $(y_t, \mathbf{x}_t')'$ is assumed to be distributed as a $(K + 1)$-multivariate normal random vector with variance–covariance matrix Σ. In the second instance, a more relaxed set of assumptions is considered; the case where X and $\mathbf{e}$ are independently distributed along with other mild conditions on their distributions. The major conclusion of this chapter's study of these stochastic regressor models is that, under general conditions, the essential results of the fixed regressor models (i.e. the classical linear regression and classical normal linear regression models of Definitions 2.2.1 and 3.2.1, respectively) remain intact even if an experimenter does not have control of the settings of the regressor matrix. There is the problem of multicollinearity, however, but that is the subject of Chapter 13.

The remainder of this chapter is organized as follows: In Section 5.2 the multivariate normal case is discussed. In Section 5.3 the independent stochastic linear regression model is presented. Section 5.4 contains a summary and guide to further readings.

5.2 Multivariate Normal Linear Regression Model

The multivariate normal linear regression model is formally specified in the following definition.

Definition 5.2.1 (The Multivariate Normal Linear Regression Model). Suppose that T independent vectors $(y_t, \mathbf{x}_t')'$, $t = 1, 2, \ldots, T$ constitute a random sample from a $(K + 1)$-multivariate normal distribution. Let the mean vector be given by

$$E\begin{bmatrix} y_t \\ \mathbf{x}_t \end{bmatrix} = \begin{bmatrix} \mu_y \\ \boldsymbol{\mu}_x \end{bmatrix} = \boldsymbol{\mu} \tag{5.2.1}$$

and the covariance matrix by

$$\Sigma = \begin{bmatrix} \sigma_y^2 & \Sigma_{\mathbf{xy}}' \\ \Sigma_{\mathbf{xy}} & \Sigma_{\mathbf{xx}} \end{bmatrix}. \tag{5.2.2}$$

The conditional distribution of $(y_t | \mathbf{x}_t)$ is normal with mean $E(y_t | \mathbf{x}_t) = \beta_0 + \mathbf{x}_t'\boldsymbol{\beta}$ and variance $\sigma^2 = \sigma_y^2 - \Sigma_{\mathbf{xy}}'\Sigma_{\mathbf{xx}}^{-1}\Sigma_{\mathbf{xy}} = \sigma_y^2(1 - \rho^2)$, where ρ^2 is the population multiple correlation coefficient, i.e., $\rho^2 = \Sigma_{\mathbf{xy}}'\Sigma_{\mathbf{xx}}^{-1}\Sigma_{\mathbf{xy}}/\sigma_y^2$. The vector $\boldsymbol{\beta}$ is defined as $\boldsymbol{\beta} = \Sigma_{\mathbf{xx}}^{-1}\Sigma_{\mathbf{xy}}$ and β_0 is defined as $\beta_0 = \mu_y - \boldsymbol{\mu}_x'\boldsymbol{\beta}$. In the multivariate normal linear regression model, the regression function of interest is $E(y_t | \mathbf{x}_t) = \beta_0 + \mathbf{x}_t'\boldsymbol{\beta}$ and the parameters to be estimated are β_0, $\boldsymbol{\beta}$, and σ^2.

Now let the corresponding sample mean and covariance matrices be given by

$$\begin{bmatrix} \bar{y} \\ \bar{\mathbf{x}} \end{bmatrix} \tag{5.2.3}$$

and

$$\begin{bmatrix} s_y^2 & S_{\mathbf{xy}}' \\ S_{\mathbf{xy}} & S_{\mathbf{xx}} \end{bmatrix}, \tag{5.2.4}$$

respectively, where $S_{\mathbf{xx}} = \sum \mathbf{x}_t\mathbf{x}_t' - T\bar{\mathbf{x}}\bar{\mathbf{x}}'$, $S_{\mathbf{xy}} = \sum \mathbf{x}_t y_t - T\bar{\mathbf{x}}\bar{y}$, and $s_y^2 = \sum y_t^2 - T(\bar{y})^2$.

Given T sample observations, the maximum likelihood estimators of $\boldsymbol{\beta}$, and β_0, and σ^2 in the multivariate normal linear regression model are, respectively,

$$\tilde{\boldsymbol{\beta}} = S_{\mathbf{xx}}^{-1}S_{\mathbf{xy}}, \tag{5.2.5}$$

$$\tilde{\beta}_0 = \bar{y} - \bar{\mathbf{x}}'\tilde{\boldsymbol{\beta}}, \tag{5.2.6}$$

and

$$\tilde{\sigma}^2 = T^{-1}(s_y^2 - S_{\mathbf{xy}}'S_{\mathbf{xx}}^{-1}S_{\mathbf{xy}}). \tag{5.2.7}$$

PROOF. See Anderson (1958, pp. 44–51). □

These estimators of $\tilde{\boldsymbol{\beta}}$ and $\tilde{\beta}_0$ are, in fact, identical to the ordinary least squares estimators one would obtain conditional on X. It follows immediately from Theorem 4.2.1 that these estimators are consistent, asymptotically efficient and normally distributed since they are maximum likelihood estimators from a regular distribution. In addition, it is known (see Graybill (1961)) that the estimates $\tilde{\beta}_0$ and $\tilde{\boldsymbol{\beta}}$ are unbiased and minimum variance unbiased. Finally, the usual tests of hypotheses (using t- and F-statistics) and confidence intervals developed for the classical normal linear regression model where X is assumed fixed (Definition 3.2.1), are equally applicable to the multivariate normal linear regression model. See Graybill (1961) and Sampson (1974) for details concerning these results. Intuitively, the hypothesis testing results hold because the confidence coefficient $(1 - \alpha)$ does not depend on X. If a confidence interval encompasses a parameter for *any* given X with probability $(1 - \alpha)$, then it will do the same for a randomly selected X. In summary, the inferential framework of the classical normal linear regression model with fixed X is equally applicable to the multivariate normal linear regression model.

The requirements of this model are, however, very stringent. First, the requirement in the multivariate normal linear regression model that the observations $(y_t, \mathbf{x}_t')'$ be independently observed is not likely to be achieved in most economic settings. For example, explanatory variables like gross national product, income, etc., are most certainly correlated over time. Secondly, the requirement of multivariate normality does not apply when any of the variables are qualitative in nature (e.g., dummy variables and qualitative, censored, or truncated variables). As a result, it is desirable to study the properties of stochastic regression under less stringent conditions.

5.3 Independent Stochastic Linear Regression Model

Before formally defining what Goldberger (1964) has called the independent stochastic linear regression model, let us determine the results we can obtain from the following assumptions:

(1) Assume for any X, the assumptions of the classical linear regression model hold.
(2) X is stochastic but distributed independently of $\mathbf{e}$.

What properties of the ordinary least squares estimators $\hat{\boldsymbol{\beta}} = (X'X)^{-1}X'\mathbf{y}$, $\hat{\sigma}^2 = \hat{\mathbf{e}}'\hat{\mathbf{e}}/(T - K)$ and $\hat{\sigma}^2(X'X)^{-1}$ are retained? Are these estimators unbiased and/or consistent?

The following property of conditional expectations will prove useful. Assume that u and v are jointly distributed random variables. Then (see

Exercise 5.1) $E[h(u, v)] = E_u[E_{v|u}h(u, v)]$, where $E_{v|u}$ represents the expectation taken over the conditional distribution of v given u and E_u represents the expectation taken over the marginal distribution of u. Thus, the expectation of a function $h(u, v)$ over the joint density of u and v can be computed in two separate steps: the expectation of $h(u, v)$ taken over the conditional distribution of v given u and then the expectation of the result over the marginal distribution of u.

Returning to our "extended" model, let E_x denote the expectation with respect to the marginal distribution of X and $E(\cdot|X)$ denote the expectation of the argument $\cdot$ for given X. Thus,

$$\begin{aligned} E(\mathbf{y}|X) &= E[(X\boldsymbol{\beta} + \mathbf{e})|X] \\ &= X\boldsymbol{\beta} + E(\mathbf{e}|X) = X\boldsymbol{\beta}, \end{aligned} \tag{5.3.1}$$

and the conditional mean is still linear in X. Also we can establish the unbiasedness of the ordinary least squares estimators $\hat{\boldsymbol{\beta}}$, $\hat{\sigma}^2$, and $\hat{\sigma}^2(X'X)^{-1}$. First, the ordinary least squares estimator $\hat{\boldsymbol{\beta}} = (X'X)^{-1}X'\mathbf{y}$ is unbiased given the above assumptions since

$$\begin{aligned} E\hat{\boldsymbol{\beta}} &= E_X\{E[(\boldsymbol{\beta} + (X'X)^{-1}X'\mathbf{e})|X]\} \\ &= E_X[\boldsymbol{\beta} + (X'X)^{-1}X'E(\mathbf{e}|X)] \\ &= E_X(\boldsymbol{\beta}) = \boldsymbol{\beta}. \end{aligned} \tag{5.3.2}$$

The variance–covariance matrix of $\hat{\boldsymbol{\beta}}$ is slightly different from previous models, however.

$$\begin{aligned} E(\hat{\boldsymbol{\beta}} - \boldsymbol{\beta})(\hat{\boldsymbol{\beta}} - \boldsymbol{\beta})' &= E_X\{E[(X'X)^{-1}X'\mathbf{ee}'X(X'X)^{-1}|X]\} \\ &= E_X\{(X'X)^{-1}X'E(\mathbf{ee}'|X)X(X'X)^{-1}\} \\ &= E_X\{(X'X)^{-1}X'\sigma^2 IX(X'X)^{-1}\} \\ &= \sigma^2 E_X(X'X)^{-1}, \end{aligned} \tag{5.3.3}$$

provided, of course, that $E_x(X'X)^{-1}$ exists. The variance–covariance matrix of $\hat{\boldsymbol{\beta}}$ is σ^2 times the expected value of $(X'X)^{-1}$ since $(X'X)^{-1}$ takes different values with new random samples.

The ordinary least squares estimator of the error variance,

$$\hat{\sigma}^2 = \hat{\mathbf{e}}'\hat{\mathbf{e}}/(T - K)$$

remains unbiased since

$$E\hat{\sigma}^2 = E_X[E(\hat{\sigma}^2|X)] = E_x(\sigma^2) = \sigma^2. \tag{5.3.4}$$

Also, the ordinary least squares estimator of the variance–covariance matrix of $\hat{\boldsymbol{\beta}}$ is unbiased.

$$\begin{aligned} E\hat{\sigma}^2(X'X)^{-1} &= E_X\{E[\hat{\sigma}^2(X'X)^{-1}|X]\} \\ &= E_X\{\sigma^2(X'X)^{-1}\} \\ &= \sigma^2 E_X(X'X)^{-1}. \end{aligned} \tag{5.3.5}$$

Since the joint density of X and $\mathbf{e}$, say $j(X, \mathbf{e})$, can be factored as

$$j(X, \mathbf{e}) = g(\mathbf{e} | X) \cdot f(X), \tag{5.3.6}$$

where $g(\mathbf{e}|X)$ is the conditional distribution of $\mathbf{e}$ given X and $f(X)$ is the marginal distribution of X, the unconditional maximum likelihood estimators of $\boldsymbol{\beta}$ and σ^2 are the same as the conditional maximum likelihood estimators of $\boldsymbol{\beta}$ and σ^2 obtained by maximizing the conditional likelihood $g(\mathbf{e}|X)$. By the independence assumption, $f(X)$ is not dependent upon $\boldsymbol{\beta}$ and σ^2 and $f(X)$ does not affect the solutions of the normal equations for $\boldsymbol{\beta}$ and σ^2. Thus, if $\mathbf{e}$ is distributed $N(\mathbf{0}, \sigma^2 I)$, the estimators $\hat{\boldsymbol{\beta}}$ and $\tilde{\sigma}^2 = \hat{\mathbf{e}}'\hat{\mathbf{e}}/T$ are the maximum likelihood estimators of $\boldsymbol{\beta}$ and σ^2 in the "extended" model. By Theorem 4.2.1 these estimators are consistent and asymptotically efficient.

Likewise, the construction of confidence intervals and hypothesis tests are unaffected by the presence of stochastic but independent X. For example, for a given X and assuming $\mathbf{e} \sim N(\mathbf{0}, \sigma^2 I)$, the following probability statement holds:

$$\Pr(\hat{\beta}_i - t \cdot \mathrm{se}(\hat{\beta}_i) < \beta_i < \hat{\beta}_i + t \cdot \mathrm{se}(\hat{\beta}_i)) = 1 - \alpha, \tag{5.3.7}$$

where $\hat{\beta}_i$ denotes the ordinary least squares estimator of the ith regression coefficient β_i, t is the t-random variable with $(T - K)$ degrees of freedom, and $\mathrm{se}(\hat{\beta}_i)$ denotes the standard error of $\hat{\beta}_i$. Since (5.3.7) holds for *any* given X, it must hold for all X and (5.3.7) is an unconditional probability statement as well.

In the absence of normally distributed errors and the results of maximum likelihood estimation, the consistent estimation of $\boldsymbol{\beta}$, σ^2, and $\sigma^2 E_x(X'X)^{-1}$ cannot be established given just the independence of X and $\mathbf{e}$ and the classical linear regression model assumptions conditional on X. More information about the stochastic nature of X is needed. This leads us to formally define the independent stochastic linear regression model specified by Goldberger (1964). But first we must briefly outline the properties of stationary multivariate stochastic processes. For a detailed discussion of stationary univariate and multivariate stochastic processes see Goldberger (1964).

A multivariate stochastic process is a family of random $K \times 1$ vectors $\{\mathbf{x}_t\}$ where

$$\mathbf{x}_t = \begin{pmatrix} x_{t1} \\ \vdots \\ x_{tK} \end{pmatrix}. \tag{5.3.8}$$

Let the mean of the stochastic process be

$$E\mathbf{x}_t = \boldsymbol{\mu} = \begin{pmatrix} \mu_1 \\ \mu_2 \\ \vdots \\ \mu_K \end{pmatrix} \tag{5.3.9}$$

and the variance–covariance matrix be

$$E(\mathbf{x}_t - \boldsymbol{\mu})(\mathbf{x}_t - \boldsymbol{\mu})' = \Sigma = \begin{pmatrix} \sigma_{11} & \cdots & \sigma_{1K} \\ & \vdots & \\ \sigma_{K1} & \cdots & \sigma_{KK} \end{pmatrix}. \tag{5.3.10}$$

Let the covariance between the random vectors $\mathbf{x}_t$ and $\mathbf{x}_{t+\tau}$, where τ is an integer, be denoted

$$E(\mathbf{x}_t - \boldsymbol{\mu})(\mathbf{x}_{t+\tau} - \boldsymbol{\mu})' = \Gamma_\tau = \begin{pmatrix} \gamma_{\tau 11} & \cdots & \gamma_{\tau 1K} \\ & \vdots & \\ \gamma_{\tau K1} & \cdots & \gamma_{\tau KK} \end{pmatrix}. \tag{5.3.11}$$

If $\mathbf{x}_t$ and $\mathbf{x}_{t+\tau}$ are uncorrelated, then $\gamma_{\tau ij} = 0$ for $i, j = 1, 2, \ldots, K$. The present multivariate process is said to be "stationary" if: (i) the distribution of $\mathbf{x}_t$ is invariant under translations along the time axis; and (ii) the dependence between $\mathbf{x}_t$ and $\mathbf{x}_{t+\tau}$ decreases sufficiently fast as $\tau \to \pm\infty$. Time invariance requires that, for *any* choice of $t = \cdots -1, 0, 1, \ldots$, $E\mathbf{x}_t = \boldsymbol{\mu}$ and

$$E(\mathbf{x}_t - \boldsymbol{\mu})(\mathbf{x}_t - \boldsymbol{\mu})' = \Sigma.$$

Also for a given τ, $E(\mathbf{x}_t - \boldsymbol{\mu})(\mathbf{x}_{t+\tau} - \boldsymbol{\mu})' = \Gamma_\tau$ is invariant with respect to the value of t. That is, the mean, contemporaneous variance, and lagged covariance remain unaltered through time. It is beyond the scope of our discussion to define "sufficiently diminishing dependence between $\mathbf{x}_t$ and subsequent realizations of $\mathbf{x}_{t+\tau}$" precisely, but, heuristically speaking, what is required is that $\Gamma_\tau \to 0$ as $\tau \to \pm\infty$ faster than $1/\tau \to \pm 0$.

Suppose that the rows $\mathbf{x}_t'$ of the matrix X of observations on the explanatory variables, constitute realizations of a stationary multivariate stochastic process. Let the sample mean vector be

$$\bar{\mathbf{x}} = \begin{pmatrix} \bar{x}_1 \\ \vdots \\ \bar{x}_K \end{pmatrix} \tag{5.3.12}$$

and the sample contemporaneous variance–covariance matrix be

$$S = \begin{pmatrix} s_{11} & \cdots & s_{1K} \\ & \vdots & \\ s_{K1} & \cdots & s_{KK} \end{pmatrix} = T^{-1}X'X - \bar{\mathbf{x}}\bar{\mathbf{x}}'. \tag{5.3.13}$$

Then, under the present conditions, plim $\bar{\mathbf{x}} = \boldsymbol{\mu}$ and plim $S = \Sigma$. Also the sample second moment matrix $T^{-1}X'X$ has a probability limit of

$$\begin{aligned} \operatorname{plim} T^{-1}X'X &= \operatorname{plim}(S + \bar{\mathbf{x}}\bar{\mathbf{x}}') = \operatorname{plim} S + \operatorname{plim} \bar{\mathbf{x}}\bar{\mathbf{x}}' = \Sigma + \boldsymbol{\mu}\boldsymbol{\mu}' \\ &= E\mathbf{x}_t\mathbf{x}_t' \equiv \Sigma_{xx}. \end{aligned}$$

Now let us formally define the independent stochastic linear regression model.

Definition 5.3.1 (Independent Stochastic Linear Regression Model). The independent stochastic linear regression model is defined by

$$\mathbf{y} = X\boldsymbol{\beta} + \mathbf{e},$$

where

(i) $\mathbf{e}$ is a vector of unobserved errors with mean $\mathbf{0}$ and variance–covariance matrix $\sigma^2 I$,
(ii) X is a sample from a stationary multivariate stochastic process with nonsingular contemporaneous moment matrix $\Sigma_{xx} = E\mathbf{x}_t\mathbf{x}_t'$ and expectation $E_x(X'X)^{-1}$ which exists, and
(iii) The stochastic process generating X is independent of the stochastic process generating $\mathbf{e}$.

Note, that unlike the multivariate normal linear regression model, the successive rows of X need not be mutually independent or normally distributed; rather the dependence between rows of X is assumed to diminish sufficiently rapidly with distance in time. From assumption (ii) we know that $\text{plim}(X'X/T)^{-1} = \Sigma_{xx}^{-1}$ and the probability is zero that there will be an exact linear relationship between the explanatory variables. The independence assumption (iii) implies that $\text{plim}(X'\mathbf{e}/T) = \mathbf{0}$. This follows from the fact that $E(X'\mathbf{e}) = \mathbf{0}$ for any sample size T and thus $\lim_{T\to\infty} E(X'\mathbf{e}/T) = \mathbf{0}$. And $\lim_{T\to\infty} \text{var}(X'\mathbf{e}/T) = 0$. By convergence in quadratic mean, $\text{plim}(X'\mathbf{e}/T) = \mathbf{0}$. (See Exercise 5.2.)

Thus, in addition to the previously derived results of unbiasedness and the invariance of confidence intervals and hypothesis tests, the properties of consistency of the ordinary least squares estimators can now be established. For example, the ordinary least squares estimator $\hat{\boldsymbol{\beta}}$ is consistent since,

$$\begin{aligned}\text{plim}\,\hat{\boldsymbol{\beta}} &= \text{plim}(\boldsymbol{\beta} + (X'X)^{-1}X'\mathbf{e}) \\ &= \boldsymbol{\beta} + \text{plim}\left(\frac{X'X}{T}\right)^{-1} \text{plim}\left(\frac{X'\mathbf{e}}{T}\right) \\ &= \boldsymbol{\beta} + \Sigma_{xx}^{-1} \cdot \mathbf{0} = \boldsymbol{\beta}. \qquad (5.3.14)\end{aligned}$$

Likewise, it can be shown (see Exercises 5.3 and 5.4) that $\text{plim}\,\hat{\sigma}^2 = \sigma^2$ and that $\hat{\sigma}^2(X'X)^{-1}$ is a consistent estimator of $T^{-1}\sigma^2\,\text{plim}(X'X/T)^{-1} = T^{-1}\sigma^2\Sigma_{xx}^{-1}$, the asymptotic variance–covariance matrix of $\hat{\boldsymbol{\beta}}$.

We, therefore, have

Theorem 5.3.1. *In the Independent Stochastic Linear Regression model the ordinary least squares estimators $\hat{\boldsymbol{\beta}}$, $\hat{\sigma}^2$, and $\hat{\sigma}(X'X)^{-1}$ are consistent and unbiased estimators. Given the normality of* $\mathbf{e}$, *the usual confidence intervals and tests of hypothesis hold unconditionally.*

Of course, the case opposite that of independent X and $\mathbf{e}$ is when they are dependent. This dependence can take two forms, one of contemporaneous dependence and the other of noncontemporaneous dependence. In the former case, one of the stochastic regressors at time t is correlated with the regression's error term of the same time period, i.e., $Ex_{tk}e_t \neq 0$. Three such circumstances discussed in this book are: the lagged dependent variable–serial correlation model (Chapter 11), unobservable variables (Chapter 12) and simultaneous equations (Chapter 19). Noncontemporaneous dependence appears in the autoregressive (lagged dependent variable) linear model discussed in Chapter 11. For this model dependence between a regressor and error term is one of correlation between a current stochastic regressor and errors from *previous* periods, not the current period. Issues of estimation and inference in the dependent $(X, \mathbf{e})$ stochastic regressors case are addressed as they appear in more specific contexts.

5.4 Summary and Guide to Further Readings

In this chapter we explored the ramifications of relaxing the assumption of a nonstochastic design matrix X in the linear model. Two distinct models with stochastic X were analyzed; the multivariate normal linear regression model and the independent stochastic linear regression model. In the multivariate normal case the ordinary least squares estimator $\hat{\boldsymbol{\beta}}$ is the maximum likelihood estimator and therefore consistent and asymptotically efficient. It is also unbiased and minimum variance unbiased. In addition, all inferential procedures, tests of hypotheses and confidence intervals, derived for the classical normal linear regression model with fixed X are appropriate for the multivariate normal linear regression model as well. The most prominent difference is the consideration of the power of the test procedures. As discussed by Sampson (1974), the power functions of the classical normal linear regression and multivariate normal linear regression models differ, though the appropriate statistical test procedures and critical values are the same. Sampson suggests that the unconditional power function is preferred when interest centers on planning experiments. Unfortunately, opportunities to plan experiments in economics are rare.

The basic premise of the multivariate normal linear regression model, multivariate normality, is not likely to be applicable in many economic contexts. As a result, the independent stochastic linear regression model was considered. Under the assumptions of the independent stochastic linear regression model it was shown that the classical results derived in the fixed regressor case essentially carry over intact to the independent stochastic regressor case. The properties of unbiasedness and consistency hold. Given normality of the errors in the independent stochastic linear regression model, traditional confidence intervals and tests of hypotheses apply since, for example, if a given confidence interval encompasses an unknown parameter $(1 - \alpha)100\,\%$ of the time for a given X, then it will encompass the parameter

$(1 - \alpha)100\%$ of the time for all X. Similarly, with normality of the errors in the independent stochastic linear regression model, the ordinary least squares estimators $\hat{\boldsymbol{\beta}} = (X'X)^{-1}X'\mathbf{y}$ are maximum likelihood estimators and are minimum variance unbiased. Strictly speaking, however, $\hat{\boldsymbol{\beta}}$ is not best linear unbiased since it is nonlinear in both $\mathbf{y}$ and X.

From the point of view of an econometrician who has to work with nonexperimental data, these results provide limited comfort. Though working in a stochastic regressor world, the econometrician can conceptualize, construct, and evaluate aspects of statistical inference as though living in a fixed regressor (repeated sampling) world. To the theoretician deriving properties of estimators, it is a theoretical convenience. To the decisionmaker using the statistical methodology of the linear model, it is a inferential convenience.

Of course, not all stochastic regressor problems involve independent X and $\mathbf{e}$. There do exist econometric models where X and $\mathbf{e}$ are dependent. Both types of dependency, contemporaneous and noncontemporaneous, are addressed in more detail when they appear in later chapters, 11, 12, and 19.

Research in stochastic regressor models continues. In addition to the vast literature on simultaneous equations models, some of which will be discussed in Chapter 19 and beyond, Kinal and Lahiri (1981) investigated the exact sampling distribution of the omitted variable estimator in the context of stochastic regressor models. They show that certain conclusions concerning the omission of a relevant variable in the nonstochastic regressor case do not carry over to the stochastic regressor case. Though the parallels between conditional and unconditional regression models are numerous and strong, there exist distinctions which additional research will probably continue to uncover.

5.5 Exercises

5.1. Let u and v denote random variables with density function $h(u, v)$ such that $E[h(u, v)]$ exists. Show that $E[h(u, v)] = E_u\{E_{v|u}h(u, v)\}$, where $E_{v|u}$ is the expectation taken with respect to the conditional distribution of v given u and E_u is the expectation taken with respect to the marginal distribution of u. (Hint: Use the result that $h(u, v) = k(v|u)g(u)$ where $k(v|u)$ is the conditional distribution of v given u and $g(u)$ is the marginal distribution of u.)

5.2. In the independent stochastic linear regression model show that $\text{plim}(X'\mathbf{e}|T) = \mathbf{0}$. (Hint: Examine the ith element of $EX'\mathbf{e}$, $E(\sum x_{ti}e_t)$, and show that it is zero. Then it follows that $\lim_{T\to\infty} E(X'\mathbf{e}/T) = \mathbf{0}$. Examine the (k, l)th element of $E(T^{-1}X'\mathbf{ee}'X)$, $T^{-1}\sum_{t=1}^{T}\sum_{s=1}^{T} Ex_{tk}x_{sl}e_te_s$. Show that it is equal to $\sigma_{kl}\sigma^2$, where σ_{kl} is the (k, l)th element of Σ_{xx}. Thus $E(T^{-1}X'\mathbf{ee}'X) = \sigma^2\Sigma_{xx}$. Conclude that $\lim_{T\to\infty} \text{var}(X'\mathbf{e}/T) = 0$.)

5.3. In the independent stochastic linear regression model show that $\operatorname{plim} \hat{\sigma}^2 = \sigma^2$. (Hint: First, show that

$$\operatorname{plim} \tilde{\sigma}^2 = \operatorname{plim}\left(\frac{\mathbf{e}'\mathbf{e}}{T} - \frac{\mathbf{e}'X}{T}\left(\frac{X'X}{T}\right)^{-1}\left(\frac{X'\mathbf{e}}{T}\right)\right) = \sigma^2, \quad \text{where } \tilde{\sigma}^2 = \hat{\mathbf{e}}'\hat{\mathbf{e}}/T.$$

Use the facts that $\operatorname{plim}(\mathbf{e}'\mathbf{e}/T) = \sigma^2$ (see Khintchine's theorem (Theorem 2.4.3)),

$$\operatorname{plim} \frac{X'\mathbf{e}}{T} = \mathbf{0} \quad \text{and} \quad \operatorname{plim}\left(\frac{X'X}{T}\right)^{-1} = \Sigma_{xx}^{-1}.$$

Finally, noting that $\lim_{T\to\infty}(T/(T-K)) = 1$, show that $\operatorname{plim} \tilde{\sigma}^2 = \operatorname{plim} \hat{\sigma}^2$.)

5.4. In the independent stochastic linear regression model show that $\hat{\sigma}^2(X'X)^{-1}$ is a consistent estimator of $T^{-1}\sigma^2\Sigma_{xx}^{-1}$, the asymptotic variance–covariance matrix of $\hat{\boldsymbol{\beta}}$. (Hint: The asymptotic variance–covariance matrix is obtained by evaluating $T^{-1} \operatorname{plim}[\sqrt{T}(\hat{\boldsymbol{\beta}} - \boldsymbol{\beta})\sqrt{T}(\hat{\boldsymbol{\beta}} - \boldsymbol{\beta})']$. Note $\hat{\sigma}^2(X'X)^{-1}$ can be written as

$$T^{-1}\sigma^2\left(\frac{X'X}{T}\right)^{-1}.$$

Conclude by claiming $\operatorname{plim} \hat{\sigma}^2 = \sigma^2$ and $\operatorname{plim}(X'X/T)^{-1} = \Sigma_{xx}^{-1}$.)

5.5. Verify the maximum likelihood estimators of (5.2.5), (5.2.6), and (5.2.7).

5.6 References

Anderson, T. W. (1958). *An Introduction to Multivariate Statistical Analysis*. New York: Wiley.

Graybill, F. A. (1961). *An Introduction to Linear Statistical Models*. New York: McGraw-Hill.

Goldberger, A. S. (1964). *Econometric Theory*. New York: Wiley.

Judge, G. G. and Bock, M. E. (1978). *The Statistical Implications of Pre-Test and Stein-Rule Estimators in Econometrics*. Amsterdam: North-Holland.

Kinal, T. and Lahiri, K. (1981). Exact sampling distribution of the omitted variable estimator. *Economics Letters*, **8**, 121–127.

Sampson, A. R. (1974). A tale of two regressions. *Journal of the American Statistical Association*, **69**, 682–689.

Schmidt, P. (1976). *Econometrics*. New York: Marcel Dekker.

CHAPTER 6

Use of Prior Information

6.1 Introduction

Econometric models are estimated in order to learn about unknown economic parameters. In many cases, however, the investigator begins the statistical analysis not only with sample information but other information as well. It may be known from theoretical arguments that the marginal propensity to consume lies between zero and one. Or it may be known from past experience that the demand for wheat is price inelastic. If the information is correct, it would seem useful to combine it with the sample information in subsequent analysis and statistical estimation. Such information may be valuable in increasing the precision of estimates, especially when the sample information is limited.

Sources of nonsample or prior information on economic parameters include economic theory, previous empirical work, experience with the data, and finally from a Bayesian viewpoint, subjective information about the parameters in the form of probability distributions. Methods of explicitly introducing this information into the estimation process for the standard linear model are essentially of four types. The first is the restricted least squares approach, i.e., minimizing the sum of squared residuals subject to exact linear equality restrictions on the parameters. A second approach, identical to the first in the limit, is called mixed estimation. In this approach the additional prior information is in the form of linear stochastic restrictions on the parameters and is treated the same as additional sample information. The sample data are augmented and estimation proceeds by direct application of generalized least squares methods. The third approach is to incorporate prior information by inequality restrictions. Finally, the fourth approach is Bayesian, where information on the parameters is represented by prior probability density functions. The Bayesian approach requires a change in viewpoint. However, given an appropriate interpretation, the restricted least squares and mixed estimation methods can be viewed as being Bayesian estimators. In general, however, our treatment of prior information concentrates on the classical statistical approach to parameter estimation.

The availability of nonsample information raises a number of important econometric questions: How is the information which is implied by the restrictions evaluated? Does the use of the prior information improve the efficiency of estimation or does it worsen matters? How does the estimator that incorporates the restrictions compare to the ordinary least squares or generalized least squares estimators based only on the sample data? These and other important questions are addressed in the remainder of this chapter.

The major topic in this chapter is how prior information may be used to improve point estimates of unknown parameters. First, the restricted least squares model is presented. This is followed by the mixed estimation model and its relationship to the restricted least squares model. Sections on inequality restricted least squares and Bayesian estimation follow. In addition, in Section 6.4, conventional hypothesis testing is extended to cover several mean square error criteria. A summary of the results and guide to further readings conclude the chapter.

6.2 Restricted Least Squares: Exact General Linear Restrictions

6.2.1 Dimension of Parameter Space

In the classical framework, prior information may be explicitly incorporated into the analysis in one of two ways, either by augmenting the sample information, through the likelihood function, or by modifying the parameter space. Stochastic prior information is incorporated in the former manner and equality and inequality restrictions through the latter. The parameter space is modified in different ways when equality and inequality restrictions are employed. In both cases, the new (restricted) parameter space is a subspace of the original one. However, for exact restrictions, the new parameter space is of reduced dimensionality while for inequality restrictions the number of parameters to be estimated is not reduced.

For the remainder of Section 6.2, information which reduces the dimensionality of the parameter space will be considered. The dimensionality reduction is the source of the gain in the precision of the parameter estimates. The available information is in a sense concentrated on the smaller set of parameters. The potential danger of applying exact restrictions that are incorrect is also made clear.

6.2.2 Correct Restrictions

Exact prior information on linear combinations of the parameters can be expressed as

$$R\boldsymbol{\beta} = \mathbf{r}, \tag{6.2.1}$$

where R is a matrix of dimension $J \times K$ with $J \leq K$, $\boldsymbol{\beta}$ is a $K \times 1$ vector of unknown parameters and $\mathbf{r}$ is a $J \times 1$ vector of known constants. In addition, it is assumed that R has rank J. This assumption is made at no loss in generality since it implies that the J equations do not contain redundant information on $\boldsymbol{\beta}$.

The assumptions on the model and sampling process are those of the classical linear regression model described in Definition 2.2.1. Namely, it is assumed that

$$\mathbf{y} = X\boldsymbol{\beta} + \mathbf{e},$$

with X nonstochastic and of full rank, the elements of $\mathbf{e}$ are independently and identically distributed with zero mean and variance σ^2. Under these assumptions, the ordinary least squares estimator of $\boldsymbol{\beta}$ is

$$\hat{\boldsymbol{\beta}} = (X'X)^{-1}X'\mathbf{y}$$

with covariance matrix

$$\text{var}(\hat{\boldsymbol{\beta}}) = \sigma^2(X'X)^{-1}.$$

The estimator $\hat{\boldsymbol{\beta}}$ is best linear unbiased. Also, the estimator

$$\hat{\sigma}^2 = (\mathbf{y} - \hat{\mathbf{y}})'(\mathbf{y} - \hat{\mathbf{y}})/(T - K)$$

is unbiased and consistent.

The *restricted least squares* estimator $\boldsymbol{\beta}^*$ is obtained by minimizing the the sum of squared residuals, subject to the condition $\mathbf{r} = \mathrm{R}\boldsymbol{\beta}$. That is, the restricted least squares problem is

$$\min_{\boldsymbol{\beta}}(\mathbf{y} - X\boldsymbol{\beta})'(\mathbf{y} - X\boldsymbol{\beta}) \quad \text{subject to } \mathbf{r} = R\boldsymbol{\beta}. \tag{6.2.2}$$

The Lagrangian for this minimization problem is

$$L = (\mathbf{y} - X\boldsymbol{\beta})'(\mathbf{y} - X\boldsymbol{\beta}) - 2\boldsymbol{\lambda}'(R\boldsymbol{\beta} - \mathbf{r}), \tag{6.2.3}$$

where $\boldsymbol{\lambda}$ is a $J \times 1$ vector of Lagrangian multipliers. Setting the partial derivatives with respect to $\boldsymbol{\beta}$ to zero gives,

$$\frac{1}{2}\frac{\partial L}{\partial \boldsymbol{\beta}} = -X'\mathbf{y} + X'X\boldsymbol{\beta}^* - R'\boldsymbol{\lambda}^* = \mathbf{0}$$

or, more simply

$$\boldsymbol{\beta}^* = \hat{\boldsymbol{\beta}} + (X'X)^{-1}R'\boldsymbol{\lambda}^*. \tag{6.2.4}$$

The derivatives with respect to $\boldsymbol{\lambda}$ simply yield $R\boldsymbol{\beta}^* = \mathbf{r}$, so that the restricted least squares estimator does, in fact, satisfy the restrictions.

The Lagrangian multipliers may be eliminated by using the fact that $R\boldsymbol{\beta} = \mathbf{r}$ must hold. Premultiplying Equation (6.2.4) by R yields the expression

$$R\boldsymbol{\beta}^* = R\hat{\boldsymbol{\beta}} + R(X'X)^{-1}R'\boldsymbol{\lambda}^*. \tag{6.2.5}$$

Imposing the restrictions for the estimated values ($R\boldsymbol{\beta}^* = \mathbf{r}$) yields

$$\mathbf{r} = R\hat{\boldsymbol{\beta}} + R(X'X)^{-1}R'\boldsymbol{\lambda}^*. \tag{6.2.6}$$

Solving (6.2.6) for $\boldsymbol{\lambda}^*$ gives

$$\boldsymbol{\lambda}^* = [R(X'X)^{-1}R']^{-1}(\mathbf{r} - R\hat{\boldsymbol{\beta}}). \tag{6.2.7}$$

Finally, inserting (6.2.7) into (6.2.4) gives

$$\boldsymbol{\beta}^* = \hat{\boldsymbol{\beta}} + (X'X)^{-1}R'[R(X'X)^{-1}R']^{-1}(\mathbf{r} - R\hat{\boldsymbol{\beta}}). \tag{6.2.8}$$

If the restrictions are true within the sample, then $\mathbf{r} = R\hat{\boldsymbol{\beta}}$, and $\boldsymbol{\beta}^* = \hat{\boldsymbol{\beta}}$. This is, of course, a highly unlikely situation. Usually, it is assumed that the restrictions are correct, $R\boldsymbol{\beta} = \mathbf{r}$, and, thus, that the ordinary least squares estimators satisfy the restrictions on average, i.e., $E(R\hat{\boldsymbol{\beta}}) = \mathbf{r}$. This need not always be the case, but for the present, we assume that it is.

If the restrictions are correct, it is easily shown that $\boldsymbol{\beta}^*$ is unbiased. Specifically, substituting $\hat{\boldsymbol{\beta}} = \boldsymbol{\beta} + (X'X)^{-1}X'\mathbf{e}$ into (6.2.8) and using the condition $\mathbf{r} - R\boldsymbol{\beta} = \mathbf{0}$ yields

$$\begin{aligned}\boldsymbol{\beta}^* &= \boldsymbol{\beta} + (X'X)^{-1}X'\mathbf{e} - (X'X)^{-1}R'[R(X'X)^{-1}R']^{-1}[R(X'X)^{-1}X'\mathbf{e}]\\ &= \boldsymbol{\beta} + \{I - (X'X)^{-1}R'[R(X'X)^{-1}R']^{-1}R\}(X'X)^{-1}X'\mathbf{e}.\end{aligned} \tag{6.2.9}$$

Clearly, then, $E(\boldsymbol{\beta}^*) = \boldsymbol{\beta}$.

The covariance matrix for the estimator $\boldsymbol{\beta}^*$ is

$$\begin{aligned}\operatorname{var}(\boldsymbol{\beta}^*) &= E(\boldsymbol{\beta}^* - \boldsymbol{\beta})(\boldsymbol{\beta}^* - \boldsymbol{\beta})'\\ &= E\{I - (X'X)^{-1}R'[R(X'X)^{-1}R']^{-1}R\}(X'X)^{-1}X'\mathbf{e}\\ &\quad \times \mathbf{e}'X(X'X)^{-1}\{I - (X'X)^{-1}R'[R(X'X)^{-1}R']^{-1}R\}'\\ &= \sigma^2(X'X)^{-1}\{I - R'[R(X'X)^{-1}R']^{-1}R(X'X)^{-1}\}\\ &= \operatorname{var}(\hat{\boldsymbol{\beta}}) - \operatorname{var}(\hat{\boldsymbol{\beta}})R'[R\operatorname{var}(\hat{\boldsymbol{\beta}})R']^{-1}R\operatorname{var}(\hat{\boldsymbol{\beta}}).\end{aligned} \tag{6.2.10}$$

Since $\operatorname{var}(\hat{\boldsymbol{\beta}})$ is positive definite and R is of full rank, it follows that $R\operatorname{var}(\hat{\boldsymbol{\beta}})R'$ is positive definite. So also is its inverse, $[R\operatorname{var}(\boldsymbol{\beta})R']^{-1}$. Finally,

$$\operatorname{var}(\hat{\boldsymbol{\beta}})R'[R\operatorname{var}(\hat{\boldsymbol{\beta}})R']^{-1}R\operatorname{var}(\hat{\boldsymbol{\beta}})$$

is positive semidefinite (see Exercises 6.1–6.4 for the necessary matrix results). Thus, the difference between $\operatorname{var}(\hat{\boldsymbol{\beta}})$ and $\operatorname{var}(\boldsymbol{\beta}^*)$ is a positive semidefinite matrix, implying that each diagonal element of var($\boldsymbol{\beta}^*$) is less than or equal to the corresponding element of var($\hat{\boldsymbol{\beta}}$). This result holds whether or not the restrictions are true (see Exercise 6.22).

The gain in estimation efficiency offered by the restricted least squares estimator can be viewed in a stronger light as a generalization of the best linear unbiased result for the ordinary least squares estimator.

Theorem 6.2.1. *Let the assumptions of the classical linear regression model hold (Definition 2.2.1), but, in addition, assume the restrictions $R\boldsymbol{\beta} = \mathbf{r}$ are correct. Then the restricted least squares estimator $\boldsymbol{\beta}^*$ is best linear unbiased in the sense that it has the minimum variance within the class of all unbiased estimators that are linear functions of* **y** *and* **r**.

PROOF. The proof is similar to that for the Gauss–Markov theorem. □

If, in addition, the error term of the classical linear regression model is normally distributed and $R\boldsymbol{\beta} = \mathbf{r}$, then Theorem 6.2.2 obtains:

Theorem 6.2.2. *If, in the classical normal linear regression model (Definition 3.2.1), the restrictions $R\boldsymbol{\beta} = \mathbf{r}$ are also true, then the restricted least squares estimator $\boldsymbol{\beta}^*$ is minimum variance unbiased and asymptotically efficient for the class of estimators using the sample information* **y** *and* **r**.

PROOF. This theorem is established using a new Cramér–Rao lower bound in the presence of the information $R\boldsymbol{\beta} = \mathbf{r}$. Then minimum variance unbiased and asymptotic efficiency follow from the fact that the Cramér–Rao bound is attained by the restricted least squares estimator (Rothenberg (1973)). □

6.2.3 Alternative Views of Restricted Least Squares

Nonsample information is not always most naturally expressed in the form $R\boldsymbol{\beta} = \mathbf{r}$. Exact information may relate the unknown parameters $\boldsymbol{\beta}$ to another set of parameters, say $\boldsymbol{\alpha}$, where $\boldsymbol{\alpha}' = (\alpha_1, \ldots, \alpha_M)$, and $M < K$. If the relationships are linear, they may be expressed as

$$\boldsymbol{\beta} = H\boldsymbol{\alpha}, \tag{6.2.11}$$

where H is a known $K \times M$ matrix of constants. Applying the restrictions to the model, by substitution, yields

$$\mathbf{y} = X\boldsymbol{\beta} + \mathbf{e} = XH\boldsymbol{\alpha} + \mathbf{e} = Z\boldsymbol{\alpha} + \mathbf{e}. \tag{6.2.12}$$

Restricted least squares estimation is then ordinary least squares estimation of $\boldsymbol{\alpha}$ in (6.2.12), giving $\hat{\boldsymbol{\alpha}} = (Z'Z)^{-1}Z'\mathbf{y}$, and $\boldsymbol{\beta}^*$ is calculated as

$$\boldsymbol{\beta}^* = H\hat{\boldsymbol{\alpha}}, \tag{6.2.13}$$

which has covariance matrix $\mathrm{var}(\boldsymbol{\beta}^*) = \sigma^2 H(Z'Z)^{-1}H'$. Though not immediately obvious, $\boldsymbol{\beta}^*$, in this form, is an restricted least squares estimator based on homogeneous linear restrictions.

That $\boldsymbol{\beta}^*$ in (6.2.13) is in fact a restricted least squares estimator is proved in Exercise 17.3, where the parametrization $\boldsymbol{\beta} = H\boldsymbol{\alpha}$ arises in Almon distributed lags. In short, the restrictions implied by (6.2.11) are of the form of the homogeneous linear restrictions $R^*\boldsymbol{\beta} = \mathbf{0}$ where $R^* = (I - H(H'H)^{-1}H')$ is a $K \times K$ matrix of rank $(K - M)$ which corresponds to the number of restrictions J. Thus, M rows of R^* are dependent upon the remaining $(K - M)$ rows and their deletion produces a $J \times K$ restriction matrix R of rank J. The imposition of the restrictions $R\boldsymbol{\beta} = \mathbf{0}$ produces estimates identical to (6.2.13).

That, in general, exact restrictions of the form $R\boldsymbol{\beta} = \mathbf{r}$ reduce the dimensionality of the estimation problem can be seen by an argument made by Mantell (1973). Linear restrictions can be applied *either* directly, as in (6.2.8), or substituted out by solving $R\boldsymbol{\beta} = \mathbf{r}$ for J of the parameters as

$$\boldsymbol{\beta}_1 = R_1^{-1}[\mathbf{r} - R_2\boldsymbol{\beta}_2], \tag{6.2.14}$$

where $R = [R_1 \vdots R_2]$ is partitioned, with rearrangement of variables if necessary, so that R_1 is $J \times J$ and nonsingular, and $X = [X_1 \vdots X_2]$ and $\boldsymbol{\beta}' = (\boldsymbol{\beta}_1', \boldsymbol{\beta}_2')$ are conformably partitioned. Then $\boldsymbol{\beta}_1$ may be substituted into $\mathbf{y} = X_1\boldsymbol{\beta}_1 + X_2\boldsymbol{\beta}_2 + \mathbf{e}$ to obtain

$$\mathbf{y} = X_1[R_1^{-1}(\mathbf{r} - R_2\boldsymbol{\beta}_2)] + X_2\boldsymbol{\beta}_2 + \mathbf{e}$$

or, equivalently,

$$\mathbf{y}^* = X^*\boldsymbol{\beta}_2 + \mathbf{e}, \tag{6.2.15}$$

where $\mathbf{y}^* = (\mathbf{y} - X_1R_1^{-1}\mathbf{r})$ and $X^* = (-X_1R_1^{-1}R_2 + X_2)$. Ordinary least squares estimates of $\boldsymbol{\beta}_2$ obtained from (6.2.15) as well as the estimates of $\boldsymbol{\beta}_1$ obtainable from (6.2.14) are identical to the restricted least squares estimates one would obtain from applying (6.2.8) directly. The J independent restrictions $R\boldsymbol{\beta} = \mathbf{r}$ reduce the estimation space from dimension K with parameters $\boldsymbol{\beta}$ to an estimation space of dimension $(K - J)$ with parameters $\boldsymbol{\beta}_2$.

6.2.4 Incorrect Restrictions

There always exists the possibility that the restrictions $R\boldsymbol{\beta} = \mathbf{r}$ are not correct in that $\mathbf{r} - R\boldsymbol{\beta} = \boldsymbol{\delta} \neq \mathbf{0}$. Then the restricted least squares estimator is biased, since

$$E\boldsymbol{\beta}^* = \boldsymbol{\beta} + (X'X)^{-1}R'[R(X'X)^{-1}R']^{-1}\boldsymbol{\delta}.$$

The covariance matrix, however, is unaffected. Consequently, we are faced with a decision. Should the unbiased ordinary least squares estimator be used, or the biased restricted least squares estimator that has smaller variance? One way to evaluate the tradeoff between bias and variance reduction is to use a loss function. After briefly developing the concepts of loss and risk functions, we will return to the problem of interest.

Assume that interest centers on estimating the unknown parameter vector $\boldsymbol{\beta}$ by means of an estimator $\tilde{\boldsymbol{\beta}}$. A *loss* function $L(\tilde{\boldsymbol{\beta}}, \boldsymbol{\beta})$ reflects the loss incurred by incorrectly guessing $\boldsymbol{\beta}$ using the estimator $\tilde{\boldsymbol{\beta}}$. Most certainly this measure is going to be positively related to the discrepancy $\tilde{\boldsymbol{\beta}} - \boldsymbol{\beta}$. For this reason we restrict our attention to loss functions of the form

$$L(\tilde{\boldsymbol{\beta}}, \boldsymbol{\beta}; W) = (\tilde{\boldsymbol{\beta}} - \boldsymbol{\beta})'W(\tilde{\boldsymbol{\beta}} - \boldsymbol{\beta}),$$

where W is a positive semidefinite weighting matrix. These are called *weighted quadratic loss functions*. In the special case that $W = I$, it is simply called the *squared error loss*. In Section 6.4 both of these loss functions are considered further.

Of course, $\tilde{\boldsymbol{\beta}}$ is a random variable and, hence, the loss $L(\tilde{\boldsymbol{\beta}}, \boldsymbol{\beta})$ is also random. As a result, in evaluating an estimator, consideration of *expected* loss is likely to be more suitable. Such expected loss functions,

$$E[L(\tilde{\boldsymbol{\beta}}, \boldsymbol{\beta}; W)] = \mathscr{R}(\tilde{\boldsymbol{\beta}}, \boldsymbol{\beta}; W),$$

are called *risk* functions. One way of measuring estimator "goodness" is to compare the risk of two estimators, with the weighting matrix W being chosen to suit the problem at hand. The estimator with the smaller risk for $\boldsymbol{\beta}$ is then preferred.

To illustrate these concepts, the squared error loss function is chosen. Let $\boldsymbol{\delta} = \mathbf{r} - R\boldsymbol{\beta}$ denote the specification errors in the prior restrictions and, for expository convenience, assume that $X'X = I_K$ and $R = I_K$. The restricted least squares estimator for this orthonormal model is $\boldsymbol{\beta}^* = \mathbf{r}$. The risk function for the restricted least squares estimator is then

$$E(\boldsymbol{\beta}^* - \boldsymbol{\beta})'(\boldsymbol{\beta}^* - \boldsymbol{\beta}) = E[\operatorname{tr}(\boldsymbol{\beta}^* - \boldsymbol{\beta})(\boldsymbol{\beta}^* - \boldsymbol{\beta})'], \tag{6.2.16}$$

which for the orthonormal linear model and $R = I_K$ is

$$E(\boldsymbol{\beta}^* - \boldsymbol{\beta})'(\boldsymbol{\beta}^* - \boldsymbol{\beta}) = \boldsymbol{\delta}'\boldsymbol{\delta}. \tag{6.2.17}$$

In this model the risk of the restricted least squares estimator is equal to the sum of squares of the restriction specification errors. The risk of the least squares estimator $\hat{\boldsymbol{\beta}} = (X'X)^{-1}X'\mathbf{y} = X'\mathbf{y}$ is simply $\sigma^2 K$ since it is unbiased and unrelated to the prior information. If the two risk functions are viewed as functions of $\boldsymbol{\delta}$, the risks are equal where $\boldsymbol{\delta}'\boldsymbol{\delta} = \sigma^2 K$ or when $\boldsymbol{\delta}'\boldsymbol{\delta}/2\sigma^2 = K/2$. These risk functions are plotted in Figure 6.2.1.

As the figure indicates, under squared error loss the restricted least squares estimator can be good relative to the ordinary least squares estimator, providing a maximum reduction in risk of $\sigma^2 K$, or it can be poor since the

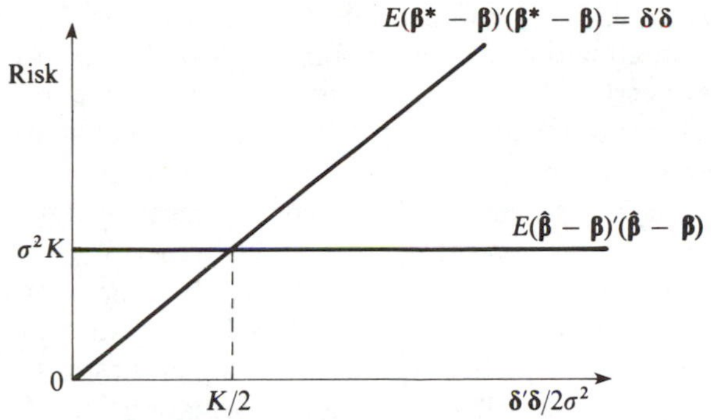

Figure 6.2.1 Risk functions for the ordinary least squares ($\hat{\boldsymbol{\beta}}$) and restricted least squares ($\boldsymbol{\beta}^*$) estimators for the orthonormal regression model.

risk is unbounded as $\boldsymbol{\delta}'\boldsymbol{\delta}/2\sigma^2 \to \infty$. That is, if the prior information is "bad" in the sense that the specification error $\boldsymbol{\delta} = \mathbf{r} - R\boldsymbol{\beta}$ is large ($\boldsymbol{\delta}'\boldsymbol{\delta}/2\sigma^2 > K/2$), the restricted least squares estimator is inferior to ordinary least squares. On the other hand, if the information is "good" in that the specification error is small, the restricted least squares estimator offers a gain over ordinary least squares. Note that the region for which the restricted least squares estimator is superior is dependent on the unknown population parameters $\boldsymbol{\beta}$ and σ^2 through the function $\boldsymbol{\delta}'\boldsymbol{\delta}/2\sigma^2$.

At first, it may appear that the estimator choice problem could be adequately addressed by a test of the hypotheses that $H_0: \boldsymbol{\delta} = \mathbf{0}$ versus $H_1: \boldsymbol{\delta} \neq \mathbf{0}$ or possibly $H_0: \boldsymbol{\delta}'\boldsymbol{\delta}/2\sigma^2 < (K/2)$ versus $H_1: \boldsymbol{\delta}'\boldsymbol{\delta}/2\sigma^2 \geq (K/2)$. In the first case the test is whether the imposed restrictions $R\boldsymbol{\beta} = \mathbf{r}$ are correct. The second is a test of whether the restrictions $R\boldsymbol{\beta} = \mathbf{r}$ are incorrect, but, only to the extent that the restricted least squares estimator is still superior to ordinary least squares. On further examination, however, it is clear that this "preliminary test" defines the "hybrid" estimator

$$\tilde{\boldsymbol{\beta}} = I_{[0,c)}(u)\boldsymbol{\beta}^* + I_{[c,\infty)}(u)\hat{\boldsymbol{\beta}},$$

where $I_{[0,c)}(u)$ is an indicator function which takes the value one if the test statistic u falls in the interval $[0, c)$ and zero otherwise with c being a critical value of the F-distribution. The indicator function $I_{[c,\infty)}(u)$ is defined in a similar way. The point to note is that the use of an hypothesis test for the purpose of estimator selection leads to a "preliminary test" estimator that is a stochastic linear combination of the restricted least squares and ordinary least squares estimators. The sampling properties of this estimator are naturally different from that of either the restricted least squares estimator or the ordinary least squares estimator. Hence, when one chooses between ordinary least squares or restricted least squares on the basis of an hypothesis test, the usual standard errors associated with ordinary least squares or restricted least squares are no longer appropriate. A complete discussion of preliminary test estimation is contained in the next chapter. Suffice it to say, when there is uncertainty as to the quality of prior information, the problem of estimator choice is not completely solved by the use of an hypothesis test.

In the discussion above we chose the orthonormal regression model ($X'X = I_K$) with $R = I_K$ for expository convenience. However, the conclusions obtained hold for nonorthogonal regressors ($X'X \neq I_K$) and general linear restrictions with $R \neq I_K$. That is, when the prior information is unbiased, or at least "nearly so," $\boldsymbol{\delta} = \mathbf{r} - R\boldsymbol{\beta} \doteq \mathbf{0}$, the restricted least squares estimator offers a gain over the ordinary least squares estimator in terms of risk. On the other hand, when the prior information includes substantial specification error, the risk of the restricted least squares estimator may exceed that of the ordinary least squares estimator. These conclusions are examined for various risk functions in Section 6.4. Nonetheless, an appropriate choice between restricted least squares and ordinary least squares estimators is dependent upon the values of unknown population parameters.

6.3 Mixed Estimation: Stochastic Linear Restrictions

6.3.1 Nature of Stochastic Restrictions

Theil and Goldberger (1961) have provided a generalization of the exact restricted least squares estimator. This estimator utilizes stochastic linear restrictions that do not hold exactly. Let the stochastic linear restrictions be denoted

$$\mathbf{r} = R\boldsymbol{\beta} + \mathbf{v}, \tag{6.3.1}$$

where $\mathbf{v}$ is a random error term with mean $E(\mathbf{v}) = \mathbf{0}$ and known covariance matrix $E\mathbf{v}\mathbf{v}' = \Psi$. The matrix R is known and nonstochastic. Two important characteristics of this prior information should be noted. First, the assumption $E(\mathbf{v}) = \mathbf{0}$ implies that the information being incorporated is unbiased, though stochastic. Secondly, since the information is stochastic, the restriction on the dimension of R (and $\mathbf{r}$) previously used ($J \leq K$) need not be imposed.

The prior information (6.3.1) may be statistical and from an independent sample, possibly the work of another investigator. In this case $\mathbf{r}$ would contain prior parameter estimates and Ψ would be consistently estimated by the estimated covariance matrix. Alternatively, (6.3.1) could represent subjective information. Nagar and Kakwani (1964) describe a situation where the first two elements of $\boldsymbol{\beta}$ fall within certain bounds. Suppose we know that with 95% probability β_1 falls between 0 and 1, and β_2 lies between $\frac{1}{4}$ and $\frac{3}{4}$.

Then, applying the two-sigma rule, the range of β_1 is $\frac{1}{2} \pm 2\sqrt{1/16}$ and that of β_2 is $\frac{1}{2} \pm 2\sqrt{1/64}$. Thus

$$\begin{aligned} \tfrac{1}{2} &= \beta_1 + v_1, \qquad Ev_1 = 0, \qquad Ev_1^2 = \tfrac{1}{16}, \\ \tfrac{1}{2} &= \beta_2 + v_2, \qquad Ev_2 = 0, \qquad Ev_2^2 = \tfrac{1}{64}, \end{aligned}$$

and

$$\mathbf{r} = \begin{bmatrix} \frac{1}{2} \\ \frac{1}{2} \end{bmatrix}, \qquad R = \begin{bmatrix} 1 & 0 & \cdots & 0 \\ 0 & 1 & \cdots & 0 \end{bmatrix}, \qquad \mathbf{v} = \begin{bmatrix} v_1 \\ v_2 \end{bmatrix},$$

$$\Psi = \begin{bmatrix} \frac{1}{16} & 0 \\ 0 & \frac{1}{64} \end{bmatrix}.$$

The term "mixed" estimator then refers to the mixing of sample information with stochastic prior information of the form (6.3.1).

As pointed out by Swamy and Mehta (1983, p. 368), this example contains a conceptual error. Do the elements $r_1 = r_2 = \frac{1}{2}$ remain the same in repeated samples? If so, the errors v_1 and v_2 are not random as previously claimed and the properties of the estimator to be proposed do not hold. However, this conceptual problem can be overcome by using a normal random number generator to generate values for the random errors v_1 and v_2 having zero mean and desired standard deviation and add them to $\frac{1}{2}$ to obtain random realizations of r_1 and r_2 as required by specification (6.3.1).

With the nature of the stochastic linear restrictions (6.3.1) explained, consider the problem of estimation. Assume that the present sample is described by $\mathbf{y} = X\boldsymbol{\beta} + \mathbf{e}$, where $E(\mathbf{e}) = \mathbf{0}$ and $E\mathbf{ee}' = \Omega$ and for the present, that Ω is known.

The mixed estimator is obtained from the augmented generalized least squares model

$$\begin{bmatrix} \mathbf{y} \\ \mathbf{r} \end{bmatrix} = \begin{bmatrix} X \\ R \end{bmatrix} \boldsymbol{\beta} + \begin{bmatrix} \mathbf{e} \\ \mathbf{v} \end{bmatrix}. \tag{6.3.2}$$

From the previous assumptions

$$E\begin{bmatrix} \mathbf{e} \\ \mathbf{v} \end{bmatrix} = \mathbf{0} \quad \text{and} \quad E\begin{bmatrix} \mathbf{e} \\ \mathbf{v} \end{bmatrix}[\mathbf{e}'\mathbf{v}'] = \begin{bmatrix} \Omega & 0 \\ 0 & \Psi \end{bmatrix}. \tag{6.3.3}$$

The generalized least squares estimator is thus

$$\hat{\boldsymbol{\beta}}^* = \left([X'R']\begin{bmatrix} \Omega & 0 \\ 0 & \Psi \end{bmatrix}^{-1}\begin{bmatrix} X \\ R \end{bmatrix}\right)^{-1}\left([X'R']\begin{bmatrix} \Omega & 0 \\ 0 & \Psi \end{bmatrix}^{-1}\begin{bmatrix} \mathbf{y} \\ \mathbf{r} \end{bmatrix}\right), \tag{6.3.4}$$

or

$$\hat{\boldsymbol{\beta}}^* = [X'\Omega^{-1}X + R'\Psi^{-1}R]^{-1}[X'\Omega^{-1}\mathbf{y} + R'\Psi^{-1}\mathbf{r}]. \tag{6.3.5}$$

The covariance matrix of $\hat{\boldsymbol{\beta}}^*$,

$$\operatorname{var}(\hat{\boldsymbol{\beta}}^*) = [X'\Omega^{-1}X + R'\Psi^{-1}R]^{-1}, \tag{6.3.6}$$

is obtained by substituting $X\boldsymbol{\beta} + \mathbf{e}$ for $\mathbf{y}$ and $R\boldsymbol{\beta} + \mathbf{v}$ for $\mathbf{r}$ and evaluating $E(\hat{\boldsymbol{\beta}}^* - E\hat{\boldsymbol{\beta}}^*)(\hat{\boldsymbol{\beta}}^* - E\hat{\boldsymbol{\beta}}^*)'$. It can easily be shown that $\text{var}(\hat{\boldsymbol{\beta}}) - \text{var}(\hat{\boldsymbol{\beta}}^*)$ is positive semidefinite and, therefore, the variances of the mixed estimators are no greater than the variances of the ordinary least squares estimators. (See Exercise 6.6.) The additional stochastic linear restrictions (6.3.1) reduce the variability of the estimators.

Finally, the mixed estimator has been developed under the assumption that the current sample information and the stochastic prior information are statistically independent. Of course, this may not be true. Mixed estimation can be modified to permit dependence between the sample and prior information as illustrated by Theil (1974). (See Exercise 6.19.)

6.3.2 Implications of Biased Restrictions

If the stochastic linear restrictions (6.3.1) are unbiased, $E\mathbf{v} = \mathbf{0}$, the mixed estimator is unbiased. In contrast, if the restrictions are biased,

$$E\mathbf{v} = E(\mathbf{r} - R\boldsymbol{\beta}) = \boldsymbol{\delta} \neq \mathbf{0},$$

then the mixed estimator has bias $(X'\Omega^{-1}X + R'\Psi^{-1}R)^{-1}R'\Psi^{-1}\boldsymbol{\delta}$. To examine how the mixed estimator is affected by bias in the stochastic restrictions, let us return to the expository case of an orthonormal linear model ($X'X = I_K$) with $R = I_K$, $\Omega = \sigma^2 I$, $E\mathbf{v} = \boldsymbol{\delta}$, and $E\mathbf{v}\mathbf{v}' = c\sigma^2 I$, where c is a positive constant. That is, the stochastic linear restrictions are of the form $\mathbf{r} = \boldsymbol{\beta} + \mathbf{v}$. Assume the risk function is the expected squared error loss $E(\hat{\boldsymbol{\beta}}^* - \boldsymbol{\beta})'(\hat{\boldsymbol{\beta}}^* - \boldsymbol{\beta})$. It can be shown in Exercise 6.7 that the risk for the mixed estimator is less than that of the ordinary least squares estimator, namely $\sigma^2 K$, when

$$\boldsymbol{\delta}'\boldsymbol{\delta}/[2\sigma^2(c + 1)] < K/2,$$

equal to that of the ordinary least squares estimator when

$$\boldsymbol{\delta}'\boldsymbol{\delta}/[2\sigma^2(c + 1)] = K/2,$$

and greater than that of the ordinary least squares estimator when

$$\boldsymbol{\delta}'\boldsymbol{\delta}/[2\sigma^2(c + 1)] > K/2.$$

The risk function for this mixed estimator is depicted in Figure 6.3.1.

Obviously, if the stochastic prior information (6.3.1) is poor in the sense that the specification error $\boldsymbol{\delta} = E(\mathbf{r} - R\boldsymbol{\beta})$ is large, then $(\boldsymbol{\delta}'\boldsymbol{\delta})/[2\sigma^2(c + 1)] > K/2$, and the mixed estimator is inferior to the ordinary least squares estimator. On the other hand, if the prior information is good, so that $\boldsymbol{\delta}$ is close to $\mathbf{0}$, the mixed estimator can offer a gain over ordinary least squares.

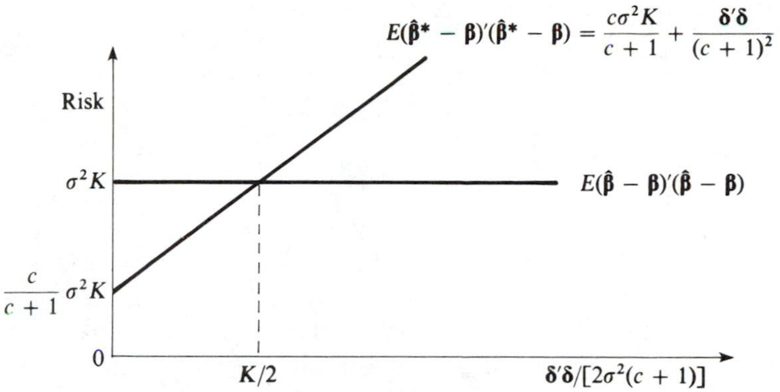

Figure 6.3.1 Risk functions for the ordinary least squares ($\hat{\boldsymbol{\beta}}$) and mixed estimator ($\hat{\boldsymbol{\beta}}^*$) for the orthonormal model.

Once again, as for the restricted least squares estimator, the region for which the mixed estimator is superior is dependent on unknown values of population parameters.

For the same reasons cited in Section 6.2.4, the choice of estimators is not made easier by an hypothesis test of H_0: $\boldsymbol{\delta} = \mathbf{0}$ versus H_1: $\boldsymbol{\delta} \neq \mathbf{0}$ or, for that matter, H_0: $\boldsymbol{\delta}'\boldsymbol{\delta}/[2\sigma^2(c + 1)] < K/2$ versus H_1: $\boldsymbol{\delta}'\boldsymbol{\delta}/[2\sigma^2(c + 1)] \geq K/2$. The associated "preliminary test" estimators have properties that are not those ascribed to ordinary least squares or mixed estimation.

There are striking similarities between the risk functions in Figures 6.2.1 and 6.3.1. If $c = 0$ the risk function of the mixed estimator in Figure 6.3.1 would look exactly like that of the restricted least squares estimator in Figure 6.2.1. As $c \to 0$ the risk of the mixed estimator approaches zero at $\boldsymbol{\delta} = \mathbf{0}$ and the intersection point between the risk of the mixed estimator and that of ordinary least squares occurs at $K/2 = \boldsymbol{\delta}'\boldsymbol{\delta}/2\sigma^2$ as in the restricted least squares case. This is intuitively obvious since as $c \to 0$ the stochastic restriction $\mathbf{r} = \boldsymbol{\beta} + \mathbf{v}$ becomes the exact restriction $\mathbf{r} = \boldsymbol{\beta}$. The variance of $\mathbf{v}$ is zero in the limit.

6.3.3 Feasible Mixed Estimation

In the previous discussion, we assumed that the error covariance matrices Ω and Ψ were known. In this instance the mixed estimator has all the properties of generalized least squares estimators; it is best, linear, unbiased and minimum variance unbiased in the presence of normally distributed errors. However, this is not the usual situation. It is most likely that the relative value (variability) of the sample information to the prior information is unknown. To illustrate, assume for simplicity that $\Omega = \sigma^2 I$ and $\Psi = \gamma^2 I$ where σ^2 is unknown (as usual in the classical linear model) but γ^2 is known.

The associated mixed estimator is

$$\begin{aligned}\hat{\boldsymbol{\beta}}^* &= (\sigma^{-2}X'X + \gamma^{-2}R'R)^{-1}(\sigma^{-2}X'\mathbf{y} + \gamma^{-2}R'\mathbf{r}) \\ &= (X'X + \tau R'R)^{-1}(X'\mathbf{y} + \tau R'\mathbf{r}),\end{aligned}$$

where $\tau = (\sigma^2/\gamma^2)$. Unfortunately, τ is unknown since σ^2 is unknown and, therefore, $\hat{\boldsymbol{\beta}}^*$ is not a feasible (practical) estimator. To make $\hat{\boldsymbol{\beta}}^*$ a feasible estimator, the relative variance σ^2/γ^2 must be consistently estimated by, say, $\hat{\tau} = \hat{\sigma}^2/\gamma^2$, where $\hat{\sigma}^2 = (\mathbf{y} - X\hat{\boldsymbol{\beta}})'(\mathbf{y} - X\hat{\boldsymbol{\beta}})/(T - K)$ is an unbiased estimator of σ^2. However, once $\hat{\tau}$ is used in place of τ, we have a feasible generalized least squares estimator, rather than the generalized least squares estimator. Feasible generalized least squares is discussed in Chapter 8. Suffice it to say that the feasible generalized least squares estimator

$$\hat{\hat{\boldsymbol{\beta}}}^* = (X'X + \hat{\tau}R'R)^{-1}(X'\mathbf{y} + \hat{\tau}R'\mathbf{r})$$

is "essentially" the same as the generalized least squares estimator $\hat{\boldsymbol{\beta}}^*$ for large sample sizes. For a more thorough discussion of the asymptotic properties of the feasible mixed estimator, see Chapter 8 and Theil (1963), Nagar and Kakwani (1964), and Yancey *et al.* (1974).

6.3.4 Restricted Least Squares and Ordinary Least Squares as Limiting Cases of Mixed Estimation

As suggested by Durbin (1953) and Theil and Goldberger (1961), there is a direct connection between restricted least squares and mixed estimation. In fact, it can be shown that restricted least squares is a special case of mixed estimation (see Exercise 6.23). As the variance of the stochastic prior information (6.3.1) goes to zero, $\text{var}(\mathbf{v}) \to 0$, the mixed estimator approaches the restricted least squares estimator implied by the exact restrictions, $R\boldsymbol{\beta} = \mathbf{r}$. In contrast, as the stochastic restrictions become less certain, $\text{var}(\mathbf{v}) \to \infty$, the mixed estimator approaches the ordinary least squares estimator $\hat{\boldsymbol{\beta}}$, assuming $E\mathbf{ee}' = \sigma^2 I$.

Figures 6.2.1 and 6.3.1 provide some insight to these limiting cases. In Figure 6.3.1 the risk functions for the ordinary least squares and mixed estimators in the orthonormal model are displayed ($X'X = I_K$, $R = I_K$, $\Omega = \sigma^2 I$, $E\mathbf{v} = \boldsymbol{\delta}$ and $E\mathbf{vv}' = c\sigma^2 I$). The extremes of mixed estimation are exhibited when $c = 0$ and $c = \infty$. In the former case the risk function of the mixed estimator is that of the restricted least squares estimator as the restrictions $\mathbf{r} = \boldsymbol{\beta}$ are imposed with certainty. In the latter case, the mixed estimator risk function coincides with the ordinary least squares risk function since $\lim_{c \to \infty}[c/(c + 1)] = 1$. The mixed estimator coincides with the ordinary least squares estimator as the restrictions $\mathbf{r} = \boldsymbol{\beta}$ are held with total uncertainty.

6.3.5 A Reformulation of the Mixed Estimation Model

In Chapter 3, a test statistic for the general linear hypothesis $R\boldsymbol{\beta} = \mathbf{r}$ was developed using the likelihood ratio method. This was the case, however, of *exact* linear restrictions. How would one proceed to test the *stochastic* linear restrictions $R\boldsymbol{\beta} + \mathbf{v} = \mathbf{r}$? The answer has been provided by Judge *et al.* (1973b). They show that the stochastically restricted least squares (mixed estimation) model can be reformulated as an exactly restricted least squares model on an *extended parameter space*. Once the mixed model has been reformulated as a restricted least squares model, the conventional F-statistic for the test of the general linear hypothesis can be used to examine the validity of the stochastic restrictions. To develop the reformulation, recall that the model is

$$\begin{bmatrix} \mathbf{y} \\ \mathbf{r} \end{bmatrix} = \begin{bmatrix} X \\ R \end{bmatrix} \boldsymbol{\beta} + \begin{bmatrix} \mathbf{e} \\ \mathbf{v} \end{bmatrix}.$$

This model can be rewritten as

$$\begin{bmatrix} \mathbf{y} \\ \mathbf{r} \end{bmatrix} = \begin{bmatrix} X & 0 \\ 0 & I_J \end{bmatrix} \begin{bmatrix} \boldsymbol{\beta} \\ \boldsymbol{\mu} \end{bmatrix} + \begin{bmatrix} \mathbf{e} \\ \mathbf{v} \end{bmatrix} \tag{6.3.7}$$

with the restriction

$$[R \,\vdots\, -I_J] \begin{bmatrix} \boldsymbol{\beta} \\ \boldsymbol{\mu} \end{bmatrix} = R\boldsymbol{\beta} - \boldsymbol{\mu} = \mathbf{0}. \tag{6.3.8}$$

The restriction implies simply that $\boldsymbol{\mu} = R\boldsymbol{\beta}$. It is easily seen that, on substituting this restriction into Equation (6.3.7), the original model results.

The mean and covariance assumptions (used by Judge *et al.* (1973b)) are

$$E\begin{bmatrix} \mathbf{e} \\ \mathbf{v} \end{bmatrix} = \begin{bmatrix} \mathbf{0} \\ \boldsymbol{\delta} \end{bmatrix} \tag{6.3.9}$$

and

$$E\begin{bmatrix} \mathbf{e} \\ \mathbf{v} \end{bmatrix}(\mathbf{e}'\mathbf{v}') = \begin{bmatrix} \sigma^2 I & 0 \\ 0 & \Psi \end{bmatrix} = \sigma^2 \begin{bmatrix} I & 0 \\ 0 & m\Psi \end{bmatrix}, \tag{6.3.10}$$

where Ψ and, for the moment, $m = (1/\sigma^2)$ are assumed known. In addition, assume that $\mathbf{e}$ and $\mathbf{v}$ are normally distributed. Note the parameter $\boldsymbol{\delta}$ represents the specification error (bias) potentially inherent in the stochastic restrictions $R\boldsymbol{\beta} + \mathbf{v} = \mathbf{r}$.

To diagonalize the error covariance matrix, the model is rewritten again as

$$\begin{bmatrix} \mathbf{y} \\ G\mathbf{r} \end{bmatrix} = \begin{bmatrix} X & 0 \\ 0 & G \end{bmatrix} \begin{bmatrix} \boldsymbol{\beta} \\ \boldsymbol{\mu} \end{bmatrix} + \begin{bmatrix} \mathbf{e} \\ G\mathbf{v} \end{bmatrix} \tag{6.3.11}$$

and

$$G[R \,\vdots\, -I_J] \begin{bmatrix} \boldsymbol{\beta} \\ \boldsymbol{\mu} \end{bmatrix} = \mathbf{0}, \tag{6.3.12}$$

where G is defined so that

$$mG\Psi G' = I_J.$$

Note that G' is simply the matrix whose columns are the eigenvectors of $m\Psi$ scaled by the square root of the reciprocal of the corresponding eigenvalue.

A last transformation makes the model equivalent to a conventional restricted least squares problem. The bias $E(\mathbf{v}) = \boldsymbol{\delta}$ is removed from the error term $\mathbf{v}$ yielding

$$\begin{bmatrix} \mathbf{y} \\ G\mathbf{r} \end{bmatrix} = \begin{bmatrix} X & 0 \\ 0 & G \end{bmatrix} \begin{bmatrix} \boldsymbol{\beta} \\ \boldsymbol{\mu} + \boldsymbol{\delta} \end{bmatrix} + \begin{bmatrix} \mathbf{e} \\ \mathbf{w} \end{bmatrix} \tag{6.3.13}$$

subject to

$$G[R \vdots -I_J] \begin{bmatrix} \boldsymbol{\beta} \\ \boldsymbol{\mu} + \boldsymbol{\delta} \end{bmatrix} = -G\boldsymbol{\delta}$$

or equivalently

$$[R \vdots -I_J] \begin{bmatrix} \boldsymbol{\beta} \\ \boldsymbol{\mu} + \boldsymbol{\delta} \end{bmatrix} = -\boldsymbol{\delta}, \tag{6.3.14}$$

where $\mathbf{e}$ and $\mathbf{w}$ are distributed independently as multivariate normal vectors with zero means and constant variances $\sigma^2 I$.

The model (6.3.13) and (6.3.14) can be expressed more compactly as

$$\mathbf{Y} = Z\boldsymbol{\phi} + \boldsymbol{\xi} \tag{6.3.15}$$

subject to

$$H\boldsymbol{\phi} = \mathbf{h}, \tag{6.3.16}$$

where,

$$H = [R \vdots -I_J], \quad \boldsymbol{\phi} = \begin{bmatrix} \boldsymbol{\phi}_1 \\ \boldsymbol{\phi}_2 \end{bmatrix} = \begin{bmatrix} \boldsymbol{\beta} \\ \boldsymbol{\mu} + \boldsymbol{\delta} \end{bmatrix}, \qquad \boldsymbol{\xi} = \begin{bmatrix} \mathbf{e} \\ \mathbf{w} \end{bmatrix}$$

and $\mathbf{h} = -\boldsymbol{\delta}$.

Using (6.3.15) and (6.3.16), the equality restricted least squares estimator on the extended parameter space becomes

$$\tilde{\boldsymbol{\phi}} = \hat{\boldsymbol{\phi}} - (Z'Z)^{-1}H'[H(Z'Z)^{-1}H']^{-1}H\hat{\boldsymbol{\phi}} = \begin{bmatrix} \tilde{\boldsymbol{\phi}}_1 \\ \tilde{\boldsymbol{\phi}}_2 \end{bmatrix}, \tag{6.3.17}$$

where

$$\hat{\boldsymbol{\phi}} = (Z'Z)^{-1}Z'\mathbf{Y} = \begin{bmatrix} (X'X)^{-1}X'\mathbf{y} \\ \mathbf{r} \end{bmatrix} = \begin{bmatrix} \hat{\boldsymbol{\beta}} \\ \mathbf{r} \end{bmatrix}$$

is the unrestricted least squares estimator for Equation (6.3.15). The variance estimator is

$$\hat{\sigma}^2 = \frac{\mathbf{Y}'[I_{T+J} - Z(Z'Z)^{-1}Z']\mathbf{Y}}{T + J - K - J} = \frac{\mathbf{y}[I_T - X(X'X)^{-1}X']\mathbf{y}}{T - K}. \quad (6.3.18)$$

The estimator $\tilde{\boldsymbol{\phi}}$, however, can be rewritten as (see Exercise 6.10),

$$\tilde{\boldsymbol{\phi}} = \begin{bmatrix} \tilde{\boldsymbol{\phi}}_1 \\ \tilde{\boldsymbol{\phi}}_2 \end{bmatrix} = \begin{bmatrix} \hat{\boldsymbol{\beta}} \\ \mathbf{r} \end{bmatrix} - \begin{bmatrix} (X'X)^{-1}R'[R(X'X)^{-1}R' + m\Psi]^{-1}(R\hat{\boldsymbol{\beta}} - \mathbf{r}) \\ -m\Psi[R(X'X)^{-1}R' + m\Psi]^{-1}(R\hat{\boldsymbol{\beta}} - \mathbf{r}) \end{bmatrix}. \quad (6.3.19)$$

Under the assumptions of the original model, $\tilde{\boldsymbol{\phi}}_1$ is the same as the standard mixed estimator $\hat{\boldsymbol{\beta}}^*$, Equation (6.3.5). (See Exercise 6.11.) That is,

$$\tilde{\boldsymbol{\phi}} = \begin{bmatrix} \tilde{\boldsymbol{\phi}}_1 \\ \tilde{\boldsymbol{\phi}}_2 \end{bmatrix} = \begin{bmatrix} \hat{\boldsymbol{\beta}}^* \\ \tilde{\boldsymbol{\phi}}_2 \end{bmatrix}.$$

Since the stochastically restricted least squares estimator can be written as a generalized restricted least squares problem, all the results for testing hypotheses developed in Chapter 3 can be applied. For example, suppose that a test of whether the stochastic restrictions $R\boldsymbol{\beta} + \mathbf{v} = \mathbf{r}$ are unbiased or not is desired. That is, we want to know if $E\mathbf{v} = E(\mathbf{r} - R\boldsymbol{\beta}) = \boldsymbol{\delta} = \mathbf{0}$. The hypotheses $H_0: \boldsymbol{\delta} = \mathbf{0}$ versus $H_1: \boldsymbol{\delta} \neq \mathbf{0}$ can easily be translated into

$$H_0: H\boldsymbol{\phi} = \mathbf{0}$$

versus $H_1: H\boldsymbol{\phi} \neq \mathbf{0}$ in the generalized (extended parameter space) restricted least squares formulation of (6.3.15) and (6.3.16). Under the null hypothesis, the conventional test statistic, Equation (3.4.17), becomes

$$\begin{aligned} u &= \hat{\boldsymbol{\phi}}'H'[H(Z'Z)^{-1}H']^{-1}H\hat{\boldsymbol{\phi}}/J\hat{\sigma}^2 = (\text{SSE}_{\hat{\beta}*} - \text{SSE}_{\hat{\beta}})/J\hat{\sigma}^2 \\ &= (R\hat{\boldsymbol{\beta}} - \mathbf{r})'[R(X'X)^{-1}R' + m\Psi]^{-1}(R\hat{\boldsymbol{\beta}} - \mathbf{r})/J\hat{\sigma}^2, \end{aligned} \quad (6.3.20)$$

where $\text{SSE}_{\hat{\beta}*} = (\mathbf{y} - X\hat{\boldsymbol{\beta}}^*)'(\mathbf{y} - X\hat{\boldsymbol{\beta}}^*)$ and $\text{SSE}_{\hat{\beta}} = (\mathbf{y} - X\hat{\boldsymbol{\beta}})'(\mathbf{y} - X\hat{\boldsymbol{\beta}})$. This statistic has an F-distribution with J (the number of rows of R) and $(T - K)$ degrees of freedom. The only difference in the test statistics between the previous case of exact restrictions $R\boldsymbol{\beta} = \mathbf{r}$ and stochastic restrictions $R\boldsymbol{\beta} + \mathbf{v} = \mathbf{r}$ is the appearance of the additional term $m\Psi$.

Recall that during this discussion it was conveniently assumed that $m = (1/\sigma^2)$ was known so that the small sample test statistic results of Chapter 3 could be applied. If m is unknown, it can be consistently estimated by $\hat{m} = 1/\hat{\sigma}^2$, where $\hat{\sigma}^2$ is the unbiased estimator of σ^2. Necessarily, the statistic u of (6.3.20) is no longer distributed as an F random variable for small samples. However, the resulting statistic, say $\hat{u}$, is *asymptotically* distributed as an F random variable with J and $T - K$ degrees of freedom.

In addition, Yancey *et al.* (1974) report that in Monte Carlo studies the F-distribution was a reasonable approximation of the distribution of u in small samples.

In a manner similar to that of Section 4.4 on nonnormal disturbances, it can be shown that the assumption of normality of $\mathbf{e}$ and $\mathbf{v}$ is not essential for asymptotic justification of the above-mentioned test procedure. All that is required is that the error properties of $\mathbf{e}$ and $\mathbf{v}$ satisfy the specification (6.3.10). The generalization of the test statistic (6.3.20) for the case where the sample information is from a generalized least squares model rather than the classical linear regression model, $E\mathbf{ee}' = \sigma^2\Omega$ rather than $E\mathbf{ee}' = \sigma^2 I$, is straightforward. (See Exercise 6.12.)

Finally, we note that Theil (1963) has developed a "compatibility" statistic which is asymptotically equivalent to the F-statistic of (6.3.20). Like the F-statistic, the purpose of the compatibility statistic is to test the unbiasedness of the stochastic prior information $R\boldsymbol{\beta} + \mathbf{v} = \mathbf{r}$; that is, $H_0: \boldsymbol{\delta} = \mathbf{0}$ versus $\boldsymbol{\delta} \neq \mathbf{0}$. Under the null hypothesis,

$$\begin{aligned} \operatorname{var}(R\hat{\boldsymbol{\beta}} - \mathbf{r}) &= E(R\hat{\boldsymbol{\beta}} - \mathbf{r})(R\hat{\boldsymbol{\beta}} - \mathbf{r})' \\ &= \sigma^2 R(X'X)^{-1}R' + \Psi \equiv \Upsilon. \end{aligned} \tag{6.3.21}$$

If the stochastic prior information is biased (not compatible), some elements of $(R\hat{\boldsymbol{\beta}} - \mathbf{r})$ will be "too large" to fit the description of zero mean and variance–covariance matrix Υ. To test this hypothesis consider the quadratic form

$$(R\hat{\boldsymbol{\beta}} - \mathbf{r})'\Upsilon^{-1}(R\hat{\boldsymbol{\beta}} - \mathbf{r}). \tag{6.3.22}$$

If $\mathbf{e}$ and $\mathbf{v}$ are normally distributed then the quadratic form is distributed as χ^2 with J degrees of freedom under the null hypothesis.

Since σ^2 is unknown in most instances, Υ is likewise unknown. Therefore, to make (6.3.22) operational, Theil (1963) has suggested that the unbiased estimate $\hat{\sigma}^2$ be used instead. The resulting statistic is thus *asymptotically* distributed as a χ^2 random variable with J degrees of freedom. Yancey *et al.* (1974) also report that in Monte Carlo experiments the χ^2-distribution was adequate in small samples. It is left as an exercise to show that Theil's compatibility statistic (6.3.22) and the F-statistic (6.3.20) derived by reformulating mixed estimation as a restricted least squares problem on an extended parameter space are asymptotically equivalent (Exercise 6.13).

To this point we have developed test statistics for testing the correctness of the exact linear restrictions $R\boldsymbol{\beta} = \mathbf{r}$ as well as the unbiasedness of the stochastic linear restrictions $R\boldsymbol{\beta} + \mathbf{v} = \mathbf{r}$. But it is obvious from the risk functions depicted in Figures 6.2.1 and 6.3.1 that there is a bias-variance "tradeoff." The restrictions imposed do not have to be unbiased to offer a risk gain over ordinary least squares estimation. If the bias in the prior information is sufficiently small, the reduction in estimator variance may more than compensate for the bias thus resulting in reduced risk. Why not test the hypothesis $H_0: 0 \leq \boldsymbol{\delta}'\boldsymbol{\delta}/2\sigma^2 < K/2$ rather than $H_0: \boldsymbol{\delta} = 0$ in Figure 6.2.1? That is, why not test for risk improvement rather than unbiasedness? This is the topic of the next section.

6.4 Mean Square Error Criteria

To generalize hypothesis testing for incorrect *a priori* information, a method must be developed to gauge whether or not, statistically speaking, the restricted least squares estimator $\boldsymbol{\beta}^*$ has smaller risk than the ordinary least squares estimator $\hat{\boldsymbol{\beta}}$. Similar comparisons between the mixed estimator $\hat{\boldsymbol{\beta}}^*$ and the ordinary least squares estimator are required.

There are, of course, as many risk functions as there are loss functions, an infinite number. In Section 6.2, we defined $L(\tilde{\boldsymbol{\beta}}, \boldsymbol{\beta})$ as the loss incurred by incorrectly guessing $\boldsymbol{\beta}$ using the estimator $\tilde{\boldsymbol{\beta}}$. Ideally, a loss function should reflect the circumstances of the problem being investigated. However, mathematical statisticians usually restrict attention to quadratic loss functions $L(\tilde{\boldsymbol{\beta}}, \boldsymbol{\beta}; W) = (\tilde{\boldsymbol{\beta}} - \boldsymbol{\beta})'W(\tilde{\boldsymbol{\beta}} - \boldsymbol{\beta})$, where W is a positive semidefinite weighting matrix.

The bias–variance tradeoff of an estimator is illustrated by the squared error loss function $L(\tilde{\boldsymbol{\beta}}, \boldsymbol{\beta}; I) = (\tilde{\boldsymbol{\beta}} - \boldsymbol{\beta})'(\tilde{\boldsymbol{\beta}} - \boldsymbol{\beta})$. The corresponding risk function is $E[L(\tilde{\boldsymbol{\beta}}, \boldsymbol{\beta}; I)] = E(\tilde{\boldsymbol{\beta}} - \boldsymbol{\beta})'(\tilde{\boldsymbol{\beta}} - \boldsymbol{\beta}) = \sum_i E(\tilde{\beta}_i - \beta_i)^2$, the sum of the expected losses for each term. Each of the terms $E(\tilde{\beta}_i - \beta_i)^2$ can be written as

$$E(\tilde{\beta}_i - \beta_i)^2 = E(\tilde{\beta}_i - E\tilde{\beta}_i)^2 + (\beta_i - E\tilde{\beta}_i)^2, \tag{6.4.1}$$

i.e., as the sum of the variance and the squared bias for $\tilde{\beta}_i$.

In the remainder of this section we define three separate measures of estimator goodness using the concept of risk. In turn, these measures will be used to determine when the restricted least squares estimator is "better" than the ordinary least squares estimator. Corresponding tests of hypotheses are also developed. First, a word of warning. The term risk is sometimes referred to in the literature as mean square error. These terms are synonymous and are often used interchangeably.

Until the work of Toro-Vizcarrondo and Wallace (1968), the major way of statistically comparing the restricted least squares and ordinary least squares estimators was on the basis of unbiasedness. That is, the null and alternative hypotheses concerned $H_0: R\boldsymbol{\beta} = \mathbf{r}$ versus $H_1: R\boldsymbol{\beta} \neq \mathbf{r}$. However, regardless of the specification error $\boldsymbol{\delta} = \mathbf{r} - R\boldsymbol{\beta}$, the variance–covariance matrix of $\boldsymbol{\beta}^*$ is "less than" the variance–covariance matrix of $\hat{\boldsymbol{\beta}}$ in the sense that the matrix difference $E(\hat{\boldsymbol{\beta}} - \boldsymbol{\beta})(\hat{\boldsymbol{\beta}} - \boldsymbol{\beta})' - E(\boldsymbol{\beta}^* - E\boldsymbol{\beta}^*)(\boldsymbol{\beta}^* - E\boldsymbol{\beta}^*)'$ is positive semidefinite. This raises an interesting possibility as the following definition will show.

Definition 6.4.1. The *mean square error matrix* of an estimator $\tilde{\boldsymbol{\beta}}$ is defined as

$$\begin{aligned}\text{MSE}(\tilde{\boldsymbol{\beta}}) &\equiv E(\tilde{\boldsymbol{\beta}} - \boldsymbol{\beta})(\tilde{\boldsymbol{\beta}} - \boldsymbol{\beta})' \\ &= E(\tilde{\boldsymbol{\beta}} - E\tilde{\boldsymbol{\beta}})(\tilde{\boldsymbol{\beta}} - E\tilde{\boldsymbol{\beta}})' + (E\tilde{\boldsymbol{\beta}} - \boldsymbol{\beta})(E\tilde{\boldsymbol{\beta}} - \boldsymbol{\beta})'.\end{aligned} \tag{6.4.2}$$

The first matrix on the right-hand side of (6.4.2) is the variance–covariance matrix of $\tilde{\boldsymbol{\beta}}$ while the second matrix is the squared bias matrix. This provides the motivation for Definition 6.4.2.

Definition 6.4.2. Let $\boldsymbol{\beta}^*$ and $\hat{\boldsymbol{\beta}}$ be two alternative estimators of the $K \times 1$ parameter vector $\boldsymbol{\beta}$. Then $\boldsymbol{\beta}^*$ is "better" than $\hat{\boldsymbol{\beta}}$ in the *strong mean square error* sense when

$$E(\mathbf{l}'\boldsymbol{\beta}^* - \mathbf{l}'\boldsymbol{\beta})^2 \leq E(\mathbf{l}'\hat{\boldsymbol{\beta}} - \mathbf{l}\boldsymbol{\beta})^2 \tag{6.4.3}$$

for every $K \times 1$ vector $\mathbf{l} \neq \mathbf{0}$.

The adjective "strong" is used because of the stringent requirement that *every* linear combination must be equally or more precisely estimated by $\boldsymbol{\beta}^*$. Note that the strong mean square error criterion can be stated in two other equivalent ways:

(a) $\boldsymbol{\beta}^*$ is superior to $\hat{\boldsymbol{\beta}}$ in strong mean square error iff the mean square error matrix difference $E(\hat{\boldsymbol{\beta}} - \boldsymbol{\beta})(\hat{\boldsymbol{\beta}} - \boldsymbol{\beta})' - E(\boldsymbol{\beta}^* - \boldsymbol{\beta})(\boldsymbol{\beta}^* - \boldsymbol{\beta})'$ is a positive semidefinite matrix.

(b) $\boldsymbol{\beta}^*$ is superior to $\hat{\boldsymbol{\beta}}$ in strong mean square error iff $E(\boldsymbol{\beta}^* - \boldsymbol{\beta})'W(\boldsymbol{\beta}^* - \boldsymbol{\beta}) \leq E(\hat{\boldsymbol{\beta}} - \boldsymbol{\beta})'W(\hat{\boldsymbol{\beta}} - \boldsymbol{\beta})$ for *any* choice of symmetric, positive semidefinite weight matrix W.

It is left as an exercise for the reader (see Exercise 6.14) to show these equivalences. Equivalence (b) makes it clear that an estimator $\boldsymbol{\beta}^*$ is superior to a competing estimator $\hat{\boldsymbol{\beta}}$ if and only if the risk of $\boldsymbol{\beta}^*$ is less than or equal to the risk of $\hat{\boldsymbol{\beta}}$ for *any* choice of quadratic loss function.

Before moving on to weaker measures of estimator superiority, let us examine under what conditions the restricted least squares estimator is superior to the ordinary least squares estimator in the strong mean square error sense. The mean square error matrix difference $\text{MSE}(\hat{\boldsymbol{\beta}}) - \text{MSE}(\boldsymbol{\beta}^*)$ can be written as (see Exercise 6.15),

$$\sigma^2(X'X)^{-1}R'[R(X'X)^{-1}R']^{-1}[B][R(X'X)^{-1}R']^{-1}R(X'X)^{-1}, \tag{6.4.4}$$

where,

$$B = \left[R(X'X)^{-1}R' - \frac{1}{\sigma^2}(R\boldsymbol{\beta} - \mathbf{r})(R\boldsymbol{\beta} - \mathbf{r})'\right]. \tag{6.4.5}$$

Expression (6.4.4), is positive semidefinite if and only if B is positive semidefinite. From the definition of positive definite matrices we have B positive semidefinite if and only if for all $\mathbf{l} \neq \mathbf{0}$

$$\mathbf{l}'\left[R(X'X)^{-1}R' - \frac{1}{\sigma^2}(R\boldsymbol{\beta} - \mathbf{r})(R\boldsymbol{\beta} - \mathbf{r})'\right]\mathbf{l} \geq 0. \tag{6.4.6}$$

Viewed as a ratio, the inequality (6.4.6) can be written,

$$Q = \frac{\mathbf{l}'(R\boldsymbol{\beta} - \mathbf{r})(R\boldsymbol{\beta} - \mathbf{r})'\mathbf{l}}{\sigma^2\mathbf{l}'R(X'X)^{-1}R'\mathbf{l}} \leq 1, \tag{6.4.7}$$

since $R(X'X)^{-1}R'$ is positive definite. This is the ratio of a quadratic form in the bias to a quadratic form in the variance of $R\hat{\boldsymbol{\beta}}$.

Now by a form of the Cauchy–Schwartz inequality (Rao (1973, p. 60), see Exercise 6.16) the ratio Q satisfies

$$\operatorname*{Sup}_{\mathbf{l}} Q = (R\boldsymbol{\beta} - \mathbf{r})'[R(X'X)^{-1}R']^{-1}(R\boldsymbol{\beta} - \mathbf{r})/\sigma^2 \tag{6.4.8}$$

and the supremum is attained when $\mathbf{l}$ takes the value

$$\mathbf{l}^0 = [R(X'X)^{-1}R']^{-1}(R\boldsymbol{\beta} - \mathbf{r}). \tag{6.4.9}$$

What remains to be shown is that the term (6.4.5) is positive semidefinite *if and only if*

$$\frac{(R\boldsymbol{\beta} - \mathbf{r})'[R(X'X)^{-1}R']^{-1}(R\boldsymbol{\beta} - \mathbf{r})}{\sigma^2} \leq 1. \tag{6.4.10}$$

To prove this assertion, note B positive semidefinite implies inequality (6.4.7) for all $\mathbf{l}$ not equal zero, and

$$\mathbf{l}^0 = [R(X'X)^{-1}R']^{-1}(R\boldsymbol{\beta} - \mathbf{r})$$

in particular. Now assume the inequality (6.4.10) is true. Since the left-hand side of Equation (6.4.10) is the supremum of Q then the inequality (6.4.10) must be true for all $\mathbf{l}$. As a final step divide Sup Q by 2 to obtain

$$\lambda = \frac{(R\boldsymbol{\beta} - \mathbf{r})'[R(X'X)^{-1}R']^{-1}(R\boldsymbol{\beta} - \mathbf{r})}{2\sigma^2} \leq \frac{1}{2}. \tag{6.4.11}$$

As the condition (6.4.11) shows, the restricted least squares estimator is superior to the ordinary least squares estimator only over a limited portion of the parameter space $(\boldsymbol{\beta}, \sigma^2)$, i.e., when $\lambda \leq \frac{1}{2}$. When the bias in the prior information is "small" then $R\boldsymbol{\beta} - \mathbf{r} \doteq \mathbf{0}$ and $\lambda \leq \frac{1}{2}$. On the other hand, when $R\boldsymbol{\beta} - \mathbf{r}$ is substantially different from $\mathbf{0}$, the mean square error matrix of $\boldsymbol{\beta}^*$ is "bigger" than the mean square error matrix of $\hat{\boldsymbol{\beta}}$ and the restricted least squares estimator is less efficient. Obviously, the region where the restricted least squares estimator is superior to the ordinary least squares estimator is dependent upon the unknown parameter λ. Therefore, the best that can be hoped for is that a statistical test can be constructed which will tell us whether, statistically speaking, the mean square error of the restricted least squares estimator $\boldsymbol{\beta}^*$ appears, to be less than the mean square error of the ordinary least squares estimator $\hat{\boldsymbol{\beta}}$.

Equation (6.4.11) is important since λ can be shown to be the non-centrality parameter of a well-known distribution. The following lemmas, stated without proof, will be used.

Lemma 6.4.1. *If* $\mathbf{x} \sim N(\boldsymbol{\mu}, \sigma^2 I_P)$ *and* A *is a real symmetric matrix of* rank r *then* $Q = \mathbf{x}'A\mathbf{x}/\sigma^2 \sim \chi^2_{(r,\lambda)}$ *iff* $A^2 = A$ *where* $\lambda = \boldsymbol{\mu}'A\boldsymbol{\mu}/2\sigma^2$.

Lemma 6.4.2. *Let* $\mathbf{x} \sim N(\boldsymbol{\mu}, \Sigma)$ *and* C *and* D *denote real symmetric matrices, then* $Q_1 = \mathbf{x}'C\mathbf{x}$ *and* $Q_2 = \mathbf{x}'D\mathbf{x}$ *are independent iff* $C\Sigma D = 0$, *where* 0 *is the null matrix.*

Using these lemmas it is easy to show (see Exercise 6.17) that the statistic

$$u = \frac{(\mathbf{r} - R\hat{\boldsymbol{\beta}})'[R(X'X)^{-1}R']^{-1}(\mathbf{r} - R\hat{\boldsymbol{\beta}})/J}{(\mathbf{y} - X\hat{\boldsymbol{\beta}})'(\mathbf{y} - X\hat{\boldsymbol{\beta}})/(T - K)} \tag{6.4.12}$$

has a noncentral F-distribution with parameters, J, $T - K$ and λ under the assumption that $R\boldsymbol{\beta} \neq \mathbf{r}$. In contrast, the "classical" F-test described in Chapter 3 is a test of the hypothesis that the prior information is unbiased, $R\boldsymbol{\beta} = \mathbf{r}$, i.e., $\lambda = 0$. If one is interested in whether $\boldsymbol{\beta}^*$ is better than the ordinary least squares estimator in the strong mean square error sense, then the appropriate hypothesis is $H_0\colon \lambda \leq \frac{1}{2}$. Values of the $F_{(J, T-K, 1/2)}$ distribution are tabled in Wallace and Toro-Vizcarrondo (1969). The procedure for the test is to compute the value of the test statistic u in (6.4.12) and compare it to the appropriate critical value for the selected level of type I error α, say u_α. If $u \geq u_\alpha$, the hypothesis that $\boldsymbol{\beta}^*$ is better than $\hat{\boldsymbol{\beta}}$ in strong mean square error is rejected.

The hypothesis implied by the inequality (6.4.3) is very stringent. As a consequence, a weaker criterion was proposed by Wallace (1972) and refined by Judge *et al.* (1973a).

Definition 6.4.3. $\boldsymbol{\beta}^*$ is better than $\hat{\boldsymbol{\beta}}$ in the *first weak mean square error* sense if

$$\operatorname{tr} \mathrm{MSE}(\boldsymbol{\beta}^*) \leq \operatorname{tr} \mathrm{MSE}(\hat{\boldsymbol{\beta}}), \tag{6.4.13}$$

where $\operatorname{tr} \mathrm{MSE}(\boldsymbol{\beta}^*) = \operatorname{tr} E(\boldsymbol{\beta}^* - \boldsymbol{\beta})(\boldsymbol{\beta}^* - \boldsymbol{\beta})' = \sum_{i=1}^K \mathrm{MSE}(\beta_i^*)$ and $\operatorname{tr} \mathrm{MSE}(\hat{\boldsymbol{\beta}})$ is similarly defined.

The interpretation of this norm is that it represents the average squared Euclidean distance between the estimator and $\boldsymbol{\beta}$. This is simply the expectation of the squared error loss measure introduced earlier. A sufficient condition and the lowest bound for the hypothesis in (6.4.13) to hold is that

$$\lambda \leq \frac{1}{2d_s} \operatorname{tr}\{(X'X)^{-1}R'[R(X'X)^{-1}R']^{-1}R(X'X)^{-1}\}, \tag{6.4.14}$$

where d_s is the smallest eigenvalue of the expression associated with the trace operator. See Judge *et al.* (1973a) for a proof of this result. This inequality may be tested by noting that under the null hypothesis the statistic u in (6.4.12) is distributed as noncentral F with J and $(T - K)$ degrees of freedom and noncentrality parameter λ given in (6.4.11).

The last measure of estimator goodness to be discussed here is the second weak mean square error proposed by Wallace (1972).

Definition 6.4.4. The estimator $\boldsymbol{\beta}^*$ is defined to be a better estimator than $\hat{\boldsymbol{\beta}}$ in the *second weak mean square error* sense if and only if

$$E(X\boldsymbol{\beta}^* - X\boldsymbol{\beta})'(X\boldsymbol{\beta}^* - X\boldsymbol{\beta}) \leq E(X\hat{\boldsymbol{\beta}} - X\boldsymbol{\beta})'(X\hat{\boldsymbol{\beta}} - X\boldsymbol{\beta})$$

or, equivalently,

$$E(\boldsymbol{\beta}^* - \boldsymbol{\beta})'X'X(\boldsymbol{\beta}^* - \boldsymbol{\beta}) \leq E(\hat{\boldsymbol{\beta}} - \boldsymbol{\beta})'X'X(\hat{\boldsymbol{\beta}} - \boldsymbol{\beta}). \tag{6.4.15}$$

This norm can be interpreted as a comparison of the mean square errors of predicting the conditional mean $X\boldsymbol{\beta}$. In other words, the second weak mean square error is a prediction norm, a comparison of how well the mean of $\mathbf{y}$ is predicted by $X\boldsymbol{\beta}^*$ versus $X\hat{\boldsymbol{\beta}}$ given the values X. Wallace (1972) shows that a necessary and sufficient condition for $\boldsymbol{\beta}^*$ to be better than $\hat{\boldsymbol{\beta}}$ in the second weak mean square error sense is that

$$\lambda = \frac{(R\boldsymbol{\beta} - \mathbf{r})'[R(X'X)^{-1}R']^{-1}(R\boldsymbol{\beta} - \mathbf{r})}{2\sigma^2} \leq \frac{J}{2}. \tag{6.4.16}$$

The test of the restricted hypothesis estimator is carried out again using the statistic u from Equation (6.4.12), which has a noncentral F-distribution with J and $(T - K)$ degrees of freedom and noncentrality parameter given by λ in Equation (6.4.16). Critical values for this test are tabled in Goodnight and Wallace (1972).

Now it is easy to see why the terms "strong" and "weak" have been coined in the literature. If an estimator $\boldsymbol{\beta}^*$ is superior to an estimator $\hat{\boldsymbol{\beta}}$ in the strong mean square error sense, then likewise it is superior in the first and second weak mean square error senses as well. However, superiority in either or both of the weak mean square error measures does not ensure that superiority obtains in the strong mean square error sense.

Since the mixed estimator $\hat{\boldsymbol{\beta}}^*$, Equation (6.3.5), can be viewed as a restricted least squares estimator on an extended parameter space (see Section 6.3.3), it follows naturally that the degree of bias introduced by incorporating the stochastic prior information $R\boldsymbol{\beta} + \mathbf{v} = \mathbf{r}$ can likewise be investigated using the results in this section. The only mean square error comparison of interest permitted, however, is that of strong mean square error. This follows from the fact that the reformulated restricted least squares estimator

$$\tilde{\boldsymbol{\phi}} = \begin{bmatrix} \tilde{\boldsymbol{\phi}}_1 \\ \tilde{\boldsymbol{\phi}}_2 \end{bmatrix} = \begin{bmatrix} \hat{\boldsymbol{\beta}}^* \\ \tilde{\boldsymbol{\phi}}_2 \end{bmatrix}$$

of (6.3.19) has two component vectors, the first being the mixed estimator and the second being an extraneous estimator $\tilde{\boldsymbol{\phi}}_2$ of the additional parameters $\boldsymbol{\mu}$ used to construct the generalized (extended parameter space) restricted least squares formulation of the mixed estimation model. In most cases the weak mean square error comparisons, $E(\tilde{\boldsymbol{\phi}} - \boldsymbol{\phi})'(\tilde{\boldsymbol{\phi}} - \boldsymbol{\phi})$ versus

$$E(\hat{\boldsymbol{\phi}} - \boldsymbol{\phi})'(\hat{\boldsymbol{\phi}} - \boldsymbol{\phi})$$

and $E(\tilde{\boldsymbol{\phi}} - \boldsymbol{\phi})'X'X(\tilde{\boldsymbol{\phi}} - \boldsymbol{\phi})$ versus $E(\hat{\boldsymbol{\phi}} - \boldsymbol{\phi})'X'X(\hat{\boldsymbol{\phi}} - \boldsymbol{\phi})$, would not be of interest. Instead, primary interest will often center on the mean square comparisons of the individual elements of $\tilde{\boldsymbol{\phi}}$, i.e., $\hat{\boldsymbol{\beta}}^*$, and the individual elements of $\hat{\boldsymbol{\phi}}$, i.e., $\hat{\boldsymbol{\beta}}$. It follows that the result $\text{MSE}(\hat{\beta}_i^*) \leq \text{MSE}(\hat{\beta}_i)$, $i = 1, 2, \ldots, K$, obtains if $\tilde{\boldsymbol{\phi}}$ is superior to $\hat{\boldsymbol{\phi}}$ in strong mean square error.

A test for the strong mean square error superiority of $\tilde{\boldsymbol{\phi}}$ over $\hat{\boldsymbol{\phi}}$ and hence $\hat{\boldsymbol{\beta}}^*$ over $\hat{\boldsymbol{\beta}}$ can be straightforwardly conducted by using the statistic of Equation (6.3.20) and comparing it to an α-level critical value of the noncentral F-distribution $F_{(J, T-K, 1/2)}$ tabled in Wallace and Toro-Vizcarrondo (1969). Recall that these results are only asymptotically justified if the relative variability of the sample to prior information has to be estimated, i.e., if feasible mixed estimation is required.

6.5 Inequality Restricted Least Squares

6.5.1 Derivation of Inequality Restricted Least Squares Estimator

In Sections 6.2. and 6.3 the constraints considered took the form of exact linear restrictions (restricted least squares) and stochastic linear restrictions (mixed estimation.) In this section a third vehicle for introducing prior information is considered: linear inequality restrictions. Inequality restrictions may arise when an investigator knows, for example, that the own price elasticity of a certain commodity cannot be positive or that a marginal propensity to consume must be in the unit interval. This nonsample information, indicating that a linear combination of parameters has an upper and/or lower bound can be expressed as the system of linear inequalities

$$R\boldsymbol{\beta} \geq \mathbf{r}, \tag{6.5.1}$$

or

$$R\boldsymbol{\beta} + \boldsymbol{\delta} = \mathbf{r}, \tag{6.5.2}$$

where $\boldsymbol{\delta} \leq \mathbf{0}$. Information of the form

$$\mathbf{r}_0 \leq R^*\boldsymbol{\beta} \leq \mathbf{r}_1$$

can be represented as in (6.5.1) by setting

$$R = \begin{bmatrix} R^* \\ -R^* \end{bmatrix} \quad \text{and} \quad \mathbf{r} = \begin{bmatrix} \mathbf{r}_0 \\ \mathbf{r}_1 \end{bmatrix}.$$

The problems of making use of inequality information have been considered by Zellner (1961), Judge and Takayama (1966), Lovell and Prescott (1970), O'Hagan (1973), Jansen (1975), Liew (1976) and Judge and Yancey (1978, 1979). Here we follow the results of Judge and Yancey.

The prior and sample information may be combined to estimate the parameters of the linear model

$$\mathbf{y} = X\boldsymbol{\beta} + \mathbf{e} \tag{6.5.3}$$

by minimizing the quadratic form, with respect to $\boldsymbol{\beta}$,

$$q = (\mathbf{y} - X\boldsymbol{\beta})'(\mathbf{y} - X\boldsymbol{\beta}) = \mathbf{y}'\mathbf{y} - 2\mathbf{y}'X\boldsymbol{\beta} + \boldsymbol{\beta}'X'X\boldsymbol{\beta} \tag{6.5.4}$$

subject to the system of linear inequality constraints (6.5.1). Because of the inequality nature of the restrictions, the usual constrained optimization procedures cannot be used. The expression (6.5.4) can be rewritten, however, since $\mathbf{y}'\mathbf{y}$ is a known scalar, as

$$q^* = \boldsymbol{\beta}'D\boldsymbol{\beta} + \mathbf{c}'\boldsymbol{\beta}, \tag{6.5.5}$$

where $D = \frac{1}{2}X'X$ and $\mathbf{c}' = -\mathbf{y}'X$. The minimization problem can be solved iteratively as a quadratic programming problem. In certain instances, however, $\boldsymbol{\beta}$ can be solved for in closed form when R is of full row rank and $X'X$ is positive definite, and, thus, nonsingular.

The Lagrangian associated with the minimization of (6.5.5) subject to (6.5.1) is

$$L(\boldsymbol{\beta}, \boldsymbol{\lambda}) = \tfrac{1}{2}\boldsymbol{\beta}'X'X\boldsymbol{\beta} - \boldsymbol{\beta}'X'\mathbf{y} + \boldsymbol{\lambda}'(\mathbf{r} - R\boldsymbol{\beta}). \tag{6.5.6}$$

The solution must satisfy the Kuhn–Tucker conditions

$$\partial L/\partial\boldsymbol{\beta} = \mathbf{0}, \tag{6.5.7a}$$

$$\partial L/\partial\boldsymbol{\lambda} = \mathbf{0}, \tag{6.5.7b}$$

$$\boldsymbol{\lambda}'[\partial L/\partial\boldsymbol{\lambda}] = 0, \tag{6.5.7c}$$

$$\boldsymbol{\lambda} \geq \mathbf{0}. \tag{6.5.7d}$$

Let the value $(\boldsymbol{\beta}^+, \boldsymbol{\lambda}^+)$ represent the optimal solution of the minimization problem. This implies $(\boldsymbol{\beta}^+, \boldsymbol{\lambda}^+)$ must satisfy

$$X'X\boldsymbol{\beta} - X'\mathbf{y} - R'\boldsymbol{\lambda} = \mathbf{0}, \tag{6.5.8a}$$

$$R\boldsymbol{\beta} \geq \mathbf{r}, \tag{6.5.8b}$$

$$\boldsymbol{\lambda}'(\mathbf{r} - R\boldsymbol{\beta}) = 0, \tag{6.5.8c}$$

$$\boldsymbol{\lambda} \geq \mathbf{0}. \tag{6.5.8d}$$

Using (6.5.8a), the inequality restricted least squares estimator may be written as

$$\boldsymbol{\beta}^+ = \hat{\boldsymbol{\beta}} + (X'X)^{-1}R'\boldsymbol{\lambda}^+,$$

where $\hat{\boldsymbol{\beta}} = (X'X)^{-1}X'\mathbf{y}$.

If $\hat{\boldsymbol{\beta}}$ satisfies the restrictions, i.e., $R\hat{\boldsymbol{\beta}} \geq \mathbf{r}$, then $(\boldsymbol{\beta}^+, \boldsymbol{\lambda}^+) = (\hat{\boldsymbol{\beta}}, \mathbf{0})$ is the solution. If the maximum likelihood estimator, $\hat{\boldsymbol{\beta}}$, does *not* satisfy the constraints then another representation is necessary.

Assume, without loss of generality, that the first J^* constraints are satisfied and the last $J - J^*$ are violated. Then

$$R_1\hat{\boldsymbol{\beta}} \geq \mathbf{r}_1 \quad \text{and} \quad R_2\hat{\boldsymbol{\beta}} < \mathbf{r}_2, \tag{6.5.9}$$

where R and $\mathbf{r}$ have been partitioned into

$$R = \begin{bmatrix} R_1 \\ R_2 \end{bmatrix} \quad \text{and} \quad \mathbf{r} = \begin{bmatrix} \mathbf{r}_1 \\ \mathbf{r}_2 \end{bmatrix}$$

with R_1 and $\mathbf{r}_1$ having J^* rows and R_2 and $\mathbf{r}_2$ having $J - J^*$ rows. Now the elements of $\boldsymbol{\lambda}$ are such that $\lambda_i = 0, i = 1, \ldots, J^*$, and the remaining elements, say $\bar{\boldsymbol{\lambda}}' = (\lambda_{J^*+1}, \ldots, \lambda_J)$ are obtained by solving

$$\mathbf{r}_2 - R_2\boldsymbol{\beta}^+ = \mathbf{0}, \tag{6.5.10}$$

or

$$\mathbf{r}_2 - R_2\hat{\boldsymbol{\beta}} - R_2(X'X)^{-1}R_2'\bar{\boldsymbol{\lambda}} = \mathbf{0}. \tag{6.5.11}$$

Therefore,

$$\boldsymbol{\beta}^+ = \hat{\boldsymbol{\beta}} + (X'X)^{-1}R_2'[R_2(X'X)^{-1}R_2']^{-1}(\mathbf{r}_2 - R_2\hat{\boldsymbol{\beta}}). \tag{6.5.12}$$

The complete set of alternatives then can be written as

$$\boldsymbol{\beta}^+ = \begin{cases} \hat{\boldsymbol{\beta}} & \text{if } R\hat{\boldsymbol{\beta}} \geq \mathbf{r}, \quad (6.5.13a) \\ \hat{\boldsymbol{\beta}} + (X'X)^{-1}R_2'[R_2(X'X)^{-1}R_2']^{-1}(\mathbf{r}_2 - R_2\hat{\boldsymbol{\beta}}) & \text{if } R_2\hat{\boldsymbol{\beta}} < \mathbf{r}_2, \quad (6.5.13b) \\ \hat{\boldsymbol{\beta}} + (X'X)^{-1}R'[R(X'X)^{-1}R']^{-1}(\mathbf{r} - R\hat{\boldsymbol{\beta}}) & \text{if } R\hat{\boldsymbol{\beta}} < \mathbf{r}. \quad (6.5.13c) \end{cases}$$

However, it is not true that one may *always* obtain the inequality restricted least squares estimators simply by modifying the maximum likelihood estimates as in (6.5.13). If only some of the constraints are violated, it is possible that their imposition will result in other, previously satisfied, constraints being violated. To avoid the possibility that $R\boldsymbol{\beta}^+ \ngeq \mathbf{r}$ some conditions must be placed on the restrictions so that $\boldsymbol{\beta}^+$ represents a feasible solution to the original problem. In order to obtain *sufficient* conditions for $\boldsymbol{\beta}^+$ to be a feasible solution examine the constraint evaluated at each of the closed form solutions in (6.5.13).

If (6.5.13a) holds, the unrestricted ordinary least squares estimator $\hat{\boldsymbol{\beta}}$ clearly is a feasible solution. If (6.5.13c) holds then $R\boldsymbol{\beta}^+ = \mathbf{r}$ and is an optimal solution if $\boldsymbol{\lambda}^+ = [R(X'X)^{-1}R']^{-1}(\mathbf{r} - R\hat{\boldsymbol{\beta}}) \geq \mathbf{0}$. If (6.5.13b) holds, then

$$R_1\boldsymbol{\beta}^+ = R_1\hat{\boldsymbol{\beta}} + [R_1(X'X)^{-1}R_2'][R_2(X'X)^{-1}R_2']^{-1}(\mathbf{r}_2 - R_2\hat{\boldsymbol{\beta}}), \quad (6.5.14)$$

$$R_2\boldsymbol{\beta}^+ = R_2\hat{\boldsymbol{\beta}} + [R_2(X'X)^{-1}R_2'][R_2(X'X)^{-1}R_2']^{-1}(\mathbf{r}_2 - R_2\hat{\boldsymbol{\beta}}) = \mathbf{r}_2. \quad (6.5.15)$$

Now for $\boldsymbol{\beta}^+$ to be a feasible solution, it must be true that $R_1\boldsymbol{\beta}^+ \geq \mathbf{r}_1$. Since $R_1\hat{\boldsymbol{\beta}} \geq \mathbf{r}_1$, a sufficient condition for $R_1\boldsymbol{\beta}^+ \geq \mathbf{r}_1$ is that

$$[R_1(X'X)^{-1}R_2']\,[R_2(X'X)^{-1}R_2']^{-1}(\mathbf{r}_2 - R_2\hat{\boldsymbol{\beta}}) \geq \mathbf{0}$$

which will be true, for example, if $R_1(X'X)^{-1}R_2'$ is composed of all positive elements and $[R_2(X'X)^{-1}R_2']^{-1}(\mathbf{r}_2 - R_2\hat{\boldsymbol{\beta}}) \geq \mathbf{0}$.

6.5.2 Sampling Properties of Inequality Restricted Least Squares Estimator

While obtaining inequality restricted least squares estimates is not a difficult problem, there has been much uncertainty about the sampling properties of the estimator and how it compares to other estimators under accepted measures of performance. To this end, consider the special case of the orthonormal linear regression model where $X'X = I_K$. The results of Judge and Yancey (1978), which are generalized to the usual linear regression model in Judge and Yancey (1979), will be summarized. In the orthonormal model the maximum likelihood estimator $\hat{\boldsymbol{\beta}} = (X'X)^{-1}X'\mathbf{y} = X'\mathbf{y}$ is multivariate normal with mean vector $\boldsymbol{\beta}$ and covariance $\sigma^2 I_K$. Thus, each element of $\hat{\boldsymbol{\beta}}$ is statistically independent and can be considered separately.

Assume that the information available on the ith coefficient can be written

$$\mathbf{R}_i'\boldsymbol{\beta} \geq r_i, \quad \text{for any } 1 = 1, \ldots, K, \quad (6.5.16)$$

where $\mathbf{R}_i'$ is a $1 \times K$ vector with a one in the ith position and zeros elsewhere. The inequality restricted estimator β_i^+ then takes the value r_i or $\hat{\beta}_i$ depending on whether the maximum likelihood estimator does or does not violate (6.5.16). Thus, the estimator for the ith coefficient which combines the sample and prior information can be written

$$\beta_i^+ = I_{(-\infty, r_i)}(\hat{\beta}_i)r_i + I_{[r_i, \infty)}(\hat{\beta}_i)\hat{\beta}_i, \quad (6.5.17)$$

where $I_{(-\infty, r_i)}(\hat{\beta}_i)$ and $I_{[r_i, \infty)}(\hat{\beta}_i)$ are indicator functions which take the value one if the random variable $\hat{\beta}_i$ falls in the stated interval and zero otherwise.

Let $r_i = \beta_i + \delta_i$, where δ_i, $-\infty < \delta_i < \infty$, is the constraint specification error. Then, when $\delta_i < 0$, *and thus the direction of the inequality* is correct, Judge and Yancey (1978) show that the mean of β_i^+ is

$$E(\beta_i^+) = \beta_i + (\delta_i/2)\Pr[\chi_1^2 \geq \delta_i^2/\sigma^2] + (\sigma/\sqrt{2\pi})\Pr[\chi_2^2 \geq \delta_i^2/\sigma^2], \quad (6.5.18)$$

where χ_1^2 and χ_2^2 represent distributions with one and two degrees of freedom, respectively. As the specification error $\delta_i \to -\infty$, it is clear that $E(\beta_i^+) \to \beta_i$. The inequality estimator becomes unbiased since the maximum likelihood estimator is always used. As $\delta_i \to 0$, so that $r_i \to \beta_i$, $E(\beta_i^+) \to \beta_i + \sigma/\sqrt{2\pi}$.

When $\delta_i \geq 0$ and $r_i > \beta_i$ the mean of β_i^+ is

$$E(\beta_i^+) = \beta_i + \delta_i - (\delta_i/2)\Pr[\chi_1^2 \geq \delta_i^2/\sigma^2] + (\sigma/\sqrt{2\pi})\Pr[\chi_2^2 \geq \delta_i^2/\sigma^2]. \tag{6.5.19}$$

As $\delta_i \to \infty$, $E(\beta_i^+) \to \beta_i + \delta_i = r_i$, the restricted least squares estimator. Again, as $\delta_i \to 0$, $E(\beta_i^+) \to \beta_i + \sigma/\sqrt{2\pi}$.

These results indicate that β_i^+ *is always biased and the bias is an increasing function of* δ_i/σ.

Judge and Yancey (1978) also show that

(i) the mean square error of β_i^+, $E(\beta_i^+ - \beta_i)^2$, is a function of δ_i/σ. When $\delta_i < 0$, $E(\beta_i^+ - \beta_i)^2 \to \sigma^2$, as $\delta_i \to -\infty$, and $E(\beta_i^+ - \beta_i)^2 \to \sigma^2/2$, as $\delta_i \to 0$. Thus, when $\beta_i = r_i$, the inequality restricted estimator risk is half the maximum likelihood estimator risk, σ^2.

(ii) When $\delta_i \geq 0$, $E(\beta_i^+ - \beta_i)^2 \to \delta_i^2$, as $\delta_i \to \infty$, and $E(\beta_i^+ - \beta_i)^2 \to \sigma^2/2$ as $\delta_i \to 0$.

(iii) Using these results it can be shown that the variance of the inequality restricted least squares estimator is less than or equal to the variance of the maximum likelihood estimator over the whole parameter space. As $\delta_i \to -\infty$, the variance of β_i^+ approaches σ^2, the variance of the maximum likelihood estimator and, as $\delta_i \to \infty$, it approaches the variance of the restricted least squares estimator, zero.

Summarizing, when the direction of the inequality restriction is correct, the risk of the inequality restricted least squares estimator is less than or equal to that of the maximum likelihood over the whole range of the δ_i^2/σ^2 parameter space. On the other hand, if the direction of the inequality constraint is incorrect the risk function of the inequality restricted least squares estimator crosses that of the maximum likelihood estimator at a point where $(\delta_i/\sigma) < 1$ and reapproaches it as $\delta_i \to \infty$. Thus, if the direction of the inequality restriction is incorrect the estimator β_i^+ is inferior to the maximum likelihood estimator over a large portion of the parameter space. For a discussion of the case of nonorthogonal regressors, see Judge and Yancey (1979).

6.5.3 Comparison of Restricted Least Squares and Mixed Estimation with Inequality Restricted Least Squares

The restricted least squares, mixed estimation, and inequality restricted least squares methods of incorporating prior information are similar in that the use of correct information, correct or unbiased restrictions and correct directions of inequalities, offers an unequivocal gain in small sample efficiency over the maximum likelihood estimator. However, the use of incorrect information can provide only limited opportunities for gain (when the information is not "too" incorrect) and worse yet, inferior estimation relative to the maximum likelihood estimator over a large portion of the parameter space.

The major dissimilarity between the restricted least squares and mixed estimators on the one hand and the inequality restricted least squares estimator on the other is the difference in the value of valid prior information in infinite samples. As remarked earlier in Theorem 6.2.2, when the restrictions $R\boldsymbol{\beta} = \mathbf{r}$ are valid, the Cramér–Rao lower bound must be modified. That is, if V denotes the asymptotic Cramér–Rao lower bound matrix for the maximum likelihood estimator $\hat{\boldsymbol{\beta}}$ of the linear model $\mathbf{y} = X\boldsymbol{\beta} + \mathbf{e}$, where no linear restrictions are assumed, then in the presence of the valid restrictions $R\boldsymbol{\beta} = \mathbf{r}$, the restricted maximum likelihood estimator $\boldsymbol{\beta}^*$ attains the asymptotic Cramér–Rao lower bound, say V^*, where $V - V^*$ is a positive semidefinite matrix ($V^* \leq V$). In fact, in Chapter 4, it was shown that

$$V = \lim_{T\to\infty} \sigma^2\left(\frac{X'X}{T}\right)^{-1} = \sigma^2 Q^{-1}$$

is the asymptotic Cramér–Rao bound. In the absence of any prior information, $R\boldsymbol{\beta} = \mathbf{r}$, the maximum likelihood estimator $\hat{\boldsymbol{\beta}}$ attains this lower bound and is, therefore, efficient. On the other hand, Rothenberg (1973, p. 23) has shown that the asymptotic Cramér–Rao lower bound in the presence of the information $R\boldsymbol{\beta} = \mathbf{r}$ is $V^* = V - VR'(RV^{-1}R')^{-1}RV$. This lower bound is attained by the restricted least squares estimator and is, thus, efficient relative to the ordinary least squares estimator $\hat{\boldsymbol{\beta}}$ when the restrictions $R\boldsymbol{\beta} = \mathbf{r}$ apply.

In a similar manner, Rothenberg (1973) has also shown that if the stochastic prior information $R\boldsymbol{\beta} + \mathbf{v} = \mathbf{r}$ is "of the same order of magnitude as the sample information," that is, $\lim_{T\to\infty}(R'\Psi^{-1}R/T)$ is a finite and nonsingular matrix, the mixed estimator $\hat{\boldsymbol{\beta}}^*$ attains an asymptotic Cramér–Rao lower bound, say $\bar{V}$, such that $V^* \leq \bar{V} \leq V$.

This brings us to the point of the dissimilarity. As Rothenberg (1973, p. 50) states, despite the presence of prior information that restricts $\boldsymbol{\beta}$ to lie in a subspace of the total parameter space ($-\infty < \boldsymbol{\beta} < \infty$), *the asymptotic Cramér–Rao lower bound remains unchanged as long as the restricted parameter space has full dimension. The unconstrained maximum likelihood estimator remains efficient in this case.* Therefore, asymptotically, the inequality restricted least squares and maximum likelihood estimators are equally efficient. However, in small samples there is a gain if the direction of the inequalities are correct or at least not "too" incorrect. The relevance of the large sample result concerning inequality least squares estimation is that when the sample size is very large, say for a cross-section data set with thousands of observations, and the appropriate computer software is not available, little efficiency is lost when not being able to impose inequality restrictions.

6.6 Bayesian Procedures and Prior Information

While this book deals primarily with the classical approach to inference and analysis of sampling distributions of statistics, we would be remiss in this chapter on the use and analysis of prior information if a discussion of the Bayesian approach to econometric problems was not presented. While many persuasive arguments for the use of Bayesian methods have been made (Zellner (1971a, 1971b)), we note the following. First, Bayesian analysis is explicitly couched in a decision theoretic framework. In economics, which is concerned with decisionmaking, it is an apparent advantage, for example, to make explicit the relationship between the decisions to be made and the information at hand, both prior and sample. Classical procedures do not do this and, in fact, generally ignore the decision aspects of econometric estimation. Second, and perhaps more relevant to discussions in previous sections, the Bayesian approach provides a logical, consistent way to characterize prior sample and/or subjective information and to combine it with sample data.

6.6.1 Basic Concepts in Bayesian Analysis

The degree of belief we currently hold concerning any proposition depends upon the information currently available to us. If the degree of belief in a proposition is expressed as a probability, then that probability is always a conditional one, based upon the amount of information currently available. As the information about a proposition changes, our belief or probability is revised, representing learning behavior. The statistical process may be viewed in Figure 6.6.1 (Zellner (1971b, p. 10)).

In this scheme the initial information I_0, based upon previous observation, statistical theories or hunches, is expressed as a prior probability distribution $P(H \mid I_0)$ concerning the proposition H and based on the initial information

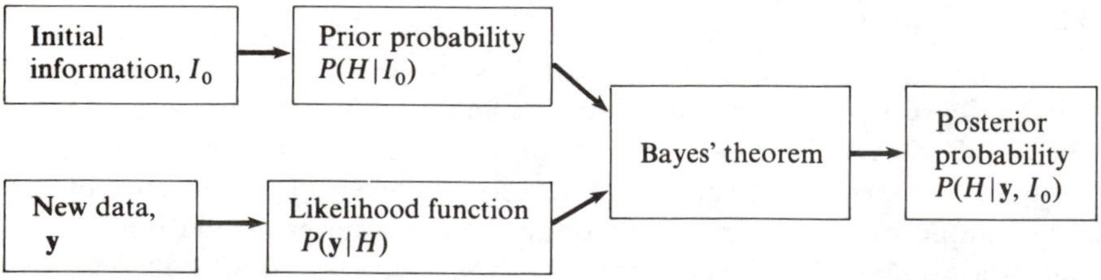

Figure 6.6.1 The process of revising probabilities given new data.

I_0. The new data, $\mathbf{y}$, have density function $P(\mathbf{y}|H)$ which is the likelihood function. There the prior probability density and the likelihood function are combined by Bayes' theorem to yield a posterior probability density function, $P(H|\mathbf{y}, I_0)$. The posterior density combines both the sample and prior information. It characterizes the revision that has occurred because of the sample data and is the basis for subsequent decisionmaking.

The notions can be expressed algebraically if we define $p(\mathbf{y}, \boldsymbol{\theta})$ as the joint probability density function for a random vector $\mathbf{y}$ and a parameter vector $\boldsymbol{\theta}$. Then, by usual operations,

$$p(\mathbf{y}, \boldsymbol{\theta}) = p(\mathbf{y}|\boldsymbol{\theta})p(\boldsymbol{\theta}), \tag{6.6.1}$$

so that

$$p(\boldsymbol{\theta}|\mathbf{y}) = \frac{p(\boldsymbol{\theta})p(\mathbf{y}|\boldsymbol{\theta})}{p(\mathbf{y})}, \tag{6.6.2}$$

with $p(\mathbf{y}) \neq 0$. Now $p(\mathbf{y})$ is the reciprocal of the normalizing constant for the density function $p(\boldsymbol{\theta}|\mathbf{y})$ and is usually not carried in the analysis. It can always be determined. Hence, (6.6.2) can be written

$$\begin{aligned} p(\boldsymbol{\theta}|\mathbf{y}) &\propto p(\boldsymbol{\theta})p(\mathbf{y}|\boldsymbol{\theta}) \\ &\propto \text{prior density} \times \text{likelihood function}, \end{aligned} \tag{6.6.3}$$

where $\propto$ denotes proportionality, $p(\boldsymbol{\theta}|\mathbf{y})$ is the *posterior* probability density function for $\boldsymbol{\theta}$, $p(\boldsymbol{\theta})$ is the prior probability density function for $\boldsymbol{\theta}$ and $p(\mathbf{y}|\boldsymbol{\theta})$, viewed as a function of $\boldsymbol{\theta}$, is the likelihood function, which is often written $L(\boldsymbol{\theta}|\mathbf{y})$ to emphasize that it is not a probability density function and is a function of $\boldsymbol{\theta}$. Equation (6.6.3) is a statement of Bayes' theorem. The posterior probability density function contains all the available information, both sample and prior. The likelihood function contains all the evidence from the sample.

Before continuing, a comment concerning the appropriateness of Bayesian analysis is in order. It is sometimes claimed that Bayesians view parameters as random variables where they are by definition fixed constants. As Rothenberg (1973, p. 138) states,

> The Bayesian analysis does not require θ to represent a random outcome of some actual experiment. We do not have to pretend that the real world is "drawn" from the set of all possible worlds with a certain probability. Bayesian decision theory merely argues that people who wish to decide consistently in uncertain situations would act *as though* θ were a random variable with a certain distribution function. It is convenient to use the terminology of random experiments even if there is no experiment in mind.

Thus the randomness of the parameters in the Bayesian world may be considered a convenient supposition for those who believe in fixed parameters.

From Equation (6.6.3), the Bayesian approach yields a posterior probability density function for the parameter vector $\boldsymbol{\theta}$. To characterize this distribution economically, measures such as skewness, dispersion, and central tendency may be considered, with the latter to serve as a point estimate. To choose the single measure of central tendency for the point estimate, we proceed as follows. Let $L = L(\hat{\boldsymbol{\theta}}, \boldsymbol{\theta})$ be our loss function, and $\hat{\boldsymbol{\theta}} = \hat{\boldsymbol{\theta}}(\mathbf{y})$ a point estimate depending upon the sample of observations $\mathbf{y}$. Since $\boldsymbol{\theta}$ is considered random, L is random. The principle used to generate point estimates is to find the value of $\hat{\boldsymbol{\theta}}$ that minimizes the *expected* loss. That is,

$$\operatorname*{Min}_{\hat{\boldsymbol{\theta}}} EL(\hat{\boldsymbol{\theta}}, \boldsymbol{\theta}) = \operatorname*{Min}_{\hat{\boldsymbol{\theta}}} \int L(\hat{\boldsymbol{\theta}}, \boldsymbol{\theta}) p(\boldsymbol{\theta} | \mathbf{y})\, d\boldsymbol{\theta}, \tag{6.6.4}$$

where it is assumed $EL(\hat{\boldsymbol{\theta}}, \boldsymbol{\theta})$ is finite and that a minimum exists. An important example is the case of a weighted squared error loss function.

$$L = (\hat{\boldsymbol{\theta}} - \boldsymbol{\theta})' Q (\hat{\boldsymbol{\theta}} - \boldsymbol{\theta}), \tag{6.6.5}$$

where Q is a known nonstochastic positive definite and symmetric matrix. Then

$$\begin{aligned} EL &= E(\hat{\boldsymbol{\theta}} - \boldsymbol{\theta})' Q (\hat{\boldsymbol{\theta}} - \boldsymbol{\theta}) \\ &= E[(\hat{\boldsymbol{\theta}} - E\boldsymbol{\theta}) - (\boldsymbol{\theta} - E\boldsymbol{\theta})]' Q [(\hat{\boldsymbol{\theta}} - E\boldsymbol{\theta}) - (\boldsymbol{\theta} - E\boldsymbol{\theta})] \\ &= E(\hat{\boldsymbol{\theta}} - E\boldsymbol{\theta})' Q (\hat{\boldsymbol{\theta}} - E\boldsymbol{\theta}) + (\boldsymbol{\theta} - E\boldsymbol{\theta})' Q (\boldsymbol{\theta} - E\boldsymbol{\theta}). \end{aligned} \tag{6.6.6}$$

the second term of which is independent of $\hat{\boldsymbol{\theta}}$. The first term is nonstochastic and minimized if $\hat{\boldsymbol{\theta}} = E\boldsymbol{\theta}$. Thus, for positive definite squared error loss functions the mean $E\boldsymbol{\theta}$ of the posterior probability density function $p(\boldsymbol{\theta} | \mathbf{y})$ is an optimal point estimator if it exists.

6.6.2 Relationship Between Bayesian and Sampling Theory Approaches

The relationship between Bayesian and sampling theory approaches can be illustrated by letting $\tilde{\boldsymbol{\theta}} = \tilde{\boldsymbol{\theta}}(\mathbf{y})$ be a sampling theory estimator which is, of course, a random variable. The risk function associated with $\tilde{\boldsymbol{\theta}}$ is

$$\mathscr{R}(\boldsymbol{\theta}) = \int L(\tilde{\boldsymbol{\theta}}, \boldsymbol{\theta}) p(\mathbf{y} | \boldsymbol{\theta})\, d\mathbf{y}, \tag{6.6.7}$$

where $L(\tilde{\boldsymbol{\theta}}, \boldsymbol{\theta})$ is a loss function, $p(\mathbf{y} | \boldsymbol{\theta})$ is a probability density function for $\mathbf{y}$, given $\boldsymbol{\theta}$, and the integral is assumed to converge. It is impossible to find a $\tilde{\boldsymbol{\theta}}$ which minimizes $R(\boldsymbol{\theta})$ for all possible values of $\boldsymbol{\theta}$ so consider the estimator that minimizes average risk, where average risk is

$$E\mathscr{R}(\boldsymbol{\theta}) = \int p(\boldsymbol{\theta}) \mathscr{R}(\boldsymbol{\theta})\, d\boldsymbol{\theta} \tag{6.6.8}$$

and $p(\boldsymbol{\theta})$ is a weighting function used to weight the performance of $\tilde{\boldsymbol{\theta}}$ over the parameter space.

The problem here is to find the estimator $\tilde{\boldsymbol{\theta}}$ which minimizes average risk. That is

$$\min_{\tilde{\boldsymbol{\theta}}} E\mathscr{R}(\boldsymbol{\theta}) = \min_{\tilde{\boldsymbol{\theta}}} \iint p(\boldsymbol{\theta}) L(\tilde{\boldsymbol{\theta}}, \boldsymbol{\theta}) p(\mathbf{y} \mid \boldsymbol{\theta}) \, d\mathbf{y} \, d\boldsymbol{\theta}. \tag{6.6.9}$$

Given that the order of integration can be changed and using $p(\boldsymbol{\theta})p(\mathbf{y} \mid \boldsymbol{\theta}) = p(\mathbf{y})p(\boldsymbol{\theta} \mid \mathbf{y})$, (6.6.9) can be written

$$\min_{\tilde{\boldsymbol{\theta}}} E\mathscr{R}(\boldsymbol{\theta}) = \min_{\tilde{\boldsymbol{\theta}}} \int \left[\int L(\tilde{\boldsymbol{\theta}}, \boldsymbol{\theta}) p(\boldsymbol{\theta} \mid \mathbf{y}) \, d\boldsymbol{\theta} \right] p(\mathbf{y}) \, d\mathbf{y}.$$

Note that the $\tilde{\boldsymbol{\theta}}$ that minimizes the term in brackets will minimize the expected risk and if the double integral in (6.6.10) converges, it will also be a solution of (6.6.4). The resulting estimator is a *Bayes' estimator* and, based on the average risk criterion, is best in repeated sampling. For application of these principles to simple and multiple regression, systems of equations and other econometric problems see Zellner (1971b) and Maddala (1977).

6.7 Summary and Guide to Further Readings

The major purpose of this chapter has been to present various ways of incorporating prior information into the linear model and to study the implications of its use. The first method discussed was exact restricted least squares. This estimator is derived by choosing the estimator which minimizes the sum of squared residuals $(\mathbf{y} - X\boldsymbol{\beta})'(\mathbf{y} - X\boldsymbol{\beta})$ subject to the constraint $R\boldsymbol{\beta} = \mathbf{r}$. If the prior information is correct ($R\boldsymbol{\beta} = \mathbf{r}$), the restricted least squares estimator is unbiased and has smaller variance than the ordinary least squares estimator. In fact, the restricted least squares estimator is best linear unbiased for unbiased estimators which are linear in $\mathbf{y}$ and $\mathbf{r}$. In the presence of normally distributed errors, the restricted least squares estimator is also minimum variance unbiased and asymptotically efficient as it is the maximum likelihood estimator. In contrast, if the prior information is incorrect ($R\boldsymbol{\beta} \neq \mathbf{r}$), the restricted least squares estimator is biased. The restricted least squares estimator is better than the ordinary least squares estimator in strong mean square error if the noncentrality parameter λ is less than $\frac{1}{2}$. This superiority condition is dependent upon unknown population parameters, however.

Though the restricted least squares estimator results are based upon constraining the ordinary least squares model, similar results obtain for the generalized least squares model. The restricted generalized least squares estimator can be derived by minimizing the weighted sum of squared residuals, $(\mathbf{y} - X\boldsymbol{\beta})'\Omega^{-1}(\mathbf{y} - X\boldsymbol{\beta})$ subject to the constraints $R\boldsymbol{\beta} = \mathbf{r}$ (Exercise 6.18).

As pointed out in Section 6.2.3, reparametrizations of the form $\boldsymbol{\beta} = H\boldsymbol{\alpha}$, where $\boldsymbol{\alpha}$ is of smaller dimension than $\boldsymbol{\beta}$, can equivalently be viewed as restricted least squares problems involving homogeneous linear restrictions of the form $R\boldsymbol{\beta} = \mathbf{0}$. The recognition of this equivalency makes the determination of resulting sampling properties much easier since we have already established the properties of the restricted least squares estimator. Also in Section 6.2.3 another interesting view of restricted least squares was discussed; the constraints $R\boldsymbol{\beta} = \mathbf{r}$ can be thought of as reducing the dimension of the parameter space.

Mixed estimation can be viewed as a method of augmenting the sample data with additional observations obtained from a sample of an outside source (possibly another experimenter) or from introspection (subjective judgment). If the stochastic prior information is unbiased ($E\mathbf{v} = \mathbf{0}$) and the relative variance between the sample and prior information is known, then the mixed estimator exhibits all of the optimal properties of a generalized least squares estimator linear in the observations $\mathbf{y}$ and $\mathbf{r}$. On the other hand, if the stochastic prior information is biased ($E\mathbf{v} \neq \mathbf{0}$), the mixed estimator is likewise biased. For sufficiently small specification errors the mixed estimator offers a gain over ordinary least squares estimation but at the same time the mixed estimator is inferior to the ordinary least squares estimator over a large portion of the parameter space. Like the restricted least squares estimator, the region where the mixed estimator is superior to ordinary least squares is dependent upon unknown population parameters.

The relative variance between the sample and prior information in mixed estimation is not always known and as a result feasible mixed estimation must be used. The discussion of the properties of this estimator is more appropriately deferred until Chapter 8 on feasible generalized least squares. Suffice it to say, the feasible mixed estimator behaves similarly to the mixed estimator in large samples.

In Section 6.3.4, it is shown that the mixed estimator is bounded between the restricted least squares estimator implied by the exact restrictions $R\boldsymbol{\beta} = \mathbf{r}$ on the one hand and the ordinary least squares estimator on the other. As the stochastic restrictions $R\boldsymbol{\beta} + \mathbf{v} = \mathbf{r}$ are imposed with ever increasing certainty, the mixed estimator approaches the restricted least squares estimator until in the limit they are algebraically identical. In the opposite case, as the stochastic restrictions are imposed with ever-increasing uncertainty the mixed estimator approaches the ordinary least squares estimator until in the limit they are algebraically identical. Thus, restricted least squares and ordinary least squares estimation can be viewed as special cases of mixed estimation.

A reformulation of the mixed estimation model as a restricted least squares model on an extended parameter space provides a means of constructing an F-statistic, much like the F-statistic for testing the exact restrictions $R\boldsymbol{\beta} = \mathbf{r}$, for testing the unbiasedness of the stochastic restrictions $R\boldsymbol{\beta} + \mathbf{v} = \mathbf{r}$. Conventional F-tables are therefore applicable. Also it is pointed out that

Theil's compatibility statistic and the present F-statistic are asymptotically equivalent.

In Section 6.4 we discussed various measures of risk which allow comparisions between unbiased and biased estimators. Since risk comparisions between restricted least squares and ordinary least squares estimation and between mixed and ordinary least squares estimation depend upon unknown population parameters, tests are discussed which allow statistical comparisons of risk. These tests lead to statistics which have noncentral F-distributions. These distributions are tabled in Wallace and Toro-Vizcarrondo (1969) and Goodnight and Wallace (1972).

The use of mean square error tests for evaluating the bias inherent in prior information and the resulting risk comparision between ordinary least squares and the corresponding restricted estimator is one matter. Another matter is the use of hypothesis tests to choose between two estimators such as ordinary least squares and restricted least squares. Such preliminary testing creates "hybrid" estimators that have sampling properties unlike those of the ordinary least squares or restricted least squares estimators. The properties of the preliminary test estimators will be discussed in more detail in the next chapter.

Unlike the restricted least squares estimator, the inequality least squares estimator does not reduce the dimension of the parameter space; it only constrains the parameter space through inequality restrictions. The inequality restricted least squares estimator minimizes the sum of squared residuals subject to the constraint $R\boldsymbol{\beta} \geq \mathbf{r}$, where R can be chosen to include positive and negative constraints as well as interval constraints. The inequality restricted least squares estimator is always biased yet if the inequality constraints are in the correct directions, its mean square error is less than that of the ordinary least squares estimator. If the inequality constraints are in the incorrect directions, the mean square error function crosses that of the ordinary least squares estimator. Small bias in the restrictions still yields a gain while with large biases the inequality restricted least squares estimator is inferior to ordinary least squares. As in the case of restricted least squares and mixed estimation, the introduction of prior information is advantageous only if it is sufficiently correct.

A major distinction between restricted least squares and mixed estimation and inequality restricted least squares is that inequality restrictions lose their potency in infinite samples. As shown by Rothenberg (1973), prior information offers an asymptotic gain in efficiency only if such information reduces the dimension of the parameter space.

In Section 6.6 the use of Bayes' theorem to introduce prior information was discussed. Though Bayesians are not generally interested in repeated sampling properties, it is shown that the Bayes' estimator minimizes average risk and thus provides one means of handling the unknown population parameter problem which so often troubles sampling theorists using potentially biased estimation techniques.

The literature on prior information in regression analysis is very extensive. As a result we have examined only the major points here. However, a guide to further readings follows.

The "new" Cramér–Rao lower bound for the linear model subject to constraints is thoroughly developed in Rothenberg (1973). In addition, Rothenberg has a very good discussion of the comparative asymptotic properties of restricted least squares and inequality least squares estimators and examines linear estimation under the constraint that the parameter vector lies in a convex set. Rothenberg's convex set theorem (p. 51) is quite general with linear inequalities which form a convex set being a special case.

The finite sample properties of mixed estimation are analyzed in Nagar and Kakwani (1964), Swamy and Mehta (1969), Mehta and Swamy (1970) and Yancey *et al.* (1972). Swamy and Mehta (1977) analyze the robustness of mixed estimators for departures from normality of the prior estimators. Applications of mixed estimation are numerous including Husby (1971) and Paulus (1975). For a criticism of mixed estimation from a Bayesian point of view see Zellner (1971a).

The Kuhn–Tucker theorem is a fundamental tool in inequality least squares. The seminal reference is Kuhn and Tucker (1951). An exposition of nonlinear programming techniques can be found in most mathematical economics textbooks, e.g., Intriligator (1971). In addition to the seminal papers by Judge and Yancey (1978, 1979), Thomson (1979) has further examined the mean square error properties of the inequality least squares estimator in the nonorthonormal ($X'X \neq I$) model.

In addition to Zellner (1971b), good comprehensive reviews of the Bayesian methodology are contained in Lindley (1971) and Edwards *et al.* (1963). For a historical perspective on the controversies surrounding the Bayesian and classical methods see Weber (1973). For good discussions of the comparisons between these methodologies, see Zellner (1971a) and Rothenberg (1971) and the accompanying comments on their articles by Kaufman and Pratt. Also see Barnett (1973).

6.8 Exercises

6.1. Prove the following matrix proposition.

Proposition. *If Σ is a positive definite matrix of* rank *K and R is a $J \times K$ matrix of* rank *$J \leq K$, then the matrix $R\Sigma R'$ is a positive definite matrix.*

6.2. Prove the following matrix proposition.

Proposition. *If Σ is a positive definite matrix, then Σ^{-1} is also positive definite.*

6.3. Prove the following matrix proposition.

Proposition. *Let Σ and R be defined as in Exercise* 6.1. *except let Σ have rank J. Then the matrix $R'\Sigma R$ is positive semidefinite.*

6.4. Prove the following matrix proposition.

Proposition. *If A is a symmetric, positive definite matrix and B is a positive semidefinite matrix, then ABA is a positive semidefinite matrix.*

6.5. Verify the following matrix proposition.

Proposition. *If $A = B + C$, where B is positive definite and C is positive semidefinite then $B^{-1} - A^{-1}$ is positive semidefinite.*

6.6. Using the proposition of Exercise 6.5, show that $\operatorname{var} \hat{\boldsymbol{\beta}} - \operatorname{var} \boldsymbol{\beta}^*$ is a positive semidefinite matrix.

6.7. Consider the mixed estimation model $\mathbf{y} = X\boldsymbol{\beta} + \mathbf{e}$ subject to $R\boldsymbol{\beta} + \mathbf{v} = \mathbf{r}$, where $X'X = I_K$, $R = I_K$, $E\mathbf{e} = \mathbf{0}$, $E\mathbf{ee}' = \sigma^2 I$, $E\mathbf{v} = \boldsymbol{\delta}$, and $E\mathbf{vv}' = \Psi = c\sigma^2 I$ and c is assumed to be a known positive constant. Show that

$$E(\hat{\boldsymbol{\beta}}^* - \boldsymbol{\beta})'(\hat{\boldsymbol{\beta}}^* - \boldsymbol{\beta}) = \frac{c\sigma^2 K}{c + 1} + \frac{\boldsymbol{\delta}'\boldsymbol{\delta}}{(c + 1)^2}.$$

6.8. Verify the following matrix proposition. This proposition is commonly called the binomial inverse theorem.

Proposition. *Assume that A and B are $p \times p$ and $q \times q$ nonsingular matrices, U is $p \times q$ and V is $q \times p$. Then*

$$(A + UBV)^{-1} = A^{-1} - A^{-1}UB(B + BVA^{-1}UB)^{-1}BVA^{-1}.$$

6.9. Show that $\operatorname{var} \hat{\boldsymbol{\beta}}^* - \operatorname{var} \boldsymbol{\beta}^*$ is a positive semidefinite matrix and that when $\operatorname{var} \mathbf{v} = \Psi \to 0$, $\operatorname{var} \hat{\boldsymbol{\beta}}^* = \operatorname{var} \boldsymbol{\beta}^*$.

6.10. Using partitioned matrix multiplication verify Equation (6.3.19).

6.11. Using the binomial inverse theorem (Exercise 5.8), show that $\tilde{\boldsymbol{\phi}}_1 = \hat{\boldsymbol{\beta}}^*$ in Equation (6.3.19).

6.12. Assume the mixed estimation model, $\mathbf{y} = X\boldsymbol{\beta} + \mathbf{e}$ subject to $R\boldsymbol{\beta} + \mathbf{v} = \mathbf{r}$, where $E\mathbf{e} = \mathbf{0}$, $E\mathbf{ee}' = \Omega$, $E\mathbf{v} = \mathbf{0}$, and $E\mathbf{vv}' = \Psi$. Rewrite the test statistic (6.3.20) using these assumptions.

6.13. Using the result that the distribution χ_J^2/J converges to the distribution $F_{J,T-K}$ as $T \to \infty$, show that Theil's compatibility statistic (6.3.22) and the statistic (6.3.20) provide asymptotically equivalent tests of the hypothesis $H_0\colon \boldsymbol{\delta} = \mathbf{0}$.

6.14. Show the equivalence of the three definitions of strong mean square error. (Hint: Use the definition of positive semidefinite matrix to show the equivalence of (b) and Definition 6.4.2. Use the fact that there exists a matrix A such that $W = A'A$, to show the equivalence of (c) and Definition 6.4.2.)

6.15. Derive the mean square error matrices $\operatorname{MSE}(\hat{\boldsymbol{\beta}})$ and $\operatorname{MSE}(\boldsymbol{\beta}^*)$ and verify that $\operatorname{MSE}(\hat{\boldsymbol{\beta}}) - \operatorname{MSE}(\boldsymbol{\beta}^*)$ is that of Equation (6.4.4).

6.16. Prove the following matrix proposition.

Proposition. *Let A be a positive definite symmetric $m \times m$ matrix and $\mathbf{u}$ a $m \times 1$ vector. Then*

$$\sup_{\mathbf{x} \in E_m} \frac{(\mathbf{u}'\mathbf{x})^2}{\mathbf{x}'A\mathbf{x}} = \mathbf{u}'A^{-1}\mathbf{u}$$

and the supremum is attained at $\mathbf{x}_* = A^{-1}\mathbf{u}$. *The vector* $\mathbf{x}$ *is an arbitrary vector belonging to m-dimensional Euclidean space,* E_m. (Hint: Show that this is a restatement of the Cauchy–Schwartz inequality. (See Rao (1973, p.54).))

6.17. Using Lemmas 6.4.1 and 6.4.2, and the definition of a noncentral F-distribution, show that the statistic (6.4.12) has a noncentral F-distribution with J and $(T - K)$ degrees of freedom and λ noncentrality parameter described in (6.4.11).

6.18. (Constrained Generalized Least Squares Estimation). Assume the generalized least squares model $\mathbf{y} = X\boldsymbol{\beta} + \mathbf{e}$, where $E\mathbf{e} = \mathbf{0}$, and $E\mathbf{ee}' = \Omega$ subject to the restrictions $R\boldsymbol{\beta} = \mathbf{r}$. Derive the implied restricted least squares estimator $\boldsymbol{\beta}^* = \hat{\boldsymbol{\beta}} + (X'\Omega^{-1}X)^{-1}R'[R(X'\Omega^{-1}X)^{-1}R']^{-1}(\mathbf{r} - R\hat{\boldsymbol{\beta}})$ with variance–covariance matrix $(X'\Omega^{-1}X)^{-1} - (X'\Omega^{-1}X)^{-1}R'[R(X'\Omega^{-1}X)^{-1}R']^{-1}R(X'\Omega^{-1}X)^{-1}$. (Hint: Transform the generalized least squares model to an ordinary least squares model and then apply the previously derived formulas.)

6.19. (Mixed Estimation and Quasi-Prior Information). For Equation (6.3.2) the generalized least squares estimator based on the sample data alone is $\tilde{\boldsymbol{\beta}} = (X'\Omega^{-1}X)^{-1}X'\Omega^{-1}\mathbf{y}$. The sampling error for $\tilde{\boldsymbol{\beta}}$ is $\tilde{\boldsymbol{\beta}} - \boldsymbol{\beta} = (X'\Omega^{-1}X)^{-1}X'\Omega^{-1}\mathbf{e}$. Thus, the difference between the estimator and the systematic part of the prior information is,

$$R(\tilde{\boldsymbol{\beta}} - \boldsymbol{\beta}) = R(X'\Omega^{-1}X)^{-1}X'\Omega^{-1}\mathbf{e}.$$

Now let the disturbance term for the prior information be defined as

$$\mathbf{v} = \mathbf{v}_0 + \Delta R(X'\Omega^{-1}X)^{-1}X'\Omega^{-1}\mathbf{e},$$

where $\mathbf{v}_0$ has the same distributional assumptions as $\mathbf{v}$ in Equation (6.3.3). Also let Δ be diagonal with elements in the unit interval. Show that the mixed estimator for this problem is

$$\begin{aligned}\tilde{\boldsymbol{\beta}}^* &= [X'\Omega^{-1}X + R'(I - \Delta)'\Psi^{-1}(I - \Delta)R]^{-1} \\ &\quad \times [X'\Omega^{-1}\mathbf{y} + R'(I - \Delta)'\Psi^{-1}(\mathbf{r} - \Delta R\hat{\boldsymbol{\beta}})]\end{aligned}$$

and

$$\operatorname{var}(\tilde{\boldsymbol{\beta}}^*) = [X'\Omega^{-1}X + R'(I - \Delta)'\Psi^{-1}(I - \Delta)R]^{-1}.$$

Discuss the limiting cases for the elements of $\tilde{\boldsymbol{\beta}}^*$, i.e., when $\Delta = 0$ and $\Delta = I$.

6.20. (Testing Stochastic Restrictions). Consider the data in Exercise 3.20 and the "unrestricted" cost function

$$\ln C = \beta_1 + \beta_2 \ln Y + \beta_3 \ln P_L + \beta_4 \ln P_K + \beta_5 \ln P_F + e.$$

Consider the stochastic prior information

$$r = \beta_3 + \beta_4 + \beta_5 + v,$$

where v is a random variable which is independent of e and has mean $Ev = 0$ and variance $\sigma_v^2 = 0.04$. Thus $Er = \beta_3 + \beta_4 + \beta_5$. Assume $r = 1.0$ is randomly realized.

(a) Test the null hypothesis

$$H_0\colon Er = \beta_3 + \beta_4 + \beta_5 \quad \text{(i.e. } Ev = 0\text{)}.$$

(b) Repeat part (a), except assume $\sigma_v^2 = 0.01$.
(c) Repeat part (a), except assume $\sigma_v^2 = 1.0$.
(d) Compare the F-statistics that you obtained in parts (a), (b), and (c) above. What conclusion can you draw with respect to the stringency (size of σ_v^2) of the stochastic prior information and the magnitude of the F-statistic? What is the value of the F-statistic when $\sigma_v^2 = 0$? $\sigma_v^2 = \infty$?
(e) Assuming that $\sigma_v^2 = 0.04$, test for a strong mean square error gain in estimation efficiency using the stochastic prior information. Use the tables in Wallace and Toro-Vizcarrando (1969).
(f) Assuming that $\sigma_v^2 = 0.04$, test for a second weak mean square error gain in estimation efficiency using the stochastic prior information. Use the tables in Goodnight and Wallace (1972).

6.21. (Inequality Least Squares). Consider the data and Tufte's presidental election equation of Exercise 3.19.
(a) Obtain the inequality least squares estimator of the Tufte model assuming the inequalities $\beta_2 > 0$ and $\beta_3 > 0$.
(b) Multiply all observations on yearly change in real per capita disposable income (x_{t2}) by -1 and reestimate the Tufte equation. Subject to the inequality restrictions $\beta_2 > 0$ and $\beta_3 > 0$, what are the inequality least squares estimates of β_2 and β_3?
(c) Given the original observations on the variables x_{t2} and x_{t3}, what are the inequality least squares estimates of β_2 and β_3 subject to $\beta_2 > 0$ and $\beta_3 < 0$?
(d) Suppose, for the moment, that x_{t2} and x_{t3} are orthonormal thus resulting in the model having a design matrix which is orthonormal ($X'X = I$). Describe the properties of the inequality least squares estimates of β_2 and β_3 subject to the constraints $\beta_2 > 0$ and $\beta_3 > 0$ when in fact $\beta_2 > 0$ but $\beta_3 < 0$. How is your conclusion modified if $X'X \neq I$? (Hint: see Thomson (1982).

6.22. Show that the covariance matrix of the restricted least squares estimator (6.2.8) is the same whether the restrictions $R\boldsymbol{\beta} = \mathbf{r}$ are true or false.

6.23. (Limiting Cases of Mixed Estimation). Assume the mixed estimation model (6.3.2) with $E\mathbf{ee}' = \sigma^2 I$ and $E\mathbf{vv}' = \gamma^2 I$. Also, for simplicity, assume σ^2 is known.
(a) Show that, as $\gamma \to \infty$, the mixed estimator becomes the ordinary least squares estimator.
(b) Use the binomial inverse theorem of Exercise 6.8 to reexpress the mixed estimator as

$$\hat{\boldsymbol{\beta}}^* = \hat{\boldsymbol{\beta}} - \sigma^2 S^{-1} R' F^{-1}(R\hat{\boldsymbol{\beta}} - \mathbf{r}),$$

where $S = X'X$ and $F = \sigma^2 R S^{-1} R' + \gamma^2 I$. Show that, as $\gamma \to 0$, the mixed estimator becomes the restricted least squares estimator.

6.24. Consider the simple regression model

$$y_t = \alpha + \beta x_t + e_t, \qquad t = 1, 2, \ldots, T.$$

Show that the variance of the restricted least squares estimator of β subject to $\alpha = 0$ is $\sigma^2/\sum x_t^2$. Assuming $\alpha \neq 0$, show that the ordinary least squares estimator of β has variance $\sigma^2/\sum (x_t - \bar{x}_t)^2$. Prove that the former variance is never larger than the latter, and argue along intuitive lines why this must be so.

6.25. Let x be an unbiased estimator of θ with variance σ^2. Consider the estimator $x^* = ax$, where a is a scalar. Show that $\text{MSE}(x^*) < \text{MSE}(x)$ when

$$\frac{1 - v^2}{1 + v^2} < a < 1,$$

where $v = \sigma/\theta$ is the coefficient of variation of x.

6.26. Let $\boldsymbol{\beta}^* = c\hat{\boldsymbol{\beta}}$, where $\hat{\boldsymbol{\beta}}$ is the ordinary least squares estimator and c is a scalar. Show that $E(\boldsymbol{\beta}^* - \boldsymbol{\beta})'(\boldsymbol{\beta}^* - \boldsymbol{\beta}) \leq E(\hat{\boldsymbol{\beta}} - \boldsymbol{\beta})'(\hat{\boldsymbol{\beta}} - \boldsymbol{\beta})$ for c satisfying

$$\frac{\boldsymbol{\beta}'\boldsymbol{\beta} - \sigma^2 \operatorname{tr}(X'X)^{-1}}{\boldsymbol{\beta}'\boldsymbol{\beta} + \sigma^2 \operatorname{tr}(X'X)^{-1}} \leq c \leq 1.$$

6.27. Let $\boldsymbol{\beta}^* = A\mathbf{y}$ denote an arbitrary linear estimator of $\boldsymbol{\beta}$ in the classical linear regression model. Show that the estimator

$$\boldsymbol{\beta}^{**} = \boldsymbol{\beta}\boldsymbol{\beta}'X'(X\boldsymbol{\beta}\boldsymbol{\beta}'X' + \sigma^2 I)^{-1}\mathbf{y}$$

is the best linear estimator in the class of estimators defined by the norm

$$E(\boldsymbol{\beta}^* - \boldsymbol{\beta})(\boldsymbol{\beta}^* - \boldsymbol{\beta})'.$$

6.28. Suppose the model of interest is

$$y_t = \mu + e_t, \qquad t = 1, 2, \ldots, T,$$

where $e_t \sim N(0, 1)$. The best, linear, unbiased estimator of μ is $\hat{\beta} = \bar{y} = \sum (y_t/T)$.
(a) Prove $E(\bar{y} - \mu)^2 = T^{-1}$.
Let $\beta^* = \mathbf{l}'\mathbf{y}$, where $\mathbf{l}'$ is an arbitrary vector of dimension $1 \times T$.
(b) Show that of all the estimators β^*,

$$\beta^{**} = \frac{T\mu^2}{1 + T\mu^2}\,\bar{y}$$

has the smallest mean square error.

6.29. Consider the model of Exercise 6.28 and the *feasible* estimator

$$\tilde{\beta} = \frac{T\bar{y}^3}{1 + T\bar{y}^2} = h(\bar{y}),$$

where $\bar{y}$ is used as an estimate of μ. Using a Taylor series expansion around the value $\bar{y} = \mu$, the following approximations for the mean and variance of $\tilde{\beta}$

$$E\tilde{\beta} = h(\mu) + \frac{1}{2}\frac{\partial^2 h}{\partial \bar{y}^2}(\mu)E(\bar{y} - \mu)^2,$$

$$\operatorname{var}\tilde{\beta} = E\left[\frac{\partial h}{\partial \bar{y}}(\mu)(\bar{y} - \mu) + \frac{1}{6}\frac{\partial^3 h}{\partial \bar{y}^3}(\mu)(\bar{y} - \mu)^3 + \frac{1}{2}\frac{\partial^2 h}{\partial^2 \bar{y}^2}(\mu)\{(\bar{y} - \mu)^2 - E(\bar{y} - \mu)^2\}\right]^2,$$

can be used to compute an *approximate* mean square error for $\tilde{\beta}$.
(a) Let $z = T\mu^2$. Show that

$$E\tilde{\beta} = (1 + z)^{-3}(3z + 2z^3 + z^4)\mu.$$

(b) Show that

$$\operatorname{var} \tilde{\beta} = (1 + z)^{-8}(z^8 + 10z^7 + 45z^6 + 72z^5 - 46z^4 - 346z^3 + 537z^2 - 144z + 15)T^{-1}.$$

(c) Show that the *approximate* mean square error of $\tilde{\beta}$ is less than or equal that of $\hat{\beta}$ if and only if

$$g(z) = -3z^7 - 26z^6 - 34z^5 + 112z^4 + 417z^3 - 505z^2 + 148z - 14 \geq 0.$$

(d) Using $g(z)$ determine at least one region of z where $g(z) \geq 0$.

6.30. Considering the results of Exercises 6.25–6.29, answer the following:
(a) Describe the so-called "unknown population parameters" problem that arises frequently in biased estimation.
(b) Compare and contrast the operability of best, linear, unbiased estimators with best linear "estimators."
(c) Compare and contrast the existence theorems of biased estimators with nuisance parameters (e.g. β^{**} of Exercise 6.28) and their "feasible" counterparts (e.g., $\tilde{\beta}$ of Exercise 6.29).

6.9 References

Barnett, V. (1973). *Comparative Statistical Inference*. New York: Wiley.
Brook, R. and Wallace, T. D. (1973). A note on extraneous information in regression. *Journal of Econometrics*, **1**, 315–316.
Durbin, J. (1953). A note on regression when there is extraneous information about one of the coefficients. *Journal of the American Statistical Association*, **48**, 799–808.
Edwards, W., Lindman, H., and Savage, L. J. (1963). Bayesian statistical inference for psychological research. *Psychological Review*, **70**, 193–242.
Goodnight, J. and Wallace, T. D. (1972). Operational techniques and tables for making weak MSE tests for restrictions in regression. *Econometrica*, **40**, 699–710.
Husby, R. D. (1971). A nonlinear consumption function estimated from time-series and cross-section data. *Review of Economics and Statistics*, **53**, 76–79.
Intriligator, M. D. (1971). *Mathematical Optimization and Economic Theory*. Englewood Cliffs, NJ: Prentice-Hall.
Jansen, R. (1975). Effects of linear inequality constraints of distributions of parameter estimates in the standard linear model. Report 7509, Erasmus University, Netherlands School of Economics, Rotterdam.
Judge, G. G. and Takayama, T. (1966). Inequality restrictions in regression analysis. *Journal of the American Statistical Association*, **61**, 166–181.
Judge, G. G. and Yancey, T. A. (1978). Inequality restricted estimation under squared error loss. Working Paper, University of Georgia, Athens.
Judge, G. G. and Yancey, T. A. (1979). Some sampling properties of a linear inequality restricted estimator. Working Paper, College of Commerce, University of Illinois, Urbana.
Judge, G. G., Bock, M. E., and Yancey, T. A. (1973a). Testing linear restrictions in regression: a tighter bound. *Econometrica*, **41**, 1203–1206.
Judge, G. G., Yancey, T. A., and Bock, M. E. (1973b). Properties of estimators after preliminary tests of significance when stochastic restrictions are used in regression. *Journal of Econometrics*, **1**, 29–47.

Judge, G. G., Griffiths, W. E., Hill, R. C., and Lee, T. C. (1980). *The Theory and Practice of Econometrics*. New York: Wiley.

Kuhn, H. W. and Tucker, A. W. (1951). Nonlinear programming. In *Proceedings of the Second Symposium on Mathematical Statistics and Probability*. Edited by J. Neyman. Berkeley, CA: University of California Press.

Liew, C. K. (1976). Inequality constrained least squares estimation. *Journal of the American Statistical Association*, **71**, 746–751.

Lindley, D. V. (1971). *Bayesian Statistics, A Review*. Regional Conference Series in Applied Mathematics. Philadelphia, PA: Society for Industrial and Applied Mathematics. Contains extensive bibliography.

Lovell, M. C. and Prescott, E. (1970). Multiple regression with inequality constraints: pre-testing bias, hypothesis testing and efficiency. *Journal of the American Statistical Association*, **65**, 913–925.

Maddala, G. S. (1977). *Econometrics*. New York: McGraw-Hill.

Mantel, E. H. (1973). Exact linear restrictions on parameters in the classical linear regression model. *The American Statistician*, **27**, 86–87.

Mehta, J. S. and Swamy, P. A. V. B. (1970). The finite sample distribution of Theil's mixed regression estimator and a related problem. *Review of the International Statistical Institute*, **37**, 202–209.

Nagar, A. L. and Kakwani, N. C. (1964). The bias and moment matrix of a mixed regression estimator. *Econometrica*, **32**, 389–402.

O'Hagan, A. (1973). Bayes estimation of a convex quadratic. *Biometrika*, **60**, 565–567.

Paulus, J. D. (1975). Mixed estimation of a complete system of consumer demand equations. *Annals of Economic and Social Measurement*, **4**, 117–131.

Press, S. J. (1972). *Applied Multivariate Analysis*. New York: Holt, Rinehart, & Winston.

Rao, C. R. (1973). *Linear Statistical Inference and Its Application*. New York: Wiley.

Rothenberg, T. J. (1971). The Bayesian approach and alternatives in Econometrics—II. In *Frontiers in Quantitative Economics*, Edited by M. D. Intriligator. Amsterdam: North-Holland. Pp. 194–204.

Rothenberg, T. J. (1973). *Efficient Estimation with A Priori Information*. Cowles Commission Monograph No. 23. New Haven, CT: Yale University Press.

Swamy, P. A. V. B. and Mehta, J. S. (1969). On Theil's mixed regression estimator. *Journal of the American Statistical Association*, **64**, 273–276.

Swamy, P. A. V. B. and Mehta, J. S. (1977). Robustness of Theil's mixed regression estimators. *The Canadian Journal of Statistics*, C, **5**, 93–109.

Swamy, P. A. V. B. and Mehta, J. S. (1983). Ridge regression estimation of the Rotterdam model. *Journal of Econometrics*, **22**, 365–390.

Theil, H. (1963). On the use of incomplete prior information in regression analysis. *Journal of the American Statistical Association*, **58**, 401–414.

Theil, H. (1974). Mixed estimation based on quasi-prior judgments. *European Economic Review*, **5**, 33–40.

Theil, H. and Goldberger, A. S. (1961). On pure and mixed statistical estimation in economics. *International Economic Review*, **2**, 65–78.

Thomson, M. (1982). Some results on the statistical properties of an inequality constrained least squares estimator in a linear model with two regressors. *Journal of Econometrics*, **19**, 215–231.

Toro-Vizcarrondo, C. and Wallace, T. D. (1968). A test of the mean square error criterion for restrictions in linear regression. *Journal of the American Statistical Association*, **63**, 558–576.

Wallace, T. D. (1972). Weaker criteria and tests for linear restrictions in regression. *Econometrica*, **40**, 689–698.

Wallace, T. D. and Toro-Vizcarrondo, C. E. (1969). Tables for the mean square error test for exact linear restrictions in regression. *Journal of the American Statistical Association*, **64**, 1949–1663.

Weber, J. D. (1973). *Historical Aspects of the Bayesian Controversy*. Tucson, AZ: University of Arizona. Contains extensive bibliography.

Yancey, T. A., Bock, M. E., and Judge, G. G. (1972). Some finite sample results for Theil's mixed regression estimator. *Journal of the American Statistical Association*, **67**, 176–179.

Yancey, T. A., Judge, G. G., and Bock, M. E., (1974). A mean square error test when stochastic restrictions are used in regression. *Communications in Statistics*, **3**, 755–768.

Zellner, A. (1961). Linear regression with inequality constraints on the coefficients: an application of quadratic programming and linear decision rules. Report 6109, International Center for Management Science, Rotterdam.

Zellner, A. (1971a). The Bayesian approach and alternatives in econometrics—I. In *Frontiers of Quantitative Economics*. Edited by M. D. Intriligator. Amsterdam: North-Holland. Pp. 178–193.

Zellner, A. (1971b). *An Introduction to Bayesian Inference in Econometrics*. New York: Wiley.

CHAPTER 7

Preliminary Test and Stein-Rule Estimators

7.1 Introduction

In the previous chapter procedures for augmenting the available sample information were considered. Consequences of incorporating nonsample information were seen to depend on the quality of information introduced. As one would expect, only the use of good information provides positive benefits. Unfortunately, we seldom are sure of the quality of the information to be introduced. In this chapter we examine the consequences of that uncertainty. First of all, investigators are in the habit of checking their prior nonsample information against the data using statistical tests of the type outlined in Chapter 6. The nonsample information is then either adopted or not depending upon the outcome of the test. The resulting estimation rule is called a preliminary test estimator since its form depends upon the outcome of a (preliminary) hypothesis test. This estimator is superior to the estimator based on sample information alone only over a relatively small portion of the parameter space, which reflects the fact that classical statistical procedures are not designed to aid the choice of a model specification. These results are discussed in Section 7.2.

Given that combining uncertain prior information with sample information may not be desirable, investigators have begun to consider nontraditional estimators which do use prior information to modify the ordinary least squares estimator, but in a way such that the resulting estimator dominates the ordinary least squares estimator over the entire parameter space. That is, these estimators dominate the ordinary least squares estimator regardless of how correct the prior information is. Development of these estimators followed from the results of Stein (1956) and others who worked on improved estimation of the mean vector of a multinormal random variable. They are called

Stein-rule estimators. These estimators are introduced and their various forms surveyed in Sections 7.3 and 7.4 of this chapter. Section 7.5 summarizes the results of this chapter and offers suggestions for further readings.

7.2 Pretest Estimators

Initially, a simplified regression model with orthonormal regressors will be used to examine the properties of the pretest estimator. Results for the general model will then be stated. This section borrows heavily from Judge and Bock (1978, Part II) and the reader is directed to this source for a more complete treatment of pretest estimators.

7.2.1 The Orthonormal Linear Statistical Model

Consider the classical normal linear regression model

$$\mathbf{y} = X\boldsymbol{\beta} + \mathbf{e}, \tag{7.2.1}$$

where $\mathbf{y}$ is $T \times 1$, X is $T \times K$, nonstochastic and of full rank, $\boldsymbol{\beta}$ is $K \times 1$ and $\mathbf{e}$ is $T \times 1$ and distributed $N(\mathbf{0}, \sigma^2 I)$. Recall that $X'X$ is a positive definite, symmetric matrix and, therefore, the following matrix result applies.

If Q is an $n \times n$ positive definite matrix, there exists a positive definite matrix, denoted $Q^{-1/2}$, such that $Q^{-1/2}QQ^{-1/2} = I$ and $Q^{-1/2}Q^{-1/2} = Q^{-1}$. It also follows that if $Q^{1/2} = (Q^{-1/2})^{-1}$ that $Q^{1/2}Q^{1/2} = Q$. If A is an orthonormal matrix ($A'A = AA' = I$) such that $A'QA = \Lambda$, where Λ is a diagonal matrix of eigenvalues $\lambda_1, \ldots, \lambda_n$ and $\Lambda^{1/2} = \operatorname{diag}(\lambda_1^{1/2}, \ldots, \lambda_n^{1/2})$ then $Q^{1/2} = A\Lambda^{1/2}A'$.

If $S = X'X$ then model (7.2.1) can be reparametrized as

$$\mathbf{y} = X\boldsymbol{\beta} + \mathbf{e} = XS^{-1/2}S^{1/2}\boldsymbol{\beta} + \mathbf{e} = Z\boldsymbol{\theta} + \mathbf{e}, \tag{7.2.2}$$

where $Z'Z = S^{-1/2}X'XS^{-1/2} = I_K$ and $\boldsymbol{\theta} = S^{1/2}\boldsymbol{\beta}$. The ordinary least squares estimator of $\boldsymbol{\theta}$ is $\hat{\boldsymbol{\theta}} = Z'\mathbf{y} = S^{1/2}\hat{\boldsymbol{\beta}}$ where $\hat{\boldsymbol{\beta}} = (X'X)^{-1}X'\mathbf{y}$ is the ordinary least squares estimator of $\boldsymbol{\beta}$. Under a squared error loss criterion, this estimator has risk

$$\mathscr{R}(\hat{\boldsymbol{\theta}}, \boldsymbol{\theta}) = E(\hat{\boldsymbol{\theta}} - \boldsymbol{\theta})'(\hat{\boldsymbol{\theta}} - \boldsymbol{\theta}) = \sigma^2 \operatorname{tr} I_K = \sigma^2 K. \tag{7.2.3}$$

This transformation is especially convenient since the risk in the $\boldsymbol{\theta}$-space,

$$\begin{aligned}\mathscr{R}(\hat{\boldsymbol{\theta}}, \boldsymbol{\theta}) &= E(\hat{\boldsymbol{\theta}} - \boldsymbol{\theta})'(\hat{\boldsymbol{\theta}} - \boldsymbol{\theta}) = E[(S^{1/2}\hat{\boldsymbol{\beta}} - S^{1/2}\boldsymbol{\beta})'(S^{1/2}\hat{\boldsymbol{\beta}} - S^{1/2}\boldsymbol{\beta})] \\ &= E[(\hat{\boldsymbol{\beta}} - \boldsymbol{\beta})'S^{1/2}S^{1/2}(\hat{\boldsymbol{\beta}} - \boldsymbol{\beta})] = E[(\hat{\boldsymbol{\beta}} - \boldsymbol{\beta})'S(\hat{\boldsymbol{\beta}} - \boldsymbol{\beta})] \\ &= E(\hat{\boldsymbol{\beta}} - \boldsymbol{\beta})'X'X(\hat{\boldsymbol{\beta}} - \boldsymbol{\beta}) = E(X\hat{\boldsymbol{\beta}} - X\boldsymbol{\beta})'(X\hat{\boldsymbol{\beta}} - X\boldsymbol{\beta}) \\ &= E(\hat{\mathbf{y}} - E\mathbf{y})'(\hat{\mathbf{y}} - E\mathbf{y}),\end{aligned} \tag{7.2.4}$$

is equivalent to the squared error of prediction risk in the $\boldsymbol{\beta}$-space. This means that anytime we wish to consider the performance of a parameter estimator in the $\boldsymbol{\beta}$-space under a squared error of prediction loss, we may equivalently, and without loss of generality, consider the estimator of $\boldsymbol{\theta}$ under our unweighted squared error loss function.

7.2.2 The Pretest Estimator

In order to keep the development simple consider the orthonormal linear statistical model (7.2.2) and the case where the investigator has uncertain prior information of the form $R\boldsymbol{\theta} = \boldsymbol{\theta} = \mathbf{r}$, where $\mathbf{r}$ is a known $K \times 1$ vector of constants. This does not constitute a serious loss of generality. The restricted least squares estimator, that combines both sample and nonsample information, is $\boldsymbol{\theta}^* = \mathbf{r}$. Thus, $\boldsymbol{\theta}^*$ is distributed with mean $E\boldsymbol{\theta}^* = \boldsymbol{\theta} - \boldsymbol{\delta}$, where $\boldsymbol{\delta} = \boldsymbol{\theta} - \mathbf{r}$, and covariance matrix $E(\boldsymbol{\theta}^* - E\boldsymbol{\theta}^*)(\boldsymbol{\theta}^* - E\boldsymbol{\theta}^*)' = \sigma^2(0_K)$ and mean square error $E(\boldsymbol{\theta}^* - \boldsymbol{\theta})(\boldsymbol{\theta}^* - \boldsymbol{\theta})' = \boldsymbol{\delta}\boldsymbol{\delta}'$. If the restrictions $\boldsymbol{\theta} = \mathbf{r}$ are correct, the estimator $\boldsymbol{\theta}^*$ is unbiased and has smaller sampling error than the ordinary least squares estimator $\boldsymbol{\theta}$. If the hypotheses are incorrect ($\boldsymbol{\delta} \neq \mathbf{0}$), under squared error loss the risk function for $\boldsymbol{\theta}^*$ is

$$E(\boldsymbol{\theta}^* - \boldsymbol{\theta})'(\boldsymbol{\theta}^* - \boldsymbol{\theta}) = \boldsymbol{\delta}'\boldsymbol{\delta}. \tag{7.2.5}$$

Under this criterion the estimator $\boldsymbol{\theta}^*$ has a smaller risk, and is, therefore, "better," than the ordinary least squares estimator if $\boldsymbol{\delta}'\boldsymbol{\delta}$ is less than $\sigma^2 K$. Recall from Section 6.2, that the risk of the restricted and unrestricted estimators may be written in terms of $\lambda = \boldsymbol{\delta}'\boldsymbol{\delta}/2\sigma^2$ and compared for each point in the parameter space. In particular $\mathscr{R}(\hat{\boldsymbol{\theta}}, \boldsymbol{\theta}) - \mathscr{R}(\boldsymbol{\theta}^*, \boldsymbol{\theta}) = \sigma^2 K - \boldsymbol{\delta}'\boldsymbol{\delta} \geq 0$ only when

$$\boldsymbol{\delta}'\boldsymbol{\delta}/\sigma^2 = (\boldsymbol{\theta} - \mathbf{r})'(\boldsymbol{\theta} - \mathbf{r})/\sigma^2 \leq K. \tag{7.2.6}$$

Since $\lambda = \boldsymbol{\delta}'\boldsymbol{\delta}/2\sigma^2 = (\boldsymbol{\theta} - \mathbf{r})'(\boldsymbol{\theta} - \mathbf{r})/2\sigma^2$, the condition (7.2.6) is equivalent to $\lambda \leq K/2$. The risk functions of $\boldsymbol{\theta}^*$ and $\hat{\boldsymbol{\theta}}$, in terms of λ are depicted in Figure 7.2.1. As is clear from that figure, as the specification error $\boldsymbol{\delta}$ increases in magnitude, the risk of the restricted least squares estimator $\boldsymbol{\theta}^*$ increases without limit.

To prevent use of the estimator $\boldsymbol{\theta}^*$ when $\boldsymbol{\theta}^*$ is inferior to $\hat{\boldsymbol{\theta}}$, investigators have traditionally checked the prior information $\boldsymbol{\theta} = \mathbf{r}$ against the data by considering $\boldsymbol{\theta} = \mathbf{r}$ an hypothesis which is tested by usual likelihood ratio procedures against the alternative hypothesis that $\boldsymbol{\theta} \neq \mathbf{r}$. The appropriate test statistic is

$$u = (\hat{\boldsymbol{\theta}} - \mathbf{r})'(\hat{\boldsymbol{\theta}} - \mathbf{r})/K\hat{\sigma}^2, \tag{7.2.7}$$

where $\hat{\sigma}^2 = (\mathbf{y} - Z\hat{\boldsymbol{\theta}})'(\mathbf{y} - Z\hat{\boldsymbol{\theta}})/(T - K)$.

If u is greater than or equal to some critical value c, then the null hypothesis is rejected. The statistic u has a noncentral F-distribution with K and $(T - K)$

degrees of freedom and noncentrality parameter $\lambda = (\boldsymbol{\theta} - \mathbf{r})'(\boldsymbol{\theta} - \mathbf{r})/K\sigma^2$, or $F_{(K, T-K, \lambda)}$. The noncentrality parameter is zero if and only if $\boldsymbol{\theta} = \mathbf{r}$ and the null hypothesis is true. Therefore the hypotheses under consideration may also be expressed in terms of λ, specifically $H_0: \lambda = 0$ and $H_1: \lambda > 0$. The traditional procedure of comparing u in (7.2.7) to a critical value c and adopting $\boldsymbol{\theta}^*$ or $\hat{\boldsymbol{\theta}}$ depending upon the outcome of the test, will be called the *traditional preliminary test procedure*.

Note that hypothesis tests can be carried out under other loss functions, such as the strong or weak mean square error criteria as described by Toro-Vizcarrondo and Wallace (1968) and Wallace (1972) (see Section 6.4). In the latter instance, for example, Wallace proposed using u to test whether λ was small enough to ensure that the risk of $\boldsymbol{\theta}^*$ is less than that for $\hat{\boldsymbol{\theta}}$. Consequently, Wallace proposed testing whether λ was less than $K/2$, with the alternative that λ was greater than or equal to $K/2$. H_0 is rejected if $u \geq c^*$ where c^* is chosen so that $\int_{c^*}^{\infty} F_{(K, T-K, (\lambda = K/2))} = \alpha$. By accepting H_0 we take $\boldsymbol{\theta}^*$ as our estimator and $\hat{\boldsymbol{\theta}}$ otherwise. The conventional test procedure may be thought of as the Wallace test under a different level of significance, and vice versa. The same can be said, of course, for the Toro-Vizcarrondo and Wallace test.

7.2.3 Properties of the Pretest Estimator

The estimator or decision rule which emerges from the traditional preliminary test procedure is $\tilde{\boldsymbol{\theta}}$, where

$$\tilde{\boldsymbol{\theta}} = \begin{cases} \boldsymbol{\theta}^* & \text{if } u < c, \\ \hat{\boldsymbol{\theta}} & \text{if } u \geq c, \end{cases} \tag{7.2.8}$$

which can be conveniently written as

$$\tilde{\boldsymbol{\theta}} = I_{[0, c)}(u)\boldsymbol{\theta}^* + I_{[c, \infty)}(u)\hat{\boldsymbol{\theta}}, \tag{7.2.9}$$

where $I_{[0, c)}(u)$ is an indicator function which takes the value one if $0 \leq u < c$ and zero otherwise, and $I_{[c, \infty)}(u)$ is an indicator function which is one if $u \geq c$ but zero otherwise.

Note that the pretest estimator $\tilde{\boldsymbol{\theta}}$ is a function of the data, the hypotheses *and* the level of significance α of the preliminary test. The latter feature is an aspect of the preliminary test process which is frequently overlooked. The level of the test is of great importance in determining the nature of the estimator. If $\alpha = 1$ the corresponding value of $c = 0$ and the hypotheses $\boldsymbol{\theta} = \mathbf{r}$ would always be rejected so that $\tilde{\boldsymbol{\theta}}$ would always equal $\hat{\boldsymbol{\theta}}$, the maximum likelihood estimator. If $\alpha = 0$ the corresponding value of $c = \infty$ and $\tilde{\boldsymbol{\theta}}$ would always be equal to the restricted estimator $\boldsymbol{\theta}^*$. Since α is generally chosen between these extremes, $\tilde{\boldsymbol{\theta}}$ in a repeated sampling context is a mixture of $\hat{\boldsymbol{\theta}}$ and $\boldsymbol{\theta}^*$ since sometimes the null hypothesis would be rejected and sometimes not, the frequency depending upon the value of α.

Now we describe some of the properties of $\tilde{\boldsymbol{\theta}}$ as discussed by Judge and Bock (1978, Ch. 3). The risk function of the pretest estimator is $\mathscr{R}(\tilde{\boldsymbol{\theta}}, \boldsymbol{\theta}) = E(\tilde{\boldsymbol{\theta}} - \boldsymbol{\theta})'(\tilde{\boldsymbol{\theta}} - \boldsymbol{\theta})$ and, for the orthonormal case it can be shown to equal

$$\mathscr{R}(\tilde{\boldsymbol{\theta}}, \boldsymbol{\theta}) = \sigma^2 K + 2(\boldsymbol{\delta}'\boldsymbol{\delta} - \sigma^2 K)h_\lambda(2) - \boldsymbol{\delta}'\boldsymbol{\delta}h_\lambda(4), \qquad (7.2.10)$$

where $h_\lambda(l) = \Pr[(\chi^2_{(K+l,\lambda)})/\chi^2_{(T-K)} \leq cK/(T-K)]$, $\lambda = \boldsymbol{\delta}'\boldsymbol{\delta}/2\sigma^2$ and $1 > h_\lambda(2) > h_\lambda(4) > 0$. Judge and Bock note the following characteristics of the risk function (7.2.10):

(i) If the hypotheses are *correct* the risk of the pretest estimator is $\sigma^2 K[1 - h_0(2)]$, and, since $h_0(2) < 1$, is less than the risk of $\hat{\boldsymbol{\theta}}$, $\sigma^2 K$.
(ii) As $\lambda \to \infty$, $h_\lambda(l)$ and $\boldsymbol{\delta}'\boldsymbol{\delta}h_\lambda(l)$ approach zero and thus the risk $\mathscr{R}(\tilde{\boldsymbol{\theta}}, \boldsymbol{\theta}) \to \mathscr{R}(\hat{\boldsymbol{\theta}}, \boldsymbol{\theta}) = \sigma^2 K$.
(iii) As $\lambda \to \infty$, $\mathscr{R}(\tilde{\boldsymbol{\theta}}, \boldsymbol{\theta})$ grows monotonically, reaches a maximum after crossing the function $\mathscr{R}(\boldsymbol{\theta}^*, \boldsymbol{\theta})$ and then monotonically decreases, approaching the risk of $\hat{\boldsymbol{\theta}}$.
(iv) The equality of the risk functions of $\tilde{\boldsymbol{\theta}}$ and $\hat{\boldsymbol{\theta}}$ occurs within the bounds $K/4 \leq \lambda \leq K/2$.
(v) Recall that $h_\lambda(2)$ and $h_\lambda(4)$ are probabilities that depend on c and thus α. As $\alpha \to 0$, $c \to \infty$ and $h_\lambda(l) \to 1$, and the risk of the pretest estimator approaches that of $\boldsymbol{\theta}^*$, the restricted estimator. As $\alpha \to 1$, $c \to 0$ and $h_\lambda(l) \to 0$ and the risk of $\tilde{\boldsymbol{\theta}}$ approaches that of the maximum likelihood estimator $\hat{\boldsymbol{\theta}}$.

Features (i)–(v) are depicted graphically in Figures 7.2.1 and 7.2.2. Finally, the mean and covariance matrix of $\tilde{\boldsymbol{\theta}}$ have also been determined.

(vi) The mean of $\tilde{\boldsymbol{\theta}}$ is given by

$$E(\tilde{\boldsymbol{\theta}}) = \boldsymbol{\theta} - h_\lambda(2)\boldsymbol{\delta}.$$

Thus if $\boldsymbol{\delta} = \mathbf{0}$ the pretest estimator is unbiased. Otherwise, since $0 < h_\lambda(2) < 1$ the bias of the pretest estimator is always less than the bias of the restricted estimator $\boldsymbol{\theta}^*$.

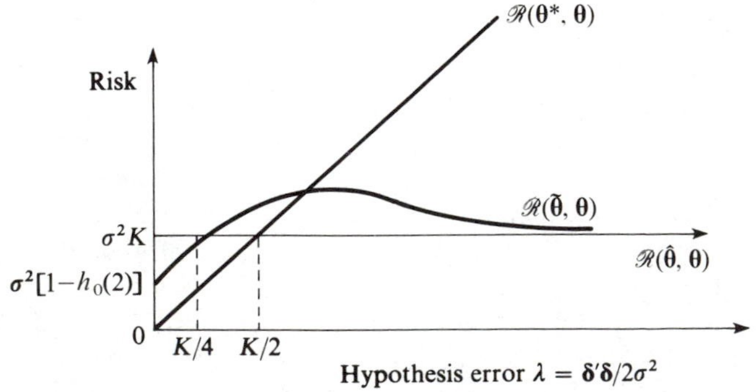

Figure 7.2.1 Risk functions for the ordinary least squares, restricted least squares and pretest estimators.

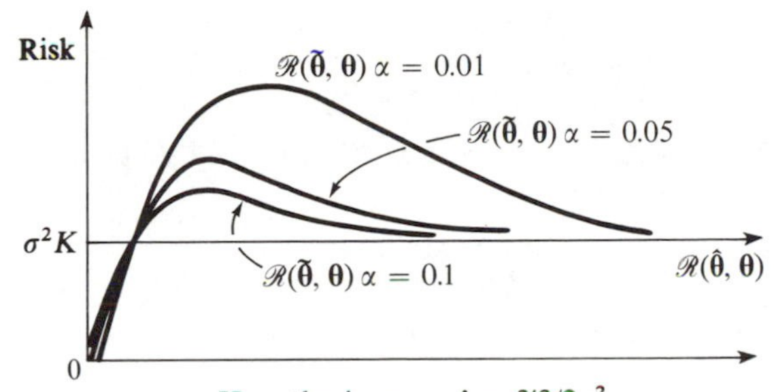

Figure 7.2.2 Effect of critical value α on the risk function of the pretest estimator.

(vii) The covariance matrix of $\tilde{\boldsymbol{\theta}}$ is

$$\begin{aligned}\Sigma_{\tilde{\boldsymbol{\theta}}} &= E[(\tilde{\boldsymbol{\theta}} - E\tilde{\boldsymbol{\theta}})(\tilde{\boldsymbol{\theta}} - E\tilde{\boldsymbol{\theta}})'] \\ &= \sigma^2(1 - h_\lambda(2))I_K + [h_\lambda(4) - 2h_\lambda(2) - h_\lambda^2(2)]\boldsymbol{\delta}\boldsymbol{\delta}'.\end{aligned}$$

Thus the covariance matrix of $\tilde{\boldsymbol{\theta}}$ depends on the variance of $\hat{\boldsymbol{\theta}}$, the probabilities $h_\lambda(l)$ and the specification error $\boldsymbol{\delta}$. Variances of each element of $\tilde{\boldsymbol{\theta}}$ are greater than or equal to the variances of the restricted estimator $\boldsymbol{\theta}^*$ and less than or equal the variances of the maximum likelihood estimator $\hat{\boldsymbol{\theta}}$. Note, however, that $\Sigma_{\tilde{\boldsymbol{\theta}}}$ depends upon unknown population parameters and cannot be used in conventional ways to perform hypothesis tests or construct interval estimates.

7.2.4 The Choice of the Optimal Value of α for Pretesting

We have noted several times that the properties of the estimator $\tilde{\boldsymbol{\theta}}$ depend upon the value of α, the level of significance of the preliminary test. Since α is under our control, we face a statistical decision problem: the optimum value of α depends upon the optimality criterion chosen. Recall that the risk functions of the restricted and unrestricted estimators cross at $\lambda = K/2$. We wish to choose a value of α that brings the risk function of $\tilde{\boldsymbol{\theta}}$ as "close" as possible, under some definition of close, to that of $\boldsymbol{\theta}^*$ over the interval λ in $[0, K/2)$ and to $\hat{\boldsymbol{\theta}}$ over the interval λ in $[K/2, \infty)$.

One way to define close is to choose the value of α that minimizes the maximum difference between the risk of the pretest estimator and "boundry" risk function $I_{[0, K/2)}(\lambda)\mathscr{R}(\boldsymbol{\theta}^*, \boldsymbol{\theta}) + I_{[K/2, \infty)}(\lambda)\mathscr{R}(\hat{\boldsymbol{\theta}}, \boldsymbol{\theta})$ over the range of λ. Sawa and Hiromatsu (1973) call this the minimax regret solution. For a single hypothesis they found the optimum value of c to be about 1.8. Brook (1976) derived minimax regret optimal values of c for multiple hypotheses of about 2.0. Toyoda and Wallace (1976) show that using the criterion of minimizing the average relative risk,

$$\int_0^\infty \frac{1}{\sigma^2} \{\mathscr{R}(\tilde{\boldsymbol{\theta}}, \boldsymbol{\theta}) - \min[\mathscr{R}(\hat{\boldsymbol{\theta}}, \boldsymbol{\theta}), \mathscr{R}(\boldsymbol{\theta}^*, \boldsymbol{\theta})]\} \, dc,$$

leads to a choice of the ordinary least squares estimator unless the number of hypotheses is greater than 5. When the number of hypotheses is large their criterion suggests optimal critical values of about 2.0.

7.2.5 The Pretest Estimator in the General Linear Statistical Model

In this section we consider the pretest estimator arising from the analysis of the general linear model. The same general conclusions found for the orthonormal linear model continue to hold but the results are more difficult to summarize neatly because the risk properties are affected by both the choice of weight matrix for the loss function and the specific form of the regressor matrix X. The analytical differences which appear for this model result from the fact that we now wish to consider estimation in the $\boldsymbol{\beta}$-space under an arbitrarily weighted risk function

$$\mathscr{R}(\hat{\boldsymbol{\beta}}, \boldsymbol{\beta}) = E(\hat{\boldsymbol{\beta}} - \boldsymbol{\beta})'Q(\hat{\boldsymbol{\beta}} - \boldsymbol{\beta}), \tag{7.2.11}$$

where Q is *any* known positive definite weight matrix. Consequently, although we can transform the general model with general restrictions to the orthonormal model with exclusion restrictions (Judge and Bock (1978, pp. 82–83)) the transformation does not leave us with a simple squared error loss function in the $\boldsymbol{\theta}$-space, but rather with a weighted risk function, making the analysis a bit more messy than in the orthonormal case.

Our starting point is the classical normal linear regression model $\mathbf{y} = X\boldsymbol{\beta} + \mathbf{e}$, where X is of full rank and $\mathbf{e} \sim N(\mathbf{0}, \sigma^2 I_T)$. In addition to the sample information there exist J independent linear hypotheses in the usual form $R\boldsymbol{\beta} = \mathbf{r}$. Recall that these linear hypotheses represent nonsample information about which we are uncertain. The restricted least squares estimator is $\boldsymbol{\beta}^* = \hat{\boldsymbol{\beta}} - (X'X)^{-1}[R(X'X)^{-1}R']^{-1}(R\hat{\boldsymbol{\beta}} - \mathbf{r})$. The "quality" of the nonsample information is assumed to be checked using the likelihood ratio test statistic

$$u = (R\hat{\boldsymbol{\beta}} - \mathbf{r})'[R(X'X)^{-1}R']^{-1}(R\hat{\boldsymbol{\beta}} - \mathbf{r})/J\hat{\sigma}^2, \tag{7.2.12}$$

where $\hat{\sigma}^2 = (\mathbf{y} - X\hat{\boldsymbol{\beta}})'(\mathbf{y} - X\hat{\boldsymbol{\beta}})/(T - K)$. The statistic u has a noncentral F-distribution with J and $(T - K)$ degrees of freedom and noncentrality parameter

$$\lambda = \frac{\boldsymbol{\delta}'[R(X'X)^{-1}R']^{-1}\boldsymbol{\delta}}{2\sigma^2}, \tag{7.2.13}$$

where $\boldsymbol{\delta} = R\boldsymbol{\beta} - \mathbf{r}$. The traditional pretest estimator is then

$$\tilde{\boldsymbol{\beta}} = I_{[0,c)}(u)\boldsymbol{\beta}^* + I_{[c,\infty)}(u)\hat{\boldsymbol{\beta}}. \tag{7.2.14}$$

This estimator takes the value of the restricted estimator $\boldsymbol{\beta}^*$ if $u < c$, where c is the critical value corresponding to the upper-α percentile of the central F-distribution of u under the assumption that the hypothesis $R\boldsymbol{\beta} = \mathbf{r}$ is true. If $u \geq c$, implying that the null hypothesis is rejected at the chosen level of significance, $\tilde{\boldsymbol{\beta}}$ takes the value of the ordinary least squares estimator $\hat{\boldsymbol{\beta}} = (X'X)^{-1}X'\mathbf{y}$.

The weighted risk function (7.2.11) of $\tilde{\boldsymbol{\beta}}$ is

$$\begin{aligned}\mathscr{R}(\tilde{\boldsymbol{\beta}}, \boldsymbol{\beta}) &= E(\tilde{\boldsymbol{\beta}} - \boldsymbol{\beta})'Q(\tilde{\boldsymbol{\beta}} - \boldsymbol{\beta})\\ &= \sigma^2 \operatorname{tr} S^{-1}Q - \sigma^2 \operatorname{tr} V[h_\lambda(2) + 2(h_\lambda(4) - 2h_\lambda(2))\gamma/\operatorname{tr} V],\end{aligned} \tag{7.2.15}$$

where $h_\lambda(l)$ is defined as for (7.2.10), $S = X'X$,

$$\gamma = \boldsymbol{\delta}'(RS^{-1}R')^{-1}RS^{-1}QS^{-1}R'(RS^{-1}R')^{-1}\boldsymbol{\delta}/2\sigma^2,$$

and

$$V = RS^{-1}QS^{-1}R'(RS^{-1}R')^{-1}.$$

Thus, the risk of the preliminary test estimator $\tilde{\boldsymbol{\beta}}$ depends on γ, λ, and α. Unlike the situation for the orthonormal model, knowing λ does not completely determine the risk function of $\tilde{\boldsymbol{\beta}}$. One must also know the value of the scalar γ. Bounds on the risk of $\tilde{\boldsymbol{\beta}}$ for given λ can be established, however, by noting that

$$\eta_S\lambda \leq \gamma \leq \eta_L\lambda, \tag{7.2.16}$$

where η_S and η_L are respectively the smallest and largest characteristic values of the matrix V. Since $h_\lambda(2) > h_\lambda(4)$ the risk function $\mathscr{R}(\tilde{\boldsymbol{\beta}}, \boldsymbol{\beta})$, is largest, for given λ, when $\gamma = \eta_L\lambda$ and smallest when $\gamma = \eta_S\lambda$. Using these limits on γ then boundary risk functions of λ alone can be constructed providing the inequality

$$\begin{aligned}\mathscr{R}_L &= \sigma^2 \operatorname{tr} S^{-1}Q - \sigma^2 \operatorname{tr} V[h_\lambda(2) + 2(h_\lambda(4) - 2h_\lambda(2))\eta_L\lambda/\operatorname{tr} V]\\ &\geq \sigma^2 \operatorname{tr} S^{-1}Q - \sigma^2 \operatorname{tr} V[h_\lambda(2) + 2(h_\lambda(4) - 2h_\lambda(2))\eta_S\lambda/\operatorname{tr} V] = \mathscr{R}_S.\end{aligned} \tag{7.2.17}$$

The bounding risk functions $\mathscr{R}_L$ and $\mathscr{R}_S$ have the same general properties as the risk function for $\tilde{\boldsymbol{\theta}}$ in the orthonormal case. Specifically, when $\lambda = 0$, $\mathscr{R}_L = \mathscr{R}_S$ and the risk of $\tilde{\boldsymbol{\beta}}$ is less than that of $\hat{\boldsymbol{\beta}}$ the ordinary least squares estimator but is greater than that of the corresponding restricted estimator. As λ increases $\mathscr{R}_L$ and $\mathscr{R}_S$ increase monotonically, attain their maxima and then approach the risk of the ordinary least squares estimator $\mathscr{R}(\hat{\boldsymbol{\beta}}, \boldsymbol{\beta}) = \sigma^2 \operatorname{tr} S^{-1}Q$. Since $\mathscr{R}(\tilde{\boldsymbol{\beta}}, \boldsymbol{\beta})$ falls between the bounding functions it too has those characteristics.

The risk function $\mathscr{R}(\tilde{\boldsymbol{\beta}}, \boldsymbol{\beta})$ is affected by the choice of α in the same manner as that of $\tilde{\boldsymbol{\theta}}$ in the orthonormal model. Specifically as $\alpha \to 1$, $c \to 0$ and the

$\mathscr{R}(\tilde{\boldsymbol{\beta}}, \boldsymbol{\beta}) \to \mathscr{R}(\hat{\boldsymbol{\beta}}, \boldsymbol{\beta})$. As $\alpha \to 0$, $c \to \infty$ and $\mathscr{R}(\tilde{\boldsymbol{\beta}}, \boldsymbol{\beta}) \to \mathscr{R}(\boldsymbol{\beta}^*, \boldsymbol{\beta})$. For more detailed results concerning the risk function of $\tilde{\boldsymbol{\beta}}$ the reader is referred to Judge and Bock (1978, Ch. 4).

7.2.6 Some General Remarks About the Consequences and Scope of Preliminary Test Procedures

The results from Section 7.2.5 have very serious consequences for procedures economists frequently apply in empirical work. The scope of preliminary testing is illustrated by the following examples:

(1) Deleting a variable from a model because the t-value for its estimated coefficient is small and reapplying least squares procedures.
(2) Using any of the mechanistic variable selection procedures for selecting the "best" subset of regressors. This includes stepwise regression in all its many forms (Draper and Smith 1966)), using Mallows (1973) C_P criterion, Amemiya's (1980) PC Criterion, the Akaike (1974) Information Criterion, or Sawa's (1977) BIC Criterion, just to name a few. All these criteria can be shown (see Judge *et al.* (1980, Ch. 11)) to be functions of the error sum of squares from the full model and can all be related to the statistic u commonly used to test hypotheses.
(3) Testing for the presence of autocorrelation or heteroscedasticity and choosing the ordinary least squares or generalized least squares estimator depending upon the outcome of the test.
(4) Pooling or not pooling on the basis of a "Chow" test for structural change.
(5) Checking the compatibility of stochastic prior information and sample information before a mixed estimation process is employed. (Judge *et al.* (1973) and Judge and Bock (1978, Ch. 6).)
(6) Principal components regression when the number of components chosen to delete is based upon an hypothesis test.
(7) Almon distributed lags where the polynomial degree is chosen on the basis of an hypothesis test.

While this list could be extended, the point has been made.

Many of the practices of applied economists produce estimators whose properties are unknown. The origin of the practices is, of course, that economists have only vague knowledge of the structure underlying the process generating their data. Consequently, economists "peek" at the data to aid in model specification. Unfortunately, classical statistics presumes that the investigator knows the process generating the data. Does this mean we cannot or should not use any of the tests listed above? The answer to that is easy. We should not use hypothesis tests to help specify our models. If we do, the resulting estimator is inferior to the maximum likelihood estimator over a large part of the parameter space in a repeated sampling context and has an unknown sampling distribution, making usual hypothesis tests inappropriate.

The next question is: Why are sampling properties important? Again the answer to that is easy. The repeated sampling properties of statistical decision rules, procedures and estimators are the only way we have to evaluate them. Classical statistics provides us no other way to choose from among the decision rules which might be used. What has been shown is that the traditional pretest estimator is inferior to the maximum likelihood estimator over a large part of the parameter space. Consequently, it is not, in general, a good estimator. What it does do is prevent potentially large average losses which would occur if the restricted estimator were employed when in fact the restrictions are severe misspecifications.

The final question then is: What do we do then when we are uncertain about the nature of the process generating the data? The answer to that is not easy. The best solution is to improve the theory so the problem can be addressed with a clearer understanding of the underlying economic structure. As always, good economic theory can make for good econometrics. Unfortunately, the converse is not generally true. This is of little comfort, since economic theory is a long way from that state of development, but that is all that can be said. Those who continue to search through data to aid model specification and for significant results to report should at least be aware of the statistical properties of their results in a repeated sampling context. These results are conditional upon the model being correct. Thus, standard errors are conditional and can *substantially understate* the unconditional standard errors of the multistep estimator. Consequently, results appear stronger, on the basis of magnitudes of t-values and the like, than they actually are.

7.3 Stein-Rule Estimators for the Orthonormal Linear Regression Model

In this section we consider a family of improved estimators that dominate the usual maximum likelihood estimator for the orthonormal linear regression model over the entire parameter space, as well as selected refinements. These results follow from the work of Stein (1956) and James and Stein (1961) and others who have considered the problem of estimating the mean vector of a multivariate normal random vector. In the succeeding section these results are extended to the general linear model. These sections rely heavily upon Judge and Bock (1978, Chs. 8 and 10).

7.3.1 The James and Stein Estimator

As in the Section 7.2.5 we will consider the transformed normal regression model

$$\mathbf{y} = X\boldsymbol{\beta} + \mathbf{e} = XS^{-1/2}S^{1/2}\boldsymbol{\beta} + \mathbf{e} = Z\boldsymbol{\theta} + \mathbf{e}, \qquad (7.3.1)$$

where all vectors and matrices have the usual dimensions and $\mathbf{e} \sim N(\mathbf{0}, \sigma^2 I)$. Note that $Z'Z = I_K$ so we can transform the model once more as

$$Z'\mathbf{y} = Z'Z\boldsymbol{\theta} + Z'\mathbf{e}, \tag{7.3.2}$$

or

$$\mathbf{z} = \boldsymbol{\theta} + \boldsymbol{\omega}, \tag{7.3.3}$$

where $\mathbf{z} = Z'\mathbf{y}$ and $\boldsymbol{\omega} = Z'\mathbf{e}$. The form (7.3.3) is convenient because it shows that the "K-mean" problem usually analyzed in the statistical literature is equivalent to the reparametrized regression model. The maximum likelihood estimator of $\boldsymbol{\theta}$ in (7.3.1) is $\hat{\boldsymbol{\theta}} = Z'\mathbf{y} = \mathbf{z}$. If $\hat{\boldsymbol{\theta}}$ is evaluated under a squared error risk function,

$$\begin{aligned}\mathscr{R}(\hat{\boldsymbol{\theta}}, \boldsymbol{\theta}) &= E[(\hat{\boldsymbol{\theta}} - \boldsymbol{\theta})'(\hat{\boldsymbol{\theta}} - \boldsymbol{\theta})] = E(\hat{\boldsymbol{\beta}} - \boldsymbol{\beta})'X'X(\hat{\boldsymbol{\beta}} - \boldsymbol{\beta}) \\ &= E[\hat{\mathbf{y}} - E\mathbf{y}]'[\hat{\mathbf{y}} - E\mathbf{y}] = \sigma^2 K,\end{aligned} \tag{7.3.4}$$

then, as noted above, we may equivalently consider the squared error of prediction loss function in the $\boldsymbol{\beta}$-space. Recall that $\hat{\boldsymbol{\theta}}$ is a minimax estimator, in decision theoretic terms, since it minimizes the maximum risk over the entire parameter space. (See Judge *et al.* (1980, p. 25).)

When σ^2 is unknown, the usual case for analysis of the regression model, the James and Stein (1961) estimator for $\boldsymbol{\theta}$ is

$$\hat{\boldsymbol{\theta}}^* = [1 - as/(\hat{\boldsymbol{\theta}}'\hat{\boldsymbol{\theta}})]\hat{\boldsymbol{\theta}}, \tag{7.3.5}$$

where a is a constant such that

$$0 \leq a \leq 2(K - 2)/(T - K + 2), \tag{7.3.6}$$

and $s = \mathbf{y}'M\mathbf{y} = (T - K)\hat{\sigma}^2$, where $M = I - X(X'X)^{-1}X'$. The risk minimizing choice of a is $a = (K - 2)/(T - K + 2)$ so that the optimal James–Stein estimator is

$$\hat{\boldsymbol{\theta}}^* = [1 - ((K - 2)/(T - K + 2))s/\hat{\boldsymbol{\theta}}'\hat{\boldsymbol{\theta}}]\hat{\boldsymbol{\theta}}. \tag{7.3.7}$$

This estimator has smaller risk than the ordinary least squares estimator for all values of $\boldsymbol{\theta}$ such that $\boldsymbol{\theta}'\boldsymbol{\theta} < \infty$ if $K \geq 3$. When $\boldsymbol{\theta} = \mathbf{0}$ the optimal estimator (7.3.7) has risk $[K - (T - K)(K - 2)/(T - K + 2)]$ which increases to $\sigma^2 K$, the maximum likelihood risk as $\boldsymbol{\theta}'\boldsymbol{\theta} \to \infty$. Plotted as a function of $\lambda = \boldsymbol{\theta}'\boldsymbol{\theta}/2\sigma^2$, a typical risk function for $\hat{\boldsymbol{\theta}}^*$ is shown in Figure 7.3.1. In order to more easily interpret this estimator and to see how it "works" to provide a risk improvement over ordinary least squares let us rewrite (7.3.7). Recall that $s/\sigma^2 = (T - K)\hat{\sigma}^2/\sigma^2 \sim \chi^2_{(T-K)}$ and is independent of $\hat{\boldsymbol{\theta}}'\hat{\boldsymbol{\theta}}/\sigma^2 \sim \chi^2_{(K,\lambda)}$ where $\lambda = \boldsymbol{\theta}'\boldsymbol{\theta}/2\sigma^2$. Therefore, (7.3.7) can be written

$$\hat{\boldsymbol{\theta}}^* = [1 - c/u]\hat{\boldsymbol{\theta}}, \tag{7.3.8}$$

where $c = (T - K)(K - 2)/((T - K + 2)K)$ and $u = \hat{\boldsymbol{\theta}}'\hat{\boldsymbol{\theta}}/K\hat{\sigma}^2$ is the likelihood ratio test statistic, for the hypothesis $\boldsymbol{\theta} = \mathbf{0}$ against the alternative $\boldsymbol{\theta} \neq \mathbf{0}$, and has an F-distribution with K and $(T - K)$ degrees of freedom and noncentrality parameter $\lambda = \boldsymbol{\theta}'\boldsymbol{\theta}/2\sigma^2$.

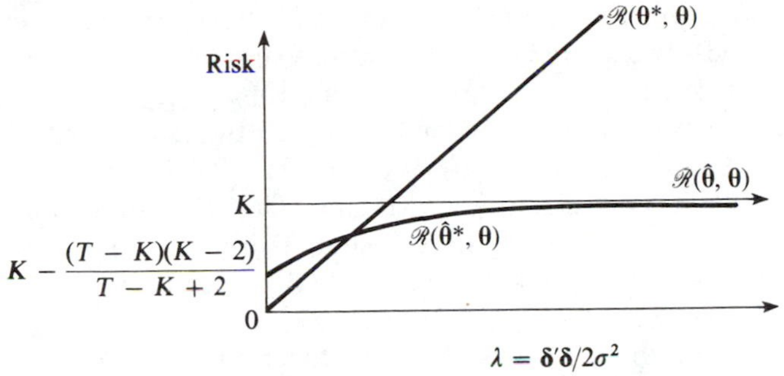

Figure 7.3.1 Risk function of the Stein-rule.

In this form, the James–Stein estimator is seen to use the test statistic u to combine the sample information with the hypothesis $\theta = 0$. In this respect it is like the traditional pretest estimator. But whereas the pretest estimator uses the statistic u to choose between the restricted (hypothesis) estimator and the unrestricted estimator, the James–Stein estimator uses the statistic u to "shrink" the estimator $\hat{\theta}$ toward the restricted estimator, in this case the null vector. The larger the value of u, and thus the less compatible the hypothesis $\theta = 0$ with the data, the larger is the shrinkage factor $1 - c/u$ and thus the less $\hat{\theta}$ is shrunk toward 0. In fact, as $u \to \infty$, $\hat{\theta}^* \to \hat{\theta}$. The smaller u is, as long as $u > c$, the greater the amount of shrinkage, with $\hat{\theta}^*$ taking the value zero if $u = c$. Furthermore, note that if $u < c$ the James–Stein estimator actually reverses the sign of the maximum likelihood estimator $\hat{\theta}$. This feature is given more attention below when the "positive" rule estimator is considered.

There is no reason why $\hat{\theta}$ must be shrunk toward the origin. In general we may shrink $\hat{\theta}$ toward any hypothesis vector θ_1. In this case the optimum James–Stein estimator is

$$\hat{\theta}_1^* = \left[1 - \frac{c_1}{u_1}\right](\hat{\theta} - \theta_1) + \theta_1$$

$$= \hat{\theta} - \frac{c_1}{u_1}(\hat{\theta} - \theta_1), \tag{7.3.9}$$

where $u_1 = (\hat{\theta} - \theta_1)'(\hat{\theta} - \theta_1)/K\hat{\sigma}^2$ and

$$c_1 = (K - 2)(T - K)/(K(T - K + 2)).$$

The statistic u_1 is the likelihood ratio test statistic for the test of the hypothesis $\theta = \theta_1$ against $\theta \neq \theta_1$. Hence $\hat{\theta}_1^*$ uses u_1 to combine the sample and prior information. Again, the estimator $\hat{\theta}_1^*$ is minimax and has lower risk than the maximum likelihood estimator $\hat{\theta}$ regardless of the true parameter value θ and how correct or incorrect the hypothesis vector θ_1, as long as $K \geq 3$.

This does not mean, however, that the James–Stein estimator is the answer to all econometric worries. Consider the following points. First, the

James–Stein estimator is biased and nonlinear. Furthermore, its covariance matrix depends on the unknown population parameters. These features, for the present, rule out using the James–Stein estimator for testing hypotheses or making interval estimates. Second, although the estimator $\boldsymbol{\theta}_1^*$ has lower risk than $\hat{\boldsymbol{\theta}}$ regardless of the value of $\boldsymbol{\theta}_1$ chosen, the closer $\boldsymbol{\theta}_1$ is to the true parameter vector $\boldsymbol{\theta}$ the greater the risk gain. Thus the point chosen toward which $\hat{\boldsymbol{\theta}}$ is shrunk is an important decision. Third, the James–Stein results depend upon the assumption of a normally distributed error term. Fourth, while the James–Stein estimator improves upon the maximum likelihood estimator, it does so with respect to a loss function which sums the squared loss of estimation from each parameter. We know nothing about *component-wise* improvement. Finally, there is the disquieting feature of $\hat{\boldsymbol{\theta}}_1^*$ and $\hat{\boldsymbol{\theta}}^*$ that if $u_1 < c_1$ or $u < c$ the estimator $\hat{\boldsymbol{\theta}}$ is shrunk *beyond* the hypothesis vector. This final point will be addressed further in the next section.

7.3.2 The James–Stein Positive Rule Estimator

While the James–Stein estimators considered above are minimax and have lower risk than the maximum likelihood estimator over the entire parameter space, they are inadmissible. That is, there are other estimators which have risk at least as small as the James–Stein estimators over the entire parameter space. Again for the case where σ^2 is unknown, the positive rule of the James–Stein estimator (7.3.7) may be written

$$\begin{aligned}\boldsymbol{\theta}^+ &= I_{[a_1,\,\infty)}(s/\hat{\boldsymbol{\theta}}'\hat{\boldsymbol{\theta}})\left[1 - \frac{a_1 s}{\hat{\boldsymbol{\theta}}'\hat{\boldsymbol{\theta}}}\right]\hat{\boldsymbol{\theta}} \\ &= I_{[c^*,\,\infty)}(u)\left[1 - \frac{c^*}{u}\right]\hat{\boldsymbol{\theta}}, \qquad (7.3.10)\end{aligned}$$

where u is the likelihood ratio test statistic for the hypothesis $\boldsymbol{\theta} = \boldsymbol{\theta}_1 = \mathbf{0}$ and $a_1 = c^*K/(T - K)$. For minimaxity $K \geq 3$ and

$$\frac{(K-2)(T-K)}{(T-K+2)K} < c^* \leq \frac{2(K-2)(T-K)}{(T-K+2)K}.$$

This estimator prevents changing the sign of the maximum likelihood estimator $\hat{\boldsymbol{\theta}}$. Now if u is small ($u < c^*$) the positive rule estimator assumes the value of the restricted estimator, the null vector. A typical risk function comparison between $\boldsymbol{\theta}^+$, $\hat{\boldsymbol{\theta}}^*$ and $\hat{\boldsymbol{\theta}}$ is depicted in Figure 7.3.2. Again the ordinary least squares estimator need not be shrunk toward the null vector. If $\boldsymbol{\theta}_1$ is any K-dimensional hypothesis vector. Then the positive-rule estimator for (7.3.10) that shrinks $\hat{\boldsymbol{\theta}}$ toward $\boldsymbol{\theta}_1$ is

$$\boldsymbol{\theta}_1^+ = I_{[c^*,\,\infty)}(u_1)\left(1 - \frac{c^*}{u_1}\right)(\hat{\boldsymbol{\theta}} - \boldsymbol{\theta}_1) + \boldsymbol{\theta}_1, \qquad (7.3.11)$$

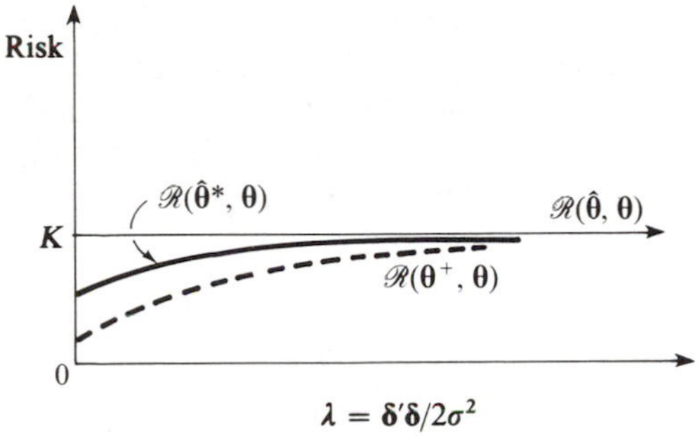

Figure 7.3.2 Risk of the positive rule.

where $u_1 = (\hat{\boldsymbol{\theta}} - \boldsymbol{\theta}_1)'(\hat{\boldsymbol{\theta}} - \boldsymbol{\theta}_1)/K\hat{\sigma}^2$. For a general formulation of positive rule estimators see Judge and Bock (1978, Ch. 8).

It is in some sense remarkable that although the results of James and Stein have been available for almost a quarter of a century there has been little if any actual application of their ideas, and those they spawned, until relatively recently. The extent of the turmoil surrounding the James–Stein results largely reflects the heavy investment classical statisticians have in analysis of small sample properties and minimum variance unbiased efficiency as discussed in Chapter 3. The best, linear, unbiased and minimum variance unbiased properties of traditional estimators shown by Gauss, Markov, Fisher, Rao, Blackwell, Lehmann, Scheffe, and others, are seemingly pushed into the background by the attributes of the biased, nonlinear James–Stein estimator. In fact the very measure of "goodness" of an estimator is called into question as the importance of unbiasedness diminishes.

One's intuition about how the Stein-rule estimator works can be greatly enhanced by considering the example provided by Efron and Morris (1977). We urge the reader to study Efron and Morris' paper and will very briefly sketch their example. Suppose we are baseball fans and wish to predict the batting averages of $K \geq 3$ baseball players, say $\boldsymbol{\theta}' = (\theta_1, \theta_2, \ldots, \theta_K)$. A player's batting average is equal to the ratio of the number of base hits the player achieves to his or her total number of official times at bat at any point in the baseball season. It is always a number between zero and one. Efron and Morris consider $K = 18$ baseball players in the 1970 baseball season. The available data were the averages of the 18 players after 45 times at bat, which in our notation is $\hat{\boldsymbol{\theta}}$. Our objective is to choose an estimator for the player's season average based on $\hat{\boldsymbol{\theta}}$ where our measure of goodness is squared error loss. For the classical statistician the best linear unbiased and minimax estimator for $\boldsymbol{\theta}$, the true, season long, averages of the 18 players, is $\hat{\boldsymbol{\theta}}$, that is their arithmetic average after 45 at bats. The appropriate James–Stein estimator, assuming σ^2 unknown, is $\hat{\boldsymbol{\theta}}_1^*$ in (7.3.9) (In Efron and Morris' example they actually assume σ^2 known but this modification does not change the usefulness of the example.) Suppose in the absence of authoritative information on the batting skills of each individual we choose to shrink each player's average toward 0.265, our best estimate of the batting average of *all* major league players. Thus our vector $\boldsymbol{\theta}_1$ is an 18×1 vector and each element is 0.265. Furthermore, the term $1 - c/u$ in (7.3.9) is 0.212 for their example. Then, under the squared-error loss function the best estimate of the season long batting average of the ith player is

$$\theta_i^* = (0.212)(\hat{\theta}_i - 0.265) + 0.265. \tag{7.3.12}$$

Thus, each average is shrunk about 80% of the distance between it and our presumed overall average of 0.265.

Now let us consider some specific cases. In 1970 after 45 times at bat the late Roberto Clemente had a batting average of 0.400. The Stein-rule estimate of Clemente's season long average is $\theta_i^* = (0.212)(0.400 - 0.265) + 0.265 = 0.294$. The late Thurman Munson was batting only 0.178 after 45 at bats in 1970 and the Stein-rule estimate of his season's long average is

$$\theta_i^* = 0.212(0.178 - 0.265) + 0.265 = 0.247.$$

Thus the Stein-rule pulls up averages which are below our "prior information" average of 0.265 and pulls down averages above 0.265. Different results, however, would be obtained if a different prior vector $\boldsymbol{\theta}_1$ had been used.

Let us examine the shrinkage factor $1 - c/u$ again. Holding everything else constant, the shrinking factor is smaller the greater the value of u. Recall that

$$u = \frac{(\hat{\boldsymbol{\theta}} - \boldsymbol{\theta}_1)'(\hat{\boldsymbol{\theta}} - \boldsymbol{\theta}_1)/K}{\hat{\sigma}^2}.$$

Now $\hat{\sigma}^2$ is the estimated variability in the data. It is constant for a given set of data. Thus for a given set of data and if K is fixed, only $\boldsymbol{\theta}_1$ can affect u and thus the amount of shrinkage. The Stein-rule assumes initially that the true but unobservable values $\boldsymbol{\theta}$ are near the vector of prior estimates $\boldsymbol{\theta}_1$. If the data support this guess in the sense that all the observed averages $\hat{\boldsymbol{\theta}}$ are not too far from $\boldsymbol{\theta}_1$, then *all* the estimates are shrunk further toward the vector $\boldsymbol{\theta}_1$. On the other hand, if the observed averages are far away from $\boldsymbol{\theta}_1$ then the data does not support the initial conjecture as strongly and less shrinkage is allowed.

The amount of shrinkage toward $\boldsymbol{\theta}_1$ is also affected by the number of observations T upon which the averages are based and K the number of means to be estimated. The larger the value of K the more drastic the shrinkage is allowed since then it is less likely that the distance between $\hat{\boldsymbol{\theta}}$ and $\boldsymbol{\theta}_1$ is random. The larger the value of T the less the shrinkage is, which reflects the consistency of the maximum likelihood estimator $\hat{\boldsymbol{\theta}}$.

7.3.3 Sclove's Modified Positive-Part Rule

At this point let us briefly reconsider the traditional pretest estimator (7.2.9). Recall that this estimator chooses between the restricted estimator $\boldsymbol{\theta}^*$ and the maximum likelihood estimator $\hat{\boldsymbol{\theta}}$ on the basis of whether the test statistic $u < c$ or $u \geq c$, respectively. In Section 7.3.2 it was observed that the James and Stein positive rule estimator $\boldsymbol{\theta}^+$ in (7.3.10) dominates the maximum likelihood estimator $\hat{\boldsymbol{\theta}}$ if $K \geq 3$. It is not surprising then that if $\boldsymbol{\theta}^+$ replaces $\hat{\boldsymbol{\theta}}$ in (7.2.9), giving

$$\tilde{\boldsymbol{\theta}}^+ = I_{[0,c)}(u)\hat{\boldsymbol{\theta}}^* + I_{[c,\infty)}(u)\boldsymbol{\theta}^+, \tag{7.3.13}$$

the resulting estimator dominates the traditional pretest estimator $\tilde{\boldsymbol{\theta}}$ under squared error loss. This was shown by Sclove *et al.* (1972). Therefore, the pretest estimator (7.2.9) is inadmissible given squared error loss.

7.4 Stein-Rule Estimators for the General Linear Model

To generalize the results of Sections 7.2 and 7.3, consider the general linear model $\mathbf{y} = X\boldsymbol{\beta} + \mathbf{e}$, $X'X$ no longer being the identity matrix, with matrices and vectors having usual dimensions and $\mathbf{e} \sim N(\mathbf{0}, \sigma^2 I)$. We seek an estimator for $\boldsymbol{\beta}$ and adopt the weighted risk function

$$\mathscr{R}(\tilde{\boldsymbol{\beta}}, \boldsymbol{\beta}) = E(\tilde{\boldsymbol{\beta}} - \boldsymbol{\beta})'Q(\tilde{\boldsymbol{\beta}} - \boldsymbol{\beta})/\sigma^2, \tag{7.4.1}$$

where Q is a known $K \times K$ positive definite and symmetric matrix. Under this loss function the maximum likelihood estimator $\hat{\boldsymbol{\beta}} = (X'X)^{-1}X'\mathbf{y}$ is minimax and has constant risk, $\text{tr}(X'X)^{-1}Q$.

Judge and Bock (1978) offer a family of minimax estimators which dominate the maximum likelihood estimator if $K \geq 3$ and under certain design related conditions. This family of estimators has the form

$$\boldsymbol{\delta}(\hat{\boldsymbol{\beta}}, s) = \left[I_K - h\left(\frac{\hat{\boldsymbol{\beta}}'B\hat{\boldsymbol{\beta}}}{s}\right)C\right]\hat{\boldsymbol{\beta}}, \tag{7.4.2}$$

where B and C are known and chosen so that $Q^{1/2}CQ^{-1/2}$ and $Q^{-1/2}BQ^{-1/2}$ are positive definite matrices that commute with each other and with $Q^{1/2}(X'X)^{-1}Q^{1/2}$. Two matrices U and V are said to commute if $UV = VU$. The function $h(x) = a/x$ is a differentiable function which must obey some fairly specific conditions (Judge and Bock (1978, p. 235)), and a is a constant which for minimaxity must obey

$$0 < a \leq \frac{2[\text{tr}(C(X'X)^{-1}Q) - 2\lambda_{\max}(C(X'X)^{-1}Q)]}{(T - K + 2)\lambda_{\max}(C'QCB^{-1})}, \tag{7.4.3}$$

where $\lambda_{\max}(\cdot)$ denotes the maximum characteristic root of the matrix in parentheses.

A member from the class (7.4.2) which is like the traditional James–Stein estimator is obtained by setting $Q = C = I$ and $B = X'X$. Then (7.4.2) becomes

$$\boldsymbol{\delta}_1(\hat{\boldsymbol{\beta}}, s) = \left[1 - \frac{as}{\hat{\boldsymbol{\beta}}'X'X\hat{\boldsymbol{\beta}}}\right]\hat{\boldsymbol{\beta}}. \tag{7.4.4}$$

For $K \geq 3$ and if

$$0 \leq a \leq 2\,\frac{\{\mathrm{tr}(X'X)^{-1} - 2\lambda_{\max}[(X'X)^{-1}]\}}{(T - K + 2)\lambda_{\max}[(X'X)^{-1}]}, \tag{7.4.5}$$

the estimator (7.4.4) dominates the maximum likelihood estimator $\hat{\boldsymbol{\beta}}$. This estimator shrinks each element of the maximum likelihood estimator toward the origin. Like the simple James–Stein estimator, however, the rule in (7.4.4) can change the sign of the maximum likelihood estimator. The positive part rule which corresponds to $\boldsymbol{\delta}_1(\hat{\boldsymbol{\beta}}, s)$ is

$$\boldsymbol{\delta}_1^+(\hat{\boldsymbol{\beta}}, s) = \left(1 - \frac{as}{\hat{\boldsymbol{\beta}}'X'X\hat{\boldsymbol{\beta}}}\right)I_{[a,\infty)}\left(\frac{\hat{\boldsymbol{\beta}}'X'X\hat{\boldsymbol{\beta}}}{s}\right)\hat{\boldsymbol{\beta}}. \tag{7.4.6}$$

This estimator has risk which is less than or equal to that of $\boldsymbol{\delta}_1(\hat{\boldsymbol{\beta}}, s)$. The estimator (7.4.6) is such that if the ratio $\hat{\boldsymbol{\beta}}'X'X\hat{\boldsymbol{\beta}}/s \leq a$, which would result in in $\boldsymbol{\delta}_1(\hat{\boldsymbol{\beta}}, s)$ changing the signs of $\hat{\boldsymbol{\beta}}$, then $\boldsymbol{\delta}_1^+(\hat{\boldsymbol{\beta}}, s) = \mathbf{0}$, which in this case corresponds to the restricted estimator.

The estimator (7.4.4) may be generalized so that the shrinkage is toward any point, say $\boldsymbol{\beta}_1$. In this case the estimator is

$$\boldsymbol{\delta}_2(\hat{\boldsymbol{\beta}}, s) = \left[1 - \frac{as}{(\hat{\boldsymbol{\beta}} - \boldsymbol{\beta}_1)'X'X(\hat{\boldsymbol{\beta}} - \boldsymbol{\beta}_1)}\right](\hat{\boldsymbol{\beta}} - \boldsymbol{\beta}_1) + \boldsymbol{\beta}_1$$

and corresponding positive rule

$$\boldsymbol{\delta}_2^+(\hat{\boldsymbol{\beta}}, s) = \left[1 - \frac{as}{(\hat{\boldsymbol{\beta}} - \boldsymbol{\beta}_1)'X'X(\hat{\boldsymbol{\beta}} - \boldsymbol{\beta}_1)}\right]I_{[a,\infty)}\left[\frac{(\hat{\boldsymbol{\beta}} - \boldsymbol{\beta}_1)'X'X(\hat{\boldsymbol{\beta}} - \boldsymbol{\beta}_1)}{s}\right] \times (\hat{\boldsymbol{\beta}} - \boldsymbol{\beta}_1) + \boldsymbol{\beta}_1.$$

In all cases the constant a must obey (7.4.3) and $K \geq 3$ for these estimators to provide improvement over the usual maximum likelihood estimator. Alternatively, the ordinary least squares estimator can be shrunk toward the general restricted least squares estimator

$$\boldsymbol{\beta}^* = \hat{\boldsymbol{\beta}} - (X'X)^{-1}R'(RS^{-1}R')^{-1}(R\hat{\boldsymbol{\beta}} - \mathbf{r}).$$

In this case the general minimax estimator becomes

$$\boldsymbol{\delta}_3(\hat{\boldsymbol{\beta}}, s) = \left[1 - \frac{as}{(\mathbf{r} - R\hat{\boldsymbol{\beta}})'[R(X'X)^{-1}R']^{-1}(\mathbf{r} - R\hat{\boldsymbol{\beta}})}\right](\hat{\boldsymbol{\beta}} - \boldsymbol{\beta}^*) + \boldsymbol{\beta}^*$$

with corresponding positive rule

$$\boldsymbol{\delta}_3^+(\hat{\boldsymbol{\beta}}, s) = \left[1 - \frac{as}{(\mathbf{r} - R\hat{\boldsymbol{\beta}})'[R(X'X)^{-1}R']^{-1}(\mathbf{r} - R\hat{\boldsymbol{\beta}})}\right] \times I_{[a,\infty)}\left[\frac{(\mathbf{r} - R\hat{\boldsymbol{\beta}})'[R(X'X)^{-1}R']^{-1}(\mathbf{r} - R\hat{\boldsymbol{\beta}})}{s}\right](\hat{\boldsymbol{\beta}} - \boldsymbol{\beta}^*) + \boldsymbol{\beta}^*.$$

In this case, where the maximum likelihood estimator is shrunk toward the restricted least squares estimator, $\boldsymbol{\delta}_3$ and $\boldsymbol{\delta}_3^+$ provide improvement over the maximum likelihood estimator if $J \geq 3$ (J being the number of linear constraints on the parameter space) and if

$$0 \leq a \leq \frac{2}{T - K + 2}\left[\frac{\operatorname{tr}[(RS^{-1}R')^{-1}RS^{-1}QS^{-1}R']}{\eta_L} - 2\right],$$

where η_L is the largest characteristic root of $(RS^{-1}R')^{-1}RS^{-1}QS^{-1}R'$ (Mittelhammer (1981)). See Exercise 7.1 for discussion of how to obtain η_L.

The estimator $\boldsymbol{\delta}_3^+(\hat{\boldsymbol{\beta}}, s)$ then allows the implementation of uncertain prior information of the form $R\boldsymbol{\beta} = \mathbf{r}$ in a way such that when the information is biased it will not be weighted very heavily, as reflected by the inverse relationship between the size of the shrinkage factor $(1 - (a/u))$ and the likelihood ratio statistic u, whereas when the information is unbiased the information is strongly imposed. This stochastic (data based) weighting scheme, unlike the use of restricted least squares, insures that invalid prior information will not impose large losses in estimator efficiency relative to ordinary least squares.

7.5 Summary and Guide to Further Readings

In this chapter some of the statistical consequences of dealing with uncertain prior information have been considered. It has been noted that the frequently used practice of testing uncertain prior information as a hypothesis, and then using an estimator that either employs the information or not depending upon the outcome of the test, produces an estimator that is inferior to the usual maximum likelihood estimator based on the sample information alone over a large portion of the parameter space. Furthermore, the traditional preliminary test estimator is inadmissible under squared error loss as another estimator exists that has lower risk for all possible parameter values.

How to use uncertain nonsample information in a way that unambiguously provides a risk improvement over the usual maximum likelihood estimator is a problem that has been solved, however. The Stein-rule and its variants combine sample and nonsample information in a superior way. A risk improvement over the maximum likelihood estimator under a variety of loss functions is guaranteed *regardless* of the correctness of the nonsample information. The drawbacks of the improved estimators are that they are nonlinear, biased, have unknown small sample distributions, have covariance matrices depending on unknown population parameters and, in many cases, they improve upon the maximum likelihood estimator only if design related conditions like (7.4.5) hold. The consequences of these design related conditions will be more fully explored in Chapter 13 on multicollinearity. These estimators do, however, provide superior point estimates of parameters, under squared error loss.

By far the most useful summary of the properties of pretest estimators is found in Judge and Bock (1978). They present proofs of basic theorems and investigate the properties of the pretest estimator for the orthonormal and general regression models. In addition, the pretest estimator that arises when stochastic nonsample information is evaluated using the compatibility statistic is investigated in their Chapter 6. The autocorrelation pretest estimator, that chooses between ordinary least squares and feasible generalized least squares depending on a test for autocorrelation, is also studied. Fomby and Guilkey (1978) further investigate the properties of the autocorrelation pretest estimator and, in particular, study the effect of changing the level of significance of the test for autocorrelation. Greenberg (1980) and Ohtani and Toyoda (1980) study the properties of the pretest estimator obtained after a test for possible heteroscedasticity. Han and Bancroft (1978) and Farebrother (1978) consider the preliminary test decision to pool or not pool data.

Judge and Bock (1978), Vinod and Ullah (1981) and Greenberg and Webster (1983) also survey the literature related to Stein-rules. Examples of the application of Stein-rules can be found in Aigner and Judge (1977) and Hill *et al.* (1978). Hill and Ziemer (1982) and Oman (1978) consider the effects of multicollinearity (see Chapter 13) on the performance of Stein-like rules. Vinod (1980) considers a generalization of the Stein-like and applies it to multicollinear data.

7.6 Exercises

7.1. Note that the matrix $(RS^{-1}R')^{-1}RS^{-1}QS^{-1}R'$ is not symmetric. While computer software is widely available to compute the characteristic roots and vectors of symmetric matrices, software to do the same for nonsymmetric matrices is less readily available since roots of nonsymmetric matrices are not necessarily real. In this case, however, the difficulty is resolved by using the fact that the characteristic roots of A are those of BAB^{-1}, where A and B are nonsingular matrices. Show that this result is true and apply it to the current problem. (Hint: Let $B = (RS^{-1}R')^{1/2}$.)

7.2. (Class Exercise). Carry out a Monte Carlo experiment to numerically generate the risk functions, as in Figure 7.3.2, for $\hat{\boldsymbol{\theta}} = Z'\mathbf{y}$, the maximum likelihood estimator, $\boldsymbol{\theta}^*$, the Stein-rule estimator (7.3.7), and $\boldsymbol{\theta}^+$, the positive-rule estimator (7.3.10).

Assume the squared error loss measure. The steps involved are:

(1) Construct a $T \times K$ design matrix Z such that $Z'Z = I$ using, for example, the transformation in Section 7.2.1. Choose $T = 20$ and $K = 4$. (The choices are unimportant as long as $K \geq 3$.)
(2) Select sets of parameter vectors $\boldsymbol{\theta}$ such that their squared length $\boldsymbol{\theta}'\boldsymbol{\theta}$ varies from zero to, say, 100. So that the portions of the risk function near the origin may be carefully plotted, select $\boldsymbol{\theta}$'s so that $\boldsymbol{\theta}'\boldsymbol{\theta} = 0, 1, \ldots, 10, 20, \ldots, 100$. Assign one parameter vector to each student in class.
(3) Each student should generate 100 samples of size T using the model $\mathbf{y} = Z\boldsymbol{\theta} + \mathbf{e}$, where the random disturbances are generated from a random number generator such that $\mathbf{e} \sim N(\mathbf{0}, I)$.
(4) For each sample construct $\hat{\boldsymbol{\theta}}$, $\boldsymbol{\theta}^*$ and $\boldsymbol{\theta}^+$. Measure the empirical risk for each estimator, for example, as

$$\sum_{i=1}^{100} (\hat{\boldsymbol{\theta}}_{(i)} - \boldsymbol{\theta})'(\hat{\boldsymbol{\theta}}_{(i)} - \boldsymbol{\theta})/100,$$

where $\hat{\boldsymbol{\theta}}_{(i)}$ is the estimator for the ith sample.
(5) Plot the empirical risk for each estimator as a function of $\lambda = \boldsymbol{\delta}'\boldsymbol{\delta}/2\sigma^2 = \boldsymbol{\theta}'\boldsymbol{\theta}/2$.

7.3. In Chapter 17, finite distributed lag models are discussed. These models have the form

$$y_t = \bar{\beta} + \sum_{i=0}^{n} \beta_i x_{t-i} + e_t, \qquad t = n+1, \ldots, T.$$

Restrictions are frequently placed on the parameters β_i so that they fall on a relatively low-order polynomial. That is, restrictions of the form

$$\beta_i = \sum_{j=0}^{q} \alpha_j i^j, \qquad i = 0, \ldots, n$$

are imposed, where q is the degree of the polynomial.

Almon (1965) used this model to study the relationship between capital expenditures in time t (y_t) by manufacturing firms and their capital appropriations (x_t). Let $n = 8$ so that the vector of unknown parameters is $\boldsymbol{\beta}' = (\bar{\beta}, \beta_0, \beta_1, \ldots, \beta_8)$

(a) Using the data in Table 7.6.1 for 1953–1969, obtain ordinary least squares estimates $\hat{\boldsymbol{\beta}}$, of the parameters.
(b) Without being concerned at this point by the source of the restrictions, let $\mathbf{r} = \mathbf{0}$,

$$R = \begin{bmatrix} 0 & 1 & -8 & 28 & -56 & 70 & -56 & 38 & -8 & 1 \\ 0 & -1 & 6 & -14 & 14 & 0 & -14 & 14 & -6 & 1 \\ 0 & 4 & -17 & 22 & 1 & -20 & 1 & 22 & -17 & 4 \\ 0 & -4 & 11 & -4 & -9 & 0 & 9 & 4 & -11 & 4 \\ 0 & 14 & -21 & -11 & 9 & 18 & 9 & -11 & -21 & 14 \\ 0 & -14 & 7 & 13 & 9 & 0 & -9 & -13 & -7 & 14 \end{bmatrix}$$

and impose the restrictions $R\boldsymbol{\beta} = \mathbf{r}$ using the restricted least squares estimator. The restricted least squares estimates $\boldsymbol{\beta}^*$ will fall on a polynomial of degree 2.

Table 7.6.1 Capital expenditures (y_t) and appropriations (x_t) for U.S. manufacturing firms, seasonally adjusted and in real 1958 dollars.*

Year Qtr.	y_t, Millions of constant dollars	x_t, Millions of constant dollars	Year Qtr.	y_t, Millions of constant dollars	x_t, Millions of constant dollars
1953 I	2494	2127	1964 I	3002	3923
1953 II	2500	2455	1964 II	3148	4408
1953 III	2501	2707	1964 III	3359	4621
1953 IV	2459	2426	1964 IV	3642	4099
1954 I	2456	2191	1965 I	3854	4793
1954 II	2447	2177	1965 II	4046	5187
1954 III	2327	2208	1965 III	4308	5207
1954 IV	2340	2672	1965 IV	4536	5688
1955 I	2261	3147	1966 I	4903	6079
1955 II	2353	3804	1966 II	5048	6193
1955 III	2327	2208	1966 III	5289	5402
1955 IV	2703	4540	1966 IV	5449	5417
1956 I	3044	4475	1967 I	5452	5367
1956 II	3329	4068	1967 II	5308	5271
1956 III	3456	3633	1967 III	4995	5161
1956 IV	3661	3620	1967 IV	5071	5176
1957 I	3780	3755	1968 I	4945	5183
1957 II	3724	3293	1968 II	4875	4941
1957 III	3624	2465	1968 III	5032	5451
1957 IV	3308	2337	1968 IV	5750	6040
1958 I	2770	1964	1969 I	5170	5760
1958 II	2375	1940	1969 II	5363	6488
1958 III	2147	2200	1969 III	5651	6255
1958 IV	2023	2217	1969 IV	5750	6040
1959 I	2075	2642	1970 I	5570	5401
1959 II	2191	2877	1970 II	5528	5144
1959 III	2223	3048	1970 III	5419	4943
1959 IV	2378	3058	1970 IV	5100	4502
1960 I	2582	2795	1971 I	4926	4396
1960 II	2666	2444	1971 II	4658	4226
1960 III	2656	2206	1971 III	4482	4471
1960 IV	2570	2633	1971 IV	4577	4516
1961 I	2439	2335	1972 I	4373	4916
1961 II	2378	2381	1972 II	4438	5288
1961 III	2360	2616	1972 III	4434	5312
1961 IV	2456	2590	1972 IV	4643	6238
1962 I	2461	2878	1973 I	4962	7191
1962 II	2404	2418	1973 II	5166	7914
1962 III	2491	2708	1973 III	5556	8409
1962 IV	2475	3029	1973 IV	5929	8577
1963 I	2501	2648	1974 I	6472	8791
1963 II	2548	3127	1974 II	6915	9937
1963 III	2731	3495	1974 III	7495	10420
1963 IV	2823	3777	1974 IV	7999	7718

* SOURCE: The Conference Board.

(c) Assume $Q = X'X$ and obtain the general minimax and positive-rule estimates $\boldsymbol{\delta}_3$ and $\boldsymbol{\delta}_3^+$. Can these rules be applied if $Q = I$?
(d) Obtain post-sample predictions, using the data in Table 7.6.1 for 1970–1974, for each of the estimators and compare.
(e) See Trivedi (1978) for further reading on this problem.

7.4. Write the model presented in Exercise 7.3 as $\mathbf{y} = X\boldsymbol{\beta} + \mathbf{e}$. To combat multicollinearity (see Chapter 13) principal components regression is sometimes advocated. Let $A'X'XA = \Lambda = \text{diag}(\lambda_1, \ldots, \lambda_K)$ such that $\lambda_1 \geq \lambda_2 \geq \cdots \geq \lambda_K$. Principal components regression can then be shown to be equivalent to applying restricted least squares using the restrictions $R\boldsymbol{\beta} = \mathbf{0}$ where $R = A_2'$, where A is partitioned as $A = (A_1 \vdots A_2)$. Let A_2 contain the characteristic vectors associated with the six smallest characteristic roots of $X'X$. Obtain the restricted least squares estimates, $\boldsymbol{\beta}^*$, as well as $\boldsymbol{\delta}_3$ and $\boldsymbol{\delta}_3^+$ for $Q = X'X$, using the data in Table 7.6.1 for 1953–1969. For each estimator obtain the predicted values of y_t for 1970–1974 and compare.

7.7 References

Aigner, D. J., and Judge, G. G. (1977). Application of pre-test and Stein estimators to economic data. *Econometrica*, **45**, 1279–1280.

Akaike, H. (1974). A new look at the statistical identification model. *I.E.E.E.: Transactions on Automatic Control*, **19**, 716–723.

Almon, S. (1965). The distributed lag between capital appropriations and expenditures. *Econometrica*, **33**, 178–196.

Amemiya, T. (1980). Selection of regressors. *International Economic Review*, **21**, 331–354.

Brook, R. J. (1976). On the use of a regret function to set significance points in prior tests of estimation. *Journal of the American Statistical Association*, **71**, 126–131.

Draper, N. and Smith, H. (1966). *Applied Regression Analysis*. New York: Wiley.

Efron, R. and Morris, C. (1977). Stein's paradox in statistics. *Scientific American*, **236**, 119–127.

Farebrother, R. W. (1978). Estimating regression coefficients under conditional specification: comment. *Communications in Statistics*, A, **7**, 193–196.

Fomby, T. B. and Guilkey, D. K. (1978). On choosing the optimal level of significance for the Durbin–Watson test and the Bayesian alternative. *Journal of Econometrics*, **8**, 203–214.

Greenberg, E. (1980). Finite sample moments of a preliminary test estimator in the case of possible heteroscedasticity. *Econometrica*, **48**, 1805–1814.

Greenberg, E. and Webster, C. (1983). *Advanced Econometrics: A Bridge to the Literature*. New York: Wiley.

Han, C. and Bancroft, T. A. (1978). Estimating regression coefficients under conditional specification. *Communications in Statistics*, A, **7**, 47–56.

Hill, R. C. and Ziemer, R. (1982). The application of generalized ridge and Stein-like general minimax rules to multicollinear data. *Communications in Statistics*, **A, 11**, 623–638.

Hill, R. C., Judge, G. G., and Fomby, T. B. (1978). On testing the adequacy of the regression equation. *Technometrics*, **20**, 491–494.

James, W. and Stein, C. (1961). Estimation with quadratic loss, *Proceedings of the Fourth Berkeley Symposium on Mathematical Statistics and Probability*, **1**, 361–379.

Judge, G. and Bock, M. (1978). *Statistical Implications of Pretest and Stein-Rule Estimators in Econometrics*. Amsterdam: North-Holland.

Judge, G., Yancey, T., and Bock, M. (1973). Properties of estimators after preliminary tests of significance when stochastic restrictions are used in regression. *Journal of Econometrics*, **1**, 29–48.

Judge, G., Griffiths, W., Hill, R. and Lee, T. (1980). *The Theory and Practice of Econometrics*. New York: Wiley.

Mallows, C. (1973). Some comments on *Cp*. *Technometrics*, **15**, 661–676.

Mittlehammer, R. (1981). Unpublished mimeo, Washington State University.

Ohtani, K. and Toyoda, T. (1980). Estimation of regression coefficients after a preliminary test for homoscedasticity. *Journal of Econometrics*, **12**, 151–160.

Oman, S. D. (1978). A Bayesian comparison of some estimators used in linear regression with multicollinear data. *Communications in Statistics*, A, **7**, 517–534.

Sawa, T. (1977). Information criteria for discriminating among alternative regression models. Faculty Working Paper 455, University of Illinois.

Sawa, T. and Hiromatsu, T. (1973). Minimax regret significance points for a preliminary test in regression analysis. *Econometrica*, **41**, 1093–1101.

Sclove, S., Morris, C., and Radharkrishnan, R. (1972). Non-optimality of preliminary test estimators for the mean of a multivariate normal distribution. *The Annals of Mathematical Statistics*, **43**, 1481–1490.

Stein, C. (1956). Inadmissibility of the usual estimator for the mean of a multivariate normal distribution. *Proceedings of the Third Berkeley Symposium*, **1**, 197–206.

Toro-Vizcarrondo, C. and Wallace, T. (1968). A test of the mean square error criterion for restrictions in linear regression. *Journal of the American Statistical Association*, **63**, 558–572.

Toyoda, T. and Wallace, T. (1976). Optimal critical values for pretesting in regression. *Econometrica*, **44**, 365–376.

Trivedi, P. K. (1978). Estimation of a distributed lag model under quadratic loss. *Econometrica*, **46**, 1181–1192.

Vinod, H. D. (1980). Improved Stein-rule estimator for regression problems. *Journal of Econometrics*, **12**, 143–150.

Vinod, H. D. and Ullah, H. (1981). *Recent Advances in Regression Methods*. New York: Marcel Dekker.

Wallace, T. (1972). Weaker criteria and tests for linear restrictions in regression. *Econometrica*, **40**, 689–698.

PART II

VIOLATIONS OF BASIC ASSUMPTIONS

The following five chapters constitute Part II of this book. The classical linear regression model and its extension, the classical normal linear regression model, represent the classical assumptions of regression analysis. According to Aitken's theorem (Chapter 2), the use of ordinary least squares in the presence of nonspherical errors causes a loss of estimation efficiency and provides an inappropriate framework for statistical inference. Naturally the violation of the spherical error assumption of the classical regression models is a cause for concern and, when appropriate, adjustments should be made. Two basic characterizations of nonspherical disturbances are heteroscedasticity and autocorrelation. Estimation and tests of hypotheses for errors with these properties are the subjects of Chapters 9 and 10. The estimation method used to correct for both heteroscedasticity and autocorrelation is called feasible generalized least squares. The term "feasible" describes the fact that the unknown error parameters are replaced by consistent estimates thus making operational what would otherwise be a nonoperational generalized least squares estimator. The method of feasible generalized least squares and its properties are discussed in Chapter 8.

Another violation of the classical linear regression model is that of contemporaneous correlation between the error term and an explanatory variable. In such circumstances, the ordinary least squares estimator is inconsistent and inefficient. Two occasions where the contemporaneous correlation condition arises are when coefficients must be estimated in the lagged dependent variable–serial correlation model and in the unobservable variables model. Consistent and efficient methods of estimation for these models are presented in Chapters 11 and 12.

CHAPTER 8

Feasible Generalized Least Squares Estimation

8.1 Introduction

There are instances in econometric modeling when an investigator is willing to specify the structure of the error variance–covariance matrix, Ω, of a generalized least squares model up to a few unknown parameters, say $\theta_1, \theta_2, \ldots, \theta_p$. This would occur, for example, when correlation in the errors of a time series regression model is suspected or when cross-sections of data are expected to satisfy a regression relationship with varying precisions. These parametrizations of Ω, which previously have been discussed in general form, will be discussed in detail in the following chapters. For the present, we will continue to discuss Ω in general terms, not limiting our discussion in any way except that the parametrization of Ω is assumed to be parasimonious enough to allow estimation.

The major discussion of this chapter will center around the estimation of Ω when it is unknown and the consequences of this estimation on the properties of the estimators of the parameters of the generalized least squares model. In Section 8.2 the feasible generalized least squares estimator is defined. In Section 8.3 the properties of feasible generalized least squares estimators are examined in two contexts, one without normality of the errors assumed and the other with normality assumed. The first-order conditions and information matrix of the maximum likelihood estimators of the generalized least squares model with unknown Ω are also developed. The model of seemingly unrelated regressions is introduced in Section 8.4 to illustrate a basic application of the feasible generalized least squares method. The large sample and small sample properties of the feasible generalized least squares estimator of the seemingly unrelated regressions model are developed in Sections 8.5 and 8.6. Under the standard conditions of seemingly unrelated regressions, the feasible generalized least squares estimator has all the properties previously developed in Section 8.3. Though the small sample properties of feasible generalized least squares estimators are, in general, unknown, some of the known small sample properties of the feasible generalized least squares estimator of the seemingly unrelated regressions model are discussed and interpreted. The results of the chapter are summarized in Section 8.7 and a guide to further readings is provided.

8.2 Definition of Feasible Generalized Least Squares

Before formally defining terms, let us motivate the issue by considering the following example. Recall that the generalized least squares model is of the form

$$\mathbf{y} = X\boldsymbol{\beta} + \mathbf{e}, \tag{8.2.1}$$

where X is a $T \times K$ matrix of nonstochastic elements of rank K satisfying the limit condition

$$\lim_{T\to\infty}\left(\frac{X'\Omega^{-1}X}{T}\right) = Q_\Omega, \tag{8.2.2}$$

Q_Ω being a $K \times K$ finite and nonsingular matrix. The error vector $\mathbf{e}$ satisfies the properties

$$E\mathbf{e} = \mathbf{0} \tag{8.2.3}$$

and

$$E\mathbf{e}\mathbf{e}' = \sigma^2\Omega. \tag{8.2.4}$$

Suppose, for example, that rather than being independently and identically distributed with zero mean and variance σ^2, the errors e_t follow the first-order autoregressive process

$$e_t = \rho e_{t-1} + u_t, \qquad |\rho| < 1, \tag{8.2.5}$$

with the u_t being independently and identically distributed with zero mean and finite variance σ_u^2. In Chapter 10 it will be shown that $E\mathbf{e}\mathbf{e}' = \sigma_u^2\Omega$ where

$$\sigma_u^2\Omega = \frac{\sigma_u^2}{1-\rho^2}\begin{bmatrix} 1 & \rho & & \cdots & \rho^{T-1} \\ \rho & 1 & \rho & \cdots & \rho^{T-2} \\ \rho^2 & \rho & 1 & & \vdots \\ \vdots & \vdots & & \ddots & \rho \\ \rho^{T-1} & \rho^{T-2} & \cdots & \rho & 1 \end{bmatrix} \tag{8.2.6}$$

and Ω is implicitly defined in (8.2.6).

To this point, it has been assumed that the error covariance matrix is known up to a scalar multiple. However, the most prevalent case is when Ω is *unknown* and Ω can be thought of as defining a class of error structures, with the appropriate member yet to be determined. The members of this class are often indexed by a set of unknown parameters. For example, the serial correlation coefficient ρ in (8.2.6) indexes the covariance structure. Note σ_u^2 is not needed to index Ω as generalized least squares estimation only requires that the error covariance be known up to a scalar multiple.

Now we present some relevant definitions.

Definition 8.2.1. If Ω depends on a finite number of parameters $\theta_1, \theta_2, \ldots, \theta_p$, and if $\hat{\Omega}$ depends on consistent estimators $\hat{\theta}_1, \hat{\theta}_2, \ldots, \hat{\theta}_p$, then $\hat{\Omega}$ is called a *consistent estimator* of Ω.

Definition 8.2.2. Let $\hat{\Omega}$ be a consistent estimator of Ω. Then the feasible generalized least squares estimator of $\boldsymbol{\beta}$ is

$$\tilde{\tilde{\boldsymbol{\beta}}} = (X'\hat{\Omega}^{-1}X)^{-1}X'\hat{\Omega}^{-1}\mathbf{y}. \tag{8.2.7}$$

In terms of estimating Ω, a first reaction might be to use the ordinary least squares residuals directly. A proposed estimator could be

$$\hat{\Omega} = (\mathbf{y} - X\hat{\boldsymbol{\beta}})(\mathbf{y} - X\hat{\boldsymbol{\beta}})'.$$

Unfortunately, several problems arise with such a procedure. First, the rank of $\hat{\Omega}$ is one and hence $\hat{\Omega}$ is singular. Therefore, $\hat{\Omega}^{-1}$ cannot be computed and hence $\tilde{\tilde{\boldsymbol{\beta}}}$ cannot be calculated. Second, in general, there are $T(T+1)/2$ distinct elements in Ω and only T observations. Therefore the number of parameters in the unstructured generalized least squares model is

$$T(T+1)/2 + K > T$$

and insufficient degrees of freedom persist no matter what the sample size. Obviously, a structure must be assumed for Ω such that the following minimal properties will hold:

(i) rank $\hat{\Omega} = T$ (thus $\hat{\Omega}^{-1}$ exists),
(ii) the number of parameters in Ω, say p, must be small enough so that $K + p \leq T$ and
(iii) consistent estimates of the parameters in Ω must exist, i.e., plim $\hat{\theta}_i = \theta_i$, $i = 1, 2, \ldots, p$.

In chapters to follow, various parametrization schemes for Ω will be discussed which will allow estimation of Ω and the other parameters of the generalized least squares model.

8.3 Properties of Feasible Generalized Least Squares Estimators

Under the conditions of the generalized least squares model, the generalized least squares (Aitken) estimator is the best linear unbiased estimator of $\boldsymbol{\beta}$. If, in addition, the error terms are normally distributed, the generalized least squares estimator takes on the additional property of minimum variance unbiased, where the class of estimators being compared includes nonlinear as well as linear ones. In the following two subsections we will discuss what properties of the generalized least squares estimators are retained and which are lost when the estimation of Ω becomes necessary. First, the properties of the feasible generalized least squares estimator $\tilde{\tilde{\boldsymbol{\beta}}}$ in the absence of normally distributed errors are discussed.

8.3.1 Feasible Generalized Least Squares in the Absence of Normal Errors

Consider the generalized least squares model of Definition 2.5.1. No specific distribution for the error terms need be assumed to derive many useful properties of feasible generalized least squares estimators. Obviously, Aitken's theorem (Theorem 2.5.1) no longer applies since Ω is unknown and must be estimated. Thus, the feasible generalized least squares estimator $\tilde{\tilde{\boldsymbol{\beta}}}$ of Definition 8.2.2 is not best linear unbiased. But as Kakwani (1967) has shown, $\tilde{\tilde{\boldsymbol{\beta}}}$ is still unbiased under general conditions. Also, as shown by Zellner (1962) and discussed in detail by Schmidt (1976), most of the properties of generalized least squares estimation remain intact in large samples when the need to implement feasible generalized least squares estimation arises. Consider the results summarized in the following theorem:

Theorem 8.3.1 (Feasible Generalized Least Squares in the Absence of Normally Distributed Errors). *Assume the conditions of the generalized least squares model* (*Definition* 2.5.1) *are satisfied but, in addition, assume that*

(i) *there exists a* P' *matrix such that* $PP' = \Omega^{-1}$ *and the elements of* $P'\mathbf{e}$ *are independently and identically distributed*;

(ii)
$$\operatorname{plim} \frac{X'\hat{\Omega}^{-1}X}{T} = \operatorname{plim} \frac{X'\Omega^{-1}X}{T} = Q_{\Omega}, \tag{8.3.1}$$

where Q_{Ω} *is finite and nonsingular*;

(iii)
$$\operatorname{plim} \frac{X'\hat{\Omega}^{-1}\mathbf{e}}{T} = \operatorname{plim} \frac{X'\Omega^{-1}\mathbf{e}}{T} = \mathbf{0}; \tag{8.3.2}$$

and

(iv)
$$\operatorname{plim} \frac{1}{T} \mathbf{e}'\hat{\Omega}^{-1}\mathbf{e} = \operatorname{plim} \frac{1}{T} \mathbf{e}'\Omega^{-1}\mathbf{e} = \sigma^2. \tag{8.3.3}$$

The feasible generalized least squares estimator $\tilde{\tilde{\boldsymbol{\beta}}}$ *is consistent,* $\sqrt{T}(\tilde{\tilde{\boldsymbol{\beta}}} - \boldsymbol{\beta})$ *is distributed, asymptotically,* $N(\mathbf{0}, \sigma^2 Q_\Omega^{-1})$ *and*

$$\tilde{\tilde{\sigma}}^2 = \frac{(\mathbf{y} - X\tilde{\tilde{\boldsymbol{\beta}}})'\hat{\Omega}^{-1}(\mathbf{y} - X\tilde{\tilde{\boldsymbol{\beta}}})}{(T - K)}$$

is a consistent estimator of σ^2. *From the result of asymptotic normality, the statistic*

$$t = \frac{\tilde{\tilde{\beta}}_s - \beta_s^0}{\sqrt{q_{ss}}}, \tag{8.3.4}$$

where β_s *is the* sth *element of* $\boldsymbol{\beta}$ *and* q_{ss} *is the* sth *diagonal element of* $\tilde{\tilde{\sigma}}^2(X'\hat{\Omega}^{-1}X)^{-1}$, *is asymptotically distributed as a* $N(0, 1)$ *random variable under the null hypothesis* $H_0\colon \beta_s = \beta_s^0$. *Since the t-distribution converges to the* $N(0, 1)$ *distribution as* $T \to \infty$, *the conventional t-test of coefficient significance obtains. Similarly, the test of the general linear hypothesis* $R\boldsymbol{\beta} = \mathbf{r}$ *also obtains in that the statistic*

$$\frac{(R\tilde{\tilde{\boldsymbol{\beta}}} - \mathbf{r})'[R(X'\hat{\Omega}^{-1}X)^{-1}R']^{-1}(R\tilde{\tilde{\boldsymbol{\beta}}} - \mathbf{r})/J}{(\mathbf{y} - X\tilde{\tilde{\boldsymbol{\beta}}})'\hat{\Omega}^{-1}(\mathbf{y} - X\tilde{\tilde{\boldsymbol{\beta}}})/(T - K)} \tag{8.3.5}$$

is asymptotically distributed as an F random variable with J and $T - K$ *degrees of freedom under the null hypothesis* $H_0\colon R\boldsymbol{\beta} = \mathbf{r}$.

PROOF. See Zellner (1962) and Schmidt (1976) for details. □

In summary, the asymptotic properties of the feasible generalized least squares estimators are the same as their generalized least squares counterparts. In large samples, the conventional tests of hypotheses obtain. What is lost when Ω is not known, is the property of best linear unbiased provided by Aitken's theorem and the minimum variance unbiased property, both of which are small sample properties.

Though Aitken's theorem does not hold when Ω is unknown, it does suggest efficiency gains which are obtained when the errors of the feasible generalized least squares model are normally distributed.

8.3.2 Feasible Generalized Least Squares in the Presence of Normal Errors

In this section, the assumptions of Theorem 8.3.1 are assumed to hold and additionally, the errors $\mathbf{e}$ are assumed to have a multivariate normal distribution. Magnus (1978) gives a complete discussion of maximum likelihood estimation of the generalized least squares model with unknown error covariance matrix. Without loss of generality, Magnus assumes $\sigma^2 = 1$ and that $E\mathbf{ee}' = \Omega$, where Ω is positive definite with elements which are twice differentiable functions of $\theta_1, \theta_2, \ldots, \theta_p$. In addition, his paper analyzes the case where X is a *nonstochastic* matrix (this rules out lagged dependent variables) of full rank and $T > K$ and the parameters $\boldsymbol{\beta}$ are assumed independent of $\theta_1, \theta_2, \ldots, \theta_p$. The following theorem provides the general first-order conditions for the feasible generalized least squares model with normally distributed errors and unknown error covariance matrix Ω.

Theorem 8.3.2 (Magnus: Feasible Generalized Least Squares with Normally Distributed Errors). *With the above assumptions, the solutions for the first-order maximum likelihood conditions for* $\boldsymbol{\beta}$ *and* $\boldsymbol{\theta}' = (\theta_1, \theta_2, \ldots, \theta_p)$ *are*:

$$\check{\boldsymbol{\beta}} = (X'\check{\Omega}^{-1}X)^{-1}X'\check{\Omega}^{-1}\mathbf{y}, \tag{8.3.6}$$

$$\operatorname{tr}\left(\frac{\partial\Omega^{-1}}{\partial\theta_h}\Omega\right)_{\boldsymbol{\theta}=\check{\boldsymbol{\theta}}} = \check{\mathbf{e}}'\left(\frac{\partial\Omega^{-1}}{\partial\theta_h}\right)_{\boldsymbol{\theta}=\check{\boldsymbol{\theta}}}\check{\mathbf{e}}, \qquad h = 1, 2, \ldots, p, \tag{8.3.7}$$

where $\check{\mathbf{e}} = \mathbf{y} - X\check{\boldsymbol{\beta}}$. *Equations* (8.3.7) *will hereafter be referred to as the* $\boldsymbol{\theta}$-equations. *Further, if* $|\Omega|$ *does not depend on* θ_h, *the hth equation of* (8.3.7) *reduces to*

$$\check{\mathbf{e}}'\left(\frac{\partial\Omega^{-1}}{\partial\theta_h}\right)_{\boldsymbol{\theta}=\check{\boldsymbol{\theta}}}\check{\mathbf{e}} = 0. \tag{8.3.8}$$

PROOF. The likelihood function is

$$L = |2\pi|^{-T/2}|\Omega|^{-1/2}\exp[-\tfrac{1}{2}(\mathbf{y} - X\boldsymbol{\beta})'\Omega^{-1}(\mathbf{y} - X\boldsymbol{\beta})],$$

$$\ln L = -\frac{T}{2}\ln 2\pi - \tfrac{1}{2}\ln|\Omega| - \tfrac{1}{2}(\mathbf{y} - X\boldsymbol{\beta})'\Omega^{-1}(\mathbf{y} - X\boldsymbol{\beta}). \tag{8.3.9}$$

The first-order conditions are

$$\begin{aligned}
\frac{\partial \ln L}{\partial\boldsymbol{\beta}} &= \frac{\partial}{\partial\boldsymbol{\beta}}[-\tfrac{1}{2}(\mathbf{y} - X\boldsymbol{\beta})'\Omega^{-1}(\mathbf{y} - X\boldsymbol{\beta})] \\
&= \frac{\partial}{\partial\boldsymbol{\beta}}[-\tfrac{1}{2}\mathbf{y}'\Omega^{-1}\mathbf{y} + \tfrac{1}{2}\boldsymbol{\beta}'X'\Omega^{-1}\mathbf{y} + \tfrac{1}{2}\mathbf{y}'\Omega^{-1}X\boldsymbol{\beta} - \tfrac{1}{2}\boldsymbol{\beta}'X'\Omega^{-1}X\boldsymbol{\beta}] \\
&= X'\Omega^{-1}\mathbf{y} - X'\Omega^{-1}X\boldsymbol{\beta}, \qquad (8.3.10) \\
\frac{\partial \ln L}{\partial\theta_h} &= \frac{\partial}{\partial\theta_h}[-\tfrac{1}{2}\ln|\Omega| - \tfrac{1}{2}(\mathbf{y} - X\boldsymbol{\beta})'\Omega^{-1}(\mathbf{y} - X\boldsymbol{\beta})] \\
&= \frac{\partial}{\partial\theta_h}(\tfrac{1}{2}\ln|\Omega^{-1}|) - \tfrac{1}{2}(\mathbf{y} - X\boldsymbol{\beta})'\frac{\partial\Omega^{-1}}{\partial\theta_h}(\mathbf{y} - X\boldsymbol{\beta}) \\
&= \tfrac{1}{2}\operatorname{tr}\left(\frac{\partial\Omega^{-1}}{\partial\theta_h}\Omega\right) - \tfrac{1}{2}\mathbf{e}'\left(\frac{\partial\Omega^{-1}}{\partial\theta_h}\right)\mathbf{e} \qquad (8.3.11)
\end{aligned}$$

for $h = 1, 2, \ldots, p$. The last equality follows from the fact that

$$\frac{\partial \ln |V|}{\partial \theta_h} = \operatorname{tr}\left(V^{-1}\frac{\partial V}{\partial \theta_h}\right),$$

where V is an arbitrary nonsingular matrix which is a function of θ_h. It follows that the maximum likelihood estimator of $\boldsymbol{\beta}$ is

$$\check{\boldsymbol{\beta}} = (X'\check{\Omega}^{-1}X)^{-1}X'\check{\Omega}^{-1}\mathbf{y}$$

and the maximum likelihood estimators, $\check{\theta}_1, \check{\theta}_2, \ldots, \check{\theta}_p$, satisfy the p equations

$$\operatorname{tr}\left(\frac{\partial\Omega^{-1}}{\partial\theta_h}\Omega\right)_{\boldsymbol{\theta}=\check{\boldsymbol{\theta}}} = \check{\mathbf{e}}'\left(\frac{\partial\Omega^{-1}}{\partial\theta_h}\right)_{\boldsymbol{\theta}=\check{\boldsymbol{\theta}}}\check{\mathbf{e}}, \qquad h = 1, 2, \ldots, p.$$

Obviously, if $|\Omega|$ does not depend on θ_h, the normal equation for θ_h becomes

$$\check{\mathbf{e}}'\left(\frac{\partial\Omega^{-1}}{\partial\theta_h}\right)_{\boldsymbol{\theta}=\check{\boldsymbol{\theta}}}\check{\mathbf{e}} = 0. \qquad \square$$

Given Ω, the normal equations for $\check{\boldsymbol{\beta}}$ are linear and hence are easily solved. However, the $\boldsymbol{\theta}$-equations are highly nonlinear and in most cases the maximum likelihood estimators $\check{\theta}_h$ cannot be solved for analytically. In such cases, the following iterative maximum likelihood procedure is operational.

(i) Choose $\boldsymbol{\theta} = \boldsymbol{\theta}_0 \in \boldsymbol{\Theta}$, the class of admissible values of $\boldsymbol{\theta}$.
(ii) Calculate $\Omega_0^{-1} = \Omega^{-1}(\boldsymbol{\theta}_0)$

$$\mathbf{b}_0 = (X'\Omega_0^{-1}X)^{-1}X'\Omega_0^{-1}\mathbf{y},$$

$$\mathbf{e}_0 = \mathbf{y} - X\mathbf{b}_0.$$

(iii) Substitute $\mathbf{e}_0$ into the $\boldsymbol{\theta}$-equations (8.3.11). This gives p (nonlinear) equations in p unknowns $\theta_1, \theta_2, \ldots, \theta_p$. The value of $\boldsymbol{\theta}$, say $\boldsymbol{\theta}_1$, which satisfies these equations is obtained.
(iv) Calculate $\Omega_1^{-1} = \Omega^{-1}(\boldsymbol{\theta}_1)$

$$\mathbf{b}_1 = (X'\Omega_1^{-1}X)^{-1}X'\Omega_1^{-1}\mathbf{y}$$

and continue until convergence.

Given a strictly concave likelihood function (as shown by a strictly negative definite second-order derivative matrix) the above iterative procedure will converge to the global maximum which is the consistent root desired. For a general nonlinear maximum likelihood function, however, there is the possibility of local maxima.

Given the likelihood function (8.3.9), the maximum likelihood information matrix is given in the following theorem.

Theorem 8.3.3. *The information matrix of the likelihood function* (8.3.9) *is*

$$I = \begin{bmatrix} X'\Omega^{-1}X & 0 \\ 0 & \frac{1}{2}\Psi \end{bmatrix},$$

where Ψ *is a symmetric* $p \times p$ *matrix with typical element*

$$(\Psi)_{ij} = \operatorname{tr}\left(\frac{\partial \Omega^{-1}}{\partial \theta_i}\,\Omega\,\frac{\partial \Omega^{-1}}{\partial \theta_j}\,\Omega\right), \qquad i, j = 1, 2, \ldots, p.$$

Proof. Evaluation of $-E[\partial^2 \ln L/\partial \boldsymbol{\theta}\, \partial \boldsymbol{\theta}']$ provides the required result. See Exercise 8.2. □

It follows that the asymptotic covariance matrix for the maximum likelihood estimates $\check{\boldsymbol{\beta}}$ and $\check{\boldsymbol{\theta}}$ obtained from the iterative procedure is

$$\frac{1}{T} \lim_{T\to\infty} \left(\frac{I}{T}\right)^{-1}.$$

A consistent estimate of this asymptotic covariance matrix is

$$\check{I}^{-1} = \begin{bmatrix} (X'\check{\Omega}^{-1}X)^{-1} & 0 \\ 0 & 2\check{\Psi}^{-1} \end{bmatrix},$$

where all the unknown parameters of Ω and Ψ have been replaced by their maximum likelihood estimates.

From the basic maximum likelihood theorem (Theorem 4.2.1), it follows that $\check{\boldsymbol{\beta}}$ and $\check{\boldsymbol{\theta}}$ are consistent, asymptotically efficient, and are distributed asymptotically normal. Then $\check{I}^{-1}$ can be used in conjunction with the normal distribution to provide asymptotic tests of hypotheses.

The iterative maximum likelihood procedure discussed above is unnecessary, asymptotically speaking. As shown in Theorem 8.3.1, the generalized least squares estimator $\tilde{\boldsymbol{\beta}}$ and the feasible generalized least squares estimator $\tilde{\tilde{\boldsymbol{\beta}}}$ using a consistent estimate of $\hat{\Omega}$ (not necessarily the maximum likelihood estimate $\check{\Omega}$) have the same asymptotic distribution. In the presence of normality, they are both asymptotically efficient since both are consistent, distributed uniformly asymptotically normal and attain the asymptotic Cramer–Rao lower bound, $\sigma^2 Q_\Omega^{-1}/T$. Given the asymptotic efficiency of $\tilde{\tilde{\boldsymbol{\beta}}}$, the asymptotic distributions of $\check{\boldsymbol{\beta}}$ and $\tilde{\tilde{\boldsymbol{\beta}}}$ are the same, namely $N(\boldsymbol{\beta}, Q_\Omega^{-1}/T)$, (note $\sigma^2 = 1$ is assumed here). Thus, under appropriate circumstances, *it does not pay to iterate, as far as asymptotic efficiency is concerned*. The benefits of iteration in small samples, however, have not, in general, been determined.

8.4 An Example of Feasible Generalized Least Squares: Seemingly Unrelated Regressions

This section examines a basic econometric model which utilizes the concept of feasible generalized least squares estimation, seemingly unrelated regressions proposed by Zellner (1962). In later sections we will analyze methods of consistently estimating the error covariance matrix Ω and examine other facets of feasible generalized least squares.

For the present, let us illustrate the basic principles behind the seemingly unrelated regressions model by analyzing the Grunfeld (1958) investment data used by Zellner (1962). Grunfeld's investment theory specifies that a firm's investment in a given year is determined, at least in part, by the profit the firm expects to make in the same year. Since "expected profit" is not directly observable, Grunfeld assumed that the "market value at the end of the year," F_t, was a measurable substitute. Then desired capital stock, C_{t+1}^*, in the succeeding year is assumed to be linearly related to F_t by

$$C_{t+1}^* = \alpha_0 + \alpha_1 F_t.$$

Desired net investment, then, is

$$C_{t+1}^* - C_t = \alpha_0 + \alpha_1 F_t - C_t,$$

where C_t denotes the capital stock at time t. Assuming that only a certain proportion, p_1, of desired net investment is realized in a given year, then actual net investment is

$$p_1(C_{t+1}^* - C_t) = p_1\alpha_0 + p_1\alpha_1 F_t - p_1 C_t.$$

In addition, Grunfeld assumed that some investment consisted of maintenance and replacement, in amount equal to a constant proportion of the existing capital stock, $p_2 C_t$. Therefore, gross investment in the upcoming year, I_{t+1}, by a firm is described by

$$I_{t+1} = p_1(C_{t+1}^* - C_t) + p_2 C_t = p_1\alpha_0 + p_1\alpha_1 F_t + (p_2 - p_1)C_t.$$

Assuming this to be an inexact relationship, a stochastic error term is added resulting in the stochastic specification

$$I_t = \beta_1 + \beta_2 F_{t-1} + \beta_3 C_{t-1} + e_t.$$

Zellner (1962) focused on the nature of the error term e_t when the firms under investigation are operating in similar environments (e.g., in the same industry). Consider the case of the investment behavior of General Electric and Westinghouse. Let us denote their investment functions by

$$I_{ti} = \beta_{1i} + \beta_{2i} F_{t-1,i} + \beta_{3i} C_{t-1,i} + e_{ti}, \tag{8.4.1}$$

where $i = 1, 2$ denotes the investment functions of General Electric and Westinghouse and there are $t = 1, 2, \ldots, T$ observations on each firm.

Of interest is the form of the error covariance matrix

$$Ee_* e_*' = E\begin{bmatrix} \mathbf{e}_1 \\ \mathbf{e}_2 \end{bmatrix}[\mathbf{e}_1' \quad \mathbf{e}_2'], \tag{8.4.2}$$

where $\mathbf{e}_i = (e_{1i}, e_{2i}, \ldots, e_{Ti})'$, $i = 1, 2$. One conceivable form of (8.4.2) might be

$$Ee_* e_*' = \begin{bmatrix} \sigma_{11} I_T & 0_{T \times T} \\ 0_{T \times T} & \sigma_{22} I_T \end{bmatrix}, \tag{8.4.3}$$

where $Ee_{ti}^2 = \sigma_{ii}$ for $t = 1, 2, \ldots, T$ and $i = 1, 2$, $Ee_{si}e_{ti} = 0, s \neq t$, $Ee_{si}e_{tj} = 0$ for $i \neq j$ and all $s, t = 1, 2, \ldots, T$, and I_T represents a $T \times T$ identity matrix. In this instance the errors for each equation are independent and identically distributed and the errors of the separate equations are not related. However, it is possible that random exogenous factors such as government policies, international events, general level of economic activity, or other omitted effects may similarly affect the investment of *both* firms apart from the specified systematic variables. Then the errors of the equations in (8.4.1) may be contemporaneously correlated in that

$$Ee_{ti}e_{tj} = \sigma_{ij}, \qquad i, j = 1, 2; \quad t = 1, 2, \ldots, T. \tag{8.4.4}$$

If the error assumption (8.4.4) is appropriate, the correct error covariance matrix is

$$\Omega = \begin{bmatrix} \sigma_{11} I_T & \sigma_{12} I_T \\ \sigma_{21} I_T & \sigma_{22} I_T \end{bmatrix}. \tag{8.4.5}$$

The reason for the label "seemingly" unrelated regressions should now be clear. Though initially it may appear that the investment equation for General Electric is not in any way related to the investment equation for Westinghouse, in fact there may be random effects which are pertinent to both. The commonality of the random effects is reflected in the covariance of the two equation's error terms, $E(e_{ti}e_{tj}) = \sigma_{ij}$.

Let us now generalize the seemingly unrelated regressions model to M equations rather than just two and define the *standard conditions for seemingly unrelated regressions*. These conditions are sufficient to insure that the seemingly unrelated regressions model meets the requirements of generalized least squares estimation. Consider the M regression equations

$$\begin{aligned} \mathbf{y}_1 &= X_1 \boldsymbol{\beta}_1 + \mathbf{e}_1, \\ \mathbf{y}_2 &= X_2 \boldsymbol{\beta}_2 + \mathbf{e}_2, \\ &\vdots \\ \mathbf{y}_M &= X_M \boldsymbol{\beta}_M + \mathbf{e}_M, \end{aligned} \tag{8.4.6}$$

where each $\mathbf{y}_i$ $(i = 1, 2, \ldots, M)$ is of dimension $T \times 1$, X_i is $T \times K_i$, $\boldsymbol{\beta}_i$ is $K_i \times 1$ and $\mathbf{e}_i$ is $T \times 1$. These M equations can be written in the combined form

$$\mathbf{y}_* = \begin{bmatrix} \mathbf{y}_1 \\ \mathbf{y}_2 \\ \vdots \\ \mathbf{y}_M \end{bmatrix}, \qquad X_* = \begin{bmatrix} X_1 & & & 0 \\ & X_2 & & \\ & 0 & \ddots & \\ & & & X_M \end{bmatrix},$$

$$\boldsymbol{\beta}_* = \begin{bmatrix} \boldsymbol{\beta}_1 \\ \boldsymbol{\beta}_2 \\ \vdots \\ \boldsymbol{\beta}_M \end{bmatrix}, \qquad \mathbf{e}_* = \begin{bmatrix} \mathbf{e}_1 \\ \mathbf{e}_2 \\ \vdots \\ \mathbf{e}_M \end{bmatrix},$$

with

$$\mathbf{y}_* = X_* \boldsymbol{\beta}_* + \mathbf{e}_*. \tag{8.4.7}$$

Definition 8.4.1. Assume that the seemingly unrelated regressions system (8.4.7) satisfies the conditions:

(i) $E(\mathbf{e}_*) = \mathbf{0}$,
(ii) $E(\mathbf{e}_* \mathbf{e}_*') = \Omega$,
where $\Omega = \Sigma \otimes I$ and $\Sigma = [\sigma_{ij}]$, $i, j = 1, 2, \ldots, M$.
(iii) The matrix X_* is nonstochastic, $(X_*'\Omega^{-1}X_*)^{-1}$ is nonsingular, and

$$\lim_{T \to \infty} \left(\frac{X_*'\Omega^{-1}X_*}{T} \right)^{-1} = Q_*$$

is finite and nonsingular.

These assumptions are called the *standard conditions for seemingly unrelated regressions.*

In more detail, the variance–covariance matrix of $\mathbf{e}_*$ is $E\mathbf{e}_*\mathbf{e}_*' = \Omega$, where

$$\Omega = \Sigma \otimes I = \begin{bmatrix} \sigma_{11}I & \sigma_{12}I & \cdots & \sigma_{1M}I \\ \sigma_{21}I & \sigma_{22}I & & \vdots \\ \vdots & & \ddots & \\ \sigma_{M1}I & & \cdots & \sigma_{MM}I \end{bmatrix}, \tag{8.4.8}$$

and

$$\Sigma = \begin{bmatrix} \sigma_{11} & \sigma_{12} & \cdots & \sigma_{1M} \\ \sigma_{21} & \sigma_{22} & & \vdots \\ \vdots & & \ddots & \\ \sigma_{M1} & & \cdots & \sigma_{MM} \end{bmatrix}. \tag{8.4.9}$$

The symbol $\otimes$ denotes the Kronecker product operator and is defined for arbitrary matrices $A = [a_{ij}]$ of dimension $m \times n$ and $B = [b_{ij}]$ of dimension $p \times q$ to be

$$A \otimes B = \begin{bmatrix} a_{11}B & a_{12}B & \cdots & a_{1n}B \\ a_{21}B & a_{22}B & \ddots & \vdots \\ a_{m1}B & & \cdots & a_{mn}B \end{bmatrix}. \tag{8.4.10}$$

Thus, $A \otimes B$ is of dimension $mp \times nq$. The operator $\otimes$ is a shorthand method of "stacking" the B matrix into the A matrix.

For the present, let us examine the estimation of the seemingly unrelated regressions system (8.4.7) in the instance where Ω is assumed *known*. The case of unknown Ω is reserved for the next section. It then immediately follows that:

Theorem 8.4.1. *Under the standard conditions for seemingly unrelated regressions, a best linear unbiased, consistent, and normally distributed (asymptotically) estimator of* $\boldsymbol{\beta}_*$ *is*

$$\tilde{\boldsymbol{\beta}}_* = (X'_*\Omega^{-1}X_*)^{-1}X'_*\Omega^{-1}\mathbf{y}_* \tag{8.4.11}$$

with covariance matrix

$$(X'_*\Omega^{-1}X_*)^{-1} \tag{8.4.12}$$

and asymptotic covariance matrix

$$\frac{1}{T}\lim_{T\to\infty}\left(\frac{X'_*\Omega^{-1}X_*}{T}\right)^{-1}. \tag{8.4.13}$$

If, in addition, $\mathbf{e}_*$ *is normally distributed, then* $\tilde{\boldsymbol{\beta}}_*$ *is minimum variance unbiased and asymptotically efficient.*

PROOF. The seemingly unrelated regression estimator $\tilde{\boldsymbol{\beta}}_*$ satisfies the conditions required in generalized least squares estimation. Therefore, these results follow directly from developments in Chapters 3 and 4. □

The generalized least squares estimator $\tilde{\boldsymbol{\beta}}_*$ is more efficient, in general, than the ordinary least squares estimator

$$\begin{aligned} \hat{\boldsymbol{\beta}}_* &= (X'_*X_*)^{-1}X'_*\mathbf{y}_* \\ &= \begin{bmatrix} X'_1X_1 & & & \\ & X'_2X_2 & 0 & \\ & & \ddots & \\ & 0 & & X'_MX_M \end{bmatrix}^{-1} \begin{bmatrix} X'_1\mathbf{y}_1 \\ X'_2\mathbf{y}_2 \\ \vdots \\ X'_M\mathbf{y}_M \end{bmatrix} = \begin{bmatrix} (X'_1X_1)^{-1}X'_1\mathbf{y}_1 \\ (X'_2X_2)^{-1}X'_2\mathbf{y}_2 \\ \vdots \\ (X'_MX_M)^{-1}X'_M\mathbf{y}_M \end{bmatrix} \\ &= \begin{bmatrix} \hat{\boldsymbol{\beta}}_1 \\ \hat{\boldsymbol{\beta}}_2 \\ \vdots \\ \hat{\boldsymbol{\beta}}_M \end{bmatrix}, \end{aligned} \tag{8.4.14}$$

where $\hat{\boldsymbol{\beta}}_i = (X_i'X_i)^{-1}X_i'\mathbf{y}_i$, $i = 1, 2, \ldots, M$ represents the ordinary least squares estimator of the ith equation. This follows directly from Aitken's theorem (Theorem 2.5.1).

There are, however, two cases in which these estimators are identical (and hence equally efficient). Theorem 8.4.2 follows immediately from the result that (see Exercise 8.3)

$$\tilde{\boldsymbol{\beta}}_* = \begin{bmatrix} \sigma^{11}X_1'X_1 & \cdots & \sigma^{1M}X_1'X_M \\ \vdots & & \vdots \\ \sigma^{M1}X_M'X_1 & \cdots & \sigma^{MM}X_M'X_M \end{bmatrix}^{-1} \begin{bmatrix} \sum_{j=1}^{M} \sigma^{1j}X_1'\mathbf{y}_j \\ \vdots \\ \sum_{j=1}^{M} \sigma^{Mj}X_M'\mathbf{y}_j \end{bmatrix}, \tag{8.4.15}$$

where σ^{ij} represents the (i, j)th element of Σ^{-1}.

Theorem 8.4.2. *If* $\sigma_{jk} = 0$, *for* $j \neq k$, *then* $\tilde{\boldsymbol{\beta}}_* = \hat{\boldsymbol{\beta}}_*$ *and ordinary least squares is fully efficient.*

Therefore, the equations of the system (8.4.7) are truly unrelated when the disturbances of the various equations are uncorrelated and nothing is lost by using an estimator which ignores the possibility of contemporaneously correlated error terms.

The other case where the generalized least squares estimator $\tilde{\boldsymbol{\beta}}_*$ and ordinary least squares estimator $\hat{\boldsymbol{\beta}}_*$ are numerically equivalent and hence equally efficient is when the regressor matrices X_i, $i = 1, 2, \ldots, M$, are *numerically* identical. Formally,

Theorem 8.4.3. *Consider the set of equations*

$$\begin{aligned} \mathbf{y}_1 &= X\boldsymbol{\beta}_1 + \mathbf{e}_1, \\ \mathbf{y}_2 &= X\boldsymbol{\beta}_2 + \mathbf{e}_2, \\ &\vdots \\ \mathbf{y}_M &= X\boldsymbol{\beta}_M + \mathbf{e}_M. \end{aligned}$$

In this case ordinary least squares is fully efficient in that $\tilde{\boldsymbol{\beta}}_* = \hat{\boldsymbol{\beta}}_*$.

PROOF. The proof of this proposition is left as Exercise 8.4. □

Note that when the *numerical* values of the M design matrices are *identical*, i.e., $X_1 = X_2 = \cdots = X_M = X$, this theorem holds regardless of the degree of contemporaneous correlation among the error terms. Numerical coincidence should not be viewed, however, as meaning "the same explanatory variables." For example, the investment equations described above have the same explanatory variables yet different values for the observations on these variables. In such a case, the generalized least squares estimator $\tilde{\boldsymbol{\beta}}_*$ can offer a gain in efficiency if $\sigma_{12} \neq 0$.

The above exceptions, $\sigma_{ij} = 0$ and $X_1 = X_2 = \cdots = X_M = X$, point to the following conjecture. Is the gain of the generalized least squares estimator $\tilde{\boldsymbol{\beta}}_*$ over the ordinary least squares estimator $\hat{\boldsymbol{\beta}}_*$ affected directly by the degree of contemporaneous correlation between the errors of separate equations and the degree of "unrelatedness" of the regressors of the separate equations? Zellner and Huang (1962) address this issue in their paper. Consider a two-equation seemingly unrelated regressions system, where, for simplicity, it is assumed that each equation has the same number of explanatory variables $(K_1 = K_2)$. Let $\hat{\boldsymbol{\beta}}_1 = (X_1'X_1)^{-1}X_1'\mathbf{y}_1$, denote the ordinary least squares estimator of the regression coefficients $\boldsymbol{\beta}_1$ of the first equation and $\tilde{\boldsymbol{\beta}}_1$ denote the generalized least squares estimator of the same coefficients. Zellner and Huang show that

$$|\mathrm{var}(\tilde{\boldsymbol{\beta}}_1)| = \frac{(1-\rho^2)^{K_1}|\mathrm{var}(\hat{\boldsymbol{\beta}}_1)|}{\prod_{i=1}^{K_1}(1-\rho^2 r_i^2)}, \tag{8.4.16}$$

where $0 \leq r_i^2 \leq 1$ denotes the square of the ith canonical correlation between the regressor matrices of the two equations, X_1 and X_2, $|\cdot|$ denotes the determinant of the designated matrix and ρ is the contemporaneous correlation between the error terms of the two equations $(\rho = \sigma_{12}/(\sigma_{11}\sigma_{22})^{1/2})$. For a review of canonical correlations see Anderson (1958). Briefly, if X_1 and X_2 are orthogonal $(X_1'X_2 = 0)$, it can be shown that $r_1 = r_2 = \cdots = r_K = 0$ and thus, for a given degree of correlation ρ between the error terms of the two equations, the gain in estimation efficiency obtained by using generalized least squares is maximized. When any of the columns of X_1 are collinear with the columns of X_2, $r_1 = 1$ and the variance of the generalized least squares estimator is infinite (undefined). Between these extremes, $0 < r_i^2 < 1$, and, for a given relationship between X_1 and X_2, the greater the correlation between the error terms of the two equations, the greater the gain in estimation efficiency obtained by using generalized least squares.

8.5 Seemingly Unrelated Regressions Estimation: Asymptotic Results

In this section we consider the estimation of the seemingly unrelated regressions system (8.4.6) where $\Omega = \Sigma \otimes I = E\mathbf{e}_*\mathbf{e}_*'$ is unknown and must be estimated. In his original paper Zellner (1962) suggested that the error variances and covariances σ_{ii} and σ_{ij} be replaced by consistent estimates

$$s_{ij} = \frac{1}{T}\hat{\mathbf{e}}_i'\hat{\mathbf{e}}_j, \qquad i, j = 2, \ldots, M, \tag{8.5.1}$$

where $\hat{\mathbf{e}}_i = \mathbf{y}_i - X_i(X_i'X_i)^{-1}X_i'\mathbf{y}_i$ represents the ordinary least squares residuals from the ith equation. Let

$$\hat{\Sigma} = \begin{bmatrix} s_{11} & s_{12} & \cdots & s_{1M} \\ \vdots & \vdots & & \vdots \\ s_{M1} & s_{M2} & \cdots & s_{MM} \end{bmatrix} \tag{8.5.2}$$

and $\hat{\Omega} = \hat{\Sigma} \otimes I$. A feasible generalized least squares estimator of the seemingly unrelated regressions system is, therefore,

$$\tilde{\tilde{\boldsymbol{\beta}}}_* = (X_*'\hat{\Omega}^{-1}X_*)^{-1}X_*'\hat{\Omega}^{-1}\mathbf{y}_*. \tag{8.5.3}$$

The following theorem establishes the properties of this feasible generalized least squares estimator.

Theorem 8.5.1 (Zellner (1962)). *The (Zellner two-step) feasible generalized least squares estimator*

$$\tilde{\tilde{\boldsymbol{\beta}}}_* = (X_*'\hat{\Omega}^{-1}X_*)^{-1}X_*'\hat{\Omega}^{-1}\mathbf{y}_*$$

has the same asymptotic distribution as the generalized least squares estimator

$$\tilde{\boldsymbol{\beta}}_* = (X_*'\Omega^{-1}X_*)^{-1}X_*'\Omega^{-1}\mathbf{y}_*.$$

In the presence of the standard seemingly unrelated regressions conditions, $\tilde{\tilde{\boldsymbol{\beta}}}_*$ is consistent and normally distributed. If, in addition, $\mathbf{e}_*$ is normally distributed, $\tilde{\tilde{\boldsymbol{\beta}}}_*$ is also asymptotically efficient.

PROOF. This result follows directly from Theorems 8.3.1 and 8.3.3. □

Notice that asymptotic tests of hypotheses for seemingly unrelated regressions do not require the normality of $\mathbf{e}_*$ although the claim of asymptotic efficiency does. A consistent estimator of the covariance matrix of $\tilde{\tilde{\boldsymbol{\beta}}}_*$ is given by $(X_*'\hat{\Omega}^{-1}X_*)^{-1}$. The standard errors so derived can be used, along with the result of normality, to provide tests of hypotheses utilizing (8.3.4) or (8.3.5).

As pointed out in Theorem 8.3.2, the $\boldsymbol{\theta}$-equations in the general feasible generalized least squares model are often highly nonlinear and as a result a closed form solution for them may not be available. Fortunately, the $\boldsymbol{\theta}$-equations for the seemingly unrelated regressions system with normally distributed errors have the closed form solution given in the following theorem.

Theorem 8.5.2. *The* $\boldsymbol{\theta}$-equations *for seemingly unrelated regressions, assuming normality, are given by*

$$\Sigma = \frac{1}{T} E'E,$$

where $E = [\mathbf{e}_1, \mathbf{e}_2, \ldots, \mathbf{e}_M]$. *The information matrix for* $\boldsymbol{\beta}_*$ *and* Σ *is*

$$I = \begin{bmatrix} X'_*\Omega^{-1}X_* & 0 \\ 0 & \frac{1}{2}\Psi \end{bmatrix},$$

where Ψ *is a* $T \times T$ *matrix defined in Magnus* (1978, *p.* 300).

PROOF. See Magnus (1978). □

Upon convergence, further iteration of Zellner's two-step estimator (along the lines of the discussion following Theorem 8.3.2) leads to Zellner's iterative estimator (Zellner (1962, p. 363)) which is the maximum likelihood estimator of the seemingly unrelated regressions system. For further discussion of the equivalence between Zellner's iterative estimator and the maximum likelihood estimator, see Dhrymes (1971).

From the point of view of asymptotic efficiency, nothing can be gained by further iteration of Zellner's two-step feasible generalized least squares estimator. However, there still remains the question of potential gain from further iteration in small (finite) samples. Kmenta and Gilbert (1968) addressed this question in a Monte Carlo experiment. They found that Zellner's two-step and iterative estimators were very similar in their small sample performances. Their qualified conclusion was that *iteration does not offer substantial gains in small samples.*

8.6 Seemingly Unrelated Regressions Estimation: Small Sample Results

In the general case of feasible generalized least squares, only the result of unbiasedness (if the mean exists) when $\hat{\Omega}$ is an even function of $\mathbf{e}$ is available at present (Kakwani (1967)). Obviously, the lack of a specific structure for Ω is a principle reason for this lack of small sample determinancy. Even with the assumption of normally distributed errors, definitive small sample properties are not available when the specific nature of Ω is left unspecified. There have been a few rare cases, however, where, in conjunction with a specific parametric distribution for the errors, most frequently the normal distribution, the small sample properties of the feasible generalized least squares estimator are available for specific forms of Ω. One of these cases is the two-equation seemingly unrelated regressions model with normal errors and orthogonal regressors, $X'_1X_2 = 0$. (For another instance in which small sample results are available for feasible generalized least squares estimators with specific forms of Ω, see Section 9.3 on grouped heteroscedasticity and the results of Taylor (1978).)

The major purpose of the discussion in this section is to highlight, using the two-equation seemingly unrelated regressions model with orthogonal regressors, the fact that there are instances in which the feasible generalized least squares estimator is less efficient than the ordinary least squares estimator in small samples. The basic principle that has arisen in the literature is: The closer the error covariance matrix Ω comes to being spherical (that is, proportional to the identity matrix), the more likely the estimation of Ω will be "expensive," in the sense that an estimator, like ordinary least squares, that ignores the structure of Ω, is more efficient than a feasible generalized least squares estimator which attempts to use an estimate of Ω.

Before pursuing the small sample properties of the feasible generalized least squares estimator $\tilde{\hat{\boldsymbol{\beta}}}_*$ in the orthogonal two-equation seemingly unrelated regressions model, we need to define two distinct estimators of Ω, the unrestricted and restricted estimators. In establishing the asymptotic efficiency of his two-step technique, Zellner proposed $\hat{\Sigma}$ as a consistent estimator of Σ (Equation (8.5.2)). $\hat{\Sigma}$ is constructed from the ordinary least squares residuals of each separate equation,

$$\hat{\mathbf{e}}_i = \mathbf{y}_i - X_i\hat{\boldsymbol{\beta}}_i, \qquad i = 1, 2, \ldots, M.$$

As discussed by Zellner (1963), however, an alternative consistent estimator of Σ can be derived by regressing the $\mathbf{y}_i$ on all numerically distinct regressors of the system and computing the corresponding residuals.

Assume, for the moment, that all of the regressors $X_1, X_2, \ldots, X_M$ are numerically distinct. Consider the system

$$\begin{bmatrix} \mathbf{y}_1 \\ \mathbf{y}_2 \\ \vdots \\ \mathbf{y}_M \end{bmatrix} = \begin{bmatrix} (X_1, X_{D1}) & 0 & & 0 \\ 0 & (X_2, X_{D2}) & & 0 \\ 0 & 0 & \ddots & \\ & & & (X_M, X_{DM}) \end{bmatrix} \begin{bmatrix} \boldsymbol{\beta}_1 \\ \boldsymbol{\beta}_{10} \\ \cdots \\ \boldsymbol{\beta}_2 \\ \boldsymbol{\beta}_{20} \\ \cdots \\ \vdots \\ \cdots \\ \boldsymbol{\beta}_M \\ \boldsymbol{\beta}_{M0} \end{bmatrix} + \begin{bmatrix} \mathbf{u}_1 \\ \mathbf{u}_1 \\ \vdots \\ \mathbf{u}_M \end{bmatrix}, \tag{8.6.1}$$

where the $\boldsymbol{\beta}_i$ are the coefficients associated with X_i and the $\boldsymbol{\beta}_{i0}$ are the coefficients corresponding to $X_{Di} = (X_1, X_2, \ldots, X_{i-1}, X_{i+1}, \ldots, X_M)$, the matrix of distinct regressors from all equations except the ith. The dimension of $\boldsymbol{\beta}_{i0}$, given the notation of (8.4.6), is $(\Sigma_{j \neq i} K_j) \times 1$. The corresponding residuals of the system are

$$\hat{\mathbf{u}}_i = \mathbf{y}_i - [X_i \quad X_{Di}]\begin{bmatrix} \hat{\boldsymbol{\beta}}_i \\ \hat{\boldsymbol{\beta}}_{i0} \end{bmatrix}, \tag{8.6.2}$$

where $\hat{\boldsymbol{\beta}}_i$ and $\hat{\boldsymbol{\beta}}_{i0}$ denote the ordinary least squares estimates of $\boldsymbol{\beta}_i$ and $\boldsymbol{\beta}_{i0}$.

These residuals can be used to compute

$$s_{uij} = \frac{\hat{\mathbf{u}}_i'\hat{\mathbf{u}}_j}{T}, \qquad i, j = 1, 2, \ldots, M$$

and therefore the $MT \times MT$ matrix

$$\hat{\Omega}_u = \hat{\Sigma}_u \otimes I = \begin{bmatrix} s_{u11}I_T & s_{u12}I_T & \cdots & s_{u1M}I_T \\ s_{u21}I_T & s_{u22}I_T & & \vdots \\ \vdots & & \ddots & \\ s_{uM1}I_T & & \cdots & s_{uMM}I_T \end{bmatrix}. \tag{8.6.3}$$

The matrix $\hat{\Sigma}_u$ is called the *unrestricted* estimator of Σ and is a consistent estimator of Σ. Notice that $\hat{\Sigma}$ can be derived from (8.6.1) by imposing the restrictions $\boldsymbol{\beta}_{i0} = \mathbf{0}$ for $i = 1, 2, \ldots, M$. For this reason $\hat{\Sigma}$ is often called the *restricted* estimator of Σ. The equation system (8.6.1) can easily be modified to accommodate the case where some but not all regressors are distinct. The dimensions of the $\boldsymbol{\beta}_{i0}$ are correspondingly reduced.

Definition 8.6.1. $\hat{\Sigma}_u$ and $\hat{\Sigma}$ are, respectively, the *unrestricted* and *restricted* estimators of Σ. $\hat{\Omega}_u = \hat{\Sigma}_u \otimes I$ and $\hat{\Omega} = \hat{\Sigma} \otimes I$ are, respectively, the *unrestricted* and *restricted* estimators of Ω.

Obviously, it does not matter asymptotically which estimator of Σ is used in constructing a feasible generalized least squares estimator. This is not necessarily the case in small samples, however. Zellner (1963, p. 988) suggested that the restricted estimator $\hat{\Sigma}$ is probably superior to the unrestricted estimator $\hat{\Sigma}_u$ in small samples in that $\hat{\Sigma}$ incorporates more *a priori* information. However, counter to intuition, Revankar (1976) has shown that this need not be the case. There exist parameter configurations where the unrestricted estimator $\hat{\Sigma}_u$ leads to more efficient estimation in small samples than $\hat{\Sigma}$.

Zellner (1963) investigated the small sample properties of the *unrestricted* two-step estimator

$$\tilde{\tilde{\boldsymbol{\beta}}}_{*u} = (X_*'(\hat{\Sigma}_u \otimes I)^{-1}X_*)^{-1}X_*'(\hat{\Sigma}_u \otimes I)^{-1}\mathbf{y}_* \tag{8.6.4}$$

in the context of a two-equation seemingly unrelated regressions model with orthogonal regressors ($X_1'X_2 = 0$) and normally distributed errors. First, Zellner showed that $\tilde{\tilde{\boldsymbol{\beta}}}_{*u}$ is unbiased. Second, Zellner investigated the relative efficiency of the ordinary least squares estimator of $\boldsymbol{\beta}_1$, namely

$$\hat{\boldsymbol{\beta}}_1 = (X_1'X_1)^{-1}X_1'\mathbf{y}_1$$

to the unrestricted estimator $\tilde{\tilde{\boldsymbol{\beta}}}_{1u}$ of $\boldsymbol{\beta}_1$. (What is true for the relative efficiency in estimating $\boldsymbol{\beta}_1$ is also true with regard to $\boldsymbol{\beta}_2$ as the choice of equation for inspection is arbitrary). Zellner (1963, 1967) shows that

$$\text{var}(\tilde{\tilde{\boldsymbol{\beta}}}_{1u}) = \sigma_{11}(1 - \rho^2)[1 + 1/(T^* - 2)](X_1'X_1)^{-1},$$

where $T^* = T - K_1 - K_2$ (>2) and $\rho = \sigma_{12}/(\sigma_{11}\sigma_{22})^{1/2}$. Then

$$\text{var}(\tilde{\tilde{\boldsymbol{\beta}}}_{1\,u}) \lesseqgtr \text{var}(\hat{\boldsymbol{\beta}}_1) \quad \text{as} \quad (1 - \rho^2)[1 + 1/(T^* - 2)] \lesseqgtr 1.$$

The feasible generalized least squares estimator $\tilde{\tilde{\boldsymbol{\beta}}}_{1u}$ is more efficient than the ordinary least squares estimator only when

$$\left(\frac{1}{T^* - 1}\right)^{1/2} < |\rho| < 1. \tag{8.6.5}$$

These values of ρ are shown in Table 8.6.1 for various values of T^*. Given the asymptotic efficiency of the feasible generalized least squares estimator $\tilde{\tilde{\boldsymbol{\beta}}}_{1u}$, it naturally follows that $\tilde{\tilde{\boldsymbol{\beta}}}_{1u}$ is more efficient than the ordinary least squares estimator $\hat{\boldsymbol{\beta}}_1$ over the entire parameter space as the sample size approaches infinity. But, for small samples, the estimation of the parameters σ_{11}, σ_{22}, and σ_{12} is "expensive" when ρ is near zero and more efficient estimation can be achieved by assuming *a priori* that $\rho = 0$. Note the basic outcome: For any given sample size T, the closer the error covariance matrix Ω is to being spherical (i.e., $\sigma^2\mathbf{I}$), the greater the possibility that ordinary least squares estimation will be superior to feasible generalized least squares estimation in small samples. This lesson will be repeated again when we examine autocorrelated and heteroscedastic errors in the next two chapters. The only comfort that can be taken in these circumstances is that, for many practical cases, feasible generalized least squares provides substantial improvement

Table 8.6.1 Regions for which the unrestricted two-step feasible generalized least squares estimator is more efficient than ordinary least squares. (Orthogonal two-equation seemingly unrelated regressions model with normal errors.)

T^*	$\left(\frac{1}{T^*-1}\right)^{1/2} < \lvert\rho\rvert$		
3	(−1, −0.707)	and	(0.707, 1)
5	(−1, −0.500)	and	(0.500, 1)
10	(−1, −0.333)	and	(0.333, 1)
15	(−1, −0.267)	and	(0.267, 1)
20	(−1, −0.229)	and	(0.229, 1)
30	(−1, −0.186)	and	(0.186, 1)
40	(−1, −0.160)	and	(0.160, 1)
50	(−1, −0.143)	and	(0.143, 1)
100	(−1, −0.101)	and	(0.101, 1)
1000	(−1, −0.032)	and	(0.032, 1)
⋮	⋮		⋮
∞	0		0

over ordinary least squares for a large portion of the parameter space while, when inferior, the loss in using it is not too great. This conclusion has been supported, to date, by studies on seemingly unrelated regressions, autocorrelation, and heteroscedasticity (see, for example, Mehta and Swamy (1976), Rao and Griliches (1969), and Taylor (1978)).

8.7 Summary and Guide to Further Readings

In the case of purely exogeneous X so that the regressors and errors are guaranteed not to be contemporaneously correlated, the feasible generalized least squares estimator is unbiased (if its mean exists), consistent, and distributed asymptotically normal. The usual generalized least squares tests of hypotheses hold asymptotically. Therefore, the absence of the exact knowledge of Ω is not crucial in large samples. However, the assumption of no contemporaneous correlation is necessary for the stated results. An example of where this condition is not met is discussed in Chapter 11. There the implications of this correlation is examined in full.

With normally distributed errors the feasible generalized least squares estimator using the maximum likelihood estimator of Ω is the maximum likelihood estimator of $\boldsymbol{\beta}$. The maximum likelihood equations of the parameters Ω, called $\boldsymbol{\theta}$-equations, were presented and an iterative maximum likelihood procedure for estimating $\boldsymbol{\beta}$ and $\boldsymbol{\theta}$ was discussed. In addition, the information matrix for feasible generalized least squares under normality was derived. Corresponding asymptotic t- and F-statistics can be based on this matrix and the result of asymptotic normality. Though the assumption of normally distributed errors is necessary for claims of asymptotic efficiency, it is not necessary for asymptotic hypothesis testing.

To illustrate that feasible generalized least squares estimators need not be more efficient than ordinary least squares in small samples, the small sample properties of feasible generalized least squares in seemingly unrelated regressions were discussed. As shown, there exist costs in small samples of not knowing Ω exactly. In the cases where Ω is "near" I, the estimation of Ω from the data and its implementation in feasible generalized least squares becomes "expensive" in that ordinary least squares, which ignores the possible presence of nonsphericalness, is more efficient that feasible generalized least squares. Certainly there is value in *a priori* information of the form $\Omega \approx I$. Some comfort can be derived, however, from the fact that, in seemingly unrelated regressions (as well as other cases studied later) feasible generalized least squares provides substantial improvement over ordinary least squares for a large portion of the parameter space while, when inferior, the loss in using it is not too great.

We have chosen to leave some of the detailed proofs of the properties of feasible generalized least squares estimators to other references. Schmidt

(1976) has an excellent discussion of this topic. A good perspective on the development of feasible generalized least squares methods can be obtained by reading Zellner's (1962) article.

There is an extensive literature on the finite sample properties of seemingly unrelated regressions estimation. For a good review article see Srivastava and Dwivedi (1979). Revankar (1976) examines the relative merits of using the restricted and unrestricted estimates of Σ. He shows that the use of one is not strictly preferred over the other. Mehta and Swamy (1976) examine the finite sample performance of Zellner's unrestricted two-step estimator relative to ordinary least squares in the context of a two-equation model with normally distributed errors and nonorthogonal regressors ($X_1'X_2 \neq 0$).

Analysis of seemingly unrelated regressions outside of the traditional framework presented by Zellner (1962) includes the study by Schmidt (1977) of the seemingly unrelated regressions model when there are unequal numbers of observations in the equations. Guilkey and Schmidt (1973) extend the traditional error specification of the seemingly unrelated regressions model to include vector autoregressive errors. Guilkey (1974) suggests appropriate test statistics for examining this specification.

8.8 Exercises

8.1. In the context of Theorem 8.3.3 show that $\sqrt{T}(\tilde{\tilde{\boldsymbol{\beta}}} - \boldsymbol{\beta}) \overset{\text{asy}}{\sim} N(\mathbf{0}, \sigma^2 Q_\Omega^{-1})$ and that $\tilde{\tilde{\sigma}}^2$ is a consistent estimator of σ^2.

8.2. Derive the information matrix of Theorem 8.3.3.

8.3. Using partitioned matrix multiplication and the Kronecker product property $(A \otimes B)^{-1} = (A^{-1} \otimes B^{-1})$, derive Equation (8.4.15).

To answer the following questions use the data at the end of this exercise section.

8.4. Using the General Electric and Westinghouse data:
 (a) Compute the seemingly unrelated regressions estimates of the investment equations for General Electric and Westinghouse using the restricted estimator of Σ. Compare these estimates and their standard errors to those obtained by applying ordinary least squares to each equation. Which standard errors are smaller and why?
 (b) Compute the unrestricted seemingly unrelated regression and Zellner's iterative estimates of the General Electric and Westinghouse equations. Do they differ substantially from the estimates obtained in part (a)?
 (c) Test the null hypothesis $H_0\colon \boldsymbol{\beta}_1 = \boldsymbol{\beta}_2$ that the regression coefficients of the General Electric and Westinghouse equations are the same, assuming the error covariance matrix is $E\mathbf{e}_*\mathbf{e}_*' = \Sigma \otimes I$.
 (d) Compare the results of your test in part (c) with those obtain assuming $E\mathbf{e}_*\mathbf{e}_*' = \Sigma \otimes I$ but $\sigma_{12} = 0$.

8.5. Using the Westinghouse and General Motors data:

(a) Compute the seemingly unrelated regressions estimates of the investment equations for Westinghouse and General Motors using the restricted estimator of Σ. Compare these estimates and their standard errors to those obtained by applying ordinary least squares to each equation.

(b) Use the restricted (ordinary least squares) residuals to compute the estimated contemporaneous correlation between the equations' errors, $\hat{\rho} = \hat{\sigma}_{12}/(\hat{\sigma}_{11}\hat{\sigma}_{22})^{1/2}$. Compute $\hat{\rho}$ for the General Electric and Westinghouse data. Compare the relative sizes of these correlations and the extent to which the standard errors of the regression coefficients are affected in moving from ordinary least squares to seemingly unrelated regressions estimation.

8.6. Assume that the estimated contemparaneous correlations $\hat{\rho}$ between Westinghouse and General Motors, on the one hand, and Westinghouse and General Electric on the other, equal their corresponding population values. (These estimates are obtained in Exercise 8.5(b).) Furthermore, assume for the moment, that the corresponding regressors of the equations are orthogonal ($X_1'X_2 = 0$). Use Table 8.6.1 to determine whether seemingly unrelated regressions estimation (in the sense of using unrestricted two-step feasible generalized least squares estimation) of the Westinghouse and General Motors equations provides a gain in estimation efficiency. Answer the same question with respect to the Westinghouse and General Electric equations.

Grunfeld Investment Data*

	Westinghouse			General Electric			General Motors		
	I	F_{-1}	C_{-1}	I	F_{-1}	C_{-1}	I	F_{-1}	C_{-1}
1935	12.93	191.5	1.8	33.1	1170.6	97.8	317.6	3078.5	2.8
1936	25.90	516.0	0.8	45.0	2015.8	104.4	391.8	4661.7	52.6
1937	35.05	729.0	7.4	77.2	2803.3	118.0	410.6	5387.1	156.9
1938	22.89	560.4	18.1	44.6	2039.7	156.2	257.7	2792.2	209.2
1939	18.84	519.9	23.5	48.1	2256.2	172.6	330.8	4313.2	203.4
1940	28.57	628.5	26.5	74.4	2132.2	186.6	461.2	4643.9	207.2
1941	48.51	537.1	36.2	113.0	1834.1	220.9	512.0	4551.2	255.2
1942	43.34	561.2	60.8	91.9	1588.0	287.8	448.0	3244.1	303.7
1943	37.02	617.2	84.4	61.3	1749.4	319.9	499.6	4053.7	264.1
1944	37.81	626.7	91.2	56.8	1687.2	321.3	547.5	4379.3	201.6
1945	39.27	737.2	92.4	93.6	2007.7	319.6	561.2	4840.9	265.0
1946	53.46	760.5	86.0	159.9	2208.3	346.0	688.1	4900.9	402.2
1947	55.56	581.4	111.1	147.2	1656.7	456.4	568.9	3526.5	761.5
1948	49.56	662.3	130.6	146.3	1604.4	543.4	529.2	3254.7	922.4
1949	32.04	583.8	141.8	98.3	1431.8	618.3	555.1	3700.2	1020.1
1950	32.24	635.2	136.7	93.5	1610.5	647.4	642.9	3755.6	1099.0
1951	54.38	723.8	129.7	135.2	1819.4	671.3	755.9	4833.0	1207.7
1952	71.78	864.1	145.5	157.3	2079.7	726.1	891.2	4924.9	1430.5
1953	90.08	1193.5	174.8	179.5	2371.6	800.3	1304.4	6241.7	1777.3
1954	68.60	1188.9	213.5	189.6	2759.9	888.9	1486.7	5593.6	2226.3

* SOURCE: Grunfeld (1958).

8.9 References

Anderson, T. W. (1958), *An Introduction to Multivariate Statistical Analysis*, New York: Wiley.

Dhrymes, P. J. (1971). Equivalence of iterative Aiken and maximum likelihood estimators for a system of regression equations. *Australian Economics Papers*, **10**, 20–24.

Grunfeld, Y. (1958). The determinants of corporate investment. Unpublished Ph.D. Thesis, University of Chicago.

Guilkey, D. K. (1974). Alternative tests for a first-order vector autoregressive error specification. *Journal of Econometrics*, **2**, 95–104.

Guilkey, D. K., and Schmidt, P. (1973). Estimation of seemingly unrelated regressions with vector autoregressive errors. *Journal of the American Statistical Association*, **68**, 642–647.

Kakwani, N. C. (1967). The unbiasedness of Zellner's seemingly unrelated regression equation estimators. *Journal of the American Statistical Association*, **82**, 141–142.

Kmenta, J. and Gilbert, R. F. (1968). Small sample properties of alternative estimators of seemingly unrelated regressions. *Journal of the American Statistical Association*, **63**, 1180–1200.

Magnus, J. R. (1978). Maximum likelihood estimation of the GLS model with unknown parameters in the disturbance covariance matrix. *Journal of Econometrics*, **7**, 281–312.

Mehta, J. S., and Swamy, P. A. V. B. (1976). Further evidence on the relative efficiencies of Zellner's seemingly unrelated regressions estimator. *Journal of the American Statistical Association*, **71**, 634–639.

Rao, P. and Griliches, Z. (1969). Small sample properties of several two-stage regression methods in the context of autocorrelated errors. *Journal of the American Statistical Association*, **64**, 253–272.

Revankar, N. S. (1976). Use of restricted residuals in SUR systems: some finite sample results. *Journal of the American Statistical Association*, **71**, 183–188.

Schmidt, P. (1976). *Econometrics*. New York: Marcel Dekker.

Schmidt, P. (1977). Estimation of seemingly unrelated regressions with unequal numbers of observations. *Journal of Econometrics*, **5**, 365–377.

Srivastava, V. K., and Dwivedi, T. D. (1979). Estimation of seemingly unrelated regression equations: a brief survey. *Journal of Econometrics*, **10**, 15–32.

Taylor, W. E. (1978). The heteroscedastic linear model: exact finite sample results. *Econometrica*, **46**, 663–675.

Zellner, A. (1962). An efficient method of estimating seemingly unrelated regressions and tests for aggregation bias. *Journal of the American Statistical Association*, **57**, 348–368.

Zellner, A. (1963). Estimators for seemingly unrelated regression equations: some exact finite sample results. **58**, 977–992.

Zellner, A. (1967). Corrigenda. *Journal of the American Statistical Association*, **67**, 255.

Zellner, A. and Huang, D. (1962). Further properties of efficient estimators for seemingly unrelated regression equations. *International Economic Review*, **3**, 300–313.

CHAPTER 9

Heteroscedasticity

9.1 Introduction

There are certain circumstances in which the assumption of constant error variance, homoscedasticity, in the linear model is not tenable. For example, in cross-sectional analysis in economics, the units under investigation are usually firms, households, or individuals, and the degree to which the linear equation explains their behavior may depend upon their specific characteristics. We illustrate this point by the use of three examples.

EXAMPLE 9.1.1. Suppose that, for a given year and a given industry, interest centers on the profit performance of individual firms as it relates to advertising expenditures and research and development expenditures. The hypothesized equation is

$$\Pi_i = a_1 + a_2 A_i + a_3 R_i + e_i, \qquad i = 1, 2, \ldots, n, \tag{9.1.1}$$

where $\Pi_i \equiv$ profit of ith firm,
$A_i \equiv$ advertising expenditures of ith firm,
$R_i \equiv$ research and development expenditures of ith firm,
$n \equiv$ number of firms being studied.

Though it seems reasonable that the means of the error terms of (9.1.1) are zero, the variances of the error terms associated with large firms may be larger than those of the small firms. This could arise because the small firms are unlikely to engage in extensive research and development while the large firms have the leverage (assets, liquidity, economies of scale) to more extensively use this competitive strategy. Because there is greater risk (more variable returns) associated with research and development, we would

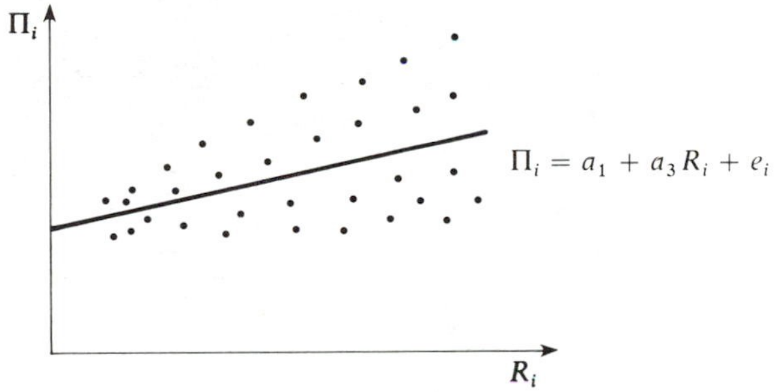

Figure 9.1.1

expect the variation around the mean profit rate of the large firms to be greater than the corresponding variation for small firms. Graphically, for given advertising expenditures, we might expect the variances of the e_i to be monotonically related to R_i (Figure 9.1.1).

In this instance we would want to weight the information related to large firms less heavily than that of small firms since the postulated linear relationship holds more exactly for small firms than for large firms. In the next section we will discuss how one goes about weighting the information associated with each individual observation.

EXAMPLE 9.1.2. Like firms, households vary in their size, where size can be measured by income or number of members. Suppose housing expenditures are explained by the following equation

$$E_i = b_1 + b_2 Y_i + b_3 N_i + e_i,$$

where $E_i \equiv$ housing expenditures,
$Y_i \equiv$ household's total disposable income,
$N_i \equiv$ number of people in household.

Because higher levels of income offer a household more discretion with respect to consumption and saving, it might be expected that the greater the income of a household the greater the variability of expenditure patterns. A relatively wealthy household has the discretion of enlarging their house with a swimming pool or instead buying a camper and spending their weekends on the beaches. A plot of some sample observations of E_i on Y_i would probably be similar to the plot in Figure 9.1.1. Prais and Houthakker (1955) found such results in their study of family budgets and expenditures.

EXAMPLE 9.1.3. In his book *Schooling, Experience, and Earnings*, Jacob Mincer (1974) analyzed the individual's acquisition of earning power as a function of years of school, S, and experience, XPR, in one's vocation. Using Mincer's theoretical development of the economics of human capital, Mincer's equation is

$$\ln Y_i = \alpha_0 + \alpha_1 (XPR)_i - \alpha_2 (XPR)_i^2 + \alpha_3 S_i + \boldsymbol{\phi}_i' \boldsymbol{\alpha}_4 + e_i,$$

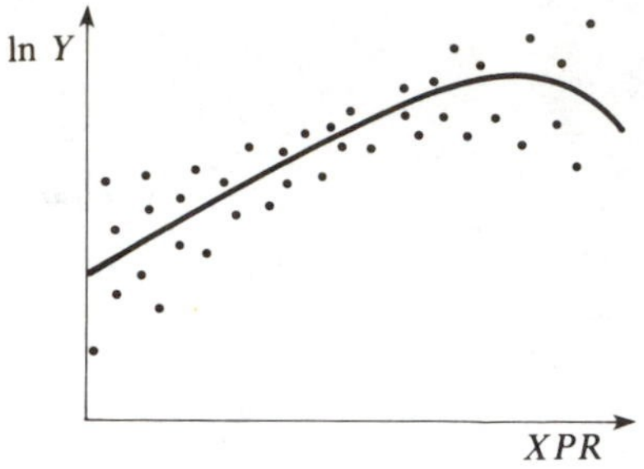

Figure 9.1.2

where $Y_i \equiv$ hourly earnings of ith individual,
$(XPR)_i \equiv$ experience of ith individual as measured by age minus schooling (in years),
$S_i \equiv$ schooling (in years) of ith individual,
$\boldsymbol{\phi}_i \equiv$ any number of other variables such as: occupation, race, union–nonunion, size of city, industry, region (south, north, etc.)

For a given level of schooling and other variables in $\boldsymbol{\phi}$, heteroscedasticity can appear in the experience profile as graphically depicted in Figure 9.1.2. That is, the error variance is approximately quadratic in experience, $\sigma_e^2 = a + b(XPR) + c(XPR)^2$, as represented in Figure 9.1.3.

There are, of course, several reasons why we might expect the error variance to be greater at the ends of the experience profile. First, at the entry level, there may be substantial discretion as to the choice of an apprenticeship period with lower starting salary but substantial upward mobility versus a high starting salary with little upward mobility. For example, a recent medical graduate may opt for a low-paying start in a partnership with someone from whom valuable surgical techniques can be learned, while another medical graduate may choose a lucrative beginning as a general practitioner with less than proportionate increases in income thereafter.

Secondly, at the exit stage, pre-retirement plans of individuals vary substantially. Some individuals may turn down promotions because they do not want to move to another city; they do not want a stressful job, or maybe

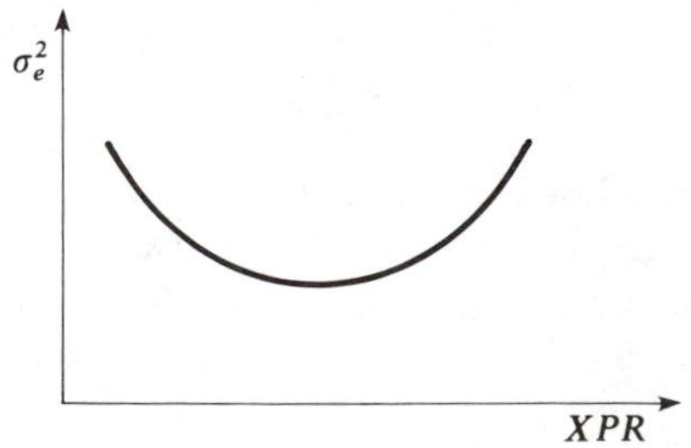

Figure 9.1.3

they do not want to operate in a managerial capacity. Years of accumulated wealth give them discretion in their choices. In addition, possibilities of early retirement vary according to individual firm retirement plans and the circumstances of the age–health–productivity interaction could also cause greater variability in the latter stages of the experience profile.

In summary, there are many instances where one would not necessarily expect the error variance of a linear model to be the same over all units being observed. From Aitken's theorem (Theorem 2.5.1), it is easy to see that ordinary least squares, though unbiased, is not efficient. The appropriate loss function we should consider is $\mathbf{e}'\Omega^{-1}\mathbf{e}$ instead of $\mathbf{e}'\mathbf{e}$. Rather than letting each errors, $e_1, e_2, \ldots, e_T$ (and hence each observation) have equal weight in determining an estimate of our regression coefficients, we should weight them inversely (as signified by Ω^{-1}) according to their variability. The more variable the e_t, the less the observation $(y_t, \mathbf{x}_t')$ should be used in determining the fitted regression equation. One of the purposes of this chapter is to examine various possible weighting schemes which arise from different forms of heteroscedasticity (compare Examples 9.1.1 and 9.1.2 with 9.1.3) and to discuss the implemention of this information in generalized least squares estimation so as to achieve not only unbiased estimators of the regression coefficients but estimators with increased efficiency. In addition, when constructing tests of hypotheses, the appropriate covariance matrix $\sigma_e^2(X'\Omega^{-1}X)^{-1}$ should be used rather than the incorrect one specified by ordinary least squares so that the true significance levels will coincide with those specified.

One might naively propose that heteroscedasticity be specified in the general form

$$\Omega = \begin{bmatrix} \sigma_1^2 & & & 0 \\ & \sigma_2^2 & & \\ & & \ddots & \\ 0 & & & \sigma_T^2 \end{bmatrix}.$$

However, generalized least squares estimation using this general form of Ω is prohibited by the fact that there would be insufficient degrees of freedom since there are $(T + K)$ parameters to estimate, $\beta_1, \beta_2, \ldots, \beta_K$ and $\sigma_1^2, \sigma_2^2, \ldots, \sigma_T^2$, while only T observations on y are available. This is clearly an impossible task and one must be willing to impose further structure on Ω before estimation becomes tractible. Section 9.2 discusses various possible parametrizations coinciding with many forms of heteroscedasticity one might encounter in practice and the corresponding implied methods of estimation. These methods are essentially generalized least squares techniques when all the parameters of a given parametrization are known and feasible generalized least squares techniques when the parameters of the parametrization are unknown (see Chapters 3 and 8).

Section 9.3 discusses various tests of heteroscedasticity while Section 9.4 investigates the effects of heteroscedasticity on the Chow test (test of structural change) often used in economics. A summary and guide to further readings is contained in Section 9.5.

9.2 Estimation Under Various Forms of Heteroscedasticity

9.2.1 Grouped Heteroscedasticity

In many instances it might be possible to identify various groups of observations where within a given group the error variance is the same whereas between groups the error variance differs. For example, in the study of housing expenditures, it may be possible to divide the observations into groups according to income classes, say \$0–20,000, \$20,001–40,000, and \$40,001 and above. Within each of these income classes the error variance may essentially be the same while the error variances of the three different groups could be quite different.

Let T be the number of observations available for a regression model and suppose that there exist G groups of observations on the dependent variable with $T_1, T_2, \ldots, T_G$ observations in each group such that $T_1 + T_2 + \cdots + T_G = T$. Furthermore, assume for all g that $T_g > K$ with K = the number of independent variables in the linear model.

In matrix form we have

$$\begin{aligned} \mathbf{y}_1 &= X_1\boldsymbol{\beta} + \mathbf{e}_1, \\ \mathbf{y}_2 &= X_2\boldsymbol{\beta} + \mathbf{e}_2, \\ &\vdots \\ \mathbf{y}_G &= X_G\boldsymbol{\beta} + \mathbf{e}_G, \end{aligned} \tag{9.2.1}$$

where $\mathbf{y}_g$, X_g, and $\mathbf{e}_g$ denote, respectively, the observations on the dependent and explanatory variables of the gth group and the random errors in the gth group. The vector of coefficients, which is the same for each group, is $\boldsymbol{\beta}' = (\beta_1, \beta_2, \ldots, \beta_K)$. In compressed form, the *grouped heteroscedasticity model* can be written as

$$\mathbf{y} = X\boldsymbol{\beta} + \mathbf{e}, \tag{9.2.2}$$

where $\mathbf{y}' = (\mathbf{y}_1', \mathbf{y}_2', \ldots, \mathbf{y}_G')$, $\mathbf{e}' = (\mathbf{e}_1', \mathbf{e}_2', \ldots, \mathbf{e}_G')$, and $X' = (X_1', X_2', \ldots, X_G')$. The error specification for the grouped heteroscedasticity model is assumed to be

$$E\mathbf{e} = \mathbf{0} \tag{9.2.3}$$

and

$$E\mathbf{e}\mathbf{e}' = E\begin{bmatrix} \mathbf{e}_1\mathbf{e}_1' & \mathbf{e}_1\mathbf{e}_2' & \cdots & \mathbf{e}_1\mathbf{e}_G' \\ \mathbf{e}_2\mathbf{e}_1' & \mathbf{e}_2\mathbf{e}_2' & \cdots & \mathbf{e}_2\mathbf{e}_G' \\ & & \vdots & \\ \mathbf{e}_G\mathbf{e}_1' & \mathbf{e}_G\mathbf{e}_2' & \cdots & \mathbf{e}_G\mathbf{e}_G' \end{bmatrix}$$

$$= \begin{bmatrix} \sigma^2 I_{T_1} & & & 0 \\ & \sigma_2^2 I_{T_2} & & \\ & 0 & \ddots & \\ & & & \sigma_G^2 I_{T_G} \end{bmatrix}, \tag{9.2.4}$$

where $E\mathbf{e}_g\mathbf{e}_g' = \sigma_g^2 I_{T_g}$, $g = 1, 2, \ldots, G$. That is σ_g^2 is the homoscedastic error variance within the gth group.

If the variances σ_g^2, $g = 1, 2, \ldots, G$, are known, the corresponding generalized least squares estimator of (9.2.2) is easily constructed. The generalized least squares transformation is of the form

$$P' = \begin{bmatrix} \frac{1}{\sigma_1} I_{T_1} & & 0 \\ & \ddots & \\ 0 & & \frac{1}{\sigma_G} I_{T_G} \end{bmatrix}. \tag{9.2.5}$$

Using this transformation matrix, we can form the transformed equation

$$P'\mathbf{y} = P'X\boldsymbol{\beta} + P'\mathbf{e}$$

or

$$\mathbf{y}^* = X^*\boldsymbol{\beta} + \mathbf{e}^*, \tag{9.2.6}$$

where $\mathbf{y}^* = P'\mathbf{y}$, $X^* = P'X$, and $\mathbf{e}^* = P'\mathbf{e}$. Equation (9.2.6) has homoscedastic error variance in that $E\mathbf{e}^*\mathbf{e}^{*\prime} = I_T$. The application of ordinary least squares to the transformed equation (9.2.6) is equivalent to generalized least squares estimation of (9.2.2). The resulting estimator for $\boldsymbol{\beta}$ is consistent, best linear unbiased and in the presence of normal errors minimum variance unbiased (see Chapters 3 and 4).

In most circumstances, however, the variances σ_g^2 will not be known and must be estimated. Let $\hat{\boldsymbol{\beta}}_g = (X_g'X_g)^{-1}X_g'\mathbf{y}_g$ denote the ordinary least squares estimator of $\boldsymbol{\beta}$ obtained from applying ordinary least squares to the gth group of observations. Then a consistent, unbiased estimator of the gth group error variance, σ_g^2, is

$$\hat{\sigma}_g^2 = \frac{(\mathbf{y}_g - X_g\hat{\boldsymbol{\beta}}_g)'(\mathbf{y}_g - X_g\hat{\boldsymbol{\beta}}_g)}{T_g - K}. \tag{9.2.7}$$

Let

$$\hat{P}' = \begin{bmatrix} \frac{1}{\hat{\sigma}_1} I_{T_1} & & 0 \\ & \ddots & \\ 0 & & \frac{1}{\hat{\sigma}_G} I_{T_G} \end{bmatrix}.$$

Then the estimator

$$\tilde{\tilde{\boldsymbol{\beta}}} = [(\hat{P}'X)'(\hat{P}'X)]^{-1}(\hat{P}'X)'\hat{P}'\mathbf{y} \tag{9.2.8}$$

is a feasible generalized least squares estimator of the grouped heteroscedasticity model. This estimator is consistent and is distributed as an asymptotic normal random variable. Tests of hypotheses concerning $\boldsymbol{\beta}$ can be based on this asymptotic normality and the result that the asymptotic covariance matrix of the feasible generalized least squares estimator $\tilde{\tilde{\boldsymbol{\beta}}}$ is consistently estimated by

$$[(\hat{P}'X')'(\hat{P}'X)]^{-1}. \tag{9.2.9}$$

In the presence of normal errors, the resulting estimator is also asymptotically efficient (see Chapters 4 and 8).

To determine whether, in an application, the grouped heteroscedasticity model is appropriate, the likelihood ratio test may be applied. See Section 9.3 for a discussion of this test.

9.2.2 Heteroscedasticity as a Function of Exogenous Variables

Frequently a given form of heteroscedasticity can be expressed as a function of one or more exogenous variables. Consider the following three examples:

(a) Recall the Mincer equation of Example 9.1.3. In that context the heteroscedasticity was expected to be of the form

$$\sigma_i^2 = a + b(XPR)_i + c(XPR)_i^2, \tag{9.2.10}$$

which is *linear* in $(XPR)_i$ and $(XPR)_i^2$. That is, the *variance is a linear function of exogenous variables.*

(b) Prais and Houthakker (1955) found that the error variances of their tea consumption equations were approximately proportional to the square of the mean of the regression function. That is,

$$\begin{aligned}\sigma_i^2 &= \sigma^2(Ey_i)^2 \\ &= \sigma^2(\beta_1 x_{i1} + \cdots + \beta_K x_{iK})^2,\end{aligned} \tag{9.2.11}$$

where σ^2 is an unknown constant. Of course, (9.2.11) can equivalently be written as

$$\begin{aligned}\sigma_i &= \sigma(\beta_1 x_{i1} + \cdots + \beta_K x_{iK}) \\ &= \beta_1^* x_{i1} + \cdots + \beta_K^* x_{iK}.\end{aligned} \tag{9.2.12}$$

In this case the *standard deviation is a linear function of exogenous variables.*

(c) Recall the profit equation of Example 9.1.1. There the variance was expected to be directly related to research and development expenditures. This relationship could be represented by

$$\sigma_i^2 = \sigma^2(R_i)^\lambda, \tag{9.2.13}$$

where σ^2 *and* λ are both unknown real constants. Here the error variance is *multiplicative* in the parameter λ.

Certainly these examples are not exhaustive, but they do illustrate three prevalent types of heteroscedasticity discussed in the econometric literature. They are:

$$\sigma_i^2 = \mathbf{z}_i'\boldsymbol{\alpha}, \tag{9.2.14}$$

$$\sigma_i^2 = (\mathbf{z}_i'\boldsymbol{\alpha})^2, \tag{9.2.15}$$

and

$$\sigma_i^2 = \exp(\mathbf{z}_i'\boldsymbol{\alpha}), \tag{9.2.16}$$

where $\mathbf{z}_i' = (z_{i1}, z_{i2}, \ldots, z_{ip})$ is a $p \times 1$ vector of observations on a set of exogenous variables which are usually, though not necessarily, related to the regressors and $\boldsymbol{\alpha}' = (\alpha_1, \alpha_2, \ldots, \alpha_p)$ is a $p \times 1$ vector of parameters. The first element of $\mathbf{z}_i$ is here always assumed to be one, i.e., $z_{i1} \equiv 1$ for all i. For the three examples discussed above, the $\mathbf{z}_i'$ and $\boldsymbol{\alpha}$ vectors are, respectively,

$$\mathbf{z}_i' = (1, (XPR)_i, (XPR)_i^2), \qquad \boldsymbol{\alpha}' = (a, b, c); \tag{9.2.17}$$

$$\mathbf{z}_i' = (1, \ldots, x_{iK}), \qquad \boldsymbol{\alpha}' = (\beta_1^*, \ldots, \beta_K^*); \tag{9.2.18}$$

and

$$\mathbf{z}_i' = (1, \ln R_i), \qquad \boldsymbol{\alpha}' = (\ln \sigma^2, \lambda). \tag{9.2.19}$$

We now turn to estimation of linear models with the above heteroscedasticity schemes.

9.2.2a *Variance as a Linear Function of Exogenous Variables:* $\sigma_i^2 = \mathbf{z}_i'\boldsymbol{\alpha}$

When the error variance can be specified as a linear function of exogenous variables the linear model can be expressed as

$$y_i = \mathbf{x}_i'\boldsymbol{\beta} + e_i, \qquad i = 1, 2, \ldots, T, \tag{9.2.20}$$

with

$$E(e_i) = 0, \qquad E(e_i^2) = \sigma_i^2 = \mathbf{z}_i'\boldsymbol{\alpha}, \qquad E(e_i e_j) = 0, \qquad i \neq j. \tag{9.2.21}$$

In addition assume the errors e_i are normally distributed. Let D_1 be the diagonal matrix with ith diagonal element $\mathbf{z}_i'\boldsymbol{\alpha}$. The generalized least squares estimator is

$$\begin{aligned}\tilde{\boldsymbol{\beta}} &= (X'D_1^{-1}X)^{-1}X'D_1^{-1}\mathbf{y} \\ &= \left(\sum_{i=1}^{T}(\mathbf{z}_i'\boldsymbol{\alpha})^{-1}\mathbf{x}_i\mathbf{x}_i'\right)^{-1}\sum_{i=1}^{T}(\mathbf{z}_i'\boldsymbol{\alpha})^{-1}\mathbf{x}_i y_i \qquad (9.2.22)\end{aligned}$$

which has mean $\boldsymbol{\beta}$ and covariance matrix

$$(X'D_1^{-1}X)^{-1} = \left(\sum_{i=1}^{T}(\mathbf{z}_i'\boldsymbol{\alpha})^{-1}\mathbf{x}_i\mathbf{x}_i'\right)^{-1}. \qquad (9.2.23)$$

In most cases, however, the parameter vector $\boldsymbol{\alpha}$ is unknown and must be estimated consistently in order that feasible generalized least squares may be implemented.

From an intuitive point of view, one alternative might be to replace σ_i^2 in the equation $\sigma_i^2 = \mathbf{z}_i'\boldsymbol{\alpha}$ with the consistent estimate $\hat{e}_i^2$, the square of the ordinary least squares residual. That is, $\hat{e}_i^2 = (y_i - \mathbf{x}_i'\hat{\boldsymbol{\beta}})^2$, where $\hat{\boldsymbol{\beta}} = (X'X)^{-1}X'\mathbf{y}$ is the ordinary least squares estimator. The resulting equation is

$$\hat{e}_i^2 = \mathbf{z}_i'\boldsymbol{\alpha} + v_i, \qquad i = 1, 2, \ldots, T, \qquad (9.2.24)$$

where

$$v_i = \hat{e}_i^2 - \sigma_i^2. \qquad (9.2.25)$$

However, the mean of v_i is (see Exercise 9.1)

$$Ev_i = \mathbf{x}_i'(X'X)^{-1}X'D_1X(X'X)^{-1}\mathbf{x}_i - 2\mathbf{x}_i'(X'X)^{-1}X'\mathbf{d} \neq 0, \qquad (9.2.26)$$

where $\mathbf{d}' = (0, \ldots, 0, \sigma_i^2, 0, \ldots, 0)$ is a $1 \times T$ vector with σ_i^2 as its ith element and zeros elsewhere. The fact the v_i have a nonzero mean which changes with i implies that ordinary least squares estimation of $\boldsymbol{\alpha}$ via equation (9.2.24) will be biased in small samples. It is left as an exercise (see Exercise 9.2) to show that the v_i are also heteroscedastic and autocorrelated. However, if the sample size is sufficiently large, ordinary least squares applied to (9.2.24) can, at least, provide consistent estimates of $\boldsymbol{\alpha}$. This is, of course, all that is required for feasible generalized least squares. To see that consistent estimation obtains, we need only consider

$$\text{plim}(\hat{e}_i - e_i) = 0, \qquad (9.2.27)$$

which will be proved in Lemma 10.8.3 of Chapter 10. That is, in large samples, the ordinary least squares residuals behave as if they were the unobservable random errors. Likewise, the $\hat{e}_i$ are independently distributed in *large* samples and have heteroscedastic variance $\sigma_i^2 = \mathbf{z}_i'\boldsymbol{\alpha}$. It follows that the $\hat{e}_i^2$ converge to a random variable e_i^{*2} which is distributed as $\sigma_i^2\chi_1^2$. Therefore, $Ee_i^{*2} = \sigma_i^2$ and $\text{var}(e_i^{*2}) = 2\sigma_i^4$ and as a result the error v_i converges to a random variable $v_i^* = (e_i^{*2} - \sigma_i^2)$ which has a zero mean and constant variance $2\sigma_i^4$. In summary, Equation (9.2.24) can be treated, in large samples, as a heteroscedastic linear model with $Ev_i^2 = 2\sigma_i^4$, $i = 1, 2, \ldots, T$.

Goldfeld and Quandt (1972) suggested the ordinary least squares estimator of $\boldsymbol{\alpha}$ obtained from Equation (9.2.24),

$$\hat{\boldsymbol{\alpha}} = \left(\sum_{i=1}^{T} \mathbf{z}_i\mathbf{z}_i'\right)^{-1} \sum_{i=1}^{T} \mathbf{z}_i\hat{e}_i^2 = (Z'Z)^{-1}Z'\hat{\mathbf{e}}^2, \tag{9.2.28}$$

where $Z' = (\mathbf{z}_1, \mathbf{z}_2, \ldots, \mathbf{z}_T)$ and $\hat{\mathbf{e}}^2 = (\hat{e}_1^2, \hat{e}_2^2, \ldots, \hat{e}_T^2)'$. Let Σ_1 denote the diagonal matrix which has as its ith diagonal element $2\sigma_i^4$. Then $\hat{\boldsymbol{\alpha}}$ is normally distributed, asymptotically, with mean $\boldsymbol{\alpha}$ (i.e., $\hat{\boldsymbol{\alpha}}$ is consistent) and covariance matrix

$$V_1 = (Z'Z)^{-1}Z'\Sigma_1 Z(Z'Z)^{-1}. \tag{9.2.29}$$

The covariance matrix V_1 is easily recognized as the covariance of an ordinary least squares estimator when the linear model has the generalized least squares error structure Σ_1 (see Chapter 3).

The feasible generalized least squares estimator using $\hat{\boldsymbol{\alpha}}$ is

$$\begin{aligned} \tilde{\tilde{\boldsymbol{\beta}}} &= (X'\hat{D}_1^{-1}X)^{-1}X'\hat{D}_1^{-1}\mathbf{y} \\ &= \left(\sum_{i=1}^{T} (\mathbf{z}_i'\hat{\boldsymbol{\alpha}})^{-1}\mathbf{x}_i\mathbf{x}_i'\right)^{-1} \sum_{i=1}^{T} (\mathbf{z}_i'\hat{\boldsymbol{\alpha}})^{-1}\mathbf{x}_i y_i, \end{aligned} \tag{9.2.30}$$

where $\hat{D}_1$ represents a diagonal matrix with the ith diagonal element being $\mathbf{z}_i'\hat{\boldsymbol{\alpha}}$. This estimator, given the results of Chapter 8, is consistent, distributed asymptotically normal, and in the presence of normally distributed e_i is asymptotically efficient. Its asymptotic covariance matrix is consistently estimated by

$$(X'\hat{D}_1^{-1}X)^{-1} = \left(\sum_{i=1}^{T} (\mathbf{z}_i'\hat{\boldsymbol{\alpha}})^{-1}\mathbf{x}_i\mathbf{x}_i'\right)^{-1}. \tag{9.2.31}$$

Though all that is required for two-step feasible generalized least squares estimators to attain full efficiency in the present model is that $\boldsymbol{\alpha}$ be estimated consistently, there is some reason to believe that a more efficient estimator of $\boldsymbol{\alpha}$ which takes into account the asymptotic heteroscedasticity of the estimating Equation (9.2.24) could provide feasible generalized least squares estimates which would perform better in small samples. This is exactly the tenor of a suggestion by Amemiya (1977). He proposed the following three-step procedure for estimating $\boldsymbol{\alpha}$:

(1) Obtain the ordinary least squares estimator $\hat{\boldsymbol{\alpha}}$ from Equation (9.2.28).
(2) Construct $\hat{\Sigma}_1$, where $\hat{\Sigma}_1$ is a diagonal matrix with ith diagonal element $2\hat{\sigma}_i^4 = 2(\mathbf{z}_i'\hat{\boldsymbol{\alpha}})^2$.
(3) Construct the feasible generalized least squares estimator of $\boldsymbol{\alpha}$,

$$\begin{aligned}\hat{\hat{\boldsymbol{\alpha}}} &= (Z'\hat{\Sigma}_1^{-1}Z)^{-1}Z'\hat{\Sigma}_1^{-1}\hat{\mathbf{e}}^2 \\ &= \left(\sum_{i=1}^{T}(\mathbf{z}_i'\hat{\boldsymbol{\alpha}})^{-2}\mathbf{z}_i\mathbf{z}_i'\right)^{-1}\sum_{i=1}^{T}(\mathbf{z}_i'\hat{\boldsymbol{\alpha}})^{-2}\mathbf{z}_i\hat{e}_i^2.\end{aligned} \tag{9.2.32}$$

Amemiya (1977) has shown that $\hat{\hat{\boldsymbol{\alpha}}}$ is distributed asymptotically normal with a zero mean and covariance matrix

$$V_2 = (Z'\Sigma_1^{-1}Z)^{-1}. \tag{9.2.33}$$

As Amemiya demonstrates, this is the same as the asymptotic covariance (Cramér–Rao lower bound) of the maximum likelihood estimator of $\boldsymbol{\alpha}$. Therefore, in the presence of normally distributed e_i's, $\hat{\hat{\boldsymbol{\alpha}}}$ is an asymptotically efficient estimator of $\boldsymbol{\alpha}$. Logically, $\hat{\boldsymbol{\alpha}}$ is not asymptotically efficient in that $V_1 - V_2$ is a positive semidefinite matrix. This occurs because $\hat{\boldsymbol{\alpha}}$ does not take into account the heteroscedasticity of the estimating equation.

Though no finite sample properties are analytically available, it seems reasonable that the suggested feasible generalized least squares estimator for heteroscedasticity of the type $\sigma_i^2 = \mathbf{z}_i'\boldsymbol{\alpha}$ should be

$$\begin{aligned}\tilde{\tilde{\boldsymbol{\beta}}} &= (X'\hat{\hat{D}}_1^{-1}X)^{-1}X'\hat{\hat{D}}_1\mathbf{y} \\ &= \left(\sum_{i=1}^{T}(\mathbf{z}_i'\hat{\hat{\boldsymbol{\alpha}}})^{-1}\mathbf{x}_i\mathbf{x}_i'\right)^{-1}\sum_{i=1}^{T}(\mathbf{z}_i'\hat{\hat{\boldsymbol{\alpha}}})^{-1}\mathbf{x}_i y_i,\end{aligned} \tag{9.2.34}$$

where $\hat{\hat{D}}$ represents a diagonal matrix with the ith diagonal element being $\mathbf{z}_i'\hat{\hat{\boldsymbol{\alpha}}}$. Like the feasible generalized least squares estimator using $\hat{\boldsymbol{\alpha}}$ (Equation (9.2.30)), this estimator is consistent, distributed asymptotically normal, and, in the presence of normal errors, is asymptotically efficient. However, as $\hat{\hat{\boldsymbol{\alpha}}}$ is superior to $\hat{\boldsymbol{\alpha}}$, the present estimator is likely to outperform its counterpart in small samples. Finally, the asymptotic covariance matrix for the estimator (9.2.34) is consistently estimated by

$$(X'\hat{\hat{D}}_1^{-1}X)^{-1} = \left(\sum_{i=1}^{T}(\mathbf{z}_i'\hat{\hat{\boldsymbol{\alpha}}})^{-1}\mathbf{x}_i\mathbf{x}_i'\right)^{-1}. \tag{9.2.35}$$

9.2.2b *Standard Deviation as a Linear Function of Exogenous Variables:* $\sigma_i = \mathbf{z}_i'\boldsymbol{\alpha}$

The linear model of interest in this section is

$$y_i = \mathbf{x}_i'\boldsymbol{\beta} + e_i, \qquad i = 1, 2, \ldots, T, \tag{9.2.36}$$

with

$$E(e_i) = 0, \qquad E(e_i^2) = \sigma_i^2 = (\mathbf{z}_i'\boldsymbol{\alpha})^2, \qquad E(e_i e_j) = 0, \qquad i \neq j, \quad (9.2.37)$$

and the e_i being normally distributed. Let D_2 be the diagonal matrix with ith diagonal element $(\mathbf{z}_i'\boldsymbol{\alpha})^2$. The generalized least squares estimator is

$$\begin{aligned}\tilde{\boldsymbol{\beta}} &= (X'D_2^{-1}X)^{-1}X'D_2^{-1}\mathbf{y} \\ &= \left(\sum_{i=1}^{T} (\mathbf{z}_i'\boldsymbol{\alpha})^{-2}\mathbf{x}_i\mathbf{x}_i'\right)^{-1} \sum_{i=1}^{T} (\mathbf{z}_i'\boldsymbol{\alpha})^{-2}\mathbf{x}_i y_i \qquad (9.2.38)\end{aligned}$$

which has mean $\boldsymbol{\beta}$ and covariance matrix

$$(X'D_2^{-1}X)^{-1} = \left(\sum_{i=1}^{T} (\mathbf{z}_i'\boldsymbol{\alpha})^{-2}\mathbf{x}_i\mathbf{x}_i'\right)^{-1}. \qquad (9.2.39)$$

Obviously, the discussion of feasible generalized least squares estimation of the model (9.2.36)–(9.2.37) is going to parallel that of the previous section except there will be a different estimating equation for $\boldsymbol{\alpha}$. By assumption, $\sigma_1^{-1}e_1, \sigma_2^{-1}e_2, \ldots, \sigma_T^{-1}e_T$ are independently and identically distributed with zero mean and variance one. It follows (see Exercise 9.3) that the mean of the absolute value of these standardized random variables, $\phi = \sigma_i^{-1}|e_i|$, is

$$E\phi = 2\int_0^{\infty} wf(w)\, dw \equiv c, \qquad (9.2.40)$$

where $f(w)$ denotes the probability density function of $w = e_i/\sigma_i$, c is a constant which is independent of i and depends on the particular density $f(w)$, and it has been assumed that $f(w)$ is symmetric about zero and has domain $-\infty < w < \infty$ (i.e., $(-\infty, \infty)$ is the assumed domain of e_i). For example, it follows from (9.2.40) (see Exercise 9.4) that if $e_i \sim N(0, \sigma_i^2)$ then $c = (2/\pi)^{1/2}$. Therefore, as $E|e_i| = c\sigma_i = c\mathbf{z}_i'\boldsymbol{\alpha}$, a logical linear estimating equation becomes

$$|\hat{e}_i| = c\mathbf{z}_i'\boldsymbol{\alpha} + v_i, \qquad (9.2.41)$$

where $\hat{e}_i = y_i - \mathbf{x}_i'\hat{\boldsymbol{\beta}}$ is the ith ordinary least squares residual, and $v_i = |\hat{e}_i| - c\sigma_i$. Gleisjer (1969) suggested estimating $c\boldsymbol{\alpha}$ by applying ordinary least squares to (9.2.41) and obtaining

$$\widehat{c\boldsymbol{\alpha}} = \left(\sum_{i=1}^{T}\mathbf{z}_i\mathbf{z}_i'\right)^{-1} \sum_{i=1}^{T}\mathbf{z}_i|\hat{e}_i| = (Z'Z)^{-1}Z'|\hat{\mathbf{e}}|, \qquad (9.2.42)$$

where $Z' = (\mathbf{z}_1, \mathbf{z}_2, \ldots, \mathbf{z}_T)$ and $|\hat{\mathbf{e}}| = (|\hat{e}_1|, |\hat{e}_2|, \ldots, |\hat{e}_T|)'$. The fact that $c\boldsymbol{\alpha}$ has been estimated rather than $\boldsymbol{\alpha}$ does not affect the feasible generalized least squares estimation of $\boldsymbol{\beta}$ as all that is required is that the error covariance structure be estimated up to a scalar multiple. The corresponding feasible generalized linear squares estimator is

$$\tilde{\tilde{\boldsymbol{\beta}}} = \left(\sum_{i=1}^{T} (\mathbf{z}_i'\widehat{c\boldsymbol{\alpha}})^{-2}\mathbf{x}_i\mathbf{x}_i'\right)^{-1} \sum_{i=1}^{T} (\mathbf{z}_i'\widehat{c\boldsymbol{\alpha}})^{-2}\mathbf{x}_i y_i. \qquad (9.2.43)$$

Of course, $\widehat{c\boldsymbol{\alpha}}$ is a biased and inefficient estimator of $c\boldsymbol{\alpha}$ in small samples as it can be shown (see Exercise 9.5) that the v_i are heteroscedastic, autocorrelated and have different nonzero means. However, in a manner analogous to the previous section, the error terms v_i have an asymptotic zero mean and are independently distributed with heteroscedastic variance

$$\begin{aligned} E(v_i^2) &= E(|\hat{e}_i|^2) - (E|\hat{e}_i|)^2 = E(|e_i|^2) - (E|e_i|)^2 \\ &= \sigma_i^2 - (c\sigma_i)^2 = (1 - c^2)\sigma_i^2 \\ &= (1 - c^2)(\mathbf{z}_i'\boldsymbol{\alpha})^2, \end{aligned} \tag{9.2.44}$$

since $\text{plim}(\hat{e}_i - e_i) = 0$ and the ordinary least squares residuals behave as if they were the unobservable errors e_i.

Therefore, asymptotically, the estimating equation (9.2.41) is heteroscedastic and the ordinary least squares estimator $\widehat{c\boldsymbol{\alpha}}$ is an asymptotically inefficient estimator of $c\boldsymbol{\alpha}$ (and hence $\hat{\boldsymbol{\alpha}}$ is also inefficient if c is known). The more efficient alternative is feasible generalized least squares estimation of $c\boldsymbol{\alpha}$. The estimation steps are:

(1) Obtain the ordinary least squares estimate $\widehat{c\boldsymbol{\alpha}}$. For *known* c, $\hat{\boldsymbol{\alpha}} = \widehat{c\boldsymbol{\alpha}}/c$.
(2) Construct $\hat{\Sigma}_2$, a consistent estimate of the error covariance Σ_2 of the estimating equation (9.2.41). $\hat{\Sigma}_2$ is a diagonal matrix with ith diagonal element $(1 - c^2)(\mathbf{z}_i'\hat{\boldsymbol{\alpha}})^2$.
(3) Construct the feasible generalized least squares estimator of $c\boldsymbol{\alpha}$

$$\widehat{\widehat{c\boldsymbol{\alpha}}} = (Z'\hat{\Sigma}_2^{-1}Z)^{-1}Z'\hat{\Sigma}_2^{-1}|\hat{\mathbf{e}}|. \tag{9.2.45}$$

The corresponding feasible generalized least squares for $\boldsymbol{\beta}$ is then

$$\tilde{\tilde{\boldsymbol{\beta}}} = \left(\sum_{i=1}^{T} (\mathbf{z}_i'\widehat{\widehat{c\boldsymbol{\alpha}}})^{-2}\mathbf{x}_i\mathbf{x}_i'\right)^{-1} \sum_{i=1}^{T} (\mathbf{z}_i'\widehat{\widehat{c\boldsymbol{\alpha}}})^{-2}\mathbf{x}_i y_i. \tag{9.2.46}$$

Notice, a requirement of this estimation procedure, unlike that of (9.2.42), is that c be *known*. That is, the investigator must be willing to specify the functional form of e_i.

With respect to the estimation of $c\boldsymbol{\alpha}$, Harvey (1974) shows that $\widehat{c\boldsymbol{\alpha}}$ and $\widehat{\widehat{c\boldsymbol{\alpha}}}$ are consistent estimates of $c\boldsymbol{\alpha}$ and have the respective covariance matrices

$$V_3 = (Z'Z)^{-1}Z'\Sigma_2 Z(Z'Z)^{-1} \tag{9.2.47}$$

and

$$V_4 = (Z'\Sigma_2^{-1}Z)^{-1}, \tag{9.2.48}$$

where Σ_2 is the diagonal matrix with ith diagonal element $(1 - c^2)(\mathbf{z}_i'\boldsymbol{\alpha})^2$. Equation (9.2.47) represents the covariance matrix of an ordinary least squares estimator when a generalized least squares error specification is appropriate while Equation (9.2.48) represents the generalized least squares covariance matrix. In the presence of normal e_i's the latter equation also represents the Cramér–Rao lower bound matrix for $c\boldsymbol{\alpha}$. As

$$(Z'Z)^{-1}Z'\Sigma_2 Z(Z'Z)^{-1} - (Z'\Sigma_2^{-1}Z)^{-1}$$

is a positive definite matrix, $\hat{\hat{c\boldsymbol{\alpha}}}$ is asymptotically more efficient than $\widehat{c\boldsymbol{\alpha}}$.

Though, in the presence of normal e_i, both feasible generalized least squares estimators ((9.2.43) and (9.2.46)) are asymptotically efficient, it seems reasonable to prefer feasible generalized least squares using $\hat{\hat{c\boldsymbol{\alpha}}}$ as the small properties of $\hat{\hat{c\boldsymbol{\alpha}}}$ are likely to be better than those of $\widehat{c\boldsymbol{\alpha}}$. Likewise, tests of hypotheses concerning $\boldsymbol{\beta}$ would probably be best carried out using the estimated covariance matrix.

$$\frac{1}{c^2}\left(\sum_{i=1}^{T}(\mathbf{z}_i'\hat{\hat{c\boldsymbol{\alpha}}})^{-2}\mathbf{x}_i\mathbf{x}_i'\right)^{-1} = \left(\sum_{i=1}^{T}(\mathbf{z}_i'\hat{\hat{\boldsymbol{\alpha}}})^{-2}\mathbf{x}_i\mathbf{x}_i'\right)^{-1}. \tag{9.2.49}$$

9.2.2c *Multiplicative Heteroscedasticity:* $\sigma_i^2 = \exp(\mathbf{z}_i'\boldsymbol{\alpha})$

Harvey (1976) proposed and investigated a general formulation of heteroscedasticity called multiplicative heteroscedasticity. His specification of the linear model was

$$y_i = \mathbf{x}_i'\boldsymbol{\beta} + e_i, \qquad i = 1, 2, \ldots, T, \tag{9.2.50}$$

with

$$E(e_i) = 0, \qquad E(e_i^2) = \sigma_i^2 = \exp(\mathbf{z}_i'\boldsymbol{\alpha}), \qquad E(e_ie_j) = 0, \qquad i \neq j, \tag{9.2.51}$$

and the e_i being normally distributed. Unlike the "additive" heteroscedasticity of $\sigma_i^2 = \mathbf{z}_i'\boldsymbol{\alpha}$ or $\sigma_i = \mathbf{z}_i'\boldsymbol{\alpha}$, the present heteroscedasticity is multiplicative in that $\sigma_i^2 = \exp(z_{i1}\alpha_1)\cdots\exp(z_{ip}\alpha_p)$. One example is $\boldsymbol{\alpha} = (\ln\sigma^2, \lambda_1, \lambda_2)'$ and $\mathbf{z}_i' = (1, \ln x_{i1}, \ln x_{i2})$ with error variances $\sigma_i^2 = \sigma^2 x_{i1}^{\lambda_1}x_{i2}^{\lambda_2}$.

Let D_3 be the diagonal matrix with ith diagonal element $\exp(\mathbf{z}_i'\boldsymbol{\alpha})$. The generalized least squares estimator is

$$\begin{aligned}\tilde{\boldsymbol{\beta}} &= (X'D_3^{-1}X)^{-1}X'D_3^{-1}\mathbf{y}\\ &= \left(\sum_{i=1}^{T}[\exp(\mathbf{z}_i'\boldsymbol{\alpha})]^{-1}\mathbf{x}_i\mathbf{x}_i'\right)^{-1}\sum_{i=1}^{T}[\exp(\mathbf{z}_i\boldsymbol{\alpha})]^{-1}\mathbf{x}_iy_i\end{aligned} \tag{9.2.52}$$

which has mean $\boldsymbol{\beta}$ and covariance matrix

$$(X'D_3^{-1}X)^{-1} = \left(\sum_{i=1}^{T}[\exp(\mathbf{z}_i'\boldsymbol{\alpha})]^{-1}\mathbf{x}_i\mathbf{x}_i'\right)^{-1}. \tag{9.2.53}$$

In most cases, however, the parameter vector $\boldsymbol{\alpha}$ must be estimated consistently in order that feasible generalized least squares may be implemented.

Applying a natural logarithmic transformation to $\sigma_i^2 = \exp(\mathbf{x}_i'\boldsymbol{\alpha})$ provides

$$\ln \sigma_i^2 = \mathbf{z}_i'\boldsymbol{\alpha}. \tag{9.2.54}$$

A logical estimating equation for $\boldsymbol{\alpha}$ becomes

$$\ln \hat{e}_i^2 = \mathbf{z}_i'\boldsymbol{\alpha} + v_i \tag{9.2.55}$$

where, as before, $\hat{e}_i$ is the ith ordinary least squares residual and $v_i = \ln(\hat{e}_i^2/\sigma_i^2)$. The distribution of v_i converges to the distribution of v_i^*, say, which is distributed as the natural logarithm of a χ^2 random variable of one degree of freedom. Moreover (see Exercise 9.6) $Ev_i^* = -1.2704$ and var $v_i^* = 4.9348$. Application of ordinary least squares to (9.2.55) provides

$$\hat{\boldsymbol{\alpha}} = \left(\sum_{i=1}^{T} \mathbf{z}_i\mathbf{z}_i'\right)^{-1} \sum_{i=1}^{T} \mathbf{z}_i \ln \hat{e}_i^2. \tag{9.2.56}$$

Let $\hat{\alpha}_1$ denote the first element of $\hat{\boldsymbol{\alpha}}$. Because of the *constant* nonzero mean of v_i^*, $\hat{\alpha}_1$ is an inconsistent estimator of α_1 in that plim $\hat{\alpha}_1 = \alpha_1 - 1.2704$. However, the other $p - 1$ elements in $\hat{\alpha}$ are consistent estimators of the corresponding parameters in $\boldsymbol{\alpha}$ (see Exercise 9.7). Since α_1 merely introduces a factor of proportionality, the feasible generalized least squares estimator

$$\tilde{\tilde{\boldsymbol{\beta}}} = \left(\sum_{i=1}^{T} [\exp(\mathbf{z}_i'\hat{\boldsymbol{\alpha}})]^{-1}\mathbf{x}_i\mathbf{x}_i'\right)^{-1} \sum_{i=1}^{T} [\exp(\mathbf{z}_i'\hat{\boldsymbol{\alpha}})]^{-1}\mathbf{x}_i y_i \tag{9.2.57}$$

constructed from $\hat{\boldsymbol{\alpha}}$ will be consistent, distributed asymptotically normal, and, in the presence of normal errors, asymptotically efficient.

Harvey (1976) also shows that the asymptotic covariance matrix for $\hat{\boldsymbol{\alpha}}$ is

$$\text{var}(\hat{\boldsymbol{\alpha}}) = 4.9348\left[\sum_{i=1}^{T} \mathbf{z}_i\mathbf{z}_i'\right]^{-1}. \tag{9.2.58}$$

We will compare this to the asymptotic covariance matrix of the maximum likelihood estimator of $\boldsymbol{\alpha}$ below.

With the assumption of normal errors the linear model with multiplicative heteroscedasticity (9.2.50)–(9.2.51) can be estimated by the method of maximum likelihood. The likelihood function of this model is

$$L(\mathbf{y}|X) = \prod_{i=1}^{T} \frac{1}{(2\pi\sigma_i^2)^{1/2}} \exp\left\{-\frac{1}{2\sigma_i^2}(y_i - \mathbf{x}_i'\boldsymbol{\beta})^2\right\} \tag{9.2.59}$$

with the natural logarithm of the likelihood function being

$$\ln L = -\frac{T}{2}\ln 2\pi - \frac{1}{2}\sum_{i=1}^{T} \mathbf{z}_i'\boldsymbol{\alpha} - \frac{1}{2}\sum_{i=1}^{T} \exp(-\mathbf{z}_i'\boldsymbol{\alpha})(y_i - \mathbf{x}_i'\boldsymbol{\beta})^2. \tag{9.2.60}$$

However, this likelihood function is nonlinear in the parameters. The "method of scoring" (see the Appendix of this book) which is a means of linearizing the maximum likelihood first-order conditions by means of a vector Taylor series expansion, provides a fairly straightforward means of obtaining estimators which are asymptotically equivalent to maximum likelihood estimators and hence are asymptotically efficient.

Following Harvey (1976), the iterative equations for estimating $\boldsymbol{\beta}$ and $\boldsymbol{\alpha}$ can be written as

$$\hat{\boldsymbol{\beta}}^{(t+1)} = \hat{\boldsymbol{\beta}}^{(t)} + \left\{ E\left[\frac{\partial^2 \ln L}{\partial \boldsymbol{\beta}\, \partial \boldsymbol{\beta}'}\right]_{\substack{\boldsymbol{\beta} = \hat{\boldsymbol{\beta}}^{(t)} \\ \boldsymbol{\alpha} = \hat{\boldsymbol{\alpha}}^{(t)}}} \right\}^{-1} \left[\frac{\partial \ln L}{\partial \boldsymbol{\beta}}\right]_{\substack{\boldsymbol{\beta} = \hat{\boldsymbol{\beta}}^{(t)} \\ \boldsymbol{\alpha} = \hat{\boldsymbol{\alpha}}^{(t)}}}$$

$$= \hat{\boldsymbol{\beta}}^{(t)} + \left(\sum_{i=1}^{T} \exp(-\mathbf{z}_i' \hat{\boldsymbol{\alpha}}^{(t)}) \mathbf{x}_i \mathbf{x}_i' \right)^{-1} \times \sum_{i=1}^{T} \mathbf{x}_i \exp(-\mathbf{z}_i' \hat{\boldsymbol{\alpha}}^{(t)})(y_i - \mathbf{x}_i' \hat{\boldsymbol{\beta}}^{(t)}) \tag{9.2.61}$$

and

$$\hat{\boldsymbol{\alpha}}^{(t+1)} = \hat{\boldsymbol{\alpha}}^{(t)} + \left\{ E\left[\frac{\partial^2 \ln L}{\partial \boldsymbol{\alpha}\, \partial \boldsymbol{\alpha}'}\right]_{\substack{\boldsymbol{\beta} = \hat{\boldsymbol{\beta}}^{(t)} \\ \boldsymbol{\alpha} = \hat{\boldsymbol{\alpha}}^{(t)}}} \right\}^{-1} \left[\frac{\partial \ln L}{\partial \boldsymbol{\alpha}}\right]_{\substack{\boldsymbol{\beta} = \hat{\boldsymbol{\beta}}^{(t)} \\ \boldsymbol{\alpha} = \hat{\boldsymbol{\alpha}}^{(t)}}}$$

$$= \hat{\boldsymbol{\alpha}}^{(t)} + \left(\sum_{i=1}^{T} \mathbf{z}_i \mathbf{z}_i' \right)^{-1} \sum_{i=1}^{T} \mathbf{z}_i [\exp(-\mathbf{z}_i' \hat{\boldsymbol{\alpha}}^{(t)})(y_i - \mathbf{x}_i' \hat{\boldsymbol{\beta}}^{(t)})^2 - 1], \tag{9.2.62}$$

where (t) represents the tth iteration. As discussed in the Appendix, if we substitute consistent estimates for $\hat{\boldsymbol{\beta}}^{(1)}$ and $\hat{\boldsymbol{\alpha}}^{(1)}$ then $\hat{\boldsymbol{\beta}}^{(2)}$ and $\hat{\boldsymbol{\alpha}}^{(2)}$ are consistent and asymptotically efficient. Further iteration, though it may be performed until successive changes are small, does not offer any gains in asymptotic efficiency though possible gains in small sample efficiency are still open to question.

In the present case let $\hat{\boldsymbol{\beta}}^{(1)} = \hat{\boldsymbol{\beta}}$, the ordinary least squares estimator of the original equation $y_i = \mathbf{x}_i' \boldsymbol{\beta} + \mathbf{e}_i$. Provided that α_1 is estimated by $\hat{\alpha}_1 + 1.2704$, the estimate $\hat{\boldsymbol{\alpha}}$ from (9.2.56) is a consistent estimate of $\boldsymbol{\alpha}$. Substitution in Equation (9.2.62) yields an efficient estimate of $\boldsymbol{\alpha}$

$$\boldsymbol{\alpha}^* = \hat{\boldsymbol{\alpha}} + \boldsymbol{\phi} + 0.2807 \left[\sum_{i=1}^{T} \mathbf{z}_i \mathbf{z}_i' \right]^{-1} \sum_{i=1}^{T} \mathbf{z}_i \exp(-\mathbf{z}_i' \hat{\boldsymbol{\alpha}}) \hat{e}_i^2, \tag{9.2.63}$$

where $\boldsymbol{\phi}$ is a $p \times 1$ vector with its first element equal to 0.2704 and the remaining elements are zero and $\hat{\boldsymbol{\alpha}}$ is that of (9.2.56).

Though the feasible generalized least squares estimator utilizing $\hat{\boldsymbol{\alpha}}$ obtained from (9.2.56) is asymptotically efficient, there remains the question as to whether the small sample estimation efficiency might not be enhanced by a *three-step* feasible generalized least squares estimator which utilizes $\hat{\boldsymbol{\alpha}}$ to obtain $\boldsymbol{\alpha}^*$ by the method of scoring and then using $\boldsymbol{\alpha}^*$ in feasible generalized least squares estimation of $\boldsymbol{\beta}$. To address this question, let us investigate to what extent $\hat{\boldsymbol{\alpha}}$ is inefficient. This can be done by comparing the covariance matrix of (9.2.58) with the asymptotic Cramér–Rao lower bound (see Chapter 4) which the estimate $\boldsymbol{\alpha}^*$ would obtain. As can be shown (see Exercise 13.7) the inverse of the information matrix is

$$\left\{ -E \begin{bmatrix} \dfrac{\partial^2 \ln L}{\partial \boldsymbol{\beta}\, \partial \boldsymbol{\beta}'} & \dfrac{\partial^2 \ln L}{\partial \boldsymbol{\beta}\, \partial \boldsymbol{\alpha}'} \\ \dfrac{\partial^2 \ln L}{\partial \boldsymbol{\alpha}\, \partial \boldsymbol{\beta}'} & \dfrac{\partial^2 \ln L}{\partial \boldsymbol{\alpha}\, \partial \boldsymbol{\alpha}'} \end{bmatrix} \right\}^{-1} = \begin{bmatrix} \left(\sum_{i=1}^{T} \sigma_i^{-2} \mathbf{x}_i \mathbf{x}_i' \right)^{-1} & 0 \\ 0 & 2\left(\sum_{i=1}^{T} \mathbf{z}_i \mathbf{z}_i' \right)^{-1} \end{bmatrix}. \tag{9.2.64}$$

Comparing the variance of $\hat{\boldsymbol{\alpha}}$ in (9.2.58) with the covariance matrix $2(\sum_{i=1}^{T} \mathbf{z}_i \mathbf{z}_i')^{-1}$ of $\boldsymbol{\alpha}^*$ makes it clear that the estimator $\hat{\boldsymbol{\alpha}}$ is inefficient relative to $\boldsymbol{\alpha}^*$. The variance of $\hat{\boldsymbol{\alpha}}$ will exceed those of $\boldsymbol{\alpha}^*$ by almost two and one-half fold. It, therefore, seems reasonable that a feasible generalized least squares estimator using $\boldsymbol{\alpha}^*$ rather than $\hat{\boldsymbol{\alpha}}$ will have better small sample properties. Of course, the estimator for $\boldsymbol{\beta}$ derived from the method of scoring using $\hat{\boldsymbol{\beta}}^{(1)} = \hat{\boldsymbol{\beta}}$ and $\hat{\boldsymbol{\alpha}}^{(1)} = \boldsymbol{\alpha}^*$ is also a viable alternative. Likewise, for the purpose of testing hypotheses concerning $\boldsymbol{\beta}$, a consistent estimate of the covariance matrix of the feasible generalized least squares estimator using $\boldsymbol{\alpha}^*$ is

$$\left(\sum_{i=1}^{T} [\exp(\mathbf{z}_i' \boldsymbol{\alpha}^*)]^{-1} \mathbf{x}_i \mathbf{x}_i' \right)^{-1}. \tag{9.2.65}$$

9.2.2d *Heteroscedasticity of Known but General Functional Form: Maximum Likelihood Estimation*

There may be cases where none of the three forms of heteroscedasticity previously discussed are appropriate. Let $f(\mathbf{z})$ denote a one-to-one function of $\mathbf{z} = (z_1, \ldots, z_p)'$ to the positive real line. Assume heteroscedasticity of the form,

$$\sigma_i^2 = f(\mathbf{z}_i), \tag{9.2.66}$$

where $\mathbf{z} = (z_{i1}, z_{i2}, \ldots, z_{ip})$ denotes the ith observation on the p exogenous variables $z_1, \ldots, z_p$ and $i = 1, 2, \ldots, T$. For example, $f(\mathbf{z}_i)$ might be of the form

$$f(\mathbf{z}_i) = \frac{a + bz_{i1}}{(c + dz_{i2})^{1/2}}. \tag{9.2.67}$$

The linear model of concern is

$$\mathbf{y} = X\boldsymbol{\beta} + \mathbf{e}, \tag{9.2.68}$$

where $E\mathbf{e} = \mathbf{0}$ and

$$\Omega = E\mathbf{e}\mathbf{e}' = \begin{bmatrix} f(\mathbf{z}_1) & & & 0 \\ & f(\mathbf{z}_2) & & \\ & & \ddots & \\ 0 & & & f(\mathbf{z}_T) \end{bmatrix}. \tag{9.2.69}$$

Once the error term has been parametrized and maximum likelihood methods are called into play, the estimation procedure is straightforward. The likelihood function, assuming normal errors, is

$$L = \left(\frac{1}{\sqrt{2\pi}}\right)^T |\Omega|^{-1/2} \exp\{-\tfrac{1}{2}(\mathbf{y} - X\boldsymbol{\beta})'\Omega^{-1}(\mathbf{y} - X\boldsymbol{\beta})\} \tag{9.2.70}$$

which is maximized with respect to $\boldsymbol{\beta}$ and the parameters of the function $f(\mathbf{z})$. As discussed in Chapter 4, asymptotic variances and covariances for the normally distributed maximum likelihood estimates can be obtained from the inverse of the information matrix. Methods of maximizing nonlinear likelihood functions and obtaining numerical approximations of the information matrix are discussed in the Appendix of this book.

9.3 Tests for Heteroscedasticity

In the previous section it was assumed that the specific heteroscedasticity was known *a priori*. Instead, the more typical case occurs when a particular form or forms of heteroscedasticity is suspected yet its existence is not known with certainty. One approach to such uncertainty is to examine tests of hypotheses of the parameters describing a given heteroscedastic scheme and determine if the data support the supposition. If it does, the heteroscedastic correction could be implemented. If it does not, ordinary least squares could be used. Of course, the choice of an error specification based upon a test of hypothesis leads to a choice between the ordinary least squares and feasible generalized least squares estimators by means of a *preliminary test*. Therefore, the resulting estimator is a preliminary test estimator. The effects of preliminary tests on estimation under heteroscedasticity will be discussed in Section 9.5. The present section describes the tests of hypotheses which may be used given the heteroscedastic schemes discussed in Section 9.2, namely grouped heteroscedasticity and heteroscedasticity as a function of exogenous variables. Also in Section 9.3.3 some "nonspecific" tests of heteroscedasticity are presented. By nonspecific, we mean tests which are designed to detect heteroscedasticity yet the investigator does not possess *a priori* knowledge of a *specific* form of heteroscedasticity.

9.3.1 Likelihood Ratio Test for Grouped Heteroscedasticity

Given the grouped heteroscedasticity model of (9.2.2)–(9.2.4), a test for homoscedasticity versus grouped heteroscedasticity would be of the form:

$$H_0: \sigma_1^2 = \sigma_2^2 = \cdots = \sigma_G^2 = \sigma^2,$$
$$H_1: \text{not all } \sigma_i^2 = \sigma^2. \tag{9.3.1}$$

Assume the e_i are normally distributed. From Theorem 4.2.4 we know that the likelihood ratio statistic, $l = L(\hat{\omega})/L(\hat{\Omega})$, can provide an asymptotic test of (9.3.1) as $-2 \ln l \overset{\text{asy}}{\approx} \chi_q^2$. Here Ω represents the $(K + G)$-dimensional universal parameter set $\{\beta_1, \ldots, \beta_K, \sigma_1^2, \ldots, \sigma_G^2\}$, and ω represents the $[(K + G) - (G - 1)]$-dimensional subset of Ω, $\{\beta_1, \ldots, \beta_K, \sigma^2\}$, corresponding to the null hypothesis.

To compute the likelihood ratio statistic, we construct

$$L(\omega) = L(\mathbf{y} \mid X, \boldsymbol{\beta}; \sigma_1^2 = \sigma_2^2 = \cdots = \sigma_G^2 = \sigma^2)$$
$$= \frac{1}{(2\pi)^{T/2}\sigma^T} \exp\left\{-\frac{1}{2\sigma^2}(\mathbf{y} - X\boldsymbol{\beta})'(\mathbf{y} - X\boldsymbol{\beta})\right\}. \tag{9.3.2}$$

But

$$L(\hat{\omega}) = \frac{1}{(2\pi)^{T/2}\tilde{\sigma}^T} \exp\left\{-\frac{1}{2\tilde{\sigma}^2}(\mathbf{y} - X\hat{\boldsymbol{\beta}})'(\mathbf{y} - X\hat{\boldsymbol{\beta}})\right\}, \tag{9.3.3}$$

where the constrained maximum likelihood estimators are

$$\hat{\boldsymbol{\beta}} = (X'X)^{-1}X'\mathbf{y} \tag{9.3.4}$$

and

$$\tilde{\sigma}^2 = \frac{(\mathbf{y} - X\hat{\boldsymbol{\beta}})'(\mathbf{y} - X\hat{\boldsymbol{\beta}})}{T}. \tag{9.3.5}$$

Also

$$L(\Omega) = L(\mathbf{y} \mid X, \boldsymbol{\beta}, \sigma_1^2, \sigma_2^2, \ldots, \sigma_G^2)$$
$$= \frac{1}{(2\pi)^{T/2}\sigma_1^{T_1}\sigma_2^{T_2}\cdots\sigma_G^{T_G}} \exp\left\{-\frac{1}{2}\sum_{g=1}^{G}\frac{1}{\sigma_g^2}(\mathbf{y}_g - X_g\boldsymbol{\beta})'(\mathbf{y}_g - X_g\boldsymbol{\beta})\right\} \tag{9.3.6}$$

and

$$L(\hat{\Omega}) = \frac{1}{(2\pi)^{T/2}\tilde{\sigma}_1^{T_1}\tilde{\sigma}_2^{T_2}\cdots\tilde{\sigma}_G^{T_G}} \exp\left\{-\frac{1}{2}\sum_{g=1}^{G}\frac{1}{\tilde{\sigma}_g^2}(\mathbf{y}_g - X_g\tilde{\tilde{\boldsymbol{\beta}}})'(\mathbf{y}_g - X_g\tilde{\tilde{\boldsymbol{\beta}}})\right\}, \tag{9.3.7}$$

where the unconstrained maximum likelihood estimators for $\boldsymbol{\beta}$ and $\sigma_1^2, \ldots, \sigma_G^2$ are

$$\tilde{\tilde{\boldsymbol{\beta}}} = (X'S^{-1}X)^{-1}X'S^{-1}\mathbf{y}, \tag{9.3.8}$$

where

$$S = \begin{bmatrix} \tilde{\sigma}_1^2 I_{T_1} & & & 0 \\ & \tilde{\sigma}_2^2 I_{T_2} & & \\ & & \ddots & \\ 0 & & & \tilde{\sigma}_G^2 I_{T_G} \end{bmatrix} \tag{9.3.9}$$

and

$$\tilde{\sigma}_g^2 = \frac{(\mathbf{y}_g - X_g\tilde{\tilde{\boldsymbol{\beta}}})'(\mathbf{y}_g - X_g\tilde{\tilde{\boldsymbol{\beta}}})}{T_g}, \qquad g = 1, 2, \ldots, G. \tag{9.3.10}$$

Using $\hat{\boldsymbol{\beta}}_g = (X'_g X_g)^{-1} X'_g \mathbf{y}_g$, an initial starting value for $\tilde{\sigma}_g^2$ in (9.3.10) can be obtained with final values of $\tilde{\tilde{\boldsymbol{\beta}}}$ and $\tilde{\sigma}_g^2$ resulting from continued iteration between (9.3.8) and (9.3.10) until successive differences are arbitrarily small.

Given the above developments, the likelihood ratio statistic is

$$l = \frac{L(\hat{\omega})}{L(\hat{\Omega})} = \frac{\dfrac{1}{(2\pi)^{T/2}\tilde{\sigma}^T} \exp\left\{-\dfrac{1}{2\hat{\sigma}^2}(\mathbf{y} - X\hat{\boldsymbol{\beta}})'(\mathbf{y} - X\hat{\boldsymbol{\beta}})\right\}}{\dfrac{1}{(2\pi)^{T/2}\tilde{\sigma}_1^{T_1}\tilde{\sigma}_2^{T_2}\cdots\tilde{\sigma}_G^{T_G}} \exp\left\{-\dfrac{1}{2}\sum_{g=1}^{G}\dfrac{1}{\tilde{\sigma}_g^2}(\mathbf{y}_g - X_g\tilde{\tilde{\boldsymbol{\beta}}})'(\mathbf{y}_g - X_g\tilde{\tilde{\boldsymbol{\beta}}})\right\}}$$

$$= \frac{\tilde{\sigma}_1^{T_1}\tilde{\sigma}_2^{T_2}\cdots\tilde{\sigma}_G^{T_G}}{\tilde{\sigma}^T} \tag{9.3.11}$$

and the statistic

$$-2\ln l = 2[T\ln\tilde{\sigma} - (T_1\ln\tilde{\sigma}_1 + T_2\ln\tilde{\sigma}_2 + \cdots + T_G\ln\tilde{\sigma}_G)] \tag{9.3.12}$$

is asymptotically distributed as a χ^2 random variable with $G - 1$ degrees of freedom. If one does not have access to computer software with which to carry out an iterative maximum likelihood computation, the estimates $\tilde{\sigma}_1, \tilde{\sigma}_2, \ldots, \tilde{\sigma}_G$ in (9.3.12) may be replaced by the consistent, though inefficient, estimates $\hat{\sigma}_1, \hat{\sigma}_2, \ldots, \hat{\sigma}_G$ obtained from using $\hat{\boldsymbol{\beta}}_g = (X'_g X_g)^{-1} X'_g \mathbf{y}_g$ in (9.3.10). Though such a statistic is likewise asymptotically distributed as a χ^2_{G-1} random variable, its power is probably less, in small samples, than that of (9.3.12).

9.3.2 Tests for Heteroscedasticity Which Are Specific Functions of Exogenous Variables

9.3.2a *Tests of Variance as a Linear Function of Exogenous Variables:* $\sigma_i^2 = \mathbf{z}_i'\boldsymbol{\alpha}$

The heteroscedastic specification of interest is

$$\sigma_i^2 = \mathbf{z}_i'\boldsymbol{\alpha}. \tag{9.3.13}$$

A test that the error variance is homoscedastic versus that the error variance follows the specification (9.3.13) is equivalent to

$$\begin{aligned} &H_0: \alpha_2 = \alpha_3 = \cdots = \alpha_p = 0, \\ &H_1: \text{not } H_0. \end{aligned} \tag{9.3.14}$$

There are two possible ways to proceed. First, the ordinary least squares estimator $\hat{\boldsymbol{\alpha}}$ described by Equation (9.2.28) is distributed asymptotically normal with covariance matrix

$$V_1 = (Z'Z)^{-1}Z'\Sigma_1 Z(Z'Z)^{-1}, \tag{9.3.15}$$

where Σ_1 is a diagonal matrix with ith diagonal element $2\sigma_i^4 = 2(\mathbf{z}_i'\boldsymbol{\alpha})^2$. Under the null hypothesis, $V_1 = 2\alpha_1^2(Z'Z)^{-1}$. A logical way to proceed is to construct the quadratic form

$$l_1 = \hat{\boldsymbol{\alpha}}_0'(V_1^0)^{-1}\hat{\boldsymbol{\alpha}}_0, \tag{9.3.16}$$

where $\hat{\boldsymbol{\alpha}}_0 = (\hat{\alpha}_2, \ldots, \hat{\alpha}_p)'$ and V_1^0 denotes the $(p-1) \times (p-1)$ matrix obtained by dropping the first row and column of $2\hat{\alpha}_1^2(Z'Z)^{-1}$. Under the null hypothesis H_0 of (9.3.14), the statistic l_1 is asymptotically distributed as a χ_{p-1}^2 random variable. Recall that if $\mathbf{x}$ is a $q \times 1$ random vector which is distributed as a multivariate normal distribution with mean $\mathbf{0}$ and covariance matrix Σ, then $\mathbf{x}'\Sigma^{-1}\mathbf{x}$ is distributed as a χ^2 distribution with q degrees of freedom.

Alternatively, the feasible generalized least squares estimator $\hat{\hat{\boldsymbol{\alpha}}}$ of (9.2.32) is distributed asymptotically normal with covariance matrix

$$V_2 = (Z'\Sigma_1^{-1}Z)^{-1}. \tag{9.3.17}$$

An alternative statistic to l_1 would be

$$l_2 = \hat{\hat{\boldsymbol{\alpha}}}_0'(V_2^0)^{-1}\hat{\hat{\boldsymbol{\alpha}}}_0, \tag{9.3.18}$$

where $\hat{\hat{\boldsymbol{\alpha}}}_0 = (\hat{\hat{\alpha}}_2, \ldots, \hat{\hat{\alpha}}_p)'$ and V_2^0 denotes the $(p-1) \times (p-1)$ matrix obtained by dropping the first row and column of $2\hat{\hat{\alpha}}_1^2(Z'Z)^{-1}$. Under the null hypothesis H_0 of homoscedasticity, l_2 is asymptotically distributed as a χ_{p-1}^2 random variable. We, therefore, have two asymptotically equivalent tests. Again it seems reasonable, in the absence of other knowledge, to give preference to the latter statistic l_2 as the relative efficiency of $\hat{\hat{\boldsymbol{\alpha}}}$ is likely to lend greater power to the associated test. (Note that an asymptotically equivalent test to (9.3.18) would be the test of overall significance (an F-test) on the transformed heteroscedasticity estimating equation used to obtain $\hat{\hat{\boldsymbol{\alpha}}}$.)

9.3.2b *Tests of Standard Deviation as a Linear Function of Exogenous Variables:* $\sigma_i = \mathbf{z}_i'\boldsymbol{\alpha}$

As before, a test of homoscedasticity against the alternative of $\sigma_i = \mathbf{z}_i'\boldsymbol{\alpha}$ involves a test of $\alpha_2 = \alpha_3 = \cdots = \alpha_p = 0$. In a similar manner, there are two estimates of $\boldsymbol{\alpha}$ available, the ordinary least squares estimator $\hat{\boldsymbol{\alpha}}$ and feasible generalized least squares estimator $\hat{\hat{\boldsymbol{\alpha}}}$ derivable from (9.2.42) and (9.2.45), respectively, for known c. Corresponding covariance matrices for $\hat{\boldsymbol{\alpha}}$ and $\hat{\hat{\boldsymbol{\alpha}}}$ are

$$\frac{1}{c^2} V_3 = \frac{1}{c^2}(Z'Z)^{-1}Z'\hat{\Sigma}_2 Z(Z'Z)^{-1} \tag{9.3.19}$$

and

$$\frac{1}{c^2} V_4 = \frac{1}{c^2}(Z'\hat{\hat{\Sigma}}_2^{-1}Z)^{-1}, \tag{9.3.20}$$

where $\hat{\Sigma}_2$ and $\hat{\hat{\Sigma}}_2$ are diagonal matrices with respective ith diagonal elements $(1 - c^2)(\mathbf{z}_i'\hat{\boldsymbol{\alpha}})^2$ and $(1 - c^2)(\mathbf{z}_i'\hat{\hat{\boldsymbol{\alpha}}})^2$. Corresponding statistics under H_0 are

$$l_3 = \hat{\boldsymbol{\alpha}}_0'(V_3^0)^{-1}\hat{\boldsymbol{\alpha}}_0 \tag{9.3.21}$$

and

$$l_4 = \hat{\hat{\boldsymbol{\alpha}}}_0'(V_4^0)^{-1}\hat{\hat{\boldsymbol{\alpha}}}_0, \tag{9.3.22}$$

where $\hat{\boldsymbol{\alpha}}_0 = (\hat{\alpha}_2, \ldots, \hat{\alpha}_p)'$, $\hat{\hat{\boldsymbol{\alpha}}}_0 = (\hat{\hat{\alpha}}_2, \ldots, \hat{\hat{\alpha}}_p)'$ and V_3^0 and V_4^0 denote $(p - 1) \times (p - 1)$ matrices obtained from deleting the first row and column of $[(1 - c^2)\hat{\alpha}_1^2/c^2](Z'Z)^{-1}$ and $[(1 - c^2)\hat{\hat{\alpha}}_1^2/c^2](Z'Z)^{-1}$, respectively. The statistics l_3 and l_4 are both distributed asymptotically as χ^2_{p-1} under the null hypothesis, however, l_4 is probably suggested as the associated estimates $\hat{\hat{\boldsymbol{\alpha}}}_0$ are more efficient than $\hat{\boldsymbol{\alpha}}_0$.

9.3.2c *Tests for Multiplicative Heteroscedasticity:* $\sigma_i^2 = \exp(\mathbf{z}_i'\boldsymbol{\alpha})$

The multiplicative heteroscedastic parameter $\boldsymbol{\alpha}$ in $\sigma_i^2 = \exp(\mathbf{z}_i'\boldsymbol{\alpha})$ can be estimated in two distinct ways. First, the ordinary least squares estimator $\hat{\boldsymbol{\alpha}}$ of Equation (9.2.56) provides consistent though inefficient estimates of α_2, $\alpha_3, \ldots, \alpha_p$. As in the other cases the test for heteroscedasticity consists of determining if $\alpha_2 = \alpha_3 = \cdots = \alpha_p = 0$. Let V_5 denote the covariance matrix of (9.2.58) and V_5^0 be the $(p - 1) \times (p - 1)$ matrix obtained by deleting the first row and column of V_5. Under the null hypothesis of homoscedasticity

$$l_5 = \hat{\boldsymbol{\alpha}}_0'(V_5^0)^{-1}\hat{\boldsymbol{\alpha}}_0, \tag{9.3.23}$$

where $\hat{\boldsymbol{\alpha}}_0 = (\hat{\alpha}_2, \ldots, \hat{\alpha}_p)'$, is distributed asymptotically as a χ^2_{p-1} random variable.

Alternatively, the asymptotically efficient estimate $\boldsymbol{\alpha}^*$ of (9.2.63) derived by the method of scoring has asymptotic covariance matrix

$$V_6 = 2\left(\sum_{i=1}^{T} \mathbf{z}_i\mathbf{z}_i'\right)^{-1}. \tag{9.3.24}$$

Let V_6^0 be the $(p - 1) \times (p - 1)$ matrix obtained by deleting the first row and column of V_6. Under the null hypothesis of homoscedasticity

$$l_6 = \boldsymbol{\alpha}_0'^*(V_6^0)^{-1}\boldsymbol{\alpha}_0^*, \tag{9.3.25}$$

where $\boldsymbol{\alpha}_0^* = (\alpha_2^*, \ldots, \alpha_p^*)'$, is distributed asymptotically as a χ^2_{p-1} random variable.

As before the small sample power of these two asymptotically test statistics l_5 and l_6 are likely to be determined by the efficiency in the estimation of $\boldsymbol{\alpha}_0$. For this reason the statistic l_6 is probably to be preferred over l_5.

Finally, Harvey (1976) discusses another asymptotically equivalent test for homoscedasticity in the multiplicative heteroscedasticity model, the likelihood ratio test. We report it here because it is obtainable in closed form in this setting unlike many likelihood ratio tests. The test statistic is

$$-2 \ln l = T \ln \tilde{\sigma}^2 - \sum_{i=1}^{T} \mathbf{z}_i'\tilde{\boldsymbol{\alpha}}, \tag{9.3.26}$$

where $\tilde{\sigma}^2 = \sum_{i=1}^{T} (y_i - \mathbf{x}_i'\hat{\boldsymbol{\beta}})^2/T$, $\hat{\boldsymbol{\beta}} = (X'X)^{-1}X'\mathbf{y}$, and $\tilde{\boldsymbol{\alpha}}$ is the maximum likelihood estimator for $\boldsymbol{\alpha}$. The statistic $-2 \ln l$ is distributed as a χ^2 random variable with $p - 1$ degrees of freedom under the null hypothesis of homoscedasticity. Operationally, $\boldsymbol{\alpha}^*$ could serve as a possible substitute for $\tilde{\boldsymbol{\alpha}}$ to avoid an iterative solution of the maximum likelihood first-order conditions. Which of these asymptotically equivalent tests for heteroscedasticity is to be preferred in small samples is still open to question.

9.3.2d *Tests Involving Heteroscedasticity of Known but General Functional Form: Maximum Likelihood Methods*

There may be cases where the three previous forms of heteroscedasticity are not appropriate. Let $\sigma_i^2 = f(\mathbf{z}_i)$ denote the form of the specified heteroscedasticity where $f(\mathbf{z}_i)$ is a specific function not of the previous forms. Given the nature of the problem, if one can specify the distribution of the random errors e_i then the tools of maximum likelihood tests are available.

Though there are other alternatives such as the Lagrangian multiplier test and the Wald statistic (see Aitchison and Silvey (1960)), two fundamental methods are available for testing for homoscedasticity versus heteroscedasticity of the form $\sigma_i^2 = f(\mathbf{z}_i)$. Let $\boldsymbol{\alpha}_0$ denote the g parameters of $f(\mathbf{z}_i)$ which determine the heteroscedasticity up to a proportional constant, $\tilde{\boldsymbol{\alpha}}_0$ denote the corresponding maximum likelihood estimators and A denote the associated portion of the inverse of the information matrix. Then under the null hypothesis of homoscedasticity ($\boldsymbol{\alpha}_0 = \mathbf{0}$),

$$\eta = \tilde{\boldsymbol{\alpha}}_0'\hat{A}^{-1}\tilde{\boldsymbol{\alpha}}_0, \tag{9.3.27}$$

where $\hat{A}^{-1}$ denotes a consistent estimate of A^{-1} obtained by replacing all unknown population parameters with their maximum likelihood estimates, is distributed asymptotically as a χ_g^2 random variable.

Secondly, the likelihood ratio statistic l can be used to test homoscedasticity, $\boldsymbol{\alpha}_0 = \mathbf{0}$. Let $\boldsymbol{\theta}$ represent the parameters of the function $f(\mathbf{z}_i)$ and the coefficient vector $\boldsymbol{\beta}$. Let $\boldsymbol{\theta}_0$ denote the $\boldsymbol{\theta}$ parameter vector except the elements of $\boldsymbol{\alpha}_0$ have been set equal to zero. Then $l = L(\hat{\boldsymbol{\theta}}_0)/L(\hat{\boldsymbol{\theta}})$, where $\hat{\boldsymbol{\theta}}_0$ and $\hat{\boldsymbol{\theta}}$ denote the restricted and unrestricted maximum likelihood estimators of $\boldsymbol{\theta}$ respectively. Therefore, (see Chapter 4), $-2 \ln l$ is distributed asymptotically as a χ^2_g random variable under the null hypothesis of $\boldsymbol{\alpha}_0 = \mathbf{0}$.

As these two methods lead to asymptotically equivalent tests one cannot be preferred over the other *ex ante*. However, computational complexity and the availability of certain computer software and expediency may make the choice more clear cut.

9.3.3 Nonspecific Tests for Heteroscedasticity

There may be instances when the form of the heteroscedasticity is not known, but nevertheless, it is known that the error variance is monotonically related (either increasing or decreasing) to the size of a known exogenous variable z by which observations on the dependent variable y can be ordered. Two frequently used tests in this instance are the Goldfeld–Quandt test and Peak test. Perhaps it is believed that the broader class of heteroscedasticity $\sigma_i^2 = h(\mathbf{z}_i'\boldsymbol{\alpha})$, where $h(\cdot)$ is a *general* function independent of i, is applicable. (Obviously, the specifications discussed above, $\sigma_i^2 = \mathbf{z}_i'\boldsymbol{\alpha}$, $\sigma_i^2 = (\mathbf{z}_i'\boldsymbol{\alpha})^2$ and $\sigma_i^2 = \exp(\mathbf{z}_i'\boldsymbol{\alpha})$, are special cases.) If so, the Breush–Pagan test is appropriate. If nothing is known *a priori* other than the heteroscedastic variances $\sigma_i^2 = E(e_i^2)$ are uniformly bounded, White's test is applicable. These "nonspecific" heteroscedasticity tests are presented in order below.

9.3.3a *Goldfeld–Quandt Test*

A very popular test for determining the presence of heteroscedasticity which is monotonically related to an exogenous variable by which observations on the dependent variable can be ordered is the Goldfeld–Quandt (1965) test. The steps of this test are as follows:

(1) Order the observations by the values of the variable z.
(2) Choose p central observations and omit them.
(3) Fit separate regressions (by ordinary least squares) to the two groups, provided $(T - p)/2 > K$.
(4) Let SSE_1 and SSE_2 denote the sum of squared residuals based on the small variance group and the large variance group, respectively. For example, when σ_i^2 increases with z then SSE_1 is the sum of squared residuals associated with the group of observations which have small values of z. Form the statistic

$$F = SSE_2/SSE_1 \tag{9.3.28}$$

This statistic is distributed as an F-random variable with $\nu = (T - p - 2K)/2$ numerator and denominator degrees of freedom under the null hypothesis of homoscedasticity.

Values of F will tend to be large under heteroscedasticity. To conduct the Goldfeld–Quandt test, a level of significance, α, is chosen, then the observed F-statistic is compared to the appropriate critical value. If this value is not exceeded by F, then homoscedasticity is accepted, otherwise heteroscedasticity is indicated.

Some comments on the Goldfeld–Quandt test are appropriate at this point. First, the power of the test will depend upon p but this relationship is not trivial. For large values of p the power of the test will tend to be reduced by few observations per partition but at the same time the inclusion of the centrally located observations will cause the residual variances to differ from each other by less than they would if p were relatively large. Therefore, the choice of p is rather subjective. Second, the power of the test will also depend on the spread of the z_i relative to its mean. The greater the coefficient of variation of z_i (standard deviation to mean) the greater the test's power. Third, when $p = 0$, the Goldfeld–Quandt test is asymptotically equivalent to the likelihood ratio statistic (9.3.12) for the grouped heteroscedasticity test when there are two groups ($G = 2$). Finally, like the likelihood ratio statistic, the error terms e_i are assumed to be normal in the construction of the Goldfeld–Quandt test statistic. Therefore, the Goldfeld–Quandt test is a small sample test in that the distribution of F is *exact* for any finite sample size T. If normally is not tenable, then reliance must be placed on asymptotic results or some nonparametric test might be proposed. One nonparametric test is the peak test constructed by Goldfeld and Quandt (1965).

9.3.3b *Peak Test*

The peak test is an attempt to formalize heuristic graphical procedures that might be used when the error variance is monotonically related to an exogeneous variable. This is a nonparametric test and as such does not depend on normality of the disturbances. The following discussion of the test procedure will assume that the error variance is monotonically *increasing* with the variable z. However, this procedure easily extends to the case where the monotonicity is decreasing with z. The steps of the peak test are as follows:

(1) Estimate the linear regression model by ordinary least squares.
(2) Let $\hat{e}_i$ denote the ith residual corresponding to the ith observation of z, z_i.
(3) Define a peak as occurring at the jth observation when $|\hat{e}_j| \geq |\hat{e}_i|$ for all $i < j$. The first residual, $\hat{e}_1$, does not constitute a peak.
(4) To test whether the number of peaks indicates heteroscedasticity a table in the Goldfeld–Quandt (1972) book, p. 121 must be consulted. This table contains the cumulative distribution of the number of peaks under the hypothesis of homoscedasticity. If the errors, e_i, are heteroscedastic, the number of observed peaks will tend to be large. Heteroscedasticity is indicated if this number exceeds the critical value in the Goldfeld–Quandt table. Otherwise, homoscedasticity is indicated.

Some comments on the peak test are appropriate. First, though this test does not assume normality, it is an asymptotic test in that, strictly speaking, it is valid only in large samples. This occurs because, as shown in Lemma 10.8.2 of Chapter 10, ordinary least squares residuals are not independently distributed in finite samples. In contrast, Goldfeld and Quandt's table assumes independence of observations. However, evidence presented by Goldfeld and Quandt (1972) suggests that, as a practical matter, the test can be used for sample sizes greater than 15. Second, sampling experiments conducted by Goldfeld and Quandt (1972) indicate that the power of the peak test compares favorably with that of the Goldfeld–Quandt test described above. In the presence of normal errors one would expect the parametric test to outperform the nonparametric one.

9.3.3c *Breush–Pagan Test*

Breush and Pagan (1979) assume a broader class of heteroscedasticity defined by

$$\sigma_i^2 = h(\mathbf{z}_i'\boldsymbol{\alpha}), \tag{9.3.29}$$

where $h(\cdot)$ is a general function independent of i and $\mathbf{z}_i'\boldsymbol{\alpha}$ is defined as in Section 9.2. The specifications $\sigma_i^2 = \mathbf{z}_i'\boldsymbol{\alpha}$, $\sigma_i^2 = (\mathbf{z}_i'\boldsymbol{\alpha})^2$ and $\sigma_i^2 = \exp(\mathbf{z}_i'\boldsymbol{\alpha})$ are obviously special cases of (9.3.29). Grouped heteroscedasticity is likewise a special case if, in $\sigma_i^2 = \mathbf{z}_i'\boldsymbol{\alpha}$, $\mathbf{z}_i'$ contains appropriate dummy variables. Breush and Pagan consider the general estimating equation

$$\frac{\hat{e}_i^2}{\tilde{\sigma}^2} = \mathbf{z}_i'\boldsymbol{\alpha} + v_i, \tag{9.3.30}$$

where $\hat{e}_i$ represents the ith ordinary least squares residual and $\tilde{\sigma}^2 = \sum_{i=1}^T \hat{e}_i^2/T$. The ordinary least squares estimator $\hat{\boldsymbol{\alpha}}$ obtained from (9.3.30) is consistent but, unless the *specific* form of $h(\cdot)$ is known, feasible generalized least squares cannot be applied.

Though efficient estimation is prohibited in the absence of knowledge of $h(\cdot)$, a test for heteroscedasticity is still possible. Since the first element of $\mathbf{z}_i'$ is unity, the null hypothesis of homoscedasticity $\boldsymbol{\alpha}_0 = (\alpha_2, \alpha_3, \ldots, \alpha_p)' = \mathbf{0}$ can be tested, if the e_i are normally distributed. Let RSS denote the regression sum of squares obtained in an ordinary least squares estimation of (9.3.30). (Let $y_i = \hat{e}_i^2/\tilde{\sigma}^2$, $\bar{y} = \sum_{i=1}^T y_i/T$, and $\hat{y}_i = \mathbf{z}_i'\hat{\boldsymbol{\alpha}}$. Then RSS $= \sum_{i=1}^T (\hat{y}_i - \bar{y})^2$.) Breush and Pagan show, if $\boldsymbol{\alpha}_0 = \mathbf{0}$, then

$$\tfrac{1}{2}\text{RSS} \overset{\text{asy}}{\sim} \chi^2_{p-1}. \tag{9.3.31}$$

Therefore, if there is some uncertainty as to which of the three forms of heteroscedasticity is appropriate, $\sigma_i^2 = \mathbf{z}_i'\boldsymbol{\alpha}$, $\sigma_i^2 = (\mathbf{z}_i'\boldsymbol{\alpha})^2$ or $\sigma_i^2 = \exp(\mathbf{z}_i'\boldsymbol{\alpha})$ or, if one is willing only to specify $\sigma_i^2 = h(\mathbf{z}_i'\boldsymbol{\alpha})$, a test of homoscedasticity is still possible.

There are, however, costs associated with using the statistic (9.3.31) for the broader class of heteroscedasticity forms $\sigma_i^2 = h(\mathbf{z}_i'\boldsymbol{\alpha})$. If the investigator lacks knowledge concerning the specific form of $h(\cdot)$, then likewise there is a lack of knowledge concerning the heteroscedastic nature of v_i in the estimating equation (9.3.30). As a result more efficient estimates of $\boldsymbol{\alpha}$ (like the $\hat{\hat{\boldsymbol{\alpha}}}$'s constructed in Section 9.2) cannot be obtained and there is a loss of small sample power for the statistic (9.3.31).

9.3.3d *White's General Heteroscedasticity Test*

White (1980) addresses the case where nothing is known about the structure of the heteroscedasticity other than the heteroscedastic variances $\sigma_i^2 = E(e_i^2)$ are uniformly bounded. As pointed out before, it is impossible to estimate each σ_i^2 as this would require estimating T different parameters given only T observations. However, as White shows, this does not preclude the consistent estimation of the variance–covariance matrix of the ordinary least squares estimator $\hat{\boldsymbol{\beta}}$, namely $(X'X)^{-1}(X'\Omega X)(X'X)^{-1}$ (see Chapter 2) when the generalized least squares error structure $E\mathbf{ee}' = \Omega = \text{diag}(\sigma_1^2, \sigma_2^2, \ldots, \sigma_T^2)$ is appropriate. Under general conditions, $\hat{V} = \sum_{i=1}^T \hat{e}_i^2 \mathbf{x}_i \mathbf{x}_i'$, where $\mathbf{x}_i'$ denotes the ith row of X and $\hat{e}_i^2 = (y_i - \mathbf{x}_i'\hat{\boldsymbol{\beta}})^2$, is a consistent estimator of $(X'\Omega X)$. As a result, the variance–covariance matrix of the ordinary least squares estimator is consistently estimated by $(X'X)^{-1}\hat{V}(X'X)^{-1}$. Inferences concerning $\boldsymbol{\beta}$ are still possible by means of ordinary least squares estimation even when the specific structure of Ω is not specified as $\hat{\boldsymbol{\beta}}$ is normally distributed asymptotically. More generally, White shows that tests of the general linear hypotheses H_0: $R\boldsymbol{\beta} = \mathbf{r}$ versus H_1: $R\boldsymbol{\beta} \neq \mathbf{r}$ can be conducted by noting that under the null hypothesis H_0

$$(R\hat{\boldsymbol{\beta}} - \mathbf{r})'[R(X'X)^{-1}\hat{V}(X'X)^{-1}R']^{-1}(R\hat{\boldsymbol{\beta}} - \mathbf{r}) \overset{\text{asy}}{\approx} \chi_J^2, \tag{9.3.32}$$

where J denotes the number of restrictions imposed.

In an analogous manner White derives a test for heteroscedasticity which consists of comparing the elements of $\hat{V}$ and $\hat{\sigma}^2(X'X)$, thus indicating whether or not the usual ordinary least squares formula $\hat{\sigma}^2(X'X)^{-1}$ is a consistent covariance matrix estimator. Large discrepancies between $\hat{V}$ and $\hat{\sigma}^2(X'X)$ support the contention of heteroscedasticity while small discrepancies support homoscedasticity. Let

$\boldsymbol{\psi}_i = [K(K+1)/2 \times 1]$ vector consisting of the elements of the lower triangle (including the main diagonal) of $\mathbf{x}_i\mathbf{x}_i'$,

$\boldsymbol{\psi} = [K(K+1)/2 \times 1]$ vector of elements of the lower triangle of $X'X/T$,

$$B = \sum_{i=1}^{T} (\hat{e}_i^2 - \hat{\sigma}^2)^2(\boldsymbol{\psi}_i - \boldsymbol{\psi})(\boldsymbol{\psi}_i - \boldsymbol{\psi})',$$

$\mathbf{d} = [K(K+1)/2 \times 1]$ vector of elements of the lower triangle of the matrix difference $\hat{V} - \hat{\sigma}^2(X'X)$.

Then under the null hypothesis of homoscedasticity H_0: $E(e_i^2) = \sigma^2$ for all i,

$$\mathbf{d}'B^{-1}\mathbf{d} \overset{\text{asy}}{\sim} \chi^2_{K(K+1)/2}. \qquad (9.3.33)$$

Two points deserve comment. Naturally, the hypothesis tests developed by White have reduced power relative to appropriate specific heteroscedasticity tests because less information is utilized. However, this may be the only alternative in the absence of *a priori* information. Secondly, even given that $(X'\Omega X)$ can be consistently estimated, feasible generalized least squares is precluded in this general case of heteroscedasticity since, in order to construct $(X'\hat{\Omega}^{-1}X)^{-1}X'\hat{\Omega}^{-1}\mathbf{y}$, individual consistent estimates of the σ_i^2, $i = 1, 2, \ldots, T$, are needed yet cannot be obtained. As a result, the lack of specific knowledge concerning the form of the heteroscedasticity precludes efficient estimation of the regression coefficients.

9.4 Chow Test Under Heteroscedasticity

There are many instances when economists wish to determine if the behavior or performance of one group is distinct from that of another group as predicted by economic theory. Or possibly interest centers on a structural change of an economic relationship over a span of time. The following two examples will illustrate what we mean.

EXAMPLE 9.4.1. In an article concerning the property rights theory of the firm, Crain and Zardkoohi (1978) investigate the comparative performance of publicly owned versus privately owned water utilities in the United States during 1974. Let Y = output (measured in millions of gallons of water per year), K = capital input, L = labor input, P_K = price of capital, P_L = wage rate, C = operating costs. After postulating the reduced form cost function of a generalized Cobb–Douglas production function and imposing restrictions which arise from *a priori* economic theory, Crain and Zardkoohi obtained the estimating equations for private and public utilities

$$(\ln C - \ln P_K) = \gamma_1 + \gamma_2 \ln Y + \gamma_3(\ln P_L - \ln P_K) + u \qquad (9.4.1)$$

and

$$(\ln C - \ln P_K) = \gamma_1' + \gamma_2' \ln Y + \gamma_3'(\ln P_L - \ln P_K) + u', \qquad (9.4.2)$$

where the primes (′) on the parameters of the second equation indicate that, *a priori*, they are distinct from those of the first equation. In testing the difference in the performance of the private versus public utilities (and hence the equality of the structural equations (9.4.1) and (9.4.2)) the test of the hypotheses

$$\begin{aligned} &H_0: \gamma_1 = \gamma_1'; \gamma_2 = \gamma_2'; \gamma_3 = \gamma_3'; \\ &H_1: \text{not } H_0. \end{aligned} \qquad (9.4.3)$$

is of prime importance.

Example 9.4.2. The effect that credit cards may have had on consumer spending patterns after their introduction could possibly be analyzed by the following two consumption equations based in part on Duesenberry's (1949) relative income hypothesis

$$C_t = \tau_1 + \tau_2 Y_t + \tau_3 C_{t-1} + v, \tag{9.4.4}$$

$$C_t = \tau_1' + \tau_2' Y_t + \tau_3' C_{t-1} + v'. \tag{9.4.5}$$

Let the first equation represent the yearly consumption (C_t) before the implementation of credit cards as a function of present disposable income and last year's consumption (Y_t and C_{t-1}, respectively) while the second equation represents consumer expenditures after credit cards. A test that consumption behavior before cards is distinct from that after might be:

$$\begin{aligned} &H_0: \tau_1 = \tau_1'; \tau_2 = \tau_2'; \tau_3 = \tau_3'; \\ &H_1: \text{not } H_0. \end{aligned} \tag{9.4.6}$$

The first example involved a test of structural distinction in cross-sections of data whereas the last example examines structural change in a time series. These structural tests form an integral part of present day economic analysis and since 1960 have become known as "Chow" tests in the economics literature after Chow (1960).

To make our examples more formal and to define the Chow test explicitly, consider the model

$$\begin{aligned} \mathbf{y}_1 &= X_1\boldsymbol{\beta}_1 + \mathbf{e}_1, \\ \mathbf{y}_2 &= X_2\boldsymbol{\beta}_2 + \mathbf{e}_2, \end{aligned} \tag{9.4.7}$$

where $\mathbf{y}_i$ and X_i are $T_i \times 1$ and $T_i \times K$ observation matrices on the dependent and independent variables respectively, $\boldsymbol{\beta}_i$ are possibly distinct $K \times 1$ coefficient vectors and the $\mathbf{e}_i$ are $T_i \times 1$ error vectors which are distributed as

$$\begin{aligned} &\mathbf{e}_1 \sim N(\mathbf{0}, \sigma_1^2 I_{T_1}), \\ &\mathbf{e}_2 \sim N(\mathbf{0}, \sigma_2^2 I_{T_2}), \\ &E\mathbf{e}_1\mathbf{e}_2' = 0, \end{aligned} \tag{9.4.8}$$

where σ_1^2 and σ_2^2 need not be equal.

In structural analysis the test of interest is

$$\begin{aligned} &H_0: \boldsymbol{\beta}_1 = \boldsymbol{\beta}_2, \\ &H_1: \boldsymbol{\beta}_1 \neq \boldsymbol{\beta}_2. \end{aligned} \tag{9.4.9}$$

In the instance that $\sigma_1^2 = \sigma_2^2$, the classical F-test discussed in Chapter 3, Equation (3.4.17) is appropriate. The corresponding statistic, which is distributed as $F_{K,(T_1+T_2-2K)}$, is

$$u = \frac{(\text{SSE}_\text{r} - \text{SSE}_\text{u})/K}{\text{SSE}_\text{u}/(T_1 + T_2 - 2K)}, \tag{9.4.10}$$

where SSE_u represents the unrestricted sum of squared errors (residuals) obtained from applying ordinary least squares to the equation system

$$\mathbf{y} = \begin{bmatrix} \mathbf{y}_1 \\ \mathbf{y}_2 \end{bmatrix} = \begin{bmatrix} X_1 & 0 \\ 0 & X_2 \end{bmatrix} \begin{bmatrix} \boldsymbol{\beta}_1 \\ \boldsymbol{\beta}_2 \end{bmatrix} + \begin{bmatrix} \mathbf{e}_1 \\ \mathbf{e}_2 \end{bmatrix} = X\boldsymbol{\beta} + \mathbf{e}, \tag{9.4.11}$$

i.e., $\text{SSE}_u = (\mathbf{y} - X\hat{\boldsymbol{\beta}})'(\mathbf{y} - X\hat{\boldsymbol{\beta}})$, $\hat{\boldsymbol{\beta}} = (X'X)^{-1}X'\mathbf{y}$, while SSE_r represents the restricted sum of squared errors (residuals) obtained from the restricted model

$$\mathbf{y} = \begin{bmatrix} \mathbf{y}_1 \\ \mathbf{y}_2 \end{bmatrix} = \begin{bmatrix} X_1 \\ X_2 \end{bmatrix} \boldsymbol{\beta}_. + \begin{bmatrix} \mathbf{e}_1 \\ \mathbf{e}_2 \end{bmatrix} = X_. \boldsymbol{\beta}_. + \mathbf{e}, \tag{9.4.12}$$

where $\boldsymbol{\beta}_.$ is the $K \times 1$ vector imposed by $\boldsymbol{\beta}_1 = \boldsymbol{\beta}_2$ and $\text{SSE}_r = (\mathbf{y} - X_.\hat{\boldsymbol{\beta}}_.)'(\mathbf{y} - X_.\hat{\boldsymbol{\beta}}_.)$, $\hat{\boldsymbol{\beta}}_. = (X_.'X_.)^{-1}X_.'\mathbf{y}$. The estimator $\hat{\boldsymbol{\beta}}_.$ is the restricted least squares estimator (see Chapter 6).

An examination of the quadratic form theory used in the proof of the distribution of u in Chapter 3, makes it obvious that an implicit assumption of the analysis is that the errors $\mathbf{e}_1$ and $\mathbf{e}_2$ are independent, have zero means *and are homoscedastic* (i.e., $\sigma_1^2 = \sigma_2^2$). There is some question, however, as to whether this homoscedasticity assumption is approriate in every case. As stated by Toyoda (1974, p. 601):

> The Chow test, which aims to test equality of sets of coefficients in two regressions, is now widely used in econometric and other research. However, without checking a maintained hypothesis of the test that variances of error terms are common between separate sample regimes, it is sometimes misused.

Analysis by Toyoda (1974) and Schmidt and Sickles (1977) provides the following basic conclusions concerning the Chow test under heteroscedasticity.

(1) Usually the true probability of a type one error is greater than the level specified. For example, the true α may be 0.10 when the investigator has seemingly assigned $\alpha = 0.05$. There a few cases, as Schmidt and Sickles note, however, where the true α is less than the assigned α. In general, the true versus assigned levels of significance exhibit greater departure as $\tau = \sigma_1^2/\sigma_2^2$ moves away from one. The greater the disparity between σ_1^2 and σ_2^2, the greater the error in the assigned level of significance.
(2) Increasing one sample size, while the other sample size remains fixed, does not, in general, improve the reliability of the Chow test.

9.4.1 Jayatissa's Test

Jayatissa (1977) has constructed an appropriate small sample test statistic for the Chow test under heteroscedasticity. Again consider the model and notation of (9.4.7). Let $\hat{\boldsymbol{\beta}}_i = (X_i'X_i)^{-1}X_i'\mathbf{y}_i$ and $\hat{\mathbf{e}}_i = M_i\mathbf{y}_i$, where $M_i = I_{T_i} - X_i(X_i'X_i)^{-1}X_i' = Z_i'Z_i$ with $Z_i'X_i = 0$ and $Z_i'Z_i = I_{(T_i - K)}$. Note that

Z_i is a $[T_i \times (T_i - K)]$ orthonormal matrix with its columns being the eigenvectors of M_i associated with unit eigenvalues. The steps of the Jayitissa test are as follows:

(i) Compute $\mathbf{d} = (\hat{\boldsymbol{\beta}}_1 - \hat{\boldsymbol{\beta}}_2)$.
(ii) Compute Z_i, $i = 1, 2$.
(iii) Compute $r =$ the largest integer less than or equal to

$$\min[(T_1 - K)/K, (T_2 - K)/K].$$

(iv) Compute the $(T_i - K) \times 1$ vectors $Z_i'\hat{\mathbf{e}}_i$, $i = 1, 2$. Choose *any* r subvectors of $Z_1'\hat{\mathbf{e}}_1$ and *any* r subvectors of $Z_2'\hat{\mathbf{e}}_2$ each of dimension $K \times 1$ and denote them $\mathbf{e}_{1(1)}^*, \mathbf{e}_{1(2)}^*, \ldots, \mathbf{e}_{1(r)}^*$ and $\mathbf{e}_{2(1)}^*, \mathbf{e}_{2(2)}^*, \ldots, \mathbf{e}_{2(r)}^*$, respectively.
(v) Compute the $K \times K$ matrices Q_i such that $Q_i'Q_i = (X_i'X_i)^{-1}$.
(vi) Form $\boldsymbol{\eta}_j$ which is defined as

$$\boldsymbol{\eta}_j = Q_1'\mathbf{e}_{1(j)}^* + Q_2'\mathbf{e}_{2(j)}^*, \qquad j = 1, 2, \ldots, r.$$

(vii) Form S which is defined as

$$S = \frac{1}{r}\sum_{j=1}^{r} \boldsymbol{\eta}_j\boldsymbol{\eta}_j'.$$

Then under the null hypothesis that $\boldsymbol{\beta}_1 = \boldsymbol{\beta}_2$ where $\sigma_1^2 \neq \sigma_2^2$ and *provided* that $r \geq K$, the statistic

$$J = \frac{\mathbf{d}'S^{-1}\mathbf{d}}{r} \cdot \frac{(r - K + 1)}{K}, \tag{9.4.13}$$

is distributed as $F_{K,(r-K+1)}$.

Some comments on Jayittisa's test are appropriate. The restriction $r \geq K$, which provides positive degrees of freedom for the numerator of the F-statistic, can be binding. For example, let $T_1 = 20$, $T_2 = 10$, and $K = 5$ then $r = \min(3, 1) = 1$ and $r < K$. The Jayitissa test cannot be applied in this case. In such instances there exist three basic alternatives:

(1) Apply the standard Chow test realizing that the assigned significance is probably inaccurate. *Rough* estimates of this inaccuracy can be garnered from tables in Schmidt and Sickles (1977).
(2) Specify *a priori* the value $\tau = \sigma_1^2/\sigma_2^2$ and for given X_1 and X_2 compute, using the Imhof (1961) numerical integration technique, the exact level of significance desired.
(3) Let $\hat{\sigma}_i^2 = (\mathbf{y}_i - X_i\hat{\boldsymbol{\beta}}_i)'(\mathbf{y}_i - X_i\hat{\boldsymbol{\beta}}_i)/(T_i - K)$ denote the ordinary least squares estimates of the σ_i^2 in each sample. Multiply the observations in $\mathbf{y}_i$ and X_i by $1/\hat{\sigma}_i$, $i = 1, 2$. Application of the coventional Chow test statistic (9.4.10) to this transformed data will be *asymptotically* valid in that u is asymptotically distributed as $F_{K,(T_1+T_2-2K)}$.

9.5 Summary and Guide to Further Readings

The literature on heteroscedasticity and related problems is voluminous yet this chapter has covered the standard forms discussed in the present econometric literature. These forms necessitate the use of feasible generalized squares estimation procedures whose properties are documented, in general, in Chapter 8. In the presence of normally distributed errors, the described estimation methods are consistent, distributed asymptotically normal, and are asymptotically efficient, given the appropriateness of the heteroscedastic specification.

Though the large sample properties of the feasible generalized least squares estimators in heteroscedasticity models are well defined, their small sample properties are not. A notable exception is Taylor's (1978) work on feasible generalized least squares estimation in the grouped heteroscedasticity model. He derives the small sample properties in the case of two groups and shows that, as in other instances in feasible generalized least squares estimation (see seemingly unrelated regression in Chapter 9 for example) there are instances where a correction for a nonspherical error structure Ω can lead to less efficient estimation than that provided by ordinary least squares estimation. However, Taylor found that the loss of efficiency to be less than 17% when there are more than five degrees of freedom per subsample. Therefore, generally, though feasible generalized least squares in the grouped heteroscedasticity model does exhibit some inefficiency when $\tau = \sigma_1^2/\sigma_2^2$ is near one, there is much to gain and little to lose from correcting for heteroscedasticity.

In Section 9.3 tests for heteroscedasticity were discussed. These tests can be broken down into two groups, those dealing with specific functional forms and those addressing unspecified functional forms. In the case of specific functional forms, auxiliary heteroscedasticity estimating equations provide the means of testing the significance of relevant heteroscedasticity parameters. The Goldfeld–Quandt test, Peak test, Breush–Pagan test and White's general heteroscedasticity test are concerned with unspecified functional forms. Though consistent tests for heteroscedasticity are provided, they possess less power than specific form heteroscedasticity tests and at the same time the lack of specific form precludes efficient estimation by feasible generalized least squares.

As noted in Chapter 7, the distinction between model verification by means of hypothesis tests and the choice of estimators by means of hypothesis tests should be kept firmly in mind. If a choice between the ordinary least squares estimator and a feasible generalized least squares estimator implementing a heteroscedastic correction is made on the basis of an hypothesis test, the resulting estimator is a preliminary test estimator whose sampling properties are distinct from either those of the ordinary least squares estimator or the feasible generalized least squares estimator. The properties of preliminary test estimation in the grouped heteroscedasticity model have been investigated by Greenberg (1980). The preliminary test estimator is unbiased and has a variance which is essentially between that of ordinary least squares and feasible generalized least squares. The preliminary test estimator offers a compromise between the poor performance of ordinary least squares for extreme values of τ, 0 and ∞, and the "mediocre" performance of feasible generalized least squares when τ is approximately one. It should be noted that hypothesis tests based upon the preliminary test estimator are not available as its sampling distribution is dependent on the choice of significance level and unknown parameters.

The usual discussions of the Chow test in the literature implicitly impose homoscedastic error variance both within and between groups. This may not be the case in certain applications and as a result the derived inferences may be misleading. Jayatissa (1977) has developed a small sample test when the variances of the two groups differ. Insufficient numbers of observations in a group can, however, limit its usefulness in which case asymptotic tests must be used.

Finally, the tools gained here will prove useful in other contexts. For example, in Chapter 14 random coefficient linear models can be viewed as generalized least squares problems with heteroscedastic error variances. Error components models in Chapter 15, which arise in pooling cross-section and time series data, can also be viewed as special forms of heteroscedasticity. In these contexts, feasible generalized least squares again displays an adeptness in attacking econometric estimation problems.

9.6 Exercises

9.1. Verify the result of Equation (9.2.26).

9.2. Show that the error term v_i defined in Equation (9.2.25) is heteroscedastic and autocorrelated.

9.3. Assume x represents a random variable with a zero mean, variance one and has a symmetric distribution with probability density function $f(x)$ and domain $-a < x < a$. Show that $E|x| = 2 \int_0^a xf(x) \equiv c$, where $|x|$ represents the absolute value of x. Hint: Use the Jacobian technique to obtain the probability density function of $|x|$ from the probability density function of x.

9.4. Consider the result of the previous exercise. Assume $x \sim N(0, 1)$. Show that $c = (2/\pi)^{1/2}$.

9.5. Show that the error term v_i defined in Equation (9.2.41) is heteroscedastic, autocorrelated, and has a nonzero mean.

9.6. Let v^* denote a random variable which is distributed as the natural logarithm of a χ^2 random variable with one degree of freedom. Show that $Ev^* = -1.2704$ and $\operatorname{var} v^* = 4.9348$.

9.7. Suppose that the assumptions of the classical linear regression model hold except $E(e_t) = \mu$ for all t. Show that, if one of the regressors is a constant term, $\hat{\sigma}^2$ and all the elements of $\hat{\boldsymbol{\beta}}$ except the coefficient of the constant term are unbiased and consistent. Show that $E\hat{\beta}_1 = \beta_1 + \mu = \text{plim } \hat{\beta}_1$.

9.8. Derive the information matrix of (9.2.64).

9.9. Consider the three artificial data sets presented below. These data sets have been generated using either the multiplicative or additive heteroscedasticity schemes: $\sigma_i^2 = \sigma^2 X_i^\lambda$ or $\sigma_i^2 = a + bX_i + cX_i^2$.

(a) Fit a linear regression of Y on $X1$, $X2$, and $X3$ in each case and plot the residuals *as a function of* $X2$.

(b) Using the residual plots, specify a particular heteroscedasticity scheme and test for the presence of heteroscedasticity.

(c) Reestimate each equation using an appropriate correction for heteroscedasticity.

Data Set A

Y	$X1$	$X2$	$X3$
8.075	8	5	25
8.160	8	10	100
8.585	8	15	225
8.620	8	20	400
8.895	8	25	625
8.860	8	30	900
7.975	9	5	25
8.510	9	10	100
8.595	9	15	225
8.930	9	20	400
8.945	9	25	625
9.130	9	30	900
8.405	10	5	25
8.500	10	10	100
8.925	10	15	225
8.970	10	20	400
9.235	10	25	625
9.200	10	30	900

Data Set B

Y	$X1$	$X2$	$X3$
9.729	12	5	25
9.654	12	10	100
10.129	12	15	225
10.134	12	20	400
10.459	12	25	625
10.314	12	30	900
10.299	12	35	1225
9.856	13	5	25
10.001	13	10	100
10.236	13	15	225
10.241	13	20	400
10.566	13	25	625
10.661	13	30	900
10.406	13	35	1225
9.623	14	5	25
9.868	14	10	100
10.143	14	15	225
10.348	14	20	400
10.673	14	25	625
10.528	14	30	900
10.813	14	35	1225

Data Set C

Y	$X1$	$X2$	$X3$
9.550	16	5	25
9.800	16	10	100
10.078	16	15	225
10.208	16	20	400
10.493	16	25	625
10.403	16	30	900
9.520	17	5	25
9.920	17	10	100
10.188	17	15	225
10.390	17	20	400
10.378	17	25	625
10.615	17	30	900
9.630	18	5	25
9.860	18	10	100
10.105	18	15	225
10.290	18	20	400
10.573	18	25	625
10.484	18	30	900

9.10. Using the data sets of Exercise 9.9:

(a) test for heteroscedasticity using the Breush–Pagan test;

(b) test for heteroscedasticity using White's general test for heteroscedasticity;

(c) obtain a consistent estimate of the variance–covariance matrix of the ordinary least squares estimator for Data Set A. Compare the standard errors obtained by using a specific heteroscedasticity scheme in Exercise 9.9. Which standard errors are smaller and why?

9.11. Consider the data sets of Exercise 9.9. Using $X2$ as the variable associated with the heteroscedasticity error variance:
  (a) Apply the Goldfeld–Quandt test and peak test. Do you obtain the same conclusions that you obtained with the tests of the previous two exercises?
  (b) Why is the heteroscedasticity of Data Set B not likely to be detected by either the Goldfeld–Quandt test or the peak test?

9.7 References

Aitchison, J. and Silvey, S. D. (1960). Maximum-likelihood estimation procedures and associated tests of significance. *Journal of The Royal Statistical Society*, B, **22**, 154–171.

Amemiya, T. (1977). A note on a heteroscedastic model. *Journal of Econometrics*, **6**, 365–370.

Breush, T. S. and Pagan, A. R. (1979). A simple test for heteroscedasticity and random coefficient variation. *Econometrica*, **47**, 1287–1294.

Chow, G. C. (1960). Tests of equality between sets of coefficients in two linear regressions. *Econometrica*, **28**, 591–605.

Crain, W. M. and Zardkoohi, A. (1978). A test of the property-rights theory of the firm: water utilities in the United States. *Journal of Law and Economics*, **21**, 395–408.

Duesenberry, J. S. (1949). *Income, Saving and the Theory of Consumer Behavior*. Cambridge, MA: Harvard University Press.

Gleisjer, H. (1969). A new test for heteroscedasticity. *Journal of The American Statistical Association*, **64**, 316–323.

Goldfeld, S. M. and Quandt, R. E. (1965). Some tests for homoscedasticity. *Journal of the American Statistical Association*, **60**, 539–547.

Goldfeld, S. M. and Quandt, R. E. (1972). *Nonlinear Methods in Econometrics*. Amsterdam: North Holland.

Greenberg, E. (1980). Finite sample moments of a preliminary test estimator in the case of possible heteroscedasticity. *Econometrica*, **48**, 1805–1813.

Harvey, A. C. (1974). Estimation of parameters in a heteroscedastic regression model. Paper presented at the European Meeting of The Econometric Society, Grenoble, September.

Harvey, A. C. (1976). Estimating regression models with multiplicative heteroscedasticity. *Econometrica*, **44**, 461–465.

Imhof, J. P. (1961). Computing the distribution of quadratic forms in normal variables. *Biometrika*, **48**, 419–426.

Jayatissa, W. A. (1977). Tests of equality between sets of coefficients in two linear regressions when disturbance variances are unequal. *Econometrica*, **45**, 1291–1292.

Mincer, J., (1974). *Schooling, Experience, and Earnings*. New York: National Bureau of Economic Research.

Prais, S. J. and Houthakker, H. S. (1955). *The Analysis of Family Budgets*. New York: Cambridge University Press.

Schmidt, P. and Sickles, R. (1977). Some further evidence on the use of the Chow test under heteroscedasticity. *Econometrica*, **45**, 1293–1298.

Taylor, W. E. (1978). The heteroscedastic linear model: exact finite sample results. *Econometrica*, **46**, 663–675.

Toyoda, T. (1974). Use of the Chow test under heteroscedasticity. *Econometrica*, **42**, 601–608.

White, H. (1980). A heteroscedasticity-consistent covariance matrix estimator and a direct test for heteroscedasticity. *Econometrica*, **48**, 817–838.

CHAPTER 10

Autocorrelation

10.1 Introduction

In this chapter we deal with statistical inference in the linear model when it is not appropriate to assume that the random disturbances are uncorrelated. The phenomenon of correlated errors in linear regression models involving time series data is called autocorrelation. Results to follow show that there is much to gain and little to lose by considering alternatives to the independent error assumption of the classical linear regression model. These results are discussed in the context of feasible generalized least squares of Chapter 8.

The outline of this chapter is as follows: In Section 10.2 the first-order autoregressive, AR(1), error structure is studied and the generalized least squares transformation matrix presented. A maximum likelihood search procedure is discussed in Section 10.3 as well as some asymptotically equivalent techniques. In Section 10.4 several two-step feasible generalized least squares estimators and their relative efficiencies are examined. In Section 10.5 the extent to which feasible generalized least squares techniques outperform ordinary least squares in small samples is discussed. In Section 10.6 the concept of a general stationary correlation structure is described and the processes, autoregressive of order p, AR(p), moving average of order q, MA(q), and combined autoregressive moving average of order p and q, ARMA(p, q), are defined. Feasible generalized least squares estimators using the generalized squares transformations for AR(2) and MA(1) error processes are presented in Section 10.7 and estimation of the general ARMA(p, q) process is discussed. Tests for AR(1) errors are presented and compared with respect to their power in Section 10.8. In Section 10.9 the use of the residual autocorrelation, likelihood ratio and coefficient tests for determining the order of ARMA(p, q) processes is discussed. An "adequacy of fit" statistic is also presented. Section 10.10 summarizes the results obtained and provides a guide to further readings.

10.2 Autoregressive Error Structure AR(1)

The existence of autocorrelated errors has been rationalized in a variety of ways, but, as noted by Maddala (1977), caution must be used when using these arguments. It is often asserted, for example, that autocorrelation occurs because omitted variables are autocorrelated. Suppose, for example, that the "true" relationship is of the form

$$y_t = \beta_1 + \beta_2 x_{t2} + \beta_3 z_t + e_t,$$

but instead the regression relationship is postulated to be

$$y_t = \beta_1 + \beta_2 x_{t2} + u_t,$$

where $u_t = \beta_3 z_t + e_t$. If z_t is autocorrelated, has no time trend, and is distributed independently of x_{t2}, then u_t is autocorrelated and most importantly, is independent of x_{t2}. Then, the correction techniques of this chapter are applicable. However, if, instead, the omitted variable z_t is contemporaneously correlated with x_{t2} then estimation, whether it proceeds by means of ordinary least squares or techniques to be subsequently discussed, will yield biased and inconsistent results. It is thus very important that we first ascertain the source of the autocorrelation of the errors. If the autocorrelation arises because of autocorrelated omitted variables which are, in turn, contemporaneously related with the present explanatory variables, we should first seek to include the omitted variables, or, at least, in the instance of their exclusion, document the potential biases arising from such an exclusion. In the present discussion we assume that the autocorrelated errors under investigation are not contemporaneously related to the included explanatory variables but, instead, represent independent persistent shocks arising from inertia in economic processes.

One way to represent this type of error dependency is to consider the linear model

$$\mathbf{y} = X\boldsymbol{\beta} + \mathbf{e} \tag{10.2.1}$$

but where

$$e_t = \rho e_{t-1} + u_t, \qquad t = 1, 2, \ldots, T. \tag{10.2.2}$$

We assume that the parameter ρ is such that $|\rho| < 1$, u_t are independent and identically distributed with zero mean and variance σ_u^2, and the stationary stochastic process generating e_t began in the infinite past.

Making successive backward substitutions gives

$$e_t = \sum_{i=0}^{\infty} \rho^i u_{t-i}. \qquad (10.2.3)$$

From the assumptions on u_t it follows that,

$$E(e_t) = \sum_{i=0}^{\infty} \rho^i E(u_{t-i}) = 0. \qquad (10.2.4)$$

The variance of e_t is obtained as

$$E(e_t^2) = E(u_t^2) + \rho^2 E(u_t^2) + \rho^4 E(u_t^2) + \cdots = \sigma_u^2/(1-\rho^2) = \sigma_e^2,$$

where the sum of a convergent geometric series and independence of the u_t have been used.

The covariance of e_t with e_{t-i} is

$$\begin{aligned} E(e_t e_{t-i}) &= E([u_t + \rho u_{t-1} + \rho^2 u_{t-2} + \cdots] \\ &\quad \times [u_{t-i} + \rho u_{t-i-1} + \rho^2 u_{t-i-2} + \cdots]) \\ &= \rho^i \sigma_e^2. \end{aligned} \qquad (10.2.5)$$

In summary, the variance–covariance matrix of $\mathbf{e}$ can be written as

$$E\mathbf{ee}' = \sigma_u^2 \Omega = \sigma_u^2 \frac{1}{1-\rho^2} \begin{bmatrix} 1 & \rho & \cdots & & \rho^{T-1} \\ \rho & 1 & & & \vdots \\ \vdots & & & \ddots & \rho \\ \rho^{T-1} & \rho^{T-2} & \cdots & \rho & 1 \end{bmatrix}, \qquad (10.2.6)$$

Ω being defined implicitly.

Since the covariance matrix of $\mathbf{e}$ is nonspherical (i.e., not a scalar multiple of the identity matrix), ordinary least squares, though unbiased, is inefficient relative to generalized least squares by Aitken's theorem. The generalized least squares estimator is

$$\tilde{\boldsymbol{\beta}} = (X'\Omega^{-1}X)^{-1}X'\Omega^{-1}\mathbf{y}, \qquad (10.2.7)$$

where

$$\Omega^{-1} = \begin{bmatrix} 1 & -\rho & & & & 0 \\ -\rho & (1+\rho^2) & -\rho & & & \\ & -\rho & (1+\rho^2) & \ddots & & \\ & & \ddots & \ddots & \ddots & \\ & & & \ddots & (1+\rho^2) & -\rho \\ 0 & & & & -\rho & 1 \end{bmatrix}. \qquad (10.2.8)$$

In the case that Ω is known, the generalized least squares model can be transformed to

$$P'\mathbf{y} = P'X\boldsymbol{\beta} + P'\mathbf{e}, \tag{10.2.9}$$

where

$$P' = \begin{bmatrix} (1-\rho^2)^{1/2} & & & & \\ -\rho & 1 & & 0 & \\ & -\rho & 1 & & \\ 0 & & \ddots & \ddots & \\ & & & -\rho & 1 \end{bmatrix} \tag{10.2.10}$$

is the $T \times T$ Prais–Winsten (1954) transformation matrix. The error terms of the transformed model are independent and identically distributed and thus ordinary least squares applied to (10.2.9) produces generalized least squares estimates of $\boldsymbol{\beta}$. Of course, if ρ is known, the generalized least squares estimator can easily be computed and under normality has the small sample property of minimum variance unbiased and large sample property of asymptotic efficiency. More frequently, however, ρ is unknown and must be estimated consistently by an estimate $\hat{\rho}$. Replacement of ρ with $\hat{\rho}$ in the generalized least squares formula provides a feasible generalized least squares estimator.

10.3 Maximum Likelihood Estimation of AR(1)

10.3.1 Maximum Likelihood Search

Dhrymes (1971, pp. 69–70) discussed the maximum likelihood estimation of $\boldsymbol{\beta}$, ρ, and σ_u^2 in the present model. The natural logarithm of the likelihood function for $y_1, y_2, \ldots, y_T$ is

$$\begin{aligned} \ln L(\mathbf{y}; X, \beta, \sigma_u^2, \rho) &= -\frac{T}{2}\ln(2\pi) - \tfrac{1}{2}\ln|\sigma_u^2\Omega| \\ &\quad - \frac{1}{2\sigma_u^2}(\mathbf{y} - X\boldsymbol{\beta})'\Omega^{-1}(\mathbf{y} - X\boldsymbol{\beta}) \\ &= -\frac{T}{2}\ln(2\pi) - \frac{T}{2}\ln(\sigma_u^2) + \tfrac{1}{2}\ln(1-\rho^2) \\ &\quad - \frac{1}{2\sigma_u^2}(\mathbf{y}^* - X^*\boldsymbol{\beta})'(\mathbf{y}^* - X^*\boldsymbol{\beta}), \end{aligned} \tag{10.3.1}$$

where $\mathbf{y}^* = P'\mathbf{y}$, $X^* = P'X$, and using the result that $|\sigma_u^2\Omega| = (\sigma_u^2)^T/(1-\rho^2)$. Maximizing partially with respect to $\boldsymbol{\beta}$ and σ_u^2 leads to

$$\boldsymbol{\beta}(\rho) = (X^{*\prime}X^*)^{-1}X^{*\prime}\mathbf{y}^* = (X'\Omega^{-1}X)^{-1}X'\Omega^{-1}\mathbf{y} \tag{10.3.2}$$

and

$$\sigma_u^2(\rho) = \frac{1}{T}[\mathbf{y}^* - X^*\boldsymbol{\beta}(\rho)]'[\mathbf{y}^* - X^*\boldsymbol{\beta}(\rho)]. \tag{10.3.3}$$

Substituting the relationships (10.3.2) and (10.3.3) back into (10.3.1) provides the concentrated likelihood function

$$\begin{aligned} L^*(\rho; \mathbf{y}, X) &= -\frac{T}{2}\{\ln(2\pi) + 1\} + \tfrac{1}{2}\ln(1-\rho^2) - \frac{T}{2}\ln\sigma_u^2(\rho) \\ &= \frac{T}{2}\{\ln(2\pi) + 1\} - \frac{T}{2}\ln\left[\frac{\sigma_u^2(\rho)}{(1-\rho^2)^{1/T}}\right]. \end{aligned} \tag{10.3.4}$$

Thus globally maximizing the log likelihood function is equivalent to globally minimizing $\sigma_u^2(\rho)/(1-\rho^2)^{1/T}$.

The maximum likelihood estimators of $\boldsymbol{\beta}$, ρ, and σ_u^2 are consistent and asymptotically efficient. This follows from the properties of maximum likelihood estimation. The information matrix is (see Exercise 10.1)

$$I = \begin{bmatrix} \dfrac{1}{\sigma_u^2}X'\Omega^{-1}X & 0 & 0 \\ 0 & \dfrac{1}{1-\rho^2}\left(T - 1 + \dfrac{2\rho^2}{1-\rho^2}\right) & \dfrac{\rho}{\sigma_u^2(1-\rho^2)} \\ 0 & \dfrac{\rho}{\sigma_u^2(1-\rho^2)} & \dfrac{T}{2\sigma_u^4} \end{bmatrix} \tag{10.3.5}$$

from which asymptotic standard errors may be obtained.

One way to maximize (10.3.1) is to maximize (10.3.4) with respect to ρ and to use that value in (10.3.2) and (10.3.3) to obtain maximum likelihood estimates of $\boldsymbol{\beta}$ and σ_u^2. There are other procedures for maximizing (10.3.1) including those suggested by Magnus (1978, p. 365) and Beach and MacKinnon (1978a, pp. 52–53).

10.3.2 Cochrane–Orcutt Iterative Procedure

Correction for serial correlation (AR(1)) has not always been obtained by using the Prais–Winsten transformation matrix of (10.2.9). Cochrane and Orcutt (1949) suggested using the transformation

$$G = \begin{bmatrix} -\rho & 1 & & & 0 \\ & -\rho & 1 & & \\ & & \ddots & \ddots & \\ 0 & & & -\rho & 1 \end{bmatrix}_{(T-1)\times T} \tag{10.3.6}$$

which omits the first observation.

The Cochrane–Orcutt transformed system is

$$\begin{aligned} y_t - \rho y_{t-1} = \beta_1(x_{t1} - \rho x_{t-1,1}) + \cdots \\ + \beta_K(x_{tK} - \rho x_{t-1,K}) + e_t - \rho e_{t-1}, \qquad t = 2, 3, \ldots, T, \end{aligned}$$

or in matrix notation,

$$G\mathbf{y} = GX\boldsymbol{\beta} + G\mathbf{e}, \tag{10.3.7}$$

where $\mathbf{y}$, X, and $\mathbf{e}$, which are of dimension $T \times 1$, $T \times K$ and $T \times 1$, represent the observations on the original dependent variable, design matrix, and error vector. The estimator

$$\tilde{\boldsymbol{\beta}}_G = (X'G'GX)^{-1}X'G'G\mathbf{y} \tag{10.3.8}$$

is the maximum likelihood estimator of $\boldsymbol{\beta}$ for known ρ conditional on given y_1.

In the presence of unknown ρ, Cochrane and Orcutt (1949) suggested an iterative procedure for estimating $\boldsymbol{\beta}$ in (10.3.7). Let

$$\hat{e}_t = y_t - (x_{t1}\hat{\beta}_1 + \cdots + x_{tK}\hat{\beta}_K)$$

denote the least squares residuals for model (10.2.1). A consistent estimator of ρ is given by $\hat{\rho} = \sum_{t=2}^{T} \hat{e}_t\hat{e}_{t-1}/\sum_{t=2}^{T} \hat{e}_{t-1}^2$. This estimator can be used to form the feasible generalized least squares estimator

$$\tilde{\tilde{\boldsymbol{\beta}}}_G = (X'\hat{G}'\hat{G}X)^{-1}X'\hat{G}'\hat{G}\mathbf{y}, \tag{10.3.9}$$

where $\hat{G}$ denotes the G matrix with ρ replaced by $\hat{\rho}$. Then using $\tilde{\tilde{\boldsymbol{\beta}}}_G$, a new estimate of ρ is given by $\hat{\hat{\rho}} = \sum_{t=2}^{T} \hat{\hat{e}}_t\hat{\hat{e}}_{t-1}/\sum_{t=2}^{T} \hat{\hat{e}}_{t-1}^2$, where $\hat{\hat{e}}_t = y_t - (x_{t1}\tilde{\tilde{\beta}}_1 + \cdots + x_{tK}\tilde{\tilde{\beta}}_K)$ and $\tilde{\tilde{\beta}}_i$, $i = 1, 2, \ldots, K$ is the ith element of $\tilde{\tilde{\boldsymbol{\beta}}}_G$. Using $\hat{\hat{\rho}}$, another feasible generalized least squares estimate of $\boldsymbol{\beta}$ could be obtained, say $\tilde{\tilde{\tilde{\boldsymbol{\beta}}}}_G$, and, in turn, used to obtain another estimate of ρ, say $\hat{\hat{\hat{\rho}}}$, and so on. This procedure continues until successive estimates of ρ and $\boldsymbol{\beta}$ differ by arbitrarily small amounts.

10.3.3 Hildreth–Lu Search Procedure

Rather than proceeding in an iterative manner from an initial estimate of ρ, Hildreth and Lu (1960) suggested partitioning the interval of ρ, $(-1, 1)$, by points ρ_i, $i = 1, 2, \ldots, n$. Then for every ρ_i there is a corresponding sum of squared errors

$$\begin{aligned} \text{SSE}(\rho_i) = \sum_{t=2}^{T} [(y_t - \rho_i y_{t-1}) - \beta_1(\rho_i)(x_{t1} - \rho_i x_{t-1,1}) - \cdots \\ - \beta_K(\rho_i)(x_{tK} - \rho_i x_{t-1,K})]^2 \end{aligned} \tag{10.3.10}$$

for the Cochrane–Orcutt transformation, where $\beta_1(\rho_i)$, $\beta_2(\rho_i)$, ..., $\beta_K(\rho_i)$ are the conditional generalized least squares estimators

$$\tilde{\boldsymbol{\beta}}_G(\rho_i) = \begin{pmatrix} \beta_1(\rho_i) \\ \vdots \\ \beta_K(\rho_i) \end{pmatrix} = (X'G'GX)^{-1}X'G'G\mathbf{y} \tag{10.3.11}$$

with G being formed using the value of $\rho = \rho_i$. The Hildreth and Lu estimate of ρ, say $\tilde{\rho}$, is that ρ_i which minimizes $\text{SSE}(\rho_i)$ and the corresponding estimates of $\beta_1, \beta_2, \ldots, \beta_K$ are $\beta_1(\tilde{\rho}), \beta_2(\tilde{\rho}), \ldots, \beta_K(\tilde{\rho})$.

The Cochrane–Orcutt and Hildreth–Lu procedures are asymptotically equivalent with the Hildreth–Lu procedure being a maximum likelihood search for $\boldsymbol{\beta}$ and ρ based on $(T - 1)$ observations with y_1 assumed fixed. In small samples, however, these procedures can lead to substantially different estimates with the Cochrane–Orcutt procedure potentially finding only a local minima rather than a global minimum of $\text{SSE}(\rho_i)$; see, for example, Oxley and Roberts (1982).

Also, though the Prais–Winsten and Cochrane–Orcutt transformations are different, disregarding the first observation makes no difference asymptotically. However, this may not be the case in small samples.

10.4 Two-Step Methods

Consider the two distinct generalized least squares estimators (10.3.2) and (10.3.8) arising from the Prais–Winsten and Cochrane–Orcutt transformations. These estimators become feasible generalized least squares estimators when ρ is replaced by a consistent estimator, say $\hat{\rho}$. There are several ways of consistently estimating ρ, however. Some of these estimators are:

(i) Cochrane–Orcutt Method: A least squares estimator of ρ is determined by replacing the unobservable variables e_t in the equation

$$e_t = \rho e_{t-1} + u_t, \qquad t = 2, 3, \ldots, T$$

with ordinary least squares residuals $\hat{e}_i$ and applying ordinary least squares on the autoregressive equation that results. The least squares estimate is

$$\hat{\rho} = \frac{\sum_{t=2}^{T} \hat{e}_t \hat{e}_{t-1}}{\sum_{t=2}^{T} \hat{e}_{t-1}^2}. \tag{10.4.1}$$

This estimator is consistent (for a proof see Press (1972, pp. 273–276)) but is biased in small samples (Rao and Griliches (1969, pp. 255–256)).

(ii) Theil's estimator:

$$\hat{\rho} = \frac{\dfrac{1}{T-1}\sum_{t=2}^{T} \hat{e}_t \hat{e}_{t-1}}{\dfrac{1}{T-K}\sum_{t=1}^{T} \hat{e}_t^2} = \frac{\sum_{t=2}^{T} \hat{e}_t \hat{e}_{t-1}}{(T-1)\hat{\sigma}^2}. \tag{10.4.2}$$

See Theil (1971, p. 254) and a proof of its consistency on p. 407.

(iii) The Durbin Estimator:
Let

$$y_t = \beta_1 + \beta_2 x_{t2} + \cdots + \beta_K x_{tK} + e_t,$$

where

$$e_t = \rho e_{t-1} + u_t.$$

The autoregressive error model can be transformed to

$$\begin{aligned} y_t &= \beta_1 + \beta_2 x_{t2} + \cdots + \beta_K x_{tK} + \rho e_{t-1} + u_t \\ &= \beta_1 + \beta_2 x_{t2} + \cdots + \beta_K x_{tK} \\ &\quad + \rho(y_{t-1} - \beta_1 - \beta_2 x_{t-1,2} - \cdots - \beta_K x_{t-1,K}) + u_t \\ &= \rho y_{t-1} + (1-\rho)\beta_1 + \beta_2 x_{t2} - \beta_2 \rho x_{t-1,2} + \cdots \\ &\quad + \beta_K x_{tK} - \beta_K \rho x_{t-1,K} + u_t. \end{aligned} \tag{10.4.3}$$

Equation (10.4.3) is called the "Durbin Equation." Durbin (1960) suggested obtaining a consistent estimator of ρ by applying ordinary least squares to the Durbin equation and then taking $\hat{\rho}$ to be the estimated coefficient of y_{t-1}. If the u_t are normally distributed this estimate is also asymptotically efficient (see Rothenberg (1973, p. 27)).

Obviously, there exist many feasible generalized least squares estimators for the model at hand since there exist two choices of transformations and many consistent estimates of ρ. All of these estimators are asymptotically equivalent. The relative performance of these estimators in small samples is another matter, however, and will be considered below in Section 10.5.

The choice between the Prais–Winsten and Cochrane–Orcutt transformations should be made on *a priori* grounds. The former should be used in those instances when *it can be assumed that the stochastic error process started in the infinite past*. Utilizing the likelihood function of (10.3.1) (and hence the Prais–Winsten transformation) offers two advantages. First, because of the term $(1-\rho^2)^{1/2}(y_1 - \mathbf{x}_1'\boldsymbol{\beta})$, it is ensured that the initial observation will have some effect upon the estimates. Second, the maximum likelihood procedure constrains the stationary condition ($|\rho| < 1$) to hold via the term $\frac{1}{2}\ln(1-\rho^2)$, which is not the case if the first observation is deleted. On purely theoretical grounds, then, if the process started in the infinite past, the maximum likelihood procedure should be preferred.

However, if the error process began in the finite past, this information should be used. Thornton (1982) has shown that the appropriate transformation matrix to diagonalize Ω, where $E\mathbf{ee}' = \sigma_u^2\Omega$, is

$$P' = \begin{bmatrix} \left(\dfrac{1-\rho^{2(q+1)}}{1-\rho^{2q}} - \rho^2\right)^{1/2} & 0 & & 0 \\ -\rho & 1 & & \\ & -\rho & \ddots & \\ 0 & & \ddots & \ddots \\ & & -\rho & 1 \end{bmatrix}, \tag{10.4.4}$$

where the error process is assumed to have begun $q - 1$ periods prior to the first observation. Thus, $PP' = \Omega^{-1}$ and $P'\Omega P = I$. Note that, if $q \to \infty$, the usual Prais–Winsten transformation (10.2.10) obtains while $q = 1$ (i.e. the process starts concurrently with the first observation) requires that the first observation be unweighted.

Since the AR(1) model with unknown ρ is a feasible generalized least squares model, the usual tests of hypotheses (see Section 8.3), even in the absence of normality, are asymptotically valid. However, once the assumption of normality is dropped, asymptotic efficiency can no longer be claimed.

10.5 Small Sample Estimation in the AR(1) Model

The asymptotic equivalence of the previous estimators naturally leads to the question of which is to be preferred in small samples. Also are there values of ρ near 0 for which feasible generalized least squares is less efficient in small samples than ordinary least squares? Which transformation is to be preferred in small samples?

Rao and Griliches (1969) investigated the small sample properties of several feasible generalized least squares estimators in the autocorrelated error model through a Monte Carlo experiment. The model used to generate the observations for the sampling experiment was

$$\begin{aligned} y_t &= 1.0x_t + e_t, \\ x_t &= \lambda x_{t-1} + v_t, \qquad |\lambda| < 1, \\ e_t &= \rho e_{t-1} + u_t, \qquad |\rho| < 1, \quad t = 1, 2, \ldots, 20. \end{aligned}$$

For given ρ and λ, 50 samples were drawn with independent x_t and e_t series. The variances of v_t and u_t were adjusted so as to make $R^2 \doteq 0.90$. The specific estimators that Rao and Griliches investigated were:

(i) ordinary least squares;
(ii) the Cochrane–Orcutt transformation with Cochrane–Orcutt $\hat{\rho}$ (10.4.1) and Durbin $\hat{\rho}$;
(iii) the Prais–Winsten transformation with Cochrane–Orcutt $\hat{\rho}$ and Durbin $\hat{\rho}$;
(iv) the nonlinearly constrained least squares estimator of β and ρ in the Durbin equation, namely,

$$y_t = \rho y_{t-1} + \beta x_t - \beta\rho x_{t-1} + u_t, \qquad t = 2, 3, \ldots, 20,$$

with imposed nonlinear constraint

$$\widehat{\beta\rho} = \hat{\beta} \cdot \hat{\rho}.$$

Method (iv) is asymptotically equivalent to maximum likelihood and hence is asymptotically efficient.

Before examining the estimation of β, Rao and Griliches first reviewed the sampling properties of the Durbin, Cochrane–Orcutt, and nonlinearly constrained estimates of ρ. They found the Durbin estimator to be slightly inferior, in terms of mean square error, to the other two estimates in the range of negative ρ's while the Durbin estimator was significantly more efficient for positive ρ. In general, it was found that the two-step procedures using the Durbin $\hat{\rho}$ proved to be superior to those using other estimates of ρ. (This is consistent with the Rothenberg (1973) finding that the Durbin $\hat{\rho}$ is asymptotically efficient.)

The major conclusions by Rao and Griliches concerning the estimation of β were:

(i) The ordinary least squares estimator is less efficient than all other methods considered for moderate and high values of ρ ($|\rho| \geq 0.3$).
(ii) There is a definite gain to be obtained from using feasible generalized least squares when $|\rho| \geq 0.3$ and very little loss from using such methods otherwise.
(iii) All of the feasible generalized least squares techniques were not very far apart in their performance.
(iv) Among the various estimators examined, the two-step estimator based on the Prais–Winsten transformation and the Durbin $\hat{\rho}$ was recommended since the authors felt that it is likely to do better over a wide range of parameters than the other estimators examined.

Of course, it is not surprising that the Prais–Winsten transformation performed better in the Rao and Griliches' experiments since the error terms were generated using the assumption that the stochastic process began in the infinite past. Likewise, Beach and MacKinnon (1978a) found the full information maximum likelihood procedure to perform substantially better than maximum likelihood conditional on y_1.

10.6 Other Correlated Error Structures

The correlation between the error terms in the model

$$\mathbf{y} = X\boldsymbol{\beta} + \mathbf{e}, \tag{10.6.1}$$

where $E\mathbf{e} = \mathbf{0}$ and $E\mathbf{ee}' = \sigma^2\Omega$, can take many forms, the first-order autoregressive error described in previous sections being one special case. A more general stationary correlation structure can be written as

$$\sigma_e^2\Omega = \sigma_e^2\begin{bmatrix} 1 & \rho_1 & & \cdots & \rho_{T-1} \\ \rho_1 & 1 & \rho_1 & \cdots & \rho_{T-2} \\ \rho_2 & \rho_1 & \ddots & \ddots & \vdots \\ \vdots & \vdots & \ddots & \ddots & \rho_1 \\ \rho_{T-1} & \rho_{T-2} & \cdots & \rho_1 & 1 \end{bmatrix}, \tag{10.6.2}$$

where

$$\rho_s = \frac{E(e_t e_{t-s})}{\sigma_e^2} = \frac{E(e_t e_{t+s})}{\sigma_e^2}, \qquad s = 1, 2, \ldots,$$

and ρ_s is the correlation between two error terms s periods apart. For example, in the first-order autoregressive process, $e_t = \rho e_{t-1} + u_t$, $\rho_s = \rho^s$, and $\sigma_e^2 = \sigma_u^2/(1 - \rho^2)$.

More general stationary error process specifications include:

(a) An autoregressive process of order p, AR(p),

$$e_t = \theta_1 e_{t-1} + \theta_2 e_{t-2} + \cdots + \theta_p e_{t-p} + u_t, \tag{10.6.3}$$

with $Eu_t = 0$, $Eu_t^2 = \sigma_u^2$ and, $Eu_t u_{t-s} = 0$, $s = 1, 2, \ldots; t = 1, 2, \ldots,$

(b) A moving-average process of order q, MA(q),

$$e_t = u_t + \alpha_1 u_{t-1} + \alpha_2 u_{t-2} + \cdots + \alpha_q u_{t-q}, \tag{10.6.4}$$

(c) A combined autoregressive moving-average process of order (p, q), ARMA(p, q),

$$\begin{aligned} e_t = \theta_1 e_{t-1} + \theta_2 e_{t-2} + \cdots + \theta_p e_{t-p} \\ + u_t + \alpha_1 u_{t-1} + \alpha_2 u_{t-2} + \cdots + \alpha_q u_{t-q}. \end{aligned} \tag{10.6.5}$$

These specifications are general enough to accommodate a wide range of alternatives. For example, the MA(1) process, $e_t = u_t + \alpha_1 u_{t-1}$, provides (see Exercise 10.2),

$$\begin{aligned} \rho_1 &= \alpha_1/(1 + \alpha_1^2), \\ \rho_s &= 0, \qquad s \geq 2 \end{aligned} \tag{10.6.6}$$

and $\sigma_e^2 = \sigma_u^2(1 + \alpha_1^2)$.

The MA(1) process illustrates the basic moving-average characteristic that the correlation between MA(q) errors vanishes after q periods.

In the ARMA(1, 1) process, $e_t = \theta_1 e_{t-1} + \alpha_1 u_{t-1} + u_t$ we have (see Exercise 10.3),

$$\begin{aligned} \rho_1 &= \frac{(1 + \theta_1\alpha_1)(\theta_1 + \alpha_1)}{(1 + \alpha_1^2 + 2\alpha_1\theta_1)}, \\ \rho_s &= \theta_1 \rho_{s-1}, \qquad s > 1, \end{aligned} \tag{10.6.7}$$

and

$$\sigma_e^2 = \frac{(1 + \alpha_1^2 + 2\alpha_1\theta_1)}{(1 - \theta_1^2)}\,\sigma_u^2.$$

In general, the AR(p) processes have geometrically declining correlations, the MA(q) processes have a finite nonzero correlation structure while the ARMA processes exhibit both characteristics.

Before turning to the discussion of feasible generalized least squares estimation in the presence of these general error schemes, some discussion of the *stationarity* and *invertibility* conditions for AR, MA, and ARMA processes is needed. Stationarity requires that the correlation structure of an error process be invariant with respect to time, i.e.,

$$E(e_t e_{t+s}) = E(e_{t+m} e_{t+s+m}), \qquad m = 1, 2, \ldots. \tag{10.6.8}$$

If q is finite, the MA(q) process is stationary. For the AR(p) and ARMA(p, q) processes to be stationary the roots of the polynomial in r

$$\theta(r) = 1 - \theta_1 r - \theta_2 r^2 - \cdots - \theta_p r^p = 0 \tag{10.6.9}$$

must be greater than one in absolute value. (If a root is complex, $r = a + bi$, then its modulus $|r| = \sqrt{a^2 + b^2}$ must be greater than one.) For example, the stationarity conditions for AR(2) are $\theta_1 + \theta_2 < 1$, $\theta_2 - \theta_1 < 1$ and $-1 < \theta_2 < 1$.

In addition, the MA and ARMA processes are assumed to satisfy the *invertibility* condition. Essentially this condition permits the MA processes to be written as AR processes of infinite order and is required for model identification (see Box and Jenkins (1970, p. 195)). This condition will be satisfied if the polynomial in r

$$\alpha(r) = 1 + \alpha_1 r + \alpha_2 r^2 + \cdots + \alpha_q r^q = 0 \tag{10.6.10}$$

has roots greater than one in absolute value. For example, in the MA(1) process, $e_t = u_t + \alpha_1 u_{t-1}$, the invertibility condition requires that $|\alpha_1| < 1$.

10.7 Feasible Generalized Least Squares for AR(2), MA(1), and ARMA(p, q)

In Chapter 2 the generalized least squares model was introduced as

$$\mathbf{y} = X\boldsymbol{\beta} + \mathbf{e}, \tag{10.7.1}$$

where $E\mathbf{e} = \mathbf{0}$ and $E\mathbf{ee}' = \sigma^2\Omega$ and Ω is known. Letting $PP' = \Omega^{-1}$ the transformed system

$$P'\mathbf{y} = P'X\boldsymbol{\beta} + P'\mathbf{e} \tag{10.7.2}$$

or

$$\mathbf{y}^* = X^*\boldsymbol{\beta} + \mathbf{e}^*$$

provided a means of proving that the generalized least squares estimator, $\tilde{\boldsymbol{\beta}} = (X'\Omega^{-1}X)^{-1}X'\Omega^{-1}\mathbf{y}$, is the best linear unbiased estimator of $\boldsymbol{\beta}$. In contrast, as outlined in Chapter 8, when Ω is unknown, it may be consistently estimated by Ω, then feasible generalized least squares can be utilized to estimate $\boldsymbol{\beta}$. In the case where X is nonstochastic, the feasible generalized least squares estimator, $\tilde{\tilde{\boldsymbol{\beta}}} = (X'\hat{\Omega}^{-1}X)^{-1}X'\hat{\Omega}^{-1}\mathbf{y}$, is asymptotically efficient under normality. What remains to be done here is to illustrate the use of feasible generalized least squares in particular cases of the more generalized ARMA processes.

10.7.1 Estimation for AR(2) Process

The linear model under consideration is

$$y_t = x_{t1}\beta_1 + x_{t2}\beta_2 + \cdots + x_{tK}\beta_K + e_t, \tag{10.7.3}$$

$$e_t = \theta_1 e_{t-1} + \theta_2 e_{t-2} + u_t, \qquad t = 1, 2, \ldots, T, \tag{10.7.4}$$

where $Eu_t = Eu_t u_{t-s} = 0$, $s = 1, 2, \ldots$, and $Eu_t^2 = \sigma_u^2$. The stationarity conditions are $\theta_1 + \theta_2 < 1$, $\theta_2 - \theta_1 < 1$, and $-1 < \theta_2 < 1$ while the autocorrelations are (see Exercise 10.4),

$$\begin{aligned} \rho_1 &= \theta_1/(1 - \theta_2), \\ \rho_2 &= \theta_2 + \theta_1^2/(1 - \theta_2), \quad \text{and} \\ \rho_s &= \theta_1\rho_{s-1} + \theta_2\rho_{s-2}, \qquad s > 2, \end{aligned} \tag{10.7.5}$$

with variance

$$\sigma_e^2 = \frac{(1-\theta_2)\sigma_u^2}{(1+\theta_2)[(1-\theta_2)^2 - \theta_1^2]}. \tag{10.7.6}$$

Let $E(\mathbf{ee}') = \sigma_u^2 \Psi$ then it can be verified (see Exercise 10.5) that

$$\Psi^{-1} = \begin{bmatrix} 1 & -\theta_1 & -\theta_2 & & & & 0 \\ -\theta_1 & 1+\theta_1^2 & -\theta_1+\theta_1\theta_2 & \ddots & & & \\ -\theta_2 & -\theta_1+\theta_1\theta_2 & 1+\theta_1^2 & \ddots & \ddots & & \\ & -\theta_2 & \ddots & \ddots & \ddots & \ddots & -\theta_2 \\ & 0 & & \ddots & \ddots & 1+\theta_1^2 & -\theta_1 \\ & & & & -\theta_2 & -\theta_1 & 1 \end{bmatrix}. \tag{10.7.7}$$

As before, let P be $PP' = \Psi^{-1}$, the generalized least squares transformation matrix. For the AR(2) process

$$P' = \begin{bmatrix} \sigma_u/\sigma_e & 0 & 0 & 0 & \cdots \\ -\rho_1\sqrt{1-\theta_1^2} & \sqrt{1-\theta_2^2} & 0 & 0 & \cdots \\ -\theta_2 & -\theta_1 & 1 & 0 & \cdots \\ 0 & -\theta_2 & -\theta_1 & 1 & \cdots \\ & & \ddots & \ddots & \ddots \\ 0 & \cdots & -\theta_2 & -\theta_1 & 1 \end{bmatrix}, \tag{10.7.8}$$

where

$$\sigma_u/\sigma_e = \{(1+\theta_2)[(1-\theta_2)^2 - \theta_1^2]/(1-\theta_2)\}^{1/2}.$$

If θ_1 and θ_2 were known, then the generalized least squares estimator of $\boldsymbol{\beta}$ in (10.7.3) would be $\tilde{\boldsymbol{\beta}} = (X'PP'X)^{-1}X'PP'\mathbf{y}$ with covariance matrix $\sigma_u^2(X'PP'X)^{-1}$ and the best linear unbiased estimator. Under an assumption of normally distributed u_t, $\tilde{\boldsymbol{\beta}}$, would also be minimum variance unbiased. Unfortunately, the usual case is that where θ_1 and θ_2 are unknown and must be estimated.

The logical approach is to use the ordinary least squares residuals $\hat{\mathbf{e}} = \mathbf{y} - X\hat{\boldsymbol{\beta}}$ to obtain sample correlation coefficients

$$r_s = \frac{\sum_{t=s+1}^{T} \hat{e}_t \hat{e}_{t-s}}{\sum_{t=1}^{T} \hat{e}_t^2}, \qquad s = 1, 2, \tag{10.7.9}$$

to estimate ρ_1 and ρ_2 of (10.7.5). This provides

$$\begin{aligned} r_1 &= \hat{\theta}_1/(1 - \hat{\theta}_2), \\ r_2 &= \hat{\theta}_2 + \hat{\theta}_1^2/(1 - \hat{\theta}_2), \end{aligned} \tag{10.7.10}$$

and solving for $\hat{\theta}_1$ and $\hat{\theta}_2$ yields

$$\begin{aligned} \hat{\theta}_1 &= r_1(1 - r_2)/(1 - r_1^2), \\ \hat{\theta}_2 &= (r_2 - r_1^2)/(1 - r_1^2). \end{aligned} \tag{10.7.11}$$

As an alternative, one could apply least squares to the equation

$$\hat{e}_t = \theta_1 \hat{e}_{t-1} + \theta_2 \hat{e}_{t-2} + \hat{u}_t, \qquad t = 3, 4, \ldots, T, \tag{10.7.12}$$

and likewise obtain consistent estimates for θ_1 and θ_2.

Whether (10.7.11) or (10.7.12) is used, the resulting consistent estimate of $\hat{P}'$ provides the feasible generalized least squares estimator,

$$\tilde{\tilde{\boldsymbol{\beta}}} = (X'\hat{P}\hat{P}'X)^{-1}X'\hat{P}\hat{P}'\mathbf{y},$$

which has asymptotic covariance matrix

$$\sigma_u^2 \lim \frac{1}{T}\left(\frac{X'PP'X}{T}\right)^{-1} = \frac{1}{T}\sigma_u^2 Q_{\Psi}^{-1}$$

whose consistent estimate is $\tilde{\tilde{\sigma}}_u^2(X'\hat{P}\hat{P}'X)^{-1}$ with

$$\tilde{\tilde{\sigma}}_u^2 = (\mathbf{y} - X\tilde{\tilde{\boldsymbol{\beta}}})'\hat{\Psi}^{-1}(\mathbf{y} - X\tilde{\tilde{\boldsymbol{\beta}}})/(T - K).$$

In the presence of normal u_t's, feasible generalized least squares is asymptotically efficient.

As an alternative to feasible generalized least squares, one could estimate the AR(2) model using maximum likelihood estimation in a manner similar to that outlined for the AR(1) process in Section 10.3. Beach and MacKinnon (1978b) outline a search algorithm based upon a concentrated likelihood function. As there is no lagged dependent variable present, feasible generalized least squares and maximum likelihood estimation are equally efficient asymptotically.

10.7.2 Estimation for MA(1) Process

In this section we consider the model

$$y_t = x_{t1}\beta_1 + x_{t2}\beta_2 + \cdots + x_{tK}\beta_K + e_t, \tag{10.7.13}$$

$$e_t = u_t + \alpha_1 u_{t-1}, \tag{10.7.14}$$

where $Eu_t = Eu_t u_{t-s} = 0$, $s = 1, 2, \ldots$, and $Eu_t^2 = \sigma_u^2$. The invertibility condition requires that $|\alpha_1| < 1$.

Let $E(\mathbf{ee}') = \sigma_u^2\Psi$ where $\sigma_e^2 = \sigma_u^2(1 + \alpha_1^2)$ and the correlations are $\rho_1 = \alpha_1/(1 + \alpha_1^2)$ and $\rho_s = 0$ for $s \geq 2$. The form of Ψ is

$$\Psi = \begin{bmatrix} 1 + \alpha_1^2 & \alpha_1 & 0 & \cdots & 0 \\ \alpha_1 & 1 + \alpha_1^2 & \alpha_1 & & \vdots \\ 0 & \alpha_1 & 1 + \alpha_1^2 & \ddots & 0 \\ \vdots & \vdots & \ddots & \ddots & \alpha_1 \\ 0 & \cdots & 0 & \alpha_1 & 1 + \alpha_1^2 \end{bmatrix}. \tag{10.7.15}$$

Of course, for known α the generalized least squares estimator

$$\tilde{\boldsymbol{\beta}} = (X'\Psi^{-1}X)^{-1}X'\Psi^{-1}\mathbf{y}$$

is the best linear unbiased estimator for the MA(1) model. With normality, $\tilde{\boldsymbol{\beta}}$ becomes minimum variance unbiased. The usual case, however, is when α is unknown and must be estimated.

Following Pesaran (1973), let A denote the matrix of eigenvectors of Ψ, whose jth column, $\mathbf{a}_j$, is given by

$$\mathbf{a}_j' = (2/(T + 1))^{1/2}\left(\sin\frac{j\pi}{(T + 1)}, \sin\frac{2j\pi}{(T + 1)}, \ldots, \sin\frac{Tj\pi}{(T + 1)}\right) \tag{10.7.16}$$

with corresponding eigenvalues

$$\lambda_j = \alpha_1^2 + 2\alpha_1 \cos(j\pi/(T + 1)) + 1, \qquad j = 1, 2, \ldots, T. \tag{10.7.17}$$

Then if we denote $\Lambda = (\lambda_1, \lambda_2, \ldots, \lambda_T)$, $PP' = \Psi^{-1}$, where $P = A\Lambda^{-1/2}$. The transformed model becomes

$$P'y = P'X\boldsymbol{\beta} + P'\mathbf{e},$$

$$\mathbf{y}^* = X^*\boldsymbol{\beta} + \mathbf{e}^*$$

with typical element

$$y_t^* = \lambda_t^{-1/2}(2/(T + 1))^{1/2} \sum_{j=1}^{T} y_j \sin\left(\frac{jt\pi}{T + 1}\right). \tag{10.7.18}$$

The problem remains to obtain a consistent estimate of α_1. One possible method is to use the sample autocorrelation coefficient

$$r_1 = \frac{\sum_{t=2}^{T} \hat{e}_t \hat{e}_{t-1}}{\sum_{t=1}^{T} \hat{e}_t^2} \tag{10.7.19}$$

and obtain an estimate $\hat{\alpha}_1$ from

$$r_1 = \hat{\alpha}_1/(1 + \hat{\alpha}_1^2) \tag{10.7.20}$$

as we know $\rho_1 = \alpha_1/(1 + \alpha_1^2)$. Solving (10.7.20) for $\hat{\alpha}_1$ yields

$$\hat{\alpha}_1 = \frac{1 - \sqrt{1 - 4r_1^2}}{2r_1}. \tag{10.7.21}$$

The invertibility condition requires $|\alpha_1| < 1$ which in turn implies $|\rho_1| < 0.5$. Thus, $\hat{\alpha}_1$ is only meaningful when $|r_1| \leq 0.5$. Since r_1 is consistent, $\hat{\alpha}_1$ is consistent by Slutsky's theorem.

To use feasible generalized least squares, $\hat{\alpha}$ is used to construct $\hat{P}$ which, in turn, provides the estimator

$$\tilde{\tilde{\boldsymbol{\beta}}} = (X'\hat{P}\hat{P}'X)^{-1}X'\hat{P}\hat{P}'\mathbf{y} \tag{10.7.22}$$

which is asymptotically efficient in the presence of normality and nonstochastic X. Relying upon asymptotic normality, the estimated covariance matrix $\tilde{\tilde{\sigma}}_u^2(X'\hat{P}\hat{P}'X)^{-1}$, where $\tilde{\tilde{\sigma}}_u^2 = (\mathbf{y} - X\tilde{\tilde{\boldsymbol{\beta}}})'\hat{\Psi}^{-1}(\mathbf{y} - X\tilde{\tilde{\boldsymbol{\beta}}})/(T - K)$, can be used in tests of hypotheses. Though $\hat{\alpha}_1$ of (10.7.21) is easy to construct, it is inefficient relative to the maximum likelihood estimator as it ignores the constraint $|\rho_1| < 0.5$ (see Fuller (1976, pp. 343–348)). This does not affect the asymptotic efficiency of the feasible generalized least squares estimator, but there still remains the question of small sample performance.

10.7.3 Estimation for General ARMA(p, q) Process

The linear model with ARMA(p, q) error process can be written

$$y_t = x_{t1}\beta_1 + \cdots + x_{tK}\beta_K + e_t, \tag{10.7.23}$$

$$e_t = \theta_1 e_{t-1} + \cdots + \theta_p e_{t-p} + u_t + \alpha_1 u_{t-1} + \cdots + \alpha_q u_{t-q}, \tag{10.7.24}$$

where $Eu_t = Eu_t u_{t-s} = 0$, $s = 1, 2, \ldots$, and $Eu_t^2 = \sigma_u^2$, $t = 1, 2, \ldots, T$. Except where Tiao and Ali (1971) derived the P matrix for the ARMA(1, 1), no general expression for the P transformation of an ARMA(p, q) process has been derived. As a result estimation usually proceeds by nonlinear least squares or by maximum likelihood estimation (Pierce (1971)) both of which are asymptotically efficient given normality of the errors u_t. For a survey of nonlinear methods, see the Appendix of this book.

10.8 Testing for AR(1) Error Process

10.8.1 The Durbin–Watson Test

The most extensively used test for AR(1) errors is the Durbin–Watson bounds test developed by Durbin and Watson (1950, 1951). In these papers the authors specialized the von Neumann–Hart ratio of the mean square of successive differences to the examination of least squares residuals for an independence hypothesis. We will briefly present the basic results (for proofs, see Durbin and Watson (1950)) concerning the von Neumann–Hart ratio and thereafter specialize them to the AR(1) problem in regression analysis. This will provide a basis for understanding why the Durbin–Watson test is a "bounds test."

Lemma 10.8.1. *Let* $\mathbf{z}$ *and* $\mathbf{e}$ *be* $T \times 1$ *normal random vectors such that* $\mathbf{z} = M\mathbf{e}$, *where* $M = I - X(X'X)^{-1}X'$ *and* X *is a* $T \times K$ *nonstochastic matrix of* rank K. *Furthermore, let* $r = \mathbf{z}'A\mathbf{z}/\mathbf{z}'\mathbf{z}$, *where* A *is a real symmetric matrix. Then*

(a) *There exists an orthogonal transformation* $\mathbf{e} = H\boldsymbol{\delta}$ *such that*

$$r = \frac{\sum_{i=1}^{T-K} v_i \delta_i^2}{\sum_{i=1}^{T-K} \delta_i^2}, \tag{10.8.1}$$

where $v_1, v_2, \ldots, v_{T-K}$ *are the* $T - K$ *nonzero eigenvalues of* MA, *the rest being zero and* $\delta_i \sim N(0, 1)$.

(b) *If s of the columns of X are linear combinations of s of the eigenvectors of A and if the eigenvalues of A associated with the remaining* $T - s$ *eigenvalues of A are renumbered so that*

$$\lambda_1 \le \lambda_2 \le \cdots \le \lambda_{T-s}$$

then

$$\lambda_i \le v_i \le \lambda_{i+K-s} \qquad (i = 1, 2, \ldots, T - K).$$

From the above lemma the following corollary can be deduced:

Corollary 10.8.1. $r_L \le r \le r_U$, *where*

$$r_L = \sum_{i=1}^{T-K} \lambda_i \delta_i^2 \Big/ \sum_{i=1}^{T-K} \delta_i^2 \tag{10.8.2}$$

and

$$r_U = \sum_{i=1}^{T-K} \lambda_{i+K-s} \delta_i^2 \Big/ \sum_{i=1}^{T-K} \delta_i^2. \tag{10.8.3}$$

The importance of this result is that it sets bounds on r which are independent of X. The bounds, r_L and r_U, are attained when the columns of X coincide with certain eigenvectors of A.

We now turn to the test of the AR(1) error process in the linear model

$$y_t = x_{t1}\beta_1 + \cdots + x_{tK}\beta_K + e_t, \tag{10.8.4}$$

$$e_t = \rho e_{t-1} + u_t, \qquad t = 1, 2, \ldots, T, \tag{10.8.5}$$

where $Eu_t = Eu_t u_{t-s} = 0$, $s = 1, 2, \ldots$, and $Eu_t^2 = \sigma_u^2$.

The Durbin–Watson d-statistic can be written as

$$d = \frac{\sum_{t=2}^{T} (\hat{e}_t - \hat{e}_{t-1})^2}{\sum_{t=1}^{T} \hat{e}_t^2} = \frac{\hat{\mathbf{e}}' A \hat{\mathbf{e}}}{\hat{\mathbf{e}}'\hat{\mathbf{e}}}, \tag{10.8.6}$$

where

$$A = \begin{bmatrix} 1 & -1 & 0 & \cdots & & & \cdots & 0 \\ -1 & 2 & -1 & & & & & \vdots \\ 0 & -1 & 2 & -1 & & & & \\ \vdots & & & & \ddots & & & 0 \\ & & & & & -1 & 2 & -1 \\ 0 & \cdots & & & \cdots & 0 & -1 & 1 \end{bmatrix}.$$

The eigenvalues of A are

$$\lambda_i = 2\left\{1 - \cos\frac{\pi(i-1)}{T}\right\}, \qquad i = 1, 2, \ldots, T.$$

The eigenvector of A corresponding to the zero eigenvalue λ_1 is $\{1, 1, \ldots, 1\}$, which is the regression vector corresponding to a constant term in the regression model. (Notice that in this discussion, as well as in the statistical table derived by Durbin and Watson (1951), the existence of a constant term in (10.8.4) is implicitly assumed.) From Corollary 10.8.1 and using the fact that $\hat{\mathbf{e}} = M\mathbf{e}$, from Chapter 2, we have

$$d_L \le d \le d_U, \tag{10.8.7}$$

where

$$d_L = \sum_{i=1}^{T-K} \lambda_i \delta_i^2 \Big/ \sum_{i=1}^{T-K} \delta_i^2 \tag{10.8.8}$$

and

$$d_U = \sum_{i=1}^{T-K} \lambda_{i+K-1} \delta_i^2 \Big/ \sum_{i=1}^{T-K} \delta_i^2. \tag{10.8.9}$$

Since the λ_i are the same in any regression model with T observations and K regressors including the constant term, the distributions of d_L and d_U can be enumerated for various values of T and K. Durbin and Watson (1951) have computed critical values of d_L and d_U for various combinations of T, K, and type I error, α. It should be noted that the Durbin–Watson bounds test is a *small* sample test in the case where u_t is assumed normally distributed.

Three hypotheses of interest with respect to AR(1) error processes are

(i) $H_0: \rho = 0$ versus $H_1: \rho > 0$;
(ii) $H_0: \rho = 0$ versus $H_1: \rho < 0$; and
(iii) $H_0: \rho = 0$ versus $H_1: \rho \neq 0$.

For test (i) the null hypothesis of independence is accepted if $d \geq d_U$ and rejected if $d \leq d_L$. No conclusion can be drawn if $d_L < d < d_U$. The region (d_L, d_U) is called the "inconclusive" region. For test (ii) the null hypothesis is accepted if $d \leq 4 - d_U$ and rejected if $d \geq 4 - d_L$. Otherwise no conclusion can be drawn. Finally, for test (iii) the null hypothesis is accepted if $d_U \leq d \leq 4 - d_U$ and rejected if $d \leq d_L$ or $d \geq 4 - d_L$. Otherwise, no conclusion can be drawn. These tests are summarized visually in Figure 10.8.1.

It is important to emphasize that: (a) the statistical tables of Durbin and Watson (1951) assume the existence of a constant term, (b) no allowance is made for missing observations, and (c) the Durbin–Watson test was derived under the assumption that X is nonstochastic and thus is not applicable, for example, when lagged values of the dependent variable appear among the regressors. Farebrother (1980) has created tables for the Durbin–Watson

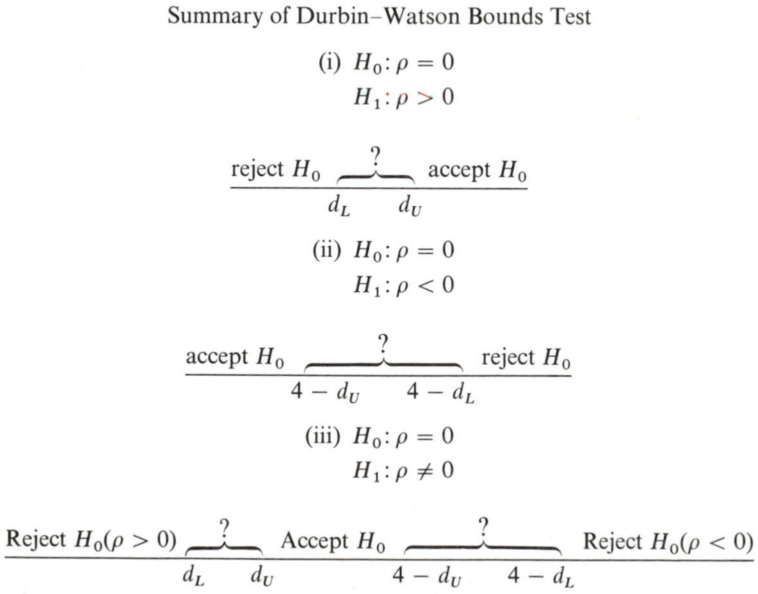

Figure 10.8.1

test when there is no intercept in the regression. Savin and White (1978) develop several statistics which may be used to test for autocorrelation in time series with missing observations. Tests for autocorrelation in the case where lagged dependent variables appear as regressors are discussed in the next chapter. Finally, note that Savin and White (1977) have extended the original Durbin–Watson tables to include cases of extreme sample sizes (6 to 200 observations) and many regressors (less than or equal to 20).

10.8.2 The Inconclusive Region

The "inconclusive region" of the Durbin–Watson test is seen to be a drawback by many researchers. Attempts to circumvent this problem have generally followed one of four different tacts: (a) approximate methods, (b) nonparametric tests, (c) tests involving transformations of the least squares residuals, and (d) use of the Imhof (1961) technique.

10.8.2a *Approximate Methods*

The *approximate* methods include:

(a) the fitting of a beta distribution to that of d (Durbin and Watson (1951) and Henshaw (1966));
(b) using the critical values of d_U as the sole critical point of the distribution of d. Theil and Nagar (1961) and Hannan and Terrell (1968) argue that if X is slowly changing, a typical characteristic of economic time series, the distribution of d_U closely approximates that of d;
(c) the use of significance points derived by Theil and Nagar (1961) obtained by fitting a beta distribution based on approximate moments; and
(d) Durbin and Watson's (1971) $a + bd_U$ approximation. As Durbin and Watson (1971) suggest, in terms of accuracy and ease of computation, the $a + bd_U$ approximation is to be preferred to the above techniques. We will pursue their method in more detail.

Durbin and Watson (1971) propose approximating the distribution of d by that of $a + bd_U$ where a and b are determined by solving the equations

$$E(d) = a + bE(d_U), \tag{10.8.10}$$

$$\operatorname{var}(d) = b^2 \operatorname{var}(d_U) \tag{10.8.11}$$

for a and b. This yields

$$a = E(d) - \sqrt{\operatorname{var}(d)/\operatorname{var}(d_U)} \cdot E(d_U) \tag{10.8.12}$$

and

$$b = \sqrt{\operatorname{var}(d)/\operatorname{var}(d_U)}. \tag{10.8.13}$$

The hypothesis of no positive serial correlation is rejected if

$$d < a + bd_U^*, \tag{10.8.14}$$

where d_U^* denotes the appropriate significance point of d_U obtained from the Durbin–Watson bounds test tables (1951). $E(d)$ and $\text{var}(d)$ are

$$E(d) = \text{tr}\, MA/(T - K),$$

$$\text{var}(d) = \frac{2\,\text{tr}(MA)^2 - (T - K)[E(d)]^2}{(T - K)(T - K + 2)},$$

where M and A are as defined above. The expressions for $E(d_U)$ and $\text{var}(d_U)$ are given by

$$E(d_U) = 2 + \frac{2}{T - K} \sum_{j=1}^{K-1} \cos(\pi j/T)$$

and

$$\text{var}(d_U) = \frac{4\left[T - 2 - 2\sum_{j=1}^{K-1} \cos^2(\pi j/T) - 2\left\{\sum_{j=1}^{K-1} \cos(\pi j/T)\right\}^2 /(T - K)\right]}{(T - K)(T - K + 2)}.$$

10.8.2b *Nonparametric Test*

Geary (1970) suggested a nonparametric test for testing the independence of errors in an AR(1) process. This test is based on a simple sign count in the residuals. Using the assumption of independent observations, Geary shows that the probability of τ sign changes is

$$\Pr(\tau) = \frac{\Gamma(T - 1)}{\tau\Gamma(\tau)\Gamma(T - \tau)} \Big/ (2^{T-1} - 1), \tag{10.8.15}$$

where Γ represents the gamma function. The cumulative distribution is

$$\Pr(\tau \le \tau') = \sum_{\tau=0}^{\tau'} \Pr(\tau). \tag{10.8.16}$$

Using this expression, the probability of τ' or less sign changes given T observations can be calculated under the null hypothesis $\rho = 0$. The results are tabled in Habibagahi and Pratschke (1972) for various rejection levels and sample sizes.

For the remainder of this section we will show, using two lemmas and a proposition, that Geary's assumption of independent residuals is appropriate only as sample size increases to infinity and therefore that Geary's test is an asymptotic rather than finite sample test.

Lemma 10.8.2. *$E\hat{e}\hat{e}' = \sigma^2 M$, where $M = I - X(X'X)^{-1}X'$ and the ordinary least squares residuals are not independently distributed for finite sample size.*

PROOF. Since $\hat{\mathbf{e}} = M\mathbf{e}$, $E\hat{\mathbf{e}}\hat{\mathbf{e}}' = EM\mathbf{e}\mathbf{e}'M' = \sigma^2 MM' = \sigma^2 M$. □

Lemma 10.8.3. *Let $\hat{e}_t$ represent the tth least squares residual. Then*

$$\text{plim}(\hat{e}_t - e_t) = 0,$$

i.e., $\hat{e}_t$ and e_t, asymptotically, have the same distribution, and $\hat{e}_t$ and $\hat{e}_s$, $s \neq t$, are uncorrelated in the limit.

PROOF.
$$E(\hat{\mathbf{e}} - \mathbf{e}) = E(M\mathbf{e} - \mathbf{e}) = \mathbf{0}$$

and

$$\begin{aligned} E(\hat{\mathbf{e}} - \mathbf{e})(\hat{\mathbf{e}} - \mathbf{e})' &= E\hat{\mathbf{e}}\hat{\mathbf{e}}' - E\mathbf{e}\hat{\mathbf{e}}' - E\hat{\mathbf{e}}\mathbf{e}' + E\mathbf{e}\mathbf{e}' \\ &= \sigma_e^2 M - \sigma_e^2 M - \sigma_e^2 M + \sigma_e^2 I \\ &= \sigma_e^2(I - M) = \sigma_e^2 X(X'X)^{-1}X'. \end{aligned}$$

$\hat{e}_t - e_t$ has zero mean and variance

$$\text{var}(\hat{e}_t - e_t) = \sigma_e^2(x_{t1} \cdots x_{tK})(X'X)^{-1}\begin{bmatrix} x_{t1} \\ \vdots \\ x_{tK} \end{bmatrix}.$$

By assumption $\lim_{T\to\infty}(X'X/T)^{-1} = Q^{-1}$ and therefore $\lim_{T\to\infty} \text{var}(\hat{e}_t - e_t) = 0$. By convergence in quadratic mean, $\text{plim}(\hat{e}_t - e_t) = 0$. □

Consider the following proposition from Rao (1973):

Proposition. *Let (x_n, y_n), $n = 1, 2, \ldots$ be a sequence of pairs of random variables. If $x_n - y_n$ converges in probability to zero and if y_n has a limiting distribution then x_n has the same limiting distribution.*

It follows that $\hat{e}_t$ and e_t have the same limiting distribution. That is $\hat{e}_t \overset{\text{asy}}{\sim} N(0, \sigma_e^2)$.

Finally,

$$E\hat{e}_t\hat{e}_s = \frac{\sigma_e^2}{T}(x_{t1} \cdots x_{tK})\left(\frac{X'X}{T}\right)^{-1}\begin{pmatrix} x_{s1} \\ \vdots \\ x_{sK} \end{pmatrix}$$

and

$$\begin{aligned} \lim_{T\to\infty} E\hat{e}_t\hat{e}_s &= \lim_{T\to\infty} \frac{\sigma_e^2}{T}\left[(x_{t1} \cdots x_{tK})\left(\frac{X'X}{T}\right)^{-1}\begin{pmatrix} x_{s1} \\ \vdots \\ x_{sK} \end{pmatrix}\right] \\ &= \lim_{T\to\infty} \frac{\sigma_e^2}{T}(x_{t1} \cdots x_{tK})Q^{-1}\begin{pmatrix} x_{s1} \\ \vdots \\ x_{sK} \end{pmatrix} \\ &= 0. \end{aligned}$$

Therefore $\hat{e}_t$ and $\hat{e}_s$ are uncorrelated in the limit.

Two essential characteristics of nonparametric tests deserve comment. First, as is obvious from the Geary test, nonparametric tests are largely based on counting rules (permutations and combinations) applied to independent observations whose distribution has no specified parametric form. Second, as less information is specified, parametric tests, such as the t-test, exhibit more power *when* the distributions specified by the parametric tests are correct. When parametric form is uncertain, nonparametric tests are often used.

10.8.2c *Transformations of Ordinary Least Squares Residuals*

We turn now to tests of AR(1) processes which involve transformations of the ordinary least squares residuals. From Lemma 10.8.2, ordinary least squares residuals are correlated and as a result give rise to inconclusive regions or reliance upon large sample independence. Theil (1965, 1971) suggested constructing new residuals which are transformations of the ordinary least squares residuals and which have the properties of independence and homoscedasticity. He suggested using the von Neumann ratio in conjunction with these new best linear unbiased scalar (BLUS) residuals in testing AR(1) processes. As the least squares residuals are subject to K constraints, only $T - K$ independent BLUS residuals can be constructed. There is some arbitrariness as to which $(T - K)$ of the T BLUS residuals to choose, however. Abrahamse and Koerts (1969) proposed a modification of Theil's BLUS test which is uniquely defined and thus overcomes this arbitrariness. For a more detailed description of BLUS residuals and how they are constructed, see Theil (1971, pp. 209–213).

10.8.2d *Imhof Technique*

Recall that the Durbin–Watson d-statistic is of the form

$$d = \hat{\mathbf{e}}'A\hat{\mathbf{e}}/\hat{\mathbf{e}}'\hat{\mathbf{e}}. \tag{10.8.17}$$

Substituting $\hat{\mathbf{e}} = M\mathbf{e}$ into (10.8.17) provides

$$d = \mathbf{e}'MAM\mathbf{e}/\mathbf{e}'M\mathbf{e}. \tag{10.8.18}$$

Under the null hypothesis, $\rho = 0$, the distribution of $\mathbf{e}$ is $N(\mathbf{0}, \sigma_e^2 I)$ so that d is a ratio of quadratic forms in normal variables. Using the algebraic results in Koerts and Abrahamse (1968) and the theoretical results of Imhof (1961), the significance points of d, say d_*, can be computed by solving $\Pr(d \le d_*) = \alpha$ by numerical integration. For a detailed description of the Imhof procedure see L'Esperance and Taylor (1975). Essentially the Imhof procedure provides a means, though a fairly capital intensive one, of determining the *exact* significance point of the Durbin–Watson d-statistic. However, for each different X matrix the exact significance point must be calculated anew as from (10.8.18) it can be seen that the distribution of d depends upon X through M.

10.8.3 Power Comparisons of Various AR(1) Tests

In one of the first studies of the relative powers of the Durbin–Watson bounds test and the BLUS procedure, Koerts and Abrahamse (1968) found the bounds test to have less power because of the occurrence of many inconclusive outcomes. Later, Abrahamse and Koerts (1969) compared the power of the BLUS procedure with the Durbin–Watson exact (using the Imhof method) test and found the following ranking: Durbin–Watson bounds $\leq$ BLUS $\leq$ Durbin–Watson exact where $\leq$ denotes the power of the right-hand side test is greater than the power of the left-hand side test. Relatedly, Johnston (1972, p. 258) found the Hannan–Terrell (d_U) method to outperform the BLUS procedure. In comparing the Durbin–Watson bounds test, a BLUS procedure, a test devised by Abrahamse, Koerts and Louter, and the Durbin–Watson exact test, L'Esperance and Taylor (1975) found the Durbin–Watson exact test to be superior.

In a series of studies by Habibagahi and Pratschke (1972), Harrison (1975), and Schmidt and Guilkey (1975), the Geary test was found to be inferior to the Durbin–Watson exact test. This is not surprising in that the Durbin–Watson exact test is a parametric one and, in the presence of normality (the setup of the experiments), should outperform a corresponding nonparametric test.

In total the Durbin–Watson exact test appears to be a superior method of testing AR(1) errors. Of course, the lack of general availability of the Durbin–Watson exact routine in present standard computer software limits its recommendation. From the standpoint of computational ease and the ability to deal with the inconclusive region of the Durbin–Watson bounds test, the Durbin–Watson (1971) $a + bd_U$ approximation or Hannan–Terrell (1968) d_U approximation seems to be a second best choice.

10.9 Testing ARMA (p, q) Processes

Every AR, MA, and ARMA process can be characterized by the behavior of its autocorrelation function, $\rho_s = E(e_t e_{t-s})/Ee_t^2$, $s = 1, 2, \ldots$. For an AR(p) process the autocorrelation function exhibits either a damped exponential or sine wave pattern while for a MA(q) process the autocorrelation function becomes zero after q periods. The autocorrelation function for a complete ARMA(p, q) process exhibits an irregular pattern for the first $(q - p)$ periods (due to the fact that the first q theoretical autocorrelations are determined by both autoregressive and moving-average parameters) but thereafter has the autoregressive characteristic of damped exponential or sine wave autocorrelations. (See Box and Jenkins (1970, Ch. 3).) One alternative is to estimate ρ_s with sample autocorrelations

$$r_s = \sum_{t=1}^{T-s} \hat{e}_t \hat{e}_{t+s} \bigg/ \sum_{t=1}^{T} \hat{e}_t^2,$$

where the $\hat{e}_t$ are the least squares residuals $\hat{e}_t = y_t - x_{t1}\hat{\beta}_1 - \cdots - x_{tK}\hat{\beta}_K$, and $\hat{\boldsymbol{\beta}} = (X'X)^{-1}X'\mathbf{y}$ is the ordinary least squares estimator and determine the parameters p and q by means of the identification methods described by Box and Jenkins (1970). The degree of validity in this approach is conditioned by how fast the distribution of $\hat{e}_t$ converges to the distribution of e_t (see Lemma 10.8.3). In small samples the $\hat{e}_t$ are correlated (Lemma 10.8.2) and hence the r_s may exhibit substantial small sample bias (Malinvaud (1970, p. 519)). In large samples, however, this approach can be quite useful when the ARMA process is of small order ($p, q \leq 2$).

The use of the sample autocorrelation function to identify p and q is by no means a simple task since sample statistics are being used to infer population values. The sample autocorrelation function does have the redeeming feature, however, of highlighting correlations that might otherwise go undetected by such standard tests as the Durbin–Watson test. For example, under the null hypothesis that $\rho_s = 0$, $s = 1, 2, \ldots$, Box and Pierce (1970) have shown that the residual autocorrelations are approximately uncorrelated, normally distributed random variables with zero mean and variance $1/T$. A more general test of autocorrelation would then involve comparing r_s with $2/T^{1/2}$ and rejecting the null hypothesis of no autocorrelation if $r_s > 2/T^{1/2}$ for any s.

The number and significance of the θ_i's and/or α_i's can be investigated in other ways. For example, once given the model

$$y_t = x_{t1}\beta_1 + \cdots + x_{tK}\beta_K + e_t,$$

$$e_t = \theta_1 e_{t-1} + \cdots + \theta e_{t-p} + u_t + \alpha_1 u_{t-1} + \cdots + \alpha_q u_{t-q},$$

for *given* p and q, asymptotic standard errors can be constructed from the information matrix. In the case where the ARMA(p, q) process is of higher order $p, q > 1$ and the information matrix is not derivable in closed form, numerical methods can be used to obtain an "approximate" information matrix of the nonlinear maximum likelihood function (see the Appendix of this book).

Likelihood ratio tests offer a means of hypothesis testing on the θ_i and α_i parameters of the ARMA(p, q) process also. Let Ω denote the universal parameter set of dimension n while ω represents the $(n - p)$-dimensional subset of Ω corresponding to the null hypothesis. Then from Theorem 4.2.4 we know that $-2 \ln l \overset{\text{asy}}{\approx} \chi_q^2$, where $l = L(\hat{\omega})/L(\hat{\Omega})$. Notice that for the likelihood ratio test to be operational, the models must be nested. For example

H_0 may represent ARMA(1, 1) while H_1 represents ARMA(1, 2). However H_0: ARMA(1, 0) and H_1: ARMA(0, 1) are not compatible. When $p = 1$, the likelihood ratio test is asymptotically equivalent to testing the significance of the relevant coefficient via the information matrix approach.

If the chosen model is the correct one, the "final" residual autocorrelations calculated from the residuals

$$\tilde{\tilde{e}}_t = y_t - x_{t1}\tilde{\tilde{\beta}}_1 - \cdots - x_{tK}\tilde{\tilde{\beta}}_K, \tag{10.9.1}$$

where $\tilde{\tilde{\beta}}_1, \ldots, \tilde{\tilde{\beta}}_K$ are the feasible generalized least squares estimators based upon estimates $\tilde{\theta}_1, \ldots, \tilde{\theta}_p$ and $\tilde{\alpha}_1, \ldots, \tilde{\alpha}_q$, will be asymptotically uncorrelated and normally distributed with zero mean and variance $1/T$. Let these final residual autocorrelations of period s be denoted by r_s^*, where

$$r_s^* = \sum_{t=1}^{T-s} \tilde{\tilde{e}}_t \tilde{\tilde{e}}_{t+s} \Big/ \sum_{t=1}^{T} \tilde{\tilde{e}}_t^2. \tag{10.9.2}$$

Pierce (1971) suggests using the following "adequacy of fit" statistic

$$Q \equiv T \sum_{s=1}^{d} r_s^{*2}, \tag{10.9.3}$$

where d is determined by the type and number of observations. For example, if quarterly data were used $d = 8$ may be a reasonable number to choose. Then, if the ARMA(p, q) error process is "adequate," the statistic Q has an approximate χ^2_{d-p-q} distribution.

10.10 Summary and Guide to Further Readings

Though a "universal" strategy cannot be specified for handling autocorrelated errors, some general suggestions and comments seem to be warranted given the present state of the literature. In testing AR(1) errors, the use of the Durbin–Watson exact test (using the Imhof method) seems to be one of the more powerful tests. In the absence of the necessary computer software, the use of the Durbin–Watson (1971) $a + bd_U$ approximation or Hannan–Terrell d_U approximation appears to be a good second best solution to the inconclusive region of the Durbin–Watson bounds test.

The choice of the level of significance for the Durbin–Watson exact test is another matter. In the context of AR(1) errors, Fomby and Guilkey (1978) investigated the effect of the choice of the significance level (α) on the efficiency of the usual preliminary test estimator

$$\boldsymbol{\beta}^* = I_{(d>d^*)}\hat{\boldsymbol{\beta}} + I_{(d \le d^*)}\tilde{\tilde{\boldsymbol{\beta}}},$$

where $\hat{\boldsymbol{\beta}} = (X'X)^{-1}X'\mathbf{y}$, $\tilde{\tilde{\boldsymbol{\beta}}} = (X'\hat{\Omega}^{-1}X)^{-1}X'\hat{\Omega}^{-1}\mathbf{y}$, d^* is the critical value of the Durbin–Watson d-statistic, and $I_{(\cdot)}$ denotes the indicator function which equals one if its argument is satisfied and zero otherwise. Using

Monte Carlo methods, they found that the choice of $\alpha \approx 0.50$ was much nearer the optimal choice of significance rather than the conventional choices of $\alpha = 0.01$ or 0.05. This finding is consistent with the Monte Carlo results of Rao and Griliches (1969) which showed that there is much to gain and little to lose from using feasible generalized least squares as an alternative to ordinary least squares. In a similar vein Nakamura and Nakamura (1978) examined the effect of preliminary tests on tests of hypotheses and also recommended high significance levels for the Durbin–Watson test. These results point to the conclusion that investigators should probably begin to put more weight on the possibility of autocorrelated errors when investigating economic time series data.

In the presence of autocorrelation processes of small order ($p, q \leq 1$) feasible generalized least squares is asymptotically efficient and from a computational standpoint easiest to apply. However, in the absence of computer software limitations, the use of maximum likelihood methods to estimate $\boldsymbol{\beta}$, $\boldsymbol{\theta}$ and $\boldsymbol{\alpha}$ might be preferred as the θ_i's and α_i's are more efficiently estimated via maximum likelihood than usual consistent estimation methods. Though feasible generalized least squares and maximum likelihood estimation of $\boldsymbol{\beta}$ are equally efficient in the nonstochastic X case, the question of which is more efficient in small samples is still open to question. Where the autocorrelation process is of higher order ($p, q > 1$), maximum likelihood becomes a virtual necessity. The crucial problem becomes the choice of p and q for starting values in the iterative solution of the nonlinear maximum likelihood equations.

Methods abound for determining the order (p, q) of an ARMA process. Use of the residual autocorrelation function may prove useful in determining autocorrelation processes of the type not detectable by the Durbin–Watson test. The use of likelihood ratio and tests of parameter significance can also be useful but the preliminary test aspects of the sequential use of such procedures (as well as the autocorrelation fuction) are complicated and to present no means of determining the unconditional levels of significance or sampling properties of the estimators produced by such procedures have been determined. At best, the practitioner must rest his case on the usefulness of the final model in addressing individual econometric problems at hand.

10.11 Exercises

10.1. Derive the information matrix in Equation (10.3.5).

10.2. Derive the variance–covariance structure of the MA(1) error process—Equation (10.6.6).

10.3. Derive the variance–covariance structure of the ARMA(1, 1) error process—Equation (10.6.7).

10.4. Derive the variance–covariance structure of the AR(2) error process—Equations (10.7.5) and (10.7.6).

10.5. Verify Equation (10.7.7).

10.6. Trace through the proofs of the following results adding additional details and explanations where necessary:
(i) the result that $\hat{\rho}$ is consistent—see Equation (10.4.1) and the Press (1972) reference; and
(ii) the result that the Durbin $\hat{\rho}$ obtained from (10.4.3) is asymptotically efficient—see the Rothenberg (1973) reference.
Notice the integral role that Lemma 10.8.4 of this chapter plays in the proof of (i) and the use of the Cramér–Rao lower bound for constrained estimators in the proof of (ii).

Frohman *et al.* (1981) examine the costs of uncertainty due to high rates of inflation. They postulate that current high rates of inflation engender greater uncertainty with respect to future rates of inflation than low rates of inflation. To test this hypothesis consider the following regression model:

$$y_{t+1} = \beta_1 + \beta_2 x_t + e_t, \tag{1}$$

where $y_{t+1} \equiv$ standard deviation of expert's forecasts of the inflation rate 12 months from now and $x_t \equiv$ current annual rate of inflation as measured by the Consumer Price Index. The data are contained in the table at end of this exercise section.

To answer the following questions use the data at the end of this exercise section.

10.7. Using any standard regression package examine the Frohman *et al.* hypothesis. Use the Durbin–Watson statistic to determine if an autocorrelation correction is needed. Compare the results you obtain when using the Cochrane–Orcutt iterative technique versus those obtained by a Hildreth–Lu search procedure.

10.8. Plot the residuals as a function of time. Do they appear to be positively or negatively correlated? Calculate consistent estimates of ρ using the Cochrane–Orcutt, Theil and Durbin methods. Do they differ substantially? Perform the Geary test for autocorrelation.

10.9. Using the Prais–Winsten transformation and the Cochrane–Orcutt, Theil, and Durbin estimates of ρ, estimate Equation (1). Do the estimates differ substantially? Do they differ from those obtained from your computer regression package (Exercise 10.7)?

10.10. Assume that, instead of beginning in the infinite past, the autoregressive error process of Equation (1) began in 1946 immediately after World War II. That is, assume that the error process began $q - 1 = 16$ periods prior to the first observation (2 periods, June and Dec., per year for 8 years). Chose any consistent estimate of ρ and the transformation (10.4.4) to obtain feasible generalized least squares estimates of Equation (1). Do they differ substantially from those obtained using the Prais–Winsten transformation? Assume $q - 1 = 0$ and again compare the results.

10.11. Consider the time spans June 1954–Dec. 1964 and June 1965–Dec. 1975. Use the Chow test to test for a possible structural change in the postulated relationship (1) due to the "Vietnam War Era." Assume that the autoregressive error process does not change over the break. Thus, you should use the dummy variable approach in obtaining the restricted versus unrestricted sum of squared errors (residuals) rather than making separate regression runs.

10.12. Consider Exercise 10.11. Suppose that there is a possible structural break in the autoregressive error process as well as a break in the regression relationship (1). How would you test both of these breaks simultaneously? Use the above data to test for such a simultaneous break.

10.13. Using the above data, test for the presence of AR(2) errors. (Hint: One possible way to proceed is to construct an asymptotic test of $H_0: \theta_1 = \theta_2 = 0$ using the estimating equation $\hat{e}_t = \theta_1 \hat{e}_{t-1} + \theta_2 \hat{e}_{t-2} + \hat{u}_t$.)

10.14. Assume that the observations for June and Dec. 1961 are missing. Using one of the methods outlined by Savin and White (1978), test for the presence of AR(1) errors.

Survey month	y_{t+1}	x_t	Survey month	y_{t+1}	x_t
June 1954	1.32	0.76	June 1965	0.59	1.40
Dec. 1954	0.94	−0.87	Dec. 1965	0.59	1.72
June 1955	0.87	−0.25	June 1966	0.97	2.87
Dec. 1955	1.11	0.37	Dec. 1966	1.13	3.79
June 1956	1.23	0.50	June 1967	0.84	2.48
Dec. 1956	2.11	2.48	Dec. 1967	0.99	2.54
June 1957	1.30	3.85	June 1968	0.87	4.04
Dec. 1957	1.53	2.91	Dec. 1968	0.86	4.65
June 1958	1.10	3.59	June 1969	1.36	5.43
Dec. 1958	0.79	2.12	Dec. 1969	0.84	5.58
June 1959	0.74	0.23	June 1970	1.35	5.98
Dec. 1959	0.65	1.50	Dec. 1970	0.94	5.82
June 1960	0.65	1.96	June 1971	1.15	4.34
Dec. 1960	0.74	1.38	Dec. 1971	0.69	3.64
June 1961	0.64	0.90	June 1972	0.86	3.41
Dec. 1961	0.62	0.79	Dec. 1972	0.66	3.43
June 1962	0.73	1.34	June 1973	1.22	5.15
Dec. 1962	0.56	1.34	Dec. 1973	1.67	7.90
June 1963	0.48	0.88	June 1974	1.98	10.10
Dec. 1963	0.47	1.21	Dec. 1974	1.74	12.01
June 1964	0.74	1.53	June 1975	1.31	10.22
Dec. 1964	0.52	1.19	Dec. 1975	1.29	7.58

SOURCES OF DATA: The dependent variable consists of standard deviations of experts forecasts of inflation (as measured by the CPI) published by J. A. Livingston in the *Philadelphia Inquirer* on the above indicated survey month. The Livingston data are compiled and reported in Carlson (1977). Computation of the actual annual rates of inflation (x_t) were computed using the formula $((\text{CPI}_{t-2} - \text{CPI}_{t-14})/\text{CPI}_{t-14}) \times 100$, where the CPI data was obtained from *Business Statistics 1977*, U.S. Department of Commerce. The two month lag in the computation of actual inflation represents the time lag between the expert's response to Livingston's inquiry and the publication date.

10.12 References

Abrahamse, A. P. J. and Koerts, J. (1969). A comparison of the Durbin–Watson test and the Blus test. *Journal of the American Statistical Association*, **64**, 938–948.

Abrahamse, A. P. J. and Koerts, J. (1971). New estimates of disturbances in regression analysis. *Journal of the American Statistical Association*, **66**, 71–74.

Beach, C. M. and MacKinnon, J. G. (1978a). A maximum likelihood procedure for regression with autocorrelated errors. *Econometrica*, **46**, 51–58.

Beach, C. M. and MacKinnon, J. G. (1978b). Full maximum likelihood estimation of second-order autoregressive error models. *Journal of Econometrics*, **7**, 187–198.

Box, G. E. P. and Jenkins, G. M. (1970). *Time Series Analysis, Forecasting and Control*. San Francisco: Holden Day.

Box, G. E. P. and Pierce, D. A. (1970). Distribution of residual autocorrelations in autoregressive moving average time series models. *Journal of the American Statistical Association*, **65**, 1509–1526.

Carlson, J. A. (1977). A study of price forecasts. *Annals of Economic and Social Measurements*, **6**, 27–56.

Cochrane, D. and Orcutt, G. H. (1949). Application of least squares regressions to relationships containing autocorrelated error terms. *Journal of the American Statistical Association*, **44**, 32–61.

Dhrymes, P. J. (1971). *Distributed Lags: Problems of Estimation and Formulation*. San Francisco: Holden Day.

Durbin, J. (1960). Estimation of parameters in time series regression models. *Journal of the Royal Statistical Society*, B, **22**, 139–153.

Durbin, J. and Watson, G. S. 1950. Testing for serial correlation in least squares regression–I. *Biometrika*, **37**, 409–428.

Durbin, J. and Watson, G. S. (1951). Testing for serial correlation in least squares regression—II. *Biometrika*, **38**, 159–178.

Durbin, J. and Watson, G. S. (1971). Test for serial correlation in least squares regression—III. *Biometrika*, **58**, 1–42.

Farebrother, R. W. (1980). The Durbin–Watson test for serial correlation when there is no intercept in the regression. *Econometrica*, **48**, 1553–1563.

Fomby, T. B. and Guilkey, D. K. (1978). On choosing the optimal level of significance for the Durbin–Watson test and the Bayesian alternative. *Journal of Econometrics*, **8**, 203–214.

Frohman, D. A., Laney, L. O., and Willet, T. D. (1981). Uncertainty costs of high inflation. *Voice* (of the Federal Reserve Bank of Dallas), July, 1–9.

Fuller, W. A. (1976). *Introduction to Statistical Time Series*. New York: Wiley.

Geary, R. C. (1970). Relative efficiency of count of sign changes for assessing residual autoregression in least squares regression. *Biometrika*, **57**, 123–127.

Habibagahi, H. and Pratschke, J. L. (1972). A comparison of the power of the von Neumann ratio, Durbin–Watson, and Geary tests. *Review of Economics and Statistics*, **54**, 179–185.

Hannan, E. J. and Terrell, R. D. (1968). Testing for serial correlation after least squares regression. *Econometrica*, **36**, 133–150.

Harrison, M. J. (1975). The power of the Durbin–Watson and Geary tests: comment and further evidence. *Review of Economics and Statistics*, **57**, 377–379.

Henshaw, R. C. (1966). Testing single-equation least-squares regression models for autocorrelated disturbances. *Econometrica*, **34**, 646–660.

Hildreth, C. and Lu, J. Y. (1960). Demand relationships with autocorrelated disturbances. Michigan State University Agricultural Experiment Station Bulletin 276, East Lansing, Michigan.

Imhof, J. P. (1961). Computing the distribution of quadratic forms in normal variables. *Biometrika*, **48**, 419–426.

Johnston, J. (1972). *Econometric Methods*, 2nd ed. New York: McGraw-Hill.
Koerts, J. and Abrahamse, A. P. J. (1968). On the power of the BLUS procedure. *Journal of the American Statistical Association*, **63**, 1227–1236.
L'Esperance, W. L. and Taylor, D. (1975). The power of four tests of autocorrelation in the linear regression model. *Journal of Econometrics*, **3**, 1–21.
Maddala, G. S. (1977). *Econometrics*. New York: McGraw-Hill.
Magnus, J. R. (1978). Maximum likelihood estimation of the GLS model with GLS model with unknown parameters in the disturbance covariance matrix. *Journal of Econometrics*, **7**, 281–312.
Malinvaud, E. (1970). *Statistical Methods in Econometrics*. Amsterdam: North-Holland.
Nakamura, A. and Nakamura, M. (1978). On the impact of the tests for serial correlation upon the test of significance for the regression coefficient. *Journal of Econometrics*, **7**, 199–210.
Oxley, L. T. and Roberts, C. T. (1982). Pitfalls in the application of the Cochrane-Orcutt technique. *Oxford Bulletin of Economics and Statistics*, **44**, 227–240.
Pesaran, M. H. (1973). Exact maximum likelihood estimation of a regression equation with first-order moving-average error. *Review of Economic Studies*, **40**, 529–536.
Pierce, D. A. (1971). Distribution of residual autocorrelations in the regression model with autoregressive-moving average errors. *Journal of the Royal Statistical Society*, B, **33**, 140–146.
Prais, S. J. and Winsten, C. B. (1954). Trend estimators and serial correlation. Cowles Commission Discussion Paper No. 383, Chicago.
Press, S. J. (1972). *Applied Multivariate Analysis*. New York: Holt, Rinehart, & Winston.
Rao, C. R. (1973). *Linear Statistical Inference and Its Applications*, 2nd ed. New York: Wiley.
Rao, P. and Griliches, Z. (1969). Small sample properties of several two-stage regression methods in the context of autocorrelated errors. *Journal of the American Statistical Association*, **64**, 253–272.
Rothenberg, T. J. (1973). *Efficient Estimation with A Priori Information*. Cowles Commission Monograph No. 23. New Haven, CT.: Yale University Press.
Savin, N. E. and White, K. J. (1977). The Durbin–Watson test for serial correlation with extreme sample sizes or many regressors. *Econometrica*, **45**, 1989–1996.
Savin, N. E. and White, K. J. (1978). Testing for autocorrelation with missing observations. *Econometrica*, **46**, 59–67.
Schmidt, P. and Guilkey, D. K. (1975). Some further evidence on the power of the Durbin–Watson and Geary tests. *Review of Economics and Statistics*, **57**, 379–382.
Theil, H. (1965). The analysis of disturbances in regression analysis. *Journal of the American Statistical Association*, **60**, 1067–1079.
Theil, H. (1971). *Principles of Econometrics*. New York: Wiley.
Theil, H. and Nagar, A. L. (1961). Testing the independence of regression disturbances. *Journal of the American Statistical Association*, **56**, 793–806.
Thornton, D. L. (1982). The appropriate autocorrelation transformation when the autocorrelation process has a finite past. Federal Reserve Bank of St. Louis Working Paper 82–002.
Tiao, G. C. and Ali, M. M. (1971). Analysis of correlated random effects: linear model with two random components. *Biometrika*, **58**, 37–51.

CHAPTER 11
Lagged Dependent Variables and Autocorrelation

11.1 Introduction

One of the major purposes of the present chapter is to investigate the effects on ordinary least squares of, first, correlation between a linear model's regressors and *previous* error terms and, second, the impact of *contemporaneous* correlation between the regressors and error term. In the instance of contemporaneous correlation, the sweeping results concerning two-step feasible generalized least squares established in Chapter 8 for the nonstochastic X-case are modified substantially. In particular, estimator efficiency is affected by the choice of $\hat{\Omega}$ and the usual generalized least squares formula $\tilde{\tilde{\sigma}}^2(X'\hat{\Omega}^{-1}X)^{-1}$ understates the variance of the two-step feasible generalized least squares estimator $\tilde{\tilde{\boldsymbol{\beta}}} = (X'\hat{\Omega}^{-1}X)^{-1}X'\hat{\Omega}^{-1}\mathbf{y}$.

The outline of the present chapter is as follows: In Section 11.2 the general form and assumptions of the lagged dependent variable model are presented and the properties of ordinary least squares in the absence of autocorrelation are discussed. The ramifications of autocorrelation on ordinary least squares estimation of the lagged dependent variable model are developed in Section 11.3. A discussion of feasible generalized least squares is contained in Section 11.4, while Hatanaka's two-step "residual-adjusted" estimator for the lagged dependent variable, AR(1) error model is introduced in Section 11.5. A summary and guide to further readings is presented in Section 11.6. Finally, the appendix in Section 11.7 develops the details of instrumental variable estimation.

11.2 Lagged Dependent Variable Model (Autoregressive Linear Model)

Definition 11.2.1 (Lagged Dependent Variable Model). The general form of the lagged dependent variable model is given by

$$y_t = \sum_{l=1}^{G} \alpha_l y_{t-l} + \mathbf{z}_t' \boldsymbol{\gamma} + e_t, \qquad t = 1, \ldots, T, \tag{11.2.1}$$

where the y_t are observations on the dependent variable y, the α_l are scalar parameters, $\mathbf{z}_t'$ is a $(K - G) \times 1$ vector of the tth observations on $(K - G)$ nonstochastic explanatory variables, $\boldsymbol{\gamma}$ is the $(K - G) \times 1$ vector of corresponding parameters, and e_t are the random disturbances.

The essential assumptions used in developing the properties of the estimators of the parameters of the lagged dependent variable model (11.2.1) are as follows:

(i) The e_t are independent and identically distributed with zero mean and variance σ_e^2. Normality will be assumed when necessary.
(ii) All G roots of the polynomial equation in λ

$$\lambda^G - \alpha_1 \lambda^{G-1} - \alpha_2 \lambda^{G-2} - \cdots - \alpha_{G-1}\lambda - \alpha_G = 0 \tag{11.2.2}$$

are less than one in absolute value.
(iii) The following assumption guarantees the convergence of moment matrices of the nonstochastic variables. Let $\eta = 0, 1, 2, \ldots$. The matrix

$$\lim_{T \to \infty} \frac{1}{T - \eta} \sum_{t=1}^{T-\eta} \mathbf{z}_t \mathbf{z}_{t+\eta}' = Q_\eta \tag{11.2.3}$$

exists for all η and is nonsingular for $\eta = 0$.
(iv) The elements z_{ti} are uniformly bounded in absolute value; that is

$$|z_{ti}| < c,$$

where $i = 1, 2, \ldots, G$, $t = 1, 2, \ldots, \infty$, and c is a finite constant.

The essence of the above assumptions, other than providing sufficient conditions for the proofs of theorems to follow, is to insure that the lagged dependent variable model (11.2.1) is dynamically stable. Dynamic stability may be interpreted heuristically in the following manner. For simplicity, let $e_t = 0$, $t = \cdots, -1, 0, 1, \ldots$ in (11.2.1). Assume that the elements of $\mathbf{z}_t'$ are held at the values $\bar{\mathbf{z}}_t'$ for an infinite span of time and that the resulting equilibrium value of y is $\bar{y}$. For one time period, change the exogenous variables of $\mathbf{z}_t'$ then return them to the values $\bar{\mathbf{z}}_t'$. The value of y will be displaced from $\bar{y}$. The model is dynamically stable if y eventually returns to $\bar{y}$ and remains there. The model is unstable if y never converges to $\bar{y}$.

We can write the model (11.2.1) in the familiar notation

$$\mathbf{y} = X\boldsymbol{\beta} + \mathbf{e}, \tag{11.2.4}$$

where $\mathbf{y}' = (y_1, \ldots, y_T)$, $\boldsymbol{\beta}' = (\alpha_1, \ldots, \alpha_G, \gamma_1, \ldots, \gamma_{(K-G)})$, $\mathbf{e}' = (e_1, \ldots, e_T)$, and

$$X = \begin{bmatrix} y_0 & y_{-1} & \cdots & y_{-G+1} & \vdots & z_{11} & z_{12} & \cdots & z_{1(K-G)} \\ y_1 & y_0 & \cdots & y_{-G+2} & \vdots & z_{21} & z_{22} & \cdots & z_{2(K-G)} \\ \vdots & \vdots & & \vdots & & \vdots & \vdots & & \vdots \\ y_{T-1} & y_{T-2} & \cdots & y_{T-G} & \vdots & z_{T1} & z_{T2} & \cdots & z_{T(K-G)} \end{bmatrix}.$$

Note that the total number of observations on y_t is $T + G$.

In what follows the pre-sample values $y_0, \ldots, y_{-G+1}$ will be treated as fixed with all probability statements conditioned on these values.

We now turn to the discussion of the properties of the ordinary least squares estimator in the lagged dependent variable model.

Theorem 11.2.1. *The ordinary least squares estimator of* $\boldsymbol{\beta}$ *in the lagged dependent variable model is biased in small samples.*

PROOF.
$$\hat{\boldsymbol{\beta}} = \boldsymbol{\beta} + (X'X)^{-1}X'\mathbf{e}.$$

Since $E(X'X)^{-1}X'\mathbf{e} \neq \mathbf{0}$ then $E\hat{\boldsymbol{\beta}} \neq \boldsymbol{\beta}$. □

Notice that though e_t is independent of the tth row of X, $\mathbf{x}_t'$ (i.e., there is *no contemporaneous* correlation between regressors and errors), the vector $\mathbf{e}$ is *not* independent of all observations in X; that is, $E(e_t|\mathbf{x}_t') = E(e_t) = 0$ but $E(\mathbf{e}|X) \neq \mathbf{0}$. This follows as $\mathbf{x}_t'$ contains $y_{t-1}, \ldots, y_{t-G}$ and, therefore, $\mathbf{x}_t'$ is not independent of $e_{t-1}, \ldots, e_{t-G}, \ldots$.

Consider the model

$$y_t = \alpha_1 y_{t-1} + e_t. \tag{11.2.5}$$

Let $\hat{\alpha}_1 = \sum y_t y_{t-1} / \sum y_{t-1}^2$. White (1961) has shown that the small sample bias (to order T^{-2}) for $\hat{\alpha}_1$ is $E(\hat{\alpha}_1 - \alpha_1) \doteq -2(\alpha_1/T)$. This small sample bias exists because there is *partial* dependence between y_{t-1} and disturbances *prior* to e_t, namely, $e_{t-1}, e_{t-2}, \ldots$. However, this bias does disappear asymptotically since $\lim_{T\to\infty} -2\alpha_1/T = 0$ and $\hat{\alpha}_1$ is consistent. Therefore, if we are to find some desirable properties for the ordinary least squares estimator in the lagged dependent variable model, they must be *asymptotic*.

The following lemma provides a basis for establishing the asymptotic properties shown subsequently.

Lemma 11.2.1. *The matrix*

$$Q = \operatorname{plim}\left(\frac{X'X}{T}\right)$$

(*notice we are now using* plim *instead of* lim *as some of the regressors of* X *are stochastic*) *is finite and nonsingular and* $X'\mathbf{e}/\sqrt{T} \overset{\text{asy}}{\sim} N(\mathbf{0}, \sigma_e^2 Q)$.

PROOF. By using the assumptions detailed above for the lagged dependent variable model, Schmidt (1976, pp. 98–99, 259) directly applies the central limit theorem for dependent variables by Schönfeld (1971) to prove the desired result. Theil (1971, pp. 409–411) proves the result for the special case $y_t = \alpha_1 y_{t-1} + e_t$. □

The following theorems detail the principal results concerning ordinary least squares estimation in the lagged dependent variable model.

Theorem 11.2.2. *Assume the above-stated assumptions concerning the lagged dependent variable model hold except that we* only *require that the e_t be independent identically distributed with zero mean, positive variance σ_e^2, and finite moments of every order. Also the presample values $y_0, \ldots, y_{-G+1}$ are regarded as constants. Then the ordinary least squares estimators $\hat{\boldsymbol{\beta}} = (X'X)^{-1}X'\mathbf{y}$ and $\hat{\sigma}_e^2 = \hat{\mathbf{e}}'\hat{\mathbf{e}}/(T - K)$ are consistent estimators of $\boldsymbol{\beta}$ and σ_e^2, respectively. In addition $\sqrt{T}(\hat{\boldsymbol{\beta}} - \boldsymbol{\beta})$ has a limiting distribution of $N(\mathbf{0}, \sigma_e^2 Q^{-1})$.*

PROOF. We will prove that $\hat{\boldsymbol{\beta}}$ is consistent and that $\sqrt{T}(\hat{\boldsymbol{\beta}} - \boldsymbol{\beta}) \overset{\text{asy}}{\approx} N(\mathbf{0}, \sigma_e^2 Q^{-1})$. That $\hat{\sigma}_e^2$ is a consistent estimator of σ_e^2 is left as an exercise for the reader. Since

$$\hat{\boldsymbol{\beta}} = \boldsymbol{\beta} + \left(\frac{X'X}{T}\right)^{-1} \frac{X'\mathbf{e}}{T},$$

then

$$\operatorname{plim} \hat{\boldsymbol{\beta}} = \boldsymbol{\beta} + Q^{-1} \cdot \mathbf{0} = \boldsymbol{\beta}$$

and $\hat{\boldsymbol{\beta}}$ is consistent. Also

$$\sqrt{T}(\hat{\boldsymbol{\beta}} - \boldsymbol{\beta}) = \left(\frac{X'X}{T}\right)^{-1} \frac{X'\mathbf{e}}{\sqrt{T}}.$$

By Lemma 11.2.1, $X'\mathbf{e}/\sqrt{T} \overset{\text{asy}}{\approx} N(\mathbf{0}, \sigma_e^2 Q)$ and $\operatorname{plim}(X'X/T)^{-1} = Q^{-1}$. Therefore, $\sqrt{T}(\hat{\boldsymbol{\beta}} - \boldsymbol{\beta}) \overset{\text{asy}}{\approx} N(\mathbf{0}, \sigma_e^2 Q^{-1} Q Q^{-1}) = N(\mathbf{0}, \sigma_e^2 Q^{-1})$. □

This theorem implies that the usual test of hypotheses are *asymptotically* justified in the lagged dependent variable model under the assumption that the e_t are independent identically distributed with zero mean and variance σ_e^2. Notice normality is not required and, therefore, is superfluous to hypothesis testing in the lagged dependent variable model.

Theorem 11.2.3. *The ordinary least squares estimator of $\boldsymbol{\beta}$ is the maximum likelihood estimator conditional on $y_0, \ldots, y_{-G+1}$. Thus, the ordinary least squares estimator is asymptotically efficient.*

PROOF. The log likelihood function of $e_1, \ldots, e_T$ is

$$\ln L(\boldsymbol{\beta}, \sigma_e^2; \mathbf{e}) = c - \frac{T}{2} \ln \sigma_e^2 - \tfrac{1}{2}\sigma_e^{-2} \sum_{t=1}^{T} e_t^2. \tag{11.2.6}$$

However, (11.2.6) is a function of the *unobservable* variables e_t and, as such, cannot be used for purposes of estimation. To allow estimation we can transform the log likelihood function (11.2.6) to a function of the *observable* variables $y_1, y_2, \ldots, y_T$. Recall that

$$y_t = \sum_{l=1}^{G} \alpha_l y_{t-l} + \mathbf{z}_t'\boldsymbol{\gamma} + e_t. \tag{11.2.7}$$

The likelihood function of $y_1, \ldots, y_T$ given $y_0, \ldots, y_{-G+1}$, denoted $L(\boldsymbol{\beta}, \sigma_e^2; \mathbf{y})$ can be obtained from the likelihood function of $e_1, \ldots, e_T$, $L(\boldsymbol{\beta}, \sigma_e^2; \mathbf{e})$, by the Jacobian technique:

$$L(\boldsymbol{\beta}, \sigma_e^2; \mathbf{y}) = L(\boldsymbol{\beta}, \sigma_e^2; e_1(\cdot), \ldots, e_T(\cdot))|J|, \tag{11.2.8}$$

where $e_t(\cdot)$ denotes the inverse function

$$e_t(y_1, y_2, \ldots, y_T) = y_t - \sum_{l=1}^{G} \alpha_l y_{t-l} - \mathbf{z}_t'\boldsymbol{\gamma}$$

and $|J|$ denotes the absolute value of the Jacobian determinant, J, defined as the determinant of the matrix of partial derivatives $[\partial e_i/\partial y_j]$, $i = 1, 2, \ldots, T$ and $j = 1, 2, \ldots, T$. That is,

$$|J| = \text{abs } J = \text{abs det}\left[\frac{\partial e_i}{\partial y_j}\right]$$

$$= \text{abs det}\begin{bmatrix} \dfrac{\partial e_1}{\partial y_1} & \dfrac{\partial e_1}{\partial y_2} & \cdots & \dfrac{\partial e_1}{\partial y_T} \\ & & \vdots & \\ \dfrac{\partial e_T}{\partial y_1} & \dfrac{\partial e_T}{\partial y_2} & \cdots & \dfrac{\partial e_T}{\partial y_T} \end{bmatrix}.$$

For the case at hand,

$$|J| = \text{abs det}\begin{bmatrix} 1 & & & & & \\ -\alpha_1 & 1 & & & 0 & \\ -\alpha_2 & -\alpha_1 & 1 & & & \\ \vdots & \ddots & \ddots & \ddots & & \\ -\alpha_G & & & & & \\ 0 & -\alpha_G & \cdots & -\alpha_2 & -\alpha_1 & 1 \end{bmatrix}$$

$$= \text{abs}[1] = 1.$$

Therefore, from (11.2.8), $L(y_1, \ldots, y_T | y_0, \ldots, y_{-G+1}) = L(e_1(\cdot), \ldots, e_T(\cdot))$. It follows directly that

$$\ln L(\boldsymbol{\beta}, \sigma_e^2; \mathbf{y}) = c - \frac{T}{2} \ln \sigma_e^2 - \frac{1}{2} \sigma_e^{-2} \sum_{t=1}^{T} \left(y_t - \sum_{l=1}^{G} \alpha_l y_{t-l} - \mathbf{z}_t'\boldsymbol{\gamma}\right)^2. \tag{11.2.9}$$

Then the maximum likelihood estimates of $\boldsymbol{\beta}$ correspond to the ordinary least squares estimator $\hat{\boldsymbol{\beta}} = (X'X)^{-1}X'\mathbf{y}$ obtained by minimizing the above sum of squares. It follows from Theorem 4.2.1 on the general properties of maximum likelihood estimation that ordinary least squares is consistent and asymptotically efficient, as we set out to prove. □

Note that normality of the e_t, though superfluous to asymptotic hypotheses tests in the lagged dependent variable model, is essential for the claim of asymptotic efficiency. Also note, given a dynamically stable lagged dependent variable model, the method of treating the initial conditions makes no difference *asymptotically*. Suppose, rather than having $T + G$ observations, we have only T observations, the values $y_0, y_1, \ldots, y_{-G+1}$ not being available. We get the same asymptotic results of consistency, normality and/or asymptotic efficiency whether we drop the first G-observations and run ordinary least squares on the remaining $T - G$ observations *or* simply assign arbitrary values (possibly zero) to $y_0, \ldots, y_{-G+1}$.

The proof of Theorem 11.2.3 offers some insights into the method of maximum likelihood. First, a likelihood function is useful for estimation purposes only if it is a function of *observations* and not of unobservable variables. This is why we often transform from e_t to y_t before using the likelihood function. Second, in the case of Theorem 3.2.1, where $\hat{\boldsymbol{\beta}}$ was shown to be the maximum likelihood estimator in the classical normal linear model, the distribution of y_t was directly deducible and the definition of the multivariate normal distribution could have been directly applied to derive the likelihood function of $\mathbf{y}$ rather than applying the Jacobian technique in transforming from e_t to y_t. However, in the lagged dependent variable case, the distribution of y_t is not directly deducible because the regressors $\mathbf{x}_t'$ are no longer nonstochastic. Thus, the Jacobian technique becomes an essential ingredient in analyzing the maximum likelihood properties of $\hat{\boldsymbol{\beta}}$ in the lagged dependent variable model.

11.3 Lagged Dependent Variable Models with Autocorrelated Errors

11.3.1 Inconsistency of Ordinary Least Squares

Consider the model

$$y_t = \alpha_1 y_{t-1} + e_t, \qquad t = 2, \ldots, T, \tag{11.3.1}$$

where $e_t = \rho e_{t-1} + u_t$ and the u_t are independent, identically distributed with zero mean variance σ_u^2, and finite third and fourth moments. The ordinary least squares estimator of α_1 is

$$\hat{\alpha}_1 = \sum_{t=2}^{T} y_t y_{t-1} \Big/ \sum_{t=2}^{T} y_{t-1}^2. \tag{11.3.2}$$

We want to investigate the consistency of ordinary least squares when *contemporaneous* correlation exists between the regressor y_{t-1} and error e_t.

By repeated substitution

$$y_t = e_t + \alpha_1 e_{t-1} + \alpha_1^2 e_{t-2} + \cdots = e_t^*. \tag{11.3.3}$$

Therefore,

$$\begin{aligned} Ey_{t-1}e_t &= Ee_{t-1}^* e_t = E(e_{t-1} + \alpha_1 e_{t-2} + \cdots)e_t \\ &= \frac{\sigma_u^2}{1-\rho^2}[\rho + \alpha_1\rho^2 + \alpha_1^2\rho^3 + \cdots] \\ &= \frac{\sigma_u^2}{1-\rho^2}[\rho(1 + \alpha_1\rho + \alpha_1^2\rho^2 + \cdots)] \\ &= \sigma_u^2\rho/((1-\rho^2)(1-\alpha_1\rho)) \neq 0 \end{aligned} \tag{11.3.4}$$

and there exists contemporaneous correlation between the regressor and error term of model (11.3.1). This contrasts with the model (11.2.1) where the regressors are related only to error terms of the *previous* periods. To determine the effect of such correlation on the consistency of $\hat{\alpha}_1$ we need to evaluate

$$\begin{aligned} \operatorname{plim}(\hat{\alpha}_1 - \alpha_1) &= \operatorname{plim} \frac{\sum_{t=2}^{T} y_{t-1}e_t}{\sum_{t=2}^{T} y_{t-1}^2} = \frac{\operatorname{plim} \sum_{t=2}^{T} y_{t-1}e_t/T}{\operatorname{plim} \sum_{T=2}^{T} y_{t-1}^2/T} \\ &= \frac{\rho(1-\alpha_1^2)}{1+\alpha_1\rho} \neq 0. \end{aligned} \tag{11.3.5}$$

This follows from the results $\operatorname{plim} \sum_{t=2}^{T} y_{t-1}e_t/T = \sigma_u^2\rho/((1-\rho^2)(1-\alpha_1\rho))$ and $\operatorname{plim} \sum_{t=2}^{T} y_{t-1}^2/T = \sigma_u^2(1+\alpha_1\rho)/((1-\rho^2)(1-\alpha_1^2)(1-\alpha_1\rho))$. (See Exercise 11.2.)

The ordinary least squares estimator of α_1 is not only biased but also *inconsistent*. When a lagged dependent variable model exhibits contemporaneous correlation, ordinary least squares is no longer consistent. This stands in contrast to the well-behaved autoregressive linear model without contemporaneous correlation. There consistency and, in the presence of normality, asymptotic efficiency obtains.

11.3.2 Durbin h-test

Tests for serial correlation (AR(1) errors), like ordinary least squares estimation, are also affected by the presence of contemporaneous correlation. In the context of model (11.3.1), let $\hat{\rho}$ denote the standard Cochrane–Orcutt estimate of ρ

$$\hat{\rho} = \frac{\sum_{t=3}^{T} \hat{e}_{t-1}\hat{e}_t}{\sum_{t=3}^{T} \hat{e}_{t-1}^2}, \tag{11.3.6}$$

where $\hat{e}_t = y_t - \hat{\alpha}_1 y_{t-1}$ and $\hat{\alpha}_1$ is defined by (11.3.2). Then (see Exercise 11.4)

$$\operatorname{plim} \hat{\rho} = \frac{\rho\alpha_1(\alpha_1 + \rho)}{1 + \alpha_1\rho}. \tag{11.3.7}$$

Therefore, $\hat{\rho}$ converges to a value between $-|\rho|$ and $|\rho|$ which means that the ordinary least squares residuals show *less* correlation than the disturbances do. The Durbin–Watson d-statistic, which is based on these residuals, is asymptotically biased toward the acceptance of the null hypothesis of independence and the power of this statistic is low in the presence of lagged dependent variables.

Durbin (1970) has provided a *large sample* test for serial correlation in the lagged dependent variable model.

$$y_t = \sum_{l=1}^{G} \alpha_l y_{t-l} + \mathbf{z}_t'\gamma + e_t, \qquad t = 1, 2, \ldots, T, \tag{11.3.8}$$

where now

$$e_t = \rho e_{t-1} + u_t, |\rho| < 1 \tag{11.3.9}$$

and u_t is independent identically distributed with mean zero and variance σ_u^2. Durbin's h-statistic is

$$h = \hat{\rho}\sqrt{\frac{T}{1 - Tv}}, \tag{11.3.10}$$

where $\hat{\rho}$ is defined by (11.3.6) and v is the estimated variance of the ordinary least squares estimator of α_1, the coefficient of y_{t-1} in (11.3.8). The h-statistic is asymptotically distributed as a $N(0, 1)$ random variable under the null hypothesis $H_0: \rho = 0$.

If $Tv > 1$, the h-test is not applicable. As Durbin (1970) shows, an asymptotically equivalent test consists of running an ordinary least squares regression of $\hat{e}_t$ on $y_{t-1}, \ldots, y_{t-G}$, $\mathbf{z}_t'$ *and* $\hat{e}_{t-1}$, where $\hat{e}_t$ denotes the least squares residuals of (11.3.8), and testing the significance of the coefficient on $\hat{e}_{t-1}$ by ordinary least squares procedures.

In addition to the above two asymptotically equivalent tests, Durbin (1970) also presented an asymptotically equivalent likelihood ratio test.

Maddala and Rao (1973) conducted a Monte Carlo study of the relative performance of these three tests in small samples. In most instances none of the tests showed any distinct superiority. But when the X-series was purely autoregressive without trend, the likelihood ratio test seemed to exhibit some advantage.

Though in large samples the Durbin h-test is clearly superior to the Durbin–Watson bounds test, the relative performances of these two tests in small samples is inconclusive at this stage. See Kenkel (1974, 1975, 1976) and Park (1975, 1976) for discussions of this point.

11.3.3 Estimation of the Lagged Dependent Variable Model with Autocorrelated Errors

Let us turn to the estimation problem posed by a lagged dependent variable model with autocorrelated errors. Such models arise in the context of the dynamic demand model employed extensively in the empirical work of Houthakker and Taylor (1966).

Consider the model

$$y_t = \beta x_t + \alpha y_{t-1} + e_t, \qquad t = 2, 3, \ldots, T, \tag{11.3.11}$$

where $e_t = \rho e_{t-1} + u_t$ and u_t is normal independent identically distributed with zero mean and variance σ_u^2. If ρ is *known* and the error process began in the infinite past, then transform (11.3.11) to

$$\sqrt{1-\rho^2}\, y_2 = \beta x_2\sqrt{1-\rho^2} + \alpha y_1\sqrt{1-\rho^2} + e_2\sqrt{1-\rho^2}, \tag{11.3.12}$$

$$y_t - \rho y_{t-1} = \beta(x_t - \rho x_{t-1}) + \alpha(y_{t-1} - \rho y_{t-2}) + u_t, \qquad t = 3, 4, \ldots, T, \tag{11.3.13}$$

or equivalently

$$P'\mathbf{y} = P'X\boldsymbol{\beta} + P'\mathbf{e}, \tag{11.3.14}$$

where $\mathbf{y}' = (y_2, \ldots, y_T)$, $\boldsymbol{\beta}' = (\beta, \alpha)$, $\mathbf{e}' = (e_2, \ldots, e_T)$,

$$X = \begin{bmatrix} x_2 & y_1 \\ \vdots & \vdots \\ x_T & y_{T-1} \end{bmatrix} \tag{11.3.15}$$

and P' is the $(T-1) \times (T-1)$ Prais–Winsten matrix

$$P' = \begin{bmatrix} \sqrt{1-\rho^2} & 0 & \cdots & \cdots & 0 \\ -\rho & 1 & 0 & \cdots & \vdots \\ 0 & -\rho & & & \vdots \\ \vdots & 0 & \ddots & 1 & 0 \\ \vdots & \vdots & & \ddots & 0 \\ 0 & 0 & \cdots\ 0 & -\rho & 1 \end{bmatrix} \tag{11.3.16}$$

Ordinary least squares applied to (11.3.14) will provide consistent and asymptotically efficient estimates for $\boldsymbol{\beta}$.

On the other hand, if ρ is *unknown* then a maximum likelihood search procedure patterned exactly after the search procedure of Section 10.3 can be used. Let

$$\begin{aligned}(T-1)\sigma_u^2(\rho) &= (\sqrt{1-\rho^2}\,y_2 - \beta x_2\sqrt{1-\rho^2} - \alpha y_1\sqrt{1-\rho^2})^2 \\ &\quad + \sum_{t=3}^{T} [(y_t - \rho y_{t-1}) - \beta(x_t - \rho x_{t-1}) - \alpha(y_{t-1} - \rho y_{t-2})]^2.\end{aligned} \tag{11.3.17}$$

Then a grid search of ρ over the interval $(-1, 1)$ so as to minimize

$$\frac{\sigma_u^2(\rho)}{(1-\rho^2)^{1/(T-1)}} \tag{11.3.18}$$

will provide the maximum likelihood estimate of ρ, say $\check{\rho}$. The maximum likelihood estimates of $\boldsymbol{\beta} = (\beta, \alpha)'$ and σ_u^2 are given by

$$\boldsymbol{\beta}(\check{\rho}) = (X'\check{P}\check{P}'X)^{-1}X'\check{P}\check{P}'\mathbf{y} = (X'\check{\Omega}^{-1}X)^{-1}X'\check{\Omega}^{-1}\mathbf{y}$$

and $\sigma_u^2(\check{\rho}) = [1/(T-1)][\check{P}'\mathbf{y} - \check{P}'X\boldsymbol{\beta}(\check{\rho})]'[\check{P}'\mathbf{y} - \check{P}'X\boldsymbol{\beta}(\check{\rho})]$, where $\check{P}'$ denotes that $\check{\rho}$ has been substituted for ρ in (11.3.16). Asymptotically equivalent estimates could be derived by minimizing $\sigma_u^2(\rho)$ and proceeding as before since $\lim_{T\to\infty} \sigma_u^2(\rho)/(1-\rho^2)^{1/(T-1)} = \sigma_u^2(\rho)$ or, since treatment of the first observation is not important asymptotically, an asymptotically efficient estimate of ρ could be obtained by minimizing

$$\sum_{t=3}^{T} [(y_t - \rho y_{t-1}) - \beta(x_t - \rho x_{t-1}) - \alpha(y_{t-1} - \rho y_{t-2})]^2$$

instead and proceeding as before.

The information matrix for β, α, ρ, and σ_u^2 is

$$I[(\beta, \alpha, \rho, \sigma_u^2)'] = I(\boldsymbol{\theta}) = -E\left[\frac{\partial^2 \ln L}{\partial\boldsymbol{\theta}\,\partial\boldsymbol{\theta}'}\right]$$

$$= \left[\begin{array}{cc:c:c} \dfrac{\mathbf{x}_{.1}'\Omega^{-1}\mathbf{x}_{.1}}{\sigma_u^2} & \dfrac{\mathbf{x}_{.1}'\Omega^{-1}\bar{\mathbf{y}}_{-1}}{\sigma_u^2} & 0 & 0 \\ \dfrac{\bar{\mathbf{y}}_{-1}'\Omega^{-1}\mathbf{x}_{.1}}{\sigma_u^2} & \dfrac{\bar{\mathbf{y}}_{-1}'\Omega^{-1}\bar{\mathbf{y}}_{-1}}{\sigma_u^2} + \dfrac{(1+\alpha\rho)}{(1-\alpha^2)(1-\alpha\rho)} + \dfrac{(T-1)}{1-\alpha^2} & \dfrac{2\rho^2}{(1-\rho^2)(1-\alpha\rho)} + \dfrac{(T-2)}{(1-\alpha\rho)} & 0 \\ \hdashline 0 & \dfrac{2\rho^2}{(1-\rho^2)(1-\alpha\rho)} + \dfrac{(T-2)}{1-\alpha\rho} & \dfrac{1}{1-\rho^2}\left(T-2+\dfrac{2\rho^2}{1-\rho^2}\right) & 0 \\ \hdashline 0 & 0 & 0 & \dfrac{(T-1)}{2\sigma_u^4} \end{array}\right], \tag{11.3.19}$$

where $\mathbf{x}'_{.1} = (x_2, \ldots, x_T)$, and $\bar{\mathbf{y}}_{-1} = (\bar{y}_1, \ldots, \bar{y}_{T-1})'$, with

$$\bar{y}_t = \beta(x_t + \alpha x_{t-1} + \alpha^2 x_{t-2} + \cdots), \qquad t = 1, \ldots, T-1.$$

This latter notation is convenient in that, after repeated substitution, the lagged dependent variable model (11.3.11) can be written as

$$y_t = \bar{y}_t + e_t^*, \tag{11.3.20}$$

where $e_t^* = e_t + \alpha e_{t-1} + \alpha^2 e_{t-2} + \cdots$. This simplifies the process of evaluating expectations.

The asymptotic covariance matrix of the maximum likelihood estimates $(\check{\beta}, \check{\alpha}, \check{\rho}, \check{\sigma}_u^2)'$ is given by (hereafter let $T_1 \equiv T - 1$)

$$\frac{1}{T_1} \lim_{T\to\infty} \left(\frac{I(\boldsymbol{\theta})}{T}\right)^{-1}$$

$$= \frac{1}{T_1} \begin{bmatrix} \lim\limits_{T\to\infty} \dfrac{\mathbf{x}'_{.1}\Omega^{-1}\mathbf{x}_{.1}}{\sigma_u^2 T} & \lim\limits_{T\to\infty} \dfrac{\mathbf{x}'_{.1}\Omega^{-1}\bar{\mathbf{y}}_{-1}}{\sigma_u^2 T} & 0 & 0 \\ \lim\limits_{T\to\infty} \dfrac{\bar{\mathbf{y}}'_{-1}\Omega^{-1}\mathbf{x}_{.1}}{\sigma_u^2 T} & \lim\limits_{T\to\infty} \dfrac{\bar{\mathbf{y}}'_{-1}\Omega^{-1}\bar{\mathbf{y}}_{-1}}{\sigma_u^2 T} + \dfrac{1}{1-\alpha^2} & \dfrac{1}{1-\alpha\rho} & 0 \\ 0 & \dfrac{1}{1-\alpha\rho} & \dfrac{1}{1-\rho^2} & 0 \\ 0 & 0 & 0 & \dfrac{1}{2\sigma_u^4} \end{bmatrix}^{-1}. \tag{11.3.21}$$

A consistent estimate of this covariance matrix can be obtained by dropping the limit operator (lim) and replacing all the unknown population parameters by their consistent estimates. As a further simplification

$$\lim_{T\to\infty} \frac{1}{T\sigma_u^2} \begin{bmatrix} \mathbf{x}'_{.1}\Omega^{-1}\mathbf{x}_{.1} & \mathbf{x}'_{.1}\Omega^{-1}\bar{\mathbf{y}}_{-1} \\ \bar{\mathbf{y}}'_{-1}\Omega^{-1}\mathbf{x}_{.1} & \bar{\mathbf{y}}'_{-1}\Omega^{-1}\bar{\mathbf{y}}_{-1} + \dfrac{T\sigma_u^2}{1-\alpha^2} \end{bmatrix}$$

$$= \operatorname{plim} \frac{1}{T\hat{\sigma}_u^2} (X'\hat{\Omega}^{-1}X)$$

$$= \operatorname{plim} \frac{1}{T\sigma_u^2} (X'\Omega^{-1}X) \equiv V, \tag{11.3.22}$$

where $\hat{\Omega}$ and $\hat{\sigma}^2$ are consistent estimates of Ω and σ^2. Therefore, (11.3.21) can be simplified to

$$\frac{1}{T_1}\left[\begin{array}{cc:c:c} \multicolumn{2}{c:}{\multirow{2}{*}{V}} & 0 & 0 \\ & & \dfrac{1}{1-\alpha\rho} & 0 \\ \hdashline 0 & \dfrac{1}{1-\alpha\rho} & \dfrac{1}{1-\rho^2} & 0 \\ \hdashline 0 & 0 & 0 & \dfrac{1}{2\sigma_u^4} \end{array}\right]^{-1} \tag{11.3.23}$$

A consistent estimate of the asymptotic covariance matrix of the maximum likelihood estimates $(\check{\beta}, \check{\alpha}, \check{\rho}, \check{\sigma}_u^2)'$ is obtained by replacing the unknown parameters of (11.3.23) with the estimates $\check{\beta}$, $\check{\alpha}$, $\check{\rho}$, and $\check{\sigma}_u^2$.

The next issue of interest is the following: What is the asymptotic covariance matrix of the *marginal* distribution of $\begin{pmatrix}\check{\beta}\\ \check{\alpha}\end{pmatrix}$ and how does it compare to the asymptotic covariance matrix of the generalized least squares estimator, namely V^{-1}/T_1? The 2×2 submatrix in the upper left-hand corner of (11.3.23) is (see Exercise 11.7)

$$\begin{aligned} \frac{V^*}{T_1} &= \frac{1}{T_1}\left[V - (1-\rho^2)\begin{pmatrix} 0 \\ \dfrac{1}{1-\alpha\rho}\end{pmatrix}\begin{pmatrix} 0 & \dfrac{1}{1-\alpha\rho}\end{pmatrix}\right]^{-1} \\ &= \frac{1}{T_1}\left[V - \begin{pmatrix} 0 & 0 \\ 0 & c\end{pmatrix}\right]^{-1}, \end{aligned} \tag{11.3.24}$$

where $c \equiv (1-\rho^2)/(1-\alpha\rho)^2$.

Expanding (11.3.24) leads to (see Exercise 11.8)

$$\frac{V^*}{T_1} = \frac{1}{T_1} V^{-1}\begin{pmatrix} 1 & 0 \\ \dfrac{cv^{21}}{1-cv^{22}} & \dfrac{1}{1-cv^{22}}\end{pmatrix}, \tag{11.3.25}$$

where v^{ij} is the (i, j)th element of V^{-1}. Letting v_{ij}^* be the (i, j)th element of V^*, it follows that (see Exercise 11.9)

$$v_{ii}^* > v^{ii}. \tag{11.3.26}$$

The meaning of (11.3.26) is that the conditional asymptotic variances v^{ii}/T_1 based on given ρ *understate* the asymptotic variances v_{ii}^*/T_1 when ρ must be estimated. The practical impact of the result (11.3.26) is that the practitioner must be careful to base tests of hypotheses on V^*/T_1 rather than V/T_1. Some computer programs (e.g. Shazam, White (1978)) allow for the estimation of ρ and provide an unconditional covariance matrix. The appropriate consistent estimate of the asymptotic covariance matrix of $\check{\beta}$ and $\check{\alpha}$ is then

$$\left[\frac{1}{\check{\sigma}_u^2} X'\check{P}\check{P}'X - \begin{pmatrix} 0 & 0 \\ 0 & \dfrac{T_1(1-\check{\rho}^2)}{(1-\check{\alpha}\check{\rho})^2} \end{pmatrix}\right]^{-1}$$

not $\check{\sigma}_u^2(X'\check{P}\check{P}'X)^{-1}$. The result of asymptotic normality provides the basis for the usual t- and F-tests.

11.4 Feasible Generalized Least Squares and Contemporaneous Correlation

As you will recall a common problem encountered in econometric analysis is the estimation of the generalized least squares model

$$\mathbf{y} = X\boldsymbol{\beta} + \mathbf{e}, \tag{11.4.1}$$

where $E\mathbf{ee}' = \sigma^2\Omega$ and Ω is unknown. In the case where all of the regressors of X are nonstochastic, it follows from Theorems 8.3.1–8.3.3 that the feasible two-step generalized least squares estimator

$$\tilde{\tilde{\boldsymbol{\beta}}} = (X'\hat{\Omega}^{-1}X)^{-1}X'\hat{\Omega}^{-1}\mathbf{y}$$

is consistent and asymptotically efficient (in the presence of normality) upon the substitution of a consistent estimate $\hat{\Omega}$ for Ω. This feasible generalized least squares estimator has the same asymptotic covariance matrix as the generalized least squares estimator which assumes Ω is known. In short, ignorance concerning the appropriate member Ω_0 of Ω in large samples is not "costly" and further iteration "does not pay." In contrast, feasible two-step generalized least squares does not fare as well in the context of lagged dependent variables and contemporaneous correlation.

Maddala (1971) considers the case of feasible generalized least squares in the presence of lagged dependent variables for the purpose of identifying sources of inefficiency and possible solutions to the problem. Though feasible generalized squares estimates are still consistent, they do not have the same asymptotic covariance matrix as the generalized least squares estimator. This is shown, in general, by Maddala (1971, pp. 24–25). In the lagged dependent variable–serial correlation model, Equation (11.3.21) makes it clear that even maximum likelihood estimates, assuming Ω unknown, do not achieve the efficiency of the generalized least squares estimator. Instead, the relevant comparison for establishing efficiency should concentrate on the relative efficiency of different estimators of $\boldsymbol{\beta}$ with Ω estimated (assumed unknown) rather than using the generalized least squares estimator as an efficiency benchmark.

The important characteristics of feasible generalized least squares in the context of lagged dependent variables can best be demonstrated by using a particular generalized least squares problem. For this purpose the lagged dependent variable—serial correlation model of (11.3.11) will be used.

The first point to note is that the maximum likelihood estimation of the structural coefficient α is not asymptotically independent of the estimation of the error structure parameter ρ in the sense that the absence of *a priori* knowledge of ρ results in a larger asymptotic covariance matrix for (β, α) than if ρ were known. This lack of independence is reflected in the information matrix which is no longer block diagonal as in the case of a nonstochastic design matrix. The element in the information matrix associated with (α, ρ) is nonzero. As a result, the asymptotic covariance matrix of the structural parameters is not $(\sigma_u^2/T_1)\ \mathrm{plim}(X'PP'X/T)^{-1} = V^{-1}/T_1$ but the appropriate upper left-hand corner submatrix of $(1/T_1)[\mathrm{plim}(1/T)I(\beta, \alpha, \rho, \sigma_u^2)']^{-1}$, namely V^*/T_1. From (11.3.26) it follows that $V^*/T_1 > V^{-1}/T_1$ for $\rho \neq 0$.

The second important point is that, relative to maximum likelihood estimation with Ω unknown, there is a loss in efficiency if any consistent estimator of Ω (other than one asymptotically equivalent to the maximum likelihood estimator) is used *without iteration*. This result is best illustrated by the Wallis two-step estimator of model (11.3.11). Wallis (1967) proposed the use of a two-step estimator where the first step obtains a consistent estimate of Ω from instrumental variables (see the appendix of this chapter for a discussion of instrumental variable estimation) while the second step involves feasible generalized least squares. Specifically, an instrumental variable estimator $\mathbf{b}_{\mathrm{IV}} = (Z'X)^{-1}Z'\mathbf{y} = (\tilde{\beta}, \tilde{\alpha})'$ (say using x_{t-1} as an instrument for y_{t-1}) is used to obtain the residuals

$$\tilde{e}_t = y_t - \tilde{\beta}x_t - \tilde{\alpha}y_{t-1}, \qquad t = 2, 3, \ldots, T, \tag{11.4.2}$$

which are used to compute the consistent estimator

$$\tilde{\rho} = \sum_{t=3}^{T} \tilde{e}_t \tilde{e}_{t-1} \Big/ \sum_{t=3}^{T} \tilde{e}_{t-1}^2. \tag{11.4.3}$$

Upon substitution of $\tilde{\rho}$ into the Prais–Winsten transformation matrix P' yielding $\tilde{P}'$, the Wallis two-step feasible generalized least squares estimator, $\tilde{\tilde{\boldsymbol{\beta}}} = (X'\tilde{P}\tilde{P}'X)^{-1}X'\tilde{P}\tilde{P}'\mathbf{y}$ is obtained.

As shown by Wallis (1972), however, there is a positive semidefinite matrix difference between the covariance matrix of this two-step estimator and the maximum likelihood estimator assuming Ω unknown. Hence the Wallis two-step estimator is *not fully efficient* relative to maximum likelihood estimation (though the two-step procedure is more efficient than the instrumental variables method alone (i.e., $\mathbf{b}_{\mathrm{IV}}$)). Intuitively, the loss in efficiency is due to the fact that the estimation of the structural coefficient of y_{t-1} is not independent of the estimation of the error structure parameter ρ. This lack of independence implies that the *quality* of the estimate of Ω (in this case ρ) is crucial in determining the efficiency of two-step feasible generalized least squares estimators in the presence of lagged dependent variables.

As noted by Maddala (1971), however, further iteration often pays in the presence of lagged dependent variables. In the lagged dependent variable–serial correlation problem, suppose a consistent estimate $\hat{\rho}$ is used to construct a two-step feasible generalized least squares estimator,

$$\tilde{\tilde{\boldsymbol{\beta}}} = (X'\hat{P}\hat{P}'X)^{-1}X'\hat{P}\hat{P}'\mathbf{y}.$$

Assuming convergence, further iteration of $\tilde{\tilde{\boldsymbol{\beta}}}$ results in the minimization of the sum of squared errors function $\sigma_u^2(\rho)$. Asymptotically this amounts to maximum likelihood estimation since this provides an approximate solution of the relevant maximum likelihood equation $\sigma_u^2(\rho)/(1 - \rho^2)^{1/(T-1)}$.

In summary, we should be conscious of the fact that, in the absence of an asymptotically efficient estimate of Ω, two-step feasible generalized least squares estimators are asymptotically less efficient than maximum likelihood estimators when lagged dependent variables are present and are contemporaneously correlated with the error term. As stated by Maddala (1971, p. 33):

> This nondiagonality of the information matrix implies that the efficiency of $\hat{\Omega}$ is important for the efficiency of the estimates of the regression parameters; i.e., any consistent estimate $\hat{\Omega}$ of Ω will not do. This makes some commonly used two-step procedures nonoptimal. In general, however, this deficiency can be remedied by further iteration. Often, an iterated two-step GLS procedure based on a consistent estimate of Ω amounts to an iterative solution of the relevant ML equations. Thus, the solution to the inefficiency problem is further iteration; it pays to iterate.

Other examples of the inefficiency of two-step feasible generalized least squares when lagged dependent variables are present and contemporaneously correlated with the error term will be presented in the discussion of the estimation of the lagged dependent variable (autoregressive) form of the geometric distributed lag (Chapter 17).

11.5 Hatanaka's Estimator

Although Maddala (1971) has shown that in the presence of lagged dependent variables and contemporaneous correlation that iteration of two-step feasible generalized least squares estimators pays, it is still possible that there exists *some* two-step estimator (not of the feasible generalized least squares class) which is asymptotically efficient. Hatanaka (1974) has provided such an estimator.

For illustration the lagged dependent variable–serial correlation model (11.3.11) will be chosen to describe Hatanaka's method. This method, however, can easily be applied to a model with more lagged dependent and nonstochastic variables.

The following steps constitute Hatanaka's two-step "residual adjusted" estimator:

(i) Use the instrumental variable technique to obtain consistent estimates $\tilde{\alpha}$ and $\tilde{\beta}$. The instrument *suggested* is

$$\tilde{y}_{t-1} = a_0 + a_1 x_{t-1} + a_2 x_{t-2} + \cdots + a_p x_{t-p},$$

where $a_0, a_1, \ldots, a_p$ denote the least squares estimates obtained from regressing y_{t-1} on $x_{t-1}, \ldots, x_{t-p}$ and a constant term. The number of x's to be used can be decided by trial and error and use of the adjusted R^2 technique. Asymptotically, x_{t-1} alone would be an adequate instrument though the small sample properties of $\tilde{y}_{t-1}$ might be more desirable because of the higher correlation between $\tilde{y}_{t-1}$ and y_{t-1} as compared to x_{t-1} and y_{t-1}. The instrumental variable estimator of β and α is of the form

$$\mathbf{b}_{\mathrm{IV}} = (Z'X)^{-1}Z'y = (\tilde{\beta}, \tilde{\alpha})'.$$

(ii) Construct the consistent estimate of ρ,

$$\tilde{\rho} = \sum_{t=3}^{T} \tilde{e}_t \tilde{e}_{t-1} \Big/ \sum_{t=3}^{T} \tilde{e}_{t-1}^2,$$

where $\tilde{e}_t = y_t - \tilde{\beta}x_t - \tilde{\alpha}y_{t-1}$.

(iii) Let $y_t - \tilde{\rho}y_{t-1}$ be the dependent variable while $x_t - \tilde{\rho}x_{t-1}$, $y_{t-1} - \tilde{\rho}y_{t-2}$, and $\tilde{e}_{t-1}$ are the independent variables. Let $\hat{\beta}$, $\hat{\alpha}$, and $\tilde{\tilde{\rho}}$ be the ordinary least squares coefficients on $x_t - \tilde{\rho}x_{t-1}$, $y_{t-1} - \tilde{\rho}y_{t-2}$, and $\tilde{e}_{t-1}$. Let $\hat{\rho} = \tilde{\rho} + \tilde{\tilde{\rho}}$.

The estimators that Hatanaka proposes are $\hat{\beta}$, $\hat{\alpha}$, and $\hat{\rho}$. These estimators are asymptotically equivalent to the maximum likelihood estimators and hence are consistent and asymptotically efficient in the presence of normality.

The asymptotic covariance matrix of the Hatanaka estimators $\hat{\beta}$, $\hat{\alpha}$, and $\hat{\rho}$ is given by

$$\frac{1}{T}\sigma_u^2[\operatorname{plim} T^{-1}X(\beta, \alpha, \rho)'X(\beta, \alpha, \rho)]^{-1},$$

where

$$X(\beta, \alpha, \rho) = [\mathbf{x}^*(\rho), \mathbf{y}^*(\rho), \tilde{\mathbf{e}}^*(\beta, \alpha)]$$

and

$$\mathbf{x}^*(\rho)' = (x_3 - \rho x_2, \ldots, x_T - \rho x_{T-1}),$$
$$\mathbf{y}^*(\rho)' = (y_2 - \rho y_1, \ldots, y_{T-1} - \rho y_{T-2}),$$
$$\tilde{\mathbf{e}}^*(\beta, \alpha)' = (\tilde{e}_2, \ldots, \tilde{e}_{T-1}).$$

This covariance matrix is consistently estimated by

$$\hat{\sigma}_u^2[X(\hat{\beta}, \hat{\alpha}, \hat{\rho})'X(\hat{\beta}, \hat{\alpha}, \hat{\rho})]^{-1},$$

where the estimates $\hat{\sigma}_u^2$, $\hat{\beta}$, $\hat{\alpha}$, and $\hat{\rho}$ have been substituted for the unknown population parameters σ_u^2, β, α, and ρ. This matrix, along with the asymptotic normality which obtains, provides the framework for tests of hypotheses.

Of course, the above results reflect the large sample properties of various estimators of the lagged dependent variable–serial correlation model. For an extensive review of alternative sampling theory estimators of this model and an accompanying Monte Carlo evaluation of their relative performances, see Swamy and Rappoport (1978).

11.6 Summary and Guide to Further Readings

In the absence of autocorrelation, ordinary least squares estimation of a dynamically stable lagged dependent variable (autoregressive) linear model provides: (i) a biased but consistent and asymptotically normal estimator of $\boldsymbol{\beta}$ and (ii) with normal errors an asymptotically efficient one. In the presence of autocorrelation, however, ordinary least squares is inconsistent and asymptotically inefficient. The Durbin–Watson d statistic is also affected so as to be asymptotically biased toward the acceptance of no autocorrelation in the presence of serially correlated (AR(1)) errors. These results arise because of the contemporaneous correlation between the lagged dependent variables and the autocorrelated errors. Durbin's h-test provides a means of testing the presence of serial correlation in lagged dependent variable models in large samples. Though other asymptotically equivalent tests exist, the Durbin h-test has the advantage of computational simplicity as well as acceptable small sample performance relative to the others (Maddala and Rao (1973)).

Maximum likelihood estimation of the lagged dependent variable–serial correlation model can be achieved by a straightforward search procedure similar to the one discussed for the AR(1) model with nonstochastic X in Chapter 10. Hatanaka (1974) has provided a two-step estimator (not of the feasible generalized least squares type) which is also asymptotically efficient. From a small sample point of view, the Monte Carlo results of Hatanaka (1974) seem to provide no strong recommendations for one method over the other.

As illustrated by the lagged dependent variable–serial correlation model, the existence of contemporaneous correlation between lagged dependent variables and the error term render the usual two-step feasible generalized least squares methods inefficient. Either further iteration or asymptotically efficient estimates of the error parameters are needed to obtain asymptotic efficiency. The major reason for this is that estimation of the regression coefficients is no longer independent of estimation of the error parameters and as a result some consistent estimates of Ω will not be as good as others in ameliorating the effects of ignorance concerning Ω.

Some additional readings in the literature include the following references. Aigner (1971) considered the estimation of lagged dependent variable models with higher order autocorrelation. Fomby and Guilkey (1983) examined the small sample performance of several two-step estimators in the lagged dependent variable–serial correlation problem and found that: (i) the first observation correction is important and (ii) the $\hat{\rho}$ obtained from unconstrained estimation of the Durbin equation no longer provides an efficient estimate of ρ and the two-step feasible generalized least squares estimator using such an estimate does not improve on the Hatanaka or Wallis two-step estimators. Recently Betancourt and Kelejian (1981) examined the use of the Cochrane–Orcutt iterative procedure when lagged endogenous variables are present. They found that the Cochrane–Orcutt procedure can have more than one fixed point and thus, when used by itself, could provide inconsistent estimation. Instead they suggest using a search procedure (such as the maximum likelihood search procedure described in Section 11.3.3) to avoid the possibly of systematically missing the global minimum of the residual sum of squares. Finally, for a good perspective on the early literature on the lagged dependent variable–serial correlation problem see Griliches (1961). He derived the asymptotic bias of ordinary least squares and examined this bias as a function of the parameters.

11.7 Appendix: Instrumental Variables

11.7.1 Motivation

Frequently in linear models describing economic processes, one or more of the regressors are contemporaneously correlated with the error term. That is, $\text{plim}(X'\mathbf{e}/T) \neq \mathbf{0}$, and the ordinary least squares estimator is not consistent. Let us consider some examples.

Consider the lagged dependent variable–serial correlation model

$$y_t = \beta x_t + \alpha y_{t-1} + e_t, \tag{11.7.1}$$

where

$$e_t = \rho e_{t-1} + u_t, \tag{11.7.2}$$

$|\rho| < 1$, $|\alpha| < 1$, and the u_t are independent identically distributed with zero mean and variance σ_u^2. In this model y_{t-1} and e_t are contemporaneously correlated hence application of ordinary least squares to (11.7.1) will yield inconsistent estimators of β and α. Moreover, the Cochrane–Orcutt estimator of ρ,

$$\hat{\rho} = \frac{\sum_{t=3}^{T} \hat{e}_t \hat{e}_{t-1}}{\sum_{t=3}^{T} \hat{e}_{t-1}^2} \tag{11.7.3}$$

using the ordinary least squares residuals $\hat{e}_t$ from (11.7.1) is an inconsistent estimator of ρ. Even if we were to apply ordinary least squares to, for instance, the Cochrane–Orcutt transformed system

$$y_t - \hat{\rho} y_{t-1} = \beta(x_t - \hat{\rho} x_{t-1}) + \alpha(y_{t-1} - \hat{\rho} y_{t-2}) + u_t$$

we would not obtain consistent estimates for β and α since $\hat{\rho}$ is inconsistent.

Another example of the contemporaneous correlation problem is exemplified by the geometric lag model

$$y_t = \beta \sum_{i=0}^{\infty} \lambda^i x_{t-i} + e_t \tag{11.7.4}$$

or written in autoregressive form

$$y_t = \beta x_t + \lambda y_{t-1} + (e_t - \lambda e_{t-1}). \tag{11.7.5}$$

The application of ordinary least squares to (11.7.5) would yield inconsistent estimates of β and λ since the regressor y_{t-1} is contemporaneously correlated with the error $(e_t - \lambda e_{t-1})$.

There are other instances where the contemporaneous correlation problem arises in econometric. Simultaneous equation and unobservable variables models are two such areas; see Chapters 12 and 19. Needless to say, it is quite important that we devise a means of handling the difficulties which arise because of contemporaneous correlation.

11.7.2 Theoretical Results

In order to properly motivate instrumental variable estimation we should examine ordinary least squares estimation from a different perspective. The normal equations for ordinary least squares are

$$\begin{aligned} X'\mathbf{y} &= X'X\hat{\boldsymbol{\beta}} \\ &= X'X\boldsymbol{\beta} + X'\mathbf{e}. \end{aligned} \tag{11.7.6}$$

If we divide both sides of Equation (11.7.6) by T and take probability limits, we obtain

$$\operatorname{plim}\left(\frac{X'\mathbf{y}}{T}\right) = \operatorname{plim}\left(\frac{X'X}{T}\right)\boldsymbol{\beta} + \operatorname{plim}\left(\frac{X'\mathbf{e}}{T}\right) \tag{11.7.7}$$

and

$$Q_{xy} = Q_{xx}\boldsymbol{\beta}, \tag{11.7.8}$$

if $\text{plim}\,(X'\mathbf{e}/T) = \mathbf{0}$ and Q_{xy} and Q_{xx} are the probability limits of $(X'\mathbf{y}/T)$, and $(X'X/T)$, respectively. Thus,

$$\boldsymbol{\beta} = Q_{xx}^{-1}Q_{xy}. \tag{11.7.9}$$

If we estimate the population cross moments Q_{xx} and Q_{xy} by $(X'X/T)$ and $(X'\mathbf{y}/T)$, we have the consistent estimator

$$\hat{\boldsymbol{\beta}} = (X'X)^{-1}X'\mathbf{y}. \tag{11.7.10}$$

However, suppose that X is contemporaneously correlated with the errors, $\text{plim}(X'\mathbf{e}/T) \neq \mathbf{0}$, and the ordinary least squares estimator is not consistent. Assume there exists a set of T observations on K variables, Z, which is uncorrelated with $\mathbf{e}$, $\text{plim}(Z'\mathbf{e}/T) = \mathbf{0}$, and at the same time is correlated with the original variables X, $\text{plim}(Z'X/T) = Q_{zx} \neq 0$. Now consider the "normal" equations

$$Z'\mathbf{y} = Z'X\boldsymbol{\beta} + Z'\mathbf{e}. \tag{11.7.11}$$

Dividing by T and taking probability limits provides

$$\text{plim}\left(\frac{Z'\mathbf{y}}{T}\right) = \text{plim}\left(\frac{Z'X}{T}\right)\boldsymbol{\beta} + \text{plim}\left(\frac{Z'\mathbf{e}}{T}\right) \tag{11.7.12}$$

and

$$Q_{zy} = Q_{zx}\boldsymbol{\beta}, \tag{11.7.13}$$

where Q_{zy} and Q_{zx} are the probability limits of $(Z'\mathbf{y}/T)$ and $(Z'X/T)$. Thus,

$$\boldsymbol{\beta} = Q_{zx}^{-1}Q_{zy}. \tag{11.7.14}$$

Estimating Q_{zx} and Q_{zy} with the sample moments $(Z'X/T)$ and $(Z'\mathbf{y}/T)$, we have the estimator

$$\mathbf{b}_{\text{IV}} = (Z'X)^{-1}Z'\mathbf{y}. \tag{11.7.15}$$

This estimator is easily seen to be consistent since

$$\begin{aligned}
\text{plim } b_{\text{IV}} &= \text{plim}\left(\frac{Z'X}{T}\right)^{-1}\left(\frac{Z'\mathbf{y}}{T}\right) \\
&= \text{plim}\left(\frac{Z'X}{T}\right)^{-1}\left(\frac{Z'X\boldsymbol{\beta}}{T} + \frac{Z'\mathbf{e}}{T}\right) \\
&= \boldsymbol{\beta} + \text{plim}\left(\frac{Z'X}{T}\right)^{-1}\text{plim}\left(\frac{Z'\mathbf{e}}{T}\right) \\
&= \boldsymbol{\beta} + Q_{zx}^{-1}\cdot\mathbf{0} = \boldsymbol{\beta}.
\end{aligned} \tag{11.7.16}$$

This discussion motivates the following definition.

Definition 11.7.1. The $T \times K$ matrix Z is an instrumental variable matrix for X if

$$\operatorname{plim}\left(\frac{Z'X}{T}\right) = Q_{zx} \tag{11.7.17}$$

is finite and nonsingular and $Z'\mathbf{e}/\sqrt{T}$ converges in distribution to $N(\mathbf{0}, \Psi)$, i.e.

$$\frac{Z'\mathbf{e}}{\sqrt{T}} \overset{\text{asy}}{\approx} N(\mathbf{0}, \Psi). \tag{11.7.18}$$

Examples of how the instrumental variable matrix Z might be obtained will be discussed below, but first let us develop the properties of the *instrumental variable* estimator.

Theorem 11.7.1. *Let Z be an instrumental variable matrix for X. Then the instrumental variable estimator*

$$\mathbf{b}_{\text{IV}} = (Z'X)^{-1}Z'\mathbf{y} \tag{11.7.19}$$

is consistent and the asymptotic distribution of $\sqrt{T}(\mathbf{b}_{\text{IV}} - \boldsymbol{\beta})$ is

$$N(\mathbf{0}, Q_{zx}^{-1}\Psi Q_{zx}^{-1'}). \tag{11.7.20}$$

PROOF. We have previously shown that $\mathbf{b}_{\text{IV}}$ is consistent. Since $\sqrt{T}(\mathbf{b}_{\text{IV}} - \boldsymbol{\beta}) = (Z'X/T)^{-1}(Z'\mathbf{e}/\sqrt{T})$ is asymptotically distributed as $Q_{zx}^{-1}(Z'\mathbf{e}/\sqrt{T})$ and $(Z'\mathbf{e}/\sqrt{T}) \overset{\text{asy}}{\approx} N(\mathbf{0}, \Psi)$, the distribution of $\sqrt{T}(\mathbf{b}_{\text{IV}} - \boldsymbol{\beta})$ is an asymptotic normal random vector with variance–covariance matrix $Q_{zx}^{-1}\Psi Q_{zx}^{-1'}$. □

If the distribution is nonspherical in that $E\mathbf{ee}' = \sigma^2\Omega$, it would seem that generalized least squares would be suggested. Given the "normal" equations

$$Z'\mathbf{y} = Z'X\boldsymbol{\beta} + Z'\mathbf{e}, \tag{11.7.21}$$

the variance of the error term $Z'\mathbf{e}$ is, roughly speaking,

$$\operatorname{var}(Z'\mathbf{e}) = Z'\sigma^2\Omega Z. \tag{11.7.22}$$

However, since (11.7.21) only represents K observations and there are K parameters in $\boldsymbol{\beta}$, there are no degrees of freedom remaining to allow for an adjustment of the nonspherical error term $Z'\mathbf{e}$. Thus, the application of generalized least squares ignores the error structure as can be seen from

$$\begin{aligned}\tilde{\boldsymbol{\beta}} &= [(Z'X)'(Z'\sigma^2\Omega Z)^{-1}(Z'X)]^{-1}(Z'X)'(Z'\sigma^2\Omega Z)^{-1}Z'\mathbf{y} \\ &= (Z'X)^{-1}(Z'\sigma^2\Omega Z)(X'Z)^{-1}(Z'X)'(Z'\sigma^2\Omega Z)^{-1}Z'\mathbf{y} \\ &= (Z'X)^{-1}Z'\mathbf{y} = \mathbf{b}_{\text{IV}}.\end{aligned} \tag{11.7.23}$$

Though the instrumental variable estimator is the same whether $\operatorname{var}(\mathbf{e}) = \sigma^2\Omega$ or $\operatorname{var}(\mathbf{e}) = \sigma^2 I$, its asymptotic variance–covariance matrix is affected. When $\operatorname{var}(\mathbf{e}) = \sigma^2 I, \Psi = \sigma^2 \operatorname{plim}(Z'Z/T)$. When

$$\operatorname{var}(\mathbf{e}) = \sigma^2\Omega, \qquad \Psi = \sigma^2 \operatorname{plim}(Z'\Omega Z/T).$$

For the purpose of hypothesis testing, a consistent estimator of the asymptotic variance–covariance matrix of $\mathbf{b}_{IV}$ is $(Z'X)^{-1}\hat{\Psi}((Z'X)^{-1})'$. When $\text{var}(\mathbf{e}) = \sigma^2 I$, a consistent estimator of Ψ is $\hat{\Psi} = s^2 Z'Z$ and

$$s^2 = (\mathbf{y} - X\mathbf{b}_{IV})'(\mathbf{y} - X\mathbf{b}_{IV})/(T - K).$$

When $\text{var}(\mathbf{e}) = \sigma^2\Omega$, a consistent estimator of Ψ is $\hat{\Psi} = s^2\hat{\Omega}$, where $s^2\hat{\Omega}$ represents a consistent estimator of $\sigma^2\Omega$. The use of the consistent estimator of the asymptotic variance–covariance matrix in conjunction with the asymptotic normality of $\mathbf{b}_{IV}$ provides the basis for conventional hypothesis testing valid in large samples. For example, an asymptotic test of the general linear hypothesis $R\boldsymbol{\beta} = \mathbf{r}$ can be based on the fact that

$$\sqrt{T}(R\mathbf{b}_{IV} - \mathbf{r}) \overset{\text{asy}}{\approx} N(\mathbf{0}, V) \tag{11.7.24}$$

under the null hypothesis where $V = RQ_{zx}^{-1}\Psi Q_{zx}^{-1'}R'$. Thus, under the null hypothesis, the statistic

$$(R\mathbf{b}_{IV} - \mathbf{r})'\hat{V}^{-1}(R\mathbf{b}_{IV} - \mathbf{r}), \tag{11.7.25}$$

where $\hat{V} = R(Z'X)^{-1}\hat{\Psi}(Z'X)^{-1'}R'$ is a consistent estimator of V, is asymptotically distributed as a chi-square random variable with J degrees of freedom (J being the number of rows of R).

11.7.3 Criteria for Selection of Z

The question naturally arises as to what objectives should be followed when choosing instrumental variables. When there are two distinct matrices of instruments which one should be chosen? In general, the instrument matrix we should choose is that one which is *uncorrelated with the error term* **e** *but at the same time has the highest correlation with the elements of the X matrix.* To see this point, consider the case of a single explanatory variable regression equation

$$y_t = x_t\beta + e_t, \tag{11.7.26}$$

where x_t and e_t are contemporaneously correlated. Let z_t denote the instrument for x_t. The instrumental variable estimator of β is

$$b_{IV} = \frac{\sum_t z_t y_y}{\sum_t x_t z_t}. \tag{11.7.27}$$

For simplicity, assume that the errors, e_t, of (11.7.26) are independent and identically distributed with zero mean and variance 1. The asymptotic variance of $\sqrt{T}(b_{\mathrm{IV}} - \beta)$ is

$$\frac{\operatorname{plim} \frac{\sum_t z_t^2}{T}}{\left(\operatorname{plim} \frac{\sum_t z_t x_t}{T}\right)^2}. \tag{11.7.28}$$

If z_t is uncorrelated with x_t, then $\operatorname{plim}(\sum_t z_t x_t/T) \doteq 0$ and the asymptotic variance of the instrumental variable estimator becomes infinitely large.

In general, the efficiency argument can be seen by noticing the form of the asymptotic covariance matrix of $\sqrt{T}(\mathbf{b}_{\mathrm{IV}} - \boldsymbol{\beta})$, namely $Q_{zx}^{-1}\Psi Q_{zx}^{-1'}$. The greater the correlation of the elements of Z with X the larger Q_{zx} is and hence the smaller Q_{zx}^{-1} is. Of course, the smaller Q_{zx}^{-1}, the smaller the asymptotic covariance matrix $Q_{zx}^{-1}\Psi Q_{zx}^{-1'}$, Ψ being held constant. For more discussion on this point, see Dhrymes (1974, pp. 296–298) in which he relates the generalized variance of the instrumental variable estimator with what he calls the sample coefficient of vector correlation between the instrumental variable matrix, Z, and the original regressor matrix X.

11.7.4 Lagged Variables as Instruments

To this point we have not suggested how the instrumental variable matrix Z might be chosen. In general, the selection of Z will be conditioned by the problem under examination and thus it is best to discuss the selection of instruments as each respective contemporaneous correlation problem arises—for example, the selection of instruments for the errors in variables problem is discussed in Chapter 12. In this chapter, the lagged dependent variable–serial correlation problem gives rise to the contemporaneous correlation problem. Below we discuss how lagged variables can be used as instruments to overcome this problem.

Consider the regression model of (11.7.1) and (11.7.2). Let the regressor matrix X be the $(T-1) \times 2$ matrix of observations on x_t and y_{t-1}. Consider the $(T-1) \times 2$ matrix Z made up of observations on x_t and x_{t-1}

$$Z = \begin{bmatrix} x_2 & x_1 \\ x_3 & x_2 \\ \vdots & \vdots \\ x_T & x_{T-1} \end{bmatrix}. \tag{11.7.29}$$

Then

$$\operatorname{plim} \frac{1}{T} Z'X = \operatorname{plim} \frac{1}{T} \begin{bmatrix} \sum x_t^2 & \sum x_t x_{t-1} \\ \sum x_t x_{t-1} & \sum x_{t-1} y_{t-1} \end{bmatrix}$$

is finite and nonsingular and x_t is exogenous in that the random vector

$$\frac{1}{\sqrt{T}}\begin{bmatrix}\sum x_t e_t \\ \sum x_{t-1} e_t\end{bmatrix}$$

is asymptotically normally distributed with zero mean and covariance matrix Ψ, and, therefore, Z is an instrumental variable matrix for X. Likewise, consistent estimates of β and α can be obtained from the instrumental variable estimator $\mathbf{b}_{IV} = (Z'X)^{-1}Z'\mathbf{y}$. In the case that the geometric lag model (11.7.5) is of interest, consistent estimates of β and λ can be obtained by using the same instrumental variable and observations matrices.

The use of x_{t-1} as an instrumental variable for the "troubling" variable y_{t-1} in the lagged dependent variable–serial correlation model (11.7.1)–(11.7.2) is not the only possibility. One could form the instrument $\tilde{y}_{t-1}$ obtained from

$$\tilde{y}_{t-1} = a_0 + a_1 x_{t-1} + a_2 x_{t-2} + \cdots + a_p x_{t-p}, \tag{11.7.30}$$

where $a_0, a_1, \ldots, a_p$ are the least squares estimators obtained from regressing y_{t-1} on $x_{t-1}, x_{t-2}, \ldots, x_{t-p}$ and a constant term. As far as consistency is concerned, x_{t-1} alone would be an adequate instrument though the sampling properties obtained from using $\tilde{y}_{t-1}$ might be more desirable because of the higher correlation between $\tilde{y}_{t-1}$ and y_{t-1} as compared to x_{t-1} and y_{t-1}. The instrumental variable matrix then becomes

$$Z = \begin{bmatrix} x_{p+1} & \tilde{y}_p \\ x_{p+2} & \tilde{y}_{p+1} \\ \vdots & \vdots \\ x_T & \tilde{y}_{T-1} \end{bmatrix}, \tag{11.7.31}$$

which has $(T - p)$ observations. The cost of the higher correlation is the loss of $p - 1$ degrees of freedom, however, and there is no clear preference for $\tilde{y}_{t-1}$ over x_{t-1} as a choice for an instrumental variable.

11.7.5 Asymptotic Inefficiency of Instrumental Variable Estimators

In general, the instrumental variable estimator $\mathbf{b}_{IV}$ is not asymptotically efficient. This is clearly illustrated when one considers the lagged dependent variable–serial correlation model (11.7.1)–(11.7.2) and the autoregressive form of the geometric lag model (11.7.5). As noted before, the instrumental variable estimator using Z defined by say (11.7.29) and the observation matrix X made up of $T - 1$ observations on x_t and y_{t-1} is a consistent estimator of the parameters of *both* models. In this instance it is obvious that the instrumental variable estimator ignores the difference in the covariance structures of the two models—the former model has an AR(1) error process while the latter model has a MA(1) error process. Certainly the maximum likelihood estimators of the two models would be different each taking into account the explicit form of the respective error processes. Naturally, since the instrumental variable estimator ignores some information, it is not likely to be asymptotically efficient. This conclusion is punctuated by many instances in the literature where instrumental variable estimators have been shown to be inefficient relative to maximum likelihood estimators. One example is that of Wallis (1972) where it is shown that the instrumental variable estimates are inefficient in the lagged dependent variable–serial correlation model.

11.7.6 Case of Surplus Instruments

Recall the "normal" equations suggested by instrumental variable estimation:

$$Z'\mathbf{y} = Z'X\boldsymbol{\beta} + Z'\mathbf{e}. \tag{11.7.32}$$

If there are as many instruments for X as there are variables in X (i.e., K), the system (11.7.32) represents K observations on a linear regression model with K regressors. There are no degrees of freedom left to estimate the variance–covariance structure of the error vector $Z'\mathbf{e}$. The generalized least squares and ordinary least squares estimators are numerically identical when there are zero degrees of freedom (see (11.7.23)). When there are more instruments available than required, the definition of the instrumental variable estimator changes to reflect the fact that the variance–covariance structure can be utilized in the estimation of $\boldsymbol{\beta}$ in (11.7.32).

Suppose that Z is of dimension $T \times L$, where $L > K$ and $L - K$ is the number of "surplus" instruments available. Furthermore, throughout the remainder of the section we will assume that $E\mathbf{ee}' = \sigma^2 I$. This error specification is the most commonly encountered in the case of "surplus" instruments. For example, in Chapter 21 the case of "surplus" instruments arises in two-stage least squares estimation when the equation being estimated is over-identified. The assumed error specification is of the form $E\mathbf{ee}' = \sigma^2 I$. Given this spherical error specification, $\text{var}(Z'\mathbf{e}) = E(Z'\mathbf{ee}'Z) = \sigma^2 Z'Z$. A generalized least squares estimator of $\boldsymbol{\beta}$ in the transformed model (11.7.32) is

$$\begin{aligned}\tilde{\boldsymbol{\beta}} &= [(Z'X)'(\sigma^2 Z'Z)^{-1}(Z'X)]^{-1}(Z'X)'(\sigma^2 Z'Z)^{-1}Z'\mathbf{y} \\ &= [X'Z(Z'Z)^{-1}Z'X]^{-1}(X'Z)(Z'Z)^{-1}Z'\mathbf{y} \\ &= \mathbf{b}_{\text{IV}}.\end{aligned} \tag{11.7.33}$$

When $L = K$, (11.7.33) reduces to the previously defined instrumental variable estimator $\mathbf{b}_{\text{IV}} = (Z'X)^{-1}Z'\mathbf{y}$. Naturally, by Aitken's theorem (2.5.1) (and assuming Z is nonstochastic), the instrumental variable estimator defined in (11.7.33) is more efficient than applying ordinary least squares estimation to (11.7.32) when $L > K$. Thus, the definition (11.7.33) is essential when dealing with a surplus number of instruments.

Likewise, the test statistic discussed in Equation (11.7.25) must be modified. Again assume $E\mathbf{e}\mathbf{e}' = \sigma^2 I$. In the case of $L > K$, the random vector $\sqrt{T}(\mathbf{b}_{\text{IV}} - \boldsymbol{\beta})$ has an asymptotic normal distribution with mean $\mathbf{0}$ and variance–covariance matrix $\sigma^2(Q'_{zx}Q_{zz}^{-1}Q_{zx})^{-1}$. This follows from the fact that $\sqrt{T}(\mathbf{b}_{\text{IV}} - \boldsymbol{\beta})$ has the same asymptotic distribution as the random vector $(Q'_{zx}Q_{zz}^{-1}Q_{zx})^{-1}Q'_{zx}Q_{zz}^{-1}Z'\mathbf{e}/\sqrt{T}$. Correspondingly, the random vector $\sqrt{T}(R\mathbf{b}_{\text{IV}} - \mathbf{r})$ has, under the null hypothesis, the asymptotic distribution $N(\mathbf{0}, V)$, where $V = R(\cdot)R'$ and $(\cdot)$ represents $\sigma^2(Q'_{zx}Q_{zz}^{-1}Q_{zx})^{-1}$. An appropriate test statistic would be

$$T \cdot (R\mathbf{b}_{\text{IV}} - \mathbf{r})'\hat{V}^{-1}(R\mathbf{b}_{\text{IV}} - \mathbf{r}), \tag{11.7.34}$$

where $\hat{V} = T \cdot Rs^2[X'Z(Z'Z)^{-1}Z'X]^{-1}R'$ and $s^2 = (\mathbf{y} - X\mathbf{b}_{\text{IV}})'(\mathbf{y} - X\mathbf{b}_{\text{IV}})/(T - K)$. This statistic is distributed asymptotically as a χ^2 random variable with J degrees of freedom.

Another interesting point to note is the following. Consider the case where $E\mathbf{e}\mathbf{e}' = \sigma^2 I$. Let $\hat{X}$ represent the fitted values of X obtained after regressing X on the matrix of instrumental variables Z, $\hat{X} = ZB = Z(Z'Z)^{-1}Z'X$. Then

$$\begin{aligned}
\mathbf{b}_{\text{IV}} &= (\hat{X}'\hat{X})^{-1}\hat{X}'\mathbf{y} \\
&= [X'Z(Z'Z)^{-1}Z'Z(Z'Z)^{-1}Z'X]^{-1}X'Z(Z'Z)^{-1}Z'\mathbf{y} \\
&= [X'Z(Z'Z)^{-1}Z'X]^{-1}X'Z(Z'Z)^{-1}Z'\mathbf{y},
\end{aligned}$$

which is exactly the same as (11.7.33) above. The instrumental variable estimator can be derived by running ordinary least squares on a "purged" equation, $\mathbf{y} = \hat{X}\boldsymbol{\beta} + \mathbf{u}$, with the regressors being the projections of Z on X and $\mathbf{u} = (X - \hat{X})\boldsymbol{\beta} + \mathbf{e}$. The matrix of regressors is "purged" of its contemporaneous correlation in the sense that

$$\begin{aligned}
\text{plim}\left(\frac{\hat{X}'\mathbf{u}}{T}\right) = \text{plim}\left(\frac{\hat{X}'\mathbf{e}}{T}\right) &= \text{plim}\left(\frac{X'Z}{T}\right)\left(\frac{Z'Z}{T}\right)^{-1}\left(\frac{Z'\mathbf{e}}{T}\right) \\
&= Q'_{zx}Q_{zz}^{-1} \cdot \mathbf{0} = \mathbf{0}
\end{aligned} \tag{11.7.35}$$

and $\hat{X}$ is uncorrelated with $\mathbf{u}$ in the limit.

Consider the "restricted least squares" instrumental variable estimator

$$\mathbf{b}_{\text{IV}}^* = \mathbf{b}_{\text{IV}} - (\hat{X}'\hat{X})^{-1}R'[R(\hat{X}'\hat{X})^{-1}R']^{-1}(R\mathbf{b}_{\text{IV}} - \mathbf{r}) \tag{11.7.36}$$

which is obtained by minimizing the sum of squared residuals $\hat{\mathbf{e}}'\hat{\mathbf{e}} = (\mathbf{y} - \hat{X}\mathbf{b}_{\text{IV}}^*)'(\mathbf{y} - \hat{X}\mathbf{b}_{\text{IV}}^*)$ subject to the restriction that $R\mathbf{b}_{\text{IV}}^* = \mathbf{r}$ (see Section

6.2.2 for a discussion of restricted least squares estimation). Under the null hypothesis $H_0: R\boldsymbol{\beta} = \mathbf{r}$, the asymptotic distribution of

$$\frac{(\mathbf{y} - \hat{X}\mathbf{b}_{\text{IV}}^*)'(\mathbf{y} - \hat{X}\mathbf{b}_{\text{IV}}^*) - (\mathbf{y} - \hat{X}\mathbf{b}_{\text{IV}})'(\mathbf{y} - \hat{X}\mathbf{b}_{\text{IV}})}{s^2} \tag{11.7.37}$$

is that of a χ^2 random variable with J degrees of freedom. This follows from the fact that (11.7.37) and (11.7.34) are algebraically equivalent (see Exercise 11.11). Note that s^2 is calculated from the residuals derived from using X, not $\hat{X}$, as the regressor matrix. This is required because, in general,

$$\text{plim}(\mathbf{y} - \hat{X}\mathbf{b}_{\text{IV}})'(\mathbf{y} - \hat{X}\mathbf{b}_{\text{IV}})/(T - K) \neq \sigma^2 \tag{11.7.38}$$

(see Exercise 11.12).

Since, asymptotically, an F random variable with J numerator degrees of freedom and $T - K$ denominator degrees of freedom is distributed as a χ^2 random variable with J degrees of freedom divided by J, X_J^2/J, the statistic,

$$u = \frac{(\text{SSE}_{\text{r}} - \text{SSE}_{\text{u}})/J}{s^2}, \tag{11.7.39}$$

where $\text{SSE}_{\text{r}} = (\mathbf{y} - \hat{X}\mathbf{b}_{\text{IV}}^*)'(\mathbf{y} - \hat{X}\mathbf{b}_{\text{IV}}^*)$ and $\text{SSE}_{\text{u}} = (\mathbf{y} - \hat{X}\mathbf{b}_{\text{IV}})'(\mathbf{y} - \hat{X}\mathbf{b}_{\text{IV}})$, is, asymptotically, distributed as an F random variable with J and $T - K$ degrees of freedom under the null hypothesis. This statistic is very similar to the F statistic developed for the general linear hypothesis in the classical normal linear regression model in Chapter 3, Equation (3.4.19). The numerator consists of a per restriction comparison of the restricted versus unrestricted sum of squared residuals obtained from the "purged" model, $\mathbf{y} = \hat{X}\boldsymbol{\beta} + \mathbf{u}$. However, the denominator is different in that the sum of squared residuals (and likewise the estimator of σ^2) is computed using the actual values of the explanatory variables, X, rather than the purged values, $\hat{X}$.

11.8 Exercises

11.1. Show that the determinant of a lower (or upper) triangular matrix is the product of its diagonal elements.

11.2. In (11.3.5) show that $\text{plim} \sum_{t=2}^T y_{t-1}e_t/T = \sigma_u^2\rho((1 - \rho^2)(1 - \alpha_1\rho))$ and $\text{plim} \sum_{t=2}^T y_{t-1}^2/T = \sigma_u^2(1 + \alpha_1\rho)/((1 - \rho^2)(1 - \alpha_1^2)(1 - \alpha_1\rho))$ by using convergence in quadratic mean. Explain in detail the conditions needed for convergence.

11.3. Examine the asymptotic bias of the ordinary least squares estimator in (11.3.5). When is this bias minimized? When it is maximized?

11.4. In the context of model (11.3.1), show that $\text{plim}\,\hat{\rho} = \rho\alpha_1(\alpha_1 + \rho)/(1 + \alpha_1\rho)$, where $\hat{\rho}$ is the Cochrane–Orcutt estimator of ρ.

11.5. Verify the information matrix (11.3.19).

11.6. Let

$$\begin{bmatrix} A & \mathbf{a} \\ \mathbf{a}' & c \end{bmatrix} = L$$

denote a $n \times n$ matrix where A is a $(n-1) \times (n-1)$ nonsingular matrix, $\mathbf{a}$ is an $n \times 1$ vector and c is a scalar. Prove that

$$L^{-1} = \begin{bmatrix} \left(A - \dfrac{\mathbf{a}\mathbf{a}'}{c}\right)^{-1} & -\dfrac{A^{-1}\mathbf{a}}{c - \mathbf{a}'A^{-1}\mathbf{a}} \\ -\dfrac{\mathbf{a}'A^{-1}}{c - \mathbf{a}'A^{-1}\mathbf{a}} & \dfrac{1}{(c - \mathbf{a}'A^{-1}\mathbf{a})} \end{bmatrix}.$$

11.7. Using Exercise 11.6, verify (11.3.24).

11.8. Verify (11.3.25) by using $[(I - CV^{-1})V]^{-1} = V^{-1}(I - CV^{-1})^{-1}$, where

$$C = \begin{pmatrix} 0 & 0 \\ 0 & c \end{pmatrix},$$

and simplifying.

11.9. Given the requirements of stability: $0 < |\alpha| < 1$ and $0 < |\rho| < 1$, verify (11.3.26). (Hint: You should prove along the way: (i) $0 < c < 1$, (ii), $1 - cv^{22} > 0$, (iii) $0 < cv^{22} < 1$, and (iv) $1/(1 - cv^{22}) > 1$.)

11.10. Prove that the Wallis two-step estimator is inefficient relative to maximum likelihood estimation. See Wallis (1972) for a start.

11.11. Show the equivalence of the expressions (11.7.34) and (11.7.37).

11.12. Prove that (11.7.38) is, in general, true and thus that the residuals derived from ordinary least squares estimation of the purged equation cannot be used to construct a consistent estimator of σ^2.

According to the simple adaptive expectations hypothesis, expectations adjust by a constant proportion of the previous discrepancy:

$$\Pi_{t+1}^e = \Pi_t^e + \lambda(\Pi_t - \Pi_t^e), \qquad 0 \le \lambda \le 1, \tag{1}$$

where Π_t is the series being predicted and Π_t^e is the expectation of Π_t formed at time $t - 1$. This model has received some support in the field of inflation rate expectations. See Lahiri (1976) and Turnovsky (1970).

The unrestricted form of Equation (1) is

$$\Pi_{t+1}^e = \beta_1 + \beta_2 \Pi_t^e + \beta_3 \Pi_t, \tag{2}$$

where the adaptive expectations hypothesis postulates $\beta_1 = 0$ and $\beta_2 + \beta_3 = 1$. Assume that (2) is an inexact relationship and its stochastic form is represented by

$$\Pi_{t+1}^e = \beta_1 + \beta_2 \Pi_t^e + \beta_3 \Pi_t + e_t. \tag{3}$$

Use the following inflation expectations data to complete the next six exercises. The observations on Π_t^e are the expected annual rates of inflation of experts obtained from the Livingston survey and tabulated by Carlson (1977). These expectations were formed in the previous year $t - 1$. The actual annual rates of inflation, Π_t, were computed using the formula

$$\left[\left(\frac{\mathrm{CPI}_t}{\mathrm{CPI}_{t-14}}\right)^{12/14} - 1\right] \times 100.$$

These are annualized percentage rates of inflation adjusted for the 2 month time lag between the time the experts received the Livingston questionnaires and the time the results of the questionnaires were published. CPI_t represents the consumer price index at time t, while CPI_{t-14} represents the consumer price index 14 months earlier. The CPI figures were obtained from various issues of the *Survey of Current Business*. Two base years were used (1947–1949 and 1957–1959) to make the CPI figures compatible with those being forecasted by the experts at the time.

Time	Π_t	Π_t^e	Time	Π_t	Π_t^e
June 1954	−0.15	−0.11	June 1965	2.82	1.07
June 1955	1.50	0.27	June 1966	2.66	2.08
June 1956	3.94	0.50	June 1967	4.15	2.40
June 1957	3.15	1.19	June 1968	5.48	3.10
June 1958	0.69	0.32	June 1969	5.94	3.44
June 1959	1.80	1.00	June 1970	4.65	3.64
June 1960	0.95	0.70	June 1971	3.41	4.12
June 1961	1.14	1.15	June 1972	5.56	3.80
June 1962	1.14	1.06	June 1973	10.53	4.21
June 1963	1.45	1.05	June 1974	10.04	6.84
June 1964	1.83	1.24	June 1975	6.18	5.62

11.13. Consider the lagged dependent variable model (3).
   (a) Use the Durbin h-statistic to test for first-order serial correlation among the errors e_t.
   (b) Use Durbin's residual regression to test for first-order serial correlation among the errors e_t. This test is asymptotically equivalent to the Durbin h-test and involves the ordinary least squares regression of $\hat{e}_t$ on Π_{t-1}^e, a constant term, Π_{t-1} and $\hat{e}_{t-1}$, where $\hat{e}_t$ represents the ordinary least squares residual at time t.
   (c) Given the results of these tests, discuss the probable properties of the ordinary least squares estimates of the present model. Consider the issues of unbiasedness, consistency and efficiency.

11.14. Regardless of the outcome of the Durbin h-test performed in Exercise 11.13, estimate Equation (3) assuming the e_t have first order serial correlation and using:
   (a) Hatanaka's estimator (where for simplicity let the instrument for Π_t^e be Π_{t-1});
   (b) Wallis' two-step estimator (let the instrument for Π_t^e be Π_{t-1});
   (c) Maximum likelihood estimator obtained from a grid search over the interval $-1 < \rho < 1$.

   Compare the various estimates. Are they substantially affected by the choice of estimation method?

11.15. Assume the errors of Equation (3) are serially uncorrelated. Test the following hypotheses:

(a) $H_0: \beta_2 + \beta_3 = 1$ versus $H_1: \beta_2 + \beta_3 \neq 1$.
(b) $H_0: \beta_1 = 0$ and $\beta_2 + \beta_3 = 1$ versus H_1: not H_0.

11.16. Assume the errors of Equation (3) have first-order serial correlation. Test the hypotheses of Exercise 11.15, using Hatanaka's estimator. (Hint: For the joint test construct a χ^2 statistic of the form $(R\mathbf{b} - \mathbf{r})'\hat{V}^{-1}(R\mathbf{b} - \mathbf{r})$, where $\hat{V}$ is a consistent estimator of the variance–covariance matrix of $R\mathbf{b}$ and $\mathbf{b}$ is Hatanaka's estimator.)

11.17. Given the results of Exercises 11.13–11.16, what conclusion can be drawn about the appropriateness of the adaptive expectations model for the above Livingston data?

11.18. Consider the two time spans June 1954–June 1964 and June 1965–June 1975. Assume that the errors of Equation (3) have first-order serial correlation. Consider the dummy variable equation

$$\Pi_{t+1}^e = \beta_1 + \beta_1' D_t + \beta_2 \Pi_t^e + \beta_2'(\Pi_t^e \cdot D_t) + \beta_3 \Pi_t + \beta_3'(\Pi_t \cdot D_t) + e_t, \quad (4)$$

where D_t represents a dummy variable which is zero for the first time span and one for the second time span. Use Hatanaka's estimator to estimate the parameters of Equation (4) and its variance–covariance matrix to construct a χ^2 statistic of the form $(\mathbf{Rb} - \mathbf{r})'\hat{V}^{-1}(\mathbf{Rb} - \mathbf{r})$ to test for a structural change over these two time periods ($\hat{V}$ is the consistent estimator of the variance-covariance matrix of $R\mathbf{b}$ and $\mathbf{b}$ is Hatanaka's estimator.)

11.9 References

Aigner, D. J. (1971). A compendium on estimation of the autoregressive moving average model from time series data. *International Economic Review*, **12**, 348–371.

Betancourt, R. and Kelejian, H. (1981). Lagged endogenous variables and the Cochrane–Orcutt method. *Econometrica*, **49**, 1073–1078.

Carlson, J. A. (1977). A study of price forecasts. *Annals of Economic and Social Measurement*, **6**, 27–56.

Dhrymes, P. J. (1974). *Econometrics*. New York: Springer-Verlag.

Durbin, J. (1970). Testing for serial correlation in least-squares regression when some of the regressors are lagged dependent variables. *Econometrica*, **38**, 410–421.

Fomby, T. B. and Guilkey, D. K. (1983). An examination of two-step estimators for models with lagged dependent variables and autoregressive errors. *Journal of Econometrics*, **22**, 291–300.

Griliches, Z. (1961). A note on the serial correlation bias in estimates of distributed lags. *Econometrica*, **29**, 65–73.

Hatanaka, M. (1974). An efficient two-step estimator for the dynamic adjustment model with auto-correlated errors. *Journal of Econometrics*, **2**, 199–220.

Houthakker, H. S. and Taylor, L. D. (1966). *Consumer Demand in the United States, 1929–1970*. Cambridge, MA: Harvard University Press.

Kenkel, J. L. (1974). Some small-sample properties of Durbin's tests for serial correlation in regression models containing lagged dependent variables. *Econometrica*, **42**, 763–769.

Kenkel, J. L. (1975). Small sample tests for serial correlation in models containing lagged dependent variables. *Review of Economics and Statistics*, **57**, 383–386.

Kenkel, J. L. (1976). Comment on the small-sample power of Durbin's *h*-test. *Journal of the American Statistical Association*, **71**, 96–97.

Lahiri, K. (1976). Inflationary expectations: their formation and interest rate effects. *American Economic Review*, **66**, 124–131.

Maddala, G. S. (1971). Generalized least squares with an estimated variance–covariance matrix. *Econometrica*, **39**, 23–33.

Maddala, G. S. and Rao, A. S. (1973). Tests for serial correlation in regression models with lagged dependent variables and serially correlated errors. *Econometrica*, **41**, 761–774.

Park, S. (1975). On the small-sample power of Durbin's *h*-test. *Journal of the American Statistical Association*, **70**, 60–63.

Park, S. (1976). Rejoinder. *Journal of the American Statistical Association*, **71**, 97–98.

Reiersol, O. (1945). Confluence analysis by means of instrumental sets of variables. *Arkiv for Matematik, Astronomi och Fysik*. Uppsala: Almquist and Wicksells Boktryckeri-AB. Pp. 1–119.

Schmidt, P. (1976). *Econometrics*. New York: Marcel Dekker.

Schönfeld, P. (1971). A useful control limit theorem for *m*-dependent random variables. *Metrika*, **17**, 116–128.

Swamy, P. A. V. B. and Rappoport, P. N. (1978). Relative efficiencies of some simple Bayes estimators of coefficients in a dynamic equation with serially correlated errors—II. *Journal of Econometrics*, **7**, 245–258.

Theil, H. (1971). *Principles of Econometrics*. New York: Wiley.

Turnovsky, S. J. (1970). Empirical evidence of the formation of price expectations. *Journal of the American Statistical Association*, **65**, 1441–1454.

Wallis, K. F. (1967). Lagged dependent variables and serially correlated errors: a reappraisal of three-pass least squares. *Review of Economics and Statistics*, **49**, 555–567.

Wallis, K. F. (1972). The efficiency of the two-step estimator. *Econometrica*, **40**, 769–770.

White, J. S. (1961). Asymptotic expansions for the mean and variance of the serial correlation coefficient. *Biometrika*, **48**, 85–94.

White, K. J. (1978). A general computer program for econometric methods—SHAZAM, *Econometrica*, **46**, 239–240.

CHAPTER 12

Unobservable Variables

12.1 Introduction

As pointed out by Stamp (1929, pp. 258–259) long ago, the data that economists must work with often leaves much to be desired.

> The Government are very keen on amassing statistics—they collect them, add them, raise them to the nth power, take the cube root and prepare wonderful diagrams. But what you must never forget is that every one of those figures come in the first instance from the village watchman, who just puts down what he damn pleases.

The errors-in-variables problem is concerned with the statistical implications of using data observed with error. Measuring the dependent variable of a linear regression model with error causes no statistical problems because the error term, e_t, is capable of accounting for this as well as for independent omitted variable effects. However, observing one or more of the explanatory variables of a regression model with error has much more serious consequences. To see this point, consider the following true proportionate relationship between the unobserved variables y_t^* and x_t^*:

$$y_t^* = \beta x_t^*. \tag{12.1.1}$$

Assume that both y_t^* and x_t^* are observed with error and that their observed counterparts, y_t and x_t, satisfy the following relationships:

$$y_t = y_t^* + e_t, \tag{12.1.2}$$

$$x_t = x_t^* + u_t, \tag{12.1.3}$$

where e_t and u_t are measurement errors satisfying the properties:

$$Ee_t = 0, \qquad Ee_t^2 = \sigma_e^2, \tag{12.1.4}$$

$$Eu_t = 0, \qquad Eu_t^2 = \sigma_u^2, \tag{12.1.5}$$

$$Ee_t u_t = Ey_t^* e_t = Ex_t^* u_t = Ey_t^* u_t = Ex_t^* e_t = 0. \tag{12.1.6}$$

The observed relationship that the economist must work with is then

$$y_t = \beta x_t + (e_t - \beta u_t) = \beta x_t + v_t, \tag{12.1.7}$$

where $v_t = (e_t - \beta u_t)$. Estimating the observed regression Equation (12.1.7) by means of ordinary least squares will unfortunately run awry due to the contemporaneous correlation problem. Since

$$\begin{aligned} E(x_t v_t) &= E(x_t^* + u_t)(e_t - \beta u_t) \\ &= -\beta\sigma_u^2 \neq 0, \end{aligned}$$

the observed regressor, x_t, and the equation's error term, v_t, are correlated and the ordinary least squares estimator will be inconsistent. It is easy to show (see Exercise 12.1) that

$$\text{plim } \hat{\beta} = \beta - \frac{\beta\sigma_u^2}{\sigma_x^2}, \tag{12.1.8}$$

where $\sigma_x^2 = \text{plim} \sum x_t^2/T$. Thus, the ordinary least squares estimator of the regression coefficient, β, will be asymptotically biased toward zero. Note that when the explanatory variable, x_t, is measured without error, $\sigma_u^2 = 0$, the ordinary least squares estimator is no longer inconsistent. Thus errors in measurement are important only when it involves one or more of the explanatory variables of the regression equation.

Figure 12.1.1 pictorally represents the errors-in-variables problem. The ordinary least squares procedure minimizes the vertical distance from a regression to an observation, O. This procedure of fitting is appropriate when the only reason for deviation from the true relationship is measurement error in y and/or omitted variables effects which are independent of x. However,

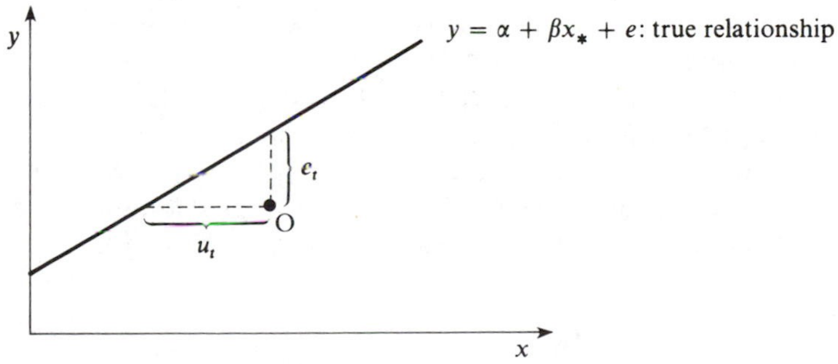

Figure 12.1.1

in the errors-in-variables context, the observation O could arise because of the combination of two random effects, u_t and e_t. Thus some procedure should be used which weights both of these deviations according to their relative importance. If $\sigma_u^2 = 0$, then vertical distance should be minimized. If $\sigma_e^2 = 0$, horizontal distance should be minimized and the reciprocal regression, $x = \gamma + \eta y + w_t$ should be estimated by ordinary least squares. Orthogonal regression which minimizes the orthogonal distance from O to the regression line is one such way that both effects could be weighted. Unfortunately, orthogonal regression is consistent only if $\sigma_u^2 = \sigma_e^2$ (Malinvaud (1970)).

Several postulated relationships in economics have involved unobservable variables. For example, Friedman's (1957) permanent income theory of consumption specifies that permanent consumption, c_{p}, is proportional to permanent income, y_{p},

$$c_{\mathrm{p}} = \beta y_{\mathrm{p}}. \tag{12.1.9}$$

However, Equation (12.1.9) is unobservable so that some assumptions must be made which will allow observations on observed consumption, c, and observed income, y, to substantiate the theory. Friedman assumed that observed consumption consists of two components, permanent consumption and transitory consumption, c_{T}, such that

$$c = c_{\mathrm{p}} + c_{\mathrm{T}}. \tag{12.1.10}$$

Also, observed income is assumed to consist of two components, permanent income and transitory income such that

$$y = y_{\mathrm{p}} + y_{\mathrm{T}}. \tag{12.1.11}$$

Hence the relationship between the observed variables is

$$\begin{aligned} c &= \beta(y - y_{\mathrm{T}}) + c_{\mathrm{T}} \\ &= \beta y + v_t, \end{aligned} \tag{12.1.12}$$

where $v_t = -\beta y_T + c_{\mathrm{T}}$. This classical errors-in-variables problem has arisen not because observed income is measured with error but because the true relationship (12.1.9) consists of variables which are unobservable.

One possible solution to this problem is to postulate an "incidental" equation describing a relationship between the unobserved explanatory variable, y_{p}, and observable variables. Let $z_1, z_2, \ldots, z_p$ represent p incidental, observable variables such as value of home, educational attainment, age, etc. Assume permanent income is related to these variables by the incidental equation

$$y_{\mathrm{p}} = \pi_1 z_1 + \cdots + \pi_p z_p, \tag{12.1.13}$$

where $\pi_1, \ldots, \pi_p$ are the incidental parameters.

Substitution of (12.1.13) in (12.1.11) results in the auxiliary stochastic equation

$$y = \pi_1 z_1 + \cdots + \pi_p z_p + y_T \tag{12.1.14}$$

which, when substituted into the observable equation (12.1.12), provides

$$c = \beta\pi_1 z_1 + \cdots + \beta\pi_p z_p + v_t. \tag{12.1.15}$$

Assuming the transitory components, y_T and c_T, have the classical properties described in (12.1.4)–(12.1.6) and further assuming the z's are independent of these components, ordinary least squares can be applied to (12.1.15) to obtain unbiased forecasts of consumption. If the marginal propensity of consumption is of intrinsic interest, however, some other method must be used since β is not identified.

One possible solution to the identification problem would be to estimate the auxiliary equation (12.1.14) by ordinary least squares and obtain consistent estimates, $\hat{\pi}_1, \hat{\pi}_2, \ldots, \hat{\pi}_p$ and, in turn, a consistent estimate of y,

$$\hat{y} = \hat{\pi}_1 z_1 + \cdots + \hat{\pi}_p z_p. \tag{12.1.16}$$

Substitution of $\hat{y}$ for y in Equation (12.1.12) and estimation of the resulting equation by ordinary least squares will provide a consistent estimate of β.

This last method for dealing with unobservable variables will likewise offer a solution to the classical errors-in-variables problem given that enough information is available to allow the specification of an incidental equation for each explanatory variable measured with error. Conceptually, the unobservable variables problem and errors-in-variables problem are inseparable.

The outline for the remainder of this chapter is as follows: In the next section the maximum likelihood solution to the errors-in-variables problem is discussed. In Section 12.3 two popular methods for estimating equations with errors-in-variables are shown to be instrumental variable methods, each giving rise to a distinct choice of instruments. In Section 12.4 the use of incidental equations for handling errors-in-variables (unobservable variables) is examined. Finally, Section 12.5 concludes with a summary and guide to further readings.

12.2 Maximum Likelihood Approach

A maximum likelihood approach to the errors-in-variables problem is to assume that the unobserved variables and their measurement errors have a multivariate normal distribution. To illustrate the basic concepts, consider the simple bivariate regression

$$y_t^* = \alpha + \beta x_t^*, \tag{12.2.1}$$

where

$$y_t^* = y_t + e_t \tag{12.2.2}$$

and

$$x_t^* = x_t + u_t. \tag{12.2.3}$$

The variables y_t^* and x_t^* are measured with error and have measurement errors e_t and u_t. Assume the vector $(x_t^*, y_t^*, u_t, e_t)'$ is distributed as a multivariate normal random variable with mean vector $(\mu_x, \alpha + \beta\mu_x, 0, 0)'$ and variance–covariance matrix

$$\Sigma = \begin{pmatrix} \sigma_{x^*}^2 & \sigma_{xy} & 0 & 0 \\ \sigma_{xy} & \sigma_{y^*}^2 & 0 & 0 \\ 0 & 0 & \sigma_u^2 & 0 \\ 0 & 0 & 0 & \sigma_e^2 \end{pmatrix}, \tag{12.2.4}$$

where $\sigma_{xy} = \beta\sigma_{x^*}^2$ and $\sigma_{y^*}^2 = \beta^2\sigma_{x^*}^2 + \sigma_e^2$.

The assumptions (12.2.1)–(12.2.4) imply that the observable random vector $(x_t, y_t)'$ has a bivariate normal distribution with mean vector $(\mu_x, (\alpha + \beta\mu_x))'$ and variance–covariance matrix

$$D = \begin{pmatrix} \sigma_{x^*}^2 + \sigma_u^2 & \beta\sigma_{x^*}^2 \\ \beta\sigma_{x^*}^2 & \sigma_{y^*}^2 + \sigma_e^2 \end{pmatrix}. \tag{12.2.5}$$

It is well known (see, for example, Anderson (1958, pp. 48–49)) that the maximum likelihood equations for the bivariate normal case are:

$$\hat{\mu}_x = \bar{x}, \tag{12.2.6}$$

$$\hat{\mu}_y = \bar{y}, \tag{12.2.7}$$

$$\hat{\sigma}_x^2 = \sum (x_t - \bar{x})^2/T, \tag{12.2.8}$$

$$\hat{\sigma}_y^2 = \sum (y_t - \bar{y})^2/T, \tag{12.2.9}$$

and

$$\hat{\sigma}_{xy} = \sum (x_t - \bar{x})(y_t - \bar{y})/T, \tag{12.2.10}$$

where $\bar{x}$ and $\bar{y}$ represent the sample means of x and y, respectively. In terms of the six parameters, μ_x, α, β, $\sigma_{x^*}^2$, σ_u^2, and σ_e^2 of the errors-in-variables model (12.2.1)–(12.2.3), the maximum likelihood equations are:

$$\hat{\mu}_x = \bar{x}, \tag{12.2.11}$$

$$\hat{\alpha} + \hat{\beta}\bar{x} = \bar{y}, \tag{12.2.12}$$

$$\hat{\sigma}_{x^*}^2 + \hat{\sigma}_u^2 = \sum (x_t - \bar{x})/T, \tag{12.2.13}$$

$$\hat{\beta}^2\hat{\sigma}_{x^*}^2 + \hat{\sigma}_e^2 = \sum (y_t - \bar{y})/T, \tag{12.2.14}$$

and

$$\hat{\beta}\hat{\sigma}_{x^*}^2 = \sum (x_t - \bar{x})(y_t - \bar{y})/T. \tag{12.2.15}$$

We thus have five equations in six unknowns. Except for μ_x, the parameters of the normally distributed errors-in-variables model are unidentified. Some additional information is needed. Assuming α and β are unknown, this means we must have *a priori* knowledge of σ_u^2 or σ_e^2 or the ratio $\lambda = \sigma_u^2/\sigma_e^2$. This information is not likely to be known in most applications, thus the practictioner is not likely to find the maximum likelihood approach very useful when confronted with the errors-in-variables problem. See Dhrymes (1978, Ch. 5) for more on the maximum likelihood approach.

12.3 Instrumental Variable Methods

Once the errors-in-variables problem is recognized as one where the regressor measured with error is contemporaneously correlated with the error term, the first estimation method that comes to mind is the instrumental variable method (Section 11.7). This method offers consistent estimation in the presence of the contemporaneous correlation problem.

It is not typically recognized that Wald's (1940) grouping method and Durbin's (1954) use of ranks are both instrumental variable methods. These two methods are discussed in the next two subsections, the emphasis being the recognition of these methods as instrumental variable methods and the specific forms that the instrumental variables take.

12.3.1 Wald's Grouping Method

Consider the simple regression model

$$y_t = \alpha + \beta x_t^* + e_t, \tag{12.3.1}$$

where x_t^* is measured with error, $x_t = x_t^* + u_t$. Wald (1940) suggested dividing the observations (x_t, y_t) into two groups of equal size according to the magnitude of the observed explanatory variable, x_t. Should there be an odd number of observations, the middle observation is deleted. Denote the sample means of the two groups by $(\bar{x}(1), \bar{y}(1))$, and $(\bar{x}(2), \bar{y}(2))$. Then an estimator of the slope is

$$\bar{\beta} = \frac{\bar{y}(2) - \bar{y}(1)}{\bar{x}(2) - \bar{x}(1)} \tag{12.3.2}$$

and an estimator of the intercept is

$$\bar{\alpha} = \bar{y} - \bar{x}\bar{\beta} = \bar{y}(1) - \bar{\beta}\bar{x}(1) = \bar{y}(2) - \bar{\beta}\bar{x}(2), \tag{12.3.3}$$

where $\bar{y}$ and $\bar{x}$ are the overall sample means of y and x. These estimators can be shown (see Exercise 12.2) to be equivalent to using instrumental variable estimation with the instrument, z_t, taking the values

$$z_t = \begin{cases} 1 & \text{if } (x_t, y_t) \text{ belongs to group one,} \\ 0 & \text{otherwise.} \end{cases} \tag{12.3.4}$$

Wald demonstrates that these estimators are consistent provided that: (1) the grouping is independent of the errors, e_t, and (2) the method of grouping ensures $\text{plim}|\bar{x}(2) - \bar{x}(1)| \neq 0$. To fulfill these conditions, the grouping cannot be assigned randomly because the second condition would be violated though the first would be satisfied. Strictly speaking, the first condition is violated, though the second is not, when assignment to groups is made according to the size of the observed explanatory variable. The grouping is not independent of the errors. Equivalently stated, the instrumental variable, z_t, is not independent of the error. One might hand wave on this issue by claiming, *a priori*, that the true explanatory values, x_t^*, are far enough apart relative to the error of measurement, u_t, so that the ranking obtained by using the observed values is the same as that which would have been obtained had the x_t^* been available. This is stringent prior information.

As an alternative to the Wald suggestion for grouping, other forms of information might be brought to bear. For example, in his permanent income hypothesis study, Friedman (1957) suggested connecting the means across dissimilar groups such as consumers across cities or occupations. This type of prior information amounts to specifying a dummy (instrumental) variable across two groups, the two groups being distinct and independent of the model's errors.

12.3.2 Durbin's Ranking Procedure

Assume that the ranking provided by the observed values, x_t, is always the same as that which would be obtained by using x_t^*. Durbin (1954) suggested using the ranks, $1, 2, \ldots, T$, of the observed values of the explanatory variable rather than the observations themselves. Assume for simplicity that the observations, x_t, are distinct. Let the instrumental variable, z_t, take the value of the rank of x_t. The estimator suggested for the slope coefficient is

$$\tilde{\beta} = \frac{\sum_i iy(i)}{\sum_i ix(i)}, \tag{12.3.5}$$

where $i = 1, 2, \ldots, T$, represents the rank of the ordered pairs $(x(i), y(i))$. An estimator of the intercept is

$$\tilde{\alpha} = \bar{y} - \tilde{\beta}\bar{x}. \tag{12.3.6}$$

Given that the ranking is independent of the equation's error term, these estimators are consistent.

12.4 The Use of Incidental Equations

A shortcoming of the grouping and ranking methods is the potential bias that may result from the lack of independence between the instrument chosen and the error terms of the equation. An alternative approach using information more attuned to economic theory is desirable. As illustrated in the introduction to this chapter, powerful identifying information may be incorporated in the errors-in-variables problem by specifying an additional equation which links the explanatory variable measured with error and observable variables. For example, permanent income could be specified as being largely determined by wealth, age, educational attainment, etc. Suppose that the observed regression equation is of the form

$$\mathbf{y} = \beta\mathbf{x} + \mathbf{e}, \tag{12.4.1}$$

where $\mathbf{y}$ and $\mathbf{x}$ are $T \times 1$ vectors of observations on the dependent and explanatory variables. Assume further that

$$\mathbf{x} = \mathbf{x}^* + \mathbf{u} \tag{12.4.2}$$

and

$$\mathbf{x}^* = Z\pi, \tag{12.4.3}$$

where Z is a $T \times p$ matrix of observations on p incidental variables and $\boldsymbol{\pi}$ is a $p \times 1$ vector of incidental parameters. Equation (12.4.3) is the incidental equation with its stochastic representation in terms of the observable variable being

$$\mathbf{x} = Z\pi + \mathbf{u}. \tag{12.4.4}$$

To illustrate this notation, consider (12.4.1) as Friedman's permanent income, consumption function with permanent income, x^*, being measured with error and reported as observed income, x. The matrix Z represents observations on the incidental variables, age, wealth, and education.

The present model can be written as the simultaneous equation system

$$\mathbf{y} = \beta\mathbf{x} + \mathbf{e}, \tag{12.4.5}$$

$$\mathbf{x} = Z\pi + \mathbf{u}. \tag{12.4.6}$$

(When the reader studies Chapter 19, an analogy will be seen between the incidental equation approach to errors-in-variables and simultaneous equations models.) One way to obtain an instrument for $\mathbf{x}$, $\hat{\mathbf{x}}$, is to apply ordinary least squares to Equation (12.4.6), obtain a consistent estimate of π, $\hat{\pi} = (Z'Z)^{-1}Z'\mathbf{x}$, and use this estimate to obtain a "purged" value of $\mathbf{x}$, $\hat{\mathbf{x}} = Z\hat{\pi}$. Instrumental variable estimation of the original equation (12.4.5) would then proceed by applying ordinary least squares to the "purged" equation

$$\mathbf{y} = \beta\hat{\mathbf{x}} + \mathbf{v}, \tag{12.4.7}$$

where $\mathbf{v} = \beta\mathbf{x} - \beta\hat{\mathbf{x}} + \mathbf{e}$. An estimator of β is then

$$\tilde{\beta} = (\hat{\mathbf{x}}'\hat{\mathbf{x}})^{-1}\hat{\mathbf{x}}'\mathbf{y} = \frac{\sum_t \hat{x}_t y_t}{\sum_t \hat{x}_t^2}. \tag{12.4.8}$$

This estimator, of course, will be consistent since a general property of instrumental variable estimators is consistency (Chapter 11). However, efficiency is not likewise guaranteed. To overcome this objection, Zellner (1970) describes a generalized least squares method of estimating the system (12.4.5)–(12.4.6) which is not only consistent but also is efficient. Briefly his procedure consists of minimizing the weighted sum of squares

$$S = \frac{1}{\sigma_u^2}(\mathbf{x} - Z\boldsymbol{\pi})'(\mathbf{x} - Z\boldsymbol{\pi}) + \frac{1}{\sigma_e^2}(\mathbf{y} - Z\boldsymbol{\pi}\beta)'(\mathbf{y} - Z\boldsymbol{\pi}\beta). \tag{12.4.9}$$

For further discussion of this method see Zellner (1970) and Judge *et al.* (1980).

12.5 Summary and Guide to Further Readings

In the simple bivariate regression model, the ordinary least squares estimator of the slope coefficient is asymptotically biased toward zero when the explanatory variable is measured with error. Levi (1973) extended the bivariate case to the multiple regression case where one explanatory variable is measured with error while the remaining explanatory variables are measured without error. He found that the ordinary least squares estimator of the coefficient of the variable measured with error is unambiguously biased toward zero despite the inclusion of the other explanatory variables measured without error. Also the direction of bias of the ordinary least squares estimators of the coefficients of the variables measured without error can be calculated given knowledge of the variance–covariance matrix of the observations. When more than one explanatory variable is measured with error, however, the direction of bias of the ordinary least squares estimators is not determinable in general.

The maximum likelihood approach to the errors-in-variables problem encounters an identification problem. The number of normal equations is exceeded by the number of unknown parameters. Only the availability of esoteric information on the population variance of the measurement errors allows estimation. The grouping method of Wald (1940) and the ranking method of Durbin (1954) are both instrumental variable methods. The most difficult task of these methods is the proper ordering of the observations.

Proper ordering will provide group selection (ranking) which maintains independence between the group (rank) of an observation and the model's error term. The best grouping and rank methods utilize economic reasoning to determine proper ordering.

An alternative to group and rank methods is the specification of an incidental equation which relates the variable measured with error to observable variables measured without error and specified by economic theory. Consistent estimation can proceed by purging the measurement error from the explanatory variable and applying ordinary least squares to the purged equation. This is simply an instrumental variable method but one where the instrument is, *a priori*, independent of the error term. Zellner (1970) describes an efficient method of estimation which minimizes a generalized sum of squares.

The Hausman (1978) test discussed in Section 18.3.3 can be used to determine if errors-in-variables bias might be a substantive problem in a given model. For the appropriate test statistic see Equation (18.3.16). The tests proposed by Wu (1973, 1974) for testing the independence of the regressors and error terms of a model are likewise applicable.

Goldberger (1972) discusses a maximum likelihood approach for estimating errors-in-variables models with incidental equations. Goldberger (1974) also has shown that alternative models of errors-in-variables can be treated as factor analysis models.

For some applications of errors-in-variables methods to the specification of economic relationships see Crockett (1960), Miller and Modigliani (1966), Chamberlain and Griliches (1974, 1975), and Roll (1969). The methodology of errors-in-variables extends to distributed lag problems. See Nerlove (1967) and Grether and Nerlove (1970) for further details.

12.6 Exercises

12.1. In the context of the simple errors-in-variables model, $y_t = \beta x_t^* + e_t$, where $x_t = x_t^* + u_t$, show that the ordinary least squares estimator of β is inconsistent:

$$\operatorname{plim} \hat{\beta} = \beta - \frac{\beta \sigma_u^2}{\sigma_x^2},$$

where $\sigma_x^2 = \operatorname{plim} \sum x_t^2/T$.

12.2. Show that the Wald estimators (12.3.2) and (12.3.3) are equivalent to instrumental variable estimators using the instrument defined in (12.3.4).

12.3. Verify that the estimator defined in (12.3.5) is the instrumental variable estimator of β where the instrument is the rank of the observations on the explanatory variable.

A very important model in finance (called the Market Model) is represented by

$$R_{jt} = a_j + \beta_j R^*_{\mathrm{mt}} + e_{jt},$$

where R_{jt} = the return on a security (stock) j for period t including both dividends and capital gains expressed as a fraction of the price of the security at the beginning of the period,

R^*_{mt} = "true" market return,

a_j = the risk free rate of return, and

β_j = beta coefficient of security j. If $\beta_j > 1$, the security is more volatile (riskier) than the market as a whole; if $\beta_j < 1$, the security is less volatile than the market; and $\beta_j = 1$ implies that security j has the same volatility as the market.

Roll (1969) has considered the effect of measurement error in the Market Model. Market indices such as Standard & Poor's 500 stock index are generally used as proxies for the "true" market return, but clearly they do not include all assets such as home mortgages and intangibles like human capital investment in education. Thus, Roll postulates

$$R_{\mathrm{mt}} = R^*_{\mathrm{mt}} + u_t,$$

where R_{mt} = the return on the Standard & Poor's 500 index.

Consider the following monthly data on the returns to Adolph Coors stock, R_{jt}, and Standard & Poor's 500 stock index, R_{mt}, for the period 2/77 through 9/79. Use this data to answer the following two questions.

Returns to Coors' Stock and Standard and Poor's 500 Index*

R_{jt}	R_{mt}	R_{jt}	R_{mt}
−1.895	−2.350	11.800	−1.372
−3.955	−0.050	1.020	5.798
3.575	−1.187	7.910	3.008
0.755	0.063	0.950	−0.322
−8.645	0.873	−27.620	−8.780
−4.335	1.284	7.840	2.110
−3.765	−2.126	2.190	1.920
−1.525	−1.156	8.150	6.063
−8.865	−2.212	−3.550	−4.767
0.075	0.968	0.150	5.853
−5.285	−0.102	6.880	0.670
−7.400	−4.420	1.050	−2.140
0.150	−2.050	1.930	4.250
1.180	2.950	10.680	1.310
3.180	8.968	6.490	5.730
1.130	0.848	−8.810	0.440

*SOURCE: Tables 2 and 3 in Mannino, K. (1980). Testing the efficient market theory; examining whether mutual funds 'beat the market'. Term paper submitted to the Department of Economics, Southern Methodist University, Dallas, TX.

12.4. Using the Coors data:
  (a) estimate the beta coefficient for Coors stock using ordinary least squares.
  (b) estimate the beta coefficient using Wald's method.
  (c) estimate the beta coefficient using Durbin's method.
  (d) test the hypotheses $H_0: \beta_j = 1$ versus $H_1: \beta_j \neq 1$ using the above three methods. Do your conclusions differ? How? Which method is to be preferred?

12.5. Use the Coors data and Hausman's test (see Equation (18.3.16)) to determine whether errors-in-variables bias appears to be a significant problem.

12.7 References

Anderson, T. W. (1958). *An Introduction to Multivariate Statistical Analysis*. New York: John Wiley.

Chamberlain, G. and Griliches, Z. (1974). Returns to schooling of brothers and ability as an unobservable variance component. Harvard Institute of Economic Research, Discussion Paper No. 340, Cambridge, MA.

Chamberlain, G. and Griliches, Z. (1975). Unobservables with a variance-components structure: ability, schooling, and the economic success of brothers. *International Economic Review*, **16**, 422–449.

Crockett, J. (1960). Technical note. In *Proceedings of the Conference on Consumption and Saving*. Edited by I. Friend and R. Jones. pp. 213–222. University of Pennsylvania, Philadelphia.

Dhrymes, P. (1978). *Introductory Econometrics*. New York: Springer-Verlag.

Durbin, J. (1954). Errors in variables. *Review of the International Statistics Institute*, **1**, 23–32.

Friedman, M. (1957). *A Theory of the Consumption Function*. Princeton, NJ: Princeton University Press.

Goldberger, A. S. (1972). Maximum likelihood estimation of regressions containing unobservable independent variables. *International Economic Review*, **13**, 1–15.

Goldberger, A. S. (1974). Unobservable variables in econometrics. In *Frontiers of Econometrics*. Edited by P. Zarembka. New York: Academic Press. Pp. 193–213.

Grether, D. M. and Nerlove, M. (1970). Some properties of "optimal" seasonal adjustment. *Econometrica*, **38**, 682–703.

Hausman, J. A. (1978). Specification tests in econometrics. *Econometrica*, **46**, 1251–2171.

Judge, G. G., Griffiths, W. E., Hill, R. C., and Lee, T. C. (1980). *The Theory and Practice of Econometrics*. New York: Wiley.

Levi, M. D. (1973). Errors in the variables bias in the presence of correctly measured variables. *Econometrica*, **41**, 985–986.

Malinvaud, E. (1970). *Statistical Methods of Econometrics*, 2nd ed. Amsterdam: North-Holland.

Miller, M. H. and Modigliani, F. (1966). Some estimates of the cost of capital to the electric utility industry, 1954–57. *American Economic Review*, **56**, 333–391.

Nerlove, M. (1967). Distributed lags and unobserved components in economic time series. In *Ten Economic Studies in the Tradition of Irving Fisher*. Edited by W. Fellner, New York: W. Fellner, C. A. Hall, Jr., T. C. Koopmans, J. P. Miller, M. Nerlove, R. Ruggles, P. A. Samuelson, H. Scarf, J. Tobin and H. C. Wallich.

Roll, R. (1969). Bias in fitting the Sharpe model to time series data. *Journal of Financial and Quantitative Analysis*, **4**, 271–289.

Stamp, J. (1929). *Some Economic Factors in Modern Life*. London: King and Son.

Wald, A. (1940). The fitting of straight lines if both variables are subject to errors. *Annals of Mathematical Statistics*, **11**, 284–300.

Wu, D. M. (1973). Alternative tests of independence between stochastic regressors and disturbances. *Econometrica*, **41**, 733–750.

Wu, D. M. (1974). Alternative tests of independence between stochastic regressors and disturbances: finite sample results. *Econometrica*, **42**, 529–546.

Zellner, A. (1970). Estimation of regression relationships containing unobservable independent variables. *International Economic Review*, **11**, 441–454.

PART III
SPECIAL TOPICS

The following six chapters constitute Part III of this book. This part will complete our discussion of the single equation linear regression model begun in Part I and continued in Part II. Unlike Part II on violations of the basic assumptions of the linear regression model, the topics discussed in this part are "special" in that there is little commonality among them. The subjects discussed are: extensions of the classical linear regression model (varying coefficient models and pooling time series and cross-sectional data models); methods used in special data circumstances (multicollinearity, qualitative and censored dependent variables, and distributed lags); and uncertainty in model specification and selection (Box–Cox transformation and the generalized likelihood ratio method.)

CHAPTER 13
Multicollinearity

13.1 Introduction

When using the linear statistical model, economists and other social scientists face a variety of problems that are caused by the nonexperimental nature of their disciplines. Several problems of this sort are discussed in this book and include uncertainty about model specification, both the form of the relationship between the variables and which variables should be included in the model (Chapter 18), the nature of the error process (Chapters 9 and 10), structural changes in the process generating the data (Chapters 14 and 15), and the problem discussed in the current chapter, multicollinearity.

Multicollinearity is a problem associated with the fact that nonexperimental scientists *observe* the values that both the independent and dependent variables take. This is in marked contrast to an experimental setting in which the values of the independent variables are *set* by the experimenter and the resulting values of only the dependent variable are observed. A regression analysis is, of course, an attempt to explain the variation in the dependent variable by the variation in the explanatory variables. In the experimental setting the researcher can set the values of the explanatory variables so that the values of each variable vary independently of the values of each of the other variables. In such a case the separate effects of each variable can be estimated precisely if sufficient care is taken in designing and executing the experiment. Frequently in nonexperimental situations, some explanatory variables exhibit little variation, or the variation they do exhibit is systematically related to variation in other explanatory variables. While it is usually the second of these cases that is labeled as multicollinearity, we will not distinguish between them as there is really no essential difference.

More formally, we will say that multicollinearity exists when one or more exact, or nearly exact, linear relationships exist among the sets of values we observe for the explanatory variables in a regression model. That is, there are one or more exact or nearly exact linear dependencies among the columns of the matrix X.

The primary statistical consequence of multicollinearity is that one or more of the estimated coefficients of the linear model may have large standard errors. Consequently the confidence intervals for the affected coefficients are wide and this means that the statistical analysis has left us uncertain about the effects of specific explanatory variables on the dependent variable. In fact, individual explanatory variables are often found to have no statistically significant effect on the dependent variable, though collectively they seem important given an overall test of significance. This reduces the usefulness of the estimated model. These consequences *may be* the result of a sample that is multicollinear and which simply does not permit us to obtain precise parameter estimates, despite the fact that the ordinary least squares estimator is still the best linear unbiased estimator and consistent if none of the other usual assumptions are violated.

In this chapter we will consider all the aspects of the multicollinearity problem. These include a careful consideration of the nature of multicollinearity and its statistical consequences, a survey of methods for determining when multicollinearity is present and severe, and a discussion of techniques that have been proposed for ameliorating the effects of working with multicollinear data sets.

13.2 The Nature and Statistical Consequences of Multicollinearity

As in previous chapters we denote the classical linear regression model (Definition 2.2.1) as

$$\mathbf{y} = X\boldsymbol{\beta} + \mathbf{e}, \tag{13.2.1}$$

where $\boldsymbol{\beta}$ is a $T \times 1$ vector of observations on the dependent variable, X is a nonstochastic $T \times K$ matrix of observations on K explanatory variables and $\mathbf{e}$ is a $T \times 1$ vector of independent and identically distributed random disturbances with means zero and variances σ^2, conditional on the values of X. Two features of these assumptions warrant comment. First, the X matrix is assumed to be nonstochastic. In the present context, however, one should recognize that nonexperimental scientists can not literally fix X in repeated trials. Faced with random X, scientists can assume the classical assumptions hold conditional on a specific realization of a random X, and proceed. Also note that we have not assumed the X matrix to be of full column rank. We will begin this section with a brief discussion of the case when X is *not* of full column rank K.

13.2.1 Exact Multicollinearity

Let the columns of the X matrix be denoted $\mathbf{x}_i$, $i = 1, \ldots, K$. Then *exact multicollinearity* is said to exist when there is *at least* one relation of the form

$$c_1\mathbf{x}_1 + c_2\mathbf{x}_2 + \cdots + c_K\mathbf{x}_K = \mathbf{0}, \tag{13.2.2}$$

where the constants c_i are not all equal to zero. The probability of observing a set of sample values for the explanatory variables for which relations like (13.2.2) hold is negligible in practice, though it would occur if "too many" dummy variables were included in a regression model or if $T < K$. If one or more relations like (13.2.2) do hold exactly then the X matrix is not of full column rank and the normal equations

$$X'X\boldsymbol{\beta} = X'\mathbf{y} \tag{13.2.3}$$

do not have a unique solution. Consequently the least squares estimation procedure breaks down in the sense that unique best linear unbiased estimators are not available for all of the K regression parameters. It is interesting that in this case unique best unbiased estimates do exist for certain linear functions of the parameters like $\mathbf{w}'\boldsymbol{\beta}$, where $\mathbf{w}$ is a $K \times 1$ vector of constants. It is shown in Theil (1971, pp. 147–152) that the unique best linear unbiased estimator of $\mathbf{w}'\boldsymbol{\beta}$ is $\mathbf{w}'\mathbf{b}^*$ where $\mathbf{b}^*$ is *any* solution to the normal equations, if $\mathbf{w}'$ is a linear combination of the rows of X. This situation is also considered in detail by Silvey (1969) who gives convenient expressions for determining whether or not the function $\mathbf{w}'\boldsymbol{\beta}$ is estimable and the variance of the estimate $\mathbf{w}'\mathbf{b}^*$ of such a function.

13.2.2 Near Exact Multicollinearity

It is unusual to encounter situations of exact multicollinearity in practice. More frequently the matrix X of observations on the explanatory variables is of full rank K but one or more *nearly* exact linear relations exist among the columns of X so that

$$c_1\mathbf{x}_1 + c_2\mathbf{x}_2 + \cdots + c_K\mathbf{x}_K \doteq \mathbf{0}. \tag{13.2.4}$$

The consequence of such relations is that, although unique best linear unbiased estimators exist for all the parameters $\boldsymbol{\beta}$, their estimated standard errors may be large, causing great uncertainty about the values of one or more parameters.

To see this, let A be the matrix whose columns are the orthonormal characteristic vectors of $X'X$ so that

$$A'X'XA = \Lambda, \tag{13.2.5}$$

where Λ is a diagonal matrix with nonzero characteristic roots $\lambda_1 \geq \lambda_2 \geq \cdots \geq \lambda_K$ along the diagonal. Since $A' = A^{-1}$, $AA' = A'A = I$. It follows that

$$X'X = A\Lambda A' \tag{13.2.6}$$

and

$$(X'X)^{-1} = A\Lambda^{-1}A' = \sum_{i=1}^{K} \lambda_i^{-1}\mathbf{a}_i\mathbf{a}_i'. \tag{13.2.7}$$

The last equality in (13.2.7) can be verified by defining $A = (\mathbf{a}_1, \mathbf{a}_2, \ldots, \mathbf{a}_K)$, where $\mathbf{a}_i$ is the characteristic vector associated with the characteristic root λ_i.

Using these results we can rewrite the covariance matrix of the ordinary least squares estimator as

$$\operatorname{cov}(\hat{\boldsymbol{\beta}}) = \sigma^2(X'X)^{-1} = \sigma^2 A\Lambda^{-1}A' = \sigma^2 \sum_{i=1}^{K} \lambda_i^{-1}\mathbf{a}_i\mathbf{a}_i'. \tag{13.2.8}$$

Using this expression, the variance of $\hat{\beta}_j$ can be written

$$\operatorname{var}(\hat{\beta}_j) = \sigma^2\left(\frac{a_{j1}^2}{\lambda_1} + \frac{a_{j2}^2}{\lambda_2} + \cdots + \frac{a_{jK}^2}{\lambda_K}\right). \tag{13.2.9}$$

Equation (13.2.9) summarizes what can be said about the precision of estimation of a specific parameter by ordinary least squares. Note that several factors are involved in determining the precision of estimation. First, the precision of estimation of any parameter is inversely related to the error variance σ^2. This is not surprising and simply reflects the fact that the greater the noise in the regression equation the less certain any statistical results will be.

Second, the variability in the values of the explanatory variables, as reflected in the values of the characteristic roots of $X'X$, affects the precision of estimation in two ways. If we measure the total variability of the explanatory variables by tr $X'X = \sum_{i=1}^{K} \lambda_i$, then an increase in total variability, everything else remaining constant including the relative magnitudes of the characteristic roots, will improve the precision of estimation by least squares. This can be seen by examining Equation (13.2.9) and simply imagining the value of any one characteristic root increasing holding everything else in the expression constant. How such a change might be achieved will be examined below. Also, the values of the characteristic roots affect the precision of estimation by their relative equality or inequality. Given that the total variability in the explanatory variables is fixed, the greater the relative inequality of the characteristic roots, the greater the potential loss of precision in estimation. That is, if λ_K is very small relative to the other characteristic roots, then the term $\sigma^2 a_{jK}^2/\lambda_K$ *may be* very large, implying that $\text{var}(\hat{\beta}_j)$ may be large also. Why some characteristic roots might be small and how the precision of estimation is affected will be thoroughly discussed. Finally, as is obvious from the preceding discussion, the other factor affecting the precision of estimation of a specific parameter are the magnitudes of the elements a_{jk}^2. Since A is orthonormal $\sum_{k=1}^{K} a_{jk}^2 = 1$, the question is how this weight is distributed among the individual elements. Note that this is important since a small value of a_{jk}^2 will offset the effect of a small λ_k. Our task in the sections below is to investigate the relations between these factors so that the nature of the multicollinearity problem is thoroughly understood.

13.2.3 Principal Components

In this and the following section we define and present the geometry of principal components. For convenience we will assume, unless otherwise stated, that the total variability in the explanatory variables is constant. A simple way to achieve this is to assume that the explanatory variables have been scaled so that $\mathbf{x}_i'\mathbf{x}_i = 1$ and thus tr $X'X = \sum_{i=1}^{K} \lambda_i = K$.

The matrix $Z = XA$ is called the matrix of principal components. The ith column of Z, $\mathbf{z}_i$, is called the ith principal component and has the property that $\mathbf{z}_i'\mathbf{z}_i = \lambda_i$. Due to the orthogonality of A we can write

$$X = ZA'$$

so that

$$\begin{aligned}\mathbf{x}_j &= Z\mathbf{a}_{(j)}' \\ &= a_{j1}\mathbf{z}_1 + a_{j2}\mathbf{z}_2 + \cdots + a_{jK}\mathbf{z}_K, \qquad j = 1, \ldots, K, \qquad (13.2.10)\end{aligned}$$

where $\mathbf{a}_{(j)}$ is the jth *row* of A.

Each column of X can be thought of as a vector in T dimensional space. Since A is nonsingular, the subspace spanned by the columns of X is also spanned by the columns of Z. Equation (13.2.10) indicates that each vector $\mathbf{x}_j$ can be written as a linear combination of the columns of Z with weights given by the appropriate elements from the jth *row* of A. Note that these elements are the same ones that appear in (13.2.9). Also recall that if the characteristic root λ_K, for example, is near zero then

$$\mathbf{z}_K = X\mathbf{a}_K \doteq \mathbf{0}.$$

This expression has two useful interpretations. First, since $X\mathbf{a}_K \doteq \mathbf{0}$ it follows that

$$a_{1K}\mathbf{x}_1 + a_{2K}\mathbf{x}_2 + \cdots + a_{KK}\mathbf{x}_K \doteq \mathbf{0}, \qquad (13.2.11)$$

so that the characteristic vector associated with a relatively small characteristic root specifies a near exact dependence among the columns of X and thus may indicate which variables are involved in the multicollinear relation. Alternatively, since $\mathbf{z}_K = \mathbf{X}\mathbf{a}_K$, if λ_K is small it implies that $\mathbf{z}_K \doteq \mathbf{0}$. From

(13.2.10) this implies that the columns of X almost fall in a $(K - 1)$-dimensional subspace.

Finally, note that if $\mathbf{z}_K$ is approximately a null vector, and if $|a_{jK}|$ is large relative to the other a_{jk}'s (recall that $\sum_{k=1}^{K} a_{jk}^2 = 1$) then from (13.2.10) $\mathbf{x}_j$ is almost a null vector and has little variation. Then from (13.2.9) $\hat{\beta}_j$ will have a relatively large sampling variance. On the other hand, if $|a_{jK}|$ is relatively small then $\mathbf{x}_j$ is unaffected by $\mathbf{z}_K$ and the near singularity of X does not affect the precision of estimation of β_j. The same reasoning extends to the case when more than one characteristic root is small. This points out that the presence of multicollinearity does not necessarily imply that all the estimated coefficients will be unreliable nor that regression analysis is futile. In the next section we will pursue in more detail the question of when multicollinearity is harmful.

13.2.4 The Geometry of Principal Components

Our analysis is still somewhat mechanical in the sense that the elements of the characteristic vectors and the characteristic roots have little intuitive meaning. This difficulty can be overcome with an alternative perspective on the problem. Since A is orthogonal we can reparametrize the linear statistical model as

$$\mathbf{y} = X\boldsymbol{\beta} + \mathbf{e} = XAA'\boldsymbol{\beta} + \mathbf{e} = Z\boldsymbol{\theta} + \mathbf{e}, \tag{13.2.12}$$

where $\boldsymbol{\theta} = A'\boldsymbol{\beta}$ and Z is the matrix of principal components. (Note that the principal components model (13.2.12) is not the same as the orthonormal reparameterization of Equation (7.2.2). In the orthonormal model the columns of Z have unit length such that $Z'Z = I$, while in the principal components model $Z'Z = \Lambda$.) The least squares estimator of $\boldsymbol{\theta}$ is

$$\hat{\boldsymbol{\theta}} = (Z'Z)^{-1}Z'\mathbf{y} = \Lambda^{-1}Z'\mathbf{y}. \tag{13.2.13}$$

The covariance matrix of $\hat{\boldsymbol{\theta}}$ is

$$E(\hat{\boldsymbol{\theta}} - \boldsymbol{\theta})(\hat{\boldsymbol{\theta}} - \boldsymbol{\theta})' = \sigma^2\Lambda^{-1}, \tag{13.2.14}$$

so that $\text{var}(\hat{\theta}_i) = \sigma^2\lambda_i^{-1}$. Consequently, in this reparametrized statistical model the variances of the $\hat{\theta}_i$ are inversely related to the values of the characteristic roots. Furthermore, if $\lambda_i > \lambda_j$ then θ_i will be more precisely estimable, relatively speaking, than θ_j since $\text{var}(\hat{\theta}_i)/\text{var}(\hat{\theta}_j) = \lambda_j/\lambda_i$.

Naturally the precision of estimation of the θ_i's directly affects the precision of estimation of the β_i's. Since $\boldsymbol{\theta} = A'\boldsymbol{\beta}$, $\boldsymbol{\beta} = A\boldsymbol{\theta}$, and

$$\hat{\boldsymbol{\beta}} = A\hat{\boldsymbol{\theta}} = (X'X)^{-1}X'\mathbf{y}$$

so

$$\text{cov}(\hat{\boldsymbol{\beta}}) = A\,\text{cov}(\hat{\boldsymbol{\theta}})A'.$$

Consequently (13.2.9) can be rewritten as

$$\operatorname{var}(\hat{\beta}_j) = a_{j1}^2 \operatorname{var}(\hat{\theta}_1) + a_{j2}^2 \operatorname{var}(\hat{\theta}_2) + \cdots + a_{jK}^2 \operatorname{var}(\hat{\theta}_K). \quad (13.2.15)$$

Now let us examine the geometry of the reparameterized statistical model and see what light is shed on the multicollinearity problem.

The relation $Z = XA$ is a linear mapping of the T rows of X, which we will now think of as "points" in a K-dimensional space, into a new K-dimensional space spanned by the basis vectors $\mathbf{a}_1, \mathbf{a}_2, \ldots, \mathbf{a}_K$. The rows of Z are the coordinates of the corresponding rows (points) of X using basis vectors $\mathbf{a}_1, \mathbf{a}_2, \ldots, \mathbf{a}_K$. That is, since $X' = AZ'$,

$$\begin{aligned} \mathbf{x}'_{(j)} &= A\mathbf{z}'_{(j)} \\ &= z_{j1}\mathbf{a}_1 + z_{j2}\mathbf{a}_2 + \cdots + z_{jK}\mathbf{a}_K. \end{aligned} \quad (13.2.16)$$

So that we may view this graphically, let $K = 2$ and consider Figure 13.2.1.

In Figure 13.2.1(a) we show the point $\mathbf{x}_{(1)} = (x_{11}, x_{12})$ in terms of the original and new coordinate systems. The vectors $\mathbf{e}_1$ and $\mathbf{e}_2$ are the unit basis vectors in the original coordinate system. In the new coordinate system, relative to axes $\mathbf{a}_1$ and $\mathbf{a}_2$, $\mathbf{x}_{(1)}$ has the coordinates $\mathbf{z}_{(1)} = (z_{11}, z_{12})$. In Figure 13.2.1(b) we consider the new coordinate system alone.

If all T sample points are plotted, and assuming for the moment that the variables have zero means (or have been adjusted for their means), though this is not essential, the sample scatter might resemble that in Figure 13.2.2. The scatter in panel (a) of Figure 13.2.2 represents a case where the values of the two regressor variables are positively correlated. We will call that scatter the data ellipse (or ellipsoid if $K > 2$). The new coordinate system with basis vectors $\mathbf{a}_1$ and $\mathbf{a}_2$ is convenient since the axes are in the direction of the major and minor axes of the data ellipse.

This representation of the X matrix is useful because it shows that the variation in the data need not be equal in all directions in the observation

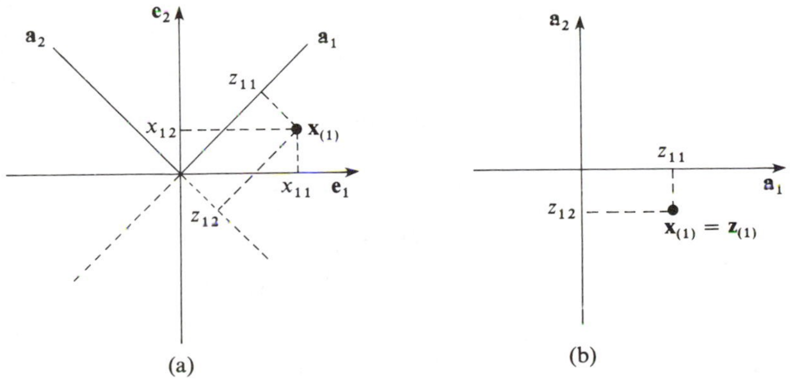

Figure 13.2.1 The point $\mathbf{x}_{(1)}$ in the old and new coordinate systems.

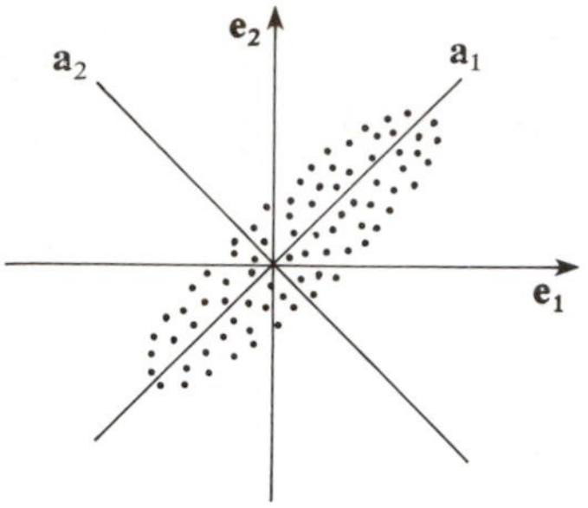

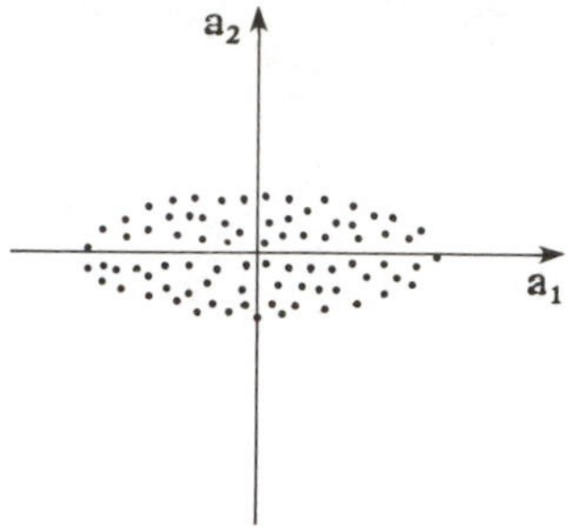

Figure 13.2.2 A sample scatter in the original and new spaces.

space. The nature of the variation in the data is revealed by the characteristic values of the $X'X$ matrix. Recall that

$$X'X\mathbf{a}_i = \lambda_i \mathbf{a}_i$$

so

$$\mathbf{a}_i' X'X\mathbf{a}_i = \lambda_i$$

or

$$\mathbf{z}_i'\mathbf{z}_i = \lambda_i.$$

Thus $\lambda_i = \sum_{t=1}^T z_{ti}^2$, and this can be represented geometrically as the sum of squares of the projections of the T points $\mathbf{x}_{(1)}, \ldots, \mathbf{x}_{(T)}$ onto the $\mathbf{a}_i$ axis. Thus the characteristic roots of $X'X$ measure the variability of the data *in the directions* of the axes of the ellipsoid.

Now let us return again to the interpretation of the elements of the characteristic vectors of $X'X$. Assume that $T = 4$ and $K = 2$ and the data scatter is as illustrated in Figure 13.2.3(a). If we are interested in estimating the parameters of the transformed model (13.2.12) then we must consider the data scatter relative to the coordinate axes $\mathbf{a}_1$ and $\mathbf{a}_2$, as shown in Figure 13.2.3(b). In this case, λ_2, the variability of the data scatter in the direction of $\mathbf{a}_2$, is small relative to λ_1. If we were concerned with estimating the parameters of the transformed model, θ_1 and θ_2, it is clear that θ_1 would be estimated relatively precisely as compared to θ_2. In the β-space

$$\operatorname{var}(\hat{\beta}_1) = \sigma^2\left(\frac{a_{11}^2}{\lambda_1} + \frac{a_{12}^2}{\lambda_2}\right), \tag{13.2.17a}$$

$$\operatorname{var}(\hat{\beta}_2) = \sigma^2\left(\frac{a_{21}^2}{\lambda_1} + \frac{a_{22}^2}{\lambda_2}\right). \tag{13.2.17b}$$

The relative precision of estimation of β_1 and β_2 depends on the magnitudes of the a_{ij}'s. The point $\mathbf{a}_1$ in Figure 13.2.3 has coordinates (a_{11}, a_{21}). Since $\mathbf{a}_1$ has unit length, a_{11} is the cosine of the angle between $\mathbf{e}_1$ and $\mathbf{a}_1$, and a_{21} is the

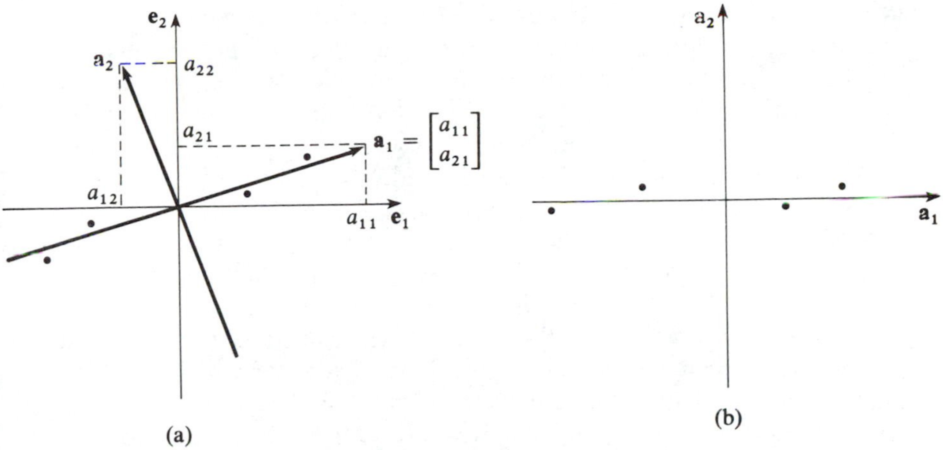

13.2.3 A sample of data.

cosine of the angle between $\mathbf{e}_2$ and $\mathbf{a}_1$. In general it follows that a_{ij} is the cosine between $\mathbf{e}_i$ and $\mathbf{a}_j$. The closer a_{ij} is to 1, i.e., the larger the cosine, the smaller the angle between $\mathbf{e}_i$ and $\mathbf{a}_j$. Thus, in Figure 13.2.3, a_{22} is large since $\mathbf{a}_2$ and $\mathbf{e}_2$ point in nearly the same direction. This combined with the fact that λ_2 is relatively small, means that β_2 will be less precisely estimated than β_1 (since a_{11} is large and a_{12} small). Thus, the parameter β_2 is estimated relatively imprecisely because $\mathbf{e}_2$ is strongly oriented in the direction of a minor axis of the data ellipse, $\mathbf{a}_2$.

Consider now the data scatter in Figure 13.2.4. The scatter is such that $\mathbf{a}_1$ forms a 45° angle with $\mathbf{e}_1$. While the data are in the same relation to $\mathbf{a}_1$ and $\mathbf{a}_2$, so the values of λ_1 and λ_2 are the same as in Figure 13.2.3, and thus the total variability in the data is unchanged, the values of the elements of the characteristic vectors must change. Specifically, since the "points" $\mathbf{a}_1$ and $\mathbf{a}_2$ must fall on the unit circle, $\mathbf{a}_1 = (\sqrt{2}/2, \sqrt{2}/2)$ and $\mathbf{a}_2 = (-\sqrt{2}/2, \sqrt{2}/2)$. Thus, $\text{var}(\hat{\beta}_1) = \text{var}(\hat{\beta}_2)$ using (13.2.17). Even though the coefficients are estimated equally precisely, due to the "equal" orientation of the data in the

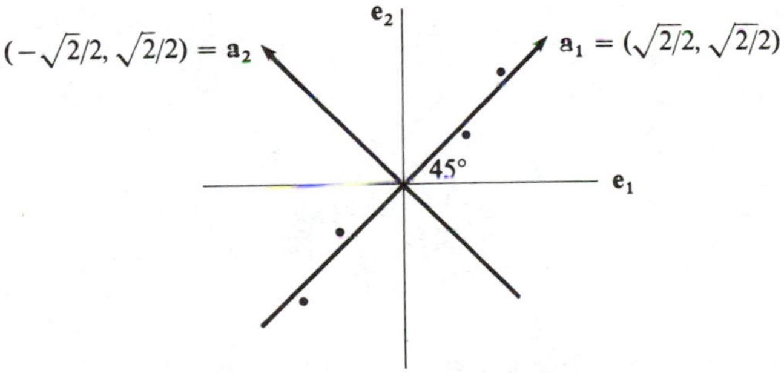

Figure 13.2.4 A sample of data.

original observation space, multicollinearity must still be considered a potential source of difficulty due to the nonsphericalness of the data ellipsoid.

These examples illustrate that it is the presence of relatively unequal characteristic roots of the $X'X$ matrix that indicate poor overall sample design. This is shown most clearly by the fact that the parameters θ_i of the transformed model cannot be estimated equally precisely if the characteristic roots are not all equal. The examples also make the following comments pertinent. First, note that multicollinearity need not be a problem even if the data scatter is very elongated. If a parameter of interest is associated with a variable such that a "long" axis of the data ellipse is oriented in its direction, then it will be relatively precisely estimated. The same holds for any linear combination of parameters that involves only relatively precisely estimated parameters θ_i in the transformed space. That is, the linear combination of parameters $\mathbf{c}'\boldsymbol{\beta}$ can be estimated relatively precisely if the transformed linear combination $\mathbf{v}'\boldsymbol{\theta}$, where $\mathbf{c}'\boldsymbol{\beta} = \mathbf{c}'AA'\boldsymbol{\beta} = \mathbf{c}'A\boldsymbol{\theta} = \mathbf{v}'\boldsymbol{\theta}$ involves primarily θ_i's that can be estimated relatively precisely.

Second, a word must be said about what "relatively precisely estimated" means. We have said that if $\lambda_i > \lambda_j$ then θ_i will be relatively more precisely estimated by ordinary least squares than θ_j. The other factor that affects the precision of estimation is σ^2, which measures the variation in the dependent variable about its expectation. If σ^2 is large relative to the characteristic roots then *none* of the coefficients may be estimated very precisely. Since the variation in the data matrix X is measured by the characteristic roots we can say that if the variation in the dependent variable, as measured by σ^2, is large relative to the variation in the explanatory variables, as measured perhaps by $|X'X| = \prod_{i=1}^{K} \lambda_i$ or $\operatorname{tr}(X'X) = \sum_{i=1}^{K} \lambda_i$, then least squares estimates may not be precise but this does *not* imply that multicollinearity is a source of difficulty. Conversely, this also means that the presence of "small" characteristic roots does not by itself imply multicollinearity. It is the inequality of the characteristic roots that characterizes multicollinearity.

A note of caution must be injected at this point. Characteristic roots and vectors can be affected by changing the scale in which independent variables are measured as well as by other reparameterizations. One should not believe, however, that the fundamental difficulties associated with the use of multicollinear data can be "solved" by simply rescaling the variables or otherwise reparameterizing the model. To facilitate our discussion of different patterns of multicollinearity, and to avoid the problem just mentioned, it is useful to think of the regressor variables as being scaled so that $\mathbf{x}_j'\mathbf{x}_j = 1$ and thus $\operatorname{tr}(X'X) = \sum_{i=1}^{K} \lambda_i = K$.

The two simple cases illustrated in Figures 13.2.3 and 13.2.4 had "equal" multicollinearity since the characteristic roots for the two data scatters were the same, though the data had different orientations. The rotation of the data scatter maintained constant variability but forced a change in the characteristic vectors, indicating changes in the parameters and linear combinations of parameters that could be estimated relatively precisely. A consequence of this observation is, of course, that it is possible to change the scatter of data without altering its orientation in the observation space. Consider, for example, adding another point to the data scatter represented in panel (b) of Figure 13.2.3. Add the point so that it, say $\mathbf{x}_{T+1}$, lies *on* the $\mathbf{a}_1$ axis. That is, let $\mathbf{x}_{T+1} = l\mathbf{a}_1$, where l is a constant. It can be shown, see Exercise 13.2.1, that the new characteristic root associated with $\mathbf{a}_1$ is $\lambda_1 + l^2$, and $\mathbf{a}_1$ is still the associated characteristic vector of the new, augmented design matrix, and thus points in the direction of the major axis of the rotated data ellipsoid. This also makes clear that if one had the option of adding a single observation in a multicollinear situation, one could improve the estimation of a particular parameter θ_i of the transformed model by adding the point along the associated characteristic vector, and as far out as possible. This would leave all the characteristic roots but the one unaffected, improving the precision of estimation of the selected θ_i.

To summarize then, multicollinearity is a condition manifested by the data ellipsoid being nonspherical. Its consequences are that if a variable, $\mathbf{x}_i$, and its basis vector, $\mathbf{e}_i$, are oriented in a direction of little variation, say $\mathbf{a}_K$, then the corresponding parameter, β_i, will be estimated relatively imprecisely. For example, if $\mathbf{e}_1$ is strongly oriented toward $\mathbf{a}_2$, and λ_2 is relatively small, then β_1 will be estimated relatively imprecisely. The actual precision of estimation depends in addition on the relation between the variation in the dependent variable and the total variation in the explanatory variables. The greater the variation in the data relative to σ^2, other things staying the same, the more precise ordinary least squares estimators will be.

13.3 Detection of the Presence and Form of Multicollinearity

A great many techniques have been proposed for detecting the presence and form of multicollinearity. In this section we discuss this important aspect of the multicollinearity problem. Our objective is to determine if relationships among the explanatory variables in the model cause ordinary least squares estimators of the regression parameters to be so imprecise that they do not provide sufficiently reliable estimates for decisionmaking purposes. Given the results of the previous section, the analysis of the characteristic roots and vectors of $X'X$ will reveal all the information that exists in the data about the relative precision of estimation of the parameters of the model. Before considering this analysis, however, we briefly note and critique traditional approaches for examining multicollinearity.

By far the most common technique for detecting multicollinearity is inspection of the simple sample correlations between the explanatory variables. If any pairwise correlation is large, say 0.8 or 0.9, then multicollinearity is deemed to be present. This sort of reasoning does not provide much useful information. Only pairwise relations can be detected by this method and not the more general interrelationships among variables. Also no clue is given by the simple correlations to the effect of the multicollinearity on the precision of estimation. A second popular technique is to consider the determinant of the sample correlation matrix of the explanatory variables. This determinant has a value between zero, when there exists one or more perfect linear dependences among the variables, and one, when all the correlations between regressors are zero. Multicollinearity is taken to be more serious the closer the determinant is to zero. Once again this technique provides little usable information since a small value of the determinant can be produced by many types and forms of interdependencies. Another, and somewhat more useful technique is to estimate auxiliary regressions. That is, regress each of the explanatory variables on all, or subsets of, the other $(K - 1)$ regressors. If the R^2 from one or more of these regressions is high then the linear dependencies between the regressors are indicated. If there is but a single linear dependence, the fitted regressions may in fact indicate which variables are involved. If more than a single linear dependence exists, however, the auxiliary regressions themselves may suffer from multicollinearity so that the nature of the relations among the variables can not be sorted out from the coefficients of the auxiliary regressions. These techniques are of course quickly and easily used but do not represent a systematic and exhaustive approach to the problem. We now turn to such an analysis.

Recall that a specific parameter, say β_j, will be relatively imprecisely estimated when $\mathbf{e}_j$ is oriented in the observation space in a direction of little variation in the data ellipsoid. Also recall that a_{jk} is the direction cosine between $\mathbf{e}_j$, the axis of the variable $\mathbf{x}_j$, and $\mathbf{a}_k$, the basis vector associated with λ_k. Consequently if $|a_{jk}|$ is relatively large and λ_k relatively small then $\mathbf{x}_j$ is oriented in a direction of little variation and β_j will be estimated relatively imprecisely. It is often useful also, however, to investigate which independent variables are linearly related. This may be possible in some cases by simply considering the independent variables directly. In cases where the relationships are complex, however, inspection of the variables may not be sufficient.

A useful starting point is to arrange the squares of the elements of the characteristic vectors in a table as illustrated below. Each column

	β_1	β_2	$\cdots$	β_K
λ_1	a_{11}^2	a_{21}^2	$\cdots$	a_{K1}^2
λ_2	a_{12}^2	a_{22}^2	$\cdots$	a_{K2}^2
λ_3	a_{13}^2	a_{23}^2	$\cdots$	a_{K3}^2
$\vdots$			$\vdots$	
λ_K	a_{1K}^2	a_{2K}^2	$\cdots$	a_{KK}^2

in this table contains the squares of the elements of the columns of A', and thus the elements of A that enter the expressions for the variances of specific coefficients as indicated by the column headings. The rows of the matrix are the squares of the elements of the characteristic vector associated with the indicated characteristic root. Recall that the sum of any row or column is one. A specific coefficient, say β_j, will be relatively imprecisely estimated when one or more of the elements a_{jk}^2 is relatively large *and* associated with a characteristic root λ_k that is relatively small. This information then is provided by examining the columns of the table. By examining the *rows* of the table we may learn about the nature of the relationships between explanatory variables. Consider for a moment a situation when there is but one relatively small characteristic root, λ_K. Suppose further that a_{1K}^2, a_{2K}^2 and a_{KK}^2 were large relative to the other elements in the last row of the table and their sum near one. This would imply that it is a near linear dependence between $\mathbf{x}_1$, $\mathbf{x}_2$ and $\mathbf{x}_K$ that is the source of the multicollinearity problem since, using (13.2.11), $a_{1K}\mathbf{x}_1 + a_{2K}\mathbf{x}_2 + a_{KK}\mathbf{x}_K \doteq \mathbf{0}$. This expression then reveals a relation among $\mathbf{x}_1$, $\mathbf{x}_2$ and $\mathbf{x}_K$ that can be inspected to determine whether there is a systematic relation among those variables that can be explained or whether the relation is a sampling "accident" and does not represent important and useful information.

The format in the above table can be made easier to use as follows. Recall from Equation (13.2.9) that

$$\operatorname{var}(\hat{\beta}_j) = \sigma^2 \sum_{k=1}^{K} \frac{a_{jk}^2}{\lambda_k} = \sigma^2 \phi_j, \tag{13.3.1}$$

where ϕ_j is implicitly defined in (13.3.1) as $\operatorname{var}(\hat{\beta}_j)/\sigma^2$. Then if each element in the jth column is divided by its corresponding characteristic root, and then divided by ϕ_j, the resulting table indicates the proportions of the variance of each coefficient that are associated with a particular characteristic root. For example, the term in the kth row and the jth column of the resulting table would be

$$\frac{\dfrac{a_{jk}^2}{\lambda_k}}{\displaystyle\sum_{k=1}^{K} \frac{a_{jk}^2}{\lambda_k}} = \frac{a_{jk}^2}{\lambda_k \phi_j}. \tag{13.3.2}$$

If multicollinearity is adversely affecting the precision of estimation of a particular parameter, then the terms like (13.3.2) in the rows of the table corresponding to small characteristic roots will be large. See Belsley *et al.* (1980) for further discussion and examples of how to use this diagnostic technique.

The same sort of reasoning *may be* usefully carried out for two or more relatively small characteristic roots although it is usually the case that the specific linear relations like (13.2.11) become difficult to interpret. The reason for this is that the characteristic vectors associated with the relatively small, and presumably near zero, characteristic roots span a subspace ("nearly" the null space of $X'X$) that contains the vectors of constants $\mathbf{c}' = (c_1, \ldots, c_K)$ that define the relations among the variables that "produced" the small characteristic roots. Thus, while the elements of the characteristic vectors will indicate which variables are involved in the several linear relations, the exact relations are unlikely to be directly identifiable from the elements of the relevant characteristic vectors. This is especially true when the linear relations "overlap" in the sense that one or more of the explanatory variables are involved in one or more separate relationships, which is what we would generally expect to occur with economic variables that are related in a variety of ways.

The above analysis is complete in the sense that using it one can identify the extent and severity of multicollinearity and whether the nonsphericalness of the data ellipsoid permits relatively precise estimation of specific parameters. A more difficult task is to determine, from the data alone, the nature of the relationships that exist between the explanatory variables that are the source of the multicollinearity. Inspection of the elements of the characteristic vectors associated with relatively small characteristic roots, or the use of auxiliary regressions, can identify the set of variables that are involved in the dependencies but not, usually, their exact form. Now, given that the form and extent of the multicollinearity has been examined and it has been concluded to be harmful to the analysis, we must examine what, if anything, can be done to improve the parameter estimates.

13.4 Improved Estimation in the Context of Multicollinearity

When multicollinearity is determined to be a problem, in the sense that ordinary least squares estimates of important parameters are considered too imprecise to be useful, the conventional remedy is to add more information to the existing sample. The information may be additional sample observations or in the form of restrictions on the parameter space. In this section we review two well-known estimation techniques, principal components and ridge regression, that have been proposed specifically for dealing with multicollinearity. As we shall see, they do not provide complete satisfactory solutions to the problem. Before turning to these specialized estimation techniques, let us briefly review the more traditional ways of dealing with multicollinearity.

The most obvious solution to the multicollinearity problem is to obtain more sample data. Using the analysis in Section 13.2 it can be determined what values the explanatory variables should take in order to increase specific characteristic roots of the design matrix and thus improve the precision of estimation. Unfortunately, economists usually have difficulty obtaining more sample data and even if they can, they rarely have the ability to specify the values of the independent variables. Consequently, this remedy is not always possible.

An alternative to using additional sample information is to use nonsample information in the form of restrictions on single parameters or linear combinations of parameters. The sampling consequences of these remedies are well known for our study of the various forms of restricted least squares in Chapter 6. See Fomby and Hill (1978) for an example of the effects of using nonsample information to deal with multicollinearity. Recall that combining restrictions on the parameter space with the sample data, using the restricted least squares estimator, mixed estimation or inequality restricted least squares, produces estimators with smaller risk than ordinary least squares over the portion of the parameter space where the restrictions are true, or nearly so, but with larger risk over the remainder of the parameter space. Since nonsample information is uncertain, its use may or may not improve estimator performance in repeated sampling, though its use does ensure that the variances of the parameter estimates are reduced. Recall also that deciding to use or not use the nonsample information using a hypothesis test of some sort is not a good solution to the problem, since the resulting pretest estimator has risk greater than the ordinary least squares estimator over a large portion of the parameter space. One especially dangerous approach to "curing" multicollinearity is to delete, on the basis of t-values, one or more variables involved in a multicollinear relation from a model, a stepwise regression routine of some sort or simply on an *ad hoc* basis. While the standard errors of the parameter estimates in the reduced model will certainly be lower (but only conditionally correct), the omission of relevant explanatory variables simply because the data will not allow precise estimation of their parameters is unsatisfactory. Using data to help specify a model that is going to be estimated using the same data is not a good statistical procedure, though, of course, it is widely done. For further discussion of model specification procedures that use sample data see Chapter 18.

Having made these comments, and recalling the properties of the Stein-like rules discussed in Chapter 7, it would be logical to assume that using a Stein-rule to combine uncertain, nonsample information with the data would be a potential remedy for multicollinearity since it is known to provide a risk improvement over the ordinary least squares estimator. While this is true, using a Stein-rule when multicollinearity is present is not without its difficulties. Recall that the Stein-rule's shrinkage factor "a" must fall in a specific interval (see Section 7.4) for minimaxity. Under squared error loss, the upper bound of that interval varies directly with the magnitude of the smallest characteristic root of $X'X$. Thus, if multicollinearity is severe, and λ_K is relatively small, then the Stein-rule will not be very different from the ordinary least squares estimator, implying that it may provide little risk improvement over ordinary least squares. Furthermore, the uneven magnitudes of the characteristic roots of $X'X$ may prevent the necessary condition, that $\lambda_K \operatorname{tr} \Lambda^{-1} > 2$ from being satisfied so that the application of a Stein-rule is not feasible. These comments apply directly only to Stein-like estimator (7.4.4) under squared error loss. For other loss functions, or for different members from the class of minimax estimators, the problem may not hold.

For further discussion of the effects of multicollinearity on members from the class of minimax estimators, see Judge *et al.* (1980, Chapter 12) and Hill and Ziemer (1982, 1984).

13.4.1 Principal Components Regression

One estimation technique that is widely discussed as a means for dealing with multicollinear data is principal components regression. As in Section 13.2, consider the transformed regression model

$$\mathbf{y} = X\boldsymbol{\beta} + \mathbf{e} = XAA'\boldsymbol{\beta} + \mathbf{e} = Z\boldsymbol{\theta} + \mathbf{e}, \tag{13.4.1}$$

where A is the $K \times K$ matrix whose columns are the orthonormal characteristic vectors of $X'X$ and ordered according to the magnitudes of the characteristic roots $\lambda_1 \geq \lambda_2 \geq \cdots \geq \lambda_K$, and $Z = XA$ is the matrix of principal components. The ith principal component is $\mathbf{z}_i = X\mathbf{a}_i$, the ith column of Z, and has the property that

$$\mathbf{z}_i'\mathbf{z}_i = \mathbf{a}_i'X'X\mathbf{a}_i = \lambda_i. \tag{13.4.2}$$

Suppose for a moment that the columns of X obey J linearly independent restrictions so that X has rank $K - J$ and consequently

$$\lambda_{K-J+1} = \cdots = \lambda_K = 0. \tag{13.4.3}$$

This means of course that the matrix X is only of rank $K - J$ and thus least squares can not be used to produce best linear unbiased estimator for all K regression parameters. In the transformed model (13.4.1) partition Z into two parts according to whether the associated characteristic roots are zero or not as $Z = [Z_1 \vdots Z_2]$. Using (13.4.2) the last J principal components must be null vectors. Consequently the transformed model (13.4.1) can be written as

$$\begin{aligned}\mathbf{y} = Z\boldsymbol{\theta} + \mathbf{e} &= [Z_1 \quad Z_2]\begin{bmatrix}\boldsymbol{\theta}_1 \\ \boldsymbol{\theta}_2\end{bmatrix} + \mathbf{e} \\ &= [Z_1 \quad 0]\begin{bmatrix}\boldsymbol{\theta}_1 \\ \boldsymbol{\theta}_2\end{bmatrix} + \mathbf{e} \\ &= \mathbf{Z}_1\boldsymbol{\theta}_1 + \mathbf{e}.\end{aligned} \tag{13.4.4}$$

The least squares estimator of $\boldsymbol{\theta}_1$ is $\hat{\boldsymbol{\theta}}_1 = (Z_1'Z_1)^{-1}Z_1'\mathbf{y}$ and is best linear unbiased, but $\boldsymbol{\theta}_2$ can not be estimated as it does not appear in the model. The deletion of the variables Z_2 from the model can equivalently be thought of as specifying $\boldsymbol{\theta}_2$ to be zero. Consequently, since

$$\boldsymbol{\theta} = A'\boldsymbol{\beta}$$

or

$$\begin{bmatrix}\boldsymbol{\theta}_1 \\ \boldsymbol{\theta}_2\end{bmatrix} = \begin{bmatrix}A_1' \\ A_2'\end{bmatrix}\boldsymbol{\beta},$$

specifying $\boldsymbol{\theta}_2$ to be zero implies $\mathbf{A}_2'\boldsymbol{\beta} = \mathbf{0}$. These J restrictions on the parameter vector $\boldsymbol{\beta}$ can be used along with the sample data to obtain parameter estimates for the complete $\boldsymbol{\beta}$ vector with the usual properties of restricted least squares estimators. Alternatively, since

$$\boldsymbol{\beta} = A\boldsymbol{\theta} = [A_1 \quad A_2]\begin{bmatrix}\boldsymbol{\theta}_1 \\ \boldsymbol{\theta}_2\end{bmatrix} = A_1\boldsymbol{\theta}_1 + A_2\boldsymbol{\theta}_2$$

we can obtain the estimates of $\boldsymbol{\beta}$ as

$$\hat{\boldsymbol{\beta}} = A_1\hat{\boldsymbol{\theta}}_1 + A_2\mathbf{0} \tag{13.4.5}$$

since $\boldsymbol{\theta}_2$ has been assumed to be zero. It is not difficult to show that this estimator is equivalent to

$$\hat{\boldsymbol{\beta}} = (X'X)^+X'\mathbf{y} = (A\Lambda^+A')X'\mathbf{y},$$

where

$$\Lambda^+ = \begin{bmatrix}\Lambda_1^{-1} & 0 \\ 0 & 0\end{bmatrix}$$

is a generalized inverse of Λ and Λ_1 is a diagonal matrix whose elements are the nonzero characteristic roots of $X'X$ and $(X'X)^+ = A\Lambda^+A'$ is the generalized inverse of $X'X$.

To summarize then, if exact multicollinearity is present in the design matrix X then principal components regression represents a way to obtain estimates of the complete parameter vector. The estimation rule is biased for $\boldsymbol{\beta}$ *unless* $\boldsymbol{\theta}_2 = \mathrm{A}_2'\boldsymbol{\beta} = \mathbf{0}$. Essentially principal components regression in this case represents a mechanical way of augmenting the sample data with enough restrictions on the parameter space to obtain estimates of the complete $\boldsymbol{\beta}$ vector.

Suppose, however, that the X matrix is of full rank but one or more *near* exact linear dependencies exist and ordinary least squares will produce best linear unbiased estimates. Suppose in the absence of any other nonsample information, we again partition the matrix of principal components into two parts and again delete the J principal components contained in Z_2. Again this is equivalent to assuming that $\boldsymbol{\theta}_2 = \mathbf{0}$. The estimator $\hat{\boldsymbol{\theta}}_1$ is still best linear unbiased due to the orthogonality of Z_1 and Z_2. The estimator (13.4.5) for $\boldsymbol{\beta}$ thus is the principal components estimator and is simply the restricted least squares estimator of $\boldsymbol{\beta}$ subject to the ad hoc restrictions $A_2'\boldsymbol{\beta} = \mathbf{0}$, where A_2 are the characteristic vectors associated with the deleted components Z_2. Unfortunately the restrictions $A_2'\boldsymbol{\beta} = \mathbf{0}$ are not likely to be true and thus the principal components estimator is likely to be biased. Nevertheless, if the restrictions are "nearly" true, the principal components estimator may have lower risk than the least squares estimator as discussed in Chapter 6. In fact it is not difficult to show that, if J components are deleted the principal components estimator has smaller mean square error if

$$\sum_{i=K-J+1}^{K} \frac{\lambda_i\theta_i^2 - \sigma^2}{\lambda_i} < 0, \tag{13.4.6}$$

where the indexing here simply refers to the deleted components and not necessarily those associated with the smallest characteristic roots (see Exercise 13.4). The difficulty with (13.4.6) is of course that it is unlikely that one would know *a priori* that this condition holds.

Given this discussion it becomes apparent that the decision of whether and how to delete one or more principal components is the difficult question. It should also be obvious, given the discussion in Chapter 6, that there are *no* criteria for deleting principal components, and thus imposing restrictions on the $\boldsymbol{\beta}$ space, that *guarantee* a risk improvement over least squares since the true $\boldsymbol{\beta}$ values are unknown. Keeping these reservations in mind let us discuss the two primary methods that have been proposed for selecting which principal components to delete. First, one might delete components associated with relatively small characteristic roots. The motivation for this rule is twofold. Small characteristic roots imply a near exact linear dependence in the *sample*, and, it is hoped, the associated characteristic vector provides a restriction on the parameter space that is nearly true. Also, since the variation in the data is measured by the characteristic roots, deletion of components associated with only the smallest characteristic roots preserves as much variation in the data as possible. Despite the reasonableness of this criteria, the decision to delete one or more principal components on this basis in no way guarantees that the resulting restrictions will be good ones, in the sense of providing a risk improvement.

A second procedure is to test the restrictions implied by the deletion of one or more components using a classical or mean square error test. One strategy in fact, would be to sequentially test restrictions implied by the deletion of components associated with increasingly larger characteristic roots. Components implying restrictions that cannot be accepted as hypotheses, of course, would not be deleted. The negative aspects of such a pretesting scheme are clear from the discussion in Chapter 7. One advantage of the pretesting scheme, however, is that at least the pretest estimator does not have unbounded risk. Another potential way to use principal components regression is to combine the sample information with a set of ad hoc principal component restrictions using a Stein-like rule. If the necessary characteristic root conditions are satisfied, the resulting estimator will have lower risk than the least squares estimator. The qualifications associated with this procedure are the data specific nature of the restrictions and the fact that the necessary conditions for the Stein-rules to be minimax may not be satisfied for some choices of loss functions when multicollinearity is severe.

13.4.2 Ridge Regression

Perhaps the most widely discussed biased estimation technique is ridge regression, proposed by Hoerl and Kennard (1970a, 1970b). Surveys of the literature devoted to ridge regression may be found in Vinod (1978), Judge *et al.* (1980, Section 12.6) and Vinod and Ullah (1981), so the discussion here will be relatively brief. The ridge *family* of estimators for the parameter vector $\boldsymbol{\beta}$ in the linear model (13.2.1) is given by

$$\mathbf{b}(k) = (X'X + kI)^{-1}X'\mathbf{y}, \tag{13.4.7}$$

where $k \geq 0$ is the *nonstochastic* parameter that defines the family of ridge estimators. Note that, if $k = 0$, the resulting ridge estimator is the least squares estimator. The characteristic of the ridge family is that it is a shrinkage estimator, shrinking the least squares estimates toward zero by an amount directly related to the magnitude of the constant k. It is a biased estimator with total bias *directly* related to the magnitude of k but total estimator variance that is *inversely* related to k. Given this tradeoff Hoerl and Kennard (1970a) show that there always exists a $k > 0$ such that a ridge estimator has lower mean squared error than the least squares estimator. In fact, they show that a sufficient condition for a mean square error improvement is that $k < \sigma^2/\theta_{\max}^2$, where $\theta_{\max}$ is the largest θ_i in the transformed model (13.4.1). (See Exercise 13.5.)

This condition for mean square error improvement is, of course, the difficulty with ridge regression. Selecting an appropriate constant k requires knowledge of all of the parameters $\boldsymbol{\beta}$ and σ^2. Faced with this problem investigators did the natural thing, and adopted a variety of techniques that use the sample data to aid in the selection of a value of k. Unfortunately, these attempts face a major problem. Methods of selecting k based on the data, specifically on the vector of values of the dependent variable $\mathbf{y}$, produces an estimate of k that is *stochastic*, and therefore, the theorem provided by Hoerl and Kennard no longer applies. Consequently, for progress to be made using these techniques, new work was required to determine conditions under which the ridge estimator based on a stochastic shrinkage factor would provide a risk improvement. We now investigate this approach.

It is possible to generalize ridge regression by considering the transformed model (13.4.1). Define the generalized ridge estimator of $\boldsymbol{\theta}$ as

$$\hat{\boldsymbol{\theta}}(D) = [Z'Z + D]^{-1}Z'\mathbf{y}, \tag{13.4.8}$$

where D is a diagonal matrix with constant elements $d_i \geq 0$. The corresponding estimator for $\boldsymbol{\beta}$ is

$$\hat{\boldsymbol{\beta}}(D) = [X'X + ADA']^{-1}X'\mathbf{y} = [I + C]^{-1}\hat{\boldsymbol{\beta}}, \tag{13.4.9}$$

where $\hat{\boldsymbol{\beta}}$ is the ordinary least squares estimator and $C = (X'X)^{-1}ADA'$. For this estimator, the optimal values of the d_i's under mean square error loss are (σ^2/θ_i^2). Once again this knowledge is of little practical value since to apply it one would have to know the true parameters $\boldsymbol{\beta}$ and σ^2.

Recently, however, work by Casella (1977), Thisted (1977), and Strawderman (1978) has recognized the stochastic nature of the shrinkage factors in ridge and generalized ridge regression. They derive conditions under which the resulting estimators are minimax and dominate the least squares estimator under a variety of standard loss functions. To indicate the nature of these estimators and the types of conditions under which they are minimax consider the estimator discussed by Strawderman.

Strawderman considers rules of the form

$$\boldsymbol{\delta}(\hat{\boldsymbol{\beta}}, s) = [I + k(\mathbf{y})C]^{-1}\hat{\boldsymbol{\beta}},$$

where C is a nonstochastic matrix, $k(\mathbf{y})$ is a stochastic shrinkage factor that is a function of $\mathbf{y}$ and s the sum of squared least squares residuals $s = \mathbf{y}'M\mathbf{y}$, where $M = I - X(X'X)^{-1}X'$. Strawderman proves that under weighted squared error loss,

$$L(\boldsymbol{\beta}, \boldsymbol{\delta}) = (\boldsymbol{\beta} - \boldsymbol{\delta})'Q(\boldsymbol{\beta} - \boldsymbol{\delta})/\sigma^2,$$

where Q is an arbitrary positive definite and symmetric matrix, and with the usual assumptions of the classical *normal* linear regression model the estimator

$$\boldsymbol{\delta}(\hat{\boldsymbol{\beta}}, s) = [I + k(\mathbf{y})Q^{-1}X'X]\hat{\boldsymbol{\beta}}, \tag{13.4.10}$$

is minimax and dominates the usual ordinary least squares estimator, when $k(\mathbf{y}) = as/(\hat{\boldsymbol{\beta}}'X'X\hat{\boldsymbol{\beta}} + gs + h)$, a is a constant such that

$$0 \leq a \leq \frac{2(K-2)}{(T-K+2)} \frac{1}{\lambda_{\max}[Q^{-1}X'X]},$$

h is a constant that is nonnegative and $g \geq 2K/(T - K + 2)$. Also $\lambda_{\max}[\cdot]$ is the largest characteristic root of the matrix argument. It is interesting to note that the usual ridge estimator occurs for the loss function $Q = (X'X)^2$, which is not a loss function that is generally adopted.

Despite the risk improvement that the estimator (13.4.10) provides over the ordinary least squares estimator it is *not* the solution to the multicollinearity problem. Note that if $Q = I$, the upper bound of the shrinkage constant a is

$$\frac{2(K-2)}{(T-K+2)\lambda_1}.$$

Consequently, the larger λ_1 the smaller a must be and the closer $\boldsymbol{\delta}(\hat{\boldsymbol{\beta}}, s)$ must resemble the ordinary least squares estimator. A relatively large value of λ_1 is associated with multicollinearity. That is, it implies that a large proportion of the variation in the data is oriented in a single direction in the observation space. The lack of difference between the ridge estimator and the usual ordinary least squares estimator under such circumstances implies that little risk improvement will be provided by the ridge-type estimator.

13.5 Summary and Guide to Further Readings

In this chapter we have considered the multicollinearity problem. The nonexperimental nature of most economic data, and the general interdependence of most economic variables, often produces values of explanatory variables that do not exhibit enough independent variation to provide ordinary least squares estimators that are useful. The interrelationships among the explanatory variables are manifested by relatively unequal characteristic roots of the cross-product matrix $X'X$. The elements of the characteristic vectors of $X'X$ indicate, to the extent possible, which explanatory variables are involved in the "troublesome" linear dependencies.

Methods for dealing with multicollinear data have traditionally been to augment the sample data with exact or stochastic nonsample information. The difficulty is that if the nonsample information is uncertain, then its imposition can result in an estimator whose performance is worse than ordinary least squares in repeated sampling. This uncertainty, of course, carries over to estimators that use *ad hoc* or sample specific information like the principal components regression estimator or the ridge regression estimator. Use of these estimators in the traditional way does not guarantee mean square error improvement over least squares.

New classes of estimators that guarantee mean square error improvement have been suggested by James and Stein and others. Unfortunately the conditions on these estimators are usually such that severe multicollinearity eliminates all or most of any potential mean square error improvement.

Our conclusions then are as follows. Nonexperimental scientists frequently must work with data that are not "good" enough to provide useful estimates of all parameters in a regression equation. If nonsample information exists about which we are relatively certain, then it can be used in conjunction with the sample data to obtain more precise estimators. If the nonsample information is *not* certain then the symptoms associated with multicollinearity *cannot* be eliminated in any completely satisfactory way.

The literature devoted to the multicollinearity problem and various ways of dealing with its consequences is extensive. Useful general references include Judge *et al.*(1980), Vinod and Ullah (1981), Belsley and Klema (1974), Belsley *et al.* (1980), Farrar and Glauber (1967), Haitovsky (1969), Kumar (1975), Mason *et al.* (1975), O'Hagen and McCabe (1975), Silvey (1969), and Willan and Watts (1978). Principal components regression as a method for dealing with multicollinearity is discussed by Fomby *et al.* (1978), Greenberg (1975), Hill *et al.* (1977), Johnson *et al.* (1973), and Massey (1965). The literature on ridge regression is vast. Useful summaries of this literature can be found in Judge *et al.* (1980), Casella (1977), Thisted (1977), and Vinod (1978).

13.6 Exercises

13.1. Agricultural supply response has been difficult to estimate. The static theory would argue that a supply function specified in terms of current price would be appropriate. This is not the case however, since production of most agricultural commodities requires that decisions be made with considerable lead time. It is also argued that producers may look at prices lagged several periods to make decisions regarding output. Consider the supply function of the form

$$y_t = f(x_t, x_{t-1}, x_{t-2}, x_{t-3}),$$

where y_t is annual output and x_t is the price. A series of data is provided.

(a) Estimate the linear supply function using ordinary least squares.
(b) Investigate the presence and nature of multicollinearity.
(c) Apply principal components regression to the model.
(d) Apply ridge regression to the model.

y	x_t	x_{t-1}	x_{t-2}	x_{t-3}
58.3	1.11	1.29	1.35	1.30
67.1	1.18	1.11	1.29	1.35
66.5	1.09	1.18	1.11	1.29
55.8	1.00	1.09	1.18	1.11
56.2	1.10	1.00	1.09	1.18
60.3	1.12	1.10	1.00	1.09
58.0	1.11	1.12	1.10	1.00
58.2	1.17	1.11	1.12	1.10
60.4	1.16	1.17	1.11	1.12
66.5	1.24	1.16	1.17	1.11
61.6	1.03	1.24	1.16	1.17
62.0	1.08	1.03	1.24	1.16
65.6	1.15	1.08	1.03	1.24
71.9	1.33	1.15	1.08	1.03
67.0	1.08	1.33	1.15	1.08
71.9	1.57	1.08	1.33	1.15
77.8	2.55	1.57	1.08	1.33
78.2	3.03	2.55	1.57	1.08

$$\begin{aligned} y &= \text{Corn, adjusted acres planted (millions)}, \\ x_t &= \text{Corn Price (\$/bu)}, \\ x_{t-1}, x_{t-2}, x_{t-3} &= \text{Lagged Corn Prices}. \end{aligned}$$

13.2. Verify that $X'X = \sum_{i=1}^{K} \mathbf{x}_i\mathbf{x}_i' = \sum_{i=1}^{K} \lambda_i \mathbf{a}_i \mathbf{a}_i'$.

13.3. Prove that $X'X$ and $(X'X)^{-1}$ have characteristic roots that are reciprocals of one another and identical characteristic vectors.

13.4. Let X be a $T \times K$ matrix of regressors. Let $\mathbf{x}_{T+1} = l\mathbf{a}_1$, where $\mathbf{a}_1$ is the characteristic vector of $X'X$ associated with the largest characteristic root, λ_1. Show that the new design matrix, X^*, formed by adding the row $\mathbf{x}'_{T+1}$ to X is such that the characteristic roots of the new matrix are identical to that of the old matrix except that $\lambda_1^* = \lambda_1 + l^2$, and the associated characteristic vector is $\mathbf{a}_1^* = \mathbf{a}_1$.

13.5. Derive Equation (13.4.6).

13.6. Show that the ridge estimator, (13.4.7), has smaller mean square error than the ordinary least squares estimator if $k < \sigma^2/\theta_{\max}^2$, where $\theta_{\max}$ is the largest θ_i in (13.4.1).

13.7. In Chapter 7, data is presented on capital expenditures (y_t) and capital appropriations (x_t). Assume the model

$$y_t = \alpha_0 + \sum_{i=0}^{8} \beta_i x_{t-i} + e_t.$$

Investigate the nature and form of the multicollinearity.

13.8. There are several classic data sets that are used to illustrate multicollinearity. These include the Longley data (1967), Jeffer's pitprop data (1967) and the Gorman and Toman (1966) data that were used by Hoerl and Kennard (1970b) to illustrate the use of ridge regression. Obtain one of these data sets and analyze the multicollinearity that is present.

13.9. Consider the following model

$$y_t = \beta x_t + e_t,$$

where x_t is nonstochastic and e_t is independent and identically distributed with zero mean and variance σ^2.

(a) Derive the mean square error of the ordinary least squares estimator $\hat{\beta}$ of β (β is a scalar).

(b) Calculate the mean square error of the following ridge estimator of β:

$$\tilde{\beta} = \sum x_t y_t / \sum (x_t + k)^2, \qquad k > 0.$$

(c) Show that $0 < k < 2\sigma^2/\beta$ is a sufficient condition for mean square error$(\tilde{\beta}) <$ mean square error$(\hat{\beta})$.

(d) Let $k_0 = \sigma^2/\beta^2$ and consider the "estimator" with k set equal to k_0. Is this estimator really an estimator? Explain.

(e) Given your answer to part (d), describe the "unknown parameter" problem in the biased estimation literature.

13.7 References

Belsley, D. and Klema, V. (1974). Detecting and assessing the problems caused by multicollinearity: a use of the singular value decomposition. Working Paper No. 66, National Bureau of Economic Research, Cambridge, MA.

Belsley, D., Kuh, E., and Welsh, R. (1980). *Regression Diagnostics*. New York: Wiley.

Casella, G. (1977). *Minimax Ridge Estimation*. Unpublished Ph.D. Dissertation, Purdue University, Lafayette, IN.

Farrar, D. and Glauber, R. (1967). Multicollinearity in regression analysis: the problem revisited. *Review of Economics and Statistics*, **49**, 92–107.

Fomby, T. and Hill, R. (1978). Multicollinearity and the value of *a priori* information. *Communications in Statistics*, A, **8**, 477–486.

Fomby, T., Hill, R., and Johnson, S. (1978). An optimality property of principal components regression. *Journal of the American Statistical Association*, **73**, 191–193.

Gorman, J. W. and Toman, R. J. (1966). Selection of variables for fitting equations to data. *Technometrics*, **8**, 27–51.

Greenberg, E. (1975). Minimum variance properties of principal components regression. *Journal of the American Statistical Association*, **70**, 194–197.

Haitovsky, T. (1969). Multicollinearity in regression analysis: comment. *Review of Economics and Statistics*, **51**, 486–489.

Hill, R., Fomby, T., and Johnson, S. (1977). Component selection norms for principal components regression. *Communications in Statistics*, A, **6**, 309–333.

Hill, R. C. and Ziemer, R. F. (1982). Small sample performance of the Stein-rule in non-orthogonal designs. *Economics Letters*, **10**, 285–292.

Hill, R. C. and Ziemer, R. F. (1984). The risk of general Stein-like estimators in the presence of multicollinearity, *Journal of Econometrics*, forthcoming.

Hoerl, A. and Kennard, R. (1970a). Ridge regression: biased estimation of nonorthogonal problems. *Technometrics*, **12**, 55–67.

Hoerl, A. and Kennard, R. (1970b). Ridge regression: applications to nonorthogonal problems. *Technometrics*, **12**, 69–82.

Johnson, S., Reimer, S., and Rothrock, T. (1973). Principal components and the problem of multicollinearity. *Metroeconomica*, **25**, 306–317.

Jeffers, J. M. R. (1967). Two case studies in the application of principal component analysis. *Applied Statistics*, **16**, 225–236.

Judge, G., Griffiths, W., Hill, R., and Lee, T. (1980). *The Theory and Practice of Econometrics*. New York: Wiley.

Kumar, T. (1975). Multicollinearity in regression analysis. *Review of Economics and Statistics*, **57**, 365–366.

Longley, J. W. (1967). An appraisal of least squares programs for the electronic computer from the point of view of the user. *Journal of the American Statistical Association*, **62**, 819–841.

Mason, R., Gunst, R., and Webster, J. (1975). Regression analysis and problems of multicollinearity. *Communications in Statistics*, A, **4**, 277–292.

Massey, W. (1965). Principal components regression in exploratory statistical research. *Journal of the American Statistical Association*, **60**, 234–256.

O'Hagen, J. and McCabe, B. (1975). Tests for the severity of multicollinearity in regression analysis: a comment. *Review of Economics and Statistics*, **57**, 368–370.

Silvey, S. (1969). Multicollinearity and imprecise estimation. *Journal of the Royal Statistical Society*, B, **35**, 67–75.

Strawderman, W. (1978). Minimax adaptive generalized ridge regression estimators. *Journal of the American Statistical Association*, **73**, 623–627.

Theil, H. (1971). *Principles of Econometrics*. New York: Wiley.

Thisted, R. (1977). *Ridge Regression, Minimax Estimation and Empirical Bayes Methods*. Unpublished Ph.D. Dissertation, Stanford University, Stanford, CA.

Vinod, H. (1978). A survey of ridge regression and related techniques for improvements over ordinary least squares. *Review of Economics and Statistics*, **60**, 121–131.

Vinod, H. and Ullah, A. (1981). *Recent Advances in Regression Methods*. New York: Marcel Dekker.

Willan, A. and Watts, D. (1978). Meaningful multicollinearity measures. *Technometrics*, **20**, 407–412.

CHAPTER 14

Varying Coefficient Models

14.1 Introduction

In this and the following chapter we consider ways to combine sets of data for the purpose of estimation that may violate a basic assumption of the linear regression model. Specifically, we will study cases when it cannot be assumed that the structural parameters are identical for all observations in a sample of data. Frequently these problems occur when a data set consists of series of observations over time on cross-sectional units. Many of the topics discussed in this chapter can or do apply directly to the pooling of time series and cross-sectional data, but the primary discussion of that topic is contained in Chapter 15. In this chapter we focus on models with parameters that vary in some systematic and/or random way across partitions of the sample data, even from observation to observation.

The motivation for attempting to model parameter variation is straightforward. If usual statistical procedures are employed to analyze observations that were generated by a process with changing structural parameters, then parameter estimates, and inferences based on them, will be meaningless. If, however, there is some way to model the parameter variation, whether it be deterministic or random, relatively simple model specifications can be used to study the changing relationships between the variables involved.

Consequently we will present an array of models in this chapter that have been used to incorporate parameter variation or, more generally, structural changes. The models are presented in an order that reflects increasing generality and flexibility. In Section 14.2 structural changes that can be modeled with dummy variables are considered, including seasonality models. In Section 14.3 we consider regression models where structural shifts can be described as switching from one regression regime to another, usually in a time series context. The point at which the structural change occurs can be assumed to be known or it can be treated as an unknown parameter. One characteristic of these models is that the transition from one structure to another can be assumed to be "smooth" rather than abrupt.

In Section 14.4, models are characterized that explain the parameter variation by assuming that regression coefficients, or their means, change in response to changes in some auxiliary explanatory variables. Consequently, the changes in economic structure are themselves actually modeled. In Section 14.5 a related set of models is presented. In these models it is assumed that the coefficients are random, and either have means that are constant, or follow a stochastic process, which may be stationary or nonstationary. The former models are primarily used in analysis of cross-sectional data while the latter models of "evolving parameters" are useful for time series models.

14.2 Dummy Variables and Sets of Regression Equations

There are many cases in which the sample can be divided into two or more partitions in which some or all of the regression coefficients may differ. Common situations include seasonality models, in which explanatory variables can have different effects depending upon the season of the year, models that allow behavioral differences in geographical regions, models that permit different response coefficients during unusual time periods, such as war years, and so on.

To make matters concrete consider the model

$$y_t = x_{t1}\beta_1 + x_{t2}\beta_2 + \cdots + x_{tK}\beta_K + e_t, \qquad t = 1, \ldots, T, \quad (14.2.1)$$

where e_t obeys the assumption of the classical linear regression model. In the absence of structural change the parameters β_i, $i = 1, \ldots, K$ are fixed for all T observations and best linear unbiased parameter estimates are obtained by applying least squares. Suppose, however, we believe that there is a difference in some, or all, of the regression coefficients for a subset of the observations. To keep matters simple, but perfectly general, let us assume that the regression structure is different for observations $t = 1, \ldots, t_0$ (the first partition) and $t = t_0 + 1, \ldots, T$ (the second partition). Furthermore, suppose that the structural change is confined to parameters β_i, $i = p + 1, \ldots, K$ where $p \in \{0, \ldots, (K - 1)\}$ and let $K = p + q$.

The standard dummy variable approach is to define a dichotomous variable

$$D_t = \begin{cases} 0 & \text{if } t = 1, \ldots, t_0, \\ 1 & \text{if } t = t_0 + 1, \ldots, T. \end{cases} \quad (14.2.2)$$

Then consider the model

$$y_t = \sum_{k=1}^{K} x_{tk}\beta_k + (x_{t,p+1} \cdot D_t)\delta_{p+1} + \cdots + (x_{t,K} \cdot D_t)\delta_K + e_t,$$

$$t = 1, \ldots, T. \qquad (14.2.3)$$

For observations in the first partition

$$Ey_t = \sum_{k=1}^{K} x_{tk}\beta_k$$

and for observations in the second partition

$$Ey_t = \sum_{k=1}^{p} x_{tk}\beta_k + \sum_{k=p+1}^{K} x_{tk}(\beta_k + \delta_k).$$

Thus δ_k represents the incremental change in the structural parameter associated with x_{tk} in the second sample partition. Best linear unbiased estimates of the δ_k are obtained by applying least squares to (14.2.3) and a test of the hypothesis that no structural change occurred is carried out by testing the joint hypothesis $H_0 : \delta_{p+1} = \cdots \delta_K = 0$.

While the dummy variable approach is simple and effective, there is value in approaching the problem from a different, but equivalent, point of view. Let us write our partitioned data set, and model, as

$$\begin{bmatrix} \mathbf{y}_1 \\ \mathbf{y}_2 \end{bmatrix} = \begin{bmatrix} X_{11} & X_{12} & 0 & 0 \\ 0 & 0 & X_{21} & X_{22} \end{bmatrix} \begin{bmatrix} \boldsymbol{\beta}_{11} \\ \boldsymbol{\beta}_{12} \\ \boldsymbol{\beta}_{21} \\ \boldsymbol{\beta}_{22} \end{bmatrix} + \begin{bmatrix} \mathbf{e}_1 \\ \mathbf{e}_2 \end{bmatrix}, \qquad (14.2.4)$$

where $\mathbf{y}_1$ and $\mathbf{y}_2$ are vectors of t_0 and $(T - t_0)$ observations on the dependent variable for the first and second partitions; X_{11} and X_{21} are $t_0 \times p$ and $(T - t_0) \times p$ matrices of observations on variables $k = 1, \ldots, p$ for the first and second partitions, X_{12} and X_{22} are $t_0 \times q$ and $(T - t_0) \times q$ matrices of observations on variables $k = p + 1, \ldots, K$ for the first and second partitions. The parameter vectors $\boldsymbol{\beta}_{11}$ and $\boldsymbol{\beta}_{21}$ correspond to X_{11} and X_{21}, respectively, and $\boldsymbol{\beta}_{12}$ and $\boldsymbol{\beta}_{22}$ to X_{12} and X_{22}. The error vector is partitioned into $\mathbf{e}_1$ and $\mathbf{e}_2$ to conform to the sample partition.

As (14.2.4) is written, the coefficients on all K explanatory variables can change across the sample partition. If we restrict the coefficients of the first p variables to be the same for the two sample partitions, so $\boldsymbol{\beta}_{11} = \boldsymbol{\beta}_{21} = \boldsymbol{\beta}_{.1}$, we have

$$\begin{bmatrix} \mathbf{y}_1 \\ \mathbf{y}_2 \end{bmatrix} = \begin{bmatrix} X_{11} & X_{12} & 0 \\ X_{21} & 0 & X_{22} \end{bmatrix} \begin{bmatrix} \boldsymbol{\beta}_{.1} \\ \boldsymbol{\beta}_{12} \\ \boldsymbol{\beta}_{22} \end{bmatrix} + \begin{bmatrix} \mathbf{e}_1 \\ \mathbf{e}_2 \end{bmatrix}. \qquad (14.2.5)$$

Estimation of this model by least squares is equivalent (see Chapter 6) to estimating the model (14.2.4), which we simply denote

$$\mathbf{y} = X\boldsymbol{\beta} + \mathbf{e} \tag{14.2.6}$$

subject to the linear constraints $R\boldsymbol{\beta} = \mathbf{0}$ where $R = [-I_p \quad 0 \quad I_p \quad 0]$, and I_p is a $p \times p$ identity matrix. The parameter estimates of (14.2.5) are equivalent to those from the dummy variable specification (14.2.3), which in the current matrix notation can be written

$$\begin{bmatrix} \mathbf{y}_1 \\ \mathbf{y}_2 \end{bmatrix} = \begin{bmatrix} X_{11} & X_{12} & 0 \\ X_{21} & X_{22} & X_{22} \end{bmatrix} \begin{bmatrix} \boldsymbol{\beta}_{.1} \\ \boldsymbol{\beta}_{.2} \\ \boldsymbol{\delta} \end{bmatrix} + \begin{bmatrix} \mathbf{e}_1 \\ \mathbf{e}_2 \end{bmatrix}, \tag{14.2.7}$$

where $\boldsymbol{\beta}'_{.1} = (\beta_1, \ldots, \beta_p)$, $\boldsymbol{\beta}'_{.2} = (\beta_{p+1}, \ldots, \beta_K)$ and $\boldsymbol{\delta}' = (\delta_{p+1}, \ldots, \delta_K)$.

To see that formulations (14.2.5) and (14.2.7) are in fact equivalent consider the reparametrized model

$$\mathbf{y} = XA_1A_1^{-1}\boldsymbol{\beta} = Z_1\boldsymbol{\gamma}_1 + \mathbf{e}_1 \tag{14.2.8}$$

where $Z_1 = XA_1, \boldsymbol{\gamma}_1 = A_1^{-1}\boldsymbol{\beta}$ and

$$A_1^{\pm 1} = \begin{bmatrix} I & 0 & 0 & 0 \\ 0 & I & 0 & 0 \\ \pm I & 0 & I & 0 \\ 0 & 0 & 0 & I \end{bmatrix}.$$

In particular (14.2.8) is

$$\mathbf{y} = Z_1\boldsymbol{\gamma}_1 + \mathbf{e} = \begin{bmatrix} X_{11} & X_{12} & 0 & 0 \\ X_{21} & 0 & X_{21} & X_{22} \end{bmatrix} \begin{bmatrix} \boldsymbol{\beta}_{11} \\ \boldsymbol{\beta}_{12} \\ \boldsymbol{\beta}_{12} - \boldsymbol{\beta}_{21} \\ \boldsymbol{\beta}_{22} \end{bmatrix} + \mathbf{e}. \tag{14.2.9}$$

To obtain the restriction matrix that yields model (14.2.5) we apply the same transformation. So,

$$R\boldsymbol{\beta} = RA_1A_1^{-1}\boldsymbol{\beta} = R_1\boldsymbol{\gamma}_1 = [0 \quad 0 \quad I \quad 0]\boldsymbol{\gamma}_1 = \mathbf{0} \tag{14.2.10}$$

which implies $\boldsymbol{\beta}_{11} - \boldsymbol{\beta}_{21} = \mathbf{0}$ as required. Thus Equation (14.2.9) subject to the constraints in (14.2.10) is identical to (14.2.5) except for a change in notation.

The dummy variable formulation can be obtained from (14.2.6) by applying the transformation

$$y = XA_2A_2^{-1}\boldsymbol{\beta} + \mathbf{e} = Z_2\boldsymbol{\gamma}_2 + \mathbf{e}, \tag{14.2.11}$$

where

$$A_2^{\pm 1} = \begin{bmatrix} I & 0 & 0 & 0 \\ 0 & I & 0 & 0 \\ \pm I & 0 & I & 0 \\ 0 & \pm I & 0 & I \end{bmatrix},$$

and observing that the necessary restriction on $\gamma_2' = (\gamma_{21}', \gamma_{22}', \gamma_{23}', \gamma_{24}')$ is that $\gamma_{23} = \mathbf{0}$ (see Exercise 14.1), or $R_2\gamma_2 = [0 \quad 0 \quad I \quad 0]\gamma_2 = \mathbf{0}$.

To see the equivalence of (14.2.10) subject to $R_1\gamma_1 = \mathbf{0}$ and (14.2.11) subject to $R_2\gamma_2 = \mathbf{0}$ simply note that $A_2 = A_1Q$ where Q is nonsingular and

$$Q^{\pm 1} = \begin{bmatrix} I & 0 & 0 & 0 \\ 0 & I & 0 & 0 \\ 0 & 0 & I & 0 \\ 0 & \pm I & 0 & I \end{bmatrix}.$$

Then the two formulations are simply nonsingular transformations of one another. That is,

$$\begin{aligned} \mathbf{y} = X\boldsymbol{\beta} + \mathbf{e} &= XA_1A_1^{-1}\boldsymbol{\beta} + \mathbf{e} = Z_1\gamma_1 + \mathbf{e} \\ &= Z_1QQ^{-1}\gamma_1 + \mathbf{e} = Z_2\gamma_2 + \mathbf{e}, \end{aligned}$$

and the restrictions

$$\begin{aligned} \mathbf{0} = R\boldsymbol{\beta} &= RA_1A_1^{-1}\boldsymbol{\beta} = R_1\gamma_1 \\ &= R_1QQ^{-1}\gamma_1 = R_2\gamma_2, \end{aligned}$$

where $R_1 = R_2 = [0 \quad 0 \quad I \quad 0]$.

Thus the "sets of equations" formulation (14.2.5) and the "dummy variable" formulation (14.2.7) represent alternative representations of the same model, and use of one rather than the other produces no loss of information or efficiency. Use of one model rather than the other should depend upon ease of use or interpretation in a specific situation.

In this section we have considered the simplest varying coefficient model, where a subset of coefficients differs across two sample partitions. The same format could easily be extended to more sample partitions. One of obvious interest is a four-partition model where each partition represents observations on a particular quarter of the year. This is a straightforward approach to the problem of testing for, or allowing for seasonal effects in estimation.

The use of the dummy variable or sets of regression equations approach to modeling structural change requires the assumption that the data *can* be partitioned into regimes, where the parameters are constant within each regime. It also is assumed that structural changes occur immediately and abruptly. In the next section we consider models where these assumptions can be weakened.

14.3 Switching Regression Models

The models discussed in this section are generalizations of those discussed in Section 14.2 in one way or another. We first consider cases where the sample partitions are known, as they were in the previous section. Several ways of "smoothing" the transition between regimes are considered. Next we consider situations where the points at which transition between one regime and another are not known exactly. In the switching regression literature (Quandt (1958), McGee and Carlton (1970)), the points where the transitions occur are called "join" points, presumably because those are the points where the regimes are joined together. These models are often called "piecewise" regression functions when the data are time series and the regimes represent intervals of time for which the structure is unchanging. Over the whole sample of time series observations the regression function is piecewise continuous. For convenience, and ease of interpretation, we will adopt the time series context for the discussion in this section.

14.3.1 Piecewise Regression Models: Known Join Point

To simplify matters somewhat let us assume there are two sample partitions, or regimes, and that (14.2.4) can be written

$$\begin{bmatrix} \mathbf{y}_1 \\ \mathbf{y}_2 \end{bmatrix} = \begin{bmatrix} X_1 & 0 \\ 0 & X_2 \end{bmatrix} \begin{bmatrix} \boldsymbol{\beta}_1 \\ \boldsymbol{\beta}_2 \end{bmatrix} + \begin{bmatrix} \mathbf{e}_1 \\ \mathbf{e}_2 \end{bmatrix}, \tag{14.3.1}$$

and we do not consider the possibility that some of the regression parameters may be the same across the regimes. Although, as we have seen above, this is not a difficult problem to handle. The model (14.3.1) separates the linear regression model into two pieces and these pieces are not necessarily joined. If the T observations are sequential in time we can impose the constraint that the regression functions are joined at $t = t_0$ by imposing the constraint that $E(y_{t_0}) = \mathbf{x}'_{t_0}\boldsymbol{\beta}_1 = \mathbf{x}'_{t_0}\boldsymbol{\beta}_2$, or $\mathbf{x}'_{t_0}(\boldsymbol{\beta}_1 - \boldsymbol{\beta}_2) = \mathbf{0}$, where $\mathbf{x}'_{t_0}$ is the $1 \times K$ vector of observations on the explanatory variables at time $t = t_0$. This constraint implies that the two regression functions join at t_0.

As illustrated by Poirier (1973, 1976) it is sometimes possible to join the regression functions more smoothly than is achieved by the above technique. To see this suppose the two regression functions in (14.3.1) are cubic polynomials in the single explanatory variable time, t. *Cubic splines* have been used extensively as approximating functions by physical scientists. Cubic splines are simply cubic regression functions that are joined smoothly at known transition points, called "knots" in the spline literature. Smoothness at the join points is characterized by the constraints that the regression functions meet at those points and have first and second derivatives that are equal there as well. In particular let the cubic regression functions be

$$g_i(t) = a_i t^3 + b_i t^2 + c_i t + d_i, \qquad i = 1, 2.$$

Then the regression model (14.3.1) can be written

$$y_t = \begin{cases} g_1(t) + e_t, & t = 1, \ldots, t_0, \\ g_2(t) + e_t, & t = t_0 + 1, \ldots, T. \end{cases}$$

The smoothness conditions require that at t_0

$$g_1(t_0) = g_2(t_0), \qquad g_1'(t_0) = g_2'(t_0), \qquad g_1''(t_0) = g_2''(t_0).$$

These constraints can be written as linear equality constraints on the coefficients of the cubic polynomials. The resulting restricted least squares problem has been shown by Buse and Lim (1977) to be equivalent to the formulation originally presented by Poirier (1973).

14.3.2 Piecewise Regression Models: Unknown Join Point

The models we have considered so far have assumed that the point, or points, of structural change are known. If this is not true then the join points can be treated as parameters to be estimated. This problem is surveyed by Goldfeld and Quandt (1973). Given the model (14.3.1) they assume that $e_{t1} \sim N(0, \sigma_1^2)$ and $e_{t2} \sim N(0, \sigma_2^2)$ and that no autocorrelation is present. Then, they note that the likelihood function, conditional on t_0, is

$$L(\boldsymbol{\beta}_1, \boldsymbol{\beta}_2, \sigma_1^2, \sigma_2^2 | t_0) = (2\pi)^{-T/2} \sigma_1^{-t_0} \sigma_2^{-(T-t_0)}$$
$$\times \exp\left\{ -\frac{1}{2\sigma_1^2} \sum_{t=1}^{t_0} (y_t - \mathbf{x}_t'\boldsymbol{\beta}_1)^2 - \frac{1}{2\sigma_1^2} \sum_{t=t_0+1}^{T} (y_t - \mathbf{x}_t'\boldsymbol{\beta}_2)^2 \right\}. \tag{14.3.2}$$

An estimate of t_0 is chosen by searching over values of t_0 and choosing the value that maximizes the value of the likelihood function. A likelihood ratio test for the hypothesis of no structural change is performed by comparing the maximum value of the likelihood function (14.3.2) to the restricted likelihood function based on the assumption that a single regression function is appropriate for the entire sample. A search procedure that is similar in spirit is suggested by Brown *et al.* (1975).

An alternative test for structural shifts, when the join point is unknown, is suggested by Farley and Hinich (1970) and Farley *et al.* (1975). They approximate a discrete structural change at an unknown point by a continuous linear shift. That is assume the model $y_t = \mathbf{x}_t'\boldsymbol{\beta}_t + \mathbf{e}_t$ where $\boldsymbol{\beta}_t = \boldsymbol{\beta} + t\boldsymbol{\delta}$. Substituting for $\boldsymbol{\beta}_t$ the model becomes $y_t = \mathbf{x}_t'\boldsymbol{\beta} + t\mathbf{x}_t'\boldsymbol{\delta} + \mathbf{e}_t$. A test for no structural change is then carried out by testing the joint hypothesis that $\boldsymbol{\delta} = \mathbf{0}$. Farley *et al.* (1975) note, that this test is not very powerful unless the sample size is large or the structural shift is large.

The analysis above is appropriate when the switching phenomenon is determined by a single variable. It is possible to generalize the process by allowing a set of explanatory variables to affect the switching process.

Goldfeld and Quandt (1973) assume that nature selects the regime according to whether $\mathbf{z}_t'\gamma \leq 0$ or $\mathbf{z}_t'\gamma > 0$, where $\mathbf{z}_t' = (z_{t1}, \ldots, z_{tm})$ is a vector of values on m explanatory variables and $\boldsymbol{\gamma}$ is an $m \times 1$ vector of unknown parameters. Specifically, let $D_t = 0$ if $\mathbf{z}_t'\boldsymbol{\gamma} \leq 0$ and $D_t = 1$ if $\mathbf{z}_t'\boldsymbol{\gamma} > 1$. Then the two regimes can be written together as

$$y_t = \mathbf{x}_t'[(1 - D_t)\boldsymbol{\beta}_1 + D_t\boldsymbol{\beta}_2] + (1 - D_t)e_{t1} + D_t e_{t2}, \qquad (14.3.3)$$

where $\boldsymbol{\beta}_1$, $\boldsymbol{\beta}_2$, σ_1^2, σ_2^2 and D_t, and thus $\boldsymbol{\gamma}$, must be estimated. To model the process that determines the choice of regime let D_t be approximated by the probit function $D_t = F(\mathbf{z}_t'\boldsymbol{\gamma})$, where $F(\cdot)$ is the cumulative distribution function of a standard normal random variable. The likelihood function then depends on $\boldsymbol{\beta}_1$, $\boldsymbol{\beta}_2$, $\boldsymbol{\gamma}$, σ_1^2, σ_2^2 and maximum likelihood estimates of the parameters can be obtained numerically. One difficulty with this approach of course is that predicted values of D_t, say $\hat{D}_t = F(\mathbf{z}_t'\hat{\boldsymbol{\gamma}})$, are not likely to be exactly zero or one, so that observations must be classified to one regime or the other according to whether $\hat{D}_t \geq 0.5$. Goldfeld and Quandt then suggest that separate regressions could be run on the separate sample partitions and the hypothesis of no switching tested using a test of equality of the regressions.

The models described above assume that the process that determines the switching is nonstochastic, or deterministic. For example, in the model just presented, the switch occurs when the nonstochastic function $\mathbf{z}_t'\boldsymbol{\gamma}$ crosses the threshold value, assumed to be zero. The alternative is to allow a regime to be chosen with a certain probability, which may depend on exogenous variables. A simple version of this stochastic process for regime selection is to let the choice of the first or second regimes be made on the basis of the unknown probabilities λ and $(1 - \lambda)$. The density function of y_t is then

$$g(y_t | \mathbf{x}_t) = \lambda f_1(y_t | \mathbf{x}_t) + (1 - \lambda) f_2(y_t | \mathbf{x}_t),$$

where $f_i(\cdot)$ is the density function of y_t for the ith regime. The likelihood function can then be maximized with respect to the $\boldsymbol{\beta}_i$'s, σ_i^2 and λ. Other modifications and extensions can be found in Goldfeld and Quandt (1973).

14.4 Systematically Varying Parameter Models

The models considered to this point have assumed that the sample could be partitioned into subsets for which different structures existed. Taking this idea a step further, we can allow for the possibility that the structure changes for every cross sectional and/or time series observation. To represent such a model we can write

$$y_{it} = \mathbf{x}_{it}'\boldsymbol{\beta}_{it} + e_{it}, \qquad i = 1, \ldots, N; \quad t = 1, \ldots, T; \qquad (14.4.1)$$

where y_{it} is an observation on the dependent variable in the ith cross-section during the tth time period; $\mathbf{x}'_{it}$ is a $1 \times K$ nonstochastic vector of explanatory variables and $\boldsymbol{\beta}_{it}$ is the corresponding parameter vector for the ith cross-sectional unit in the tth time period. The e_{it} are assumed to be normally and independently distributed with zero means and variances σ^2. This formulation allows the regression coefficients to vary for each cross-sectional and time series observation. The obvious problem is that there are KNT + 1 parameters to estimate from NT observations. In order to proceed some structure must be placed on how the coefficients vary. In this and the next section alternative ways of imposing a structure are considered.

Belsley (1973) suggested imposing the nonsample information

$$\boldsymbol{\beta}_{it} = Z_{it}\boldsymbol{\gamma}, \tag{14.4.2}$$

where Z_{it} is a $K \times M$ matrix of observations on variables that explain the parameter variation, where M could be greater than K, and $\boldsymbol{\gamma}$ is a vector of associated coefficients. This model is flexible and can be used to represent many forms of parameter variation. For example, (14.4.2) could be specified to be a simple switching regression model by setting $Z_{it} = [I_K \quad 0_K]$, where 0_K is a $K \times K$ matrix of zeros, for $t \le t_0$ and $Z_{it} = [0_K \quad I_K]$ for $t > t_0$ and $\boldsymbol{\gamma}' = (\boldsymbol{\gamma}'_1, \boldsymbol{\gamma}'_2)$. Alternatively, Z_{it} could contain variables already in $\mathbf{x}_{it}$, implying that y_{it} is not linear in the original explanatory variables, or Z_{it} could contain other exogenous variables. In any case, estimation is easily carried out by substituting (14.4.2) into (14.4.1) to obtain

$$y_{it} = \mathbf{x}'_{it} Z_{it}\boldsymbol{\gamma} + e_{it} = \mathbf{w}'_{it}\boldsymbol{\gamma} + e_{it}. \tag{14.4.3}$$

Under the assumptions we have made $\boldsymbol{\gamma}$ can be estimated by ordinary least squares. As long as Z_{it} is known, and nonstochastic, no real problems occur. On the other hand, if Z_{it} is not known with certainty, all the difficulties associated with model specification must be faced.

It is, of course, possible to make (14.4.2) stochastic by adding a $K \times 1$ vector of random disturbances, $\mathbf{v}_{it}$. The resulting model is

$$y_{it} = \mathbf{w}'_{it}\boldsymbol{\gamma} + u_{it}, \tag{14.4.4}$$

where $u_{it} = \mathbf{x}'_{it}\mathbf{v}_{it} + e_{it}$, which is heteroscedastic. Models of this form are discussed in the next section, and in the next chapter. More specifically, if $T = 1$, so only cross-sectional observations are available, and if $Z_i = I_K$, the resulting model is that of Hildreth and Houck, presented in the next section. If $Z_{it} = I_K$ and $\boldsymbol{\beta}_{it} = \boldsymbol{\beta}_i$, $\mathbf{v}_{it} = \mathbf{v}_i$ we obtain the Swamy random coefficient model which is also presented in the next section. When $N = 1$, so only time series observations are considered, and Z_t contains functions of calendar time, Singh *et al.* (1976) propose estimation techniques for the resulting time varying parameter model. Finally if Z_{it} is constructed so that only the constant term varies, and if the random disturbance $\mathbf{v}_{it}$ is composed of separate errors reflecting time specific factors, cross-section specific factors and an overall error, the error components model of Chapter 15 is produced.

14.5 Random Coefficient Models

In this section we consider models in which the coefficients are assumed to be realizations of a random process. These models can be used for cross-sectional, time series and cross-sectional or pure time series data. We will review models that are representative for each of these cases. The first two models considered are the Hildreth–Houck (1968) and Swamy (1970, 1971) random coefficient models. These are designed for cross-sectional and pooled time series and cross-sectional data respectively. They are similar in that both assume the stochastic processes generating the coefficients are stationary and in both the objective is to estimate common mean values of the coefficients and relevant variances and covariances. Finally we briefly present the Harvey and Phillips (1982) and Cooley and Prescott (1973, 1976) models which are appropriate for use with time series data. In the former the stochastic process generating the parameters is stationary while in the latter it is nonstationary.

14.5.1 The Hildreth–Houck Random Coefficient Model

The model we consider is (14.4.1) with $T = 1$ and the error term suppressed,

$$y_i = \mathbf{x}_i' \boldsymbol{\beta}_i, \qquad i = 1, \ldots, N. \tag{14.5.1}$$

The model of the coefficients is $\boldsymbol{\beta}_i = Z_i \boldsymbol{\gamma} + \mathbf{v}_i$, where $Z_i = I_K$ and $\boldsymbol{\gamma} = \bar{\boldsymbol{\beta}}$, so

$$\boldsymbol{\beta}_i = \bar{\boldsymbol{\beta}} + \mathbf{v}_i. \tag{14.5.2}$$

This is the random coefficient model of Hildreth and Houck (1968). The vector $\boldsymbol{\beta}_i$ contains the response coefficients for the ith individual, $\bar{\boldsymbol{\beta}}$ is the population mean response factor and $\mathbf{v}_i$ is a vector of random disturbances and $\mathbf{v}_i \sim (\mathbf{0}, V)$ and independently of $\mathbf{v}_j$, $i \neq j$. Note that the equation error can not be distinguished from the random disturbance for the intercept parameter v_{1i}, and is thus omitted from (14.5.1).

The parameters of this model are $\bar{\boldsymbol{\beta}}$ and V. In order to estimate them combine (14.5.1) and (14.5.2) as

$$y_i = \mathbf{x}_i' \bar{\boldsymbol{\beta}} + e_i, \tag{14.5.3}$$

where $e_i = \mathbf{x}_i' \mathbf{v}_i$ and $e_i \sim (0, \sigma_i^2 = \mathbf{x}_i' V \mathbf{x}_i)$. If V were known the appropriate estimation technique is generalized least squares. However, since V is not likely to be known we must consider ways to estimate its elements. To that end, let $\mathbf{w}$ contain the unique elements of V and write $\sigma_i^2 = \mathbf{z}_i' \mathbf{w}$. Here $\mathbf{z}_i$ will contain the explanatory variables, their squares and cross products. The procedures outlined in Section 9.2.2a for feasible generalized least squares estimates of such models are appropriate. The testing procedures in Sections

9.3.2a and 9.3.3 are relevant for testing for the presence of random coefficients of this form. From the point of view of estimation the problem is somewhat different than the usual case, since the elements of $\mathbf{w}$ are variances and covariances and thus must obey the constraint that V is positive semidefinite. Since such constraints are nonlinear they are frequently omitted. Unconstrained estimates of course are not necessarily going to satisfy the constraint. Various methods for estimating V are presented in Hildreth and Houck (1968), Swamy and Mehta (1975) and Srivastava *et al.* (1981).

Finally, note that there may be cases where we wish individual estimates, or more accurately, predictions of the $\boldsymbol{\beta}_i$. The predictor

$$\hat{\boldsymbol{\beta}}_i = \hat{\bar{\boldsymbol{\beta}}} + V\mathbf{x}_i(\mathbf{x}_i'V\mathbf{x}_i)^{-1}(y_i - \mathbf{x}_i'\hat{\bar{\boldsymbol{\beta}}})$$

is best linear and unbiased (Griffiths (1972), Swamy and Mehta (1975), and Lee and Griffiths (1979)). It is unbiased in the sense that $E(\hat{\boldsymbol{\beta}}_i - \boldsymbol{\beta}_i) = \mathbf{0}$ and best in the sense that the covariance matrix of the prediction error of $(\hat{\boldsymbol{\beta}}_i - \boldsymbol{\beta}_i)$ is smaller than that of any other linear unbiased predictor.

14.5.2 The Swamy Random Coefficient Model

The Swamy (1970, 1971) random coefficient model is similar in spirit to the Hildreth–Houck model presented in the previous section, but it is appropriate for the pooling time series and cross-sectional model (14.4.1). In particular, let the T observations on the ith cross-sectional unit (individual) be written

$$\mathbf{y}_i = X_i\boldsymbol{\beta}_i + \mathbf{e}_i, \tag{14.5.4}$$

$\mathbf{e}_i \sim (\mathbf{0}, \sigma_i^2 I)$, $E(\mathbf{e}_i\mathbf{e}_j') = 0$ if $i \neq j$, $\boldsymbol{\beta}_i = \bar{\boldsymbol{\beta}} + \mathbf{v}_i$, $\mathbf{v}_i \sim (\mathbf{0}, V)$ and $E\mathbf{v}_i\mathbf{v}_j' = 0, i \neq j$. Thus each individual in the sample has a unique coefficient vector $\boldsymbol{\beta}_i$, but each individual's responses are constant over time, and the $\boldsymbol{\beta}_i$ have a common mean $\bar{\boldsymbol{\beta}}$. For this model we are interested in estimating $\bar{\boldsymbol{\beta}}$ and V, testing the hypothesis that $V = 0$, and obtaining predictions for $\boldsymbol{\beta}_i$.

To estimate $\bar{\boldsymbol{\beta}}$ write all NT observations as

$$\mathbf{y} = \tilde{X}\bar{\boldsymbol{\beta}} + X\mathbf{v} + \mathbf{e},$$

where $\mathbf{y}' = (\mathbf{y}_1', \ldots, \mathbf{y}_N')$, and $\mathbf{v}$ and $\mathbf{e}$ are similarly defined. The matrix $\tilde{X}$ is the matrix of stacked X_i's, $\tilde{X}' = (X_1', X_2', \ldots, X_N')$ and X is a block diagonal matrix, $X = \text{diag}(X_1, X_2, \ldots, X_N)$. The covariance matrix of the composite error term $X\mathbf{v} + \mathbf{e}$ is Ω, which is block diagonal with ith block $\Omega_{ii} = X_i'VX_i + \sigma_i^2 I$. The generalized least squares estimator can be conveniently written as

$$\hat{\bar{\boldsymbol{\beta}}} = (\tilde{X}'\Omega^{-1}\tilde{X})^{-1}\tilde{X}'\Omega^{-1}\mathbf{y} = \sum_{i=1}^{N} W_i\mathbf{b}_i,$$

where

$$W_i = \left\{ \sum_{j=1}^{N} [V + \sigma_j^2 (X_j' X_j)^{-1}]^{-1} \right\}^{-1} [V + \sigma_i^2 (X_i' X_i)^{-1}]^{-1},$$

and $\mathbf{b}_i = (X_i' X_i)^{-1} X_i' \mathbf{y}_i$. The term in braces, { }, is $X' \Omega^{-1} X$, which provides a convenient basis for computing the covariance matrix.

In order to obtain feasible generalized least squares estimates we must obtain consistent estimates of V and σ_i^2. Swamy (1970) shows that σ_i^2 is consistently estimated by

$$\hat{\sigma}_i^2 = (\mathbf{y}_i - X_i \mathbf{b}_i)'(\mathbf{y}_i - X_i \mathbf{b}_i)/(T - K),$$

and a consistent estimator of V is

$$\hat{V} = S/(N - 1) - \frac{1}{N} \sum_{i=1}^{N} \hat{\sigma}_i^2 (X_i' X_i)^{-1},$$

where

$$S = \sum_{i=1}^{N} (\mathbf{b}_i - \bar{\mathbf{b}})(\mathbf{b}_i - \bar{\mathbf{b}})',$$

and $\bar{\mathbf{b}} = (1/N) \sum_{i=1}^{N} \mathbf{b}_i$. One difficulty here is that $\hat{V}$ is not guaranteed to be positive semidefinite. Swamy (1971) considers this problem and suggests as an alternative the use of $S/(N - 1)$. This estimator is always positive semidefinite and consistent.

To test for the presence of random coefficients the null hypothesis $\boldsymbol{\beta}_1 = \boldsymbol{\beta}_2 = \cdots = \boldsymbol{\beta}_N = \bar{\boldsymbol{\beta}}$ is of interest. Swamy (1970) suggests the test statistic

$$h = \sum_{i=1}^{N} (\mathbf{b}_i - \tilde{\bar{\boldsymbol{\beta}}})' X_i' X_i (\mathbf{b}_i - \tilde{\bar{\boldsymbol{\beta}}})/\hat{\sigma}_i^2,$$

where $\tilde{\bar{\boldsymbol{\beta}}}$ is the estimator of $\bar{\boldsymbol{\beta}}$ under the hypothesis, namely

$$\tilde{\bar{\boldsymbol{\beta}}} = \left(\sum_{i=1}^{N} (\hat{\sigma}_i^2)^{-1} X_i' X_i \right)^{-1} \sum_{i=1}^{N} (\hat{\sigma}_i^2)^{-1} X_i' X_i \mathbf{b}_i.$$

Under the hypothesis $h \overset{\text{asy}}{\rightarrow} \chi^2_{K(N-1)}$.

Finally, how can the specific $\boldsymbol{\beta}_i$ be predicted? Lee and Griffiths (1979) show that

$$\hat{\boldsymbol{\beta}}_i = \hat{\bar{\boldsymbol{\beta}}}_i + V X_i' (X_i' V X_i + \sigma_i^2 I)^{-1} (\mathbf{y}_i - X_i \hat{\bar{\boldsymbol{\beta}}})$$

is the best linear unbiased predictor within the class of predictors where sampling properties are considered over time and individuals.

14.5.3 Models with Coefficients That Evolve Over Time

In this section we briefly present two models that have been proposed for use with time series data where the coefficients cannot be assumed constant over time. The models are considerably different in that the "return to normality" model of Harvey and Phillips (1982) proposes that the coefficients follow a stationary stochastic process about a constant mean, whereas in the Cooley–Prescott (1976) model the coefficients follow a nonstationary process.

Harvey and Phillips write the regression model as

$$y_t = \mathbf{x}_t' \boldsymbol{\beta}_t, \qquad t = 1, \ldots, T, \tag{14.5.5a}$$

$$\boldsymbol{\beta}_t - \bar{\boldsymbol{\beta}} = \Phi(\boldsymbol{\beta}_{t-1} - \bar{\boldsymbol{\beta}}) + \mathbf{e}_t, \tag{14.5.5b}$$

where $\bar{\boldsymbol{\beta}}$ is the mean coefficient vector and Φ is a $K \times K$ parameter matrix with roots less than one in absolute value. Note that if $\Phi = 0$, then this model reduces to a Hildreth–Houck type model. Substituting (14.5.5b) into (14.5.5a) we obtain

$$y_t = \mathbf{x}_t' \bar{\boldsymbol{\beta}} + v_t,$$

where $v_t = \mathbf{x}_t'\Phi(\boldsymbol{\beta}_{t-1} - \bar{\boldsymbol{\beta}}) + \mathbf{x}_t'\mathbf{e}_t$. This model is a linear regression with fixed coefficients but the error is heteroscedastic and serially correlated. Harvey and Phillips (1982) suggest an estimation procedure based on the Kalman filter (see Harvey (1981, Chapter 4 and Section 7.3)).

The Cooley and Prescott model (1973, 1976) proposes a less restrictive structure on the parameter variation. In their model the parameters follow a nonstationary, random walk process. Starting with (14.5.5a) they assume $\boldsymbol{\beta}_t$ is composed of two components exhibiting different kinds of parameter variation, permanent and transitory. Specifically, they hypothesize that

$$\boldsymbol{\beta}_t = \boldsymbol{\beta}_t^p + \mathbf{u}_t, \tag{14.5.6a}$$

$$\boldsymbol{\beta}_t^p = \boldsymbol{\beta}_{t-1}^p + \mathbf{v}_t, \tag{14.5.6b}$$

where $\boldsymbol{\beta}_t^p$ is the permanent component of the parameter vector and $\mathbf{u}_t$ and $\mathbf{v}_t$ are vectors of independent random disturbances with means zero and covariance matrices $(1 - \gamma)\sigma^2\Sigma_u$ and $\gamma\sigma^2\Sigma_v$, respectively. This parametrization is such that the parameter γ reflects the degree of permanent and transitory change. If γ is close to one the permanent changes are large relative to the transitory ones.

Maximum likelihood estimation of the parameters of this model is not feasible since the parameter generating process is not stationary. Cooley and Prescott show, however, that if one particular parameter vector is of interest, $\boldsymbol{\beta}_{T+1}^p$ in their case, a well-defined likelihood function can be constructed. They also develop a procedure for testing hypotheses about γ. The reader is referred to their papers for further details.

14.6 Summary and Guide to Further Readings

In this chapter we have reviewed a variety of models that have been developed for situations when it cannot be assumed that the coefficients of the regression model are constant for the entire sample. Such situations arise for two basic reasons. First the model may be properly specified but the coefficients are simply not the same for some subsets of the observations. In this case it is important to account for these differences because use of standard regression models will not lead to accurate information about the economic structure and will not provide a good basis for forecasting. Another reason often given for using varying parameter models is that the structural models we use are simple abstractions of the true data generation process, and the specification errors we make in making the approximations can be captured, in some sense, and offset by using random or varying coefficient models. This reasoning is potentially misleading, for while varying parameter models add flexibility and may improve the fit of the model, they may simply hide the true nature of the structural model.

In Section 14.2 we reviewed the use of dummy variables to account for structural shifts that occur for known subsets of observations. The equivalence between the dummy variable approach and a corresponding sets of equations approach was shown.

In Section 14.3 we considered other switching regression models where the observations can be partitioned *a priori* into different structural regimes. If the observations cannot be separated into regimes because of uncertainty about when transitions occurred, then the switching or "join" points can be treated as unknown parameters and estimated. As might be expected, Bayesian investigators have considered how *a priori* information might be incorporated. Useful references are Ferreira (1975), Holbert (1982), and Ohtani (1982).

In Section 14.4 models in which the parameters varied systematically in response to sets of explanatory variables were presented. This model is potentially useful in its own right and it can also be used to relate the models discussed in this chapter, from switching regressions to the Swamy random coefficient model, to one another.

Finally, in Section 14.5, we considered models in which the coefficients can usefully be characterized as random variables. The first model discussed was the Hildreth and Houck (1968) model of random coefficients. In addition to the references cited in the chapter, the reader can consult Griffiths *et al.* (1979) and Liu (1981) for Bayesian treatments of the problem. A second model, useful for the analysis of time series and cross-sectional data, is the Swamy (1970, 1971) random coefficient model. Mundlak (1978a, b) considers the interesting question of whether the coefficients should be treated as fixed, and estimated in a sets of equations framework, or estimated in the random coefficient framework. In addition to the references cited in the chapter, estimation of related models has been considered by Swamy and Mehta (1977) and Singh and Ullah (1974). Rosenberg (1973) and Johnson and

Rausser (1975) suggest models where the parameters also change systematically over time. Hsiao (1974, 1975) constructs an error components structure by adding a time specific error so that $\beta_{kit} = \bar{\beta}_k + \mu_{ki} + \lambda_{kt}$ measures the response of the dependent variable to the kth explanatory variable for the ith individual in the tth time period.

Finally, we considered models in which the regression coefficients are thought to evolve over time, following a stochastic process that can be either stationary or nonstationary. In addition to references cited in the chapter for the case where the parameter process is stationary, the reader can consult Burnett and Guthrie (1970), Rosenberg (1972, 1973), Pagan (1980), Swamy and Tinsley (1980), and Liu and Hanssens (1981). Models similar to the random walk model of Cooley and Prescott (1973, 1976) are discussed by Sarris (1973), Cooper (1973), Sant (1977), Belsley (1973), and Rausser, Mundlak, and Johnson (1983).

14.7 Exercises

14.1. Show that for the reparametrized model (14.2.11) the restriction $\boldsymbol{\gamma}_{23} = \mathbf{0}$ gives the dummy variable formulation.

14.2. Using the Grunfeld data in Chapter 8:
  (a) Obtain the dummy variable and sets of equations estimates for the General Electric and Westinghouse equations assuming the slope coefficients are different for observations 1939–1945.
  (b) Using the sets of equations format, test the hypothesis that the slope coefficients are equal and show that this test is identical to the test of the hypothesis that $\boldsymbol{\delta} = \mathbf{0}$ in the dummy variable format.

14.3. Using the data in Exercise 3.21, assume a structural shift occurs at observation $t_0 = 1955$. Obtain parameter estimates of the two regimes under the assumption that $E(y_{t_0}) = \mathbf{x}'_{t_0}\boldsymbol{\beta}_1 = \mathbf{x}'_{t_0}\boldsymbol{\beta}_2$ and test this hypothesis.

14.4. Using the data in Exercise 3.21, assume S is a function of time alone and estimate a cubic spline with a knot at 1954. Test the smoothness restrictions.

14.5. Using the data referred to in Exercise 14.3, assume t_0 is unknown and estimate it on the basis of the likelihood function (14.3.2).

14.6 Estimate the parameters of the General Electric and Westinghouse equations, see Exercise 14.2, under the assumption that the Swamy random coefficients model is correct. Test for the presence of parameter variation.

14.8 References

Belsley, C. (1973). On the determination of systematic parameter variation in the linear regression model. *Annals of Economic and Social Measurement*, **2**, 487–494.

Brown, R., Durbin, J., and Evans, J. (1975). Techniques for testing the constancy of regression relationships over time. *Journal of the Royal Statistical Society*, Series **B**, 149–163.

Burnett, T. D. and Guthrie, D. (1970). Estimation of stationary stochastic regression parameters. *Journal of the American Statistical Association*, **65**, 1547–1553.

Buse, A. and Lim, L. (1977). Cubic splines as a special case of restricted least squares. *Journal of the American Statistical Association*, **72**, 64–68.

Cooley, T. and Prescott, E. (1973). Varying parameter regression, a theory and some applications. *Annals of Economic and Social Measurement*, **2**, 463–474.

Cooley, T. and Prescott, E. (1976). Estimation in the presence of stochastic parameter variation. *Econometrica*, **44**, 167–184.

Cooper, J. (1973). Time-varying regression coefficients: a mixed estimation approach and operational limitations of the general Markov structure. *Annals of Economic and Social Measurement*, **2**, 525–530.

Farley, J. and Hinich, M. (1970). Testing for a shifting slope coefficient in a linear model. *Journal of the American Statistical Association*, **65**, 1320–1329.

Farley, J., Hinich, M., and McGuire, T. (1975). Some comparisons of tests for a shift in the slopes of a multivariate linear time series model. *Journal of Econometrics*, **3**, 297–318.

Ferreira, P. (1975). A Bayesian analysis of a switching regression model: Known number of regimes. *Journal of the American Statistical Association*, **70**, 370–374.

Goldfeld, S. and Quandt, R. (1973). The estimation of structural shifts by switching regressions. *Annals of Economic and Social Measurement*, **2**, 475–485.

Griffiths, W. E. (1972). Estimation of actual response coefficients in the Hildreth–Houck random coefficients model. *Journal of the American Statistical Association*, **67**, 633–635.

Griffiths, W. E., Drynan, R., and Prakash, S. (1979). Bayesian estimation of a random coefficient model. *Journal of Econometrics*, **10**, 201–220.

Harvey, A. C. (1981). *Time Series Models*. Oxford: Halsted Press.

Harvey, A. and Phillips, G. (1982). Estimation of regression models with time varying parameters. In *Games, Economic Dynamics and Time Series Analysis*, Edited by M. Deistler, E. Fürst, and G. Schwödianer. Wien–Würzburg: Physica-Verlag. Pp. 306–321.

Hildreth, C. and Houck, J. P. (1968). Some estimators for a linear model with random coefficients. *Journal of the American Statistical Association*, **63**, 584–595.

Holbert, D. (1982). A Bayesian analysis of a switching linear model. *Journal of Econometrics*, **19**, 77–87.

Hsiao, C. (1974). Statistical inference for a model with both random cross-sectional and time effects. *International Economic Review*, **15**, 12–30.

Hsiao, C. (1975). Some estimation methods for a random coefficient model. *Econometrica*, **43**, 305–325.

Johnson, S. R. and Rausser, G. C. (1975). An estimating method for models with stochastic, time varying parameters. American Statistical Association, Proceedings of the Business and Economics Statistics Section, 356–361.

Lee, L. F. and Griffiths, W. E. (1979). The prior likelihood and best linear unbiased prediction in stochastic coefficient linear models. University of New England Working Papers in Econometrics and Applied Statistics No. 1, Armidale, Australia.

Liu, L. (1981). Estimation of random coefficient regression models. *Journal of Statistical Computation and Simulation*, **13**, 27–39.

Liu, L. and Hanssens, D. (1981). A Bayesian approach to time varying cross-sectional regression models. *Journal of Econometrics*, **15**, 341–356.

McGee, V. E. and Carlton, W. T. (1970). Piecewise regression. *Journal of the American Statistical Association*, **65**, 1109–1124.

Mundlak, Y. (1978a). On the pooling of time series and cross-sectional data. *Econometrica*, **46**, 69–86.

Mundlak, Y. (1978b). Models with variable coefficients: Interpretation and extension. *Annales de l'Insee*, **30/31**, 483–510.

Ohtani, K. (1982). Bayesian estimation of the switching regression model with autocorrelated errors. *Journal of Econometrics*, **18**, 251–261.

Pagan, A. (1980). Some identification and estimation results for regression models with stochastically varying coefficients. *Journal of Econometrics*, **13**, 341–363.

Poirier, D. (1973). Piecewise regressions using cubic splines. *Journal of the American Statistical Association*, **68**, 515–524.

Poirier, D. (1976). *The Economics of Structural Change*. Amsterdam: North-Holland.

Quandt, R. (1958). The estimation of the parameters of a linear regression system obeying two separate regimes. *Journal of the American Statistical Association*, **53**, 873–880.

Rausser, G., Mundlak, Y., and Johnson, S. (1983). Structural change, updating, and forecasting in G. Rausser ed. *New Directions in Econometric Modeling and Forecasting in U.S. Agriculture*. Amsterdam: North-Holland. Pp. 659–718.

Rosenberg, B. (1972). The estimation of stationary stochastic regression parameters reexamined. *Journal of the American Statistical Association*, **67**, 650–654.

Rosenberg, B. (1973). The analysis of a cross-section of time series by stochastically convergent parameter regression. *Annals of Economic and Social Measurement*, **2**, 399–428.

Sant, D. (1977). Generalized least squares applied to time varying parameter models. *Annals of Economic and Social Measurement*, **6**, 301–314.

Sarris, A. (1973). A Bayesian approach to estimation of time varying regression coefficients. *Annals of Economic and Social Measurement*, **2**, 501–523.

Singh, B. and Ullah, A. (1974). Estimation of seemingly unrelated regressions with random coefficients. *Journal of the American Statistical Association*, **69**, 191–195.

Singh, B., Nagar, A. L., Choudhry, N. K., and Raj, B. (1976). On the estimation of structural change: A generalization of the random coefficients regression model. *International Economic Review*, **17**, 340–361.

Srivastava, V., Mishva, G., and Chaturvedi, A. (1981). Estimation of linear regression model with random coefficients ensuring almost non-negativity of variance estimators. *Biometric Journal*, **23**, 3–8.

Swamy, P. A. V. B. (1970). Efficient inference in a random coefficient regression model. *Econometrica*, **38**, 311–323.

Swamy, P. A. V. B. (1971). *Statistical Inference in Random Coefficient Regression Models*. New York: Springer-Verlag.

Swamy, P. A. V. B. and Mehta, J. S. (1975). Bayesian and non-Bayesian analysis of switching regressions and of random coefficient regression models. *Journal of the American Statistical Association*, **70**, 593–602.

Swamy, P. A. V. B. and Mehta, J. S. (1977). Estimation of linear models with time and cross-sectionally varying coefficients. *Journal of the American Statistical Association*, **72**, 890–898.

Swamy, P. and Tinsley, P. (1980). Linear prediction and estimation methods for regression models with stationary stochastic coefficients. *Journal of Econometrics*, **12**, 103–142.

CHAPTER 15

Models That Combine Time-Series and Cross-Section Data

15.1 Introduction

In the previous chapter we considered models that can be used when the economic structure generating the data are thought to vary from observation to observation. Such situations arise naturally in the context of time series data, where structural changes can occur over time, but random coefficient models have also been found useful when using cross-sectional data and individual decision making units are thought to respond differently to changes in independent variables. It is not surprising then, that with the growing availability of time-series of cross-section data, specialized models have developed that allow for possible changes in the economic structure generating the data.

In this chapter we will consider special cases of the general linear model

$$y_{it} = \sum_{k=1}^{K} \beta_{kit} x_{kit} + e_{it}, \qquad i = 1, \ldots, N; \quad t = 1, \ldots, T; \qquad (15.1.1)$$

where N is the number of cross-section observations and T is the number of time series observations. Note that the parameters of this general model are indexed by both a time-series and a cross-section index, so that each observation can be generated by a different economic structure. Since the estimation of KNT regression coefficients, plus any error process parameters, is intractable given only NT observations, restrictions of some sort must be placed on the extent of structural change. In the following sections models of increasing generality are presented that have been suggested as suitable for combining time-series and cross-section data.

15.2 Models in Which All Variation Is Contained in the Error Term

In this section we consider model (15.1.1) under the assumption that $\beta_{kit} = \beta_k$ for all k, i and t. Thus all economic units in all economic periods are assumed to respond in an identical fashion to a change in an independent variable. Under this assumption the observations for each cross-section can be written

$$\mathbf{y}_i = X_i\boldsymbol{\beta} + \mathbf{e}_i, \qquad i = 1, \ldots, N, \tag{15.2.1}$$

where

$$\mathbf{y}_i \equiv \begin{bmatrix} y_{i1} \\ y_{i2} \\ \vdots \\ y_{iT} \end{bmatrix}, \qquad X_i \equiv \begin{bmatrix} 1 & x_{2i1} & \cdots & x_{Ki1} \\ 1 & x_{2i2} & \cdots & x_{Ki2} \\ \vdots & \vdots & & \\ 1 & x_{2iT} & \cdots & x_{KiT} \end{bmatrix},$$

$$\boldsymbol{\beta} \equiv \begin{bmatrix} \beta_1 \\ \beta_2 \\ \vdots \\ \beta_K \end{bmatrix}, \qquad \mathbf{e}_i \equiv \begin{bmatrix} e_{i1} \\ e_{i2} \\ \vdots \\ e_{iT} \end{bmatrix}.$$

Writing all the observations together we have

$$\mathbf{y} = X\boldsymbol{\beta} + \mathbf{e}, \tag{15.2.2}$$

where

$$\mathbf{y} \equiv \begin{bmatrix} \mathbf{y}_1 \\ \mathbf{y}_2 \\ \vdots \\ \mathbf{y}_N \end{bmatrix}, \qquad X \equiv \begin{bmatrix} X_1 \\ X_2 \\ \vdots \\ X_N \end{bmatrix}, \qquad \mathbf{e} \equiv \begin{bmatrix} \mathbf{e}_1 \\ \mathbf{e}_2 \\ \vdots \\ \mathbf{e}_N \end{bmatrix}.$$

The model (15.2.2) could be estimated by least squares to obtain estimators with good properties if $E(\mathbf{e}) = \mathbf{0}$ and $E(\mathbf{ee}') = \sigma^2 I_{NT}$. Unfortunately, when dealing with time-series and cross-sectional data, we may face heteroscedasticity, autocorrelation, and contemporaneous covariance. Their presence implies that the least squares estimator is no longer the best, linear, unbiased estimator. To allow for these possibilities let us assume that

$$E(\mathbf{ee}') = \Omega, \tag{15.2.3}$$

where

$$\Omega = \begin{bmatrix} \Omega_{11} & \cdots & \Omega_{1N} \\ \vdots & & \vdots \\ \Omega_{N1} & \cdots & \Omega_{NN} \end{bmatrix}.$$

The form of the submatrices Ω_{ij} depends on which of the following assumptions are made:

(i) $E(e_{it}^2) = \sigma_i^2$ (heteroscedasticity);

(ii) $E(e_{is}e_{jt}) = \begin{cases} \sigma_{ij} & \text{if } s = t, \\ 0 & \text{otherwise} \end{cases}$ (contemporaneous covariance);

and

(iii) $e_{it} = \rho_i e_{i,t-1} + u_{it}$ (first-order autocorrelation);

where

$$u_{it} \sim (0, \phi_{ii})$$

and

$$E(u_{is}u_{jt}) = \begin{cases} \phi_{ij} & \text{if } s = t, \\ 0 & \text{otherwise.} \end{cases}$$

In order to develop the generalized least squares estimator we can express the contemporaneous covariance σ_{ij} in terms of ϕ_{ij}. The e_{it} can be written

$$e_{it} = u_{it} + \rho_i u_{i,t-1} + \rho_i^2 u_{i,t-2} + \cdots = \sum_{s=0}^{\infty} \rho_i^s u_{i,t-s},$$

by repeated substitution. Consequently,

$$\begin{aligned} E(e_{it}e_{jt}) &= E\left[\left(\sum_{s=0}^{\infty} \rho_i^s u_{i,t-s}\right)\left(\sum_{w=0}^{\infty} \rho_j^w u_{j,t-w}\right)\right] \\ &= E\left[\sum_{s=0}^{\infty} (\rho_i \rho_j)^s u_{i,t-s} u_{j,t-s}\right] \\ &= \phi_{ij} \sum_{s=0}^{\infty} (\rho_i \rho_j)^s \\ &= \frac{\phi_{ij}}{1 - \rho_i \rho_j} \quad \text{if } |\rho_i \rho_j| < 1. \end{aligned}$$

Furthermore, it follows similarly that

$$E(e_{it}, e_{j,t+s}) = \rho_j^s \frac{\phi_{ij}}{1 - \rho_i \rho_j},$$

and thus

$$\Omega_{ij} = \frac{\phi_{ij}}{1 - \rho_i \rho_j} \begin{bmatrix} 1 & \rho_j & & \cdots & \rho_j^{T-1} \\ \rho_i & 1 & \rho_j & \cdots & \rho_j^{T-2} \\ \vdots & & & \ddots & \vdots \\ \rho_i^{T-1} & \rho_i^{T-2} & & \cdots & 1 \end{bmatrix}.$$

Under these assumptions the best, linear, unbiased estimator of $\boldsymbol{\beta}$ is

$$\tilde{\boldsymbol{\beta}} = (X'\Omega^{-1}X)^{-1}X'\Omega^{-1}\mathbf{y}, \tag{15.2.4}$$

the generalized least squares estimator.

Since Ω in (15.2.4) is generally unknown, a consistent estimator for it must be obtained to apply feasible generalized least squares (Chapter 8). We can proceed as follows. Apply ordinary least squares to (15.2.2) to obtain the residuals

$$\hat{\mathbf{e}} = \mathbf{y} - X\hat{\boldsymbol{\beta}} = \mathbf{y} - X(X'X)^{-1}X'\mathbf{y}.$$

The residuals $\hat{e}_{it}$, $t = 1, \ldots, T$, can be used to obtain a consistent estimator for ρ_i, as discussed in Chapter 10, say $\hat{\rho}_i$. Then we can apply the Prais–Winston transformation matrix,

$$P_i = \begin{bmatrix} \sqrt{1-\hat{\rho}_i^2} & 0 & 0 & \cdots & 0 \\ -\hat{\rho}_i & 1 & 0 & \cdots & 0 \\ 0 & -\hat{\rho}_i & 1 & \cdots & 0 \\ \vdots & & \ddots & \ddots & \vdots \\ 0 & 0 & 0 \;\cdots & -\hat{\rho}_i & 1 \end{bmatrix},$$

to each cross-section equation (15.2.1) to obtain

$$\mathbf{y}_i^* = P_i\mathbf{y}_i = P_iX_i\boldsymbol{\beta} + P_i\mathbf{e}_i = X_i^*\boldsymbol{\beta} + \mathbf{u}_i, \qquad i = 1, \ldots, N, \tag{15.2.5}$$

where $\mathbf{u}_i' = (u_{i1}, \ldots, u_{iT})$. If the transformed observations are stacked we have

$$\mathbf{y}^* = X^*\boldsymbol{\beta} + \mathbf{u}, \tag{15.2.6}$$

where asymptotically $E(\mathbf{uu}') = \Phi \otimes I_T$ and Φ is the $N \times N$ contemporaneous covariance matrix whose elements are ϕ_{ij}. Applying ordinary least squares to (15.2.6) yields residuals

$$\mathbf{u}_i^* = \mathbf{y}_i^* - X_i^*(X_i^{*\prime}X_i^*)^{-1}X_i^{*\prime}\mathbf{y}_i^*.$$

Consistent estimates of the contemporaneous covariances can be obtained (see Section 8.5) as

$$\hat{\phi}_{ij} = \mathbf{u}_i^{*\prime}\mathbf{u}_j^*/T. \tag{15.2.7}$$

Finally then, a consistent feasible generalized least squares estimator for $\boldsymbol{\beta}$ is

$$\tilde{\tilde{\boldsymbol{\beta}}} = (X'\hat{\Omega}^{-1}X)^{-1}X'\hat{\Omega}^{-1}\mathbf{y} = [X^{*\prime}(\hat{\Phi}^{-1} \otimes I)X^*]^{-1}X^{*\prime}(\hat{\Phi}^{-1} \otimes I)\mathbf{y}^*. \tag{15.2.8}$$

The asymptotic distribution of $\sqrt{T}(\tilde{\tilde{\boldsymbol{\beta}}} - \boldsymbol{\beta})$ is $N(\mathbf{0}, \operatorname{plim} T(X'\Omega^{-1}X)^{-1})$ so that for finite samples the asymptotic covariance matrix of $\tilde{\tilde{\boldsymbol{\beta}}}$ can be approximated by $(X'\hat{\Omega}^{-1}X)^{-1}$.

The model above is easy to employ and may be applicable to a wide range of situations. However the underlying assumption, that all structural differences are captured within the error term, must be held firmly in mind. In the next sections we present models where some, or all, structural changes are in the regression parameters.

15.3 Models Where All Structural Change Is Captured by the Intercept

In this section we consider the model (15.1.1) under the restriction that all structural variation across time series and cross-sectional units is confined to the intercept. That is, we will restrict (15.1.1) so that $\beta_{kit} = \beta_k$ for $k = 2, \ldots, K$ but that β_{1it} may vary over individuals, over time or both. The estimation procedure depends on whether the intercept varies in a fixed or random manner. In the former case dummy variable models are appropriate and in the latter "error components" models are produced.

15.3.1 Dummy Variable Models

15.3.1a *Dummy Variable Models Where the Intercept Varies Over Individuals*

Consider the first case where the N cross-sectional relations are identical except for the fact that the intercept is possibly different for each cross-section. That is,

$$y_{it} = \beta_{1i} + \sum_{k=2}^{K} \beta_k x_{kit} + e_{it}, \qquad i = 1, \ldots, N, \quad t = 1, \ldots, T. \quad (15.3.1)$$

Note that by the specification of Equation 15.3.1 we are assuming that the intercept term does not vary over time for any individual. Each cross-section relation can be written

$$\mathbf{y}_i = \beta_{1i}\mathbf{j}_T + X_{.i}\boldsymbol{\beta}_. + \mathbf{e}_i, \qquad i = 1, \ldots, N, \qquad (15.3.2)$$

where $\mathbf{j}_T$ is a $T \times 1$ vector of ones, $X_{.i} = (\mathbf{x}_{2i.}, \mathbf{x}_{3i.}, \ldots, \mathbf{x}_{Ki.})$ is the $T \times (K-1)$ matrix of observations for the ith cross-section on independent variables other than the intercept and $\boldsymbol{\beta}'_. = (\beta_2, \ldots, \beta_K)$. It is also assumed that the error terms are well behaved, that is

$$E(\mathbf{e}_i) = \mathbf{0},$$
$$E(\mathbf{e}_i\mathbf{e}_i') = \sigma_e^2 I_T, \qquad (15.3.3)$$

and $$E(\mathbf{e}_i\mathbf{e}_j') = 0 \quad \text{if } i \neq j.$$

These assumptions can be relaxed in the manner of the previous section with little difficulty. Observations on all the cross-sections can be written as

$$\begin{bmatrix} \mathbf{y}_1 \\ \mathbf{y}_2 \\ \vdots \\ \mathbf{y}_N \end{bmatrix} = \begin{bmatrix} \mathbf{j}_T & \mathbf{0} & \cdots & \mathbf{0} & X_{.1} \\ \mathbf{0} & \mathbf{j}_T & \cdots & \mathbf{0} & X_{.2} \\ \vdots & \vdots & & \vdots & \vdots \\ \mathbf{0} & \mathbf{0} & \cdots & \mathbf{j}_T & X_{.N} \end{bmatrix} \begin{bmatrix} \beta_{11} \\ \beta_{12} \\ \vdots \\ \beta_{1N} \\ \boldsymbol{\beta}_. \end{bmatrix} + \begin{bmatrix} \mathbf{e}_1 \\ \mathbf{e}_2 \\ \vdots \\ \mathbf{e}_N \end{bmatrix}, \tag{15.3.4}$$

or in more compact notation

$$\mathbf{y} = [I_N \otimes \mathbf{j}_T \quad X_.] \begin{bmatrix} \boldsymbol{\beta}_1 \\ \boldsymbol{\beta}_. \end{bmatrix} + \mathbf{e}, \tag{15.3.5}$$

where $\boldsymbol{\beta}_1' = (\beta_{11}, \beta_{12}, \ldots, \beta_{1N})$ and the definition of $X_.$ is implied by (15.3.4). If the number of regression parameters, $N + (K - 1)$, is not too large for computation, ordinary least squares provides best linear unbiased estimators under the assumptions (15.3.3). Furthermore, under the assumption of normally distributed errors, the hypothesis of structural homogeneity, $H_0: \beta_{11} = \beta_{12} = \cdots = \beta_{1N}$, can be tested by methods described in Chapter 3, or given a sufficiently large sample with the asymptotic tests in Chapter 4.

It should also be noted that an alternative, but completely equivalent, formulation is often employed. In (15.3.4) each cross-sectional intercept is a distinct parameter. Often one parameter is defined as the "benchmark" value and then all other intercepts represented as deviations from that value. For example, if $N = 2$ we might formulate the model as

$$\begin{bmatrix} \mathbf{y}_1 \\ \mathbf{y}_2 \end{bmatrix} = \begin{bmatrix} \mathbf{j}_T & \mathbf{0} & X_{.1} \\ \mathbf{j}_T & \mathbf{j}_T & X_{.2} \end{bmatrix} \begin{bmatrix} \beta_{11} \\ \delta_2 \\ \boldsymbol{\beta}_. \end{bmatrix} + \begin{bmatrix} \mathbf{e}_1 \\ \mathbf{e}_2 \end{bmatrix}. \tag{15.3.6}$$

Here β_{11} is the "benchmark" intercept, as well as the intercept for the first cross-section and δ_2 is the incremental difference between β_{11} and the intercept of the second cross-section. That is, $\beta_{12} = \beta_{11} + \delta_2$. There is no difference in the resulting estimates of the original parameters and the standard errors of the intercept estimates may be easily computed from the covariance matrix of the estimates in (15.3.6). The hypothesis of structural homogeneity in the second formulation is that $\delta_2 = 0$. In the general case with N cross-sectional units the second formulation is written

$$\mathbf{y} = \left[\mathbf{j}_{NT} \quad \begin{bmatrix} \mathbf{0}' \\ I_{N-1} \end{bmatrix} \otimes \mathbf{j}_T \quad X_. \right] \begin{bmatrix} \beta_{11} \\ \boldsymbol{\delta} \\ \boldsymbol{\beta}_. \end{bmatrix} + \mathbf{e}, \tag{15.3.7}$$

where $\boldsymbol{\delta}' = (\delta_2, \ldots, \delta_N)$.

If the number of parameters in (15.3.5) or (15.3.7) is so large that the inversion of the $N + (K - 1)$ order matrix is computationally burdensome, the magnitude of the problem can be greatly reduced by considering the estimator of $\boldsymbol{\beta}_.$ alone from the partitioned model (15.3.5). See Exercise (15.1) for proof that

$$\hat{\boldsymbol{\beta}}_. = [X_.'(I_N \otimes D_T)X_.]^{-1}X_.'(I_N \otimes D_T)\mathbf{y}$$
$$= \left(\sum_{i=1}^{N} X_{i.}' D_T X_{i.}\right)^{-1} \sum_{i=1}^{N} X_{i.}' D_T \mathbf{y}_i, \tag{15.3.8}$$

where $D_T = I_T - \mathbf{j}_T\mathbf{j}_T'/T$. For future reference, note that D_T is an idempotent matrix that transforms the tth observation so that it is a deviation about the mean for that individual. That is,

$$X_{i.}' D_T X_{i.} = X_{i.}' D_T D_T X_{i.}$$

and the tth row of $D_T X_{i.}$ is

$$(x_{2it} - \bar{x}_{2i.}, \ldots, x_{Kit} - \bar{x}_{Ki.}),$$

and $\bar{x}_{ki.} = \sum_{t=1}^{T} x_{kit}/T$. The advantage of (15.3.8) is that it requires an inversion only of order $(K - 1)$. Following Exercise 15.2 it can be shown that the estimates of the intercepts can be computed as

$$\hat{\beta}_{1i} = \bar{y}_{i.} - \sum_{k=2}^{K} \hat{\beta}_k \bar{x}_{ki.}, \tag{15.3.9}$$

and their variances computed directly from knowledge of the variances of $\bar{y}_{i.}$ and the $\hat{\beta}_k$.

15.3.1b *Dummy Variable Models Where the Intercept Varies Over Individuals and Time*

In this section we generalize the previous model to allow the intercept to vary over individuals and time. That is, the model we consider is

$$y_{it} = \beta_{1it} + \sum_{k=2}^{K} \beta_k x_{kit} + e_{it}. \tag{15.3.10}$$

As in the previous model, the slope coefficients of this model are assumed to be constant for all time periods and cross-section units, and only the intercept is allowed to vary.

For this model it is convenient to think of β_{1it} as composed of three components. That is, let

$$\beta_{1it} = \bar{\beta}_1 + \mu_i + \lambda_t,$$

where μ_i represents the difference between β_{1it} and the common factor $\bar{\beta}_1$ that is due to a cross-section influence and λ_t is the difference attributable to a time series influence.

With the model as defined, one of the μ_i or λ_t is redundant. That is, for a particular cross-section the model is

$$\mathbf{y}_i = (\bar{\beta}_1 + \mu_i)\mathbf{j}_T + I_T\boldsymbol{\lambda} + X_{i.}\boldsymbol{\beta}_. + \mathbf{e}_i, \tag{15.3.11}$$

where $\boldsymbol{\lambda}' = (\lambda_1, \lambda_2, \ldots, \lambda_T)$. Thus the columns $\mathbf{j}_T$ and $I_T\boldsymbol{\lambda}$ are exactly collinear. One solution is to omit one of the time related dummy variables so that the model for the ith cross-section is

$$\mathbf{y}_i = \beta_{1i}\mathbf{j}_T + \begin{bmatrix} I_{T-1} \\ \mathbf{0}' \end{bmatrix}\boldsymbol{\lambda}^* + X_.\boldsymbol{\beta}_. + \mathbf{e}_i,$$

where $\beta_{1i} = \bar{\beta}_1 + \mu_i$ and $\boldsymbol{\lambda}^{*\prime} = (\lambda_1, \ldots, \lambda_{T-1})$. Thus, the observations over all N cross-sections are

$$\mathbf{y} = \left\{ I_N \otimes \mathbf{j}_T \quad \mathbf{j}_N \otimes \begin{bmatrix} I_{T-1} \\ \mathbf{0}' \end{bmatrix} \quad X_. \right\} \begin{bmatrix} \boldsymbol{\beta}_1 \\ \boldsymbol{\lambda}^* \\ \boldsymbol{\beta}_. \end{bmatrix} + \mathbf{e}. \tag{15.3.12}$$

If $E(\mathbf{e}) = \mathbf{0}$ and $E(\mathbf{ee}') = \sigma_e^2 I_{NT}$, the ordinary least squares estimator is best linear unbiased. If the total number of parameters, $N + (T - 1) + (K - 1)$, is not too large, ordinary least squares can be applied directly. Otherwise $\hat{\boldsymbol{\beta}}_.$ can be obtained by partitioning the model as in the previous section. See Exercise 15.3 for proof that

$$\hat{\boldsymbol{\beta}}_. = (X_.'QX_.)^{-1}X_.'Q\mathbf{y}, \tag{15.3.13}$$

where

$$Q = I_{NT} - \left(I_N \otimes \frac{\mathbf{j}_T\mathbf{j}_T'}{T}\right) - \left(\frac{\mathbf{j}_N\mathbf{j}_N'}{N} \otimes I_T\right) + \frac{\mathbf{j}_{NT}\mathbf{j}_{NT}'}{NT}. \tag{15.3.14}$$

The matrix Q is idempotent and transforms $X_.$ to contain typical element $x_{kit} - \bar{x}_{ki.} - \bar{x}_{k.t} + \bar{x}_{k..}$, where

$$\bar{x}_{ki.} = \sum_{t=1}^{T} x_{kit}/T,$$

$$\bar{x}_{k.t} = \sum_{i=1}^{N} x_{kit}/N,$$

and

$$\bar{x}_{k..} = \sum_{t=1}^{T}\sum_{i=1}^{N} x_{kit}/NT.$$

Once $\hat{\boldsymbol{\beta}}_.$ is obtained, the remaining parameters are estimated as

$$\hat{\mu}_i = (\bar{y}_{i.} - \bar{y}_{..}) - \sum_{k=2}^{K} \hat{\beta}_k(\bar{x}_{ki.} - \bar{x}_{k..}),$$

$$\hat{\lambda}_t = (\bar{y}_{.t} - \bar{y}_{..}) - \sum_{k=2}^{K} \hat{\beta}_k(\bar{x}_{k.t} - \bar{x}_{k..}),$$

and

$$\hat{\bar{\beta}}_1 = \bar{y}_{..} - \sum_{k=2}^{K} \hat{\beta}_k \bar{x}_{k..}.$$

15.3.2 Error Components with Variation Only Over Individuals

Once again we will consider model (15.3.1), but now we will treat the intercept β_{1i} as random. In this context we consider the cross-section observations to be random draws from a larger population. All the members of the population are assumed to have identical responses to changes in $(K - 1)$ explanatory variables. The value of the intercept, however, is random with mean $\bar{\beta}_1$. That is, we can represent β_{1i} as

$$\beta_{1i} = \bar{\beta}_1 + \mu_i, \tag{15.3.15}$$

where $\bar{\beta}_1$ is the mean intercept of the cross-section population and μ_i is a random variable with $E(\mu_i) = 0$ and $E(\mu_i^2) = \sigma_\mu^2$, $E(\mu_i \mu_j) = 0$ for $i \neq j$, and the e_{it}'s are not correlated with μ_i. Under these assumptions (15.3.1) becomes

$$\mathbf{y}_i = X_i\boldsymbol{\beta} + \mu_i\mathbf{j}_T + \mathbf{e}_i, \tag{15.3.16}$$

where $\boldsymbol{\beta}' = (\bar{\beta}_1, \beta_2, \ldots, \beta_K)$. The composite error term has covariance matrix

$$\begin{aligned}
\Omega_i &= E[(\mu_i\mathbf{j}_T + \mathbf{e}_i)(\mu_i\mathbf{j}_T + \mathbf{e}_i)'] \\
&= \sigma_\mu^2\mathbf{j}_T\mathbf{j}_T' + \sigma_e^2 I_T \\
&= \begin{bmatrix} \sigma_\mu^2 & \sigma_\mu^2 & \cdots & \sigma_\mu^2 \\ \sigma_\mu^2 & \sigma_\mu^2 & \cdots & \sigma_\mu^2 \\ \vdots & \vdots & & \vdots \\ \sigma_\mu^2 & \sigma_\mu^2 & \cdots & \sigma_\mu^2 \end{bmatrix} + \begin{bmatrix} \sigma_e^2 & & & 0 \\ & \sigma_e^2 & & \\ & & \ddots & \\ 0 & & & \sigma_e^2 \end{bmatrix}.
\end{aligned} \tag{15.3.17}$$

Thus for each individual equation the error term is homoscedastic but there are identical covariances between disturbances across time.

15.3.2a *Generalized Least Squares Estimation*

If all the equations (15.3.16) are written together then

$$\mathbf{y} = X\boldsymbol{\beta} + \boldsymbol{\mu} \otimes \mathbf{j}_T + \mathbf{e}, \tag{15.3.18}$$

where $\boldsymbol{\mu}' = (\mu_1, \ldots, \mu_N)$. The covariance matrix of $\mathbf{e}$ is

$$E(\mathbf{e}\mathbf{e}') = \Omega = I_N \otimes \Omega_i, \tag{15.3.19}$$

a block diagonal matrix. If σ_μ^2 and σ_e^2 are known the generalized least squares estimator for $\boldsymbol{\beta}$ is

$$\tilde{\boldsymbol{\beta}} = (X'\Omega^{-1}X)^{-1}X'\Omega^{-1}\mathbf{y}, \tag{15.3.20}$$

which is best linear unbiased.

As with many generalized least squares problems it is convenient to find a transformation matrix so that ordinary least squares can be applied to the transformed model. Fuller and Battese (1973) suggest

$$P = I_N \otimes P_i, \tag{15.3.21}$$

where

$$P_i = I_T - \left(1 - \frac{\sigma_e}{\sigma_1}\right)\frac{\mathbf{j}_T\mathbf{j}_T'}{T}, \tag{15.3.22}$$

where $P_i'P_i = \sigma_e^2\Omega_i^{-1}$ and $\sigma_1^2 = T\sigma_\mu^2 + \sigma_e^2$, so that $P'P = \sigma_e^2\Omega^{-1}$. Multiplying both sides of (15.3.18) by P yields observations of the form

$$(y_{it} - \alpha\bar{y}_{i.}) = (1 - \alpha)\beta_1 + \sum_{k=2}^{K} \beta_k(x_{kit} - \alpha\bar{x}_{ki.}) + v_{it}, \tag{15.3.23}$$

where $\alpha = 1 - \sigma_e/\sigma_1$ and the v_{it} are homoscedastic and uncorrelated with variance σ_e^2. If α were known, applying ordinary least squares to (15.3.23) would yield generalized least squares estimates.

15.3.2b *Estimation of the Variance Components*

Since σ_μ^2 and σ_e^2 are unknown, they must be estimated consistently so feasible generalized least squares can be applied. Maddala (1971) suggests the following estimators. If $\hat{\mathbf{e}} = (I_N \otimes D_T)\mathbf{y} - (I_N \otimes D_T)X_{.}\hat{\boldsymbol{\beta}}_{.}$, then an unbiased estimator of σ_e^2 is

$$\hat{\sigma}_e^2 = \hat{\mathbf{e}}'\hat{\mathbf{e}}/(N(T - 1) - (K - 1)). \tag{15.3.24}$$

Then, define

$$\boldsymbol{\beta}_{.}^{*} = (X_{.}'Q_1X_{.})^{-1}X_{.}'Q_1\mathbf{y}, \tag{15.3.25}$$

where

$$Q_1 = \left(I_N \otimes \frac{\mathbf{j}_T\mathbf{j}_T'}{T}\right) - \frac{\mathbf{j}_{NT}\mathbf{j}_{NT}'}{NT} \tag{15.3.26}$$

is an idempotent matrix such that

$$Q_1X_{.} = \begin{bmatrix} \bar{x}_{21.} - \bar{x}_{2..} & \cdots & \bar{x}_{K1.} - \bar{x}_{K..} \\ \vdots & \ddots & \vdots \\ \bar{x}_{2N.} - \bar{x}_{2..} & \cdots & \bar{x}_{KN.} - \bar{x}_{K..} \end{bmatrix} \otimes \mathbf{j}_T. \tag{15.3.27}$$

If $\mathbf{e}^* = Q_1\mathbf{y} - Q_1X_{.}\boldsymbol{\beta}_{.}^{*}$, then an unbiased estimator of σ_1^2 is

$$\hat{\sigma}_1^2 = \frac{\mathbf{e}^{*\prime}\mathbf{e}^*}{(N-K)}. \tag{15.3.28}$$

The variance σ_μ^2 may then be estimated as

$$\hat{\sigma}_\mu^2 = \begin{cases} (\hat{\sigma}_1^2 - \hat{\sigma}_e^2)/T & \text{if } \sigma_\mu^2 > 0, \\ 0 & \text{otherwise.} \end{cases} \tag{15.3.29}$$

Alternative estimators for the variance components are suggested by Fuller and Battese (1973).

The properties of the resulting feasible generalized least squares estimators are explored by Fuller and Battese (1973). They show that under the usual type regularity conditions the feasible generalized least squares and generalized least squares estimators have the same asymptotic distribution.

15.3.3 Error Components Models with Variation Over Individuals and Time

In this section we generalize the type of variation permitted to randomness in the intercept over individuals and time. Consider the model (15.3.10) but assume the intercept β_{1it} to be random. Express it as

$$\beta_{1it} = \bar{\beta}_1 + \mu_i + \lambda_t, \tag{15.3.30}$$

where the individual effects μ_i are random with $E(\mu_i) = 0$, $E(\mu_i^2) = \sigma_\mu^2$; the time effects λ_t are random with $E(\lambda_t) = 0$ and $E(\lambda_t^2) = \sigma_\lambda^2$. It is further assumed that $E(\mu_i\mu_j) = 0$ if $i \neq j$ and $E(\lambda_t\lambda_s) = 0$ if $t \neq s$; also μ_i, λ_t, and e_{it} are all uncorrelated.

Under these assumptions the observations for the ith cross-section are

$$\mathbf{y}_i = X_i\boldsymbol{\beta} + \mu_i\mathbf{j}_T + I_T\boldsymbol{\lambda} + \mathbf{e}_i, \tag{15.3.31}$$

where $\boldsymbol{\lambda}' = (\lambda_1, \ldots, \lambda_T)$. The covariance matrix of the composite error term $(\mu_i \mathbf{j}_T + I_T\boldsymbol{\lambda} + \mathbf{e}_i)$ is

$$\Omega_{ii} = \sigma_\mu^2 \mathbf{j}_T \mathbf{j}_T' + \sigma_\lambda^2 I_T + \sigma_e^2 I_T$$

and the covariance between disturbance vectors for two individuals is

$$\Omega_{ij} = \sigma_\lambda^2 I_T.$$

Pooling all NT observations yields

$$\mathbf{y} = X\boldsymbol{\beta} + \boldsymbol{\mu} \otimes \mathbf{j}_T + (\mathbf{j}_N \otimes I_T)\boldsymbol{\lambda} + \mathbf{e}. \qquad (15.3.32)$$

The error term has covariance matrix

$$\Omega = \sigma_\mu^2(I_N \otimes \mathbf{j}_T\mathbf{j}_T') + \sigma_\lambda^2(\mathbf{j}_N\mathbf{j}_N' \otimes I_T) + \sigma_e^2 I_{NT}.$$

This matrix is not block diagonal and the disturbances corresponding to different individuals are contemporaneously correlated.

So that generalized least squares estimation can be implemented, Fuller and Battese (1974) note that

$$\Omega^{-1} = \frac{Q}{\sigma_e^2} + \frac{Q_1}{\sigma_1^2} + \frac{Q_2}{\sigma_2^2} + \frac{Q_3}{\sigma_3^2} = \Omega^{-1/2}\Omega^{-1/2},$$

where Q, Q_1 and σ_1^2 are defined above and

$$Q_2 = \left(\frac{\mathbf{j}_N\mathbf{j}_N'}{N} \otimes I_T\right) - \frac{\mathbf{j}_{NT}\mathbf{j}_{NT}'}{NT},$$

$$Q_3 = \frac{\mathbf{j}_{NT}\mathbf{j}_{NT}'}{NT},$$

$$\sigma_2^2 = \sigma_e^2 + N\sigma_\lambda^2,$$

$$\sigma_3^2 = \sigma_e^2 + T\sigma_\mu^2 + N\sigma_\lambda^2,$$

and

$$\Omega^{-1/2} = \frac{Q}{\sigma_e} + \frac{Q_1}{\sigma_1} + \frac{Q_2}{\sigma_2} + \frac{Q_3}{\sigma_3}.$$

The form of $\Omega^{-1/2}$ follows from the idempotency of Q, Q_1, Q_2, and Q_3. Consequently, if (15.3.32) is premultiplied by $\sigma_e\Omega^{-1/2}$ then the transformed errors are uncorrelated and have variances σ_e^2. The variables in the transformed model are

$$y_{it}^* = y_{it} - \alpha_1\bar{y}_{i.} - \alpha_2\bar{y}_{.t} + \alpha_3\bar{y}_{..}, \qquad (15.3.32a)$$

$$x_{kit}^* = x_{kit} - \alpha_1\bar{x}_{ki.} - \alpha_2\bar{x}_{k.t} + \alpha_3\bar{x}_{k..}, \qquad (15.3.32b)$$

where $\alpha_1 = 1 - \sigma_e/\sigma_1$, $\alpha_2 = \sigma_e/\sigma_2$ and $\alpha_3 = \alpha_1 + \alpha_3 - 1 + \sigma_e/\sigma_3$. An ordinary least squares regression of y_{it}^* on x_{kit}^* yields the generalized least squares estimator.

To implement feasible generalized least squares the variance components must be estimated. Swamy and Arora (1972) suggest the unbiased estimators

$$\hat{\sigma}_1^2 = \frac{\mathbf{e}^{*\prime}\mathbf{e}^*}{N - K},$$

$$\hat{\sigma}_2^2 = \frac{\mathbf{e}^{0\prime}\mathbf{e}^0}{T - K},$$

$$\hat{\sigma}_e^2 = \frac{\hat{\mathbf{e}}'\hat{\mathbf{e}}}{(N-1)(T-1) - (K-1)},$$

where

$$\mathbf{e}^* = Q_1\mathbf{y} - Q_1 X_. \boldsymbol{\beta}_.^*, \qquad \boldsymbol{\beta}_.^* = (X_.' Q_1 X_.)^{-1} X_.' Q_1 \mathbf{y},$$

$$\mathbf{e}^0 = Q_2\mathbf{y} - Q_2 X_. \boldsymbol{\beta}_.^0, \qquad \boldsymbol{\beta}_.^0 = (X_.' Q_2 X_.)^{-1} X_.' Q_2 \mathbf{y},$$

$$\hat{\mathbf{e}} = Q\mathbf{y} - QX_. \hat{\boldsymbol{\beta}}_., \qquad \hat{\boldsymbol{\beta}}_. = (X_.' Q X_.)^{-1} X_.' Q \mathbf{y}.$$

15.4 Models Where All Coefficients Are Allowed to Vary

If we consider the general model (15.1.1), coefficients other than the intercept may also vary. Several alternative assumptions can be made. First, the coefficients can vary across cross-sections but not time, leading to the seemingly unrelated regressions model (Chapter 8) or the Swamy random coefficient model (Chapter 14) depending on whether the coefficients are fixed or random. Alternatively the coefficients could vary across cross-sections and time, which leads to the random coefficient model proposed by Hsiao (1974, 1975). The general model is made tractable, at least conceptually, by assuming that all the coefficients can be represented as

$$\beta_{kit} = \bar{\beta}_k + \mu_{ki} + \lambda_{kt},$$

where μ_{ki} and λ_{kt} are random components with mean zero and allow for random individual and time effects, respectively. The resulting complete model has a complicated covariance matrix that depends upon the variances of the μ_{ki}, λ_{kt} and equation disturbances. Hsiao presents consistent estimators for these variances so that feasible generalized least squares can be applied.

15.5 Summary and Guide to Further Readings

In this chapter we have reviewed models that are useful for pooling time-series and cross-section data. The reason for considering such models is that one or more assumptions associated with the usual linear model are likely to be violated when pooling data. The first difficulty is that a pooled model's errors may be heteroscedastic, autocorrelated and may exhibit contemporaneous covariance. Under these circumstances generalized least squares is an appropriate estimation technique. A second potential problem when pooling time-series and cross-section data is that the parameters of the data generating process may not be the same for all observations. Not only might different individuals react differently to changes in explanatory variables, but an individual's reactions may change over time. Under either of these circumstances the usual ordinary least squares estimator is inappropriate. As is always the case we wish to specify a statistical model that is consistent with the way the data at our disposal were generated. When pooling data extra care must be taken to adapt a sufficiently general model to allow for the difficulties noted above.

An important point remains to be addressed. When should one choose the dummy variable formulation and when should one choose the error components models? On one hand the dummy variable model can be regarded as one that is conditional upon values of μ_i and λ_t that occur in the sample and thus is relevant whether the μ_i and λ_t are fixed or random. On the other hand, the error components models make specific assumptions about the μ_i and λ_t and *if* they are correct, should lead to more efficient estimators. If the assumptions are incorrect then the error components model will lead to biased estimators. Mundlak (1978) considers this problem further and concludes that the choice depends on whether the random effects are correlated with the regressors. Mundlak argues that if correlation exists, the dummy variable model is more appropriate, while if no correlation exists, the variance components estimator may be appropriate. Other useful references related to variance–components models include Nerlove (1971), Arora (1973), Amemiya (1971), and Judge *et al.* (1980, Chapter 8).

The models discussed in this chapter are appropriate under a wide variety of circumstances, and are not designed necessarily to take advantage of any special characteristics of a data set. Recently, however, substantial work has been undertaken on exploiting the large longitudinal data sources that are becoming increasingly available. These data sets are distinguished by their *short* time series on a large number of individuals. Good initial sources of references on such models include the special issue of the *Journal of Econometrics* (January, 1982) entitled *Econometric Analysis of Longitudinal Data*, edited by Heckman and Singer, and *The Econometrics of Panel Data* (1978), a special issue of *Annales de l'Insee.*

15.6 Exercises

15.1. Verify that the estimator (15.3.8) is the ordinary least squares estimator of the subvector $\boldsymbol{\beta}$ in (15.3.5) by applying the usual least squares rule but using the partitioned inverse of $X'X$.

15.2. Verify that the estimates represented in (15.3.9) are the ordinary least squares estimates of the intercepts coming from the partitioned model in Exercise 15.1.

15.3. Verify that the estimator in (15.3.3) is the ordinary least squares estimator for the subvector $\boldsymbol{\beta}$ in (15.3.12) using the partitioned inverse rule as in Exercise 15.1.

15.4. Verify that the matrix P defined in (15.3.21) transforms the model in (15.3.18) to (15.3.23).

15.7 References

Amemiya, T. (1971). The estimation of the variances in a variance-components model. *International Economic Review*, **12**, 1–13.

Arora, S. (1973). Error components regression models and their application. *Annals of Economic and Social Measurement*, **2**, 451–461.

Fuller, W. A. and Battese, G. E. (1973). Transformations for estimation of linear models with nested error structure. *Journal of the American Statistical Association*, **68**, 626–632.

Fuller, W. A. and Battese, G. E. (1974). Estimation of linear models with crossed-error structure. *Journal of Econometrics*, **2**, 67–68.

Hsiao, C. (1974). Statistical inference for a model with both random cross-sectional and time effects. *International Economic Review*, **15**, 12–30.

Hsiao, C. (1975). Some estimation methods for a random coefficient model. *Econometrica*, **43**, 305–325.

Judge, G., Griffiths, W., Hill, R., and Lee, T. (1980). *The Theory and Practice of Econometrics*. New York: Wiley.

Maddala, G. S. (1971). The use of variance components in pooling cross section and time series data. *Econometrica*, **39**, 341–358.

Mundlak, Y. (1978). On the pooling of time series and cross sectional data. *Econometrica*, **46**, 69–86.

Nerlove, M. (1971). A note on error components models. *Econometrica*, **39**, 383–396.

Swamy, P. A. V. B. and Arora, S. S. (1972). The exact finite sample properties of the estimators of coefficients in the error components regression models. *Econometrica*, **40**, 253–260.

CHAPTER 16

The Analysis of Models with Qualitative or Censored Dependent Variables

16.1 Introduction

Traditionally economists have dealt with models designed to explain the variation in a dependent variable which could be assumed continuous and normally distributed. Economics, however, as a theory of choice, can be applied not only to questions about how much to produce or consume but also "whether" to produce or consume a certain item. More generally, individual economic units often must choose between a finite set of alternatives. Economists are interested in what factors are considered by the decision making unit and in quantifying their individual effects. Some examples of situations where such choices arise are:

(i) a household must decide whether to buy or rent a suitable dwelling;
(ii) a Senator must decide on whether to vote yes or no on a particular piece of legislation;
(iii) a consumer must choose which of perhaps several shopping areas to visit and a mode of transportation;
(iv) members of a household must decide whether to take part-time or full-time employment, or whether or not to seek a second job; and
(v) a person must decide whether or not to attend college.

While the list could go on, the basic similarity of these situations is clear. In each case the decisionmaker must choose an action from a finite set of discrete alternatives, often just two as in a yes–no decision.

Another problem that has received considerable attention in recent years is the failure of usual regression procedures when the dependent variables in a model can take only a limited range of values. For example, there are many cases in economics where the dependent variable must be nonnegative. Procedures for obtaining consistent parameter estimates in these situations are presented in Section 16.5.

Finally, since extensive reference is made to maximum likelihood estimation, the method of scoring and numerical optimization techniques these, subjects are reviewed in the Appendix to this book.

16.2 A Framework for Studying Models with Binary Dependent Variables

When considering models in which the dependent variable can take only two values, say $y_i = 1$ if an event E occurs but $y_i = 0$ if the event does not occur, the discussion must be couched in terms of the probability of the event E occurring. Economic theory suggests a set of variables or factors that will be considered when a choice is to be made. However, we know that different individuals faced with identical circumstances and options will often choose differently based on their own preference structure. Moreover, a single individual in apparently identical situations will often make different choices. This can either be explained as random human behavior or by concluding that the situations were not in fact identical and that changes in other unconsidered and omitted factors caused variations in choice behavior. Consequently, as in other statistical models, the outcome of a choice experiment is random and thus y_i is random. In regression situations we assume that the expected value of the dependent variable is a function of a set of explanatory variables. The same will be true here, as we assume that the Bernoulli random variable y_i has expectation $E(y_i) = P_i$, where P_i is the probability that the event occurs. As economists, we are interested in factors that affect P_i. Thus, we assume P_i is a function of a set of explanatory variables and from knowledge of the values of these variables and observations on the values taken by y_i, we can estimate the parameters of the assumed functional relationship.

Each of the models described below differs in its assumption about the relation between P_i and the explanatory variables. As a first step, and keeping within our familiar regression framework, we might assume that P_i is a linear function of a set of explanatory variables. That is, let $Ey_i = P_i = \mathbf{x}_i'\boldsymbol{\beta}$ where $\mathbf{x}_i'$ is a $1 \times K$ vector of observations on a set of explanatory variables and $\boldsymbol{\beta}' = (\beta_1, \ldots, \beta_K)$ is the associated parameter vector. If then, as usual, we add a disturbance to account for the difference between the value of the observed random variable y_i and its mean $Ey_i = P_i$, we have

$$y_i = P_i + e_i = \mathbf{x}_i'\boldsymbol{\beta} + e_i, \qquad i = 1, \ldots, T, \tag{16.2.1}$$

y_i	e_i	$\Pr(e_i)$
1	$1 - \mathbf{x}_i'\boldsymbol{\beta}$	$(\mathbf{x}_i'\boldsymbol{\beta})$
0	$-\mathbf{x}_i'\boldsymbol{\beta}$	$(1 - \mathbf{x}_i'\boldsymbol{\beta})$

(16.2.2)

where T is the number of times the choice experiment is repeated. Since the dependent variable y_i can take only two values, the same is true of the error term e_i. The error term e_i takes the values $1 - \mathbf{x}_i'\boldsymbol{\beta}$ and $-\mathbf{x}_i'\boldsymbol{\beta}$ when y_i takes the values 1 and 0, respectively. Furthermore, if we are to maintain the assumption that $E(e_i) = 0$ so that $E(y_i) = \mathbf{x}_i'\boldsymbol{\beta}$, then the values of e_i must have the probabilities shown in (16.2.2), since

$$\begin{aligned} E(e_i) &= \sum_{i=1}^{2} e_i \Pr(e_i) \\ &= (1 - \mathbf{x}_i'\boldsymbol{\beta})(\mathbf{x}_i'\boldsymbol{\beta}) + (-\mathbf{x}_i'\boldsymbol{\beta})(1 - \mathbf{x}_i'\boldsymbol{\beta}) = 0. \end{aligned}$$

The expectation $E(y_i) = P_i = \mathbf{x}_i'\boldsymbol{\beta}$ is interpreted as the conditional probability, given $\mathbf{x}_i$, that the event E occurs. From this point of view, and that in (16.2.2), the model (16.2.1) is awkward since $\mathbf{x}_i'\boldsymbol{\beta}$ can take any value, making the probabilities associated with values of y_i and e_i greater than 1 or less than zero if $\mathbf{x}_i'\boldsymbol{\beta}$ is not contained in the unit interval.

The variance of the random variable e_i is

$$\begin{aligned} \operatorname{var}(e_i) &= \sum_{i=1}^{2} e_i^2 \Pr(e_i) \\ &= (-\mathbf{x}_i'\boldsymbol{\beta})^2(1 - \mathbf{x}_i'\boldsymbol{\beta}) + (1 - \mathbf{x}_i'\boldsymbol{\beta})^2(\mathbf{x}_i'\boldsymbol{\beta}) \\ &= (\mathbf{x}_i'\boldsymbol{\beta})(1 - \mathbf{x}_i'\boldsymbol{\beta}) \\ &= (Ey_i)(1 - Ey_i). \end{aligned}$$

Thus if all T observations are written

$$\mathbf{y} = X\boldsymbol{\beta} + \mathbf{e}$$

it follows that the covariance matrix of $\mathbf{e}$ is

$$\operatorname{Cov}(\mathbf{e}) = E\mathbf{e}\mathbf{e}' = \Omega,$$

where Ω is a diagonal matrix with ith diagonal element $Ey_i(1 - Ey_i)$. Since the error term e_i is heteroscedastic, ordinary least squares estimation is inefficient relative to generalized least squares.

How generalized least squares estimation is implemented depends upon the nature of the available sample data. It will often be the case that the number of choice outcomes y_i observed for each set of explanatory variables $\mathbf{x}_i$, say n_i, will be just one. That is, we only observe one value of the random variable y_i for each different $\mathbf{x}_i$, so that $n_i = 1$. In that case feasible generalized least squares can be carried out by estimating (16.2.1) by ordinary least squares which, though inefficient, is consistent and constructing $\hat{\Omega}$ to be a diagonal matrix with elements

$$\mathbf{x}_i'\hat{\boldsymbol{\beta}}(1 - \mathbf{x}_i'\hat{\boldsymbol{\beta}}) = \hat{y}_i(1 - \hat{y}_i). \tag{16.2.3}$$

Since $\hat{\Omega}$ is diagonal, feasible generalized least squares is easily applied using weighted least squares. That is, multiplication of each observation on the dependent and independent variables by the square root of the reciprocal of (16.2.3) yields a transformed model, ordinary least squares estimation of which produces feasible generalized least squares estimates.

While this estimation procedure is consistent, an obvious difficulty exists. If $\mathbf{x}_i'\hat{\boldsymbol{\beta}}$ falls outside the (0, 1) interval, the $\hat{\Omega}$ matrix has negative or undefined elements on its diagonal. If this occurs one must modify $\hat{\Omega}$, either by deleting the observations for which the problem occurs or setting the value of $\mathbf{x}_i'\hat{\boldsymbol{\beta}}$ to say 0.01 or 0.99, and proceeding. While this does not affect the asymptotic properties of the feasible generalized least squares procedure, it is clearly an awkward position to be in, especially since predictions based on the feasible generalized least squares estimates, $\hat{\hat{P}}_i = \mathbf{x}_i'\hat{\hat{\boldsymbol{\beta}}}$, may also fall outside the (0, 1) interval.

An alternative exists when, for each vector of explanatory variables $\mathbf{x}_i$, repeated observations on y_i are available. That is, let $n_i > 1$ and y_i now be the *number* of occurrences of the event E in n_i choice experiments with the values of the vector of explanatory variable given by $\mathbf{x}_i$. The sample proportion of the number of occurrences of E is then $p_i = y_i/n_i$. Since $E(p_i) = P_i = \mathbf{x}_i'\boldsymbol{\beta}$ the model (16.2.1) can be rewritten as

$$p_i = P_i + e_i = \mathbf{x}_i'\boldsymbol{\beta} + e_i, \qquad i = 1, \ldots, T, \tag{16.2.4}$$

where e_i is now the difference between p_i and its expectation P_i. The full set of T observations is then written

$$\mathbf{p} = X\boldsymbol{\beta} + \mathbf{e}.$$

Since the sample proportions p_i are related to the true proportions P_i by

$$p_i = P_i + e_i, \qquad i = 1, \ldots, T,$$

the error term e_i has zero mean and variance $P_i(1 - P_i)/n_i$, the same as the sample proportion based on n_i Bernoulli trials. The covariance matrix of $\mathbf{e}$ is

$$\Omega = E\mathbf{e}\mathbf{e}' = \begin{bmatrix} P_1(1 - P_1)/n_1 & & & 0 \\ & P_2(1 - P_2)/n_2 & & \\ & 0 & \ddots & \\ & & & P_T(1 - P_T)/n_T \end{bmatrix}, \tag{16.2.5}$$

and the appropriate estimator for $\boldsymbol{\beta}$ is

$$\tilde{\boldsymbol{\beta}} = (X'\Omega^{-1}X)^{-1}X'\Omega^{-1}\mathbf{p}, \tag{16.2.6}$$

the generalized least squares estimator. If the true proportions P_i are not known then a feasible generalized least squares estimator is

$$\tilde{\tilde{\boldsymbol{\beta}}} = (X'\hat{\Omega}^{-1}X)^{-1}X'\hat{\Omega}^{-1}\mathbf{p}, \tag{16.2.7}$$

where the diagonal elements of $\hat{\Omega}$ are $\hat{P}_i(1 - \hat{P}_i)/n_i$, and $\hat{P}_i$ is a suitable consistent estimate of P_i. One alternative is to use $\hat{P}_i = p_i$, the sample proportion. This alternative has the advantage of simplicity and that p_i falls in the interval [0, 1]. This makes "adjustment" of the elements of $\hat{\Omega}$ unnecessary unless $p_i = 0$ or 1. Another alternative is to let $\hat{P}_i = \mathbf{x}_i'\hat{\boldsymbol{\beta}}$ where

$$\hat{\boldsymbol{\beta}} = (X'X)^{-1}X'\mathbf{p}.$$

Alternatively one could use $\hat{\hat{P}}_i = \mathbf{x}_i'\hat{\hat{\boldsymbol{\beta}}}$ where $\hat{\hat{\boldsymbol{\beta}}}$ is the feasible generalized least squares estimation based on p_i. Asymptotically the choice does not matter since $\sqrt{T}(\tilde{\boldsymbol{\beta}} - \boldsymbol{\beta})$ and $\sqrt{T}(\tilde{\tilde{\boldsymbol{\beta}}} - \boldsymbol{\beta})$ have the same asymptotic distributions under conditions outlined in Section 8.3. However, since the feasible generalized least squares predictor takes into account the error covariance matrix Ω, it may be advocated in small samples.

Unfortunately, one must still face the difficulty that the predictor obtained from feasible generalized least squares estimation can fall outside the zero–one interval. To ensure that the predicted proportion of successes will fall within the unit interval, at least over a range of $\mathbf{x}_i$ of interest, one may employ inequality restrictions of the form $0 \le \mathbf{x}_i'\boldsymbol{\beta} \le 1$. See Judge *et al.* (1980, Ch. 14) for further details.

As a practical matter the number of repetitions n_i must be large enough so that the sample proportion p_i is a reliable estimate of the probability P_i. In most cases this means that n_i must be at least five or six, and preferably 20 to 30, for the model (16.2.4) to be used effectively.

The difficulty with the *linear probability model* $P_i = \mathbf{x}_i'\boldsymbol{\beta}$ is that while $\mathbf{x}_i'\boldsymbol{\beta}$ can take any value, P_i must fall in the interval [0, 1]. The situation is illustrated in Figure 16.2.1 for the case when $\mathbf{x}_i'\boldsymbol{\beta} = \beta_1 + \beta_2 x_{i2}$. While the linearity assumption may be appropriate over a range of values of the explanatory variable, it is certainly not appropriate for either extremely large

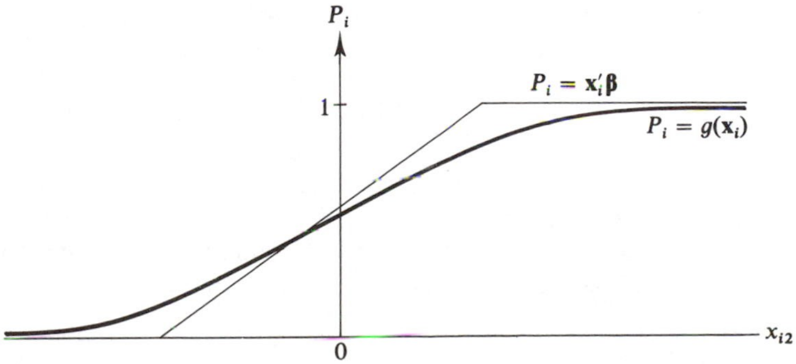

Figure 16.2.1 Linear and nonlinear probability models.

or small values. As an alternative to the linear probability model, the probabilities P_i may be assumed to be a nonlinear function of the explanatory variables. In the next sections two particular nonlinear probability models are discussed, first when repeated observations are available and feasible generalized least squares can be applied and then when $n_i = 1$, or is small, and maximum likelihood estimation must be used.

16.3 Feasible Generalized Least Squares Estimation of Probit and Logit Models When Repeated Observations Are Available

Two choices of the nonlinear function $P_i = g(\mathbf{x}_i)$ are the cumulative density functions of normal and logistic random variables. The former gives rise to the probit model and the latter to the logit model. We may think of the probit model arising as follows. The event E is an action taken by an individual decision maker if its expected utility is high enough. What "high enough" is of course, depends on the individual. Then let $I_i = \mathbf{x}_i'\boldsymbol{\beta}$ be a latent index variable, that is linear in $\boldsymbol{\beta}$, such that the larger the index variable the greater the probability of the event E in question occurring. Since that probability must fall between zero and one, the monotonic relationship between I_i and $\Pr[E|I_i]$ must assume the general form of a cumulative density function, as shown in Figure 16.2.1. Note that we are assuming all individuals weight the explanatory factors $\mathbf{x}_i$ identically, that is the $\boldsymbol{\beta}$ vector is constant across all individuals, and that of all individuals faced with a particular $\mathbf{x}_i'\boldsymbol{\beta}$, some will choose event E and other will choose not-E because of personal preferences.

The following argument for the choice of a normal cumulative distribution function is often made: Each individual makes a choice between E and not-E by comparing the value of I_i to some threshold level, say I_*, so that if $I_i \geq I_*$ then E occurs. For each individual the value of the threshold I_* is determined by many independent factors and thus can be assumed normally distributed distributed by the central limit theorem. Therefore

$$P_i = \Pr(E|I_i) = \Pr(I_* \leq I_i) = F(I_i) = F(\mathbf{x}_i'\boldsymbol{\beta}), \qquad (16.3.1)$$

where $F(\cdot)$ is the value of the standard normal cumulative distribution function evaluated at the argument.

A frequently used alternative to the probit model is the logit model. The logit model is based on the logistic cumulative distribution function and

$$P_i = \Pr(I_* \leq \mathbf{x}_i'\boldsymbol{\beta}) = \frac{1}{1 + \exp(-\mathbf{x}_i'\boldsymbol{\beta})}, \qquad -\infty < \mathbf{x}_i'\boldsymbol{\beta} < \infty. \qquad (16.3.2)$$

This cumulative distribution function closely approximates that of a normal random variable and has some convenient properties. More will be said in sections below about why the logistic cumulative distribution function has been widely used and also its weaknesses.

Estimation of the resulting models may be carried out by feasible generalized least squares if several observations are available on each individual, i.e. several choice decisions are observed for each observation vector $\mathbf{x}_i$, or maximum likelihood estimation which is applicable whether repeated observations are available or not. Only the former case is discussed in this section.

16.3.1 Feasible Generalized Least Squares Estimation of the Probit Model

Assume that for each vector $\mathbf{x}_i$ there are $n_i > 1$ observations and y_i of those resulted in event E. Thus the sample proportion p_i is $p_i = y_i/n_i$, and is related to the true proportion P_i by

$$p_i = P_i + e_i, \tag{16.3.3}$$

where $E(e_i) = 0$ and $\text{var}(e_i) = P_i(1 - P_i)/n_i$, the latter following directly from the assumption that the sample proportion p_i is based on n_i independent Bernoulli trials.

The discussion above implies that

$$\Pr(E \mid I_i) = P_i = \int_{-\infty}^{I_i} \frac{1}{\sqrt{2\pi}} e^{-(t^2/2)}\, dt = F(I_i). \tag{16.3.4}$$

Following Zellner and Lee (1965) we note that

$$F^{-1}(p_i) = F^{-1}(P_i + e_i), \tag{16.3.5}$$

where $F^{-1}(\cdot)$ is the inverse of the standard normal cumulative distribution function. Expanding $F^{-1}(P_i + e_i)$ by a Taylor's series about P_i we obtain

$$F^{-1}(p_i) = F^{-1}(P_i) + e_i \frac{dF^{-1}(P_i)}{dP_i} + R_i. \tag{16.3.6}$$

The derivative of the inverse function is

$$\frac{dF^{-1}(P_i)}{dP_i} = \frac{1}{f[F^{-1}(P_i)]}, \tag{16.3.7}$$

where $f(\cdot)$ is the value of the standard normal density evaluated at its argument, and R_i is a remainder that goes to zero in probability as $n_i \to \infty$. Therefore,

$$F^{-1}(p_i) \doteq F^{-1}(P_i) + \frac{e_i}{f[F^{-1}(P_i)]},$$

or

$$v_i = \mathbf{x}_i'\boldsymbol{\beta} + u_i, \qquad i = 1, \ldots, T, \tag{16.3.8}$$

where $v_i = F^{-1}(p_i)$ is the "observed" probit and the random disturbance u_i has $E(u_i) = 0$ and

$$\operatorname{var}(u_i) = \frac{P_i(1 - P_i)}{n_i f[F^{-1}(P_i)]^2}. \tag{16.3.9}$$

If (16.3.8) is written as

$$\mathbf{v} = X\boldsymbol{\beta} + \mathbf{u}, \tag{16.3.10}$$

the appropriate estimator for $\boldsymbol{\beta}$ is

$$\tilde{\boldsymbol{\beta}} = (X'\Omega^{-1}X)^{-1}X'\Omega^{-1}\mathbf{v}, \tag{16.3.11}$$

where Ω is a diagonal matrix whose ith diagonal element is (16.3.9). Since Ω is unknown, a feasible generalized squares estimator is

$$\tilde{\tilde{\boldsymbol{\beta}}} = (X'\hat{\Omega}^{-1}X)^{-1}X'\hat{\Omega}^{-1}\mathbf{v}, \tag{16.3.12}$$

where $\hat{\Omega}$ is based on estimates of P_i; using the sample proportion, the ordinary least squares predictions $\hat{P} = X(X'X)^{-1}X'\mathbf{p}$, the predictions from the linear probability model, or predictions based on ordinary least squares estimation of $\boldsymbol{\beta}$ in (16.3.10) and obtained from

$$\tilde{P}_i = \int_{-\infty}^{\hat{v}_i} f(t)\, dt,$$

where $\hat{v}_i = \mathbf{x}_i'(X'X)^{-1}X'\mathbf{v}$ and $f(t)$ is a $N(0, 1)$ probability density function. The advantage of this latter approach is, of course, that not only are the $\tilde{P}_i$ confined to the zero–one interval but they also based on the information provided by the structure (16.3.10).

Since the remainder R_i in (16.3.6) vanishes in probability, the usual results of feasible generalized least squares hold. Namely, under some general conditions the feasible generalized least squares estimators of (16.3.12) are consistent and have an asymptotic normal distribution. Therefore, the usual tests of hypotheses can be based on the consistent estimate $(X'\hat{\Omega}^{-1}X)^{-1}$.

16.3.2 Feasible Generalized Least Squares Estimation of the Logit Model

Again assuming that the sample and true proportions are related by

$$p_i = P_i + e_i,$$

the "odds ratio" is

$$\frac{p_i}{1 - p_i} = \frac{P_i + e_i}{1 - P_i - e_i} = \frac{P_i}{1 - P_i} \cdot \frac{1 + (e_i/P_i)}{1 - (e_i/(1 - P_i))}$$

and the "log-odds" ratio is

$$\ln\left[\frac{p_i}{1-p_i}\right] = \ln\left[\frac{P_i}{1-P_i}\right] + \ln\left[1 + \frac{e_i}{P_i}\right] - \ln\left[1 - \frac{e_i}{1-P_i}\right].$$

Expanding the last two terms about e_i/P_i and $e_i/(1 - P_i)$, respectively, and deleting higher order terms gives

$$\ln\left[\frac{p_i}{1-p_i}\right] \doteq \ln\left[\frac{P_i}{1-P_i}\right] + \frac{e_i}{P_i} + \frac{e_i}{(1-P_i)}$$

$$= \mathbf{x}_i'\boldsymbol{\beta} + \frac{e_i}{P_i(1-P_i)}, \tag{16.3.13}$$

since $\ln[P_i/(1 - P_i)] = \mathbf{x}_i'\boldsymbol{\beta}$ if the logistic structure (16.3.2) is placed on P_i. The model (16.3.13) can be written

$$v_i = \mathbf{x}_i'\boldsymbol{\beta} + u_i, \qquad i = 1, \ldots, T, \tag{16.3.14}$$

where $v_i = \ln(p_i/(1 - p_i))$ is called the "observed logit" and $Eu_i = 0$, $\operatorname{var}(u_i) = 1/(n_i P_i(1 - P_i))$. In matrix notation this model is

$$\mathbf{v} = X\boldsymbol{\beta} + \mathbf{u}, \tag{16.3.15}$$

and the appropriate generalized least squares estimator is

$$\tilde{\boldsymbol{\beta}} = (X'\Omega^{-1}X)^{-1}X'\Omega^{-1}\mathbf{v},$$

where the covariance matrix Ω is diagonal with diagonal elements $1/(n_i P_i(1 - P_i))$. Once again since Ω is unknown the appropriate feasible generalized least squares estimator is

$$\tilde{\tilde{\boldsymbol{\beta}}} = (X'\hat{\Omega}^{-1}X)^{-1}X'\hat{\Omega}^{-1}\mathbf{v}, \tag{16.3.16}$$

where $\hat{\Omega}$ is based on estimates of P_i. Candidates for these estimators range from using the sample proportion p_i, to using predictions from the linear probability model or predictions based on ordinary least squares estimation of (16.3.15) and computing

$$\hat{P}_i = 1/(1 + \exp(-\hat{v}_i)),$$

where $\hat{v}_i = \mathbf{x}_i'(X'X)^{-1}X'\mathbf{v}$.

Again the usual results of feasible generalized least squares hold, namely they are consistent and have an asymptotic normal distribution. Therefore, the usual tests of hypotheses can be based on a consistent estimate $(X'\hat{\Omega}^{-1}X)^{-1}$.

The advantage of the logit model over probit is that the inverse of the normal cumulative distribution function need not be calculated. This is no longer a major consideration given modern computer software.

16.3.3 An Interpretive Note

Finally, we note the interpretation of the estimated coefficients in logit and probit models. Estimated coefficients do not indicate the increase in the probability of the event occurring given a one unit increase in the corresponding independent variable. Rather, the coefficients reflect the effect of a change in an independent variable upon $F^{-1}(P_i)$ for the probit model and upon $\ln(P_i/(1 - P_i))$ for the logit model. In both cases the amount of the increase in the probability depends upon the original probability and thus upon the initial values of all the independent variables and their coefficients. This is true since $P_i = F(\mathbf{x}_i'\boldsymbol{\beta})$ and $\partial P_i/\partial x_{ij} = f(\mathbf{x}_i'\boldsymbol{\beta}) \cdot \beta_j$, where $f(\cdot)$ is the probability density function associated with $F(\cdot)$. For the logit model

$$\frac{\partial P_i}{\partial x_{ij}} = \frac{\exp(-\mathbf{x}_i'\boldsymbol{\beta})}{[1 + \exp(-\mathbf{x}_i'\boldsymbol{\beta})]^2}\,\beta_j$$

and for the probit model

$$\begin{aligned}\frac{\partial P_i}{\partial x_{ij}} &= \frac{\partial}{\partial x_{ij}} \int_{-\infty}^{\mathbf{x}_i'\boldsymbol{\beta}} \frac{1}{\sqrt{2\pi}} \exp(-\tfrac{1}{2}t^2)\, dt \\ &= \frac{1}{\sqrt{2\pi}} \exp(-\tfrac{1}{2}\mathbf{x}_i'\boldsymbol{\beta})^2 \cdot \beta_j.\end{aligned}$$

Having examined binary dependent variable models when repeated observations are available we will now consider the binary choice model where only one or a few observations are available on each choicemaker.

16.4 Maximum Likelihood Estimation of Logit and Probit Models

When the number of repeated observations on the choice experiment n_i is small and P_i cannot be reliably estimated using the sample proportion, then maximum likelihood estimation of the logit and probit models can be carried out. If P_i is the probability that the event E occurs on the ith trial of the experiment then the random variable y_i, which is one if the event occurs but zero otherwise, has the probability function

$$y_i = \begin{cases} 1 & \text{with probability } P_i, \\ 0 & \text{with probability } 1 - P_i. \end{cases} \tag{16.4.1}$$

Consequently, if T observations are available then the likelihood function is

$$L = \prod_{i=1}^{T} P_i^{y_i}(1 - P_i)^{1-y_i}. \tag{16.4.2}$$

The logit or probit model arises when P_i is specified to be given by the logistic or normal cumulative distribution function evaluated at $\mathbf{x}_i'\boldsymbol{\beta}$. If $F(\mathbf{x}_i'\boldsymbol{\beta})$ denotes either of the cumulative distribution functions evaluated at $\mathbf{x}_i'\boldsymbol{\beta}$, then the likelihood function for both models is

$$L = \prod_{i=1}^{T} [F(\mathbf{x}_i'\boldsymbol{\beta})]^{y_i}[1 - F(\mathbf{x}_i'\boldsymbol{\beta})]^{1-y_i} \tag{16.4.3}$$

and the log likelihood function is

$$\ln L = \sum_{i=1}^{T} y_i \ln[F(\mathbf{x}_i'\boldsymbol{\beta})] + (1 - y_i) \ln[1 - F(\mathbf{x}_i'\boldsymbol{\beta})]. \tag{16.4.4}$$

Whether $F(\cdot)$ is chosen to be the logistic or standard normal cumulative distribution function, the first-order conditions for a maximum will be nonlinear, so maximum likelihood estimates must be obtained numerically. From the Appendix on nonlinear optimization, we know that the Newton–Raphson iterative procedure for maximizing a nonlinear objective function leads to the recursive relation

$$\tilde{\boldsymbol{\beta}}_{n+1} = \tilde{\boldsymbol{\beta}}_n - \left[\frac{\partial^2 \ln L}{\partial \boldsymbol{\beta}\, \partial \boldsymbol{\beta}'}\right]^{-1}_{\boldsymbol{\beta}=\tilde{\boldsymbol{\beta}}_n} \cdot \left[\frac{\partial \ln L}{\partial \boldsymbol{\beta}}\right]_{\boldsymbol{\beta}=\tilde{\boldsymbol{\beta}}_n}, \tag{16.4.5}$$

where $\tilde{\boldsymbol{\beta}}_n$ is the nth round estimate and the matrix of second partials and the gradient vector are evaluated at the nth round estimate. This is convenient since, under the usual regularity conditions, the maximum likelihood estimator, say $\tilde{\boldsymbol{\beta}}$, is consistent and

$$\sqrt{T}(\tilde{\boldsymbol{\beta}} - \boldsymbol{\beta}) \overset{\text{asy}}{\to} N\left(\mathbf{0}, -T\left[E\,\frac{\partial^2 \ln L}{\partial \boldsymbol{\beta}\, \partial \boldsymbol{\beta}'}\right]^{-1}\right),$$

For finite samples, the asymptotic distribution of $\tilde{\boldsymbol{\beta}}$ can be approximated by $N(\boldsymbol{\beta}, -[(\partial^2 \ln L)/(\partial \boldsymbol{\beta}\, \partial \boldsymbol{\beta}')]^{-1}_{\boldsymbol{\beta}=\tilde{\boldsymbol{\beta}}})$.

Thus, in order to carry out optimization the first and second derivatives of the log likelihood function are required. While derivatives could be approximated numerically there is no reason to do so for the logit and probit models since they are quite tractable analytically. For the logit model $P_i = F(\mathbf{x}_i'\boldsymbol{\beta})$, where

$$F(t) = \frac{1}{1 + e^{-t}}, \tag{16.4.6a}$$

and

$$f(t) = \frac{e^{-t}}{(1 + e^{-t})^2}. \tag{16.4.6b}$$

Also note that

$$1 - F(t) = \frac{e^{-t}}{1 + e^{-t}} = F(-t), \tag{16.4.7a}$$

$$\frac{f(t)}{F(t)} = 1 - F(t) \tag{16.4.7b}$$

and

$$f'(t) = -f(t) \cdot F(t) \cdot (1 - e^{-t}). \tag{16.4.7c}$$

Using the definitions (16.4.6) and the relations (16.4.7) it is not difficult to show that for the logit model

$$\begin{aligned}\frac{\partial \ln L}{\partial \boldsymbol{\beta}} &= \sum_{i=1}^{T} y_i \frac{1}{1 + \exp(\mathbf{x}_i'\boldsymbol{\beta})} \mathbf{x}_i - \sum_{i=1}^{T} (1 - y_i) \frac{1}{1 + \exp(-\mathbf{x}_i'\boldsymbol{\beta})} \cdot \mathbf{x}_i \\ &= \sum_{i=1}^{T} [y_i F(-\mathbf{x}_i'\boldsymbol{\beta}) - (1 - y_i)F(\mathbf{x}_i'\boldsymbol{\beta})]\mathbf{x}_i \end{aligned} \tag{16.4.8}$$

and

$$\begin{aligned}\frac{\partial^2 \ln L}{\partial \boldsymbol{\beta}\, \partial \boldsymbol{\beta}'} &= -\sum_{i=1}^{T} \frac{\exp(-\mathbf{x}_i'\boldsymbol{\beta})}{[1 + \exp(-\mathbf{x}_i'\boldsymbol{\beta})]^2} \cdot \mathbf{x}_i \mathbf{x}_i' \\ &= -\sum_{i=1}^{T} f(\mathbf{x}_i'\boldsymbol{\beta})\mathbf{x}_i \mathbf{x}_i'. \end{aligned} \tag{16.4.9}$$

For the probit model $P_i = F(\mathbf{x}_i'\boldsymbol{\beta})$ where

$$f(t) = \frac{1}{\sqrt{2\pi}} \exp(-\tfrac{1}{2}t^2) \tag{16.4.10a}$$

and

$$F(t) = \int_{-\infty}^{t} f(v)\, dv. \tag{16.4.10b}$$

Also note that

$$f'(t) = -t \cdot f(t) \tag{16.4.11a}$$

and

$$F(-t) = 1 - F(t). \tag{16.4.11b}$$

Then

$$\frac{\partial \ln L}{\partial \boldsymbol{\beta}} = \sum_{i=1}^{T} \left[y_i \frac{f(\mathbf{x}_i'\boldsymbol{\beta})}{F(\mathbf{x}_i'\boldsymbol{\beta})} - (1 - y_i) \frac{f(\mathbf{x}_i'\boldsymbol{\beta})}{1 - F(\mathbf{x}_i'\boldsymbol{\beta})} \right] \mathbf{x}_i \tag{16.4.12}$$

and

$$\frac{\partial^2 \ln L}{\partial \boldsymbol{\beta}\, \partial \boldsymbol{\beta}'} = -\sum_{i=1}^{T} f(\mathbf{x}_i'\boldsymbol{\beta})\left[y_i \cdot \frac{f(\mathbf{x}_i'\boldsymbol{\beta}) + (\mathbf{x}_i'\boldsymbol{\beta})F(\mathbf{x}_i'\boldsymbol{\beta})}{[F(\mathbf{x}_i'\boldsymbol{\beta})]^2}\right.$$
$$\left. + (1 - y_i)\frac{f(\mathbf{x}_i'\boldsymbol{\beta}) - (\mathbf{x}_i'\boldsymbol{\beta})(1 - F(\mathbf{x}_i'\boldsymbol{\beta}))}{[1 - F(\mathbf{x}_i'\boldsymbol{\beta})]^2}\right] \cdot \mathbf{x}_i\mathbf{x}_i'. \quad (16.4.13)$$

Using these derivatives and the recursive relation (16.4.5), maximum likelihood estimates can be obtained given some initial estimates $\tilde{\boldsymbol{\beta}}_1$. For probit and logit models the choice of the initial estimates do not matter since it can be shown (see Dhrymes (1978, pp. 344–347)) that, for both of these models, the matrix of second partials $\partial^2 \ln L/\partial \boldsymbol{\beta}\, \partial \boldsymbol{\beta}'$ is negative definite for *all* values of $\boldsymbol{\beta}$. Consequently, the Newton–Raphson procedure will converge, ultimately, to the unique maximum likelihood estimates regardless of the initial estimates. Computationally, of course, the choice does matter since the better the initial estimates the fewer iterations required to attain the maximum of the likelihood function. While several alternatives for initial estimates exist, one can simply use the ordinary squares estimates of $\boldsymbol{\beta}$ obtained by regressing y_i on the explanatory variables.

The interpretation and evaluation of these models deserves comment. First, the comments in Section 16.3.4 about the interpretation of the estimates coefficients still hold. Specifically, the estimated coefficients do not determine the change in the probability of the event E occurring given a one unit change in an explanatory variable. Rather those partial derivatives are

$$\frac{\partial P_i}{\partial x_{ij}} = f(\mathbf{x}_i'\boldsymbol{\beta}) \cdot \beta_j,$$

where $f(\cdot)$ is the appropriate probability density function. Thus, while the sign of the coefficient does indicate the *direction* of the change, the magnitude depends upon $f(\mathbf{x}_i'\boldsymbol{\beta})$, which, of course, reflects the *steepness* of the cumulative distribution function at $\mathbf{x}_i'\boldsymbol{\beta}$. Naturally, the steeper the cumulative distribution function the greater the impact of a change in the value of an explanatory variable will be.

Second, usual tests about individual coefficients and confidence intervals can be constructed from the estimate of the asymptotic covariance matrix, the negative of the inverse of the matrix of second partials evaluated at the maximum likelihood estimates, and relying on the asymptotic normality of the maximum likelihood estimator. Third, tests of general linear hypotheses $H\boldsymbol{\beta} = \mathbf{h}$ can be constructed as described in the Appendix. The hypothesis H_0: $\beta_2 = \beta_3 = \cdots = \beta_K = 0$ can be easily carried out using the likelihood ratio procedure since the value of the log likelihood function under the hypothesis is easily attained analytically. If n is the number of successes ($y_i = 1$) observed in the T observations, then for both the logit and probit model the maximum value of the log likelihood function under the null hypothesis H_0 is

$$\ln L(\hat{\omega}) = n \ln\left(\frac{n}{T}\right) + (T - n) \ln\left(\frac{T - n}{T}\right). \tag{16.4.14}$$

Consequently, if the hypothesis is true, then asymptotically

$$-2 \ln l = -2[\ln L(\hat{\omega}) - \ln L(\hat{\Omega})]$$

has a $\chi^2_{(K-1)}$ distribution, where $\ln L(\hat{\Omega})$ is the value of the log likelihood function evaluated at $\tilde{\boldsymbol{\beta}}$. Acceptance of this hypothesis would, of course, imply that the explanatory variables have no effect on the probability of E occurring. In this case the probability that $y_i = 1$ is estimated by $\hat{P}_i = n/T$, which is simply the sample proportion. A related summary measure that is often reported is the pseudo-R^2, defined as

$$\rho^2 = 1 - \frac{\ln L(\hat{\Omega})}{\ln L(\hat{\omega})}.$$

This measure is 1 when the model is a perfect predictor, in the sense that $\hat{P}_i = F(\mathbf{x}_i'\tilde{\boldsymbol{\beta}}) = 1$ when $y_i = 1$ and $\hat{P}_i = 0$ when $y_i = 0$, and is 0 when $\ln L(\hat{\Omega}) = \ln L(\hat{\omega})$. Between these limits the value of ρ^2 had no obvious intuitive meaning. However, Hauser (1977) shows that ρ^2 can be given meaning in an information theoretic context. Specifically, ρ^2 measures the percent of the "uncertainty" in the data explained by the empirical results. See Judge *et al.* (1980, pp. 602–605) for further discussion.

Finally, logit and probit models might be usefully used as an alternative to discriminant analysis for classifying individuals into one population or another. Specifically if $\hat{P}_i \geq 0.5$ a set of characteristics $\mathbf{x}_i$ may be asserted to "predict" that $y_i = 1$. See Press and Wilson (1978) for a discussion of the relation between discrimination based on logistic models and a discriminant function. However, from a summary point of view, it is frequently worth while to report the in-sample predictive success of the model. The number of "correct" predictions can be reported, where a prediction is correct when $\hat{P}_i \geq 5$ and $y_i = 1$ or $\hat{P}_i < 0.5$ and $y_i = 0$. It is an interesting feature of the logit model that the predicted share of occurrences of the event E, that is the number of times $\hat{P}_i \geq 0.5$ over T, is equal to the actual share n/T.

16.5 General Choice Models

In the section above models appropriate when only two alternatives were available to the decisionmaker were considered and estimation techniques presented for the case when repeated observations on individuals existed. In this section the problem is generalized so that more alternatives are available and maximum likelihood estimation methods are outlined which allow estimation even when only a single observation per individual is available.

Let each individual face J alternatives from which one must be chosen. Let the probability that the ith individual chooses the jth alternative be P_{ij} and denote the choice of the ith individual by $\mathbf{y}_i' = (y_{i1}, y_{i2}, \ldots, y_{iJ})$ where $y_{ij} = 1$ if the jth alternative is selected and all other elements of $\mathbf{y}_i$ are zero. If each individual is observed only a single time, the likelihood function of the sample of values $\mathbf{y}_1, \ldots, \mathbf{y}_T$ is

$$L = \prod_{i=1}^{T} P_{i1}^{y_{i1}} P_{i2}^{y_{i2}} \cdots P_{iJ}^{y_{iJ}}. \tag{16.5.1}$$

The problem of interest is to allow the selection probabilities to depend upon characteristics of the available alternatives and the individual decision-makers.

To model individual decisionmaking, assume the existence of an "average" decisionmaker. Assume that "average" individual i derives utility $\bar{U}_{ij}$, if the jth alternative is chosen, and that $\bar{U}_{ij}$ can be expressed

$$\bar{U}_{ij} = \mathbf{x}_{ij}'\boldsymbol{\beta},$$

where $\mathbf{x}_{ij}$ is a $K \times 1$ vector of observations on variables that are *specific* to the ith individual and the jth alternative. These variables are functions of the characteristics of the individual decision maker *and* the available alternatives. The parameter vector $\boldsymbol{\beta}$ is assumed to be constant across the entire population.

Then, in order to separate the individual from the average, a stochastic component is added to the "average" utility so that the utility derived by the ith individual from the selection of the jth alternative is

$$U_{ij} = \bar{U}_{ij} + e_{ij} = \mathbf{x}_{ij}'\boldsymbol{\beta} + e_{ij},$$

where e_{ij} is a random variable. The usual justifications for the addition of e_{ij}'s are made, namely that e_{ij} represents the combined effects of unobserved factors and random individual behavior.

Now if each individual is a utility maximizer, the probability that individual i chooses, say, the first alternative is

$$\begin{aligned} P_{i1} &= \Pr[U_{i1} > U_{i2} \text{ and } U_{i1} > U_{i3} \text{ and } \cdots U_{i1} > U_{iJ}] \\ &= \Pr[e_{i2} - e_{i1} > \bar{U}_{i1} - \bar{U}_{i2} \text{ and } \cdots e_{iJ} - e_{i1} > \bar{U}_{i1} - \bar{U}_{iJ}]. \end{aligned}$$

Similar expressions hold for all P_{ij}'s and become well defined once a joint density is chosen for the e_{ij}'s.

The multiple logit model is based on the assumption that the e_{ij} are independently and identically distributed with Weibull density functions. The probit model is based on the assumption that the e_{ij} have a multivariate normal distribution. Of the two, the multiple logit model has received more attention than its probit counterpart due to estimation difficulties associated with the latter. Only the logit model will be discussed here. For discussions of the probit model see Hausman and Wise (1978), Albright *et al.* (1977) and Judge *et al.* (1980).

As noted above the logit model is based on the assumption that the errors e_{ij} are independent and identically distributed Weibull random variables. McFadden (1974) has shown that the "random utility" model presented above yields a logit model if and only if the errors have Weibull distributions. The difference between any two random variables with Weibull distributions has a logistic distribution function, giving rise to the multiple logit model.

The probabilities arising from this model can be expressed as

$$P_{ij} = \frac{\exp(\mathbf{x}'_{ij}\boldsymbol{\beta})}{\sum_{j=1}^{J} \exp(\mathbf{x}'_{ij}\boldsymbol{\beta})}, \qquad (16.5.2)$$

which is a general form of the logistic distribution function. Recall that $\boldsymbol{\beta}$ is an unknown $K \times 1$ vector of parameters common to all members of the population and $\mathbf{x}_{ij}$ is a $K \times 1$ vector of observations on variables which are functions of the characteristics of the alternatives and the individual decision-makers. Now note some consequences of this specification.

First, consider the effect on the odds of choosing alternative 1 rather than alternative 2 where the number of alternatives facing the individual are increased from J to J^*. The odds of alternatives 1 being chosen rather than 2 where J alternatives are available is

$$\frac{P_{i1}}{P_{i2}} = \frac{\exp(\mathbf{x}'_{i1}\boldsymbol{\beta}) \Big/ \sum_{i=1}^{J} \exp(\mathbf{x}'_{ij}\boldsymbol{\beta})}{\exp(\mathbf{x}'_{i2}\boldsymbol{\beta}) \Big/ \sum_{i=1}^{J} \exp(\mathbf{x}'_{ij}\boldsymbol{\beta})} = \frac{\exp(\mathbf{x}'_{i1}\boldsymbol{\beta})}{\exp(\mathbf{x}'_{i2}\boldsymbol{\beta})}.$$

The odds when J^* alternatives are available is *still*

$$\frac{P_{i1}}{P_{i2}} = \frac{\exp(\mathbf{x}'_{i1}\boldsymbol{\beta})}{\exp(\mathbf{x}'_{i2}\boldsymbol{\beta})},$$

since the denominators of (16.5.2) divide out. Thus, for this model the odds of a particular choice are *unaffected* by the presence of additional alternatives. This property is called the *independence of irrelevant alternatives* and can represent a serious weakness in the logit model. Suppose, for example, members of a population, when offered a choice between a pony and a bicycle, choose the pony in two-thirds of the cases. If an additional alternative is made available, say an additional bicycle just like the first except of a different color, then one would still expect two-thirds of the population to choose the pony and the remaining one-third to split their choices among the bicycles according to their color preference. In the logit model, however, the proportion choosing the pony must fall to one-half if the odds relative to either bicycle is to remain two-to-one in favor of the pony. This illustrates the point that when two or more of the J alternatives are close substitutes, the conditional logit model may not produce reasonable results. On the other hand, there are many circumstances where the alternatives are distinct enough for this feature of the logit model not to be a negative factor.

Second, in this formulation none of the K variables represented in $\mathbf{x}_{ij}$ can be constant across all alternatives since then the associated parameter would not be identified. For example, consider again the odds of choosing alternative 1 rather than alternative 2,

$$\frac{P_{i1}}{P_{i2}} = \frac{\exp(\mathbf{x}'_{i1}\boldsymbol{\beta})}{\exp(\mathbf{x}'_{i2}\boldsymbol{\beta})} = \exp(\mathbf{x}'_{i1} - \mathbf{x}'_{i2})\boldsymbol{\beta}.$$

If any corresponding elements of $\mathbf{x}_{i1}$ and $\mathbf{x}_{i2}$ are equal, the associated variable has no influence on the odds. If this is the case for all alternatives, then the variable in question does not contribute to the explanation of why one alternative is chosen over another and its parameter cannot be estimated. Intuitively, if the parameter vector $\boldsymbol{\beta}$ is to remain constant across all alternatives, only factors which change from alternative to alternative can help explain why one is chosen rather than another. Consequently, variables like age, sex, income, or race which are constant across alternatives provide no information about the choice process given this model. Variables which *would* provide information about the choices made include the cost of a particular alternative to each individual (for instance the cost of transportation by car, bus, train or taxi to a particular destination) or the return to an individual from each available alternative. These factors vary across alternatives for each individual.

Unfortunately, economists rarely have data that varies over both the individual in the sample and over each alternative faced by an individual. Such data are both costly to collect and difficult to characterize. The data economists usually have access to vary across individuals but not across alternatives, so that for any individual $\mathbf{x}_{i1} = \mathbf{x}_{i2} = \cdots = \mathbf{x}_{iJ} = \mathbf{x}_i$. Given this circumstance, the model must be modified in some way before it can be used to characterize choice behavior. One possible modification is to allow the explanatory variables to have differential impacts upon the odds of choosing one alternative rather than another. That is the coefficient vector must be made alternative specific. That is, let the selection probabilities be given by

$$P_{ij} = \frac{\exp(\mathbf{x}'_{ij}\boldsymbol{\beta}_j)}{\sum_{j=1}^{J} \exp(\mathbf{x}'_{ij}\boldsymbol{\beta}_j)}, \tag{16.5.3}$$

where now the parameter vector is indexed by j, indicating that explanatory variables may have differential impacts depending upon the alternative.

Now the odds of the kth alternatives relative to the first are

$$\begin{aligned}\frac{P_{ik}}{P_{i1}} &= \frac{\exp(\mathbf{x}'_{ik}\boldsymbol{\beta}_k)}{\exp(\mathbf{x}'_{i1}\boldsymbol{\beta}_1)} \\ &= \exp(\mathbf{x}'_{ik}\boldsymbol{\beta}_k - \mathbf{x}'_{i1}\boldsymbol{\beta}_1), \qquad k = 2, \ldots, J.\end{aligned} \tag{16.5.4}$$

If the vectors $\mathbf{x}_{ik}$ and $\mathbf{x}_{i1}$ contain variables that are constant across alternatives then $\mathbf{x}_{ik} = \mathbf{x}_{i1} = \mathbf{x}_i$, for all $k = 2, \ldots, J$, and (16.5.4) becomes

$$\frac{P_{ik}}{P_{i1}} = \exp[\mathbf{x}_i'(\boldsymbol{\beta}_k - \boldsymbol{\beta}_1)]. \tag{16.5.5}$$

Some sort of normalization rule is clearly needed, and a convenient one is to assume $\boldsymbol{\beta}_1 = \mathbf{0}$. This condition, together with the $(J - 1)$ equations in (16.5.5), uniquely determines the selection probabilities and guarantees they sum to 1 for each i.

Now the selection probabilities are

$$P_{i1} = \frac{1}{1 + \sum_{j=2}^{J} \exp(\mathbf{x}_i'\boldsymbol{\beta}_j)},$$

and

$$P_{ij} = \frac{\exp(\mathbf{x}_i'\boldsymbol{\beta}_j)}{1 + \sum_{j=2}^{J} \exp(\mathbf{x}_i'\boldsymbol{\beta}_j)}, \qquad j = 2, \ldots, J. \tag{16.5.6}$$

Maximum likelihood estimates of the parameters may be obtained as follows. Insert the selection probabilities (16.5.6) into the likelihood function (16.5.1) to obtain

$$\begin{aligned}
L &= \prod_{i=1}^{T} P_{i1}^{y_{i1}} P_{i2}^{y_{i2}} \cdots P_{iJ}^{y_{iJ}} \\
&= \prod_{i=1}^{T} \left\{ \left[\frac{1}{1 + \sum_{j=2}^{J} \exp(\mathbf{x}_i'\boldsymbol{\beta}_j)} \right]^{y_{i1}} \cdot \prod_{j=2}^{J} \left[\frac{\exp(\mathbf{x}_i'\boldsymbol{\beta}_j)}{1 + \sum_{j=2}^{J} \exp(\mathbf{x}_i'\boldsymbol{\beta}_j)} \right]^{y_{ij}} \right\} \\
&= \prod_{i=1}^{T} \left[\frac{1}{1 + \sum_{j=2}^{J} \exp(\mathbf{x}_i'\boldsymbol{\beta}_j)} \right] \cdot \prod_{i=1}^{T} \left[1^{y_{i1}} \left[\prod_{j=2}^{J} \exp(\mathbf{x}_i'\boldsymbol{\beta}_j)^{y_{ij}} \right] \right] \\
&= \prod_{i=1}^{T} \left[\frac{1}{1 + \sum_{j=2}^{J} \exp(\mathbf{x}_i'\boldsymbol{\beta}_j)} \right] \cdot \prod_{i=1}^{T} \prod_{j=2}^{J} \exp(\mathbf{x}_i'\boldsymbol{\beta}_j)^{y_{ij}}.
\end{aligned} \tag{16.5.7}$$

The log likelihood function is

$$\begin{aligned}
\ln L &= \sum_{i=1}^{T} - \ln\left(1 + \sum_{j=2}^{J} \exp(\mathbf{x}_i'\boldsymbol{\beta}_j)\right) + \sum_{i=1}^{T} \sum_{j=2}^{J} (y_{ij}\mathbf{x}_i'\boldsymbol{\beta}_j) \\
&= \sum_{i=1}^{T} \left[\sum_{j=2}^{J} y_{ij}\mathbf{x}_i'\boldsymbol{\beta}_j - \ln\left(1 + \sum_{j=2}^{J} \exp(\mathbf{x}_i'\boldsymbol{\beta}_j)\right) \right].
\end{aligned} \tag{16.5.8}$$

The likelihood function and its logarithm are nonlinear in $\boldsymbol{\beta}_j$ as are the first order conditions. Consequently, (16.5.8) must be maximized numerically.

Fortunately ln L is strictly concave in the $\boldsymbol{\beta}_j$'s and thus any nonlinear optimization procedure that converges, such as the Newton–Raphson method, will yield maximum likelihood estimates at any point where the first order conditions are satisfied. For a brief review of some nonlinear optimization techniques the reader is referred to the Appendix. The Newton–Raphson method requires use of the following derivatives (see Exercise 16.4).

$$\frac{\partial \ln L}{\partial \boldsymbol{\beta}_j} = \sum_{i=1}^{T} \left[y_{ij} - \frac{\exp(\mathbf{x}_i'\boldsymbol{\beta}_j)}{1 + \sum_{j=2}^{J} \exp(\mathbf{x}_i'\boldsymbol{\beta}_j)} \right] \mathbf{x}_i, \qquad j = 2, \ldots, J, \quad (16.5.9)$$

$$\begin{aligned} \frac{\partial^2 \ln L}{\partial \boldsymbol{\beta}_j \, \partial \boldsymbol{\beta}_k'} = I_{jk} &= \sum_{i=1}^{T} \left[\frac{\exp(\mathbf{x}_i'\boldsymbol{\beta}_j) \exp(\mathbf{x}_i'\boldsymbol{\beta}_k)}{\left[1 + \sum_{j=2}^{J} \exp(\mathbf{x}_i'\boldsymbol{\beta}_j)\right]^2} \right] \mathbf{x}_i \mathbf{x}_i' \\ &= \sum_{i=1}^{T} P_{ij} P_{ik} \mathbf{x}_i \mathbf{x}_i', \quad \text{for } j \neq k, \end{aligned} \qquad (16.5.10)$$

and

$$\begin{aligned} \frac{\partial^2 \ln L}{\partial \boldsymbol{\beta}_j \, \partial \boldsymbol{\beta}_j'} = I_{jj} &= -\sum_{i=1}^{T} \left[\frac{\exp(\mathbf{x}_i'\boldsymbol{\beta}_j)}{1 + \sum_{j=2}^{J} \exp(\mathbf{x}_i'\boldsymbol{\beta}_j)} - \left\{ \frac{\exp(\mathbf{x}_i'\boldsymbol{\beta}_j)}{1 + \sum_{j=2}^{J} \exp(\mathbf{x}_i'\boldsymbol{\beta}_j)} \right\}^2 \right] \mathbf{x}_i \mathbf{x}_i' \\ &= -\sum_{i=1}^{T} (P_{ij} - P_{ij}^2) \mathbf{x}_i \mathbf{x}_i'. \end{aligned} \qquad (16.5.11)$$

Furthermore, if $\boldsymbol{\beta}^*$ is the maximum likelihood estimator, we know that under general conditions $\sqrt{T}(\boldsymbol{\beta}_T^* - \boldsymbol{\beta}) \overset{\text{asy}}{\to} N(\mathbf{0}, \lim_{T \to \infty} T[I(\boldsymbol{\beta})]^{-1})$, where $I(\boldsymbol{\beta})$ is the information matrix $-E(\partial^2 \ln L / \partial \boldsymbol{\beta} \, \partial \boldsymbol{\beta}')$. We may then approximate the distribution of $\boldsymbol{\beta}^*$ for finite samples as $N(\boldsymbol{\beta}, I(\boldsymbol{\beta}^*)^{-1})$ where the information matrix in this problem is given by

$$I = \begin{bmatrix} -I_{22} & \cdots & -I_{2J} \\ \vdots & & \vdots \\ -I_{J2} & \cdots & -I_{JJ} \end{bmatrix},$$

and the P_{ij} in (16.5.10) and (16.5.11) are replaced by their estimates.

A convenient property of these models is that the basic log-odds equations for (P_{ik}/P_{i1}) can be used to construct other comparisons since

$$\ln(P_{ij}/P_{ik}) = \ln(P_{ij}/P_{i1}) - \ln(P_{ik}/P_{i1}).$$

Thus, the coefficients of the resulting equations are simply differences of the coefficients in the original equations, which also means their variances can be calculated from the original covariance matrix I^{-1}.

16.6 Analysis of Models with Censored Dependent Variables

Data available to economists is often incomplete in one way or another. Frequently values of the dependent variable can only be observed for a limited range or in a limited way, i.e., whether an event occurs or not as in logit or probit analysis. In this section we consider the former problem.

Within the limited dependent variable framework there are two special cases to consider. How the data limitation is dealt with depends upon how the data were collected. A *censored* sample is one in which some observations on the dependent variable corresponding to *known* sets of independent variables are not observable. A *truncated* sample results when knowledge of the independent variables is available only when the dependent variable is observed. Thus, for some trials of an experiment neither dependent *nor* independent variables are observed. A familiar example is Tobin's (1958) model for consumer durables, in which a purchase is made if a consumer's desire is high enough, where a measure of that desire is provided by the dollar amount spent on the purchase. On the other hand, no measure is available if no purchase is made, so that the sample is incomplete. This situation gives rise to a censored sample if values of independent variables are available for both those who make purchases and those who do not, while the sample is truncated if values of explanatory variables are recorded only for those who make a purchase.

It is not surprising that the truncated sample is more difficult to deal with than the censored sample since less information is available. Relatively simple two-step procedures for the censored sample problem have been suggested by Heckman (1976, 1979) and Amemiya (1973). Amemiya's (1973) procedure is based on the method of scoring and is applicable to both censored and truncated sample problems.

16.6.1 Heckman's Analysis of Censored Samples

Let us consider a model in which the dependent variable is observed *only* if it is nonnegative and otherwise takes the value zero. This is the Tobit model mentioned above which can be written

$$\begin{aligned} y_j &= \mathbf{x}_j'\boldsymbol{\beta} + e_j \quad && \text{if } y_j \geq 0, \\ &= 0 && \text{otherwise.} \end{aligned} \tag{16.6.1}$$

Furthermore assume that, of T observations, the last s y_j's are zero. Then the regression function can be written

$$E(y_j \mid \mathbf{x}_j, y_j \geq 0) = \mathbf{x}_j'\boldsymbol{\beta} + E(e_j \mid y_j \geq 0), \qquad j = 1, \ldots, T - s.$$

If the conditional expectation of the error term is zero there is no problem, since then an ordinary squares regression on the $(T - s)$ available observations will provide an unbiased estimate of $\boldsymbol{\beta}$. This, unfortunately, is not the case. If the e_j are independent and normally distributed random variables, then

$$E(e_j | y_j \geq 0) = E(e_j | e_j \geq -\mathbf{x}_j'\boldsymbol{\beta}) = \frac{\sigma^2}{(\sigma^2)^{1/2}} \lambda_j, \tag{16.6.2}$$

where

$$\lambda_j = \frac{f(\psi_j)}{1 - F(\psi_j)},$$
$$\psi_j = -\mathbf{x}_j'\boldsymbol{\beta}/(\sigma^2)^{1/2}, \tag{16.6.3}$$

and $f(\cdot)$ and $F(\cdot)$ are, respectively, the density and cumulative distribution function of a standard normal random variable evaluated at the argument. Thus, the regression function can be written

$$E(y_j | \mathbf{x}_j, y_j \geq 0) = \mathbf{x}_j'\boldsymbol{\beta} + \frac{\sigma^2}{(\sigma^2)^{1/2}} \lambda_j, \qquad j = 1, \ldots, T - s. \tag{16.6.4}$$

The difficulty with ordinary least squares is that it omits the second term on the right-hand side of (16.6.4). If λ_j were known, σ^2 and $\boldsymbol{\beta}$ could be estimated consistently using ordinary least squares. Since λ_j is not known, however, it must be estimated and this is the importance of having a censored rather than a truncated sample. It is a relatively simple matter to estimate λ_j for censored samples, but not for a truncated sample.

Let y_j^* be a random variable that is 1 when y_j is observed and zero otherwise. Then the likelihood function for the sample is

$$\begin{aligned} L &= \prod_{j=1}^{T} [\Pr(e_j < -\mathbf{x}_j'\boldsymbol{\beta})]^{1-y_j^*} [\Pr(e_j \geq -\mathbf{x}_j'\boldsymbol{\beta})]^{y_j^*} \\ &= \prod_{j=1}^{T} \Pr\left[\frac{e_j}{(\sigma^2)^{1/2}} < \frac{-\mathbf{x}_j'\boldsymbol{\beta}}{(\sigma^2)^{1/2}}\right]^{1-y_j^*} \Pr\left[\frac{e_j}{(\sigma^2)^{1/2}} \geq \frac{-\mathbf{x}_j'\boldsymbol{\beta}}{(\sigma^2)^{1/2}}\right]^{y_j^*} \\ &= \prod_{j=1}^{T} F\left(\frac{\mathbf{x}_j'\boldsymbol{\beta}}{(\sigma^2)^{1/2}}\right)^{y_j^*} \left[1 - F\left(\frac{\mathbf{x}_j'\boldsymbol{\beta}}{(\sigma^2)^{1/2}}\right)\right]^{1-y_j^*}, \end{aligned} \tag{16.6.5}$$

since $F(-t) = 1 - F(t)$ for the normal distribution. This is the likelihood function for probit estimation of the model

$$Ey_j^* = \mathbf{x}_j'\boldsymbol{\beta}/(\sigma^2)^{1/2}.$$

Thus, the first step of Heckman's two-step procedure is to estimate a probit model where the dependent variable is 1 or 0 depending on whether y_j is observed or not. This provides consistent estimates of $\boldsymbol{\beta}/(\sigma^2)^{1/2}$, which can be used to consistently estimate ψ_j and λ_j. The consistent estimates of λ_j are then inserted into (16.6.4) and the second step of the two-step procedure is the application of ordinary least squares to the resulting equation. The estimate of $\boldsymbol{\beta}$ produced by this process is consistent and asymptotically normally distributed. See Heckman (1976, 1979) for the proofs, expressions for the asymptotic covariance matrix and other generalizations.

16.6.2 Maximum Likelihood Estimation of Models with Censored Samples

Consider again the "Tobit" model

$$\begin{aligned} y_j &= \mathbf{x}_j'\boldsymbol{\beta} + e_j \quad \text{if } e_j \geq -\mathbf{x}_j'\boldsymbol{\beta}, \\ &= 0 \qquad\qquad\quad e_j < -\mathbf{x}_j'\boldsymbol{\beta}, \quad j = 1, \ldots, T, \end{aligned} \tag{16.6.6}$$

where the e_j are independent and $N(0, \sigma^2)$. Our objective now is to estimate $\boldsymbol{\beta}$ and σ^2 using T observations via maximum likelihood procedures. Since the likelihood function is highly nonlinear, we will, following Amemiya (1973), seek a consistent estimator with which to begin an iterative search process. The availability of a consistent initial estimator will also allow use of the linearized maximum likelihood estimator, which is known to have the same asymptotic distribution as the maximum likelihood estimator if the intial estimator is consistent.

Let S be a s-element subset of the T integers $\{1, 2, \ldots, \mathrm{T}\}$ such that $y_j = 0$ for j in S. Let $\bar{S}$ be the set of $(T - s)$ elements such that $y_j > 0$ for j in $\bar{S}$. The likelihood function is defined as

$$L = \prod_S G(-\mathbf{x}_j'\boldsymbol{\beta}, \sigma^2) \cdot \prod_{\bar{S}} g(y_j - \mathbf{x}_j'\boldsymbol{\beta}, \sigma^2), \tag{16.6.7}$$

where $G(\cdot)$ and $g(\cdot)$ are the cumulative distribution function and probability density function of a $N(0, \sigma^2)$ random variable respectively. The likelihood function can be simplified since $G(-\mathbf{x}_j'\boldsymbol{\beta}, \sigma^2) = 1 - G(\mathbf{x}_j'\boldsymbol{\beta}, \sigma^2) = 1 - G_j$.

$$L = \prod_S [1 - G_j] \cdot \prod_{\bar{S}} \frac{1}{\sqrt{2\pi}\sigma} \exp\left(-\frac{1}{2\sigma^2}(y_j - \mathbf{x}_j'\boldsymbol{\beta})^2\right). \tag{16.6.8}$$

This likelihood function is a mixture of normal cumulative distribution functions (discrete probabilities) and density functions. The log likelihood function, apart from constants, is

$$\ln L = \sum_S \ln(1 - G_j) - \frac{T - s}{2} \ln \sigma^2 - \frac{1}{2\sigma^2} \sum_{\bar{S}} (y_j - \mathbf{x}_j'\boldsymbol{\beta})^2. \tag{16.6.9}$$

The normal equations (see Exercise 16.5) are highly nonlinear and thus a root must be obtained numerically. Furthermore, because of the nature of the likelihood function usual theorems about the asymptotic normality and consistency of the maximum likelihood estimator do not hold. Amemiya (1973) shows that a root $\hat{\boldsymbol{\theta}}$ of the normal equations $\partial \ln L/\partial\boldsymbol{\theta} = \mathbf{0}$, where $\boldsymbol{\theta} = (\boldsymbol{\beta}', \sigma^2)'$, is consistent and asymptotically

$$\sqrt{T}(\hat{\boldsymbol{\theta}} - \boldsymbol{\theta}) \overset{\text{asy}}{\to} N\left(\mathbf{0}, \left[-\frac{\partial^2 Q(\boldsymbol{\theta})}{\partial\boldsymbol{\theta}\,\partial\boldsymbol{\theta}'}\right]^{-1}\right), \tag{16.6.10}$$

where

$$\frac{\partial^2 Q(\boldsymbol{\theta})}{\partial\boldsymbol{\theta}\,\partial\boldsymbol{\theta}'} = -\lim \frac{1}{T}\begin{bmatrix} \sum_1^T a_j \mathbf{x}_j \mathbf{x}_j' & \sum_1^T b_j \mathbf{x}_j \\ \sum_1^T b_j \mathbf{x}_j' & \sum c_j \end{bmatrix}, \tag{16.6.11}$$

and

$$\begin{aligned} a_j &= -\frac{1}{\sigma^2}\left(z_j f_j - \frac{f_j^2}{1 - F_j} - F_j\right), \\ b_j &= \frac{1}{2\sigma^2}\left(z_j^2 f_j + f_j - \frac{z_j f_j^2}{1 - F_j}\right), \\ c_j &= -\frac{1}{4\sigma^4}\left(z_j^3 f_j + z_j f_j - \frac{z_j^2 f_j^2}{1 - F_j} - 2F_j\right), \end{aligned} \tag{16.6.12}$$

where $z_j = \mathbf{x}_j'\boldsymbol{\beta}/\sigma$, $F(\mathbf{x}_j'\boldsymbol{\beta}/\sigma) = F_j$, and $f(\mathbf{x}_j'\boldsymbol{\beta}/\sigma) = f_j$. This means that the finite sample distribution of $\hat{\boldsymbol{\theta}}$ may be approximated by

$$N\left(\boldsymbol{\theta}, \left[-T\left(\frac{\partial^2 Q(\boldsymbol{\theta})}{\partial\boldsymbol{\theta}\,\partial\boldsymbol{\theta}'}\right)^{-1}_{\boldsymbol{\theta}=\hat{\boldsymbol{\theta}}}\right]\right),$$

after the limit sign in (16.6.11) is removed.

Since the normal equations are nonlinear, their solution may be obtained by an iterative process. The method of Newton gives the second round estimate

$$\hat{\boldsymbol{\theta}}_2 = \hat{\boldsymbol{\theta}}_1 - \left[\left(\frac{\partial^2 \ln L(\boldsymbol{\theta})}{\partial\boldsymbol{\theta}\,\partial\boldsymbol{\theta}'}\right)_{\boldsymbol{\theta}=\hat{\boldsymbol{\theta}}_1}\right]^{-1}\left(\frac{\partial \ln L(\boldsymbol{\theta})}{\partial\boldsymbol{\theta}}\right)_{\boldsymbol{\theta}=\hat{\boldsymbol{\theta}}_1}, \tag{16.6.13}$$

where

$$\frac{\partial \ln L}{\partial \boldsymbol{\beta}} = -\sum_{S} \frac{g_j}{1 - G_j} \mathbf{x}_j + \frac{1}{\sigma^2} \sum_{\bar{S}} (y_j - \mathbf{x}_j' \boldsymbol{\beta}) x_j,$$

$$\frac{\partial \ln L}{\partial \sigma^2} = \frac{1}{2\sigma^2} \sum_{S} \frac{\mathbf{x}_j' \boldsymbol{\beta} g_j}{1 - G_j} - \frac{T - s}{2\sigma^2} + \frac{1}{2\sigma^4} \sum_{\bar{S}} (y_j - \mathbf{x}_j' \boldsymbol{\beta})^2,$$

$$\frac{\partial^2 \ln L}{\partial \boldsymbol{\beta}\, \partial \boldsymbol{\beta}'} = -\sum_{S} \frac{g_j}{(1 - G_j)^2} \left[g_j - \frac{1}{\sigma^2} (1 - G_j) \mathbf{x}_j' \boldsymbol{\beta} \right] \mathbf{x}_j \mathbf{x}_j' - \frac{1}{\sigma^2} \sum_{\bar{S}} \mathbf{x}_j \mathbf{x}_j',$$

$$\frac{\partial^2 \ln L}{\partial \sigma^2\, \partial \boldsymbol{\beta}} = -\frac{1}{2\sigma^2} \sum_{S} \frac{g_j}{(1 - G_j)^2} \left[\frac{1}{\sigma^2} (1 - G_j)(\mathbf{x}_j' \boldsymbol{\beta})^2 - (1 - G_j) - \mathbf{x}_j' \boldsymbol{\beta} g_j \right] \mathbf{x}_j$$
$$- \frac{1}{\sigma^4} \sum_{\bar{S}} (y_j - \mathbf{x}_j' \boldsymbol{\beta}) \mathbf{x}_j,$$

$$\frac{\partial^2 \ln L}{(\partial \sigma^2)^2} = \frac{1}{4\sigma^4} \sum_{S} \frac{g_j}{(1 - G_j)^2} \left[\frac{1}{\sigma^2} (1 - G_j)(\mathbf{x}_j' \boldsymbol{\beta})^3 - 3(1 - G_j) \mathbf{x}_j' \boldsymbol{\beta} - (\mathbf{x}_j' \boldsymbol{\beta})^2 g_j \right]$$
$$+ \frac{T - s}{2\sigma^4} - \frac{1}{\sigma^6} \sum_{\bar{S}} (y_j - \mathbf{x}_j' \boldsymbol{\beta})^2, \tag{16.6.14}$$

where the following results have been used

$$\frac{\partial G_j}{\partial \boldsymbol{\beta}} = g_j \mathbf{x}_j; \qquad \frac{\partial G_j}{\partial \sigma^2} = -\frac{1}{2\sigma^2} \mathbf{x}_j' \boldsymbol{\beta} g_j;$$
$$\frac{\partial g_j}{\partial \boldsymbol{\beta}} = -\frac{1}{\sigma^2} \mathbf{x}_j' \boldsymbol{\beta} g_j \mathbf{x}_j; \qquad \frac{\partial g_j}{\partial \sigma^2} = \frac{(\mathbf{x}_j' \boldsymbol{\beta})^2 - \sigma^2}{2\sigma^4} g_j. \tag{16.6.15}$$

In order for the second-round estimator to be consistent a consistent initial estimator must be used. To derive a consistent estimator consider the truncated normal density,

$$h(\lambda) = \frac{1}{G_j} \frac{1}{\sqrt{2\pi\sigma^2}} \exp\left(-\frac{1}{2} \left(\frac{\lambda}{\sigma} \right)^2 \right), \qquad -\mathbf{x}_j' \boldsymbol{\beta} < \lambda < \infty,$$
$$= 0 \qquad \text{elsewhere.} \tag{16.6.16}$$

Then we have

$$y_j = \mathbf{x}_j' \boldsymbol{\beta} + e_j^* \quad \text{for } j \text{ in } \bar{S}, \tag{16.6.17}$$

where the random disturbance follows the distribution $h(\lambda)$. The moments of e_j^* are, conditional on j in $\bar{S}$,

$$Ee_j^* = \sigma^2 \frac{g_j}{G_j},$$

$$Ee_j^{*2} = \sigma^2 - \sigma^2 \mathbf{x}_j'\boldsymbol{\beta} \frac{g_j}{G_j},$$

$$Ee_j^{*3} = \sigma^2 \frac{g_j}{G_j} [(\mathbf{x}_j'\boldsymbol{\beta})^2 + 2\sigma^2],$$

$$Ee_j^{*4} = \sigma^2\left[3\sigma^2 - 3\sigma^2\mathbf{x}_j'\boldsymbol{\beta}\frac{g_j}{G_j} - (\mathbf{x}_j'\boldsymbol{\beta})^3 \frac{g_j}{G_j}\right], \tag{16.6.18}$$

where g_j and G_j are understood to be evaluated at their true parameter values. Now

$$Ey_j = \mathbf{x}_j'\boldsymbol{\beta} + \sigma^2 \frac{g_j}{G_j}, \qquad j \text{ in } \bar{S}, \tag{16.6.19}$$

and

$$Ey_j^2 = (\mathbf{x}_j'\boldsymbol{\beta})^2 + \sigma^2\mathbf{x}_j'\boldsymbol{\beta}\frac{g_j}{G_j} + \sigma^2, \qquad j \text{ in } \bar{S}. \tag{16.6.20}$$

Therefore,

$$Ey_j^2 = (Ey_j)\mathbf{x}_j'\boldsymbol{\beta} + \sigma^2, \qquad j \text{ in } \bar{S}. \tag{16.6.21}$$

Hence,

$$y_j^2 = y_j\mathbf{x}_j'\boldsymbol{\beta} + \sigma^2 + \eta_j, \qquad j \text{ in } \bar{S}, \tag{16.6.22}$$

where

$$\eta_j = \mathbf{x}_j'\boldsymbol{\beta}(Ey_j - y_j) + y_j^2 - Ey_j^2.$$

Now define

$$\hat{y}_j = \mathbf{x}_j'\left(\sum_{\bar{S}} \mathbf{x}_j\mathbf{x}_j'\right)^{-1} \sum_{\bar{S}} \mathbf{x}_j y_j. \tag{16.6.23}$$

Use $(\hat{y}_j\mathbf{x}_j', 1)$ as $(K + 1)$ instrumental variables in (16.6.22) and define the instrumental variable estimator

$$\hat{\boldsymbol{\theta}}_1 = \begin{bmatrix}\hat{\boldsymbol{\beta}}_1 \\ \hat{\sigma}^2\end{bmatrix} = \left[\sum_{\bar{S}} \begin{bmatrix}\hat{y}_j\mathbf{x}_j \\ 1\end{bmatrix}(y_j\mathbf{x}_j', 1)\right]^{-1} \sum_{\bar{S}} \begin{bmatrix}\hat{y}_j\mathbf{x}_j \\ 1\end{bmatrix} y_j^2. \tag{16.6.24}$$

Amemiya (1973) shows this estimator to be consistent and asymptotically normal, and, therefore, a suitable first-round estimator for use in the two-step estimator (16.5.20).

16.6.3 An Interpretive Note

As with the probit and logit models, the estimated coefficients in a Tobit model must be interpreted with care. McDonald and Moffitt (1980) explore the interpretation and use of the estimated Tobit coefficients. They show that

$$\frac{\partial Ey_i}{\partial x_{ij}} = F(z_i)\frac{\partial Ey_i^*}{\partial x_{ij}} + Ey_i^* \frac{\partial F(z_i)}{\partial x_{ij}}, \tag{16.6.25}$$

where $z_i = \mathbf{x}_i'\boldsymbol{\beta}/\sigma$, Ey_i^* is the expected value of the value of the dependent variable y_i given that $y_i > 0$, and $F(\cdot)$ is the cumulative standard normal distribution function. Furthermore,

$$\frac{\partial Ey_i^*}{\partial x_{ij}} = \beta_j[1 - z_i f(z_i)/F(z_i) - (f(z_i))^2/(F(z_i))^2], \tag{16.6.26}$$

where $f(\cdot)$ is the value of the standard normal density, and

$$Ey_i^* = \mathbf{x}_i'\boldsymbol{\beta} + \sigma f(z_i)/F(z_i), \tag{16.6.27}$$

$$Ey_i = F(z_i) \cdot Ey_i^*. \tag{16.6.28}$$

Thus, the total change in Ey_i in (16.6.25) is disaggregated into two parts: first the change in y for those above the limit, weighted by the probability of being above the limit and second, the change in probability of being above the limit, weighted by the expected value of y_i given that it is above the limit. These values, of course, depend upon the parameter estimates for $\boldsymbol{\beta}$ and σ^2 as well as the values of the explanatory variables $\mathbf{x}_i$. For the purposes of reporting the results, one might choose $\mathbf{x}_i$ to be the mean values of the explanatory variables. Also note that the coefficient β_j is *not* $\partial y_i^*/\partial x_{ij}$. See the McDonald and Moffitt paper for examples of the use of this decomposition.

16.7 Summary and Guide to Further Readings

In this chapter we have considered a variety of models for situations in which the outcomes of an experiment, the dependent variable, is only incompletely observed. That is, the dependent variable may be such that it may take only a finite number of values, in which case a binary or general choice model is appropriate; or the dependent variable may be continuous but observable only over a limited range, in which case a model for a censored or truncated variable is called for.

For the binary choice model the appropriate estimation technique depends upon the nature of the sample data that are available. If repeated observations exist on individual decisionmakers, a feasible generalized least squares estimation procedure can be used. Several alternative models exist and differ by the assumption of how the choice probabilities are related to the explanatory variables. If only one or a few observations exist for each decisionmaker, maximum likelihood estimation is possible for the two models, logit and probit, that relate the choice probabilities to the unknown parameters in a nonlinear way. A similar maximum likelihood estimation procedure can be used when the number of choice alternatives facing an individual is greater than two but still relatively few.

For models where the dependent variable is not observed over its full range of values, use of the usual ordinary least squares estimator is not appropriate. The correct estimation framework depends upon whether the sample is censored, where the value of the dependent variable is not observed for some individual's whose characteristics are known, or truncated, where the characteristics of the decisionmaker are observed only when the value of the dependent variable is observed. Both situations lead to a maximum likelihood estimation procedure.

During recent years there has been great interest in models with qualitative or limited dependent variables and consequently much published research. While not all the literature on these topics can be reviewed here, we will list some of the works appearing in journals devoted to economics. For a complete overall summary of this literature see Maddala (1983).

Excellent survey papers on qualitative dependent variable models have been written by Amemiya (1975, 1981), McFadden (1974, 1976a), and Nerlove and Press (1973). Textbook treatments appear in Judge *et al.* (1980), Dhrymes (1978), Maddala (1977), and Pindyck and Rubinfeld (1976), among others. To discuss the more specific literature or qualitative dependent variable models, we will classify such models into three categories: those with binary or dichotomous dependent variables, those multiresponse models where more than two options are available to each choice-maker, and, finally, those that deal with two or more jointly determined, or endogeneous, qualitative variables. References relevant to each category will be discussed in turn.

The survey papers listed above cover the basic binary dependent variable model thoroughly. In addition, however, Gourieroux and Monfort (1981) discuss the theoretical properties of the maximum likelihood estimator for this model. Predictions from binary dependent variable models and their aggregation is discussed by Westin (1974), while Press and Wilson (1978), McFadden (1976b), and Amemiya and Powell (1980) consider predictions from such models as alternatives to discriminant analysis. Zellner and Lee (1965) survey models useful when repeated observations are available.

Multiresponse logit models are discussed by McFadden (1974, 1976a), Nerlove and Press (1973), Domencich and McFadden (1975), and Schmidt and Strauss (1975b). Multiresponse probit models are discussed by Hausman and Wise (1978), Albright *et al.* (1977) and Daganzo (1979). A comparison in the bivariate case is provided by Morimune (1979). Multiresponse models where the alternatives are ordered are considered by McKelvey and Zavonia

(1975) and Akin *et al.* (1979). When responses are sequential, in the sense that earlier choices must be made before later ones, the sequential logit model of Kahn and Morimune (1979) may be useful.

Multivariate models, in the qualitative variable context, are those with jointly determined or endogenous qualitative or categorical variables. These models have been thought of in several ways. First, one could visualize a contingency table with the various cells having probabilities that are to be "explained" by a model. This is the framework of the multivariate logistic model of Nerlove and Press (1973) and the multivariate probit model discussed in Ashford and Sowden (1970). More recently, however, as typified by Heckman (1978), these models have been generalized to simultaneous equations systems with some or all of the endogenous variables being qualitative. In this context the qualitative variables serve to produce an endogenous shift or endogenous switching between different simultaneous equation regimes. The literature related to these types of models includes Schmidt and Strauss (1975a), Guilkey and Schmidt (1979), McFadden (1977, 1978), Lee (1979, 1981), Amemiya (1978a, 1978b) (discussed in Chapter 25, Section 3), Maddala and Trost (1981), Poirier and Ruud (1981), and Gourieroux *et al.* (1980) and Manski and McFadden (1981).

As in the case with qualitative dependent variables, substantial additions to the literature on models with censored or truncated dependent variables have appeared. One part of the new literature extends and refines to idea of Tobin's (1958). This includes the already mentioned works by Amemiya (1973), Heckman (1974, 1976, 1979), and McDonald and Moffitt (1980). Wales and Woodland (1980) offer an excellent exposition of Heckman-type models in the context of estimating a labor supply function. Also Greene (1981a, 1981b) corrects and simplifies Heckman's (1979) work and Olson (1980b) considers a generalization of the assumptions of the Heckman model. Goldberger (1981) examines the effects of various forms of truncation when the explanatory variables are multivariate normal. Olson (1980a) suggests a simply applied, although inconsistent, approximation to the maximum likelihood estimator. Nelson (1981) offers a Hausman specification error test for use with Tobit models. Hurd (1979) considers the effects of heteroscedasticity upon the maximum likelihood estimator in truncated samples. He shows that, unlike the usual regression case, if the heteroscedasticity is ignored the maximum likelihood estimator is inconsistent.

A second theme is the literature involving limited dependent variable models is to generalize the simultaneous equations framework so that some or all of the endogenous variables can be limited. One of these models has been suggested by Nelson and Olson (1978) and revised by Amemiya (1979). In addition to these important contributions, another related topic concerns modeling two regimes (that may themselves involve single or simultaneous Tobit systems) where the choice of regime is based on a probit or Tobit criterion function. Relevant references include Lee and Trost (1978), Kenny *et al.* (1979), Lee *et al.* (1980), and Lee (1978a, 1978b, 1979).

16.8 Exercises

16.1. Given the logit model, derive expressions (16.4.8) and (16.4.9).

16.2. Given the probit model, derive expressions (16.4.12) and (16.4.13).

16.3. Derive the maximum of the log likelihood for the binary logit and probit models under the null hypothesis that $\beta_2 = \beta_3 = \cdots = \beta_K$ as shown in (16.4.14).

16.4. Verify the derivatives in (16.5.9), (16.5.10), and (16.5.11).

16.5. Verify the derivatives in (16.6.14).

16.6. Amemiya's initial consistent estimator (16.6.24) can also be used for situations when the sample is truncated rather than censored. Recall that a truncated sample is said to exist when the values of the explanatory variables are known only if $y_j \geq 0$. The log likelihood function, apart from constants is,

$$\ln k\alpha = \sum_{j=1}^{T-s} \ln G_j - \frac{T-s}{2} \ln \sigma^2 - \frac{1}{2\sigma^2} \sum_{j=1}^{T-s} (y_j - \mathbf{x}_j'\boldsymbol{\beta}).$$

Obtain the first and second partials of ln l with respect to $\boldsymbol{\theta}' = (\boldsymbol{\beta}', \sigma^2)$.

16.7. Verify the partitioning of the partial derivative (16.6.25) for the Tobit model.

16.9 References

Akin, J. S., Guilkey, D. R., and Sickles, R. (1979). A random coefficient probit model with an application to a study of migration. *Journal of Econometrics*, **11**, 233–246.

Albright, R. L., Lerman, S. R., and Manski, C. F. (1977). Report on the development of an estimation program for the multinomial probit model. Prepared for the Federal Highway Administration.

Amemiya, T. (1973). Regression analysis when the dependent variable is truncated normal. *Econometrica*, **42**, 999–1012.

Amemiya, T. (1975). Qualitative response models. *Annals of Economic and Social Measurement*, **4**, 363–372.

Amemiya, T. (1978a). On a two-step estimator of a multivariate logit model. *Journal of Econometrics*, **8**, 13–21.

Amemiya, T. (1978b). The estimation of a simultaneous equation generalized probit model. *Econometrica*, **46**, 1193–1206.

Amemiya, T. (1979). The estimation of a simultaneous-equation tobit model. *International Economic Review*, **20**, 169–182.

Amemiya, T. (1981). Qualitative response models: a survey. *Journal of Economic Literature*, **19**, 1483–1536.

Amemiya, T. and Powell, J. L. (1980). A comparison of the logit model and normal discriminant analysis when independent variables are binary. Technical Report No. 320, Institute for Mathematical Studies in the Social Sciences, Stanford Univ., Stanford, CA.

Ashford, J. R. and Sowden, R. R. (1970). Multivariate probit analysis. *Biometrics*, **26**, 535–456.

Daganzo, C. (1979). *Multinomial Probit*. New York: Academic Press.

Dhrymes, P. J. (1978). *Introductory Econometrics*, New York: Springer-Verlag.

Domencich, T. and McFadden, D. (1975). *Urban Travel Demand: A Behavioral Analysis*. Amsterdam: North-Holland.

Goldberger, A. S. (1981). Linear regression after selection. *Journal of Econometrics*, **15**, 357–366.

Gourieroux, C., Laffont, J. J., and Monfort, A. (1980). Coherancy conditions in simultaneous linear equation models with endogenous switching regimes. *Econometrica*, **48**, 675–695.

Gourieroux, C. and Monfort, A. (1981). Asymptotic properties of the maximum likelihood estimator in dichotomous logit models. *Journal of Econometrics*, **17**, 83–98.

Greene, W. H. (1981a). On the asymptotic bias of the ordinary least squares estimator of the tobit model. *Econometrica*, **49**, 505–514.

Greene, W. H. (1981b). Sample selection bias as a specification error. *Econometrica*, **49**, 795–798.

Guilkey, D. K. and Schmidt, P. (1979). Some small sample properties of estimators and test statistics in the multivariate logit model. *Journal of Econometrics*, **10**, 33–42.

Hauser, J. R. (1977). Testing the accuracy, usefulness and significance of probabilistic choice models: an information theoretic approach. *Operations Research*, **26**, 406–421.

Hausman, J. A. and Wise, D. A. (1978). A conditional probit model for qualitative choice: discrete decisions recognizing interdependence and heterogeneous preferences. *Econometrica*, **46**, 403–426.

Heckman, J. (1974). Shadow prices, market wages, and labor supply. *Econometrica*, **42**, 679–694.

Heckman, J. (1976). The common structure of statistical models of truncation, sample selection and limited dependent variables and a simple estimator for such models. *Annals of Economic and Social Measurement*, **5**, 475–492.

Heckman, J. (1978). Dummy endogenous variables in a simultaneous equation system. *Econometrica*, **47**, 153–161.

Heckman, J. (1979). Sample bias as specification error. *Econometrica*, **47**, 153–162.

Hurd, M. (1979). Estimation in truncated samples when there is heteroscedasticity. *Journal of Econometrics*, **11**, 247–258.

Judge, G. G., Griffiths, W. E., Hill, R. C., Lee, T. C. (1980). *The Theory and Practice of Econometrics*. New York: Wiley.

Kahn, L. M. and Morimune, K. (1979). Unions and employment stability: a sequential logit approach. *International Economic Review*, **20**, 217–235.

Kenny, L. W., Lee, L. F., Maddala, G. S., and Trost, R. P. (1979). Returns to college education: an investigation of self-selection bias based on project talent data. *International Economic Review*, **20**, 775–790.

Lee, L. F. (1978a). Unionism and wage rates: a simultaneous equations model with qualitative and limited dependent variables. *International Economic Review*, **19**, 415–434.

Lee, L. F. (1978b). On the estimation of probit choice model with censored dependent variables and Amemiya's principle. Discussion Paper 78–99, Center For Economic Research, University of Minnesota, Minneapolis.

Lee, L. F. (1979). Identification and estimation in binary choice models with limited (censored) dependent variables. *Econometrica*, **47**, 977–996.

Lee, L. F. (1981). Fully recursive probability models and multivariate log-linear probability models for the analysis of qualitative data. *Journal of Econometrics*, **16**, 51–70.

Lee, L. F. and Trost, R. P. (1978). Estimation of some limited dependent variable models with application to housing demand. *Journal of Econometrics*, **8**, 357–382.

Lee, L. F., Maddala, G. S., and Trost, R. P. (1980). Asymptotic covariance matrices of two-stage probit and two-stage tobit methods for simultaneous equations models with selectivity. *Econometrica*, **48**, 491–503.

Maddala, G. S. (1977). *Econometrics.* New York: McGraw-Hill.

Maddala, G. S. (1983). *Limited-Dependent and Qualitative Variables in Econometrics.* Cambridge: Cambridge University Press.

Maddala, G. S. and Trost, R. S. (1981). Alternative formulations of the Nerlove–Press models. *Journal of Econometrics*, **16**, 35–50.

Manski, C. F. and McFadden, D. (1981). *Structural Analysis of Discrete Data with Econometric Applications.* Cambridge: The MIT Press.

McDonald, J. F. and Moffitt, R. A. (1980). The uses of tobit analysis. *Review of Economics and Statistics*, **62**, 318–321.

McFadden, D. (1974). Conditional logit analysis of qualitative choice behavior. In *Frontiers in Econometrics.* Edited by P. Zarembka. New York: Academic Press.

McFadden, D. (1976a). Quantal choice analysis: a survey. *Annals of Economic and Social Measurement*, **5**, 363–390.

McFadden, D. (1976b). A comment on discriminant analysis "versus" logit analysis. *Annals of Economic and Social Measurement*, **5**, 511–523.

McFadden (1977). Quantitative methods for analyzing travel behavior of individuals: some recent developments. Cowles Foundation Discussion Paper No. 474, New Haven.

McFadden (1978). Modelling the choice of residential location. In *Spatial Interaction Theory and Residential Location.* Edited by A. Karlquist, L. Lundquist, F. Snickars, and J. Weibull. North Holland, Amsterdam. Pp. 75–96.

McKelvey, R. D. and Zavonia, W. (1975). A statistical model for the analysis of ordinal level dependent variables. *Journal of Mathematical Sociology*, **4**, 103–120.

Morimune, K. (1979). Comparisons of normal and logistic models in the bivariate dichotomous analysis. *Econometrica*, **47**, 957–975.

Nelson, F. and Olson, L. (1978). Specification and estimation of a simultaneous-equation model with limited dependent variables. *International Economic Review*, **19**, 695–710.

Nerlove, M. and Press, S. J. (1973). Univariate and multivariate log-linear and logistic models. Rand Corporation, R-1306-EDA/NIH, Santa Monica, CA.

Nelson, F. D. (1981). A test for misspecification in the censored normal model. *Econometrica*, **49**, 1317–1330.

Olson, R. J. (1980a). Approximating a truncated regression with the method of moments. *Econometrica*, **48**, 1099–1106.

Olson, R. J. (1980b). A least squares correction for selectivity bias. *Econometrica*, **48**, 1815–1820.

Pindyck, R. S. and Rubinfield, D. L. (1976). *Econometric Models and Economic Forecasts.* New York: McGraw-Hill.

Poirier, D. J. and Ruud, P. A. (1981). On the appropriateness of endogenous switching. *Journal of Econometrics*, **16**, 249–256.

Press, S. J. and Wilson, S. (1978). Choosing between logistic regression and discriminant analysis. *Journal of the American Statistical Association*, **73**, 699–705.

Schmidt, P. (1978). Estimation of a simultaneous equations model with jointly dependent continuous and qualitative variables: the union–earnings question revisited. *International Economic Review*, **19**, 453–466.

Schmidt, P. and Strauss, R. P. (1975a). Estimation of models with jointly dependent qualitative variables: a simultaneous logit approach. *Econometrica*, **43**, 745–756.

Schmidt, P. and Strauss, R. P. (1975b). The prediction of occupation using multiple logit models. *International Economic Review*, **16**, 471–486.

Tobin, J. (1958). Estimation of relationships for limited dependent variables. *Econometrica*, **26**, 24–36.

Wales, T. J. and Woodland, A. D. (1980). Sample selectivity and estimation of labor supply functions. *International Economic Review*, **21**, 437–468.

Westin, R. B. (1974). Predictions from binary choice models. *Journal of Econometrics*, **2**, 1–16.

Zellner, A. and Lee, T. H. (1965). Joint estimation of relationships involving discrete random variables. *Econometrica*, **33**, 382–394.

CHAPTER 17
Distributed Lags

17.1 Introduction

Economic data are generated by systems of economic relations that are dynamic, stochastic, and simultaneous. In this chapter we consider dynamic aspects of single equation models. Distributed lag models are those that contain independent variables that are observed at different points in time. They are motivated by the fact that effects of changes in an independent variable are not always completely exhausted within one time period but are "distributed" over several, and perhaps many, future periods. These lagged effects may arise from habit persistence, institutional or technological constraints. They may also be the consequence of how individual decision maker's expectations are linked with experience. For more extensive justification of dynamic models see Cagan (1956), Nerlove (1956), and Muth (1961).

In the absence of any information about how long the effect of a change in an independent variable persists, the *general infinite distributed lag* might be considered. It is written

$$y_t = \sum_{i=0}^{\infty} \beta_i x_{t-i} + e_t, \qquad t = 1, 2, \ldots, \tag{17.1.1}$$

where the unknown regression parameters, β_i, are called distributed lag weights (or parameters) in this context. The difficulties with model (17.1.1) are obvious. An infinite number of parameters cannot be estimated with a finite amount of data. Progress can be made only by augmenting the sample information with additional information about the relation between the distributed lag weights, or alternatively, about how the effects of a change in an explanatory variable are distributed over time. One approach to this problem is to take advantage of the similarity between the normalized lag weights and probabilities associated with discrete random variables. Assuming that the lag weights are generated by a probability function means that instead of an infinite number of parameters only a small number, usually two or three, must be estimated. Much of the work on infinite distributed lags has relied on this linkage. The specification and estimation of infinite distributed lags is discussed in Sections 17.3 and 17.4.

An alternative to the infinite distributed lag specification is to assume that the effects of changes in independent variables do not persist for infinite time but are, essentially, exhausted after a finite length of time. That is, the restrictions

$$\beta_{n+j} = 0, \qquad j = 1, 2, \ldots, \infty, \tag{17.1.2}$$

are imposed for some specified integer n. The result is the *finite* distributed lag model

$$y_t = \sum_{i=0}^{n} \beta_i x_{t-i} + e_t, \qquad t = n + 1, \ldots, T, \tag{17.1.3}$$

where the integer n is called the length of the distributed lag.

The implication of this specification can be seen by writing out several observations,

$$Ey_{n+1} = \beta_0 x_{n+1} + \cdots + \beta_n x_1,$$
$$Ey_{n+2} = \beta_0 x_{n+2} + \beta_1 x_{n+1} + \cdots + \beta_n x_2, \text{ etc.}$$

Suppose $x_1, x_2, \ldots, x_n, x_{n+2}, \ldots$ are all the same value and only x_{n+1} is a different value. Then in time period $n + 1$ the value of x_{n+1} is given weight, β_0. In time period $n + 2$, the value of x_{n+1} is given weight β_1, and so on. The effect of the value of x_{n+1} persists $n + 1$ periods. The form of (17.1.3) is that of the usual linear regression model with $n + 1$ parameters that can be estimated by ordinary least squares. Usually, however, two difficulties arise in the estimation of the regression parameters of (17.1.3). First, the $(n + 1)$ explanatory variables x_{t-i}, $i = 0, \ldots, n$, are often highly correlated since economic time series are frequently strong autoregressive processes. Consequently, due to this multicollinearity, the parameters β_i may be imprecisely estimated and thus the pattern of influence of the explanatory variables may not be easily discerned. This may have serious practical consequences if, for example, the explanatory variable is subject to policy decision and if the timing of the consequences of a policy action is of concern. A second difficulty is that the lag length, n, is usually not known. Misspecification of the parameter n can have serious consequences. Procedures for dealing with the problems associated with the finite distributed lag specification (17.1.3) are discussed in Section 17.2.

17.2 Finite Distributed Lags

Initially we will assume that the lag length n in (17.1.3) is known and correct. The only remaining difficulty with the estimation of the distributed lag weights $\beta_0, \ldots, \beta_n$ is the potential lack of precision of the ordinary least squares estimates due to multicollinearity. The traditional approach for dealing with multicollinearity in this context is to reduce the number of parameters that must be estimated by assuming that relationships hold among the distributed lag parameters $\beta_0, \ldots, \beta_n$. These relations imply, or allow, the delayed, or lagged, effects of the explanatory variable to be more important during some subsequent periods than others. In this section it will be shown that commonly used assumptions imply relations among the parameters that can be recast as linear restrictions and consequently that finite distributed models and estimates can be studied in the context of restricted least squares discussed in Chapter 6.

17.2.1 The Arithmetic Lag

As a beginning, an "arithmetic" distributed lag will be considered. While we will subsequently generalize this model, consideration of the arithmetic lag will allow us to develop all the essential features and problems associated with finite distributed lags. An arithmetic lag arises when it is assumed that the effect of a change in an independent variable declines linearly over succeeding periods. That is, the size of the distributed lag weights diminishes linearly from β_0 to β_n. More specifically, assume that the distributed lag weights are given by

$$\beta_i = (n + 1 - i)\beta = (n + 1)\beta - i\beta, \qquad i = 0, \ldots, n, \qquad (17.2.1)$$

where β is an unknown scalar. Thus the lag weights β_i are taken to be points on a straight line with intercept $(n + 1)\beta$ and slope $-\beta$. This pattern of lag weights is depicted in Figure 17.2.1. Note that the distributed lag weights diminished in each succeeding period and vanish after n time periods.

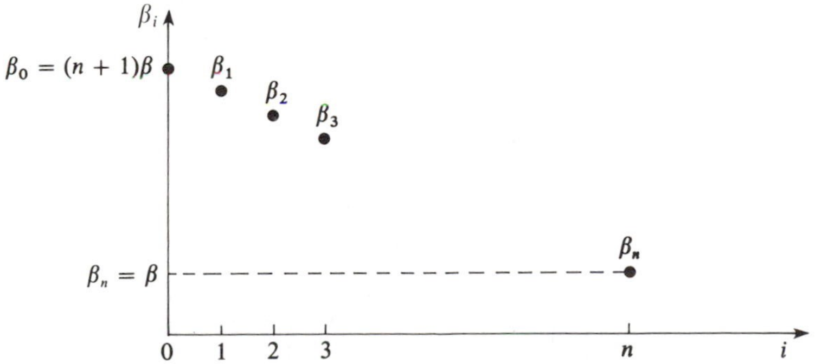

Figure 17.2.1 The arithmetic distributed lag.

Estimation of the unknown parameter β of the arithmetic distributed lag is simple. Substitute (17.2.1) into (17.1.3) to obtain

$$\begin{aligned} y_t &= \sum_{i=0}^{n} (n + 1 - i)\beta x_{t-i} + e_t \\ &= \beta \sum_{i=0}^{n} (n + 1 - i)x_{t-i} + e_t \\ &= \beta z_t + e_t, \end{aligned} \tag{17.2.2}$$

where $z_t = \sum_{i=0}^{n} (n + 1 - i)x_{t-i}$. If the e_t are normally and independently distributed random variables with zero means and constant variances σ^2 then the maximum likelihood estimator for β is

$$\hat{\beta} = \frac{\sum_{t=n+1}^{T} z_t y_t}{\sum_{t=n+1}^{T} z_t^2}.$$

This estimator is minimum variance unbiased if the model specification is correct, and specifically if the relations (17.2.1) are correct. Estimates of the distributed lag weights are then obtained as

$$\hat{\beta}_i = (n + 1 - i)\hat{\beta}, \qquad i = 0, \ldots, n.$$

The estimates $\hat{\beta}_i$ are normally distributed with mean β_i and variance

$$(n + 1 - i)^2\sigma^2\left(\sum_{t=n+1}^{T} z_t^2\right)^{-1}.$$

Note, however, that the number of parameters that has been estimated has been reduced from $(n + 1)$ to one. This has occurred because n linearly independent restrictions have been imposed on $\beta_0, \ldots, \beta_n$. Using (17.2.1) these restrictions are given by

$$\begin{aligned} \beta_0 &= (n + 1)\beta = (n + 1)\beta_n, \\ \beta_1 &= n\beta = n\beta_n, \\ &\vdots \\ \beta_{n-1} &= 2\beta = 2\beta_n. \end{aligned} \tag{17.2.3}$$

Consequently, if (17.1.3) is written in matrix form as

$$\mathbf{y} = X\boldsymbol{\beta} + \mathbf{e}, \tag{17.2.4}$$

where

$$X = \begin{bmatrix} x_{n+1} & x_n & \cdots & x_1 \\ x_{n+2} & x_{n+1} & \cdots & x_2 \\ \vdots & \vdots & \ddots & \vdots \\ x_T & x_{T-1} & \cdots & x_{T-n} \end{bmatrix}, \tag{17.2.5}$$

$\mathbf{y}' = (y_{n+1}, \ldots, y_T)$, $\boldsymbol{\beta}' = (\beta_0, \ldots, \beta_n)$ and $\mathbf{e}' = (e_{n+1}, \ldots, e_T)$, then the relations (17.2.3) may be rewritten as

$$R\boldsymbol{\beta} = \mathbf{0}, \tag{17.2.6}$$

where, R is the $n \times (n + 1)$ matrix

$$R = \begin{bmatrix} 1 & 0 & 0 & \cdots & 0 & -(n+1) \\ 0 & 1 & 0 & \cdots & 0 & -n \\ \vdots & \vdots & \vdots & \ddots & \vdots & \vdots \\ 0 & 0 & 0 & \cdots & 1 & -2 \end{bmatrix}. \tag{17.2.7}$$

The estimates of β_i *from* (17.2.2) *are equivalent to the restricted least estimates of* $\boldsymbol{\beta}$ *in* (17.2.4) *subject to the n, homogeneous restrictions in* (17.2.6).

From the results in Chapters 6 and 7, we know that even when (17.2.4) is correctly specified and $\mathbf{e} \sim N(\mathbf{0}, \sigma^2 I)$, if the restrictions (17.2.6) are incorrect, the resulting estimators are biased, have smaller sampling variances than the ordinary least squares estimators, and have a smaller mean square error only on that portion of the parameter space where the restrictions are "close" to being correct.

If we are uncertain about the correctness of the nonsample information, it has been customary to treat the restrictions as hypotheses and test their compatibility with the sample data using a classical hypothesis test or one of the mean square error criteria. As shown in Chapter 7 the resulting pretest estimator is inferior to ordinary least squares under a squared error loss function over much of the parameter space. The good alternative would appear to be to combine the sample information with the uncertain nonsample information using the positive-part Stein-like rule discussed in Chapter 7.

A remaining problem is, of course, that the above discussion presumed that the lag length n was known. This is rarely the case. Methods that have been suggested for determining the lag length using the data, and the other difficulties that arise with the arithmetic lag that are common to all finite distributed lag schemes, will be discussed below.

17.2.2 Lag Operators and Restrictions on Polynomial Distributed Lags

In the following sections we will use a lag operator L, defined such that

$$Lx_t = x_{t-1} \tag{17.2.8}$$

Dhrymes (1971) thoroughly explores the algebra of lag operators, so we will simply note some of their useful properties. From (17.2.8), observe that

$L^i x_t = x_{t-i}$, and if we define $L^0 = 1$, then the infinite distributed lag model can be written

$$\begin{aligned} y_t &= \sum_{i=0}^{\infty} \beta_i L^i x_t + e_t \\ &= W(L)x_t + e_t, \end{aligned}$$

where $W(L) = \sum_{i=0}^{\infty} \beta_i L^i$. The finite distributed lag model is written in the same way as

$$y_t = \sum_{i=0}^{n} \beta_i L^i x_t + e_t.$$

We can use the lag operator to develop a more general procedure for deriving restrictions on finite distributed lag weights. A straight line can be characterized as a polynomial of degree one. Consequently the arithmetic distributed lag is a special case of a polynomial distributed lag, discussed completely in the next section, where the finite distributed lag weights are constrained to fall on a polynomial of a specified degree.

At this time it will be useful to explore some properties of polynomials. First, note that if L is the lag operator then $D = 1 - L$ is a difference operator. That is,

$$Dx_t = (1 - L)x_t = x_t - x_{t-1}, \tag{17.2.9}$$

and

$$D^2 x_t = D \cdot (Dx_t) = (x_t - x_{t-1}) - (x_{t-1} - x_{t-2}),$$

etc. Polynomials have the property that if f_i is a polynomial of degree n whose domain is the integers, then the first difference $Df_i = (1 - L)f_i$ is expressible as a polynomial of degree $n - 1$ in i. (See Exercise 17.4.) Consequently, the nth difference $D^n f_i$ is a constant function and the $(n + 1)$st difference $D^{n+1} f_i$ is the zero function.

This property can be used to define restrictions on polynomial distributed lag weights. As an example, let us reexamine the arithmetic lag. Since a straight line is a first degree polynomial, second differences yield the zero function. That is

$$\begin{aligned} D^2\beta_i = D[\beta_i - \beta_{i-1}] &= (\beta_i - \beta_{i-1}) - (\beta_{i-1} - \beta_{i-2}) \\ &= \beta_i - 2\beta_{i-1} + \beta_{i-2} \end{aligned} \tag{17.2.10}$$

should equal zero. To see this note that the next to the last inequality in (17.2.10) amounts to differences between slopes at different points of the line, which are, of course, zero for a straight line. The difference operator works in the same way for higher order polynomials.

If we apply (17.2.10) to all lag weights $\beta_0, \ldots, \beta_n$ we have $(n-1)$ homogeneous relations that can be written $R\boldsymbol{\beta} = \mathbf{0}$ where

$$R = \begin{bmatrix} 1 & -2 & 1 & 0 & & \cdots & & 0 \\ 0 & 1 & -2 & 1 & 0 & & \cdots & 0 \\ \vdots & & & & & & & \vdots \\ 0 & \cdots & 0 & & & 1 & -2 & 1 \end{bmatrix}. \tag{17.2.11}$$

The use of this matrix or (17.2.7) in a restricted least squares estimator will yield arithmetic distributed lag weights, though unlike the restrictions (17.2.7), the line will not necessarily cross the i-axis at $i = n + 1$. The advantage of the procedure we have outlined here is that it can be used to generate restrictions for any polynomial degree and any lag length.

17.2.3 The Almon Polynomial Distributed Lag

The Almon (1965) lag imposes much less structure on the pattern of the lag effects than the arithmetic lag or the inverted-V lag (see Exercise 17.2). With the Almon method, a general polynomial structure is imposed on lag parameters and the sample data determine the specific shape. Those who use a polynomial lag structure usually assume that a polynomial of relatively low degree is sufficiently flexible to characterize the lag.

Let the degree of the polynomial lag structure be q so that the lag weights can be written as

$$\begin{aligned} \beta_i &= \alpha_0 + \alpha_1 i + \alpha_2 i^2 + \cdots + \alpha_q i^q \\ &= \sum_{j=0}^{q} \alpha_j i^j, \qquad i = 0, \ldots, n, \end{aligned} \tag{17.2.12}$$

or

$$\boldsymbol{\beta} = H\boldsymbol{\alpha}, \tag{17.2.13}$$

where $\boldsymbol{\alpha}' = (\alpha_0, \ldots, \alpha_q)$, $\boldsymbol{\beta}' = (\beta_0, \ldots, \beta_n)$, and

$$H = \begin{bmatrix} 1 & 0 & 0 & \cdots & 0 \\ 1 & 1 & 1 & \cdots & 1 \\ 1 & 2 & 2^2 & \cdots & 2^q \\ \vdots & \vdots & \vdots & \ddots & \vdots \\ 1 & n & n^2 & \cdots & n^q \end{bmatrix}$$

The parameters $\boldsymbol{\alpha}$ of the polynomial distributed lag can be estimated by substituting (17.2.13) into (17.2.4) to obtain

$$\mathbf{y} = XH\boldsymbol{\alpha} + \mathbf{e} = Z\boldsymbol{\alpha} + \mathbf{e}. \tag{17.2.14}$$

The ordinary least squares estimator of $\boldsymbol{\alpha}$ is $\hat{\boldsymbol{\alpha}} = (Z'Z)^{-1}Z'\mathbf{y}$ and the estimator for the $(n + 1)$ polynomial distributed lag parameters is $\hat{\boldsymbol{\beta}} = H\hat{\boldsymbol{\alpha}}$. It has distribution $N(\boldsymbol{\beta}, \sigma^2 H(Z'Z)^{-1}H')$ if the lag length n is known, $\mathbf{e} \sim N(\mathbf{0}, \sigma^2 I)$ and the relations (17.2.13) are correct. The properties of the polynomial lag estimator follow immediately from its restricted least squares nature. Note that the reparameterization from $\boldsymbol{\beta}$ to $\boldsymbol{\alpha}$ has reduced the number of parameters that must be estimated from $(n + 1)$ to $(q + 1)$, implying that $(n - q)$ independent restrictions have been applied. These restrictions can be identified in several equivalent ways, but the most direct uses the difference operator presented in the previous section.

If the β_i fall on a polynomial of degree q, then the $(q + 1)$st differences equal zero, defining $(n - q)$ restrictions on the parameters. For example, if the polynomial distributed lag is of degree two, then

$$\begin{aligned} D^3\beta_i &= (1 - L)^3\beta_i \\ &= (1 - 3L + 3L^2 - L^3)\beta_i \\ &= \beta_i - 3\beta_{i-1} + 3\beta_{i-2} - \beta_{i-3} = 0, \qquad i = (q + 1), \ldots, n. \end{aligned}$$

Consequently the restriction matrix R has the form

$$R = \begin{bmatrix} 1 & -3 & 3 & -1 & 0 & \cdots & & & 0 \\ 0 & 1 & -3 & 3 & -1 & \cdots & & & 0 \\ & & & & \vdots & & & & \\ 0 & & \cdots & & & 1 & -3 & 3 & -1 \end{bmatrix}.$$

This matrix has $n - q = n - 2$ linearly independent rows. The restricted least squares estimator of (17.2.4) subject to the homogeneous linear restrictions $R\boldsymbol{\beta} = \mathbf{0}$ will produce polynomial distributed lag estimates that fall on a polynomial of the desired degree. See Exercises 17.3–17.6 for frequently used alternative formulations of the restriction matrix.

Given that we have formulated the polynomial distributed lag problem in a restricted least squares format, how can this be used? First, given a choice of n and an uncertain choice of the polynomial degree q one might test the "hypothesis" $R\boldsymbol{\beta} = \mathbf{0}$ and decide on the basis of that test whether or not to employ the restrictions. The resulting pretest estimator has the properties we examined in Chapter 7. A better alternative for point estimation is the positive-part rule that combines sample and nonsample information also discussed in Chapter 7.

Second, given a fixed lag length n, the sequence of nested restrictions corresponding to polynomials of degree $n - 1, \ldots, 1, 0$ could be tested sequentially to determine the order of the polynomial. That is, we wish to test the sequence of hypotheses

$$\begin{aligned} H_1&: q = n - 1, \\ H_2&: q = n - 2, \\ &\ \vdots \\ H_n&: q = 0. \end{aligned} \tag{17.2.15}$$

This sequence is nested in that each subsequent hypothesis adds one more restriction and if H_k is true, H_{k-j} is also true, $j > 0$. Thus, one could test H_1, H_2, etc., until some H_k is rejected. If H_k is the first hypothesis rejected, $q = n - k + 1$ would be chosen as the degree of the polynomial. Using this process, care should be taken when the significance level of each test is chosen. The type I error for testing H_2 is the probability of rejecting H_1 *or* H_2 incorrectly. The probability of this event is greater than the probability that H_2 alone is rejected. It can be shown that the type I error for the kth test in the sequence is

$$\alpha_k = \begin{cases} \gamma_1 & \text{if } k = 1, \\ \gamma_k(1 - \alpha_{k-1}) + \alpha_{k-1} & \text{if } k = 2, 3, \ldots, n, \end{cases} \qquad (17.2.16)$$

where γ_k is the significance level of the kth test in the sequence. If γ_k is chosen to be a constant for all tests, say 0.01 or 0.05, the probability of a type I error will grow (Anderson (1971)).

All of the discussion above has been predicated upon knowledge of the lag length, n. If n is not known, there are costs incurred whether n is chosen to be longer or shorter than the true lag length. Trivedi and Pagan (1976) show that if the polynomial degree is chosen correctly, overstating the true lag length by more than the degree of the polynomial ensures that the polynomial distribution lag estimator will be biased, and if the lag length is understated the polynomial distributed lag estimator is generally biased. Since the length of the lag is rarely known, several data dependent procedures have been developed for determining the lag length. It is unfortunate for testing purposes that for a given polynomial degree the restriction sets that imply shorter lag lengths are *not* conveniently "nested." To see this, let N be the maximum lag length to be considered. So the finite distributed lag model is

$$y_t = \sum_{i=0}^{N} \beta_i x_{t-i} + e_t, \qquad t = N + 1, \ldots, T. \qquad (17.2.17)$$

Now we seek a set of restrictions that forces the parameters to fall on a polynomial of specified degree with lag length $N - r$, where $N - r + 1 \geq q + 1$ and $r \geq 0$. Thus we are requiring that $\beta_{N-r+1} = \beta_{N-r+2} = \cdots = \beta_N = 0$ and that $\beta_0, \ldots, \beta_{N-r}$ fall on a polynomial of degree q. The former requires r restrictions and the latter requires $N - r + q$. Thus a total of $N - q$ restrictions are required in order to specify a polynomial of degree q, regardless of the choice of r and thus the implied lag length.

Consequently what has been suggested is the following. Using (17.2.17) as a starting point, sequentially test the hypotheses

$$\begin{aligned} H_{(0)}&: \beta_N = 0, \\ H_{(1)}&: \beta_N = \beta_{N-1} = 0, \\ &\vdots \\ H_{(r)}&: \beta_N = \beta_{N-1} = \cdots = \beta_{N-r} = 0, \end{aligned}$$

and select the appropriate lag length based upon the first hypothesis that is rejected. Thus if $H_{(r)}$ is rejected one would select $N - r$ as the appropriate lag length and then proceed as if the lag length were known. While expedient and easy to carry out, the statistical consequences of such repeated pretest have not been investigated. Pagano and Hartley (1981) develop a convenient orthogonal reparameterization of the problem that makes use of simple t-statistics to test the sequential hypotheses concerning both lag length and polynomial degree. Alternatives to usual hypothesis testing procedures that have been suggested include use of the specification error tests of Ramsey (1969, 1970, 1974) by Harper (1977) and Griffiths and Kerrison (1978) and subset model selection procedures, such as Mallows C_p-statistic, by Pagano and Hartley (1981) and Gweke and Meese (1979). It should be noted, however, that both the lag length and polynomial degree testing procedures appear very sensitive to the presence of autocorrelation. See Griffiths and Kerrison (1978) and Pagano and Hartley (1981) for more on this problem.

17.2.4 Summary and Guide to Further Readings on Finite Lags

To summarize then, imposing a finite polynomial distributed lag means one must face some difficult practical problems. Two parameters of the model, the lag length n and the polynomial degree q cannot be estimated directly, but rather are only implicit in restrictions placed on the distributed lag weights. Consequently, all the difficulties associated with the use of uncertain nonsample information must be dealt with. In this light, all the literature on multicollinearity, the use of exact and stochastic nonsample information and specification error tests becomes relevant and can be straightforwardly applied to this problem.

Surveys of the polynomial distributed lag literature are provided in Dhrymes (1971), Maddala (1977), Judge *et al.* (1980) and papers by Trivedi and Pagan (1976) and Hendry and Pagan (1980). The topic of how to specify the lag length and polynomial degree parameters has drawn a great deal of attention. Godfrey and Poskitt (1975), Amemiya and Morimune (1974), and Schmidt and Sickles (1975) consider the problem of choosing the polynomial degree given the lag length. Papers by Schmidt and Waud (1973), Frost (1975), Terasvirta (1976), Carter *et al.* (1976), Sargan (1980), Pagano and Hartley (1981), Harper (1977), and Griffiths and Kerrison (1978) consider the consequences of and methods for having to search for the lag length as well. To present, no adequate decision-theoretic framework has been developed for simultaneously choosing n and q and, at the same time, allowing unconditional inference on the parameters.

Generalizations of the Almon lag include Shiller's (1973) smoothness priors, which has been related to mixed estimation by Taylor (1974), who showed that Shiller's estimator could be thought of as a polynomial distributed lag model with stochastic, rather than exact, restrictions. Fomby (1979) noted that usual mean square error tests could be applied given Taylor's formulation. Poirier (1976) suggested increasing the flexibility of the polynomial distributed lag by employing cubic splines instead of a single polynomial. Alternatives to polynomial distributed lag models for the finite distributed lag model have been suggested by Hamlen and Hamlen (1978), who develop a trigonometric approximation, and Maddala (1974), who considers addressing the multicollinearity problem using a ridge estimator. This latter reference should remind us that any technique designed to deal with multicollinearity, such as principal components regression, could be applied directly to the finite lag model.

17.3 Geometric Lag Structures

17.3.1 Model Formulation

The general infinite lag structure may be written

$$y_t = \alpha + \sum_{i=0}^{\infty} \beta_i^* x_{t-i} + e_t.$$

Since this model has an infinite number of parameters the model is not useful as is. If the β_i^* are nonnegative and have a finite sum, say

$$\sum_{i=0}^{\infty} \beta_i^* = \beta,$$

we can normalize the lag structure as

$$y_t = \alpha + \beta \sum_{i=0}^{\infty} \beta_i x_{t-i} + e_t, \tag{17.3.1}$$

where $\beta_i = \beta_i^*/\beta$. Since $\beta_i \in [0, 1]$ and $\sum_{i=0}^{\infty} \beta_i = 1$, we may associate the set of lag weights with mass functions of discrete random variables that depend on one or, perhaps, two parameters. Then, by an appropriate substitution, we may reduce the estimation problem from one of estimating an infinite number of lag parameters to just one or two. This association also permits calculation of the mean and variance of the lag distribution, which are useful descriptive measures. It should be noted in passing that choosing a parameterized lag structure is equivalent to imposing an infinite number of restrictions on the parameters of the original model. Consequently lag structures that are extremely flexible, yet parsimonious, are advantageous.

One commonly adopted lag structure is the geometric lag structure. That is

$$\beta_i = (1 - \lambda)\lambda^i, \qquad i = 0, 1, 2, \ldots, \tag{17.3.2}$$

where the unknown lag parameter $\lambda \in (0, 1)$. This structure is normalized since $\sum_{i=0}^{\infty} \lambda^i = 1/(1 - \lambda)$. Substituting (17.3.2) into (17.3.1) we obtain

$$y_t = \alpha + \beta(1 - \lambda) \sum_{i=0}^{\infty} \lambda^i x_{t-i} + e_t \tag{17.3.3a}$$

or

$$y_t = \alpha + \beta^* W(L)x_t + e_t, \tag{17.3.3b}$$

where $W(L)$ is a polynomial in the lag operator and defined as

$$W(L) = 1 + \lambda L + \lambda^2 L^2 + \cdots = (1 - \lambda L)^{-1}$$

and $\beta^* = \beta(1 - \lambda)$. Making use of $[W(L)]^{-1} = 1 - \lambda L$ we can rewrite (17.3.3b) as

$$(1 - \lambda L)y_t = (1 - \lambda L)\alpha + \beta^* x_t + (1 - \lambda L)e_t$$

or

$$y_t = \alpha^* + \beta^* x_t + \lambda y_{t-1} + e_t^*, \tag{17.3.4}$$

where $\alpha^* = (1 - \lambda)\alpha$ and $e_t^* = e_t - \lambda e_{t-1}$. We will call (17.3.3) the *direct* form of the geometric lag model and (17.3.4) the *autoregressive* form.

The popularity of the geometric lag stems from the fact that two important economic hypotheses lead to models of the form (17.3.4), and thus the geometric lag. The partial adjustment and adaptive expectations models have commonly been used for investigating such topics as supply response, inventory investment, and demand based on expected prices. These models are formulated by specifying auxiliary equations that describe adjustment processes and relationships between observable and unobservable variables. Some applications in supply response are Nerlove (1958), Jones (1962), Hill (1971), and Anderson (1974). Examples in inventory adjustment are Burrows (1971), Burrows and Godfrey (1973), and Park (1974). Cagan (1956) used adaptive expectations to investigate the demand for money as a function of "expected price."

17.3.1a *Partial Adjustment Models*

The first model to be investigated is the *partial adjustment* model. One rationale for such a model has been discussed by Griliches (1967). Assume that the firm incurs two types of costs: (1) a cost of being out of equilibrium (e.g., foregone profits from having too much or too little inventory), and (2) a cost of change (e.g., the cost of acquiring new storage facilities or finding a rentor for unused ones). Let y_t^* represent the desired level of some variable of interest y (e.g., optimal level of inventory) at time t and y_t be the actual value of y at time t. If both of the above costs can be approximated by quadratic terms, the firm's cost function can be written as

$$c_t = a(y_t - y_t^*)^2 + b(y_t - y_{t-1})^2.$$

To minimize this cost the first order condition is

$$\frac{\partial c_t}{\partial y_t} = 2a(y_t - y_t^*) + 2b(y_t - y_{t-1}) = 0.$$

Therefore,

$$y_t = \frac{a}{a+b} y_t^* + \frac{b}{a+b} y_{t-1}$$

or equivalently

$$y_t - y_{t-1} = \gamma(y_t^* - y_{t-1}), \tag{17.3.5}$$

where $\gamma = a/(a + b)$ is the adjustment coefficient. Then minimization of costs requires that adjustment to the optimal level of inventories (y^*) only be partial hence the name *partial adjustment* model. Notice the adjustment coefficient depends on the relative importance of (marginal) out-of-equilibrium costs to the (marginal) adjustment costs. Not surprisingly, the higher the adjustment costs, the slower the rate of adjustment.

Assuming the actual level of y is stochastic but that the desired level is deterministic, and that expectations are formed in a consistent manner, a random perturbation is added to (17.3.5) to obtain

$$y_t - y_{t-1} = \gamma(y_t^* - y_{t-1}) + e_t. \tag{17.3.6}$$

As it stands, (17.3.6) is not an estimable relationship since y_t^* is unobservable. There needs to be a linkage between this unobservable variable and one or more observable variables. Suppose the optimal level of inventories is related to present sales by the equation

$$y_t^* = \alpha + \beta x_t, \tag{17.3.7}$$

where x_t represents sales at time t. Substituting (17.3.7) into (17.3.6) results in

$$y_t - y_{t-1} = \gamma(\alpha + \beta x_t - y_{t-1}) + e_t \tag{17.3.8}$$

or

$$y_t = \alpha\gamma + \beta\gamma x_t + (1 - \gamma)y_{t-1} + e_t. \tag{17.3.9}$$

This lagged dependent variable model has resulted from a partial adjustment hypothesis and an auxiliary relationship between unobservable and observable variables. Thus, except for the specification of the error term, the partial adjustment assumption (17.3.5) leads to the autoregressive form of a geometric distributed lag model.

17.3.1b *Adaptive Expectations Models*

Now let us turn to the consideration of the *adaptive expectations* model. Suppose a simple regression model is modified so that $E(y_t)$ is a linear function, not of x_t, but of the "expected" level of x at time t, say, x_t^*. One example might be a demand relationship that is a function of expected price. Under such a specification

$$y_t = \alpha + \beta x_t^* + e_t, \tag{17.3.10}$$

Assume the formation of expectations follows

$$x_t^* - x_{t-1}^* = \eta(x_t - x_{t-1}^*), \tag{17.3.11}$$

where $0 \leq \eta < 1$. Now

$$x_t^* = \eta x_t + (1 - \eta)x_{t-1}^*$$

which in turn implies

$$x_t^* = \eta(x_t + (1 - \eta)x_{t-1} + (1 - \eta)^2 x_{t-2} + \cdots). \tag{17.3.12}$$

Substituting (17.3.12) into (17.3.10) yields

$$y_t = \alpha + \beta\eta\left(\sum_{i=0}^{\infty} (1 - \eta)^i x_{t-i}\right) + e_t \tag{17.3.13a}$$

or, in the autoregressive form,

$$y_t = \alpha\eta + \beta\eta x_t + (1 - \eta)y_{t-1} + u_t, \tag{17.3.13b}$$

where $u_t = e_t - (1 - \eta)e_{t-1}$. This model is identical to (17.3.4) with $\lambda = (1 - \eta)$. We now turn to problems of estimating the geometric lag model.

17.3.2 Estimation of the Geometric Lag

17.3.2a *Estimation of the Autoregressive Form of the Geometric Lag*

Since (17.3.4) is in the form of a lagged dependent variable model, the ordinary least squares estimator might be considered as it is consistent if the errors are uncorrelated. The validity of this latter assumption, however, must be carefully considered. First, for the partial adjustment model (17.3.9), if e_t are assumed to be independent and identically distributed with mean zero and constant variance σ^2, the ordinary least squares estimator will have the desired properties. However, for the adaptive expectations model (17.3.13), if the e_t in (17.3.10) are independent and identically distributed with mean zero and variance σ_e^2 then the $u_t = e_t - (1 - \eta)e_{t-1}$ are serially correlated. In fact, the u_t follow a MA(1) process as described in Chapter 10. If $(1 - \eta)$ were known, generalized least squares could be applied directly to (17.3.13) with all the usual small and large sample properties obtaining.

Since $(1 - \eta)$ is not likely to be known, one might consider applying ordinary least squares to (17.3.13) and choosing the estimated coefficient of y_{t-1} as an estimate of $(1 - \eta)$ to be used in a feasible generalized least squares procedure. Such a procedure would lead to inconsistent estimation of $(1 - \eta)$, however, since y_{t-1} is contemporaneously correlated with u_t. This follows since

$$\begin{aligned} Eu_t y_{t-1} &= [(e_t - (1 - \eta)e_{t-1})(\alpha + \beta\eta(x_{t-2} + (1 - \eta)x_{t-3} + \cdots) + e_{t-1})] \\ &= -(1 - \eta)\sigma_e^2 \neq 0. \end{aligned}$$

Given that $(1 - \eta)$ is estimated inconsistently, the resulting feasible generalized least squares is also inconsistent.

In Section 10.7.2, where the MA(1) process is discussed in detail, a procedure is discussed whereby a consistent though inefficient estimate of η can be obtained. In turn use of such an estimate of $(1 - \eta)$ in two-step feasible generalized least squares estimation would result in consistent but, unfortunately, asymptotically inefficient estimation of (17.3.13). The same can be said for instrumental variable estimation of $1 - \eta$, discussed below. Correlation between lagged dependent variables and autocorrelated errors results in inefficient two-step feasible generalized least squares estimation when the error covariance matrix, say Ω, is inefficiently estimated. To emphasize an important point, when there exists contemporaneous correlation between the errors and regressors of a generalized least squares model, the quality of the first step estimate $\hat{\Omega}$ is extremely important in determining the asymptotic efficiency of the two-step feasible generalized least squares extimator $\hat{\hat{\boldsymbol{\beta}}}$. Not just any estimate of Ω will do; an efficient estimate of Ω is needed.

An estimation technique that does not require any distributional assumption about e_t^* in the autoregressive form of the geometric lag (17.3.4) is the instrumental variable technique. The troublesome variable (17.3.4) is y_{t-1} since this regressor is contemporaneously correlated with the error term e_t^*, thus making ordinary least squares inconsistent. To overcome this problem Liviatan (1963) suggested using an instrument for y_{t-1}, namely x_{t-1}. The matrix of instruments is then

$$Z = \begin{bmatrix} 1 & x_2 & x_1 \\ 1 & x_3 & x_2 \\ \vdots & \vdots & \vdots \\ 1 & x_T & x_{T-1} \end{bmatrix}_{(T-1)\times 3}.$$

Let the matrix of observations on the explanatory variables be

$$X = \begin{bmatrix} 1 & x_2 & y_1 \\ 1 & x_3 & y_2 \\ \vdots & \vdots & \vdots \\ 1 & x_T & y_{T-1} \end{bmatrix}_{(T-1)\times 3},$$

then the instrumental variable estimator

$$\mathbf{b}_{\mathrm{IV}} = (Z'X)^{-1}Z'\mathbf{y}$$

provides consistent estimates of the relevant parameters. As shown by Dhrymes (1971), however, if the e_t^* are independent and identically distributed $N(0, \sigma_{e^*}^2)$, the instrumental variable estimator is inefficient relative to the maximum likelihood estimator presented below.

17.3.2b *Estimation of the Direct Form of the Geometric Lag*

In order to estimate the direct form of the geometric lag observe that

$$\begin{aligned}(1-\lambda)\sum_{i=0}^{\infty}\lambda^i x_{t-i} &= (1-\lambda)\sum_{i=0}^{t-1}\lambda^i x_{t-i} + (1-\lambda)\lambda^t \sum_{i=0}^{\infty}\lambda^i x_{-i} \\ &= w_t(\lambda) + (1-\lambda)\lambda^t \sum_{i=0}^{\infty}\lambda^i x_{-i}\end{aligned}$$

and since

$$E(y_0) = \alpha + \beta(1-\lambda)\sum_{i=0}^{\infty}\lambda^i x_{-i}$$

then

$$E(y_0) - \alpha = \beta(1-\lambda)\sum_{i=0}^{\infty}\lambda^i x_{-i} = \eta_0 \tag{17.3.14}$$

which will be called the *truncation remainder.*

The geometric lag model can then be expressed as a function of the truncation remainder, namely,

$$y_t = \alpha + \beta w_t(\lambda) + \eta_0\lambda^t + e_t. \tag{17.3.15}$$

Estimation of this direct form of the geometric lag can be carried out in several ways, depending upon the treatment of the truncation remainder.

It will be shown that maximum likelihood estimation of α, β, and λ amounts to minimizing the sum of squares

$$\sum_{t=1}^{T}(y_t - \alpha - \beta w_t(\lambda) - \eta_0\lambda^t)^2 \tag{17.3.16}$$

with respect to α, β, λ, and η_0.

It should be clear, that as the sample size (T) becomes large, the influence of the truncation remainder becomes negligible. In particular, Dhrymes (1971) has shown that asymptotically it makes no difference whether η_0 is neglected or not. However, it may make a difference in small samples.

The log likelihood function of the observation is

$$\ln L(\alpha, \beta, \lambda, \eta_0, \sigma^2; \mathbf{y}, X) = -\frac{T}{2}\ln(2\pi) - \frac{T}{2}\ln(\sigma^2) - \frac{1}{2\sigma^2}(y - X\mathbf{a})'(\mathbf{y} - X\mathbf{a}), \tag{17.3.17}$$

where

$$X = (\mathbf{x}_1, \mathbf{x}_2, \mathbf{x}_3), \qquad \mathbf{x}_1' = (1, 1, \ldots, 1),$$
$$\mathbf{x}_2' = (w_1(\lambda), w_2(\lambda), \ldots, w_T(\lambda)), \quad \text{where } w_t(\lambda) = \sum_{i=0}^{t-1} \lambda^i x_{t-i}, \tag{17.3.18}$$
$$\mathbf{x}_3' = (\lambda, \lambda^2, \ldots, \lambda^t) \quad \text{and} \quad \mathbf{a}' = (\alpha, \beta, \eta_0).$$

It is clear that, for given λ, the X matrix is easily computed from the observations by the following simple recursive scheme,

$$w_1(\lambda) = x_1, w_t(\lambda) = \lambda w_{t-1}(\lambda) + x_t, \qquad t = 2, 3, \ldots, T,$$

provided that, for example, $w_0(\lambda) = 0$.

Maximizing the above log likelihood function partially with respect to **a** and σ^2 leads to

$$\hat{\mathbf{a}}(\lambda) = (X'X)^{-1}X'\mathbf{y}, \hat{\sigma}^2(\lambda) = \frac{(\mathbf{y} - X\hat{\mathbf{a}}(\lambda))'(\mathbf{y} - X\hat{\mathbf{a}}(\lambda))}{T}. \tag{17.3.19}$$

Inserting these expressions into the log likelihood function yields the *concentrated* log likelihood function

$$L(\lambda, \mathbf{y}, X) = -\frac{T}{2}[\ln(2\pi) + 1] - \frac{T}{2}\ln\hat{\sigma}^2(\lambda) \tag{17.3.20}$$

and it is clear that the global maximum of the concentrated log likelihood function corresponds to the global minimum of $\hat{\sigma}^2(\lambda)$ with respect to λ.

Conditions of the problem require that $\lambda \in [0, 1)$. Estimation can proceed as with the AR(1) autocorrelated errors model. Partition the admissible range of λ by the points λ_i, $i = 1, 2, \ldots, n$. For each λ_i compute the elements of X and then obtain $\mathbf{a}(\lambda_i)$ and $\sigma^2(\lambda_i)$. Choose the estimator of λ, say $\hat{\lambda}$, such that

$$\sigma^2(\hat{\lambda}) = \min_i \sigma^2(\lambda_i). \tag{17.3.21}$$

The maximum likelihood estimators of $\mathbf{a}$ and σ^2 are then

$$\hat{\mathbf{a}} = \mathbf{a}(\hat{\lambda}) \quad \text{and} \quad \hat{\sigma}^2 = \sigma^2(\hat{\lambda}). \tag{17.3.22}$$

The triplet $(\hat{\mathbf{a}}, \hat{\lambda}, \hat{\sigma}^2)$ globally maximizes the log likelihood and hence the maximum likelihood estimators are $\hat{\mathbf{a}}$, $\hat{\lambda}$, and $\hat{\sigma}^2$.

Alternatively, since omission of the truncation remainder does not matter asymptotically, set $\eta_0 = 0$ and then minimize

$$\sum_{t=1}^{T} [y_t - \alpha - \beta w_t(\lambda)]^2 \tag{17.3.23}$$

with respect to α, β, and λ and obtain nonlinear least squares estimates for α, β, and λ.

Another alternative has been suggested by Peseran (1973). Instead of estimating η_0, one can drop y_1 and write

$$y_t = \alpha + \beta w_t^*(\lambda) + \eta_1 \lambda^{t-1} + e_t, \qquad t = 2, \ldots, T, \tag{17.3.24}$$

where

$$w_t^*(\lambda) = (1 - \lambda) \sum_{i=0}^{t-2} \lambda^i x_{t-i} \quad \text{and} \quad \eta_1 = E(y_1) - \alpha$$

is a constant. Equation (17.3.24) results from the following manipulation

$$\sum_{i=0}^{\infty} \lambda^i x_{t-i} = \sum_{i=0}^{t-2} \lambda^i x_{t-i} + \lambda^{t-1} \sum_{i=0}^{\infty} \lambda^i x_{-i+1},$$

$$y_1 = \alpha + \beta(1 - \lambda)\left(\sum_{i=0}^{\infty} \lambda^i x_{-i+1}\right) + e_1,$$

$$E(y_1) - \alpha = \beta(1 - \lambda) \sum_{i=0}^{\infty} \lambda^i x_{-i+1} = \eta_1.$$

Then

$$\begin{aligned} y_t &= \alpha + \beta(1 - \lambda)\left(\sum_{i=0}^{\infty} \lambda^i x_{t-i}\right) + e_t \\ &= \alpha + \beta(1 - \lambda)\left(\sum_{i=0}^{t-2} \lambda^i x_{t-i}\right) + \eta_1 \lambda^{t-1} + e_t \\ &= \alpha + \beta w_t^*(\lambda) + \eta_1 \lambda^{t-1} + e_t. \end{aligned}$$

This is just the result specified in Equation (17.3.24). If η_1 is replaced by y_1, then β and λ can be estimated by minimizing the sum of squares

$$\sum_{t=2}^{T} [y_t - \alpha - \lambda^{t-1} y_1 - \beta w_t^*(\lambda)]^2.$$

All three of the above methods give consistent estimates of α, β, and λ. In the presence of normally distributed errors these estimates are also asymptotically efficient. In contrast, the small sample properties of these methods are not analytically available.

Schmidt (1975) investigated the relative performance of these estimators in small samples via a Monte Carlo experiment. For various values of η_0, λ, and T, $\alpha = 0$, $\beta = 1$, $\sigma_e^2 = 1$ and x's generated from an autoregressive process, the mean square errors for the various estimates of λ and β were compared to determine whether it is worth while to take account of the initial value parameters as suggested by Maddala and Rao (1971). Schmidt finds that even in samples as large as 100, it is worthwhile including the truncation remainders. As far as maximum likelihood versus Peseran's alternative, there seems to be little difference in their performance.

Tests of hypotheses in the geometric lag model can be carried out using the developments of maximum likelihood estimation. For simplicity assume $\alpha = 0$. In order to obtain asymptotic variances of the estimates, the information matrix is needed. With η_0 treated as a parameter, the information matrix is of the form

$$I = \frac{1}{\sigma_e^2} \sum_{t=1}^{T} \mathbf{z}_t \mathbf{z}_t', \tag{17.3.25}$$

where

$$\mathbf{z}_t' = (w_t(\lambda), \beta R_t + t\eta_0 \lambda^{t-1}, \lambda^t),$$
$$R_t = d(w_t(\lambda))/d\lambda.$$

The rows and columns of I correspond to β, λ, and η_0 in that order. The row and column corresponding to σ_e^2 are omitted, since the matrix is block diagonal.

To test the null hypothesis that $\beta = c$, the test statistic

$$(\hat{\beta} - c)/\sqrt{(\hat{I}^{-1})_{11}}, \tag{17.3.26}$$

where $\hat{I}^{-1}$ indicates the inverse of the information matrix evaluated at the corresponding maximum likelihood estimates and $(\hat{I}^{-1})_{11}$ denotes the first diagonal element. The asymptotic distribution of this test statistic, under the null hypothesis, is $N(0, 1)$. Hypotheses concerning λ would be tested in exactly the same way, except that the second element of I^{-1} would be used.

From Monte Carlo investigations by Schmidt and Guilkey (1976), it appears that $T = 50$ is needed for the performance of the information matrix to be reliable. In addition, in the same paper Schmidt and Guilkey investigate two other asymptotically equivalent tests. They find little difference in the three tests but recommend the full information test (i.e., not dropping the truncation remainder) with degrees of freedom correction in estimating σ_e^2.

17.3.3 Summary and Guide to Further Readings on Geometric Lags

In this section we saw how two separate economic hypotheses, partial adjustment and adaptive expectations, led to nearly identical estimating equations. However, the stochastic properties of the errors terms which arise in these models are distinct and thus condition the choice of appropriate estimation technique. In the former case the equation to be estimated is a lagged dependent variable model with independent and identically distributed errors. Ordinary least squares provides biased though consistent and asymptotically efficient results given normality of the errors. The resulting model arising from adaptive expectations presents a greater estimation challenge.

There are two algebracially equivalent versions of the adaptive expectations model, the direct form and the autoregressive form. The direct form is that of a geometric distributed lag while the autoregressive form is a lagged dependent variable model with a first-order moving average, MA(1), error process. The estimation of the autoregressive form is difficult in that contemporaneous correlation between the errors and regressors causes plausible two-step feasible generalized least squares estimators to be inefficient. Maximum likelihood estimation of the direct form of the geometric lag was discussed and found to be preferable to the estimation of the autoregressive form.

The literature on geometric lags and associated problems is extensive. A comprehensive and detailed discussion of all the basic issues can be found in Dhrymes (1971, Chs. 4–7). Other good textbook treatments are to be found in Kmenta (1971), Maddala (1977) and Judge *et al.* (1980), the latter containing an extensive list of references as well. One generalization of the geometric lag that should be noted is that proposed by Schmidt (1974a) and Schmidt and Mann (1977). In this lag scheme the lag weights are given by $\beta_i = \lambda^i \sum_{j=0}^{m} \gamma_i i^j$, thus combining the geometric and polynomial lag schemes. This lag scheme is flexible, in the sense that it can approximate any lag structure arbitrarily well.

17.4 Other Infinite Lag Structures

In this chapter we have given detailed attention to polynomial finite lag models and geometric infinite lag models. The justification for our approach is that these are the most frequently adopted models. There are other infinite lag structures, however, that are well known, some of which are quite new, that are flexible and can be useful. These we wish to mention briefly, if only for the sake of completeness.

17.4.1 The Pascal Lag

Solow (1960) suggested a family of lag structures based on the Pascal distribution. The lag coefficients are specified as

$$\beta_i = \beta\binom{r+i-1}{i}(1-\lambda)^r\lambda^i, \qquad i = 0, 1, 2, \ldots, \tag{17.4.1}$$

where $\lambda \in (0, 1)$ and r is an integer. Inserting (17.4.1) into the general infinite lag model yields

$$\begin{aligned} y_t &= \beta(1-\lambda)^r \sum_{i=0}^{\infty} \binom{r+i-1}{i}\lambda^i x_{t-i} + e_t \\ &= \beta(1-\lambda)^r(1-\lambda L)^{-r}x_t + e_t \end{aligned} \tag{17.4.2}$$

since

$$\sum_{i=0}^{\infty}\binom{r+i-1}{i}\lambda^i L^i = (1-\lambda L)^{-r}.$$

If $r = 1$ the Pascal lag reduces to a geometric lag, but for $r \geq 2$ the lag distribution is "humped," suggesting that the maximum effect of the lagged variable need not occur for $i = 0$. For a given value of r a variety of estimation techniques can be used, including maximum likelihood and use of instrumental variables. Maddala and Rao (1971) suggest that alternative values of r be tried and the one yielding the highest $\bar{R}^2$ selected. Schmidt (1973) suggests rewriting the Pasdal lag, relaxing the integer restriction on r and searching over λ and a range of r values.

17.4.2 The Rational Distributed Lag

Jorgenson (1966) proposed the general rational lag structure

$$y_t = \frac{A(L)}{B(L)}x_t + e_t, \tag{17.4.3}$$

where $A(L)$ and $B(L)$ are polynomials in the lag operator of degree m and n, respectively. This structure contains the Pascal lag as a special case, with $n = 0$, and has the property that it can approximate any lag structure arbitrarily well with sufficiently high choices of m and n.

For estimation purposes note that the rational lag has autoregressive form

$$\begin{aligned} y_t = a_0 x_t + a_1 x_{t-1} + \cdots + a_m x_{t-m} - b_1 y_{t-1} \\ - b_2 y_{t-2} - \cdots - b_n y_{t-n} + e_t^*. \end{aligned} \tag{17.4.4}$$

If the e_t^* were not autocorrelated, (17.4.4) could be estimated by ordinary least squares, but since $e_t^* = B(L)e_t$ one should assume serial correlation.

Several estimation techniques for the general case exist, including maximum likelihood, described by Maddala and Rao (1971). Other estimation techniques are discussed in Judge *et al.* (1980, Ch. 16) and Dhrymes (1971, Ch. 9).

17.4.3 The Gamma Distributed Lag

Tsurumi (1971) proposed a gamma distributed lag where the lag weights are specified as

$$\beta_i = \frac{\beta}{\Gamma(s)} i^{s-1} \exp(-i), \qquad i = 0, 1, 2, \ldots, \tag{17.4.5}$$

where β and s are parameters to be estimated. For $s \geq 2$ the gamma lag distribution is peaked and unimodal. Tsurumi offers several modifications as does Schmidt (1974b).

17.4.4 The Exponential Lag

The rational lag and Schmidt's geometric-polynomial lag allow approximation of any lag structure arbitrarily well, but they do not guarantee that estimated lag weights will be nonnegative. Lütkepohl (1981) proposes a class of lag structures that avoids sign changes and can approximate any lag structure to any desired degree of accuracy. The family of lag structures is called *exponential*. The lag weights have the form

$$\beta_i = \beta \exp[P(i)], \qquad i = 0, 1, 2, \ldots,$$

where β is a parameter and $P(i) = \sum_{j=1}^{m} \gamma_j i^j$ is a polynomial in i of degree m. The parameters of this model can be estimated by partitioning the infinite sum into a finite sum and a truncation remainder, as for the geometric lag. The resulting model is estimated by nonlinear least squares. See Lütkepohl (1981) for further details.

17.5 Exercises

17.1. The restrictions that characterize the polynomial distributed lag estimator can be parameterized in many different, but equivalent ways. To see that many different restriction matrices can produce the same estimator, show that if A is a nonsingular matrix, then the matrices $R^* = AR$ and $\mathbf{r}^* = A\mathbf{r}$ may be substituted for R and $\mathbf{r}$ in the restricted least squares problem without affecting the results.

17.2. De Leeuw (1962) suggested use of an "inverted-V" finite distributed lag. This is characterized by weights satisfying

$$\beta_i = \begin{cases} (i+1)\alpha & 0 \le i \le s, \\ (n-i+1) & i \ge s+1, \\ 0 & \text{otherwise,} \end{cases}$$

where $s = n/2$ and n is even. Show that α may be estimated by applying ordinary least squares to $y = \alpha z_t + e_t$, where

$$z_t = \sum_{i=0}^{s} (i+1)x_{t-i} + \sum_{i=s+1}^{n} (n-i+1)x_{t-i}.$$

Show that the β_i may also be estimated directly by applying restricted least squares to the original model with restrictions $R\boldsymbol{\beta} = \mathbf{0}$ and $R = [I_n^* \vdots \mathbf{m}]$, where I_n^* is a matrix containing all but the last row of an nth-order identity matrix and $-\mathbf{m}' = (1, 2, \ldots, (s+1), (n-s), (n-s-1), \ldots, 2)$.

17.3. Using Equation (17.2.13), $\boldsymbol{\beta} = H\boldsymbol{\alpha}$, it has been suggested that the appropriate restrictions can be obtained as follows: premultiply both sides of the equation by $(H'H)^{-1}H'$ to obtain

$$\boldsymbol{\alpha} = (H'H)^{-1}H'\boldsymbol{\beta}.$$

Therefore

$$\boldsymbol{\beta} - H\boldsymbol{\alpha} = \mathbf{0}$$

and thus

$$\boldsymbol{\beta} - H(H'H)^{-1}H'\boldsymbol{\beta} = \mathbf{0}$$

implies

$$(I - H(H'H)^{-1}H')\boldsymbol{\beta} = \mathbf{0}$$

which defines a set of homogeneous restrictions on $\boldsymbol{\beta}$. Show that the matrix $I - H(H'H)^{-1}H'$ is *not* a suitable restriction matrix.

17.4. Prove that the first difference of a polynomial of degree q, whose domain is the integers, can be expressed as a polynomial of degree $q - 1$.

17.5. In Almon's (1965) original work, she formulated the problem using Lagrangian interpolation polynomials. She specified the original $n + 1$ lag weights in terms of $q + 1$ weights, by using the relations

$$\beta_i = \sum_{k=0}^{q} L_k(i)\beta_k, \qquad i = 0, \ldots, n,$$

where

$$L_k(i) = \prod_{\substack{j=0 \\ j \ne k}}^{q} \frac{i-j}{k-j}, \qquad i = 0, \ldots, n, \quad k = 0, \ldots, q,$$

are the Lagrangian interpolation polynomials. Show that for $i = 0, \ldots, q$ the relations specify that $\beta_i = \beta_i$, and that for $\beta_{q+1}, \ldots, \beta_n$ the relations can be written

$$R\boldsymbol{\beta} = [L : -I_{n-q}]\boldsymbol{\beta} = \mathbf{0}$$

where

$$L = \begin{bmatrix} L_0(q+1) & L_1(q+1) & \cdots & L_q(q+1) \\ L_0(q+2) & L_1(q+2) & \cdots & L_q(q+2) \\ \vdots & \vdots & & \vdots \\ L_0(n) & L_1(n) & \cdots & L_q(n) \end{bmatrix}.$$

Show that the restricted least squares estimator $R\boldsymbol{\beta} = \mathbf{0}$ is the Almon polynomial distributed lag estimator.

17.6. A convenient alternative to standard methods for constructing restriction matrices for the polynomial distributed lag estimator involves the use of orthogonal polynomials. Suppose we have $(n + 1)$ observations (z_i, y_i), $i = 0, \ldots, n$, where z is the independent variable and y is the dependent variable and we wish to fit the polynomial model

$$y_i = \beta_0 + \beta_1 z_i + \beta_2 z_i^2 + \cdots + \beta_p z_i^p + e_i,$$

or in matrix terms

$$\mathbf{y} = Z\boldsymbol{\beta} + \mathbf{e}.$$

The matrix Z is not orthogonal, so if the polynomial is raised by one degree, say z^{p+1}, all the ordinary least squares coefficients must be re-estimated. This problem can be avoided by using *orthogonal polynomials.* Consider the rth order polynomial

$$H_r(z_i) = \alpha_{0,r} + \alpha_{1,r} z_i + \cdots + \alpha_{r-1,r} z_i^{r-1} + \alpha_{r,r} z_i^r.$$

These polynomials can be constructed so that they are orthogonal, that is

$$\sum_{i=0}^{n} H_j(z_i) H_m(z_i) = 0, \qquad j \neq m.$$

Then the polynomial regression model can be rewritten as

$$y_i = a_0 H_0(z_i) + a_1 H_1(z_i) + \cdots + a_p H_p(z_i) + e_i$$

or in matrix terms

$$\mathbf{y} = H\mathbf{a} + \mathbf{e}.$$

Now $H'H$ is diagonal matrix with elements $A_{jj} = \sum_{i=0}^{n} \{H_j(z_i)\}^2$, so the ordinary least squares estimates of the coefficients a_j are

$$\hat{a}_j = \frac{\sum_{i=0}^{n} y_i H_j(z_i)}{A_{jj}}, \qquad j = 0, \ldots, p.$$

Note that adding another term $a_{p+1} H_{p+1}(z_i)$ to the polynomial model requires no recomputation of coefficients already obtained due to the orthogonality of the polynomials.

The $H_j(z_i)$ can be constructed for any z_i, but if the z_i are equally spaced the values of $H_j(\cdot)$ have already been tabled in many places. See Delury (1950) for example. Also many computer packages, such as SAS, contain functions that generate these values. The point is that the $H_j(z_i)$ are readily available. As an example, if $n + 1 = 5$

	z_0	z_1	z_2	z_3	z_4
$H_1(z_i)$	-2	-1	0	1	2
$H_2(z_i)$	2	-1	-2	-1	2
$H_3(z_i)$	-1	2	0	-2	1
$H_4(z_i)$	1	-4	6	-4	1

To see how these values, also called the "coefficients" of the orthogonal polynomials, relate to our problem, consider the case where the observation y_i in the regression model *do* come from a qth degree polynomial and that there is no random disturbance. In this case the coefficients $\hat{a}_j$ will yield precisely the true polynomial. *All* $\hat{a}_j, j > q$, *will be zero.* That is,

$$\sum_{i=0}^{n} y_i H_j(z_i) = 0 \quad \text{for all } j > q.$$

This property allows the construction of homogeneous equations that can serve as restrictions for a restricted least squares problem. These restrictions are *orthogonal*, already tabled and have a clear interpretation.

Show that to constrain the estimated parameters β_i to fall on a polynomial of degree q or less, one would impose the restrictions.

$$\sum_{i=0}^{n} H_{q+1}(z_i)\beta_i = 0,$$

$$\sum_{i=0}^{n} H_{q+2}(z_i)\beta_i = 0,$$

$$\vdots$$

$$\sum_{i=0}^{n} H_n(z_i)\beta_i = 0.$$

These restrictions in turn force $\hat{a}_{q+1}, \ldots, \hat{a}_n$ to *zero, preventing* the polynomial from being that value. Thus, for example, if $n + 1 = 5$ and a polynomial of degree $q = 2$ is desired $n - q = 2$ restrictions must be imposed that eliminate the quartic and cubic components of the model. These restrictions would be

$$\begin{bmatrix} -1 & 2 & 0 & -2 & 1 \\ 1 & -4 & 6 & -4 & 1 \end{bmatrix} \begin{bmatrix} \beta_0 \\ \beta_1 \\ \beta_2 \\ \beta_3 \\ \beta_4 \end{bmatrix} = \begin{bmatrix} 0 \\ 0 \end{bmatrix}.$$

Furthermore, these restrictions have the convenient property that they are nested. That is, to allow a polynomial of one higher degree, here a cubic, simply *remove* the "cubic" restriction from the R matrix, leaving the restriction that prevents a fourth degree polynomial.

17.7. For the Adaptive Expectations model, use (17.3.13) and the expectational model

$$x_t^* - x_{t-1}^* = (1 - \lambda)(x_{t-1} - x_{t-1}^*)$$

to derive a geometric lag model. Comment on this alternative formulation and its effects.

17.8. For the Partial Adjustment model, assume (17.3.6) is appropriate, but that

$$y_t^* = \alpha + \beta x_{t-1}.$$

Obtain the corresponding geometric lag model and comment on the effect of using this alternative formulation.

17.9. Estimating the unrestricted model (17.3.9),

$$\begin{aligned} y_t &= \alpha\gamma + \beta\gamma x_t + (1 - \gamma)y_{t-1} + e_t \\ &= \beta_1 + \beta_2 x_t + \beta_3 y_{t-1} + e_t \end{aligned}$$

yields estimates of β_1, β_2, and β_3. Discuss how one would obtain estimates of the original parameters. Also discuss the properties of these estimators under the assumption first that the e_t are independent and identically distributed with mean zero and variance σ^2 and second that in addition the e_t are normal.

17.10. Verify the information matrix in (17.3.25).

17.11. In Chapter 7, Table 7.6.1, quarterly data is reported on capital expenditures (y_t) and capital appropriations (x_t) for all manufacturing, from 1953 to 1974.

(a) Fit a declining arithmetic lag (17.2.1) to this data, assuming that $n = 8$. Evaluate the resulting parameter estimates.

(b) Fit an inverted-V lag (Exercise 17.2), assuming that the lag length is $n = 8$.

(c) Assuming $n = 8$ and $q = 2$, show that the restriction formulations discussed in Chapter 17.2, Exercises 17.3, 17.5, and 17.6 are numerically equivalent in that they produce identical parameter estimates. Evaluate the resulting estimates using an F-test.

(d) Assume $n = 8$. Use a pretesting scheme to determine the "best" polynomial degree.

(e) Assume the maximum lag length you are willing to consider is $N = 12$. Choose the "best" lag length and polynomial degree. How did you choose the level of type I error for each test and why?

(f) How would you test for and/or correct for first order autocorrelation in a finite lag model?

17.12. Fit a geometric lag to the capital expenditures (y_t)—capital appropriations (x_t) data presented in Table 7.6.1 by estimating the direct form of the lag, first omitting the truncation remainder and then by retaining it. Test the hypothesis that $\lambda = 0.75$.

17.6 References

Almon, S. (1965). The distributed lag between capital appropriations and expenditures. *Econometrica*, **33**, 178–196.

Amemiya, T. and Morimune, K. (1974). Selecting the optimal order of polynomial in the Almon distributed lag. *Review of Economic and Statistics*, **56**, 378–386.

Anderson, T. (1971). *The Statistical Analysis of Time Series*. New York: Wiley.

Anderson, T. (1974). Distributed lags and barley acreage response analysis. *The Australian Journal of Agricultural Economics*, **18**, 119–132.

Burrows, P. (1971). Explanatory and forecasting models of inventory investment in Britain. *Applied Economics*, **3**, 275–290.

Burrows, P. and Godfrey, L. (1973). Identifying and estimating the parameters of a symmetrical model of inventory investment. *Applied Economics*, **5**, 193–197.

Cagan, P. (1956). The monetary dynamics of hyperinflations. In *Studies in the Quantity Theory of Money*. Edited by M. Friedman. Chicago: University of Chicago Press.

Carter, R., Nager, A., and Kirkham, P. (1976). The estimation of misspecified polynomial distributed lag models. Research Report 7525, Department of Economics, University of Western Ontario.

Cooper, J. (1972). The approaches to polynomial distributed lags estimation: an expository note and comment. *American Statistician*, **26**, 32–35.

DeLeeuw, F. (1962). The demand for capital goods by manufactures: a study of quarterly time series. *Econometrica*, **30**, 407–423.

Delury, D. (1950). *Values and Integrals of Orthogonal Polynomials Up to $n = 26$*. Toronto: University of Toronto Press.

Dhrymes, P. (1971). *Distributed Lags: Problems of Estimation and Formulation*. San Francisco: Holden Day.

Fomby, T. (1979). Mean square error evaluation of Shiller's smoothness priors. *International Economic Review*, **20**, 203–216.

Frost, P. A. (1975). Some properties of the Almon lag technique when one searches for degree of polynomial and lag. *Journal of the American Statistical Association*, **70**, 606–612.

Fuller, W. (1976). *Introduction to Statistical Time Series*. New York: Wiley.

Geweke, J. and Meese, R. (1979). Estimating distributed lags of unknown order. Presented at North American Econometrics Society Meetings, Montreal.

Godfrey, L. G. and Poskitt, D. S. (1975). Testing the restrictions of the Almon lag technique. *Journal of the American Statistical Association*, **70**, 105–108.

Griffiths, W. and Kerrison, R. (1978). Using specification error tests to choose between alternative polynomial lag distributions: an application to investment functions. Working Paper, University of New England, Armidale, Australia.

Griliches, Z. (1967). Distributed lags: a survey. *Econometrica*, **35**, 16–49.

Hamlen, S. and Hamlen, W. (1978). Harmonic alternatives to the Almon polynomial technique. *Journal of Econometrics*, **6**, 57–66.

Harper, C. P. (1977). Testing for the existence of a lagged relationship within Almon's method. *Review of Economics and Statistics*, **50**, 204–210.

Hendry, D. and Pagan, A. (1980). Distributed lags: a survey of some recent developments. Unpublished mimeo.

Hill, B. E. (1971). Supply responses in crop and livestock production. *Journal of Agricultural Economics*, **22**, 287–293.

Jones, G. T. (1962). The response of the supply of agricultural products in the United Kingdom to price, Part II. *Farm Economist*, **10**, 1–28.

Jorgenson, D. (1966). Rational distributed lag functions. *Econometrica*, **34**, 135–149.

Judge, G., Griffiths, W., Hill, R., and Lee, T. (1980). *The Theory and Practice of Econometrics*. New York: Wiley.

Kmenta, J. (1971). *Elements of Econometrics.* New York: Macmillan.
Liviatan, N. (1963). Consistent estimation of distributed lags. *International Economic Review*, **4**, 44–52.
Lütkepohl, H. (1981). A model for nonnegative and nonpositive distributed lag functions. *Journal of Econometrics*, **16**, 211–219.
Maddala, G. (1974). Ridge estimators for distributed lag models. Working Paper No. 69, National Bureau of Economic Research.
Maddala, G., (1977). *Econometrics.* New York: McGraw-Hill.
Maddala, G. and Rao, A. (1971). Maximum likelihood estimation of Solow's and Jorgenson's distributed lag models. *Review of Economics and Statistics*, **53**, 80–88.
Muth, J. (1961). Rational expectations and the theory of price movements. *Econometrica*, **29**, 313–335.
Nerlove, M. (1956). Estimates of the elasticities of supply of selected agricultural commodities. *Journal of Farm Economics*, **38**, 496–509.
Nerlove, M. (1958). *Distributed Lags and Demand Analysis.* Agriculture Handbook No. 141. U.S. Department of Agriculture.
Pagan, A. (1978). Rational and polynomial lags: the finite connection. *Journal of Econometrics*, **8**, 247–254.
Pagano, M. and Hartley, M. (1981). On fitting distributed lag models subject to polynomial restrictions. *Journal of Econometrics*, **16**, 171–198.
Park, S. (1974). Maximum likelihood estimation of a distributed lag model. *Proceedings of the Business and Economic Statistics Section of the American Statistical Association.* Washington: American Statistical Association. Pp. 510–513.
Peseran, M. (1973). The small sample problem of truncation remainders in the estimation of distributed lag models with autocorrelated errors. *International Economic Review*, **14**, 120–131.
Poirier, D. (1976). *The Economics of Structural Change with Special Emphasis on Spline Functions.* Amsterdam: North-Holland.
Ramsey, J. (1969). Tests for specification errors in classical linear least squares regression analysis. *Journal of Royal Statistical Society*, B, **31**, 350–371.
Ramsey, J. (1970). Models, specification error and inference: a discussion of some problems in econometric methodology. *Bulletin of Oxford University Institute of Economics and Statistics*, **32**, 301–318.
Ramsey, J. (1974). Classical model selection through specification error tests. In *Frontiers in Econometrics.* Edited by Paul Zarembka. New York: Academic Press.
Sargan, J. (1980). The consumer price equation in the post-war British economy: an exercise in equation specification testing. *Review of Economic Studies*, **47**, 113–135.
Schmidt, P. (1973). On the difference between conditional and unconditional asymptotic distributions of estimates in distributed lag models with integer-valued parameters. *Econometrica*, **41**, 165–169.
Schmidt, P. (1974a). A modification of the Almon distributed lag. *Journal of the American Statistical Association*, **69**, 679–681.
Schmidt, P. (1974b). An argument for the usefulness of the gamma distributed lag model. *International Economic Review*, **15**, 246–250.
Schmidt, P. (1975). The small sample effects of various treatments of truncation remainders in the estimation of distributed lag models. *Review of Economics and Statistics*, **57**, 387–389.
Schmidt, P. and Guilkey, D. (1976). The effects of various treatments of truncation remainders in tests of hypotheses in distributed lag models. *Journal of Econometrics*, **4**, 211–230.
Schmidt, P. and Mann, W. (1977). A note on the approximation of arbitrary distributed lag structures by the modified Almon lag. *Journal of the American Statistical Association*, **72**, 442–443.

Schmidt, P. and Sickles, R. (1975). On the efficiency of the Almon lag technique. *International Economic Review*, **16**, 792–795.

Schmidt, P. and Waud, R. (1973). The Almon lag technique and the monetary vs. fiscal policy debate. *Journal of the American Statistical Association*, **68**, 11–19.

Shiller, R. (1973). A distributed lag estimator derived from smoothness priors. *Econometrica*, **41**, 775–788.

Solow, R. (1960). On a family of lag distributions. *Econometrica*, **28**, 393–406.

Taylor, W. (1974). Smoothness priors and stochastic prior restrictions in distributed lag estimation. *International Economic Review*, **15**, 803–804.

Terasvirta, T. (1976). A note on the bias in the Almon distributed lag estimator. *Econometrica*, **44**, 1317–1322.

Trivedi, P. and Pagan, A. (1976). Polynomial distributed lags: a unified treatment. Working Paper, Australian National University, Canberra.

Tsurumi, H. (1971). A note on gamma distributed lags. *International Economic Review*, **12**, 317–323.

CHAPTER 18

Uncertainty in Model Specification and Selection

18.1 Introduction

What are econometric models and how is economic science advanced by their use? Gaver and Geisel (1974, p. 50) define an econometric model in the following manner:

> ... an econometric or statistical model is fundamentally a characterization (in terms of parameters and exogeneous variables) of the probability distribution of some random variable(s) of interest.

But why propose an econometric model? There are essentially two major reasons: *control* and *prediction* of economic events. In the former instance, a probabilistic characterization of certain random variables allows one to judge which variables are most important in determining economic outcomes and, therefore, how appropriate modification of these variables may lead to a desired outcome or goal. Economic modeling can also aid in prediction of future economic events. Given the relevance of certain economic variables, perceived future changes in these variables should aid in forming judgments about the probabilities of future events. In contrast, naive forecasting methods using such rules as "no change from last period" or "the same change for the future as occurred in the past," will usually not perform as well since important causal factors are ignored. The commonality between control and prediction problems is that the better our understanding of the structure of economic relationships, the better should be our decisions in the world of uncertain economic events.

In the majority of cases discussed thus far, (for two major exceptions see the discussion of ordinary least squares estimation in the context of the generalized least squares model in Chapter 2 and preliminary testing and Stein-rules in Chapter 7) the model under consideration has been taken to be true and properties of parameter estimates have been conditioned by this assumption. However, rarely is the true (or more appropriately "best") probability model for characterizing an economic relationship known *a priori*. This brings us to the following question: "Which one of many possible hypotheses should we maintain in order to most effectively address a decision problem involving prediction or control?" This question is the central one to be addressed in this chapter.

Within the context of regression probability models, the phenomenon of many possible hypotheses can be translated into such questions as: What variables should be included in the regression equation? What functional form should the regression model take? Is the equation linear in the variables or their logarithms? What is the appropriate variance-covariance structure for the errors of the regression model? Are the errors normally distributed or best characterized by some nonnormal distribution? The task of the econometrician is to answer these questions as best as possible. The purpose of this chapter is to provide a discussion of selected facets of the difficult tasks of model verification and selection.

In the next section we will investigate the implications of omitting relevant variables or including irrelevant variables in a regression equation. In Section 18.3 the idea of specification error tests is discussed. In Section 18.4 the concepts of nested and nonnested models are introduced and various tests for discriminating between competing models are presented. The Box–Cox transformation is defined in Section 18.5. This transformation characterizes a class of functional forms by means of an additional parameter and thus reduces some of the arbitrariness of functional form specification. A summary and guide to further readings is contained in Section 18.6.

18.2 Classical Specification Analysis

18.2.1 Effects of Omitting Relevant Variables or Including Irrelevant Variables

Frequently economists are uncertain about the specification of linear regression models. *A priori* it may not be clear which exogenous variables best characterize the behavior of an endogenous variable. Is a certain exogenous variable important in explaining the movement of the endogenous variable or is it independent of the changes in the endogenous variable? Even if a relevant variable is known but no observations are available, what is the effect of its omission? These questions can be answered by the method of *specification analysis* developed by Theil (1957).

Consider the regression model

$$\begin{aligned} \mathbf{y} &= X\boldsymbol{\beta} + \mathbf{e}, \\ &= X_1\boldsymbol{\beta}_1 + X_2\boldsymbol{\beta}_2 + \mathbf{e} \end{aligned} \tag{18.2.1}$$

where, for purposes to be explained in a moment, the $T \times K$ matrix of regressors is partitioned into two parts, the matrix X_1, being $T \times K_1$ and X_2, being $T \times K_2$, with $K_1 + K_2 = K$. Likewise, the regression coefficient vector $\boldsymbol{\beta}$ is partitioned into two parts, the $K_1 \times 1$ vector $\boldsymbol{\beta}_1$ associated with the K_1 variables of X_1 and the $K_2 \times 1$ vector $\boldsymbol{\beta}_2$ associated with the K_2 variables of X_2. Assume throughout the rest of our discussion that the errors of (18.2.1) are independent and identically distributed with zero mean and constant variance σ^2. Consider the case where $\boldsymbol{\beta}_1 \neq \mathbf{0}$ and $\boldsymbol{\beta}_2 \neq \mathbf{0}$ and all included variables are relevant. Ordinary least squares estimation would then provide consistent and unbiased estimators of $\boldsymbol{\beta}_1$ and $\boldsymbol{\beta}_2$, which are best linear unbiased and, when the errors are normally distributed, minimum variance unbiased. Likewise, the same result would obtain for the ordinary least squares estimators if $\boldsymbol{\beta}_2 = \mathbf{0}$ and in fact X_2 was excluded in the estimation process. The cases of interest here are when $\boldsymbol{\beta}_2 \neq \mathbf{0}$ but for some reason the variables of X_2 are excluded or when $\boldsymbol{\beta}_2 = \mathbf{0}$ but for some reason the variables of X_2 are included. What are the effects of either the omission of relevant variables or inclusion of irrelevant variables? This question can be answered directly given the results of Chapter 6.

When X_2 is inappropriately omitted, the ordinary least squares estimates $\boldsymbol{\beta}_1^*$ are biased but have smaller sampling variance and possibly smaller mean square error. In addition, it can be shown, see Exercise 18.1, that the error variance estimator $\overset{*}{\hat{\sigma}}{}^2 = (\mathbf{y} - X_1\boldsymbol{\beta}_1^*)'(\mathbf{y} - X_1\boldsymbol{\beta}_1^*)/(T - K_1)$ is biased upward.

On the other hand, if X_2 is inadvertently included, the ordinary least squares estimates of the relevant parameters $\boldsymbol{\beta}_1$ are unbiased and consistent but inefficient relative to the efficient estimator $\boldsymbol{\beta}_1^*$. This result of efficiency can be shown by comparing the variance–covariance matrix of the restricted estimator $\boldsymbol{\beta}_1^*$, namely $\sigma^2(X_1'X_1)^{-1}$, with the variance–covariance matrix of the ordinary least squares estimator $\hat{\boldsymbol{\beta}}_1$ obtained from the incorrect model $\mathbf{y} = X_1\boldsymbol{\beta}_1 + X_2\boldsymbol{\beta}_2 + \mathbf{e}$, namely $\sigma^2 L$, where L denotes the upper left-hand $K_1 \times K_1$ submatrix of $(X'X)^{-1}$. It can be shown, see Exercise 18.2, that $\sigma^2 L - \sigma^2(X_1'X_1)^{-1}$ is a positive semidefinite matrix with equality between L and $(X_1'X_1)^{-1}$ occurring only when $X_1'X_2 = 0$. That is, the restricted estimator $\boldsymbol{\beta}_1^*$ and the ordinary least squares estimator $\hat{\boldsymbol{\beta}}_1$ are equally efficient only in the rare case that the irrelevant observations X_2 are orthogonal to the relevant observations X_1. It is left as Exercise 18.3 for the reader to show that the ratio of the generalized variance of $\boldsymbol{\beta}_1^*$ to the generalized variance of $\hat{\boldsymbol{\beta}}_1$ is

$$\frac{|\mathrm{var}(\boldsymbol{\beta}_1^*)|}{|\mathrm{var}(\hat{\boldsymbol{\beta}}_1)|} = \prod_{i=1}^{K_1} \left(\frac{1}{1 - r_i^2} \right), \tag{18.2.2}$$

where r_i^2 is the square of the ith canonical correlation coefficient between, the relevant variables, X_1 and, the irrelevant variables, X_2 and it is understood that if $K_2 < K_1$, $r_i^2 = 0$ for $i > K_2$. See Anderson (1958) for a discussion of canonical correlation coefficients and Fomby (1981). Equation (18.2.2) shows that the degree of the efficiency loss in estimating the relevant parameters $\boldsymbol{\beta}_1$ arising from the inclusion of the irrelevant variables X_2 is conditioned by the collinearity between X_1 and X_2. This collinearity is measured by the magnitudes of the canonical correlations, $0 \leq r_i \leq 1$. In the case of orthogonality of X_1 and X_2, $r_i = 0$ for all i and $\boldsymbol{\beta}_1^*$ and $\hat{\boldsymbol{\beta}}_1$ are equally efficient. In contrast, if any column of X_2 is expressible as a linear combination of the columns of X_1, $r_1 = 1$, and $\hat{\boldsymbol{\beta}}_1$ is infinitely inefficient. In summary, the more collinear the irrelevant variables are to the relevant variables, the greater the loss of efficiency in estimating the relevant parameters. The effects of incorrectly including or excluding variables are summarized in the Table 18.2.1.

One question should be of particular interest to the practitioner. What is the *direction* of the bias for particular included coefficients when relevant variables are omitted and what determines the *degree* of this bias? In order to address this question, let us introduce some new notation. Let the true model be represented by $\mathbf{y} = X\boldsymbol{\beta} + \mathbf{e}$ where now all of the variables of X are relevant. Let $\bar{X}$ denote a matrix of dimension $T \times \bar{K}$, where $\bar{X}$ and X have certain columns in common. In the case of omitted variables, $\bar{X}$ will

Table 18.2.1 Effects of specification error in including or excluding variables in a regression model.

		True Model	
		$\mathbf{y} = X_1\boldsymbol{\beta}_1 + X_2\boldsymbol{\beta}_2 + \mathbf{e}$; $\boldsymbol{\beta}_2 = \mathbf{0}$	$\mathbf{y} = X_1\boldsymbol{\beta}_1 + X_2\boldsymbol{\beta}_2 + \mathbf{e}$; $\boldsymbol{\beta}_2 \neq \mathbf{0}$
Model Adopted	$\mathbf{y} = X_1\boldsymbol{\beta}_1 + X_2\boldsymbol{\beta}_2 + \mathbf{e}$; $\boldsymbol{\beta}_2 = \mathbf{0}$	Ordinary least squares estimates $\boldsymbol{\beta}_1^*$ and $\overset{*}{\sigma}{}^2$ are unbiased and efficient.	Ordinary least squares estimates $\boldsymbol{\beta}_1^*$ and $\overset{*}{\sigma}{}^2$ are biased. $\boldsymbol{\beta}_1^*$ has smaller sampling variance than ordinary least squares $\hat{\boldsymbol{\beta}}_1$ and possibly smaller mean square error. $\overset{*}{\sigma}{}^2$ is biased upward.
	$\mathbf{y} = X_1\boldsymbol{\beta}_1 + X_2\boldsymbol{\beta}_2 + \mathbf{e}$; $\boldsymbol{\beta}_2 \neq \mathbf{0}$	Ordinary least squares estimates $\hat{\boldsymbol{\beta}}_1$, $\hat{\boldsymbol{\beta}}_2$, and $\hat{\sigma}^2$ are unbiased but inefficient.	Ordinary least squares estimates $\hat{\boldsymbol{\beta}}_1$, $\hat{\boldsymbol{\beta}}_2$, and $\hat{\sigma}^2$ are unbiased and efficient.

contain only some of the columns of X, the rest being omitted. Let $\bar{\mathbf{b}} = (\bar{X}'\bar{X})^{-1}\bar{X}'\mathbf{y}$ denote the corresponding ordinary least squares estimator. Substituting $\mathbf{y} = X\boldsymbol{\beta} + \mathbf{e}$ we obtain

$$\begin{aligned} \bar{\mathbf{b}} &= (\bar{X}'\bar{X})^{-1}\bar{X}'\mathbf{y} = (\bar{X}'\bar{X})^{-1}\bar{X}'(X\boldsymbol{\beta} + \mathbf{e}) \\ &= A\boldsymbol{\beta} + (\bar{X}'\bar{X})^{-1}\bar{X}'\mathbf{e} \end{aligned} \tag{18.2.3}$$

and, therefore,

$$E(\bar{\mathbf{b}}) = A\boldsymbol{\beta}. \tag{18.2.4}$$

The matrix A is called the auxiliary regression matrix. That is, the ith column of A, $A_{.i}$, represents the estimated least squares coefficients of the regression of $X_{.i}$, the ith column of X, on $\bar{X}$ and $A_{.i} = (\bar{X}'\bar{X})^{-1}\bar{X}'X_{.i}$. Equivalently,

$$x_{ti} = a_{1i}\bar{x}_{t1} + a_{2i}\bar{x}_{t2} + \cdots + a_{\bar{K}i}\bar{x}_{t\bar{K}} + \hat{u}_{ti}, \tag{18.2.5}$$

where $a_{1i}, \ldots, a_{\bar{K}i}$ are the corresponding elements of $A_{.i}$ and $\hat{u}_{ti}$ is the least squares residual.

To illustrate the usefulness of (18.2.4), consider the case where $\bar{X}$ differs from X only in that the last $K - p$ columns of X have been omitted. Then

$$A = \begin{bmatrix} 1 & 0 & \cdots & 0 & a_{1,p+1} & \cdots & a_{1,K} \\ & & & & \vdots & & \\ 0 & 1 & & & \cdot & & \vdots \\ \vdots & & \ddots & 0 & & & \\ 0 & \cdots & 0 & 1 & a_{p,p+1} & \cdots & a_{p,K} \end{bmatrix}$$

and likewise

$$E\bar{b}_j = \beta_j + a_{j,p+1}\beta_{p+1} + \cdots + a_{j,K}\beta_K, \qquad j = 1, 2, \ldots, p. \tag{18.2.6}$$

Therefore, when $K - p$ relevant variables are omitted, the jth ordinary least squares estimator $\bar{b}_j$ is biased by an amount dependent on the true coefficients of the $K - p$ omitted variables and the auxiliary regression coefficients between the $K - p$ omitted variables and the jth included variable. In the instance that the omitted variables are orthogonal to the included variables then $E\bar{b}_j = \beta_j$, $j = 1, 2, \ldots, p$ since in that case $a_{j,p+1} = a_{j,p+2} = \cdots = a_{j,K} = 0$ and the ordinary least squares estimators of the included coefficients are unbiased. In the more transparent case of only one omitted variable, say the Kth, the bias of the jth coefficient is then determined simply by $a_{j,K}\beta_K$. For example, if the effect of the omitted variable is positive ($\beta_K > 0$) and the relationship between the Kth (omitted) variable and the jth included variable is positive after "correction" for the other $K - 2$ included variables ($a_{j,K} > 0$) the bias of the jth ordinary least square estimator is positive reflecting the fact that the ordinary least squares procedure incorrectly gives some of the credit of the Kth variable's causal effect to the jth variable.

The auxiliary regression notation of (18.2.4) is equally applicable to the case of inclusion of irrelevant variables. Let $\bar{X}$ be of dimension $T \times \bar{K}$, where $\bar{K} = K + r$ and $\bar{X}$ differs from X only in that r irrelevant variables are included as the last r columns of $\bar{X}$. Then it can be shown, see Exercise 18.4, that the auxiliary regression matrix is of the form

$$A = \begin{bmatrix} I_K \\ 0 \end{bmatrix},$$

where 0 is a zero matrix of order $r \times K$. Therefore, as stated before, the ordinary least squares estimators of the relevant (nonzero) coefficients are unbiased.

18.2.2 Other Forms of Misspecification in Regression Variables

The exclusion of relevant variables and inclusion of irrelevant variables are obvious forms of misspecification that may be encountered in regression analysis. There are, however, other forms of misspecification in the variables. For example, the dependent variable may be of the form $\ln(y)$ rather than y or an explanatory (exogenous) variable may properly be of the form $(1/x)$ rather than x. The variables chosen for a regression may be appropriate but the selected functional form may be inappropriate. To illustrate the bias in estimation induced by an incorrect choice of functional form, we focus on two separate cases: misspecification of the functional form of a regressor and misspecification of the functional form of the dependent variable.

Let us first investigate the case of a misspecified explanatory variable. Suppose that, instead of the specified linear relationship

$$y_t = \beta_1 x_{t1} + \beta_2 x_{t2} + \cdots + \beta_K x_{tK} + e_t, \tag{18.2.7}$$

the true relationship (unknown to the investigator) is

$$y_t = \beta_1 x_{t1} + \beta_2 x_{t2} + \cdots + \beta_K x_{tK}^* + e_t, \tag{18.2.8}$$

where x_{tK}^* is some function of x_{tK}, $f(x_{tK})$, other than the identity function $x_{tK}^* \equiv x_{tK}$. For example, $f(x_{tK})$ could be of the form $f(x_{tK}) = 1/x_{tK}$. We would like to know the effect of applying ordinary least squares to the misspecified model (18.2.7) when in fact the correct model is (18.2.8), the focus being on the properties of the estimators of the β_i. Again the result of Equation (18.2.4) is useful. The form of the auxiliary regression matrix is

$$A = \begin{bmatrix} 1 & 0 & \cdots & 0 & a_{1K} \\ 0 & 1 & & & a_{2K} \\ & & \ddots & & \\ & & & 1 & \vdots \\ 0 & & \cdots & 0 & a_{KK} \end{bmatrix},$$

where the a_{iK}'s, $i = 1, 2, \ldots, K$, are the coefficients in the auxiliary regression

$$x_{tK}^* = \sum_{i=1}^{K-1} a_{iK} x_{ti} + a_{KK} x_{tK} + \hat{u}_t,$$

and $\hat{u}_t$ is the least squares residual. Therefore, the expectations of the ordinary least squares estimators obtained from the misspecified equation (18.2.7) are

$$\begin{aligned} E\bar{b}_j &= \beta_j + a_{jK}\beta_K, \qquad j = 1, 2, \ldots, K-1 \\ &= a_{KK}\beta_K, \qquad j = K. \end{aligned} \tag{18.2.9}$$

The ordinary least squares estimators are, in general, biased except when the appropriately specified explanatory variables $x_{t1}, \ldots, x_{t,K-1}$ and the misspecified variable x_{tK} are orthogonal to x_{tK}^*.

Misspecification of the dependent variable can, as well, lead to biased ordinary least squares estimators. Consider the simple case of the specified model

$$y_t = \beta x_t + e_t \tag{18.2.10}$$

when in fact the true model is

$$\ln y_t = \beta x_t + e_t, \tag{18.2.11}$$

where the e_t are normally and independently distributed with zero mean and variance σ^2. For simplicity of exposition, assume $\sum x_t/T = \bar{x} = 0$. The ordinary least squares estimator of β derived from the misspecified model is

$$\hat{\beta} = \frac{\sum x_t y_t}{\sum x_t^2} = \frac{\sum x_t \exp(\beta x_t + e_t)}{\sum x_t^2}. \tag{18.2.12}$$

Then

$$\begin{aligned} E\hat{\beta} &= E\left[\frac{\sum x_t \exp(\beta x_t) \exp e_t}{\sum x_t^2}\right] \\ &= \frac{\sum x_t \exp(\beta x_t)}{\sum x_t^2} \exp(\sigma^2/2) \neq \beta, \end{aligned} \tag{18.2.13}$$

where the fact that, see Exercise 18.5, $E[\exp(e_t)] = \exp(\sigma^2/2)$ when $e_t \sim N(0, \sigma^2)$ is used. Thus the incorrect application of ordinary least squares to the model (18.2.10) with a misspecified dependent variable leads to estimator bias.

Of course, it is to be expected that the simultaneous occurrence of the misspecification of the functional form of an explanatory variable as well as the dependent variable, likewise does not offer optimistic circumstances for ordinary least squares estimation. In general, ordinary least squares estimation applied in such instances leads to biased estimators. For example, suppose that the demand equation for a commodity is iso-elastic of the form

$$y_t = \exp(\beta_1) x_t^{\beta_2} \exp(e_t)$$

or in familiar log form

$$\ln y_t = \beta_1 + \beta_2 \ln x_t + e_t, \tag{18.2.14}$$

where $y_t \equiv$ quantity demanded, $x_t \equiv$ price, and e_t are independently, normally distributed errors with zero mean and constant variance σ^2. Instead, assume that the investigator utilizes ordinary least squares estimation in the linear demand equation

$$y_t = \gamma_1 + \gamma_2 x_t + e_t, \tag{18.2.15}$$

to obtain an estimate of γ_2 and in turn an estimate of the own price elasticity of demand evaluated at the mean: $\hat{\gamma}_2(\bar{x}/\bar{y})$, where $\bar{x} = \sum x_t/T$ and $\bar{y} = \sum y_t/T$. As Theil (1971, pp. 553–555) shows,

$$\text{plim}\ \hat{\gamma}_2\left(\frac{\bar{x}}{\bar{y}}\right) = \beta_2 + \tfrac{1}{2}\beta_2(\beta_2 - 1)\left(\frac{m_3}{m_2}\right) + \cdots,$$

where $m_r = (1/T)\sum (x_t - \bar{x})^r/\bar{x}^r$, $r = 1, 2, \ldots$, and the ordinary least squares estimate of the true elasticity β_2 is inconsistent when derived using the misspecified Equation (18.2.15), except when β_2 is zero ($\beta_2 = 1$ is excluded *a priori* if the inverse relationship between price and quantity demanded holds as specified by the law of demand.)

As the bias of ordinary least squares estimators is very sensitive to functional form misspecification, it would seem desirable to have a procedure which would allow the data to indicate the appropriate functional form to use in obtaining estimates of regression parameters. Such a procedure, the Box–Cox transformation, does exist and will be examined in Section 18.5 below.

18.3 Specification Error Tests

In the previous section we examined the statistical implications of included irrelevant variables, omitted relevant variables and incorrect functional form. The inclusion of irrelevant variables causes inefficient though unbiased estimation while omitted relevant variables and incorrect functional form cause bias and inconsistency. In the first subsection below the traditional F-test for relevant variables is discussed. In the next subsection we examine three popular methods for detecting functional form misspecification when the alternative model is not specified. Finally, in the last subsection Hausman's general specification error test is presented. This test is appropriate for examining possible misspecification errors which lead to a shift in the central tendency of the estimator; i.e. if an estimator were unbiased, then specification error leads to bias; or if an estimator were biased, but consistent, the error leads to a different bias and inconsistency. Examples of such specification errors include omitted variables, incorrect functional form and contemporaneous correlation bias prevalent in the lagged dependent variable-serial correlation model (Chapter 11), the errors-in-variables model (Chapter 12), and the simultaneous equations model (Chapter 19). The Hausman test requires a specific alternative hypothesis and thus can offer greater power than specification error tests having no specific alternative hypotheses.

18.3.1 Traditional Tests for Relevant Variables

When there is uncertainty with respect to the functional form of a regression model, the traditional practice has been to specify a given model as the maintained hypothesis, say,

$$y_t = x_{t1}\beta_1 + \cdots + x_{tK}\beta_K + e_t \tag{18.3.1}$$

such that $Ee_t = 0$, $Ee_s e_t = 0$, $s \neq t$, and $e_t \sim N(0, \sigma^2)$ for all t, and then test the relevance (significance) of various variables by utilizing the t-distribution to test the hypotheses

$$\left.\begin{aligned} H_0\colon \beta_i &= 0 \\ H_1\colon \beta_i &\neq 0 \end{aligned}\right\} \qquad i = 1, 2, \ldots, K.$$

Also the "overall significance" of the regression equation with an included constant term can be examined by testing the hypotheses

$$H_0\colon \beta_2 = \beta_3 = \cdots = \beta_K = 0,$$

$$H_1\colon \text{not } H_0,$$

using the F-distribution with $K - 1$ and $T - K$ degrees of freedom.

These procedures are well accepted given that the investigator *begins* with the maintained hypothesis (18.3.1) and *concludes* the analysis with the outcome of the test. However, if the above tests are used in an iterative, "data mining" way to determine an "acceptable" model, the usual reported standard errors are no longer appropriate as preliminary testing changes the sampling distributions of the implied estimates. See Chapter 7 for a thorough discussion of this point. Needless to say, the most that can be inferred from the statistics of a model obtained from preliminary testing is that any probability statements made must be considered to be *conditional* on the validity of the final model chosen and as a result the significance of the coefficients and overall regression are certain to be overstated as the process of model selection has not been considered. Even so, the practice of iterative model building continues to be used in applications because the construction of hypothesis tests and the calculation of standard errors given preliminary test estimators are yet to be established. At minimum an investigator should be aware of the caveats of preliminary tests and as a result always attempt to come into a statistical problem with a well formulated maintained hypothesis based upon solid theoretical economic reasoning and *a priori* judgment.

18.3.2 Tests for Omitted Variables and Incorrect Functional Form When the Alternatives Are Nonspecific

In the previous section we discussed the use of the classical F-test for the appropriate choice of functional form. The use of this test, however, necessarily requires the specification of a specific alternative hypothesis. For example, consider the linear model

$$y_t = \beta_1 + x_{t2}\beta_2 + e_t. \tag{18.3.2}$$

Under the specific alternative hypothesis that the model is instead a second degree polynomial in x_{t2}

$$y_t = \beta_1 + x_{t2}\beta_2 + (x_{t2})^2\beta_3 + e_t, \tag{18.3.3}$$

the competing functional forms can be tested by examining the hypotheses $H_0\colon \beta_3 = 0$ versus $H_1\colon \beta_3 \neq 0$.

In some instances, however, the problem at hand may not lend itself to the specification of specific alternatives. Instead, it may be suspected that the relevant regression equation is of the form

$$y_t = x_{t1}\beta_1 + x_{t2}\beta_2 + \cdots + x_{tK}\beta_K + f + e, \tag{18.3.4}$$

where f is some function of the x_{ti}'s or possibly some function of variables yet to be specified. It is tests of functional forms in these nonspecific instances that we now address.

In this section we will discuss three popular methods of detecting functional form misspecification when the alternative is not specific: Examination of residuals, Durbin–Watson test, and Ramsey's RESET test. These tests, of course, do not exhaust all of the available tests for functional misspecification but they are representative.

The examination of the residuals $\hat{e}_t$ of a regression is a well-established practice. The various tests involving residuals like the Durbin–Watson test (Chapter 10) and White's test (Chapter 9) for heteroscedasticity are standard fare when examining different proposed covariance structures for a regression model's disturbances. However, residuals can also be examined for the purpose of detecting omitted variables and incorrect functional form. For example, consider the models (18.3.2) and (18.3.3). If $\beta_3 > 0$ then (18.3.3) differs from (18.3.2) in that the former has a concave shape rather than a linear one. If Equation (18.3.2) is fit to the data but instead model (18.3.3) is appropriate then the estimated residuals are likely to exhibit a pattern much like that of Figure 18.3.1.

In the presence of functional form misspecification, the residuals exhibit certain patterns. It is the recognition of this pattern that is the major purpose

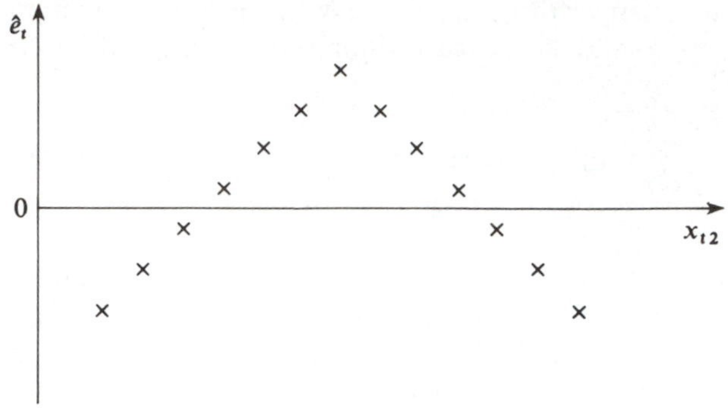

Figure 18.3.1 Pattern of residuals obtained from using a linear model to fit polynomial data.

of the visual examination of residuals. In a similar vein, residuals displaying discrete jumps like those displayed in Figure 18.3.2 could signify the need for seasonal adjustment or dummy variables reflecting structural change.

A common practice in residual analysis is the analysis of the sign patterns of the residuals. For example, the sign pattern of Figure 18.3.2 is:

$$(+)(+)(+)(-)(-)(-)(+)(+)(+)(-)(-)(-).$$

This pattern exhibits "runs" in that there are series of signs which are the same. Draper and Smith (1966, pp. 95–97) recommend the use of a nonparametric *runs* test to determine if the sign pattern is random or instead is systematic in some way. Also Harvey and Collier (1977) discuss other nonparametric tests designed to detect function misspecification. For additional discussion concerning the use of residual plots for detecting misspecification see Draper and Smith (1966 Chapter 3) and Anscombe and Tukey (1963).

Though the Durbin–Watson (1950) test for serial correlation was designed to detect error dependence in time series data it can just as well be used to detect systematic patterns of residuals in cross-section regression equations subject to misspecification. For example, the residual pattern of Figure 18.3.1

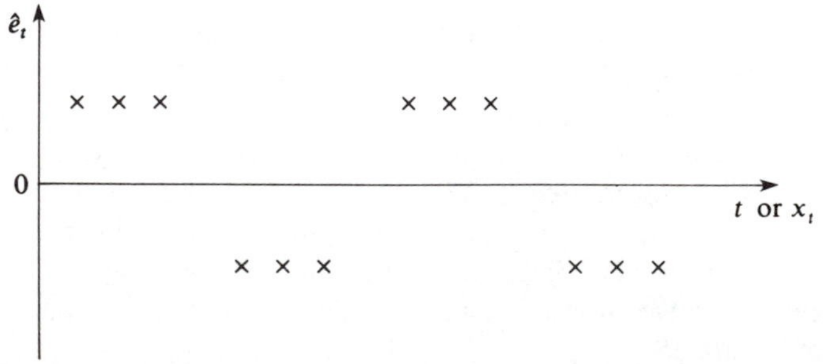

Figure 18.3.2 Residual pattern reflecting need for seasonal adjustment or allowance for structural change.

is consistent with a low Durbin–Watson d-statistic as the residuals exhibit a positive correlation pattern as a function of x_{t2}. Therefore, if it is felt that the misspecification function f in Equation (18.3.4) is related to a variable z (possibly one of the regressors), then the ordered residuals, ordered according to z, can be examined via the Durbin–Watson d-statistic to determine if residual dependences exist because of functional misspecification.

Ramsey (1969, 1974) developed a general test to detect specification errors arising from omitted variables, functional misspecification and/or contemporaneous correlation. This test is called RESET (Regression Specification Error Test). RESET uses the Theil (1965) BLUS (Best Linear Unbiased Scalar) residuals. Forsaking the details of a theoretical development of BLUS residuals, the relationship between the ordinary least squares residuals $\hat{\mathbf{e}}$ and the BLUS residuals $\tilde{\mathbf{e}}$ is given by

$$\tilde{\mathbf{e}} = HQ\hat{\mathbf{e}}, \tag{18.3.5}$$

where Q is an orthonormal basis for the eigenvectors of

$$M = I - X(X'X)^{-1}X'$$

and H extracts the $(T - K)$ rows of Q that correspond to the nonzero eigenvalues of M. The BLUS residuals are then $(T - K)$ "new" residuals which have zero means and, unlike the ordinary least squares residuals, are uncorrelated with each other. That is, under the null hypothesis that the classical normal linear regression model, see Definition 3.2.1,

$$y_t = x_{t1}\beta_1 + \cdots + x_{tK}\beta_K + e_t$$

with $\mathbf{e} \sim N(\mathbf{0}, \sigma^2 I)$ is correct then

$$H_0: \tilde{\mathbf{e}} \sim N(\mathbf{0}, \sigma^2 I_{T-K}). \tag{18.3.6}$$

However, Ramsey (1969) has shown that, in the presence of quite general specification error bias, the mean vector of $\tilde{\mathbf{e}}$ can be approximated by

$$A'\boldsymbol{\xi} \doteq \alpha_0 \mathbf{i} + \alpha_1 \mathbf{q}_1 + \alpha_2 \mathbf{q}_2 + \cdots, \tag{18.3.7}$$

where $\boldsymbol{\xi}$ is a nonstochastic vector, the precise definition of which depends upon the particular misspecification, A' is a $(T - K) \times T$ matrix satisfying

$$A'X = 0, \qquad A'A = I_{T-K}, \tag{18.3.8}$$

the $(T - K) \times 1$ vectors $\mathbf{q}_j$, $j = 1, 2, \ldots$ are defined by

$$\mathbf{q}_j = A'\hat{\mathbf{y}}^{(j+1)'}, \qquad j = 1, 2, \ldots, \tag{18.3.9}$$

with the $1 \times T$ vector $\hat{\mathbf{y}}^{(j+1)'} = (\hat{y}_1^{j+1}, \hat{y}_2^{j+1}, \ldots, \hat{y}_T^{j+1})$; i.e., the vector $\hat{\mathbf{y}}^{(j+1)}$ is the vector obtained by raising each element of the estimated vector of the conditional mean of the regressand to the $j + 1$ power. And $\mathbf{i}$ denotes a column of ones. In summary, under the alternative hypothesis of the presence of biasing specification error, $H_1: \tilde{\mathbf{e}} \sim N(A'\boldsymbol{\xi}, \bar{\sigma}^2 I)$, where $\bar{\sigma}^2$ is the variance of the $\tilde{e}_i$ under H_1 and $A'\boldsymbol{\xi}$ is defined above.

In essence Ramsay's approach to testing the presence of biasing specification error is to analyze the distribution of the BLUS residuals under the competing hypotheses: $H_0: \tilde{\mathbf{e}} \sim N(\mathbf{0}, I_{T-K})$ versus $H_1: \tilde{\mathbf{e}} \sim N(A'\boldsymbol{\xi}, \bar{\sigma}^2 I)$. In particular, Ramsey's RESET test involves the inspection of the regression equation

$$\tilde{\mathbf{e}} = \alpha_0 \mathbf{i} + \alpha_1 \mathbf{q}_1 + \alpha_2 \mathbf{q}_2 + \cdots + \alpha_p \mathbf{q}_p + \mathbf{u}, \tag{18.3.10}$$

where a "suitable" order of approximation p is chosen and $\mathbf{u}$ is assumed to have the distribution $\mathbf{u} \sim N(\mathbf{0}, \sigma^2 I)$. The RESET test procedure then is simply to apply the usual F test for the hypothesis that *all* the α's are zero. Under the null hypothesis H_0, the F-statistic is distributed as a central F with $p + 1$ and $(T - K - p - 1)$ degrees of freedom. Under the alternative hypothesis, the F-statistic is distributed approximately as noncentral F. Therefore, in the event that at least one of the α's is significant, some type of biasing error should be suspected.

In passing we should mention that Harvey and Collier (1977) have proposed a test for functional form misspecification which appears promising. This test uses recursive residuals and a simple t-statistic. The power of their test seems to compare favorably with the Durbin–Watson test and other tests commonly used to detect functional misspecification from residuals. The interested reader should consult their article for additional details. Also in Section 5 we will discuss the Box–Cox transformation which allows tests for functional form specification.

18.3.3 Hausman's Test

In the previous section the primary focus was on those errors in model specification which lead to a shift in the central tendency of the estimator. One should note the RESET test's potential inability to detect specification bias because of the lack of precisely specified alternative hypotheses. What is causing the estimation bias—errors in the variables, simultaneous equation bias or other features of the true versus specified model? The lack of specificity of the alternative hypotheses could result in reduced power of the test relative to a test with a specific alternative. Because of this consideration it is worth while that we discuss Hausman's (1978) specification error test.

To set the stage for Hausman's test, the regression model under consideration is of the form

$$\mathbf{y} = X\boldsymbol{\beta} + \mathbf{e}, \tag{18.3.11}$$

where

$$E(\mathbf{e} \mid X) = \mathbf{0} \quad \text{or in large samples}$$

$$\operatorname{plim} \frac{1}{T} X'\mathbf{e} = \mathbf{0} \tag{18.3.12}$$

and

$$E(\mathbf{ee}'|X) = \sigma^2 I. \tag{18.3.13}$$

Failure of assumption (18.3.12), sometimes called the orthogonality assumption, leads to biased estimation while failure of the second assumption, sometimes called the sphericality assumption, leads to a loss of efficiency though the central tendency of the estimator is still correct. Hausman's test focuses on detecting violations of the orthogonality assumption.

The principle behind the Hausman test is quite straightforward. Under the null hypothesis of no misspecification, there will exist a consistent, asymptotically normal and asymptotically efficient estimator, $\hat{\boldsymbol{\beta}}_0$ where efficiency means attaining the asymptotic Cramér–Rao lower bound (that is, of course, if a suitable distribution for $\mathbf{e}$ has been specified which satisfies the regularity conditions of maximum likelihood estimation). Under the alternative hypothesis of misspecification $\hat{\boldsymbol{\beta}}_0$ will, however, be biased and inconsistent. In order to construct Hausman's test for misspecification another estimator $\hat{\boldsymbol{\beta}}_1$ must be found which is consistent under both the null and alternative hypotheses. Naturally, $\hat{\boldsymbol{\beta}}_1$ will be inefficient under the null hypothesis and, therefore, its variance will not attain the asymptotic Cramér–Rao lower bound. The test then consists of analyzing the difference $\hat{\mathbf{q}} = \hat{\boldsymbol{\beta}}_1 - \hat{\boldsymbol{\beta}}_0$ under the null and alternative hypotheses. Under the null hypothesis of no misspecification plim $\hat{\mathbf{q}} = \mathbf{0}$ while under the alternative hypothesis of misspecification plim $\hat{\mathbf{q}} \neq \mathbf{0}$ and, if the power of the test is high, $\hat{\mathbf{q}}$ will be large in absolute value relative to its standard error.

The theoretical foundations of the Hausman test are established by the following two theorems. For proofs of these theorems see Hausman (1978).

Theorem 18.3.1. *Consider two estimators $\hat{\boldsymbol{\beta}}_0$ and $\hat{\boldsymbol{\beta}}_1$ which are both consistent and asymptotically normally distributed with $\hat{\boldsymbol{\beta}}_0$ attaining the asymptotic Cramér–Rao bound so that $\sqrt{T}(\hat{\boldsymbol{\beta}}_0 - \boldsymbol{\beta}) \overset{\text{asy}}{\sim} N(\mathbf{0}, V_0)$ and $\sqrt{T}(\hat{\boldsymbol{\beta}}_1 - \boldsymbol{\beta}) \overset{\text{asy}}{\sim} N(\mathbf{0}, V_1)$, where V_0 is the inverse of the information matrix. Let $\hat{\mathbf{q}} = \hat{\boldsymbol{\beta}}_1 - \hat{\boldsymbol{\beta}}_0$ and $V(\hat{\mathbf{q}}) = V_1 - V_0$. Then under the null hypothesis H_0, the test statistic.*

$$m = T\hat{\mathbf{q}}'[\hat{V}(\hat{\mathbf{q}})]^{-1}\hat{\mathbf{q}} \overset{\text{asy}}{\sim} \chi^2_K, \tag{18.3.14}$$

where $\hat{V}(\hat{\mathbf{q}})$ is a consistent estimator (under H_0) of $V(\hat{\mathbf{q}})$ and K is the number of parameters in $\boldsymbol{\beta}$.

Theorem 18.3.2. *Under the alternative hypothesis H_1, the statistic m of* (18.3.14) *is distributed as a noncentral χ^2 random variable with noncentrality parameter $\delta^2 = T\bar{\mathbf{q}}'[V(\hat{\mathbf{q}})]^{-1}\bar{\mathbf{q}}$, where $\bar{\mathbf{q}} = \text{plim}(\hat{\boldsymbol{\beta}}_1 - \hat{\boldsymbol{\beta}}_0)$.*

Given these two theorems, it is easily seen that an asymptotic test of misspecification under a specific alternative hypothesis can be based on the χ^2 distribution and a quadratic form in a discrepancy vector between two estimators one of which is consistent and efficient under H_0 but inconsistent under H_1 while the other is consistent under both hypotheses. The power of the test is naturally conditioned by the degree of specification bias induced on $\hat{\boldsymbol{\beta}}_0$ under the alternative hypothesis. The more bias induced, the greater the power of the test.

The beauty of the Hausman test is that it is designed for investigating specific alternatives and thus avoids the need to rely upon approximations of specification bias which sometimes may not be appropriate as in the Ramsey RESET test approximation, $A'\boldsymbol{\xi}$. The Hausman test is widely applicable as it can be applied for detecting errors in variables and simultaneous equations bias as well as determining the appropriateness of error components versus fixed effects time-series–cross-section error specifications. Though Hausman discusses his test principle for each of these applications, we focus here on a test for errors in variables bias for the sake of simplicity.

Consider the simple model

$$y_t = \beta x_t + e_{t1}, \tag{18.3.15}$$

where e_{t1} is independent and identically distributed as a normal random variable with zero mean. Under the null hypothesis that x_t is measured without error, x_t and e_{t1} are orthogonal in large samples, that is

$$\text{plim}(1/T)X'\mathbf{e}_1 = \mathbf{0}.$$

Under the alternative hypothesis that $x_t = x_t^* + e_{t2}$ is measured with error the ordinary least squares estimator $\hat{\beta}_0$ is biased and inconsistent. On the other hand, the instrumental variable estimator $\hat{\beta}_1 = (\mathbf{z}'\mathbf{x})^{-1}\mathbf{z}'\mathbf{y}$ is consistent under both the null and alternative hypotheses. To form the test statistic, note that under the null hypothesis $\sqrt{T}\,\hat{q} = \sqrt{T}\,(\hat{\beta}_1 - \hat{\beta}_0) \overset{\text{asy}}{\sim} N(0, D)$, where $D = V(\hat{q}) = \sigma^2[\text{plim}((1/T)\hat{\mathbf{x}}'\hat{\mathbf{x}})^{-1} - \text{plim}((1/T)\mathbf{x}'\mathbf{x})^{-1}]$, and $\hat{\mathbf{x}} = \mathbf{z}(\mathbf{z}'\mathbf{z})^{-1}\mathbf{z}'\mathbf{x}$. Then, given the result of Theorem 18.3.1,

$$m = T\hat{q}'\hat{D}^{-1}\hat{q} \overset{\text{asy}}{\sim} \chi_1^2, \tag{18.3.16}$$

where $\hat{D}$ is a consistent estimate of D obtained by consistently estimating σ^2 (under H_0) with $\hat{\sigma}^2$, the ordinary least squares estimator of σ^2. The extension of this errors in variables test to regression equations with several variables, one or more of which are measured with error is straightforward. $\mathbf{x}$ and $\mathbf{z}$ become matrices and the degrees of freedom of the χ^2-distribution of m coincide with the dimension of $\boldsymbol{\beta}$.

18.4 Choice Between Competing Nonnested Models

There are times when comparisons between regression models with different variables and functional forms are of interest. These comparisons arise in economics when competing economic theories give rise to different sets of relevant variables and the probability distributions (possibly in the form of conditional linear regression models) chosen to characterize these economic relationships are likewise distinct. In these cases the data must be used to discriminate between competing hypotheses. For example, Friedman and Meiselman (1963) compare simple quantity theory models with simple Keynesian models. Jorgenson and Siebert (1968) compare alternative investment theories.

In this section we will be interested in methods used to discriminate between *nested* and *nonnested* linear models *having the same dependent variable*. First, let us define the terms nested and nonnested. Consider the following competing regression equations:

$$\mathbf{y} = X_1\boldsymbol{\beta}_1 + X_2\boldsymbol{\beta}_2 + \mathbf{e}_1 \tag{18.4.1}$$

and

$$\mathbf{y} = X_1\boldsymbol{\beta}_1 + \mathbf{e}_2, \tag{18.4.2}$$

where X_1 and X_2 are $T \times K_1$ and $T \times K_2$ observation matrices on the explanatory variables. Obviously, Equation (18.4.2) is a special case of Equation (18.4.1) when $\boldsymbol{\beta}_2 = \mathbf{0}$. The model of Equation (18.4.2) is *nested* within the model of Equation (18.4.1). Therefore, two models are nested if one of them can be considered a special case of the other. On the other hand, consider the model

$$\mathbf{y} = Z\boldsymbol{\gamma} + \mathbf{u}, \tag{18.4.3}$$

where Z is a $T \times G$ matrix of observations on some explanatory variables which are distinct from X_1 and X_2. Obviously, the model of Equation (18.4.3) cannot be written as a special case of either (18.4.1) or (18.4.2) and thus a comparison between, say, Equations (18.4.2) and (18.4.3) would involve *nonnested* models.

Methods for testing nested linear models have been treated elsewhere in Section 18.3.1. In the following sections, we focus on methods frequently used to discriminate between nonnested linear models.

18.4.1 Mechanical Nesting

The following illustration discussed in Gaver and Geisel (1974) is useful in illustrating the method of mechanically nesting two competing nonnested linear models. Consider the following two competing theories of the consumption function,

$$\text{Model 1:} \quad C_t = \beta_1 + \beta_2 Y_t + \beta_3 Y_{t-1} + e_t, \tag{18.4.4}$$

$$\text{Model 2:} \quad C_t = \beta_1^* + \beta_2^* Y_t + \beta_3^* C_{t-1} + e_t^*, \tag{18.4.5}$$

where C_t and Y_t represent, respectively, levels of consumption and income at time t. One can form a general model

$$C_t = \beta_1^{**} + \beta_2^{**} Y_t + \beta_3^{**} Y_{t-1} + \beta_4^{**} C_{t-1} + e_t^{**}, \tag{18.4.6}$$

by embedding models 1 and 2 into one comprehensive model. Then the two competing models can be examined by testing separately $\beta_3^{**} = 0$ and $\beta_4^{**} = 0$. If $\beta_3^{**} = 0$ is accepted yet all other variables are significant, then model 2 is indicated. On the other hand, if $\beta_4^{**} = 0$ is accepted yet all other variables are significant, then model 1 is indicated.

Obviously, there are some drawbacks to the mechanical nesting procedure. First, an indeterminate outcome is a likely possibility. In the process of embedding the specific models into a comprehensive model, the number of variables under investigation increases arithmetically. Multicollinearity problems are a distinct possibility with the coefficients being imprecisely estimated. See Section 18.2.1 for a discussion of the effects of including irrelevant variables. In the case of Equation (18.4.6) it is distinctly possible that $\beta_3^{**} = 0$ and $\beta_4^{**} = 0$ will *both* be accepted or rejected thus leading to no conclusive outcome of the test.

Moreover, there is a lack of symmetry of hypotheses in the following respect. Suppose model 1 is chosen as the reference hypothesis and that all of its coefficients are significant. A t-test (equivalently an F-test) measuring the incremental contribution of C_{t-1} to the regression sum of squares may find it to be insignificant and hence model 1 is chosen. However, suppose model 2 had instead been chosen as the reference hypothesis and that all of its coefficients were significant. It is quite possible (especially given the presence of multicollinearity) that a t-test measuring the incremental contribution of Y_{t-1} to the regression sum of squares might have found it to be insignificant and hence model 2 would have instead been chosen. The choice of the reference hypothesis could determine the outcome of the choice of model. Thus, though the mechanical nesting procedure has great appeal, it does incur statistical problems. Multicollinearity compounded by small sample size reduces its discriminatory power. Asymmetry of the hypotheses implies that great care must be exercised in interpreting the results of tests.

18.4.2 Residual Variance (Adjusted R^2) Criterion

Theil (1957) provides a means for selecting between nonnested linear models (and for that matter between nested models). His procedure is based upon choosing the model which, given the data, minimizes the residual variance. Let $\mathbf{y}$ be the common dependent variable and X and Z be the competing sets of regressors. The two competing models are then

$$\mathbf{y} = X\boldsymbol{\beta} + \mathbf{e} \tag{18.4.7}$$

and

$$\mathbf{y} = Z\boldsymbol{\gamma} + \mathbf{u}, \tag{18.4.8}$$

with $E\mathbf{e} = \mathbf{0}$ and $E\mathbf{ee}' = \sigma^2 I$. The residual variance estimators are

$$\hat{\sigma}_e^2 = \mathbf{y}'M_x\mathbf{y}/(T - K_1) \tag{18.4.9}$$

and

$$\hat{\sigma}_u^2 = \mathbf{y}'M_z\mathbf{y}/(T - K_2), \tag{18.4.10}$$

where $M_x = (I - X(X'X)^{-1}X')$ and K_1 is the number of variables in X. M_z and K_2 are similarly defined. Assume that (18.4.7) is the correct model. It follows that $E\hat{\sigma}_e^2 = \sigma^2$ and

$$\begin{aligned} E\hat{\sigma}_u^2 &= E(\mathbf{y}'M_z\mathbf{y}/(T - K_2)) \\ &= [\boldsymbol{\beta}'X'M_zX\boldsymbol{\beta} + 2E(\boldsymbol{\beta}'X'M_z\mathbf{e}) + E(\mathbf{e}'M_z\mathbf{e})]/(T - K_2) \\ &= [\boldsymbol{\beta}'X'M_zX\boldsymbol{\beta} + (T - K_2)\sigma^2]/(T - K_2) \\ &\geq \sigma^2 = E\hat{\sigma}_e^2, \end{aligned} \tag{18.4.11}$$

since $E(\boldsymbol{\beta}'X'M_z\mathbf{e}) = 0$ and $E(\mathbf{e}'M_z\mathbf{e}) = E\operatorname{tr}(\mathbf{e}'M_z\mathbf{e}) = E\operatorname{tr} M_z\mathbf{ee}' = \operatorname{tr} M_z\sigma^2 = (T - K_2)\sigma^2$. Therefore, *on average*, the residual variance estimate of the incorrect specification exceeds the residual variance estimate of the correct specification. Notice the phrase "on average." There is a positive probability that the incorrect model will be chosen. In fact, the probability of selecting the correct model becomes progressively smaller as the number of competing models increases.

The minimum residual variance criterion has also been called the "maximum adjusted R-squared ($\bar{R}^2$) criterion." Recall that the R-square (R^2) value, the coefficient of determination or squared multiple correlation coefficient, is given by

$$R^2 = 1 - \frac{\hat{\sigma}^2(T - K)}{\hat{\sigma}_y^2(T - 1)}, \tag{18.4.12}$$

where $\hat{\sigma}^2$ is the unbiased estimator of σ^2,

$$\hat{\sigma}^2 = (\mathbf{y} - X\hat{\boldsymbol{\beta}})'(\mathbf{y} - X\hat{\boldsymbol{\beta}})/(T - K),$$

and $\hat{\sigma}_y^2 = \sum (y_t - \bar{y})^2/(T - 1)$ is the sample variance of y. The usual interpretation of R^2 is "the proportion of the total variation of y explained by the regression adjusted for the mean." Attempting to maximize R^2 by the addition of variables, some of which are likely irrelevant, is generally regarded as unacceptable practice as the addition of variables can never lower R^2. A more reasonable procedure would be to maximize the explained variation of y relative to the unexplained variation of y with appropriate adjustment for the degrees of freedom lost with the addition of variables. To meet this objective the adjusted (corrected) R^2 is defined by

$$\bar{R}^2 = 1 - (1 - R^2)\frac{(T - 1)}{(T - K)}. \tag{18.4.13}$$

$\bar{R}^2$ is not a monotonic function in K as R^2 is. It can be shown, see Exercise 18.6, that the selection of a competing model with the smallest residual variance estimate is equivalent to the selection of the model with the maximum adjusted R-square value.

Besides the fact that in the presence of many competing models the probability of selecting the correct model is likely to be low, an obvious limitation of the minimum residual variance criterion is that it does not apply when *both* models are incorrect. There is nothing inherent in the test which would indicate that neither model is suitable. In contrast, the Cox procedure, popularized by Peseran (1974) and discussed in the next section, does offer the possibility of rejecting both models.

18.4.3 The Cox Generalized Likelihood Ratio Procedure: Peseran's Results

In Chapter 3 the likelihood ratio principle was used to generate the u-test statistic of (3.4.17) for testing the general linear hypotheses $H_0: R\boldsymbol{\beta} = \mathbf{r}$ versus $H_1: R\boldsymbol{\beta} \neq \mathbf{r}$. The hypothesis $R\boldsymbol{\beta} = \mathbf{r}$ is *nested* in that the model implied by it is a special case of the original model $\mathbf{y} = X\boldsymbol{\beta} + \mathbf{e}$. Imposing these restrictions on the original model provides the restricted model. The application of the likelihood ratio principle is not restricted, however, to the construction of tests of nested hypotheses. To the contrary, it can be used to generate test statistics for separate (nonnested) families of hypotheses. For example, Hogg and Craig (1970, p. 278) illustrate the use of the likelihood ratio principle for discriminating between disparate probability families by posing the following problem. Let $X_1, \ldots, X_T$ denote a random sample from an unknown probability density function which is positive only on the set of nonnegative integers. Suppose that it is desired to test whether the random sample comes from the Poisson process

$$H_0: f(X) = \frac{e^{-1}}{X!}, \qquad X = 0, 1, 2, \ldots,$$

or the alternative probability density function

$$H_1: g(X) = (\tfrac{1}{2})^{X+1}, \qquad X = 0, 1, 2, \ldots.$$

Hogg and Craig then proceed to construct a test of H_0 versus H_1 using the likelihood ratio

$$\frac{f(X_1, X_2, \ldots, X_T)}{g(X_1, X_2, \ldots, X_T)} = \frac{e^{-T}/(X_1!\,X_2!\ldots X_T!)}{(\frac{1}{2})^T(\frac{1}{2})^{X_1+X_2+\cdots+X_T}}$$

to discriminate between the two hypotheses (and thus the two competing distributions of X).

In this same vein, Cox (1961, 1962) has developed the theory of tests of separate families of distributions (nonnested hypotheses). In subsequent work Peseran (1974) and Peseran and Deaton (1978) develop tests using the results established by Cox to discriminate between linear as well as nonlinear nonnested regression models. Here we discuss only the Peseran (1974) results for discriminating between nonnested *linear* models.

The problem then is to discriminate between the two models

$$\begin{aligned} H_0 &: \mathbf{y} = X\boldsymbol{\beta}_0 + \mathbf{e}_0;\ \mathbf{e}_0 \sim N(\mathbf{0}, \sigma_0^2 I); \\ H_1 &: \mathbf{y} = Z\boldsymbol{\beta}_1 + \mathbf{e}_1;\ \mathbf{e}_1 \sim N(\mathbf{0}, \sigma_1^2 I). \end{aligned} \tag{18.4.14}$$

The basic assumptions are that

$$\lim\left(\frac{1}{T} X'X\right) = Q_{XX}, \tag{18.4.15}$$

$$\lim\left(\frac{1}{T} Z'Z\right) = Q_{ZZ}, \tag{18.4.16}$$

$$\lim\left(\frac{1}{T} X'Z\right) = Q_{XZ} \tag{18.4.17}$$

are finite and that Q_{XX} and Q_{ZZ} are nonsingular while $Q_{XZ} \neq 0$.

Before deriving the specific test statistic for the hypotheses of (18.4.14), we must state the basic results obtained by Cox. Let the log likelihood functions of the separate distributions under H_0 and H_1 be $L_0(\boldsymbol{\alpha}_0)$ and $L_1(\boldsymbol{\alpha}_1)$, respectively. Also let $L_0(\hat{\boldsymbol{\alpha}}_0)$ and $L(\hat{\boldsymbol{\alpha}}_1)$ denote the maximized log likelihoods under their respective hypotheses with $\hat{\boldsymbol{\alpha}}_0$ and $\hat{\boldsymbol{\alpha}}_1$ denoting the respective maximum likelihood estimates. Then $\hat{L}_{10} = L_0(\hat{\boldsymbol{\alpha}}_0) - L_1(\hat{\boldsymbol{\alpha}}_1)$ denotes the logarithm of the maximum likelihood ratio. The statistic proposed by Cox for the test of the null model is

$$T_0 = \hat{L}_{10} - T\left[\operatorname*{plim}_{T\to\infty}{}_0(\hat{L}_{10}/T)\right]_{\boldsymbol{\alpha}_0 = \hat{\boldsymbol{\alpha}}_0}, \tag{18.4.18}$$

where plim_0 denotes the probability limit when H_0 is true and the notation $[\cdot]_{\boldsymbol{\alpha}_0 = \hat{\boldsymbol{\alpha}}_0}$ denotes the substitution of the maximum likelihood estimates for the unknown parameters $\boldsymbol{\alpha}_0$ in the expression. Under general conditions Cox shows that, given H_0 is the true model, T_0 will be asymptotically, normally distributed with zero mean and variance $V_0(T_0)$. Define $L_{10} = L_0(\boldsymbol{\alpha}_0) - L_1(\boldsymbol{\alpha}_{10})$, where $\boldsymbol{\alpha}_{10}$ is the asymptotic expectation of $\hat{\boldsymbol{\alpha}}_1$ under H_0. Then Cox (1962) shows that

$$V_0(T_0) = V_0(L_{10}) - \frac{1}{T}\boldsymbol{\eta}'Q^{-1}\boldsymbol{\eta}, \tag{18.4.19}$$

where $Q = -\text{plim}_0(1/T)\partial^2(L_0(\boldsymbol{\alpha}_0))/\partial\boldsymbol{\alpha}_0\,\partial\boldsymbol{\alpha}_0'$ is the asymptotic information matrix of H_0 and

$$\boldsymbol{\eta} = T\,\frac{\partial[\text{plim}_0(\hat{L}_{10}/T)]}{\partial\boldsymbol{\alpha}_0}.$$

Using these basic results, Peseran (1974) derives specific expressions for T_0 and $V_0(T_0)$. To this end, let the log likelihood functions of H_0 and H_1 of (18.4.14) be

$$L_0(\boldsymbol{\alpha}_0) = -\frac{T}{2}\ln(2\pi\sigma_0^2) - \frac{1}{2\sigma_0^2}(\mathbf{y} - X\boldsymbol{\beta}_0)'(\mathbf{y} - X\boldsymbol{\beta}_0), \quad (18.4.20)$$

$$L_1(\boldsymbol{\alpha}_1) = -\frac{T}{2}\ln(2\pi\sigma_1^2) - \frac{1}{2\sigma_1^2}(\mathbf{y} - Z\boldsymbol{\beta}_1)'(\mathbf{y} - Z\boldsymbol{\beta}_1), \quad (18.4.21)$$

where $\boldsymbol{\alpha}_0' = (\boldsymbol{\beta}_0', \sigma_0^2)$ and $\boldsymbol{\alpha}_1' = (\boldsymbol{\beta}_1', \sigma_1^2)$. It is left as an exercise for the reader, see Exercise 18.7, to show that:

$$\hat{L}_{10} = \frac{T}{2}\ln(\hat{\sigma}_1^2/\hat{\sigma}_0^2), \quad (18.4.22)$$

where $\hat{\sigma}_0^2 = \hat{\mathbf{e}}_0'\hat{\mathbf{e}}_0/T$ and $\hat{\sigma}_1^2 = \hat{\mathbf{e}}_1'\hat{\mathbf{e}}_1/T$ and $\hat{\mathbf{e}}_0$ and $\hat{\mathbf{e}}_1$ are the ordinary least squares residual vectors of models H_0 and H_1, respectively. The asymptotic expectation of $\hat{\sigma}_1^2$ under H_0 (i.e., σ_{10}^2) is

$$\sigma_{10}^2 = \sigma_0^2 + \boldsymbol{\beta}_0' H \boldsymbol{\beta}_0, \quad (18.4.23)$$

where $H = Q_{XX} - Q_{XZ}Q_{ZZ}^{-1}Q_{XZ}'$. Finally,

$$T\,\text{plim}_0(\hat{L}_{10}/T) = \frac{T}{2}\ln\left[\frac{(\sigma_0^2 + \boldsymbol{\beta}_0' H \boldsymbol{\beta}_0)}{\sigma_0^2}\right]. \quad (18.4.24)$$

Using the results of (18.4.22)–(18.4.24), it follows that

$$T_0 = \frac{T}{2}\ln\left(\frac{\hat{\sigma}_1^2}{\hat{\sigma}_0^2 + \frac{1}{T}\hat{\boldsymbol{\beta}}_0' X' M_Z X \hat{\boldsymbol{\beta}}_0}\right), \quad (18.4.25)$$

where $\hat{\boldsymbol{\beta}}_0 = (X_0'X_0)^{-1}X_0'\mathbf{y}$ is the ordinary least squares estimator of $\boldsymbol{\beta}_0$ in model H_0 and $M_Z = (I - Z(Z'Z)^{-1}Z')$.

In a similar manner, see Exercise 18.8, the following result holds:

$$L_{10} = \frac{T}{2}\ln\left(\frac{\sigma_{10}^2}{\sigma_0^2}\right) - \frac{1}{2\sigma_0^2}\mathbf{e}_0'\mathbf{e}_0 + \frac{1}{2\sigma_{10}^2}(X\boldsymbol{\beta}_0 - Z\boldsymbol{\beta}_{10} + \mathbf{e}_0)'(X\boldsymbol{\beta}_0 - Z\boldsymbol{\beta}_0 + \mathbf{e}_0)$$

$$(18.4.26)$$

(recall that $L_{10} = L_0(\boldsymbol{\alpha}_0) - L_1(\boldsymbol{\alpha}_{10})$, with $\boldsymbol{\alpha}_{10}$ being the asymptotic expectation of $\boldsymbol{\alpha}_1$ under H_0) where σ_{10}^2 is defined in (18.4.23) and $\boldsymbol{\beta}_{10} = Q_{ZZ}^{-1}Q_{XZ}'\boldsymbol{\beta}_0$.

Note $\boldsymbol{\beta}_{10}$ is directly derivable from the auxiliary regression equation expression (18.2.4) in Section 18.2.

$$\begin{aligned} V_0(L_{10}) &= V_0\left[\frac{1}{2}\left(\frac{1}{\sigma_{10}^2} - \frac{1}{\sigma_0^2}\right)\mathbf{e}_0'\mathbf{e}_0 + \frac{1}{\sigma_{10}^2}(X\boldsymbol{\beta}_0 - Z\boldsymbol{\beta}_{10})'\mathbf{e}_0\right] \\ &= \frac{T}{2}\left(\frac{1}{\sigma_{10}^2} - \frac{1}{\sigma_0^2}\right)^2\sigma_0^4 + \frac{\sigma_0^2}{\sigma_{10}^4}(X\boldsymbol{\beta}_0 - Z\boldsymbol{\beta}_{10})'(X\boldsymbol{\beta}_0 - Z\boldsymbol{\beta}_{10}). \end{aligned} \tag{18.4.27}$$

$$\boldsymbol{\eta} = T\frac{\partial\left[\operatorname*{plim}_{0\,T\to\infty}(\hat{L}_{10}/T)\right]}{\partial\boldsymbol{\alpha}_0} = \frac{T}{\sigma_{10}^2}\begin{bmatrix} H\boldsymbol{\beta}_0 \\ -\dfrac{\boldsymbol{\beta}_0' H\boldsymbol{\beta}_0}{2\sigma_0^2}\end{bmatrix} \tag{18.4.28}$$

$$\operatorname*{plim}_{0\,T\to\infty}\left[-\frac{1}{T}\frac{\partial^2 L_0(\boldsymbol{\alpha}_0)}{\partial\boldsymbol{\alpha}_0\,\partial\boldsymbol{\alpha}_0'}\right]^{-1} = \begin{bmatrix}\sigma_0^2 Q_{XX}^{-1} & \mathbf{0} \\ \mathbf{0}' & 2\sigma_0^4\end{bmatrix}. \tag{18.4.29}$$

$$\frac{1}{T}\boldsymbol{\eta}' Q^{-1}\boldsymbol{\eta} = \frac{T}{\sigma_{10}^4}\left[\sigma_0^2\boldsymbol{\beta}_0' H Q_{XX}^{-1} H\boldsymbol{\beta}_0 + \tfrac{1}{2}(\boldsymbol{\beta}_0' H\boldsymbol{\beta}_0)^2\right]. \tag{18.4.30}$$

Therefore, a consistent estimate of $V_0(T_0)$ can then be obtained by using (18.4.27) and (18.4.30) in (18.4.19) and replacing the unknowns by their consistent estimates, i.e.,

$$\hat{V}_0(T_0) = \frac{\hat{\sigma}_0^2}{\hat{\sigma}_{10}^4}\hat{\boldsymbol{\beta}}_0' X' M_Z M_X M_Z X\hat{\boldsymbol{\beta}}_0, \tag{18.4.31}$$

where $\hat{\sigma}_{10}^4 = (\hat{\sigma}_{10}^2)^2 = (\hat{\sigma}_0^2 + \hat{\boldsymbol{\beta}}_0' H\hat{\boldsymbol{\beta}}_0)^2$ and $M_X = (I - X(X'X)^{-1}X')$. It then follows from Cox's results that the statistic

$$N_0 = T_0/[V_0(T_0)]^{1/2} \tag{18.4.32}$$

is asymptotically distributed as a $N(0, 1)$ random variable when H_0 is true. A significant negative value of N_0 can be interpreted as strong evidence rejecting H_0 in favor of H_1 while a significant positive value is strong evidence against H_0 in favor of an alternative which differs from H_0 in some sense opposite to that which H_1 differs from H_0. A nonsignificant value of N_0, of course, favors H_0.

Now for some comments on Peseran's test. The small sample distribution of T_0 is, in general, not known so that the test statistic has only asymptotic justification. However, Monte Carlo experiments conducted by Peseran (1974) show the normal distribution to be a good approximation in relatively small samples ($T = 20$). Second, it should be pointed out that the above test is defined only as long as

$$\lim_{T\to\infty}\left[\frac{1}{T}X' M_Z M_X M_Z X\right] \neq 0. \tag{18.4.33}$$

This means that the test is not valid when the models are nested or when the competing explanatory variables are orthogonal to each other ($X'Z = 0$). But in these cases the classical F-test is applicable.

One problem with the Cox procedure (and thus Peseran's test) is that the test is *not symmetric* in the hypotheses. When H_1 instead of H_0 is made the reference hypothesis, different conclusions may result. Great care should, therefore, be exercised in interpreting the results of the test. Also the test does not readily generalize to the cases of more than two alternative models.

Finally, Peseran (1974) conducts an interesting Monte Carlo investigation of the relative power of the N_0-test (Equation 18.4.32) and the classical F-test procedure applied to the mechanically nested model. See Section 18.4.1 for a discussion of mechanical nesting. Taking into account the lack of determinancy of some outcomes and the lack of symmetry in the hypotheses of both procedures, Peseran concludes that the N_0-test is preferrable to the F-test procedure applied to a mechanically nested model especially when the sample size is small ($T \leq 40$) and the correlation between the competing sets of explanatory variables (measured by their canonical correlation coefficients) is large. Of course, Peseran's conclusions are limited by the fact that the power comparisons are derived by experiment rather than analytical solutions. They are, however, suggestive.

18.4.4 Other Work on Discriminating Between Alternative Models

The procedures discussed in Sections 18.4.1–18.4.3 certainly do not exhaust all of the sampling theory methods presently available for discriminating between alternative models. Two recent methods have been motivated by Cox's (1961, 1962) suggestions for embedding separate hypotheses into a single model.

Atkinson (1970) suggests choosing between two linear models by *exponentially* forming a probability density function for the general model as

$$\mathbf{f}(y_t; \boldsymbol{\theta}_1, \boldsymbol{\theta}_2, \lambda) \propto \{f_1(y_t; \boldsymbol{\theta}_1)\}^{\lambda}\{f_2(y_t; \boldsymbol{\theta}_2)\}^{1-\lambda}, \qquad (18.4.34)$$

where inferences about the two specific models are made through the new parameter λ. Alternatively, Quandt (1972) suggests forming a general probability density function as a *linear* combination of the separate probability density functions

$$f(y_t; \boldsymbol{\theta}_1, \boldsymbol{\theta}_2, \lambda) = \lambda f_1(y_t; \boldsymbol{\theta}_1) + (1 - \lambda) f_2(y_t; \boldsymbol{\theta}_2), \qquad 0 \leq \lambda \leq 1. \quad (18.4.35)$$

Several problems plague these alternatives to the Cox generalized likelihood-ratio procedure. In the case of normal disturbances, Atkinson's exponential procedure can be shown to be equivalent to the procedure of mechanical nesting discussed in Section 18.4.1. It is, therefore, susceptible to the same problems. The greater the multicollinearity between the competing sets of variables the greater the probability of an inconclusive outcome. Also care must be exercised in interpreting the results of the test as there is an asymmetry in the choice of the reference hypothesis.

Quandt's formulation has the peculiar characteristic of implying the view that the "correct" model changes from one observation to the next while other formulations usually assume the existence of a *stable* "correct" model. In addition, it is possible, in certain circumstances, that λ will not be identified and maximum likelihood estimators will not exist. Also the estimation procedure entails a high dimensional nonlinear search problem which can be quite time consuming.

As yet there does not seem to have been adequate evaluation of the Atkinson and Quandt's procedures. As a result, the Peseran method has much to recommend it, especially since it has been generalized to the comparison of competing nonlinear models (Peseran and Deaton (1978)). Davidson and MacKinnon (1981) recently suggested several discrimination procedures which are closely related, but not identical, to the nonnested hypothesis tests proposed by Peseran and Deaton. Peseran (1982) showed that the asymptotic power of the orthodox F-test (using mechanical nesting) against local alternatives is strictly less than the Peseran N_0 test and the J test proposed by Davidson and MacKinnon unless the number of nonoverlapping variables of alternative hypothesis over the null hypothesis is unity, in which case all three tests are asymptotically equivalent. Theoretical and Monte Carlo comparisons between the Peseran N_0 test and the Davidson and MacKinnon J test are too scant at present to be conclusive.

Of course, there exists a Bayesian method for discriminating between alternative models, posterior odds analysis. The advantage of the Bayesian approach is that the problem of discriminating between alternative models is treated formally as a decision problem with explicit recognition given to the losses incurred in incorrectly choosing a model. For a formal discussion of this method Zellner (1971) and Gaver and Geisel (1974) should be consulted. Zellner (1971) also provides some examples of applications.

18.5 Choice of Functional Form: Box–Cox Transformation

18.5.1 Motivation

A common characteristic of the model discrimination techniques discussed to present is that the competing linear models are assumed to have the same dependent variable y. However, there are instances where the competing models of interest do not have the same dependent variable; instead the two dependent variables are functionally related, e.g., ln y and y. This is the case, for example, when the two competing models are demand functions, one being linear in the variable q, p and p_s, where $q \equiv$ quantity demanded, $p \equiv$ own price, and $p_s \equiv$ price of substitute

$$q = \beta_1 + \beta_2 p + \beta_3 p_s + e_1, \tag{18.5.1}$$

the other being the isoelastic demand curve linear in the logarithms of the same variables

$$\ln q = \gamma_1 + \gamma_2 \ln p + \gamma_3 \ln p_s + e_2. \tag{18.5.2}$$

In this case the methods of the previous Section 18.4 do not apply.

The Box–Cox (1964) transformation, popularized in economics by Zarembka (1968, 1974), provides a method of choosing among a *family* of competing models not necessarily having the same dependent variable. This relaxation of requirements is important in two ways. First, as was shown in Section 18.2.2, the misspecification of the dependent variable can lead to biased regression coefficient estimates just as easily as omitted explanatory variables. Therefore, scrutiny of the dependent variable is important. Second, in the methods of Section 18.4, comparisons were possible between only *two* models at a time. Using these methods in a sequential manner for the purpose of discriminating between more than two models results in the ambiguity of significance levels and standard errors. Therefore, a method allowing multiple comparisons of a *family* of models all at one time without disturbing significance levels and standard errors would enjoy distinct advantages. The Box–Cox transformation analysis allows such multiple comparisons.

The Box–Cox procedure utilizes the following definitions and logic. Consider the power transformation

$$Z^{(\lambda)} = \begin{cases} \dfrac{Z^\lambda - 1}{\lambda}, & \lambda \neq 0, \\ \ln Z, & \lambda = 0, \end{cases} \tag{18.5.3}$$

of the random variable Z. Then $Z^{(1)} \equiv (Z - 1)$, $Z^{(-1)} \equiv -1/Z + 1$, while $Z^{(0)} \equiv \ln Z$ as $\lim_{\lambda \to 0}[(Z^\lambda - 1)/\lambda] = \ln Z$ by l'Hôpital's rule. The utility of this transformation can be seen by considering the following simple model:

$$y_t^{(\lambda_1)} = \beta_1 + \beta_2 x_t^{(\lambda_2)} + e_t, \tag{18.5.4}$$

where (18.5.4) is assumed to hold for some values of λ_1 and λ_2. For the special case $\lambda_1 = \lambda_2 = 1$ we have

$$y_t - 1 = \beta_1 + \beta_2(x_t - 1) + e_t$$

or

$$\begin{aligned} y_t &= (\beta_1 - \beta_2 + 1) + \beta_2 x_t + e_t \\ &= \beta_1^* + \beta_2 x_t + e_t, \end{aligned} \tag{18.5.5}$$

a model linear in the variables y_t and x_t. For $\lambda_1 = \lambda_2 = 0$ we have

$$\ln y_t = \beta_1 + \beta_2 \ln x_t + e_t, \tag{18.5.6}$$

a model linear in the logarithms $\ln y_t$ and $\ln x_t$. Other possibilities include $\lambda_1 = 1, \lambda_2 = 0$ and $\lambda_1 = 1, \lambda_2 = -1$ which provide the models

$$\begin{aligned} y_t &= (\beta_1 + 1) + \beta_2 \ln x_t + e_t \\ &= \beta_1^{**} + \beta_2 \ln x_t + e_t, \end{aligned} \tag{18.5.7}$$

$$\begin{aligned} y_t &= (\beta_1 + \beta_2 + 1) + \beta_2\left(-\frac{1}{x_t}\right) + e_t \\ &= \beta_1^{***} + \beta_2^{*}\left(\frac{1}{x_t}\right) + e_t \end{aligned} \tag{18.5.8}$$

which are linear-log and linear-inverse models, respectively. Of course, other well-known functional forms involving the various combinations of $\lambda = 0$, 1, and -1 can be formed, though the transformation itself does not restrict the value of λ to be solely of these values. For example, it is feasible that the appropriate model within the Box–Cox family (18.5.4) is specified by $\lambda_1 = \sqrt{2}$, $\lambda_2 = \frac{1}{2}$. The Box–Cox transformation offers very flexible functional forms.

Logically, the Box–Cox transformation can be applied to regressions with more than two explanatory variables, i.e.,

$$y_t^{(\lambda_1)} = \beta_1 + \beta_2 x_{t2}^{(\lambda_2)} + \beta_3 x_{t3}^{(\lambda_3)} + \cdots + \beta_K x_{tK}^{(\lambda_K)} + e_t, \tag{18.5.9}$$

though the need to estimate more parameters may become costly. For much of the remainder of this section we will confine our discussion, for expository reasons, to the special case of $\lambda_1 = \lambda_2 = \cdots = \lambda_K = \lambda$. At the end of this section we will discuss the relaxation of this assumption.

Before proceeding to the discussion of the details of the estimation of the Box–Cox parameter λ and corresponding methods of inference, let us indicate a point of contention that has arisen in the Box–Cox transformation literature (see, for example, Huang and Grawe (1980), Huang and Kelingos (1979), Poirer (1978), and Poirer and Melino (1978)). Obviously, for the transformation (18.5.9) to be meaningful, all values of y must be positive, $y_t > 0, t = 1, 2, \ldots, T$, since the logarithmic transformation is defined only over the positive real line. If there were nonpositive (zero or negative) values of y_t then the Box–Cox transformation would not be defined for $\lambda = 0$. In addition, it will be shown later that the likelihood function chosen for estimating λ as well as the other parameters $\boldsymbol{\beta}$ and σ^2 contains terms of the form $\ln y_t$ and thus the likelihood function is undefined for negative values of y_t and maximum likelihood methods are not applicable. Of course, the same can be said for the explanatory variables if they are transformed via the Box–Cox transformation. The transformation is not defined for $\lambda = 0$ if the x_{ti}'s take on nonpositive values.

The important point to note is that the distribution of the error term e_t of the Box–Cox model (18.5.9) is *necessarily truncated*. To see this consider the Box–Cox model of (18.5.9). Let $Z_t = (y_t^{\lambda_1} - 1)/\lambda_1$. Then $y_t = (Z_t + 1/\lambda_1)^{1/\lambda_1}$ and the requirement of positive y_t implies $Z_t + 1/\lambda_1 > 0$ for all t. But $Z_t = \beta_1 + \beta_2 x_{t2}^{(\lambda_2)} + \cdots + \beta_K x_{tK}^{(\lambda_K)} + e_t$ and

$$e_t > -\frac{1}{\lambda_1} - \beta_1 - \beta_2 x_{t2}^{(\lambda_2)} - \cdots - \beta_K x_{tK}^{(\lambda_K)}. \qquad (18.5.10)$$

Hence, the error term e_t necessarily has a truncated domain. This requirement is worrisome especially if, as is conventional, it is assumed that e_t is normally distributed for the purpose of estimation via the method of maximum likelihood.

As shown by Draper and Cox (1969), however, the Box–Cox procedure leads to "a consistent estimate of nearly the correct transformation" when the distribution of e_t is reasonably symmetric and thus not too badly truncated. That is, in the absence of a significant truncation, the Box–Cox procedure leads to approximately consistent estimates of λ. Hereafter, we assume that the random errors e_t are independently distributed as (approximately) normal random variables with zero means and constant variances and that the effects of truncation are negligible.

18.5.2 Maximum Likelihood Estimation

The model of interest is

$$y_t^{(\lambda)} = \beta_1 + \beta_2 x_{t2}^{(\lambda)} + \cdots + \beta_K x_{tK}^{(\lambda)} + e_t, \qquad (18.5.11)$$

where, for simplicity, the transformations on the dependent and explanatory variables are assumed the same. Equation (18.5.11) can be written in matrix form

$$\mathbf{y}^{(\lambda)} = X^{(\lambda)}\boldsymbol{\beta} + \mathbf{e}, \qquad (18.5.12)$$

where $\mathbf{y}^{(\lambda)} = (y_1^{(\lambda)}, y_2^{(\lambda)}, \ldots, y_T^{(\lambda)})'$, $X^{(\lambda)} = (\mathbf{i}, \mathbf{x}_2^{(\lambda)}, \mathbf{x}_3^{(\lambda)}, \ldots, \mathbf{x}_K^{(\lambda)})$, $\mathbf{i}$ is a $T \times 1$ vector of ones and $\mathbf{x}_2^{(\lambda)}, \mathbf{x}_3^{(\lambda)}, \ldots, \mathbf{x}_K^{(\lambda)}$ are each $T \times 1$ vectors of observations on $x_{t2}^{(\lambda)}, x_{t3}^{(\lambda)}, \ldots, x_{tK}^{(\lambda)}$, respectively. The error vector $\mathbf{e}$ is assumed to have the following properties: $E\mathbf{e} = \mathbf{0}$, $E\mathbf{ee}' = \sigma^2 I$, and $\mathbf{e}$ is assumed (provisionally) to be normally distributed. To derive the joint probability density function of the original observations y_t given the joint probability density function of the e_t's, we must obtain the Jacobian matrix J of the transformation $e_t = y_t^{(\lambda)} - \beta_1 - \beta_2 x_{t2}^{(\lambda)} - \cdots - \beta_K x_{tK}^{(\lambda)}$. The Jacobian is defined by

$$J = \det \begin{bmatrix} \frac{\partial e_1}{\partial y_1} & \frac{\partial e_1}{\partial y_2} & \cdots & \frac{\partial e_1}{\partial y_T} \\ \frac{\partial e_2}{\partial y_1} & \frac{\partial e_2}{\partial y_2} & \cdots & \frac{\partial e_2}{\partial y_T} \\ \vdots & & & \\ \frac{\partial e_T}{\partial y_1} & \frac{\partial e_T}{\partial y_2} & \cdots & \frac{\partial e_T}{\partial y_T} \end{bmatrix}$$

$$= \det \begin{bmatrix} y_1^{\lambda-1} & & & 0 \\ & y_2^{\lambda-1} & & \\ & 0 & \ddots & \\ & & & y_T^{\lambda-1} \end{bmatrix} = \prod_{t=1}^{T} y_t^{\lambda-1}, \tag{18.5.13}$$

where det[·] denotes the determinant of the matrix [·]. Therefore, the probability density function of $\mathbf{y}$ is

$$(2\pi\sigma^2)^{-T/2} \exp\left(- \frac{(\mathbf{y}^{(\lambda)} - X^{(\lambda)}\boldsymbol{\beta})'(\mathbf{y}^{(\lambda)} - X^{(\lambda)}\boldsymbol{\beta})}{2\sigma^2} \right) \text{abs } J, \tag{18.5.14}$$

where abs J denotes the absolute value of the Jacobian. The log likelihood function is then

$$\begin{aligned} L(\boldsymbol{\beta}, \lambda, \sigma^2 | \mathbf{y}, X) = &- \frac{T}{2} \ln(2\pi) - \frac{T}{2} \ln \sigma^2 \\ &- \frac{1}{2\sigma^2} (\mathbf{y}^{(\lambda)} - X^{(\lambda)}\boldsymbol{\beta})'(\mathbf{y}^{(\lambda)} - X^{(\lambda)}\boldsymbol{\beta}) \\ &+ (\lambda - 1) \sum_{t=1}^{T} \ln y_t \end{aligned} \tag{18.5.15}$$

and $y_t > 0$, $t = 1, 2, \ldots, T$ is assumed.

Differentiating (18.5.15) with respect to $\boldsymbol{\beta}$ and σ^2 and setting these derivatives to zero provides

$$\hat{\boldsymbol{\beta}}(\lambda) = (X^{(\lambda)\prime}X^{(\lambda)})^{-1}X^{(\lambda)\prime}\mathbf{y}^{(\lambda)} \tag{18.5.16}$$

and

$$\hat{\sigma}^2(\lambda) = (\mathbf{y}^{(\lambda)} - X^{(\lambda)}\hat{\boldsymbol{\beta}}(\lambda))'(\mathbf{y}^{(\lambda)} - X^{(\lambda)}\hat{\boldsymbol{\beta}}(\lambda))/T. \tag{18.5.17}$$

If λ were known, then $\hat{\boldsymbol{\beta}}(\lambda)$ and $\hat{\sigma}^2(\lambda)$ would represent the maximum likelihood estimators of $\boldsymbol{\beta}$ and σ^2. However, since λ is unknown, we can concentrate the likelihood by substituting (18.5.16) and (18.5.17) for $\boldsymbol{\beta}$ and σ^2 in (18.5.15) and obtain

$$L(\lambda \mid \mathbf{y}, X) = \text{const} + (\lambda - 1)\sum_{t=1}^{T} \ln y_t - \frac{T}{2} \ln \hat{\sigma}^2(\lambda). \qquad (18.5.18)$$

Then the maximum likelihood estimate $\hat{\lambda}$ of λ is that value of λ which maximizes (18.5.18) and can be obtained by a grid search over the range of λ. Maximum likelihood estimates of $\boldsymbol{\beta}$ and σ^2, $\hat{\boldsymbol{\beta}}(\hat{\lambda})$ and $\hat{\sigma}^2(\hat{\lambda})$ can in turn be obtained by substituting $\hat{\lambda}$ into (18.5.16) and (18.5.17).

Approximate large sample confidence intervals for λ can be based on the asymptotic likelihood ratio statistic, see Theorem 4.2.4, where $-2 \ln l \overset{\text{asy}}{\approx} \chi^2_q$, l denotes the likelihood ratio statistic and q is the number of restrictions imposed by the null hypothesis. For example, the result that $2(L(\hat{\lambda} \mid \mathbf{y}, X) - L(\lambda_0 \mid \mathbf{y}, X)) \overset{\text{asy}}{\approx} \chi^2_1$, where λ_0 is the value of λ under the null hypothesis, can be used to construct confidence intervals for λ and test the significance of linear functional forms $\lambda = 1$ and log linear functional forms $\lambda = 0$. Similarly, the asymptotic likelihood ratio can be used to conduct tests of hypotheses on $\boldsymbol{\beta}$ and σ^2. Notice the tests on $\boldsymbol{\beta}$ and σ^2 are not contaminated by pretest bias since $\boldsymbol{\beta}$, σ^2, and λ have been estimated simultaneously and not in a stepwise manner.

An alternative approach to testing hypotheses concerning the parameters $\boldsymbol{\beta}$, λ, and σ^2, which is asymptotically equivalent to using the statistic $-2 \ln l$, is the use of the information matrix $I_\theta = [-E[\partial^2 L(\boldsymbol{\theta} \mid \mathbf{y}, X)/\partial\boldsymbol{\theta}\, \partial\boldsymbol{\theta}']$, where $\boldsymbol{\theta} = (\boldsymbol{\beta}', \lambda, \sigma^2)'$. Asymptotically, $\sqrt{T}(\hat{\boldsymbol{\theta}} - \boldsymbol{\theta}) \overset{\text{asy}}{\approx} N[\mathbf{0}, \lim_{T\to\infty} (I_\theta/T)^{-1}]$. Approximate standard errors can be constructed from

$$[-\partial^2 L(\boldsymbol{\theta} \mid \mathbf{y}, X)/\partial\boldsymbol{\theta}\, \partial\boldsymbol{\theta}']^{-1}_{\boldsymbol{\theta}=\hat{\boldsymbol{\theta}}}$$

and tests can be based on the result of asymptotic normality. To illustrate this approach assume the model

$$y_t^{(\lambda)} = \beta_1 + \beta_2 x_t^{(\lambda)} + e_t, \qquad t = 1, 2, \ldots, T, \qquad (8.5.19)$$

is of interest. For the purpose of notational brevity let $L(\boldsymbol{\theta} \mid \mathbf{y}, X) = L$ and

$$\begin{aligned}
e_t &= y_t^{(\lambda)} - \beta_1 - \beta_2 x_t^{(\lambda)}, \\
B_{yt} &= \partial y_t^{(\lambda)}/\partial\lambda = (\lambda y_t^\lambda \ln y_t - y_t^\lambda + 1)/\lambda^2, \\
B_{xt} &= \partial x_t^{(\lambda)}/\partial\lambda = (\lambda x_t^\lambda \ln x_t - x_t^\lambda + 1)/\lambda^2, \\
B_t &= \partial e_t/\partial\lambda = B_{yt} - \beta_2 \beta_{xt}, \\
C_{yt} &= \partial B_{yt}/\partial\lambda = [y_t^\lambda (\ln y_t)^2 - 2B_{yt}]/\lambda, \\
C_{xt} &= \partial B_{xt}/\partial\lambda = [x_t^\lambda (\ln x_t)^2 - 2B_{xt}]/\lambda, \\
C_t &= \partial B_t/\partial\lambda = C_{yt} - \beta_2 C_{xt}.
\end{aligned}$$

Then, it can be shown, see Exercise 18.9, that

$$\frac{\partial^2 L}{\partial^2 \beta_1} = -\frac{T}{\sigma^2}, \tag{18.5.20}$$

$$\frac{\partial^2 L}{\partial \beta_2 \partial \beta_1} = -\frac{1}{\sigma^2} \sum_{t=1}^{T} x_t^{(\lambda)} \tag{18.5.21}$$

$$\frac{\partial^2 L}{\partial \lambda\, \partial \beta_1} = \frac{1}{\sigma^2} \sum_{t=1}^{T} B_t, \tag{18.5.22}$$

$$\frac{\partial^2 L}{\partial \sigma^2\, \partial \beta_1} = -\frac{1}{\sigma^4} \sum_{t=1}^{T} e_t, \tag{18.5.23}$$

$$\frac{\partial^2 L}{\partial \lambda\, \partial \beta_2} = \frac{1}{\sigma^2} \sum_{t=1}^{T} (x_t^{(\lambda)})^2, \tag{18.5.24}$$

$$\frac{\partial^2 L}{\partial \lambda\, \partial \beta_2} = \frac{1}{\sigma^2} \sum_{t=1}^{T} (B_t x_t^{(\lambda)} + e_t B_{xt}), \tag{18.5.25}$$

$$\frac{\partial^2 L}{\partial \sigma^2\, \partial \beta_2} = -\frac{1}{\sigma^4} \sum_{t=1}^{T} e_t x_t^{(\lambda)}, \tag{18.5.26}$$

$$\frac{\partial^2 L}{\partial^2 \lambda^2} = \frac{1}{\sigma^2} \sum_{t=1}^{T} (B_t^2 + e_t C_t), \tag{18.5.27}$$

$$\frac{\partial^2 L}{\partial \lambda\, \partial \sigma^2} = \frac{1}{\sigma^4} \sum_{t=1}^{T} (e_t B_t), \tag{18.5.28}$$

$$\frac{\partial^2 L}{\partial^2 \sigma^2} = \frac{T}{2\sigma^4} - \frac{1}{\sigma^6} \sum_{t=1}^{T} e_t^2. \tag{18.5.29}$$

Then $[-\partial^2 L/\partial \boldsymbol{\theta}\, \partial \boldsymbol{\theta}']_{\boldsymbol{\theta}=\hat{\boldsymbol{\theta}}}$ is a consistent estimator of the asymptotic variance–covariance matrix of the maximum likelihood estimators $(\hat{\boldsymbol{\beta}}', \hat{\lambda}, \hat{\sigma}^2)' = \hat{\boldsymbol{\theta}}$.

To this point, we have assumed for expository convenience that $\lambda_1 = \lambda_2 = \cdots = \lambda_K$ and that the dependent and explanatory variables are restricted to be of the same functional form. This requirement is quite restrictive, however, and greater flexibility (and reality) is offered by allowing the λ_i's to be different. See the generalized Box–Cox model (18.5.9). In this case, the maximum likelihood estimates for $\boldsymbol{\beta}$ and σ^2 can still be solved for *conditional* on given values of $\lambda_1, \lambda_2, \ldots, \lambda_K$. Denote these estimates by

$$\hat{\boldsymbol{\beta}}(\boldsymbol{\lambda}) = (X^{(\boldsymbol{\lambda}_{(2)})'} X^{(\boldsymbol{\lambda}_{(2)})})^{-1} X^{(\boldsymbol{\lambda}_{(2)})'} \mathbf{y}^{(\lambda_1)} \tag{18.5.30}$$

and

$$\tilde{\sigma}^2(\boldsymbol{\lambda}) = (\mathbf{y}^{(\lambda_1)} - X^{(\boldsymbol{\lambda}_{(2)})} \hat{\boldsymbol{\beta}}(\boldsymbol{\lambda}))' (\mathbf{y}^{(\lambda_1)} - X^{(\boldsymbol{\lambda}_{(2)})} \hat{\boldsymbol{\beta}}(\boldsymbol{\lambda}))/T, \tag{18.5.31}$$

where $\boldsymbol{\lambda}' = (\lambda_1, \lambda_2, \ldots, \lambda_K)$ and $\boldsymbol{\lambda}'_{(2)} = (\lambda_2, \lambda_3, \ldots, \lambda_K)$. Concentration of the likelihood function then provides

$$L(\lambda_1, \lambda_2, \ldots, \lambda_K | \mathbf{y}, X) = \text{const} + (\lambda_1 - 1) \sum_{t=1}^{T} \ln y_t - \frac{T}{2} \ln \tilde{\sigma}^2(\boldsymbol{\lambda}). \quad (18.5.32)$$

The maximum likelihood estimates of $\lambda_1, \lambda_2, \ldots, \lambda_K$ then are obtained by a grid search over the K-dimensional space of $\boldsymbol{\lambda}$ with the maximum likelihood estimates corresponding to the maximum of (18.5.32). Naturally this leads to a substantial increase in computational burden and is the reason why many previous studies have specified *a priori* that $\lambda_1 = \lambda_2 = \cdots = \lambda_K = \lambda$. Hypothesis testing in the generalized Box–Cox model can proceed by using the asymptotic likelihood ratio statistic $-2 \ln l$ or the information matrix.

18.5.3 Overstatement of Significance by the Ordinary Least Squares Covariance Matrix

After obtaining the maximum likelihood estimates $\hat{\boldsymbol{\beta}}, \hat{\sigma}^2$, and $\hat{\lambda}$ from Equations (18.5.16)–(18.5.18), the practice has frequently been to estimate the variance–covariance matrix of $\hat{\boldsymbol{\beta}}$ by $\tilde{\sigma}^2(X^{(\hat{\lambda})\prime}X^{(\hat{\lambda})})^{-1}$ rather than by utilizing the appropriate submatrix of the inverse of the information matrix. The following matrix lemma will allow us to determine what effect this has on statistical inference.

Lemma 18.5.1. *Let A be an $n \times n$ positive definite matrix partitioned as follows:*

$$A = \begin{bmatrix} A_{11} & A_{12} \\ A_{21} & A_{22} \end{bmatrix},$$

where A_{ij} is of dimension $n_i \times n_j$, $i, j = 1, 2$ and $n_1 + n_2 = n$. Let A^{-1} be the inverse of A partitioned conformably with A as follows

$$A^{-1} = \begin{bmatrix} A^{11} & A^{12} \\ A^{21} & A^{22} \end{bmatrix},$$

where A^{ij}, $i, j = 1, 2$ are of dimension $n_i \times n_j$ and denote the submatrices of A^{-1}. Then $A^{11} - (A_{11})^{-1}$ is a positive semidefinite matrix, where $(A_{11})^{-1}$ is the inverse of A_{11}.

PROOF. See Exercise 18.10. □

Now consider the model (18.5.19), for example. Let

$$A_{11} = \frac{1}{\sigma^2}\begin{pmatrix} T & \sum x_t^{(\lambda)} \\ \sum x_t^{(\lambda)} & \sum (x_t^{(\lambda)})^2 \end{pmatrix} = \frac{1}{\sigma^2} X^{(\lambda)\prime} X^{(\lambda)},$$

$$A_{21} = A'_{12} = -\begin{pmatrix} \dfrac{\partial^2 L}{\partial\lambda\, \partial\beta_1} & \dfrac{\partial^2 L}{\partial\lambda\, \partial\beta_2} \\ \dfrac{\partial^2 L}{\partial\sigma^2\, \partial\beta_1} & \dfrac{\partial^2 L}{\partial\sigma^2\, \partial\beta_2} \end{pmatrix},$$

$$A_{22} = -\begin{pmatrix} \dfrac{\partial^2 L}{\partial^2\lambda} & \dfrac{\partial^2 L}{\partial\lambda\, \partial\sigma^2} \\ \dfrac{\partial^2 L}{\partial\lambda\, \partial\sigma^2} & \dfrac{\partial^2 L}{\partial^2\sigma^2} \end{pmatrix}.$$

It then follows directly from Lemma 18.5.1 that $A^{11} - \sigma^2(X^{(\lambda)\prime}X^{(\lambda)})^{-1}$ is a positive semidefinite matrix. Thus, the asymptotic convariance matrix for the maximum likelihood esimator $\hat{\boldsymbol{\beta}}$, namely A^{11}, is "larger" than the ordinary least squares covariance matrix taken conditional on λ. Therefore, if standard errors of the coefficient estimates in the Box–Cox model are taken for $\hat{\sigma}^2$ $(X^{(\hat{\lambda})\prime}X^{(\hat{\lambda})})^{-1}$, they will overstate the significance of the coefficients since the standard errors are underestimated. The ordinary least squares covariance matrix does not take into account the lack of independence between the estimation of $\boldsymbol{\beta}$ and the estimation of λ. Note that the same conclusion holds in the generalized Box–Cox model. The ordinary least squares covariance matrix $\tilde{\sigma}^2(X^{(\hat{\boldsymbol{\lambda}}_{(2)})\prime}X^{(\hat{\boldsymbol{\lambda}}_{(2)})})^{-1}$ understates the standard errors of the maximum likelihood estimates $\hat{\boldsymbol{\beta}}(\hat{\boldsymbol{\lambda}})$ and thus overstates their significance.

Interestingly, an analogous result occurs when the usual generalized least squares covariance matrix formula $\sigma^2(X'\Omega^{-1}X)^{-1}$ is used in the lagged dependent variable–serial correlation problem (see Chapter 11). The generalized least squares formula does not admit the dependence between the estimation of $\boldsymbol{\beta}$ and the error parameter ρ. As a consequence, the generalized least squares formula understates the standard errors of $\hat{\boldsymbol{\beta}}$ and overstates the significance of the coefficient estimates.

18.6 Summary and Guide to Further Readings

The discussion in this chapter has centered around four major topics: classical specification analysis, tests for correct specification including Hausman's (1978) test, tests for discriminating between nonnested models, and the Box–Cox transformation. Classical specification analysis emphasizes the importance of beginning any regression analysis with the correct model specification. Hausman's specification error test is widely applicable to many problems in econometrics which give rise to a violation of the orthogonality condition $\text{plim}(X'\mathbf{e}/T) \neq \mathbf{0}$, for example, errors in variables (Chapter 12) and simultaneous equations (Chapter 19). The Cox likelihood procedure (1961, 1962) for testing disparate likelihoods, has been extended by Peseran (1974) and Peseran and Deaton (1978) to discriminating between nonnested linear and nonlinear regression models.

The Box–Cox procedure provides a means of examining a very flexible family of functional forms which, unlike the Cox procedure, does not restrict our examination of alternative regression models to those having the same dependent variable. Also the uncertainty of model specification is reflected directly in the derivation of the standard errors of the regression coefficients. The small sample properties of the Box–Cox procedure have been investigated by Spitzer (1978) and Williams (1980). A good primer on Box–Cox estimation can be found in Spitzer (1982).

Recent advancements have been made in generalizing the Box–Cox transformation to include the possibility of autocorrelation (Savin and White (1978)) and heteroscedasticity (Gaudry and Dagenais (1979)). Essentially, the maximum likelihood method is applied to an extended parameter space, the additional parameters representing the autocorrelation and heteroscedasticity effects.

Several other developments not discussed here should be noted. In recent work Shiller (1982) has suggested the use of smoothness priors in the linear regression model to allow for "simple" nonlinearity in an explanatory variable. Akaike (1973) has proposed an information criterion for discriminating between alternative models. The adequacy of an approximation to the true distribution of a random variable is measured by the distance between the "model of reality" and the true model. Finally, White (1982) examines the consequences and detection of model misspecification when using maximum likelihood methods. A quasi-maximum likelihood estimator is defined. The properties of the quasi-maximum likelihood estimator and the information matrix are exploited to yield several tests for model misspecification.

18.7 Exercises

18.1. Consider the model of Equation (18.2.1) with $\boldsymbol{\beta}_1 \neq \mathbf{0}$ and $\boldsymbol{\beta}_2 \neq \mathbf{0}$. Show that the estimator $\overset{*}{\sigma}{}^2 = (\mathbf{y} - X_1\boldsymbol{\beta}_1^*)'(\mathbf{y} - X_1\boldsymbol{\beta}_1^*)/(T - K_1)$ is biased upward.

18.2. Consider the model of Equation (18.2.1) with $\boldsymbol{\beta}_1 \neq \mathbf{0}$ but $\boldsymbol{\beta}_2 = \mathbf{0}$. Partition $X'X$ into

$$\begin{pmatrix} X_1'X_1 & X_1'X_2 \\ X_2'X_1 & X_2'X_2 \end{pmatrix}.$$

Then use Lemma 18.5.1 to show that the relevant coefficients $\boldsymbol{\beta}_1$ are inefficiently estimated by $\hat{\boldsymbol{\beta}}_1$ obtained from $\hat{\boldsymbol{\beta}} = (\hat{\boldsymbol{\beta}}_1', \hat{\boldsymbol{\beta}}_2')' = (X'X)^{-1}X'\mathbf{y}$, i.e., the inclusion of irrelevant variables leads to inefficient estimates of the relevant regression coefficients.

18.3. Verify Equation (18.2.2).

18.4. In the case of irrelevant explanatory variables show that the auxiliary regression matrix A defined in Equation (18.2.3) is of the form $A = [I_K 0]'$ and therefore that the ordinary least squares estimators are unbiased.

18.5. Using the moment generating function, show that $E[\exp(e_t)] = \exp(\sigma^2/2)$ when $e_t \sim N(0, \sigma^2)$.

18.6. Using Equations (18.4.12) and (18.4.13) show that choosing a regression equation with minimum residual variance from a set of competing regression equations is equivalent to choosing the regression equation having the maximum adjusted R^2, $\bar{R}^2$.

18.7. Verify Equation (18.4.22).

18.8. Verify Equation (18.4.26).

18.9. Verify Equations (18.5.20)–(18.5.29).

18.10. Prove Lemma 18.5.1. Hint: Use the partitioned inverse theorem (Graybill (1969), p. 165)

$$A^{-1} = \begin{bmatrix} [A_{11} - A_{12}A_{22}^{-1}A_{21}]^{-1} & -A_{11}^{-1}A_{12}[A_{22} - A_{21}A_{11}^{-1}A_{12}]^{-1} \\ -A_{22}^{-1}A_{21}[A_{11} - A_{12}A_{22}^{-1}A_{21}]^{-1} & [A_{22} - A_{21}A_{11}^{-1}A_{12}]^{-1} \end{bmatrix}$$

and the matrix proposition of Exercise 6.5.

18.11. Consider the regression model

$$y_t = \beta_1 + \beta_2 x_{t2} + \beta_3 x_{t3} + e_t$$

and the following data:

y	x_2	x_3
290	1	8
131	2	5
40	3	2
27	4	1
180	5	6
96	6	4
243	7	7
63	8	3
381	9	9
458	10	10

Check for the omission of a quadratic term in one of the explanatory variables by examining the residuals (both visually and with the Durbin–Watson statistic) of regressions on ordered values of x_2 and x_3. Add the appropriate quadratic term and re-estimate the equation. Re-examine the residuals of the "new" equation.

18.12. Two competing consumption models are

$$\text{(A)} \quad c = \beta_1 + \beta_2 y + \beta_3 w + e,$$

$$\text{(B)} \quad c = \gamma_1 + \gamma_2 y + \gamma_3 c_{-1} + e,$$

where $c \equiv$ consumption, $y \equiv$ income, $w \equiv$ wealth and $c_{-1} \equiv$ last period's consumption. Consider the data provided by Peseran and Deaton (1978, pp. 693–694).

(a) Use the mechanical nesting technique to determine which model receives the support of the data.
(b) Use Peseran's N_0 statistic (Equation (18.4.32)) to discriminate between these two models.
(c) Compare the results you obtained from parts (a) and (b) and the sensitivity of your results to the choice of the reference hypothesis.

18.13. The following three artificial data sets were each generated using one of the models:

(i) $Q = \beta_1 - \beta_2 P + e$;
(ii) $\ln Q = \beta_1 - \beta_2 \ln P + e$;
(iii) $Q = \beta_1 - \beta_2 \ln P + e$;

where $Q \equiv$ quantity demanded and $P \equiv$ price.

Data Set A

P	1	2	3	4	5	6	7	8	9	10
Q	164	67	54	34	33	24	22	18	16	13

Data Set B

P	1	2	3	4	5	6	7	8	9	10
Q	10	8.6	7.8	7.2	6.8	6.4	6.0	5.8	5.6	5.4

Data Set C

P	1	2	3	4	5	6	7	8	9	10
Q	9.7	8.8	8.7	7.8	7.7	6.8	6.7	6.2	5.7	5.2

(a) Use the Box–Cox transformation to match these data sets with their appropriate "parents" and in each case calculate an estimate of the price elasticity and its standard error. In the nonisoelastic cases compute the elasticity at the sample mean of P.

(b) Once the appropriate transformation is determined for each data set, run a conditional ordinary least squares regression with the appropriate transformation taken as given. Compare the standard errors of your estimates with the standard errors obtained from the Box–Cox transformation. Explain the observed relationship.

18.8 References

Akaike, H. (1973). Information theory and the extension of the maximum likelihood principle. In *Proceedings of the Second International Symposium on Information Theory*. Edited by B. N. Petrov and F. Csaki. Budapest: Akailseoniai-Kindo. Pp. 267–281.

Anderson, T. W. (1958). *An Introduction to Multivariate Statistical Analysis*. New York: Wiley.

Anscombe, F. J. and Tukey, J. W. (1963). The examination and analysis of residuals. *Technometrics*, **5**, 141–160.

Atkinson, A. C. (1970). A method for discriminating between models. *Journal of the Royal Statistical Society*, B, **32**, 323–353.

Box, G. E. P. and Cox, D. R. (1964). An analysis of transformations. *Journal of the Royal Statistical Society*, B, **26**, 211–234.

Cox, D. R. (1961). Tests of separate families of hypotheses. In *Proceedings of the Fourth Berkeley Symposium in Mathematical Statistics and Probability*, Vol. 1. Edited by Jerzy Neyman. Berkeley: University of California Press. Pp. 105–123.

Cox, D. R. (1962). Further results on tests of separate hypotheses. *Journal of the Royal Statistical Society*, B, **24**, 406–424.

Davidson, R. and MacKinnon, J. G. (1981). Several tests for model specification in the presence of alternative hypotheses. *Econometrica*, **49**, 781–793.

Draper, N. R. and Cox, D. R. (1969). On distributions and their transformation to normality. *Journal of the Royal Statistical Society*, B, **31**, 472–476.

Draper, N. R. and Smith, H. (1966). *Applied Regression Analysis*. New York: Wiley.

Durbin, J. and Watson, G. S. (1950). Testing for serial correlation in least squares regression—I. *Biometrika*, **37**, 409–428.

Fomby, T. B. (1981). Loss of efficiency in regression analysis due to irrelevant variables: a generalization. *Economics Letters*, **7**, 319–322.

Friedman, M. and Meiselman, D. (1963). The relativity stability of monetary velocity and the investment multiplier in the United States 1897–1958. In *Stabilization Policies*. Commission on Money and Credit Research Study. Edited by E. Cary Brown, Robert M. Solow, A. Ando, J. Karenken, M. Friedman, D. Meiselman, L. E. Thompson, A. M. Okun, M. H. Miller, A. H. Meltzer, O. Brownlee, and A. Conrad. Englewood Cliffs, NJ: Prentice-Hall.

Gaudry, J. I. and Dagenais, G. (1979). Heteroscedasticity and the use of Box–Cox transformations. *Economics Letters*, **2**, 225–229.

Gaver, K. M. and Geisel, M. S. (1974). Discriminating among alternative models: Bayesian and non-Bayesian methods. In *Frontiers in Econometrics*. Edited by P. Zarembka. New York: Academic Press. Pp. 13–47.

Graybill, F. A. (1969). *Introduction to Matrices with Applications in Statistics*. Belmont, Cal.: Wadsworth.

Harvey, A. C. and Collier, P. (1977). Testing for functional misspecification in regression analysis. *Journal of Econometrics*, **6**, 103–119.

Hausman, J. A. (1978). Specification tests in econometrics. *Econometrica*, **46**, 1251–1271.
Hogg, R. V. and Craig, A. T. (1970). *Introduction to Mathematical Statistics*, 3rd ed. New York: Macmillan.
Huang, C. J. and Grawe, O. R. (1980). Functional forms and the demand for meat in the United States—A comment. *Review of Economics and Statistics*, **62**, 144–146.
Huang, C. J. and Kelingos, J. A. (1979). Conditional mean function and a general specification of the disturbance in regression analysis. *Southern Economic Journal*, **45**, 710–717.
Jorgenson, D. W. and Siebert, C. D. (1968). A comparison of alternative theories of corporate investment behavior. *American Economic Review*, **58**, 681–712.
Peseran, M. H. (1974). On the general problem of model selection. *Review of Economic Studies*, **41**, 153–171.
Peseran, M. H. (1982). Comparison of local power of alternative tests of nonnested regression models. *Econometrica*, **50**, 1287–1305.
Peseran, M. H. and Deaton, A. (1978). Testing non-nested nonlinear regression models. *Econometrica*, **46**, 677–694.
Poirer, D. J. (1978). The use of the Box–Cox transformation in limited dependent variable models. *Journal of the American Statistical Association*, **73**, 284–287.
Poirer, D. J. and Melino, A. (1978). A note on the interpretation of regression coefficients within a class of truncated distributions. *Econometrica*, **46**, 1207–1209.
Quandt, R. E. (1972). Testing nonnested hypotheses. Memorandum No. 140, Econometric Research Program, Princeton University, Princeton, NJ.
Ramsey, J. B. (1969). Tests for specification errors in classical linear least squares regression analysis. *Journal of Royal Statistical Society*, B, **31**, 350–371.
Ramsey, J. B. (1974). Classical model selection through specification error tests. In *Frontiers in Econometrics*. Edited by P. Zarembka. New York: Academic Press. Pp. 13–47.
Savin, N. E. and White, K. J. (1978). Estimation and testing for functional form and autocorrelation. *Journal of Econometrics*, **8**, 1–12.
Shiller, R. J. (1982). Smoothness priors and nonlinear regression. Technical Working Paper No. 25, National Bureau of Economic Research, Cambridge, MA.
Spitzer, J. J. (1978). A Monte Carlo investigation of the Box–Cox transformation in small samples. *Journal of the American Statistical Association*, **73**, 488–495.
Spitzer, J. J. (1982). A primer on Box–Cox estimation. *The Review of Economics and Statistics*, **64**, 307–313.
Theil, H. (1957). Specification errors and the estimation of economic relationships. *Review of the International Statistical Institute*, **25**, 41–51.
Theil, H. (1965). The analysis of disturbances in regression analysis. *Journal of the American Statistical Association*, **60**, 1067–1079.
Theil, H. (1971). *Principles of Econometrics*. New York: Wiley.
White, H. (1982). Maximum likelihood estimation of misspecified models. *Econometrica*, **50**, 1–25.
Williams, M. E. (1980). Properties and performance of the Box–Cox transformation. Unpublished Doctoral Dissertation, Department of Economics, Southern Methodist University, Dallas, TX.
Zarembka, P. (1968). Functional form in the demand for money. *Journal of the American Statistical Association*, **63**, 502–511.
Zarembka, P. (1974). Transformation of variables in econometrics. In *Frontiers in Econometrics*. Edited by P. Zarembka. New York: Academic Press. Pp. 81–104.
Zellner, A. (1971). *An Introduction to Bayesian Inference in Econometrics*. New York: Wiley.

PART IV

SIMULTANEOUS EQUATIONS MODELS

The following six chapters constitute Part IV of this book. Part IV is the first of two parts on simultaneous equations models in econometrics and confines itself to developing basic results. In Chapter 19 the notation and basic assumptions of simultaneous equations models are introduced. The simultaneous equation bias which arises when using ordinary least squares to estimate equations in these models is described. In Chapter 20 the identification problem is defined and necessary and sufficient conditions for identification are presented. In Chapter 21 consistent single equation methods are analyzed. These methods are called limited information methods since only the identifying information specific to the equation to be estimated is used. Full information methods are discussed in Chapter 22. These methods use the identifying information of all equations and all equations are estimated jointly. Comparisons are drawn between limited information methods and full information methods. In Chapter 23 the restricted reduced form is distinguished from the unrestricted reduced form and efficient estimation methods are discussed. In Chapter 24 the concepts of a final form and dynamic multipliers are introduced. Sufficient conditions for the stability of a dynamic simultaneous equations model are described and a test for stability is presented. A discussion of standard errors of simulation forecasts and the technique of optimal control concludes the chapter.

CHAPTER 19

Introduction to Simultaneous Equations Models

19.1 Introduction

The purpose of this chapter is to provide an informal introduction to the unique estimation problems arising in economic models where the values of several variables are determined simultaneously. Some examples include the usual Keynesian and monetary macroeconomic models as well as supply and demand equations of microeconomic markets. The models addressed to this point are appropriate when the conditional expectation, $E(\mathbf{y}|X)$, is approximately linear and the stochastic process which generates the regressor X operates independently of the error e_t. This assumption allows the determination of X to be treated independently of $\mathbf{y}$. In some cases, however, it is more appropriate to treat X and $\mathbf{y}$ as jointly determined.

The outline of this chapter is as follows: Section 19.2 discusses the simultaneous equation problem in the context of the simple Keynesian model. The basic notation and assumptions to be used in our discussion of simultaneous equation models will be introduced in Section 19.3, while Section 19.4 contains a discussion of ordinary least squares estimation of the reduced form.

19.2 The Simultaneous Equations Problem

Economic data are often generated by a set of processes that are interdependent. Modeling such interdependent processes leads to the consideration of systems of simultaneous equations. These equations have the characteristic that *each* may contain several dependent variables that also occur in other equations.

Let us begin with the simple Keynesian model

$$c_t = \beta y_t + e_t, \tag{19.2.1}$$

$$y_t = c_t + i_t, \tag{19.2.2}$$

where $t = 1, 2, \ldots, T$ represent successive annual observations. These equations are called *structural* equations because they are designed to describe part of the structure of the economy. The first equation is the consumption function. Total consumption, c_t, is proportional to total income, apart from a random disturbance. This is a *behavioral* equation since it describes the behavior of an economic unit. The second equation is definitional and states that consumption plus investment equals income every year. This is an *identity*. It has no random disturbance and all its coefficients are known. Our objective is to estimate β on the basis of T observations under the assumption that e_t's are uncorrelated random variables with zero mean and constant variance.

To investigate one assumption of the usual linear model, is it reasonable to assume that values of the explanatory variable y_t are independent of the disturbances e_t, so that we can operate conditionally on y_t values? Let there be a perturbation in e_t. The consequences of this are a "pip" in c_t, which, from Equation (19.2.2) causes a "pip" in y_t given i_t remains unchanged. Thus, in Equation (19.2.1) the assumption of independence between the (stochastic) regressor y_t and the disturbance e_t cannot be maintained. We will see that this implies that ordinary least squares applied to Equation (19.2.1) produces a biased and inconsistent estimator of β.

Equations (19.2.1) and (19.2.2), because they together describe the economic system, must be treated jointly. In this system there are three variables, c, y, and i and only two equations. Accordingly, one objective of the equation system is to describe a subset of its variables in terms of the remaining variables. The former group contains those variables whose values are determined by the system given the values of the variables in the second group. Consequently the former variables are said to be *endogenous* and are *jointly* and *simultaneously* determined by the system. The remaining variables are called *exogenous* since their values are not determined within the system but rather somewhere *outside*, that is, by a process which is independent of the process described in the system. The statistical equivalent of this difference is to say the exogenous variables are stochastically independent of the disturbances of the system. This assumption allows us to operate conditionally on the values of the exogenous variables so we may regard them as constants.

In Equations (19.2.1) and (19.2.2) assume i_t is exogenous and c_t and y_t are endogenous. If $\beta \neq 1$, we can solve for c_t and y_t as

$$c_t = \frac{\beta}{1-\beta} i_t + \frac{1}{1-\beta} e_t, \tag{19.2.3}$$

$$y_t = \frac{1}{1-\beta} i_t + \frac{1}{1-\beta} e_t. \tag{19.2.4}$$

The covariance between y_t and e_t is

$$E(y_t - Ey_t)e_t = E\left(\frac{e_t^2}{1-\beta}\right) = \frac{\sigma^2}{1-\beta} > 0 \tag{19.2.5}$$

if $Ee_t^2 = \sigma^2$ and $0 \le \beta < 1$. Thus the general stochastic linear regression model (Chapter 5) is not appropriate for the first structural equation. Ordinary least squares will not provide a consistent estimator. Explicitly, the ordinary least squares estimator for β is

$$\begin{aligned}\hat{\beta} &= \frac{\sum c_t(y_t - \bar{y})}{\sum (y_t - \bar{y})^2} = \frac{\sum (\beta y_t + e_t)(y_t - \bar{y})}{\sum (y_t - \bar{y})^2} \\ &= \frac{\beta \sum y_t(y_t - \bar{y})}{\sum (y_t - \bar{y})^2} + \frac{\sum e_t(y_t - \bar{y})}{\sum (y_t - \bar{y})^2}.\end{aligned} \tag{19.2.6}$$

But $\sum y_t(y_t - \bar{y}) = \sum (y_t - \bar{y})^2$, therefore,

$$\hat{\beta} = \beta + \frac{\sum e_t(y_t - \bar{y})/T}{\sum(y_t - \bar{y})^2/T}. \tag{19.2.7}$$

The sample covariance between e_t and y_t is $\sum e_t(y_t - \bar{y})/T$ and under general conditions

$$\operatorname{plim}\left(\sum e_t(y_t - \bar{y})/T\right) = Ee_t(y_t - Ey_t) = \frac{\sigma^2}{1-\beta}. \tag{19.2.8}$$

Similarly, the sample variance $\sum (y_t - \bar{y})^2/T$ is a consistent estimate for $E(y_t - Ey_t)^2 = \sigma_y^2$. Thus,

$$\operatorname{plim} \hat{\beta} = \beta + \frac{(1-\beta)^{-1}\sigma^2}{\sigma_y^2}. \tag{19.2.9}$$

The ordinary least squares estimator is not consistent. In fact, since $0 \le \beta < 1$ we know $\operatorname{plim}(\hat{\beta}) > \beta$. Intuitively, the ordinary least squares regression of c_t on y_t gives credit to income for the effect of disturbances since the disturbances are positively correlated with income. Hence, the effect of y_t on c_t is overstated.

The equation system of (19.2.1) and (19.2.2) is said to be *complete* when it can be solved for the endogenous variables. That is, there are as many equations as endogenous variables. We will consider only complete systems. The solution for endogenous variables solely in terms of exogenous variables and disturbances is called the *reduced form* and each equation is called a reduced form equation (see Equations (19.2.3) and (19.2.4)).

The economic interpretation of the structural equations is simpler and more direct than that of the reduced form. On the other hand, the reduced form is convenient if one wants to calculate the effect of a change in an exogenous variable on the endogenous variables. In fact, the usual Keynesian multipliers $\partial c_t/\partial i_t = \beta/(1-\beta)$ and $\partial y_t/\partial i_t = 1/(1-\beta)$ can be obtained from the reduced form equations. Also note that the values of i_t on the right-hand side of the reduced form equations are nonstochastic. Thus, the reduced form equations are closer to the usual single equation linear model than the structural equations.

A more elaborate simultaneous model is Klein's (1950) model of the U.S. economy. It is a six equation model based on annual data. Furthermore, it is *dynamic* in the sense that it is formulated in terms of variables belonging to different points in time.

The three behavioral equations are

$$c_t = \beta_0 + \beta_1 p_t + \beta_2 p_{t-1} + \beta_3(w_t + w_t') + e_t, \tag{19.2.10}$$

$$i_t = \beta_0' + \beta_1' p_t + \beta_2' p_{t-1} + \beta_3' k_{t-1} + e_t', \tag{19.2.11}$$

$$w_t = \beta_0'' + \beta_1'' x_t + \beta_2'' x_{t-1} + \beta_3''(t - 1931) + e_t'', \tag{19.2.12}$$

where $c_t \equiv$ aggregate consumption, $p_t \equiv$ total profits, $w_t \equiv$ total private wage bill, $w_t' \equiv$ government wage bill, $k_t \equiv$ total capital stock, $x_t \equiv$ total production, $i_t \equiv$ net investments, and $t \equiv$ time by year. These equations represent the consumption, investment and demand for labor functions, respectively. To make the system complete, the model contains the following identities

$$x_t = c_t + i_t + g_t, \tag{19.2.13}$$

$$p_t = x_t - w_t - b_t, \tag{19.2.14}$$

$$k_t = k_{t-1} + i_t, \tag{19.2.15}$$

where $g_t \equiv$ government nonwage expenditure and $b_t \equiv$ business taxes. The first identity states that total production consists of consumption, net investment, and nonwage government expenditures. The second identity specifies profits as a residual and the third identity defines net investment.

This model has six equations and eleven variables (including the constant term and the time trend). Which of these variables is exogenous? We will assume g_t, b_t, w_t', t and the constant are exogenous. Then c_t, p_t, w_t, i_t, k_t, and x_t are endogenous.

Now it is impossible to express each of the current endogenous variables solely as a function of current exogenous variables and current disturbances. This is due to the lagged endogenous variables p_{t-1}, k_{t-1}, and x_{t-1}. For example, solving for total production x_t

$$x_t = h(\text{constant}, g_t, b_t, w_t', t, p_{t-1}, k_{t-1}, x_{t-1}) + v_t,$$

where $h(\cdot)$ denotes a linear function in the indicated variables. This equation will still be called a reduced form equation. The notion is that lagged endogenous variables are "like" exogenous variables in that they are independent of the *current* operation of the system, as long as there is not autocorrelation in the errors.

Thus, current endogenous variables are called jointly dependent variables. They are left-hand variables in the reduced form. All other variables, exogenous, lagged exogenous, and lagged endogenous, are called *predetermined* variables. Therefore, the reduced form describes the behavior of the jointly dependent variables in terms of the predetermined variables and the disturbances.

19.3 Notation and Assumptions

Consider a system of G simultaneous equations

$$\sum_{j=1}^{G} y_{tj}\Gamma_{ji} + \sum_{j=1}^{K} x_{tj}\Delta_{ji} + e_{ti} = 0, \qquad i = 1, 2, \ldots, G, \quad t = 1, \ldots, T, \tag{19.3.1}$$

or written out for a particular time period t

$$\begin{aligned} y_{t1}\Gamma_{11} + y_{t2}\Gamma_{21} + \cdots + y_{tG}\Gamma_{G1} + x_{t1}\Delta_{11} + x_{t2}\Delta_{21} \\ + \cdots + x_{tK}\Delta_{K1} + e_{t1} = 0, \\ y_{t1}\Gamma_{12} + y_{t2}\Gamma_{22} + \cdots + y_{tG}\Gamma_{G2} + x_{t1}\Delta_{12} + x_{t2}\Delta_{22} \\ + \cdots + x_{tK}\Delta_{K2} + e_{t2} = 0, \\ \vdots \\ y_{t1}\Gamma_{1G} + y_{t2}\Gamma_{2G} + \cdots + y_{tG}\Gamma_{GG} + x_{t1}\Delta_{1G} + x_{t2}\Delta_{2G} \\ + \cdots + x_{tK}\Delta_{KG} + e_{tG} = 0. \end{aligned} \tag{19.3.2}$$

Note there are G equations determining the G endogenous variables $y_{t1}, \ldots, y_{tG}$, K predetermined variables $x_{t1}, \ldots, x_{tK}$ and a random disturbance for each equation $e_{t1}, e_{t2}, \ldots, e_{tG}$. There are a total of T observations on each variable. The Γ_{ji}'s and Δ_{ji}'s are the structural coefficients.

All T observations can be written in matrix form as

$$\underset{(T \times G)(G \times G)}{Y\Gamma} + \underset{(T \times K)(K \times G)}{X\Delta} + \underset{(T \times G)}{E} = \underset{(T \times G)}{0}. \tag{19.3.3}$$

More explicitly

$$\begin{bmatrix} y_{11} & y_{12} & \cdots & y_{1G} \\ y_{21} & y_{22} & \cdots & y_{2G} \\ \vdots & \vdots & & \vdots \\ y_{T1} & y_{T2} & \cdots & y_{TG} \end{bmatrix} \begin{bmatrix} \Gamma_{11} & \Gamma_{12} & \cdots & \Gamma_{1G} \\ \Gamma_{21} & \Gamma_{22} & \cdots & \Gamma_{2G} \\ \vdots & \vdots & & \vdots \\ \Gamma_{G1} & \Gamma_{G2} & \cdots & \Gamma_{GG} \end{bmatrix}$$

$$+ \begin{bmatrix} x_{11} & x_{12} & \cdots & x_{1K} \\ x_{21} & x_{22} & \cdots & x_{2K} \\ \vdots & \vdots & & \vdots \\ x_{T1} & x_{T2} & \cdots & x_{TK} \end{bmatrix} \begin{bmatrix} \Delta_{11} & \Delta_{12} & \cdots & \Delta_{1G} \\ \Delta_{21} & \Delta_{22} & \cdots & \Delta_{2G} \\ \vdots & \vdots & & \vdots \\ \Delta_{K1} & \Delta_{K2} & \cdots & \Delta_{KG} \end{bmatrix}$$

$$+ \begin{bmatrix} e_{11} & e_{12} & \cdots & e_{1G} \\ e_{21} & e_{22} & \cdots & e_{2G} \\ \vdots & \vdots & & \vdots \\ e_{T1} & e_{T2} & \cdots & e_{TG} \end{bmatrix} = \begin{bmatrix} 0 & 0 & \cdots & 0 \\ 0 & 0 & \cdots & 0 \\ \vdots & \vdots & & \vdots \\ 0 & 0 & \cdots & 0 \end{bmatrix}. \tag{19.3.4}$$

Thus, the equation system (19.3.2), which represents the tth observation on all equations, is generated by taking the tth row of Y, X, and E and the full coefficient matrices. That is, if $\mathbf{y}_{t.}$, $\mathbf{x}_{t.}$, and $\mathbf{e}_{t.}$ are the tth rows of Y, X, and E, respectively, then (19.3.2) is given in matrix notation by

$$\mathbf{y}_{t.}\Gamma + \mathbf{x}_{t.}\Delta + \mathbf{e}_{t.} = \mathbf{0}'. \tag{19.3.5}$$

Similiarly, all the observations on a single equation can be written as

$$Y\Gamma_{.i} + X\Delta_{.i} + \mathbf{e}_{.i} = \mathbf{0}, \tag{19.3.6}$$

where $\Gamma_{.i}$, $\Delta_{.i}$, and $\mathbf{e}_{.i}$ are the ith columns of Γ, Δ and E. Each *column* of Γ, Δ, and E is specific to an equation.

Using the notation we have adopted, the simple Keynesian model for all equations and all observations can be written as

$$\begin{bmatrix} c_1 & y_1 \\ c_2 & y_2 \\ \vdots & \vdots \\ c_T & y_T \end{bmatrix} \begin{bmatrix} 1 & 1 \\ -\beta & -1 \end{bmatrix} + \begin{bmatrix} i_1 \\ i_2 \\ \vdots \\ i_T \end{bmatrix} [0 \quad 1] + \begin{bmatrix} -e_1 & 0 \\ -e_2 & 0 \\ \vdots & \vdots \\ -e_T & 0 \end{bmatrix} = \begin{bmatrix} 0 & 0 \\ 0 & 0 \\ \vdots & \vdots \\ 0 & 0 \end{bmatrix}.$$

The standard assumptions of the simultaneous equations model (19.3.3) are:

(1) The vectors $\mathbf{e}'_{t.} = (e_{t1}, e_{t2}, \ldots, e_{tG})'$ are independently and identically distributed as $N(\mathbf{0}, \Sigma)$. That is

$$\text{(i)}\quad E[\mathbf{e}'_{t.}] = \begin{bmatrix} Ee_{t1} \\ Ee_{t2} \\ \vdots \\ Ee_{tG} \end{bmatrix} = \begin{bmatrix} 0 \\ 0 \\ \vdots \\ 0 \end{bmatrix} = \mathbf{0} \quad \text{for all } t = 1, 2, \ldots, T. \tag{19.3.7}$$

$$\text{(ii)}\quad E\begin{bmatrix} e_{t1} \\ e_{t2} \\ \vdots \\ e_{tG} \end{bmatrix} [e_{t1} \quad e_{t2} \quad \cdots \quad e_{tG}] = E\mathbf{e}'_{t.}\mathbf{e}_{t.} = E\begin{bmatrix} e_{t1}^2 & e_{t1}e_{t2} & \cdots & e_{t1}e_{tG} \\ e_{t2}e_{t1} & e_{t2}^2 & \cdots & e_{t2}e_{tG} \\ \vdots & \vdots & \ddots & \vdots \\ e_{tG}e_{t1} & e_{tG}e_{t2} & \cdots & e_{tG}^2 \end{bmatrix}$$

$$= \begin{bmatrix} \sigma_{11} & \sigma_{12} & \cdots & \sigma_{1G} \\ \sigma_{21} & \sigma_{22} & \cdots & \sigma_{2G} \\ \vdots & \vdots & \ddots & \vdots \\ \sigma_{G1} & \sigma_{G2} & \cdots & \sigma_{GG} \end{bmatrix} = \Sigma, \tag{19.3.8}$$

where σ_{ij} is the *contemporaneous* covariance between the disturbances of the ith and jth equations.

(iii) $E(e_{tj}e_{sk}) = 0$ unless $t = s$.

(2) Γ is nonsingular. This guarantees that the system is complete.

(3) In the case that the predetermined variables X consist solely of purely exogenous variables, predetermined variables which are not lagged endo-

genous variables, it is assumed that $\operatorname{plim}(X'X/T) = Q$, where Q is a finite and nonsingular matrix.

(4) If the system is dynamic, at least one of the predetermined variables is a lagged endogenous variable, it is assumed to be stable. A system of dynamic simultaneous equations is stable if the following holds: assume that the purely exogenous variables of the system are held constant for an infinite time span. Then the endogenous variables (apart from stochastic disturbances) will be at rest at their equilibrium values. Impose a change in any one of the purely exogenous variables for one period and then return it to its original value in the next period and hold it there. If the endogeneous variables, once disturbed, eventually return to their original equilibrium values, the system is stable. A discussion of a necessary and sufficient condition for stability, and a statistical test for such, is reserved for Chapter 24.

19.4 Ordinary Least Squares Estimation of the Reduced Form

The equation system $Y\Gamma + X\Delta + E = 0$ is a system of G equations in G endogenous variables plus predetermined variables and disturbances. Assuming Γ^{-1} exists, we can solve for the current endogenous variables in terms of the predetermined variables and disturbances

$$\begin{aligned} Y\Gamma\Gamma^{-1} + X\Delta\Gamma^{-1} + E\Gamma^{-1} &= 0, \\ Y &= -X\Delta\Gamma^{-1} - E\Gamma^{-1} \\ &= X\Pi + V \quad \text{(the reduced form)}, \end{aligned} \tag{19.4.1}$$

where Π is the $K \times G$ matrix of reduced form parameters and $V = -E\Gamma^{-1}$ is the $T \times G$ matrix of reduced form disturbances. Note that the ith column of Π contains the reduced form coefficients for the ith endogenous variable. That is,

$$\mathbf{y}_{.i} = X\Pi_{.i} + \mathbf{v}_{.i}$$

or

$$y_{ti} = \sum_{j=1}^{K} x_{tj}\Pi_{ji} + v_{ti}, \qquad t = 1, \ldots, T,$$

is the ith reduced form equation.

We are interested in examining the ordinary least squares estimator $\hat{\Pi} = (X'X)^{-1}X'Y$ of the reduced form parameter matrix Π. The estimator is a least squares estimator in the sense that it minimizes the sum of squares defined by $|\hat{V}'\hat{V}|$, where $\hat{V} = Y - X\hat{\Pi}$. See Goldberger (1964, p. 201) for a proof of this result. In Chapter 23 we examine other methods of estimating Π and compare their efficiency to the efficiency of the ordinary least squares estimator. First we establish the precision of the ordinary least squares estimator. The next two theorems lay the groundwork for the major result contained in Theorem 19.4.3.

Theorem 19.4.1. *Let* $\mathbf{v}_{t.}$ *be the* tth *row of* $V = -E\Gamma^{-1}$. *Then the vectors* $\mathbf{v}'_{t.}$ *($G \times 1$ column vectors) are independently and identically distributed as* $N(\mathbf{0}, \Omega)$, *where* $\Omega = (\Gamma^{-1})'\Sigma\Gamma^{-1}$.

PROOF. Note that $\mathbf{v}'_{t.} = (-\mathbf{e}_{t.}\Gamma^{-1})' = -(\Gamma^{-1})'\mathbf{e}'_{t.}$. But the $G \times 1$ vectors $\mathbf{e}'_{t.}$ are independently and identically distributed $N(\mathbf{0}, \Sigma)$. Therefore,

$$\operatorname{var}[(-\Gamma^{-1})'\mathbf{e}'_{t.}] = (-\Gamma^{-1})'\operatorname{var}(\mathbf{e}'_{t.})(-\Gamma^{-1}) = (\Gamma^{-1})'\Sigma(\Gamma^{-1}) = \Omega. \quad \square$$

Theorem 19.4.2. $Q = \operatorname{plim}(X'X/T)$ *is finite and nonsingular and* $\operatorname{vec}(X'V/\sqrt{T})$ *is asymptotically distributed as* $N(\mathbf{0}, \Omega \otimes Q)$.

PROOF. Consider the case where X *consists solely of purely exogenous variables.* Then $Q = \operatorname{plim}(X'X/T)$ is finite and nonsingular by assumption. Also

$$\operatorname{vec}\left(\frac{X'V}{\sqrt{T}}\right) = \frac{1}{\sqrt{T}}\begin{bmatrix} X'\mathbf{v}_{.1} \\ X'\mathbf{v}_{.2} \\ \vdots \\ X'\mathbf{v}_{.G} \end{bmatrix}.$$

Note

$$\operatorname{vec}(A) = \begin{bmatrix} A_{.1} \\ A_{.2} \\ \vdots \\ A_{.n} \end{bmatrix}_{mn \times 1},$$

where A is a $m \times n$ matrix with columns $A_{.1}, A_{.2}, \ldots, A_{.n}$. $\operatorname{Vec}(X'V/\sqrt{T})$ is normally distributed (since linear combinations of multivariate normal random variables are normal) with mean vector zero since

$$EX'\mathbf{v}_{.i} = \mathbf{0}, \qquad i = 1, 2, \ldots, G, \tag{19.4.2}$$

and asymptotic covariance matrix

$$\lim_{T\to\infty} E\frac{1}{T}\begin{bmatrix} X'\mathbf{v}_{.1} \\ X'\mathbf{v}_{.2} \\ \vdots \\ X'\mathbf{v}_{.G} \end{bmatrix}[\mathbf{v}'_{.1}X \quad \mathbf{v}'_{.2}X \quad \cdots \quad \mathbf{v}'_{.G}X] = \begin{bmatrix} Q\Omega_{11} & Q\Omega_{12} & \cdots & Q\Omega_{1G} \\ Q\Omega_{21} & Q\Omega_{22} & \cdots & Q\Omega_{2G} \\ \vdots & \vdots & & \vdots \\ Q\Omega_{G1} & Q\Omega_{G2} & \cdots & Q\Omega_{GG} \end{bmatrix}$$

$$= \Omega \otimes Q, \tag{19.4.3}$$

where $\otimes$ denotes the usual Kronecker product operator. The result of (19.4.3) follows from the facts that

$$E\frac{1}{T}[X'\mathbf{v}_{.i}\mathbf{v}'_{.j}X] = E\frac{1}{T}X'\begin{bmatrix} v_{1i} \\ v_{2i} \\ \vdots \\ v_{Ti} \end{bmatrix}[v_{1j} \quad v_{2j} \quad \cdots \quad v_{Tj}]X$$

$$= \frac{1}{T}X'E\begin{bmatrix} v_{1i}v_{1j} & v_{1i}v_{2j} & \cdots & v_{1i}v_{Tj} \\ v_{2i}v_{1j} & v_{2i}v_{2j} & & v_{2i}v_{Tj} \\ \vdots & & \ddots & \vdots \\ v_{Ti}v_{1j} & & \cdots & v_{Ti}v_{Tj} \end{bmatrix}X.$$

But $\mathbf{v}'_{t.}$ is independently and identically distributed $N(\mathbf{0}, \Omega)$. Therefore, $E(v_{ti}v_{sj}) = \Omega_{ij}$ if $t = s$ but zero otherwise and finally

$$E\frac{1}{T}[X'\mathbf{v}_{.i}\mathbf{v}'_{.j}X] = \frac{1}{T}X'(\Omega_{ij}I)X = \Omega_{ij}\frac{X'X}{T}.$$

When X contains lagged endogenous variables the proof is not as straightforward. For a detailed proof of this case see Schmidt (1976, pp. 122, 259). □

The following theorem describes the properties of the ordinary least squares estimator of Π.

Theorem 19.4.3. *The ordinary least squares estimator of* Π, $\hat{\Pi}$, *is consistent and*

$$\sqrt{T}\,\operatorname{vec}(\hat{\Pi} - \Pi) \overset{\text{asy}}{\sim} N(\mathbf{0}, \Omega \otimes Q^{-1}).$$

PROOF.

$$\sqrt{T}\,\operatorname{vec}(\hat{\Pi} - \Pi) = \sqrt{T}\begin{bmatrix}(X'X)^{-1}X'\mathbf{y}_{.1} - \Pi_{.1}\\ (X'X)^{-1}X'\mathbf{y}_{.2} - \Pi_{.2}\\ \vdots \\ (X'X)^{-1}X'\mathbf{y}_{.G} - \Pi_{.G}\end{bmatrix}$$

$$= \sqrt{T}\begin{bmatrix}(X'X)^{-1}X'(X\Pi_{.1} + \mathbf{v}_{.1}) - \Pi_{.1}\\ \vdots \\ (X'X)^{-1}X'(X\Pi_{.G} + \mathbf{v}_{.G}) - \Pi_{.G}\end{bmatrix}$$

$$= \begin{bmatrix}\left(\dfrac{X'X}{T}\right)^{-1}\dfrac{X'\mathbf{v}_{.1}}{\sqrt{T}}\\ \vdots \\ \left(\dfrac{X'X}{T}\right)^{-1}\dfrac{X'\mathbf{v}_{.G}}{\sqrt{T}}\end{bmatrix}$$

$$= \begin{bmatrix}\left(\dfrac{X'X}{T}\right)^{-1} & & 0\\ & \ddots & \\ 0 & & \left(\dfrac{X'X}{T}\right)^{-1}\end{bmatrix}\operatorname{vec}\left(\frac{X'V}{\sqrt{T}}\right)$$

$$= \left[I \otimes \left(\frac{X'X}{T}\right)^{-1}\right]\operatorname{vec}\left(\frac{X'V}{\sqrt{T}}\right).$$

We know that $\text{vec}(X'V/\sqrt{T}) \overset{\text{asy}}{\sim} N(\mathbf{0}, \Omega \otimes Q)$ and hence $\sqrt{T}\,\text{vec}(\hat{\Pi} - \Pi)$ is asymptotically normally distributed with mean vector $\mathbf{0}$ and variance–covariance matrix

$$\text{plim}\left[I \otimes \left(\frac{X'X}{T}\right)^{-1}\right](\Omega \otimes Q)\left[I \otimes \left(\frac{X'X}{T}\right)^{-1}\right] = \Omega \otimes Q^{-1}$$

since $\text{plim}(X'X/T)^{-1} = Q^{-1}$. □

Thus, we have shown that although the reduced form coefficients can be consistently estimated by ordinary least squares, the coefficients of any single structural equation cannot. For a detailed general proof of this latter result see Schmidt (1976, pp. 126–128). Now the question is, is it possible to deduce the parameters of the structural model given knowledge of the reduced form parameters? This is the next topic to be considered as we study the identification problem in Chapter 20.

19.5 Summary and Guide to Further Readings

Economics is a discipline in which it is recognized from first principles that variables under consideration are jointly or simultaneously determined. Econometric models that specify interdependent, simultaneous relationships pose problems for investigators who wish to give empirical content to economic theories. In particular, it is shown that application of ordinary least squares estimators to individual structural equations is unsatisfactory because of the nonzero covariance between the error term and endogenous variables on the right hand side of the equation. This violation of a basic least squares assumption renders the resulting estimator inconsistent. Reduced form equations, which express each endogenous variable solely as a function of exogenous and predetermined variables plus disturbances, however, are such that the ordinary least squares estimator yields consistent estimates.

Further readings relevant to this chapter include several classic papers. Marschak (1953) discusses the usefulness of economic models and the need for structural estimation in a clear and nontechnical way. Haavelmo (1943) discusses the consequences of simultaneous equations for ordinary least squares. Lui (1960) and Fisher (1961) consider and discuss problems associated with the fact that structural systems as specified are only approximations to reality.

Also relevant to this chapter are readings that illustrate the nature and usefulness of simultaneous equations models, which also will provide some insight into the model building process. An excellent general reference in this regard is Intriligator (1978), Chapters 12–16. Intriligator considers applications of simultaneous equations models to macroeconomics, industrial organization, labor economics, and other areas. He then discusses the uses of simultaneous equations models for structural analysis, forecasting and policy evaluation. Other sources include Girschick and Haavelmo (1953), who discuss, in general terms, simultaneous equations models and model building and develop a system of simultaneous equations for food. Wallis (1973) discusses examples of microeconomic and macroeconomic simultaneous equations systems. The *International Economic Review* published a symposium on Econometric Model Performance in the June and October 1974 issues and the February 1975 issue. These papers discuss the structure and performance of many macro-econometric models and represent a rich source of material for understanding such models.

19.6 Exercises

19.1. Put Klein's Model I, discussed in this chapter, into the notation of (19.3.2).

19.2. Strickland and Weiss (1976) specify a system of equations concerning advertising, concentration and price-cost margins. A slightly modified version is

$$\begin{aligned} Ad/S &= \beta_0 + \beta_1 C + \beta_2 M + \beta_3(CD/S) + \beta_4 Gr + \beta_5 Dur + e_1, \\ C &= \alpha_0 + \alpha_1(Ad/S) + \alpha_2(MES/S) + e_2, \\ M &= \gamma_0 + \gamma_1 C + \gamma_2 Gr + \gamma_3(Ad/S) + \gamma_4(MES/S) + \gamma_5(K/S) + \gamma_6 GD + e_3, \end{aligned}$$

where $Ad \equiv$ advertising expense,
$S \equiv$ value of shipments,
$C \equiv$ four-firm concentration ratio,
$CD \equiv$ consumer demand,
$MES \equiv$ minimum efficient scale,
$M \equiv$ price/cost margin,
$Gr \equiv$ annual rate of growth of industrial production,
$Dur \equiv$ dummy variable for durable goods industry,
$K \equiv$ capital stock,
$GD \equiv$ measure of geographic dispersion of output.

Classify these variables as endogenous or exogenous and put the three structural equations into the notation of (19.3.2).

19.7 References

Fisher, F. (1961). The cost of approximate specification in simultaneous equation estimation. *Econometrica*, **29**, 139–170.

Girschick, M. and Haavelmo, T. (1953). Statistical analysis of the demand for food: examples of simultaneous estimation of structural equations. In *Studies in Econometric Method*. Edited by N. Hood and T. Koopmans. New York: Wiley. Pp. 92–112.

Goldberger, A. (1964). *Econometric Theory*. New York: Wiley.

Haavelmo, T. (1943). The statistical implications of a system of simultaneous equations. *Econometrica*, **11**, 1–12.

Intriligator, M. (1978). *Econometric Models, Techniques and Applications*. Englewood Cliffs, NJ: Prentice-Hall.

Klein, L. (1950). *Economic Fluctuations in the United States, 1921–1941*. Cowles Commission Monograph No. 11. New York: Wiley.

Lui, T. (1960). Underidentification, structural estimation and forecasting. *Econometrica*, **29**, 855–865.

Marschak, J. (1953). Economic measurements for policy and prediction. In *Studies in Econometric Method*. Edited by W. Hood and T. Koopmans. New York: Wiley. Pp. 1–27.

Schmidt, P. (1976). *Econometrics*. New York: Marcel Dekker.

Strickland, A. and Weiss, L. (1976). Advertising, concentration and price–cost margins. *Journal of Political Economy*, **84**, 1109–1121.

Wallis, K. (1973). Simultaneous equation systems. In *Topics in Applied Econometrics*. London: Gray-Mills. Pp. 98–127.

CHAPTER 20

Identification

20.1 Introduction

Study of the identification problem is a precursor to the estimation problem in simultaneous equations. When the number of observations exceeds the number of exogenous variables in the model, ordinary least squares provides a method for consistently estimating the reduced form parameters via $\hat{\Pi} = (X'X)^{-1}X'Y$, as shown in the previous chapter. Though Π can be consistently estimated, such information cannot always be used to infer values for the structural parameters Γ and Δ. This is the essence of the identification problem. Does the investigator have enough available information to make statistical statements concerning the structure of a given simultaneous equations model?

In the following section the concept of identification is defined and the information contained in the data alone is examined. In Section 20.3 the identification problem is shown to be confined to linear transformations of the structure while in Section 20.4 the use of linear homogenous restrictions on the structural parameters is shown to be a means of identification. The identification power of covariance restrictions and the theory of recursive simultaneous equations is briefly examined in Sections 20.5 and 20.6. A summary and suggestions for further readings are in Section 20.7.

20.2 The Identification Problem

In Chapter 19 it was shown that ordinary least squares applied to each reduced form equation provides a consistent method for estimating the reduced form parameters of a simultaneous equation system. In fact, it can be argued that the estimates of Π contain all the information in the sample observations about the structural parameters Γ and Δ. Later it is shown that the data contain K independent "bits" of information. Consequently, while the K parameters of any reduced form equation can be estimated consistently, consistent estimation of $G + K$ parameters of a structural equation requires, in addition, G independent bits of nonsample information. To make these ideas more precise we introduce the following definition.

Definition 20.2.1. A structural parameter is identified if and only if its value can be deduced from knowledge of the reduced form parameters. If a parameter's value can not be inferred from knowledge of the reduced form parameters, it is unidentified. A structural equation is identified if all its parameters are identified.

The following theorem and its proof make quite clear that, without nonsample information on the structural parameters Γ and Δ, none of the parameters of any structural equation are identified.

Theorem 20.2.1. *In the absence of nonsample information about the structural parameters of an equation* none *of the structural parameters are identified.*

PROOF. The structural model $Y\Gamma + X\Delta + E = 0$ has reduced form $Y = -X\Delta\Gamma^{-1} - E\Gamma^{-1}$. Let A be any $G \times G$ nonsingular matrix of constants. Consider the structural model

$$Y\Gamma^* + X\Delta^* + E^* = 0,$$

where $\Gamma^* = \Gamma A$, $\Delta^* = \Delta A$, and $E^* = EA$. This structural model has the reduced form

$$\begin{aligned} Y &= -X\Delta^*(\Gamma^*)^{-1} - E^*(\Gamma^*)^{-1} = -X\Delta A A^{-1}\Gamma^{-1} - EAA^{-1}\Gamma^{-1} \\ &= -X\Delta\Gamma^{-1} - E\Gamma^{-1}, \end{aligned}$$

which is, of course, identical to the reduced form of the original system. Consequently, even if Π were known *exactly* and not estimated, we could not tell whether the true structural parameters were Γ and Δ or Γ^* and Δ^*, and, thus, the structural parameters are not identified in any equation. □

Now the question is, "What sort of nonsample information can be used in conjunction with the sample data to identify the structural parameters?" One answer to this question is motivated by the following series of examples.

The basic problem facing us now is that we must impose enough prior information on the structure so that "any" A matrix will not produce the same reduced form. Consider first a simple demand and supply model where $y_{t1} \equiv q_t$ is the tth observation on equilibrium quantity and $y_{t2} \equiv p_t$ is the tth observation on equilibrium price. Then the structure is

$$\begin{aligned} \Gamma_{11}q_t + \Gamma_{21}p_t + \Delta_{11} + e_{t1} &= 0 \quad \text{(demand)}, \\ \Gamma_{12}q_t + \Gamma_{22}p_t + \Delta_{12} + e_{t2} &= 0 \quad \text{(supply)}, \end{aligned} \tag{20.2.1}$$

where the first equation is the demand equation and the second is the supply equation. In this example, economic theory embodied in our structural model implies that the data points (q_t, p_t) are clustered around a supply and demand equilibrium as illustrated in Figure 20.2.1. Unfortunately, if this is *all* that economic theory says about how the data is generated, then we have no hope of estimating the slope and intercept parameters of the supply and demand relations, no matter how many observations are available.

In the context of Theorem 20.2.1 let the nonsingular matrix A be

$$A = \begin{bmatrix} a_{11} & a_{12} \\ a_{21} & a_{22} \end{bmatrix}.$$

Postmultiplying our simultaneous equation system (20.2.1) by A yields a structure with a first equation of

$$(a_{11}\Gamma_{11} + a_{21}\Gamma_{12})q_t + (a_{11}\Gamma_{21} + a_{21}\Gamma_{22})p_t + (a_{11}\Delta_{11} + a_{21}\Delta_{12}) + (a_{11}e_{t1} + a_{21}e_{t2}) = 0$$

or

$$\Gamma_{11}^* q_t + \Gamma_{21}^* p_t + \Delta_{11}^* + e_{t1}^* = 0.$$

The same result holds for the second equation. Postmultiplication of the system by A has generated a new system whose equations "look" exactly like the equations of the original system *and* each other, and whose coefficients are linear combinations of corresponding parameters from both equations in the original system. It is this result, that the equations in the transformed system can not be distinguished from the equations in the original system, that is the source of our difficulty. This notion will be formalized shortly, but for now, let us continue.

Consider the addition of the exogenous variable income y_t to the demand equation. Then the structural system is

$$\Gamma_{11}q_t + \Gamma_{21}p_t + \Delta_{11} + \Delta_{21}y_t + e_{t1} = 0,$$
$$\Gamma_{12}q_t + \Gamma_{22}p_t + \Delta_{12} + \Delta_{22}y_t + e_{t2} = 0,$$

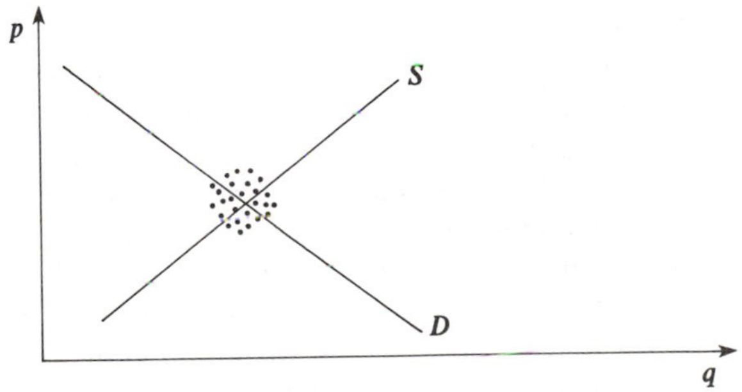

Figure 20.2.1 A supply and demand model.

or, assuming $\Delta_{22} = 0$,

$$\Gamma_{11}q_t + \Gamma_{21}p_t + \Delta_{11} + \Delta_{21}y_t + e_{t1} = 0,$$
$$\Gamma_{12}q_t + \Gamma_{22}p_t + \Delta_{12} + e_{t2} = 0.$$

By restricting income to appear only in the demand function the parameter Δ_{22} is restricted to zero. Post-multiplying the system by an arbitrary matrix A yields, for the first equation,

$$\Gamma_{11}^* q_t + \Gamma_{21}^* p_t + \Delta_{11}^* + \Delta_{21}^* y_t + e_{t1}^* = 0.$$

This equation looks just like the demand equation in the original structure. However, it is clear that it is *not* the supply curve since it contains the exogenous variable y_t. Thus, the restriction that $\Delta_{22} = 0$, based on the notion that income affects demand but not supply, has created a difference between the supply function and linear combinations of the structural equations. Alternatively, we now have an economic model that proposes that the equilibrium data points observed are generated by a shifting demand curve and a stationary supply curve (Figure 20.2.2). The data trace the supply curve and we can estimate the slope and intercept of the supply function.

Thus, the supply curve is identified because it *can* be distinguished from any linear combination of equations in the system. We have identified it by setting one of its coefficients to zero, so that the *other* equation will shift independently, producing equilibrium observations along it, which permits estimation of its slope and intercept.

Finally, consider adding an exogenous weather variable w to the supply equation but not to the demand equation. Then our system is

$$\Gamma_{11}q_t + \Gamma_{21}p_t + \Delta_{11} + \Delta_{21}y_t + \Delta_{31}w_t + e_{t1} = 0,$$
$$\Gamma_{12}q_t + \Gamma_{22}p_t + \Delta_{12} + \Delta_{22}y_t + \Delta_{32}w_t + e_{t2} = 0,$$

or

$$\begin{aligned} \Gamma_{11}q_t + \Gamma_{21}p_t + \Delta_{11} + \Delta_{21}y_t + e_{t1} &= 0, \\ \Gamma_{12}q_t + \Gamma_{22}p_t + \Delta_{12} + \Delta_{32}w_t + e_{t2} &= 0, \end{aligned} \tag{20.2.2}$$

where we have imposed the restrictions $\Delta_{31} = \Delta_{22} = 0$. Now each equation has an independent shift variable, and thus both curves can be traced out by the data. Each equation is identified. This can be verified by noting that any linear combination of the two equations does not look like either a demand or supply function. Thus, this combination of *a priori* restrictions leads to the identification of the two equations since each now can be distinguished from arbitrary linear combinations of the structural equations.

Before going on to formalize the ideas in this series of examples, we note one additional point. It is customary to write simultaneous systems like usual regression models with a single endogenous variable on the left-hand side of the equation and everything else on the right-hand side. This is achieved

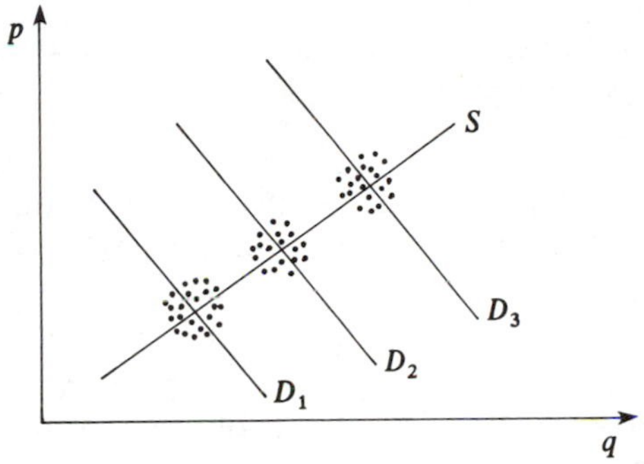

Figure 20.2.2

by "solving" each structural equation for one endogenous variable in terms of all the remaining variables in the equation *and* the error term. For instance, we can multiply the first equation in (20.2.2) by $(1/-\Gamma_{11})$ and obtain

$$q_t = -(\Gamma_{21}/\Gamma_{11})p_t - (\Delta_{11}/\Gamma_{11}) - (\Delta_{21}/\Gamma_{11})y_t - (1/\Gamma_{11})e_{t1}. \quad (20.2.3)$$

This does nothing to the validity of the structural system because it is quite clear that we could multiply a structural equation on both sides by *any* constant and not affect its correctness. This also shows that the parameters of any structural equation are in this sense arbitrary since we cannot distinguish them from any proportional set. Consequently, choosing one endogenous variable to appear on the left-hand side of an equation can be thought of as *normalizing* the parameters of an equation. That is, choosing one of the infinitely many proportional and equally "correct" parameter vectors to estimate. It should be clear that the choice of the endogenous variable to appear on the left hand side is, in most cases, completely arbitrary for each equation and can be made for the investigators convenience. When a normalization rule is selected one usually writes (20.2.3) as

$$q_t = \Gamma_{21}p_t + \Delta_{11} + \Delta_{21}y_t + e_{t1},$$

thus, only implicitly recognizing that the parameter values are *relative* to $-\Gamma_{11}$. We now turn to the matter of providing a theoretical foundation for the above informal discussion of admissable transformations.

20.3 Admissible Transformations

The system $Y\Gamma + X\Delta + E = 0$ can be written as

$$[Y : X]\begin{bmatrix}\Gamma \\ \Delta\end{bmatrix} + E = Z\mathrm{B} + E = 0. \quad (20.3.1)$$

Adopting this notation we have the following theorem:

Theorem 20.3.1. *If the structure is written* $Z\mathrm{B} + E = 0$ *then* $\boldsymbol{\beta}_{.i}$, *the* ith *column of* B, *can be distinguished from an arbitrary* $(G + K) \times 1$ *vector* $\boldsymbol{\alpha}$ *on the basis of observational information alone if and only if* $\boldsymbol{\alpha}$ is not *a linear combination of the columns of* B.

Proof. Let p be the event that $\boldsymbol{\beta}_{.i}$ can be distinguished from $\boldsymbol{\alpha}$ and $\bar{p}$ the event that $\boldsymbol{\beta}_{.i}$ cannot be distinguished from $\boldsymbol{\alpha}$, q that $\boldsymbol{\alpha}$ is not a linear combination of $\boldsymbol{\beta}_{.i}$, $i = 1, 2, \ldots G$, and $\bar{q}$ that $\boldsymbol{\alpha}$ is a linear combination of $\boldsymbol{\beta}_{.i}$, $i = 1, 2, \ldots, G$. What we want to show is that p implies $(\rightarrow)$ q and $q \rightarrow p$ or equivalently $\bar{q} \rightarrow \bar{p}$ and $\bar{p} \rightarrow \bar{q}$. Theorem 20.2.1 proves $\bar{q} \rightarrow \bar{p}$. Now to prove $\bar{p} \rightarrow \bar{q}$, we proceed as follows. Recall that all possible observational information about Δ and Γ is contained in the reduced form parameters Π. Furthermore, since $\Pi = -\Delta\Gamma^{-1}$, the data provide the matrix equation $\Pi\Gamma + \Delta = 0$ or

$$(\Pi, I)\begin{bmatrix}\Gamma \\ \Delta\end{bmatrix} = 0,$$

$$(\Pi, I)\mathrm{B} = 0 \tag{20.3.2}$$

and, thus, $(\Pi, I)\,\boldsymbol{\beta}_{.i} = \mathbf{0}$. Hence, if $\boldsymbol{\alpha}$ is to be indistinguishable from $\boldsymbol{\beta}_{.i}$ on the basis of observational information alone, it must be the case that $(\Pi, I)\,\boldsymbol{\alpha} = \mathbf{0}$. Therefore $\boldsymbol{\alpha}$ is in the null space of (Π, I). (Let A be an $m \times n$ matrix of rank k. The solutions to $A\mathbf{x} = \mathbf{0}$ form a subspace of E^n whose dimension is $n - k$. The solution subspace in this case is called the null space of A).

Since (Π, I) has $(G + K)$ columns and has rank K the null space of (Π, I) has rank G. Finally, B is of rank G and is also in the null space of (Π, I) and its columns therefore span (form a basis for) the null space of (Π, I). That is, any other vector $\boldsymbol{\alpha}$ in the null space is a linear combination of the columns of B. This proves the theorem. □

This theorem makes clear that identification is a problem of distinguishing the parameters of a particular structural equation from those of linear transformations of the structural model. What must be done now is to determine how much and what type of nonsample information must be used to identify the parameters of a structural equation. The following definition of an admissible transformation matrix is a step in that direction.

Definition 20.3.1. A linear transformation of the model $Y\Gamma + X\Delta + E = 0$, denoted by the $G \times G$ nonsingular transformation matrix A, is *admissible* if and only if

(i) $\mathrm{B}A = \begin{bmatrix}\Gamma \\ \Delta\end{bmatrix}A = \begin{bmatrix}\Gamma A \\ \Delta A\end{bmatrix}$ satisfies all *a priori* restrictions on $\mathrm{B} = \begin{bmatrix}\Gamma \\ \Delta\end{bmatrix}$ and,

(ii) $A'\Sigma A$ satisfies all *a priori* restrictions on Σ.

Note that the error vector $\mathbf{e}_{t.}A = \mathbf{e}_t^*$ of the transformed system $Y\Gamma A + X\Delta A + EA$ has the variance-covariance matrix $\mathrm{var}(\mathbf{e}_{t.}A)' = A'\Sigma A$. Thus, this definition says a transformation is admissible if the transformed model obeys the same *a priori* restrictions as the structural parameters B and the error covariance matrix Σ of the original model.

If we are considering the first equation of the structure, and if no normalization has yet been applied, then, for the parameters of the equation to be identified, any admissible transformation must change $\boldsymbol{\beta}_{.1}$ by at most a scalar multiple. As our previous examples illustrated, when this is the case, the first equation cannot be confused with other equations in the system or linear combinations of them. The following corollary to Theorem 20.3.1 states this result precisely.

Corollary 20.3.1. *The first equation in the model* $ZB + E = 0$ *is identified if and only if the first column, say* A_1, *of any admissible transformation is a vector whose first element is an arbitrary nonzero scalar and whose remaining elements are zero. That is* A_1 *must be of the form* $(c \quad \mathbf{0}')'$, *where* c *denotes a nonzero scalar, if the first equation is identified.*

Note that if a normalization rule has been applied, the admissible transformation can not change $\boldsymbol{\beta}_{.1}$ at all so that the constant c in the corollary must be one.

Let us consider what this corollary means. The first equation is

$$y_{t1}\Gamma_{11} + y_{t2}\Gamma_{21} + \cdots y_{tG}\Gamma_{G1} + x_{t1}\Delta_{11} + x_{t2}\Delta_{21} + \cdots + x_{tK}\Delta_{K1} + e_{t1} = 0.$$

First note that multiplying this equation by a nonzero scalar leaves it intact. Thus, the *most* we can ever hope for is estimating the structural parameters up to a scalar multiple as we noted earlier. Second, we have said that for the equation to be *identified* any admissible transformation (one that is consistent with *all a priori* information on the entire system) must be such that it only changes the parameters in the first equation by a scalar multiple. Third, this combination makes clear that the first equation will be identified (and distinguishable from linear combinations of all other equations) when enough *a priori* restrictions are put on the system so that the *only remaining admissible transformations* alter the first equation by multiplying it by a scalar. Fourth, since the parameters of the first equation can be known only up to a constant multiple we can "normalize" on the coefficient of one variable. Essentially one of the nonzero Γ_{i1} coefficients is divided into all the others. This "picks" out, from all the equally suitable scalar multiples, one particular parameter vector.

20.4 Identification Using Linear Homogeneous Restrictions

For the present we will consider identification of the first equation of a simultaneous equations system by linear homogeneous restrictions on $\boldsymbol{\beta}_{.1}$ of the form

$$\phi\boldsymbol{\beta}_{.1} = \mathbf{0}, \tag{20.4.1}$$

where ϕ is a known $R \times (G + K)$ matrix of rank R. Each row of ϕ represents an independent linear homogeneous restriction on $\boldsymbol{\beta}_{.1}$. A restriction is called a "zero" restriction or an "exclusion" restriction if the corresponding row of ϕ has only one nonzero element. Let $B = [\boldsymbol{\beta}_{.1}, B_{(1)}]$ and $\phi B = [\phi\boldsymbol{\beta}_{.1}, \phi B_{(1)}]$. Then rank (ϕB) = rank $[\phi B_{(1)}] \leq \min(R, G - 1)$. This follows since $\phi B = [\phi\boldsymbol{\beta}_{.1}, \phi B_{(1)}]$ and $\phi\boldsymbol{\beta}_{.1} = \mathbf{0}$. Therefore, rank ϕB = rank $\phi B_{(1)}$. Also $\phi B_{(1)}$ is of dimension $R \times (G - 1)$ and so its rank cannot exceed the minimum of R and $G - 1$.

Theorem 20.4.1 (Rank Condition). *A necessary and sufficient condition for the first equation to be identified by the* a priori *restrictions $\phi\boldsymbol{\beta}_{.1} = \mathbf{0}$ is that*

$$\text{Rank } (\phi B) = G - 1. \tag{20.4.2}$$

PROOF. Let A be a nonsingular transformation matrix with first column A_1; let A_1^* be *all* of A_1 except the first element so that

$$A_1 = \begin{bmatrix} c \\ A_1^* \end{bmatrix},$$

where c is a scalar. Then the first equation is identified if and only if $A_1^* = \mathbf{0}$ for any admissible transformation.

The transformation is admissible if and only if $\phi B A_1 = \mathbf{0}$, but

$$\phi B A_1 = [\phi\boldsymbol{\beta}_{.1}, \phi B_{(1)}]\begin{bmatrix} c \\ A_1^* \end{bmatrix} = \phi B_{(1)} A_1^* \quad \text{since } \phi\boldsymbol{\beta}_{.1} = \mathbf{0}$$

and a necessary and sufficient condition for $\phi B_{(1)} A_1^* = \mathbf{0}$ to imply $A_1^* = \mathbf{0}$ is that $\phi B_{(1)}$ have full column rank. That is $\text{rank}(\phi B_{(1)}) = G - 1$. Since rank (ϕB) = rank $(\phi B_{(1)})$ this proves the theorem. □

Corollary 20.4.1. (Order Condition). *A necessary, but not sufficient, condition for identification is that $R \geq G - 1$.*

Note that the satisfaction of the order condition could fail to identify the first equation in several ways:

First, the coefficients of *another* equation could satisfy all R restrictions on the first equation. Then rank $(\phi B) \leq G - 2$ since two or more columns of ϕB would be zero.

Second, all $G - 1$ other equations could satisfy a particular restriction on the first equation. Then a *row* of ϕB would be zero and such a restriction would not aid in identification. Intuitively, it does not serve to differentiate the first equation from all the remaining equations. An example would be when one variable is excluded from *all* the equations.

In summary, the rank condition provides the following definition.

Definition 20.4.1. The first equation is

underidentified if rank $(\phi \mathrm{B}) < G - 1$;

exactly identified if rank $(\phi \mathrm{B}) = G - 1$ and rank $(\phi) = G - 1$;

overidentified if rank $(\phi \mathrm{B}) = G - 1$ and rank $(\phi) > G - 1$.

The above results on identification under linear homogeneous restrictions can be derived another *equivalent* way, which will be useful to illustrate several points, and in particular the nature of identification as described in Definition 20.2.1.

Theorem 20.4.2. *A necessary and sufficient condition for the identification of the first equation under the restriction* $\phi \boldsymbol{\beta}_{.1} = \mathbf{0}$ *is that*

$$\operatorname{rank}\begin{bmatrix}(\Pi, I_K)\\ \phi\end{bmatrix} = G + K - 1.$$

Proof. Recall that all possible observational information is contained in the reduced form parameters. Since there is no *a priori* knowledge of Σ, all that is available is that

$$\Pi\Gamma = -\Delta \leftrightarrow (\Pi, I)\mathrm{B} = 0$$

and $\phi\boldsymbol{\beta}_{.1} = \mathbf{0}$. Now recall that (Π, I) has $G + K$ columns and rank K. Thus, the restrictions provided by the data for the first equation are

$$(\Pi, I)\boldsymbol{\beta}_{.1} = \mathbf{0}.$$

This confines $\boldsymbol{\beta}_{.1}$ to the G-dimensional null space of (Π, I). Since we wish to confine $\boldsymbol{\beta}_{.1}$ to a one-dimensional null space we must somehow reduce the dimension of the space in which $\boldsymbol{\beta}_{.1}$ lies by $G - 1$. In a sense we need $G - 1$ additional *independent* pieces of information to add to the K independent pieces of information provided by the data. It is $\phi\boldsymbol{\beta}_{.1} = \mathbf{0}$ that contains those additional $G - 1$ independent pieces of information about $\boldsymbol{\beta}_{.1}$. □

Theorem 20.4.2 above simply states that, in order for the combination of observational and *a priori* information to identify the first equation, the linear homogenous equation system

$$\begin{bmatrix}(\Pi, I_K)\\ \phi\end{bmatrix}\boldsymbol{\beta}_{.1} = \mathbf{0} \tag{20.4.3}$$

must confine $\boldsymbol{\beta}_{.1}$ to a one-dimensional vector space. In order for that to occur the rank of $\begin{bmatrix}(\Pi, I_K)\\ \phi\end{bmatrix}$ must be $G + K - 1$ since it has $G + K$ columns. If the conditions of the theorem hold along with a normalization rule for the first equation, then (20.4.3) can be solved for $\boldsymbol{\beta}_{.1}$, illustrating the link between our identification theorems and Definition 20.2.1.

The following examples should illustrate the above results. Consider the two equation system

$$y_{t1}\Gamma_{11} + y_{t2}\Gamma_{21} + x_{t1}\Delta_{11} + x_{t2}\Delta_{21} + e_{t1} = 0,$$
$$y_{t1}\Gamma_{12} + y_{t2}\Gamma_{22} + x_{t1}\Delta_{12} + x_{t2}\Delta_{22} + e_{t2} = 0.$$

EXAMPLE 20.4.1. Assume the *a priori* information $\Delta_{21} = 0$, $\Delta_{12} = 0$. For the first equation then

$$\phi = [0 \quad 0 \quad 0 \quad 1]$$

and

$$\phi\mathbf{B} = [0 \quad 0 \quad 0 \quad 1]\begin{bmatrix} \Gamma_{11} & \Gamma_{12} \\ \Gamma_{21} & \Gamma_{22} \\ \Delta_{11} & \Delta_{12} \\ \Delta_{21} & \Delta_{22} \end{bmatrix}$$
$$= [\Delta_{21} \quad \Delta_{22}] = [0 \quad \Delta_{22}].$$

Rank $(\phi\mathbf{B}) = 1 = G - 1$ and the first equation is identified (exactly) provided $\Delta_{22} \neq 0$.

Similarly for the second equation

$$\phi = [0 \quad 0 \quad 1 \quad 0],$$
$$\phi\mathbf{B} = [\Delta_{11} \quad \Delta_{12}] = [\Delta_{11} \quad 0],$$
$$\text{rank } (\phi\mathbf{B}) = 1 = G - 1 \quad \text{if } \Delta_{11} \neq 0.$$

Alternatively, for the identification of the first equation consider

$$\begin{bmatrix} \Pi, I \\ \phi \end{bmatrix} = \begin{bmatrix} \Pi_{11} & \Pi_{12} & 1 & 0 \\ \Pi_{21} & \Pi_{22} & 0 & 1 \\ 0 & 0 & 0 & 1 \end{bmatrix}.$$

This matrix has rank $G + K - 1 = 3$. Furthermore consider the equations

$$\begin{bmatrix} \Pi, I \\ \phi \end{bmatrix} \boldsymbol{\beta}_{.1} = \mathbf{0}$$

or

$$\begin{bmatrix} \Pi_{11} & \Pi_{12} & 1 & 0 \\ \Pi_{21} & \Pi_{22} & 0 & 1 \\ 0 & 0 & 0 & 1 \end{bmatrix} \begin{bmatrix} \Gamma_{11} \\ \Gamma_{21} \\ \Delta_{11} \\ \Delta_{21} \end{bmatrix} = \begin{bmatrix} 0 \\ 0 \\ 0 \end{bmatrix}.$$

This provides

$$\Pi_{11}\Gamma_{11} + \Pi_{12}\Gamma_{21} + \Delta_{11} = 0, \tag{20.4.4a}$$
$$\Pi_{21}\Gamma_{11} + \Pi_{22}\Gamma_{21} + \Delta_{21} = 0, \tag{20.4.4b}$$
$$\Delta_{21} = 0. \tag{20.4.4c}$$

Equation (20.4.4b) becomes

$$\Pi_{21}\Gamma_{11} + \Pi_{22}\Gamma_{21} = 0,$$

$$\Gamma_{21} = \left[-\frac{\Pi_{21}}{\Pi_{22}}\right]\Gamma_{11}. \tag{20.4.5}$$

Then (20.4.4a) becomes

$$\Pi_{11}\Gamma_{11} + \Pi_{12}\left[\frac{-\Pi_{21}}{\Pi_{22}}\right]\Gamma_{11} + \Delta_{11} = 0, \tag{20.4.6}$$

therefore

$$\Delta_{11} = \left[\frac{\Pi_{21}\Pi_{12}}{\Pi_{22}} - \Pi_{11}\right]\Gamma_{11}. \tag{20.4.7}$$

Now *all* the parameters of the first equation are expressed in terms of a single unknown parameter Γ_{11}. This is *exactly* what it means for the null space of $\begin{bmatrix}\Pi, I\\ \phi\end{bmatrix}$ to be of dimension 1 since $\boldsymbol{\beta}_{.1}$ is now determined up to a scalar multiple. Imposing the normalization rule $\Gamma_{11} = -1$ permits expression of the structural parameters of the first equation in terms of the reduced form parameters alone. The parameters of the second structure equation may be similarly identified.

Example 20.4.2. Suppose $\Delta_{21} = 0$, $\Delta_{22} = 0$. Then

$$\phi = [0 \quad 0 \quad 0 \quad 1],$$
$$\phi B = [\Delta_{21} \quad \Delta_{22}] = [0 \quad 0]$$

which has zero rank. Thus the first equation is underidentified *even* though the order condition is satisfied. The two equations cannot be distinguished.

Example 20.4.3. Suppose $\Delta_{11} = 0$ and $\Delta_{21} = 0$. For the identification of the first equation then

$$\phi = \begin{bmatrix} 0 & 0 & 1 & 0 \\ 0 & 0 & 0 & 1 \end{bmatrix},$$

$$\phi B = \begin{bmatrix} 0 & 0 & 1 & 0 \\ 0 & 0 & 0 & 1 \end{bmatrix}\begin{bmatrix} \Gamma_{11} & \Gamma_{12} \\ \Gamma_{21} & \Gamma_{22} \\ \Delta_{11} & \Delta_{12} \\ \Delta_{21} & \Delta_{22} \end{bmatrix} = \begin{bmatrix} \Delta_{11} & \Delta_{12} \\ \Delta_{21} & \Delta_{22} \end{bmatrix} = \begin{bmatrix} 0 & \Delta_{12} \\ 0 & \Delta_{22} \end{bmatrix}.$$

Rank $(\phi B) = 1 = G - 1$ and rank $(\phi) = 2$ so the first equation is overidentified. The consequences of this can be seen by examining

$$\begin{bmatrix} \Pi, I \\ \phi \end{bmatrix} \boldsymbol{\beta}_{.1} = \mathbf{0},$$

$$\begin{bmatrix} \Pi_{11} & \Pi_{12} & 1 & 0 \\ \Pi_{21} & \Pi_{22} & 0 & 1 \\ 0 & 0 & 1 & 0 \\ 0 & 0 & 0 & 1 \end{bmatrix} \begin{bmatrix} \Gamma_{11} \\ \Gamma_{21} \\ \Delta_{11} \\ \Delta_{21} \end{bmatrix} = \begin{bmatrix} 0 \\ 0 \\ 0 \\ 0 \end{bmatrix}$$

which gives

$$\begin{aligned} \Pi_{11}\Gamma_{11} + \Pi_{12}\Gamma_{21} + \Delta_{11} &= 0, \\ \Pi_{21}\Gamma_{11} + \Pi_{22}\Gamma_{21} + \Delta_{21} &= 0, \\ \Delta_{11} &= 0, \\ \Delta_{21} &= 0. \end{aligned}$$

On setting $\Gamma_{11} = -1$ this gives

$$\Gamma_{21} = \frac{\Pi_{11}}{\Pi_{12}} = \frac{\Pi_{21}}{\Pi_{22}}. \tag{20.4.8}$$

This does not imply a contradiction, for both values of Γ_{21} are identical. *Overidentification provides multiple solutions for structural parameters in terms of reduced form parameters.* We will return to this point when we discuss the efficiency of the indirect least squares estimation method in the overidentified case (see Chapter 21).

The prior specification and normalization rules $\Gamma_{11} = \Gamma_{22} = -1$ yield the model

$$-y_{t1} + y_{t2}\Gamma_{21} + e_{t1} = 0, \tag{20.4.9}$$

$$y_{t1}\Gamma_{12} - y_{t2} + x_{t1}\Delta_{12} + x_{t2}\Delta_{22} + e_{t2} = 0, \tag{20.4.10}$$

substituting (20.4.9) into (20.4.10) yields

$$(y_{t2}\Gamma_{21} + e_{t1})\Gamma_{12} - y_{t2} + x_{t1}\Delta_{12} + x_{t2}\Delta_{22} + e_{t2} = 0$$

or

$$y_{t2}(\Gamma_{21}\Gamma_{12} - 1) + x_{t1}\Delta_{12} + x_{t2}\Delta_{22} + e_{t2} + \Gamma_{12}e_{t1} = 0$$

and, therefore,

$$y_{t2} = \frac{-x_{t1}\Delta_{12}}{\Delta} - \frac{x_{t2}\Delta_{22}}{\Delta} - \frac{(e_{t2} + \Gamma_{12}e_{t1})}{\Delta},$$

where $\Delta = \Gamma_{21}\Gamma_{12} - 1$. Thus

$$\begin{aligned} y_{t1} &= y_{t2}\Gamma_{21} + e_{t1} \\ &= \frac{-x_{t1}\Delta_{12}}{\Delta}\Gamma_{21} - \frac{x_{t2}\Delta_{22}}{\Delta}\Gamma_{21} - \frac{(e_{t2} + \Gamma_{12}e_{t1})}{\Delta}\Gamma_{21} + e_{t1}. \end{aligned}$$

The matrix of reduced form coefficients is then

$$\Pi = \begin{bmatrix} \Pi_{11} & \Pi_{12} \\ \Pi_{21} & \Pi_{22} \end{bmatrix} = \begin{bmatrix} -\dfrac{\Delta_{12}}{\Delta}\Gamma_{21} & -\dfrac{\Delta_{12}}{\Delta} \\ -\dfrac{\Delta_{22}}{\Delta}\Gamma_{21} & -\dfrac{\Delta_{22}}{\Delta} \end{bmatrix}.$$

Thus, although Π is 2×2, it only has rank one. This is an example of overidentification. Only one prior restriction is needed to identify the first equation but we have two. The consequence is a *restriction on the reduced form*

$$\begin{bmatrix} \Pi_{11} \\ \Pi_{21} \end{bmatrix} - \begin{bmatrix} \Pi_{12} \\ \Pi_{22} \end{bmatrix}\Gamma_{21} = \begin{bmatrix} 0 \\ 0 \end{bmatrix}.$$

The result that overidentification gives rise to restrictions on the reduced form will be examined more closely when we turn to efficient estimation of the reduced form parameters (see Chapter 23).

20.5 Identification Using Covariance Restrictions

In this section we will investigate the identification power of *a priori* information that the disturbances of an equation, the first, is uncorrelated with the disturbance(s) in some other equation(s). That is $\sigma_{1j} = 0$ for some $j \neq 1$. Let

$$\begin{aligned} J_1 &= \{j \mid \sigma_{1j} \neq 0, j = 1, 2, \ldots, G\} \\ J_2 &= \{j \mid \sigma_{1j} = 0, j = 1, 2, \ldots, G\}. \end{aligned}$$

Let the equations in J_1 be the first g_1 equations, and those in J_2 be the last g_2, $g_1 + g_2 = G$. Partition Σ and any transformation matrix A conformably as

$$\Sigma = \begin{bmatrix} \Sigma_{11} & \Sigma_{12} \\ \Sigma_{21} & \Sigma_{22} \end{bmatrix}, \qquad A = \begin{bmatrix} A_{11} & A_{12} \\ A_{21} & A_{22} \end{bmatrix},$$

where Σ_{11} and A_{11} are $g_1 \times g_1$. Now if $\sigma_{1j} = 0$, $j \in J_2$, the first row of Σ_{12} and first column of Σ_{21} are zero. Any admissible transformation A is such that $A'\Sigma A$ satisfies these same restrictions. Therefore, an admissible transformation must be such that the first column of the lower left-hand block of $A'\Sigma A$ must be zero.

$$(A'_{12} \quad A'_{22})\begin{bmatrix}\Sigma_{11} & \Sigma_{12}\\ \Sigma_{21} & \Sigma_{22}\end{bmatrix}A_1 = \mathbf{0}, \tag{20.5.1}$$

where, again, A_1 is the first column of A. The covariance matrix $A'\Sigma A$ satisfies the *a priori* restrictions on Σ if and only if (20.5.1) is true.

Lemma 20.5.1. *A necessary condition for the identification of the first equation is that for every admissible transformation A*

$$\text{rank}\begin{bmatrix}\phi\text{B}\\ (A'_{12}, A'_{22})\Sigma\end{bmatrix} = G - 1. \tag{20.5.2}$$

Proof. For the first equation to be identified $A_1 = \begin{bmatrix} c \\ \mathbf{0}\end{bmatrix}$. Therefore

$$\begin{bmatrix}\phi\text{B}\\ (A'_{12}, A'_{22})\Sigma\end{bmatrix}A_1 = \mathbf{0}. \tag{20.5.3}$$

The solution space of (20.5.3) is of dimension one if and only if

$$\text{rank}\begin{bmatrix}\phi\text{B}\\ (A'_{12}, A'_{22})\Sigma\end{bmatrix} \text{ is } G - 1.$$ □

Theorem 20.5.1 (Generalized Rank Condition). *A necessary (though not sufficient) condition for identification of the first equation is that*

$$\text{rank}\begin{bmatrix}\phi\text{B}\\ (\Sigma_{21}, \Sigma_{22})\end{bmatrix} = G - 1. \tag{20.5.4}$$

Note, although this matrix is $G \times G$, its maximum rank is $G - 1$ since the first column is zero.

Proof. $A = I$ is an admissible transformation. Then $(A'_{12}, A'_{22})\Sigma = (\Sigma_{12}, \Sigma_{22})$ and the theorem follows from the above lemma. □

Corollary 20.5.1 (Generalized Order Condition). *A necessary condition for the identification of the first equation is that $R + g_2 \geq G - 1$.*

Definition 20.5.1. The ith equation of $ZB + E = 0$ is identified with respect to the jth equation if every admissible transformation A has $a_{ji} = 0$. (This requires that any linear combination of equations which is equivalent to the ith equation not include the jth equation.)

Theorem 20.5.2. *A* sufficient *condition for the identification of the first equation is that*

(i) *the generalized rank condition holds;*
(ii) *every equation in J_2 is identified with respect to every equation in J_1.*

PROOF. Condition (ii) implies that $A_{12} = 0$. For A to be an admissible transformation $A'\Sigma A$ must satisfy the current covariance restrictions. That is

$$[A'_{12}, A'_{22}]\begin{bmatrix}\Sigma_{11} & \Sigma_{12}\\ \Sigma_{21} & \Sigma_{22}\end{bmatrix}A_1 = \mathbf{0}$$

since $A_{12} = 0$

$$[0, A'_{22}]\begin{bmatrix}\Sigma_{11} & \Sigma_{12}\\ \Sigma_{21} & \Sigma_{22}\end{bmatrix}A_1 = \mathbf{0},$$

$$[A'_{22}\Sigma_{21}, A'_{22}\Sigma_{22}]A_1 = \mathbf{0},$$

$$A'_{22}[\Sigma_{21}, \Sigma_{22}]A_1 = \mathbf{0}$$

or, equivalently,

$$[\Sigma_{21}, \Sigma_{22}]A_1 = \mathbf{0}$$

since A_{22} is nonsingular. Also for admissibility $\phi \mathrm{B} A_1 = \mathbf{0}$ because the *a priori* restrictions $\phi\boldsymbol{\beta}_{.1}$ are assumed to hold. Therefore,

$$\begin{bmatrix}\phi\mathrm{B}\\ (\Sigma_{21}, \Sigma_{22})\end{bmatrix}A_1 = \mathbf{0}. \tag{20.5.5}$$

But $A_1 = [c \quad \mathbf{0}']'$ is a solution of the homogeneous system of equations (20.5.5) and is unique up to a scalar multiple if and only if the generalized rank condition holds. Recall that the first column of

$$\begin{bmatrix}\phi\mathrm{B}\\ (\Sigma_{21}, \Sigma_{22})\end{bmatrix}$$

is the zero vector and this forces the solution to be of the form $A_1 = (c \quad \mathbf{0}')'$. We now have a sufficient condition for identification in the presence of covariance restrictions. □

Some comments are now appropriate. First, Theorem 20.5.2 proves that if (ii) holds, a necessary and sufficient condition for identification of the first equation is that the generalized rank condition hold. Second, there are no *simple* necessary and sufficient conditions for analyzing identification in the presence of zero covariance restrictions as there are for the case of homogeneous linear restrictions on Γ and Δ. *Each case must be examined separately* except for cases of readily recognizable simple and block recursive systems—see Example 20.5.1 below.

The following example illustrates an important consequence of covariance restrictions.

$$y_{t1}\Gamma_{11} + y_{t2}\Gamma_{21} + y_{t3}\Gamma_{31} + x_{t1}\Delta_{11} + e_{t1} = 0,$$

$$y_{t1}\Gamma_{12} + y_{t2}\Gamma_{22} + y_{t3}\Gamma_{32} + x_{t1}\Delta_{12} + e_{t2} = 0,$$

$$y_{t1}\Gamma_{13} + y_{t2}\Gamma_{23} + y_{t3}\Gamma_{33} + x_{t1}\Delta_{13} + e_{t3} = 0.$$

Let us assume the prior information $\Gamma_{21} = \Gamma_{31} = \Gamma_{32} = 0$. For the first equation

$$\phi B = \begin{bmatrix} 0 & 1 & 0 & 0 \\ 0 & 0 & 1 & 0 \end{bmatrix} \begin{bmatrix} \Gamma_{11} & \Gamma_{12} & \Gamma_{13} \\ \Gamma_{21} & \Gamma_{22} & \Gamma_{23} \\ \Gamma_{31} & \Gamma_{32} & \Gamma_{33} \\ \Delta_{11} & \Delta_{12} & \Delta_{13} \end{bmatrix} = \begin{bmatrix} \Gamma_{21} & \Gamma_{22} & \Gamma_{23} \\ \Gamma_{31} & \Gamma_{32} & \Gamma_{33} \end{bmatrix}$$

$$= \begin{bmatrix} 0 & \Gamma_{22} & \Gamma_{23} \\ 0 & 0 & \Gamma_{33} \end{bmatrix}$$

is of rank $G - 1 = 2$ so the first equation is identified. It is easy to verify that the second and third equations are not.

Suppose, however, that $\sigma_{21} = \sigma_{12} = \sigma_{23} = \sigma_{32} = 0$. Then for the second equation

$$J_1 = \{j \mid \sigma_{2j} \neq 0, j = 1, 2, 3\} = \{2\},$$

$$J_2 = \{j \mid \sigma_{2j} = 0, j = 1, 2, 3\} = \{1, 3\},$$

For a transformation to be admissible, BA must satisfy the restriction on B.

$$\begin{bmatrix} \Gamma_{11} & \Gamma_{12} & \Gamma_{13} \\ \Gamma_{21} & \Gamma_{22} & \Gamma_{23} \\ \Gamma_{31} & \Gamma_{32} & \Gamma_{33} \\ \Delta_{11} & \Delta_{12} & \Delta_{13} \end{bmatrix} [A_1 \quad A_2 \quad A_3] = \begin{bmatrix} \Gamma^*_{11} & \Gamma^*_{12} & \Gamma^*_{13} \\ 0 & \Gamma^*_{22} & \Gamma^*_{23} \\ 0 & 0 & \Gamma^*_{33} \\ \Delta^*_{11} & \Delta^*_{12} & \Delta^*_{13} \end{bmatrix},$$

where A_i, $i = 1, 2, 3$ denotes the ith column of A. Therefore,

$$(\Gamma_{21} \quad \Gamma_{22} \quad \Gamma_{23})A_1 = 0 \Rightarrow \Gamma_{21}a_{11} + \Gamma_{22}a_{21} + \Gamma_{23}a_{31} = 0,$$

$$(\Gamma_{31} \quad \Gamma_{32} \quad \Gamma_{33})A_1 = 0 \Rightarrow \Gamma_{31}a_{11} + \Gamma_{32}a_{21} + \Gamma_{33}a_{31} = 0,$$

$$(\Gamma_{31} \quad \Gamma_{32} \quad \Gamma_{33})A_2 = 0 \Rightarrow \Gamma_{31}a_{12} + \Gamma_{32}a_{22} + \Gamma_{33}a_{32} = 0.$$

And, finally,

$$\Gamma_{33}a_{31} = 0 \Rightarrow a_{31} = 0,$$

$$\Gamma_{33}a_{32} = 0 \Rightarrow a_{32} = 0$$

$$\Gamma_{22}a_{21} + \Gamma_{23}a_{31} = 0 \Rightarrow a_{21} = 0,$$

provides

$$A = \begin{bmatrix} a_{11} & a_{12} & a_{13} \\ 0 & a_{22} & a_{23} \\ 0 & 0 & a_{33} \end{bmatrix}.$$

The covariance restrictions $\sigma_{12} = \sigma_{32} = 0$ then imply

$$\begin{bmatrix} A'_1 \\ A'_2 \\ A'_3 \end{bmatrix} \begin{bmatrix} \sigma_{11} & 0 & \sigma_{13} \\ 0 & \sigma_{22} & 0 \\ \sigma_{31} & 0 & \sigma_{33} \end{bmatrix} (A_1 \quad A_2 \quad A_3) = \begin{bmatrix} \cdot & 0 & \cdot \\ 0 & \cdot & 0 \\ \cdot & 0 & \cdot \end{bmatrix},$$

where $\cdot$ denotes a nonzero value. But $A_1'\Sigma A_2 = 0$ provides

$$[a_{11} \quad 0 \quad 0]\begin{bmatrix} \sigma_{11} & 0 & \sigma_{13} \\ 0 & \sigma_{22} & 0 \\ \sigma_{31} & 0 & \sigma_{33} \end{bmatrix}\begin{bmatrix} a_{12} \\ a_{22} \\ 0 \end{bmatrix} = 0,$$

$$[a_{11}\sigma_{11} \quad 0 \quad a_{11}\sigma_{13}]\begin{bmatrix} a_{12} \\ a_{22} \\ 0 \end{bmatrix} = a_{11}\sigma_{11}a_{12} = 0,$$

and, finally, $a_{12} = 0$. Also

$$\begin{aligned} A_3'\Sigma A_2 = [a_{13} \quad a_{23} \quad a_{33}]\begin{bmatrix} \sigma_{11} & 0 & \sigma_{13} \\ 0 & \sigma_{22} & 0 \\ \sigma_{31} & 0 & \sigma_{33} \end{bmatrix}\begin{bmatrix} a_{12} \\ a_{22} \\ 0 \end{bmatrix} = 0 \\ = a_{13}\sigma_{11}a_{12} + a_{33}\sigma_{31}a_{12} + a_{23}\sigma_{22}a_{22} \\ = a_{23}\sigma_{22}a_{22} \end{aligned}$$

and $a_{23} = 0$. Therefore

$$A = \begin{bmatrix} a_{11} & 0 & a_{13} \\ 0 & a_{22} & 0 \\ 0 & 0 & a_{33} \end{bmatrix}.$$

Now the first and second equations are identified but *not* the third. Further note that since $a_{32} = a_{12} = 0$ the second equation is identified with respect to the first and third equations. The reader should verify that the generalized rank condition holds for the second equation.

Assume, in addition, to the previous covariance restrictions that $\sigma_{13} = \sigma_{31} = 0$. The reader should verify that $a_{13} = 0$ and that the third equation is identified by the generalized rank condition. An equation system where Γ is triangular and Σ diagonal is called a *simple recursive system*. Our example above provides the basis for the following theorem.

Theorem 20.5.3. *In a simple recursive system every equation is identified.*

PROOF. For a detailed proof see Fisher (1966, p. 120). □

20.6 Ordinary Least Squares and Simple Recursive Systems

The following example is used to illustrate the consistency of ordinary least squares in the special case where a simultaneous equation system is a simple recursive one. Consider the model

$$y_{t1} = y_{t2}\Gamma_{21} + x_{t1}\Delta_{11} + e_{t1}, \tag{20.6.1}$$

$$y_{t2} = y_{t1}\Gamma_{12} + x_{t1}\Delta_{12} + e_{t2}. \tag{20.6.2}$$

Suppose we wish to investigate under what conditions y_{t1} could be treated as being exogenous in the sense that $\text{cov}(y_{t1}, e_{t2}) = 0$. Substituting the second equation into the first provides

$$y_{t1} = (y_{t1}\Gamma_{12} + x_{t1}\Delta_{12} + e_{t2})\Gamma_{21} + x_{t1}\Delta_{11} + e_{t1},$$

$$y_{t1} = \frac{x_{t1}\Delta_{12}\Gamma_{21} + x_{t1}\Delta_{11}}{1 - \Gamma_{12}\Gamma_{21}} + \frac{\Gamma_{21}e_{t2} + e_{t1}}{1 - \Gamma_{12}\Gamma_{21}}.$$

Therefore

$$\text{cov}(y_{t1}, e_{t2}) = \frac{\Gamma_{21}\sigma_{22}}{1 - \Gamma_{12}\Gamma_{21}} + \frac{\sigma_{12}}{1 - \Gamma_{12}\Gamma_{21}}. \tag{20.6.3}$$

The first term represents the effect of e_{t2} on y_{t1} by way of y_{t2} while the second term is the effect by way of e_{t1}. Then if $\Gamma_{21} = \sigma_{12} = 0$, $\text{cov}(y_{t1}, e_{t2}) = 0$ and we can take y_{t1} as predetermined in the second equation. With these conditions the system (20.6.1)–(20.6.2) is simple recursive and all equations are identified by Theorem 20.5.3. As the right-hand sides of (20.6.1) and (20.6.2) contain no variables which are contemporaneously correlated with the disturbance terms, ordinary least squares applied to each equation will provide consistent estimates of the structural parameters. This example leads to the following generalization:

Theorem 20.6.1. *Each equation in a simple recursive system can be consistently estimated by ordinary least squares.*

20.7 Summary and Guide to Further Readings

The identification problem involves trying to deduce, from the data, information concerning the structural parameters Γ, Δ, and Σ of simultaneous equation models. In the absence of any prior information in the form of linear homogenous and/or covariance restrictions, the task is impossible. Only the reduced form parameters Π and Ω can be deduced from the data alone. The rank condition (Theorem 20.4.1) provides a necessary and sufficient condition whereby the combination of data and prior information allow Γ, Δ, and Σ to be deduced from Π and Ω. The proof of the theorem involves the theory of sets of linear homogeneous equations and the conditions needed to solve for Γ and Δ in terms of Π. A discussion is also provided on how redundant restrictions result in the order condition (Corollary 20.4.2) being only a necessary condition for identification.

There is no simple identification rule when considering the identification of an equation in the presence of covariance restrictions. Every situation must be investigated on a case by case basis using the concept of admissible transformations. Theorem 20.5.2 provides a sufficient condition for identification. An example was presented to illustrate its usefulness. One exception to the above rule is the simple recursive simultaneous equations system. When Γ is triangular and Σ is diagonal, all equations are identified regardless of the number of exogenous variables present or absent in any given equation. Also in such systems, the endogenous variables on the right-hand side of any given equation can be considered predetermined and ordinary least squares provides a consistent method of estimation.

Further reading on the material contained in this chapter may be found in Fisher's book, *The Identification Problem in Econometrics* (1966) and the series of articles Fisher wrote that formed the basis of the book, which are of course referenced there. Included is not only a treatment of the material in this chapter but also consideration of the problem of nonlinearities in the variables and the *a priori* restrictions. Two classic papers on identification are Koopmans and Hood (1953) and Koopmans *et al.* (1950). These papers represent the starting point for modern thinking about identification.

The basic identification results have been generalized in a variety of ways. Wegge (1965) and Kelly (1975) consider the use of cross equation constraints to aid in the identification of blocks of equations. Richmond (1974) also considers a generalization of the usual identification problem based on the theory of estimable functions. Bowden (1973) and Rothenberg (1971) consider very general identification criteria for structural estimation problems, not confined to simultaneous equation and errors-in-variables models, and where neither the constraints nor the structural model need be linear. These general approaches will become increasingly important as nonlinear models gain wider use by econometricians.

20.8 Exercises

20.1. Consider the simultaneous equation model

$$(y_{t1} \quad y_{t2})\begin{bmatrix} -1 & \Gamma_{12} \\ \Gamma_{21} & -1 \end{bmatrix} + (x_{t1} \quad x_{t2} \quad x_{t3})\begin{bmatrix} \Delta_{11} & \Delta_{12} \\ \Delta_{21} & \Delta_{22} \\ \Delta_{31} & \Delta_{32} \end{bmatrix} + (e_{t1} \quad e_{t2}) = \mathbf{0}',$$

where $E(e_{t1} \quad e_{t2}) = (0 \quad 0)$, $\operatorname{cov}(e_{t1} \quad e_{t2})' = \Sigma$, $\Sigma = \begin{bmatrix} \sigma_{11} & \sigma_{12} \\ \sigma_{21} & \sigma_{22} \end{bmatrix}$, and $(e_{t1} \quad e_{t2})'$ are independently and identically distributed. Investigate the rank and order conditions for identifiability of each equation under each of the following sets of circumstances.

(a) $\Delta_{21} = \Delta_{31} = 0$;
(b) $\Delta_{21} = \Delta_{31} = \sigma_{12} = 0$;
(c) $\Delta_{21} = \Delta_{31} = \Delta_{22} = 0$;
(d) $\Delta_{21} = \Delta_{31} = \sigma_{12} = \Delta_{22} = 0$;
(e) $\Delta_{21} = \Delta_{31} = \Delta_{12} = 0$;
(f) $\Gamma_{12} = 0$;
(g) $\Gamma_{12} = \sigma_{12} = 0$;
(h) $\Delta_{11} + \Delta_{21} = 1$ and $\sigma_{11} = 1$.

20.2. Consider the rank and order conditions for identifiability of each equation in Exercise 19.2.

20.3. Consider the following simultaneous equations system

$$y_{t1} = y_{t2}\Gamma_{21} + y_{t-1,1}\Delta_{11} + x_t\Delta_{21} + e_{t1},$$

$$y_{t2} = y_{t1}\Gamma_{12} + y_{t-1,2}\Delta_{32} + x_t\Delta_{22} + z_t\Delta_{42} + e_{t2},$$

where x_t and z_t are purely exogenous and all usual error assumptions hold.
(a) Check the identifiability of each equation.
(b) Check the identifiability of each equation if $\Gamma_{21} = \Delta_{11} = \Delta_{32} = 0$.
(c) Check the identifiability of each equation if $\Delta_{11} = \Delta_{32} = 0$.

20.4. Consider the system of equations

$$-y_{t1} + y_{t2}\Gamma_{21} + y_{t3}\Gamma_{31} + x_{t1}\Delta_{11} + x_{t2}\Delta_{21} + x_{t3}\Delta_{31} + e_{t1} = 0,$$

$$-y_{t2} + y_{t3}\Gamma_{32} + x_{t1}\Delta_{12} + x_{t2}\Delta_{22} + e_{t2} = 0,$$

$$y_{t1}\Gamma_{13} + y_{t2}\Gamma_{23} - y_{t3} + x_{t1}\Delta_{13} + e_{t3} = 0,$$

when the usual error term asumptions hold.
(a) Determine the identification status of each equation.
(b) How does the identification status of each equation change, if at all, if $\Delta_{12} = \Delta_{13} = 0$?

20.5. Consider the system

$$y_{t1}\Gamma_{11} + y_{t2}\Gamma_{21} + x_{t1}\Delta_{11} + e_{t1} = 0,$$

$$y_{t1}\Gamma_{12} + y_{t2}\Gamma_{22} + x_{t1}\Delta_{12} + e_{t2} = 0.$$

(a) Check the identification of each equation assuming $\Gamma_{21} = 0$ via the admissible transformation approach.
(b) Check the identification of each equation assuming $\Gamma_{21} = \sigma_{12} = 0$ via the admissible transformation approach.

20.6. Check the rank and order conditions for identifiability of each each equation in Klein's Model I (see Exercise 19.1).

20.9 References

Bowden, R. (1973). The theory of parametric identification. *Econometrica*, **41**, 1069–1074.
Fisher, F. (1966). *The Identification Problem in Econometrics*. New York: McGraw-Hill.
Kelly, J. (1975). Linear cross-equation constraints and the identification problem. *Econometrica*, **43**, 125–140.
Koopmans, T. (1953). Identification problems in economic model construction. In *Studies in Econometric Method*. Edited by W. Hood and T. Koopmans, New York: Wiley. Chapter II.
Koopmans, T. and Hood, W. (1953). The estimation of simultaneous linear economic relationships. In *Studies in Econometric Method*. Edited by W. Hood and T. Koopmans. New York: Wiley. Chapter VI.

Koopmans, T., Rubin, H., and Leipnik, R. (1950). Measuring the equation systems of dynamic economics. In *Statistical Inference in Dynamic Economic Models.* Edited by T. Koopmans. New York: Chapter 2.
Richmond, J. (1974). Identifiability in linear models. *Econometrica*, **42**, 731–736.
Rothenberg, T. (1971. Identification in parametric models. *Econometrica*, **39**, 577–592.
Wegge, L. (1965). Identifiability criteria for a system of equations as a whole. *Australian Journal of Statistics*, 67–77.

CHAPTER 21
Limited Information Estimation

21.1 Introduction

In the present chapter we examine several "limited information" estimators that provide consistent estimates of the structural coefficients of the ith equation of a system of simultaneous equations. The term limited information refers to the fact that only the information *specific* to the equation under investigation is utilized in the estimation process. The *a priori* information present in other equations and the fact that the structural disturbances of various equations may be contemporaneously correlated are not used in estimation. The utilization of this additional information would constitute "full information" estimation. Such methods are discussed in the following chapter.

The outline of this chapter is as follows: In Sections 21.2, 21.3, and 21.4 the methods of indirect least squares and two-stages least squares are introduced. Their existence and relative efficiency are examined under varying degrees of identification. In Section 21.5 the asymptotic properties of the two-stage least squares estimators are examined. In Section 21.6 the k-class estimators are defined, and in Section 21.7 the limited information maximum likelihood estimator is defined and shown to be equivalent to the least generalized residual variance estimator and the least variance ratio estimator. A comparison is made between two-stage least squares and these "less" traditional estimators. A summary and guide to further readings are contained in Section 21.8.

21.2 Indirect Least Squares

Consider the following two equation system

$$y_{t1} = y_{t2}\Gamma_{21} + x_{t1}\Delta_{11} + x_{t2}\Delta_{21} + e_{t1}, \tag{21.2.1}$$

$$y_{t2} = y_{t1}\Gamma_{12} + x_{t1}\Delta_{12} + x_{t2}\Delta_{22} + e_{t2}. \tag{21.2.2}$$

Assume the prior information $\Delta_{21} = \Delta_{12} = 0$ is available. Then the information provided by the data and *a priori* reasoning for the first equation is

$$\begin{bmatrix} (\Pi \vdots I) \\ \phi \end{bmatrix} \boldsymbol{\beta}_{.1} = \begin{bmatrix} \Pi_{11} & \Pi_{12} & 1 & 0 \\ \Pi_{21} & \Pi_{22} & 0 & 1 \\ 0 & 0 & 0 & 1 \end{bmatrix} \begin{bmatrix} -1 \\ \Gamma_{21} \\ \Delta_{11} \\ \Delta_{21} \end{bmatrix}$$

$$= \begin{bmatrix} -\Pi_{11} + \Pi_{12}\Gamma_{21} + \Delta_{11} \\ -\Pi_{21} + \Pi_{22}\Gamma_{21} + \Delta_{21} \\ \Delta_{21} \end{bmatrix} = \begin{bmatrix} 0 \\ 0 \\ 0 \end{bmatrix}.$$

As a result $\Gamma_{21} = \Pi_{21}/\Pi_{22}$ and $\Delta_{11} = \Pi_{11} - \Pi_{12}(\Pi_{21}/\Pi_{22})$ and the structural parameters can be solved for in terms of the reduced form parameters. The first equation is exactly identified.

Writing the information provided by the data and *a priori* reasoning for the second equation as

$$\begin{bmatrix} (\Pi \vdots I) \\ \phi \end{bmatrix} \boldsymbol{\beta}_{.2} = \begin{bmatrix} \Pi_{11} & \Pi_{12} & 1 & 0 \\ \Pi_{21} & \Pi_{22} & 0 & 1 \\ 0 & 0 & 1 & 0 \end{bmatrix} \begin{bmatrix} \Gamma_{12} \\ -1 \\ \Delta_{12} \\ \Delta_{22} \end{bmatrix} = \begin{bmatrix} 0 \\ 0 \\ 0 \end{bmatrix}$$

and solving provides $\Gamma_{12} = \Pi_{12}/\Pi_{11}$ and $\Delta_{22} = \Pi_{22} - \Pi_{21}(\Pi_{12}/\Pi_{11})$. The structural parameters of the second equation can be solved for in terms of the reduced form parameters and the second equation is likewise exactly identified.

Since the reduced form parameters Π_{11}, Π_{21}, Π_{12}, and Π_{22} can be consistently estimated by ordinary least squares (Theorem 19.4.3), *indirect least squares* estimates of the structural parameters of (21.2.1) and (21.2.2) are $\hat{\Gamma}_{21} = \hat{\Pi}_{21}/\hat{\Pi}_{22}$,

$$\hat{\Delta}_{11} = \hat{\Pi}_{11} - \hat{\Pi}_{12}(\hat{\Pi}_{21}/\hat{\Pi}_{22}), \qquad \hat{\Gamma}_{12} = \hat{\Pi}_{12}/\hat{\Pi}_{11}$$

and

$$\hat{\Delta}_{22} = \hat{\Pi}_{22} - \hat{\Pi}_{21}(\hat{\Pi}_{12}/\hat{\Pi}_{11}).$$

These estimates are consistent by Slutsky's Theorem 4.2.2. For example, $\operatorname{plim} \hat{\Gamma}_{21} = \operatorname{plim}(\hat{\Pi}_{21}/\hat{\Pi}_{22}) = \operatorname{plim} \hat{\Pi}_{21}/\operatorname{plim} \hat{\Pi}_{22} = \Pi_{21}/\Pi_{22} = \Gamma_{21}$.

Consider the different situation that arises when one of the equations is overidentified. Assume again the two equation system of (21.2.1) and (21.2.2) but assume that the only prior information available is $\Delta_{11} = \Delta_{21} = 0$. The first equation is overidentified. As a result

$$\begin{bmatrix} (\Pi \vdots I) \\ \phi \end{bmatrix} \boldsymbol{\beta}_{.1} = \begin{bmatrix} \Pi_{11} & \Pi_{12} & 1 & 0 \\ \Pi_{21} & \Pi_{22} & 0 & 1 \\ 0 & 0 & 1 & 0 \\ 0 & 0 & 0 & 1 \end{bmatrix} \begin{bmatrix} -1 \\ \Gamma_{21} \\ \Delta_{11} \\ \Delta_{21} \end{bmatrix}$$

$$= \begin{bmatrix} -\Pi_{11} + \Pi_{12}\Gamma_{21} + \Delta_{11} \\ -\Pi_{21} + \Pi_{22}\Gamma_{21} + \Delta_{21} \\ \Delta_{11} \\ \Delta_{21} \end{bmatrix} = \begin{bmatrix} 0 \\ 0 \\ 0 \\ 0 \end{bmatrix}$$

and there exists a multiple solution $\Gamma_{21} = (\Pi_{11}/\Pi_{12}) = (\Pi_{21}/\Pi_{22})$ for a structural parameter in terms of reduced form parameters. As the reduced form estimates $\hat{\Pi}_{11}$, $\hat{\Pi}_{12}$, $\hat{\Pi}_{21}$, and $\hat{\Pi}_{22}$ need not satisfy this equality, the indirect least squares estimator is no longer unique, though regardless of which estimate, $(\hat{\Pi}_{11}/\hat{\Pi}_{12})$ or $(\hat{\Pi}_{21}/\hat{\Pi}_{22})$, is chosen, it is consistent. This "lack of uniqueness" of the indirect least squares estimates in the overidentified case can be remedied by arbitrarily dropping one of the rows of the $(\Pi \vdots I)$ matrix. For example, if we eliminate the first (second) row, the estimate $\hat{\Pi}_{21}/\hat{\Pi}_{22}$ $(\hat{\Pi}_{11}/\hat{\Pi}_{12})$ is implied. The dropping of some information (in this case a row of $(\Pi \vdots I)$) raises a question as to the efficiency of indirect least squares estimates. We will return to this issue subsequently (see Section 21.4 below).

In general, consider the problem of estimating the coefficients of the first equation

$$Y\Gamma_{.1} + X\Delta_{.1} + \mathbf{e}_{.1} = \mathbf{0}$$

or

$$(Y, X)\begin{bmatrix} \Gamma_{.1} \\ \Delta_{.1} \end{bmatrix} + \mathbf{e}_{.1} = Z\boldsymbol{\beta}_{.1} + \mathbf{e}_{.1} = \mathbf{0}.$$

Suppose the *a priori* restrictions are of the form $\phi\boldsymbol{\beta}_{.1} = \mathbf{0}$ and that a normalization rule has been chosen.

Definition 21.2.1. The indirect least squares estimator of $\boldsymbol{\beta}_{.1}$ is the solution to

$$\begin{bmatrix} (\hat{\Pi} \vdots I) \\ \phi \end{bmatrix} \boldsymbol{\beta}_{.1} = \mathbf{0},$$

where $\hat{\Pi} = (X'X)^{-1}X'Y$, if the equation is exactly identified. If the equation is overidentified, certain rows of $(\hat{\Pi} \vdots I)$ will be dropped to obtain the solution.

The above examples provide the basis for the following theorem.

Theorem 21.2.1. *The indirect least squares estimates are consistent and are unique if the equation is exactly identified.*

See Exercise 21.5 for an instrumental variable interpretation of indirect least squares.

21.3 Two-Stage Least Squares

Consider the ith structural equation

$$Y\Gamma_{.i} + X\Delta_{.i} + \mathbf{e}_{.i} = \mathbf{0}.$$

In general some elements of $\Gamma_{.i}$ and $\Delta_{.i}$ are known to be zero. Also we may normalize on the coefficient of one variable letting its value be -1. We will write, with rearrangement if necessary,

$$Y = (\mathbf{y}_i, Y_i, Y_i^*), \qquad \Gamma_{.i} = \begin{bmatrix} -1 \\ \boldsymbol{\gamma}_i \\ \mathbf{0} \end{bmatrix}, \qquad X = (X_i, X_i^*), \qquad \Delta_{.i} = \begin{bmatrix} \boldsymbol{\delta}_i \\ \mathbf{0} \end{bmatrix},$$

where Y_i^* and X_i^* denote the matrices of observations on the excluded current endogenous and predetermined variables, respectively. So the ith equation can be written as

$$\mathbf{y}_i = Y_i\boldsymbol{\gamma}_i + X_i\boldsymbol{\delta}_i + \mathbf{e}_{.i}. \tag{21.3.1}$$

Further, let the number of included endogenous variables for this equation be g and $g_* = G - g$ be the number excluded. Similarly, the number of included and excluded exogenous variables is k and $k_* = K - k$. Hence, $\boldsymbol{\gamma}_i$ is $(g - 1) \times 1$ and $\boldsymbol{\delta}_i$ is $k \times 1$.

The difficulty in estimating Equation (21.3.1) is that some of the explanatory variables are contemporaneously correlated with the error term. Since this is the source of trouble, we can eliminate it as follows.

Partition the reduced form corresponding to (21.3.1) as

$$(\mathbf{y}_i, Y_i, Y_i^*) = (X_i, X_i^*)\begin{bmatrix} \Pi_{11} & \Pi_{12} & \Pi_{13} \\ \Pi_{21} & \Pi_{22} & \Pi_{23} \end{bmatrix} + (\mathbf{v}_i, V_i, V_i^*). \tag{21.3.2}$$

Let $\Pi_{.i}$ be the ith column partition of Π and $\Pi_{j.}$ denote the jth row partition, so that, for example,

$$\Pi_{.1} = \begin{bmatrix} \Pi_{11} \\ \Pi_{21} \end{bmatrix} \quad \text{and} \quad \Pi_{1.} = [\Pi_{11}, \Pi_{12}, \Pi_{13}].$$

Now consider

$$Y_1 = (X_1, X_1^*)\Pi_{.2} + V_1 = X\Pi_{.2} + V_1, \tag{21.3.3}$$

which are the reduced form equations for the included right-hand side endogenous variables in the first equation. Thus, Y_1 is the sum of two components, one random (V_1) and the other nonrandom, or at least contemporaneously uncorrelated with the error term $\mathbf{e}_{.1}$, namely $X\Pi_{.2}$.

If $\Pi_{.2}$ were known, we could substitute $X\Pi_{.2}$ for Y_1 in (21.3.1). By using only the systematic part of Y_1 we ensure that no contemporaneous correlation exists between the error term and *any* of the explanatory variables in that equation. This would guarantee that ordinary least squares applied to such an equation would produce *consistent* parameter estimates.

Since $\Pi_{.2}$ is not known, we must rely on the fact that it *can* be estimated consistently. Thus, instead of $\Pi_{.2}$, we might use $\hat{\Pi}_{.2} = (X'X)^{-1}X'Y_1$, and instead of $X\Pi_{.2}$ use $X\hat{\Pi}_{.2}$. As the sample size increases, $\hat{\Pi}_{.2}$ converges to $\Pi_{.2}$ in probability and the estimators of the structural parameters will be consistent. This is what we will now prove.

The reduced form for the current endogenous variables appearing as the explanatory variables in $\mathbf{y}_1 = Y_1\boldsymbol{\gamma}_1 + X_1\boldsymbol{\delta}_1 + \mathbf{e}_{.1}$ is $Y_1 = X\Pi_{.2} + V_1$. The ordinary least squares estimator of $\Pi_{.2}$ is $\hat{\Pi}_{.2} = (X'X)^{-1}X'Y_1$. Define $\hat{V}_1$ by $Y_1 = X\hat{\Pi}_{.2} + \hat{V}_1$, so that $\hat{V}_1$ is the matrix of ordinary least squares residuals in the regression of Y_1 on X. Note that,

$$\begin{aligned} X'\hat{V}_1 &= X'[Y_1 - X(X'X)^{-1}X'Y_1] \\ &= X'Y_1 - (X'X)(X'X)^{-1}X'Y_1 = 0. \end{aligned} \tag{21.3.4}$$

Further, $\hat{V}_1'\hat{V}_1 = (Y_1 - X\hat{\Pi}_{.2})'\hat{V}_1 = Y_1'\hat{V}_1$ since $\hat{\Pi}_{.2}'X'\hat{V}_1 = 0$ and thus,

$$(Y_1 - \hat{V}_1)'(Y_1 - \hat{V}_1) = Y_1'Y_1 - \hat{V}_1'Y_1 - Y_1'\hat{V}_1 + \hat{V}_1'\hat{V}_1 = Y_1'Y_1 - \hat{V}_1'\hat{V}_1. \tag{21.3.5}$$

Now the equation to be estimated can be written as

$$\mathbf{y}_1 = [Y_1 - \hat{V}_1]\boldsymbol{\gamma}_1 + X_1\boldsymbol{\delta}_1 + \mathbf{e}_{.1} + \hat{V}_1\boldsymbol{\gamma}_1 = \hat{Y}_1\boldsymbol{\gamma}_1 + X_1\boldsymbol{\delta}_1 + \mathbf{e}_{.1} + \hat{V}_1\boldsymbol{\gamma}_1 \tag{21.3.6}$$

and thus expresses $\mathbf{y}_1$ in terms of that part of Y_1 which has been "purged" of its stochastic component V_1.

Let $\hat{Z}_1 = [Y_1 - \hat{V}_1, X_1]$. Then (21.3.6) can be compactly written

$$\mathbf{y}_1 = \hat{Z}_1\boldsymbol{\beta}_{.1} + \mathbf{e}_{.1} + \hat{V}_1\boldsymbol{\gamma}_1. \tag{21.3.7}$$

The two-stage least squares estimator of $\boldsymbol{\beta}_{.1}$, where $\boldsymbol{\beta}_{.1}$ now contains only the structural parameters corresponding to included right-hand side variables, is the ordinary least squares estimator applied to (21.3.7). Hence the term two-stage least squares. The first stage consists of "removing" $\hat{V}_1$ from Y_1 and the second is estimating the structural parameters.

Thus, the two-stage least squares estimator for $\boldsymbol{\beta}_{.1}$ is

$$\begin{aligned}\hat{\boldsymbol{\beta}}_{.1} &= (\hat{Z}_1'\hat{Z}_1)^{-1}\hat{Z}_1'\mathbf{y}_1\\ &= (\hat{Z}_1'\hat{Z}_1)^{-1}\hat{Z}_1'(\hat{Z}_1\boldsymbol{\beta}_{.1} + \mathbf{e}_{.1} + \hat{V}_1\boldsymbol{\gamma}_1)\\ &= \boldsymbol{\beta}_{.1} + (\hat{Z}_1'\hat{Z}_1)^{-1}\hat{Z}_1'\mathbf{e}_{.1} + (\hat{Z}_1'\hat{Z}_1)^{-1}\hat{Z}_1'\hat{V}_1\boldsymbol{\gamma}_1\end{aligned}$$

but

$$\hat{Z}_1'\hat{V}_1\boldsymbol{\gamma}_1 = \begin{bmatrix}\hat{\Pi}_{.2}'X'\hat{V}_1\boldsymbol{\gamma}_1\\ X_1'\hat{V}_1\boldsymbol{\gamma}_1\end{bmatrix} = \begin{bmatrix}\mathbf{0}\\ \mathbf{0}\end{bmatrix}$$

since $X'\hat{V}_1 = 0$. To evaluate the consistency of $\hat{\boldsymbol{\beta}}_{.1}$, we need only examine the probability limit of $(\hat{Z}_1'\hat{Z}_1)^{-1}\hat{Z}_1'\mathbf{e}_{.1}$. But

$$\operatorname{plim}(\hat{Z}_1'\hat{Z}_1)^{-1}\hat{Z}_1'\mathbf{e}_{.1} = \operatorname{plim}\left(\frac{\hat{Z}_1'\hat{Z}_1}{T}\right)^{-1}\operatorname{plim}\frac{\hat{Z}_1'\mathbf{e}_{.1}}{T}.$$

Now

$$\frac{\hat{Z}_1'\hat{Z}_1}{T} = \begin{bmatrix}\dfrac{Y_1'Y_1}{T} - \dfrac{\hat{V}_1'\hat{V}_1}{T} & \dfrac{Y_1'X_1}{T}\\[2ex] \dfrac{X_1'Y_1}{T} & \dfrac{X_1'X_1}{T}\end{bmatrix}.$$

Note that

$$\frac{\hat{V}_1'\hat{V}_1}{T} = \frac{Y_1'\hat{V}_1}{T} = \frac{Y_1'Y_1}{T} - \frac{Y_1'X}{T}\left(\frac{X'X}{T}\right)^{-1}\frac{X'Y_1}{T}$$

so that the upper left-hand term is

$$\frac{Y_1'X}{T}\left(\frac{X'X}{T}\right)^{-1}\frac{X'Y_1}{T}.$$

Also note that

$$\begin{aligned}\operatorname{plim}\frac{Y'X}{T} &= \operatorname{plim}\frac{(X\Pi + V)'X}{T}\\ &= \operatorname{plim}\frac{[\Pi'X' - (\Gamma^{-1})'E']X}{T}\\ &= \operatorname{plim}\Pi'\frac{X'X}{T} - \operatorname{plim}(\Gamma^{-1})'\frac{E'X}{T}\\ &= \Pi'Q.\end{aligned}$$

Hence,

$$\operatorname{plim}\frac{Y_1'X}{T} = \Pi_{.2}'Q \quad \text{and} \quad \operatorname{plim}\frac{Y_1'X_1}{T} = \Pi_{.2}'Q_1,$$

where $\text{plim}(X'X/T) = Q$, $\text{plim}(X'X_1/T) = Q_1$ and $\text{plim}(X_1'X_1/T) = Q_{11}$. Then

$$\text{plim}\,\frac{\hat{Z}_1'\hat{Z}_1}{T} = \begin{bmatrix} \Pi_{.2}'Q\Pi_{.2} & \Pi_{.2}'Q_1 \\ Q_1'\Pi_{.2} & Q_{11} \end{bmatrix}. \tag{21.3.8}$$

Now

$$\frac{\hat{Z}_1'\mathbf{e}_{.1}}{T} = \begin{bmatrix} \dfrac{\hat{\Pi}_{.2}'X'\mathbf{e}_{.1}}{T} \\ \dfrac{X_1'\mathbf{e}_{.1}}{T} \end{bmatrix}$$

but

$$\text{plim}\,\hat{\Pi}_{.2}'(X'\mathbf{e}_{.1}/T) = \text{plim}\,\hat{\Pi}_{.2}'\,\text{plim}(X'\mathbf{e}_{.1}/T) = \Pi_{.2}'\cdot\mathbf{0}$$

since $\text{plim}(X'\mathbf{e}_{.1}/T) = \mathbf{0}$ and, therefore $\hat{\boldsymbol{\beta}}_{.1}$ is consistent. Even though $\hat{\boldsymbol{\beta}}_{.1}$ is consistent, it will be biased, in general, because

$$E\hat{\boldsymbol{\beta}}_{.1} = \boldsymbol{\beta}_{.1} + E[(\hat{Z}_1'\hat{Z}_1)^{-1}\hat{Z}_1'\mathbf{e}_{.1}]$$

if the above expectation exists, and for finite samples $\hat{Z}_1$ may be correlated with $\mathbf{e}_{.1}$. See Exercise 21.6 for the effect of underidentification on two-stage least squares.

21.4 Two-Stage Least Squares as Aitken and Instrumental Variable Estimators

The preceding section presented an intuitive approach to two-stage least squares. It seems as though we must compute two separate regressions, but this is not so. We present two additional numerically equivalent methods for computing two-stage least squares estimates, as Aitken and instrumental variable estimation.

Again consider the first structural equation

$$\mathbf{y}_1 = Y_1\boldsymbol{\gamma}_1 + X_1\boldsymbol{\delta}_1 + \mathbf{e}_{.1}.$$

Let X be the matrix of observations on all predetermined variables in the system and consider the transformed equation

$$X'\mathbf{y}_1 = X'Y_1\boldsymbol{\gamma}_1 + X'X_1\boldsymbol{\delta}_1 + X'\mathbf{e}_{.1}. \tag{21.4.1}$$

Note that the "explanatory" variables are sample cross moments between the included and predetermined variables. If we divided by T, they would converge in probability to a nonstochastic limit and, thus, would be uncorrelated with the error term in the equation. Then if we applied an efficient estimation technique, we would expect to obtain consistent estimators of $\boldsymbol{\gamma}_1$ and $\boldsymbol{\delta}_1$.

Now for large samples,

$$\operatorname{var}(X'\mathbf{e}_{.1}) = \sigma_{11}X'X \tag{21.4.2}$$

in the sense that $X'X/T$ has as its probability limit Q. Hence, it would appear that Aitken (generalized least squares) estimation is appropriate. We will verify that the two-stage least squares estimator is an Aitken estimator. Furthermore, since Aitken estimation has some optimality properties, it is reasonable to suppose that two-stage least squares is optimal in some sense within a class of estimators which uses only information conveyed by the present equation containing $\boldsymbol{\gamma}_1$ and $\boldsymbol{\delta}_1$ and thus disregarding information in the rest of the system.

Since $X'X$ is positive definite, there exists a nonsingular matrix P such that $P'X'XP = I$ and $PP' = (X'X)^{-1}$ (see Exercise 2.6). We will use this transformation matrix to diagonalize the variance–covariance matrix of $X'\mathbf{e}_{.1}$.

$$P'X'\mathbf{y}_1 = P'X'Y_1\boldsymbol{\gamma}_1 + P'X'X_1\boldsymbol{\delta}_1 + P'X'\mathbf{e}_{.1}$$

or,

$$\mathbf{w}_1 = W_1\boldsymbol{\beta}_{.1} + \mathbf{r}_1, \tag{21.4.3}$$

where $\mathbf{w}_1 = P'X'\mathbf{y}_1$, $W_1 = (P'X'Y_1, P'X'X_1)$, and $\mathbf{r}_1 = P'X'\mathbf{e}_{.1}$. Now $E\mathbf{r}_1 = \mathbf{0}$ and $E\mathbf{r}_1\mathbf{r}_1' = \sigma_{11}I_K$.

The two-stage least squares estimator is ordinary least squares applied to Equation (21.4.3).

$$\hat{\boldsymbol{\beta}}_{.1} = (W_1'W_1)^{-1}W_1'\mathbf{w}_1$$

but

$$\begin{aligned} W_1'W_1 &= \begin{bmatrix} Y_1'XP \\ X_1'XP \end{bmatrix}[P'X'Y_1, P'X'X_1] \\ &= \begin{bmatrix} Y_1'X(X'X)^{-1}X'Y_1 & Y_1'X(X'X)^{-1}X'X_1 \\ X_1'X(X'X)^{-1}X'Y_1 & X_1'X(X'X)^{-1}X'X_1 \end{bmatrix}. \end{aligned}$$

Also

$$\begin{aligned} Y_1'X(X'X)^{-1}X'X_1 &= Y_1'X(X'X)^{-1}X'X\begin{bmatrix} I_k \\ 0 \end{bmatrix} \\ &= Y_1'X_1 \end{aligned}$$

and similarly $X_1'X(X'X)^{-1}X'X_1 = X_1'X_1$. We have also previously shown that

$$Y_1'X(X'X)^{-1}X'Y_1 = Y_1'(Y_1 - \hat{V}_1) = Y_1'Y_1 - \hat{V}_1'\hat{V}_1.$$

Thus $W_1'W_1 = \hat{Z}_1'\hat{Z}_1$. Next

$$\begin{aligned} W_1'\mathbf{w}_1 &= \begin{bmatrix} Y_1'XP \\ X_1'XP \end{bmatrix} P'X'\mathbf{y}_1 \\ &= \begin{bmatrix} Y_1'XPP'X'\mathbf{y}_1 \\ X_1'XPP'X'\mathbf{y}_1 \end{bmatrix} \\ &= \begin{bmatrix} Y_1'X(X'X)^{-1}X'\mathbf{y}_1 \\ X_1'X(X'X)^{-1}X'\mathbf{y}_1 \end{bmatrix} \\ &= \begin{bmatrix} Y_1' - \hat{V}_1' \\ X_1' \end{bmatrix} \mathbf{y}_1 = \hat{Z}_1'\mathbf{y}_1. \end{aligned}$$

Therefore, it follows that $\hat{\boldsymbol{\beta}}_{.1} = (W_1'W_1)^{-1}W_1'\mathbf{w}_1 = (\hat{Z}_1'\hat{Z}_1)^{-1}\hat{Z}_1'\mathbf{y}_1$. Hence, two-stage least squares obtained from ordinary least squares estimation of the "purged" equation $\mathbf{y}_1 = \hat{Z}_1\boldsymbol{\beta}_{.1} + \mathbf{e}_{.1} + \hat{V}_1\boldsymbol{\gamma}_1$ can equivalently be derived as the Aitken estimator of the transformed equation (21.4.1).

This latter formulation of two-stage least squares is also convenient when considering all of the equations of the system at once. Put each equation in the system (after substituting out identities) in the form

$$\mathbf{w}_i = W_i\boldsymbol{\beta}_{.i} + \mathbf{r}_i$$

where $\mathbf{w}_i = P'X'\mathbf{y}_i$, $W_i = (P'X'Y_i, P'X'X_i)$, $\boldsymbol{\beta}_{.i} = \begin{bmatrix} \boldsymbol{\gamma}_i \\ \boldsymbol{\delta}_i \end{bmatrix}$ and $\mathbf{r}_i = P'X'\mathbf{e}_{.i}$.

Define

$$\mathbf{w} = \begin{bmatrix} \mathbf{w}_1 \\ \mathbf{w}_2 \\ \vdots \\ \mathbf{w}_G \end{bmatrix}, \quad \boldsymbol{\beta} = \begin{bmatrix} \boldsymbol{\beta}_{.1} \\ \boldsymbol{\beta}_{.2} \\ \vdots \\ \boldsymbol{\beta}_{.G} \end{bmatrix}, \quad W = \begin{bmatrix} W_1 & & & 0 \\ & W_2 & & \\ & & \ddots & \\ 0 & & & W_G \end{bmatrix}, \quad \mathbf{r} = \begin{bmatrix} \mathbf{r}_1 \\ \mathbf{r}_2 \\ \vdots \\ \mathbf{r}_G \end{bmatrix}.$$

The entire system may be written as

$$\mathbf{w} = W\boldsymbol{\beta} + \mathbf{r}. \qquad (21.4.4)$$

Then the two-stage least squares estimator for *all* the structural parameters is

$$\hat{\boldsymbol{\beta}} = (W'W)^{-1}W'\mathbf{w}. \qquad (21.4.5)$$

Since $W'W$ is block diagonal, the ith subvector of $\hat{\boldsymbol{\beta}}$ is just $\hat{\boldsymbol{\beta}}_{.i}$, the two-stage least squares estimator of the ith equation. Thus, two-stage least squares estimators for the entire system are obtained by simply applying two-stage least squares to each equation. The two-stage least squares estimator will be compared to other estimators of the entire system in the next chapter.

Another numerically equivalent method of deriving two-stage least squares estimates is by the use of instrumental variables (see Section 11.7).

The troubling variables, in the sense that they are contemporaneously correlated to the error term, are contained in Y_1 in the equation

$$\mathbf{y}_1 = Y_1\boldsymbol{\gamma}_1 + X_1\boldsymbol{\delta}_1 + \mathbf{e}_{.1}.$$

Letting X_1 serve as its own instrument and $Y_1 - \hat{V}_1 = \hat{Y}_1 = X\hat{\Pi}_{.2}$ serve as an instrument for Y_1, the instrumental variable matrix is

$$Z = [\hat{Y}_1, X_1]$$

and the instrumental variable estimator of $\boldsymbol{\beta}_{.1} = \begin{bmatrix}\boldsymbol{\gamma}_1\\ \boldsymbol{\delta}_1\end{bmatrix}$ is

$$\hat{\boldsymbol{\beta}}_{.1} = \{[\hat{Y}_1, X_1]'[Y_1 X_1]\}^{-1}[\hat{Y}_1, X_1]'\mathbf{y}_1. \tag{21.4.6}$$

By showing that (see Exercise 21.1)

$$\begin{bmatrix}\hat{Y}_1'Y_1 & \hat{Y}_1'X_1\\ X_1'Y_1 & X_1'X_1\end{bmatrix} = \begin{bmatrix}\hat{Y}_1'\hat{Y}_1 & \hat{Y}_1'X_1\\ X_1'\hat{Y}_1 & X_1'X_1\end{bmatrix}$$

it can be seen that the two-stage least squares estimator, when interpreted as an instrumental variable estimator (21.4.6), is numerically equivalent to the estimator derived as the ordinary least squares estimator in the purged equation (21.3.7). In total, then, there are three numerically equivalent ways to derive two-stage least squares estimates.

Comparatively speaking, in the exactly identified case, two-stage least squares and indirect least squares are numerically identical (see Exercise 21.7), and hence, they are equally efficient. On the other hand, in the over-identified case, the indirect least squares estimates are no longer unique and some information must be ignored in order that unique estimates be determined. Intuitively, this raises the possibility that the indirect least squares estimates are not efficient in this case. In fact, this conjecture is true. In the model

$$\mathbf{y}_1 = Y_1\boldsymbol{\gamma}_1 + X_1\boldsymbol{\delta}_1 + \mathbf{e}_{.1} = Z_1\boldsymbol{\beta}_{.1} + \mathbf{e}_{.1}$$

consider the class of instrumental variable estimators

$$\hat{\boldsymbol{\beta}}_{\text{IV}} = (L'Z_1)^{-1}L'\mathbf{y}_1, \tag{21.4.7}$$

where the instrumental variable matrix L is of the form $L = XA$, X is the matrix of all predetermined variables in the system and A is a $K \times (g + k - 1)$ linear transformation matrix. Thus, (21.4.7) represents an instrumental variable estimator with instrumental variable matrix constructed solely from linear combinations of the predetermined variables. Schmidt (1976, pp. 148, 164) shows that, while both indirect least squares and two-stage least squares belong to the same class of estimators, the most asymptotically efficient instrumental variable estimator is the two-stage least squares estimator. In words, this result is obtained by showing that the instruments utilized by two-stage least squares are more highly correlated with the original variables, $Z_1 = [Y_1, X_1]$, than any other instruments that can be constructed from this class. That is, the instrument $XA = X\hat{\Pi}_{.2} = \hat{Y}_1$ used in two-stage least squares is "closer" to Y_1 than any other instrument of this class. Recall from Section 11.7 that, besides the necessity that the instruments be uncorrelated with the error term, the greater the correlation between the instruments and the original variables, the greater the efficiency of instrumental variables estimation.

Another way of looking at the inefficiency of indirect least squares relative to two-stage least squares in the overidentified case is the following. The two-stage least squares estimator can be viewed as an Aitken estimator of an appropriately transformed equation (see Equation (21.4.1)). In the case of overidentification, indirect least squares does not appropriately account for the nonsphericalness of this transformed equation and hence is less efficient, asymptotically, than the Aitken estimator.

21.5 Asymptotic Properties of Two-Stage Least Squares Estimators

We have shown that two-stage least squares estimators are consistent, but in applied work we need to be able to perform tests of significance, and, thus, we must know something about the distribution of the estimator. Unfortunately, the small sample distribution of the two-stage least squares estimator is not, in general, known. Thus, the problem of significance of empirical results is unresolved for small samples. For large samples, however, the situation is simpler, and useful results can be established.

We will begin by considering the asymptotic distribution of the two-stage least squares estimator of a single structural equation, say the first. Assume for the moment that all the predetermined variables are purely exogenous, so they may be taken as nonstochastic or at least independent of the error terms.

The two-stage least squares estimator of the first equation is

$$\hat{\boldsymbol{\beta}}_{.1} = (W_1'W_1)^{-1}W_1'\mathbf{w}_1 = \boldsymbol{\beta}_{.1} + (W_1'W_1)^{-1}W_1\mathbf{r}_1.$$

The problem is to determine the limiting distribution of the sequence $\sqrt{T}(\hat{\boldsymbol{\beta}}_{.1} - \boldsymbol{\beta}_{.1})$ as $T \to \infty$. Then the distribution of $\hat{\boldsymbol{\beta}}_{.1}$ in moderately large samples can be approximated by its asymptotic distribution.

Now $\sqrt{T}(\hat{\boldsymbol{\beta}}_{.1} - \boldsymbol{\beta}_{.1}) = ((W_1'W_1)^{-1}/T)(W_1'\mathbf{r}_1/\sqrt{T})$, but

$$\begin{aligned} W_1'\mathbf{r}_1 &= \begin{bmatrix} Y_1'XP \\ X_1'XP \end{bmatrix} P'X'\mathbf{e}_{.1} \\ &= \begin{bmatrix} Y_1'XPP'X'\mathbf{e}_{.1} \\ X_1'XPP'X'\mathbf{e}_{.1} \end{bmatrix} = (Z_1'X)(X'X)^{-1}(X'\mathbf{e}_{.1}), \end{aligned}$$

where $Z_1 = (Y_1, X_1)$. So

$$\sqrt{T}(\hat{\boldsymbol{\beta}}_{.1} - \boldsymbol{\beta}_{.1}) = \left[\frac{(W_1' W_1)}{T}\right]^{-1} \frac{Z_1'X}{T}\left(\frac{X'X}{T}\right)^{-1} \frac{X'\mathbf{e}_{.1}}{\sqrt{T}}. \tag{21.5.1}$$

All the matrices on the right-hand side of (21.5.1) have, by assumption, probability limits which are nonsingular and nonstochastic. Now,

$$\frac{X'\mathbf{e}_{.1}}{\sqrt{T}} = \frac{1}{\sqrt{T}} \sum_{s=1}^{T} \mathbf{c}_s e_{s1},$$

where $\mathbf{c}_s$ is the sth column of X' and is nonstochastic or independent of e_{s1}. The vectors $\mathbf{c}_s e_{s1}$ are mutually independent with variance–covariance matrix

$$\operatorname{var}(\mathbf{c}_s e_{s1}) = \sigma_{11}\mathbf{c}_s\mathbf{c}_s'.$$

Then we may employ the following multivariate version of the Central Limit Theorem.

Theorem 21.5.1. *Let $\{\mathbf{x}_t : t = 1, 2, \ldots\}$ be a sequence of independent random vectors with zero means and covariance matrices Φ_t. Further, suppose that*

$$\lim_{T\to\infty} \frac{1}{T} \sum_t \Phi_t = \Phi.$$

Then under a general boundedness condition, the sequence

$$\{\mathbf{z}_t : t = 1, 2, \ldots, T\} \overset{\text{asy}}{\to} N(\mathbf{0}, \Phi),$$

where $\mathbf{z}_t = \sum_{t=1}^{T} \mathbf{x}_t/\sqrt{T}$.

PROOF. See Dhrymes (1974, p. 108). □

We then conclude that $X'\mathbf{e}_{.1}/\sqrt{T}$ is asymptotically normal with zero mean vector and variance–covariance matrix

$$\Phi_1 = \sigma_{11} \lim_{T\to\infty} \frac{1}{T} \sum_{s=1}^{T} \mathbf{c}_s\mathbf{c}_s' = \sigma_{11} \lim_{T\to\infty} \left(\frac{X'X}{T}\right).$$

Thus, the asymptotic variance–covariance matrix $\sqrt{T}(\hat{\boldsymbol{\beta}}_{.1} - \boldsymbol{\beta}_{.1})$ is

$$\begin{aligned}
&\operatorname{plim}\left[\frac{W_1'W_1}{T}\right]^{-1}\left[\frac{Z_1'X}{T}\right]\left[\frac{X'X}{T}\right]^{-1}\left(\sigma_{11}\frac{X'X}{T}\right)\left[\frac{X'X}{T}\right]^{-1}\left[\frac{Z_1'X}{T}\right]'\left[\frac{W_1'W_1}{T}\right]^{-1} \\
&= \sigma_{11}\operatorname{plim}\left[\frac{W_1'W_1}{T}\right]^{-1}\frac{W_1'W_1}{T}\left[\frac{W_1'W_1}{T}\right]^{-1} = \sigma_{11}\operatorname{plim}\left[\frac{W_1'W_1}{T}\right]^{-1} \\
&= \operatorname{plim}\sigma_{11}\left[\left(\frac{Z_1'X}{T}\right)\left[\frac{X'X}{T}\right]^{-1}\left(\frac{Z_1'X}{T}\right)'\right]^{-1},
\end{aligned} \tag{21.5.2}$$

and $\sqrt{T}(\hat{\boldsymbol{\beta}}_{.1} - \boldsymbol{\beta}_{.1}) \overset{\text{asy}}{\sim} N[\mathbf{0}, \sigma_{11} \operatorname{plim}(W_1'W_1/T)^{-1}]$. Note the variance–covariance matrix of $\hat{\boldsymbol{\beta}}_{.1}$ coincides with that of an Aitken estimator of the transformed equation (21.4.1) or equivalently an ordinary least squares estimator of the homoscedastic equation (21.4.3).

The above development does not assume normality of $\mathbf{e}_{.1}$. With normality of $\mathbf{e}_{.1}$ the same conclusion holds. If lagged endogenous variables are admitted, the situation becomes more difficult, since the columns of $X'\mathbf{e}_{.1}/\sqrt{T}$ are not independent. The same results can be obtained, however, using more general Central Limit Theorems. See, for instance, Schmidt (1976, p. 259).

For the purpose of hypothesis testing when using two-stage least squares, a consistent estimator of the asymptotic covariance matrix of $\sqrt{T}(\hat{\boldsymbol{\beta}}_{.1} - \boldsymbol{\beta}_{.1})$ is

$$\hat{\sigma}_{11}\left[\frac{W_1'W_1}{T}\right]^{-1} = \hat{\sigma}_{11}T[(Z_1'X)(X'X)^{-1}(Z_1'X)']^{-1}, \tag{21.5.3}$$

where

$$\hat{\sigma}_{11} = \frac{\hat{\mathbf{e}}_{.1}'\hat{\mathbf{e}}_{.1}}{T} = \frac{(\mathbf{y}_1 - Z_1\hat{\boldsymbol{\beta}}_{.1})'(\mathbf{y}_1 - Z_1\hat{\boldsymbol{\beta}}_{.1})}{T}. \tag{21.5.4}$$

The consistency of $\hat{\sigma}_{11}$ can be established as follows.

$$\hat{\mathbf{e}}_{.1} = \mathbf{y}_1 - Z_1\hat{\boldsymbol{\beta}}_{.1} = \mathbf{e}_{.1} - Z_1(\hat{\boldsymbol{\beta}}_{.1} - \boldsymbol{\beta}_{.1})$$

and hence

$$\hat{\sigma}_{11} = \frac{\mathbf{e}_{.1}'\mathbf{e}_{.1}}{T} - \frac{\mathbf{e}_{.1}'Z_1}{T}(\hat{\boldsymbol{\beta}}_{.1} - \boldsymbol{\beta}_{.1}) - (\hat{\boldsymbol{\beta}}_{.1} - \boldsymbol{\beta}_{.1})'\frac{Z_1'\mathbf{e}_{.1}}{T}$$
$$+ (\hat{\boldsymbol{\beta}}_{.1} - \boldsymbol{\beta}_{.1})'\frac{Z_1'Z_1}{T}(\hat{\boldsymbol{\beta}}_{.1} - \boldsymbol{\beta}_{.1}).$$

Since $\hat{\boldsymbol{\beta}}_{.1}$ is consistent

$$\operatorname{plim} \hat{\sigma}_{11} = \operatorname{plim} \frac{\mathbf{e}_{.1}'\mathbf{e}_{.1}}{T} = \sigma_{11}.$$

Therefore, tests of hypotheses about individual β_{ki} may be based on the fact that

$$\frac{\sqrt{T}(\hat{\beta}_{ki} - \beta_{ki})}{W_i^{kk}} \overset{\text{asy}}{\sim} N(0, 1),$$

where W_i^{kk} is the square root of the kth diagonal element of

$$\sigma_{ii} \operatorname{plim}\left(\frac{W_i'W_i}{T}\right)^{-1}.$$

Note, that for a sample of finite size, we can utilize the statistic with

$$\frac{\hat{\beta}_{ki} - \beta_{ki}}{\hat{\sigma}_{\beta_{ki}}},$$

where $\hat{\sigma}_{\beta_{ki}}$ is the square root of the kth diagonal element of $\hat{\sigma}_{ii}(W_i' W_i)^{-1}$.

Procedures for testing joint hypotheses of the form $H\boldsymbol{\beta}_{.1} = \mathbf{h}$ are considered in Exercises 21.3 and 21.4.

Consider now the asymptotic distribution of the two-stage least squares estimators of the entire system which may be written as

$$\mathbf{w} = W\boldsymbol{\beta} + \mathbf{r}$$

with two-stage least squares estimator

$$\hat{\boldsymbol{\beta}} = (W'W)^{-1}W'\mathbf{w}.$$

Hence,

$$\sqrt{T}(\hat{\boldsymbol{\beta}} - \boldsymbol{\beta}) = \left(\frac{W'W}{T}\right)^{-1} \frac{W'\mathbf{r}}{\sqrt{T}}$$

and its asymptotic distribution is that of

$$\operatorname{plim}\left(\frac{W'W}{T}\right)^{-1} \frac{W'\mathbf{r}}{\sqrt{T}}.$$

Now

$$\frac{W'\mathbf{r}}{\sqrt{T}} = \frac{1}{\sqrt{T}}\begin{bmatrix} W_1'\mathbf{r}_1 \\ W_2'\mathbf{r}_2 \\ \vdots \\ W_G'\mathbf{r}_G \end{bmatrix}$$

$$= \begin{bmatrix} \frac{Z_1'X}{T}\left[\frac{X'X}{T}\right]^{-1} & & & 0 \\ & \frac{Z_2'X}{T}\left[\frac{X'X}{T}\right]^{-1} & & \\ & & \ddots & \\ 0 & & & \frac{Z_G'X}{T}\left[\frac{X'X}{T}\right]^{-1} \end{bmatrix}$$

$$\times \frac{1}{\sqrt{T}}(I \otimes X')\operatorname{vec}(E). \tag{21.5.5}$$

But this last term is $\operatorname{vec}(X'E/\sqrt{T})$ with asymptotic distribution (see Exercise 21.2) $N(\mathbf{0}, \Sigma \otimes Q)$, where $Q = \operatorname{plim}(X'X/T)$. Let the block diagonal matrix $\operatorname{diag}\{(Z_i'X/T)[X'X/T]^{-1}\}$ be denoted by D. Then the asymptotic covariance matrix of $[W'W/T]^{-1}(W'\mathbf{r}/\sqrt{T})$ is

$$\operatorname{plim}\left[\frac{W'W}{T}\right]^{-1} D(\Sigma \otimes Q)D'\left[\frac{W'W}{T}\right]^{-1}.$$

The product $D(\Sigma \otimes Q)D'$ can be written as

$$\operatorname{plim}\begin{bmatrix} \frac{Z_1'X}{T} & & 0 \\ & \ddots & \\ 0 & & \frac{Z_G'X}{T} \end{bmatrix}\left[I_G \otimes \left(\frac{X'X}{T}\right)^{-1}\right](\Sigma \otimes Q)\left[I_G \otimes \left(\frac{X'X}{T}\right)^{-1}\right]$$

$$\times \begin{bmatrix} \frac{X'Z_1}{T} & & 0 \\ & \ddots & \\ 0 & & \frac{X'Z_G}{T} \end{bmatrix} \quad (21.5.6)$$

but

$$\operatorname{plim}\left[I_G \otimes \left(\frac{X'X}{T}\right)^{-1}\right](\Sigma \otimes Q)\left[I_G \otimes \left(\frac{X'X}{T}\right)^{-1}\right] = \Sigma \otimes Q^{-1}.$$

Also $(X'X/T)^{-1} = \sqrt{T}PP'\sqrt{T}$. This term can be split and taken to the front and back of matrices (21.5.6) to give $W'/\sqrt{T}$ and $W/\sqrt{T}$. Therefore,

$$\sqrt{T}(\hat{\boldsymbol{\beta}} - \boldsymbol{\beta}) \overset{\text{asy}}{\sim} N\left[\mathbf{0}, \operatorname{plim}\left(\frac{W'W}{T}\right)^{-1}\frac{W'}{\sqrt{T}}(\Sigma \otimes I_K)\frac{W}{\sqrt{T}}\left(\frac{W'W}{T}\right)^{-1}\right]. \quad (21.5.7)$$

This last expression will be useful when comparing the efficiency of two-stage least squares applied to the entire system and alternative system estimation methods such as three-stage least squares (see next chapter). Similarly, the covariance matrix of (21.5.7) may be consistently estimated by

$$\left(\frac{W'W}{T}\right)^{-1}\frac{W'}{\sqrt{T}}(\hat{\Sigma} \otimes I_K)\frac{W}{\sqrt{T}}\left(\frac{W'W}{T}\right)^{-1},$$

where

$$\hat{\Sigma} = [\hat{\sigma}_{ij}], \qquad \hat{\sigma}_{ij} = \frac{\hat{\mathbf{e}}_{.i}'\hat{\mathbf{e}}_{.j}}{T}.$$

21.6 k-Class Estimators

To this point we have discussed estimation methods (indirect least squares, two-stage least squares) which have utilized only that information required in the identification of a given particular equation. No use has been made of prior information concerning other equations or the fact that there exist contemporaneous correlations among the disturbance terms of the various equations, $E\mathbf{e}'_{t.}\mathbf{e}_{t.} = \Sigma$. Such estimators are termed "limited information" estimators in that information usage is limited to the particular equation being estimated. There exist other limited information estimators, however, besides indirect least squares and two-stage least squares. The discussion of these estimators will not be exhaustive.

A general class of estimators that encompasses two-stage least squares, ordinary least squares and other limited information estimators to be discussed subsequently is the k-class. The motivation for this class of estimators is best understood by considering the expression of the two-stage least squares estimator given by

$$\begin{aligned}\hat{\boldsymbol{\beta}}_{.1} &= (\hat{Z}'_1\hat{Z}_1)^{-1}\hat{Z}'_1\mathbf{y}_1 \\ &= \begin{bmatrix} Y'_1Y_1 - \hat{V}'_1\hat{V}_1 & Y'_1X_1 \\ X'_1Y_1 & X'_1X_1 \end{bmatrix}^{-1}\begin{bmatrix} Y'_1 - \hat{V}'_1 \\ X'_1 \end{bmatrix}\mathbf{y}_1. \end{aligned} \tag{21.6.1}$$

The two-stage least squares estimator is then obtained by "purging" the contemporaneous correlation from the explanatory current endogenous variables, Y_1. Suppose that we remove, instead of $\hat{V}_1$, a proportion of it. Using this logic, the general k-class estimator is

$$\hat{\boldsymbol{\beta}}_{.1}(k) = \begin{bmatrix} Y'\,Y_1 - k\hat{V}'_1\hat{V}_1 & Y'_1X_1 \\ X'_1Y_1 & X'_1X_1 \end{bmatrix}^{-1}\begin{bmatrix} Y'_1 - k\hat{V}'_1 \\ X'_1 \end{bmatrix}\mathbf{y}_1. \tag{21.6.2}$$

When $k = 0$, $\hat{\boldsymbol{\beta}}_{.1}(0)$ is the ordinary least squares estimator while $k = 1$ yields the two-stage least squares estimator.

More generally, it has been shown that the k-class estimator is consistent if plim $k = 1$. In addition, it has the same asymptotic distribution as the two-stage least squares estimator if plim $\sqrt{T}(k - 1) = 0$. This raises the question of what circumstances might lead to a stochastic choice of k. This is the topic of the next section.

21.7 Limited Information Maximum Likelihood

Again, consider the first equation in a system of simultaneous equations

$$\mathbf{y}_1 = Y_1\boldsymbol{\gamma}_1 + X_1\boldsymbol{\delta}_1 + \mathbf{e}_{.1}. \tag{21.7.1}$$

Define

$$Y_1^0 = (\mathbf{y}_1, Y_1) \quad \text{and} \quad \boldsymbol{\gamma}^0 = \begin{bmatrix} -1 \\ \boldsymbol{\gamma}_1 \end{bmatrix}.$$

Then, (21.7.1) can be written as

$$Y_1^0\boldsymbol{\gamma}^0 + X_1\boldsymbol{\delta}_1 + \mathbf{e}_{.1} = \mathbf{0}. \tag{21.7.2}$$

In the sense of "limited information" estimation, let us determine what information is provided by the available *a priori* knowledge concerning the first equation *alone*. The reduced form equation associated with Y_1^0 is

$$(\mathbf{y}_1, Y_1) = (X_1, X_1^*)\begin{bmatrix}\Pi_{11} & \Pi_{12}\\ \Pi_{21} & \Pi_{22}\end{bmatrix} + (\mathbf{v}_1, V_1) \tag{21.7.3}$$

or

$$Y_1^0 = X\Pi^0 + V_1^0, \tag{21.7.4}$$

where Π^0 and V_1^0 are defined implicitly in (21.7.3) and X_1^* denotes those predetermined variables excluded from the first equation. Let $\Pi_{1.}^0 = (\Pi_{11}, \Pi_{12})$ and $\Pi_{2.}^0 = (\Pi_{21}, \Pi_{22})$, then (21.7.4) can be written as

$$Y_1^0 = X_1\Pi_{1.}^0 + X_1^*\Pi_{2.}^0 + V_{1}^0. \tag{21.7.5}$$

Post-multiplying the left- and right-hand sides of (21.7.5) by γ^0 provides

$$Y_1^0\gamma^0 = X_1\Pi_{1.}^0\gamma^0 + X_1^*\Pi_{2.}^0\gamma^0 + V_1^0\gamma^0 = -X_1\boldsymbol{\delta}_1 - \mathbf{e}_{.1}. \tag{21.7.6}$$

Therefore, given *a priori*, that X_1^* is excluded from the first equation, the *a priori* information concerning *only* the first equation requires that

$$\Pi_{2.}^0\gamma^0 = \mathbf{0}. \tag{21.7.7}$$

In the instance that the first equation is exactly identified, the number of rows in $\Pi_{2.}^0$, namely k_*, is equal to one less than the number of columns (g) in $\Pi_{2.}^0$. That is $k_* = g - 1$. Therefore, γ^0 can be exactly solved for in terms of $\Pi_{2.}^0$ and *there are no restrictions on the reduced form parameters*. However, in the case of overidentification, more than $g - 1$ predetermined variables are omitted from the first equation and as a result, the prior information places restrictions on the columns of $\Pi_{2.}^0$. In short, *overidentification places restrictions on the reduced form parameters of the form* (21.7.7). The implementation of these restrictions, which are specific to the first equation, is the essential ingredient in limited information maximum likelihood estimation.

We now define the limited information likelihood estimator.

Definition 21.7.1. The limited information maximum likelihood estimator of γ^0 is obtained by maximizing the likelihood function of Y_1^0 subject to the restriction $\Pi_{2.}^0\gamma^0 = \mathbf{0}$.

We will only sketch the method of obtaining limited information maximum likelihood estimates. The likelihood function of Y (see Exercise 21.11) is

$$L(Y) = (2\pi)^{-GT/2}\Omega^{-T/2}\exp\{-\tfrac{1}{2}\operatorname{tr}\Omega^{-1}(Y - X\Pi)'(Y - X\Pi)\}.$$

It follows that the log likelihood function of Y_1^0 is

$$\ln L(Y_1^0) = C + \frac{T}{2}\ln|\Omega_0^{-1}| - \tfrac{1}{2}\operatorname{tr}\Omega_0^{-1}(Y_1^0 - X\Pi^0)'(Y_1^0 - X\Pi^0), \tag{21.7.8}$$

where C denotes a constant and Ω_0 denotes the variance–covariance matrix of the reduced form disturbances V_1^0. Maximizing (21.7.8) with respect to γ^0 subject to (21.7.7) is equivalent to minimizing the generalized residual variance

$$|(Y_1^0 - X\Pi^0)'(Y_1^0 - X\Pi^0)| \tag{21.7.9}$$

subject to the same constraint. This is then the limited information maximum likelihood procedure. Some authors term the constrained minimization of (21.7.9), the *least generalized residual variance* procedure (estimator). However, the distinction is artificial as this minimization is equivalent to constrained maximization of the partial likelihood function of Y_1^0 subject to the same constraint.

The *least variance ratio* estimator of γ^0 that minimizes the variance ratio

$$l = \frac{\gamma^{0\prime}Y_1^{0\prime}M_1Y_1^0\gamma^0}{\gamma^{0\prime}Y_1^{0\prime}MY_1^0\gamma^0}, \tag{21.7.10}$$

where $M_1 = I - X_1(X_1'X_1)^{-1}X_1'$ and $M = I - X(X'X)^{-1}X'$, is numerically equivalent to limited information maximum likelihood (and hence least generalized residual variance). Therefore, all of these estimators have the same sampling distribution. But what are the properties of these estimators?

It can be shown that the least variance ratio (and hence limited information maximum likelihood and least generalized residual variance) estimator is a k-class estimator with $k = \hat{l}$ where

$$\hat{l} = \frac{\hat{\gamma}^{0\prime}Y_1^{0\prime}M_1Y_1^0\hat{\gamma}^0}{\hat{\gamma}^{0\prime}Y_1^{0\prime}MY_1^0\hat{\gamma}^0} \tag{21.7.11}$$

and $\hat{\gamma}^0$ denotes the least variance ratio (limited information maximum likelihood, least generalized residual variance) estimator of γ^0. It can be shown that plim $\hat{l} = 1$ and hence the least variance ratio (limited information maximum likelihood, least generalized residual variance) estimator is consistent. Similarly, it can be shown that plim $\sqrt{T}(\hat{l} - 1) = 0$, and hence the least variance ratio (limited information maximum likelihood, least generalized residual variance) estimator has the same asymptotic distribution as the two-stage least squares estimator. Therefore, all of these "limited" information estimators are members of the general k-class of estimators and as $T \to \infty$, their sampling distributions coincide.

21.8 Summary and Guide to Further Readings

In the present chapter, we have studied the properties of "limited information" estimators of the ith equation, $\mathbf{y}_i = Y_i\boldsymbol{\gamma}_i + X_i\boldsymbol{\delta}_i + \mathbf{e}_{.i}$, of a simultaneous equation system. The two-stage least squares estimator was shown to be more efficient than indirect least squares in the case of overidentification. The two were numerically identical (and hence have the same asymptotic distribution) in the case of exact identification. As a result, relatively speaking, the indirect least squares estimator is of interest primarily as an instructional tool. It does illustrate the identification problem and the restrictions on the reduced form that arise from overidentification.

In Section 21.6, the k-class estimator was defined and under appropriate circumstances was found to be consistent. For $k = 1$, the k-class estimator is the two-stage least squares estimator. In the next section, the limited information maximum likelihood estimator was defined. It was seen to be numerically equivalent to the least generalized residual variance and least variance ratio estimators (and hence all have the same asymptotic distribution). For appropriate selection of k, these estimators, like two-stage least squares, also belong to the k-class. Asymptotically, they have the same distribution as two-stage least squares estimates. Except for indirect least squares, the k-class provides a commonality between all the estimators discussed in this chapter.

The literature on simultaneous equations models is vast and continually expanding. Here we try to break down the literature into convenient partitions, that are by no means mutually exclusive, and suggest some recent works than can serve as a guide to additional study.

Limited information estimators are catalogued and related by several authors. Hendry (1976), extended by Anderson (1980), links almost all of the usual limited (and full) information estimators, for linear and nonlinear systems, by characterizing them as numerical approximations to the maximum likelihood estimators. Chow (1974) presents an alternative family of estimators that are modifications of maximum likelihood. Klein (1979) considers instrumental estimators, including the k-class, that are optimal under certain conditions. Nagar (1962) presents, and Ullah and Ullah (1978), and Brown *et al.* (1974) examine the properties of, the double k-class of estimators that contains both the k- and h-classes as special cases.

The simultaneous equations model is one of the most important to econometricians from theoretical and applied perspectives. It is unfortunate that the estimators employed have exact, finite-sample distributions that are difficult to derive. Thus, their properties are usually discussed only on the basis of large sample theory. Small sample properties have been studied using Monte Carlo techniques (see Johnston (1972), Dhrymes (1974), Cragg (1967), and Wagner (1958)), but these analyses can not sort out the possibly complex dependence of the distributions on unknown parameters, nor do they reveal the possibility that moments of the exact distribution do not exist, making comparisons of empirical mean square errors, biases and sampling variances meaningless. In the last two decades, however, work has been done on the analysis of exact distributions, albeit on very simple models. Useful summaries of this work are provided by Basmann (1974) and Greenberg and Webster (1983). Some specific references are listed below.

Sawa (1969) and Richardson (1968) derived the exact distribution of the ordinary least squares and two-stage least squares estimator in an equation with two endogenous variables, and Sawa presents graphs of the densities for several parameter configurations. Marino and McDonald (1979) consider the two-stage least squares estimator (and limited information maximum likelihood) in the just identified case, and Holly and Phillips (1979) use an asymptotic expansion to approximate the distribution of the two-stage least squares estimator. Anderson and Sawa (1973) derive an alternative form of the exact distributions of ordinary least squares and two-stage least squares and present approximations as well. Anderson (1977) examines the expansions further and Anderson and Sawa (1979) present tables of the exact distribution and examine the accuracy of the approximation. An alternative approach to approximation may be found in Marino (1973a), and additional work on approximation of instrumental variable estimators by Sargan and Mikhail (1971) is also pertinent. Marino and Sawa (1972) obtain the exact distribution of the limited information maximum likelihood estimator for the two endogenous variable case while Anderson (1974) provides an approximation. Anderson and Sawa (1979) compare the two-stage least squares and limited information maximum likelihood estimators and note substantial differences in small sample properties. The distribution of instrumental variable estimators is considered by Carter (1976), Phillips (1980), and Marino (1977). Sargan and Mikhail (1971), as noted above, consider approximations to the distributions of instrumental variable estimators. Exact distributions of k-class estimators are derived by Anderson and Sawa (1973) who also provide an approximation. Marino (1973b) and Holly and Phillips (1980) provide alternative approximations, and Srivastava *et al.* (1980) make numerical comparisons.

A related problem is the derivation of moments, and their approximations, of estimators. Moments of the k-class estimators are derived by Sawa (1972) and commented on by Mehta and Swamy (1978). Kinal (1980) provides necessary and sufficient conditions for the existence of moments of k-class estimators. Nagar (1969) and Kadane (1971) examine the moments of k-class estimators where error variances are small, the "small-σ" method. Marino and Sawa (1972) and Anderson (1974, 1977) discuss the limited information maximum likelihood estimator. Carter (1976), Marino (1977), and Phillips (1980) consider instrumental variable estimators.

A problem related to the distributions of estimators is the distribution of test statistics for hypothesis in both large and small samples. In addition to the references on overidentifying restrictions referred to in Exercise 21.9, see Dhrymes (1974, pp. 272–276), Maddala (1974), Berndt and Savin (1977), Morgan and Vandaele (1974), and Hatanaka (1977).

In addition to problems unique to simultaneous equations, traditional ones have been examined in the context of simultaneous equations. We mention some of these references here, although they may appear in other chapters as well. Computational methods relating to limited information estimators are considered by Jennings (1980), Phillips (1977), and Dent (1976). Problems of autocorrelation in simultaneous equations are considered in Chapter 25. In addition to references cited there, see Harvey and Phillips (1980, 1981), Dhrymes *et al.* (1974), Godfrey (1976), Berndt and Savin (1975), Dhrymes and Taylor (1976), Hendry (1979), Baillie (1981), Hatanaka (1976), and Hall and Pagan (1981). Heteroscedasticity is discussed by Harvey and Phillips (1981); Multicollinearity and design by Atkinson (1978) and Conlisk (1979); Errors-in-Variables by Hsiao (1976, 1977, 1979), Geraci (1976, 1977), and Hausman (1977); Specification errors by Hale *et al.* (1980); Error components and random coefficients by Baltagi (1981), Kelejian (1974), and Raj *et al.* (1980); incomplete observations by Dagenais (1976); goodness of fit by Knight (1980), Carter and Nagar (1977), and McElroy (1977). Disequilibrium models and models with limited endogenous variables are discussed and references given in Chapter 25. Models that are nonlinear in the parameters and/or variables are discussed by Gallant and Holly (1980), Gallant and Jorgenson (1979), Amemiya (1974), and Kelejian (1971). References on nonlinear models pertaining more specifically to full information methods are found in the next chapter.

21.9 Exercises

21.1. Show that the instrumental variable estimator for $\boldsymbol{\beta}_{.1}$ using the instrument matrix $[\hat{Y}_1, X_1]$ for $[Y_1, X_1]$ is equivalent to the two-stage least squares estimator.

21.2. Under the assumptions stated in Chapter 19 show that the asymptotic distribution of vec $X'E/\sqrt{T}$ is $N(\mathbf{0}, \Sigma \otimes Q)$ where $Q = \text{plim}(X'X/T)$.

21.3. Let $\hat{\boldsymbol{\delta}}$ be an estimator for $\boldsymbol{\delta}$ with the multivariate normal density $N(\boldsymbol{\delta}, \Sigma)$. Consider the set of linear hypotheses $H\boldsymbol{\delta} = \mathbf{h}$ where H has J linearly independent rows and, thus, is of rank J. Then $H\hat{\boldsymbol{\delta}} \sim N(H\boldsymbol{\delta}, H\Sigma H')$ or, if the hypothesis is true, as $N(\mathbf{h}, H\Sigma H')$. Consequently, $H\hat{\boldsymbol{\delta}} - \mathbf{h} \sim N(\mathbf{0}, H\Sigma H')$ if the hypothesis is true. If P is a nonsingular matrix such that $P'(H\Sigma H')P = I$, then $P'(H\hat{\boldsymbol{\delta}} - \mathbf{h}) \sim N(0, I)$. Use this result to show then that

$$(\mathbf{h} - H\hat{\boldsymbol{\delta}})'(H\Sigma H')^{-1}(\mathbf{h} - H\hat{\boldsymbol{\delta}})$$

has a χ^2_J distribution if the hypothesis $H\boldsymbol{\delta} = \mathbf{h}$ is true. How might this result be modified so that one could perform joint hypothesis tests on the coefficient vector $\boldsymbol{\beta}_{.1}$.

21.4. Dhrymes (1974, pp. 272–277) presents alternative test statistics for the significance of two-stage least squares parameter estimates, based on the transformed model (21.4.3), that have t- and F-distributions asymptotically. He shows that the number of degrees of freedom for these test statistics are the extent of overidentification for the equation under consideration. Consequently, no such tests exist when an equation is exactly identified. This illustrates the point that one *cannot* test (exclusion) restrictions that are used to identify an equation.

Using the results in Dhrymes, what is the appropriate F-statistic for the hypothesis $H\boldsymbol{\beta}_{.1} = \mathbf{h}$ based on the two-stage least squares estimates?

21.5. The reduced form parameters are consistently estimated by $\hat{\Pi} = (X'X)^{-1}X'Y$. Since

$$\Pi\Gamma_{.i} = -\Delta_{.i}$$

or

$$\Pi\begin{bmatrix}-1\\ \gamma_i\\ \mathbf{0}\end{bmatrix} = \begin{bmatrix}-\boldsymbol{\delta}_i\\ \mathbf{0}\end{bmatrix}$$

we can write

$$(X'X)^{-1}X'(\mathbf{y}_i, Y_i, Y_i^*)\begin{bmatrix}-1\\ \hat{\gamma}\\ \mathbf{0}\end{bmatrix} = \begin{bmatrix}-\hat{\boldsymbol{\delta}}_i\\ \mathbf{0}\end{bmatrix}.$$

Show that by rearrangement this can be written

$$(X'Z_i)\begin{bmatrix}\hat{\gamma}_i\\ \hat{\boldsymbol{\delta}}_i\end{bmatrix} = X'\mathbf{y}_i.$$

Also show that, if the ith equation is exactly identified, $X'Z_i$ is square and nonsingular. Then show that the resulting estimator of the structural parameters is an instrumental variables estimator with matrix of instruments X.

21.6. Show that if the order condition for identification is not met, then the two-stage least squares estimator does not exist, and that if the order condition is met but the rank condition is not, then the two-stage least squares estimator exists but is not consistent.

21.7. Show that, if an equation is identified, then two-stage least squares and indirect least squares estimators are identical.

21.8. Show that $V_1^0\gamma^0 = \mathbf{e}_{.1}$ (See Equation (21.7.6).)

21.9. (Tests of Overidentifying Restrictions). Anderson and Rubin (1949) proposed a test for the null hypothesis that the rank of $\Pi_{2.}$, the $k_* \times g$ matrix in (21.7.7), is $g - 1$, against the alternative that the rank is g. Koopmans and Hood (1953) consider the null hypothesis that $\gamma_i^* = \mathbf{0}$ and $\boldsymbol{\delta}_i^* = \mathbf{0}$, where γ_i^* is the g_* dimensional vector of coefficients on endogenous variables omitted from the ith equations and $\boldsymbol{\delta}_i^*$ is the k_*-dimensional vector of coefficients associated with exogenous variables omitted from the ith equation. If $k_* = g - 1$, the rank of $\Pi_{2.}$ is not greater than $g - 1$, and the ith equation is not identified or just identified and no test of zero restrictions is possible. If $k_* \geq g$, then the hypothesis $\gamma_i^* = \mathbf{0}$ and $\boldsymbol{\delta}_i^* = \mathbf{0}$ imply through (21.7.7) that the rank of $\Pi_{2.}$ is at most $g - 1$ since a restriction exists on the columns of $\Pi_{2.}$ for some $\boldsymbol{\gamma}^0$ not equal to zero. Thus, Koopmans and Hood suggest using the same test statistic as Anderson and Rubin for the test of this null hypothesis against its alternative. Under the null hypothesis the likelihood ratio test statistic $T \ln \hat{l}$ is distributed asymptotically as χ^2 with $k_* - (g - 1)$ degrees of freedom, which of course means the test is defined only for overidentified equations. See Basmann (1960) for a test based on the two-stage least squares estimator, and see Kadane and Anderson (1977) for an extension of the alternative hypothesis. Also, see Kadane (1974), Byron (1974), Wegge (1978), Hwang (1980), and Rhodes (1981) for extensions and refinements of the test.

21.10. Obtain the two-stage least squares and limited information maximum likelihood estimates of Klein's Model I. The data is presented in Table 21.9.1.

Table 21.9.1 Data for Klein's model I.

Year	C	P	W	I	K_{-1}	X	W'	G	T
1920	39.8	12.7	28.8	2.7	180.1	44.9	2.2	2.4	3.4
21	41.9	12.4	25.5	−0.2	182.8	45.6	2.7	3.9	7.7
22	45.0	16.9	29.3	1.9	182.6	50.1	2.9	3.2	3.9
23	49.2	18.4	34.1	5.2	184.5	57.2	2.9	2.8	4.7
24	50.6	19.4	33.9	3.0	189.7	57.1	3.1	3.5	3.8
25	52.6	20.1	35.4	5.1	192.7	61.0	3.2	3.3	5.5
26	55.1	19.6	37.4	5.6	197.8	64.0	3.3	3.3	7.0
27	56.2	19.8	37.9	4.2	203.4	64.4	3.6	4.0	6.7
28	57.3	21.1	39.2	3.0	207.6	64.5	3.7	4.2	4.2
29	57.8	21.7	41.3	5.1	210.6	67.0	4.0	4.1	4.0
1930	55.0	15.6	37.9	1.0	215.7	61.2	4.2	5.2	7.7
31	50.9	11.4	34.5	−3.4	216.7	53.4	4.8	5.9	7.5
32	45.6	7.0	29.0	−6.2	213.3	44.3	5.3	4.9	8.3
33	46.5	11.2	28.5	−5.1	207.1	45.1	5.6	3.7	5.4
34	48.7	12.3	30.6	−3.0	202.0	49.7	6.0	4.0	6.8
35	51.3	14.0	33.2	−1.3	199.0	54.4	6.1	4.4	7.2
36	57.7	17.6	36.8	2.1	197.7	62.7	7.4	2.9	8.3
37	58.7	17.3	41.0	2.0	199.8	65.0	6.7	4.3	6.7
38	57.5	15.3	38.2	−1.9	201.8	60.9	7.7	5.3	7.4
39	61.6	19.0	41.6	1.3	199.9	69.5	7.8	6.6	8.9
1940	65.0	21.1	45.0	3.3	201.2	75.7	8.0	7.4	9.6
41	69.7	23.5	53.3	4.9	204.5	88.4	8.5	13.8	11.6

21.11. The tth observation on the simultaneous equations model is

$$\mathbf{y}_{t.}\Gamma + \mathbf{x}_{t.}\Delta + \mathbf{e}_{t.} = \mathbf{0}',$$

and $\mathbf{e}_{t.}' \sim N(\mathbf{0}, \Sigma)$.

(a) Write down the joint density of $\mathbf{e}_{t.}$ and make a change of variables to $\mathbf{y}_{t.}$. Show that the Jacobian of the transformation is abs(det(Γ)). Then show that the T observations on the model have likelihood function

$$(2\pi)^{-GT/2}|\Sigma|^{-T/2}\|\Gamma\|^{T} \exp\{-\tfrac{1}{2} \operatorname{tr} \Sigma^{-1}(Y\Gamma + X\Delta)'(Y\Gamma + X\Delta)\}.$$

(b) Note that $|\Omega| = |(\Gamma^{-1})'\Sigma\Gamma^{-1}| = |\Sigma|\,\|\Gamma\|^{-2}$ and show that

$$\operatorname{tr} \Omega^{-1}(Y - X\Pi)'(Y - X\Pi) = \operatorname{tr} \Sigma^{-1}(Y\Gamma + X\Delta)'(Y\Gamma + X\Delta).$$

Use these two expressions to show that the likelihood function in (a) can be written

$$(2\pi)^{-GT/2}|\Omega|^{-T/2} \exp\{-\tfrac{1}{2} \operatorname{tr} \Omega^{-1}(Y - X\Pi)'(Y - X\Pi)\}.$$

21.10 References

Amemiya, T. (1974). The nonlinear two stage least squares estimator. *Journal of Econometrics*, **2**, 105–110.

Anderson, G. (1980). The structure of simultaneous estimators: a comment. *Journal of Econometrics*, **14**, 271–276.

Anderson, T. (1974). An asymptotic expansion of the distribution of the limited information maximum likelihood estimate of a coefficient in a simultaneous equation system. *Journal of the American Statistical Association*, **69**, 565–573.

Anderson, T. (1977). Asymptotic expansions of the distributions of estimates in simultaneous equations for alternative parmater sequences. *Econometrica*, **45**, 509–518.

Anderson, T. and Rubin, H. (1949). Estimation of the parameters of a single equation in a complete system of stochastic equations. *Annals of Mathematical Statistics*, **20**, 46–63.

Anderson, T. and Sawa, T. (1973). Distributions of estimates of coefficients of a single equation in a simultaneous system and their asymptotic expansions. *Econometrica*, **41**, 683–714.

Anderson, T. and Sawa, T. (1979). Evaluation of the distribution function of the two stage least squares estimates. *Econometrica*, **47**, 163–182.

Atkinson, S. (1978). Small sample properties of simultaneous equation estimates with multicollinearity. *Journal of the American Statistical Association*, **73**, 719–723.

Baillie, R. (1981). Prediction from the dynamic simultaneous equation model with vector autoregressive errors. *Econometrica*, **49**, 1331–1338.

Baltagi, B. (1981). Simultaneous equations with error components. *Journal of Econometrics*, **17**, 189–200.

Basmann, R. (1974). Exact finite sample distributions for some econometric estimators and test statistics: a survey and appraisal. In *Frontiers of Quantitative Economics*, vol. II. Edited by M. D. Intriligator and D. A. Kendrick. Amsterdam: North-Holland. Pp. 209–285.

Basmann, R. (1960). On finite sample distributions of generalized classical linear identifiability test statistics. *Journal of the American Statistical Association*, **55**, 650–659.

Berndt, E. and Savin, N. (1977). Conflict among criteria for testing hypotheses in a multivariate linear regression model. *Econometrica*, **45**, 1263–1278.

Berndt, E. and Savin, N. (1975). Estimation and hypothesis testing in singular equation systems with autoregressive disturbances. *Econometrica*, **43**, 937–958.

Brown, G., Kadane, J., and Ramage, J. (1974). The asymptotic bias and mean square error of double k-class estimators when disturbances are small. *International Economic Review*, **15**, 667–680.

Byron, R. (1974). Testing structural specification using unrestricted reduced form. *Econometrica*, **42**, 869–884.

Carter, R. (1976). The exact distribution of an instrumental variable estimator. *International Economic Review*, **17**, 228–233.

Carter, R. and Nagar, A. (1977). Coefficients of correlation for simultaneous equation systems. *Journal of Econometrics*, **6**, 39–50.

Chow, G. (1974). A family of estimators for simultaneous equation systems. *International Economic Review*, **15**, 654–666.

Conlisk, J. (1979). Design for simultaneous equations. *Journal of Econometrics*, **11**, 63–76.

Cragg, J. (1967). On the relative small sample properties of several structural equation estimators. *Econometrica*, **35**, 89–110.

Dagenais, M. (1976). Incomplete observations and simultaneous equation models. *Journal of Econometrics*, **4**, 231–242.

Dent, W. (1976). Information and computation in simultaneous equation estimation. *Journal of Econometrics*, **4**, 89–95.

Dhrymes, P. (1974). *Econometrics: Statistical Foundations and Applications*. New York: Springer-Verlag.

Dhrymes, P. and Taylor, J. (1976). On an efficient two-step estimator for dynamic simultaneous equations models with autoregressive errors. *International Economic Review*, **17**, 362–376.

Dhrymes, P., Berner, R., and Cummins, D. (1974). A comparison of some limited information estimators for dynamic simultaneous equations models with autocorrelated errors. *Econometrica*, **42**, 311–332.

Gallant, A. and Holly, A. (1980). Statistical inference in an implicit, nonlinear simultaneous equation model in the context of maximum likelihood estimation. *Econometrica*, **48**, 697–720.

Gallant, A. and Jorgenson, D. (1979). Statistical inference for a system of simultaneous, nonlinear, implicit equations in the context of instrumental variable estimation. *Journal of Econometrics*, **11**, 275–302.

Geraci, V. (1976). Identification of simultaneous equations models with measurement error. *Journal of Econometrics*, **4**, 263–283.

Geraci, V. (1977). Estimation of simultaneous equations models with measurement error. *Econometrica*, **45**, 1243–1257.

Godfrey, L. (1976). Testing for serial correlation in dynamic simultaneous equation models. *Econometrica*, **44**, 1077–1084.

Greenberg, E. and Webster, C. (1983). *Advanced Econometrics: A Bridge to the Current Literature*. New York: Wiley.

Hale, C., Marino, R., and Ramage, J. (1980). Finite sample analysis of misspecification in simultaneous equation models. *Journal of American Statistical Association*, **75** 418–427.

Hall, A. and Pagan, A. (1981). The LIML and related estimators of an equation with moving average disturbances. *International Economic Review*, **22**, 719–730.

Harvey, A. and Phillips, G. (1980). Testing for serial correlation in simultaneous equation models. *Econometrica*, **48**, 747–760.

Harvey, A. and Phillips, G. (1981). Testing for serial correlation in simultaneous equation models: some further results. *Journal of Econometrics*, **17**, 99–106.

Hatanaka, M. (1976). Several efficient two-step estimators for the dynamic simultaneous equations model with auto-regressive disturbances. *Journal of Econometrics*, **4**, 189–204.

Hatanaka, M. (1977). Hypothesis testing in large macroeconomic models. *International Economic Review*, **18**, 607–628.

Hausman, J. (1977). Errors in variables in simultaneous equation models. *Journal of Econometrics*, **5**, 389–401.

Hendry, D. (1976). The structure of simultaneous equations estimators. *Journal of Econometrics*, **4**, 51–88.

Hendry, D. (1979). The behavior of inconsistent instrumental variables estimators of dynamic systems with autocorrelated errors. *Journal of Econometrics*, **9**, 295–314.

Holly, A. and Phillips, P. (1979). A saddlepoint approximation to the distribution of the k-class estimator of a coefficient in a simultaneous system. *Econometrica*, **47**, 1527–1547.

Hsiao, C. (1976). Identification and estimation of simultaneous equation models with measurement error. *International Economic Review*, **17**, 319–340.

Hsiao, C. (1977). Identification for a linear dynamic simultaneous error-shock model. *International Economic Review*, **18**, 181–194.

Hsiao, C. (1979). Measurement error in dynamic simultaneous equations models with stationary disturbances. *Econometrica*, **47**, 475–494.

Hwang, H. (1980). A comparison of tests of overidentifying restrictions. *Econometrica*, **48**, 1821–1825.

Jennings, L. (1980). Simultaneous equations estimation: computational aspects. *Journal of Econometrics*, **12**, 23–41.

Johnston, J. (1972). *Econometric Methods*, 2nd ed. New York: McGraw-Hill.

Kadane, J. (1971). Comparison of k-class estimators when the disturbances are small. *Econometrica*, **39**, 723–738.

Kadane, J. (1974). Testing a subset of the overidentifying restrictions. *Econometrica*, **42**, 853–867.

Kadane, J. and Anderson, T. (1977). A comment on the test of overidentifying restrictions. *Econometrica*, **45**, 1027–1031.

Kelejian, H. (1971). Two stage least squares and econometric systems linear in parameters but nonlinear in endogenous variables. *Journal of the American Statistical Association*, **66**, 373–374.

Kelejian, H. (1974). Random parameters in a simultaneous equation framework: identification and estimation. *Econometrica*, **42**, 517–529.

Kinal, T. (1980). The existence of moments of k-class estimators. *Econometrica*, **48**, 240–249.

Klein, R. (1979). Optimal instruments when disturbances are small. *Journal of Econometrics*, **9**, 367–377.

Knight, J. (1980). The coefficient of determination and simultaneous equations systems. *Journal of Econometrics*, **14**, 265–270.

Koopmans, T. and Hood, W. (1953). The estimation of simultaneous linear economic relationships. In *Studies in Econometric Method*. Edited by W. Hood and T. Koopmans, New York: Wiley. Pp. 112–199.

Maddala, G. (1974). Some small sample evidence on tests of significance in simultaneous equation models. *Econometrica*, **42**, 841–851.

Marino, R. (1973a). Approximations to the distribution functions of the ordinary least squares and two stage least squares estimators in the case of two included endogenous variables. *Econometrica*, **41**, 67–77.

Marino, R. (1973b). Approximations to the distribution functions of Theil's k-class estimators. *Econometrica*, **41**, 715–721.

Marino, R. (1977). Finite sample properties of instrumental variable estimators of structural coefficients. *Econometrica*, **45**, 487–496.

Marino, R. and McDonald, J. (1979). A note on the distribution functions of LIML and 2SLS structural coefficients in the exactly identified case. *Journal of the American Statistical Association*, **74**, 847–848.

Marino, R. and Sawa, T. (1972). The exact finite-sample distributions of the limited-information maximum likelihood estimator in the case of two included endogenous variables. *Journal of the American Statistical Association*, **67**, 159–163.

McElroy, M. (1977). Goodness of fit for seemingly unrelated regressions: Glahn's $R_{y.x}^2$ and Hooper's $\bar{r}^2$. *Journal of Econometrics*, **6**, 381–388.
Mehta, J. and Swamy, P. (1978). The existence of moments of some simple Bayes estimators of coefficients in a simultaneous equation model. *Journal of Econometrics*, **7**, 1–13.
Morgan, A. and Vandaele, W. (1974). On testing hypotheses in simultaneous equations models. *Journal of Econometrics*, **2**, 55–65.
Nagar, A. (1959). The bias and moment matrix of the general k-class estimators of the parameters in simultaneous equations. *Econometrica*, **27**, 575–595.
Nagar, A. (1962). Double k-class estimators of parameters in simultaneous equations and their small-sample properties. *International Economic Review*, **3**, 168–188.
Phillips, G. (1977). Recursions for the two stage least squares estimators. *Journal of Econometrics*, **6**, 65–78.
Phillips, P. (1980). The exact distribution of instrumental variable estimators in an equation containing $n + 1$ endogenous variables. *Econometrica*, **48**, 861–878.
Raj, B., Srivastava, V., and Ullah, A. (1980). Generalized two stage least squares estimators for a structural equation with both fixed and random components. *International Economic Review*, **21**, 171–184.
Rhodes, G. (1981). Exact density functions and approximate critical regions for likelihood ratio identifiability test statistics. *Econometrica*, **49**, 1035–1055.
Richardson, D. (1968). The exact distribution of a structural coefficient estimator. *Journal of the American Statistical Association*, **63**, 1214–1226.
Saragan, J. and Mikhail, W. (1971). A general approximation to the distribution of instrumental variable estimates. *Econometrica*, **39**, 131–169.
Sawa, T. (1969). The exact sampling distribution of ordinary least squares and two stage least squares estimators. *Journal of the American Statistical Association*, **64**, 923–937.
Sawa, T. (1972). Finite sample properties of the k-class estimators. *Econometrica*, **40**, 653–680.
Schmidt, P. (1976). *Econometrics*. New York: Marcel Dekker.
Srivastava, V., Dwivedi, T., Belinsky, M., and Tiwari, R. (1980). A numerical comparison of exact, large sample and small sample disturbance approximations of properties of k-class estimators. *International Economic Review*, **21**, 249–252.
Ullah, A. and Ullah, S. (1978). Double k-class estimators of coefficients in linear regression. *Econometrica*, **46**, 705–722.
Wagner, H. (1958). A Monte Carlo study of estimates of simultaneous linear structural equations. *Econometrica*, **26**, 117–133.
Wegge, L. (1978). Constrained indirect least squares. *Econometrica*, **46**, 435–450.

CHAPTER 22

Full Information Estimation

22.1 Introduction

In the previous chapter, we discussed methods of estimation for systems of simultaneous equations that utilized information pertaining to a particular equation alone but not that related to other equations nor the fact that the structural disturbances of various equations are contemporaneously correlated. In this chapter, however, methods are introduced that utilize both intra- and inter-equation information. As we shall see, the utilization of this additional information leads to a gain in the efficiency of estimation. In addition, this chapter discusses the implementation and testing of linear hypotheses in simultaneous equations models that may arise from *a priori* economic reasoning. Apart from the information implicit in a simultaneous equations model itself, the utilization of linear hypotheses can lead to extra gains in efficiency.

The outline of this chapter is as follows: Sections 22.2 and 22.3 describe the three-stage least squares estimator, its asymptotic distribution, and its efficiency relative to the limited information estimators discussed in the previous chapter. In Section 22.4 the use and testing of linear hypotheses in simultaneous equation models is discussed while in Section 22.5 the full information maximum likelihood estimator is outlined and contrasted to three-stage least squares. Section 22.6 concludes with a summary and guide to further reading.

22.2 Three-Stage Least Squares

Consider again the system

$$\mathbf{y}_i = Y_i\boldsymbol{\gamma}_i + X_i\boldsymbol{\delta}_i + \mathbf{e}_{.i}, \qquad i = 1, 2, \ldots, G, \tag{22.2.1}$$

and the associated transformation

$$P'X'\mathbf{y}_i = P'X'Y_i\boldsymbol{\gamma}_i + P'X'X_i\boldsymbol{\delta}_i + P'X'\mathbf{e}_{.i}, \tag{22.2.2}$$

where $P'(X'X)P = I$. The entire transformed system can be written as

$$\mathbf{w} = W\boldsymbol{\beta} + \mathbf{r}, \tag{22.2.3}$$

where $\mathbf{w}_i = P'X'\mathbf{y}_i$, $W_i = (P'X'Y_i, P'X'X_i)$, $\mathbf{r}_i = P'X'\mathbf{e}_{.i}$, $\boldsymbol{\beta}_i = \begin{bmatrix}\boldsymbol{\gamma}_i\\ \boldsymbol{\delta}_i\end{bmatrix}$,

$$\mathbf{w} = \begin{bmatrix}\mathbf{w}_1\\ \mathbf{w}_2\\ \vdots\\ \mathbf{w}_G\end{bmatrix}, \qquad W = \begin{bmatrix}W_1 & & & 0\\ & W_2 & & \\ & & \ddots & \\ 0 & & & W_G\end{bmatrix}, \qquad \boldsymbol{\beta} = \begin{bmatrix}\boldsymbol{\beta}_1\\ \boldsymbol{\beta}_2\\ \vdots\\ \boldsymbol{\beta}_G\end{bmatrix}$$

$$\text{and} \quad \mathbf{r} = \begin{bmatrix}\mathbf{r}_1\\ \mathbf{r}_2\\ \vdots\\ \mathbf{r}_G\end{bmatrix}.$$

But $\mathbf{r} = F\ \text{vec}(E)$, where $F = I_G \otimes P'X'$, $E\ (\text{vec}\ E) = \mathbf{0}$ and $\text{var}(\text{vec}\ E) = \Sigma \otimes I_T$ by assumption. Thus, conditionally on X

$$E\mathbf{r} = \mathbf{0}, \tag{22.2.4}$$

$$\begin{aligned}\text{var}(\mathbf{r}) &= F(\Sigma \otimes I_T)F'\\ &= \Sigma \otimes P'X'XP = \Sigma \otimes I_K.\end{aligned} \tag{22.2.5}$$

Therefore, the transformed system (22.2.3) has the familiar "contemporaneous correlation" covariance matrix and we are led to consider generalized least squares as the appropriate estimation technique.

The Aitken estimator for the transformed equation is

$$\tilde{\boldsymbol{\beta}} = (W'\Phi^{-1}W)^{-1}W'\Phi^{-1}\mathbf{w}, \tag{22.2.6}$$

where $\Phi = \Sigma \otimes I_K$. A feasible generalized least squares estimator for $\boldsymbol{\beta}$ is then

$$\tilde{\tilde{\boldsymbol{\beta}}} = (W'\hat{\Phi}^{-1}W)^{-1}W'\hat{\Phi}^{-1}\mathbf{w}, \tag{22.2.7}$$

where $\hat{\Phi} = \hat{\Sigma} \otimes I_K$. A consistent estimate of Σ does exist and can be constructed from the two-stage least squares residuals. In summary the three-stage least squares procedure for estimating the entire simultaneous equation system consists of

Stage 1: Purge the explanatory variables of their endogeneity by transformation.
Stage 2: Construct a consistent estimate of Σ.
Stage 3: Obtained the desired estimates by utilizing feasible generalized least squares.

In practice, "three" stages need not be computed since $\hat{\Sigma}$ can be expressed in terms of the raw data as

$$\hat{\sigma}_{ij} = \frac{1}{T}\mathbf{y}_i' A_{ij}\mathbf{y}_j \tag{22.2.8}$$

with $A_{ij} = [I_T - Z_i(W_i'W_i)^{-1}W_i'P'X']'[I_T - Z_j(W_j'W_j)^{-1}W_j'P'X']$ and $Z_i = (Y_i, X_i)$.

22.3 Asymptotic Distribution of Three-Stage Least Squares Estimators and Relative Efficiency

The three-stage least squares estimator can be written as

$$\begin{aligned}\tilde{\tilde{\boldsymbol{\beta}}} &= \boldsymbol{\beta} + (W'\hat{\Phi}^{-1}W)^{-1}W'\hat{\Phi}^{-1}\mathbf{r} \\ &= \boldsymbol{\beta} + \left(\frac{W'\hat{\Phi}^{-1}W}{T}\right)^{-1}\frac{W'\hat{\Phi}^{-1}}{\sqrt{T}}\frac{\mathbf{r}}{\sqrt{T}}.\end{aligned} \tag{22.3.1}$$

Both of the matrices on the right-hand side of (22.3.1) have finite and nonstochastic probability limits. To see this, note that a typical element of $(W'\hat{\Phi}^{-1}W/T)$ is

$$\hat{\sigma}^{ij}\left[\frac{W_i'W_j}{T}\right] = \hat{\sigma}^{ij}\frac{Z_i'X}{T}\left(\frac{X'X}{T}\right)^{-1}\frac{X'Z_j}{T},$$

where $\hat{\sigma}^{ij}$ denotes a consistent estimator of the (i, j)th element of Σ^{-1}. By assumption, $\operatorname{plim}(X'X/T) = Q$ is finite and nonsingular. Results in Section 21.3 show that $\operatorname{plim}(Z_i'X/T)$ and $\operatorname{plim}(X'Z_j/T)$ exist and contain finite elements. Thus, $\operatorname{plim}(W'\Phi^{-1}W/T)^{-1}$ exists and contains finite elements. A typical element of $(W'\hat{\Phi}^{-1}/\sqrt{T})$ is $(Z_i'X/T)\sqrt{T}P\hat{\sigma}^{ij}$. Let $\bar{P} = \operatorname{plim}\sqrt{T}P$ be the matrix that diagonalizes $\operatorname{plim}(X'X/T) = Q$, i.e., $\bar{P}'Q\bar{P} = I$. Such a matrix exists since, for every sample size T, there exists a matrix P that diagonalizes $X'X$, $P'(X'X)P = I$. Thus, $\sqrt{T}P'(X'X/T)P\sqrt{T} = I$ and $\operatorname{plim}\sqrt{T}P'(X'X/T)P\sqrt{T} = \bar{P}'Q\bar{P} = I$. Therefore, the consistency of $\tilde{\tilde{\boldsymbol{\beta}}}$ depends on $\operatorname{plim}\mathbf{r}/\sqrt{T}$. But $\mathbf{r}/\sqrt{T} = F\operatorname{vec}(E)/\sqrt{T}$ with ith subvector

$$\frac{P'X'\mathbf{e}_{.i}}{\sqrt{T}} = \frac{\sqrt{T}P'X'\mathbf{e}_{.i}}{T}.$$

Then

$$\text{plim}(\sqrt{T}P')\ \frac{(X'\mathbf{e}_{.i})}{T} = \bar{P}'\mathbf{0} = \mathbf{0}$$

and the three-stage least squares estimates are consistent in that plim $\tilde{\tilde{\boldsymbol{\beta}}} = \boldsymbol{\beta}$. In fact, using the correspondence that $\tilde{\tilde{\boldsymbol{\beta}}}$ is a feasible generalized least squares estimator (see Chapter 8), it follows straightforwardly that

$$\sqrt{T}(\tilde{\tilde{\boldsymbol{\beta}}} - \boldsymbol{\beta}) \overset{\text{asy}}{\approx} N\left(\mathbf{0}, \underset{T\to\infty}{\text{plim}} \left(\frac{W'\Phi^{-1}W}{T}\right)^{-1}\right). \tag{22.3.2}$$

Intuitively, this result obtains from the following line of reasoning. For the entire system, two-stage least squares amounts to ordinary least squares estimation of the transformed system

$$\mathbf{w} = W\boldsymbol{\beta} + \mathbf{r}.$$

That is, the two-stage least squares estimates are given by

$$\hat{\boldsymbol{\beta}} = (W'W)^{-1}W'\mathbf{w}.$$

However, the covariance structure of the transformed error term is var($\mathbf{r}$) = $\Sigma \otimes I_K = \Phi$. The three-stage least squares estimates incorporate this information via feasible generalized least squares

$$\tilde{\tilde{\boldsymbol{\beta}}} = (W'\hat{\Phi}^{-1}W)^{-1}W'\hat{\Phi}^{-1}\mathbf{w}.$$

Under the conditions developed in Chapter 8, this feasible generalized least squares estimator has the same asymptotic distribution as the Aitken estimator which assumes Φ is known. It follows that, asymptotically speaking, the three-stage least squares estimates are more efficient than two-stage least squares estimates, and hence other limited information estimators such as limited information maximum likelihood.

We can more formally investigate the comparative "sizes" of the asymptotic covariance matrix of the two-stage least squares estimates, $\sqrt{T}(\hat{\boldsymbol{\beta}} - \boldsymbol{\beta})$, namely,

$$\text{plim}\left(\frac{W'W}{T}\right)^{-1} \frac{W'\Phi W}{T} \left(\frac{W'W}{T}\right)^{-1} \tag{22.3.3}$$

derived as (21.5.7) and the asymptotic covariance matrix of the three-stage least squares estimates, $\sqrt{T}(\tilde{\tilde{\boldsymbol{\beta}}} - \boldsymbol{\beta})$, namely,

$$\text{plim}\left(\frac{W'\Phi^{-1}W}{T}\right)^{-1}. \tag{22.3.4}$$

Note expression (22.3.3) is the asymptotic covariance matrix for ordinary least squares under a generalized least squares error structure (see Section 2.7) while (22.3.4) is the usual asymptotic covariance matrix of the Aitken (generalized least squares) estimator.

Theorem 22.3.1. *The three-stage least squares estimator is more efficient than the two-stage least squares estimator.*

PROOF. See Exercise 22.4. □

In Exercise 22.4 you are asked to show that if $\sigma_{ij} = 0$ for all $i \neq j$ then there is no efficiency gain from using three-stage least squares instead of two-stage least squares. That is, the two-stage least squares and three-stage least squares estimators have the same asymptotic distributions. This is not to say, however, that for finite samples the estimates derived using the two methods would be numerically the same. Though Σ is diagonal, $\hat{\Sigma}$ need not be. Nevertheless, the two methods are equally efficient asymptotically.

There is another circumstance when two-stage least squares and three-stage least squares are equally efficient. Generalized least squares and ordinary least squares estimators are identical in a regression context when the number of observations equals the number of regression coefficients to be estimated. This situation might be termed the "zero degrees of freedom case." The corresponding case in simultaneous equations is when each equation in the system is exactly identified. In Exercise 22.4 you are asked to show that in this case the two-stage least squares and three-stage least squares estimators are numerically identical, and thus equally efficient.

Finally, it can be shown (see Exercise 22.1) that three-stage least squares fails to exist if *any* equation in the system fails the order condition for identification. In this instance $W'\hat{\Phi}^{-1}W$ is singular and the three-stage least squares estimator cannot be computed.

22.4 Use of Linear Hypotheses in Simultaneous Equations

There are often instances where economic reasoning leads to linear restrictions on the structural parameters. See Exercise 22.5 for an example. In this section we consider use of such restrictions to improve the efficiency of estimation and how the hypotheses might be tested.

22.4.1 Restricted Three-Stage Least Squares Estimation

Again, consider the simultaneous equation system

$$\begin{aligned} \mathbf{y}_i &= Y_i \boldsymbol{\gamma}_i + X_i \boldsymbol{\delta}_i + \mathbf{e}_{.i} \\ &= Z_i \boldsymbol{\beta}_{.i} + \mathbf{e}_{.i}, \qquad i = 1, 2, \ldots, G. \end{aligned} \tag{22.4.1}$$

Assume the additional restrictions

$$H\boldsymbol{\beta} = \mathbf{h} \tag{22.4.2}$$

are available. The known matrix H is of dimension $J \times m$, $\mathbf{h}$ is a $J \times 1$ vector of constants, and the parameter vector

$$\boldsymbol{\beta} = \begin{bmatrix} \boldsymbol{\beta}_{.1} \\ \boldsymbol{\beta}_{.2} \\ \vdots \\ \boldsymbol{\beta}_{.G} \end{bmatrix}$$

is $m \times 1$, where $m = \sum_{i=1}^{G} [k_i + (g_i - 1)]$ and J is the number of independent restrictions in the entire system. (Note: Restricted estimation could always proceed by substituting out the restrictions of (22.4.2) and estimating the restricted model as in Klein's Model I. However, discussion is facilitated by using the present formulation (22.4.1)–(22.4.2).)

For convenience, let us transform the model of (22.4.1)–(22.4.2) to

$$\mathbf{w} = W\boldsymbol{\beta} + \mathbf{r} \tag{22.4.3}$$

subject to

$$H\boldsymbol{\beta} = \mathbf{h}, \tag{22.4.4}$$

where (22.4.3) is defined as before. Estimation of (22.4.3) subject to $H\boldsymbol{\beta} = \mathbf{h}$ then becomes nothing more than a restricted generalized least squares problem, or equivalently restricted least squares estimation of a homoscedastic model after appropriate transformation. The unrestricted three-stage least squares estimator is

$$\tilde{\tilde{\boldsymbol{\beta}}} = (W'\hat{\Phi}^{-1}W)^{-1}W'\hat{\Phi}^{-1}\mathbf{w}, \tag{22.4.5}$$

whereas the restricted three-stage least squares estimator is

$$\tilde{\tilde{\boldsymbol{\beta}}}^* = \tilde{\tilde{\boldsymbol{\beta}}} + CH'(HCH')^{-1}(\mathbf{h} - H\tilde{\tilde{\boldsymbol{\beta}}}), \tag{22.4.6}$$

where $C = (W'\hat{\Phi}^{-1}W)^{-1}$. $\tilde{\tilde{\boldsymbol{\beta}}}^*$ is consistent and asymptotically efficient relative to $\tilde{\tilde{\boldsymbol{\beta}}}$ if $H\boldsymbol{\beta} = \mathbf{h}$ is true. Furthermore, given $H\boldsymbol{\beta} = \mathbf{h}$,

$$\sqrt{T}(\tilde{\tilde{\boldsymbol{\beta}}}^* - \boldsymbol{\beta}) \overset{\text{asy}}{\sim} N(\mathbf{0}, \bar{C} - \bar{C}H'(H\bar{C}H')^{-1}H\bar{C}), \tag{22.4.7}$$

where $\bar{C} = \text{plim}(TC)$. The relative efficiency of the restricted three-stage least squares estimator follows from the fact that $\bar{C}$ is the asymptotic covariance matrix of $\sqrt{T}(\tilde{\tilde{\boldsymbol{\beta}}} - \boldsymbol{\beta})$ and $\bar{C}H'(H\bar{C}H')^{-1}H\bar{C}$ is a positive semidefinite matrix. Using the result of normality and the fact that the diagonal elements of

$$C - CH'(HCH')^{-1}HC$$

provide approximate asymptotic standard errors of $\tilde{\tilde{\boldsymbol{\beta}}}^*$, usual test of hypothesis concerning $\boldsymbol{\beta}$ can be conducted using restricted three-stage least squares estimates.

22.4.2 Tests of Linear Hypotheses Using Three-Stage Least Squares Estimates

One way of statistically investigating the validity of a model is to test the restrictions imposed on the model by the economic theory. For example, in Exercise 22.5, the imposed economic theory specifies certain restrictions. If the data support the model, a test of the implied linear hypotheses should be affirmative.

In general, suppose that interest centers on the test of the hypotheses

$$\begin{aligned} H_0 &: H\boldsymbol{\beta} = \mathbf{h}, \\ H_1 &: H\boldsymbol{\beta} \neq \mathbf{h} \end{aligned} \tag{22.4.8}$$

in the model $\mathbf{y}_i = Y_i\boldsymbol{\gamma}_i + X_i\boldsymbol{\delta}_i + \mathbf{e}_{.i}$, $i = 1, 2, \ldots, G$. This problem is equivalent to general linear hypothesis testing in feasible generalized least squares models (see Chapter 8). The analogous statistic is

$$u = \left(\frac{KG - m}{J}\right) \cdot \frac{(\mathbf{h} - H\tilde{\tilde{\boldsymbol{\beta}}})'[H(W'\hat{\Phi}^{-1}W)H']^{-1}(\mathbf{h} - H\tilde{\tilde{\boldsymbol{\beta}}})}{(\mathbf{w} - W\tilde{\tilde{\boldsymbol{\beta}}})'\hat{\Phi}^{-1}(\mathbf{w} - W\tilde{\tilde{\boldsymbol{\beta}}})}. \tag{22.4.9}$$

Under the null hypothesis $H\boldsymbol{\beta} = \mathbf{h}$, u is asymptotically distributed $F(J, KG - m)$. Note that the denominator degrees of freedom is the number of overidentifying restrictions in the system. As a result, this statistic is only applicable when all equations are identified (assuring three-stage least squares exists) and when, in addition, at least one equation is overidentified.

22.5 Full Information Maximum Likelihood

Unlike the limited information maximum likelihood estimator of Section 21.7, which maximizes the likelihood function of the ith equation's included endogenous variables, Y_i^0, subject to the restrictions imposed on the reduced form, $\Pi_{2.}^0\boldsymbol{\gamma}_i^0 = \mathbf{0}$, the full information likelihood estimator maximizes the likelihood function of the entire system's current endogenous variables, Y, subject to the restrictions placed on the reduced form of Y, $(\Pi, I_K)\begin{bmatrix}\Gamma \\ \Delta\end{bmatrix} = 0$, by the overidentification in all equations. Specifically, the likelihood function for Y is (see Exercise 21.11)

$$L(Y) = (2\pi)^{-GT/2}|\Omega|^{-T/2}\exp[-\tfrac{1}{2}\operatorname{tr}\Omega^{-1}(Y - X\Pi)'(Y - X\Pi)]. \tag{22.5.1}$$

Then maximizing (22.5.1) subject to

$$(\Pi, I_K)\begin{bmatrix}\Gamma \\ \Delta\end{bmatrix} = 0 \tag{22.5.2}$$

provides the maximum likelihood (full information maximum likelihood) estimates of Γ and Δ. This constrained maximization is equivalent to minimizing the generalized residual variance $|(Y - X\Pi)'(Y - X\Pi)|$ subject to (22.5.2). The analogy to the limited information maximum likelihood estimator is quite obvious. The full information maximum likelihood estimator utilizes all information, hence the term "full," whereas the limited information maximum likelihood estimator utilizes only that information particular to the given equation.

Naturally, given $L(Y)$, the full information maximum likelihood estimator possesses all the properties of a maximum likelihood estimator; consistency, asymptotic normality and asymptotic efficiency in that the asymptotic covariance matrix of the full information maximum likelihood estimator achieves the asymptotic Cramér–Rao lower bound. In addition, hypothesis tests can be based on the inverse of the information matrix.

The following results put into perspective the relative efficiencies of the three-stage least squares and full information maximum likelihood estimators. First, when there exists no prior information on the variance–covariance matrix of the structural disturbances, Σ (for example, no covariance restrictions of the form $\sigma_{ij} = 0$), the three-stage least squares and full information maximum likelihood estimators, though numerically distinct in small samples, have the same asymptotic distribution (see Schmidt (1976)). It follows that three-stage least squares, in the presence of normally distributed errors, is asymptotically efficient. In contrast, however, when prior information concerning Σ is available, the full information maximum likelihood estimator is asymptotically more efficient than three-stage least squares. See Rothenberg and Leenders (1964). The quality of the estimate of Σ is important in determining the efficiency of the estimate of $\boldsymbol{\beta}$. Not just any estimate of Σ will do when prior information of the form $\sigma_{ij} = 0$ is available. Restricted estimation of Σ utilizing the prior knowledge $\sigma_{ij} = 0$ is more efficient than unrestricted estimation of Σ. As a result, the unrestricted estimate of Σ arising from three-stage least squares is inefficient and the three-stage least squares estimate of $\boldsymbol{\beta}$ is inefficient. Finally, the full information maximum likelihood estimator is defined only when *all* equations in the system are identified.

22.6 Summary and Guide to Further Readings

As illustrated in this chapter, full information methods such as three-stage least squares and full information maximum likelihood offer a gain in large samples over limited information methods like two-stage least squares and limited information maximum likelihood. This result obtains because full information methods utilize the information concerning the contemporaneous disturbance $\mathbf{e}_{t.}$ and the overidentifying restrictions arising from other equations. Implicit in our discussion, however, is the assumption that the given simultaneous equation model has been correctly specified. In the case of incorrect specification (improper inclusion or exclusion of variables), it is not clear which estimator, limited information, full information or ordinary least squares, is to be preferred. The choice, of course, will depend on the form of the misspecification and which equations are involved. To this point, Monte Carlo studies (see Summers (1965), for example) have studied the performance of these estimators when specification error is present. In most studies, ordinary least squares is seldom recommended. However, when a given equation is correctly specified yet the other equations sustain some specification error, it is often suggested that an investigator is best served by "localizing" the potential effects of misspecification by utilizing a limited information method like two-stage least squares. The full information estimates of a particular equation can be confounded by misspecification in other equations. Therefore, though conceptually the full information methods appear the most desirable, an investigator might be wise to choose a limited information estimator for a given equation which is felt to be correctly specified and of particular importance, especially when the specifications of the remaining equations are held with less confidence. In summary, the full information methods, though more efficient under correct specification, are more sensitive to misspecification than limited information methods. The selection of estimators then must be made on a case-by-case basis reflecting the degree of confidence with which the specification of the model is held.

Finally, as shown in our discussion of restricted and mixed three-stage least squares estimation (see Exercise 22.3 for mixed three-stage least squares), the implementation of valid prior information can offer an efficiency gain in simultaneous equation estimation. Statistics were also derived to determine the "appropriateness" of linear hypotheses given the data. As in the case of single equation estimation (Chapter 6), the reward of more cogent *a priori* reasoning is more precise statistical inference concerning economic relationships.

Much of the recent work on full information estimation has been to extend three-stage least squares and full information maximum likelihood to nonlinear systems and to explore estimators that computationally and statistically approximate them. Computational aspects are discussed by Dagenais (1978), Byron (1977), Dent (1976), and Parke (1982). Extensions of full information maximum likelihood and three-stage least squares relating to linear and nonlinear systems are found in Brundy and Jorgenson (1971), Hausman (1975), Gallant and Holly (1980), Wegge (1978), Hendry (1976), Brown (1981), Amemiya (1977), Fair and Parke (1980), Belsley (1979, 1980), Jennings (1980), Gallant and Jorgenson (1979), and Gallant (1977). Autoregressive error structures are discussed by Reinsel (1979), Dhrymes and Erlat (1974), and Hendry (1976). Other useful references, that serve to modify and relate estimators, include Maasoumi (1980), Scharf (1976), Byron (1976), Maravall (1976), and Rothenberg (1973).

22.7 Exercises

22.1. Show that $W'\hat{\Phi}^{-1}W$ is singular and, therefore, the three-stage least squares estimator fails to exist if any structural equation does not satisfy the order condition.

22.2. Instead of assuming that the restrictions (22.4.2) are exact, assume that $\mathbf{h} = H\boldsymbol{\beta} + \mathbf{v}$, where $\mathbf{v} \sim N(\mathbf{0}, \Psi)$ and Ψ is known. Show that the "mixed" three-stage least squares estimator can be written

$$\tilde{\tilde{\boldsymbol{\beta}}} = \{W'(\hat{\Sigma}^{-1} \otimes I)W + H'\Psi^{-1}H\}^{-1}\{W'(\hat{\Sigma}^{-1} \otimes I)\mathbf{w} + H'\Psi^{-1}\mathbf{h}\}$$

with estimated asymptotic covariance matrix

$$\{W'(\hat{\Sigma} \otimes I)W + H'\Psi^{-1}H\}^{-1}.$$

22.3. Obtain the three-stage least squares parameter estimates for Klein's Model I.

22.4. Prove Theorem 22.3.1 using the following: define the matrix A by

$$(W'W)^{-1}W' = (W'\Phi^{-1}W)^{-1}W'\Phi^{-1} + A \tag{1}$$

and note that $AW = 0$. Also note that

$$\sqrt{T}A = \left(\frac{W'W}{T}\right)^{-1}\frac{W'}{\sqrt{T}} - \left(\frac{W'\Phi^{-1}W}{T}\right)^{-1}\frac{W'\Phi^{-1}}{\sqrt{T}}. \tag{2}$$

Since all the elements on the right-hand side of (2) have well-defined nonstochastic probability limits,

$$\operatorname{plim}\sqrt{T}A = \bar{A} \tag{3}$$

and $\bar{A}$ is nonstochastic with finite elements. Note that

$$[\sqrt{T}(W'W)^{-1}W']\Phi[\sqrt{T}W(W'W)^{-1}] = \left(\frac{W'W}{T}\right)^{-1}\frac{W'\Phi W}{T}\left(\frac{W'W}{T}\right)^{-1}. \tag{4}$$

Using (1) the expression (4) can be rewritten as

$$\begin{aligned}
&\left(\frac{W'W}{T}\right)^{-1}\frac{W'\Phi W}{T}\left(\frac{W'W}{T}\right)^{-1} \\
&= \left[\left(\frac{W'\Phi^{-1}W}{T}\right)\frac{W'}{\sqrt{T}}\Phi^{-1} + \sqrt{T}A\right]\Phi\left[\Phi^{-1}\frac{W}{\sqrt{T}}\left(\frac{W'\Phi^{-1}W}{T}\right)^{-1} + \sqrt{T}A'\right] \\
&= \left(\frac{W'\Phi^{-1}W}{T}\right)^{-1} + \sqrt{T}A\Phi(\sqrt{T}A)'.
\end{aligned}$$

Taking probability limits, we conclude that

$$\operatorname{plim}\left(\frac{W'W}{T}\right)^{-1}\frac{W'\Phi W}{T}\left(\frac{W'W}{T}\right)^{-1} = \operatorname{plim}\left(\frac{W'\Phi^{-1}W}{T}\right)^{-1} + \bar{A}\Phi\bar{A}'. \tag{5}$$

The left-hand side of (5) is the asymptotic covariance matrix of the two-stage least squares estimates while the first term on the right-hand side of (5) is the asymptotic covariance matrix of the three-stage least squares estimates. Therefore, the difference between these two covariance matrices is $\bar{A}\Phi\bar{A}'$ which is a positive semidefinite matrix since Φ is positive definite.

(a) Now, show that if $\sigma_{ij} = 0$ for all $i \neq j$, then $A = \bar{A} = 0$, and consequently there is no efficiency gain from using three-stage least squares rather than two-stage least squares.

(b) Show that if each equation is exactly identified then the matrices W_i are square and of dimension $K = k + (g - 1)$. Then show that the two-stage least squares and three-stage least squares estimators are identical.

22.5. Yeh (1976) analyzes the aggregate supply and demand for farm products in the United States. Apart from the growth term that the present authors have included, the Yeh model is of the form:

$$Q_{dt} = \alpha_d PR_t^{\lambda^0\beta_d} PR_{t-1}^{\lambda^1\beta_d} \cdots PR_{t-\infty}^{\lambda^\infty\beta_d} e^{g_d t}, \tag{1}$$

$$Q_{st} = \alpha_s \left(\frac{PR}{PDFE}\right)_t^{\mu^0\beta_s} \left(\frac{PR}{PDFE}\right)_{t-1}^{\mu^1\beta_s} \cdots \left(\frac{PR}{PDFE}\right)_{t-\infty}^{\mu^\infty\beta_s} e^{g_s t}, \tag{2}$$

$$Q_{dt} = Q_{st}(1 - DIAA_t), \tag{3}$$

where $Q_{dt} \equiv$ quantity demanded of farm products by private sector at time t;
$Q_{st} \equiv$ quantity supplied by farmers at time t;
$PR_t \equiv$ prices received by farmers at time t;
$PDFE_t \equiv$ prices paid by farmers for farm operating expense at time t;
$DIAA_t \equiv$ federal government diversion rate at time t;
$t \equiv$ time.

The aggregate demand and supply equations are geometric lags with geometric parameters λ and μ, respectively. Taking natural logarithmic transformations of the Equations (1)–(3) and applying the Koyck transformation yields

$$\ln(Q_{dt}) = (1 - \lambda)\ln\alpha_d + \lambda g_d + \beta_d \ln(PR_t) + \lambda\ln(Q_{d,t-1}) + g_d(1 - \lambda)t, \tag{4}$$

$$\begin{aligned}\ln(Q_{st}) = {} & (1 - \mu)\ln\alpha_s + \mu g_s + \beta_s \ln(PR/PDFE)_t \\ & + \mu\ln(Q_{s,t-1}) + q_s(1 - \mu)t,\end{aligned} \tag{5}$$

$$\ln(Q_{dt}) = \ln(Q_{st}) + \ln(1 - DIAA_t). \tag{6}$$

Substituting in the identity (6) and appending error terms u_t and v_t provides the model

$$\begin{aligned}\ln(Q_t) = {} & a_0 + a_1\ln(PR_t) + a_2\ln(Q_{t-1}) \\ & + a_3\ln(1 - DIAA_{t-1}) + a_4 t \\ & + a_5\ln(1 - DIAA_t) + u_t,\end{aligned} \tag{7}$$

$$\begin{aligned}\ln(Q_t) = {} & b_0 + b_1\ln(PR_t) + b_2\ln(PDFE_t) \\ & + b_3\ln(Q_{t-1}) + b_4 t + v_t,\end{aligned} \tag{8}$$

where $a_0 = (1 - \lambda)\ln\alpha_d + \lambda g_d$, $a_1 = \beta_d$, $a_2 = a_3 = \lambda$, $a_4 = g_d(1 - \lambda)$, $a_5 = 1$, $b_0 = (1 - \mu)\ln\alpha_s + \mu g_s$, $b_1 = -b_2 = \beta_s$, $b_3 = \mu$, and $b_4 = g_s(1 - \mu)$. The equilibrium quantity is $Q_t = Q_{dt} = Q_{st}$. The error terms u_t and v_t are assumed to have zero means with variances and covariances

$$E\begin{bmatrix} u_t \\ v_t \end{bmatrix}(u_t \quad v_t) = \begin{bmatrix} \sigma_{11} & \sigma_{12} \\ \sigma_{21} & \sigma_{22} \end{bmatrix}$$

and

$$Eu_t v_s = 0 \quad \text{for } t \neq s.$$

This model has two endogenous variables, $\ln(Q_t)$ and $\ln(PR_t)$, and six predetermined variables; a constant, $\ln(Q_{t-1})$, $\ln(1 - DIAA_{t-1})$, $\ln(1 - DIAA_t)$, t, and $\ln(PDFE_t)$. The reader should verify that each equation is overidentified.

What three linear restrictions can be imposed on the parameters of the structural Equations (7) and (8) in light of the assumed theory?

22.8 References

Amemiya, T. (1977). The maximum likelihood and nonlinear three-stage least squares estimator in the general nonlinear simultaneous equation model. *Econometrica*, **45**, 955–968.

Belsley, D. (1979). On the computational competitiveness of full-information maximum likelihood and three-stage least squares in the estimation of nonlinear simultaneous equations systems. *Journal of Econometrics*, **9**, 315–342.

Belsley, D. (1980). On the efficient computation of the nonlinear full information maximum likelihood estimator. *Journal of Econometrics*, **14**, 203–226.

Brown, B. (1981). Sample size requirements in full information maximum likelihood estimation. *International Economic Review*, **22**, 443–460.

Brundy, J. and Jorgensen, D. (1971). Efficient estimation of simultaneous equations by instrumental variables. *Review of Economics and Statistics*, **53**, 207–224.

Byron, R. (1976). A reinterpretation of two and three stage least squares. *International Economic Review*, **17**, 773–778.

Byron, R. (1977). Efficient estimation and inference in large econometric systems. *Econometrica*, **45**, 1499–1516.

Dagenais, M. (1978). The computation of FIML estimates as iterative generalized least squares estimates in linear and nonlinear simultaneous equation models. *Econometrica*, **46**, 1351–1363.

Dent, W. (1976). Information and computation in simultaneous equation estimation. *Journal of Econometrics*, **4**, 89–95.

Dhrymes, P. and Erlat, H. (1974). Asymptotic properties of full information estimators in dynamic autoregressive simultaneous equations models. *Journal of Econometrics*, **2**, 247–259.

Fair, R. and Parke, W. (1980). Full information estimates of a nonlinear macroeconometric model. *Journal of Econometrics*, **13**, 269–292.

Gallant, A. (1977). Three-stage least squares estimation for a system of simultaneous, nonlinear, implicit equations. *Journal of Econometrics*, **5**, 71–88.

Gallant, A. and Holly, A. (1980). Statistical inference in an implicit, nonlinear simultaneous equation model in the context of maximum likelihood estimation. *Econometrica*, **48**, 697–720.

Gallant, A. and Jorgenson, D. (1979). Statistical inference for a system of simultaneous, nonlinear, implicit equations in the context of instrumental variable estimation. *Journal of Econometrics*, **11**, 275–302.

Hausman, J. (1975). An instrumental variable approach to full information estimation for linear and certain nonlinear econometric models. *Econometrica*, **43**, 727–738.

Hendry, D. (1976). The structure of simultaneous equations estimators. *Journal of Econometrics*, **4**, 51–88.

Jennings, L. (1980). Simultaneous equations estimation: computational aspects. *Journal of Econometrics*, **12**, 23–41.

Maasoumi, E. (1980). A ridge-like method for simultaneous estimation of simultaneous equations. *Journal of Econometrics*, **12**, 161–176.

Maravall, A. (1976). A note on three stage least squares estimation. *Journal of Econometrics*, **4**, 325–330.

Parke, W. (1982). An algorithm for FIML and 3SLS estimation for large nonlinear models. *Econometrica*, **50**, 81–97.

Reinsel, G. (1979). FIML estimation of the dynamic simultaneous equation models with ARMA disturbances. *Journal of Econometrics*, **9**, 263–281.

Rothenberg, T. (1973). *Efficient Estimation with A Priori Information*. New Haven, CT: Yale University Press.

Rothenberg, T. and Leenders, C. (1964). Efficient estimation of simultaneous equation systems. *Econometrica*, **32**, 406–425.

Scharf, W. (1976). *K*-matrix class estimators and the full information maximum likelihood estimator as a special case. *Journal of Econometrics*, **4**, 41–50.

Schmidt, P. (1976). *Econometrics*. New York: Marcel Dekker.

Summers, R. (1965). A capital intensive approach to the small sample properties of various simultaneous equation estimators. *Econometrica*, **33**, 1–41.

Wegge, L. (1978). Constrained indirect least squares. *Econometrica*, **46**, 435–450.

Yeh, C. J. (1976). Prices, farm outputs, and income projections under alternative assumed demand and supply conditions. *American Journal of Agricultural Economics*, **58**, 703–711.

CHAPTER 23

Reduced Form Estimation and Prediction in Simultaneous Equations Models

23.1 Introduction

In this chapter we turn our attention from point estimation of the structural coefficients of a simultaneous equations model to the efficient estimation of the reduced form equation $Y = X\Pi + V$ and its use for forecasting future values of the endogenous variables given values (either known or forecasted) of the predetermined variables. Assuming the appropriateness of the initial model specification, efficient estimation requires the utilization of *all* available information. As we shall see, the ordinary least squares estimator, $\hat{\Pi} = (X'X)^{-1}X'Y$, of the reduced form parameters does not utilize all available information and as a result there exist more efficient ways to estimate Π. Such methods are discussed in Section 23.2.

Logically, the more efficient the estimates of the reduced form parameters, the more precise the corresponding forecasts derivable from the reduced form. Forecast confidence intervals will be developed in Section 23.3 for efficient prediction of yet unrealized values of the joint endogenous variables. In Section 23.4, we expand the traditional discussion of forecasting in simultaneous equation models to the case where the errors are autocorrelated. As in the case of forecasting in the linear model with AR(1) errors (see Section 2.6), the usual method of forecasting is modified when autocorrelation is present. The summary and guide to further reading are presented in Section 23.5.

23.2 Restricted Reduced Form

Consider the simultaneous equations model

$$Y\Gamma + X\Delta + E = 0, \tag{23.2.1}$$

where the standard assumptions concerning the errors are

$$\begin{aligned} E\mathbf{e}_{t.} &= \mathbf{0}', \qquad t = 1, 2, \ldots, T, \\ E\mathbf{e}'_{t.}\mathbf{e}_{t.} &= \Sigma \end{aligned} \tag{23.2.2}$$

and

$$E\mathbf{e}'_{s.}\mathbf{e}_{t.} = 0 \quad \text{for } s \neq t.$$

The reduced form is

$$Y = X\Pi + V, \tag{23.2.3}$$

where $\Pi = -\Delta\Gamma^{-1}$ and $V = -E\Gamma^{-1}$. The rows of V (i.e., $\mathbf{v}_{t.}$) are independent and identically distributed as $N(\mathbf{0}, \Omega)$, where $\Omega = (\Gamma^{-1})'\Sigma\Gamma^{-1}$. Consider the case when X is nonstochastic. One interpretation of (23.2.3) is that the expected values of the current endogenous are linear combinations of the predetermined variables, that is,

$$E(Y|X) = X\Pi. \tag{23.2.4}$$

Let Π_{kg} denote the reduced form coefficient for the kth predetermined variable associated with the gth current endogenous variable. This coefficient can be interpreted as the partial derivative of the conditional expectation of the current endogenous variable y_{tg} with respect to the predetermined variable x_{tk} while holding all other x_t's constant.

In Chapter 19 (Theorem 19.4.3) we saw that the ordinary least squares estimator of Π, $\hat{\Pi} = (X'X)^{-1}X'Y$, is consistent and that

$$\sqrt{T}\,\mathrm{vec}(\hat{\Pi} - \Pi) \overset{\text{asy}}{\sim} N(\mathbf{0}, \Omega \otimes Q^{-1}), \tag{23.2.5}$$

where

$$Q = \mathrm{plim}(X'X/T). \tag{23.2.6}$$

Consider, however, the following alternative means of estimating Π.

Definition 23.2.1. Let $\tilde{\Delta}$ and $\tilde{\Gamma}$ be consistent estimators of Δ and Γ. Then a *derived (restricted) reduced form* estimator of Π is

$$\tilde{\Pi} = -\tilde{\Delta}\tilde{\Gamma}^{-1}. \tag{23.2.7}$$

From Slutsky's theorem (Theorem 4.2.2), $\tilde{\Pi}$ is a consistent estimator for Π. More importantly, deriving the reduced form, rather than directly estimating it via ordinary least squares, offers a means of more efficiently estimating Π. To see this point, recall that when some of the structural equations of a simultaneous equation system are overidentified, certain restrictions are imposed on Π. There exist multiple solutions for the structural parameters Γ and Δ as functions of the elements of Π. For illustration, consider Example 20.4.3, a two-equation model with its first equation being overidentified. The restriction imposed on the reduced form by the first equation is

$$\begin{bmatrix} \Pi_{11} \\ \Pi_{21} \end{bmatrix} - \begin{bmatrix} \Pi_{12} \\ \Pi_{22} \end{bmatrix} \Gamma_{21} = \mathbf{0}. \tag{23.2.8}$$

The second equation does not impose any restrictions on the reduced form as it is unidentified. Even if it were identified, only overidentification places restrictions on the reduced form.

In general, using the notation of Section 21.7, the restrictions placed on the reduced form by overidentification of the first equation are of the form

$$\Pi_2^0 \boldsymbol{\gamma}^0 = \mathbf{0}. \tag{23.2.9}$$

For a detailed development of (23.2.9), read carefully Section 21.7. As far as the number of restrictions, the following theorem provides a specific answer. Let $\phi \boldsymbol{\beta}_{.1} = \mathbf{0}$ denote the linear homogeneous restrictions available *a priori* on the first equation and $\mathbf{B}' = [\Gamma' \Delta']$.

Theorem 23.2.1 (Fisher (1966)). *The a priori restrictions* $\phi \boldsymbol{\beta}_{.1} = \mathbf{0}$ *imply the existence of precisely* rank (ϕ) − rank $(\phi \mathrm{B})$ *linear, but not necessarily homogeneous, restrictions on the reduced form matrix* Π. *These restrictions take the form of linear dependencies among the columns of* Π.

PROOF. Note the row dimension and column rank of $\Pi_{2.}^0$ in the instance of overidentification. For a more detailed discussion see Fisher (1966). □

In summary, then, each degree of overidentification introduces an additional restriction on the reduced form parameters.

In total the restrictions placed on the reduced form parameters Π by the overidentification of equations in the entire system is represented by

$$(\Pi, I_K) \begin{bmatrix} \Gamma \\ \Delta \end{bmatrix} = 0. \tag{23.2.10}$$

As to the number of *independent* restrictions implied by the degree of overidentification in the entire system, certainly summing the terms rank (ϕ) − rank $(\phi \mathrm{B})$ for each equation gives an upper bound on that number. However, it is possible that this total may exceed the true number of independent restrictions. Fisher (1966, p. 51), provides an example of redundant restrictions on the reduced form arising from overidentification in separate equations. Regardless of the lack of uniqueness of the total number of independent restrictions on the reduced form, however, the important point of overidentification is that there are at least some restrictions placed on the reduced form.

Clearly the identity $\Pi = -\Delta\Gamma^{-1}$ places restrictions on the reduced form when some or all equations in the system are overidentified and as a result a derived reduced form estimator, $\tilde{\Pi} = -\tilde{\Delta}\tilde{\Gamma}^{-1}$, satisfies these restrictions. Since the ordinary least squares estimator $\hat{\Pi}$ does not utilize the information in such restrictions, there arises the possibility that deriving an estimator of the reduced form parameters may prove to be more efficient than the ordinary least squares estimator. By more efficient we mean that, when the asymptotic variance–covariance matrix of $\tilde{\Pi}$ is subtracted from the asymptotic variance–covariance matrix of $\hat{\Pi}$, the resulting matrix is positive semidefinite.

But which consistent estimates of Γ and Δ should be used in forming the derived reduced form? Assuming that all equations in the system are identified, two possible candidates are three-stage least squares and two-stage least squares estimates of the entire system. Of course, it was shown earlier in Chapter 22 that the three-stage least squares estimates are more efficient than the two-stage least squares estimates when at least one equation is overidentified (in the case of exact identification for all equations, two-stage least squares and three-stage least squares are equally efficient). Intuitively, it would seem that the derived reduced form using the more efficient estimates of Γ and Δ would in turn be more efficient.

Two conjectures, therefore, seem to be worthy of investigation. First, the three-stage least squares derived reduced form estimates are more efficient than the two-stage least squares derived reduced form estimates. Second, because more prior information is used, the three-stage least squares derived reduced form estimates of Π are more efficient than the ordinary least squares estimates. We now turn to these conjectures.

The asymptotic properties of derived reduced form estimates were obtained by Dhrymes (1973). We present here a sketch of the basic results. First, the following theorem will prove instrumental in understanding the following results.

Theorem 23.2.2. *Let $\tilde{\Gamma}$ and $\tilde{\Delta}$ denote consistent estimates of Γ and Δ such that*

$$\sqrt{T}\,\text{vec}\begin{bmatrix}\tilde{\Gamma} - \Gamma \\ \tilde{\Delta} - \Delta\end{bmatrix} \overset{\text{asy}}{\sim} N(\mathbf{0}, \Psi) \tag{23.2.11}$$

and $\tilde{\Pi} = -\tilde{\Delta}\tilde{\Gamma}^{-1}$. Then

$$\sqrt{T}\,\text{vec}(\tilde{\Pi} - \Pi) \overset{\text{asy}}{\sim} N(\mathbf{0}, A\Psi A'), \tag{23.2.12}$$

where $A = (\Gamma^{-1})' \otimes (\Pi, I)$.

PROOF. The following proof is due to Schmidt (1976, pp. 237–238).

$$\begin{aligned}\tilde{\Pi} - \Pi &= \tilde{\Delta}\Gamma^{-1} + \tilde{\Pi} - \tilde{\Delta}\Gamma^{-1} + \Delta\Gamma^{-1} \\ &= -\tilde{\Pi}\tilde{\Gamma}\Gamma^{-1} + \tilde{\Pi}\Gamma\Gamma^{-1} - \tilde{\Delta}\Gamma^{-1} + \Delta\Gamma^{-1} \\ &= -\tilde{\Pi}(\tilde{\Gamma} - \Gamma)\Gamma^{-1} - (\tilde{\Delta} - \Delta)\Gamma^{-1} \\ &= -(\tilde{\Pi}, I)\begin{bmatrix}\tilde{\Gamma} - \Gamma \\ \tilde{\Delta} - \Delta\end{bmatrix}\Gamma^{-1}.\end{aligned}$$

But note that for conformable matrices A, B, and C, $\text{vec}(ABC) = (C' \otimes A)\,\text{vec}(B)$. Therefore

$$\text{vec}(\tilde{\Pi} - \Pi) = -[(\Gamma^{-1})' \otimes (\tilde{\Pi}, I)]\,\text{vec}\begin{bmatrix}\tilde{\Gamma} - \Gamma \\ \tilde{\Delta} - \Delta\end{bmatrix}$$

and

$$\sqrt{T}\,\text{vec}(\tilde{\Pi} - \Pi) = -\tilde{A}\sqrt{T}\,\text{vec}\begin{bmatrix}\tilde{\Gamma} - \Gamma \\ \tilde{\Delta} - \Delta\end{bmatrix},$$

where $\tilde{A} = (\Gamma^{-1})' \otimes (\tilde{\Pi}, I)$. Since $\text{plim}\,\tilde{\Pi} = \Pi$ then

$$\sqrt{T}\,\text{vec}(\tilde{\Pi} - \Pi) \overset{\text{asy}}{\sim} N(\mathbf{0}, A\Psi A')$$

as desired. □

If any equation of the system is not identified then the three-stage least squares estimator has a singular asymptotic covariance matrix and as such the three-stage least squares estimator is undefined (see Exercise 22.1). It then logically follows that $A\Psi A'$ is also singular, given Ψ represents a singular three-stage least squares asymptotic covariance matrix. Formally:

Theorem 23.2.3. *Unless every equation in the structural system obeys the rank and order conditions for identification, the derived reduced form estimator has a singular asymptotic covariance matrix. Hence the estimator is undefined asymptotically speaking.*

Let Ψ_1 and Ψ_2 denote the asymptotic covariance matrices for two-stage least squares and three-stage least squares, respectively. From Chapter 22 we know that $\Psi_1 - \Psi_2$ is positive semidefinite. It follows that

$$A(\Psi_1 - \Psi_2)A' = A\Psi_1 A' - A\Psi_2 A'$$

is also positive semidefinite. This provides the proof for

Theorem 23.2.4. *The three-stage least squares derived reduced form estimator is asymptotically more efficient than the two-stage least squares derived reduced form estimator.*

The final major result provided by Dhrymes (1973) is the following:

Theorem 23.2.5. *The derived reduced form based on three-stage least squares structural estimates is asymptotically more efficient than the ordinary least squares estimate of the reduced form.*

PROOF. Recall that

$$\sqrt{T}\,\mathrm{vec}(\hat{\Pi} - \Pi) \overset{\text{asy}}{\sim} N(\mathbf{0}, \Omega \otimes Q^{-1}),$$

where $Q = \mathrm{plim}(X'X/T)$. Let

$$\boldsymbol{\beta} = \begin{bmatrix} \boldsymbol{\gamma}_1 \\ \boldsymbol{\delta}_1 \\ \vdots \\ \boldsymbol{\gamma}_G \\ \boldsymbol{\delta}_G \end{bmatrix}$$

denote the structural coefficients of the simultaneous equation model. Adopting the notation of Chapter 22 in general and Equation (22.2.4) in particular.

$$\tilde{\tilde{\boldsymbol{\beta}}} = (W'\hat{\Phi}^{-1}W)^{-1}W'\hat{\Phi}^{-1}\mathbf{w}$$

denotes the three-stage least squares estimates. From Chapter 22 we know that

$$\sqrt{T}(\tilde{\tilde{\boldsymbol{\beta}}} - \boldsymbol{\beta}) \overset{\text{asy}}{\sim} N\left[\mathbf{0}, \underset{T\to\infty}{\mathrm{plim}} \left(\frac{W'\Phi^{-1}W}{T}\right)^{-1}\right],$$

where $\Phi = \Sigma \otimes I_K$. Finally it can be shown (see Exercise 23.1) that

$$\Omega \otimes Q^{-1} - A \underset{T\to\infty}{\mathrm{plim}} \left(\frac{W'\Phi^{-1}W}{T}\right)^{-1} A', \tag{23.2.13}$$

where $A = (\Gamma^{-1})' \otimes (\Pi, I)$, is a positive semidefinite matrix. □

A few final comments are warranted. In the above theorems two-stage least squares can be replaced by limited information maximum likelihood and three-stage least squares can be replaced by full information maximum likelihood as these estimators have the same asymptotic distributions. However, in the presence of prior information concerning the error covariance matrix Σ (such as information of the form $\sigma_{ij} = 0$), the full information maximum likelihood derived reduced form estimator would be preferred over the three-stage least squares derived reduced form estimator since full information maximum likelihood is more efficient than three-stage least squares in this case (see Section 22.5).

Finally Dhrymes (1973) obtained the interesting result that two-stage least squares derived reduced form estimates are not necessarily asymptotically more efficient than the ordinary least squares reduced form estimates. This is seemingly a contradiction of the intuitive notation that "the more restrictions taken into account the more efficient the resulting estimators." However, this statement overlooks that there are two types of information in this context: *Sample* information and *a priori* information. Ordinary least squares uses all the sample information and none of the *a priori* information while the two-stage least squares derived reduced form estimator uses all *a priori* information on the structural parameters but, typically, only some of the relevant sample information, unless all of the equations in the system are just identified. Therefore the relative efficiency is, in general, undeterminable. Since the three-stage least squares derived reduced form estimates use all the available sample and *a priori* information, they are superior to either the ordinary least squares or two-stage least squares derived reduced form estimates.

As the next section illustrates, efficient estimation of Π plays a crucial role in efficient prediction of future values of the current endogenous variables of a simultaneous equations model.

23.3 Forecasting in Simultaneous Equations Models with Usual Error Assumptions

Let $\tilde{\Pi}$ denote a consistent estimator of the reduced form parameters Π such that

$$\sqrt{T}\,\operatorname{vec}(\tilde{\Pi} - \Pi) \overset{\text{asy}}{\sim} N(\mathbf{0}, \Theta).$$

The form of Θ is determined, of course, by the method used to estimate Π. Suppose we are interested in predicting yet to be realized values of the jointly determined endogenous variables at some future time period f,

$$\mathbf{y}_{f.} = (y_{f1}, y_{f2}, \ldots, y_{fG}),$$

given values of the predetermined variables

$$\mathbf{x}_{f.} = (x_{f1}, x_{f2}, \ldots, x_{fK}).$$

Consider the prediction $\hat{\mathbf{y}}_{f.} = \mathbf{x}_{f.}\tilde{\Pi}$ and let $\hat{\mathbf{e}}_{f.} = \mathbf{y}_{f.} - \hat{\mathbf{y}}_{f.}$ represent the vector of forecast errors and let

$$F' = \begin{bmatrix} \mathbf{x}_{f.} & & & 0 \\ & \mathbf{x}_{f.} & & \\ & & \ddots & \\ 0 & & & \mathbf{x}_{f.} \end{bmatrix} = I_G \otimes \mathbf{x}_{f.} \tag{23.3.1}$$

Theorem 23.3.1. *Under the standard assumptions of the simultaneous equations model, the asymptotic covariance matrix of the forecast error,* $\hat{\mathbf{e}}_{f.}$ *is*

$$\mathrm{T} = \frac{1}{T} F'\Theta F + \Omega, \tag{23.3.2}$$

where $\Omega = (\Gamma^{-1})'\Sigma\Gamma^{-1}$ *is the covariance matrix of the reduced form errors.* (*Note*: Do not confuse the covariance matrix T with sample size T.)

PROOF.

$$\begin{aligned}\sqrt{T}\hat{\mathbf{e}}'_{f.} &= \sqrt{T}(\mathbf{y}_{f.} - \hat{\mathbf{y}}_{f.})' = \sqrt{T}(\mathbf{x}_{f.}(\Pi - \tilde{\Pi}))' + \sqrt{T}\mathbf{v}'_{f.}\\ &= \sqrt{T}F' \operatorname{vec}(\Pi - \tilde{\Pi}) + \sqrt{T}\mathbf{v}'_{f.},\end{aligned}$$

where $\mathbf{v}_{f.} = \mathbf{e}_{f.}\Gamma^{-1}$ represents the G reduced form errors occurring at time f. Note that $\tilde{\Pi}$ must be a function of the within sample disturbances $\mathbf{e}_{t.}$, $t = 1, 2, \ldots, T$ while $\mathbf{v}_{f.}$ is a function of $\mathbf{e}_{f.}$. Given the independence of $\mathbf{e}_{t.}$ and $\mathbf{e}_{f.}$ for $t \neq f$, $\tilde{\Pi}$ and $\mathbf{v}_{f.}$ must be independent. The asymptotic covariance matrix of $\sqrt{T}F' \operatorname{vec}(\Pi - \tilde{\Pi})$ is $F'\Theta F$. The covariance matrix of $\sqrt{T}\mathbf{v}_{f.}$ is $T\Omega$ since $E\mathbf{v}'_{t.}\mathbf{v}_{t.} = \Omega$. It then follows that the asymptotic covariance matrix of $\sqrt{T}\hat{\mathbf{e}}'_{f.}$ is $F'\Theta F + T\Omega$ and the theorem is proved. □

The first term, $(1/T)F'\Theta F$, represents the asymptotic variance of the forecast $\hat{\mathbf{y}}_{f.}$ about the mean $E(\mathbf{y}_{f.}|\mathbf{x}_{f.}) = \mathbf{x}_{f.}\Pi$ whereas the second term represents the variance of $\mathbf{y}_{f.}$ about its mean $\mathbf{x}_{f.}\Pi$.

The most efficient prediction methods (methods which produce the smallest asymptotic variances of forecasts) will involve the use of a derived reduced form estimate of Π obtained from full information methods (full information maximum likelihood, three-stage least squares). This result can be seen by letting Θ_1 and Θ_2 denote efficient versus inefficient derived reduced form covariance matrices, respectively. Then

$$\begin{aligned}\mathrm{T}_2 - \mathrm{T}_1 &= \frac{1}{T}F'\Theta_2 F + \Omega - \left(\frac{1}{T}F'\Theta_1 F + \Omega\right)\\ &= \frac{1}{T}F'(\Theta_2 - \Theta_1)F\end{aligned}$$

and since $\Theta_2 - \Theta_1$ is positive semidefinite then $\mathrm{T}_2 - \mathrm{T}_1$ is also positive semidefinite.

Suppose that no *a priori* information concerning the structural error covariance matrix, $E\mathbf{e}'_{t.}\mathbf{e}_{t.} = \Sigma$, is available. Then when using the three-stage least squares derived reduced form estimates of Π, the asymptotic covariance matrix of the forecast errors is

$$\mathrm{T} = \frac{1}{T}F'A\Psi A'F + \Omega, \tag{23.3.3}$$

where Ψ is the asymptotic covariance matrix defined by $\operatorname{plim}(W'\Phi^{-1}W/T)^{-1}$. Note that Ψ is of order $G(G + K)$.

To illustrate some of the concepts of this chapter, consider Klein's Model I, discussed in Section 19.2. The model is estimated for the years 1920–1941 using three-stage least squares with the three-stage least squares derived reduced form estimate of Π being

$\tilde{\Pi} = -\tilde{\Delta}\tilde{\Gamma}^{-1} =$

	C	I	W	X	P	K
One	46.727	27.618	31.592	74.346	42.774	27.618
K_{-1}	−0.124	−0.192	−0.127	−0.316	−0.189	0.808
P_{-1}	0.746	0.744	0.597	1.490	0.893	0.744
X_{-1}	0.199	0.807 (10^{-3})	0.261	0.199	−0.062	0.807 (10^{-3})
W'	1.291	−0.010	0.513	1.281	0.768	−0.010
G	0.635	−0.013	0.650	1.622	0.972	−0.013
T	−0.196	0.015	−0.073	−0.181	−1.109	0.015
Time	0.164	0.667 (10^{-3})	0.216	0.165	−0.051	0.667 (10^{-3})

For example, the immediate (expected) change in consumption resulting from a one unit change in government nonwage expenditure (G), while holding all other predetermined variables constant, is 0.635 units, here, billions of 1934 dollars. The reader should attempt verbal descriptions of other elements of $\tilde{\Pi}$. The word "immediate" was used in describing the above reduced form parameter because in actuality Klein's Model I is a dynamic model; it contains lagged variables and a change in any purely exogenous variable will produce a series of changes in the endogenous variables through time. Therefore, reduced form parameters in a dynamic simultaneous equation model only describe immediate impacts on endogenous variables arising from a unit change in a predetermined variable not additional changes which are expected to occur in the future. In the next chapter we will discuss the estimation of subsequent impacts through the so-called final form.

Now to illustrate the use of Theorem 23.3.1. The 1947 values of the predetermined variables are

	One	K_{-1}	P_{-1}	X_{-1}	W'	G	T	Time
$\mathbf{x}_{f.} =$	1.0	197.7	26.2	94.8	8.7	8.7	9.2	11.0

Using the three-stage derived reduced form above, the forecast values for the current endogenous variables for 1947 are

	C	I	W	X	P	K
$\hat{\mathbf{y}}_{f.} = \mathbf{x}_{f.}\tilde{\Pi} =$	77.42	9.10	58.77	95.22	27.25	206.8

A consistent estimate of the asymptotic covariance matrix of the forecast errors is

$$\hat{\Upsilon} = F'\hat{A}\hat{\Psi}\hat{A}'F + \hat{\Omega} \tag{23.3.4}$$

and

$\hat{\Upsilon} =$ (23.3.5)

	C	I	W	X	P	K
C	6.02	3.14	3.93	9.16	5.22	3.14
I		2.59	2.79	5.73	2.94	2.59
W			3.93	6.72	2.79	2.79
X				14.89	8.16	5.73
P					5.37	2.94
K						2.59

where $\hat{A} \equiv (\hat{\Gamma}^{-1})' \otimes (\hat{\Pi}, I)$;

$\hat{\Sigma} \equiv$ three-stage least squares estimate of $\Sigma = E\mathbf{e}'_{t.}\mathbf{e}_{t.}$ (see (22.2.10));

$\hat{\Pi} \equiv$ three-stage least squares derived reduced form estimate of Π;

$\hat{\Gamma} \equiv$ three-stage least squares estimate of coefficients on the current endogenous variables;

$F' \equiv$ see (23.3.1);

$\hat{\Psi} \equiv$ the estimated variances and covariances of the three-stage least squares estimates arranged as indicated by (23.2.11).

The square roots of the diagonal elements of $\hat{\Upsilon}$ are the standard errors of forecasts and can be used to specify forecast confidence intervals for individual endogenous variables.

The actual 1947 values of the current endogenous variables are

	C	I	W	X	P	K
$\mathbf{y}_{f.} =$	82.8	6.4	60.7	97.9	27.9	204.1

with actual forecast error

	C	I	W	X	P	K
$\hat{\mathbf{e}}_{f.} = \mathbf{y}_{f.} - \hat{\mathbf{y}}_{f.} =$	5.37	−2.70	1.93	2.68	0.64	−2.70

Up to this point the standard errors of forecasts have been obtained assuming that the values of the predetermined variables, $\mathbf{x}_{f.}$, for the prediction period are *known constants.* However, in many instances $\mathbf{x}_{f.}$ is unknown and instead must be estimated consistently by $\hat{\mathbf{x}}_{f.}$, say. If so, the forecast of the endogenous variables at $t = f$ would be of the form $\hat{\hat{\mathbf{y}}}_{f.} = \hat{\mathbf{x}}_{f.}\tilde{\Pi}$ and the asymptotic matrix for the forecast errors $\hat{\hat{\mathbf{e}}}_{f.} = \mathbf{y}_{f.} - \hat{\hat{\mathbf{y}}}_{f.}$ would be different from that obtained *conditional* on known $\mathbf{x}_{f.}$, see (23.3.2). Some allowance must be made for the fact that $\hat{\mathbf{x}}_{f.}$ is estimated. As demonstrated by Feldstein (1971), if the uncertainty about the future values of the predetermined variables is of the same order of magnitude (as measured by relative variance) as the uncertainty about the reduced form coefficients, the asymptotic covariance matrix (23.3.2) can seriously underestimate the actual forecast standard error. Feldstein (1971) formalizes the issue of the error of forecasts when the forecast period predetermined variables are stochastic. We report his basic results though for brevity details of the proofs are omitted.

Let us first examine the problem of stochastic predetermined variables in the simpler single equation context and then generalize the results to simultaneous equations forecasting. The single equation model may be written as $\mathbf{y} = X\boldsymbol{\beta} + \mathbf{e}$. The value of the dependent variable in the forecast period is $y_f = \mathbf{x}'_f\boldsymbol{\beta} + e_f$. The problem addressed here is to estimate y_f when neither $\mathbf{x}'_f$ nor $\boldsymbol{\beta}$ is known and derive the standard error of forecast. The unknown $\boldsymbol{\beta}$ is estimated by ordinary least squares, $\hat{\boldsymbol{\beta}} = (X'X)^{-1}X'\mathbf{y}$, which has covariance matrix $\sigma^2(X'X)^{-1} = S$. Assume that $\mathbf{x}'_f$ is estimated by $\hat{\mathbf{x}}'_f$ with covariance matrix $\mathrm{Z} = E(\hat{\mathbf{x}}_f - \mathbf{x}_f)(\hat{\mathbf{x}}_f - \mathbf{x}_f)'$. For the present $\hat{\mathbf{x}}'_f$ is assumed to be an unbiased estimator. Later, when talking about simultaneous equation forecasting this requirement can be relaxed to one of consistency, plim $\hat{\mathbf{x}}'_f = \mathbf{x}'_f$. In addition the estimates of the regression coefficients and the forecast-period predetermined variables are assumed to be independent: $E(\hat{\mathbf{x}}_f - \mathbf{x}_f)(\hat{\boldsymbol{\beta}} - \boldsymbol{\beta})' = 0$. Note that this assumption holds special meaning when the regression model contains lagged dependent variables. If any estimates of these lagged dependent variables are obtained from $\hat{y}_l = \mathbf{x}'_l\hat{\boldsymbol{\beta}}$, $l = t, t-1, t-2, \ldots$, then $\hat{\mathbf{x}}'_f$ is not independent of $\hat{\boldsymbol{\beta}}$ and the above assumption is violated.

The proposed unbiased estimate of y_f is $\hat{\hat{y}}_f = \hat{\mathbf{x}}'_f\hat{\boldsymbol{\beta}}$. The variance of the forecast error is $\sigma^2_{\hat{\hat{y}}_f} = E(\hat{\hat{y}}_f - y_f)^2$. Feldstein (1971) then proves

Theorem 23.3.2. *The variance of the forecast error in the standard linear regression model when the regressors are estimated by $\hat{\mathbf{x}}'_f$ having covariance matrix $\mathrm{Z} = E(\hat{\mathbf{x}}_f - \mathbf{x}_f)(\hat{\mathbf{x}}_f - \mathbf{x}_f)'$ is*

$$\sigma^2_{\hat{\hat{y}}_f} = \mathbf{x}'_f S \mathbf{x}_f + \boldsymbol{\beta}'\mathrm{Z}\boldsymbol{\beta} + \mathrm{tr}(S\mathrm{Z}) + \sigma^2_e, \tag{23.3.6}$$

where σ^2_e is the variance of the regression error term.

Proof. The proof is straightforward. For details see Feldstein (1971, p. 56). □

As this theorem proves, the variance of the forecast error, when $\mathbf{x}'_f$ is estimated, has two additional terms, $\boldsymbol{\beta}'Z\boldsymbol{\beta}$ and tr(SZ), compared to the case where forecasts are made conditional on known $\mathbf{x}'_f$. Feldstein points out the importance of recognizing the stochastic nature of $\hat{\mathbf{x}}'_f$ by considering a simple bivariate regression model $y_t = \beta x_t + e_t$. Here $\sigma^2_{\hat{y}_f} = x_f^2\sigma^2_{\hat{\beta}} + \sigma^2_e + (\sigma^2_{\hat{\beta}} + \hat{\beta}^2)\sigma^2_{\hat{x}_f}$. If the variance of $\hat{x}_f$ is ignored (i.e., the final term is dropped) then the actual variance of the forecast error can be underestimated by a factor of 50 percent or more. The moral is that, if $\mathbf{x}'_f$ is actually estimated, proper account should be taken of this fact.

Now let us turn to the same problem in the simultaneous equation context. Let $\mathbf{y}_{f.}$ denote the yet to be realized values of the joint dependent variables at $t = f$. Then $\mathbf{y}_{f.} = \mathbf{x}_{f.}\Pi + \mathbf{v}_{f.}$ is the reduced form. Assume that $\hat{\mathbf{x}}_{f.}$ is a consistent estimate of $\mathbf{x}_{f.}$ with covariance matrix

$$Z = E(\hat{\mathbf{x}}_{f.} - \mathbf{x}_{f.})'(\hat{\mathbf{x}}_{f.} - \mathbf{x}_{f.}).$$

The predictor of interest is $\hat{\hat{\mathbf{y}}}_{f.} = \hat{\mathbf{x}}_{f.}\tilde{\Pi}$, where $\sqrt{T}\,\text{vec}(\tilde{\Pi} - \Pi) \overset{\text{asy}}{\sim} N(\mathbf{0}, \Theta)$. In addition, it is assumed that the estimates of the reduced form parameters, $\tilde{\Pi}$, are independent of the forecast period predetermined variables: $E(\tilde{\Pi}_{.i} - \Pi_{.i})(\hat{\mathbf{x}}_{f.} - \mathbf{x}_{f.}) = 0$, for $i = 1, 2, \ldots, G$, where $\Pi_{.i}$ denotes the reduced form parameters for the ith equation. Again note that in the instance of a dynamic simultaneous equation model with lagged dependent variables, $\mathbf{x}_{f.}$ will contain lagged dependent variables. If, for any of these variables, values are obtained from $\hat{Y} = X\tilde{\Pi}$ then the independence assumption is violated and the following theorem does not strictly hold.

Theorem 23.3.3. *Let the asymptotic covariance of forecast errors for the* rth *endogenous variable,* $(\hat{\hat{y}}_{rf} - y_{rf})$, *and the* sth *endogenous variable,* $(\hat{\hat{y}}_{sf} - y_{sf})$, *be denoted by* $\sigma^2_{\hat{\hat{y}}_r\hat{\hat{y}}_s}$. *Then*

$$\sigma^2_{\hat{\hat{y}}_r\hat{\hat{y}}_s} = \mathbf{x}_{f.}\Theta_{rs}\mathbf{x}'_{f.} + \Pi'_{.r}Z\Pi_{.s} + \text{tr}(\Theta_{rs}Z) + \delta_{rs}, \tag{23.3.7}$$

where Θ_{rs} *denotes the asymptotic covariance matrix for the cross product of* $\tilde{\Pi}_{.r}$ *and* $\tilde{\Pi}_{.s}$, *i.e., the asymptotic covariance between the* rth *equation's reduced form estimates and the* sth *equation's reduced form estimates, and* δ_{rs} *is the covariance between the reduced form errors* v_{rt} *and* v_{st}.

Proof. See Feldstein (1971, p. 58). As pointed out by Schmidt (1978, footnote 1), there is a small error in the Feldstein paper. In his Equations (9) and (10), the term $K^2\delta_{rs}$ should be simply δ_{rs}. □

Notice the addition of the two extra terms, $\Pi'_{.r}Z\Pi_{.s}$ and tr($\Theta_{rs}Z$), which are required once the nature of $\hat{\mathbf{x}}_{f.}$ is considered. The need to estimate the forecast period predetermined variables necessarily increases the variance of the forecast error. In line with the previous discussion the most efficient methods of estimating Π, namely full information maximum likelihood or three-stage least squares derived reduced form estimates, will provide, asymptotically, the smallest forecast error variances since the "size" of Θ is minimized.

Operationally, a consistent estimate of $\sigma^2_{\hat{\tilde{y}}_r \hat{\tilde{y}}_s}$ is provided by replacing all unknown parameters with consistent estimates and may be used to construct asymptotic confidence intervals. Using the covariance matrix specified for the values of the predetermined variables in Exercise 23.3, it is left as an exercise to recompute the asymptotic standard errors of forecast for Klein's Model I. How much larger are the standard errors in this instance?

23.4 Forecasting with an Autocorrelated Error Structure

There can be instances where the "standard" error structure specified in (23.2.2) is not appropriate for the problem at hand. For example, rather than assuming that the equation errors are not related intertemporally, i.e., $E\mathbf{e}'_{s.}\mathbf{e}_{t.} = 0$ for $s \neq t$, suppose that each equation's error terms satisfy a first order autoregressive scheme

$$e_{ti} = \rho_i e_{t-1,i} + u_{ti} \qquad (i = 1, 2, \ldots, G), \tag{23.4.1}$$

with $\mathbf{u}_{t.} = (u_{t1}, u_{t2}, \ldots, u_{TG})$ satisfying the standard assumptions

$$\begin{aligned} E\mathbf{u}_{t.} &= \mathbf{0}', \\ E\mathbf{u}'_{t.}\mathbf{u}_{t.} &= \Sigma, \\ E\mathbf{u}'_{t.}\mathbf{u}_{s.} &= 0 \quad \text{for } s \neq t. \end{aligned} \tag{23.4.2}$$

This autocorrelated error structure can be written in the matrix form

$$E = E_{-1}R + U, \tag{23.4.3}$$

where E_{-1} is a $T \times G$ matrix of one period lagged values of the structural disturbance matrix E, U is the $T \times G$ matrix of "classical" disturbances, and

$$R = \begin{bmatrix} \rho_1 & & & 0 \\ & \rho_2 & & \\ & & \ddots & \\ 0 & & & \rho_G \end{bmatrix}.$$

The question of interest here is: "Should the classical prediction procedure in simultaneous equations (discussed in the previous section) be altered when the error process is autocorrelated? If so, how?" An intuitive answer to the first question would be yes. Recall (Exercise 2.8) that the best, linear, unbiased predictor for the single equation generalized least squares model is

$$\tilde{y}_{T+1} = \mathbf{x}'_{T+1}\tilde{\boldsymbol{\beta}} + \frac{1}{\sigma_e^2}\mathbf{w}'\Omega^{-1}\tilde{\mathbf{e}}, \tag{23.4.4}$$

where $\tilde{\boldsymbol{\beta}} = (X'\Omega^{-1}X)^{-1}X'\Omega^{-1}\mathbf{y}$ is the generalized least squares (Aitken) estimator, $\tilde{\mathbf{e}} = (\mathbf{y} - X\tilde{\boldsymbol{\beta}})$, $\mathbf{w} = E\mathbf{e}e_{T+1}$, $\sigma_e^2\Omega = E\mathbf{e}\mathbf{e}'$ is the generalized least squares error covariance matrix, $\mathbf{x}'_{T+1}$ represents the $K \times 1$ vector of values of the predetermined variables at the next (future) time period $T + 1$ and $\tilde{y}_{T+1}$ is the best, linear, unbiased prediction of the yet to be realized value of the dependent variable at time $T + 1$. The usual best, linear, unbiased forecasting formula, $\hat{y}_{T+1} = \mathbf{x}'_{T+1}\hat{\boldsymbol{\beta}}$, where $\hat{\boldsymbol{\beta}} = (X'X)^{-1}X'\mathbf{y}$, is modified in the presence of a generalized least squares error structure. The appropriate best, linear, unbiased forecast incorporates not only the mean response but also information concerning the error structure. For example, in the single equation context, if the errors follow the AR(1) scheme, $e_t = \rho e_{t-1} + u_t$, the best, linear, unbiased predictor is

$$\tilde{y}_{T+1} = \mathbf{x}'_{T+1}\tilde{\boldsymbol{\beta}} + \rho\tilde{e}_T, \tag{23.4.5}$$

where $\tilde{e}_T = (y_T - \mathbf{x}'_T\tilde{\boldsymbol{\beta}})$. Let us turn to the second question of specifically how forecasting in simultaneous equations should be modified to take into an autocorrelated error structure such as (23.4.3).

Consider the following simultaneous equation system

$$Y\Gamma + X\Delta_1 + Y_{-1}\Delta_2 + E = 0 \tag{23.4.6}$$

with autocorrelated error structure

$$E = E_{-1}R + U \tag{23.4.7}$$

specified by (23.4.1) and (23.4.2). The dynamic simultaneous equation system (23.4.6) has been written in a manner distinct from the conventional form $Y\Gamma + X\Delta + E = 0$. The matrix X represents those observations on the predetermined variables which are either current or lagged *purely* exogenous variables with Δ_1 having conformable dimensions. The matrix Y_{-1} represents a $T \times G$ matrix of one period lagged values of the endogenous variables with Δ_2 being of dimension $G \times G$. Of course, Δ_2 may contain rows of zeroes which correspond to lagged dependent variables that are not present in given equations. The reduced form of this model is

$$\begin{aligned}
Y &= -X\Delta_1\Gamma^{-1} - Y_{-1}\Delta_2\Gamma^{-1} - E\Gamma^{-1} \\
&= -X\Delta_1\Gamma^{-1} - Y_{-1}\Delta_2\Gamma^{-1} - E_{-1}R\Gamma^{-1} - U\Gamma^{-1} && (23.4.8a) \\
&= -X\Delta_1\Gamma^{-1} - Y_{-1}\Delta_2\Gamma^{-1} \\
&\quad + (Y_{-1}\Gamma + X_{-1}\Delta_1 + Y_{-2}\Delta_2)R\Gamma^{-1} - U\Gamma^{-1} \\
&= -X\Delta_1\Gamma^{-1} + Y_{-1}(-\Delta_2\Gamma^{-1} + \Gamma R\Gamma^{-1}) \\
&\quad + X_{-1}\Delta_1 R\Gamma^{-1} + Y_{-2}\Delta_2 R\Gamma^{-1} - U\Gamma^{-1} \\
&= X\Pi_1 + Y_{-1}\Pi_2 + X_{-1}\Pi_3 + Y_{-2}\Pi_4 + V, && (23.4.8b)
\end{aligned}$$

where V is the matrix of reduced form errors with the same properties as before. Notice that ordinary least squares regression of Y on X and Y_{-1} in (23.4.8a) would *not* provide consistent estimates of $-\Delta_1\Gamma^{-1}$ and $-\Delta_2\Gamma^{-1}$

since Y_{-1} is contemporaneously correlated with the error term $(-E_{-1}R\Gamma^{-1} - U\Gamma^{-1})$. But ordinary least squares regression of Y on X, Y_{-1}. X_{-1} and Y_{-2} in (23.4.8b) would provide consistent estimates $\hat{\Pi}_1$, $\hat{\Pi}_2$, $\hat{\Pi}_3$, and $\hat{\Pi}_4$ of the reduced form parameters. However, in the same vein that the full information derived reduced form estimates of Section 23.2 were superior to the ordinary least squares reduced form estimates in the standard case, derived estimates

$$\begin{aligned}
\tilde{\Pi}_1 &= -\tilde{\Delta}_1\tilde{\Gamma}^{-1}, \\
\tilde{\Pi}_2 &= -\tilde{\Delta}_2\tilde{\Gamma}^{-1} + \tilde{\Gamma}\tilde{R}\tilde{\Gamma}^{-1}, \\
\tilde{\Pi}_3 &= \tilde{\Delta}_1\tilde{R}\tilde{\Gamma}^{-1}, \\
\tilde{\Pi}_4 &= \tilde{\Delta}_2\tilde{R}\tilde{\Gamma}^{-1},
\end{aligned} \tag{23.4.9}$$

where $\tilde{\Delta}_1$, $\tilde{\Delta}_2$, $\tilde{\Gamma}$, and $\tilde{R}$ represent efficient estimates, should provide more efficient estimates of the reduced form parameters since they incorporate all available *a priori* information. We will discuss a method of efficiently estimating the structural parameters Δ_1, Δ_2, Γ, and R in Section 25.5. For now we turn to forecasting in a dynamic simultaneous equation model of the form (23.4.6)–(23.4.7).

Let $\mathbf{y}_{f.} = (y_{f1}, y_{f2}, \ldots, y_{fG})$ denote yet to be realized values of the jointly determined endogenous variables at some future time period f, $\mathbf{x}_{f.} = (x_{f1}, x_{f2}, \ldots, x_{fK})$ denote given values of the K purely exogenous variables, $\mathbf{y}_{f-1.}$ and $\mathbf{y}_{f-2.}$ are $1 \times G$ vectors of given values of the endogenous variables from the two previous time periods and $\mathbf{x}_{f-1.}$ a $1 \times K$ vector of given lagged values of $\mathbf{x}_{f.}$. To forecast $\mathbf{y}_{f.}$ we use

$$\begin{aligned}
\tilde{\mathbf{y}}_{f.} = &-\mathbf{x}_{f.}\tilde{\Delta}_1\tilde{\Gamma}^{-1} + \mathbf{y}_{f-1.}(-\tilde{\Delta}_2\tilde{\Gamma}^{-1} + \tilde{\Gamma}\tilde{R}\tilde{\Gamma}^{-1}) \\
&+ \mathbf{x}_{f-1.}\tilde{\Delta}_1\tilde{R}\tilde{\Gamma}^{-1} + \mathbf{y}_{f-2.}\tilde{\Delta}_2\tilde{R}\tilde{\Gamma}^{-1}.
\end{aligned} \tag{23.4.10}$$

As in the case of prediction in the single equation generalized least squares model, forecasting in simultaneous equations with autocorrelated errors requires modifying the conditional mean with information concerning the error structure.

23.5 Summary and Guide to Further Readings

In this chapter two distinct ways of estimating the reduced form parameters Π have been discussed. The three-stage least squares derived reduced form estimator was shown to be superior to the ordinary least squares reduced form estimator. Though both estimators fully utilize the sample information, the three-stage least squares derived reduced form estimator, unlike ordinary least squares, utilizes restrictions on the reduced form imposed by overidentification of equations in the system. The utilization of this prior information provides a gain in efficiency.

Consistent forecasts of future values of the jointly dependent variables require knowledge of the reduced form parameters. The asymptotic covariance matrix for forecast errors, assuming the forecast period predetermined variables are known, was developed in Theorem 23.3.1. The asymptotic covariance matrix for forecast errors, when the forecast period predetermined variables are estimated, is provided in Theorem 23.3.3. Ignoring the stochastic nature of the forecast period variables can lead to serious underestimation of forecast error variance. In either case, the accuracy of forecasts is dependent on the efficiency of the method chosen to estimate the reduced form parameters. The greater the precision in estimating Π, the greater the accuracy of forecasts. Therefore, the most efficient forecasts are obtained when Π is estimated using full information methods (three-stage least squares or full information maximum likelihood derived reduced form estimation).

In the instance that a simultaneous equation system has an autocorrelated error structure rather than the traditional uncorrelated one, the traditional method of forecasting requires modification. As in the case of best, linear, unbiased forecasting in the single equation generalized least squares model, prediction consists of modifying the mean response to reflect the autocorrelation of previous error terms.

In addition to the literature cited in this chapter on forecasting in the context of simultaneous equation systems, the reader will find Chapter 24 and Section 25.5 relevant. There has also developed a body of literature devoted to "improved" estimation of the reduced form. The need for these estimators is based on the fact that the derived reduced form may have no finite moments, and thus undefined risk in small samples (McCarthy (1972)). Consequently efforts have been made to construct estimators of the reduced form that do have finite moments and which are superior to the unrestricted reduced form. Maasoumi (1978) has offered a modified Stein like estimator that combines the unrestricted reduced form estimator and the derived reduced form based on the three-stage least squares estimates. A Wald test statistic is used to control the shrinking mechanism. The resulting estimator has finite moments up to a certain order. An alternative approach has been based on the partially restricted reduced form (Amemiya (1966), Kakwani and Court (1972)). This estimator imposes the restrictions of a single structural equation one at a time on the reduced form coefficients. The properties of this estimator have been investigated by Knight (1977), Swamy and Mehta (1980, 1981), McCarthy (1972, 1981), and Nagar and Sahay (1978). This estimator does possess finite moments under fairly general conditions. Finally, there is sometimes the problem that the reduced form parameters can not be estimated unbiasedly due to undersized samples, which is equivalent to the case of exact multicollinearity. Swamy (1980) compares some of the estimators that have been proposed for this situation.

23.6 Exercises

23.1. Show that (23.2.13) is positive semidefinite.

23.2. The forecasting illustration in Section 23.3 is taken from Goldberger (1964, p. 373). However Goldberger defines Klein's Model I slightly differently than we have. Follow Goldberger's formulation and generate the standard errors of the forecasts for the *eight* endogenous variables in his system.

23.3. Suppose the covariance matrix of $\mathbf{x}'_{f.}$ is assumed to be

$$\text{cov}(\mathbf{x}'_{f.}) = \text{diag}(25.0 \quad 4.0 \quad 9.0 \quad 1.0 \quad 1.0 \quad 1.0 \quad 0).$$

Recompute the standard errors of the forecasts for Klein's Model I.

23.4. Below is data on the system's variables for 1948–1953. Use these data to obtain point and 95% confidence interval forecasts for the means of the endogenous variables

	C	P	W	I	K	X	W'	T	G^*
1948	104.5	33.1	77.0	16.0	235.6	117.9	11.9	7.8	19.0
1949	106.9	31.9	76.5	8.48	242.2	114.9	13.2	6.5	18.9
1950	112.9	34.5	82.3	17.0	260.7	128.0	14.1	11.1	19.9
1951	114.3	32.6	88.5	16.5	273.6	134.3	17.0	13.2	29.8
1952	117.2	32.6	93.5	11.7	280.7	137.3	19.2	11.2	35.7
1953	121.6	32.8	99.4	11.6	290.9	143.8	19.5	11.5	37.5

DATA: Said Alawad, "Klein Model I—Updated 1948–1978," Field Paper, Economics Department, Southern Methodist University, 1982. Note the data is in 1934 dollars. G^* is all government expenditure. To obtain government nonwage expenditure, the G employed in our version of Klein's Model I, subtract W'.

23.7 References

Amemiya, T. (1966). On the use of principal components of independent variables in two-stage least squares estimation. *International Economic Review*, **7**, 283–303.

Dhrymes, P. (1973). Restricted and unrestricted reduced forms: asymptotic distribution and relative efficiency. *Econometrica*, **41**, 119–134.

Feldstein, M. (1971). The error of forecast in econometric models when the forecast period exogenous variables are stochastic. *Econometrica*, **39**, 55–60.

Fisher, F. (1966). *The Identification Problem in Econometrics*. New York: McGraw-Hill.

Goldberger, A. (1964). *Econometric Theory*. New York: Wiley.

Kakwani, N. and Court, R. (1972). Reduced form coefficient estimation and forecasting from a simultaneous equation model. *The Australian Journal of Statistics*, **14**, 143–160.

Knight, J. (1977). On the existence of moments of the partially restricted reduced form estimators from a simultaneous-equation model. *Journal of Econometrics*, **5**, 315–322.

Maasoumi, E. (1978). A modified Stein-like estimator for the reduced form coefficients in simultaneous equations. *Econometrica*, **46**, 695–705.

McCarthy, M. (1972). A note on the forecasting properties of the two stage least squares restricted reduced forms—the finite sample case. *International Economic Review*, **13**, 757–761.

McCarthy, M. (1981). A note on the moments of partially restricted reduced forms. *Journal of Econometrics*, **17**, 383–387.

Nagar, A. and Sahay, S. (1978). The bias and mean square error of forecasts from partially restricted reduced forms. *Journal of Econometrics*, **7**, 227–244.

Schmidt, P. (1976). *Econometrics*. New York: Marcel Dekker.

Schmidt, P. (1978). A note on dynamic simulation forecasts and stochastic forecast-period exogenous variables. *Econometrica*, **46**, 1227–1230.

Swamy, P. (1980). A comparison of estimators for undersized samples. *Journal of Econometrics*, **14**, 161–182.

Swamy, P. and Mehta, J. (1980). On the existence of moments of partially restricted reduced form coefficients. *Journal of Econometrics*, **14**, 183–194.

Swamy, P. and Mehta, J. (1981). On the existence of moments of partially restricted reduced form estimators: a comment. *Journal of Econometrics*, **17**, 389–392.

CHAPTER 24

Properties of Dynamic Simultaneous Equations Models

24.1 Introduction

The task of modeling national economies has received much attention and considerable progress has been made. Large scale econometric models are used to make econometric forecasts, help explain the dynamic behavior of the economy and to aid economic policy decisionmaking. We examine each of these topics in this chapter.

In order to represent the cyclical behavior of economic variables, models which are dynamic and stochastic must be considered. The ability to explain cyclical variation is important from a policy point of view since decision-makers are concerned with the time patterns of effects resulting from a change in government policy. It is clear that the trends, fluctuations, and rate of convergence to a new equilibrium are all important considerations when evaluating the consequences of a policy action. Furthermore, a comparison of known time lags in policy actions to the delayed reactions predicted by the model provides valuable information for validating the model.

A static economic theory explains the behavior of a set of endogenous variables by a set of simultaneous equations without specifying how variables are related at different points in time. Rarely, however, in markets and the economy in general, is full adjustment attained in a given period of analysis, say 3 months (a quarterly model). Adjustment is fully achieved only over an extended period of time. A dynamic theory, on the other hand, specifies the relations among the variables at *different* points in time, and thus can yield time paths of endogenous variables. Consideration of the time paths of endogenous effects generated by policy action are incorporated into the analysis of the dynamic multipliers of an econometric model. This is the subject of Section 24.2.

Since the true dynamic multipliers are unknown and must be estimated from the sample, the asymptotic distributions of the estimates are developed and efficient estimation is discussed in Section 24.3. Another important characteristic is the stability of a postulated dynamic simultaneous equation model. As our economy has, to present, not shown tendencies toward divergent (explosive) time paths, it seems reasonable to postulate a stable model where endogenous variables tend to move from one equilibrium to another when subjected to exogenous policy changes. In Section 24.2, a necessary and sufficient condition for stability is discussed. This condition is based upon an unknown parameter, however, and the standard error of its estimate is developed in Section 24.4 to allow a probabilistic statement as to the likelihood of stability.

In Section 24.5, means of forecasting future values of the endogenous variables in a dynamic simultaneous equations model are discussed. Standard errors are also developed for the forecasts. Finally the problem of optimal control in dynamic simultaneous equations models is outlined in Section 24.6. Such problems are important from a policy point of view as they provide a means of optimally manipulating policy variables so as to achieve certain goals. That is, we study the determination of optimal means of achieving desired ends. Section 24.7 contains a summary and guide to further reading.

24.2 Final Form and Dynamic Multipliers

When the predetermined variables of a simultaneous equations model contain lagged variables, either dependent or purely exogenous, the model is *dynamic*. That is, a unit change in a purely exogenous variable at time t can lead to delayed as well as immediate changes in the joint dependent variables of the model. The adjustment process implied by the model is not instantaneous but rather intertemporal. When the only lags are those of purely exogenous variables, the intertemporal effects are quite easy to visualize. A one unit change in a purely exogenous variable will result in a "one shot" change in the joint dependent variables after a delay equal to the length of the lag. The more interesting intertemporal effects exist, however, when at least one of the predetermined variables is a lagged endogenous variable. Here a unit change of a purely exogenous variable causes changes in the joint dependent variables which continue to reverberate through the system into the infinite future. The changes in the joint dependent variables can be oscillatory, damped or even explosive. Hereafter we will be interested in dynamic simultaneous equations models which contain lagged dependent variables.

In order to study how the time paths of the purely exogenous variables generate the time paths of the joint dependent variables, we must derive what is called the *final form* of a simultaneous equation system. This form expresses the current endogenous variables solely as a function of current and lagged purely exogenous variables and random disturbances. First, to develop some notation.

In the remainder of this chapter we will consider only dynamic simultaneous equations with one-period lagged endogenous variables and current purely exogenous variables because the algebra is easier and exposition is facilitated. However, the concepts covered here do generalize, though the generalization may be somewhat tedious, to lags of any finite order on both the endogenous and purely exogenous variables.

Let k denote the number of purely exogenous variables in the model. The structural form of the dynamic simultaneous equation model to be investigated here is

$$\mathbf{y}_{t.}\Gamma + \mathbf{x}_{t.}\Delta_1 + \mathbf{y}_{t-1,.}\Delta_2 + \mathbf{e}_{t.} = \mathbf{0}', \tag{24.2.1}$$

where

$\mathbf{y}_{t.} \equiv 1 \times G$ vector of observations on the joint dependent variables at time t,

$\mathbf{x}_{t.} \equiv 1 \times k$ vector of observators on the k purely exogenous variables at time t,

$\Gamma \equiv G \times G$ matrix of structural coefficients associated with the joint dependent variables,

$\Delta_1 \equiv k \times G$ matrix of structural coefficients associated with the purely exogenous variables,

$\mathbf{y}_{t-1,.} \equiv 1 \times G$ vector of observations on one period lagged dependent variables,

$\Delta_2 \equiv G \times G$ matrix of structural coefficients associated with the lagged dependent variables. Notice some rows of Δ_2 may contain all zeros denoting that specific lagged dependent variables are absent from the model,

$\mathbf{e}_{t.} \equiv 1 \times G$ vector of structural disturbances with the classical error properties cited in Section 19.3.

The reduced form is then

$$\begin{aligned}\mathbf{y}_{t.} &= -\mathbf{x}_{t.}\Delta_1\Gamma^{-1} - \mathbf{y}_{t-1,.}\Delta_2\Gamma^{-1} - \mathbf{e}_{t.}\Gamma^{-1}\\ &= \mathbf{x}_{t.}\Pi_1 + \mathbf{y}_{t-1,.}\Pi_2 + \mathbf{v}_{t.},\end{aligned} \tag{24.2.2}$$

where $\Pi_1 = -\Delta_1\Gamma^{-1}$, $\Pi_2 = -\Delta_2\Gamma^{-1}$, and $\mathbf{v}_{t.} = -\mathbf{e}_{t.}\Gamma^{-1}$. The reduced form is transformed to the final form by repeated substitution.

$$\begin{aligned}\mathbf{y}_{t.} &= \mathbf{x}_{t.}\Pi_1 + (\mathbf{x}_{t-1,.}\Pi_1 + \mathbf{y}_{t-2,.}\Pi_2 + \mathbf{v}_{t-1,.})\Pi_2 + \mathbf{v}_{t.}\\ &= \mathbf{x}_{t.}\Pi_1 + \mathbf{x}_{t-1,.}\Pi_1\Pi_2 + \mathbf{y}_{t-2,.}\Pi_2^2 + \mathbf{v}_{t.} + \mathbf{v}_{t-1,.}\Pi_2.\end{aligned} \tag{24.2.3}$$

Substituting s times provides

$$\begin{aligned}\mathbf{y}_{t.} &= \mathbf{x}_{t.}\Pi_1 + \mathbf{x}_{t-1,.}\Pi_1\Pi_2 + \mathbf{x}_{t-2,.}\Pi_1\Pi_1^2 \\ &\quad + \cdots + \mathbf{x}_{t-s,.}\Pi_1\Pi_2^s + \mathbf{y}_{t-(s+1),.}\Pi_2^{s+1} \\ &\quad + \mathbf{v}_{t.} + \mathbf{v}_{t-1,.}\Pi_2 + \cdots + \mathbf{v}_{t-s,.}\Pi_2^s.\end{aligned} \tag{24.2.4}$$

Letting $s \to \infty$ and assuming $\lim \Pi_2^s = 0$, the *final form* is

$$\begin{aligned}\mathbf{y}_{t.} &= \mathbf{x}_{t.}\Pi_1 + \mathbf{x}_{t-1,.}\Pi_1\Pi_2 + \mathbf{x}_{t-2,.}\Pi_1\Pi_2^2 \\ &\quad + \cdots + \mathbf{v}_{t.}^* \\ &= \mathbf{x}_{t.}M_0 + \mathbf{x}_{t-1,.}M_1 + \mathbf{x}_{t-2,.}M_2 \\ &\quad + \cdots + \mathbf{v}_{t.}^*,\end{aligned} \tag{24.2.5}$$

where $M_0 = \Pi_1$, $M_\tau = \Pi_1\Pi_2^\tau$, $\tau = 1, 2, \ldots,$ and $\mathbf{v}_{t.}^* = \mathbf{v}_{t.} + \mathbf{v}_{t-1,.}\Pi_2 + \mathbf{v}_{t-2,.}\Pi_2^2 + \cdots$.

The matrices of interest in the final form are M_0, the impact multiplier matrix, and M_τ, the *interim* multiplier matrix of *delay* τ. The interpretation of these matrices is best understood by partial differentiation of the *expected* value of the final form. In detail, the final form can be expressed as

$$\begin{aligned}(y_{t1}, y_{t2}, \ldots, y_{tG}) &= (x_{t1}, \ldots, x_{tk})\begin{bmatrix} m_{0,1,1} & \cdots & m_{0,1,G} \\ m_{0,2,1} & \cdots & m_{0,2,G} \\ \vdots & \vdots & \vdots \\ m_{0,k,1} & \cdots & m_{0,k,G}\end{bmatrix} \\ &\quad + \sum_{\tau=1}^{\infty}(x_{t-\tau,1}, \ldots, x_{t-\tau,k})\begin{bmatrix} m_{\tau,1,1} & \cdots & m_{\tau,1,G} \\ m_{\tau,2,1} & \cdots & m_{\tau,2,G} \\ \vdots & \vdots & \vdots \\ m_{\tau,k,1} & \cdots & m_{\tau,k,G}\end{bmatrix} \\ &\quad + \mathbf{v}_{t.}^*.\end{aligned}$$

Therefore, for $g = 1, 2, \ldots, G$ and $k' = 1, 2, \ldots, k$

$$\begin{aligned}\frac{\partial E y_{tg}}{\partial x_{tk'}} &= \frac{\partial}{\partial x_{tk'}}(x_{t1}m_{0,1,g} + x_{t2}m_{0,2,g} + \cdots + x_{tk'}m_{0,k',g} + \cdots + x_{tk}m_{0,k,g}) \\ &= m_{0,k',g}.\end{aligned}$$

In other words, holding all other purely exogenous variables constant, a one unit change in the purely exogenous variable $x_{k'}$ leads to an *expected* change of $m_{0,k',g}$ units in the gth endogenous variable y_g during the *same* time period. Note the location of $m_{0,k',g}$ in the M_0 matrix, the k'th row (associated with the k'th purely exogenous variable) and the gth column (associated with the gth endogenous variable). Since the result of the exogenous variable change is immediately realized, M_0 is called the *impact* multiplier matrix. In a similar manner it can be shown that $\partial E y_{tg}/\partial x_{t-\tau,k'} = m_{\tau,k',g}$, the (k', g) element of M_τ. Therefore, holding all other purely exogenous variables constant, a one unit change in the k'th purely exogenous variable at time $t - \tau$ results in an *expected* change of $m_{\tau, k', g}$ units in the gth endogenous variable at time t. As there is a delayed impact of τ periods, the matrix M_τ is called the *interim* multiplier matrix of *delay* τ.

The impact and interim (delay) multipliers refer to "one shot" exogenous changes. They depict the expected effect on current and future values of an endogenous variable arising from raising (or lowering) a purely exogenous variable by one unit and then restoring it to its original value. In the absence of a sustained change in the exogenous variable, the endogenous variable returns to the original equilibrium (mean) level given that the system is stable. We will discuss what conditions constitute a stable system below.

The effects of sustaining a change in a purely exogenous variable for τ' time periods before returning it to its original value are given by the elements of the *cumulative* multiplier matrix

$$C_{\tau'} = \sum_{\tau=0}^{\tau'} M_\tau = \sum_{\tau=0}^{\tau'} \Pi_1 \Pi_2^\tau, \tag{24.2.6}$$

where $\Pi_2^0 = I_G$. The (k', g) element of $C_{\tau'}$, $c_{\tau', k', g} = \sum_{\tau=0}^{\tau'} m_{\tau, k', g}$, represents the *expected* cumulative effect on the gth endogenous variable of sustaining a a one unit change of the k'th purely exogenous variable for τ' time periods. Logically, the *total* (equilibrium) multiplier matrix is given by

$$\begin{aligned} \bar{C} &= \sum_{\tau=0}^{\infty} M_\tau = \sum_{\tau=0}^{\infty} \Pi_1 \Pi_2^\tau \\ &= \Pi_1(I + \Pi_2 + \Pi_2^2 + \cdots) \\ &= \Pi_1(I - \Pi_2)^{-1}, \end{aligned} \tag{24.2.7}$$

where the property $(I + \Pi_2 + \Pi_2^2 + \cdots) = (I - \Pi_2)^{-1}$ holds provided $\lim_{s\to\infty} \Pi_2^s = 0$. The elements of this matrix, $\bar{c}_{k', g}$ describe the total expected response of the gth endogenous variable to a *sustained* unit change in the k'th purely exogenous variable, holding all other exogenous variables constant.

A major assumption utilized in deriving the above multipliers is the postulated stability of the dynamic simultaneous equations model (24.2.1), i.e., that $\lim_{s\to\infty} \Pi_{2=0}^s$. We will now show how this latter condition is synonymous with the condition that, if an exogenous shock occurs to the endogenous variables of the model, the endogenous variables will, unless subjected to further shocks, return to their former equilibrium (mean) values. Of course, apart from the changes in endogenous variables resulting from changes in exogenous variables, the endogenous variables will fluctuate because of the effect of stochastic disturbances. Throughout we will consider only cases where the probability is zero that an otherwise stable system would be unstable because of random disturbances. For example, we exclude by assumption (see the error properties of Section 19.3) the possibility that the error vector $\mathbf{e}_{t.}$ has an ever increasing variance as $t \to \infty$. As a result we can, without loss of generality, analyze the stability of a dynamic simultaneous equations model as if it were a system of exact (containing no error) linear difference equations. Therefore, we set $\mathbf{e}_{t.} = (0, 0, \ldots, 0)$ for all t during the present discussion of stability.

If the exogenous variable vector $\mathbf{x}_{t.}$ is indefinitely sustained at some value $\bar{\mathbf{x}}$ then the final form is

$$\begin{aligned}\mathbf{y}_{t.} &= \bar{\mathbf{x}}M_0 + \bar{\mathbf{x}}M_1 + \bar{\mathbf{x}}M_2 + \cdots \\ &= \bar{\mathbf{x}}\sum_{\tau=0}^{\infty} M_\tau = \bar{\mathbf{x}}\bar{C} \quad \text{for all } t.\end{aligned}$$

Therefore the endogenous variable vector $\mathbf{y}_{t.}$ attains the equilibrium value

$$\bar{\mathbf{y}} = \bar{\mathbf{x}}\bar{C}. \tag{24.2.8}$$

Letting $s = t - 1$ in (24.2.4) provides

$$\mathbf{y}_{t.} = \sum_{\tau=0}^{t-1} \mathbf{x}_{t-\tau,.} M_\tau + \mathbf{y}_{0,.}\Pi_2^t, \tag{24.2.9}$$

where $\mathbf{e}_{t.} = \mathbf{v}_{t.} = \mathbf{0}'$ for all t has been imposed. But at equilibrium $\mathbf{y}_{t.} = \mathbf{y}_{0,.} = \bar{\mathbf{y}}$ and $\mathbf{x}_{t-\tau,.} = \bar{\mathbf{x}}$ for all t and τ, therefore

$$\bar{\mathbf{y}} = \bar{\mathbf{x}} \sum_{\tau=0}^{t-1} M_\tau + \bar{\mathbf{y}}\Pi_2^t. \tag{24.2.10}$$

Subtracting (24.2.10) from (24.2.9) yields

$$(\mathbf{y}_{t.} - \bar{\mathbf{y}}) = \sum_{\tau=0}^{t-1} (\mathbf{x}_{t-\tau,.} - \bar{\mathbf{x}})M_\tau + (\mathbf{y}_{0,.} - \bar{\mathbf{y}})\Pi_2^t. \tag{24.2.11}$$

The interpretation of Equation (24.2.11) is as follows: the (expected) distance of the endogenous variables from their respective equilibria at time t is a linear function of the displacement of the exogenous variables from their equilibrium values in previous time periods and the initial displacement of the endogenous variables from their equilibria. Since stability refers to the time path of the endogenous variables following an initial displacement from equilibrium without further changes in the exogenous variables, we set $(\mathbf{x}_{t-\tau,.} - \bar{\mathbf{x}}) = \mathbf{0}'$, $\tau = 0, 1, \ldots,$ in Equation (24.2.11) and obtain

$$(\mathbf{y}_{t.} - \bar{\mathbf{y}}) = (\mathbf{y}_{0,.} - \bar{\mathbf{y}})\Pi_2^t. \tag{24.2.12}$$

The (expected) distance of the endogenous variables from their equilibria following initial displacement with no exogenous change thereafter is proportional to initial displacement. Obviously, if the endogenous variables are to return to their equilibria as $t \to \infty$ (and hence for the system to be stable), $\lim_{t\to\infty} \Pi_2^t = 0$. This is the same condition we encountered before in the derivation of the dynamic multipliers.

To understand better what condition is placed on the reduced form coefficient matrix Π_2 for stability, consider the following matrix theorem.

Theorem 24.2.1 (Spectral Decomposition of Nonsymmetric Matrix). *Let A be a $n \times n$ real matrix. The determinant $|A - \lambda I| = 0$ has n roots, some of which may be complex. There exist vectors $\mathbf{p}_i$, $i = 1, 2, \ldots, n$, such that $A\mathbf{p}_i = \lambda_i \mathbf{p}_i$. Assuming all the roots are distinct and letting the columns of P be made up of the $\mathbf{p}_i$, $P = (\mathbf{p}_1, \mathbf{p}_2, \ldots, \mathbf{p}_n)$, the following representation exists:*

$$A = P\Lambda Q, \tag{24.2.13}$$

where Λ is a diagonal matrix with the λ_i along the diagonal and $Q = P^{-1}$.

Proof. See Rao (1973, p. 43). For a decomposition of A when the roots are not distinct, see references given by Rao (p. 44). Note this theorem is a generalization of the frequently used diagonalization theorem for symmetric matrices.

Not let the matrix of interest be Π_2. Then from the previous theorem $\Pi_2 = P\Lambda Q$, $\Pi_2^2 = P\Lambda Q P\Lambda Q = P\Lambda^2 Q$, and in general $\Pi_2^s = P\Lambda^s Q$. We then have the following theorem.

Theorem 24.2.2. *A necessary and sufficient condition for the dynamic simultaneous equations model* (24.2.1) *to be stable is that the characteristic roots of the reduced form coefficient matrix $\Pi_2 = -\Delta_2 \Gamma^{-1}$ be less than one in absolute value. In the instance that the characteristic roots are complex, $a + bi$, their modulus, $\sqrt{a^2 + b^2}$, must be less than one.*

Note also that the characteristic roots are instrumental in determining the "shape" of time paths of the endogenous variables. Of course, given that the system is stable, all time paths will be damped. But these paths can take on monotonic, sawtooth, sinusoidal shapes or any combination of these. Since $\Pi_2^t = P\Lambda^t Q$ by Theorem 24.2.1, we can write (24.2.12) as

$$\begin{aligned}(\mathbf{y}_{t.} - \bar{\mathbf{y}}) &= (\mathbf{y}_{0,.} - \bar{\mathbf{y}})P\Lambda^t Q \\ &= \sum_{i=1}^{G} (\mathbf{y}_{0,.} - \bar{\mathbf{y}})\mathbf{p}_i \mathbf{q}_i' \lambda_i^t,\end{aligned} \tag{24.2.14}$$

where $\mathbf{q}_i$ denotes the ith column at Q. From Equation (24.2.14) it is easy to see that each positive root contributes a monotonic component to the time path while negative and complex roots contribute sawtooth (positive, negative, positive, negative, etc.) and sinusoidal components, respectively. Which factors dominate can be determined only on a case-by-case basis, however. (See Chow (1975, Ch.2) for detailed discussion.)

To illustrate the concepts discussed in this section we turn to an empirical investigation of Klein's Model I. The impact, interim and total multipliers for each of the endogenous variables with respect to selected exogenous variables are reported in Table 24.2.1. These multipliers are derived from

Table 24.2.1 Impact, interim and equilibrium multipliers for Klein's Model I.

Lag in years	C	I	W	X	P	K
			Unit increase in W'			
0	1.291	−0.010	0.513	1.281	0.768	−0.010
1	0.829	0.574	0.794	1.403	0.609	0.564
2	0.663	0.345	0.658	1.009	0.350	0.910
3	0.349	0.866	0.357	0.436	0.078	0.996
4	0.022	−0.132	0.346	−0.110	−0.145	0.863
5	−0.237	−0.274	−0.225	−0.512	−0.286	0.589
6	−0.388	−0.327	−0.379	−0.716	−0.336	0.362
7	−0.425	−0.303	−0.420	−0.727	−0.306	−0.039
8	−0.367	−0.220	−0.367	−0.588	−0.221	−0.259
9	−0.249	−0.114	−0.252	−0.364	−0.111	−0.374
10	−0.109	−0.011	−0.114	−0.121	−0.006	−0.386
11	0.018	0.069	0.013	0.088	0.074	−0.317
12	1.112	0.116	0.107	0.229	0.121	−0.200
13	0.161	0.129	0.157	0.290	0.132	0.071
14	0.165	0.112	0.163	0.277	0.113	0.041
15	0.134	0.769	0.135	0.211	0.076	0.118
16	0.847	0.034	0.086	0.119	0.033	0.152
17	0.029	−0.004	0.031	0.024	−0.006	0.148
18	−0.018	−0.033	−0.016	−0.051	−0.035	0.114
19	−0.051	−0.048	−0.049	−0.099	−0.050	0.066
20	−0.065	−0.502	−0.064	−0.115	−0.051	0.015
Total multiplier	1.881	0	1.094	1.881	0.786	2.999
			Unit increase in G			
0	0.634	−0.012	0.649	1.621	0.972	−0.012
1	1.049	0.727	1.005	1.776	0.771	0.714
2	0.840	0.437	0.833	1.227	0.443	1.152
3	0.442	0.109	0.452	0.552	0.099	1.261
4	0.027	−0.168	0.043	−0.140	−0.184	1.093
5	−0.300	−0.347	−0.285	−0.648	−0.363	0.745
6	−0.492	0.414	−0.480	−0.906	−0.425	0.331
7	−0.538	−0.381	−0.532	−0.920	−0.387	−0.049
8	−0.465	−0.279	−0.465	−0.745	−0.279	−0.329
9	−0.316	−0.145	−0.320	−0.461	−0.141	−0.474
10	−0.138	−0.014	−0.145	−0.153	−0.008	−0.489
11	0.023	0.087	0.016	0.111	0.094	−0.401
12	0.142	0.147	0.136	0.290	0.153	0.253
13	0.203	0.163	0.199	0.367	0.167	−0.090
14	0.209	0.142	0.207	0.351	0.144	0.052
15	0.170	0.097	0.171	0.268	0.097	0.149
16	0.107	0.043	0.109	0.150	0.041	0.193

Table 24.2.1 (*Contd.*)

Lag in years	C	I	W	X	P	K
17	0.037	−0.005	0.039	0.031	−0.008	0.187
18	−0.023	−0.042	−0.020	−0.065	−0.045	0.145
19	−0.064	−0.061	−0.062	−0.126	−0.063	0.083
20	−0.082	−0.063	−0.081	−0.146	−0.064	0.019
Total Multiplier	1.381	0	1.385	2.381	9.996	3.796
			Unit increase in T			
0	−0.195	0.014	−0.072	−0.181	−1.108	0.014
1	−0.865	−0.827	−0.710	−1.693	−0.982	−0.813
2	−0.968	−0.575	−0.925	−1.544	−0.618	−1.389
3	−0.596	−0.194	−0.596	−0.791	−0.194	−1.583
4	−0.106	0.159	−0.122	0.052	0.175	−1.424
5	0.317	0.404	0.298	0.721	0.423	−1.019
6	0.585	0.511	0.570	1.096	0.526	−0.508
7	0.673	0.490	0.665	1.164	0.499	−0.017
8	0.606	0.375	0.604	0.981	0.377	0.357
9	0.432	0.212	0.436	0.645	0.208	0.570
10	0.213	0.046	0.220	0.259	0.038	0.616
11	0.004	−0.089	0.012	−0.085	−0.098	0.527
12	−0.155	−0.174	−0.147	−0.330	−0.182	0.352
13	−0.245	−0.203	−0.239	−0.449	−0.209	0.148
14	−0.263	−0.184	−0.261	−0.448	−0.187	−0.036
15	−0.224	−0.132	−0.224	−0.357	−0.133	−0.169
16	−0.149	−0.066	−0.151	−0.216	−0.064	−0.235
17	−0.062	−0.002	−0.065	−0.065	0.000	−0.238
18	0.016	0.046	0.013	0.062	0.049	−0.192
19	0.073	0.073	0.070	0.147	0.076	−0.118
20	0.101	0.080	0.099	0.181	0.082	−0.038
Total Multiplier	−0.685	0	−0.399	−0.685	−1.286	−4.904

the three-stage least squares estimates of the structural parameters. Note that the interim multipliers are not all the same sign, indicating the presence of nonmonotonic components in (24.2.14). This is verified by examining the nonzero characteristic roots of Π_2 which appear in Table 24.2.2. The roots are less than one in absolute value and thus the estimated system is stable. The imaginary roots contribute a sinusoidal pattern to the time path of the endogenous variables.

The above multipliers were calculated using the three-stage least squares *derived* reduced form estimates of Π_1 and Π_2. As shown in Section 23.2,

Table 24.2.2 Characteristic roots of Π_2 for the three-stage least squares estimates of Klein's Model I.

Real	0.34362
Imaginary	$0.77846 \pm 0.39126i$

if the specified model is correct, the full information methods provide the most efficient means of estimating the reduced form parameters. It seems logical that the efficiency of reduced form estimation is intimately linked to the efficiency of estimating the final form multiplier matrices since they are functions of the reduced form coefficient matrices Π_1 and Π_2. We formally examine these results in the following section as well as determine the asymptotic distribution of the largest characteristic root of Π_2 in Section 24.4.

24.3 Efficient Estimation and Asymptotic Distribution of Dynamic Multipliers

In this section we examine the asymptotic distributions of estimates of the impact, interim, cumulative and total multiplier matrices,

$$M_0 = \Pi_1\Pi_2^0 = \Pi_1, \tag{24.3.1}$$

$$M_\tau = \Pi_1\Pi_2^\tau, \tag{24.3.2}$$

$$C_{\tau'} = \sum_{\tau=0}^{\tau'} M_\tau = \sum_{\tau=0}^{\tau'} \Pi_1\Pi_2^\tau, \tag{24.3.3}$$

$$\bar{C} = \sum_{\tau=0}^{\infty} \Pi_1\Pi_2^\tau = \Pi_1(I - \Pi_2)^{-1}, \tag{24.3.4}$$

respectively. Logically, the asymptotic distributions and corresponding efficiency of estimates of these multiplier matrices are dependent upon the asymptotic distributions and efficiency of the estimates of the reduced form parameters Π_1 and Π_2. The following results are based on the work of Schmidt (1973).

Recall the reduced form of the dynamic simultaneous equations model (24.2.1) is

$$\mathbf{y}_{t.} = \mathbf{x}_{t.}\Pi_1 + \mathbf{y}_{t-1,.}\Pi_2 + \mathbf{v}_{t.}, \tag{24.3.5}$$

where $\Pi_1 = -\Delta_1\Gamma^{-1}$, $\Pi_2 = -\Delta_2\Gamma^{-1}$, and $\mathbf{v}_{t.} = -\mathbf{e}_{t.}\Gamma^{-1}$. Before proving the major theorems of this section, the following lemma will prove useful.

Lemma 24.3.1. *For $n \geq 1$, define*

$$A_n = \sum_{j=0}^{n-1} (\Pi_2^j)' \otimes \tilde{\Pi}_1 \tilde{\Pi}_2^{n-1-j},$$

$$D_n = (\Pi_2^n)' \otimes I_k.$$

Then

$$\operatorname{vec}(\tilde{\Pi}_1 \tilde{\Pi}_2^n - \Pi_1 \Pi_2^n) = (D_n, A_n) \begin{bmatrix} \operatorname{vec}(\tilde{\Pi}_1 - \Pi_1) \\ \operatorname{vec}(\tilde{\Pi}_2 - \Pi_2) \end{bmatrix}.$$

Proof. Let $M_n = \Pi_1 \Pi_2^n$. Then note that

$$\tilde{M}_n - M_n = \tilde{\Pi}_1(\tilde{\Pi}_2^n - \Pi_2^n) + (\tilde{\Pi}_1 - \Pi_1)\Pi_2^n.$$

But

$$\tilde{\Pi}_2^n - \Pi_2^n = \sum_{j=0}^{n-1} \Pi_2^j(\tilde{\Pi}_2 - \Pi_2)\Pi_2^{n-j-1},$$

and therefore

$$\tilde{M}_n - M_n = \sum_{j=0}^{n-1} [\tilde{\Pi}_1 \tilde{\Pi}_2^j(\tilde{\Pi}_2 - \Pi_2)\Pi_2^{n-1-j}] + I_k(\tilde{\Pi}_1 - \Pi_1)\Pi_2^n.$$

Using the matrix property that (see Nissen (1968)) for any conformable matrices A, B, C, $\operatorname{vec}(ABC) = (C' \otimes A)\operatorname{vec}(B)$,

$$\begin{aligned} \operatorname{vec}(\tilde{M}_n - M_n) &= \sum_{j=0}^{n-1} \operatorname{vec} \tilde{\Pi}_1 \tilde{\Pi}_2^j(\tilde{\Pi}_2 - \Pi_2)\Pi_2^{n-1-j} \\ &\quad + \operatorname{vec} I_k(\tilde{\Pi}_1 - \Pi_1)\Pi_2^n \\ &= \sum_{j=0}^{n-1} (\Pi_2^{n-1-j})' \otimes (\tilde{\Pi}_1 \tilde{\Pi}_2^j) \operatorname{vec}(\tilde{\Pi}_2 - \Pi_2) \\ &\quad + (\Pi_2^n)' \otimes I_k \operatorname{vec}(\tilde{\Pi}_1 - \Pi_1) \\ &= \sum_{j=0}^{n-1} (\Pi_2^j)' \otimes (\tilde{\Pi}_1 \tilde{\Pi}_2^{n-1-j}) \operatorname{vec}(\tilde{\Pi}_2 - \Pi_2) \\ &\quad + (\Pi_2^n)' \otimes I_k \operatorname{vec}(\tilde{\Pi}_1 - \Pi_1) \\ &= (D_n, A_n) \begin{bmatrix} \operatorname{vec}(\tilde{\Pi}_1 - \Pi_1) \\ \operatorname{vec}(\tilde{\Pi}_2 - \Pi_2) \end{bmatrix}. \end{aligned}$$

□

The first major result is contained in the following theorem.

Theorem 24.3.1. *Let $\tilde{\Pi}_1$ and $\tilde{\Pi}_2$ denote consistent estimators of Π_1 and Π_2 such that*

$$\sqrt{T} \begin{bmatrix} \operatorname{vec}(\tilde{\Pi}_1 - \Pi_1) \\ \operatorname{vec}(\tilde{\Pi}_2 - \Pi_2) \end{bmatrix}$$

has asymptotic distribution $N(\mathbf{0}, \Theta)$. *Define*

$$\bar{A}_n = \operatorname{plim} A_n = \sum_{j=0}^{n-1} (\Pi_2^j)' \otimes \Pi_1 \Pi_2^{n-1-j},$$

$$\bar{D}_n = \operatorname{plim} D_n = D_n.$$

Then the asymptotic distribution of $\sqrt{T}\ \mathrm{vec}(\tilde{\Pi}_1 \tilde{\Pi}_2^n - \Pi_1 \Pi_2^n)$ *is*

$$N[\mathbf{0}, (\bar{D}_n, \bar{A}_n)\Theta(\bar{D}_n, \bar{A}_n)'].$$

PROOF. The above conclusion follows from the well-known result that if G is a matrix with probability limit $\bar{G}$ and if $\mathbf{h}$ is a vector with asymptotic distribution $N(\mathbf{0}, \Omega)$, then the asymptotic distribution of $G\mathbf{h}$ is $N(\mathbf{0}, \bar{G}\Omega\bar{G}')$. □

The other major result is as follows:

Theorem 24.3.2. *Let the conditions of Theorem* 24.3.1 *hold and let*

$$C_n = \sum_{j=0}^{n} M_j = \sum_{j=0}^{n} \Pi_1 \Pi_2^j.$$

For notational purposes, define $A_0 = \bar{A}_0 = 0$, $D_0 = \bar{D}_0 = I_{kG}$, $Z_n = \sum_{j=0}^{n} (D_n, A_n)$ *and* $\bar{Z}_n = \sum_{j=0}^{n} (\bar{D}_n, \bar{A}_n)$. *Then the asymptotic distribution of* $\sqrt{T}\ \mathrm{vec}(\tilde{C}_n - C_n)$ *is* $N(\mathbf{0}, \bar{Z}_n \Theta \bar{Z}_n')$.

PROOF.

$$\begin{aligned}
\mathrm{vec}(\tilde{C}_n - C_n) &= \sum_{j=0}^{n} \mathrm{vec}(\tilde{M}_j - M_j) \\
&= \sum_{j=0}^{n} \mathrm{vec}(\tilde{\Pi}_1 \tilde{\Pi}_2^j - \Pi_1 \Pi_2^j) \\
&= [I, 0] \begin{bmatrix} \mathrm{vec}(\tilde{\Pi}_1 - \Pi_1) \\ \mathrm{vec}(\tilde{\Pi}_2 - \Pi_2) \end{bmatrix} \\
&\quad + \sum_{j=1}^{n} (D_j, A_j) \begin{bmatrix} \mathrm{vec}(\tilde{\Pi}_1 - \Pi_1) \\ \mathrm{vec}(\tilde{\Pi}_2 - \Pi_2) \end{bmatrix} \\
&= Z_n \begin{bmatrix} \mathrm{vec}(\tilde{\Pi}_1 - \Pi_1) \\ \mathrm{vec}(\tilde{\Pi}_2 - \Pi_2) \end{bmatrix}.
\end{aligned}$$

The conclusion then follows by an argument similar to that in the latter part of the proof of Theorem 24.3.1. □

Consider the meaning of these two theorems. Theorem 24.3.1 establishes the asymptotic distributions of the impact and interim multiplier matrices given the consistent estimates $\tilde{\Pi}_1$ and $\tilde{\Pi}_2$ while Theorem 24.3.2 provides the asymptotic distributions of the cumulative and total multiplier matrices.

Estimated asymptotic variances of the individual multipliers can be obtained as the diagonal elements of the above covariance matrices divided by the sample size T. The unknowns $\bar{A}_n$, $\bar{D}_n$, and $\bar{Z}_n$ must, of course, be replaced by their consistent estimates, $\tilde{A}_n$, $\tilde{D}_n$, and $\tilde{Z}_n$ which depend on the consistent estimates $\tilde{\Pi}_1$ and $\tilde{\Pi}_2$ in the same way that $\bar{A}_n$, $\bar{D}_n$, and $\bar{Z}_n$ depend upon Π_1 and Π_2.

These theorems apply for any consistent estimation method for Π_1 and Π_2. However, as shown in Theorems 23.2.4 and 23.2.5, the three-stage least squares *derived reduced form* estimates of Π_1 and Π_2 in the reduced form (24.3.5) are more efficient than similar estimates from either ordinary least squares or two-stage least squares. That is, the asymptotic covariance matrix of the three-stage least squares derived reduced form estimates is "smaller" (in the positive semidefinite sense) than the covariance matrices of the ordinary least squares or two-stage least squares reduced form estimates. Therefore, the following theorem is immediate.

Theorem 24.3.3. *The most efficient estimates of the multipliers* (24.3.1)–(24.3.4) *are obtained by utilizing full information derived reduced form estimates of* Π_1 *and* Π_2.

Proof. The asymptotic covariance matrices are quadratic forms with symmetric matrix Θ, the "smallest" Θ matrix being associated with the three-stage least squares derived reduced form estimates. □

To illustrate the previous concepts, we again consider Klein's model I. In Table 24.3.1 the standard errors of the first few interim multipliers of government nonwage expenditure and taxes on national income are reported.

Table 24.3.1 Impact and interim multipliers of nonwage government expenditure (G) and taxes (T) on national income (X) for Klein's Model I.

Lag	G	T
0	1.622	−0.181
	(0.348)	(0.401)
1	1.777	−1.693
	(0.368)	(0.477)
2	1.278	−1.544
	(0.321)	(0.398)
3	0.552	−0.791
	(0.219)	(0.274)

24.4 Stability and Standard Error of Dominant Characteristic Root

As we have previously seen, the dynamic simultaneous equations system (24.2.1) is stable if and only if the absolute value of the largest characteristic root of Π_2 is less than one. Naturally since Π_2 is unknown and must be estimated, the dominant root of Π_2 is likewise unknown and must be estimated. Consequently, one can talk about stability only in a statistical sense. That is, one can only claim, given the present sample, that the dominant root has absolute value less than one with a certain probability. We now turn to the derivation of the asymptotic standard error of the absolute value of the dominant root.

There are basically two ways that we may proceed. The appropriate standard error of the dominant characteristic root can be derived in terms of the asymptotic covariance matrix of the structural coefficients or alternatively in terms of the asymptotic covariance matrix of the reduced form estimates of Π_1 and Π_2. The first approach is pursued by Oberhofer and Kmenta (1973) while Theil and Boot (1962) and Neudecker and Van De Panne (1966) develop the second approach. We present the second approach because of expositional convenience.

Since Π_2 is not symmetric, its characteristic roots are not necessarily real. According to Theorem 24.2.1 the spectral decomposition of Π_2 provides right- and left-hand characteristic vectors $\mathbf{p}_i$ and $\mathbf{q}_i$ such that

$$(\Pi_2 - \lambda_j I)\mathbf{p}_j = \mathbf{0}, \qquad j = 1, 2, \ldots, G, \tag{24.4.1}$$

$$\mathbf{q}_j'(\Pi_2 - \lambda_j I) = \mathbf{0}', \qquad j = 1, 2, \ldots, G, \tag{24.4.2}$$

where, for simplicity, we assume that there are no multiple characteristic roots. In addition, after normalization

$$\begin{aligned} \mathbf{q}_i'\mathbf{p}_j &= 1 \quad \text{for } i = j, \quad i, j = 1, 2, \ldots, G, \\ &= 0 \quad \text{for } i \neq j. \end{aligned} \tag{24.4.3}$$

This decomposition provides a means of proving the following theorem.

Theorem 24.4.1. *Let $\tilde{\Pi}_2$ denote a consistent estimator of Π_2 such that $\sqrt{T}\,\mathrm{vec}(\tilde{\Pi}_2 - \Pi_2)$ has asymptotic distribution $N(\mathbf{0}, \Theta_2)$. Let λ_1 denote the largest characteristic root of Π_2 and $\tilde{\lambda}_1$ its corresponding consistent estimate obtained as the largest characteristic root of $\tilde{\Pi}_2$. In the case that λ_1 is real, the asymptotic variance of $\tilde{\lambda}_1$ is*

$$\frac{1}{T}\operatorname{plim}\{T(\tilde{\lambda}_1 - \lambda_1)^2\} = \mathbf{s}_1'(\Theta_2/T)\mathbf{s}_1, \tag{24.4.4}$$

where $\mathbf{s}_1' = (p_{11}\mathbf{q}_1', p_{12}\mathbf{q}_1', \ldots, p_{1G}\mathbf{q}_1')$. When the dominant root is complex, $\lambda_1 = a + bi$, the corresponding characteristic vectors $\mathbf{p}_i$ and $\mathbf{q}_i$ are also complex and hence $\mathbf{s}_1$ is also complex. The complex vector $\mathbf{s}_1$ can be separated into a *real part,* $\mathbf{s}_1^*$, *and a complex part,* $i\mathbf{s}_1^{**}$, *where* $\mathbf{s}_1^*$ *and* $\mathbf{s}_1^{**}$ *denote real vectors such that* $\mathbf{s}_1 = \mathbf{s}_1^* + i\mathbf{s}_1^{**}$. *Then the asymptotic variance of* $|\tilde{\lambda}_1|$ *is equal to*

$$\frac{1}{T}\operatorname{plim}\{T(\tilde{\lambda}_1 - \lambda_1)^2\} = (a^2 + b^2)^{-1}(a\mathbf{s}_1^{*\prime} + b\mathbf{s}_1^{**\prime})(\Theta_2/T)(a\mathbf{s}_1^* + b\mathbf{s}_1^{**}). \tag{24.4.5}$$

PROOF. First consider the case where λ_1 is real. From (24.4.1) and (24.4.2) it is obvious that λ_1 is a function of the elements of Π_2, that is,

$$\lambda_1 = f(\operatorname{vec}\Pi_2). \tag{24.4.6}$$

According to Corollary 4.2.2, we have for the asymptotic variance of λ_1

$$\frac{1}{T}\operatorname{plim}\{T(\tilde{\lambda}_1 - \lambda_1)^2\} = \left(\frac{\partial\lambda_1}{\partial\operatorname{vec}\Pi_2}\right)'(\Theta_2/T)\left(\frac{\partial\lambda_1}{\partial\operatorname{vec}\Pi_2}\right), \tag{24.4.7}$$

where $(\partial\lambda_1/(\partial\operatorname{vec}\Pi_2))$ is a column vector of derivatives of λ_1 with respect to the elements of Π_2. Totally differentiating (24.4.1), we have

$$(d\Pi_2 - d\lambda_1 I_G)\mathbf{p}_1 + (\Pi_2 - \lambda_1 I_G)\,d\mathbf{p}_1 = \mathbf{0}. \tag{24.4.8}$$

Premultiplying (24.4.8) by $\mathbf{q}_1'$

$$\mathbf{q}_1'(d\Pi_2 - d\lambda_1 I_G)\mathbf{p}_1 + \mathbf{q}_1'(\Pi_2 - \lambda_1 I_G)\,d\mathbf{p}_1 = \mathbf{0} \tag{24.4.9a}$$

and

$$\mathbf{q}_1'(d\Pi_2 - d\lambda_1 I_G)\mathbf{p}_1 = \mathbf{0}, \tag{24.4.9b}$$

since $\mathbf{q}_1'(\Pi_2 - \lambda_1 I_G) = \mathbf{0}'$ from (24.4.2). Simplifying

$$\begin{aligned} d\lambda_1 &= \mathbf{q}_1'\,d\Pi_2\,\mathbf{p}_1 \\ &= (p_{11}\mathbf{q}_1', p_{12}\mathbf{q}_1', \ldots, p_{1G}\mathbf{q}_1')\operatorname{vec}(d\Pi_2). \end{aligned} \tag{24.4.10}$$

Therefore,

$$\left(\frac{d\lambda_1}{d\operatorname{vec}\Pi_2}\right)' = (p_{11}\mathbf{q}_1', p_{12}\mathbf{q}_1', \ldots, p_{1G}\mathbf{q}_1') = \mathbf{s}_1', \tag{24.4.11}$$

as desired. The reader is referred to Neudecker and Van De Panne (1966) for a proof of the complex case. □

An estimated asymptotic variance of the dominant root can be obtained by replacing all unknown parameters with consistent estimates. That is, $\tilde{\mathbf{p}}_1$ and $\tilde{\mathbf{q}}_1$ can be obtained from the decomposition of $\tilde{\Pi}_2$ and Θ_2 consistently estimated by $\tilde{\Theta}_2$. Of course, Theorem 24.4.1 applies to *any* consistent estimate of Π_2 but, obviously from the quadratic form of the asymptotic variance of $\tilde{\lambda}_1$, the smaller Θ_2 is (i.e. the greater the efficiency of $\tilde{\Pi}_2$), the smaller the asymptotic variance of $\tilde{\lambda}_1$. Therefore, if the dynamic simultaneous equation model is specified correctly, the full information derived reduced form estimates of Π_2 will in turn provide the most efficient means of estimating the dominant root of the system.

24.5 Standard Errors of Dynamic Simulation Forecasts

Again consider the dynamic simultaneous equations model

$$\mathbf{y}_{t.}\Gamma + \mathbf{x}_{t.}\Delta_1 + \mathbf{y}_{t-1,.}\Delta_2 + \mathbf{e}_{t.} = \mathbf{0}' \tag{24.5.1}$$

with reduced form

$$\mathbf{y}_{t.} = \mathbf{x}_{t.}\Pi_1 + \mathbf{y}_{t-1,.}\Pi_2 + \mathbf{v}_{t.}, \tag{24.5.2}$$

where $\Pi_1 = -\Delta_1\Gamma^{-1}$, $\Pi_2 = -\Delta_2\Gamma^{-1}$, and $\mathbf{v}_{t.} = -\mathbf{e}_{t.}\Gamma^{-1}$. Suppose that by means of a *previous* sample consistent estimates $\tilde{\Pi}_1$ and $\tilde{\Pi}_2$ are available. Let $\mathbf{y}_{0.}$ denote the *last* observation vector on the joint dependent variables from the previous sample and $\mathbf{y}_{1.}, \mathbf{y}_{2.}, \ldots, \mathbf{y}_{h.}$ denote h consecutive future values of the joint dependent variables. Often interest centers on predicting these future values and the corresponding standard errors of the forecasts. That is, predictions of the form

$$\begin{aligned}
\tilde{\mathbf{y}}_{1.} &= \mathbf{x}_{1.}\tilde{\Pi}_1 + \mathbf{y}_{0.}\tilde{\Pi}_2, \\
\tilde{\mathbf{y}}_{2.} &= \mathbf{x}_{2.}\tilde{\Pi}_1 + \tilde{\mathbf{y}}_{1.}\tilde{\Pi}_2 = \mathbf{x}_{1.}\tilde{\Pi}_1\tilde{\Pi}_2 + \mathbf{x}_{2.}\tilde{\Pi}_1 + \mathbf{y}_{0.}\tilde{\Pi}_2, \\
&\vdots \\
\tilde{\mathbf{y}}_{h.} &= \sum_{j=1}^{h} \mathbf{x}_{j.}\tilde{\Pi}_1\tilde{\Pi}_2^{h-j} + \mathbf{y}_{0.}\tilde{\Pi}_2^{h}
\end{aligned} \tag{24.5.3}$$

may be of interest. In (24.5.1) we have implicitly assumed that the *future* values of the purely exogenous variables $\mathbf{x}_{1.}, \mathbf{x}_{2.}, \ldots, \mathbf{x}_{h.}$ are known. This may not be the case, however, and such future values may have to be forecasted. In such a case the prediction equations (24.5.3) would be modified by the replacement of $\mathbf{x}_{1.}, \mathbf{x}_{2.}, \ldots, \mathbf{x}_{h.}$ with forecasts $\tilde{\mathbf{x}}_{1.}, \tilde{\mathbf{x}}_{2.}, \ldots, \tilde{\mathbf{x}}_{h.}$. The first case where the $\mathbf{x}_{i.}$, $i = 1, 2, \ldots, h$ are known is treated by Schmidt (1974a) while the case of forecasted exogenous variables, $\tilde{\mathbf{x}}_{t.}$, $i = 1, 2, \ldots, h$ is discussed in Schmidt (1978). In what follows we present the basic results without proofs. The interested reader should, with the background established in the previous sections, be able to reconstruct proofs given in these references.

Let us first examine the case where the future values of the purely exogenous variables are *known*. The forecasts of (24.5.1) are then conditional as known $\mathbf{x}_{i.}$, $i = 1, 2, \ldots, h$ and $\mathbf{y}_{0.}$. Schmidt (1974a, pp. 304–307) shows that

Theorem 24.5.1. *Let $\tilde{\Pi}_1$ and $\tilde{\Pi}_2$ be consistent estimators such that*

$$\sqrt{T}\begin{bmatrix}\operatorname{vec}(\tilde{\Pi}_1 - \Pi_1) \\ \operatorname{vec}(\tilde{\Pi}_2 - \Pi_2)\end{bmatrix}$$

has asymptotic distribution $N(\mathbf{0}, \Theta)$. *Then the asymptotic distribution of* $\sqrt{T}(\tilde{\mathbf{y}}_{h.} - \mathbf{y}_{h.})'$, *where* $\tilde{\mathbf{y}}_{h.} - \mathbf{y}_{h.}$ *denotes the forecast error, is* $N(\mathbf{0}, \mathrm{T})$, *where*

$$\begin{aligned} \mathrm{T} &= \mathrm{T}_1 + \mathrm{T}_2, \\ \mathrm{T}_1 &= \operatorname{plim}(I \otimes W_h)R_h Q_h \Theta Q_h' R_h'(I \otimes W_h'), \\ \mathrm{T}_2 &= T \sum_{j=0}^{h-1} (\Pi_2^j)'\Omega\Pi_2^j, \end{aligned} \tag{24.5.4}$$

where W_h, R_h, Q_h *are defined in Schmidt (1974a) and* Ω *is the covariance matrix of the reduced form disturbance vector* $\mathbf{v}_{t.}$. (*T represents the sample size used to estimate* Π_1 *and* Π_2 *and has no relationship to* h.)

The asymptotic covariance matrix for the forecasts errors is then T/T. (*Note*: Do not confuse the covariance matrix T with sample size T.) The square roots of the diagonal elements of this matrix are the standard errors of the forecasts. Consistent estimates of these standard errors can in turn be obtained by replacing all unknown population parameters in T with corresponding consistent estimates.

The above Theorem 24.5.1 holds for any consistent estimates of Π_1 and Π_2. However, it is obvious, since T_1 consists of a quadratic form in Θ and T_2 is invariant to the estimation of Π_1 and Π_2, that the most efficient forecasts of $\mathbf{y}_{1.}, \mathbf{y}_{2.}, \ldots, \mathbf{y}_{h.}$ are obtained by utilizing full information derived reduced form estimates of Π_1 and Π_2.

The second case of *unknown* future values of the purely exogenous variables is probably the more realistic one in practice. Let us begin by writing the hth future value of the joint dependent variables as

$$\mathbf{y}_{h.} = \mathbf{w}_{h.} A_h + \boldsymbol{\varepsilon}_{h.}, \tag{24.5.5}$$

where

$$\mathbf{w}_{h.} = (\mathbf{x}_{1.}, \mathbf{x}_{2.}, \ldots, \mathbf{x}_{h.}, \mathbf{y}_{0.}), \tag{24.5.6}$$

$$A_h \equiv \operatorname{plim} \tilde{A}_h = \operatorname{plim} \begin{bmatrix} \tilde{\Pi}_1 \tilde{\Pi}_2^{h-1} \\ \vdots \\ \tilde{\Pi}_1 \\ \tilde{\Pi}_2^h \end{bmatrix} = \begin{bmatrix} \Pi_1 \Pi_2^{h-1} \\ \vdots \\ \Pi_1 \\ \Pi_2^h \end{bmatrix} \tag{24.5.7}$$

and

$$\boldsymbol{\varepsilon}_{h.} = \sum_{j=0}^{h-1} \mathbf{v}_{h-j,.} \Pi_0^j. \tag{24.5.8}$$

The dynamic simulation forecast with *known* $\mathbf{w}_{h.}$ is $\tilde{\mathbf{y}}_{h.} = \mathbf{w}_{h.} \tilde{A}_h$ and the asymptotic covariance matrix of the forecast error, $\tilde{\mathbf{y}}_{h.} - \mathbf{y}_{h.}$, is given by T/T of Theorem 24.5.1. Now assume that a consistent estimate of $\mathbf{w}_{h.}$,

$\tilde{\mathbf{w}}_{h.} = (\tilde{\mathbf{y}}_{0.}, \tilde{\mathbf{x}}_{1.}, \tilde{\mathbf{x}}_{2.}, \ldots, \tilde{\mathbf{x}}_{h.})$ is available, that $\mathbf{w}_{h.}$ is determined independently of Π_1 or Π_2, and that Σ denotes the asymptotic covariance matrix of $\tilde{\mathbf{w}}_{h.}$. That is,

$$\Sigma = \frac{1}{T} \operatorname{plim}\{T(\tilde{\mathbf{w}}_{h.} - \mathbf{w}_{h.})'(\tilde{\mathbf{w}}_{h.} - \mathbf{w}_{h.})\}. \tag{24.5.9}$$

The dynamic simulation forecast for the hth period ahead where the future exogenous variables have been estimates can be written

$$\tilde{\tilde{\mathbf{y}}}_{h.} = \tilde{\mathbf{w}}_{h.} \tilde{A}_h. \tag{24.5.10}$$

Schmidt then proceeds to show that

Theorem 24.5.2. *Let Π_1 and Π_2 be consistent estimators such that*

$$\sqrt{T} \begin{bmatrix} \operatorname{vec}(\tilde{\Pi}_1 - \Pi_1) \\ \operatorname{vec}(\tilde{\Pi}_2 - \Pi_2) \end{bmatrix}$$

has asymptotic distribution $N(\mathbf{0}, \Theta)$. Then the asymptotic distribution of $\sqrt{T}(\tilde{\tilde{\mathbf{y}}}_{h.} - \mathbf{y}_{h.})'$ is $N(\mathbf{0}, \mathrm{T}^*)$, where

$$\mathrm{T}^* = \mathrm{T} + TA_h'\Sigma A_h + D, \tag{24.5.11}$$

T is defined in (24.5.4), and the (r, s)th element of D is $D_{rs} = \operatorname{tr}(\Lambda_{rs}\Sigma)$, Λ_{rs} being the (r, s)th element of $\Lambda = R_h Q_h \Theta Q_h' R_h'$. The matrices R_h and Q_h are defined in Schmidt (1974a).

Notice the difference in the asymptotic variances of the forecast errors $\tilde{\mathbf{y}}_{h.} - \mathbf{y}_{h.}$ and $\tilde{\tilde{\mathbf{y}}}_{h.} - \mathbf{y}_{h.}$. The difference is the positive semidefinite matrix sum $A_h'\Sigma A_h + D/T = \mathrm{T}^*/T - \mathrm{T}/T$. Naturally, the precision of forecasts of $\mathbf{y}_{h.}$ are diminished by the need to forecast the future period exogenous variables. As in previous cases, a consistent estimate of the asymptotic variance of the forecast errors can be obtained by replacing all unknown population parameters in T^*/T by their consistent estimates. Also, it is obvious from the form of T^* that, apart from the need to estimate the future exogenous variables, the efficiency of forecasts is best served by the use of full information derived reduced form estimates of Π_1 and Π_2.

24.6 Optimal Control in Dynamic Simultaneous Equations Models

In this section we will only give a rudimentary discussion of optimal control in dynamic simultaneous equation models. For a more advanced and thorough coverage of this topic consult Chow (1975) and references therein.

Probably the most frequent use of optimal control methods has been in connection with the analysis of government policies within the context of simultaneous equation macroeconomic models; see Fair (1976, 1978) for example. Optimal control involves the optimal choice of *policy variables* such as the Federal Reserve Board's reserve ratio and the Federal Government's tax rates to obtain desired values of *target variables* such as real gross national product and inflation.

To illustrate the principles involved, assume that the model of interest is a simultaneous equation model, possibly a macroeconomic model,

$$Y\Gamma + X\Delta + E = 0, \tag{24.6.1}$$

where we have for convenience chosen not to distinguish the lagged endogenous variables from the purely exogenous variables in the set of predetermined variables, X. Write (24.6.1) in the implicit form

$$\phi_g(y_{t1}, y_{t2}, \ldots, y_{tG}, x_{t1}, \ldots, x_{tK}, \boldsymbol{\beta}_g) = e_{tg} \qquad (g = 1, 2, \ldots, G) \quad (t = 1, 2, \ldots, T) \tag{24.6.2}$$

where $\boldsymbol{\beta}_g$ denotes the structural parameter vector for the gth equation. Assume, further, that the following welfare (utility) function, h, is to be maximized:

$$W = h(y_{11}, \ldots, y_{1G}, \ldots, y_{T1}, \ldots, y_{TG}, x_{11}, \ldots, x_{1K}, \ldots, x_{T1}, \ldots, x_{TK}). \tag{24.6.3}$$

Finally, assume, without loss of generality, that $x_{t1}, t = 1, 2, \ldots, T$, is the only control (policy) variable. Given estimates of the parameter vectors $\boldsymbol{\beta}_g$, $g = 1, 2, \ldots, G$, and values of the predetermined variables at time t, x_{ti}, $i = 1, 2, \ldots, K$, the model (24.6.2) can be solved numerically for the endogenous variables at time t, y_{tg}, $g = 1, 2, \ldots, G$, after, say, all the disturbance terms, $e_{tg}, g = 1, 2, \ldots, G$, have been set equal to zero. Repeating this process for all time periods, a value of W in (24.6.3) can be computed. Given a different set of values of the control variable, the model can be resolved for all time periods and a new value of W calculated. Therefore, W can be considered as an implicit function of the T control values:

$$W = \Psi(x_{11}, x_{21}, \ldots, x_{T1}). \tag{24.6.4}$$

The control problem is then solved by choosing those values of x_{t1}, $t = 1, 2, \ldots, T$ which maximize W. Notice that in principle the time periods $t = 1, 2, \ldots, T$ need not coincide with the sample period used to estimate the parameters $\boldsymbol{\beta}_g$. When the control problem involves future periods, however, it should be noted that future values of the predetermined variables must be predicted and that constancy of the structural parameters $\boldsymbol{\beta}_g$ during future periods may be a questionable assumption. This last caveat is the usual warning given when extrapolating a model beyond the sample period used to estimate it.

In an interesting application of optimal control principles, Fair (1978) investigates the sensitivity of fiscal policy effects to various assumptions about the behavior of the Federal Reserve. The targets of the control problem involved a given level of real output and a zero rate of inflation for each quarter. Instead of maximizing a given welfare function, Fair chose to equivalently minimize a loss function. The loss function he chose was:

$$L = \sum_{t=1969\text{I}}^{1976\text{II}} \left[\left| \frac{Y_t - Y_t^*}{Y_t^*} \right|^2 + (\%PF_t)^2 \right], \qquad (24.6.5)$$

where Y_t^* is the target level of real output Y_t and $\%PF_t$ is the percentage change in the implicit price deflator at an annual rate. The econometric model used consists of 84 equations, 26 of which are stochastic. A detailed description of the model is contained in Fair (1976). The control variables of the Federal Reserve were (a) the reserve requirement ratio (b) the discount rate and (c) the amount of government securities outstanding while the control variable of the fiscal authority (government) was the real value of goods purchased by the government.

Fair then proceeded to use optimal control methods to determine to what extent the effectiveness of the fiscal authority is affected by various types of behavior by the Federal Reserve. The optimal accomodating policy by the Federal Reserve was determined by minimizing the loss function (24.6.5) for a given fiscal policy. For further details of this interesting application of optimal control one should consult Fair (1978).

In summary, the intent of optimal control theory is to choose those values of the policy (control) variables which most closely achieve target values of target variables as measured by a chosen utility (or equivalently loss) function. Detailed discussions of alternative methods of solving this problem are contained in Theil (1964, 1970), Chow (1972, 1975), and Fair (1976, 1978).

24.7 Summary and Guide to Further Readings

This chapter has discussed various facets of dynamic simultaneous equations models. The time paths of the endogenous variables as they relate to the time paths of the exogenous variables are described by the impact, interim, cumulative, and total multipliers. The impact multipliers provide the expected immediate change in an endogenous variable resulting from a one unit-one period change in an exogenous variable holding all other exogenous variables constant. The interim multipliers have a similar interpretation except, instead of the immediate expected change, they provide the change expected to take place τ-periods from now. The cumulative multipliers are the cumulative effects expected in an endogenous variable resulting from a τ-period change in an exogenous variable holding all other exogenous variables constant. The total multiplier effects represent expected changes arising from a unit change in an exogenous variable sustained forever.

The stability of a dynamic simultaneous equation model depends upon the dominant root of the reduced form coefficients matrix of the lagged endogenous variables. Of course this root is estimated and standard errors must be used to make probability statements concerning the likelihood of stability.

A methodology for primarily forecasting one period ahead was developed in Chapter 23. However, in dynamic simultaneous models, interest often centers on simulating (forecasting) the values of endogenous variables in consecutive future periods. These forecasts are dependent on previous forecasts of the endogenous variables and future values of the purely exogenous variables. Two distinct cases were discussed—when the future values of the exogenous variables are assumed *known* and when they are assumed *unknown* yet consistent estimates are available. Simulation with known values uses more knowledge than with unknown but consistently estimated values. As a result the asymptotic standard errors of the simulations in the latter case are larger than in the former case. As pointed out by Schmidt (1974a) these standard errors enable one to test the hypothesis that observed forecast errors are due solely to chance. Such information can be useful in checking model specification.

In the previous chapter it was shown that full information methods (three-stage least squares or full information maximum likelihood) provide the most efficient means of estimating the reduced form coefficients. As shown in this chapter the dynamic multipliers, dominant characteristic root, and simulation forecasts are functions of the reduced form coefficients. In addition their asymptotic variances are quadratic forms involving the asymptotic covariance matrix of the reduced form coefficients. It follows that full information methods likewise provide the most efficient means of estimating the dynamic multipliers, dominant root, and simulation forecasts.

We briefly discussed the method and purpose of optimal control in a dynamic simultaneous equations model. The purpose of optimal control is to determine the optimal time paths of policy variables given the time paths of other exogenous variables and the desired levels of target variables. This is accomplished by the maximization of a specified utility function which is an implicit function of the time paths of the policy variables.

The general optimal control problem is a nonlinear maximization problem. In certain special cases, however, solutions can be obtained in closed form. Theil (1964, 1970) and Chow (1972, 1975) have analyzed the optimal control problem in the case of quadratic loss functions and linear simultaneous equations systems. Theil's solution is called the certainty equivalence method while Chow's approach is called the linear feedback method. Norman (1974) has shown these two methods to be logically equivalent though numerical solutions may differ slightly due to numerical rounding differences.

24.8 Exercises

24.1. Consider the following cobweb model of supply and demand.

$$p_t = \beta_0 + \beta_1 q_t + \beta_2 I_t \qquad \text{(Demand)},$$
$$q_t = \alpha_0 + \alpha_1 p_{t-1} + \alpha_2 R_t \quad \text{(Supply)},$$

where $p \equiv$ price, $q \equiv$ quantity, $I \equiv$ income and $R \equiv$ rainfall. *A priori* we know that $\beta_1 < 0$, $\beta_2 > 0$, $\alpha_1 > 0$ and $\alpha_2 > 0$.

(a) Write this model in the form of Equation (24.2.1).
(b) Derive the reduced form (24.4.2).
(c) What condition must hold for the stability of the system?
(d) What are the signs of the impact multipliers?
(e) What are the signs of the 1 period delay multipliers?
(f) Can you generalize the results in (d) and (e) to determine the signs of the τ period delay multiplier, depending on whether τ is odd or even?
(g) Determine the total multiplier matrix.
(h) Graphically illustrate the workings of a cobweb market using standard supply and demand graphs.

24.2. Construct a 95% confidence interval for the dominant root of Π_2 using the three-stage least squares estimates of Klein's Model I.

24.3. Generate forecasts of the endogenous variables in Klein's Model I through 1953 using known values of the exogenous variables. Compute asymptotic standard errors of forecasts. Use the data for 1947–1953 given below.

	C	*P*	*W*	*I*	*K*	*X*	*W*	*T*	*G*
1947	82.8	27.9	60.7	6.4	204.1	97.9	8.7	9.2	8.7
1948	104.5	33.1	77.0	16.0	235.6	117.9	11.9	7.8	7.1
1949	106.9	31.9	76.5	8.48	242.4	114.9	13.2	6.6	5.7
1950	112.9	34.5	82.3	17.0	260.7	128.0	14.1	11.1	5.8
1951	114.3	32.6	88.5	16.5	273.6	134.3	17.0	13.2	12.8
1952	117.2	32.6	93.5	11.7	280.7	137.3	19.2	11.2	16.5
1953	121.6	32.8	99.4	11.6	290.9	143.8	19.5	11.5	18.4

24.9 References

Bianchi, C., Calzolari, G., and Corsi, P. (1981). Estimating asymptotic standard errors and inconsistencies of impact multipliers in nonlinear econometric models. *Journal of Econometrics*, **16**, 277–294.

Brissimis, S. and Gill, L. (1978). On the asymptotic distribution of impact and interim multipliers. *Econometrica*, **46**, 463–470.

Chow, G. C. (1972). Optimal control of linear econometric systems with finite time horizons. *International Economic Review*, **13**, 16–25.

Chow, G. C. (1975). *Analysis and Control of Dynamic Economic Systems*. New York: Wiley.
Fair, R. (1976). *A Model of Macroeconomic Activity*, vol. II. Cambridge, MA: Ballinger.
Fair, R. (1978). The sensitivity of fiscal policy effects to assumptions about the behavior of the federal reserve. *Econometrica*, **46**, 1165–1179.
Nissen, D. (1968). A note on the variance of a matrix. *Econometrica*, **36**, 603–704.
Norman, A. L. (1974). On the relationship between linear feedback control and first period certainty equivalence. *International Economic Review*, **15**, 209–215.
Nissen, D. (1968). A note on the variance of a matrix. *Econometrica*, **36**, 603–604.
Oberhofer, W. and Kmenta, J. (1973). Estimation of standard errors of the characteristic roots of a dynamic econometric model. *Econometrica*, **41**, 171–177.
Rao, C. R. (1973). *Linear Statistical Inference and Its Applications*, 2nd ed. New York: Wiley.
Schmidt, P. (1973). The asymptotic distribution of dynamic multipliers. *Econometrica*, **41**, 161–164.
Schmidt, P. (1974a). The asymptotic distribution of forecasts in the dynamic simulation of an econometric model. *Econometrica*, **42**, 303–310.
Schmidt, P. (1974b). The algebraic equivalence of the Oberhofer–Kmenta and Theil–Boot formulae for the asymptotic variance of a characteristic root of a dynamic econometric model. *Econometrica*, **42**, 591–592.
Schmidt, P. (1978). A note on dynamic simulation forecasts and stochastic forecast-period exogenous variables. *Econometrica*, **46**, 1227–1230.
Theil, H. (1964). *Optimal Decision Rules for Government and Industry*. Amsterdam: North-Holland.
Theil, H. (1970). *Economic Forecasts and Policy*, 2nd ed. Amsterdam: North-Holland.
Theil, H. and Boot, J. (1962). The final form of econometric equation systems. *Review of the International Statical Institute*, **30**, 136–152.

PART V

FRONTIERS

Chapter 25 constitutes Part V, the final part of this book. This part concludes our discussion of simultaneous equations models and contains advanced topics in the field. Each section of the chapter is dedicated to a distinct subject. These subjects are: a simultaneous equations tobit model; a simultaneous equations generalized probit model; disequilibrium econometric models; vector autoregressive error processes in simultaneous equations models; rational expectations in econometric models; and updating econometric models.

CHAPTER 25

Special Topics in Simultaneous Equations

25.1 Introduction

In this chapter we review selected special topics related to simultaneous equations. In Sections 25.2 and 25.3 we consider extensions of the tobit and probit models (Chapter 16) into the simultaneous equations framework. In Section 25.4 we consider systems of equations that describe disequilibrium situations, Section 25.5 contains a generalization of the usual error assumptions associated with simultaneous equations estimation, vector autoregressive disturbances. The important topic of rational expectations is reviewed in Section 25.6. Finally, procedures for updating parameter estimates using sample or nonsample information are considered in Section 25.7 in the context of a single equation model, and extensions to the simultaneous equations context briefly described.

25.2 A Simultaneous Equations Tobit Model

In this section we consider estimation of a simultaneous equations model in which some or all the endogenous variables are censored (see Chapter 16). Amemiya (1974) considered the situation where all the endogenous variables were censored and suggested an indirect least squares type of estimator. Nelson and Olson (1978) developed a two-step estimation procedure for the case where some of the endogenous variables were a continuous and some were censored. Subsequently, Amemiya (1979) reviewed this two-step procedure and developed a two-step alternative to the Nelson–Olson estimator that is asymptotically more efficient. In this section Amemiya's (1979) technique is considered.

Following Amemiya we define the simultaneous equations model

$$\mathbf{y}_1 = \mathbf{y}_2^*\gamma_1 + X_1\boldsymbol{\delta}_1 + \mathbf{e}_1 = Z_1\boldsymbol{\beta}_1 + \mathbf{e}_1, \tag{25.2.1}$$

$$\mathbf{y}_2^* = \mathbf{y}_1\gamma_2 + X_2\boldsymbol{\delta}_2 + \mathbf{e}_2 = Z_2\boldsymbol{\beta}_2 + \mathbf{e}_2, \tag{25.2.2}$$

where $\mathbf{y}_1$ is a $T \times 1$ vector of observable random variables, $\mathbf{y}_2^*$ is a $T \times 1$ vector of unobservable random variables y_{t2}^* such that

$$y_{t2} = \begin{cases} y_{t2}^* & \text{if } y_{t2}^* > 0, \\ 0 & \text{otherwise} \quad t = 1, \ldots, T, \end{cases} \tag{25.2.3}$$

X_1 and X_2 are $T \times K_1$ and $T \times K_2$ matrices of observations on exogenous variables with conformable parameter vectors $\boldsymbol{\delta}_1$ and $\boldsymbol{\delta}_2$, respectively. The error vectors are such that (e_{t1}, e_{t2}) are independent and identically distributed bivariate normal random disturbances.

The reduced form equations can be written.

$$\mathbf{y}_1 = X\boldsymbol{\pi}_1 + \mathbf{v}_1, \tag{25.2.4}$$

$$\mathbf{y}_2^* = X\boldsymbol{\pi}_2 + \mathbf{v}_2, \tag{25.2.5}$$

where X is a $T \times K$ matrix containing the distinct columns of X_1 and X_2, and $\boldsymbol{\pi}_1$, $\boldsymbol{\pi}_2$, $\mathbf{v}_1$, and $\mathbf{v}_2$ are vectors of reduced form parameters and disturbances, respectively. The variances and contemporaneous covariance of (v_{t1}, v_{t2}) are σ_1^2, σ_2^2, and σ_{12}.

The estimators proposed by Nelson and Olson (1978) for $\boldsymbol{\beta}_1$ and $\boldsymbol{\beta}_2$ require two steps. The first step is to obtain estimates of the reduced form parameters. The vector $\boldsymbol{\pi}_1$ is estimated by ordinary least squares and is

$$\hat{\boldsymbol{\pi}}_1 = (X'X)^{-1}X'\mathbf{y}_1 = \boldsymbol{\pi}_1 + (X'X)^{-1}X'\mathbf{v}_1. \tag{25.2.6}$$

The vector $\boldsymbol{\pi}_2$ must be estimated from the Tobit model defined by (25.2.5) and (25.2.3). From Chapter 16 the likelihood function of the Tobit model is

$$L(\boldsymbol{\pi}_2, \sigma_2^2) = \prod_{t \in \psi} [1 - F(\boldsymbol{\pi}_2'\mathbf{x}_t, \sigma_2^2)] \prod_{t \in \bar{\psi}} \frac{1}{\sqrt{2\pi\sigma_2^2}} \exp\left\{-\frac{(y_{t2} - \boldsymbol{\pi}_2'\mathbf{x}_t)^2}{2\sigma_2^2}\right\}, \tag{25.2.7}$$

where ψ is the set of observations where y_{t2} is zero and $\bar{\psi}$ the set where y_{t2} is observed, and

$$F(\boldsymbol{\pi}_2'\mathbf{x}_t, \sigma_2^2) = F_t = \int_{-\infty}^{\boldsymbol{\pi}_2'\mathbf{x}_t} \frac{1}{\sqrt{2\pi\sigma_2^2}} \exp\left\{-\frac{s^2}{2\sigma_2^2}\right\} ds.$$

Maximizing the likelihood function (25.2.7) with respect to $\boldsymbol{\pi}_2$ and σ_2^2 yields $\hat{\boldsymbol{\pi}}_2$.

To estimate $\boldsymbol{\beta}_1$, the second step is as follows. Substitute (25.2.5) into (25.2.1) to obtain

$$\begin{aligned}
\mathbf{y}_1 &= (X\boldsymbol{\pi}_2 + \mathbf{v}_2)\gamma_1 + X_1\boldsymbol{\delta}_1 + \mathbf{e}_1 \\
&= X\boldsymbol{\pi}_2\gamma_1 + X_1\boldsymbol{\delta}_1 + \mathbf{v}_2\gamma_1 + \mathbf{e}_1 \\
&= X\hat{\boldsymbol{\pi}}_2\gamma_1 + X_1\boldsymbol{\delta}_1 + \mathbf{v}_1 - X(\hat{\boldsymbol{\pi}}_2 - \boldsymbol{\pi}_2)\gamma_1 \\
&= X\hat{H}\boldsymbol{\beta}_1 + \mathbf{w}_1, \qquad (25.2.8)
\end{aligned}$$

where the next to least equality was obtained using

$$v_{1t} = \gamma_1 v_{2T} + e_{1t} \qquad (25.2.9)$$

(see Exercise 25.2.1), $\hat{H} = (\hat{\boldsymbol{\pi}}_2, J_1)$, and J_1 is a matrix of ones and zeros so that $XJ_1 = X_1$.

The Nelson–Olson estimator of $\boldsymbol{\beta}_1$ is

$$\hat{\boldsymbol{\beta}}_1 = (\hat{H}'X'X\hat{H})^{-1}\hat{H}'X'\mathbf{y}_1, \qquad (25.2.10)$$

which is the result of applying ordinary least squares to (25.2.8). This estimator is consistent and has asymptotic covariance matrix

$$V(\hat{\boldsymbol{\beta}}_1) = c(H'X'XH)^{-1} + \gamma_1^2(H'X'XH)^{-1}H'X'XV_0X'XH(H'X'XH)^{-1},$$

where $c = \sigma_1^2 - 2\gamma_1^2\sigma_{12}$, $H = (\boldsymbol{\pi}_2, J_1)$ and V_0 is the asymptotic covariance matrix of the Tobit estimator $\hat{\boldsymbol{\pi}}_2$, the expression for which is given in Chapter 16. (See Exercise 25.2.2.)

To estimate $\boldsymbol{\beta}_2$, substitute (25.2.4) into (25.2.2) to obtain

$$\begin{aligned}
\mathbf{y}_2^* &= (X\boldsymbol{\pi}_1 + \mathbf{v}_1)\gamma_2 + X_2\boldsymbol{\delta}_2 + \mathbf{e}_2 \\
&= X\boldsymbol{\pi}_1\gamma_2 + X_2\boldsymbol{\delta}_2 + \mathbf{v}_1\gamma_2 + \mathbf{e}_2 \\
&= XG\boldsymbol{\beta}_2 + \mathbf{v}_2, \qquad (25.2.11)
\end{aligned}$$

where $G = [\boldsymbol{\pi}_1, J_2]$ and J_2 is a matrix of ones and zeros such that $XJ_2 = X_2$ and we have used the equality $v_{t2} = \gamma_2 v_{t1} + e_{t2}$. (See Exercise 25.2.1.) Also note that

$$\boldsymbol{\pi}_2 = G\boldsymbol{\beta}_2. \qquad (25.2.12)$$

This follows from $\Pi(-\Gamma) = \Delta$ and

$$(\boldsymbol{\pi}_1, \boldsymbol{\pi}_2)\begin{bmatrix} -\gamma_2 \\ 1 \end{bmatrix} = \begin{bmatrix} \boldsymbol{\delta}_2 \\ \mathbf{0}_{(K_1 \times 1)} \end{bmatrix}$$

or

$$-\boldsymbol{\pi}_1\gamma_2 + \boldsymbol{\pi}_2 = \begin{bmatrix} \boldsymbol{\delta}_2 \\ \mathbf{0} \end{bmatrix}.$$

So $\boldsymbol{\pi}_2 = \boldsymbol{\pi}_1\gamma_2 + J_2\boldsymbol{\delta}_2 = G\boldsymbol{\beta}_2$.

Consequently (25.2.12) can be substituted into the likelihood function (25.2.7) so that it becomes a function of $\boldsymbol{\pi}_1$, $\boldsymbol{\beta}_2$, and σ_2^2. Therefore, if $\boldsymbol{\pi}_1$ is replaced by $\hat{\boldsymbol{\pi}}_1$ in G, so $\hat{G} = (\hat{\boldsymbol{\pi}}_1, J_2)$, then the Nelson–Olson estimator is obtained by applying Tobit to

$$\mathbf{y}_2^* = X\hat{G}\boldsymbol{\beta}_2 + \mathbf{v}_2.$$

The asymptotic covariance matrix of $\boldsymbol{\beta}_2$ is

$$V(\hat{\boldsymbol{\beta}}_2) = (G'V_0^{-1}G)^{-1} + d(G'V_0^{-1}G)^{-1}G'V_0^{-1}(X'X)^{-1}V_0^{-1}G(G'V_0^{-1}G)^{-1},$$

where $d = \gamma_2^2\sigma_1^2 - 2\gamma_2\sigma_{12}$.

Amemiya (1979) proposes two alternative estimators for $\boldsymbol{\beta}_1$ and $\boldsymbol{\beta}_2$, one of which is more efficient than the Nelson–Olson two-step estimator. The principle employed by Amemiya to derive these estimators also provides the foundation for an estimation technique presented in the next section for the simultaneous equation generalized probit model. It can be applied to any overidentified simultaneous equations system and produces the two-stage least squares estimator when applied to the usual simultaneous equations model.

Recall that our structural model is written

$$Y\Gamma + X\Delta + E = 0$$

with the ith equation given by

$$Y\Gamma_{.i} + X\Delta_{.i} + \mathbf{e}_{.i} = \mathbf{0}.$$

Also we can partition

$$Y = (\mathbf{y}_i, Y_i, Y_i^*), \qquad \Gamma_{.i} = \begin{bmatrix} -1 \\ \boldsymbol{\gamma}_i \\ \mathbf{0} \end{bmatrix}, \qquad X = (X_i, X_i^*), \qquad \Delta_{.i} = \begin{bmatrix} \boldsymbol{\delta}_i \\ \mathbf{0} \end{bmatrix},$$

so that the ith structural equation can be written

$$\mathbf{y}_i = Y_i\boldsymbol{\gamma}_i + X_i\boldsymbol{\delta}_i + \mathbf{e}_{.i}.$$

The reduced form of the structural system is

$$Y = X\Pi + V,$$

where $\Pi = -\Delta\Gamma^{-1}$ or $\Pi(-\Gamma) = \Delta$. Partition Π conformably to $\Gamma_{.i}$ and we can write

$$(\boldsymbol{\pi}_i, \Pi_i, \Pi_i^*)\begin{bmatrix} 1 \\ -\boldsymbol{\gamma}_i \\ \mathbf{0} \end{bmatrix} = \Delta_{.i} = \begin{bmatrix} \boldsymbol{\delta}_i \\ \mathbf{0} \end{bmatrix} = \begin{bmatrix} I \\ 0 \end{bmatrix}\boldsymbol{\delta}_i = J_i\boldsymbol{\delta}_i,$$

where Π_i contains the columns of Π corresponding to $\boldsymbol{\gamma}_i$.

Therefore $\boldsymbol{\pi}_i - \Pi_i\boldsymbol{\gamma}_i = J_i\boldsymbol{\delta}_i$, or

$$\boldsymbol{\pi}_i = \Pi_i\boldsymbol{\gamma}_i + J_i\boldsymbol{\delta}_i. \tag{25.2.13}$$

Then, adding and subtracting identical terms to (25.2.13), we can obtain

$$\begin{aligned}\hat{\boldsymbol{\pi}}_i &= \hat{\boldsymbol{\pi}}_i + \hat{\Pi}_i \boldsymbol{\gamma}_i - \hat{\Pi}_i \boldsymbol{\gamma}_i - \boldsymbol{\pi}_i + \Pi_i \boldsymbol{\gamma}_i + J_i \boldsymbol{\delta}_i \\ &= \hat{\Pi}_i \boldsymbol{\gamma}_i + J_i \boldsymbol{\delta}_i + (\hat{\boldsymbol{\pi}}_i - \boldsymbol{\pi}_i) - (\hat{\Pi}_i - \Pi_i)\boldsymbol{\gamma}_i \\ &= (\hat{\Pi}_i, J_i)\begin{bmatrix} \boldsymbol{\gamma}_i \\ \boldsymbol{\delta}_i \end{bmatrix} + \boldsymbol{\eta}_i \\ &= \hat{Z}_i \boldsymbol{\beta}_i + \boldsymbol{\eta}_i. \end{aligned} \tag{25.2.14}$$

Amemiya proposes ordinary least squares and generalized least squares estimators for $\boldsymbol{\beta}_i$ in (25.2.14), and it is to this analysis we now turn.

Assume the model of Equations (25.2.1) and (25.2.2) is relevant. To estimate the vector $\boldsymbol{\beta}_1$ we consider the equation

$$\begin{aligned}\hat{\boldsymbol{\pi}}_1 &= \hat{\boldsymbol{\pi}}_2 \gamma_1 + J_1 \boldsymbol{\delta}_1 + (\hat{\boldsymbol{\pi}}_1 - \boldsymbol{\pi}_1) - (\hat{\boldsymbol{\pi}}_2 - \boldsymbol{\pi}_2)\gamma_1 \\ &= \hat{Z}_1 \boldsymbol{\beta}_1 + \boldsymbol{\eta}_1. \end{aligned} \tag{25.2.15}$$

The properties of the ordinary least squares and generalized least squares estimator of $\boldsymbol{\beta}_1$ in (25.2.15) depend on the asymptotic variance of $\boldsymbol{\eta}_1 = (\hat{\boldsymbol{\pi}}_1 - \boldsymbol{\pi}_1) - (\hat{\boldsymbol{\pi}}_2 - \boldsymbol{\pi}_2)\gamma_1$. Now $\hat{\boldsymbol{\pi}}_1 - \boldsymbol{\pi}_1 = (X'X)^{-1}X'\mathbf{v}_1$, and the properties of this expression we know well. The term $(\hat{\boldsymbol{\pi}}_2 - \boldsymbol{\pi}_2)$ presents more of a problem. Remember that $\hat{\boldsymbol{\pi}}_2$ is obtained by maximizing the likelihood function (25.2.7) with respect to $\boldsymbol{\pi}_2$ and σ_2^2. Thus, if $\boldsymbol{\theta}_1' = (\boldsymbol{\pi}_2', \sigma_2^2)$, $\hat{\boldsymbol{\pi}}_2 - \boldsymbol{\pi}_2$ has the same asymptotic distribution as

$$-(I, \mathbf{0})\left[E\,\frac{\partial^2 \ln L}{\partial \boldsymbol{\theta}_1\, \partial \boldsymbol{\theta}_1'}\right]^{-1} \frac{\partial \ln L}{\partial \boldsymbol{\theta}_1},$$

where I is a Kth order identity matrix and $\mathbf{0}$ a $K \times 1$ null vector. The asymptotic covariance matrix of $\hat{\boldsymbol{\pi}}_2$ is

$$V(\hat{\boldsymbol{\pi}}_2) = -(I, \mathbf{0})\left[E\,\frac{\partial^2 \ln L}{\partial \boldsymbol{\theta}_1\, \partial \boldsymbol{\theta}_1'}\right]^{-1}\begin{bmatrix} I \\ \mathbf{0}' \end{bmatrix} = V_0. \tag{25.2.16}$$

Furthermore, using the results in Amemiya (1973),

$$E\left[\frac{\partial^2 \ln L}{\partial \boldsymbol{\theta}_1\, \partial \boldsymbol{\theta}_1'}\right] = \mathbf{X}'A\mathbf{X}, \tag{25.2.17}$$

where $\mathbf{X} = \begin{bmatrix} X & \mathbf{0} \\ 0 & \mathbf{l} \end{bmatrix}$, $\mathbf{l}$ being a $T \times 1$ vector of ones and 0 a $T \times K$ null matrix. The matrix A is

$$A = \begin{bmatrix} A_{11} & A_{12} \\ A_{12} & A_{22} \end{bmatrix}$$

and each A_{ij} is a T-dimensional diagonal matrix whose tth element $a_{ij}(t)$ is

$$a_{11}(t) = \frac{1}{\sigma_2^2}\left[\boldsymbol{\pi}_2'\mathbf{x}_t f_t - \frac{\sigma_2^2 f_t^2}{1 - F_t} - F_t\right],$$

$$a_{12}(t) = \frac{-1}{2\sigma_2^4}\left[(\boldsymbol{\pi}_2'\mathbf{x}_t)^2 f_t + \sigma_2^2 f_t - \frac{\sigma_2^2 \boldsymbol{\pi}_2'\mathbf{x}_t f_t^2}{(1 - F_t)}\right],$$

$$a_{22}(t) = \frac{1}{4\sigma_2^4}\left[\frac{(\boldsymbol{\pi}_2'\mathbf{x}_t)^4 f_t}{\sigma_2^2} + \boldsymbol{\pi}_2'\mathbf{x}_t f_t - \frac{(\boldsymbol{\pi}_2'\mathbf{x}_t f_t)^2}{1 - F_t} - 2F_t\right],$$

where F_t is the cumulative distribution function of a $N(0, \sigma^2)$ random variable evaluated at $\boldsymbol{\pi}_2'\mathbf{x}_t$ and

$$f_t = \frac{1}{\sqrt{2\pi\sigma_2^2}} \exp\left\{-\frac{(\boldsymbol{\pi}_2'\mathbf{x}_t)^2}{2\sigma_2^2}\right\}.$$

Furthermore, using the moments of the truncated normal distribution, and the fact that v_{t1} can be expressed as a function of v_{t2} as

$$v_{t1} = \frac{\sigma_{12}}{\sigma_2^2} v_{t2} + u_t$$

(see Exercise 25.2.1), Amemiya shows that

$$E\left[\frac{\partial \ln L}{\partial \boldsymbol{\theta}_1} \mathbf{v}_1'\right] = -\sigma_{12}\mathbf{X}'A\begin{bmatrix} I \\ 0 \end{bmatrix}, \tag{25.2.18}$$

where here 0 is a $T \times T$ null matrix. Using these results we can obtain the covariance matrix of $\boldsymbol{\eta}_1$ in (25.2.15)

$$\begin{aligned}
V(\boldsymbol{\eta}_1) &= \sigma_1^2(X'X)^{-1} + \gamma_1^2 V_0 + \gamma_1(X'X)^{-1}X'E\left[\mathbf{v}_1 \frac{\partial \ln L}{\partial \boldsymbol{\theta}_1'}\right] E\left[\frac{\partial^2 \ln L}{\partial \boldsymbol{\theta}_1\, \partial \boldsymbol{\theta}_1'}\right]^{-1} \begin{bmatrix} I \\ \mathbf{0}' \end{bmatrix} \\
&\quad + \gamma_1(I, \mathbf{0})E\left[\frac{\partial^2 \ln L}{\partial \boldsymbol{\theta}_1\, \partial \boldsymbol{\theta}_1'}\right]^{-1} E\left[\frac{\partial \ln L}{\partial \boldsymbol{\theta}_1} \mathbf{v}_1'\right] X(X'X)^{-1} \\
&= \sigma_1^2(X'X)^{-1} + \gamma_1^2 V_0 - \gamma_1\sigma_{12}(X'X)^{-1}X'[I, 0]A\mathbf{X}(\mathbf{X}'A\mathbf{X})^{-1}\begin{bmatrix} I \\ \mathbf{0}' \end{bmatrix} \\
&\quad - \gamma_1\sigma_{12}(I, \mathbf{0})(\mathbf{X}'A\mathbf{X})^{-1}\mathbf{X}'A\begin{bmatrix} I \\ 0 \end{bmatrix} X(X'X)^{-1} \\
&= c(X'X)^{-1} + \gamma_1^2 V_0 = V_1,
\end{aligned} \tag{25.2.19}$$

where $c = \sigma_1^2 - 2\gamma_1\sigma_{12}$ and the last equality in (25.2.19) was obtained using

$$\begin{bmatrix} I \\ 0 \end{bmatrix} X = \mathbf{X}\begin{bmatrix} I \\ \mathbf{0}' \end{bmatrix}.$$

Finally, then, the ordinary least squares estimator of $\boldsymbol{\beta}_1$ in (25.2.15) is

$$\hat{\boldsymbol{\beta}}_1^{(L)} = (\hat{Z}_1'\hat{Z}_1)^{-1}\hat{Z}_1'\hat{\boldsymbol{\pi}}_1$$

and the asymptotic covariance matrix of $\hat{\boldsymbol{\beta}}_1^{(L)}$ is

$$V(\hat{\boldsymbol{\beta}}_1^{(L)}) = (Z_1'Z_1)^{-1}Z_1'V_1Z_1(Z_1'Z_1)^{-1}.$$

The feasible generalized least squares estimator for $\boldsymbol{\beta}_1$ is

$$\hat{\boldsymbol{\beta}}_1^{(G)} = (\hat{Z}_1'\hat{V}_1^{-1}\hat{Z}_1)^{-1}\hat{Z}_1'\hat{V}_1^{-1}\hat{\boldsymbol{\pi}}_1$$

which has asymptotic covariance matrix

$$V(\hat{\boldsymbol{\beta}}_1^{(G)}) = (Z_1'V_1^{-1}Z_1)^{-1}$$

and is asymptotically more efficient than $\hat{\boldsymbol{\beta}}_1^{(L)}$ or the Nelson–Olson estimator.

To estimate the parameter vector $\boldsymbol{\beta}_2$ consider the equation

$$\begin{aligned}\hat{\boldsymbol{\pi}}_2 &= \hat{\boldsymbol{\pi}}_1\gamma_2 + J_2\boldsymbol{\delta}_2 + (\hat{\boldsymbol{\pi}}_2 - \boldsymbol{\pi}_2) - (\hat{\boldsymbol{\pi}}_1 - \boldsymbol{\pi}_1)\gamma_2 \\ &= \hat{Z}_2\boldsymbol{\beta}_2 + \boldsymbol{\eta}_2. \qquad (25.2.20)\end{aligned}$$

Again the parameter vector $\boldsymbol{\beta}_2$ can be estimated by ordinary least squares or generalized least squares. The error vector $\boldsymbol{\eta}_2$ is

$$\boldsymbol{\eta}_2 = (\hat{\boldsymbol{\pi}}_2 - \boldsymbol{\pi}_2) - (\hat{\boldsymbol{\pi}}_1 - \boldsymbol{\pi}_2)\gamma_1 = (\hat{\boldsymbol{\pi}}_2 - \boldsymbol{\pi}_2) - ((X'X)^{-1}X'\mathbf{v}_1)\gamma_1,$$

and using arguments similar to those above the covariance matrix of $\boldsymbol{\eta}_2$ is

$$V(\boldsymbol{\eta}_2) = V_2 = V_0 + d(X'X)^{-1},$$

where $d = \gamma_2^2\sigma_1^2 - 2\sigma_{12}\gamma_2$. Thus the ordinary least squares estimator of $\boldsymbol{\beta}_2$ is

$$\hat{\boldsymbol{\beta}}_2^{(L)} = (\hat{Z}_2'\hat{Z}_2)^{-1}\hat{Z}_2'\hat{\boldsymbol{\pi}}_2$$

and has asymptotic covariance matrix

$$V(\hat{\boldsymbol{\beta}}_{(2)}^{L}) = (Z_2'Z_2)^{-1}Z_2'V_2Z_2(Z_2'Z_2)^{-1}.$$

The generalized least squares estimator is

$$\hat{\boldsymbol{\beta}}_2^{(G)} = (\hat{Z}_2'\hat{V}_2^{-1}\hat{Z}_2)^{-1}\hat{Z}_2'\hat{V}_2^{-1}\hat{\boldsymbol{\pi}}_2$$

and has asymptotic covariance matrix

$$V(\hat{\boldsymbol{\beta}}_2^{G}) = (Z_2'V_2^{-1}Z_2)^{-1}.$$

Finally, the computations leading to the generalized least squares estimates must be done in several steps. Estimates of $\boldsymbol{\pi}_1, \boldsymbol{\pi}_2, \sigma_1^2$ and σ_2^2 come naturally from first stage results. Since V_1 and V_2 also depend on γ_1, γ_2, and σ_{12} these too must be estimated before the generalized least squares estimates of $\boldsymbol{\beta}_1$ and $\boldsymbol{\beta}_2$ can be obtained. The parameters γ_1 and γ_2 can be obtained from the ordinary least squares or Nelson–Olson estimator or by indirect least squares. The covariance σ_{12} is consistently estimated by

$$\hat{\sigma}_{12} = \sum_{t=1}^{T}\frac{y_{t2}\hat{v}_{t1}}{T\hat{F}_t},$$

where $\hat{v}_{t1}$ is the ordinary least squares residual from (25.2.4) and $\hat{F}_t$ is F_t with $(\hat{\boldsymbol{\pi}}_2, \hat{\sigma}_2^2)$ replacing $(\boldsymbol{\pi}_2, \sigma_2^2)$.

25.2.1 Exercises

25.2.1. Given the reduced form disturbances $V = -E\Gamma^{-1}$, where $\Gamma = \begin{bmatrix} -1 & \gamma_2 \\ \gamma_1 & -1 \end{bmatrix}$, show that

(a) $v_{t1} = \gamma_1 v_{t2} + e_{t1}$ and $v_{t2} = \gamma_2 v_{t1} + e_{t2}$.

(b) Use this result to show that

$$v_{t1} = \frac{\sigma_{12}}{\sigma_2^2} v_{t2} + u_t,$$

where $\sigma_{12} = E(v_{t1}v_{t2})$, $\sigma_2^2 = E(v_{t2}^2)$ and u_t is normal and independent of v_{t2}.

25.2.2. Verify Equation (16.6.11).

25.2.2 References

Amemiya, T. (1973). Regression analysis when the dependent variable is truncated normal. *Econometrica*, **41**, 997–1016.

Amemiya, T. (1974). Multivariate regression and simultaneous equation models when the dependent variables are truncated normal. *Econometrica*, **42**, 999–1012.

Amemiya, T. (1979). The estimation of a simultaneous equation tobit model. *International Economic Review*, **20**, 169–182.

Nelson, F. and Olson, L. (1978). Specification and estimation of a simultaneous equation model with limited dependent variables. *International Economic Review*, **19**, 695–709.

25.3 A Simultaneous Equations Generalized Probit Model

Heckman (1978) considers a simultaneous equation model in which a subset of the endogenous variables are dummy variables. In his model some of the dummy variables may appear on the right-hand side of the equation and thus serve as endogenous shift variables. Amemiya (1978) examined the two-step estimators proposed by Heckman and derived their asymptotic covariance matrix. Amemiya also proposed ordinary least squares and generalized least squares estimators for the parameters based on the principle introduced in the previous section. We will consider both the Heckman and Amemiya estimators for the two-equation case where the shift variable is not present on the right-hand side of the structural equations. The reader is referred to the original papers for a discussion of these models.

The two equation simultaneous model is

$$\mathbf{y}_1 = \mathbf{y}_2^*\gamma_1 + X_1\boldsymbol{\delta}_1 + \mathbf{e}_1 = Z_1\boldsymbol{\beta}_1 + \mathbf{e}_1, \tag{25.3.1}$$

$$\mathbf{y}_2^* = \mathbf{y}_1\gamma_2 + X_2\boldsymbol{\delta}_2 + \mathbf{e}_2 = Z_2\boldsymbol{\beta}_2 + \mathbf{e}_2, \tag{25.3.2}$$

which is, of course, identical to the model described in (25.2.1) and (25.2.2). Here, however, y_{2t} is an observable scalar random variable such that

$$y_{t2} = \begin{cases} 1 & \text{if } y_{t2}^* > 0, \\ 0 & \text{otherwise}, \ t = 1, \ldots, T, \end{cases} \tag{25.3.3}$$

which replaces (25.2.3). As before the reduced form is written

$$\mathbf{y}_1 = X\boldsymbol{\pi}_1 + \mathbf{v}_1, \tag{25.3.4}$$

$$\mathbf{y}_2^* = X\boldsymbol{\pi}_2 + \mathbf{v}_2. \tag{25.3.5}$$

In addition to the assumptions associated with (25.2.4) and (22.2.5), we assume the normalization $\sigma_2^2 = 1$. This is required since $\mathbf{y}_2^*$ is binary and $\boldsymbol{\pi}_2$ can be only estimated up to a scalar multiple.

Heckman's two-step estimation process begins by obtaining a consistent estimator $\hat{\boldsymbol{\pi}}_2$ of $\boldsymbol{\pi}_2$. This is the usual probit estimator obtained from (25.3.5) and (25.3.3). Then to estimate $\boldsymbol{\beta}_1$, insert (25.3.5) into (25.3.1) to obtain

$$\mathbf{y}_1 = X\hat{H}\boldsymbol{\beta}_1 + \mathbf{w}_1 \tag{25.3.6}$$

in exactly the same way that (25.2.8) was obtained. Recall that $\hat{H} = (\hat{\boldsymbol{\pi}}_2, J_1)$ where $XJ_1 = X_1$ and $\mathbf{w}_1 = \mathbf{v}_1 - \gamma_1 X(\hat{\boldsymbol{\pi}}_2 - \boldsymbol{\pi}_2)$. The Heckman estimator of $\boldsymbol{\beta}_1$ is obtained by applying ordinary least squares to (25.3.6) to obtain

$$\hat{\boldsymbol{\beta}}_1 = (\hat{H}'X'X\hat{H})^{-1}\hat{H}'X'\mathbf{y}_1. \tag{25.3.7}$$

This estimator is consistent and has asymptotic covariance matrix which is that of $(\hat{H}'X'X\hat{H})^{-1}\hat{H}'X'\mathbf{w}_1$. Since $X'\mathbf{w}_1$ is composed of two parts, we must be concerned with the variance structures of each and their covariances. First, the asymptotic covariance matrix of $\mathbf{v}_1$ is $\sigma_1^2 I$ and that of $X'\mathbf{v}_1$ is $\sigma_1^2 X'X$. The estimator $\hat{\boldsymbol{\pi}}_2$ is obtained by maximizing the log likelihood function

$$\ln L = \sum_t [y_{t2} \ln F_t + (1 - y_{t2}) \ln(1 - F_t)],$$

where F_t is the cumulative distribution function of a standard normal random variable evaluated at $\mathbf{x}_t'\boldsymbol{\pi}_2$. The expressions for the first- and second-order partial derivatives are given in (16.4.12) and (16.4.13). Recall that $E[\partial \ln L/\partial \boldsymbol{\pi}_2] = \mathbf{0}$, and it is not difficult to show that the information matrix is

$$-E\left[\frac{\partial^2 \ln L}{\partial \boldsymbol{\pi}_2 \, \partial \boldsymbol{\pi}_2'}\right] = \sum_t \frac{f_t^2}{F_t(1 - F_t)} \mathbf{x}_t \mathbf{x}_t', \tag{25.3.8}$$

where f_t is the value of the standard normal probability density function evaluated at $\boldsymbol{\pi}_2'\mathbf{x}_t$. Therefore the asymptotic covariance matrix of $\hat{\boldsymbol{\pi}}_2$ is $(X'AX)^{-1}$ where A is a diagonal matrix with tth element

$$a_{tt} = \frac{f_t^2}{F_t(1 - F_t)}.$$

The asymptotic variance of $\gamma_1 X'X(\hat{\boldsymbol{\pi}}_2 - \boldsymbol{\pi}_2)$ is then $\gamma_1^2 X'X(X'AX)^{-1}X'X$. Finally we need the asymptotic covariance between $X'\mathbf{v}_1$ and $X'X(\hat{\boldsymbol{\pi}}_2 - \boldsymbol{\pi}_2)$. The asymptotic distribution of $\hat{\boldsymbol{\pi}}_2 - \boldsymbol{\pi}_2$ is the same as that of

$$\left[-E\frac{\partial^2 \ln L}{\partial \boldsymbol{\pi}_2\, \partial \boldsymbol{\pi}_2'}\right] \cdot \frac{\partial \ln L}{\partial \boldsymbol{\pi}_2},$$

where

$$\frac{\partial \ln L}{\partial \boldsymbol{\pi}_2} = \sum_t \frac{(y_{t2} - F_t)f_t}{F_t(1 - F_t)} \cdot \mathbf{x}_t.$$

Furthermore, using $v_{t1} = \sigma_{12}v_{t2} + u_t$ (see Exercise 25.2.1 and recall that $\sigma_2^2 = 1$ here) and the fact that $E[y_{t2}v_{t2}] = f_t$ (see Exercise 25.3.1) the asymptotic expectation of $(\hat{\boldsymbol{\pi}}_2 - \boldsymbol{\pi}_2)\mathbf{v}_1'X$ is $\sigma_{12}I$ and thus the relevant covariance is $-\gamma_1\sigma_{12}X'X$. Combining these results we obtain

$$\begin{aligned} V(X'\mathbf{w}_1) &= \sigma_1^2 X'X + \gamma_1^2 X'X(X'AX)^{-1}X'X - 2\gamma_1\sigma_{12}X'X \\ &= cX'X + \gamma_1^2 X'X(X'AX)^{-1}X'X, \end{aligned}$$

where $c = \sigma_1^2 - 2\gamma_1\sigma_{12}$. Therefore the asymptotic variance of $\hat{\boldsymbol{\beta}}_1$ is

$$\begin{aligned} V(\hat{\boldsymbol{\beta}}_1) &= (H'X'XH)^{-1}H' \cdot V(X'\mathbf{w}_1) \cdot H(H'X'XH)^{-1} \\ &= c(H'X'XH)^{-1} + \gamma_1^2(H'X'XH)^{-1}H'X'X(X'AX)^{-1} \\ &\quad \times X'XH(H'X'XH)^{-1}, \end{aligned} \tag{25.3.9}$$

where H has replaced $\hat{H}$ since $\hat{\boldsymbol{\pi}}_2$ is consistent.

To estimate $\boldsymbol{\beta}_2$ insert (25.3.5) into (25.3.2) and solve for $\mathbf{y}_1$ to obtain

$$X\boldsymbol{\pi}_2 + \mathbf{v}_2 = \gamma_2\mathbf{y}_1 + X_2\boldsymbol{\delta}_2 + \mathbf{e}_2$$

or

$$\mathbf{y}_1 = \frac{1}{\gamma_2}X\boldsymbol{\pi}_2 - \frac{1}{\gamma_2}X_2\boldsymbol{\delta}_2 + \frac{1}{\gamma_2}(\mathbf{v}_2 - \mathbf{e}_2).$$

But $v_{t2} = \gamma_2 v_{t1} + e_{t2}$ so $\mathbf{v}_2 - \mathbf{e}_2 = \gamma_2\mathbf{v}_1$, and adding and subtracting $(1/\gamma_2)X\hat{\boldsymbol{\pi}}_2$ gives

$$\begin{aligned} \mathbf{y}_1 &= \frac{1}{\gamma_2}X\hat{\boldsymbol{\pi}}_2 - \frac{1}{\gamma_2}X\boldsymbol{\delta}_2 + \mathbf{v}_1 - \frac{1}{\gamma_2}X(\hat{\boldsymbol{\pi}}_2 - \boldsymbol{\pi}_2) \\ &= X\hat{Q}\boldsymbol{\lambda} + \mathbf{w}_2, \end{aligned} \tag{25.3.10}$$

where $\hat{Q} = (\hat{\boldsymbol{\pi}}_2, -J_2)$, $XJ_2 = X_2$ and

$$\boldsymbol{\lambda} = \begin{bmatrix} \gamma_2^{-1} \\ \gamma_2^{-1}\boldsymbol{\delta}_2 \end{bmatrix}$$

and $\mathbf{w}_2 = \mathbf{v}_1 - \gamma_2^{-1}X(\hat{\boldsymbol{\pi}}_2 - \boldsymbol{\pi}_2)$. Heckman's estimator for $\boldsymbol{\lambda}$ is obtained by applying ordinary least squares to (25.3.10). That is,

$$\hat{\lambda} = (\hat{Q}'X'X\hat{Q})^{-1}\hat{Q}'X'\mathbf{y}_1. \tag{25.3.11}$$

Since there is a one to one relation between $\boldsymbol{\beta}_2$ and $\boldsymbol{\lambda}$ one can obtain $\hat{\boldsymbol{\beta}}_2$ from $\hat{\boldsymbol{\lambda}}$. Using these relations Amemiya shows that $\hat{\boldsymbol{\beta}}_2 - \boldsymbol{\beta}_2$ has the same asymptotic distribution as $P(\hat{\boldsymbol{\lambda}} - \boldsymbol{\lambda})$, where

$$P = -\gamma_2 \begin{bmatrix} \gamma_2 & \mathbf{0}' \\ \boldsymbol{\delta}_2 & -I \end{bmatrix}.$$

Consequently,

$$V(\hat{\boldsymbol{\beta}}_2) = PV(\hat{\boldsymbol{\lambda}})P',$$

where

$$V(\hat{\boldsymbol{\lambda}}) = (Q'X'XQ)^{-1}Q'V(X'\mathbf{w}_2)Q(Q'X'XQ)^{-1}$$

and

$$V(X'\mathbf{w}_2) = \gamma_2^{-2}[dX'X + X'X(X'AX)^{-1}X'X],$$

where $d = \gamma_2^2\sigma_1^2 - 2\gamma_2\sigma_{12}$.

Now we will consider estimation of the parameters $\boldsymbol{\beta}_1$ and $\boldsymbol{\beta}_2$ using Amemiya's principle outlined in the previous section. Once again we examine the forms of Equation (25.2.14) that are relevant. For the estimation of $\boldsymbol{\beta}_1$, the relevant equation is

$$\begin{aligned} \hat{\boldsymbol{\pi}}_1 &= \hat{\boldsymbol{\pi}}_2\gamma_1 + J_1\boldsymbol{\delta}_1 + (\hat{\boldsymbol{\pi}}_1 - \boldsymbol{\pi}_1) - (\hat{\boldsymbol{\pi}}_2 - \boldsymbol{\pi}_2)\gamma_1 \\ &= \hat{Z}_1\boldsymbol{\beta}_1 + \boldsymbol{\eta}_1. \end{aligned} \tag{25.3.12}$$

which is identical to (25.2.15). The ordinary least squares estimator of $\boldsymbol{\beta}_1$ is

$$\hat{\boldsymbol{\beta}}_1^{(L)} = (\hat{Z}_1'\hat{Z}_1)^{-1}\hat{Z}_1'\hat{\boldsymbol{\pi}}_1 \tag{25.3.13}$$

and the feasible generalized least squares estimator is

$$\hat{\boldsymbol{\beta}}^{(G)} = (\hat{Z}_1'\hat{V}_1^{-1}\hat{Z}_1)^{-1}\hat{Z}_1'\hat{V}_1^{-1}\hat{\boldsymbol{\pi}}_1, \tag{25.3.14}$$

where $\hat{V}_1$ is a consistent estimator of the asymptotic covariance matrix $V_1 \equiv V(\boldsymbol{\eta}_1)$. Since $\hat{\boldsymbol{\pi}}_1 - \boldsymbol{\pi}_1 = (X'X)^{-1}X'\mathbf{v}_1$ it can be shown that

$$V_1 = c(X'X)^{-1} + \gamma_1^2(X'AX)^{-1}, \tag{25.3.15}$$

where $c = \sigma_1^2 - 2\gamma_1\sigma_{12}$ as defined above. Therefore

$$V(\hat{\boldsymbol{\beta}}_1^{(L)}) = (Z_1'Z_1)^{-1}Z_1'V_1Z_1(Z_1'Z_1)^{-1} \tag{25.3.16}$$

and

$$V(\hat{\boldsymbol{\beta}}_1^{(G)}) = (Z_1'V_1^{-1}Z_1)^{-1}. \tag{25.3.17}$$

Amemiya shows that

$$V(\hat{\boldsymbol{\beta}}_1) - V(\hat{\boldsymbol{\beta}}_1^{(G)}) = \text{psd matrix}$$

but

$$V(\hat{\boldsymbol{\beta}}_1) - V(\hat{\boldsymbol{\beta}}_1^{(L)}) = \text{indefinite}.$$

Computationally $\hat{\boldsymbol{\beta}}_1^{(G)}$ is more difficult than the others but is still quite feasible. One only needs consistent estimates of γ_1 and σ_1^2 which are easily obtainable. A consistent estimate of σ_{12} is given by

$$\hat{\sigma}_{12} = \sum_{t=1}^{T} \frac{y_{2t}\hat{v}_{1t}}{T\hat{f}_t^{-1}},$$

where $\hat{v}_{1t}$ is the residual from (25.3.4) and $\hat{f}_t$ is f_t with $\hat{\boldsymbol{\pi}}_2$ replacing $\boldsymbol{\pi}_2$.

To estimate $\boldsymbol{\beta}_2$ consider

$$\hat{\boldsymbol{\pi}}_2 = \gamma_2\hat{\boldsymbol{\pi}}_1 + J_2\boldsymbol{\delta}_2 + (\hat{\boldsymbol{\pi}}_2 - \boldsymbol{\pi}_2) - \gamma_2(\hat{\boldsymbol{\pi}}_1 - \boldsymbol{\pi}_1) = \hat{Z}_2\boldsymbol{\beta}_2 + \boldsymbol{\eta}_2. \quad (25.3.18)$$

The ordinary least squares and generalized least squares estimators of $\boldsymbol{\beta}_2$ are

$$\hat{\boldsymbol{\beta}}_2^{(L)} = (\hat{Z}_2'\hat{Z}_2)^{-1}\hat{Z}_2'\hat{\boldsymbol{\pi}}_2 \quad (25.3.19)$$

and

$$\hat{\boldsymbol{\beta}}_2^{(G)} = (\hat{Z}_2'\hat{V}_2^{-1}\hat{Z}_2)^{-1}\hat{Z}_2'\hat{V}_2^{-1}\hat{\boldsymbol{\pi}}_2. \quad (25.3.20)$$

The asymptotic covariance matrices of these estimators depend on

$$V_2 = V(\boldsymbol{\eta}_2) = d(X'X)^{-1} + (X'AX)^{-1}, \quad (25.3.21)$$

where $d = \gamma_2^2\sigma_1^2 - 2\gamma_2\sigma_{12}$ as defined above and using results established earlier. Finally then

$$V(\hat{\boldsymbol{\beta}}_2^G) = (Z_2'V_2^{-1}Z_2)^{-1}$$

and

$$V(\hat{\boldsymbol{\beta}}_2^{(L)}) = (Z_2'Z_2)^{-1}Z_2'V_2Z_2(Z_2'Z_2)^{-1}$$

which bear the same relation to $V(\hat{\boldsymbol{\beta}}_2)$ as the estimators for $\boldsymbol{\beta}_1$.

25.3.1 Exercise

25.3.1. Verify that if $y_{t2} = 1$ if $y_{t2}^* > 0$ but zero otherwise, then $E(y_{t2}v_{t2}) = f_t$.

25.3.2 References

Amemiya, T. (1978). The estimation of a simultaneous equation generalized probit model. *Econometrica*, **46**, 1193–1205.

Heckman, J. (1978). Dummy endogeneous variables in a simultaneous equations system. *Econometrica*, **46**, 931–959.

25.4 Disequilibrium Econometric Models*

In this section we consider models of demand and supply markets that are assumed to operate in a state of disequilibrium. The characteristic that distinguishes disequilibrium from equilibrium models is the relaxation of the assumption that both the quantity supplied and the quantity demanded are equal to the quantity transacted. In other words, by disequilibrium we mean that market transactions occur at prices which do not clear the market, so that some buyers and sellers are not able to trade desired quantities at the prevailing price. The simplest disequilibrium model imaginable would consist of only a demand and supply function, however such a model provides no information on what quantity will be transacted at nonequilibrium prices. See Fair and Jaffee (1972). A standard assumption is that actual transactions are dominated by the short side of the market (Clower (1965)), implying that observed quantity will be equal to the minimum of quantity demanded and quantity supplied. The resulting specification can be written

$$\begin{aligned} D_t &= \mathbf{x}_t'\boldsymbol{\alpha} + P_t\alpha^* + u_t, \\ S_t &= \mathbf{z}_t'\boldsymbol{\beta} + P_t\beta^* + v_t, \\ Q_t &= \min(D_t, S_t), \end{aligned} \tag{25.4.1}$$

where D_t and S_t are the quantities demanded and supplied in period "t," P_t is price, $\mathbf{x}_t'$ and $\mathbf{z}_t'$ denote row vectors of observations on appropriate exogenous factors, Q_t is the observed quantity transacted, $\boldsymbol{\alpha}$, $\boldsymbol{\beta}$, α^*, and β^* represent parameters, u_t and v_t are normally distributed random error terms with zero means and finite variances σ_u^2 and σ_v^2, and $t = 1, \ldots, T$.

The above model indicates the effect of disequilibrium prices on the quantity exchanged but fails to describe the nature of buyer and seller behavior in periods when the market does not clear. (See Maddala and Nelson (1974), Hartley and Mallela (1977) and Hartley (1976) for estimation procedures.) Therefore, it is customary to include a Walrasian price adjustment mechanisms in the model which can be written

$$\Delta P_t = \lambda(D_t - S_t), \qquad 0 \le \lambda \le \infty, \tag{25.4.2}$$

where ΔP_t is the change in price, usually defined as $P_t - P_{t-1}$ or $P_{t+1} - P_t$, and λ is referred to as the speed of adjustment. The larger the value of λ, the faster price adjusts to an imbalance of supply and demand; if there is no excess demand (supply), price remains the same. The limiting values for λ, zero and infinity, can be associated with the hypotheses of no adjustment and perfect or instantaneous adjustment, respectively. Equation (25.4.2) can be

* This section was written by Rod F. Ziemer, Department of Agricultural Economics, Texas A & M University, College Station, TX.

generalized to allow for different speeds of adjustment during periods of excess demand and excess supply as suggested by Laffont and Garcia (1977):

$$\Delta P_t = \lambda_1(D_t - S_t), \quad \text{if } (D_t - S_t) > 0$$
$$= \lambda_2(D_t - S_t), \quad \text{if } (D_t - S_t) < 0. \tag{25.4.3}$$

An immediate problem associated with estimating a model composed of Equations (25.4.1) and (25.4.2) or (25.4.3) is that D_t and S_t are not observable unless $Q_t = D_t = S_t$. Given Equations (25.4.1) and the price adjustment equations in (25.4.3), if $\Delta P_t > 0$,

$$Q_t = S_t = D_t - \lambda_1^*\Delta P_t = \mathbf{x}_t'\boldsymbol{\alpha} + P_t\alpha^* - \lambda_1^*\Delta P_t + u_t \tag{25.4.4}$$

and if $\Delta P_t < 0$,

$$Q_t = D_t = S_t + \lambda_2^*\Delta P_t = \mathbf{z}_t'\boldsymbol{\beta} + P_t\beta^* + \lambda_2^*\Delta P_t + v_t, \tag{25.4.5}$$

where $\lambda_i^* = 1/\lambda_i$, $i = 1, 2$. Using indicator variables, as suggested by Fair and Jaffee (1972), Equations (25.4.4) and (25.4.5) can be written:

$$Q_t = \mathbf{x}_t'\boldsymbol{\alpha} + P_t\alpha^* - \lambda_1^* d_t + u_t, \tag{25.4.6}$$

$$Q_t = \mathbf{z}_t'\boldsymbol{\beta} + P_t\beta^* + \lambda_2^* s_t + v_t, \tag{25.4.7}$$

where,

$$d_t = \begin{cases} \Delta P_t, & \text{if } \Delta P_t > 0, \\ 0, & \text{otherwise,} \end{cases}$$

$$s_t = \begin{cases} \Delta P_t, & \text{if } \Delta P_t < 0, \\ 0, & \text{otherwise,} \end{cases}$$

so that all variables are observed for $t = 1, \ldots, T$.

Equations (25.4.6) and (25.4.7) can be consistently estimated by the usual two-stage least squares estimator. If $\Delta P_t = P_{t+1} - P_t$ (for example, see Laffont and Garcia (1977)), P_t is exogenous, so that in the first stage d_t and s_t are regressed on the exogenous variables $\mathbf{x}_t'$ and $\mathbf{z}_t'$. Next, the resulting predictors, say $\hat{d}_t$ and $\hat{s}_t$, are used to obtain second-stage parameter estimates. If $\Delta P_t = P_t - P_{t-1}$, P_t is endogenous, so that in the first stage a predictor for P_t, say $\hat{P}_t$, is obtained for use in the second stage. Although the two-stage least squares estimator is consistent in this case, it is not asymptotically efficient since, as noted by Amemiya (1974), d_t and s_t are not linear functions of the exogenous variables.

Given $\Delta P_t = P_{t+1} - P_t$, if $S_t > D_t$ then

$$(\Delta P_t | Q_t) \sim N[\lambda_2(Q_t - \mathbf{z}_t'\boldsymbol{\beta} - P_t\beta^*), \lambda_2^2\sigma_v^2]$$

and

$$Q_t \sim N[(\mathbf{x}_t'\boldsymbol{\alpha} + P_t\alpha^*), \sigma_u^2],$$

while if $S_t < D_t$ then

$$(\Delta P_t | Q_t) \sim N[\lambda_1(-Q_t + \mathbf{x}_t'\alpha + P_t\alpha^*), \lambda_1^2\sigma_u^2]$$

and $Q \sim N[(\mathbf{z}_t'\boldsymbol{\beta} + P_t\beta^*), \sigma_v^2]$. Letting,

$$\begin{aligned}
A_1 &= (Q_t - \mathbf{x}_t'\boldsymbol{\alpha} - P_t\alpha^*),\\
A_2 &= (Q_t - \mathbf{z}_t'\boldsymbol{\beta} - P_t\beta^*),\\
A_3 &= [\Delta P_t - \lambda_2(Q_t - \mathbf{z}_t'\boldsymbol{\beta} - P_t\beta^*)],\\
A_4 &= [\Delta P_t + \lambda_1(Q_t - \mathbf{x}_t'\boldsymbol{\alpha} - P_t\alpha^*)],
\end{aligned}$$

the appropriate log likelihood function can then be written:

$$\begin{aligned}
L = &-T\ln(2\pi) - T_1 \ln \lambda_2 - T_2 \ln \lambda_1 - T(\ln(\sigma_u)) - T(\ln(\sigma_v))\\
&- \frac{1}{2\sigma_u^2}\sum_1 A_1^2 - \frac{1}{2\sigma_v^2}\sum_2 A_2^2 - \frac{1}{2\lambda_2^2\sigma_v^2}\sum_1 A_3^2\\
&- \frac{1}{2\lambda_1^2\sigma_u^2}\sum_2 A_4^2, \qquad (25.4.8)
\end{aligned}$$

where $\sum_1$ applies to the T_1 observations such that $\Delta P_t < 0$ and $\sum_2$ applies to the T_2 observations such that $\Delta P_t > 0$. Following a modified Amemiya (1974) algorithm, maximum likelihood parameter estimates for the case that $\Delta P_t = P_{t+1} - P_t$ can be obtained by iteratively solving the first-order equations:

$$\begin{aligned}
\bar{\boldsymbol{\alpha}} &= \left(\sum_T \bar{\mathbf{x}}_t\bar{\mathbf{x}}_t'\right)^{-1}\left(\sum_T \bar{\mathbf{x}}_t Q_t + \lambda_1^* \sum_2 \bar{\mathbf{x}}_t \Delta P_t\right),\\
\bar{\boldsymbol{\beta}} &= \left(\sum_T \bar{\mathbf{z}}_t\bar{\mathbf{z}}_t'\right)^{-1}\left(\sum_T \bar{\mathbf{z}}_t Q_t - \lambda_2^* \sum_1 \bar{\mathbf{z}}_t \Delta P_t\right),\\
\sigma_u^2 &= \left[\sum_1 (Q_t - \bar{\mathbf{x}}_t'\bar{\boldsymbol{\alpha}})^2 + \sum_2 (Q_t + \lambda_1 \Delta P_t - \bar{\mathbf{x}}_t'\bar{\boldsymbol{\alpha}})^2\right]\Big/ T,\\
\sigma_v^2 &= \left[\sum_2 (Q_t - \bar{\mathbf{z}}_t'\bar{\boldsymbol{\beta}})^2 + \sum_1 (Q_t - \lambda_2 \Delta P_t - \bar{\mathbf{z}}_t'\bar{\boldsymbol{\beta}})^2\right]\Big/ T,\\
0 &= T_1\sigma_u^2\lambda_1^2 - \lambda_1 \sum_2 \Delta P_t(Q_t - \bar{\mathbf{x}}_t'\bar{\boldsymbol{\alpha}}) - \sum_2 (\Delta P_t)^2,\\
0 &= T_2\sigma_v^2\lambda_2^2 - \lambda_2 \sum_1 \Delta P_t(Q_t - \bar{\mathbf{z}}_t'\bar{\boldsymbol{\beta}}) - \sum_1 (\Delta P_t)^2, \qquad (25.4.9)
\end{aligned}$$

where $\bar{\mathbf{x}}_t = [\mathbf{x}_t', P_t]'$, $\bar{\mathbf{z}}_t = [\bar{\mathbf{z}}_t', P_t]'$, $\bar{\boldsymbol{\alpha}} = [\boldsymbol{\alpha}', \alpha^*]'$, $\bar{\boldsymbol{\beta}} = [\boldsymbol{\beta}', \beta^*]'$ and $\sum_T$ applies to all the sample observations $1, \ldots, T$. Based on initial estimates of $\bar{\boldsymbol{\alpha}}$, $\bar{\boldsymbol{\beta}}$, σ_u^2, and σ_v^2, which can come from the two-stage least squares procedure described above, positive roots for λ_1 and λ_2 are computed from the last two quadratic equations in (25.4.9). These roots are then used to compute values of $\bar{\boldsymbol{\alpha}}$, $\bar{\boldsymbol{\beta}}$, σ_u^2, and σ_v^2 from the remaining equations in (25.4.9) which are normalized on these parameters. New roots are then computed for λ_1 and λ_2 and the procedure continued until convergence. Laffont and Garcia (1977) show that this procedure has the uphill property which guarantees a unique solution and that the equations in (25.4.9) involving λ_1 can be solved separately from those involving λ_2. Standard errors for the estimated parameters can be based on the negative of the analytical Hessian of (25.4.8) or the Berndt *et al.* (1974) approximation:

$$H = \sum_{t=1}^{T} \left(\frac{\partial L_t}{\partial \boldsymbol{\theta}}\right)\left(\frac{\partial L_t}{\partial \boldsymbol{\theta}}\right)', \tag{25.4.10}$$

where $\boldsymbol{\theta} = [\boldsymbol{\alpha}', \bar{\boldsymbol{\beta}}', \lambda_1, \lambda_2, \sigma_u^2, \sigma_v^2]'$, which is asymptotically equivalent to the information matrix $E[-\partial^2 L/\partial\boldsymbol{\theta}\,\partial\boldsymbol{\theta}']$. The approximation (25.4.10) is convenient since the gradient $[\partial L_t/\partial\boldsymbol{\theta}]$ is easily computed from the first-order equations in (25.4.9), although it is not unreasonably difficult to obtain the analytical Hessian of (25.4.8).

It may be of interest to test the hypothesis of constant upward and downward speeds of adjustment, i.e. $\lambda_1 = \lambda_2$, implied by Equations (25.4.2). Such a test is easily accomplished by deriving the maximum likelihood parameter estimates from (25.4.8) given the restriction that $\lambda_1 = \lambda_2 = \lambda$. To test this restriction, the usual likelihood ratio statistic is used:

$$\omega = -2[\ln L(\bar{\boldsymbol{\theta}}) - \ln L(\hat{\boldsymbol{\theta}})], \tag{25.4.11}$$

where $\bar{\boldsymbol{\theta}}$ is the restricted and $\hat{\boldsymbol{\theta}}$ the unrestricted maximum likelihood estimator of the true parameter vector $\boldsymbol{\theta}$, and ω has a χ^2-distribution with one degree of freedom, if the null hypothesis $H_0\colon \lambda_1 = \lambda_2$ is true.

A further test of interest concerns the hypothesis of equilibrium versus disequilibrium. Fair and Jaffee (1972) suggest that the hypothesis of perfect or continuous equilibrium can be considered by testing the null hypothesis $H_0\colon \lambda^* = 1/\lambda = 0$. An estimate of the standard error of λ^* can be based on the general asymptotic covariance matrix of a nonlinear vector function, say Ψ, of a maximum likelihood estimator $\hat{\boldsymbol{\theta}}$ (see Corollary 4.2.2):

$$D\left(-\frac{\partial^2 L}{\partial\hat{\boldsymbol{\theta}}\,\partial\hat{\boldsymbol{\theta}}'}\right)^{-1} D', \tag{25.4.12}$$

where D denotes the derivative of Ψ with respect to $\hat{\boldsymbol{\theta}}$. Based on (25.4.12), it is convenient to note that the ratio of λ to its standard error is equal to the ratio of λ^* to its standard error so that the Fair and Jaffee test is easily carried out. However, in a Monte Carlo study, Quandt (1978) concluded that the ratio of λ^* to its standard error may not be well approximated by a normal distribution and that subsequently the test leads to a high probability for type I error. Alternatively, Quandt concluded that the Fair and Jaffee test gives satisfactory inferences when the model hypothesis of equilibrium is false. Other tests of equilibrium versus disequilibrium have been suggested (see Bowden (1978b), Quandt (1978)), but there remains no generally accepted approach to the problem.

For the case that $\Delta P_t = P_t - P_{t-1}$, P_t is endogenous and maximum likelihood estimation is less straightforward than if P_t is exogenous, although certainly feasible. The appropriate likelihood function is fairly complicated relative to (25.4.8) and is presented in Laffont and Garcia (1977). Maximum likelihood estimates can be obtained following any nonlinear optimization method which guarantees convergence such as the gradient search procedure suggested by Berndt *et al.* (1974). However, given the computational burden of analytically deriving the derivatives of the likelihood function, a derivative free method of estimation should be considered.

Fair and Kelejian (1974) suggest that the price adjustment Equation (25.4.2) be specified as a stochastic multivariate function such as:

$$\Delta P_t = \lambda(D_t - S_t) + \mathbf{w}_t'\boldsymbol{\gamma} + e_t, \tag{25.4.13}$$

where e_t is a random error term, $\mathbf{w}_t'$ is a row vector of exogenous variable values, and $\boldsymbol{\gamma}$ is a conformable parameter vector. A consistent estimation technique for a model comprised of Equations (25.4.1) and (25.4.13) given $\Delta P_t = P_t - P_{t-1}$ is discussed by Fair and Kelejian (1974). Estimation of this model is not straightforward because observed quantity, Q_t, cannot be strictly identified with D_t or S_t since observed price is stochastic. The appropriate likelihood function for the model assuming e_t is normally distributed and $\boldsymbol{\gamma} = \mathbf{0}$ appears in Quandt (1978). Given the complexity of the likelihood function, a derivative-free method is again recommended for obtaining maximum likelihood parameter estimates.

An important characteristic of interest in a disequilibrium model is the speed of adjustment with which the system moves back toward equilibrium after it is disturbed. To determine the speed of adjustment over time for a disequilibrium model consisting of Equations (25.4.1) and (25.4.3), consider the reduced form of the model:

$$\Delta P_t = \lambda_i(\tilde{D}_t + P_t\alpha^* - \tilde{S}_t - P_t\beta^*); \tag{25.4.14}$$

where $\tilde{D}_t = \mathbf{x}_t'\boldsymbol{\alpha} + u_t$, $\tilde{S}_t = \mathbf{z}_t'\boldsymbol{\beta} + v_t$, $i = 1$ if $\Delta P_t > 0$ and $i = 2$ if $\Delta P_t < 0$. Assuming that $u_t = v_t$ for all t, $\tilde{D}_t = \bar{D}$, and $\tilde{S}_t = \bar{S}$ where $\bar{D}$ and $\bar{S}$ are constants implying there are not changes in the exogenous factors $\mathbf{x}_t$ and $\mathbf{z}_t$ over time, (25.4.14) can be written:

$$P_{t+1} + aP_t = k, \tag{25.4.15}$$

where,

$$a = -[1 + (\alpha^* - \beta^*)],$$
$$k = \lambda_i(\bar{D} - \bar{S})$$

if $\Delta P_t = P_{t+1} - P_t$ and,

$$a = -1/[1 - \lambda_i(\alpha^* - \beta^*)],$$
$$k = -a\lambda_i(\bar{D} - \bar{S})$$

if $\Delta P_t = P_t - P_{t-1}$. Since (25.4.15) is in the form of a nonhomogeneous first-order difference equation, its solution is straightforward and can be written:

$$P_t = (-a)^t\left(P_0 - \frac{k}{1+a}\right) + \frac{k}{1+a}, \qquad a \neq 1, \tag{25.4.16}$$

where P_0 represents an arbitrary initial price. Since the equilibrium or market clearing price is: $\bar{P}_t = (\tilde{D}_t - \tilde{S}_t)/(\beta^* - \alpha^*)$, we might define a steady-state equilibrium as: $\bar{P} = (\bar{D} - \bar{S})/(\beta^* - \alpha^*)$. It is easy to show that $\bar{P} = k/(1+a)$, so Equation (25.4.17) can be written:

$$P_t = (-a)^t(P_0 - \bar{P}) + \bar{P}. \tag{25.4.17}$$

From Equation (25.4.17), the dynamic stability of the disequilibrium system described by Equations (25.4.1) and (25.4.3) can be determined by the parameters α^*, β^*, λ_1, and λ_2 which determine the value of the term $(-a)$. If $|-a| > 1$, the system will explode given a discrepancy between P_0 and $\bar{P}$. If $|-a| < 1$, the system will converge toward equilibrium where convergence will be more rapid given smaller values of $|-a|$. If $(-a) < 0$, price adjustment will follow a cobweb path alternately rising above and falling below the equilibrium price from period to period. If $(-a) > 0$ and $|-a| < 1$, then observed price will monotonically approach the equilibrium price. For example, if $(-a) = 0.5$, 50 % of a shock from equilibrium is observed within one period, 75 % in two periods, and about 98 % of the adjustment process is complete in six periods.

A natural extension of a single market disequilibrium model is a general model which considers the possibility of many interrelated markets in disequilibrium. The majority of studies involving multimarket disequilibrium follow in the spirit of Patinkin (1956, Ch. 13), Clower (1965), and others who suggests that, within a commodity–labor market model, unsatisfied demand or supply in one market generates spillover effects on the other. Ito (1980) and Portes (1977) propose a linear commodity–labor market disequilibrium model which can be generally written for two markets as:

$$\begin{aligned}
D_{1t} &= \mathbf{x}'_{1t}\boldsymbol{\alpha}_1 + \mu_1(Q_{2t} - S^*_{2t}) + u_{1t},\\
S_{1t} &= \mathbf{z}'_{1t}\boldsymbol{\beta}_1 + \omega_1(Q_{2t} - D^*_{2t}) + v_{1t},\\
Q_{1t} &= \min(D_{1t}, S_{1t}),\\
D_{2t} &= \mathbf{x}'_{2t}\boldsymbol{\alpha}_2 + \mu_2(Q_{1t} - S^*_{1t}) + u_{2t},\\
S_{2t} &= \mathbf{z}'_{2t}\boldsymbol{\beta}_2 + \omega_2(Q_{1t} - D^*_{1t}) + v_{2t},\\
Q_{2t} &= \min(D_{2t}, S_{2t}),
\end{aligned} \tag{25.4.18}$$

where u_{t1}, u_{t2}, v_{t1} and v_{2t} are normally distributed random errors with zero means and finite variances and,

$$\begin{aligned} D_{1t}^* &= \mathbf{x}_{1t}'\boldsymbol{\alpha}_1, \\ S_{1t}^* &= \mathbf{z}_{1t}'\boldsymbol{\beta}_1, \\ D_{2t}^* &= \mathbf{x}_{2t}'\boldsymbol{\alpha}_2, \\ S_{2t}^* &= \mathbf{z}_{2t}'\boldsymbol{\beta}_2. \end{aligned} \tag{25.4.19}$$

Equations (25.4.18) define "effective" demands and supplies which take into account quantity constraints in the other market. The equations in (25.4.19) describe "notational" or unconstrained demands and supplies which do not account for spillover effects from the other market. Portes (1977) proposes an alternative specification for Equations (25.4.18) in which S_{2t}^*, D_{2t}^*, S_{1t}^*, and D_{1t}^* are replaced by S_{2t}, D_{2t}, S_{1t}, and D_{1t} so that spillover effects are dictated by effective demands and supplies in the other market rather than notational demands and supplies. With either specification, if both markets clear, demand and supply behavior is simply a function of exogenous factors relevant to that particular market and notational and effective demands and supplies are equal, i.e., there are no spillover effects between markets.

Ito (1980) suggests the following price adjustment mechanisms for this model:

$$\begin{aligned} \Delta P_{1t} &= \lambda_1(D_{1t} - S_{1t}), \quad \text{if } D_{1t} > S_{1t} \\ &= \delta_1(D_{1t} - S_{1t}), \quad \text{if } D_{1t} < S_{1t}, \\ \Delta P_{2t} &= \lambda_2(D_{2t} - S_{2t}), \quad \text{if } D_{2t} > S_{2t} \\ &= \delta_2(D_{2t} - S_{2t}), \quad \text{if } D_{2t} < S_{2t}, \end{aligned} \tag{25.4.20}$$

where P_{1t} and P_{2t} are observed prices in the two markets and $\Delta P_{it} = P_{i,t+1} - P_{it}$ or $\Delta P_{it} = P_{it} - P_{i,t-1}$ $(i = 1, 2)$, so that current prices are exogenous or endogenous, respectively. As shown by Ito (1980, p. 116) the model in (25.4.18) and (25.4.20) can be consistently estimated by applying two-stage least squares to the following reduced form equations:

$$\begin{aligned} Q_{1t} &= \mathbf{x}_{1t}'\boldsymbol{\alpha}_1 - \mu_1\mathbf{z}_{2t}'\boldsymbol{\beta}_2 + \mu_1 Q_{2t} - \lambda_1^* d_{1t} + (u_{1t} - \mu_1 v_{2t}), \\ Q_{1t} &= \mathbf{z}_{1t}'\boldsymbol{\beta}_1 - \omega_1\mathbf{x}_{2t}'\boldsymbol{\alpha}_2 + \omega_1 Q_{2t} + \delta_1^* s_{it} + (v_{1t} - \omega_1 u_{2t}), \\ Q_{2t} &= \mathbf{x}_{2t}'\boldsymbol{\alpha}_2 - \mu_2\mathbf{z}_{1t}'\boldsymbol{\beta}_1 + \mu_2 Q_{1t} - \lambda_2^* d_{2t} + (u_{2t} - \mu_2 v_{1t}), \\ Q_{2t} &= \mathbf{z}_{2t}'\boldsymbol{\beta}_2 - \omega_2\mathbf{x}_{1t}'\boldsymbol{\alpha}_1 + \omega_2 Q_{1t} + \delta_2^* s_{2t} + (v_{2t} - \omega_2 u_{1t}), \end{aligned} \tag{25.4.21}$$

where $\lambda_i^* = (1/\lambda_i)$, $\delta_i^* = (1/\delta_i)$, and

$$\begin{aligned} d_{it} &= \Delta P_{it}, \quad \text{if } \Delta P_{it} > 0, \\ &= 0, \quad \text{otherwise}, \\ s_{it} &= \Delta P_{it}, \quad \text{if } \Delta P_{it} < 0, \\ &= 0, \quad \text{otherwise}, \end{aligned} \tag{25.4.22}$$

for $i = 1, 2$. In the first stage Q_{1t}, Q_{2t}, d_{1t}, d_{2t}, s_{1t}, and s_{2t} are regressed on all the exogenous variables ($\mathbf{x}'_{1t}$, $\mathbf{x}'_{2t}$, $\mathbf{z}'_{1t}$, and $\mathbf{z}'_{2t}$) and the resulting predictions (say $\hat{Q}_{1t}$, $\hat{Q}_{2t}$, $\hat{d}_{1t}$, $\hat{d}_{2t}$, $\hat{s}_{1t}$, and $\hat{s}_{2t}$) substituted in the second stage. If P_{1t} and P_{2t} appear in $\mathbf{x}'_{1t}$, $\mathbf{x}'_{2t}$, $\mathbf{z}'_{1t}$, and $\mathbf{z}'_{2t}$ and $\Delta P_t = P_t - P_{t-1}$, so that P_t is endogenous, then predictors for P_{1t} and P_{2t} will also have to be defined for two-stage least squares estimation of (25.4.21). Maximum likelihood estimation of the model is discussed in Gourieroux *et al.* (1980) and Ito (1980).

In general, demand and supply functions for two interrelated markets in disequilibrium may be affected by either excess demand or excess supply in the other market. Such an idea is expressed in the following model in which we replace the demand and supply equations in (25.4.18) by:

$$\begin{aligned} D_{it} &= \mathbf{x}'_{it}\boldsymbol{\alpha}_i + \mu_i(Q_{jt} - S^*_{jt}) + \theta_i(Q_{jt} - D^*_{jt}) + u_{it}, \\ S_{it} &= \mathbf{z}'_{it}\boldsymbol{\beta}_i + \omega_i(Q_{jt} - S^*_{jt}) + \phi_i(Q_{jt} - D^*_{jt}) + v_{it}, \end{aligned} \tag{25.4.23}$$

where $i, j = 1, 2$ and $i \neq j$. The reduced form for this model can be written:

$$\begin{aligned} Q_{it} &= \mathbf{x}'_{it}\boldsymbol{\alpha}_i - \mu_i\mathbf{z}'_{jt}\boldsymbol{\beta}_j - \theta_i\mathbf{x}'_{jt}\boldsymbol{\alpha}_j + (\mu_i + \theta_i)Q_{jt} \\ &\quad - \lambda^*_i d_{it} + [u_{it} - (\mu_i + \theta_i)v_{jt}], \\ Q_{it} &= \mathbf{z}'_{it}\boldsymbol{\beta}_i - \omega_i\mathbf{x}'_{jt}\boldsymbol{\alpha}_j - \phi_i\mathbf{z}'_{jt}\boldsymbol{\beta}_j + (\omega_i + \phi_i)Q_{jt} \\ &\quad + \delta^*_i s_{it} + [v_{it} - (\omega_i + \phi_i)u_{jt}] \end{aligned} \tag{25.4.24}$$

for $i, j = 1, 2$ and $i \neq j$. The parameters of (25.4.24) can also be consistently estimated by two-stage least squares as was the case of the model in (25.4.21). The two-market model in (25.4.23) appears to have many applications including product–product, factor–product, and factor–factor markets. Depending on the nature of the relationship between the two markets of interest, it may be possible to make some assumptions concerning the values of the spillover coefficients μ_i, θ_i, ω_i, and ϕ_i. That θ_i and ϕ_i are assumed to be zero in labor–commodity models reflects certain assumptions concerning the factor–product relationship between the two markets (for example, see Barro and Grossman (1971), Gourieroux *et al.* (1980), Ito (1980). For the case of "n" interrelated markets in disequilibrium we might write a general model as follows:

$$\begin{aligned} D_{it} &= \mathbf{x}'_{it}\boldsymbol{\alpha}_i + \sum_{j=1}^{n} \mu_{ij}(Q_{jt} - S^*_{jt}) + \sum_{j=1}^{n} \theta_{ij}(Q_{jt} - D^*_{jt}) + u_{it}, \\ S_{it} &= \mathbf{z}'_{it}\boldsymbol{\beta}_i + \sum_{j=1}^{n} \omega_{ij}(Q_{jt} - S^*_{jt}) + \sum_{j=1}^{n} \phi_{ij}(Q_{jt} - D^*_{jt}) + v_{it}, \\ Q_{it} &= \min(D_{it}, S_{it}), \\ \Delta P_{it} &= \lambda_i(D_{it} - S_{it}) \quad \text{if } D_{it} > S_{it} \\ &= \delta_i(D_{it} - S_{it}) \quad \text{if } D_{it} < S_{it}, \end{aligned} \tag{25.4.25}$$

where $i = 1, \ldots, n$, and $i \neq j$. The parameters of (25.4.25) can be consistently estimated by applying two-stage least squares to the reduced form:

$$
\begin{aligned}
Q_{it} = {} & \mathbf{x}'_{it}\boldsymbol{\alpha}_i - \sum_{j=1}^{n} \mu_{ij}\mathbf{z}'_{jt}\boldsymbol{\beta}_j - \sum_{j=1}^{n} \theta_{ij}\mathbf{x}'_{jt}\boldsymbol{\alpha}_j \\
& + \sum_{j=1}^{n} (\mu_{ij} + \theta_{ij})Q_{jt} - \lambda_i^* d_{it} \\
& + \left[u_{it} - \sum_{j=1}^{n} (\mu_{ij} + \theta_{ij})v_{jt}\right], \\
Q_{it} = {} & \mathbf{z}'_{it}\boldsymbol{\beta}_i - \sum_{j=1}^{n} \omega_{ij}\mathbf{x}'_{jt}\boldsymbol{\alpha}_j - \sum_{j=1}^{n} \phi_{ij}\mathbf{z}'_{jt}\boldsymbol{\beta}_j \\
& + \sum_{j=1}^{n} (\omega_{ij} + \phi_{ij})Q_{jt} + \delta_i^* s_{it} \\
& + \left[v_{it} - \sum_{j=1}^{n} (\omega_{ij} + \phi_{ij})u_{it}\right],
\end{aligned}
\tag{25.4.26}
$$

where λ_i^*, δ_i^*, d_{it}, and s_{it} are as defined previously, and $i, j = 1, \ldots, n$, $i \neq j$. As in the case of the general two market model (25.4.24), it may be possible to make certain assumptions concerning the values of the spillover parameters μ_{ij}, θ_{ij}, ω_{ij}, and ϕ_{ij} depending on the economic relationship between the markets considered. For example, see Ito (1980).

Since econometric disequilibrium models are a relatively recent phenomenon, further applications are needed to determine their general usefulness. Empirical applications of simple disequilibrium market models include the market for housing starts (Bowden (1978a), Fair and Jaffee (1972), Maddala and Nelson (1974)), the U.S. labor market (Rosen and Quandt (1978)), the market for business loans (Laffont and Garcia (1977)), the market for U.S. beef (Ziemer and White (1982)), and the market for watermelons (Goldfield and Quandt (1975)). In practice, the investigator must weigh the *a priori* evidence indicating possible disequilibrium behavior with the econometric simplicity associated with an equilibrium model. If theory and/or other evidence strongly support the hypothesis of significant disequilibrium behavior, the added computational burden of a disequilibrium model may be justified.

25.4.1 References

Amemiya, T. (1974). A note on a Fair and Jaffee model. *Econometrica*, **42**, 759–762.

Barro, R. J., and Grossman, H. I. (1971). A general disequilibrium model of income and employment. *American Economic Review*, **61**, 82–93.

Berndt, E. K., Hall, B. H., Hall, R. E., and Hausman, J. A. (1974). Estimation and inference in nonlinear structural models. *Annals of Economic and Social Measurement*, **3**, 653–665.

Bowden, R. J. (1978a). *The Econometrics of Disequilibrium*. Amsterdam: North-Holland.
Bowden, R. J. (1978b). Specification, estimation and inference for model of markets in disequilibrium. *International Economic Review*, **19**, 711–726.
Clower, R. W. (1965). The Keynesian counter-revolution: a theoretical appraisal. In *The Theory of Interest Rates*. Edited by F. M. Hakn and F. P. R. Brechling. London: Macmillan.
Fair, R. C., and Jaffee, D. M. (1972). Methods of estimation for markets in disequilibrium. *Econometrica*, **40**, 497–514.
Fair, R. C., and Kelejian, H. H. (1974). Method of estimation for markets in disequilibrium: a further study. *Econometrica*, **42**, 177–190.
Goldfeld, S. M., and Quandt, R. E. (1975). Estimation in a disequilibrium model and the value of information. *Journal of Econometrics*, **3**, 325–348.
Gourieroux, C., Laffont, J. J., and Monfort, A. (1980). Disequilibrium econometrics in simultaneous equations systems. *Econometrica*, **48**, 75–96.
Hartley, M. J. (1976). The estimation of markets in disequilibrium: the fixed supply case. *International Economic Review*, **17**, 687–699.
Hartley, M. J. and Mallela, P. (1977). The asumptotic properties of a maximum likelihood estimator for a model of markets in disequilibrium. *Econometrica*, **45**, 1205–1220.
Ito, T. (1980). Methods of estimation for multi-market disequilibrium models. *Econometrica*, **48**, 97–125.
Laffont, J. J., and Garcia, R. (1977). Disequilibrium econometrics for business loans. *Econometrica*, **45**, 1187–1204.
Maddala, G. S., and Nelson, F. D. (1974). Maximum likelihood methods for models of markets in disequilibrium. *Econometrica*, **42**, 1013–1030.
Patinkin, D. (1956). *Money, Interest and Prices*. New York: Harper & Row.
Portes, R. (1977). Effective demand and spillovers in empirical two-market disequilibrium models. Harvard Institute of Economic Research Discussion Paper No. 595, Harvard University.
Quandt, R. E. (1978). Tests of equilibrium vs. disequilibrium hypotheses. *International Economic Review*, **19**, 435–452.
Rosen, H. S., and Quandt, R. E. (1978). Estimation of a disequilibrium aggregate labor market. *Review of Economics and Statistics*, **60**, 371–379.
Ziemer, R. F., and White, F. C. (1982). Disequilibrium market analysis: an application to the U.S. fed beef sector. *American Journal of Agricultural Economics*, **64**, 56–62.

25.5 Vector Autoregressive Error Processes in Simultaneous Equations Models

In their discussion of econometric forecasting and time-series analysis, Granger and Newbold (1977, p. 301) comment that

> . . . even when a model is built, it will fit the data imperfectly, producing residuals from each equation of the system, and unless these residuals are negligibly small (which typically they are not) their time series properties about which economic theory has little or nothing to say) will be of great relevance to forecasting. The econometrician ignores this factor at his peril.

Recently, the "typical" specification of serial independence of the errors in simultaneous equations models has been extended to include the possibility of autocorrelated errors. In particular, the simultaneous equations model we will consider for the remainder of this section is

$$Y\Gamma + X\Delta + Y_{-1}\mathrm{H} + E = 0 \tag{25.5.1}$$

with error specification

$$E = E_{-1}R + U, \tag{25.5.2}$$

where $E\mathbf{u}'_{t.} = \mathbf{0}$ and $E\mathbf{u}'_{t.}\mathbf{u}_{t.} = \Sigma$ and $E\mathbf{u}'_{s.}\mathbf{u}_{t.} = 0$ for $s \neq t$. To insure that our model is dynamically stable, it is assumed that the equations $\det(\Gamma - \mathrm{H}\mathbf{x}) = 0$ and $\det(I - R\mathbf{x}) = 0$ have all roots outside the unit circle. The system of Equations (25.5.1) and (25.5.2) represents a dynamic simultaneous equations model with a vector autoregressive error process. Let us examine (25.5.2) more closely. The matrix E_{-1} is a $T \times G$ matrix of lagged values of the unobservable random errors E while R is a $G \times G$ matrix of correlation coefficients representing the degree and type of autocorrelation among the errors in E. If R is the zero matrix, the above model reduces to the usual error specification described in (19.3.7) and (19.3.8), $E(E) = 0$, $E(\mathbf{e}'_{t.}\mathbf{e}_{t.}) = \Sigma$ and $E(\mathbf{e}'_{s.}\mathbf{e}_{t.}) = 0$ for $s \neq t$. If $R = \operatorname{diag}(r_{11}, r_{22}, \ldots, r_{gg})$ is a diagonal matrix, each equation has autocorrelated errors of the form:

$$e_{tg} = r_{gg}e_{t-1,g} + u_{tg}, \qquad g = 1, 2, \ldots, G.$$

This is the AR(1) error process discussed in Chapter 10 except here it is specified in the context of a simultaneous equations model. When the off-diagonal elements of R are nonzero, the autocorrelation involves the errors of other equations as well. To illustrate, consider the case of a two equation model where R is of the form

$$R = \begin{bmatrix} r_{11} & r_{12} \\ r_{21} & r_{22} \end{bmatrix}.$$

For the tth observation the error specification of the system is

$$(e_{t1} \quad e_{t2}) = (e_{t-1,1} \quad e_{t-1,2})\begin{bmatrix} r_{11} & r_{12} \\ r_{21} & r_{22} \end{bmatrix} + (u_{t1} \quad u_{t2})$$

or, equivalently,

$$e_{t1} = r_{11}e_{t-1,1} + r_{21}e_{t-1,2} + u_{t1},$$
$$e_{t2} = r_{12}e_{t-1,1} + r_{22}e_{t-1,2} + u_{t2}.$$

The remainder of the discussion in this section on vector autoregressive error processes in simultaneous equations models is divided into three subsections. The next subsection contains a detailed development of the variance–covariance structure of the errors E when they follow the vector autoregressive error process (25.5.2). In the subsequent two subsections, two-step feasible generalized least squares estimation and tests of hypotheses in the model described by (25.5.1) and (25.5.2) are discussed. In the first of these subsections, we examine the case of no lagged dependent variables (H = 0 and the model is dynamic only to the degree that X contains lagged values of purely exogenous variables). Then the estimation and tests of hypotheses for the lagged dependent variable case (H ≠ 0) are considered in the last subsection.

25.5.1 Covariance Structure of the Vector Autoregressive Error Structure

Given the error process (25.5.2), the errors for all equations at time t satisfies

$$\begin{aligned} \mathbf{e}_{t.} &= \mathbf{e}_{t-1.}R + \mathbf{u}_{t.} \\ &= (\mathbf{e}_{t-2.}R + \mathbf{u}_{t-1.})R + \mathbf{u}_{t.} \\ &= [(\mathbf{e}_{t-3.}R + \mathbf{u}_{t-2.})R + \mathbf{u}_{t-1.}]R + \mathbf{u}_{t.} \\ &= \mathbf{e}_{t-n.}R^n + \sum_{i=0}^{n} \mathbf{u}_{t-i.}R^i, \end{aligned} \tag{25.5.3}$$

where $\mathbf{e}_{t.}$ represents the tth row of E, $\mathbf{u}_{t.}$ represents the tth row of U, and R^i is the ith fold product of R. Now letting $n \to \infty$ we have

$$\begin{aligned} E(\mathbf{e}_{t.}'\mathbf{e}_{t.}) &= E\left(\sum_{i=0}^{\infty} \mathbf{u}_{t-i.}R^i\right)'\left(\sum_{i=0}^{\infty} \mathbf{u}_{t-i.}R^i\right) \\ &= \sum_{i=0}^{\infty} R^{i\prime}E(\mathbf{u}_{t-i.}'\mathbf{u}_{t-i.})R^i \\ &= \sum_{i=0}^{\infty} R^{i\prime}\Sigma R^i \\ &\equiv \Omega. \end{aligned} \tag{25.5.4}$$

Let $j \geq i$, then

$$\begin{aligned} E(\mathbf{e}_{i.}'\mathbf{e}_{j.}) &= E(\mathbf{e}_{i-1.}R + \mathbf{u}_{i.})'(\mathbf{e}_{j-1.}R + \mathbf{u}_{j.}) \\ &= E(R'\mathbf{e}_{i-1.}'\mathbf{e}_{j-1.}R + \mathbf{u}_{i.}'\mathbf{e}_{j-1.}R \\ &\quad + R'\mathbf{e}_{i-1.}\mathbf{u}_{j.} + \mathbf{u}_{i.}'\mathbf{u}_{j.}). \end{aligned}$$

Defining $R^0 = I$ and letting $j - i = v$,

$$\begin{aligned}
E(\mathbf{e}'_{i.}\mathbf{e}_{j.}) &= E\Bigg[R'\left(\sum_{\tau=0}^{\infty}\mathbf{u}_{i-1-\tau.}R^{\tau}\right)'\left(\sum_{\tau=0}^{\infty}\mathbf{u}_{j-1-\tau.}R^{\tau}\right)R \\
&\quad + \mathbf{u}'_{i.}\left(\sum_{\tau=0}^{\infty}\mathbf{u}_{j-1-\tau.}R^{\tau}\right)R \\
&\quad + R'\left(\sum_{\tau=0}^{\infty}\mathbf{u}_{i-1-\tau.}R^{\tau}\right)'\mathbf{u}_{j.}\Bigg] \\
&= R'E(\mathbf{u}'_{i-1.}\mathbf{u}_{j-(v+1).})R^{v+1} \\
&\quad + R'^2E(\mathbf{u}'_{i-2.}\mathbf{u}_{j-(v+2).})R^{v+2} \\
&\quad + \cdots + R'^nE(\mathbf{u}'_{i-n.}\mathbf{u}_{j-(v+n).})R^{v+n} + \cdots \\
&\quad + E(\mathbf{u}'_{i.}\mathbf{u}_{j-v.})R^{v} \\
&= R'\Sigma R^{v+1} + R'^2\Sigma R^{v+2} + \cdots + R'^n\Sigma R^{v+n} + \cdots \\
&\quad + \Sigma R^{v} \\
&= \sum_{i=0}^{\infty}(R'^i\Sigma R^i)R^v = \Omega R^v = \Omega R^{j-i}. \qquad (25.5.5)
\end{aligned}$$

When $i > j$, we can use the above developments to obtain

$$E(\mathbf{e}'_{i.}\mathbf{e}_{j.}) = R'^{(-v)}\Omega = R'^{(i-j)}\Omega.$$

In summary, the variance–covariance matrix for E satisfying the vector autoregressive error process (25.5.2) is

$$E\begin{bmatrix}\mathbf{e}'_{1.}\\ \mathbf{e}'_{2.}\\ \vdots \\ \mathbf{e}'_{T.}\end{bmatrix}[\mathbf{e}_{1.} \quad \mathbf{e}_{2.} \quad \cdots \quad \mathbf{e}_{T.}] = \Phi, \qquad (25.5.6)$$

where

$$\begin{aligned}
\Phi_{ii} &= \Omega, & i &= 1, 2, \ldots, T, & (25.5.7)\\
\Phi_{ij} &= \Omega R^{j-i}, & &\text{for } j \geq i, & (25.5.8)\\
&= R'^{i-j}\Omega, & &\text{for } i > j, & (25.5.9)
\end{aligned}$$

each Φ_{ij} being a square matrix of order G, G being the number of equations in the system. Obviously, in the case that the errors are uncorrelated, $R = 0$, the error variance–covariance structure takes the classical form $E\mathbf{e}'_{t.}\mathbf{e}_{t.} = \Sigma$.

Consider the simultaneous equations model

$$\mathbf{y}_* = Z_*\boldsymbol{\alpha} + \mathbf{e}_* \tag{25.5.10}$$

with

$$\mathbf{e}_* = (R' \otimes I_T)\mathbf{e}_{*,-1} + \mathbf{u}_* \tag{25.5.11}$$

which in expanded form is

$$\begin{bmatrix} \mathbf{y}_1 \\ \mathbf{y}_2 \\ \vdots \\ \mathbf{y}_G \end{bmatrix} = \begin{bmatrix} Z_1 & & & 0 \\ & Z_2 & & \\ & & \ddots & \\ 0 & & & Z_G \end{bmatrix} \begin{bmatrix} \boldsymbol{\alpha}_1 \\ \boldsymbol{\alpha}_2 \\ \vdots \\ \boldsymbol{\alpha}_G \end{bmatrix} + \begin{bmatrix} \mathbf{e}_{.1} \\ \mathbf{e}_{.2} \\ \vdots \\ \mathbf{e}_{.G} \end{bmatrix} \tag{25.5.12}$$

with $Z_i = (Y_i, X_i, Y_{-1,i})$, $\boldsymbol{\alpha}_i = (\boldsymbol{\gamma}_i', \boldsymbol{\delta}_i', \boldsymbol{\eta}_i')'$ and error specification

$$\begin{bmatrix} e_{11} \\ \vdots \\ e_{T1} \\ e_{12} \\ \vdots \\ e_{T2} \\ \vdots \\ e_{1G} \\ \vdots \\ e_{TG} \end{bmatrix} = \begin{bmatrix} r_{11}I_T & r_{21}I_T & \cdots & r_{G1}I_T \\ r_{12}I_T & r_{22}I_T & \cdots & r_{G2}I_T \\ & & \vdots & \\ r_{1G}I_T & & \cdots & r_{GG}I_T \end{bmatrix} \begin{bmatrix} e_{01} \\ \vdots \\ e_{T-1,1} \\ e_{02} \\ \vdots \\ e_{T-1,2} \\ \vdots \\ e_{0G} \\ \vdots \\ e_{T-1,G} \end{bmatrix} + \begin{bmatrix} u_{11} \\ \vdots \\ u_{T1} \\ u_{12} \\ \vdots \\ u_{T2} \\ \vdots \\ u_{1G} \\ \vdots \\ u_{TG} \end{bmatrix}. \tag{25.5.13}$$

Given the variance–covariance structure described by (25.5.6), there exists a $TG \times TG$ transformation matrix P such that $P\mathbf{e}^*$ has the classical simultaneous equation specification of contemporaneous but serially independent error variance–covariance structure $E(P\mathbf{e}_*\mathbf{e}_*'P') = \Sigma \otimes I_T$. It can be shown that P matrix is of the form

$$P = \begin{bmatrix} P_{11} & P_{12} & \cdots & P_{1G} \\ P_{21} & P_{22} & \cdots & P_{2G} \\ & & \vdots & \\ P_{G1} & P_{G2} & \cdots & P_{GG} \end{bmatrix}, \tag{25.5.14}$$

where

$$P_{ii} = \begin{bmatrix} (\Omega^{-1/2}\Sigma^{-1/2})_{ii} & & & & \\ -r_{ii} & 1 & & 0 & \\ & -r_{ii} & 1 & & \\ 0 & & \ddots & \ddots & \\ & & & -r_{ii} & 1 \end{bmatrix} \qquad i = 1, 2, \ldots, G, \tag{25.5.15}$$

and

$$P_{ij} = \begin{bmatrix} (\Omega^{-1/2}\Sigma^{-1/2})_{ij} & & & & \\ -r_{ij} & 0 & & 0 & \\ & -r_{ij} & 0 & & \\ 0 & & \ddots & \ddots & \\ & & & -r_{ij} & 0 \end{bmatrix} \quad i, j = 1, 2, \ldots, G, \quad i \neq j. \tag{25.5.16}$$

The element $(\Omega^{-1/2}\Sigma^{-1/2})_{ij}$ denotes the (i, j)th element of the product matrix $\Omega^{-1/2}\Sigma^{-1/2}$ where $\Omega^{-1/2}$ and $\Sigma^{-1/2}$ are matrices such that $\Omega^{-1/2}\Omega^{-1/2} = \Omega^{-1} = (\sum_{i=0}^{\infty} R'^i \Sigma R^i)^{-1}$ and $\Sigma^{-1/2}\Sigma^{-1/2} = \Sigma^{-1}$.

Since, asymptotically speaking, the treatment of the first observation in each equation is unimportant, we may drop these observations and form the following first-order partial differences:

$$\begin{aligned} \mathbf{y}_* - (R' \otimes I_{T-1})\mathbf{y}_{*,-1} &= Z_*\boldsymbol{\alpha} - (R' \otimes I_{T-1})Z_{*,-1}\boldsymbol{\alpha} \\ &\quad + \mathbf{e}_* - (R' \otimes I_{T-1})\mathbf{e}_{*,-1} \\ &= (Z_* - (R' \otimes I_{T-1})Z_{*,-1})\boldsymbol{\alpha} + \mathbf{u}_*. \end{aligned} \tag{25.5.17}$$

Note that $\mathbf{y}_*$, Z_*, and $\mathbf{u}_*$ now have $G(T-1)$ rows. We have transformed the vector autoregressive error model (25.5.1) and (25.5.2) into one where the error structure is of the familiar contemporaneous correlation form, $E\mathbf{u}_*\mathbf{u}_*' = \Sigma \otimes I_{T-1}$.

If Z_* contains current endogenous variables then (25.5.17) can be estimated by generalized least squares using the error variance–covariance matrix $\Sigma \otimes I_{T-1}$ and purging Z_* of its stochastic elements via $\hat{Z}_*$, say. Assuming Σ and R are *known*, the desired three-stage least squares estimates applied to the transformed model are

$$\hat{\boldsymbol{\alpha}}_R = [\hat{Z}_R'(\Sigma^{-1} \otimes I_{T-1})\hat{Z}_R]^{-1}\hat{Z}_R'(\Sigma^{-1} \otimes I_{T-1})\mathbf{y}_R, \tag{25.5.18}$$

where $\hat{Z}_R = (\hat{Z}_* - (R' \otimes I_{T-1})Z_{*,-1})$ and $\mathbf{y}_R = (\mathbf{y}_* - (R' \otimes I_{T-1})\mathbf{y}_{*,-1})$. Note in $\hat{Z}_R$, $Z_{*,-1}$ does not have to be purged since it is not contemporaneously correlated with $\mathbf{u}_*$. The asymptotic variance–covariance matrix of $\sqrt{T}(\hat{\boldsymbol{\alpha}}_R - \boldsymbol{\alpha})$ is

$$\operatorname{plim}\left[\frac{1}{T} Z_R'(\Sigma^{-1} \otimes X(X'X)^{-1}X')Z_R\right]^{-1}, \tag{25.5.19}$$

where $Z_R = (Z_* - (R' \otimes I_{T-1})Z_{*,-1})$.

Unfortunately, Σ and R are rarely known *a priori*. Thus, to make $\hat{\boldsymbol{\alpha}}_R$ a feasible estimator, Σ and R must be consistently, and where necessary, efficiently estimated. We address feasible generalized least squares estimation of the vector autoregressive error model (25.5.10) and (25.5.11) under two different circumstances; the first case, where Z_* does not contain lagged dependent variables, is discussed in the next section; the second case, where Z_* contains lagged dependent variables, is discussed in the following section.

25.5.2 Two-Step Estimation of Simultaneous Equations with Vector Autoregressive Error Structure and No Lagged Dependent Variables

In the absence of lagged dependent variables, the model in question is

$$Y\Gamma + X\Delta + E = 0 \tag{25.5.20}$$

with

$$E = E_{-1}R + U. \tag{25.5.21}$$

The following steps provide a two-step feasible generalized least squares procedure which results in consistent, and in the case of normally distributed errors, asymptotically efficient estimation:

(1) Apply two-stage least squares to the entire system (25.5.12) (equivalently, two-stage least squares equation by equation) and obtain the consistent residual estimators

$$(\hat{\mathbf{e}}_{.1}, \hat{\mathbf{e}}_{.2}, \ldots, \hat{\mathbf{e}}_{.G}) = \hat{E}, \tag{25.5.22}$$

where $\hat{\mathbf{e}}_{.i} = \mathbf{y}_i - Z_i\hat{\boldsymbol{\alpha}}_i$, and $\hat{\boldsymbol{\alpha}}_i$ is the two-stage least squares estimator of the ith equation's coefficients.

(2) Regress $\hat{E}$ on $\hat{E}_{-1}$ and obtain a consistent estimate of R, namely

$$\hat{R} = (\hat{E}'_{-1}\hat{E}_{-1})^{-1}\hat{E}'_{-1}\hat{E}. \tag{25.5.23}$$

(3) Compute consistent estimates of U in one of two asymptotically (though not numerically) equivalent ways:

$$\hat{U} = \hat{E} - \hat{E}_{-1}\hat{R} \tag{25.5.24}$$

or computing residuals from Equation (25.5.17) using two-stage least squares.

(4) Estimate Σ with

$$\hat{\Sigma} = \frac{\hat{U}'\hat{U}}{T-1}. \tag{25.5.25}$$

Note that $\hat{\Sigma} = [\hat{\sigma}_{ij}]$, where $\hat{\sigma}_{ij} = \hat{\mathbf{u}}'_{.i}\hat{\mathbf{u}}_{.j}/(T-1)$.

(5) Using the consistent estimators $\hat{R}$ and $\hat{\Sigma}$, form the feasible generalized least squares estimator

$$\hat{\hat{\boldsymbol{\alpha}}}_R = (\hat{\hat{Z}}'_R(\hat{\Sigma}^{-1} \otimes I_{T-1})\hat{\hat{Z}}_R]^{-1}\hat{\hat{Z}}'_R(\hat{\Sigma}^{-1} \otimes I_{T-1})\hat{\mathbf{y}}_R, \tag{25.5.26}$$

where $\hat{\mathbf{y}}_R = (\mathbf{y}_* - (\hat{R}' \otimes I_{T-1})\mathbf{y}_{*,-1})$, $\hat{\hat{Z}}_R = (\hat{Z}_* - (\hat{R}' \otimes I_{T-1})Z_{*,-1})$, and $\hat{Z}_* = \text{diag}(\hat{Z}_1, \hat{Z}_2, \ldots, \hat{Z}_G)$ is the block diagonal matrix of purged regressors. For example, $\hat{Z}_i = (\hat{Y}_i, X_i) = [X(X'X)^{-1}X'Y_i, X_i]$ is the matrix of purged regressors for the ith equation.

The two-step feasible generalized least squares estimator $\hat{\hat{\alpha}}_R$ is asymptotically efficient, in the presence of normally distributed errors, and does not require further iteration. This is because the estimation of the regressor coefficients is independent of the estimation of the parameters of the error structure due to the absence of lagged dependent variables in the model. Note, that in the case that $\Gamma = -I$ in (25.5.20), we have the seemingly unrelated regression model with vector autoregressive errors studied by Guilkey and Schmidt (1973). Also note that overspecification of the error structure (specification of $R \neq 0$ when, in fact, $R = 0$) does not cost us anything asymptotically. As Guilkey and Schmidt show in the seemingly unrelated regression case, R has to be quite near zero before the feasible generalized least squares estimation procedure becomes expensive in terms of inferior small sample properties relative to seemingly unrelated regression and ordinary least squares estimation. However, there is a loss asymptotically from overspecification when lagged dependent variables are present (see Dhrymes and Erlat (1974)).

25.5.3 Tests of Hypotheses $R = 0$ and $R = \text{diag}(r_{11}, \ldots, r_{GG})$ when No Lagged Dependent Variables Are Present

The following discussion is based upon developments in Guilkey (1974). What we want to ascertain is the asymptotic distribution of $\sqrt{T}\,\text{vec}(\hat{R} - R)$, where $\hat{R}$ is the ordinary least squares estimator (25.5.23). We will show that

$$\sqrt{T}\,\text{vec}(\hat{R} - R) \sim N(\mathbf{0}, V), \tag{25.5.27}$$

where

$$\begin{aligned} V &= \left(\text{plim}\,\frac{U'U}{T} \otimes \text{plim}\left(\frac{\hat{E}'_{-1}\hat{E}_{-1}}{T}\right)^{-1}\right) \\ &= \Sigma \otimes \text{plim}\left(\frac{E'_{-1}E_{-1}}{T}\right)^{-1}. \end{aligned} \tag{25.5.28}$$

A small sample estimator of the variance–covariance matrix of $\text{vec}(\hat{R} - R)$ is

$$\hat{V}/T = \hat{\Sigma} \otimes (\hat{E}'_{-1}\hat{E}_{-1})^{-1}. \tag{25.5.29}$$

Now, as $T \to \infty$

$$\begin{aligned} \hat{R} &= (\hat{E}'_{-1}\hat{E}_{-1})^{-1}\hat{E}'_{-1}\hat{E} = (\hat{E}'_{-1}\hat{E}_{-1})^{-1}\hat{E}'_{-1}(\hat{E}_{-1}R + U) \\ &= R + (\hat{E}'_{-1}\hat{E}_{-1})^{-1}\hat{E}'_{-1}U. \end{aligned}$$

Therefore,

$$\begin{aligned}\operatorname{vec}(\hat{R} - R) &= (I \otimes A)\operatorname{vec}(U)\\ &= (I \otimes A)\begin{bmatrix}\mathbf{u}_{.1}\\ \vdots\\ \mathbf{u}_{.G}\end{bmatrix},\end{aligned}$$

where $A = (\hat{E}'_{-1}\hat{E}_{-1})^{-1}\hat{E}'_{-1}$. But, the variance–covariance matrix for $\operatorname{vec}(U)$ is $\operatorname{var}[\operatorname{vec}(U)] = \Sigma \otimes I$ and thus

$$\begin{aligned}\operatorname{var}[\operatorname{vec}(\hat{R} - R)] &= (I \otimes A)\operatorname{var}[\operatorname{vec}(U)](I \otimes A)'\\ &= (I \otimes A)(\Sigma \otimes I)(I \otimes A')\\ &= \Sigma \otimes AA'\\ &= \Sigma \otimes (\hat{E}'_{-1}\hat{E}_{-1})^{-1}.\end{aligned}$$

Then, asymptotically, $\sqrt{T}\operatorname{vec}(\hat{R} - R)$ has the variance–covariance matrix $\Sigma \otimes \operatorname{plim}(\hat{E}'_{-1}\hat{E}_{-1}/T)^{-1}$.

Under the null hypothesis that $R = 0$,

$$\operatorname{vec}(\hat{R})'[\hat{\Sigma} \otimes (\hat{E}'_{-1}\hat{E}_{-1})^{-1}]^{-1}\operatorname{vec}(\hat{R}) = \operatorname{vec}(\hat{R})'[\hat{\Sigma}^{-1} \otimes \hat{E}'_{-1}\hat{E}_{-1}]\operatorname{vec}(\hat{R}) \tag{25.5.30}$$

is asymptotically distributed as a chi-square random variable with G^2 degrees of freedom. A test of the null hypothesis that $R = \operatorname{diag}(r_{11}, r_{22}, \ldots, r_{GG})$ can also be constructed. Let $\bar{R}$ be the $(G^2 - G) \times 1$ vector formed by deleting the diagonal elements of R and stacking the columns. For example, in the two equation case

$$R = \begin{bmatrix} r_{11} & r_{12}\\ r_{21} & r_{22}\end{bmatrix} \quad \text{and} \quad \bar{R} = \begin{bmatrix} r_{21}\\ r_{12}\end{bmatrix}.$$

Similarly, define $\bar{V}$ as the $(G^2 - G) \times (G^2 - G)$ matrix formed by deleting the rows and columns of V indexed by the numbers $1, G + 2, 2G + 3, 3G + 4, \ldots, G^2$. These index numbers correspond to the deletion of $r_{11}, r_{22}, \ldots, r_{GG}$ in $\operatorname{vec}(R)$. Then asymptotically, under the null hypothesis that $\bar{R} = \mathbf{0}$,

$$\hat{\bar{R}}'(\hat{\bar{V}})^{-1}\hat{\bar{R}} \sim \chi^2_{G^2 - G}. \tag{25.5.31}$$

Guilkey (1974) discusses two additional asymptotically equivalent tests for the hypotheses $R = 0$ and $\bar{R} = 0$, Anderson's U-test (the multivariate analogue of the F-test) and the likelihood ratio test. In the context of a two-equation seemingly unrelated regressions model, Guilkey conducted Monte Carlo experiments to examine the small sample properties of the three competing test statistics. There appeared to be no basis for preferring any one test over the others. Moreover, a sample size of 50 or greater appeared to be sufficient for the validity of the asymptotic approximations.

25.5.4 Two-Step Estimation of a Simultaneous Equations Model with Vector Autoregressive Error Structure and Lagged Dependent Variables

When there are no lagged dependent variables in the simultaneous equations model (25.5.1) and (25.5.2), the asymptotic Cramér–Rao lower bound matrix (the inverse of the information matrix) takes the form of the block diagonal matrix

$$\begin{bmatrix} A & 0 \\ 0 & B \end{bmatrix},$$

where A is the lower bound matrix for the regression coefficients $\boldsymbol{\alpha}$ and B is the lower bound matrix for the error parameters R and Σ. This diagonality reflects the independence in the estimation of R and Σ from the estimation of $\boldsymbol{\alpha}$. Thus, the use of *any* consistent estimators of R and Σ, regardless of their efficiency, will provide an asymptotically efficient estimator of the regression coefficients $\boldsymbol{\alpha}$. No further iteration is necessary. This result is analogous to the case of feasible generalized least squares estimation in a single equation model when there is no contemporaneous correlation between the error term and regressors. Any consistent estimator of Ω will suffice (see Chapter 8).

However, as discussed previously in Section 11.4, when any of the regressors of a single equation model are contemporaneously correlated with the error term, the estimation of the regression coefficients $\boldsymbol{\beta}$ and the error parameters Ω are no longer independent of each other (the information matrix is no longer block diagonal). Thus, the efficient estimation of Ω is a prerequisite for efficient estimation via feasible generalized least squares. An analogous situation exists in the case of a simultaneous equations model with a vector autoregressive error process and lagged dependent variables. The estimation of R and Σ is no longer independent of the estimation of $\boldsymbol{\alpha}$. In order for two-step feasible generalized least squares estimation to provide an asymptotically efficient estimator of $\boldsymbol{\alpha}$, efficient estimators of R and Σ are needed. Alternatively, given inefficient, though consistent, estimates of R and Σ, further iteration of the feasible generalized least squares estimator is necessary. We will illustrate these concepts in the following discussion by first developing a consistent though asymptotically inefficient estimator and then presenting Hatanaka's residual adjusted two-step estimator which is asymptotically efficient.

The model we will be concerned with for the remainder of this section is of the form

$$\mathbf{y}_* = Z_*\boldsymbol{\alpha} + \mathbf{e}_*$$

with

$$\mathbf{e}_* = (R' \otimes I_T)\mathbf{e}_{*,-1} + \mathbf{u}_*.$$

However, it is assumed here that Z_* contains lagged dependent variables. Also $\mathbf{e}_*$ is assumed to have a multivariate normal distribution.

In detail the G equations are of the form

$$\begin{aligned} \mathbf{y}_i &= Y_i \boldsymbol{\gamma}_i + X_i \boldsymbol{\delta}_i + Y_{-1,i} \boldsymbol{\eta}_i + \mathbf{e}_i, \qquad i = 1, 2, \ldots, G \\ &= Z_i \boldsymbol{\alpha}_i + \mathbf{e}_i, \end{aligned} \tag{25.5.32}$$

where $Z_i = [Y_i, X_i, Y_{-1,i}]$ and $\boldsymbol{\alpha}_i = (\boldsymbol{\gamma}_i', \boldsymbol{\delta}_i', \boldsymbol{\eta}_i')'$.

25.5.4a *A Wallis-Like Two-Step Estimator*

We draw upon the analogies of Section 11.4 to create an asymptotically inefficient two-step feasible generalized least squares estimator of the present model. We choose to call it the Wallis-like estimator because of the correspondence that it has with Wallis' (1967) two-step estimator of a single equation model with lagged dependent variables and autocorrelated errors. Our choice of a label for the estimator does not imply that Wallis recommends (or recommended) it. Instead our choice is to emphasize the analogy.

The appropriate reduced form for the dynamic simultaneous equation model (25.5.1) with vector autoregressive error specification (25.5.2) is

$$\begin{aligned} Y &= -X\Delta\Gamma^{-1} - Y_{-1}\mathrm{H}\Gamma^{-1} - (E_{-1}R + U)\Gamma^{-1} \\ &= -X\Delta\Gamma^{-1} - Y_{-1}\mathrm{H}\Gamma^{-1} - [-(Y_{-1}\Gamma + X_{-1}\Delta + Y_{-2}\mathrm{H})R + U]\Gamma^{-1} \\ &= -X\Delta\Gamma^{-1} + Y_{-1}(\Gamma R - \mathrm{H})\Gamma^{-1} + X_{-1}\Delta R\Gamma^{-1} \\ &\quad + Y_{-2}\mathrm{H}R\Gamma^{-1} - U\Gamma^{-1} \\ &= X\Pi_1 + Y_{-1}\Pi_2 + X_{-1}\Pi_3 + Y_{-2}\Pi_4 + V, \end{aligned} \tag{25.5.33}$$

where $\Pi_1 = -\Delta\Gamma^{-1}$, $\Pi_2 = (\Gamma R - \mathrm{H})\Gamma^{-1}$, $\Pi_3 = \Delta R\Gamma^{-1}$, $\Pi_4 = \mathrm{H}R\Gamma^{-1}$, and $V = -U\Gamma^{-1}$. Applying ordinary least squares to (25.5.33) provides a consistent estimator for Y,

$$\check{Y} = X\hat{\Pi}_1 + Y_{-1}\hat{\Pi}_2 + X_{-3}\hat{\Pi}_3 + Y_{-2}\hat{\Pi}_4,$$

when lagged dependent variables are present.

To obtain consistent estimators of R and Σ, consider the following steps. Apply the instrumental variable estimator

$$\check{\boldsymbol{\alpha}}_i = [(\check{Y}_i, X_i, \check{Y}_{-1,i})'(Y_i, X_i, Y_{-1,i})]^{-1}(\check{Y}_i, X_i, \check{Y}_{-1,i})'\mathbf{y}_i, \tag{25.5.34}$$

to obtain a consistent estimator of $\boldsymbol{\alpha}_i$. Now compute the residuals

$$\check{\mathbf{e}}_{.i} = \mathbf{y}_i - Z_i\check{\boldsymbol{\alpha}}_i, \qquad i = 1, 2, \ldots, G, \tag{25.5.35}$$

and form the matrix

$$\check{E} = (\check{\mathbf{e}}_{.1}, \check{\mathbf{e}}_{.2}, \ldots, \check{\mathbf{e}}_{.G}). \tag{25.5.36}$$

A consistent estimator of R is

$$\check{R} = (\check{E}_{-1}'\check{E}_{-1})^{-1}\check{E}_{-1}'\check{E}. \tag{25.5.37}$$

Finally, we can form

$$\check{U} = \check{E} - \check{E}_{-1}\check{R} \tag{25.5.38}$$

and a consistent estimator of Σ is

$$\check{\Sigma} = \frac{\check{U}'\check{U}}{T-1}. \tag{25.5.39}$$

In light of these consistent estimates of R and Σ, consider the generalized Cochrane–Orcutt transformation of Equation (25.5.17). A Wallis-like two-step estimator can be obtained in the following manner. Apply two-step feasible generalized least squares estimation (i.e. three-stage least squares) with estimated error variance–covariance matrix $(\check{\Sigma} \otimes I_{T-1})$, $\check{R}$ substituted for R and $\check{Y}$ used to compute the "purged" regressor matrices, say $\check{Z}_*$. Following the parallel of Equation (25.5.26), the Wallis-like two-step estimator is

$$\check{\boldsymbol{\alpha}}_R = [\check{Z}_R'(\check{\Sigma}^{-1} \otimes I_{T-1})\check{Z}_R]^{-1}\check{Z}_R'(\check{\Sigma}^{-1} \otimes I_{T-1})\check{\mathbf{y}}_R, \tag{25.5.40}$$

where $\check{Z}_R = (\check{Z}_* - (\check{R}' \otimes I_{T-1})Z_{*,-1})$ and $\mathbf{y}_R = (\mathbf{y}_* - (\check{R}' \otimes I_{T-1})\mathbf{y}_{*,-1})$. The asymptotic variance–covariance matrix of $\sqrt{T}(\check{\boldsymbol{\alpha}}_R - \boldsymbol{\alpha})$ is

$$\operatorname{plim} \frac{1}{T}[Z_R'(\Sigma^{-1} \otimes \mathbf{X}(\mathbf{X}'\mathbf{X})^{-1}\mathbf{X}')Z_R]^{-1} \tag{25.5.41}$$

where $\mathbf{X} = (X, Y_{-1})$ is the full set of predetermined variables. The Wallis-like estimator is consistent but *not* asymptotically efficient. In essence the variance–covariance matrix of Equation (25.5.41) is too "big." This result arises because of the estimation of Γ, Δ, and H are not independent of the estimation of R and Σ. Therefore, two-step estimation using inefficient estimates of R and Σ is not adequate, asymptotically speaking, when lagged dependent variables are present. Additional iteration is needed or, alternatively, we can develop a simultaneous equations generalization of Hatanaka's residual adjusted two-step estimator for the single equation lagged dependent variable model with autocorrelated errors.

25.5.4b *Hatanaka's Residual Adjusted Two-Step Estimator for Simultaneous Equations with Vector Autoregressive Error Processes*

Hatanaka (1976) has devised a method of using the previously defined consistent estimates of R and Σ, $\check{R}$ and $\check{\Sigma}$, to obtain asymptotically efficient estimates of the regression coefficients $\boldsymbol{\alpha}$ in a dynamic simultaneous equations model with vector autoregressive errors. We briefly outline the method here. The interested reader should consult Hatanaka (1976) for detailed proofs.

Specify $\mathbf{y}_* - (\check{R}' \otimes I_{T-1})\mathbf{y}_{*,-1} \equiv \check{\mathbf{y}}_R$ as the dependent variable and $\check{Z}_* - (\check{R}' \otimes I_{T-1})Z_{*,-1} \equiv Z_R$ and $(I_G \otimes \check{E}_{-1}) \equiv \check{\xi}_{-1}$ as explanatory variable matrices of dimensions $(T-1)G \times m$ (m being the total number of right-hand side variables in the simultaneous equations model) and $(T-1)G \times G^2$, respectively. In addition $\check{Z}_*$ is the diagonal matrix with elements

$$\check{Z}_i = (\check{Y}_i, X_i, Y_{-1,i}), \qquad i = 1, 2, \ldots, G,$$

on the main diagonal. Now apply generalized least squares with estimated covariance matrix $(\check{\Sigma} \otimes I_{T-1})$,

$$\begin{bmatrix} \check{\boldsymbol{\alpha}}^{(1)} \\ \text{vec}\check{R}^{(1)} \end{bmatrix} = [(\check{Z}_R, \check{\xi}_{-1})'(\check{\Sigma} \otimes I_{T-1})^{-1}(\check{Z}_R, \check{\xi}_{-1})]^{-1} \times (\check{Z}_R, \check{\xi}_{-1})'(\check{\Sigma} \otimes I_{T-1})^{-1}\check{\mathbf{y}}_R. \tag{25.5.42}$$

Finally, let vec $\check{R}^{(2)} =$ vec $\check{R}^{(1)} +$ vec $\check{R}$. Then the Hatanaka residual adjusted Aitken estimators of $\boldsymbol{\alpha}$ and vec R are $\check{\boldsymbol{\alpha}}^{(1)}$ and vec $\check{R}^{(2)}$, respectively. Unlike the Wallis-like two-step estimator, the Hatanaka estimator is asymptotically efficient in that it achieves the asymptotic Cramér–Rao lower bound

$$\operatorname*{plim}_{T\to\infty}\left[-T^{-1}E\left[\frac{\partial^2 \ln L(\boldsymbol{\theta})}{\partial\boldsymbol{\theta}\,\partial\boldsymbol{\theta}'}\right]^{-1}\right].$$

25.5.5 Final Comments

To close this section, we include some final comments. First, Hatanaka (1976) discusses two other asymptotically efficient estimators which he attributes (at least the estimation ideas) to (i) Brundy and Jorgenson (1971) and (ii) Hannan and Terrell (1973). The small sample performance of these estimators was not investigated by a Monte Carlo study. Hendry (1971) and Dhrymes and Erlat (1974) examine full information maximum likelihood estimation of the present model.

Second, as far as testing $R = 0$ and $\bar{R} = 0$ in the presence of lagged dependent variables is concerned, an approach similar to that discussed in Section 25.5.3 could be used. Assume that $\check{V}$ is a consistent estimator of the asymptotic variance–covariance matrix of the Hatanaka estimator vec $\check{R}^{(2)}$. Under the null hypothesis $R = 0$,

$$\text{vec } \check{R}^{(2)\prime}[\check{V}]^{-1} \text{ vec } \check{R}^{(2)} \sim \chi_{G^2}, \tag{25.5.43}$$

Likewise, under the null hypothesis $\bar{R} = 0$,

$$\check{\bar{R}}^{(2)\prime}[\check{\bar{V}}]^{-1}\check{\bar{R}}^{(2)} \sim \chi^2_{G^2-G}, \tag{25.5.44}$$

where the matrices $\bar{R}$ and $\bar{V}$ are defined in Section 25.5.3. For discussions of similar tests of these hypotheses, see Guilkey (1975) and Maritz (1978).

Third, as noted by Dhrymes and Erlat (1974), if $R = 0$, but this fact is not used in the estimation procedure, then there is a loss of asymptotic efficiency in estimation. This result stands in contrast to the case where there are no lagged dependent variables. In such a case overspecification of R does not result in an asymptotic loss of efficiency. Thus, misspecification of autocorrelation is more serious in lagged dependent variable models than in models with no lagged dependent variables.

Fourth, note that, in order to achieve efficient prediction in the presence of lagged dependent variables and vector autoregressive errors, the appropriate reduced form is

$$Y = X\Pi_1 + Y_{-1}\Pi_2 + X_{-1}\Pi_3 + Y_{-2}\Pi_4 + V \tag{25.5.45}$$

instead of

$$\begin{aligned} Y &= -X\Delta\Gamma^{-1} - Y_{-1}\mathrm{H}\Gamma^{-1} - (E_{-1}R + U)\Gamma^{-1} \\ &= X\Pi_1^* + Y_{-1}\Pi_2^* + V^*, \end{aligned} \tag{25.5.46}$$

where $\Pi_1^* = -\Delta\Gamma^{-1}$, $\Pi_2^* = -\mathrm{H}\Gamma^{-1}$, and $V^* = -(E_{-1}R + U)\Gamma^{-1}$. Application of ordinary least squares to Equation (25.5.46) results in inconsistent estimation of Y since Y_{-1} and V^* are contemporaneously correlated. Efficient prediction is provided by using derived reduced form estimates generated from an asymptotically efficient estimation process, for example,

$$\check{\Pi}_1 = -\check{\Delta}\check{\Gamma}^{-1}, \check{\Pi}_2 = (\check{\Gamma}\check{R} - \check{\mathrm{H}})\check{\Gamma}^{-1}, \check{\Pi}_3 = \check{\Delta}\check{R}\check{\Gamma}^{-1},$$

and $\check{\Pi}_4 = \check{\mathrm{H}}\check{R}\check{\Gamma}^{-1}$, where $\check{\Delta}$, $\check{\Gamma}$, $\check{\mathrm{H}}$, and $\check{R}$ represent Hatanaka residual adjusted estimates.

Finally, the dynamic multipliers derived in Section 24.2 are no longer appropriate in the presence of a vector autoregressive error process. The appropriate multipliers are obtained by repeated substitution for lagged values of Y in (25.5.44). Knight (1982) has derived the asymptotic distributions of the restricted reduced form and dynamic multipliers in the lagged dependent variable–vector autoregressive error case. Also Baillie (1981) has extended the work of Schmidt (1974) by deriving the asymptotic distributions of the dynamic simulation forecasts for the same case.

25.5.6 References

Baillie, R. T. (1981). Prediction from the dynamic simultaneous equation model with vector autoregressive errors. *Econometrica*, **49**, 1331–1337.

Brundy, J. M. and Jorgenson, D. W. (1971). Efficient estimation of simultaneous equations by instrumental variables. *Review of Economics and Statistics*, **53**, 207–224.

Dhrymes, P. J. and Erlat, H. (1974). Asymptotic properties of full information estimators in dynamic autoregressive simultaneous equation models. *Journal of Econometrics*, **2**, 247–259.

Fair, R. C. (1970). The estimation of simultaneous equation models with lagged endogenous variables and first order serially correlated errors. *Econometrica*, **38**, 507–516.

Granger, C. W. J. and Newbold, P. (1977). *Forecasting Economic Time Series*. New York: Academic Press.

Guilkey, D. K. (1974). Alternative tests for a first-order vector autoregressive error specification. *Journal of Econometrics*, **2**, 95–104.
Guilkey, D. K. (1975). A test for the presence of first-order vector autoregressive errors when lagged endogenous variables are present. *Econometrica*, **43**, 711–717.
Guilkey, D. K. and Schmidt, P. (1973). Estimation of seemingly unrelated regressions with vector autoregressive errors. *Journal of the American Statistical Association*, **68**, 642–647.
Hannan, E. J. and Terrell, R. D. (1973). Multiple equation systems with stationary errors. *Econometrica*, **41**, 299–320.
Hatanaka, M. (1976). Several efficient two-step estimators for the dynamic simultaneous equations model with autoregressive disturbances. *Journal of Econometrics*, **4**, 189–204.
Hendry, D. F. (1981). Maximum likelihood estimation of systems of simultaneous regression equations with errors generated by a vector autoregressive process. *International Economic Review*, **12**, 257–272.
Knight, J. L. (1982). Asymptotic distribution of restricted reduced forms and dynamic multipliers in a linear dynamic model with vector autoregressive errors. *International Economic Review*, **23**, 553–563.
Maritz, A. (1978). A note of correction to Guilkey's test for serial independence in simultaneous equations models. *Econometrica*, **46**, 471.
Schmidt, P. (1974). The asymptotic distribution of forecasts in the dynamic simulation of an econometric model. *Econometrica*, **42**, 303–309.
Wallis, K. F. (1967). Lagged dependent variables and serially correlated errors: a reappraisal of three-pass least squares. *Review of Economics and Statistics*, **49**, 555–567.

25.6 Rational Expectations

Various hypotheses have been proposed to generate unobservable expectations variables for econometric models. Futures prices (Turnovsky (1979), Peck (1976), Gardner (1976)), Delphi methods or pooled judgments (Dalkey *et al.* (1972), Carlson (1977), Mullineaux (1978)) and more structured approaches to subjective distributions on the variables in question (Johnson and Rausser (1983)) are examples of less conventional methods not involving the sample data. Alternatively, extrapolative or adaptive expectations (Nerlove (1958, 1972)) use lagged values to proxy the variables in question. Finally, rational expectations models (Muth 1961)) assume that the mechanism generating the unobservable expectations variables is consistent with the structure determining their realized values. Methods of operationalizing this approach are now available (Aoki and Canzoneri (1979), Chavas and Johnson (1983), McCallum (1976a), Nelson (1975a, 1975b), Sargent and Wallace (1975), Woglom (1979)).

25.6.1 Rationality and Model Specification

The formation of rational expectations depends on the information available to economic agents and the way it is used. For a given information set, the rational hypothesis assumes that expectations of the decisionmakers are distributed about the prediction from the theory (Muth (1961)). That is, for rationality, information is processed using the structure relevant to the economic activity in question. For applied work, this means that expectations must be consistent with the structure of the econometric model for the system under study. Thus, implementing rational expectations in applied econometrics requires special assumptions on the characteristics of agents modeled and the structure of the economic system in which they function. Information available, knowledge of the economic structure, and the intent of the modeling exercise all affect the way the rationality hypothesis is implemented.

To illustrate the consequences of rational expectations for econometric modeling, consider the standard linear model for an equation system

$$B\mathbf{y}_t + \sum_{i=1}^{M} (\Gamma_i \mathbf{y}_{t-i}) + \sum_{i=0}^{P} (\phi_i \mathbf{x}_{t-i}) + \sum_{i=1}^{N} (\Delta_i \mathbf{y}^*_{t+i|t}) + \mathbf{e}_t = \mathbf{0}, \quad (25.6.1)$$

where $\mathbf{y}_t$, $\mathbf{y}_{t-i}$ $(i = 1, \ldots, M)$, $\mathbf{x}_{t-i}$ $(i = 0, \ldots, P)$, $\mathbf{y}^*_{t+i|t}$ $(i = 1, \ldots, N)$ denote; the tth observation of the G observable endogenous variables, the lagged endogenous variables, the K observable exogenous variables contemporaneous and lagged up to P periods, and finally, the G unobservable expectations $\mathbf{y}^*_{t+i|t}$ for $\mathbf{y}_{t+i}$ formulated at time t $(i = 1, \ldots, N)$, respectively. The matrices, B, Γ_i, ϕ_i, and Δ_i are appropriately dimensioned arrays of structural parameters. Assumptions for the disturbance term $\mathbf{e}_t$ complete the definition of the simultaneous system.

$$E(\mathbf{e}_t) = \mathbf{0}$$

and

$$E(\mathbf{e}_t \mathbf{e}'_{t'}) = \begin{cases} \mathbf{0} & t \neq t', \\ \Sigma, & t = t, \end{cases}$$

with Σ a positive definite contemporaneous covariance matrix.

For simplicity of exposition and following Chavas and Johnson (1983), it is assumed that expectations are generated for N future periods. Thus, the planning period for the system is up to N periods. The value N in applied situations would be determined by the technology, institutions and/or the economic theory supporting the specification. Practically, the assumption means that expectations for variables at times greater than $t + N$ are not relevant to decisionmaking process at time t. Finally, note that since rationality implies the expectations $\mathbf{y}^*_{t+j}$ become endogenous to the structure, each unobservable expectation variable must have a counterpart endogenous variable in the system.

Now consider Equation (25.6.1) at time $t + j$. The mathematical expectation for the model based on information available at time t is

$$BE_t(\mathbf{y}_{t+j}) + \sum_{i=1}^{M} \Gamma_i E_t(\mathbf{y}_{t+j-i}) + \sum_{i=0}^{P} \phi_i E_t(\mathbf{x}_{t+j-i})$$
$$+ \sum_{i=1}^{N} \Delta_i E_t(\mathbf{y}^*_{t+j+i|t}) = \mathbf{0}. \quad (25.6.2)$$

The rationality hypothesis is based on this expected version of (25.6.1),

$$B\mathbf{y}^*_{t+j|t} + \sum_{i=1}^{M} \Gamma_i \mathbf{y}^*_{t+j-i|t} + \sum_{i=0}^{P} \phi_i \mathbf{x}^*_{t+j-i|t} + \sum_{i=1}^{N} \Delta_i \mathbf{y}^*_{t+j+i|t} = \mathbf{0}, \quad (25.6.3)$$

where $\mathbf{y}^*_{t+j-i|t} = \mathbf{y}_{t+j-i}$ when $(j - i) \leq 0$ given the assumption of weak consistency or that the rational expectation of a value at time t is the observed value. The notation adopted is to indicate the expectation at t of $\mathbf{y}_{t+j}$, $\mathbf{y}_{t+j|t}$.

Equation (25.6.3) shows that the expectations $\mathbf{y}^*_{t+j|t}$ are formed using the econometric model structure at time $t + j$, based on the information available at time t. Of course, Equation (25.6.3) contains a number of other unobservable variables. However, the assumed planning period is of length N. Thus, all expectations of variables at times greater than $t + N$ can be deleted from the model. Specifically, for values of the endogenous variables further into the future, information available for conditioning the expectation is not sufficient to influence the behavior of the agents. If the variables for the model are expressed as deviations from their unconditional means, then expectations for periods greater than $t + N$ can be replaced by zeros, truncating the expression.

From Equation (25.6.3), the model for $(j = 1, \ldots, N)$, can be written

$$\begin{bmatrix} \Delta_{n-1} & & \cdots & & \Delta_1 & & B \\ \Delta_{n-2} & & \cdots & \Delta_1 & B & & \Gamma_1 \\ \vdots & & & & & & \vdots \\ \Delta_1 & & & & & & \\ B & \Gamma_1 & \cdots & \Gamma_M & 0 & \cdots & 0 \end{bmatrix} \begin{bmatrix} \mathbf{y}^*_{t+N|t} \\ \mathbf{y}^*_{t+N-1|t} \\ \vdots \\ \\ \mathbf{y}^*_{t+1|t} \end{bmatrix}$$

$$+ \begin{bmatrix} \Gamma_1 & \Gamma_2 & \cdots & & \Gamma_M \\ \Gamma_2 & & \cdots & \Gamma_M & 0 \\ \vdots & & & & \vdots \\ \Gamma_M & 0 & \cdots & & 0 \end{bmatrix} \begin{bmatrix} \mathbf{y}_t \\ \mathbf{y}_{t-1} \\ \vdots \\ \mathbf{y}_{t-M+1} \end{bmatrix}$$

$$+ \begin{bmatrix} 0 & & \cdots & 0 & \phi_0 \\ 0 & & \cdots & \phi_0 & \phi_1 \\ \vdots & & & & \vdots \\ \phi_0 & \phi_1 & \cdots & & \end{bmatrix} \begin{bmatrix} \mathbf{x}^*_{t+N|t} \\ \\ \vdots \\ \\ \mathbf{x}^*_{t+1|t} \end{bmatrix}$$

$$+ \begin{bmatrix} \phi_1 & \phi_2 & \cdots & & \phi_P \\ \phi_2 & & \cdots & \phi_P & 0 \\ \vdots & & & & \vdots \\ \phi_P & 0 & \cdots & & 0 \end{bmatrix} \begin{bmatrix} \mathbf{x}_{t-1+1} \\ \\ \vdots \\ \\ \mathbf{x}_{t-P+1} \end{bmatrix} = \mathbf{0},$$

or more compactly,

$$C\mathbf{y}^*_t + D\mathbf{y}_{Lt} + F\mathbf{x}^*_t + G\mathbf{x}_{Lt} = \mathbf{0}. \quad (25.6.4)$$

Assuming that C (a square matrix) is nonsingular, the reduced form for Equation (25.6.4) is

$$\mathbf{y}_t^* = \Pi_1 \mathbf{y}_{Lt} + \Pi_2 \mathbf{x}_t^* + \Pi_3 \mathbf{x}_{Lt}, \tag{25.6.5}$$

where $\Pi_1 = -C^{-1}D$, $\Pi_2 = -C^{-1}F$, and $\Pi_3 = -C^{-1}G$. Equation (25.6.5) is the rational structure for generating expectations of the endogenous variables, $\mathbf{y}_t^*$.

The rational hypothesis implies that the expectations are functions of predetermined variables and the projected values of the predetermined in future periods. Implications of implementing the rationality hypothesis, Equation (25.6.1) can be rewritten as

$$[B\ \Gamma_1 \cdots \Gamma_M]\mathbf{y}_{Lt} + [\Delta_N \cdots \Delta_1]\mathbf{y}_t^* + [\phi_0 \cdots \phi_P]\mathbf{x}_{Lt} + \mathbf{e}_t = \mathbf{0}. \tag{25.6.6}$$

Substituting the reduced form equation (25.6.5) into the rewritten structural equation (25.6.6) yields,

$$[(B\ \Gamma_1 \cdots \Gamma_M) + \Delta\Pi_1]\mathbf{y}_{Lt} + (\Delta\Pi_2)\mathbf{x}_t^* + [(\phi_0 \cdots \phi_P) + \Delta\Pi_3]\mathbf{x}_{Lt} + \mathbf{e}_t = \mathbf{0}, \tag{25.6.7}$$

where $\Delta = (\Delta_N, \ldots, \Delta_1)$. Thus, expression (25.6.7) is a partial reduced form obtained by substituting the derived expressions for the expectations variables into the original structure. It relates the current endogenous variables ($\mathbf{y}_t$) to the lagged endogenous variables ($\mathbf{y}_{t-j}$), the current and lagged predetermined variables ($\mathbf{x}_{Lt}$), and the *projected values* of the predetermined variables for future periods ($\mathbf{x}_t^*$). In short, expectations of future endogenous variables have been processed by the model structure and then substituted back into the model.

The only variables concerning future time periods which remain in Equation (25.6.7) are the predetermined variables, $\mathbf{x}_t^*$. Since the economic structure underlying rational hypothesis cannot aid in identifying future exogenous or predetermined shocks, values for $\mathbf{x}_t^*$ must be generated externally. Interestingly, future values of the predetermined variables or a structure for generating them or instruments for these variables must be posited to complete the system. Otherwise the model is not complete and the rationality hypothesis will not be applicable.

25.6.2 Estimation

Expression (25.6.7) provides the basis for the design of an estimation procedure for the model (25.6.1). Alternatively, the model (25.6.7) can be expressed as

$$\alpha_1 \mathbf{y}_{Lt} + \alpha_2 \mathbf{x}_t^* + \alpha_3 \mathbf{x}_{Lt} + \mathbf{e}_t = \mathbf{0}, \tag{25.6.8}$$

where $\alpha_1 = [(B \ \Gamma_1 \cdots \Gamma_M) + \Delta\Pi_1]$, $\alpha_2 = \Delta\Pi_2$, and $\alpha_3 = [(\phi_0 \ \phi_1 \cdots \phi_P) + \Delta\Pi_3]$. Assuming $\mathbf{x}_t^*$ a vector of projectable predetermined variables, Equation (25.6.8) represents a standard form for a system of simultaneous structural equations. Thus, it can be estimated by conventional methods, given appropriate assumptions for $\mathbf{x}_t^*$ and the structural disturbances $\mathbf{e}_t$. For example, under the previously indicated assumptions, consistent estimators of α_1, α_2, and α_3 can be obtained by applying two-stage or three-stage least squares.

If the objective is to use the model for predictions, expression (25.6.8) as estimated provides the required results for incorporating rationality into the econometric model. Equation (25.6.8) is in fact a partial reduced form that suppresses the expectations determination structure. On the other hand, if the objective is to investigate the structure of the process for generating the rational expectations, then estimates for the parameters B, Δ_i, ϕ_i, and Γ_i are required. In restricted form, including the *a priori* information from the initial structural specification and the rationality hypothesis, equation (25.6.7) can be written

$$[(B \ \Gamma_1 \cdots \Gamma_M) - \Delta C^{-1}D]\mathbf{y}_{Lt} - (\Delta C^{-1}F)\mathbf{x}_t^* + [(\phi_0 \cdots \phi_P) - \Delta C^{-1}G]\mathbf{x}_{Lt} + \mathbf{e}_t = \mathbf{0}. \quad (25.6.9)$$

Observe that Equation (25.6.9) is nonlinear in the parameters (B, Δ_i, ϕ_i, and Γ_i) and, therefore, must be estimated by appropriate nonlinear methods. Error assumptions and conditions on $\mathbf{x}_t^*$ for assuring consistent estimators of the parameters are standard. Hoffman and Schmidt (1981) have investigated restrictions implied by (25.6.9) when the $\mathbf{x}_t^*$ is assumed generated by a first-order autoregressive process. They also have suggested testing for rationality based on comparisons of the unrestricted, Equation (25.6.7), and restricted, equation (25.6.9), in structural econometric models.

Generally, there are an array of methods that can be used to obtain estimators for models incorporating rational expectations. These can be understood by comparing expressions for the model (25.6.5), (25.6.7), and (25.6.9). Clearly, Equation (25.6.5) is just an expression for instrumental variables for $\mathbf{y}_t^*$ implied by the structure of the model for the economic system. Other instruments for these variables can produce consistent estimators (McCallum (1976a, 1976b), Nelson (1975a, 1975b)). Also, the unrestricted reduced form estimators can be used (Sargent (1978), Sargent and Wallace (1975)). But the full impact of the prior information implied by the rationality hypothesis can, abstracting from nonlinearity problems, be obtained only by introducing the restrictions for Π_1, Π_2 and Π_3 in Equation (25.6.5) as in Equation (25.6.9).

25.6.3 Applications

In view of the simplicity of the rationality hypothesis for standard simultaneous estimation problems, it is surprising that the approach is not more commonly applied. With time series, trended or other projections of the predetermined variables in Equations (25.6.8) and even (25.6.9) are relatively easy to estimate. In addition, problems encountered in applying the rationality hypothesis can point to important limitations of the structural models. Notice from Equation (25.6.9) that, if the conditioning on predetermined variables can not be projected with accuracy, the instruments for $\mathbf{y}_t^*$ will not be closely correlated with the realized values. Also, the fact that the $\mathbf{x}_t^*$'s may have to be projected at similar values can imply important problems of multicollinearity. All this highlights concerns about building econometric models using predetermined or exogenous variables that can not be accurately projected (Popkin (1975), Feldstein (1971)).

A final comment on rationality, tests for rationality and the frailty of the concept for applied work is in order. Tests for rationality are conditioned on the choice of a structure for projecting the predetermined variables, $\mathbf{x}_t^*$. But there is frequently no basis in theory for suggesting how these variables should be projected. As well, economic time series are of such length as to imply problems in identifying common ARIMA processes (Granger and Newbold 1977)). The result is that agents may not exhibit rationality although appearing to operate consistently with the structural model. They may be operating with a simplified version of the model more consistent with their ability to project the predetermined variables (Chavas and Johnson (1983)). These observations argue for parsimonious models.

25.6.4 Exercises

25.6.1. Consider the two equation supply and demand model

$$y_{t1}a_{11} + y_{t2}a_{21} + x_{t1}b_{11} + x_{t2}b_{21} + e_{t1} = 0,$$

$$y_{t1}a_{12} + b_{02}y_{t+1,2}^* + x_{t2}b_{22} + x_{t3}b_{32} + e_{t2} = 0,$$

where y_2 is the price. Let the first equation represent demand and the second supply. Thus, the supply is conditioned by an expected price in the period $t + 1$. Show how the model can be estimated, assuming that $y_{t+1,2}^*$ is a rational expectation. Also, show explicitly how one could test for the validity of the rationality hypothesis.

25.6.2. Consider the model in Exercise 25.6.1, again, and assume that we include a proxy variable, say $y_{t-1,2}$ for $y_{t+1,2}$ and then use lagged values of the x's to form an instrument for $y_{t-1,2}$. Will this process yield consistent estimators for the structural parameters? Compare your conclusions to those of McCallum (1976a, 1976b) and Nelson (1975a, 1975b).

25.6.3. Consider the Exercise 25.6.2 but assume that $y_{t-1,2}$ was introduced due to an adaptive expectations hypothesis (Nerlove (1958)). Compare the exprsessions for estimators of the structural parameters to those from Exercise 25.6.2. (Note, be careful about how you specify the structural covariance matrix, it is the key.)

25.6.4. Consider Exercise 25.6.1 again. Assume that the x's follow a first order autoregressive process. Then assume that the same x's follow a second order autoregressive process. How does this assumption affect the estimation method under the rationality hypothesis (see Hoffman and Schmidt (1981)).

25.6.5 References

Aoki, M. and Canzoneri, M. (1979). Reduced forms of rational expectations models. *Quarterly Journal of Economics*, **93**, 59–71.

Carlson, J. A. (1977). A study of price forecasts. *Annals of Economics and Social Measurement*, **6**, 27–56.

Chavas, J. and Johnson, S. R. (1983). Rational expectations in econometric models. In *New Directions in Econometric Modeling and Forecasting in U.S. Agriculture*. Edited by C. R. Rausser. New York: Elsevier–North Holland.

Dalkey, N. C., Rourke, D. L., Lewis, R., and Snyder, D. (1972). *Studies in the Quality of Life; Delphi Decision Making*. Lexington, MA: Lexington Books.

Feldstein, M. (1971). The error of forecast in econometric models when the forecast-period exogenous variables are stochastic. *Econometrica*, **39**, 55–60.

Gardner, B. L. (1976). Futures prices in supply analysis. *American Journal of Agricultural Economics*, **58**, 81–84.

Granger, C. W. J. and Newbold, P. (1977). *Forecasting Economic Time Series*. New York: Academic Press.

Hoffman, D. L. and Schmidt, P. (1981). Testing the restrictions implied by the rational expectations hypothesis. *Journal of Econometrics*, **15**, 265–87.

Johnson, S. R. and Rausser, G. C. (1983). Composite forecasting in commodity systems. In *New Directions in Econometric Modeling and Forecasting in U.S. Agriculture*. Edited by G. C. Rausser. New York: Elsevier North-Holland.

McCallum, B. T. (1976a). Rational expectations and the estimation of econometric models: an alternative procedure. *International Economic Review*, **17**, 485–490.

McCallum, B. T. (1976b). Rational expectations and the natural rate hypothesis: some consistent estimates. *Econometrica*, **44**, 42–52.

Mullineaux, D. J. (1978). On testing for rationality: another look at the Livingston price expectations data. *Journal of Political Economy*, **86**, 329–336.

Muth, J. F. (1961). Rational expectations and the theory of price movements. *Econometrica*, **29**, 315–335.

Nelson, C. R. (1975a). Rational expectations and the estimation of econometric models. *International Economic Review*, **16**, 555–561.

Nelson, C. R. (1975b). Rational expectations and predictive economic models. *Journal of Business*, **47**, 331–343.

Nerlove, M. (1972). Lags in economic behavior. *Econometrica*, **40**, 221–251.

Nerlove, M. (1958). Adaptive expectations and cobweb phenomena. *Quarterly Journal of Economics*, **73**, 227–240.

Peck, A. E. (1976). Futures markets, supply responses and price stability. *Quarterly Journal of Economics*, **90**, 407–423.

Popkin, J. (1975). Some avenues for the improvement of price forecasts generated by macroeconomic models. *American Journal of Agricultural Economics*, **57**, 157–163.

Sargent, T. J. (1978). Rational expectations, econometric exogeneity and consumption. *Journal of Political Economy*, **86**, 673–700.

Sargent, T. J. and Wallace, N. (1975). Rational expectations, the optimal monetary instrument and the optimal money supply rule. *Journal of Political Economy*, **83**, 241–254.

Turnovsky, S. J. (1979). Futures markets, private storage, and price stabilization. *Journal of Political Economy*, **12**, 301–327.
Woglom, J. (1979). Rational expectations and monetary policy in a simple macroeconomic model. *Quarterly Journal of Economics*, **59**, 91–105.

25.7 Updating

The updating problem is one of utilizing added sample or other prior information to improve the parameter estimates for a statistical model. For the present, the statistical model employed will be the classical normal linear model as defined in Section 2.2. The model is of the form

$$\mathbf{y} = X\boldsymbol{\beta} + \mathbf{e} \tag{25.7.1}$$

with X of full rank and the elements of $\mathbf{e}$ normally, identically and independently distributed with mean zero and variance σ^2. As before, let the sample size be T so that $\mathbf{y}$ is $T \times 1$ and assume there are K explanatory variables, $\boldsymbol{\beta}$ is $K \times 1$. Finally, let X and $\boldsymbol{\beta}$ be conformably defined.

In the econometric literature, the analysis of updating problems has dealt with the use of Kalman filtering procedures and related methods (Belsey (1973a, 1973b), Chow (1975, 1981)). These procedures and methods are derived on the basis of a result due to Kalman (1960), who showed that the filter to be discussed provides for optimal incorporation of additional sample information in estimating parameters of the linear model, Equation (25.7.1). The approach utilized for developing the result of Kalman illustrates how the concept of updating can be extended to include stochastic and deterministic linear restrictions on the parameters that may not come necessarily from additional sample information. Thus, for purposes of econometric analysis where sample data are limited, and usually passively generated, the approach indicates how added information on the model parameters, however obtained, can be used to update the estimates. The framework used to develop these results is mixed estimation (Rausser *et al.* (1983)).

25.7.1 Mixed Estimation and Kalman Filtering

Assume that in addition to the original sample observations for the model (25.7.1), there is a set of n (≥ 1) additional stochastic restrictions on the structural parameters, $\boldsymbol{\beta}$. Denote these stochastic restrictions as

$$\mathbf{y}_n = X_n\boldsymbol{\beta} + \mathbf{e}_n. \tag{25.7.2}$$

For the present assume that the elements of $\mathbf{e}_n$ have the same distribution as those of $\mathbf{e}$. The standard mixed estimation problem, combining the two sets of linear stochastic restrictions is

$$\begin{bmatrix} \mathbf{y} \\ \mathbf{y}_n \end{bmatrix} = \begin{bmatrix} X \\ X_n \end{bmatrix} \boldsymbol{\beta} + \begin{bmatrix} \mathbf{e} \\ \mathbf{e}_n \end{bmatrix} \tag{25.7.3}$$

with the corresponding estimator for $\boldsymbol{\beta}$ (see Section 6.3)

$$\hat{\boldsymbol{\beta}}_{T+n} = (X'X + X_n'X_n)^{-1}(X'\mathbf{y} + X_n'\mathbf{y}_n). \tag{25.7.4}$$

Simple extensions or adaptations of this estimator for: (1) different distributions for elements of $\mathbf{e}$ than $\mathbf{e}_n$ (Theil (1971)), (2) nonstochastic additional restrictions, the distribution of $\mathbf{e}_n$ degenerate at zero (Brook and Wallace (1973)) and (3) covariance assumptions permitting nonindependence between elements of $\mathbf{e}_n$ and $\mathbf{e}$ (Theil (1974)) can be developed. In general, they imply particular generalized least squares estimators for $\boldsymbol{\beta}_{T+n}$. Since methods of obtaining generalized least squares estimators have been reviewed in Section 2.8 and Chapter 8, respectively, the current discussion is confined to the situation where the elements of $\mathbf{e}$ and $\mathbf{e}_n$ are appropriate for the estimator (25.7.4) to be unbiased and efficient.

Using a matrix inversion lemma (Sage and Melsa (1971), Murata (1982, p. 84)) that has been applied conveniently in updating, note that the first term on the left-hand side of Equation (25.7.4) can be written,

$$\begin{aligned}(X'X &+ X_n'X_n)^{-1} \\ &= (X'X)^{-1} - (X'X)^{-1}X_n(I + X_n(X'X)^{-1}X_n')^{-1}X_n'(X'X)^{-1}.\end{aligned} \tag{25.7.5}$$

Substituting this result into Equation (25.7.4) and making appropriate algebraic simplifications yields the expression

$$\hat{\boldsymbol{\beta}}_{T+n} = \hat{\boldsymbol{\beta}}_T + K_{T+n}(\mathbf{y}_n - X_n\hat{\boldsymbol{\beta}}_T), \tag{25.7.6}$$

where $\hat{\boldsymbol{\beta}}_T$ is the ordinary least squares estimator from the original T observations and K_{T+n}, the Kalman filter, is

$$K_{T+n} = (X'X)^{-1}X_n(I + X_n(X'X)^{-1}X_n')^{-1}. \tag{25.7.7}$$

The interpretation for Equation (25.7.6) is that the additional stochastic restrictions (25.7.2) are used to "update" the estimator $\hat{\boldsymbol{\beta}}_T$ by applying the matrix of proportionality or the Kalman filter, K_{T+n}, to the prediction error $(\mathbf{y}_n - X_n\hat{\boldsymbol{\beta}}_T)$ resulting from the use of the "un-updated" estimator $\hat{\boldsymbol{\beta}}_T$.

The way that this information (prediction error) is processed by Kalman filter can be better understood by writing it alternatively. Specifically, observe that (25.7.7) can be expressed as

$$K_{T+n} = \operatorname{var}(\hat{\boldsymbol{\beta}}_T)X_n'[\sigma^2 I + X_n \operatorname{var}(\hat{\boldsymbol{\beta}}_T)X_n']^{-1}. \tag{25.7.8}$$

The term in the brackets on the right-hand side of Equation (25.7.8) is the sum of the variance of the forecast for $\mathbf{y}_n$ based on the parameter estimator

$\hat{\boldsymbol{\beta}}_T$ and the variance of $\mathbf{y}_n$. Thus, other things equal, as the variance of the forecast based on $\hat{\boldsymbol{\beta}}_T$ or the variance of $\mathbf{y}_n$ increases, the adjustment to $\hat{\boldsymbol{\beta}}_T$ based on the added information will be smaller. This effect is counterbalanced by the first term in the right-hand side of Equation (25.7.8). According to this first term, $\text{var}(\hat{\boldsymbol{\beta}}_T)$, if the reason for the result implied by the value in the brackets is a large variance for $\hat{\boldsymbol{\beta}}_T$, then other things equal, the adjustment to $\hat{\boldsymbol{\beta}}_T$ based on the prediction error $(\mathbf{y}_n - X_n\hat{\boldsymbol{\beta}}_T)$ will be larger. In the latter case, the result says simply that if one does not know much about $\boldsymbol{\beta}$ based on the T original sample observations, prediction errors will be more important in changing the estimator to $\hat{\boldsymbol{\beta}}_{T+n}$. These intuitive interpretations of the Kalman filter K_{T+n} are most unambiguously seen by letting $n = 1$.

The covariance matrix for $\hat{\boldsymbol{\beta}}_{T+n}$ in the mixed estimation context is

$$\text{var}(\hat{\boldsymbol{\beta}}_{T+n}) = \sigma^2(X'X + X_n'X_n)^{-1}.$$

Applying the inversion lemma (25.6.7) again, the covariance matrix in a form more consistent with the filtering results is,

$$\text{var}(\hat{\boldsymbol{\beta}}_{T+n}) = \text{var}(\hat{\boldsymbol{\beta}}_T) - \mathrm{K}_{T+n}DK_{T+n}', \tag{25.7.9}$$

where,

$$D = I + X_n(X'X)^{-1}X_n'.$$

Since $K_{T+n}DK_{T+n}'$ is positive semidefinite, the estimator $\hat{\boldsymbol{\beta}}_{T+n}$ has a variance at least as small as $\hat{\boldsymbol{\beta}}_T$.

25.7.2 Implications for Experimental Design

These updating results have interesting implications for evaluating contributions of additional observations (or more properly stochastic or nonstochastic linear restrictions) on the "quality" of the estimator $\hat{\boldsymbol{\beta}}_{T+n}$. Additional information for the estimation problem can be passively or experimentally generated. If data are passively generated, the question for say additional time series observations, is how frequently should the model be reestimated. Alternatively, can we tell without reestimation, whether the estimator $\hat{\boldsymbol{\beta}}_{T+n}$ will have a distribution much different from that of $\hat{\boldsymbol{\beta}}_T$? The answer is yes. In a different context, if we are at liberty to choose X_n in an experimental context, is there a systematic basis for making such choices so that $\hat{\boldsymbol{\beta}}_{T+n}$ will be somehow optimally better than $\hat{\boldsymbol{\beta}}_T$? Again, the answer is yes.

To illustrate the value of the updating results for experimentation and the evaluation of passively generated "additional" stochastic restrictions, it is useful to revert to the mixed estimation format for the updating problem.

Suppose that a variance norm for the estimators is adopted. That is, the criterion for improved estimation of the parameters $\boldsymbol{\beta}$ is a function of a smaller sampling variance. The improvement in variance resulting from the additional stochastic (or nonstochastic) restrictions can be written

$$\begin{aligned}\Delta \operatorname{var}(\hat{\boldsymbol{\beta}}_{T+n}) &= \operatorname{var}(\hat{\boldsymbol{\beta}}_{T+n}) - \operatorname{var}(\hat{\boldsymbol{\beta}}) \\ &= \sigma^2[(\mathrm{X}'\mathrm{X} + \mathrm{X}_n'X_n)^{-1} - (X'X)^{-1}], \end{aligned} \tag{25.7.10}$$

where, as previously, it has been assumed that the distribution of the elements of $\mathbf{y}_n$ is the same as that for the elements of $\mathbf{y}$. The variance norm is a natural choice in this context since it is implicitly assumed that the added observations are from the population initially sampled. Since $X'X$ cannot be changed, the improvement in $\Delta \operatorname{var}(\hat{\boldsymbol{\beta}}_{T+n})$ must come from the characteristics of $X_n'X_n$ as related to $X'X$.

Experimentation designed to improve $\hat{\boldsymbol{\beta}}_{T+N}$ over $\hat{\boldsymbol{\beta}}_T$ can then proceed by choices of the vectors forming X_n or alternatively Z_n to assure that the matrix $X'X + X_n'X_n$ is optimally augmented. To choose an optimum, a more specific definition of variance improvement must be added (Covey-Crump and Silvey (1970)). Alternatives that have received attention include maximizing the determinant of $X'X + X_n'X_n$, maximizing the minimum characteristic root of $X'X + X_n'X_n$ and others. The choice, of course, should depend upon the model applications intended. However, the upshot is that if the problem of improving the variance can be cast to lend itself to the eigenvalue formulation, it can be, in principal, straightforwardly solved. Thus, if design points for additional observations or other prior information can be chosen and a criterion for improvement of the estimators is available. An optimal augmentation to the existing design matrix, $X'X$, can be determined, see Section 13.2 and Silvey (1969), Kiefer (1958), Guttman (1971), and MacRae (1977).

25.7.3 Conclusions

Thus, the updating problem beings to focus a number of the important questions for applications in econometrics. It is interesting, however, that the Kalman filter updating methods that directed much attention in the econometrics profession to this problem can be viewed in a familiar mixed estimation context. The attention to updating methods has heightened interest in experimental design and the valuation of additional sample and nonsample information. The Kalman filter lead to computationally efficient methods of estimation but these are not of major importance given present computer technology. The importance of the results involves evolutionary concepts of estimators and the flexibility that the methods suggest for sources of information to be included in econometric estimation problems (Anderson and Moore (1979), Conard and Corrado (1979), Chow (1975, 1981)).

25.7.4 Exercises

25.7.1. Derive the Kalman filter for the situation in which

$$E\left[\begin{pmatrix}\mathbf{e}\\ \mathbf{e}_n\end{pmatrix}(\mathbf{e}'\mathbf{e}_n')\right] = \sigma^2\begin{bmatrix}\psi & 0\\ 0 & \Omega\end{bmatrix}.$$

Interpret the results. If this were the appropriate error assumption, how might one estimate Ω?

25.7.2. Show that the estimator $\hat{\boldsymbol{\beta}}_{T+1}$ in Equation (25.7.4) is equivalent to that obtained by applying ordinary least squares to the pooled "old" and "new" sample information.

25.7.3. Consider the simple one variable linear, varying parameter regression model, $y_t = x_t\beta_t + e_t$. The estimate for the coefficient (assuming data are differenced so the constant is zero) is

$$\hat{\beta} = \sum y_t x_t / \sum x_t^2.$$

Show that the expected value for the estimator $\hat{\beta}$ is a weighted average of the coefficients associated with the original obervations, i.e.,

$$E(\hat{\beta}) = \sum w_t \beta_t,$$

where $w_t = x_t^2/\sum x_t^2$ so that $\sum w_t = 1$, and $0 \leq w_t \leq 1$. Discuss the implications of this result for updating.

25.7.4. Use the expression for variance in Exercise 25.7.1. to show how in a time series context, one could *a priori* develop an updating scheme that would give more weight in estimating $\hat{\boldsymbol{\beta}}_{T+n}$ to the recent observations.

25.7.5 References

Anderson, B. D. O. and Moore, J. B. (1978). *Optimal Filtering*. Englewood Cliffs, N.J.: Prentice-Hall, Inc. 1978.

Belsey, D. A. (1973a). On the determination of systematic parameter variation in the linear regression model. *Annals of Economics and Social Measurement*, **2**, 487–494.

Belsey, D. A. (1973b). The applicability of the Kalman filter in the determination of systematic parameter variation. *Annals of Economics and Social Measurement*, **2**, 531–533.

Brook, R. and Wallace, T. D. (1973). A note on extraneous information in regression. *Journal of Econometrics*, **1**, 315–316.

Chow, G. C. (1975). *Analysis and Control of Dynamic Economic Systems*. New York: Wiley.

Chow, G. C. (1981). *Econometric Analysis by Control Methods*. New York: Wiley.

Conard, W., and Corrado, C. (1979). Applications of the Kalman filter to revisions in monthly retail sales estimates. *Journal of Economic Dynamics and Control*, **1**, 177–198.

Covey-Crump, P. A. K. and Silvey, S. D. (1970). Optimal regression designs with previous observations. *Biometrika*, **62**, 551–566.

Guttman, I. (1971). A remark on the optimal regression designs with previous observations of Covey-Crump and Silvey. *Biometrica*, **64**, 683–684.

Kalman, R. E. (1960). A new approach to linear filtering and prediction problems. *Journal of Basic Engineering*, D, **82**, 95–108.

Kiefer, J. (1958). On the nonrandomized optimality and randomized nonoptimality of symmetrical designs. *Annals of Mathematical Statistics*, **29**, 675–699.

MacRae, E. C. (1977). Optimal experimental design for dynamic econometric models. *Annals of Economic and Social Measurement*, **6**, 399–405.

Murata, Y. (1982). *Optimal Control Methods for Linear Discrete-Time Economic Systems*. New York: Springer-Verlag.

Rausser, G. C., Mundlak, Y., and Johnson, S. R. (1983). Structural change, updating and forecasting. In *New Directions in Econometric Modeling and Forecasting in U.S. Agriculture*. Edited by G. Rausser. New York: Elsevier–North Holland.

Sage, A. P., and Melsa, J. L. (1971). *Estimation Theory with Applications to Communications and Control*. New York: McGraw-Hill.

Silvey, S. D. (1969). Multicollinearity and imprecise estimation. *Journal of the Royal Statistical Society*, B, **31**, 539–552.

Theil, H. (1971). *Principles of Econometrics*. New York: Wiley.

Theil, H. (1974). Mixed estimation based on quasi-prior judgements. *European Economic Review*, **5**, 33–40.

APPENDIX

Estimation and Inference in Nonlinear Statistical Models

In this Appendix we will consider the problem of estimation and inference in nonlinear statistical models. Our discussion will be brief and the interested reader is directed to Chapter 17 of Judge *et al.* (1980) and the references cited there for a more complete treatment. Estimation in nonlinear models is complicated by the fact that whether one adopts the least squares or maximum likelihood principle, the first-order conditions of the maximization or minimization problem usually cannot be easily solved analytically. Consequently, the maximum likelihood or least squares estimates must be obtained by iterative, numerical techniques. Statistical inference in nonlinear models is based on the asymptotic distributions of the maximum likelihood and nonlinear least squares estimation rules. Our discussion will be presented in three sections: the first containing a discussion of general algorithms for maximizing or minimizing an objective function. In Section A.2 these results are specialized to maximum likelihood estimation and in Section A.3 to nonlinear least squares. A summary and guide to further readings is contained in Section A.4.

A.1 Nonlinear Optimization

Let $y = f(\theta_1, \ldots, \theta_K) = f(\boldsymbol{\theta})$ be an objective function that we wish to maximize with respect to the variables (parameters) $\boldsymbol{\theta}' = (\theta_1, \ldots, \theta_K)$. All the results below hold as well for the minimization problem as it may be thought of as maximizing the negative of the objective function. If $f(\boldsymbol{\theta})$ is continuous and has continuous first and second partial derivatives, then sufficient conditions for a local maximum are

$$\left.\frac{\partial f}{\partial \boldsymbol{\theta}}\right|_{\boldsymbol{\theta}=\boldsymbol{\theta}_*} = F_* = \mathbf{0}, \tag{A.1.1}$$

and at the point $\boldsymbol{\theta}_*$ defined by (A.1.1) that the Hessian matrix

$$\left.\frac{\partial^2 f}{\partial \boldsymbol{\theta}\, \partial \boldsymbol{\theta}'}\right|_{\boldsymbol{\theta}=\boldsymbol{\theta}_*} = H_* \tag{A.1.2}$$

is negative definite. Thus, the standard maximization problem is solved by finding all the solutions to (A.1.1) such that the Hessian is negative definite and then choosing as *the* solution the point corresponding to the global maximum.

In practice it is usually extremely difficult to solve Equations (A.1.1) analytically. Consequently, the objective function is usually maximized numerically. The numerical methods we will consider are iterative. That is, given some initial value of $\boldsymbol{\theta}$, say $\hat{\boldsymbol{\theta}}_0$, a recursive relation is used that yields, it is hoped, values that are nearer and nearer to a local maximum. The iterative process is stopped on the basis of one or more criteria. The process might be stopped when the values of the parameters, or the objective function, cease to change by an appreciable amount from one iteration to the next. Alternatively, or, in addition, the iterative process may be halted after a specified number of iterations or after a given amount of computer time has elapsed. The recursive relation can be written in general form as

$$\boldsymbol{\theta}_{n+1} = \boldsymbol{\theta}_n + \mathbf{d}_n, \tag{A.1.3}$$

where $\boldsymbol{\theta}_n$ is the approximation to the maximizing value at the nth iteration and $\mathbf{d}_n$ is a vector of constants that is added to $\boldsymbol{\theta}_n$ to obtain $\boldsymbol{\theta}_{n+1}$. The step $\mathbf{d}_n$ will be said to be acceptable if $f(\boldsymbol{\theta}_{n+1}) > f(\boldsymbol{\theta}_n)$. It is usefully written as

$$\mathbf{d}_n = t_n \boldsymbol{\delta}_n,$$

where t_n is a positive constant, the step length, and $\boldsymbol{\delta}_n$ a *direction* vector. If $\boldsymbol{\delta}_n$ is to lead to an acceptable step it must be true for t_n close to zero that

$$\begin{aligned}\left.\frac{df(\boldsymbol{\theta}_n + t_n\boldsymbol{\delta}_n)}{dt_n}\right|_{t_n=0} &= F_n'\left[\left.\frac{df(\boldsymbol{\theta}_n + t_n\boldsymbol{\delta}_n)}{dt_n}\right|_{t_n=0}\right], \\ &= F_n'\boldsymbol{\delta}_n > 0,\end{aligned} \tag{A.1.4}$$

where F_n' is the transpose of the gradient vector evaluated at $\boldsymbol{\theta}_n$. From (A.1.4) any $\boldsymbol{\delta}_n$ of the form

$$\boldsymbol{\delta}_n = C_n F_n, \tag{A.1.5}$$

where C_n is a positive definite matrix, will lead to an acceptable step. Thus, the general form of an iteration is

$$\boldsymbol{\theta}_{n+1} = \boldsymbol{\theta}_n + t_n C_n F_n. \tag{A.1.6}$$

Methods involving such iterations are called gradient methods since the direction vector is a function of the gradient vector F_n. Several gradient methods will now be considered.

A.1.1 Method of Steepest Ascent

One choice of C_n is $C_n = I$. This choice is motivated by the fact that F_n points in the direction of the most rapid increase, if $F_n \neq \mathbf{0}$, of the function $f(\cdot)$ at $\boldsymbol{\theta} = \boldsymbol{\theta}_n$. To see this let $\|\mathbf{x}\|$ be the length of the vector $\mathbf{x}$ and define $\|\mathbf{x}\| = (\mathbf{x}'\mathbf{x})^{1/2}$. Then let $\boldsymbol{\phi}$ be a vector such that $\|\boldsymbol{\phi}\| = 1$. Then, the *directional derivative* of f in the direction of $\boldsymbol{\phi}$ is

$$\frac{df}{d\boldsymbol{\phi}}(\boldsymbol{\theta}_n) = \frac{\partial f'}{\partial \boldsymbol{\theta}}(\boldsymbol{\theta}_n)\boldsymbol{\phi} = F'_n\boldsymbol{\phi}.$$

The real number $(df/d\boldsymbol{\phi})(\boldsymbol{\theta}_n)$ indicates the rate of increase, or decrease, of $f(\cdot)$ as we leave $\boldsymbol{\theta}_n$ along a ray pointing in the direction of the vector $\boldsymbol{\phi}$. If $\mathbf{x}$ and $\mathbf{y}$ are two vectors then the Schwartz inequality states that

$$|\mathbf{x}'\mathbf{y}| \leq \|\mathbf{x}\| \cdot \|\mathbf{y}\|$$

with equality holding iff there are real numbers α and β, not both zero, such that $\alpha\mathbf{x} + \beta\mathbf{y} = \mathbf{0}$. Therefore

$$\left|\frac{df}{d\boldsymbol{\phi}}(\boldsymbol{\theta}_n)\right| = |F'_n\boldsymbol{\phi}| \leq \|F_n\| \cdot \|\boldsymbol{\phi}\| = \|F_n\|$$

and equality holds only if there exist real α and β such that

$$\alpha\boldsymbol{\phi} + \beta F_n = \mathbf{0},$$

or

$$\boldsymbol{\phi} = -\frac{\beta}{\alpha}F_n.$$

Thus, the absolute value of $(df/d\boldsymbol{\phi})(\boldsymbol{\theta}_n)$ is maximized when $\boldsymbol{\phi}$ has the same, or opposite, direction as F_n.

The step size can be selected to maximize the improvement in the function at each iteration. If $f(\boldsymbol{\theta})$ can be approximated by a Taylor's series expansion then

$$f(\boldsymbol{\theta}_{n+1}) \doteq f(\boldsymbol{\theta}_n) + (\boldsymbol{\theta}_{n+1} - \boldsymbol{\theta}_n)'F_n + \tfrac{1}{2}(\boldsymbol{\theta}_{n+1} - \boldsymbol{\theta}_n)'H_n(\boldsymbol{\theta}_{n+1} - \boldsymbol{\theta}_n). \quad \text{(A.1.7)}$$

Substituting (A.1.6) into (A.1.7) and rearranging (recall that $C_n = I$) gives

$$f(\boldsymbol{\theta}_{n+1}) - f(\boldsymbol{\theta}_n) = t_nF'_nF_n + \tfrac{1}{2}t_n^2F'_nH_nF_n. \quad \text{(A.1.8)}$$

Maximizing (A.1.8) with respect to t_n gives

$$t_n = -(F'_nH_nF_n)^{-1}F'_nF_n. \quad \text{(A.1.9)}$$

Expression (A.1.9) yields a maximum only if

$$F_n' H_n F_n < 0,$$

which holds if H_n is negative definite. Since the negative definiteness of the Hessian matrix is necessary and sufficient for the concavity of $f(\boldsymbol{\theta})$ in a neighborhood of $\boldsymbol{\theta}_n$, it follows that this method will break down if $\boldsymbol{\theta}_n$ is not sufficiently close to the maximum to ensure the concavity of the function. A further theoretical difficulty is that the method of steepest ascent may converge to a saddle point rather than a maximum. Finally, if the maximum lies on a narrow ridge then there is a tendency for successive steps to oscillate back and forth across the ridge, so that convergence is slow.

A.1.2 The Method of Newton

The method of Newton, also called the Newton–Raphson method, is based on the quadratic approximation (A.1.7). Specifically, maximize the right-hand side of (A.1.7) with respect to $\boldsymbol{\theta}_{n+1}$. The first-order conditions for a maximum are

$$F_n + H_n(\boldsymbol{\theta}_{n+1} - \boldsymbol{\theta}_n) = \mathbf{0}$$

or

$$\boldsymbol{\theta}_{n+1} = \boldsymbol{\theta}_n - H_n^{-1} F_n. \tag{A.1.10}$$

If $f(\boldsymbol{\theta})$ is quadratic then (A.1.7) is exact and (A.1.10) yields a maximum in one step. If the function is not quadratic, but $\boldsymbol{\theta}_n$ is sufficiently close to the maximum so that the quadratic approximation is good, then convergence to the maximum is likely to be fast. The difficulty with this method, like the method of steepest ascent, is that if $f(\boldsymbol{\theta})$ is not concave in the region near $\boldsymbol{\theta}_n$ then the method will not converge and in fact will move in the wrong direction. Note too that the step size for this method is $t_n = 1$. It is possible when using this method for the step to be so large that the quadratic approximation at $\boldsymbol{\theta}_n$ is not valid at $\boldsymbol{\theta}_{n+1}$.

A.1.3 Method of Quadratic Hill Climbing

The method called quadratic hill climbing has been proposed by Goldfeld *et al.* (1966). It is described to illustrate modifications of gradient methods designed to cope with the weaknesses noted above. In particular this method is specifically designed to work for functions that are not concave everywhere and for initial values $\boldsymbol{\theta}_0$ that may not be near the maximum. It uses a quadratic approximation, like the method of Newton, but introduces a factor that controls the size of the step being taken. This factor is altered according to how accurate the quadratic approximation appears to be. The step size is reduced in regions where the approximation appears poor and is increased in regions where the approximation is good.

The essence of the method is that at each iteration a step is taken that maximizes the quadratic approximation of $f(\boldsymbol{\theta})$ on a sphere of suitable radius. The basic results are contained in the following two lemmas and theorems, which assume that $f(\boldsymbol{\theta})$ is a quadratic function and thus $H_n = H$ is constant

Lemma 1. *Let* $||\mathbf{x}||$ *denote the length of a vector* $\mathbf{x}$ *and define* $||\mathbf{x}|| = (\mathbf{x}'\mathbf{x})^{1/2}$. *Thus* $||\mathbf{x} - \mathbf{y}||$ *is the distance between* $\mathbf{x}$ *and* $\mathbf{y}$. *Let* α *be any number such that* $H_n - \alpha I$ *is negative definite and define*

$$\boldsymbol{\theta}_{n+1} = \boldsymbol{\theta}_n - (H_n - \alpha I)^{-1} F_n \tag{A.1.11}$$

and

$$r_\alpha = ||\boldsymbol{\theta}_{n+1} - \boldsymbol{\theta}_n||. \tag{A.1.12}$$

Then $f(\boldsymbol{\theta}_{n+1}) \geq f(\boldsymbol{\theta})$ *for all* $\boldsymbol{\theta}$ *such that* $||\boldsymbol{\theta} - \boldsymbol{\theta}_n|| = r_\alpha$.

Lemma 2. *If* $F_n \neq \mathbf{0}$ *then* r_α *defined by* (A.1.11) *and* (A.1.12) *is a strictly decreasing function of* α *on the interval* (λ_1, ∞) *where* λ_1 *is the maximum characteristic root of* H_n.

Lemma 1 provides a rule, (A.1.11), for finding the maximum value of a function, that is not necessarily concave since H_n is not required to be negative definite, on the surface of a sphere of a certain radius. Lemma 2 states that the larger the constant α, that is the more H_n must be modified to obtain a negative definite matrix, the smaller the radius of the sphere in Lemma 1. From these lemmas come the following theorems.

Theorem 1. *Let* $F_n \neq \mathbf{0}$ *and let* R_α *be the region consisting of all* $\boldsymbol{\theta}$ *such that* $||\boldsymbol{\theta} - \boldsymbol{\theta}_n|| \leq r_\alpha$. *The maximum of* $f(\boldsymbol{\theta})$ *on* R_α *is obtained at* $\boldsymbol{\theta}_{n+1}$ *if* $\alpha \geq 0$ *and in the interior of* R_α *at* $\boldsymbol{\theta}_n = H_n^{-1} F_n$ *if* $\alpha < 0$.

This theorem, which holds if $f(\boldsymbol{\theta})$ is quadratic, provides a rule for finding the maximum of $f(\boldsymbol{\theta})$ when on or inside a sphere of radius r_α and $F_n \neq \mathbf{0}$. The following theorem covers the other possibility.

Theorem 2. *If* $F_n = \mathbf{0}$ *then the maximum of* $f(\boldsymbol{\theta})$ *on the region* R_r *defined by* $||\boldsymbol{\theta} - \boldsymbol{\theta}_n|| < r$ *occurs at* $\boldsymbol{\theta}_n \pm r\mathbf{a}_1$ *if* $\lambda_1 > 0$ *and at* $\boldsymbol{\theta}_n$ *otherwise, where* λ_1 *is the maximum characteristic root of* H_n *and* $\mathbf{a}_1$ *is the corresponding characteristic vector of unit length.*

This alternative prevents convergence to a saddle point. To actually carry out this iterative procedure we proceed as follows. The ideal we seek is to use the largest spherical region at each step but at the same time having the region be small enough so that the quadratic approximation is a reasonable guide to the behavior of the function. Two cases can occur at each step.

Case 1. $F_n \neq \mathbf{0}$ according to some predetermined criterion.

In this case choose

$$\alpha = \lambda_1 + R\|F_n\|, \tag{A.1.13}$$

where R is a positive constant described below. Then

$$\boldsymbol{\theta}_{n+1} = \boldsymbol{\theta}_n - (H_n - \alpha I)^{-1}F_n \quad \text{if } \alpha \geq 0,$$

$$\boldsymbol{\theta}_{n+1} = \boldsymbol{\theta}_n - H_n^{-1}F_n \quad \text{if } \alpha < 0.$$

By Theorem 1, $\boldsymbol{\theta}_{n+1}$ is the maximum of the quadratic approximation on the spherical region R_α of radius $\|(H_n - \alpha I)^{-1}F_n\|$ with center at $\boldsymbol{\theta}_n$.

Lemma 2 shows that the larger the value of R, and thus α, the smaller the region R_α. In fact, the radius of the region R_α is less than or equal to R^{-1}. In practice, an initial value of R is specified and then modified at each iteration so that the step size increases when the quadratic approximation appears good and decreases when it is poor. Explicitly, let Δf be the change in the value of the function resulting from the change $\Delta\boldsymbol{\theta} = \boldsymbol{\theta}_{n+1} - \boldsymbol{\theta}_n$. Let ΔQ be the change in the corresponding quadratic approximation (A.1.7). Define $z = \Delta f/\Delta Q$. Then, act according to the following rules. If $z \leq 0$ then $\Delta\boldsymbol{\theta}$ implies too big a step has been taken and therefore it is not accepted. The factor R is multiplied by 4 and a new α calculated. If $z > 0$ and close to 1, i.e. $0.7 \leq z \leq 1.3$, then R is multiplied by 0.4 and a new α calculated. If $z > 2$ then R is again multiplied by 4. If $0 \leq z \leq 0.7$ or $1.3 \leq z \leq 2$ then the factor to be multiplied by R is found by linear interpolation between 0.4 and 4.0. The values listed here are those suggested by Goldfeld *et al.* (1966) and are based on their experience using numerical experiments. Given a value of α, one computes a new estimate of $\boldsymbol{\theta}$ and accepts the step if the change in the function is positive. Otherwise R is increased and a smaller step taken until an improvement is obtained.

Case 2. $F_n = \mathbf{0}$ according to the predetermined criterion.

If $F_n = \mathbf{0}$ and if H_n is negative definite ($\lambda_1 < 0$) then $\boldsymbol{\theta}_n$ is accepted as the maximum. If H_n is not negative definite ($\lambda_1 \geq 0$) then Theorem 2 is applied. This guarantees that we do not converge to a saddle point.

A.1.4 Numerical Differentiation

The methods discussed above require the evaluation of the Hessian and/or gradient at each iteration. A very real practical consideration is the effort involved in deriving and programming these derivatives. If $K = 10$ then the

Hessian consists of 55 different terms! If the objective function is complicated at all, its differentiation would be extremely tedious at a minimum. Consequently, it is often the practice to approximate the derivatives numerically. First derivatives are calculated as the slope of a secant over some interval. If $f(\cdot)$ is a function of two variables, x and y, then

$$\left.\frac{\partial f(x, y)}{\partial x}\right|_{\substack{x=a\\y=b}} = \frac{f(a + \Delta x, b) - f(a - \Delta x, b)}{2\Delta x}. \tag{A.1.14}$$

Second derivatives are computed as changes in first derivatives over some interval.

$$\left.\frac{\partial^2 f(x, y)}{\partial x^2}\right|_{\substack{x=a\\y=b}} = \frac{f(a + 2\Delta x, b) - 2f(a, b) + f(a - 2\Delta x, b)}{(2\Delta x)^2} \tag{A.1.15}$$

and

$$\begin{aligned}\left.\frac{\partial^2 f(x, y)}{\partial x\, \partial y}\right|_{\substack{x=a\\y=b}} &= [f(a + \Delta x, b + \Delta y) - f(a - \Delta x, b + \Delta y) \\ &\quad - f(a + \Delta x, b - \Delta y) + f(a - \Delta x, b - \Delta y)]/4\Delta x\, \Delta y.\end{aligned} \tag{A.1.16}$$

The question is, of course, what should the increments Δx and Δy be set to? Goldfeld *et al.* (1966) suggest that it is adequate to set the increment in the ith direction at the nth iteration equal to

$$\max[|f(\boldsymbol{\theta}_n)|\varepsilon_1, |\theta_{n,i} - \theta_{n-1,i}|\varepsilon_2, (|\theta_{n,i}|\varepsilon_3)\varepsilon_4],$$

where $\theta_{n,i}$ is the value of the ith parameter at the nth iteration and ε_1, ε_2, ε_3, and ε_4 are preassigned small constants. This rule sets the increment in the ith direction equal to a fraction of the change in the value of the variable since the last iteration, unless the absolute value of the variable or the value of the function becomes large.

Bard (1974) presents two other alternatives. The inaccuracy of the derivative comes from two sources: the *rounding error* arising when two closely spaced values of $\boldsymbol{\theta}$ are subtracted from each other and the truncation error associated with the fact that (A.1.14) is accurate only in the limit as the increment goes to zero. To minimize the maximum total error, the increment in the ith direction should be set to $(4\varepsilon|f(\boldsymbol{\theta}_n)/h_n^{ii}|)^{1/2}$, where $\varepsilon = 2^{-b}$ and b is the number of binary digits carried by the computer in use and h_n^{ii} is the ith diagonal element of H_n. Alternatively, to minimize the mean square error we would choose an increment in the ith direction equal to $(2\sqrt{2}\varepsilon|f(\boldsymbol{\theta}_n)/h_n^{ii}|)^{1/2}$. Whatever formulas are used, however, they should not be used without care. Upper and lower bounds on the increments like

$$[10^{-5}|\theta_{n,i}|, 10^{-2}|\theta_{n,i}|]$$

should be used. Finally, these formulas apply specifically to one-sided difference approximations as opposed to the symmetric, central difference scheme presented in (A.1.14) to (A.1.16). As a result they represent conservative values for the increments.

A.2 Maximum Likelihood Estimation

The *likelihood function* of a sample of T independent observations is

$$L(\boldsymbol{\theta} \mid y_1, \ldots, y_T) = f(y_1 \mid \boldsymbol{\theta}) \cdot f(y_2 \mid \boldsymbol{\theta}) \ldots \cdot f(y_T \mid \boldsymbol{\theta}). \tag{A.2.1}$$

Maximum likelihood estimates of the parameters $\boldsymbol{\theta}$ are those values, $\tilde{\boldsymbol{\theta}}$ that maximize (A.2.1) or, more typically, its logarithm, denoted $\ln L$. In Chapter 4 the properties of maximum likelihood rules are thoroughly discussed. Briefly, however, the maximum likelihood estimator of $\boldsymbol{\theta}$, say $\tilde{\boldsymbol{\theta}}$, is asymptotically normally distributed with mean $\boldsymbol{\theta}$ and covariance matrix $[I(\boldsymbol{\theta})]^{-1}$, the inverse of the information matrix, where

$$I(\boldsymbol{\theta}) = -E\left[\frac{\partial^2 \ln L}{\partial \boldsymbol{\theta}\, \partial \boldsymbol{\theta}'}\right]. \tag{A.2.2}$$

The maximum likelihood estimator is consistent and asymptotically efficient. That is, any other estimator of $\boldsymbol{\theta}$ that is consistent and uniformly asymptotically normal has an asymptotic covariance matrix which is larger than $[I(\boldsymbol{\theta})]^{-1}$ in the usual sense.

Frequently the first-order conditions for the maximum of $\ln L$ with respect to $\boldsymbol{\theta}$,

$$\frac{\partial \ln L}{\partial \boldsymbol{\theta}} = \mathbf{0},$$

cannot be solved analytically for maximum likelihood estimates. Consequently, numerical methods like those in the previous section must often be employed to obtain maximum likelihood estimates. There are several properties of the likelihood function that can be used from time to time to make the problem of obtaining maximum likelihood estimates simpler.

A.2.1 Use of the Method of Newton

The method of Newton is an especially convenient algorithm for maximum likelihood estimation, though the caveats associated with the method, and noted above, must be kept in mind. If the density $f(y_i \mid \boldsymbol{\theta})$ admits a sufficient statistic then

$$I(\tilde{\boldsymbol{\theta}}) = -E\left(\frac{\partial^2 \ln L}{\partial \boldsymbol{\theta}\, \partial \boldsymbol{\theta}'}\right)\bigg|_{\boldsymbol{\theta}=\tilde{\boldsymbol{\theta}}} = -\left(\frac{\partial^2 \ln L}{\partial \boldsymbol{\theta}\, \partial \boldsymbol{\theta}'}\right)\bigg|_{\boldsymbol{\theta}=\tilde{\boldsymbol{\theta}}}, \qquad (A.2.3)$$

where $\tilde{\boldsymbol{\theta}}$ is the maximum likelihood estimator of $\tilde{\boldsymbol{\theta}}$. See Dhrymes (1974, pp. 134–135) for a proof.

Application of the method of Newton, with $\ln L$ as the objective function, gives

$$\boldsymbol{\theta}_{n+1} = \boldsymbol{\theta}_n - H_n^{-1} F_n. \qquad (A.2.4)$$

In this situation $H = \partial^2 \ln L/\partial \boldsymbol{\theta}\, \partial \boldsymbol{\theta}'$. Therefore, instead of using $[I(\tilde{\boldsymbol{\theta}})]^{-1}$ as an estimate of the asymptotic covariance matrix, which involves taking the expectation of the matrix of second partials, one may simply use (A.2.3) and substitute the negative of the Hessian, evaluated at $\tilde{\boldsymbol{\theta}}$, for $I(\tilde{\boldsymbol{\theta}})$. This substitution is strictly correct only in the presence of a sufficient statistic, however. If a sufficient statistic is not available then the substitution can still be made in large samples since the matrix of second partials evaluated at $\tilde{\boldsymbol{\theta}}$ converges to $-I(\boldsymbol{\theta})$.

A second attractive feature of the method of Newton is embodied in the following theorem.

Theorem 3. *Let $\hat{\boldsymbol{\theta}}_0$ be an initial consistent estimator of $\boldsymbol{\theta}$ with a well-defined asymptotic distribution, then*

$$\hat{\boldsymbol{\theta}}_1 = \hat{\boldsymbol{\theta}}_0 - [H|_{\boldsymbol{\theta}=\hat{\boldsymbol{\theta}}_0}]^{-1}[F|_{\boldsymbol{\theta}=\hat{\boldsymbol{\theta}}_0}] \qquad (A.2.5)$$

has the same asymptotic distribution as the maximum likelihood estimator.

This result says that the estimator obtained after one step of the Method of Newton is asymptotically efficient if the iteration begins with a consistent estimate. This result is quite useful when iterations in the method of Newton are computationally expensive. The resulting estimator is known as the *linearized maximum likelihood* estimator.

A.2.2 Method of Scoring

The method of scoring is related to the method of Newton. The method of scoring replaces $-H_n$ in the method of Newton by $I(\boldsymbol{\theta}_n)$. Consequently an iteration using the method of scoring is

$$\boldsymbol{\theta}_{n+1} = \boldsymbol{\theta}_n + I(\boldsymbol{\theta}_n) F_n. \qquad (A.2.6)$$

If determining $I(\boldsymbol{\theta})$ is not difficult, the method of scoring may be advocated as it will usually converge to a maximum more quickly.

A.2.3 The Method of Berndt, Hall, Hall, and Hausman

In practice, using the properties of the likelihood function, it can be shown that

$$I(\boldsymbol{\theta}) = E\left[\frac{\partial \ln L}{\partial \boldsymbol{\theta}}\right]\left[\frac{\partial \ln L}{\partial \boldsymbol{\theta}}\right]' = E[Q(\boldsymbol{\theta})].$$

Berndt *et al.* (1974) suggest replacing $[I(\boldsymbol{\theta}_n)]^{-1}$ in the method of scoring by $[Q(\boldsymbol{\theta}_n)]^{-1}$. That is, to use the iterative procedure

$$\boldsymbol{\theta}_{n+1} = \boldsymbol{\theta}_n + [Q(\boldsymbol{\theta}_n)]^{-1}F_n,$$

where $Q(\boldsymbol{\theta}_n)$ is replaced by its estimate

$$\sum_{i=1}^{T}\left[\frac{\partial \ln f(y_i)}{\partial \boldsymbol{\theta}}\right]\left[\frac{\partial \ln f(y_i)}{\partial \boldsymbol{\theta}}\right]'.$$

Then a consistent estimate of the asymptotic covariance matrix of the maximum likelihood estimator $\tilde{\boldsymbol{\theta}}$ is provided by $[I(\tilde{\boldsymbol{\theta}})]^{-1}$ or $[Q(\tilde{\boldsymbol{\theta}})]^{-1}$.

A.2.4 Asymptotic Tests Based on the Maximum Likelihood Method

In this section we present three asymptotically equivalent tests procedures that can be used in conjunction with maximum likelihood estimation. The first is the Wald (1943) test. It is based on the idea that the null hypothesis can be tested by asking if the unrestricted estimates nearly satisfy the restrictions implied by the null hypothesis. The second test is the Lagrange-multiplier test developed by Aitchison and Silvey (1958) and Silvey (1959). The idea of this test is that when the null hypothesis is correct the maximum likelihood estimates constrained by the null hypotheses will be near the unrestricted maximum likelihood estimate. The third test is the familiar likelihood ratio test, which is asymptotically equivlaent to the first two. For a useful geometric interpretation, see Buse (1982).

A.2.4a *The Wald Test*

The Wald test is based on the method of scoring, Equation (A.2.6). Let the null hypothesis H_0 state that the K unknown parameters $\boldsymbol{\theta}$ obey $J \leq K$ well-behaved relationships of the form

$$h_1(\boldsymbol{\theta}) = h_2(\boldsymbol{\theta}) = \cdots = h_J(\boldsymbol{\theta}) = \mathbf{0}. \qquad \text{(A.2.7)}$$

Let $\mathbf{h}(\boldsymbol{\theta})$ denote the J-dimensional column vector whose ith component is $h_i(\boldsymbol{\theta})$ and $R'_{\boldsymbol{\theta}}$ as the $K \times J$ matrix whose (i, j)th elements is $\partial h_j(\boldsymbol{\theta})/\partial \theta_i$. $R_{\boldsymbol{\theta}}$

will be of rank J if none of the hypotheses is redundant. Wald's method of testing H_0 uses the test statistic

$$W = \mathbf{h}'(\tilde{\boldsymbol{\theta}})[R_{\tilde{\boldsymbol{\theta}}}[I(\tilde{\boldsymbol{\theta}})]^{-1}R'_{\tilde{\boldsymbol{\theta}}}]^{-1}\mathbf{h}(\tilde{\boldsymbol{\theta}}), \tag{A.2.8}$$

where $\tilde{\boldsymbol{\theta}}$ is the unrestricted maximum likelihood estimate.

Under the null hypothesis W is asymptotically distributed as $\chi^2_{(J)}$, and we reject H_0 is the value of the test statistic is greater than the upper α critical point of the $\chi^2_{(J)}$-distribution.

A.2.4b *The Lagrange-Multiplier Test*

The Lagrange-multiplier test requires the computation of the restricted maximum likelihood estimates of $\boldsymbol{\theta}$, say $\boldsymbol{\theta}^*$. Normally this requires maximization of the augmented likelihood function

$$L^* = \ln L + \boldsymbol{\lambda}'\mathbf{h}(\boldsymbol{\theta}), \tag{A.2.9}$$

where $\boldsymbol{\lambda}$ is a $J \times 1$ vector of Lagrangian multipliers. The method of scoring then takes the form

$$\begin{bmatrix} \boldsymbol{\theta}_{n+1} \\ \boldsymbol{\lambda}_{n+1} \end{bmatrix} = \begin{bmatrix} \boldsymbol{\theta}_n \\ \boldsymbol{\lambda}_n \end{bmatrix} + \begin{bmatrix} I(\boldsymbol{\theta}_n) & -R'_{\boldsymbol{\theta}_n} \\ -R_{\boldsymbol{\theta}_n} & 0 \end{bmatrix}^{-1} \begin{bmatrix} F_n + R'_{\boldsymbol{\theta}_n}\boldsymbol{\lambda}_n \\ h(\boldsymbol{\theta}_n) \end{bmatrix}.$$

The Lagrange-multiplier test is based on the test statistic

$$LM = \boldsymbol{\lambda}^{*\prime}R_{\boldsymbol{\theta}*}[I(\boldsymbol{\theta}^*)]^{-1}R'_{\boldsymbol{\theta}*}\boldsymbol{\lambda}^*, \tag{A.2.10a}$$

where $\boldsymbol{\theta}^*$ and $\boldsymbol{\lambda}^*$ are values that maximize (A.2.9). An alternative form, also called the score statistic by Rao (1973), is

$$LM = \mathbf{F}'_*[I(\boldsymbol{\theta}^*)]^{-1}\mathbf{F}_*, \tag{A.2.10b}$$

where $\mathbf{F}_*$ is the value of the gradient vector evaluated at $\boldsymbol{\theta}^*$. The test statistic LM is asymptotically distributed as a $\chi^2_{(J)}$ random variable if H_0 is true, thus we reject H_0 if the value of the test statistic is greater than the appropriate critical value.

A.2.4c *The Likelihood Ratio Test Statistic*

The likelihood ratio test is based on the statistic

$$\lambda = \frac{L(\boldsymbol{\theta}^*)}{L(\tilde{\boldsymbol{\theta}})}.$$

Asymptotically $-2 \ln \lambda$ has a $\chi^2_{(J)}$-distribution if the null hypothesis H_0 is true. The hypothesis H_0 is rejected if the value of the test statistic

$$-2 \ln \lambda = -2(\ln L(\boldsymbol{\theta}^*) - \ln L(\tilde{\boldsymbol{\theta}}))$$

is greater than the appropriate critical value. For proof of this result see Theil (1971, p. 396).

A.2.4d *Concluding Remarks*

The choice of which of the above test statistics to employ in a given instance is a difficult one since all are asymptotically equivalent but may differ in small samples. One criteria is convenience. The Wald statsitic does not require computation of restricted maximum likelihood estimates and the Lagrange-multiplier statistic does not require the unrestricted estimates. Both, however, do require the gradient and information matrix. Asymptotically, of course, one is usually justified in replacing the information matrix by the negative of the Hessian or the approximation suggested by Berndt *et al.* (1974). The likelihood ratio test requires both the restricted and unrestricted estimates. A final note of caution, and an area for future research, there are situations where *systematic* relations exist between the values of the alternative test statistics, implying that one may reach consistently different conclusions depending upon the choice of test statistic, despite their asymptotic equivalence. See, for example, Savin (1976).

A.3 Nonlinear Regression

Nonlinear regression models take the form

$$y_t = f_t(\boldsymbol{\theta}) + e_t, \qquad t = 1, \ldots, T, \tag{A.3.1}$$

where y_t is an observed response variable, $f_t(\boldsymbol{\theta})$ is some function of explanatory variables that is nonlinear in the parameters $\boldsymbol{\theta}' = (\theta_1, \ldots, \theta_K)$ and $e_t \sim N(0, \sigma^2)$ and independently of other errors. In matrix notation the model becomes

$$\mathbf{y} = \mathbf{f}(\boldsymbol{\theta}) + \mathbf{e}. \tag{A.3.2}$$

The nonlinear least squares estimates of $\boldsymbol{\theta}$ are those values, say $\boldsymbol{\theta}_{\text{LS}}$, that minimize

$$S[\boldsymbol{\theta}] = [\mathbf{y} - \mathbf{f}(\boldsymbol{\theta})]'[\mathbf{y} - \mathbf{f}(\boldsymbol{\theta})]. \tag{A.3.3}$$

It is easily shown that the nonlinear least squares estimator is identical to the maximum likelihood estimator, $\tilde{\boldsymbol{\theta}}$, given the normality of the error term.

One estimation algorithm is based on the linear expansion of $\mathbf{f}(\boldsymbol{\theta})$ around a point $\boldsymbol{\theta}_0$.

$$f(\boldsymbol{\theta}) = f(\boldsymbol{\theta}_0) + F_0(\boldsymbol{\theta} - \boldsymbol{\theta}_0),$$

where F_0 is the $T \times K$ matrix of partial derivatives

$$\frac{\partial f_t}{\partial \theta_j}; \qquad t = 1, \ldots, T; \quad j = 1, \ldots, K,$$

evaluated at $\boldsymbol{\theta} = \boldsymbol{\theta}_0$. Then minimize

$$[\mathbf{y} - \mathbf{f}(\boldsymbol{\theta}_0) - F_0(\boldsymbol{\theta} - \boldsymbol{\theta}_0)]'[\mathbf{y} - \mathbf{f}(\boldsymbol{\theta}_0) - F_0(\boldsymbol{\theta} - \boldsymbol{\theta}_0)]$$

with respect to $\boldsymbol{\theta}$ to obtain

$$F_0'[\mathbf{y} - \mathbf{f}(\boldsymbol{\theta}_0) - F_0(\boldsymbol{\theta} - \boldsymbol{\theta}_0)] = \mathbf{0}$$

or

$$\boldsymbol{\theta} = \boldsymbol{\theta}_0 + (F_0' F_0)^{-1} F_0'(\mathbf{y} - \mathbf{f}(\boldsymbol{\theta}_0)).$$

This relation may, of course, be used iteratively and written

$$\begin{aligned} \boldsymbol{\theta}_{n+1} &= \boldsymbol{\theta}_n + \boldsymbol{\delta}_n \\ &= \boldsymbol{\theta}_n + (F_n' F_n)^{-1} F_n'(\mathbf{y} - \mathbf{f}(\boldsymbol{\theta}_n)). \end{aligned} \tag{A.3.4}$$

This is called the Gauss–Newton method. Unfortunately, it may be the case that $\mathrm{SSE}(\boldsymbol{\theta}_{n+1}) \geq \mathrm{SSE}(\boldsymbol{\theta}_n)$ and, thus, (A.3.4) is not an acceptable step. Consequently, Hartley (1961) suggested that a step of less than unit length be taken, since for intermediate points between $\boldsymbol{\theta}_n$ and $\boldsymbol{\theta}_{n+1}$, sufficiently close to $\boldsymbol{\theta}_n$, improvement will occur. Consequently Hartley's algorithm is

$$\boldsymbol{\theta}_{n+1} = \boldsymbol{\theta}_n + t_n \boldsymbol{\delta}_n, \tag{A.3.5}$$

where t_n is chosen at each step so that $t_n \in (0, 1)$ and $\mathrm{SSE}(\boldsymbol{\theta}_{n+1}) \leq \mathrm{SSE}(\boldsymbol{\theta}_n)$.

Statistical inference in the nonlinear regression model is based on the asymptotic distribution of $\boldsymbol{\theta}_{\mathrm{LS}}$ which is $N(\boldsymbol{\theta}, \sigma^2(F'F)^{-1})$. A consistent estimator of σ^2 is $\hat{\sigma}^2 = \mathrm{SSE}(\boldsymbol{\theta}_{\mathrm{LS}})/(T - K)$ and an approximation of the asymptotic covariance matrix is $\hat{\sigma}^2(F_{\mathrm{LS}}' F_{\mathrm{LS}})^{-1}$.

A.4 Summary and Guide to Further Readings

In this chapter we have considered some aspects of estimation and inference in nonlinear statistical models. This topic is becoming increasingly important in econometrics, due to the increased availability of computer algorithms and software to deal with such problems and the corresponding increase in the willingness of economists to tackle problems directly that are intrinsically nonlinear, instead of avoiding the problem in one way or another. The first topic discussed in the chapter is the general problem of nonlinear optimization. Several methods of optimization were discussed including the methods of steepest ascent, Newton and quadratic-hill climbing. Excellent surveys of optimization methods can be found in Judge *et al.* (1980), Bard (1974), Fletcher (1972a, 1972b), Goldfeld and Quandt (1972), Lootsma (1972), Maddala (1977), and Himmelblau (1972). Discussions of specific algorithms can be found in Broyden (1965), Fletcher and Powell (1963), Hooke and Jeeves (1961), and Powell (1964, 1965).

The second topic of the chapter related to numerical methods and inference in the context of maximum likelihood estimation. Extensive references can be found in Chapter 4, but other useful references include Silvey (1970), Kendall and Stuart (1961), Dhrymes (1974), and Maddala (1977). Literature related to hypothesis testing includes Silvey (1970), Aitchison and Silvey (1958) and Breusch and Pagan (1980). The important topic of conflict among these criteria is discussed by Berndt and Savin (1977), Evans and Savin (1982), and Breusch (1979).

Finally, nonlinear regression methods are considered. In addition to the references already given, see Draper and Smith (1966), Gallant (1975a, 1975b), Marquardt (1963), and Malinvaud (1970a, 1970b).

A.5 References

Aitchison, J. and Silvey, S. (1958). Maximum likelihood estimation of parameters subject to restraints. *Annals of Mathematical Statistics*, **29**, 813–828.

Bard, Y. (1974). *Nonlinear Parameter Estimation*. New York: Academic Press.

Berndt, E. and Savin, N. (1977). Conflict among criteria for testing hypotheses in the multivariate linear regression model. *Econometrica*, **45**, 1263–1278.

Berndt, E., Hall, B., Hall, R., and Hausman, J. (1974). Estimation and inference in nonlinear structural models. *Annals of Economic and Social Measurement*, **3**, 653–665.

Breusch, T. (1979). Conflict among criteria for testing hypothesis: extension and comment. *Econometria*, **47**, 203–208.

Breusch, T. and Pagan, A. (1980). The Lagrange multiplier test and its applications to model specification in econometrics. *Review of Economic Studies*, **47**, 239–254.

Broyden, G. (1965). A class of methods for solving nonlinear simultaneous equations. *Mathematics of Computation*, **19**, 577–593.

Buse, A. (1982). The likelihood ratio, Wald and Lagrange multiplier tests: an expository note. *The American Statistician*, **36**, 153–157.

Dhrymes, P. (1974). *Econometrics: Statistical Foundations and Applications*. New York: Springer-Verlag.

Draper, N. and Smith, H. (1966). *Applied Regression Analysis*. New York: Wiley.

Evans, G. and Savin, N. (1982). Conflict among the criteria revisited: the W, LR and LM tests. *Econometrica*, **50**, 737–748.

Fletcher, R. (1972a). Conjugate direction methods. In *Numerical Methods for Unconstrained Optimization*. Edited by W. Murray. London: Academic Press. Pp. 73–86.

Fletcher, R. (1972b). A survey of algorithms for unconstrained optimization. In *Numerical Methods for Unconstrained Optimization*. Edited by W. Murray. London: Academic Press. Pp. 123–129.

Fletcher, R. and Powell, M. (1963). A rapidly convergent descent method for minimization. *The Computer Journal*, **6**, 163–168.

Gallant, A. (1975a). Nonlinear regression. *The American Statistician*, **29**, 73–81.

Gallant, A. (1975b). Testing a subset of the parametrics of a nonlinear regression model. *Journal of the American Statistical Association*, **70**, 927–932.

Goldfeld, S. and Quandt, R. (1972). *Nonlinear Methods in Econometrics*. Amsterdam: North-Holland.

Goldfeld, S., Quandt, R., and Trotter, H. (1966). Maximization by quadratic hill climbing. *Econometrica*, **34**, 541–551.

Hartley, H. (1961). The modified Gauss–Newton method for the fitting of non-linear regression functions by least squares. *Technometics*, **3**, 269–280.

Himmelblau, D. (1972). *Applied Nonlinear Programming*. New York: McGraw-Hill.

Hooke, R. and Jeeves, T. (1961). A direct search solution of numerical and statistical problems. *Journal of the Association for Computing Machinery*, **8**, 212–229.

Judge, G., Griffiths, W., Hill, R., and Lee, T. (1980). *The Theory and Practice of Econometrics*. New York: Wiley.

Kendall, M. and Stuart, A. (1961). *The Advanced Theory of Statistics*, Vol. 2. New York: Hafner.

Lootsma, F. (1972). *Numerical Methods for Nonlinear Optimization*. London: Academic Press.

Maddala, G. (1977). *Econometrics*, New York: McGraw-Hill.

Malinvaud, E. (1970a). *Statistical Methods of Econometrics*. Amsterdam: North-Holland.

Malinvaud, E. (1970b). The consistency of nonlinear regressions. *The Annals of Mathematical Statistics*, **41**, 956–969.

Marquardt, D. (1963). An algorithm for least squares estimation of nonlinear parameters. *Journal of the Society for Industrial and Applied Mathematics*, **11**, 431–441.

Powell, M. (1964). An efficient method for finding the minimum of a function of several variables without calculating derivatives. *The Computer Journal*, **7**, 155–162.

Powell, M. (1965). A method for minimizing a sum of squares of nonlinear functions without calculating derivatives. In *Optimization*. Edited by R. Fletcher. London: Academic Press. Pp. 283–298.

Rao, C. (1973). *Linear Statistical Reference and its Application*. New York: Wiley.

Savin, N. (1976). Conflict among testing procedures in a linear regression model with autoregressive disturbances. *Econometrica*, **44**, 1303–1315.

Silvey, S. (1959). The Lagrangian multiplier test. *Annals of Mathematical Statistics*, **30**, 389–407.

Silvey, S. (1970). *Statistical Inference*. Harmondsworth: Penguin.

Theil, H. (1971). *Principles of Econometrics*. New York: Wiley.

Wald, A. (1943). Tests of hypotheses concerning several parameters when the numbers of observations is large. *Transactions of the American Mathematical Society*, **54**, 426–482.

Index